D0037383

# Writing about Writing

A College Reader

# Writing about Writing

## A College Reader

**Second Edition**

**Elizabeth Wardle**
University of Central Florida

**Doug Downs**
Montana State University

Bedford / St. Martin's
Boston • New York

**FOR BEDFORD/ST. MARTIN'S**

*Publisher for Composition:* Leasa Burton
*Executive Editor:* John E. Sullivan III
*Senior Production Editor:* Bridget Leahy
*Assistant Production Manager:* Joe Ford
*Marketing Manager:* Emily Rowin
*Editorial Assistant:* Rachel Greenhaus
*Copy Editor:* Steve Patterson
*Indexer:* Leoni Z. McVey
*Photo Researcher:* Christine End
*Senior Art Director:* Anna Palchik
*Text Design:* Brian Salisbury
*Cover Design:* Marine Miller
*Composition:* Cenveo Publisher Services
*Printing and Binding:* RR Donnelley and Sons

*President, Bedford/St. Martin's:* Denise B. Wydra
*Editorial Director, English and Music:* Karen S. Henry
*Director of Marketing:* Karen R. Soeltz
*Production Director:* Susan W. Brown
*Director of Rights and Permissions:* Hilary Newman

Copyright © 2014, 2011 by Bedford/St. Martin's
All rights reserved. No part of this book may be reproduced, stored in a retrieval system, or transmitted in any form or by any means, electronic, mechanical, photocopying, recording, or otherwise, except as may be expressly permitted by the applicable copyright statutes or in writing by the Publisher.

Manufactured in the United States of America.

8 7 6 5 4
f e d c b

*For information, write:* Bedford/St. Martin's, 75 Arlington Street, Boston, MA 02116    (617-399-4000)

ISBN: 978-1-4576-3694-3

*Acknowledgments*

Acknowledgments and copyrights can be found at the back of the book on pages 805–09, which constitute an extension of the copyright page.

It is a violation of the law to reproduce these selections by any means whatsoever without the written permission of the copyright holder.

# Preface for Instructors

*Writing about Writing* is part of a movement that has been growing steadily for years. As composition instructors, we have always focused on teaching students how writing works and on helping them develop ways of thinking that would enable them to succeed as writers in college. We found ourselves increasingly frustrated, however, teaching traditional composition courses based on topics that had nothing to do with writing. It made far more sense to us to have students really engage with writing in the writing course; the best way to do this, we decided, was to adopt a "writing about writing" approach, introducing students directly to what writing researchers have learned about writing and challenging them to respond by writing and doing research of their own. After years of experimenting with readings and assignments, and watching our colleagues do the same, we eventually developed *Writing about Writing*, a textbook for first-year composition students that presents the subjects of composition, discourse, and literacy as its content. Here's why we think *Writing about Writing* is a smart choice for composition courses:

**Writing about Writing engages students in a relevant subject.** One of the major goals of the writing course, as we see it, is to move students' ideas about language and writing from the realm of the automatic and unconscious to the forefront of their thinking. In conventional composition courses, students are too often asked to write about either an arbitrary topic unrelated to writing or, conversely, about anything at all. In our experience, when students are asked to read and interact with academic scholarly conversations about writing and test their opinions through their own research, they become more engaged with the goals of the writing course and—most important—they learn more about writing.

**Writing about Writing engages students' own areas of expertise.** By the time they reach college, students are expert language users with multiple literacies: they are experienced student writers, and they're engaged in many other discourses as well—blogging, texting, instant messaging, posting to social networking sites like Facebook and YouTube, and otherwise using language and writing on a daily basis. *Writing about Writing* asks students to work from their own experience to consider how writing works, who they are as writers, and how they use (and don't use) writing. Students might wonder, for example, why they did so poorly on the SAT writing section or why some groups of people use writing that is so specialized it seems intended to leave others out. This book encourages students to discover how others—including Sondra Perl, Mike Rose, James Paul Gee, their instructors, and their classmates—have answered these questions and then to find out more by doing meaningful research of their own.

**Writing about Writing helps students transfer what they learn.** Teachers often assume that students can automatically and easily "apply" what they learn in a writing course to all their other writing—or at the very least, to other college writing. This assumption sees writing and reading as "basic" universal skills that work the same regardless of situation. Yet research on transfer of learning suggests that there is nothing automatic about it: David Perkins and Gavriel Salomon found that in order to transfer knowledge, students need to explicitly create general principles based on their own experience and learning; be self-reflective, so that they keep track of what they are thinking and learning as they do it; and be mindful, that is, alert to their surroundings and to what they are doing rather than just doing things automatically and unconsciously. A writing course that takes language, writing, reading, and literacy as its subjects can help students achieve these goals by teaching them to articulate general principles such as "Carefully consider what your audience needs and wants this document to do." In addition, it teaches them to reflect on their own reading, writing, and research processes.

***Writing about Writing* has been extensively class tested—and it works.** The principles of this writing-about-writing approach have been well tested and supported by the experience of writing instructors and thousands of students across the country. The first edition of *Writing about Writing* was formally class tested in a pilot at the University of Central Florida, an experiment that yielded impressive outcomes in comparative portfolio assessment with more traditional composition courses. Assessment results suggest, among other things, that the writing-about-writing approach had a statistically significant impact on higher-order thinking skills—rhetorical analysis, critical thinking about ideas, and using and integrating the ideas of others. The writing-about-writing approach also had a significant impact on how students and teachers engaged in writing as a process. The first edition of *Writing about Writing* was used in a variety of composition programs across the country. Based on positive feedback from those users, we have even greater confidence that this approach is successful.

# Features of *Writing about Writing*, Second Edition

## Topics That Matter to Writers

*Writing about Writing* is organized around concepts and principles from Writing Studies with which we think students should become familiar: how texts in general—and ideas about writing in particular—are constructed; what writing processes are and how they work; what "literacy" means and how people become literate (or multiliterate); how communities use and are shaped by discourse; and how writers can gain authority when writing in college. These issues are framed in the text as questions, each of which forms the basis of one chapter. Many of these are issues that were covered in the first edition, but some are new. All have been re-ordered to create a carefully sequenced and scaffolded learning experience for students:

- Chapter 1: Literacies: Where Do Your Ideas About Reading and Writing Come From?
- Chapter 2: Individual in Community: How Do Texts Mediate Activities?
- Chapter 3: Rhetoric: How Is Meaning Constructed in Context?
- Chapter 4: Processes: How Are Texts Composed?
- Chapter 5: Multi-Modal Composition: What Counts as Writing?

By asking students to find their own answers to these questions, we encourage them to reflect on past literacy experiences and to be mindful of present ones, making them directly responsible, in the end, for their own learning.

## Framed Around Threshold Concepts about Writing

The chapter concepts have been re-thought and re-ordered around what we think are some central "threshold concepts" related to writing. Threshold concepts are concepts that learners must become acquainted with in order to progress in that area of study—they are gateways to learning. Naming and using threshold concepts is an approach that has been used in the United Kingdom and now increasingly in the U.S. to improve teaching and learning in various disciplines and programs. Because they are central to work in a particular field but are often assumed and unstated, threshold concepts when explicitly identified can better help students come to understand ideas that are central to that field or phenomenon.

Researchers Ray Land and Jan Meyer have argued that threshold concepts are often troublesome, and can conflict with common knowledge about a phenomenon. We think that this is particularly true when it comes to writing. Much of what we have learned as a field about writing conflicts with commonly held assumptions about writing. For example, many people believe that "good writers" are people for whom writing is easy, while research about writing suggests that "good writers" are people who persist, revise, and are willing to learn from their failures.

Threshold concepts are now the organizing theme for the second edition, and we've arranged them in a sequence that we believe assists understanding of each subsequent concept.

- **Chapter 1, "Literacies: Where Do Your Ideas about Reading and Writing Come From?"** engages the threshold concept that *writing performance is informed by prior literacy experiences*, or in simpler terms, that our reading and writing past will shape our reading and writing present.

- **Chapter 2, "Individual in Community: How Do Texts Mediate Activities?"** engages the threshold concept that *writing mediates activity*. In other words, that writing gets things done, makes things happen.

- **Chapter 3, "Rhetoric: How Is Meaning Constructed in Context?"** introduces students to some underlying rhetorical concepts; for example, that good *writing is dependent on the situation, readers, and uses it's being created for.*

- **Chapter 4, "Processes: How Are Texts Composed?"** asks students to engage several threshold concepts about writing: that writing is *knowledge-making*, that making knowledge requires ongoing and repeating *processes*, and that *writing is not perfectible*.

- **Chapter 5, "Multimodal Composition: What Counts as Writing?"** emphasizes the threshold concept that *writing is by nature a technology*. Writing involves tools, and writing is not "natural" (in a biological sense).

## Challenging but Engaging Readings

Because our intention in putting this book together was to invite students directly into scholarly conversations about writing, most readings in the book are articles by rhetoric and composition scholars. In deciding which articles to include, we looked for work that was readable by undergraduates, relevant to student experience, effective in modeling how to research and write about writing, and useful for helping students frame and analyze writing-related issues. We drew not only on our own experience with students but also on feedback from a growing nationwide network of faculty using writing-about-writing approaches to composition and on the feedback of teachers who used the first edition of the book. The articles that made the final cut expose students to some of the longest-standing questions and some of the most interesting work in our field, encouraging them to wrestle with concepts we're all trying to figure out. For this second edition, eighteen readings by professional scholars are new to the print book. They range from Kevin Roozen's account of a student's developing literacy practices, to an overview of rhetoric by William Covino and David Jollife, to Charles Bazerman's analysis of speech acts, genres, and activity systems.

Of course, we don't expect first-year students to read these texts like graduate students would—that is, with a central focus on the content of the readings, for the purposes of critiquing them and extending their ideas. Instead, we intend for them to be used as springboards to exploration of students' own writing and reading experiences. The readings—and thus this book—are not the center of the course; instead, they help students develop language and ideas for thinking through the threshold concepts identified above, and begin exploring them by considering their own experiences with writing, discourse, and literacy, and their (and the field's) open questions.

While most readings are scholarly, we include a number of other sorts of texts throughout this edition. There are non-academic pieces by fiction writers (including Sherman Alexie and Junot Diaz), short pieces by academic writers (including Dorothy Winsor and Donald Murray), and research reports by the Pew Research Center and Writing in Digital Environments Research Group. These readings, combined with the others in the book, help students approach the threshold concepts about writing from a variety of perspectives.

## Online e-Pages with Additional Readings

This edition of *Writing about Writing* includes Bedford Integrated Media, more than a dozen readings presented online as e-Pages, four of which are new to this edition, at **bedfordstmartins.com/writingaboutwriting**. The e-Pages include the same apparatus that accompanies the print selections, and the e-Pages platform allows for note taking and highlighting to enhance the learning experience, making it possible to work alternatively with readings in the print book and those online. **Students** receive access to e-Pages automatically with the purchase of a new print book or Bedford e-Book. Students who buy a used book or rent a book can purchase access to online materials at bedfordstmartins .com/writingaboutwriting. **Instructors** receive access automatically with an evaluation or desk copy. Visit bedfordstmartins.com/writingaboutwriting and register as an instructor. For technical support, visit macmillanhighered.com/techsupport.

## Real Student Writing

The second edition of *Writing about Writing* also includes a greater number of student voices than the previous edition, with ten pieces of student writing, nine of which are new. For the first time, we've drawn work from *Young Scholars in Writing*, the national peer-reviewed journal of undergraduate research in writing studies and rhetoric, and from *Stylus*, the University of Central Florida Writing Program's peer-reviewed first-year student publication. Given their nature as reprinted scholarly articles, we have treated the student essays much the same as we have treated the professional essays: they are framed and introduced and accompanied by questions and activities. We want the students who use this book to see other students as participants in the ongoing conversations about writing; we hope this will enable them to see themselves as potential contributors to these conversations.

## Scaffolded Support for Learning

The material presented in this book is challenging. We've found that students need guidance in order to engage with it constructively, and many instructors appreciate support in teaching it. Therefore, we've scaffolded the material in ways that help make individual readings more accessible to students and that help them build toward mastery of often complex rhetorical concepts.

- The book begins with an expanded introduction for students that explains what the book does and why, provides extended explanation about the concepts of the book (including the idea that meaning is constructed), and explains why and how the book is organized around threshold concepts. The introduction also provides some reading strategies and an overview of John Swales' CARS model of research introductions, to help students understand how to read some of the research articles in the chapter. There you will also find a new reading by Richard Straub that helps prepare students for responding to each other's writing. Finally, the introduction includes a reading by Stuart Greene that asks students to think about this class and book as inquiry.

- Each chapter begins with a chapter introduction that summarizes its content and goals and overviews each reading and its central ideas. In some cases, as with Chapter 3, "Rhetoric: How Is Meaning Constructed in Context?," these introductions are notably robust discussions of background knowledge and principles, in order to help students better approach the threshold concepts the chapter includes.

- Each reading begins with a *Framing the Reading* section offering background on the author and the text and *Getting Ready to Read* suggestions for activities to do *before* reading and questions to ask *during* reading.

- Each reading is followed by two sets of questions: *Questions for Discussion and Journaling*, which can be used in class or for homework, and *Applying and Exploring Ideas*, which recommends medium-scale reading-related writing activities (both individual and group). These questions and activities are designed to make teachers' jobs easier by providing a variety of prompts that have been class tested by others.

- Each chapter ends with "major" assignment options. Building on one or more of the readings from the chapter, assignments are designed to help students achieve the goals outlined in the chapter introduction. Though these assignments hardly scratch the surface of what's possible, these have proven to be favorites with us, our students, and other teachers.

- The book includes a glossary of technical terms in composition that students will encounter in their readings. Terms in the glossary, such as **rhetorical situation** and **discourse**, are noted in the reading via bold print.

*A note on citation styles.* While student writings reflect current MLA or APA style guides in citation and documentation, other material in the book, all previously published, remains written in the citation styles used by the journals and books in which they were originally published, current at those times. This means you should expect to see a great deal of variation from current MLA, APA, or CMS style guidelines—a decision that we hope will provide many instructors with an excellent starting point for conversation about how citation actually works in the "real world" of academic publication over time.

## The Instructor's Edition of *Writing about Writing*

Some teachers won't need any supplements at all, including the discussion questions and major assignment options. But we have designed the book to be as accessible as possible to composition instructors with a wide range of experience, including new graduate students and very busy adjuncts. Toward that end, we provide instructor's resource material written by Deborah Weaver and Lindee Owens, two long-time teacher-trainers at the University of Central Florida, who themselves piloted an early version of this book and taught the material in it to a number of other composition teachers there. This material, bound together with the student text in a special Instructor's Edition, includes the following:

- sample course calendars
- lists of key vocabulary for each chapter
- key student outcomes for each chapter
- a list of readings that can help teach key student outcomes
- summaries and take-home points for each reading, and
- supplemental activities that help teach to each outcome.

The manual is also available for download on the instructor's resources tab at bedfordstmartins.com/writingaboutwriting.

## Acknowledgments

We came to writing-about-writing independently of one another, in different ways, and became better at it as a result of working together. David Russell was a mentor for us both. Elizabeth came to writing-about-writing as a result of her dissertation research, which Russell chaired and supported. Doug came to it as a result of questions about building better research pedagogy, directly fueled by Joseph Russell's work on the history of college research-writing instruction and his chapter in Petraglia's *Reconceiving*

*Writing*. Initially, Elizabeth's interest was theoretical ("this might be an interesting idea") while Doug's was quite practical (he designed and studied a writing-about-writing class for his dissertation). We discovered each other's common interest through dialog on the WPA-L listserv and a long-term collaboration was born. It is fair to say that neither of us would have written this book without the other, as we both seem to get a lot more done when working collaboratively. (There is a vividly remembered two hours in the sunshine at the University of Delaware, at the 2004 WPA conference, where we took our first steps at figuring out collaboration.) So, if it's not too corny, we would like to acknowledge collaboration in general, our collaboration in particular, and tenure and promotion systems at our institutions that have recognized collaborative work for the valid, challenging, and rewarding process it is.

To many, many people—colleagues, mentors, and friends—we owe a deep debt of gratitude for putting the ideas grounding *Writing about Writing* "in the air." In addition, over the five years that it took to build the first edition of this book, and the three years we planned and wrote the second edition, we met many wonderful teacher-scholars who inspired us to keep going. Over many dinners, SIGs, conference panels, e-mail discussions, and drinks, we learned and are still learning a lot from them. A partial list of people who helped us start on this path or rethink it and make it better includes Linda Adler-Kassner, Anis Bawarshi, Barb Bird, Shannon Carter, Dana Driscoll, Heidi Estrem, Deb Holdstein, Michelle LaFrance, Moriah McCracken, Laurie McMillan, Michael Michaud, Michael Murphy, Sarah Read, Kevin Roozen, David Russell, Betsy Sargent, Jody Shipka, David Slomp, Susan Thomas, Jennifer Wells, Kathi Yancey, and Leah Zuidema.

Each of us is also deeply indebted to the wonderful teachers, scholars, and students at our own institutions who have worked with this curriculum and pushed our thinking on what is possible in a writing about writing classroom. At UCF, some of these people include: Matt Bryan, Angela Rounsaville, Debbie Weaver, Lindee Owens, Mark Hall, Dan Martin, Matt McBride, Adele Richardson, Nichole Stack, Mary Tripp, and Thomas Wright. At Montana State, some of these people include: Jess Carroll, Jill Davis, ZuZu Feder, Katie Jo LaRiviere, Miles Nolte, Mark Schlenz, and Aaron Yost.

Many of these people are now on the FYC as Writing Studies listserv; members of the Writing about Writing Network founded by Betsy Sargent; or participants in or leaders of the annual CCCC Special Interest Group, The Subject Is Writing: FYC as Introduction to Writing Studies. Through such interaction, they continue to develop research projects, create conference presentations and workshops, and inspire us—and one another—with their curricular creativity. Writing-about-writing students have also been given a national platform to publish their work, thanks to the editorial board of the national, peer-reviewed undergraduate journal of Writing Studies, *Young Scholars in Writing*. Editor Laurie Grobman created a First-year Writing Feature (continued as the Spotlight on First-year Writing under the editorship of Jane Greer) co-edited over time by Shannon Carter, Doug Downs, David Elder, Heidi Estrem, Patti Hanlon-Baker, and Holly Ryan.

We are grateful to those instructors who gave us valuable feedback as we worked on this new edition: Tabetha Adkins, Texas A&M University-Commerce; Jennafer Alexander, University of Missouri-St. Louis; Dennis Bohr, Appalachian State University; Jennifer Bray, Texas A&M University-Corpus Christi; Matthew Bryan, University of Central Florida; Jonikka Charlton, University of Texas-Pan American; Paul Dahlgren, Georgia Southwestern State University; Elias Dominguez Barajas, University of Arkansas; Suellynn Duffey,

University of Missouri-St. Louis; Mia Eaker, The University of North Carolina at Charlotte; Anthony Edgington, University of Toledo; Stephen Fairbanks, University of Missouri-St. Louis; Carolyn Fitzpatrick, University of Maryland, Baltimore County; Shelly Fox, Texas A&M University-Corpus Christi; Laura Friddle, DePaul University; Alanna Frost, University of Alabama in Huntsville; Marlene Galvan, University of Texas-Pan American; Gwen Gorzelsky, Wayne State University; Andrew Green, University of Miami; Jane Greer, University of Missouri-Kansas City; Kim Gunter, Appalachian State University; Gina Hanson, California State University, San Bernardino; Sharon Alusow Hart, Appalachian State University; Carol Haviland, California State University, San Bernardino; Kellie L. Jarvis, Texas A&M University-Corpus Christi; Frances Johnson, Texas A&M University-Corpus Christi; Mitzi Jones, University of Arkansas-Fort Smith; Michelle LaFrance, University of Massachusetts-Dartmouth; Katie Jo LaRiviere, Montana State University; Eugene Launier, University of Central Florida; Jennifer Maher, University of Maryland Baltimore County; Paul Martin, University of Central Florida; Laura Martinez, University of Central Florida; Lisa J. McClure, Southern Illinois University-Carbondale; Jill McCracken, University of South Florida-St. Petersburg; Beatrice McKinsey, Grambling State University; Holly McSpadden, Missouri Southern State University; Laura Micciche, University of Cincinnati; Michael Michaud, Rhode Island College; Linda Moser, Missouri State University; Paula Patch, Elon University; Laurie A. Pinkert, Purdue University; Georgia Rhoades, Appalachian State; Jan Rieman, The University of North Carolina at Charlotte; Kevin Roozen, University of Central Florida; Travis Rountree, Appalachian State University; Albert Rouzie, Ohio University; Jody Shipka, University of Maryland, Baltimore County; Michael Sobiech, University of Louisville; Mary Tripp, University of Central Florida; Matthew Vetter, Ohio University; Elizabeth West, Appalachian State; and John Whicker, Ohio University.

We owe a massive thank you to Bedford/St Martin's, and to Leasa Burton and Joan Feinberg in particular, who had the vision to believe that this book might really find an audience if they published it. To all the Bedford crew who made it real the first time and improved the second time, we are deeply grateful. This second go-round, John Sullivan, Molly Parke, Karita dos Santos, Leasa Burton, Bridget Leahy, and Ginny Creedon have been integral to our ability to make it happen.

Ultimately, our students deserve the most acknowledgment. They have inspired us to keep teaching writing about writing. They have demonstrated that the focus is one that continues to excite and motivate, and their ideas continue to inspire and teach us.

Elizabeth Wardle
Doug Downs

# You Get More Choices

Bedford/St. Martin's offers resources and format choices that help you and your students get even more out of the book and your course. To learn more about or order any of the following products, contact your Bedford/St. Martin's sales representative, e-mail sales support (sales_support@bfwpub.com), or visit the Web site at bedfordstmartins.com /writingaboutwriting/catalog.

## Let Students Choose Their Format

Bedford/St. Martin's offers a range of affordable formats, including the portable, download-able Bedford e-Book to Go for *Writing about Writing* for about half the price of the print book. To order access cards for the Bedford e-Book to Go format, use ISBN 978-1-4576-7070-1. For details, visit bedfordstmartins.com/writingaboutwriting/formats.

## Choose the Flexible *Bedford e-Portfolio*

Students can collect, select, and reflect on their coursework and personalize and share their e-Portfolio for any audience. Instructors can provide as much or as little structure as they see fit. Rubrics and learning outcomes can be aligned to student work, so instructors and programs can gather reliable and useful assessment data. Every *Bedford e-Portfolio* comes pre-loaded with *Portfolio Keeping* and *Portfolio Teaching*, by Nedra Reynolds and Elizabeth Davis. *Bedford e-Portfolio* can be purchased separately or packaged with the book at a significant discount. An activation code is required. To order *Bedford e-Portfolio* with the print book, use ISBN 978-1-4576-7873-8. Visit bedfordstmartins.com/eportfolio.

## Watch Peer Review Work

*Eli Review* lets instructors scaffold their assignments in a clearer, more effective way for students—making peer review more visible and teachable. *Eli Review* can be purchased separately or packaged with the book at a significant discount. An activation code is required. To order *Eli Review* with the print book, use ISBN 978-1-4576-7874-5. Visit bedfordstmartins.com/eli.

## Select Value Packages

Add value to your course by packaging one of the following resources with *Writing about Writing* at a significant discount. To learn more about package options, contact your Bedford/St. Martin's sales representative or visit bedfordstmartins.com /writingaboutwriting/catalog.

- *EasyWriter,* **Fifth Edition, by Andrea Lunsford,** distills Andrea Lunsford's teaching and research into the essentials that today's writers need to make good choices in any rhetorical situation. To order *EasyWriter* packaged with *Writing about Writing* use ISBN 978-1-4576-8372-5.

- *A Pocket Style Manual,* **Sixth Edition, by Diana Hacker and Nancy Sommers,** a straightforward, inexpensive quick reference, with content flexible enough to suit the needs of writers in the humanities, social sciences, sciences, health professions, business, fine arts, education, and beyond. To order *A Pocket Style Manual* with *Writing about Writing*, use ISBN 978-1-4576-8371-8.

- ***LearningCurve for Readers and Writers,*** Bedford/St. Martin's adaptive quizzing program, quickly learns what students already know and helps them practice what they don't yet understand. Game-like quizzing motivates students to engage with their course, and reporting tools help teachers discern their students' needs. An activation code is required. To order *LearningCurve for Readers and Writers* packaged with the print book, use 978-1-4576-7878-3. For details, visit bedfordstmartins.com/englishlearningcurve.

- ***Portfolio Keeping,*** **Third Edition, by Nedra Reynolds and Elizabeth Davis,** provides all the information students need to use the portfolio method successfully in a writing course. *Portfolio Teaching*, a companion guide for instructors, provides the practical information instructors and writing program administrators need to use the portfolio method successfully in a writing course. To order *Portfolio Keeping* packaged with the print book, use ISBN 978-1-4576-7876-9.

## Try *Re:Writing 2* for Fun

What's the fun of teaching writing if you can't try something new? The best collection of free writing resources on the Web, *Re:Writing 2* gives you and your students even more ways to think, watch, practice, and learn about writing concepts. Listen to Nancy Sommers on using a teacher's comments to revise. Try a logic puzzle. Consult our resources for writing centers. All free for the fun of trying it. Visit bedfordstmartins.com/rewriting.

## Instructor Resources

**You have a lot to do in your course. Bedford/St. Martin's wants to make it easy for you to find the support you need—and to get it quickly.**

- **Teaching Central** (bedfordstmartins.com/teachingcentral) offers the entire list of Bedford/St. Martin's print and online professional resources in one place. You'll find landmark reference works, sourcebooks on pedagogical issues, award-winning collections, and practical advice for the classroom—all free for instructors.

- ***Bits*** (bedfordbits.com) collects creative ideas for teaching a range of composition topics in an easily searchable blog format. A community of teachers—leading scholars, authors, and editors, including Elizabeth Wardle and Doug Downs—discuss revision, research, grammar and style, technology, peer review, and much more.

- **Bedford Coursepacks** (bedfordstmartins.com/coursepacks) allow you to easily download digital materials from Bedford/St. Martin's for your course for the most common course management systems— Blackboard, Angel, Desire2Learn, Canvas, Moodle, or Sakai.

# About the Authors

Elizabeth Wardle is a professor and Department Chair in the Department of Writing and Rhetoric at the University of Central Florida. Her research interests center on transfer of writing-related knowledge, genre theory, composition pedagogy, and questions of disciplinarity. She is currently conducting a longitudinal study of knowledge transfer, as well as working on a book project about the "threshold concepts" of Writing Studies with Linda Adler-Kassner.

Doug Downs is an associate professor of writing studies as well as Director of Composition in the Department of English at Montana State University. His research interests center on writing, research, and reading instruction at the college level, especially related to first-year composition and undergraduate research. His most recent research projects focus on how reading practices are shifting with the increasing use of screen-based devices to read multimodal documents.

# Contents

CHAPTER 2

# Individual in Community: How Do Texts Mediate Activities?    212

**JOHN SWALES,** The Concept of Discourse Community    215
   Describes six characteristics of a discourse community and provides examples of how discourse communities function.

**LUCILLE MCCARTHY,** A Stranger in Strange Lands: A College Student Writing across the Curriculum    230
   Follows an undergraduate student, Dave, through three different classes in order to understand how he approaches and understands writing tasks in different settings.

**SEAN BRANICK,** Coaches Can Read, Too: An Ethnographic Study of a Football Coaching Discourse Community (FIRST-YEAR STUDENT TEXT)    262
   Analyzes coaching interviews and speeches in order to argue that football coaches constitute a discourse community that entails complex textual, interpersonal, and situational literacies.

**DONNA KAIN and ELIZABETH WARDLE,** Activity Theory: An Introduction for the Writing Classroom    273
   Presents a brief overview of activity theory appropriate for undergraduate students, and describes how activity theory could be used to analyze texts as they mediate activity in different contexts.

**ELIZABETH WARDLE,** Identity, Authority, and Learning to Write in New Workplaces    284
   Describes the struggle an employee faces as he tries to communicate in a new workplace setting. Uses activity theory to analyze some of his communicative failures.

**VICTORIA MARRO,** The Genres of Chi Omega: An Activity Analysis (FIRST-YEAR STUDENT TEXT)    302
   Draws on activity theory and genre theory to analyze how a sorority's genres are used across chapters in order to further the goals of the organization.

**e** **TONY MIRABELLI,** Learning to Serve: The Language and Literacy of Food Service Workers (E-PAGES)
   Draws on theories about language in communities in order to examine how workers and patrons in a diner interact through language and texts.

## CHAPTER 3

# Rhetoric: How Is Meaning Constructed in Context?    318

**e** bedfordstmartins.com/writingaboutwriting

**e** bedfordstmartins.com/writingaboutwriting

CHAPTER 5

# Multimodal Composition: What Counts as Writing? 683

# Writing about Writing

A College Reader

# Introduction to the Conversation

Have you ever wondered why every teacher seems to have a different set of rules for writing? Or why writing seems to be more difficult for some people than for others? Or why some people use big words when they don't have to? This book invites you to explore questions like these by reading research about writing, comparing your own writing experiences to those of others, and finding your own answers by conducting research of your own.

This book does not tell you how to write. It does not contain step-by-step advice about how to draft your paper or how to conduct research. Instead, it introduces you to research about writing conducted in the field of **writing studies**,[1] much as your textbooks in biology or psychology introduce you to the research of those fields. Writing studies researchers study how writing works, how people write, and how best to teach writing. From this book, then, you'll learn *about* the subject—writing—just as you would learn about biology from a biology textbook or about psychology from a psychology textbook. *Writing about Writing* asks you to think about writing as something we *know about*, not just something we *do*. It offers you these kinds of learning:

- Deeper understanding of what's going on with your own writing and how writing works
- Knowledge about writing that you can take with you to help you navigate other writing situations
- Experience engaging with scholarly articles and other research
- The ability to conduct inquiry-driven research on unanswered questions

## Why Study Writing?

You might wonder why it could be helpful to learn *about* writing rather than simply be told *how* to write. What good will this do you as a writer?

We think the answer to this question is that changing what you know *about* writing can change *the way* you write. Much of the research in this book questions everyday

---

[1] **Boldface** terms are further defined in the glossary (p. 791).

assumptions about writing—like the idea that you can't use your own **voice** in writing for school, or that writing is just easy for some people and hard for others, or that **literacy** is only about how well you can read. If you change your ideas about what writing is *supposed* to be, you're likely to do things differently—more effectively—when you write.

There are additional advantages to studying writing in a writing course:

- Writing is *relevant* to all of us. Most of us do it every day, and all of us live in a world in which writing, reading, and other related uses of language are primary means of communication.
- What you learn about writing now will be directly *useful* to you long after the class ends. In college, at work, and in everyday life, writing well can have a measurable impact on your current and future success.
- You already have a great deal of *experience* with writing and reading, so you are a more knowledgeable investigator of these subjects than you might be of a lot of others.
- Doing research on writing will give you the opportunity to *contribute new knowledge* about your subject, not simply gather and repeat what lots of other people have already said.

## Two Stories about Writing

You might be thinking that we're making writing harder than it has to be: Can't people just tell you how to write for any new situation or task? Even if studying about writing can help you write differently and better, wouldn't it be more direct to simply *tell you the rules* and let you practice and memorize them?

That would work if the traditional story about writing that most of us learn in school were accurate. In that traditional story, "writing" is a basic grammatical skill of transcribing speech to print, a skill that can "transfer" (be used again) unaltered from the situation in which you learn it (high school and college English classes, usually) to any other writing situation. Because, that story goes, the rules of English don't change. English is English, whether you're in a chemistry class or the boardroom of a bank. And, according to that story, what makes good writing is following all the rules and avoiding errors: *Just don't do anything wrong* and your writing will be okay. According to this view of writing, people who are good at writing are people who break the fewest rules and write with the greatest ease; writing is hard because following the rules is hard, so if you can learn the rules, you can write more easily and thus be a good writer. That's the story that the majority of high school graduates seem to have learned. It's likely that no one stood in front of you and told you this story directly; but instead, it is a story that you learned by what people around you did and modeled. For example, when teachers read your papers and ignored your ideas but corrected your grammatical mistakes, they were telling you this story: Writing is nothing but error-avoidance. When you took standardized tests (like the SAT) and were given a prompt you had never seen before and told to write about it in 30 minutes, and then a stranger read it and ignored your ideas and facts and instead rated you on correctness and organization, they were telling you this story: Writing is not about content; it is about correctness. If you think about the views of writing that you see on the news

("Kids today can't write! Texting is ruining their spelling!") or what you saw teachers and test-makers model, you will likely start to recognize how widespread this particular story of writing is.

But there's more than one story about writing. You'll find the college writing instructor who assigned this book probably believes a very different story, one based not on teachers' rulebooks but rather on observation of successful writers and how writing, reading, language, and texts actually work—how people actually experience them. In this other story, "writing" is much fuller and richer. Writing is not just how you say something (form) but also what you say (content), how you come up with your ideas (invention), how you go through the act of thinking and writing (process), and whether what you've said and how you've said it successfully meets the current situation (rhetoric). In this story, avoiding errors that get in the way of the readers' understanding is only one small part of writing. Writing is about communicating in ways that work, that *do something* in the world. In this view, writing is much more than grammar, and it's also much more than the final text you create; writing is the whole process of creating that text. In this story, there is not one universal set of rules for writing correctly, but rather many sets of *habits* adopted by groups of people using particular texts to accomplish particular ends or activities. For example, the habits and conventions of engineers' writing are vastly different than the habits and conventions of lawyers' writing or your writing for your history class. That means there is *no easily transferable set of rules* from one writing situation to another. What transfers is not *how to write*, but *what to ask about writing*.

This second, alternative story about writing is one we think you have also been exposed to, but maybe not in school. When you text your friends, for example, you already know that what you say and how you say it matter, and that the text will be successful if your friend reads it and understands it and responds somehow. If your friend ignores it or finds it insulting or can't quite decipher the new shorthand you devised, then it's not "good writing." You also know that when you go to your English class, or write a letter to your mother, you can't write the same way you do when you are texting your friends. You know these things even if no one has ever told them to you directly. How you know them even if no one ever taught you is an interesting question that we'll take up in Chapter 2 of this book.

This second story about writing—the one that writing scholars believe—is why we think it would not be very helpful to write a book that tries to teach you "how to write." After all, in a "how to write" book you would have to respond to every piece of advice by asking, "How to write *what*, for *whom*, in order to be used *in what way*?" This book doesn't give you easy, quick, or limited advice about how to write, but instead shows you ways of thinking about how writing works, and how to make informed and effective choices for yourself in each new writing situation.

As a writer you have likely been experiencing the two competing stories about, or "conceptions of," writing throughout much of your life. This might have led to confusing and frustrating experiences with writing. Teachers might have said they want to hear your personal voice and heartfelt opinion on something and then respond only to spelling and comma splices in your papers. School might have turned into a place where writing is simply an opportunity for you to be told that you've made mistakes. But at the same time, you might have a rich writing life through texting and Facebooking, writing fanfiction, writing on gaming chatboards, writing songs or poetry. In those worlds, writing is used to communicate, to share ideas, to get things done. These competing experiences with writing are enacting different conceptions of what writing is, and those conceptions of writing lead you to do different things. If you think that writing is avoiding error, it is unlikely you will spend much time developing ideas. If you think that a reader is going to respond and react to your ideas, you are quite likely to spend a lot of time developing them and thinking about your reader's possible reactions.

Part of the purpose of this book is to give you the language and the ideas to figure out what conceptions of writing you are experiencing and which ones might be most accurate, and what to do about it. This idea of "conceptions" is one worth talking about in a little more depth.

## Conceptions and Misconceptions about Writing

A **conception** is a belief, an idea about something. (It's the same root as the word *concept*.) Many of the readings in this book suggest that some of our cultural beliefs about reading and writing aren't exactly right, and our lives as readers and writers would make a lot more sense if we could see these beliefs as *misconceptions*—that is, as ideas and stories about writing that don't really hold up to interrogation and research.

In this book, you'll find readings that challenge many common but, research suggests, incorrect conceptions about writing and reading. It is likely that many of these are misconceptions that you learned in previous schooling or picked up from testing experiences or watching the news. Some misconceptions you'll see these readings refute include:

- The rules of writing (including grammar) are universal and do not change based on the situation; there is one single set of correct rules for all writing at all times. (See Wardle and McCarthy, both in Chapter 2; Rose in Chapter 4; and Dawkins in the e-Pages.) A more accurate conception is that rules of writing depend on the situation—**audience** (potential readers), purpose (what you are trying to accomplish), **exigence** (what caused you to write in the first place), and **context** (the situation in which the writing is taking place).
- Writing can convey facts without "spin" and thus transmit information without changing it. (See Kantz as well as Haas and Flower, both in Chapter 3.) A more accurate conception is that there is no way to directly transmit information; when we write something, we bring our own ideas, experiences, and biases to it, and when you read something, you do the same. Thus, writers and readers **construct** meaning together.
- Texts inherently "mean" something all on their own, regardless of who's reading them. (See Haas and Flower in Chapter 3, and Penrose and Geisler as well as Sosnoski, both in the e-Pages.) A more accurate conception, again, is that readers make meaning when they read a text; when two different people read the same text, they often understand it in completely different ways.
- You can write without putting yourself in the text—that is, you can write objectively or "impersonally." (See Greene in this Introduction and Murray, Villanueva, and Strasser, each in Chapter 1.) A more accurate conception is that writers can never fully take themselves out of what they are writing; their previous experiences and ideas affect what they write and how they write it, in ways small and large.

- It is easy to distinguish which ideas are a writer's "own" and which they "borrowed" from others, and failing to make this distinction is plain and simple plagiarism. (See Porter and Martin, both in Chapter 3, and Kohl in Chapter 5.) A more accurate conception is that all writers borrow language and ideas, directly or indirectly, for everything they write, and that there is no way to avoid doing so. Completely citing everything we have borrowed would not be possible.
- Writing is mostly about getting the grammar right, so what makes writing good is largely just simple and basic rules of English syntax. (See Swales in Chapter 2, Grant-Davie in Chapter 3, Winsor in Chapter 4, and Gee in the e-Pages.) A more accurate conception is that writing is about making meaning, sharing ideas, getting things done. "Rules" are actually **conventions**, agreements between groups of readers and writers that can differ by situation, and getting them right or wrong has different consequences in each situation.

Readings in this book are intended to challenge your everyday ideas about writing; they suggest that writing is much more complicated (and interesting) when we actually pay close attention to how texts work and what readers and writers are doing when they engage them. These readings also suggest that, as a writer and a reader, you usually have a great deal more power, and are less controlled by universal, mysterious rules, than you may have been taught. You can construct different ideas about writing, and construct meaning for yourself in ways that can empower you as a writer. And you can choose to operate using different constructions (conceptions) of writing.

Let's consider this word, *construct*, a little further.

## Constructs

Writers *construct* texts by using words and images to develop ideas, and readers *construct* a variety of meanings for a text by bringing their personal experiences and understandings to a text. In this usage, *construct* is a verb. It suggests actions that writers and readers take.

But *construct* is not only a verb (conSTRUCT); it is also a noun (CONstruct). **Constructs** (noun) are mental frameworks that people build in order to make sense of the world around them.

Do you remember the movie *The Matrix*? In that movie, people did not realize they were living in a constructed fantasy. One of the key features of an effective construct is that it seems "natural" or inevitable, rather than made up. The world people saw in *The Matrix* was a construct (the characters even called it that!), but they could not see their world as constructed until they took a red pill that enabled them to see things differently.

Many of the things we believe about writing are constructs, too—and we hope that this book can function as a sort of "red pill" to help you see writing constructs *as* constructs rather than believing that they are *inevitably* true or real.

The ideas in the previous bulleted list are all examples of constructs of writing. For example, most students in the United States are taught that reusing any part of any text in their own texts is **plagiarism** unless they carefully cite and document the original sources, and they're taught that their writing isn't "theirs" if anyone else works on or helps them on it. Yet in most U.S. workplaces, texts are routinely reused and copied from earlier publications with little or no acknowledgement, and collaborative writing in which individual writers' contributions aren't clearly acknowledged (ghost-writing) is routine. Our cultural construct of "plagiarism" seems out of step with this other reality.

Another construct you'll encounter is the idea that **writing** equals **grammar**, so that what makes writing "good" is the simple question of whether its grammar is correct. Yet the closer we look at writing, the more we realize that different audiences perceive different kinds of quality in the same texts, depending on the situation in which they're reading and on their identity as readers. Engineers and English professors might look at the same piece of writing and, because they value different qualities in writing, have conflicting opinions about whether it's good writing or not. Clearly, there's more at work than just grammar.

Not all constructs are negative misconceptions, though. Another construct that's heavily emphasized in this book is one we call **rhetoric**. *Rhetoric* is typically used to describe both the language that speakers and writers (or **rhetors**) use to communicate and get things done, and the *study of* that language. **Rhetorical** theory helps us understand how readers interpret texts, how rhetors (speakers and writers) construct texts persuasively, how readers and writers construct meaning from texts, and how the "rules" for writing vary with writers' and readers' **rhetorical situations** and needs. The ideas from rhetorical theory that you'll encounter throughout this book contradict nearly all the simple myths above about how writing works, and so rhetoric becomes an important construct for you to carry with you as you experience writing and reading both in other college classes and after school.

Considering constructs about writing, assessing whether your ideas about writing are misconceptions might be difficult at times, and will require you to be willing to really think through ideas that might be uncomfortable. The reason this might happen is because much of what the book is asking you to do is examine "threshold concepts" from the field of Writing Studies—that is, ideas we have about writing that people who don't think about writing for a living might not share or immediately understand. However, if you can grapple with these concepts, we think that you will be a much more effective and empowered writer.

Because the experiences you might have while reading this book may be challenging, we want to prepare you for them by assuring you that difficulty is a normal part of learning. So we'll say a little more here about the experience of learning "threshold concepts."

## Threshold Concepts

Some ideas literally change the way you experience, think about, and understand a subject. Researchers call these special ideas **threshold concepts**. Every specialized field of study (or "discipline"—like history, biology, mathematics, etc.) has threshold concepts that learners in that field must become acquainted with in order to fully understand the ideas of that field of study. People learn these threshold concepts at different times, and different people, depending on their goals, need to learn more or fewer of them. For example, an English major who is taking one biology class to fulfill her general education science requirement doesn't need to learn many of the most difficult threshold concepts of biology. But a biology major must learn more. And a biology graduate student must learn even more. In order to go out and do the work of a biologist, there are ideas that must be learned, thresholds that must be crossed. The threshold concepts in this book are ones related to writing that we think will help you even if you never take another writing class and have no intention of being a writing major. Everyone writes in some aspect of their lives, so this book focuses on the threshold concepts about writing that are relevant to every writer, not just writing majors, writing graduate students, or professional writers.

Threshold concepts, once learned, help the learner see the world differently. They can be hard to learn (what researchers Jan Meyer and Ray Land call "troublesome") for a variety of reasons, including because they might directly conflict with ideas you already have. Once you're aware of these new and troublesome threshold concepts and you really start to understand them, they are hard to unlearn—Meyer and Land say they are "irreversible." Very often, learning threshold concepts doesn't just change the way you think about the subject, but also the way you think about yourself. But what makes them most powerful is that they help you understand a whole set of other ideas that are hard to imagine without knowing the threshold concept—so they let you do a whole lot of learning at once by helping entire sets of ideas "fall into place."

Threshold concepts are discipline-specific, and we don't know what background you as a specific reader actually have, so it's hard to give examples of threshold concepts that we know most of our readers will recognize. But, here's a try: Many of you have sufficient mathematics background to have learned that fractions, ratios, decimals, and percentages aren't actually different "things," but just different ways to express *parts in relation to wholes*—and so is division (which is why fractions are basically just a frozen division problem, so that the fraction 3/4 is also literally "three divided by four"). If you can remember the moment when you realized that a fraction is, say, just another way to write a percentage, which is just another way to write division, and if learning that helped you approach math problems differently, then you know what a threshold concept is. A teacher might have tried to explain this idea to you numerous times while you stared blankly, unable to understand. One day, though, you might have had an experience that helped you start to comprehend her point. And eventually you crossed the threshold and could see this threshold concept at work whenever you were presented with math problems of various kinds.

That experience is an important one to remember about what it is like to learn threshold concepts: Learning them takes time, sometimes you might feel like you will never understand them, sometimes you might think you understand only to lose that feeling the next day. That is a normal part of learning threshold concepts, and you should be patient with yourself throughout this book; the learning will come, but sometimes it takes awhile.

You might already be able to guess, based on our earlier descriptions of conceptions and constructs, some of the threshold concepts about writing you will encounter in this book. But we'd like to go ahead and spell them out for you here so that you can be expecting them, and start to mull them over—and be prepared and not surprised if you struggle when you encounter them in the various chapters.

- Chapter 1, "Literacies: Where Do Your Ideas about Reading and Writing Come From?," engages the threshold concept that *writing performance is informed by prior literacy experiences*, or in simpler terms, your reading and writing past will shape your reading and writing present. That might seem obvious—what we've learned previously always shapes what we do now, right? But the readings in that chapter will take you beyond the obvious, to show you some influences on your current reading and writing that you probably haven't been aware of. Once you are, you'll realize how those previous influences impact you, and whether you want to seek out other experiences or try to lessen the effects of previous experiences.

- Chapter 2, "Individual in Community: How Do Texts Mediate Activities?," will help you encounter the threshold concept that *writing mediates activity*. In other words, that writing gets things done, makes things happen. Right now, you're probably used to thinking of writing (both the action and the texts it leads to) as pretty isolated—you write a text and it's just this paper that stands on its own. We're going to ask you to think about questions like this: How does the paper you write for a class actually make *the entire school system* possible? Your paper isn't standing on its own; it's participating in and creating the class you're in, the school you attend, and the degree you earn. This chapter will explain how that works.
- Chapter 3, "Rhetoric: How Is Meaning Constructed in Context?," will be your introduction to some underlying principles of rhetoric; for example, that good *writing is completely dependent on the situation, readers, and uses it's being created for*. Right now, if your teacher asked you, "What makes writing good?," how would you respond? Most people who don't have the threshold concept of rhetoric will offer answers like "clarity," "conciseness," "directness," "error-free," "correct grammar," or "flow." Once you think in terms of rhetoric, the answer is, "It depends on the readers' needs, values, and expectations, the circumstances in which the text is being written, and what it needs to be used for." Not all writing needs to be "clear," or "concise," or "error-free." *It depends* on who's using it and what they are using it for.
- Chapter 4, "Processes: How Are Texts Composed?," will lead you to a number of threshold concepts about writing: that writing is *knowledge-making*, that making knowledge requires ongoing and repeating *processes*, and that *writing is not perfectible*. Again, if you already have any of these threshold concepts under control, then you know how different writing looks once you know them than before you did. But if these are new ideas to you, you're probably asking either, "What are you talking about?" or "What's the big deal? Isn't it obvious that writing is knowledge-making?" Actually, it's not: Our culture tends to tell us that writing is knowledge-*transmitting*: You take something you already know, "write it down," and then if the ideas "get across to" your reader unaltered, so that the readers think exactly what you did, that's successful writing. To know that writing is knowledge-*making*, you have to recognize that you cannot actually write what you think without *changing* what you think in the process—the act of writing actually creates new ideas. That's just one example of the ideas about writing process you'll encounter in this chapter.
- Chapter 5, "Multimodal Composition: What Counts as Writing?," emphasizes the threshold concept that *writing is by nature a technology*. Writing involves tools, and writing is not "natural" (in a biological sense). Again, you might be asking, "Huh?" or "So what?" Most people don't think of a number 2 pencil as technology—but it is. And most people don't know how difficult and unlikely writing actually is for humans to do—unlike language and speech, which are biological and natural. As you read this chapter and start realizing all the implications of the technological nature of writing, you'll likely start understanding writing very differently.

Ultimately, *Writing about Writing* does much of its work of helping you better understand the nature and activity of writing—and thus to change your own approaches to, habits of, and strategies for writing—by bringing you in contact with a wide range of these threshold concepts.

# What's in This Book, and Where Does It Come From?

Almost all of the individual pieces in this book have been published someplace else before. In most cases, they were published in scholarly journals and books—where expert writing researchers are telling each other about studies they've conducted on writing (and literacy, language, discourse, and technology) and what they've found.

This kind of research about writing is actually relatively new, although human communication broadly has been philosophized about for thousands of years. Originally—in the oldest written records we have on the subject, which go back close to three thousand years—philosophers and rhetoricians (people who study rhetoric) studied oration and persuasion. Writing back then was extremely rare because it was difficult and expensive, done by specialists only (scribes, who were basically clerks). Writing got a lot easier throughout the late Middle Ages and Renaissance with the invention of less expensive papers and inks, and especially the printing press. In the following centuries, writing and printing got *so* cheap and easy that oratory began to take a back seat to writing. By the 1800s, schools began to de-emphasize oratory and increase the teaching of writing. Until then, there hadn't been a lot of research on writing *as writing*. But once college professors had to teach writing, it started to become clear that they needed to research the best *ways of* teaching it. They started doing that in the late 1800s and early 1900s. And in doing that, it became clear that they also needed a better understanding of writing itself—the nature of it, how it worked, what successful writers actually did.

Until that point, there wasn't a clearly identifiable "field" or "discipline" of *writing* as such. But in the early 1960s, a number of events and the publication of some major research helped the study of writing become distinct from the study of literature, the study of speech communication, and the study of language (linguistics). What did these researchers want to know about writing that they really didn't yet? Actually, many of their questions parallel the chapters in this book. What do we believe to be true about writing, and where do these beliefs come from? Do writers get their ideas through inspiration or through the world around them, or both (in what balance)? How does meaning depend on context? How does the shape a text takes depend on its rhetorical situation? How to writers actually get writing done? And how can we tell the difference between writing and other kinds of communication like photo-essays and pictorial instruction manuals—what counts as writing? You'll see these and other themes and concerns arising regularly in the articles and chapters reprinted in *Writing about Writing*.

Because anyone who writes (and that's everyone in high school and college) has direct, personal experience with writing, *everyone* has something to say and the grounds to research questions about writing, if they wish. To demonstrate that point, we've included in the book a selection of research articles written by undergraduate college students like you. Many, in fact, were written in exactly the same kind of class in which you're now reading this book. It is important for you to see what writing research can look like when it's done by student researchers and writers; but it is also important for you to see that these student-researchers are asking and answering questions that older, more experienced researchers aren't. The moral of the story is that *your ideas matter, too*, when it comes to writing research.

## Making Sense of the Readings

Reading texts that are written by expert researchers for other experts is not easy even for your instructors, and they won't be easy or quick reading for you at first, either. We've created *Writing about Writing* to make sure that the time you spend with the readings is worthwhile and will lead you to new insights and more successful writing experiences. To help you, we have some advice on how to approach the readings:

- Leave plenty of time for reading. These aren't pieces that you'll be able to sit down and skim in fifteen minutes, as you may be able to with material in a traditional textbook. Know that you'll need an hour or two, so give yourself that time. You'll find yourself less frustrated with the time reading can take if you *expect* it to take that time.
- Consciously connect at least *some* part of each piece you read to your own experience as a writer. The readings have been chosen specifically to allow you to do that. You'll understand them best in the moments you can say, "Oh, that sounds like what I do"—or, "That's actually not what I do at all—I do this instead."
- Read the backstory of each piece, which you'll find in the "Framing the Readings" sections. These introductions give you background knowledge necessary to more fully understand the pieces themselves.
- Look up any boldface terms in the glossary before you dive into the reading. Terms that we anticipate you'll need background on we include in the "Framing" section and bold so that you know you can find information on it in the glossary. Don't forget that's there.
- Use the activities and questions in the "Getting Ready to Read" section to help you focus your reading and develop additional background knowledge that may help you make the clearest sense of the texts. Often we've chosen these to get your brain turning on a specific subject so that when you encounter it in the reading, you've already been thinking about it.
- Look over the "Questions for Journaling and Discussion," "Applying and Exploring Ideas," and "Meta Moments" *before* you read, so that you can get a further sense of where we suggest you focus your attention. This should help you be *selective* in your attention, rather than trying to read every word in the article in equal depth.
- Read with your favorite search engine and Wikipedia at hand so you can get instant definitions and background, and so that you can learn more about the authors by quickly researching them.
- Don't automatically read the piece straight through in order. First, skim through it and write down any bold headings so that you can see the flow of topics in the piece. If the piece has a clearly marked introduction or opening section, start there, but then consider moving to the conclusion, if that closing section is clearly marked. Reading this way can give you the "big picture" of the piece, so that when you read the middle parts, you have a clearer sense of the overall argument the writer is trying to make, and where he or she is going.
- When you get bogged down in phrases, lines, or paragraphs that you just can't make sense of, try *reading more quickly*. Often, when you can't make sense of

a particular line, it's because you don't yet have enough information on the new subject to "connect" it to. If you skim ahead to a point in the article where things start to make sense to you again, you can more quickly build that "big picture" that will let you make more sense of the individual lines that are hard for you.

- Plan to reread parts of the article once or twice. That's good, responsible reading, not a lack of ability or success. Your brain works by hooking new knowledge to existing knowledge. If *all* the knowledge in a piece is new, you need to read a piece to make some of it "old" in order to have a place to hang the rest of the new knowledge. That's why we often have to reread.

- Don't feel like you're doing poorly just because you don't understand the piece well. Your instructors encounter readings *all the time* that they have difficulty understanding—that's how you know you're stretching your knowledge and growing. It's okay not to have complete clarity; if we couldn't accept that, we'd never be able to learn anything new. What you really want is to finish a piece, having worked hard on it, and be able to say "Here are the parts that made sense to me, and here are the parts I still don't understand and want to talk about more." Even if you write down only a few things that you understood and many more that you didn't, that's okay—you're doing what you're supposed to, and you *are* learning.

- Remember that sometimes you only learn things, or realize you've learned them, long after the initial encounter. In other words, when you finish a text with a certain level of understanding, you can expect that as you go on and read other texts, ideas in them will continue to clarify aspects of the first text that you hadn't understood yet. That, too, is a natural part of learning.

To help you get through some of the more difficult research-based readings in the text, we would like to introduce you to John Swales's "CARS model" of research introductions. John Swales is a linguist who analyzed thousands of introductions to academic research articles and discovered that they all made similar "moves" to "create a research space" (CARS). Swales wrote a book in which he explained this and other ways that academic research articles are similarly constructed. Knowing the common "moves" in research introductions will help you understand how academic writers construct the introductions to their research articles. This will help you know where to look for parts of the article that will help you quickly make sense of it.

# "Create a Research Space" (CARS) Model of Research Introductions[1]

## JOHN SWALES

Sometimes getting through the introduction of a research article can be the most difficult part of reading it. In his CARS model, Swales describes three "moves" that almost all research introductions make. We're providing a summary of Swales's model here as a kind of shorthand to help you in both reading research articles and writing them. Identifying these moves in introductions to the articles you read in this book will help you understand the authors' projects better from the outset. When you write your own papers, making the same moves yourself will help you present your own arguments clearly and convincingly. So read through the summary now, but be sure to return to it often for help in understanding the selections in the rest of the book.

## Move 1: Establishing a Territory

In this move, the author sets the context for his or her research, providing necessary background on the topic. This move includes one or more of the following steps:

### Step 1: Claiming Centrality

The author asks the **discourse community** (the audience for the paper) to accept that the research about to be reported is part of a lively, significant, or well-established research area. To claim centrality the author might write:

> "Recently there has been a spate of interest in . . ."

> "Knowledge of X has great importance for . . ."

This step is used widely across the academic disciplines, though less in the physical sciences than in the social sciences and the humanities.

and/or

### Step 2: Making Topic Generalizations

The author makes statements about current knowledge, practices, or phenomena in the field. For example:

---

[1]Adapted from John M. Swales's *Genre Analysis: English in Academic and Research Settings*. Cambridge: Cambridge UP, 1990.

"The properties of X are still not completely understood."

"X is a common finding in patients with . . ."

and/or

### Step 3: Reviewing Previous Items of Research

The author relates what has been found on the topic and who found it. For example:

"Both Johnson and Morgan claim that the biographical facts have been misrepresented."

"Several studies have suggested that . . . (Gordon, 2003; Ratzinger, 2009)."

"Reading to children early and often seems to have a positive long-term correlation with grades in English courses (Jones, 2002; Strong, 2009)."

In citing the research of others, the author may use *integral citation* (citing the author's name in the sentence, as in the first example above) or *non-integral citation* (citing the author's name in parentheses only, as in the second and third examples above). The use of different types of verbs (e.g., *reporting verbs* such as "shows" or "claims") and verb tenses (past, present perfect, or present) varies across disciplines.

## Move 2: Establishing a Niche

In this move, the author argues that there is an open "niche" in the existing research, a space that needs to be filled through additional research. The author can establish a niche in one of four ways:

### Counter-claiming

The author refutes or challenges earlier research by making a counter-claim. For example:

"While Jones and Riley believe X method to be accurate, a close examination demonstrates their method to be flawed."

### Indicating a Gap

The author demonstrates that earlier research does not sufficiently address all existing questions or problems. For example:

"While existing studies have clearly established X, they have not addressed Y."

### Question-raising

The author asks questions about previous research, suggesting that additional research needs to be done. For example:

"While Jones and Morgan have established X, these findings raise a number of questions, including . . ."

## Continuing a Tradition

The author presents the research as a useful extension of existing research. For example:

"Earlier studies seemed to suggest X. To verify this finding, more work is urgently needed."

## Move 3: Occupying a Niche

In this move, the author turns the niche established in Move 2 into the *research space* that he or she will fill; that is, the author demonstrates how he or she will substantiate the counter-claim made, fill the gap identified, answer the question(s) asked, or continue the research tradition. The author makes this move in several steps, described below. The initial step (1A or 1B) is obligatory, though many research articles stop after that step.

### Step 1A: Outlining Purposes

The author indicates the main purpose(s) of the current article. For example:

"In this article I argue . . ."

"The present research tries to clarify . . ."

or

### Step 1B: Announcing Present Research

The author describes the research in the current article. For example:

"This paper describes three separate studies conducted between March 2008 and January 2009."

### Step 2: Announcing Principal Findings

The author presents the main conclusions of his or her research. For example:

"The results of the study suggest . . ."

"When we examined X, we discovered . . ."

### Step 3: Indicating the Structure of the Research Article

The author previews the organization of the article. For example:

"This paper is structured as follows . . ."

# Another Kind of Reading: Peer Texts

In addition to reading the research about writing contained in this book, the writing class you are enrolled in is very likely to ask you to engage in another kind of reading: reading the drafts created by your classmates. This kind of reading will ask for a different sort of approach and response. You'll need to read carefully for understanding, but then also work to help your peer improve his or her text. To help you do that, we've included here a short reading by Professor Richard Straub written directly to students regarding how to respond to their classmate's writing.

# Responding—Really Responding—to Other Students' Writing

## RICHARD STRAUB

■ Straub, Richard. "Responding—Really Responding—to Other Students' Writing." *The Subject Is Writing*. Ed. Wendy Bishop. Portsmouth, NH: Boynton/Cook, 136–46. Print.

### Framing the Reading

Richard Straub was an Associate Professor of English at Florida State University prior to his untimely death in 2002. His special area of research interest was responding to student writing. He wrote a number of articles and books on how teachers can respond effectively to student writing in order to help students grow and improve. The short piece you will read here takes what Straub learned about responding to writing and explains it directly to students. It was originally published in a textbook for first-year students, so you'll see that he speaks directly to you, giving you explicit advice about what to do.

### Getting Ready to Read

*Before you read*, do the following activity:

- Consider your experiences with "peer review." What has gone wrong? What has gone well? What is your attitude about peer review?

*As you read*, consider the following question:

- Does Straub's advice set up peer review differently than your previous experiences did?

Okay. You've got a student paper you have to read and make comments on for Thursday. It's not something you're looking forward to. But that's alright, you think. There isn't really all that much to it. Just keep it simple. Read it quickly and mark whatever you see. Say something about the introduction. Something about details and examples. Ideas you can say you like. Mark any typos and spelling errors. Make your comments

brief. Abbreviate where possible: *awk. Good intro, give ex, frag.* Try to imitate the teacher. Mark what he'd mark and sound like he'd sound. But be cool about it. Don't praise anything really, but no need to get harsh or cut throat either. Get in and get out. You're okay. I'm okay. Everybody's happy. What's the problem?

This is, no doubt, a way of getting through the assignment. Satisfy the teacher   2 and no surprises for the writer. It might just do the trick. But say you want to do a *good* job. Say you're willing to put in the time and effort—though time is tight and you know it's not going to be easy—and help the writer look back on the paper and revise it. And maybe in the process learn something more yourself about writing. What do you look for? How do you sound? How much do you take up? What exactly are you trying to accomplish? Here are some ideas.

## How Should You Look at Yourself as a Responder?

Consider yourself a friendly reader. A test pilot. A roommate who's been asked   3 to look over the paper and tell the writer what you think. Except you don't just take on the role of The Nice Roommate or The Ever-faithful Friend and tell her what she wants to hear. *This all looks good. I wouldn't change a thing. There are a couple places that I think he might not like, but I can see what you're doing there. I'd go with it. Good stuff.* You're supportive. You give her the benefit of the doubt and look to see the good in her writing. But friends don't let friends think their writing is the best thing since *The Great Gatsby* and they don't lead them to think that all is fine and well when it's not. Look to help this friend, this roommate writer—okay, this person in your class—to get a better piece of writing. Point to problems and areas for improvement but do it in a constructive way. See what you can do to push her to do even more than she's done and stretch herself as a writer.

## What Are Your Goals?

First, don't set out to seek and destroy all errors and problems in the writing.   4 You're not an editor. You're not a teacher. You're not a cruise missile. And don't rewrite any parts of the paper. You're not the writer; you're a reader. One of many. The paper is not yours; it's the writer's. She writes. You read. She is in charge of what she does to her writing. That doesn't mean you can't make suggestions. It doesn't mean you can't offer a few sample rewrites here and there, as models. But make it clear they're samples, models. Not rewrites. Not edits. Not corrections. Be reluctant at first even to say what you would do if the paper were yours. It's not yours. Again; Writers write, readers read and show what they're understanding and maybe make suggestions. What to do instead: Look at your task as a simple one. You're there to play back to the writer how you read the paper: what you got from it; what you found interesting; where you were confused; where you wanted more. With this done, you can go on to point out problems, ask questions, offer advice, and wonder out loud with the writer about her ideas. Look to help her improve the writing or encourage her to work on some things as a writer.

## How Do You Get Started?

Before you up and start reading the paper, take a minute (alright, thirty sec-  5
onds) to make a mental checklist about the circumstances of the writing, the
context. You're not going to just read a text. You're going to read a text within
a certain context, a set of circumstances that accompany the writing and that
you bring to your reading. It's one kind of writing or another, designed for one
audience and purpose or another. It's a rough draft or a final draft. The writer
is trying to be serious or casual, straight or ironic. Ideally, you'll read the paper
with an eye to the circumstances that it was written in and the situation it is
looking to create. That means looking at the writing in terms of the assignment, the writer's particular interests and aims, the work you've been doing in
class, and the stage of drafting.

- *The assignment:* What kind of writing does the assignment call (or allow)
  for? Is the paper supposed to be a personal essay? A report? An analysis?
  An argument? Consider how well the paper before you meets the demands of the kind of writing the writer is taking up.
- *The writer's interests and aims:* What does the writer want to accomplish?
  If she's writing a personal narrative, say, is she trying to simply recount a
  past experience? Is she trying to recount a past experience and at the same
  time amuse her readers? Is she trying to show a pleasant experience on the
  surface, yet suggest underneath that everything was not as pleasant as it
  seems? Hone in on the writer's particular aims in the writing.
- *The work of the class:* Try to tie your comments to the concepts and
  strategies you've been studying in class. If you've been doing a lot of work
  on using detail, be sure to point to places in the writing where the writer
  uses detail effectively or where she might provide richer detail. If you've
  been working on developing arguments through examples and sample
  cases, indicate where the writer might use such methods to strengthen her
  arguments. If you've been considering various ways to sharpen the style
  of your sentences, offer places where the writer can clarify her sentence
  structure or arrange a sentence for maximum impact. The best comments
  will ring familiar even as they lead the writer to try to do something she
  hasn't quite done before, or done in quite the same way. They'll be comforting and understandable even as they create some need to do more, a
  need to figure out some better way.
- *The stage of drafting:* Is it an early draft? A full but incomplete draft?
  A nearly final draft? Pay attention to the stage of drafting. Don't try to
  deal with everything all at once if it's a first, rough draft. Concentrate on
  the large picture: the paper's focus; the content; the writer's voice. Don't
  worry about errors and punctuation problems yet. There'll be time for
  them later. If it's closer to a full draft, go ahead and talk, in addition to the
  overall content, about arrangement, pacing, and sentence style. Wait till
  the final draft to give much attention to fine-tuning sentences and dealing
  in detail with proofreading. Remember: You're not an editor. Leave these
  sentence revisions and corrections for the writer. It's her paper. And she's
  going to learn best by detecting problems and making her own changes.

## What to Address in Your Comments?

Try to focus your comments on a couple of areas of writing. Glance through 6
the paper quickly first. Get an idea whether you'll deal mostly with the overall
content and purpose of the writing, its shape and flow, or (if these are more
or less in order) with local matters of paragraph structure, sentence style, and
correctness. Don't try to cover everything that comes up or even all instances
of a given problem. Address issues that are most important to address in this
paper, at this time.

## Where to Put Your Comments?

Some teachers like to have students write comments in the margins right next 7
to the passage. Some like to have students write out their comments in an
end note or in a separate letter to the writer. I like to recommend using both
marginal comments and a note or letter at the end. The best of both worlds.
Marginal comments allow you to give a quick moment-by-moment reading of
the paper. They make it easy to give immediate and specific feedback. You still
have to make sure you specify what you're talking about and what you have
to say, but they save you some work telling the writer what you're addressing and allow you to focus your end note on things that are most important.
Comments at the end allow you to provide some perspective on your response.
This doesn't mean that you have to size up the paper and give it a thumbs up
or a thumbs down. You can use the end comment to emphasize the key points
of your response, explain and elaborate on issues you want to deal with more
fully, and mention additional points that you don't want to address in detail.
One thing to avoid: plastering comments all over the writing; in between and
over the lines of the other person's writing—up, down, and across the page.
Write in your space, and let the writer keep hers.

## How to Sound?

Not like a teacher. Not like a judge. Not like an editor or critic or shotgun 8
(Wouldn't you want someone who was giving you comments not to sound like
a teacher's red pen, a judge's ruling, an editor's impatience, a critic's wrath, a
shotgun's blast?) Sound like you normally sound when you're speaking with a
friend or acquaintance. Talk to the writer. You're not just marking up a text;
you're responding to the writer. You're a reader, a helper, a colleague. Try to
sound like someone who's a reader, who's helpful, and who's collegial. Supportive. And remember: Even when you're tough and demanding you can still
be supportive.

## How Much to Comment?

Don't be stingy. Write most of your comments out in full statements. Instead of 9
writing two or three words, write seven or eight. Instead of making only one
brief comment and moving on, say what you have to say and then go back over

the statement and explain what you mean or why you said it or note other alternatives. Let the writer know again and again how you are understanding her paper, what you take her to be saying. And elaborate on your key comments, Explain your interpretations, problems, questions, and advice.

## Is It Okay to Be Short and Sweet?

No. At least not most of the time. Get specific. Don't rely on general statements alone. How much have generic comments helped you as a writer? "Add detail." "Needs better structure." "Unclear." Try to let the writer know what exactly the problem is. Refer specifically to the writer's words and make them a part of your comments. "Add some detail on what it was like working at the beach." "I think we'll need to know more about your high school crowd before we can understand the way you've changed." "This sentence is not clear. Were *you* disappointed or were *they* disappointed?" This way the writer will see what you're talking about, and she'll have a better idea what to work on.     10

## Do You Praise or Criticize or What?

Be always of two (or three) minds about your response to the paper. You like the paper, but it could use some more interesting detail. You found this statement interesting, but these ideas in the second paragraph are not so hot. It's an alright paper, but it could be outstanding if the writer said what was really bothering her. Always be ready to praise. But always look to point to places that are not working well or that are not yet working as well as they might. Always be ready to expect more from the writer.     11

## How to Present Your Comments?

Don't steer away from being critical. Feel free—in fact, feel obliged—to tell the writer what you like and don't like, what is and is not working, and where you think it can be made to work better. But use some other strategies, too. Try to engage the writer in considering her choices and thinking about possible ways to improve the paper. Make it a goal to write two or three comments that look to summarize or paraphrase what the writer is saying. Instead of *telling* the reader what to do, *suggest* what she might do. Identify the questions that are raised for you as you reader:     12

- Play back your way of understanding the writing:
    This seems to be the real focus of the paper, the issue you seem
        most interested in.
    So you're saying that you really weren't interested in her
        romantically?

- Temper your criticisms:
    This sentence is a bit hard to follow.
    I'm not sure this paragraph is necessary.

- Offer advice:

    It might help to add an example here.

    Maybe save this sentence for the end of the paper.

- Ask questions, especially real questions:

    What else were you feeling at the time?

    What kind of friend? Would it help to say?

    Do you need this opening sentence?

    In what ways were you "a daddy's little girl"?

- Explain and follow up on your initial comments:

    You might present this episode first. This way we can see what you
        mean when you say that he was always too busy.

    How did you react? Did you cry or yell? Did you walk away?

    This makes her sound cold and calculating. Is that what you want?

- Offer some praise, and then explain to the writer why the writing works:

    Good opening paragraph. You've got my attention.

    Good detail. It tells me a lot about the place.

    I like the descriptions you provide—for instance, about your grand-
        mother cooking, at the bottom of page 1; about her house. in the
        middle of page 2; and about how she said her rosary at night:
        "quick but almost pleading, like crying without tears."

## How Much Criticism? How Much Praise?

Challenge yourself to write as many praise comments as criticisms. When you    13
praise, praise well. Think about it. Sincerity and specificity are everything when
it comes to a compliment.

## How Much Should You Be Influenced by What You Know About the Writer?

Consider the person behind the writer when you make your comments. If she's    14
not done so well in class lately, maybe you can give her a pick-me-up in your
comments. If she's shy and seems reluctant to go into the kind of personal
detail the paper seems to need, encourage her. Make some suggestions or tell
her what you would do. If she's confident and going on arrogant, see what you
can do to challenge her with the ideas she presents in the paper. Look for other
views she may not have thought about, and find ways to lead her to consider
them. Always be ready to look at the text in terms of the writer behind the text.

Good comments, this listing shows, require a lot from a reader. But you    15
don't have to make a checklist out of these suggestions and go through each
one methodically as you read. It's amazing how they all start coming together
when you look at your response as a way of talking with the writer seriously
about the writing, recording how you experience the words on the page and

giving the writer something to think about for revision. The more you see examples of thoughtful commentary and the more you try to do it yourself, the more you'll get a feel for how it's done.

Here's a set of student comments on a student paper. They were done in the 16 last third of a course that focused on the personal essay and concentrated on helping students develop the content and thought of their writing. The class had been working on finding ways to develop and extend the key statements of their essays (by using short, representative details, full-blown examples, dialogue, and multiple perspectives) and getting more careful about selecting and shaping parts of their writing. The assignment called on students to write an essay or an autobiographical story where they looked to capture how they see (or have seen) something about one or both of their parents—some habits, attitudes, or traits their parents have taken on. They were encouraged to give shape to their ideas and experiences in ways that went beyond their previous understandings and try things they hadn't tried in their writing. More a personal narrative than an essay, Todd's paper looks to capture one distinct difference in the way his mother and father disciplined their children. It is a rough draft that will be taken through one or possibly two more revisions. Readers were asked to offer whatever feedback they could that might help the writer with the next stage of writing (Figure 14–1).

This is a full and thoughtful set of comments. The responder, Jeremy, creates 17 himself not as a teacher or critic but first of all as a reader, one who is intent on saying how he takes the writing and what he'd like to hear more about:

> Good point Makes it more unlikely that you should be the one to get caught. Great passage. Really lets the reader know what you were thinking. Was there a reason you were first or did it just happen that way? Would he punish you anyway or could you just get away with things?

He makes twenty-two comments on the paper—seventeen statements in the margins and five more in the end note. The comments are written out in full statements, and they are detailed and specific. They make his response into lively exchange with the writer, one person talking with another about what he's said. Well over half of the comments are follow-up comments that explain, illustrate, or qualify other responses.

The comments focus on the content and development of the writing, in line 18 with the assignment, the stage of drafting, and the work of the course. They also view the writing rhetorically, in terms of how the text has certain effects on readers. Although there are over two dozen wording or sentence-level errors in the paper, he decides, wisely, to stick with the larger matters of writing. Yet even as he offers a pretty full set of comments he doesn't ever take control over the text. His comments are placed unobtrusively on the page, and he doesn't try to close things down or decide things for the writer. He offers praise, encouragement, and direction. What's more, he pushes the writer to do more than he has already done, to extend the boundaries of his examination. In keeping with the assignment and the larger goals of the course, he calls on Todd in several comments to explore the motivations and personalities behind his parents' different ways of disciplining:

Figure 14–1

Jeremy
Todd
ENG 1
Rick Straub
Assign 8b

"Uh, oh"

When I called home from the police station I was praying that my father would answer the phone. He would listen to what I had to say and would react comely, logical, and in a manner that would keep my mother from screaming her head off. If my Mother was to answer the phone, I would have to explain myself quickly in order to keep her from having a heart attached.

> *I like this paragraph. It immediately lets the reader relate to you and also produces a picture in the reader's mind*

When I was eleven years old I hung out with a group of boys that were almost three years older than me. The five of us did all the things that young energetic kids did playing ball, riding bikes, and getting in to trouble. [Because they were older they worried less about getting in trouble and the consequences of there actions than I did.]

> *Good point, makes it more unlikely that you should be the one to get caught*

My friends and I would always come home from school, drop our backpacks off and head out in the neighborhood to find something to do. Our favorite thing to do was to find construction cites and steal wood to make tree forts in the woods or skateboard ramps. So one day, coming home from school, we noticed a couple new houses being built near our neighborhood. It was a prime cite for wood, nails, and anything else we could get our hands on. We discussed our plan on the bus and decided that we would all meet there after dropping our stuff off at home. [I remember being a little at hesitant first because it was close to my house but beyond the boundaries my parents had set for me. Of course I went because I didn't want to be the odd man out and have to put up with all the name calling.] I dropped my bag off and I headed to the construction cite.

> *What other things did you do to get into trouble? Or is it irrelevant?*

> *great passage really lets the reader know what you were thinking*

I meet my friends there and we began to search the different houses for wood and what not. We all picked up a couple of things and were about to leave when one of my friends noticed what looked to be a big tool shed off behind of the houses. It looked promising so we decided that we should check it out. Two of the boys in the group said that they had all the wood they could carry and said they were going home. The rest of us headed down to the shed to take a look.

Once there we noticed that the shed had been broken in to previously. The lock on it had been busted on the hinges were bent. I opened the door to the shed and stepped inside to take a look while my friends waited outside. It was dark inside but I could tell the place had been ransacked, there was nothing to take so I decided to leave. I heard my friends say something so turned back around to site of them running away.

> *was there a reason you were there first or did it just happen that way*

*(continued)*

Maybe you could say more as to why you think your mom is like this. Did your dad get into trouble as a kid so he knows what it's like? Explain why he reacts as he does.

He is careful, though, not to get presumptuous and make decisions for the writer. Instead, he offers options and points to possibilities:

Perhaps more on your understanding of why your parents react as they do. What other things did you do to get into trouble? Or is it irrelevant?

From start to finish he takes on the task of reading and responding and leaves the work of writing and revising to Todd.

Jeremy's response is not in a class by itself. A set of comments to end all commentary on Todd's paper. He might have done well, for instance, to recognize how much this paper works because of the way Todd arranges the story. He could have done more to point to what's not working in the writing or what could be made to work better. He might have asked Todd for more details about his state of mind when he got caught by the policeman and while he was being held at the police station. He might have urged him more to make certain changes. He might even have said, if only in a brief warning, something about (*continued*)                                        Figure 14–1

I thought that they were playing a joke on me so I casually walked
out only to see a cop car parked near one of the houses under construction.
As soon as I saw that cop car I took off but was stopped when a big hand
pulled at the back of my shirt. I watched my friends run until they were out
of cite and then I turned around.

The cop had me sit in the cop car while he asked my questions. He
asked me if I know those kids that ran off and I said "Nnnnnooooooooo". He
asked me if I had broken into that shed and I said "Nnnnnoooooo". The cop
wrote down what I was saying all the while shaking his head. Then he told
me that I wasn't being arrested but I would have to go down to the station
to call parents and have them pick me up. Upon hearing that I nearly soiled
my undershorts. "My God, I'm dead. My mom is going to kill me".

*what else happened at the police station? how long were you there?*

At the station the officer showed me the whole station, jail cells
and everything. An obvious tactic to try and scare me, which worked. That
plus the thought of my mom answering the phone and my trying to explain
what happened nearly made me sick.

"Wwwwhhhaatttt! You're where?" She would say.

"The police station mom," uh oh, hear it comes.

"Ooooohhhh my God, my son is a criminal," so loud I would have to
pull the phone away from my ear.

*maybe you could say more as to why you think your mom is like this*

She had this uncanny ability to blow things out of proportion right
from the start. She would assume the worse and then go from there. This was
a classic example of why I could never go to her if I had any bad news. She
would start screaming, get upset, and then go bitch at my father. My father
is a pretty laid back but when ever my mother started yelling at him about
me, he would get angry and come chew me out worse than if I had just gone
to him in the first place.

If my father were to answer the phone he would respond with out
raising his voice. He would examine the situation in a logical manner and
make a decision from there.

"Uhmmm (long pause). You're at the police station."

"Yeah dad. I didn't get arrested they just had me come down here so
I had to tell you."

"Uhm, so you didn't get arrested (long pause). Well (long pause), I'll
come pick you up and will talk about then."

*Did your Dad get into trou- ble as a kid so he knows what it's like? Explain why he reacts as he does*

I feel like I can relate to my father much better than I can to my
mother. He has a cool and collective voice that can take command of any
situation. I always feel like he understands me, like he knows what I'm
thinking all the time. This comes in real handy when I get in trouble.

*would he punish you anyway or could you just get away with things*

*I like the way you use dialogue in this section to illustrate how each of your parents would reach and then explain to the reader what each of them are like, it works well.*

(*continued*)

the number of errors across the writing. But this is moot and just. Different
readers are always going to pick up on different things and respond in different
ways, and no one reading or response is going to address everything that might
well be addressed, in the way it might best be addressed. All responses are incomplete and provisional—one reader's way of reading and reacting to the text
in front of him. And any number of other responses, presented in any number
of different ways, might be as useful or maybe even more useful to Todd as he
takes up his work with the writing.

All this notwithstanding, Jeremy's comments are solid. They are full. They
are thoughtful. And they are respectful. They take the writing and the writer
seriously and address the issues that arc raised responsibly. His comments
do what commentary on student writing should optimally do. They turn the
writer back into his writing and lead him to reflect on his choices and aims, to

(*continued*)

I called home. Sweet beading on my lip.

"Hello", my mom said. Oh geez, I'm dead.

"Mom can I talk to dad?"

"Why, what's wrong?"

"Oh, nothing, I just need to talk to him," yes, this is going to work!

"Hold on," she said.

"Hello," my father said.

"Dad, I'm at the police station," I told him the whole story of what happened. He reacted exactly as I expect he would.

"Uhmm (long pause). You're at the police station..........

*I really like the ending, it tells the reader what is going to happen without having to explain it step, by step. Good paper, I like the use of dialogue. Perhaps more on your understanding of why your parents react as they do.*

consider and reconsider his intentions as a writer and the effects the words on the page will have on readers. They help him see what he can work on in revision and what he might deal with in his ongoing work as a writer.

## Sharing Ideas

- What are your experiences with responding to other students' writing? <sup>21</sup> Have you done so in other classes? How did that work out? Were you able to discuss your responses? In small groups or large groups? Which situation did you like best?

- Do you have any papers where others have responded to your writing? Collect one or more and see how the responses stack up against Rick's guidelines. Having read his essay, what would you say your respondent did well and needs to learn to do better?

- In the same way, after everyone in your small group responds to a first paper, go over those papers/responses together in a group and look at what was done and what could be done to improve the quality of responses. In addition, you might try to characterize each of you as a responder: What are your habits? What character/persona do you take on? Would you like to be responded to by the responder you find you are through this group analysis?

- Look at Hint Sheet I in this collection. How do my suggestions for response to student writers sound the same or different from Rick's suggestions? Do we come from the same "school" of responding or do we suggest different approaches? Characterize the differences or similarities you find.

- Rick shows you a responder—Jeremy—and the comments he wrote on Todd's paper. If you were Todd, how would you feel about Jeremy's responses? Do you agree with Rick's analysis of Jeremy's comments? What three or four additional things would you tell Todd about his paper?

- What are your insights into responding? What has worked for you? What do you wish people would do or not do when they respond to your writing? What would make you most inclined to listen to responses and use them to change your work?

# A Different Kind of Research and Argument

One of the biggest differences between the readings in this book and what you'd encounter in a traditional textbook is that very little of what you'll read in the rest of this book would be considered *fact*. Rather, it's *argument*. But not the kind of argument you have with a sibling over whose turn it is to take out the trash, and not the kind of argument frustrated people might have over whose fault it is that their cars collided in an intersection.

The readings here are doing a kind of research we call *scholarly inquiry*. It is, and *means to be*, imperfect, incomplete, inconclusive, and provisional. It doesn't offer easy or full answers. It is question- and problem-driven. It includes a great deal of personal opinion rather than clear, objective facts.

How can this be? The point of most scholarly inquiry isn't to gather and transmit *existing* knowledge; rather, in scholarly inquiry, researchers come together to try a lot of different approaches to the same problem, and then, through argument *as conversation*, gradually develop consensus about what the best explanation of, or solution to, the problem is.

Before you turn to Chapter 1, we'd like you to read Stuart Greene's piece "Argument as Conversation." Greene's article will help you see how the selections in the rest of the book argue differently than texts you might be more familiar with. We offer this selection as an introduction to the ongoing scholarly conversations about writing, research, and inquiry—conversations in which they, and now you, are an essential part.

# Argument as Conversation: The Role of Inquiry in Writing a Researched Argument

## STUART GREENE

■ Greene, Stuart. "Argument as Conversation: The Role of Inquiry in Writing a Researched Argument." *The Subject Is Research*. Ed. Wendy Bishop and Pavel Zemliansky. Portsmouth, NH: Boynton/Cook, 2001. 145–64. Print.

## Framing the Reading

In "Argument as Conversation," Stuart Greene explains how scholarly inquiry is a different kind of research and argument from the kinds we encounter in our everyday lives or (for most of us) in earlier schooling. The principles that Greene discusses—research as *conversational inquiry*, where an *issue* and *situation* contribute to *framing* a problem a particular way and researchers seek not to collect information but to generate new knowledge in *a social process*—are the ideas and activities that drive the entire college or university where you're studying right now. They work in every field where scholarly research is happening, from anthropology to zoology.

In this book, you'll apply these principles specifically in terms of research on writing, literacy, language, communication, and related fields. As Greene suggests in his discussion of context, you'll "weave" your experiences with research that's already been done on questions and issues related to them. The research you do on your own may even offer new insights into long-running questions about these subjects.

## Getting Ready to Read

*Before you read*, do at least one of the following activities:

- Think about how you define *argument*. How is the word used in everyday conversation? What do you think the word means in an academic setting? What's the difference between the two?
- Have a conversation with a classmate on the following topic: How would you say *argument* and *conversation* relate to each other? Can some arguments be conversational and some conversations argumentative, or is no crossover possible? Provide examples, and be sure to explain your terms as precisely as possible.

*As you read*, consider the following questions to help you focus on particularly important parts of the article:

- Who is Greene's audience? Who, in other words, is the "you" he addresses? How do you know?
- How does Greene structure his article? If you were to pull out the major headings, would the outline created from them be useful in any way?
- What kinds of support does Greene use for his claims? What other texts does he refer to? Is this support relevant to his claims and sufficient to prove them?

.................................................................................................................

Argument is very much a part of what we do every day: We confront a public issue, something that is open to dispute, and we take a stand and support what we think and feel with what we believe are good reasons. Seen in this way, argument is very much like a conversation. By this, I mean that making an argument entails providing good reasons to support your viewpoint, as well as counterarguments, and recognizing how and why readers might object to your ideas. The metaphor of conversation emphasizes the social nature of writing. Thus inquiry, research, and writing arguments are intimately related. If, for example, you are to understand the different ways others have approached your subject, then you will need to do your "homework." This is what Doug Brent (1996) means when he says that research consists of "the looking-up of facts in the context of other worldviews, other ways of seeing" (78).

In learning to argue within an academic setting, such as the one you probably find yourself in now, it is useful to think about writing as a form of inquiry in which you convey your understanding of the claims people make, the questions they raise, and the conflicts they address. As a form of inquiry, then, writing begins with problems, conflicts, and questions that you identify as important. The questions that your teacher raises and that you raise should be questions that are open to dispute and for which there are not prepackaged answers. Readers within an academic setting expect that you will advance a scholarly conversation and not reproduce others' ideas. Therefore, it is important to find out who else has confronted these problems, conflicts, and questions in order to take a stand within some ongoing scholarly conversation. You will want to read with an eye toward the claims writers make, claims that they are making with respect to you, in the sense that writers want you to think and feel in a certain way. You will want to read others' work critically, seeing if the reasons writers use to support their arguments are what you would consider good reasons. And finally, you will want to consider the possible counterarguments to the claims writers make and the views that call your own ideas into question.

*The questions that your teacher raises and that you raise should be questions that are open to dispute and for which there are not prepackaged answers.*

Like the verbal conversations you have with others, effective arguments 3
never take place in a vacuum; they take into account previous conversations
that have taken place about the subject under discussion. Seeing research as
a means for advancing a conversation makes the research process more *real*,
especially if you recognize that you will need to support your claims with evidence in order to persuade readers to agree with you. The concept and practice
of research arises out of the specific social context of your readers' questions
and skepticism.

Reading necessarily plays a prominent role in the many forms of writing 4
that you do, but not simply as a process of gathering information. This is true
whether you write personal essays, editorials, or original research based on library research. Instead, as James Crosswhite suggests in his book *The Rhetoric
of Reason*, reading "means making judgments about which of the many voices
one encounters can be brought together into productive conversation" (131).

When we sit down to write an argument intended to persuade someone to 5
do or to believe something, we are never really the first to broach the topic
about which we are writing. Thus, learning how to write a researched argument is a process of learning how to enter conversations that are already going
on in written form. This idea of writing as dialogue—not only between author
and reader but between the text and everything that has been said or written
beforehand—is important. Writing is a process of balancing our goals with the
history of similar kinds of communication, particularly others' arguments that
have been made on the same subject. The conversations that have already been
going on about a topic are the topic's historical context.

Perhaps the most eloquent statement of writing as conversation comes from 6
Kenneth Burke (1941) in an oft-quoted passage:

> Imagine that you enter a parlor. You come late. When you arrive, others have
> long preceded you, and they are engaged in a heated discussion, a discussion
> too heated for them to pause and tell you exactly what it is about. In fact the
> discussion had already begun long before any of them got there, so that no one
> present is qualified to retrace for you all the steps that had gone before. You
> listen for a while, until you decide that you have caught the tenor of the argu-
> ment; then you put in your oar. Someone answers; you answer him; another
> comes to your defense; another aligns himself against you, to either the embar-
> rassment or gratification of your opponent, depending on the quality of your
> ally's assistance. However, the discussion is interminable. The hour grows late,
> you must depart, with the discussion still vigorously in progress. (110–111)

As this passage describes, every argument you make is connected to other arguments. Every time you write an argument, the way you position yourself will
depend on three things: which previously stated arguments you share, which
previously stated arguments you want to refute, and what new opinions and
supporting information you are going to bring to the conversation. You may,
for example, affirm others for raising important issues, but assert that they
have not given those issues the thought or emphasis that they deserve. Or you
may raise a related issue that has been ignored entirely.

## Entering the Conversation

To develop an argument that is akin to a conversation, it is helpful to think of 7 writing as a process of understanding conflicts, the claims others make, and the important questions to ask, not simply as the ability to tell a story that influences readers' ways of looking at the world or to find good reasons to support our own beliefs. The real work of writing a researched argument occurs when you try to figure out the answers to the following:

- What topics have people been talking about?
- What is a relevant problem?
- What kinds of evidence might persuade readers?
- What objections might readers have?
- What is at stake in this argument? (What if things change? What if things stay the same?)

In answering these questions, you will want to read with an eye toward identifying an *issue*, the *situation* that calls for some response in writing, and framing a *question*.

### Identify an Issue

An issue is a fundamental tension that exists between two or more conflicting 8 points of view. For example, imagine that I believe that the best approach to educational reform is to change the curriculum in schools. Another person might suggest that we need to address reform by considering social and economic concerns. One way to argue the point is for each writer to consider the goals of education that they share, how to best reach those goals, and the reasons why their approach might be the best one to follow. One part of the issue is (a) that some people believe that educational reform should occur through changes in the curriculum; the second part is (b) that some people believe that reform should occur at the socioeconomic level. Notice that in defining different parts of an issue, the conflicting claims may not necessarily invalidate each other. In fact, one could argue that reform at the levels of curriculum and socioeconomic change may both be effective measures.

Keep in mind that issues are dynamic and arguments are always evolving. 9 One of my students felt that a book he was reading placed too much emphasis on school-based learning and not enough on real-world experience. He framed the issue in this way: "We are not just educated by concepts and facts that we learn in school. We are educated by the people around us and the environments that we live in every day." In writing his essay, he read a great deal in order to support his claims and did so in light of a position he was writing against: "that education in school is the most important type of education."

### Identify the Situation

It is important to frame an issue in the context of some specific situation. Whether 10 curricular changes make sense depends on how people view the problem. One kind of problem that E. D. Hirsch identified in his book *Cultural Literacy* is that students do not have sufficient knowledge of history and literature to communicate well. If that is true in a particular school, perhaps the curriculum might be changed. But there might be other factors involved that call for a different emphasis. Moreover, there are often many different ways to define an issue or frame a question. For example, we might observe that at a local high school, scores on standardized tests have steadily decreased during the past five years. This trend contrasts with scores during the ten years prior to any noticeable decline. Growing out of this situation is the broad question, "What factors have influenced the decline in standardized scores at this school?" Or one could ask this in a different way: "To what extent have scores declined as a result of the curriculum?"

The same principle applies to Anna Quindlen's argument about the home- 11 less in her commentary "No Place Like Home," which illustrates the kinds of connections an author tries to make with readers. Writing her piece as an editorial in the *New York Times*, Quindlen addresses an issue that appears to plague New Yorkers. And yet many people have come to live with the presence of homelessness in New York and other cities. This is the situation that motivates Quindlen to write her editorial: People study the problem of homelessness, yet nothing gets done. Homelessness has become a way of life, a situation that seems to say to observers that officials have declared defeat when it comes to this problem.

### Frame a Good Question

A good question can help you think through what you might be interested in 12 writing; it is specific enough to guide inquiry and meets the following criteria:

- It can be answered with the tools you have.
- It conveys a clear idea of who you are answering the question for.
- It is organized around an issue.
- It explores "how," "why," or "whether," and the "extent to which."

A good question, then, is one that can be answered given the access we have to certain kinds of information. The tools we have at hand can be people or other texts. A good question also grows out of an issue, some fundamental tension that you identify within a conversation. Through identifying what is at issue, you should begin to understand for whom it is an issue—who you are answering the question for.

## Framing as a Critical Strategy for Writing, Reading, and Doing Research

Thus far, I have presented a conversational model of argument, describing 13 writing as a form of dialogue, with writers responding to the ways others have defined problems and anticipating possible counterarguments. In this section, I want to add another element that some people call framing. This is a strategy that can help you orchestrate different and conflicting voices in advancing your argument.

Framing is a metaphor for describing the lens, or perspective, from which  14
writers present their arguments. Writers want us to see the world in one way as opposed to another, not unlike the way a photographer manipulates a camera lens to frame a picture. For example, if you were taking a picture of friends in front of the football stadium on campus, you would focus on what you would most like to remember, blurring the images of people in the background. How you set up the picture, or frame it, might entail using light and shade to make some images stand out more than others. Writers do the same with language.

For instance, in writing about education in the United States, E. D. Hirsch  15
uses the term *cultural literacy* as a way to understand a problem, in this case the decline of literacy. To say that there is a decline, Hirsch has to establish the criteria against which to measure whether some people are literate and some are not. Hirsch uses *cultural literacy* as a lens through which to discriminate between those who fulfill his criteria for literacy and those who do not. He defines *cultural literacy* as possessing certain kinds of information. Not all educators agree. Some oppose equating literacy and information, describing literacy as an *event* or as a *practice* to argue that literacy is not confined to acquiring bits of information; instead, the notion of literacy as an *event or practice* says something about how people use what they know to accomplish the work of a community. As you can see, any perspective or lens can limit readers' range of vision: readers will see some things and not others.

In my work as a writer, I have identified four reasons to use framing as a  16
strategy for developing an argument. First, framing encourages you to name your position, distinguishing the way you think about the world from the ways others do. Naming also makes what you say memorable through key terms and theories. Readers may not remember every detail of Hirsch's argument, but they recall the principle—cultural literacy—around which he organizes his details. Second, framing forces you to offer both a definition and description of the principle around which your argument develops. For example, Hirsch defines *cultural literacy* as "the possession of basic information needed to thrive in the modern world." By defining your argument, you give readers something substantive to respond to. Third, framing specifies your argument, enabling others to respond to your argument and to generate counterarguments that you will want to engage in the spirit of conversation. Fourth, framing helps you organize your thoughts, and readers', in the same way that a title for an essay, a song, or a painting does.

To extend this argument, I would like you to think about framing as a  17
strategy of critical inquiry when you read. By critical inquiry, I mean that reading entails understanding the framing strategies that writers use and using framing concepts in order to shed light on our own ideas or the ideas of others. Here I distinguish *reading as inquiry* from *reading as a search for information*. For example, you might consider your experiences as readers and

writers through the lens of Hirsch's conception of cultural literacy. You might recognize that schooling for you was really about accumulating information and that such an approach to education served you well. It is also possible that it has not. Whatever you decide, you may begin to reflect upon your experiences in new ways in developing an argument about what the purpose of education might be.

Alternatively, you might think about your educational experiences through 18 a very different conceptual frame in reading the following excerpt from Richard Rodriguez's memoir, *Hunger of Memory*. In this book, Rodriguez explains the conflicts he experienced as a nonnative speaker of English who desperately sought to enter mainstream culture, even if this meant sacrificing his identity as the son of Mexican immigrants. Notice how Rodriguez recalls his experience as a student through the framing concept of "scholarship boy" that he reads in Richard Hoggart's 1957 book, *The Uses of Literacy*. Using this notion of "scholarship boy" enables him to revisit his experience from a new perspective.

As you read this passage, consider what the notion of "scholarship boy" 19 helps Rodriguez to understand about his life as a student. In turn, what does such a concept help you understand about your own experience as a student?

Motivated to reflect upon his life as a student, Rodriguez comes across Richard Hoggart's book and a description of "the scholarship boy."

His initial response is to identify with Hoggart's description. Notice that Rodriguez says he used what he read to "frame the meaning of my academic success."

For weeks I read, speed-read, books by modern educational theorists, only to find infrequent and slight mention of students like me. . . . Then one day, leafing through Richard Hoggart's *The Uses of Literacy*, I found, in his description of the scholarship boy, myself. For the first time I realized that there were other students like me, and so I was able to frame the meaning of my academic success, its consequent price—the loss.

Hoggart's description is distinguished, at least initially, by deep understanding. What he grasps very well is that the scholarship boy must move between environments, his home and the classroom, which are at cultural extremes, opposed. With his family, the boy has the intense pleasure of intimacy, the family's consolation in feeling public alienation. Lavish emotions texture home life. *Then*, at school, the instruction bids him to trust lonely reason primarily. Immediate needs set the pace of his parents' lives. From his mother and father the boy learns to trust spontaneity and nonrational ways of knowing. *Then*, at school, there is mental calm. Teachers

The scholarship boy moves between school and home, between moments of spontaneity and reflectiveness.

emphasize the value of a reflectiveness that opens a space between thinking and immediate action.

Years of schooling must pass before the boy will be able to sketch the cultural differences in his day as abstractly as this. But he senses those differences early. Perhaps as early as the night he brings home an assignment from school and finds the house too noisy for study.

Rodriguez uses Hoggart's words and idea to advance his own understanding of the problem he identifies in his life: that he was unable to find solace at home and within his working-class roots.

He has to be more and more alone, if he is going to 'get on.' He will have, probably unconsciously, to oppose the ethos of the health, the intense gregariousness of the working-class family group. . . . The boy has to cut himself off mentally, so as to do his homework, as well as he can. (47)

In this excerpt, the idea of framing highlights the fact that other people's texts can serve as tools for helping you say more about your own ideas. If you were writing an essay using Hoggart's term *scholarship boy* as a lens through which to say something about education, you might ask how Hoggart's term illuminates new aspects of another writer's examples or your own—as opposed to asking, "How well does Hoggart's term *scholarship boy* apply to my experience?" (to which you could answer, "Not very well"). Further, you might ask, "To what extent does Hirsch's concept throw a more positive light on what Rodriguez and Hoggart describe?" or "Do my experiences challenge, extend, or complicate such a term as *scholarship boy?*"

Now that you have a sense of how framing works, let's look at an excerpt from a researched argument a first-year composition student wrote, titled "Learning 'American' in Spanish." The assignment to which she responded asked her to do the following:

Draw on your life experiences in developing an argument about education and what it has meant to you in your life. In writing your essay, use two of the four authors (Freire, Hirsch, Ladson-Billings, Pratt) included in this unit to frame your argument or any of the reading you may have done on your own. What key terms, phrases, or ideas from these texts help you teach your readers what you want them to learn from your experiences? How do your experiences extend or complicate your critical frames?

In the past, in responding to this assignment, some people have offered an overview of almost their entire lives, some have focused on a pivotal experience, and others have used descriptions of people who have influenced them. The important thing is that you use those experiences to argue a position: for example, that even the most well-meaning attempts to support students can actually hinder learning. This means going beyond narrating a simple list of experiences, or simply asserting an opinion. Instead you must use—and analyze—your experiences, determining which will most effectively convince your audience that your argument has a solid basis.

As you read the excerpt from this student's essay, ask yourself how the writer uses two framing concepts—"transculturation" and "contact zone"—from Mary Louise Pratt's article "Arts of the Contact Zone." What do these ideas help the writer bring into focus? What experience do these frames help her to name, define, and describe?

## Jennifer Farrell

The writer has not yet named her framing concept; but notice that the concrete details she gathers here set readers up to expect that she will juxtapose the culture of Guayabal and the Dominican Republic with that of the United States.

Exactly one week after graduating from high school, with thirteen years of American education behind me, I boarded a plane and headed for a Caribbean island. I had fifteen days to spend on an island surrounded with crystal blue waters, white sandy shores, and luxurious ocean resorts. With beaches to play on by day and casinos to play in during the night, I was told that this country was an exciting new tourist destination. My days in the Dominican Republic, however, were not filled with snorkeling lessons and my nights were not spent at the blackjack table. Instead of visiting the ritzy East Coast, I traveled inland to a mountain community with no running water and no electricity. The bus ride to this town, called Guayabal, was long, hot, and uncomfortable. The mountain roads were not paved and the bus had no air-conditioning. Surprisingly, the four-hour ride flew by. I had plenty to think about as my mind raced with thoughts of the next two weeks. I wondered if my host family would be welcoming, if the teenagers would be friendly, and if my work would be hard. I mentally prepared myself for life without the everyday luxuries of a flushing toilet, a hot shower, and a comfortable bed. Because Guayabal was without such basic commodities, I did not expect to see many reminders of home. I thought I was going to leave behind my American ways and immerse myself into another culture. These thoughts filled my head as the bus climbed the rocky hill toward Guayabal. When I finally got off the bus and stepped into the town square, I realized that I had thought wrong: There was no escaping the influence of the American culture.

In a way, Guayabal was an example of what author Mary Louise Pratt refers to as a contact zone. Pratt defines a contact zone as "a place where cultures

The writer names her experience as an example of Pratt's conception of a "contact zone." Further, the writer expands on Pratt's quote by relating it to her own observations. And finally, she uses this frame as a way to organize the narrative (as opposed to ordering her narrative chronologically).

The writer provides concrete evidence to support her point.

The writer offers an illustration of what she experienced, clarifying how this experience is similar to what Pratt describes. Note that Pratt's verb *clash*, used in the definition of *contact zone*, reappears here as part of the author's observation.

The author adds another layer to her description, introducing Pratt's framing concept of "transculturation."

meet, clash, and grapple with each other, often in contexts of highly asymmetrical relations of power" (76). In Guayabal, American culture and American consumerism were clashing with the Hispanic and Caribbean culture of the Dominican Republic. The clash came from the Dominicans' desire to be American in every sense, and especially to be consumers of American products. This is nearly impossible for Dominicans to achieve due to their extreme poverty. Their poverty provided the "asymmetrical relation of power" found in contact zones, because it impeded not only the Dominican's ability to be consumers, but also their ability to learn, to work, and to live healthily. The effects of their poverty could be seen in the eyes of the seven-year-old boy who couldn't concentrate in school because all he had to eat the day before was an underripe mango. It could be seen in the brown, leathered hands of the tired old man who was still picking coffee beans at age seventy.

The moment I got off the bus I noticed the clash between the American culture, the Dominican culture, and the community's poverty. It was apparent in the Dominicans' fragmented representation of American pop culture. Everywhere I looked in Guayabal I saw little glimpses of America. I saw Coca-Cola ads painted on raggedy fences. I saw knockoff Tommy Hilfiger shirts. I heard little boys say, "I wanna be like Mike" in their best English, while playing basketball. I listened to merengue house, the American version of the traditional Dominican merengue music. In each instance the Dominicans had adopted an aspect of American culture, but with an added Dominican twist. Pratt calls this transculturation. This term is used to "describe processes whereby members of subordinated or marginal groups select and invent from materials transmitted by a dominant or metropolitan culture" (80). She claims that transculturation is an identifying feature of contact zones. In the contact zone of Guayabal, the marginal group, made up of impoverished Dominicans, selected aspects of the dominant American culture, and invented a unique expression of a culture combining both Dominican and American styles. My most vivid memory of this transculturalization was on a hot afternoon when

Here again she quotes Pratt in order to bring into focus her own context here. The writer offers another example of transculturation.

I heard some children yelling, "Helado! Helado!" or "Ice cream! Ice cream!" I looked outside just in time to see a man ride by on a bicycle, ringing a hand bell and balancing a cooler full of ice cream in the front bicycle basket. The Dominican children eagerly chased after him, just as American children chase after the ice-cream truck.

Although you will notice that the writer does not challenge the framing 22 terms she uses in this paper, it is clear that rather than simply reproducing Pratt's ideas and using her as the Voice of Authority, she incorporates Pratt's understandings to enable her to say more about her own experiences and ideas. Moreover, she uses this frame to advance an argument in order to affect her readers' views of culture. In turn, when she mentions others' ideas, she does so in the service of what she wants to say.

## Conclusion: Writing Researched Arguments

I want to conclude this chapter by making a distinction between two differ- 23 ent views of research. On the one hand, research is often taught as a process of collecting information for its own sake. On the other hand, research can also be conceived as the discovery and purposeful use of information. The emphasis here is upon *use* and the ways you can shape information in ways that enable you to enter conversations. To do so, you need to demonstrate to readers that you understand the conversation: what others have said in the past, what the context is, and what you anticipate is the direction this conversation might take. Keep in mind, however, that contexts are neither found nor located. Rather, context, derived from the Latin *contexere*, denotes a process of weaving together. Thus your attempt to understand context is an active process of making connections among the different and conflicting views people present within a conversation. Your version of the context will vary from others' interpretations.

Your attempts to understand a given conversation may prompt you to do 24 research, as will your attempts to define what is at issue. Your reading and inquiry can help you construct a question that is rooted in some issue that is open to dispute. In turn, you need to ask yourself what is at stake for you and your reader other than the fact that you might be interested in educational reform, homelessness, affirmative action, or any other subject. Finally, your research can provide a means for framing an argument in order to move a conversation along and to say something new.

If you see inquiry as a means of entering conversations, then you will un- 25 derstand research as a social process. It need not be the tedious task of collecting information for its own sake. Rather, research has the potential to change readers' worldviews and your own.

## Works Cited

Bartholomae, David, and Anthony Petrosky. 1996. *Ways of Reading: An Anthology for Writers.* New York: Bedford Books.

Brent, Doug. 1996. "Rogerian Rhetoric: Ethical Growth Through Alternative Forms of Argumentation." In *Argument Revisited; Argument Redefined: Negotiating Meaning in a Composition Classroom*, 73–96. Edited by Barbara Emmel, Paula Resch, and Deborah Tenney. Thousand Oaks, CA: Sage Publications.

Burke, Kenneth. 1941. *The Philosophy of Literary Form.* Berkeley: University of California Press.

Crosswhite, James. 1996. *The Rhetoric of Reason: Writing and the Attractions of Argument.* Madison, WI: University of Wisconsin Press.

Freire, Paulo. 1970. *Pedagogy of the Oppressed.* New York: Continuum.

Hirsch, E. D. 1987. *Cultural Literacy.* New York: Vintage Books.

Ladson-Billings, Gloria. 1994. *The Dreamkeepers: Successful Teachers of African American Children.* New York: Teachers College Press.

Pratt, Mary Louise. "Arts of the Contact Zone." *Profession* 91 (1991): 33–40.

Quindlen, Anna. 1993. "No Place Like Home." In *Thinking Out Loud: On the Personal, the Public, and the Private*, 42–44. New York: Random House.

Rodriguez, Richard. 1983. *Hunger of Memory: The Education of Richard Rodriguez.* New York: Bantam Books.

## Acknowledgment

I wish to thank Robert Kachur and April Lidinsky for helping me think through the notions of argument as conversation and framing.

## Questions for Discussion and Journaling

1. What role, according to Greene, does reading play in the kind(s) of writing you will be asked to do in college?

2. Take another look at the "oft-quoted passage" by Kenneth Burke in paragraph 6. Why does Greene quote it yet again? Explain the extended metaphor that Burke uses. How would you describe the way it presents writing? What other ideas about writing might it challenge?

3. Explain the concept of *framing*. What metaphor underlies it? Why is the concept important for Greene? What does framing allow a writer to do?

## Applying and Exploring Ideas

1. What, if anything, does Greene's article leave you wondering? That is, along with whatever questions he answers, what questions does he *raise* in your mind? Pair up with another student and make a list of your questions.

2. Does Greene's article itself represent a "conversation"? If so, with whom? How does he frame his argument? Would you say, in short, that Greene practices what he preaches in "Argument as Conversation"?

3. Take another look at the passages in which Greene describes Richard Rodriguez's use of "scholarship boy" (para. 19) and a first-year college student's use of "transculturation" and "contact zone" (para. 21) as framing concepts to illuminate their own experiences. Think about some of the new concepts you've recently learned in your other classes; browse your class notes or textbooks to refresh your memory. Try to find a concept that works as a frame that illuminates your own experience, and explain how it works. After completing this exercise, consider: Why do you think Greene considers framing so significant in the process of writing and inquiry? Did you find the exercise useful?

## chapter 1

# Literacies:

## Where Do Your Ideas About Reading and Writing Come From?

If you are reading this textbook, you are a literate person. You went to school, learned to read and write, and were accepted to college where you are now being asked to write new and different kinds of texts. Experts who study **literacy** typically think about being literate as more than the ability to read and write. They generally are referring broadly to fluency or expertise in communicating and interacting with other people in many different ways. Thus, it's more accurate to speak about **literacies** than about literacy when thinking about what it means to be a literate person. This chapter, and the book as a whole, are going to ask you to think broadly about what it means to be literate. What is writing? What is reading? How do you communicate and compose? How have you been taught to

If you ever read Maurice Sendak's *Where the Wild Things Are*, you might recognize the "literacy sponsor" who so delights these children. Far from the mere ability to read, **literacy** includes these children's ideas, conveyed by their culture, that reading is fun, valuable, and important.

engage with texts and how has this influenced your understanding of writing and your relationship with writing? This chapter focuses on how individuals develop literacies and become literate learners. It asks you to think about what your literacies and your attitudes about literacies are, how they developed, how they influence one another, and who you are as a literate person.

In thinking about literacies, it might help you to start by considering your daily life. For example, every day you read and write all kinds of things that you probably rarely talk about in school and that you might not think about as **literacy practices** or forms of literacy: you check your Facebook account, you text friends, you Skype. You interpret thousands of visual images every time you turn on the television, read a magazine, or go to the mall. You also have literacies particular to your interests—you may know everything there is to know about a particular baseball player's RBIs, for example, or you may have advanced to an impressively high level in a complex, massively multiplayer online role-playing game like *World of Warcraft*. And, of course, you have home literacies that may be very different from school or hobby-related literacies. You may come from a family where languages other than English are spoken, or you may live in a community that values collaborative literacy practices (such as storytelling) that school does not.

Researchers in the discipline of Writing Studies are particularly interested in these more complex ideas about literacy because they want to understand how people acquire literacies and what literacies a society should assist people in acquiring. For example, in contemporary United States culture, schools don't educate people in highly specialized literacies—for example, those related to most hobbies, like radio-controlled vehicles or gaming. Computer literacy was once in this category; as the use of computers went mainstream in the 1980s and 1990s, however—and particularly as it grew in importance in the workplace—the school system realized it needed to commit significant resources toward educating students in computer and information literacy.

This chapter's readings focus particularly on questions of what counts as "literacy," how we become literate, and how cultures support various literacies. Deborah Brandt's piece, "Sponsors of Literacy," will start you with some definitions of literacy and some questions about how we acquire the literacies that we do. All of the other readings in the chapter can be understood in some ways as demonstrating the ideas that Brandt talks about in her piece—literacy, access to literacy, and the power that literacy can provide. The excerpts from Sherman Alexie's, Victora Villanueva's, and Malcolm X's autobiographies are short but poignant examples of how an individual's family situation, financial situation, race, home language and culture, gender, and similar identifiers influence life-long literacies, access to education, economic status, and the like. Mahiri and Sablo's study of the writing and literacy attitudes of urban African American youth similarly demonstrates the important role that writing and reading can play in the lives of students who face difficult odds in their home lives and communities. Kevin Roozen's study takes a slightly different perspective on literacy practices: he examines how literacy habits and ideas learned in one setting (in this example, from a church youth group and a prayer journal) influence an individual's literacy habits and practices in a very different setting (an English literature class). Thomas Newkirk's study of the literacy practices of young children pushes this idea of literate development even further; he argues that children naturally combine writing, pictures, and words to tell stories in **multimodal** ways, but that schooling denies this sort of creative communication (an idea revisited in Chapter 5). And, Donald Murray argues the overarching idea of this chapter: Everything you write, from how you write it to what you think of saying or whether you say it at all, is autobiographical. That is, all of your past experiences inform your writing and your identity as a writer and as a literate person.

Before you begin reading, take a few minutes to consider how you became the literate person you are today. No two people have exactly the same literacies, and yours are peculiar to your own personal history—your family, your geographic location, your culture, your hobbies, your religious training, your schooling, and so on. Consider, for example, the following questions:

- When and how did you learn to read?
- What did you read?
- Were there things you were not allowed to read?
- Where did you first or most memorably encounter texts as a child—for example, at home, at school, at a church or synagogue, at daycare, at a friend's or relative's house?
- Did you write or draw as a child? Was this encouraged or discouraged?

The **threshold concept** this chapter addresses is that your experiences have shaped your literacy practices—both what they are, and what they are not—so your answers will not be the same as other people's. All of us were shaped by what Deborah Brandt, whose work you'll read shortly, calls **literacy sponsors**—people, ideas, or institutions who helped us become literate, but literate in specific ways. If you attended private school instead of public school, for example, what were you exposed to and what literate experiences did you not have that public school kids might have had?

As you reflect on your own experiences, consider both the texts you were exposed to and those you were not exposed to, or the ones that you were explicitly denied. When you learned to write, what motivated you to want to write? Who helped you—or didn't? What kinds of things did you write, and for whom? As you grew older, did your interest in writing change? What factors impacted those changes—friends? teachers? parents? new hobbies?

This brief reflection on your literacy history should illustrate the point we are trying to make: You are a literate person, and you are an expert on your own literacy practices and history. You come to this chapter knowing a lot, and through the readings and activities you'll find here, we hope to help you uncover more of what you know, in addition to learning some things that you did not know before. We hope you will be able to see your past experiences living in your current experiences, and draw on them in creative and useful ways. We hope you will consciously consider what it means to be literate, what it means to read and write, and by so doing broaden your understandings in new ways.

## Chapter Goals

- To understand the concepts of *literacy* and *multiple literacies*
- To acquire additional vocabulary for talking about yourself as a writer and reader
- To come to greater awareness of the forces that have shaped you as a writer and reader
- To understand ways of conducting contributive research and writing about literacy that can be shared with an audience
- To strengthen your ability to read complex, research-based texts more confidently
- To gain experience writing from readings and citing sources

# Sponsors of Literacy

## DEBORAH BRANDT

■ Brandt, Deborah. "Sponsors of Literacy." *College Composition and Communication* 49.2 (1998): 165–85. Print.

## Framing the Reading

Deborah Brandt is a professor in the Department of English at the University of Wisconsin–Madison. She has written several books about literacy, including *Literacy as Involvement: The Acts of Writers, Readers and Texts* (Southern Illinois University Press, 1990); *Literacy in American Lives* (Cambridge University Press, 2001); and *Literacy and Learning: Reading, Writing, Society* (Jossey-Bass, 2009). She has also written a number of scholarly research articles about literacy, including the one you are about to read here, "Sponsors of Literacy," which describes some of the data she collected when writing *Literacy in American Lives*. In that book, Brandt examined the way literacy learning changed between 1895 and 1985, noting that literacy standards have risen dramatically. In "Sponsors of Literacy" she discusses the forces that shape our literacy learning and practices.

Brandt's breakthrough idea in this piece is that people don't become literate on their own; rather, literacy is *sponsored* by people, institutions, and circumstances that both make it possible for a person to become literate and shape the way the person actually acquires literacy. In interviewing a stunningly large number of people from all ages and walks of life, Brandt began recognizing these literacy sponsors everywhere, and thus her article here (and the book that the same research led to) is crammed with examples of them, ranging from older siblings to auto manufacturers and World War II.

While we think of the term *sponsor* as suggesting support or assistance, Brandt doesn't confine her discussion to the supportive aspects of literacy sponsors. Her research shows ways in which, while opening some doors, literacy sponsors may close others. Literacy sponsors are not always (or even, perhaps, usually) altruistic—they have self-interested reasons for sponsoring literacy, and very often only some kinds of literacy will support their goals. (If you've ever wondered why schools encourage you to read, but seem less than thrilled if you'd rather read the *Twilight* series than Ernest Hemingway, Brandt's explanation of literacy sponsorship may provide an answer.) Brandt also discusses cases where people "misappropriate" a literacy sponsor's intentions by using a particular literacy for their own ends rather than for the sponsor's.

Brandt's portrayal of the tension between people and their literacy sponsors illustrates one more important point in thinking about literacy acquisition and how each of us has become literate. We claim

in the chapter introduction that you have a combination of literacies that make you unique. While this is true, people also share many of the *same* literacy experiences. Brandt can help us understand this, too. Some literacy sponsors are organizations or institutions, like a public school system or a major corporation, whose sponsorship affects large numbers of people. In the Middle Ages prior to the invention of the printing press, the biggest literacy sponsor in Western civilization was the Roman Catholic Church, which shaped the literacies of virtually every person in feudal Europe as well as vast native populations around the world. Remember, literacy sponsors are not necessarily empowering; they can also disempower and *prevent* people from becoming literate in some ways while fostering other literacies. "Big" literacy sponsors like these have likely influenced your literacy narrative in the same way they've influenced many others, giving you something in common with others around you even as your particular literacies are unique to you.

## Getting Ready to Read

*Before you read*, do at least one of the following activities:

- Compare notes with a roommate or friend about what your school literacy experience was like. What books did the school encourage you to read and discourage you from reading? What events and activities supported reading?
- Make a list of the ways you've seen U.S. culture and your own local community encourage and emphasize reading. What are the reasons usually given for being a good reader and writer, and who gives those reasons?

*As you read*, consider the following questions:

- What are Brandt's primary terms, in addition to *literacy sponsor*, and how do they apply to you?
- Where do you see yourself in the examples Brandt gives, and where do you not? Keep your early literacy experiences in mind as you read.
- What are implications of Brandt's idea of literacy sponsors for your education *right now* as a college student?

......................................................................................

In his sweeping history of adult learning in the United States, Joseph Kett 1 describes the intellectual atmosphere available to young apprentices who worked in the small, decentralized print shops of antebellum America. Because printers also were the solicitors and editors of what they published, their workshops served as lively incubators for literacy and political discourse. By the mid-nineteenth century, however, this learning space was disrupted when the invention of the steam press reorganized the economy of the print industry. Steam presses were so expensive that they required capital outlays beyond the means of many printers. As a result, print jobs were outsourced, the processes of editing and printing were split, and, in tight competition, print apprentices became low-paid mechanics with no more access to the multi-skilled environment of the craft-shop (Kett 67–70). While this shift in working conditions may be evidence of the deskilling of workers induced by the Industrial Revolution (Nicholas and Nicholas), it also offers a site for reflecting upon the dynamic sources of literacy and literacy learning. The reading and writing skills of print apprentices in this period were the achievements not simply of teachers and learners nor of the discourse practices of the printer community. Rather, these skills existed fragilely, contingently within an economic moment. The pre-steam press economy enabled some of the most basic aspects of the apprentices' literacy, especially their access to material production and the public meaning or worth of their skills. Paradoxically, even as the steam-powered penny press made print more accessible (by making publishing more profitable), it brought an end to a particular form of literacy sponsorship and a drop in literate potential.

The apprentices' experience invites rumination upon literacy learning and teaching today. Literacy looms as one of the great engines of profit and competitive advantage in the 20th century: a lubricant for consumer desire; a means for integrating corporate markets; a foundation for the deployment of weapons and other technology; a raw material in the mass production of information. As ordinary citizens have been compelled into these economies, their reading and writing skills have grown sharply more central to the everyday trade of information and goods as well as to the pursuit of education, employment, civil rights, status. At the same time, people's literate skills have grown vulnerable to unprecedented turbulence in their economic value, as conditions, forms, and standards of literacy achievement seem to shift with almost every new generation of learners. How are we to understand the vicissitudes of individual literacy development in relationship to the large-scale economic forces that set the routes and determine the wordly worth of that literacy? 2

> *Literacy looms as one of the great engines of profit and competitive advantage in the 20th century: a lubricant for consumer desire; a means for integrating corporate markets; a foundation for the deployment of weapons and other technology; a raw material in the mass production of information.*

The field of writing studies has had much to say about individual literacy development. Especially in the last quarter of the 20th century, we have theorized, researched, critiqued, debated, and sometimes even managed to enhance the literate potentials of ordinary citizens as they have tried to cope with life as they find it. Less easily and certainly less steadily have we been able to relate what we see, study, and do to these larger contexts of profit making and competition. This even as we recognize that the most pressing issues we deal with—tightening associations between literate skill and social viability, the breakneck pace of change in communications technology, persistent inequities 3 in access and reward—all relate to structural conditions in literacy's bigger picture. When economic forces are addressed in our work, they appear primarily as generalities: contexts, determinants, motivators, barriers, touchstones. But rarely are they systematically related to the local conditions and embodied moments of literacy learning that occupy so many of us on a daily basis.[1]

This essay does not presume to overcome the analytical failure completely. But it does offer a conceptual approach that begins to connect literacy as an individual development to literacy as an economic development, at least as the two have played out over the last ninety years or so. The approach is through what I call sponsors of literacy. Sponsors, as I have come to think of them, are any agents, local or distant, concrete or abstract, who enable, support, teach, model, as well as recruit, regulate, suppress, or withhold literacy—and gain advantage by it in some way. Just as the ages of radio and television accustom us to having programs *brought* to us by various commercial sponsors, it is useful to think about who or what underwrites occasions of literacy learning and use. Although the interests of the sponsor and the sponsored do not have to converge (and, in fact, may conflict) sponsors nevertheless set the terms for access to literacy and wield powerful incentives for compliance and loyalty. Sponsors are a tangible reminder that literacy learning throughout history has always required permission, sanction, assistance, coercion, or, at minimum, contact with existing trade routes. Sponsors are delivery systems for the economies of literacy, the means by which these forces present themselves to—and through—individual learners. They also represent the causes into which people's literacy usually gets recruited.[2]

For the last five years I have been tracing sponsors of literacy across the 20th century as they appear in the accounts of ordinary Americans recalling how they learned to write and read. The investigation is grounded in more than 100 in-depth interviews that I collected from a diverse group of people born roughly between 1900 and 1980. In the interviews, people explored in great detail their memories of learning to read and write across their lifetimes, focusing especially on the people, institutions, materials, and motivations involved in the process. The more I worked with these accounts, the more I came to realize that they were filled with references to sponsors, both explicit and latent, who appeared in formative roles at the scenes of literacy learning. Patterns of sponsorship became an illuminating site through which to track the different cultural attitudes people developed toward writing vs. reading as well as the ideological congestion faced by late-century literacy learners as their sponsors proliferated and diversified (see my essays on "Remembering Reading" and "Accumulating Literacy"). In this essay I set out a case for why the concept of sponsorship is so richly suggestive for exploring economies of literacy and their effects. Then, through use of extended case examples, I demonstrate the practical application of this approach for interpreting current conditions of literacy teaching and learning, including persistent stratification of opportunity and escalating standards for literacy achievement. A final section addresses implications for the teaching of writing.

## Sponsorship

Intuitively, *sponsors* seemed a fitting term for the figures who turned up most  6
typically in people's memories of literacy learning: older relatives, teachers,
priests, supervisors, military officers, editors, influential authors. Sponsors,
as we ordinarily think of them, are powerful figures who bankroll events or
smooth the way for initiates. Usually richer, more knowledgeable, and more
entrenched than the sponsored, sponsors nevertheless enter a reciprocal relationship with those they underwrite. They lend their resources or credibility to
the sponsored but also stand to gain benefits from their success, whether by
direct repayment or, indirectly, by credit of association. *Sponsors* also proved
an appealing term in my analysis because of all the commercial references that
appeared in these 20th-century accounts—the magazines, peddled encyclopedias, essay contests, radio and television programs, toys, fan clubs, writing
tools, and so on, from which so much experience with literacy was derived. As
the 20th century turned the abilities to read and write into widely exploitable
resources, commercial sponsorship abounded.

In whatever form, sponsors deliver the ideological freight that must be borne  7
for access to what they have. Of course, the sponsored can be oblivious to or innovative with this ideological burden. Like Little Leaguers who wear the logo of
a local insurance agency on their uniforms, not out of a concern for enhancing
the agency's image but as a means for getting to play ball, people throughout
history have acquired literacy pragmatically under the banner of others' causes.
In the days before free, public schooling in England, Protestant Sunday Schools
warily offered basic reading instruction to working-class families as part of evangelical duty. To the horror of many in the church sponsorship, these families insis-
tently, sometimes riotously demanded of their Sunday Schools more instruction,
including in writing and math, because it provided means for upward mobility.[3]
Through the sponsorship of Baptist and Methodist ministries, African Americans
in slavery taught each other to understand the Bible in subversively liberatory
ways. Under a conservative regime, they developed forms of critical literacy that
sustained religious, educational, and political movements both before and after
emancipation (Cornelius). Most of the time, however, literacy takes its shape
from the interests of its sponsors. And, as we will see below, obligations toward
one's sponsors run deep, affecting what, why, and how people write and read.

The concept of sponsors helps to explain, then, a range of human relation-  8
ships and ideological pressures that turn up at the scenes of literacy learning—
from benign sharing between adults and youths, to euphemized coercions in
schools and workplaces, to the most notorious impositions and deprivations
by church or state. It also is a concept useful for tracking literacy's material:
the things that accompany writing and reading and the ways they are manufactured and distributed. Sponsorship as a sociological term is even more broadly
suggestive for thinking about economies of literacy development. Studies of
patronage in Europe and *compradrazgo* in the Americas show how patron-
client relationships in the past grew up around the need to manage scarce
resources and promote political stability (Bourne; Lynch; Horstman and Kurtz).

Pragmatic, instrumental, ambivalent, patron-client relationships integrated otherwise antagonistic social classes into relationships of mutual, albeit unequal dependencies. Loaning land, money, protection, and other favors allowed the politically powerful to extend their influence and justify their exploitation of clients. Clients traded their labor and deference for access to opportunities for themselves or their children and for leverage needed to improve their social standing. Especially under conquest in Latin America, *compradrazgo* reintegrated native societies badly fragmented by the diseases and other disruptions that followed foreign invasions. At the same time, this system was susceptible to its own stresses, especially when patrons became clients themselves of still more centralized or distant overlords, with all the shifts in loyalty and perspective that entailed (Horstman and Kurtz 13–14).

In raising this association with formal systems of patronage, I do not wish to   9
overlook the very different economic, political, and educational systems within which U.S. literacy has developed. But where we find the sponsoring of literacy, it will be useful to look for its function within larger political and economic arenas. Literacy, like land, is a valued commodity in this economy, a key resource in gaining profit and edge. This value helps to explain, of course, the lengths people will go to secure literacy for themselves or their children. But it also explains why the powerful work so persistently to conscript and ration the powers of literacy. The competition to harness literacy, to manage, measure, teach, and exploit it, has intensified throughout the century. It is vital to pay attention to this development because it largely sets the terms for individuals' encounters with literacy. This competition shapes the incentives and barriers (including uneven distributions of opportunity) that greet literacy learners in any particular time and place. It is this competition that has made access to the right kinds of literacy sponsors so crucial for political and economic well-being. And it also has spurred the rapid, complex changes that now make the pursuit of literacy feel so turbulent and precarious for so many.

In the next three sections, I trace the dynamics of literacy sponsorship   10
through the life experiences of several individuals, showing how their opportunities for literacy learning emerge out of the jockeying and skirmishing for economic and political advantage going on among sponsors of literacy. Along the way, the analysis addresses three key issues: (1) how, despite ostensible democracy in educational chances, stratification of opportunity continues to organize access and reward in literacy learning; (2) how sponsors contribute to what is called "the literacy crisis," that is, the perceived gap between rising standards for achievement and people's ability to meet them; and (3) how encounters with literacy sponsors, especially as they are configured at the end of the 20th century, can be sites for the innovative rerouting of resources into projects of self-development and social change.

## Sponsorship and Access

A focus on sponsorship can force a more explicit and substantive link between   11
literacy learning and systems of opportunity and access. A statistical correlation

between high literacy achievement and high socioeconomic, majority-race status routinely shows up in results of national tests of reading and writing performance.[4] These findings capture yet, in their shorthand way, obscure the unequal conditions of literacy sponsorship that lie behind differential outcomes in academic performance. Throughout their lives, affluent people from high-caste racial groups have multiple and redundant contacts with powerful literacy sponsors as a routine part of their economic and political privileges. Poor people and those from low-caste racial groups have less consistent, less politically secured access to literacy sponsors—especially to the ones that can grease their way to academic and economic success. Differences in their performances are often attributed to family background (namely education and income of parents) or to particular norms and values operating within different ethnic groups or social classes. But in either case, much more is usually at work.

As a study in contrasts in sponsorship patterns and access to literacy, consider the parallel experiences of Raymond Branch and Dora Lopez, both of whom were born in 1969 and, as young children, moved with their parents to the same, mid-sized university town in the midwest.[5] Both were still residing in this town at the time of our interviews in 1995. Raymond Branch, a European American, had been born in southern California, the son of a professor father and a real estate executive mother. He recalled that his first-grade classroom in 1975 was hooked up to a mainframe computer at Stanford University and that, as a youngster, he enjoyed fooling around with computer programming in the company of "real users" at his father's science lab. This process was not interrupted much when, in the late 1970s, his family moved to the midwest. Raymond received his first personal computer as a Christmas present from his parents when he was twelve years old, and a modem the year after that. In the 1980s, computer hardware and software stores began popping up within a bicycle-ride's distance from where he lived. The stores were serving the university community and, increasingly, the high-tech industries that were becoming established in that vicinity. As an adolescent, Raymond spent his summers roaming these stores, sampling new computer games, making contact with founders of some of the first electronic bulletin boards in the nation, and continuing, through reading and other informal means, to develop his programming techniques. At the time of our interview he had graduated from the local university and was a successful freelance writer of software and software documentation, with clients in both the private sector and the university community. 12

Dora Lopez, a Mexican American, was born in the same year as Raymond Branch, 1969, in a Texas border town, where her grandparents, who worked as farm laborers, lived most of the year. When Dora was still a baby her family moved to the same midwest university town as had the family of Raymond Branch. Her father pursued an accounting degree at a local technical college and found work as a shipping and receiving clerk at the university. Her mother, who also attended technical college briefly, worked part-time in a bookstore. In the early 1970s, when the Lopez family made its move to the midwest, the Mexican-American population in the university town was barely one per cent. Dora recalled that the family had to drive seventy miles to a big city to find not 13 only suitable groceries but also Spanish-language newspapers and magazines that carried information of concern and interest to them. (Only when reception was good could they catch Spanish-language radio programs coming from Chicago, 150 miles away.) During her adolescence, Dora Lopez undertook to teach herself how to read and write in Spanish, something, she said, that neither her brother nor her U.S.-born cousins knew how to do. Sometimes, with the help of her mother's employee discount at the bookstore, she sought out novels by South American and Mexican writers, and she practiced her written Spanish by corresponding with relatives in Colombia. She was exposed to computers for the first time at the age of thirteen when she worked as a teacher's aide in a federally-funded summer school program for the children of migrant workers. The computers were being used to help the children to be brought up to grade level in their reading and writing skills. When Dora was admitted to the same university that Raymond Branch attended, her father bought her a used word processing machine that a student had advertised for sale on a bulletin board in the building where Mr. Lopez worked. At the time of our interview, Dora Lopez had transferred from the university to a technical college. She was working for a cleaning company, where she performed extra duties as a translator, communicating on her supervisor's behalf with the largely Latina cleaning staff. "I write in Spanish for him, what he needs to be translated, like job duties, what he expects them to do, and I write lists for him in English and Spanish," she explained.

In Raymond Branch's account of his early literacy learning we are able to see behind the scenes of his majority-race membership, male gender, and high-end socioeconomic family profile. There lies a thick and, to him, relatively accessible economy of institutional and commercial supports that cultivated and subsidized his acquisition of a powerful form of literacy. One might be tempted to say that Raymond Branch was born at the right time and lived in the right place—except that the experience of Dora Lopez troubles that thought. For Raymond Branch, a university town in the 1970s and 1980s provided an information-rich, resource-rich learning environment in which to pursue his literacy development, but for Dora Lopez, a female member of a culturally unsubsidized ethnic minority, the same town at the same time was information- and resource-poor. Interestingly, both young people were pursuing projects of self-initiated learning, Raymond Branch in computer programming and Dora Lopez in biliteracy. But she had to reach much further afield for the material and communicative systems needed to support her learning. Also, while Raymond Branch, as the son of an academic, was sponsored by some of the most powerful agents of the university (its laboratories, newest technologies, and most educated personnel), Dora Lopez was being sponsored by what her parents could pull from the peripheral service systems of the university (the mail room, the bookstore, the second-hand technology market). In these accounts we also can see how the development and eventual economic worth of Raymond Branch's literacy skills were underwritten by late-century transformations in communication technology that created a boomtown need for programmers and software writers. Dora Lopez's biliterate skills developed and paid off much further down the

14

economic-reward ladder, in government-sponsored youth programs and commercial enterprises, that, in the 1990s, were absorbing surplus migrant workers into a low-wage, urban service economy.[6] Tracking patterns of literacy sponsorship, then, gets beyond SES shorthand to expose more fully how unequal literacy chances relate to systems of unequal subsidy and reward for literacy. These are the systems that deliver large-scale economic, historical, and political conditions to the scenes of small-scale literacy use and development.

This analysis of sponsorship forces us to consider not merely how one 15 social group's literacy practices may differ from another's, but how everybody's literacy practices are operating in differential economies, which supply different access routes, different degrees of sponsoring power, and different scales of monetary worth to the practices in use. In fact, the interviews I conducted are filled with examples of how economic and political forces, some of them originating in quite distant corporate and government policies, affect people's day-to-day ability to seek out and practice literacy. As a telephone company employee, Janelle Hampton enjoyed a brief period in the early 1980s as a fraud investigator, pursuing inquiries and writing up reports of her efforts. But when the breakup of the telephone utility reorganized its workforce, the fraud division was moved two states away and she was returned to less interesting work as a data processor. When, as a seven-year-old in the mid-1970s, Yi Vong made his way with his family from Laos to rural Wisconsin as part of the first resettlement group of Hmong refugees after the Vietnam War, his school district—which had no ESL programming—placed him in a school for the blind and deaf, where he learned English on audio and visual language machines. When a meager retirement pension forced Peter Hardaway and his wife out of their house and into a trailer, the couple stopped receiving newspapers and magazines in order to avoid cluttering up the small space they had to share. An analysis of sponsorship systems of literacy would help educators everywhere to think through the effects that economic and political changes in their regions are having on various people's ability to write and read, their chances to sustain that ability, and their capacities to pass it along to others. Recession, relocation, immigration, technological change, government retreat all can—and do—condition the course by which literate potential develops.

## Sponsorship and the Rise in Literacy Standards

As I have been attempting to argue, literacy as a resource becomes available 16 to ordinary people largely through the mediations of more powerful sponsors. These sponsors are engaged in ceaseless processes of positioning and repositioning, seizing and relinquishing control over meanings and materials of literacy as part of their participation in economic and political competition. In the give and take of these struggles, forms of literacy and literacy learning take shape. This section examines more closely how forms of literacy are created out of competitions between institutions. It especially considers how this process relates to the rapid rise in literacy standards since World War II. Resnick and Resnick lay out the process by which the demand for literacy achievement has been escalating, from basic, largely rote competence to more complex analytical and interpretive skills. More and more people are now being expected to accomplish more and more things with reading and writing. As print and its spinoffs have entered virtually every sphere of life, people have grown increasingly dependent on their literacy skills for earning a living and exercising and protecting their civil rights. This section uses one extended case example to trace the role of institutional sponsorship in raising the literacy stakes. It also considers how one man used available forms of sponsorship to cope with this escalation in literacy demands.

The focus is on Dwayne Lowery, whose transition in the early 1970s from  17
line worker in an automobile manufacturing plant to field representative for a major public employees union exemplified the major transition of the post-World War II economy—from a thing-making, thing-swapping society to an information-making, service-swapping society. In the process, Dwayne Lowery had to learn to read and write in ways that he had never done before. How his experiences with writing developed and how they were sponsored—and distressed—by institutional struggle will unfold in the following narrative.

A man of Eastern European ancestry, Dwayne Lowery was born in 1938  18
and raised in a semi-rural area in the upper midwest, the third of five children of a rubber worker father and a homemaker mother. Lowery recalled how, in his childhood home, his father's feisty union publications and left-leaning newspapers and radio shows helped to create a political climate in his household. "I was sixteen years old before I knew that goddamn Republicans was two words," he said. Despite this influence, Lowery said he shunned politics and newspaper reading as a young person, except to read the sports page. A diffident student, he graduated near the bottom of his class from a small high school in 1956 and, after a stint in the Army, went to work on the assembly line of a major automobile manufacturer. In the late 1960s, bored with the repetition of spraying primer paint on the right door checks of 57 cars an hour, Lowery traded in his night shift at the auto plant for a day job reading water meters in a municipal utility department. It was at that time, Lowery recalled, that he rediscovered newspapers, reading them in the early morning in his department's break room. He said:

> At the time I guess I got a little more interested in the state of things within the state.
> I started to get a little political at that time and got a little more information about
> local people. So I would buy [a metropolitan paper] and I would read that paper in
> the morning. It was a pretty conservative paper but I got some information.

At about the same time Lowery became active in a rapidly growing public  19
employees union, and, in the early 1970s, he applied for and received a union-sponsored grant that allowed him to take off four months of work and travel to Washington, D.C., for training in union activity. Here is his extended account of that experience:

> When I got to school, then there was a lot of reading. I often felt bad. If I had
> read more [as a high-school student] it wouldn't have been so tough. But they
> pumped a lot of stuff at us to read. We lived in a hotel and we had to some extent

homework we had to do and reading we had to do and not make written reports but make some presentation on our part of it. What they were trying to teach us, I believe, was regulations, systems, laws. In case anything in court came up along the way, we would know that. We did a lot of work on organizing, you know, learning how to negotiate contracts, contractual language, how to write it. Gross National Product, how that affected the Consumer Price Index. It was pretty much a crash course. It was pretty much crammed in. And I'm not sure we were all that well prepared when we got done, but it was interesting.

After a hands-on experience organizing sanitation workers in the west, Lowery returned home and was offered a full-time job as a field staff representative for the union, handling worker grievances and contract negotiations for a large, active local near his state capital. His initial writing and rhetorical activities corresponded with the heady days of the early 1970s when the union was growing in strength and influence, reflecting in part the exponential expansion in information workers and service providers within all branches of government. With practice, Lowery said he became "good at talking," "good at presenting the union side," "good at slicing chunks off the employer's case." Lowery observed that, in those years, the elected officials with whom he was negotiating often lacked the sophistication of their Washington-trained union counterparts. "They were part-time people," he said. "And they didn't know how to calculate. We got things in contracts that didn't cost them much at the time but were going to cost them a ton down the road." In time, though, even small municipal and county governments responded to the public employees' growing power by hiring specialized attorneys to represent them in grievance and contract negotiations. "Pretty soon," Lowery observed, "ninety percent of the people I was dealing with across the table were attorneys."

This move brought dramatic changes in the writing practices of union reps, 20 and, in Lowery's estimation, a simultaneous waning of the power of workers and the power of his own literacy. "It used to be we got our way through muscle or through political connections," he said. "Now we had to get it through legalistic stuff. It was no longer just sit down and talk about it. Can we make a deal?" Instead, all activity became rendered in writing: the exhibit, the brief, the transcript, the letter, the appeal. Because briefs took longer to write, the wheels of justice took longer to turn. Delays in grievance hearings became routine, as lawyers and union reps alike asked hearing judges for extensions on their briefs. Things went, in Lowery's words, "from quick, competent justice to expensive and long term justice."

In the meantime, Lowery began spending up to 70 hours a week at work, 21 sweating over the writing of briefs, which are typically fifteen to thirty-page documents laying out precedents, arguments, and evidence for a grievant's case. These documents were being forced by the new political economy in which Lowery's union was operating. He explained:

> When employers were represented by an attorney, you were going to have a written brief because the attorney needs to get paid. Well, what do you think if you were a union grievant and the attorney says, well, I'm going to write a brief and

Dwayne Lowery says, well, I'm not going to. Does the worker somehow feel that their representation is less now?

To keep up with the new demands, Lowery occasionally traveled to major cities for two or three-day union-sponsored workshops on arbitration, new legislation, and communication skills. He also took short courses at a historic School for Workers at a nearby university. His writing instruction consisted mainly of reading the briefs of other field reps, especially those done by the college graduates who increasingly were being assigned to his district from union headquarters. Lowery said he kept a file drawer filled with other people's briefs from which he would borrow formats and phrasings. At the time of our interview in 1995, Dwayne Lowery had just taken an early and somewhat bitter retirement from the union, replaced by a recent graduate from a master's degree program in Industrial Relations. As a retiree, he was engaged in local Democratic party politics and was getting informal lessons in word processing at home from his wife.

Over a 20-year period, Lowery's adult writing took its character from a   22 particular juncture in labor relations, when even small units of government began wielding (and, as a consequence, began spreading) a "legalistic" form of literacy in order to restore political dominance over public workers. This struggle for dominance shaped the kinds of literacy skills required of Lowery, the kinds of genres he learned and used, and the kinds of literate identity he developed. Lowery's rank-and-file experience and his talent for representing that experience around a bargaining table became increasingly peripheral to his ability to prepare documents that could compete in kind with those written by his formally-educated, professional adversaries. Face-to-face meetings became occasions mostly for a ritualistic exchange of texts, as arbitrators generally deferred decisions, reaching them in private, after solitary deliberation over complex sets of documents. What Dwayne Lowery was up against as a working adult in the second half of the 20th century was more than just living through a rising standard in literacy expectations or a generalized growth in professionalization, specialization, or documentary power—although certainly all of those things are, generically, true. Rather, these developments should be seen more specifically, as outcomes of ongoing transformations in the history of literacy as it has been wielded as part of economic and political conflict. These transformations become the arenas in which new standards of literacy develop. And for Dwayne Lowery—as well as many like him over the last 25 years—these are the arenas in which the worth of existing literate skills become degraded. A consummate debater and deal maker, Lowery saw his value to the union bureaucracy subside, as power shifted to younger, university-trained staffers whose literacy credentials better matched the specialized forms of escalating pressure coming from the other side.

In the broadest sense, the sponsorship of Dwayne Lowery's literacy experi-   23 ences lies deep within the historical conditions of industrial relations in the 20th century and, more particularly, within the changing nature of work and labor struggle over the last several decades. Edward Stevens Jr. has observed the rise in this century of an "advanced contractarian society" (25) by which formal relationships of all kinds have come to rely on "a jungle of rules and regulations" (139). For labor, these conditions only intensified in the 1960s and 1970s when a flurry of federal and state civil rights legislation curtailed the previously unregulated hiring and firing power of management. These developments made the appeal to law as central as collective bargaining for extending employee rights (Heckscher 9). I mention this broader picture, first, because it relates to the forms of employer backlash that Lowery began experiencing by the early 1980s and, more important, because a history of unionism serves as a guide for a closer look at the sponsors of Lowery's literacy.

These resources begin with the influence of his father, whose membership in 24 the United Rubber Workers during the ideologically potent 1930s and 1940s grounded Lowery in class-conscious progressivism and its favorite literate form: the newspaper. On top of that, though, was a pragmatic philosophy of worker education that developed in the U.S. after the Depression as an anti-communist antidote to left-wing intellectual influences in unions. Lowery's parent union, in fact, had been a central force in refocusing worker education away from an earlier emphasis on broad critical study and toward discrete techniques for organizing and bargaining. Workers began to be trained in the discrete bodies of knowledge, written formats, and idioms associated with those strategies. Characteristic of this legacy, Lowery's crash course at the Washington-based training center in the early 1970s emphasized technical information, problem solving, and union-building skills and methods. The transformation in worker education from critical, humanistic study to problem-solving skills was also lived out at the school for workers where Lowery took short courses in the 1980s. Once a place where factory workers came to write and read about economics, sociology, and labor history, the school is now part of a university extension service offering workshops—often requested by management—on such topics as work restructuring, new technology health and safety regulations, and joint labor-management cooperation.[7] Finally, in this inventory of Dwayne Lowery's literacy sponsors, we must add the latest incarnations shaping union practices: the attorneys and college-educated co-workers who carried into Lowery's workplace forms of legal discourse and "essayist literacy."[8]

What should we notice about this pattern of sponsorship? First, we can 25 see from yet another angle how the course of an ordinary person's literacy learning—its occasions, materials, applications, potentials—follows the transformations going on within sponsoring institutions as those institutions fight for economic and ideological position. As a result of wins, losses, or compromises, institutions undergo change, affecting the kinds of literacy they promulgate and the status that such literacy has in the larger society. So where, how, why, and what Lowery practiced as a writer—and what he didn't practice—took shape as part of the post-industrial jockeying going on over the last thirty years by labor, government, and industry. Yet there is more to be seen in this inventory of literacy sponsors. It exposes the deeply textured history that lies within the literacy practices of institutions and within any individual's literacy experiences. Accumulated layers of sponsoring influences—in families, workplaces, schools, memory—carry forms of literacy that have been shaped out of ideological and economic struggles of the past. This history, on the one hand, is a sustaining resource in the quest for literacy. It enables an older generation to pass its literacy resources onto another. Lowery's exposure to his father's newspaper-reading and supper-table political talk kindled his adult passion for news, debate, and for language that rendered relief and justice. This history also helps to create infrastructures of opportunity. Lowery found crucial supports for extending his adult literacy in the educational networks that unions established during the first half of the 20th century as they were consolidating into national powers. On the other hand, this layered history of sponsorship is also deeply conservative and can be maladaptive because it teaches forms of literacy that oftentimes are in the process of being overtaken by new political realities and by ascendent forms of literacy. The decision to focus worker education on practical strategies of recruiting and bargaining—devised in the thick of Cold War patriotism and galloping expansion in union memberships—became, by the Reagan years, a fertile ground for new forms of management aggression and cooptation.

It is actually this lag or gap in sponsoring forms that we call the rising 26 standard of literacy. The pace of change and the place of literacy in economic competition have both intensified enormously in the last half of the 20th century. It is as if the history of literacy is in fast forward. Where once the same sponsoring arrangements could maintain value across a generation or more, forms of literacy and their sponsors can now rise and recede many times within a single life span. Dwayne Lowery experienced profound changes in forms of union-based literacy not only between his father's time and his but between the time he joined the union and the time he left it, twenty-odd years later. This phenomenon is what makes today's literacy feel so advanced and, at the same time, so destabilized.

## Sponsorship and Appropriation in Literacy Learning

We have seen how literacy sponsors affect literacy learning in two powerful 27 ways. They help to organize and administer stratified systems of opportunity and access, and they raise the literacy stakes in struggles for competitive advantage. Sponsors enable and hinder literacy activity, often forcing the formation of new literacy requirements while decertifying older ones. A somewhat different dynamic of literacy sponsorship is treated here. It pertains to the potential of the sponsored to divert sponsors' resources toward ulterior projects, often projects of self-interest or self-development. Earlier I mentioned how Sunday School parishioners in England and African Americans in slavery appropriated church-sponsored literacy for economic and psychic survival. "Misappropriation" is always possible at the scene of literacy transmission, a reason for the tight ideological control that usually surrounds reading and writing instruction. The accounts that appear below are meant to shed light on the dynamics of appropriation, including the role of sponsoring agents in that process. They are also meant to suggest that diversionary tactics in literacy learning may be invited now by the sheer proliferation of literacy activity in contemporary life.

The uses and networks of literacy crisscross through many domains, exposing people to multiple, often amalgamated sources of sponsoring powers, secular, religious, bureaucratic, commercial, technological. In other words, what is so destabilized about contemporary literacy today also makes it so available and potentially innovative, ripe for picking, one might say, for people suitably positioned. The rising level of schooling in the general population is also an inviting factor in this process. Almost everyone now has some sort of contact, for instance, with college-educated people, whose movements through workplaces, justice systems, social service organizations, houses of worship, local government, extended families, or circles of friends spread dominant forms of literacy (whether wanted or not, helpful or not) into public and private spheres. Another condition favorable for appropriation is the deep hybridity of literacy practices extant in many settings. As we saw in Dwayne Lowery's case, workplaces, schools, families bring together multiple strands of the history of literacy in complex and influential forms. We need models of literacy that more astutely account for these kinds of multiple contacts, both in and out of school and across a lifetime. Such models could begin to grasp the significance of reappropriation, which, for a number of reasons, is becoming a key requirement for literacy learning at the end of the 20th century.

The following discussion will consider two brief cases of literacy diversion. 28 Both involve women working in subordinate positions as secretaries, in print-rich settings where better-educated male supervisors were teaching them to read and write in certain ways to perform their clerical duties. However, as we will see shortly, strong loyalties outside the workplace prompted these two secretaries to lift these literate resources for use in other spheres. For one, Carol White, it was on behalf of her work as a Jehovah's Witness. For the other, Sarah Steele, it was on behalf of upward mobility for her lower-middle-class family.

Before turning to their narratives, though, it will be wise to pay some attention to the economic moment in which they occur. Clerical work was the largest and fastest-growing occupation for women in the 20th century. Like so much employment for women, it offered a mix of gender-defined constraints as well as avenues for economic independence and mobility. As a new information economy created an acute need for typists, stenographers, bookkeepers, and other office workers, white, American-born women and, later, immigrant and minority women saw reason to pursue high school and business-college educations. Unlike male clerks of the 19th century, female secretaries in this century had little chance for advancement. However, office work represented a step up from the farm or the factory for women of the working class and served as a respectable occupation from which educated, middle-class women could await or avoid marriage (Anderson, Strom). In a study of clerical work through the first half of the 20th century, Mary Christine Anderson estimated that secretaries might encounter up to 97 different genres in the course of doing dictation or transcription. They routinely had contact with an array of professionals, including lawyers, auditors, tax examiners, and other government overseers (52–53). By 1930, 30% of women office workers used machines other than typewriters (Anderson 76) and, in contemporary offices, clerical workers have often been the first employees to learn to operate CRTs and personal computers and to teach others how to use them. Overall, the daily duties of 20th-century secretaries could serve handily as an index to the rise of complex administrative and accounting procedures, standardization of information, expanding communication, and developments in technological systems.

With that background, consider the experiences of Carol White and Sarah 30 Steele. An Oneida, Carol White was born into a poor, single-parent household in 1940. She graduated from high school in 1960 and, between five maternity leaves and a divorce, worked continuously in a series of clerical positions in both the private and public sectors. One of her first secretarial jobs was with an urban firm that produced and disseminated Catholic missionary films. The vice-president with whom she worked most closely also spent much of his time producing a magazine for a national civic organization that he headed. She discussed how typing letters and magazine articles and occasionally proofreading for this man taught her rhetorical strategies in which she was keenly interested. She described the scene of transfer this way:

> [My boss] didn't just write to write. He wrote in a way to make his letters appealing. I would have to write what he was writing in this magazine too. I was completely enthralled. He would write about the people who were in this [organization] and the different works they were undertaking and people that died and people who were sick and about their personalities. And he wrote little anecdotes. Once in a while I made some suggestions too. He was a man who would listen to you.

The appealing and persuasive power of the anecdote became especially important to Carol White when she began doing door-to-door missionary work for the Jehovah's Witnesses, a pan-racial, millenialist religious faith. She now uses colorful anecdotes to prepare demonstrations that she performs with other women at weekly service meetings at their Kingdom Hall. These demonstrations, done in front of the congregation, take the form of skits designed to explore daily problems through Bible principles. Further, at the time of our interview, Carol White was working as a municipal revenue clerk and had recently enrolled in an on-the-job training seminar called Persuasive Communication, a two-day class offered free to public employees. Her motivation for taking the course stemmed from her desire to improve her evangelical work. She said she wanted to continue to develop speaking and writing skills that would be "appealing," "motivating," and "encouraging" to people she hoped to convert.

Sarah Steele, a woman of Welsh and German descent, was born in 1920 into 31 a large, working-class family in a coal mining community in eastern Pennsylvania. In 1940, she graduated from a two-year commercial college. Married soon after, she worked as a secretary in a glass factory until becoming pregnant with the first of four children. In the 1960s, in part to help pay for her children's college educations, she returned to the labor force as a receptionist and bookkeeper in a law firm, where she stayed until her retirement in the late 1970s.

Sarah Steele described how, after joining the law firm, she began to model her 32 household management on principles of budgeting that she was picking up from one of the attorneys with whom she worked most closely. "I learned cash flow from Mr. B____," she said. "I would get all the bills and put a tape in the adding machine and he and I would sit down together to be sure there was going to be money ahead." She said that she began to replicate that process at home with household bills. "Before that," she observed, "I would just cook beans when I had to instead of meat." Sarah Steele also said she encountered the genre of the credit report during routine reading and typing on the job. She figured out what constituted a top rating, making sure her husband followed these steps in preparation for their financing a new car. She also remembered typing up documents connected to civil suits being brought against local businesses, teaching her, she said, which firms never to hire for home repairs. "It just changes the way you think," she observed about the reading and writing she did on her job. "You're not a pushover after you learn how business operates."

The dynamics of sponsorship alive in these narratives expose important ele- 33 ments of literacy appropriation, at least as it is practiced at the end of the 20th century. In a pattern now familiar from the earlier sections, we see how opportunities for literacy learning—this time for diversions of resources—open up in the clash between long-standing, residual forms of sponsorship and the new: between the lingering presence of literacy's conservative history and its pressure for change. So, here, two women—one Native American and both working-class— filch contemporary literacy resources (public relations techniques and accounting practices) from more-educated, higher-status men. The women are emboldened in these acts by ulterior identities beyond the workplace: Carol White with faith and Sarah Steele with family. These affiliations hark back to the first sponsoring arrangements through which American women were gradually allowed to acquire literacy and education. Duties associated with religious faith and child rearing helped literacy to become, in Gloria Main's words, "a permissable feminine activity" (579). Interestingly, these roles, deeply sanctioned within the history of women's literacy—and operating beneath the newer permissible feminine activity of clerical work—become grounds for covert, innovative appropriation even as they reinforce traditional female identities.

Just as multiple identities contribute to the ideologically hybrid charac- 34 ter of these literacy formations, so do institutional and material conditions. Carol White's account speaks to such hybridity. The missionary film company with the civic club vice president is a residual site for two of literacy's oldest campaigns—Christian conversion and civic participation—enhanced here by 20th-century advances in film and public relations techniques. This ideological reservoir proved a pleasing instructional site for Carol White, whose interests in literacy, throughout her life, have been primarily spiritual. So literacy appropriation draws upon, perhaps even depends upon, conservative forces in the history of literacy sponsorship that are always hovering at the scene of acts of learning. This history serves as both a sanctioning force and a reserve of ideological and material support.

At the same time, however, we see in these accounts how individual acts 35 of appropriation can divert and subvert the course of literacy's history, how changes in individual literacy experiences relate to larger-scale transformations.

Carol White's redirection of personnel management techniques to the cause of the Jehovah's Witnesses is an almost ironic transformation in this regard. Once a principal sponsor in the initial spread of mass literacy, evangelism is here rejuvenated through late-literate corporate sciences of secular persuasion, fund-raising, and bureaucratic management that Carol White finds circulating in her contemporary workplaces. By the same token, through Sarah Steele, accounting practices associated with corporations are, in a sense, tracked into the house, rationalizing and standardizing even domestic practices. (Even though Sarah Steele did not own an adding machine, she penciled her budget figures onto adding-machine tape that she kept for that purpose.) Sarah Steele's act of appropriation in some sense explains how dominant forms of literacy migrate and penetrate into private spheres, including private consciousness. At the same time, though, she accomplishes a subversive diversion of literate power. Her efforts to move her family up in the middle class involved not merely contributing a second income but also, from her desk as a bookkeeper, reading her way into an understanding of middle-class economic power.

## Teaching and the Dynamics of Sponsorship

It hardly seems necessary to point out to the readers of CCC that we haul a 36 lot of freight for the opportunity to teach writing. Neither rich nor powerful enough to sponsor literacy on our own terms, we serve instead as conflicted brokers between literacy's buyers and sellers. At our most worthy, perhaps, we show the sellers how to beware and try to make sure these exchanges will be a little fairer, maybe, potentially, a little more mutually rewarding. This essay has offered a few working case studies that link patterns of sponsorship to processes of stratification, competition, and reappropriation. How much these dynamics can be generalized to classrooms is an ongoing empirical question.

I am sure that sponsors play even more influential roles at the scenes of lit- 37 eracy learning and use than this essay has explored. I have focused on some of the most tangible aspects—material supply, explicit teaching, institutional aegis. But the ideological pressure of sponsors affects many private aspects of writing processes as well as public aspects of finished texts. Where one's sponsors are multiple or even at odds, they can make writing maddening. Where they are absent, they make writing unlikely. Many of the cultural formations we associate with writing development—community practices, disciplinary traditions, technological potentials—can be appreciated as make-do responses to the economics of literacy, past and present. The history of literacy is a catalogue of obligatory relations. That this catalogue is so deeply conservative and, at the same time, so ruthlessly demanding of change is what fills contemporary literacy learning and teaching with their most paradoxical choices and outcomes.[9]

In bringing attention to economies of literacy learning I am not advocating 38 that we prepare students more efficiently for the job markets they must enter. What I have tried to suggest is that as we assist and study individuals in pursuit of literacy, we also recognize how literacy is in pursuit of them. When this process stirs ambivalence, on their part or on ours, we need to be understanding.

## Acknowledgments

This research was sponsored by the NCTE Research Foundation and the Center on English Learning and Achievement. The Center is supported by the U.S. Department of Education's Office of Educational Research and Improvement, whose views do not necessarily coincide with the author's. A version of this essay was given as a lecture in the Department of English, University of Louisville, in April 1997. Thanks to Anna Syvertsen and Julie Nelson for their help with archival research. Thanks too to colleagues who lent an ear along the way: Nelson Graff, Jonna Gjevre, Anne Gere, Kurt Spellmeyer, Tom Fox, and Bob Gundlach.

## Notes

1. Three of the keenest and most eloquent observers of economic impacts on writing, teaching, and learning have been Lester Faigley, Susan Miller, and Kurt Spellmeyer.
2. My debt to the writings of Pierre Bourdieu will be evident throughout this essay. Here and throughout I invoke his expansive notion of "economy," which is not restricted to literal and ostensible systems of money making but to the many spheres where people labor, invest, and exploit energies—their own and others'—to maximize advantage, see Bourdieu and Wacquant, especially 117–120 and Bourdieu, Chapter 7.
3. Thomas Laqueur (124) provides a vivid account of a street demonstration in Bolton, England, in 1834 by a "pro-writing" faction of Sunday School students and their teachers. This faction demanded that writing instruction continue to be provided on Sundays, something that opponents of secular instruction on the Sabbath were trying to reverse.
4. See, for instance, National Assessments of Educational Progress in reading and writing (Applebee et al.; and "Looking").
5. All names used in this essay are pseudonyms.
6. I am not suggesting that literacy that does not "pay off" in terms of prestige or monetary reward is less valuable. Dora Lopez's ability to read and write in Spanish was a source of great strength and pride, especially when she was able to teach it to her young child. The resource of Spanish literacy carried much of what Bourdieu calls cultural capital in her social and family circles. But I want to point out here how people who labor equally to acquire literacy do so under systems of unequal subsidy and unequal reward.
7. For useful accounts of this period in union history, see Heckscher; Nelson.
8. Marcia Farr associates "essayist literacy" with written genres esteemed in the academy and noted for their explictness, exactness, reliance on reasons and evidence, and impersonal voice.
9. Lawrence Cremin makes similar points about education in general in his essay "The Cacophony of Teaching." He suggests that complex economic and social changes since World War Two, including the popularization of schooling and the penetration of mass media, have created "a far greater range and diversity of languages, competencies, values, personalities, and approaches to the world and to its educational opportunities" than at one time existed. The diversity most of interest to him (and me) resides not so much in the range of different ethnic groups there are in society but in the different cultural formulas by which people assemble their educational—or, I would say, literate—experience.

## Works Cited

Anderson, Mary Christine. "Gender, Class, and Culture: Women Secretarial and Clerical Workers in the United States, 1925–1955." Diss. Ohio State U, 1986.

Applebee, Arthur N., Judith A. Langer, and Ida V. S. Mullis. *The Writing Report Card: Writing Achievement in American Schools*. Princeton: ETS, 1986.

Bourdieu, Pierre. *The Logic of Practice*. Trans. Richard Nice. Cambridge: Polity, 1990.

Bourdieu, Pierre and Loic J. D. Wacquant. *An Invitation to Reflexive Sociology*. Chicago: Chicago UP, 1992.

Bourne, J. M. *Patronage and Society in Nineteenth-Century England*. London: Edward Arnold, 1986.

Brandt, Deborah. "Remembering Reading, Remembering Writing." CCC 45 (1994): 459–79.

_____. "Accumulating Literacy: Writing and Learning to Write in the 20th Century." *College English* 57 (1995): 649–68.

Cornelius, Janet Duitsman. *'When I Can Ready My Title Clear': Literacy, Slavery, and Religion in the Antebellum South*. Columbia: U of South Carolina, 1991.

Cremin, Lawrence. "The Cacophony of Teaching." *Popular Education and Its Discontents*. New York: Harper, 1990.

Faigley, Lester. "Veterans' Stories on the Porch." *History, Reflection and Narrative: The Professionalization of Composition, 1963–1983*. Eds. Beth Boehm, Debra Journet, and Mary Rosner. Norwood: Ablex, 1999. 23–38.

Farr, Marcia. "Essayist Literacy and Other Verbal Performances." *Written Communication* 8 (1993): 4–38.

Heckscher, Charles C. *The New Unionism: Employee Involvement in the Changing Corporation*. New York: Basic, 1988.

Horstman, Connie, and Donald V. Kurtz. *Compradrazgo in Post-Conquest Middle America*. Milwaukee: Milwaukee-UW Center for Latin America, 1978.

Kett, Joseph F. *The Pursuit of Knowledge Under Difficulties: From Self Improvement to Adult Education in America 1750–1990*. Stanford: Stanford UP, 1994.

Laqueur, Thomas. *Religion and Respectability: Sunday Schools and Working Class Culture 1780–1850*. New Haven: Yale UP, 1976.

*Looking at How Well Our Students Read: The 1992 National Assessment of Educational Progress in Reading*. Washington: US Dept. of Education, Office of Educational Research and Improvement, Educational Resources Information Center, 1992.

Lynch, Joseph H. *Godparents and Kinship in Early Medieval Europe*. Princeton: Princeton UP, 1986.

Main, Gloria L. "An Inquiry Into When and Why Women Learned to Write in Colonial New England." *Journal of Social History* 24 (1991): 579–89.

Miller, Susan. *Textual Carnivals: The Politics of Composition*. Carbondale: Southern Illinois UP, 1991.

Nelson, Daniel. *American Rubber Workers & Organized Labor, 1900–1941*. Princeton: Princeton UP, 1988.

Nicholas, Stephen J., and Jacqueline M. Nicholas. "Male Literacy, 'Deskilling,' and the Industrial Revolution." *Journal of Interdisciplinary History* 23 (1992): 1–18.

Resnick, Daniel P., and Lauren B. Resnick. "The Nature of Literacy: A Historical Explanation." *Harvard Educational Review* 47 (1977): 370–85.

Spellmeyer, Kurt. "After Theory: From Textuality to Attunement With the World." *College English* 58 (1996): 893–913.

Stevens, Jr., Edward. *Literacy, Law, and Social Order*. DeKalb: Northern Illinois UP, 1987.

Strom, Sharon Hartman. *Beyond the Typewriter: Gender, Class, and the Origins of Modern American Office Work, 1900–1930*. Urbana: U of Illinois P, 1992.

## Questions for Discussion and Journaling

1. How does Brandt define *literacy sponsor*? What are the characteristics of a literacy sponsor?

2. How does Brandt support her claim that sponsors always have something to gain from their sponsorship? Can you provide any examples from your own experience?

3. How do the sponsored sometimes "misappropriate" their literacy lessons?

4. Consider Brandt's claim that literacy sponsors "help to organize and administer stratified systems of opportunity and access, and they raise the literacy stakes in struggles for competitive advantage" (para. 27). What does Brandt mean by the term *stratified*? What "stakes" is she referring to?

5. Giving the examples of Branch and Lopez as support, Brandt argues that race and class impact how much access people have to literacy sponsorship. Summarize the kinds of access Branch and Lopez had—for example, in their early education, access to books and computers, parental support, and so on—and decide whether you agree with Brandt's claim.

## Applying and Exploring Ideas

1. Compare your own literacy history to those of Branch and Lopez, using categories like those in discussion question number 5 above. Then consider who your primary literacy sponsors were (people, as well as institutions like churches or clubs or school systems) and what literacies they taught you (academic, civic, religious, and so on). Would you consider the access provided by these sponsors adequate? What literacies have you not had access to that you wish you had?

2. Have you ever had literacy sponsors who withheld (or tried to withhold) certain kinds of literacies from you? For example, did your school ban certain books? Have sponsors forced certain kinds of literacies on you (for example, approved reading lists in school) or held up some literacies as better than others (for example, saying that certain kinds of books didn't "count" as reading)? Were you able to find alternative sponsors for different kinds of literacy?

3. Interview a classmate about a significant literacy sponsor in their lives, and then discuss the interview in an entry on a class wiki or blog, a brief presentation, or a one-page report. Try to cover these questions in your interview:

   a. Who or what was your literacy sponsor?

   b. What did you gain from the sponsorship?

   c. Did you "misappropriate" the literacy in any way?

   d. What materials, technologies, and so forth were involved?

   In reflecting on the interview, ask yourself the following:

   a. Did the sponsorship connect to larger cultural or material developments?

b. Does the sponsorship let you make any hypotheses about the culture of your interviewee? How would you test that hypothesis?

c. Does your classmate's account have a "So what?"—a point that might make others care about it?

**Meta Moment**

Review the goals for this chapter (p. 42): For which ones is Brandt's article relevant? Are there experiences you're currently having that Brandt's thinking seems to explain or predict?

# All Writing Is Autobiography

## DONALD M. MURRAY

■ Murray, Donald M. "All Writing Is Autobiography." *College Composition and Communication* 42.1 (1991): 66–74. Print.

## Framing the Reading

By the time you've gotten to college, it's very likely that at least one teacher has told you not to use "I" in your school papers. Push the question, and you might be told that academic writing (especially if it uses research) isn't supposed to be "personal"—rather, you should strive to be as objective as possible. The paper, after all, isn't about you—so you shouldn't be in it.

Donald Murray probably had the same voices echoing in his head when he wrote this article for the writing teachers who read *College Composition and Communication*. Having made his living as a writer (including winning a Pulitzer prize as a newspaper columnist, writing textbooks, and publishing a range of poetry and fiction), Murray disagreed. Writing, he thought, is *always* personal, whatever else it is. So he sat down to catalog the various ways that writing of any sort *includes the writer*—the ways that, in a sense, all writing is **autobiography**. This article is one result of his thinking on this topic.

Some readers object to Murray's argument because they misunderstand his use of the term *autobiography*, assuming he's referring to all writing as books in which people tell the stories of their lives. Murray makes it clear, though, that he's not thinking that research papers and workplace memos are autobiographies. Rather, Murray is referring to the autobiographical *nature* of texts, all of which necessarily contain traces of their creators. If you understand autobiography in this sense, it will be easier to fairly weigh Murray's arguments.

Murray's arguments are explicitly about writing, but his broader focus is *all* literacy activities. He is really arguing that all our past literacy experiences inform our present literacy experiences—how we write, what language we use, even (he suggests in the end) how we read. As such, he helps us connect ourselves as *writers* with the literacy work in the rest of the chapter, even when it focuses only on reading or language use. These are all fuels to a writer's fire, and the traces of our literate pasts unavoidably emerge in our writing.

This book is also about how careful research on writing—attempting to explain how writing works on the basis of actual examples of that writing, and the people doing it—actually challenges many of the commonsense "rules" we're taught about writing as young people—like, in this case, "Don't use *I* in your writing" or

"Research writing is purely factual and objective." Research like Murray's tells a more complicated story that does a better job explaining the actual writing we see around us.

## Getting Ready to Read

*Before you read* Murray's article, try the following activity:

- Think back to what you've been taught about how "personal" your school or work writing (that is, not your diary, journal, poetry, songwriting, or other "expressive" writing) can be. What kinds of rules or guidance did you get? If you have friends or classmates around, compare notes with them.

*As you read* this article, consider the following questions:

- What reasons does Murray give for his contention that all writing is autobiography?
- What **genres** (kinds) of writing does Murray discuss? Why? Does he leave any out?
- How does Murray relate writing and reading?
- Why did Murray choose to write *as* he did (for example, by using poetry), *where* he did (in the scholarly journal *College Composition and Communication*), and *for whom* he did? (You may need to do some research to answer this question.) What did he hope to accomplish?

.............................................................................................................................................

I publish in many forms—poetry, fiction, academic article, essay, newspaper  1 column, newsletter, textbook, juvenile nonfiction and I have even been a ghost writer for corporate and government leaders—yet when I am at my writing desk I am the same person. As I look back, I suspect that no matter how I tuned the lyre, I played the same tune. All my writing—and yours—is autobiographical.

To explore this possibility, I want to share a poem that appeared in the  2 March 1990 issue of *Poetry*.

### At 64, Talking Without Words

*The present comes clear when rubbed*
*with memory. I relive a childhood*
*of texture; oatmeal, the afternoon rug,*
*spears of lawn, winter finger tracing*
*frost on window glass, August nose*
*squenched against window screen. My history*
*of smell: bicycle oil, leather catcher's*
*mitt, the sweet sickening perfume of soldiers*
*long dead, ink fresh on the first edition.*
*Now I am most alone with others, companioned*
*by silence and the long road at my back,*
*mirrored by daughters. I mount the evening*
*stairs with mother's heavy, wearied*

*step, sigh my father's long complaint.*
*My beard grows to the sepia photograph*
*of a grandfather I never knew. I forget*
*if I turned at the bridge, but arrive*
*where I intended. My wife and I talk*
*without the bother of words. We know Lee*
*is 32 today. She did not stay twenty*
*but stands at each room's doorway. I place*
*my hand on the telephone. It rings.*

What is autobiographical in this poem? I was 64 when I wrote it. The child- 3
hood memories were real once I remembered them by writing. I realized I was
mirrored by daughters when the line arrived on the page. My other daughter
would have been 32 on the day the poem was written. Haven't you all had the
experience of reaching for the phone and hearing it ring?

There may even be the question of autobiographical language. We talk 4
about our own language, allowing our students their own language. In going
over this draft my spellcheck hiccupped at "squenched" and "companioned."
As an academic I gulped; as a writer I said, "Well they are now."

Then Brock Dethier, one of the most perceptive of the test readers with whom 5
I share drafts, pointed out the obvious—where all the most significant information is often hidden. He answered my question, "What is autobiographical in
this poem?" by saying, "Your thinking style, your voice." Of course.

We are autobiographical in the 6
way we write; my autobiography
exists in the examples of writing I use in this piece and in the
text I weave around them. I have
my own peculiar way of looking
at the world and my own way of
using language to communicate
what I see. My voice is the product
of Scottish genes and a Yankee environment, of Baptist sermons and
the newspaper city room, of all the language I have heard and spoken.

> *We are autobiographical in the way we write; my autobiography exists in the examples of writing I use in this piece and in the text I weave around them.*

In writing this paper I have begun to understand, better than I ever have 7
before, that all writing, in many different ways, is autobiographical, and that
our autobiography grows from a few deep taproots that are set down into our
past in childhood.

Willa Cather declared, "Most of the basic material a writer works with is 8
acquired before the age of fifteen." Graham Greene gave the writer five more
years, no more: "For writers it is always said that the first 20 years of life contain the whole of experience—the rest is observation."

Those of us who write have only a few topics. My poems, the novel I'm 9
writing, and some of my newspaper columns keep returning to my family
and my childhood, where I seek understanding and hope for a compassion

that has not yet arrived. John Hawkes has said, "Fiction is an act of revenge." I hope not, but I can not yet deny the importance of that element in my writing. Revenge against family, revenge against the Army and war, revenge against school.

Another topic I return to is death and illness, religion and war, a great tangle   10 of themes. During my childhood I began the day by going to see if my grandmother had made it through the night; I ended my day with, "Now I lay me down to sleep, I pray the Lord my soul to keep. If I should die before I wake, I pray the Lord my soul to take."

I learned to sing "Onward Christian Soldiers Marching as to War," and still   11 remember my first dead German soldier and my shock as I read that his belt buckle proclaimed God was on *his* side. My pages reveal my obsession with war, with the death of our daughter, with that territory I explored in the hours between the bypass operation that did not work and the one that did.

Recently, Boynton/Cook/Heinemann published *Shoptalk*, a book I began in   12 Junior High School that documents my almost lifelong fascination with how writing is made. I assume that many people in this audience are aware of my obsession with writing and my concern with teaching that began with my early discomfort in school that led to my dropping out and flunking out. My academic writing is clearly autobiographical.

Let's look now at a Freshman English sort of personal essay, what I like to   13 call a reflective narrative. I consider such pieces of writing essays, but I suppose others think of them in a less inflated way as newspaper columns. I write a column, *Over Sixty*, for the *Boston Globe*, and the following one was published October 10th of 1989. It was based on an experience I had the previous August.

> Over sixty brings new freedoms, a deeper appreciation of life and the time to celebrate it, but it also brings, with increasing frequency, such terrible responsibilities as sitting with the dying.
>
> Recently it was my turn to sit with my brother-in-law as he slowly left us, the victim of a consuming cancer.
>
> When I was a little boy, I wanted—hungered—to be a grown-up. Well, now I am a grown-up. And when someone had to sit with the dying on a recent Saturday, I could not look over my shoulder. I was the one. My oldest daughter will take her turn. She is a grown-up as well, but those of us over sixty have our quota of grown-upness increase. Time and again we have to confront crisis: accident, sickness, death. There is no one else to turn to. It is our lonely duty.
>
> Obligation has tested and tempered us. No one always measures up all the time. We each do what we can do, what we must do. We learn not to judge if we are wise, for our judgments boomerang. They return. At top speed and on target.
>
> Most of us, sadly and necessarily, have learned to pace ourselves. We have seen friends and relatives destroyed by obligation, who have lost themselves in serving others. There is no end to duty for those who accept it.
>
> And we have seen others who diminish by shirking responsibility. When we call them for help the door is shut. We hear silence.

We grow through the responsible acceptance of duty, obligation balanced by self-protection. We teeter along a high wire trying to avoid guilt or sancrimoniousness as we choose between duty and avoidance.

And so my mind wanders as Harry sleeps, blessedly without pain for the moment, moving steadily toward a destination he seems no longer to fear.

He would understand that as we mourn for him, we mourn for ourselves. Of course. We are learning from his dying how to live. We inevitably think of what he did that we can emulate and what we should try to avoid.

And we learn, from his courage and his example, not to fear death. I remember how horrified I was years ago when a mother of a friend of mine, in her late eighties, feeling poorly in the middle of the night, would get up, change into her best nightgown, the one saved for dying, and go back to sleep.

Now I understand. During my last heart attack I had a volcanic desire to live but no fear of dying. It was not at all like my earlier trips to the edge.

Harry continues my education. He did not want trouble while he lived and now he is dying the same way, causing no trouble, trying to smile when he wakes, trying to entertain me.

He needs the comfort of sleep and I leave the room, turning outside his door to see how quickly his eyes close. He wants nothing from us now. Not food, not drink, not, we think, much companionship. He accepts that his road is lonely and he does not even show much impatience at its length.

It is not a happy time, alone in the house with a dying man, but it is not a dreadful time either. I pat the cat who roams the house but will not go to the room where Harry lies; I read, write in my daybook, watch Harry, and take time to celebrate my living.

This house, strange to me, in an unfamiliar city, is filled with silence. No music, no TV, just the quiet in which I can hear his call. But he does not call. I cannot hear his light breathing. Every few minutes I go to the door to see if the covers still rise and fall.

He would understand as I turn from him to watch the tree branch brush the roof of the house next door, as I spend long moments appreciating the dance of shadows from the leaves on the roof, then the patterns of sunlight reflected up on the ceiling of the room where I sit, as I celebrate my remaining life.

Again I stand at the edge of the door watching, waiting, and take instruction from his dying. We should live the hours we have in our own way, appreciating their passing. And we should each die in our own way. I will remember his way, his acceptance, his not giving trouble, his lonely, quiet passing.

This is simple narrative with the facts all true, but it is really not that simple; few things are in writing or in life. The details are selective. A great deal of family history is left out. A great many details about the day, the illness, where it was taking place and why were left out. In fact, I wrote it in part for therapy, and it began as a note to myself several weeks after the experience to help me cut through a jungle of thoughts and emotions, to try to recover for myself what was happening that day. Later I saw that it might speak to others, give comfort or form to their own autobiographies. I did not write the whole truth of that day, 14 although the facts in the piece are accurate; I wrote a limited truth seeking a limited understanding, what Robert Frost called "a momentary stay of confusion."

Yes, I confess it, I wrote, and write, for therapy. Writing autobiography is 15 my way of making meaning of the life I have led and am leading and may lead.

Let's look at another autobiographical poem, one of my favorites, which, 16 I suppose, means that it was one I especially needed to write for no autobiographical reason I can identify. It has not yet been published, although a great many of the best poetry editors in the country have failed in their obligation to Western culture by rejecting it.

### Black Ice

*On the first Saturday of winter, the boy*
*skated alone on Sailor's Home Pond, circling*
*from white ice to black, further each time*
*he rode the thin ice, rising, dipping, bending*
*the skin of the water until the crack raced*
*from shore to trick him but he heard, bent*
*his weight to the turn, made it back in time.*

*That winter he saw the fish frozen in ice,*
*its great unblinking eye examining him*
*each time he circled by. He dreamt that eye*
*all summer, wondered if Alex had seen*
*the fish eye before he rode the black ice,*
*did not hear the crack sneak out from shore,*
*imagined he learned to skate on water.*

*At night, after loving you, I fall back*
*to see that fish eye staring down, watch*
*Alex in shoe skates and knickers from below*
*as he skates overhead, circling faster, faster,*
*scissor legs carrying him from white ice*
*to black. His skates sing their cutting song,*
*etching larger, larger circles in my icy sky.*

It is true that the boy, myself, skated on thin ice and that he skated at Sailor's 17 Home Pond in Quincy, Massachusetts, although the thin ice may not have been on that pond. He did not, however, see a fish in the ice until he wrote the poem, although he was obsessed with the eyes of the fish, haddock and cod, that followed him when he went to Titus's fish store in Wollaston. Readers believe that Alex is my brother, although I was an only child. There was no Alex; no one I knew had drowned by falling through the ice until I received the poem; I did not, after loving, stare up to see him skating above me until after I wrote the poem. I do now. The poem that was for a few seconds imaginary has become autobiographical by being written.

Ledo Ivo, the Latin American writer, said, "I increasingly feel that my writ- 18 ing creates me. I am the invention of my own words" (*Lives on the Line*, Ed.

Doris Meyer, U of California P, 1988). Don DeLillo explains, "Working at sentences and rhythms is probably the most satisfying thing I do as a writer. I think after a while a writer can begin to know himself through his language. He sees someone or something reflected back at him from these constructions. Over the years it's possible for a writer to shape himself as a human being through the language he uses. I think written language, fiction, goes that deep. He not only sees himself but begins to make himself or remake himself" (*Anything Can Happen,* Ed. Tom LeClair and Larry McCaffery, U of Illinois P, 1988).

We become what we write. That is one of the great magics of writing. I am best known as a nonfiction writer, but I write fiction and poetry to free myself of small truths in the hope of achieving large ones. Here are the first pages from a novel I am writing. 19

> Notebook in his lap, pen uncapped, Ian Fraser sat in the dark green Adirondack chair studying the New Hampshire scene that had so often comforted him as he put in his last years in his Washington office. The green meadow sloping unevenly over granite ledge to the lake and the point of land with its sentinel pine that marked the edge of his possession, and across the lake the hills rising into mountains touched with the reds, oranges, yellows that would flame into autumn this week or next. He was settled in at last and ready to begin the book he had so long delayed, but he could not write until he scanned this quiet scene with his infantryman's eyes for it still was, as were all his landscapes, a field of fire.
>
> He had to know where to dig in, where the enemy would attack, what was at his back. He supposed it was what had attracted him to this old farmhouse, he could hold this position, he had a good field of fire. First he scanned the lake. Left to right, far edge to near, not one boat or canoe, nothing breaking the surface, no wind trail or wake. Now right to left to see what might be missed. Nothing.
>
> The point of land, his furthest outpost. Scraggly pines, hulking ledge, ideal cover. He studied it close up, knew the pattern of shadows, where the ledge caught the light, where crevice was always dark. This is ridiculous, he thought, an old man whose wars are all over, but he could not stop the search for the enemies that had been there at the edge of other fields so long ago, so recent in memory.
>
> The woods left, on the other side from sentinel point. Sweep his eyes at the woods a half a field away, open ground any enemy would have to cross. He made himself still; anyone watching would not know his eyes were on patrol. He could have hidden a platoon in these woods, tree and bush, ledge and rock wall, but there was no shadow that moved, no unexpected sound, no leaves that danced without wind.
>
> And yet, Ian felt a presence as if he, the watcher, were being watched. He scanned the woods on the left again, moving from lake edge up. Nothing.
>
> Now the woods on the right, he had cut back from the house when he bought it, saying he needed sun for vegetables. He needed open field. More hardwoods here, more openness, the road unseen beyond. It was where someone would come in. His flood lights targeted these woods, but it was not night. He examined these familiar

woods, suddenly looking high in the old oak where a pileated woodpecker started his machine gun attack. Ian studied squirrel and crow, the pattern of light and dark, followed the trail of the quiet lake breeze that rose through the woods and was gone.

Now the field of fire itself, where a civilian would think no-one could hide. He smiled at the memory of a young paratrooper, himself, home on leave, telling Claire, who would become his first wife, to stand at the top of the field and spot him if she could as he crept up the slope, taking cover where there seemed no cover. She was patient with his soldiering—then. She knew her quarry and did not laugh as this lean young man crawled up the slope moving quickly from ledge to slight hollow to the cover of low bush blueberries that July in 1943.

He never knew if she saw him or not.

Do I have a green lawn that reaches down to a New Hampshire lake? No. 20 Do I still see when I visit a new place, forty-six years after I have been in combat, a good field of fire? Yes. Did I have another wife than Minnie Mae? Yes. Was her name Claire? No. Did I play that silly game in the field when I was home on leave? Yes. Is the setting real? Let Herman Melville answer, "It is not down on any map: true places never are."

What is true, what is documentally autobiographical, in the novel will not 21 be clear to me when I finish the last draft. I confess that at my age I am not sure about the source of most of my autobiography. I have written poems that describe what happened when I left the operating table, looked back and decided to return. My war stories are constructed of what I experienced, what I heard later, what the history books say, what I needed to believe to survive and recover—two radically different processes.

I dream every night and remember my dreams. Waking is often a release 22 from a greater reality. I read and wear the lives of the characters I inhabit. I do not know where what I know comes from. Was it dreamt, read, overheard, imagined, experienced in life or at the writing desk? I have spun a web more coherent than experience.

But of course I've been talking about fiction, a liar's profession, so let us turn 23 to the realistic world of nonfiction. That novel from which I have quoted is being written, more days than not, by a technique I call layering that I describe in the third edition of *Write to Learn:*

> One technique, I've been using, especially in writing the novel, is to layer my writing. Once I did quite a bit of oil painting and my pictures were built up, layer after layer of paint until the scene was revealed to me and a viewer. I've been writing each chapter of the novel the same way, starting each day at the beginning of the chapter, reading and writing until the timer bings and my daily stint is finished. Each day I lay down a new layer of text and when I read it the next day, the new layer reveals more possibility.
>
> There is no one way the chapters develop. Each makes its own demands, struggles towards birth in its own way. Sometimes it starts with a sketch, other times the first writing feels complete [next day's reading usually shows it is not]; sometimes I race ahead through the chapter, other times each paragraph is honed before I go on to the next one. I try to allow the text to tell me what it needs.

I start reading and when I see—or, more likely, hear—something that needs doing, I do it. One day I'll read through all the written text and move it forward from the last day's writing; another time I'll find myself working on dialogue; the next day I may begin to construct a new scene [the basic element of fiction]; one time I'll stumble into a new discovery, later have to set it up or weave references to it through the text; I may build up background description, develop the conflict, make the reader see a character more clearly; I may present more documentation, evidence, or exposition, or hide it in a character's dialogue or action.

Well, that is academic writing, writing to instruct, textbook writing. It 24 is clearly nonfiction, and to me it is clearly autobiography. And so, I might add, is the research and scholarship that instructs our profession. We make up our own history, out own legends, our own knowledge by writing our autobiography.

This has enormous implications for our students, or should have. In *Note-* 25 *books of the Mind* (U of New Mexico P, 1985), a seminal book for our discipline, Vera John-Steiner documents the importance of obsession. "Creativity requires a *continuity of concern*, an intense awareness of one's active inner life combined with sensitivity to the external world." Again and again she documents the importance of allowing and even cultivating the obsessive interest of a student in a limited area of study. I read that as the importance of encouraging and supporting the exploration of the autobiographical themes of individual students—and the importance of allowing ourselves to explore the questions that itch our lives.

I do not think we should move away from personal or reflective narrative in 26 composition courses, but closer to it; I do not think we should limit reflective narrative to a single genre; I do not think we should make sure our students write on many different subjects, but that they write and rewrite in pursuit of those few subjects which obsess them.

But then, of course, I am writing autobiographically, telling other people to 27 do what is important to me.

And so all I can do is just rest my case on my own personal experience. I 28 want to read my most recent poem in which the facts are all true. I had not seen as clearly before I wrote the poem the pattern of those facts, the way I— and a generation of children in the United States and Germany and Britain and Japan and China and Spain and France and Italy and Russia and so many other countries—was prepared for war. This piece of writing is factually true but watch out as you hear it. Writing is subversive and something dangerous may happen as you hear my autobiography.

A woman hearing this poem may write, in her mind, a poem of how she was 29 made into a docile helpmate by a society that had its own goals for her. A black may write another autobiography as mine is heard but translated by personal history. A person who has been mistreated in childhood, a person who is a Jew, a person whose courage was tested at the urging of jeering peers on a railroad bridge in Missouri, will all hear other poems, write other poems in their mind as they hear mine.

### Winthrop 1936, Seventh Grade

*December and we comb our hair wet,*
*pocket our stocking caps and run,*
*uniformed in ice helmets,*

*to read frost etched windows:*
*castle, moat, battlements, knight,*
*lady, dragon, feel our sword*

*plunge in. At recess we fence*
*with icicles, hide coal in*
*snow balls, lie freezing*

*inside snow fort, make ice balls*
*to arc against the enemy; Hitler.*
*I lived in a town of Jews,*

*relatives hidden in silences,*
*letters returned, doors shut,*
*curtains drawn. Our soldier*

*lessons were not in books taught*
*by old women. In East Boston,*
*city of Mussolinis, we dance*

*combat, attack and retreat, sneak,*
*hide, escape, the companionship*
*of blood. No school, and side*

*staggered by icy wind we run*
*to the sea wall, wait*
*for the giant seventh wave*

*to draw back, curl mittens*
*round iron railing, brace*
*rubber boots, watch*

*the entire Atlantic rise*
*until there is no sky. Keep*
*mittens tight round iron rail,*

*prepare for the return of ocean,*
*that slow, even sucking back,*
*the next rising wave.*

I suspect that when you read my poem, you wrote your own autobiography. 30
That is the terrible, wonderful power of reading: the texts we create in our own
minds while we read—or just after we read—become part of the life we believe
we lived. Another thesis: all reading is autobiographical.

## Questions for Discussion and Journaling

1. Remember that one of the goals of this book is to help you consider **threshold concepts** about writing that help you rethink how writing actually works. What threshold concept is Murray asking you to consider here?

2. In what ways, according to Murray, is writing autobiography? Can you categorize the ways that Murray believes writing is autobiography?

3. Murray's article was published in a peer-reviewed, scholarly journal, yet it does not share the typical features of that genre. Murray's writing is more informal, more "literary," and easier to read in some ways. Make a list of the ways that Murray's article is different from the other scholarly articles in this chapter. Then consider some reasons why Murray would have wanted to break out of the usual "rules" for writing in the scholarly article genre.

4. If you've answered the third question, you have already considered the ways in which this piece is unusual for a scholarly article. Now consider the opposite question: Make a list of the features that mark Murray's article as belonging to the genre of "scholarly article."

5. Consider the implications of Murray's arguments: If he's right, how do his ideas change the way you think about writing? Would they encourage you to write any differently than you currently do?

6. Consider the last few texts that you have written, whether for school, work, or personal reasons. Consider the ways that these texts are—or are not—autobiography in the sense that Murray describes.

## Applying and Exploring Ideas

1. Write a one- to two-page response to Murray that explains your reaction to his piece and gives reasons for your thinking. You could write this piece a number of different ways: as a letter to Murray, or to a friend; as an article in the same style as Murray's; or as a review of the article (like a review of a new album or film).

2. If you've heard before that writing—especially academic writing—should be impersonal and keep the writer out, Murray's article might inspire you to argue against that point of view. Take one to two pages and freewrite comments you might make to a teacher or other authority figure who told you in the past to write "objectively" and keep yourself out of the text.

---

**Meta Moment**

Quickly name two or three ways that understanding Murray's claims here can have a positive impact on you as a writer and/or on your attitude about writing.

# Draw Me a Word, Write Me a Picture

## THOMAS NEWKIRK

■ Newkirk, Thomas. "Draw Me a Word, Write Me a Picture." *More Than Stories: The Range of Children's Writing*. Portsmouth, NH: Heinemann 1989. 35–66. Print.

## Framing the Reading

Thomas Newkirk is a literacy researcher who, throughout his career, has focused on how children learn to read and write, and especially on the texts that they are reading and writing. This piece is an example of his research. (Newkirk has also studied boys' reading habits and play around literacy—one of his most famous books is *Misreading Masculinity: Boys, Literacy, and Popular Culture*.) Instead of accepting common assumptions about how children acquire reading and writing, Newkirk gathers concrete examples of their literacy practices and looks closely at the texts children create. In doing so, he learns a number of surprising things about the way children read and write. Newkirk has spent most of his very long career as a professor at the University of New Hampshire, where he's also focused extensively on the teaching of writing at the high-school and college levels.

The piece that follows is a chapter from his book *More Than Stories: The Range of Children's Writing*, which is an excellent example of his commitment to drawing conclusions about how we come to writing as children by looking at many, many actual examples of that writing. Based on how young children blend drawing and writing into multimodal texts that include both pictures and words, Newkirk asks us to look at our assumptions about how pictures relate to language in written texts, and the notion that pictures are "easier" than alphabetic text, so that kids draw only until they can write alphabetically because there's somehow greater sophistication in writing words than in drawing pictures. His analysis raises questions about this traditional assumption.

## Getting Ready to Read

*Before you read*, do at least one of the following activities:

- Find, if you can, some of your childhood drawings. How many of them incorporate alphabetic writing? (If you don't have these where you're going to school, you might see if your family saved any.)

- In the kinds of texts you see that include both alphabetic print and images, how do the images usually relate to the alphabetic writing? What is the print there to do, and what are the images there to do?
- Find an online reference to the book from which this chapter is taken. What else does Newkirk do in that book?

*As you read*, consider the following questions:

- What might have prompted Newkirk to think along these lines—to ask these questions and do this particular study—to begin with?
- How is the chapter enacting its title: "Draw me a word, write me a picture"? Why do these characterizations of writing and drawing and words and pictures sound a little strange to us?

It was writing time in Anna Sumida's first-grade classroom, and, as usual, 1 Jason, Gregg, and Alan were drawing. Each had drawn a space-age tank that was being assaulted by varieties of spacecraft. Laser beams threaded through the sky. At first glance, the three pictures seemed distinct—that is until Jason showed me the hinge at the end of each paper that attached the three drawings. At times, they would swap papers because each child specialized in a particular type of plane: Gregg, for example, was a master at drawing small jets. All the while as they were drawing the three kept up a running commentary, complete with explosive sound effects, elaborating the story of the ongoing battle. I watched as Gregg created a magnetic field (a series of wavelike lines) that sucked one of the bigger planes into the hold of his tank. When the alarm clock rang indicating the end of writing period, Jason quickly wrote "Spae Invadrs" at the top of his paper.

I asked permission to photocopy the three papers and enthusiastically ex- 2 plained their complexity to a teacher standing by the machine. "Yes," she sighed. "Now if we could only get them to write that."

In a way, this teacher's observation is right. Schools are far more concerned 3 about verbal competence than graphic competence. In fact, it is easy to feel impatient with students like Jason, Gregg, or Alan who spend their time drawing when they could be writing, who clearly view the written message as marginal. School culture is word centered; while we might admire the drawing of young children, we're not terribly concerned (as a culture) when the interest in drawing gives way to an interest in print.

Fortunately, early research on the writing processes of young children has 4 confirmed the interrelationship of writing and drawing. Donald Graves and his associates have shown that when children draw before they write, the drawing helps them to discover what they would like to write. According to Graves (1983), the drawing serves as a "rehearsal" for the writing. But when I think of Jason, Gregg, and Alan, I have difficulty thinking of their drawing as a rehearsal for the minimal message that Jason eventually (and grudgingly) wrote. The drawing-as-rehearsal concept seems to me to be inadequate for three reasons:

- It gets the priorities wrong. A rehearsal is a preliminary to the more important performance and has significance because it prepares the actor for that performance. But, for many children, the drawing is more important, taking up most of the paper, with the writing squeezed into any free space.
- It suggests a greater separation between drawing and writing than the children actually intend. When you ask a child to show you his or her "writing," the child will display both the picture and the caption or label. The "writing" is the whole production, text and picture—even the running commentary is part of it. To be sure, as writers mature, the writing becomes more self-sufficient or, as David Olson (1977) terms it, more "autonomous." But this view of writing as text, separate from pictures and oral commentary, is too stripped down for the beginning writer.
- The word "rehearsal" suggests that the drawing is a cognitive crutch to help students find things to write about. But students actually may be working within a genre that they know well — the picture book. They interpret the request to "write" as a request to reproduce the "writing" that they've seen before. I've noticed that, when young children change genre — for example, when they write birthday announcements or letters —they tend not to give the drawing the central position. Their desire to draw before writing in school may show their understanding of the picture-book genre rather than their cognitive need to produce a picture so that they can find something to write.

The idea of drawing-as-rehearsal is just one more example of the word- 5 centered view that reigns in our educational system. The child's drawing is reduced to a preliminary, a kind of prewriting, rather than being accepted as an important communicative symbol system in its own right. Of course, a host of researchers have taken children's drawing seriously — among them, Rhoda Kellogg (1970), Jacqueline Goodnow (1977), and Howard Gardner (1980)— but usually as it represents the development of artistic abilities. Less frequently explored is the relationship between drawing and the development of literate ability. To borrow Ann Dyson's beautiful expression, children like Jason, Gregg, and Alan are "symbol-weaving" (1986), constantly shifting among mutually supporting systems of representation—talking, drawing, and, in a minimal way, producing written text. Their "writing" is a fabric formed of all these strands.

While symbol-weaving may describe more satisfactorily the relationship 6 between drawing and emerging print literacy, it is also considerably more complex than regarding drawing as rehearsal. I first thought one could begin to analyze this weaving process by looking at the writing and drawing (and talking) that children did during writing time in school. Yet because children seemed so primed to use writing to label pictures, I began to wonder how their early experience of learning to talk and, particularly, learning to talk about picture books set the stage for learning to read and write. Labelling pictures is not new for most schoolchildren; it has solid roots in early language-learning interactions with parents. So, in the first part of this chapter, I will look at the way this early learning prepares the way for literacy learning.

Next, I will address the question of genre. In the last chapter, I argued that the dominant theories of writing development underestimate the *range* of children's writing; even beginning writers seem able to appropriate a variety of non-narrative forms. Can the same be said of their pictures? Do children draw narrative pictures and expository pictures, that is, pictures that show a frozen moment in a series of ongoing actions (a narrative picture) and static pictures that seem to be graphic lists perhaps showing the members of the child's family in a family portrait (an expository picture)? 7

Finally, I will examine how children allocate informativeness among the symbol systems available. The written text, the picture, and the oral commentary each make their own contribution to the woven fabric. What guides the child's choice of pattern? 8

## The Achievement of Labelling

Anyone who has read Helen Keller's autobiography or seen *The Miracle Worker* remembers the scene where Annie Sullivan takes six-year-old Helen to the water pump, runs water over one of her hands, and signs "water" into the other. Suddenly Helen understands that words name things, and her chaotic world stabilizes. Like Adam, she gains dominion over her new world by *naming* it. The linguist Ernst Cassirer (1984) has written eloquently about the importance of this discovery:

> The idea of drawing-as-rehearsal is just one more example of the word-centered view that reigns in our educational system. The child's drawing is reduced to a preliminary, a kind of prewriting, rather than being accepted as an important communicative symbol system in its own right. 9

> By learning to name things a child does not simply add a list of artificial signs to his previous knowledge of ready-made empirical objects. He learns rather to form concepts of those objects, to come to terms with the objective world. Henceforth the child stands on firmer ground. His vague, uncertain, fluctuating perceptions, and his dim feelings begin to assume a new shape. They may be said to crystallize around the name as a fixed center, a focus of thought. Without the help of the name every new advance made in the process of objectification would always run the risk of being lost again in the nest moment. (110)

So readily—indeed, voraciously—do children around the age of two take to naming objects that it is tempting to view this development as a natural unfolding of linguistic ability. Yet, as Jerome Bruner (1983) put it, parents provide a "Language Acquisition Support System," a regularized pattern of interaction that helps children learn to label, although, as parents, we are often unaware of our systematic assistance.

While we might consider labelling to be fairly straightforward, a fundamental ambiguity exists. Suppose I point to my telephone and ask, "What's that?" A number of answers are possible—"dial," "numbers," "letters"—in addition to "telephone." For you to answer the question, we must first agree on whether we are referring to a part (e.g., the dial) or a whole (e.g., the telephone). It is even possible to answer by stating the *type* of object to which I am referring) (e.g., a "nuisance" or "means of communication"), although children are unlikely to err in this direction. Bruner's colleague, Anat Ninio (1980), demonstrated that labelling can only proceed under a tacit agreement about the level of specification required, furnishing convincing evidence of this systematic agreement.

Studying forty mother-infant pairs, Ninio found that parents consistently elicited a label for the whole and that, if they asked for an attribute label, they consistently did so after the whole had been identified. For example, the mother might say, "Do you see a baby? A baby, yes. What else? Shoes. The baby wears shoes." Scollon and Scollon (1979) have called this kind of interaction a "vertical buildup." The main name is elicited first, and, next, an attribute of that whole is requested. A child might be asked to identify an animal and then to describe the sound that the animal makes. There is nothing inevitable about this order, it could as easily move from parts to a whole. But parents act, in Bruner's words (1983), as "agents of the culture," where discourse regularly moves from whole to parts, from assertions to reasons, from terms to definitions, from generalizations to specifics. And this education begins not too far from the crib.

Once children learn that things have names, they often want to name everything, pointing to anything in a room and asking "whazat?" Yet, in many homes, picture books play a special role in the achievement of labelling. First, we point to a picture and say something like, "Do you see the bunny? Point to the bunny." As the child builds a vocabulary of labels, we shift more of the burden to him to him or her; reversing roles, *we* ask the "whazat?" questions. Again, much of this instruction seems natural and unpremiditated. Yet Ninio and Bruner (1978) argue that this simple act of identifying a picture may be more complex than it first appears:

> Pictures, being two-dimensional representations of three-dimensional objects, have special visual properties: they can be perceived both as a two-dimensional object AND as representing a three-dimensional visual scene. This poses a conflict for the child, one which he solves increasingly by assigning a privileged, autonomous status to pictures as visual objects. There is steadily less evidence of the child trying to manipulate, grasp, or scratch pictured objects on the page. This process might be one of the stepping stones to grasping the arbitrary symbolic representation in language, since visual representations are themselves arbitrary in the sense of a crucial property, i.e. graspability is missing. (5)

In other words, children who can accept the fiction that a two-dimensional picture of a telephone can represent the actual object may be on their way to accepting the fiction that the word "telephone" can represent the object as well.

Children not only learn routines for talking about pictures in books, they soon begin to develop hypotheses about the relationship of the print to the pictures or objects connected to the print. A number of researchers (Ferreiro and Teberosky, 1982; Harste, Woodward, and Burke, 1984; Snow, 1983) have shown that children initially tend to view all print as a label for an object. Snow offers the following example of Nathaniel, age thirty-one months, who often played with a toy cargo truck with the initials KLM (for the airline) on the side of it. The toy regularly was referred to as "the airport truck." One day, Nathaniel decided that he could read the letters on the side of the truck: [13]

> NATHANIEL [*pointing to* KLM *on toy truck*]: That say airport truck.
> MOTHER: No, that says KLM.
> NATHANIEL [*insistently*]: That says de airport truck.
> MOTHER: KLM cargo.
> NATHANIEL [*more insistently*]: That says airport truck.
> MOTHER [*patiently*]: In the airport the trucks have to carry cargo from the planes to other planes, or into the city and that's what this truck does.
> NATHANIEL [*pointing to* KLM]: Who's this?
> MOTHER: Where?
> NATHANIEL: That says . . . de airport . . .
> MOTHER [*interrupting*]: KLM, Nathaniel, this says KLM. (176)

Nathaniel clearly prefers a straightforward relationship in which words label objects and resists his mother's attempts to suggest that the letters may not represent his choice for the truck's label. The mother's role in this exchange is also interesting. After correcting him twice, she shifts to the identification-plus-attribute pattern that we have seen before. In this case, she explains the function of the truck. But Nathaniel's not buying because he doesn't accept the notion that an object may have more than one designation.

Labelling, and talking about labels, comes so easily to most children who have been read to regularly that we underestimate the difficulty of apparently simple "what?" questions for children with no book reading experience. Gordon Wells (1986) provides a painful instance of this difficulty in his case study to Rosie. Rosie had virtually no experience with books in her home, so, when asked the simple "what?" question in school, she seemed to be at a loss. In the following excerpt from a transcript, Rosie is in nursery school making a calendar from a Christmas card showing Santa Claus skiing down a hill. The teacher is attempting to get Rosie to identify elements of the picture on the card and is interrupted several times in the process: [14]

> CHILD: Miss, I done it.
> TEACHER [*to Rosie*]: Will you put it at the top?
> CHILD: Miss, I done it, look.
> [*Several seconds' pause*]

TEACHER [*to Rosie, pointing with finger at card*]: What are those things?

CHILD: Miss, I done it. Miss, I done it.

[*Rosie drops something, then picks it up.*]

TEACHER [*to Rosie*]: What are those things?

CHILD: Miss, I done it.

TEACHER [*referring to skis in picture*]: D'you know what they're called? [*Rosie shakes her head.*] What d'you think he uses them for? [*Rosie looks at the card. The teacher turns to the other child's calendar.*] It's very nice. After play, we'll put some ribbons at the top.

CHILD: What?

TEACHER: Ribbon at the top to hang them up by. Would you put all the cards together now? Put the cards together.

CHILD: Oh.

TEACHER [*to Rosie, pointing at the skis on the card*]: What's—what are those? [*Rosie looks blank.*] What d'you think he uses them for?

ROSIE [*rubbing her eye with the back of her hand*]: Go down.

TEACHER: Go down—yes, you're right; go on. [*Rosie rubs both of her eyes with the backs of her hands.*] What's the rest of it? [*Puts down card*] You have a little think and I'll get—er, get the little calendar for you. . . . (96–97)

Children like Rosie are generally described as nonverbal or even linguistically deprived, but these terms really say very little. Why does this exchange go so badly? In part, because the teacher is distracted and consequently listens poorly to what Rosie is saying. She insists that Rosie identify the skis even after Rosie says she doesn't know that word. But, surely, Rosie's bafflement is due to more than her ignorance of this single label.

Because Rosie is unfamiliar with the rituals associated with talking about pictures, she is probably confused by the entire pattern of questioning, beginning with the opening question, "What are those things?" To answer this question, Rosie would have to understand that, for the purposes of this question, the picture is the thing—the expected answer is "skis" and not "pictures," "lines," "colors," or "calendar," which to Rosie may be as reasonable. 15

Rosie may also be wondering why the teacher is asking the question in the first place: Surely, this woman towering above her *knows* the answer to the question she is asking? The most perplexing moment probably comes when the teacher says "go on." What can this mean? Rosie knows she should say something—but what? The teacher's "go on" presumes that Rosie is familiar with the talk that usually goes on at reading time when a child is asked to elaborate on the original identification (Heath, 1982). Rosie could have responded to the teacher's request for elaboration by giving more specific information about the skis, identifying other things in the picture, predicting what will happen to Santa Claus as he skis down the hill, or, depending on the flexibility of the teacher, by offering personal reactions or associations that might relate to the picture. That is what the request minimally coded in "go on" asks for. And that is what more "verbal" children would do, not simply because they have bigger vocabularies or are more talkative, but because they are familiar with the routines for labelling pictures and providing elaborative information about the 16 labels. Shirley Brice Heath (1982) claims that familiarity with these routines gives some children a powerful advantage in school:

> Close analysis of how mainstream school-oriented children come to learn to take from books at home suggests that such children learn not only how to take meaning from books, but also how to talk about it. In doing the latter, they repeatedly practice routines which parallel those of classroom interaction. By the time they enter school, they have had continuous experience as information-givers; they have learned how to perform in those interactions which surround literate sources throughout school. They have had years of practice in interaction situations that are the heart of reading—both learning to read and reading to learn in school. (56)

For Rosie, who never had those encounters, these routines remain a mystery.

Heath's essay is entitled "What No Bedtime Story Means: Narrative Skills at  17 Home and School." It is clear, though, that she believes these encounters with books promote more than narrative skills. In effect, the bedtime story becomes a staging area, where the child engages in book talk. When my daughter and I read *Miss Nelson Is Back*, I might pause to comment on the inept principal, Mr. Blandsford: "Don't you think Blandsford is dumb?" And Sarah might say, "Yeah, him and his dumb ballpoint pen collection." This kind of exchange is a precursor to more extended character evaluation. In the next chapter, I will show how the label-plus-attribute request (which Rosie failed to understand) anticipates the early informative writing that children attempt. These early routines help students learn what to "go on" means.

Thus, it is hardly surprising that, when children begin to write, they often  18 do so by attaching labels to the pictures that they draw—not because they need the drawings to rehearse for the writings, but because they have often had thousands of literacy experiences that centered around pictures. Children have mastered routines that they apply to school situations. The psychologist Larry Gross (1974) has also commented on the importance of these routines:

> One achieves competence in a medium by slowly building on the routines which have been performed over and over until they have become tacit and habitual. This basic repetitious activity can be easily seen in children who derive enormous satisfaction from performing over and over some action which results in a predictable effect. The felling of efficacy . . . is the basic and initial form of satisfaction in competence. It is on the basis of a repertoire of often repeated actions that the child can begin to introduce and perceive slight variations and thus extend the range of his perceptual intellectual competence to more complex forms of organized behavior. (73)

The beginning writer seems to rely on the routine of labelling and then extending labels by explaining attributes.

Heath's work (1982), in particular, suggests that a modification should be  19 made to the speech-dependency model of literacy learning that claims that the development of literacy skills is built on a foundation of oral language ability (see, in particular, Moffett and Wagner, 1983). If, for example, early writing is talk written down, one would expect that a child who talks fluently would be well prepared for writing. The problem with this position is that it fails to account for the difficulty many talkative, expressive children have with literacy learning in school settings. Heath describes in wonderful detail the rich oral culture of a working-class black community in the Piedmont mountains. Yet, when she followed children from this community into schools, she found that they had problems not because they were not expressive, but because they did not have access to certain literate routines that had become habitual to the mainstream or middle-class children. It all relates to the request made to Rosie to "go on," which was not simply a request for her to keep talking in a certain way—a game that she did not know how to play. Similarly, I would argue that children do not begin to write by working outside literate tradition, writing down preformal speech. They are working within literate traditions, even before they begin to draw, even as they learn to talk around books.

## The Drawing as Genre

One day I was reading to my younger daughter (age five years, five months at the time) from an informational book on trucks. Each page pictured different categories of trucks—those that carried things, those that helped in emergencies, and so on. On one page was a picture of a logging truck with "Logging Truck" printed below it. "What do you think this says?" I asked. Abby thought a minute and then said, "I bet it says 'carrying.'" 20

Her answer surprised me because I had expected the object label. As I thought about my question, I realized that I had asked for more than a simple identification. Abby had the option of determining whether the picture focused on ongoing action or on the identification of the object in the picture. As it turned out, she was drawn to the ongoing action—to the implied verb rather than the implied noun. She read the picture as a narrative (as action), not as a description. 21

I realize that, in using "narrative" and "description," I am applying verbal terms to something graphic and visual. This is intentional. In this section, I will argue that the written forms that children use—both narrative and expositional—have clear counterparts in the drawings that they attempt. They can emphasize the continity of action, in effect, drawing one frame of a reel of film, but, if they are skillful and resourceful, a frame that suggests what went on before and what will follow. Or children can emphasize permanence, capturing a timeless moment—a family portrait, for example—that seems to be extracted from the onward flow of events. Each option poses its own graphic challenge and the narrative, in particular, requires the child to suggest many pictures with one. 22

I will also look at the minimal writing that often accompanies these pictures. These short messages usually are referred to indiscriminately as "labels," as many indeed are. But some of these messages more appropriately are called "captions" because they focus on the action of the picture: I expected a label from Abby, and she responded with a caption. 23

## Narrative Pictures

The young writer/artist who wants to draw action immediately confronts a 24 problem—a picture cannot move. Movement must be suggested by the child so that the observer can infer the action. This section will examine how children circumvent the immobility of the picture. Most of the drawings reproduced were done by kindergarten children in Hawaiian schools (Lindberg, 1988). As a result, this sample may have a regional flavor, but most of the drawings will, I believe, seem quite familiar—even Hawaiian children draw houses with smoke coming out of slanted chimneys.

*Strategy 1: The initiating state.* When selecting which slice of the action 25 to depict, a child may choose the opening moment. For example, the child's family may be shown standing outside a house, ready to take a trip. Such a picture represents the starting point of the commentary that accompanies it. The advantage of this strategy is that the child does not have to deal with the graphic challenge of depicting action. The commentary, written or oral, suggests the narrative.

Figure 2–1 is a fairly typical portrait of a family at the moment before the 26 action is about to begin. The child, when asked to tell about the picture, said, "I at the beach. My brothers and sisters went with me. We going swimming." Similarly, Figure 2–2 shows the author-artist and friend Gaylene facing us directly beneath five clouds. The child explained the picture: "Gaylene and me going to the pool and then shopping at Pay-n-Save. Then back home."

FIGURE 2–1 *Initiating state: "I at the beach. My brothers and sisters went with me. We going swimming."*

FIGURE 2–2 *Initiating state:* "*Gaylene and me going to the pool and then shopping at Pay-n-Save. Then back home.*"

*Strategy 2: The midaction picture.*    While strategy 1 yields drawings that   27
seem static, the midaction picture is dynamic; the author-artist has found a
visual language to suggest ongoing action. One method might be called the
"gravity technique." Because objects cannot remain aloft permanently, we
mentally complete the action of an object's return to earth when we see it in
midair. It's for this reason that we find pictures of people falling so terrifying. In
Figure 2–3, the fish in midair adds a sense of movement to the picture. In Figure
2–4, the ball in midair suggests the activity of the catcher because we mentally
complete the ball's flight. This figure also uses wavy lines to denote action, a
technique that will be discussed later.

  Children can also create dynamic tension between objects or people in   28
their pictures; from this tension, we infer action, imagining the effect that one
thing might have on another. If, for example, we see someone with an uplifted
knife standing behind an unsuspecting victim, we mentally complete the action. Many of the Hawaiian children experimented with this kind of action
picture soon after they saw the Bigfoot show at Aloha Stadium. Bigfoot was a
huge truck with wheels about seven feet in diameter. The highlight of the show
was when Bigfoot drove over a series of cars—a delicious power fantasy for
many of the boys. In their drawings, the author-artists often successfully created the illusion of action by showing the results of Bigfoot's power. In several
drawings, we see Bigfoot on top of a car crushed so thoroughly that it is little
more than a shadow. (See Figure 2–5.) In Figure 2–6, we also anticipate action

**FIGURE 2–3** *Midaction state: Gravity technique—fish in midair.*

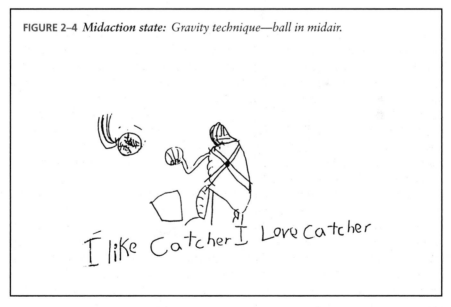

**FIGURE 2–4** *Midaction state: Gravity technique—ball in midair.*

because of what we know about dogs. The child has drawn himself pulling his dog's tail, and we mentally complete the action by imagining the dog turning toward the child.

FIGURE 2–5 *Midaction state:* Tension between objects—Bigfoot crushing a car.

FIGURE 2–6 *Midaction state:* Tension between objects—child and dog.

FIGURE 2–7 *Wedding scene:* *Figures in profile.*

One difficulty that children face in showing people interacting is the prob-    29
lem of profile. Children almost invariably draw human figures facing forward,
looking at us, the viewers, and not at each other. To create a sense of dramatic
interaction, however, it is often necessary to break out of this face-forward
pattern and show the figures in profile so that we see only the side of the face
(Sowers, 1985b). We get some sense of this possibility in Figure 2–4, where the
catcher is clearly facing away from us. We also see the effect of profile drawing
in Figure 2–7, where the bride and groom are looking toward the ringbearer,
who in turn is watching them. The effect is considerably more dynamic than a
face-forward presentation.

Another way to create the illusion of action is to use wavy lines to show    30
dirt flying, wind blowing, firecrackers exploding. The author-artist of
Figure 2–8 clearly wants to suggest as much action as he can. He describes
his picture: "One motorcycle and fire on the motorcycle. All wind coming
blowing—all dark. This all my three smokes." Figure 2–9 was drawn just

**FIGURE 2–8** *Midaction state:* Action lines, "One motorcycle and fire on the motorcycle. All wind coming blowing—all dark. This all my three smokes."

**FIGURE 2–9** *Midaction state:* ActionLines-fireworks.

after the New Year's celebration in Honolulu, when fireworks crackled throughout the city (there were about fifty fires in the city that night). The author uses wavy lines to show the trajectories and explosions of the fireworks.

These examples of action demonstrate the children's awareness of graphic 31 conventions—or codes—that allow an observer mentally to transform something static into something active. Hubbard (1988) claims that devices like action lines are used commonly in Western culture to indicate action. By contrast, non-Western cultures do not denote action in the same way. Hubbard (1973), which involved showing the same cartoon picture of a dog to rural Zulus and Western subjects in South Africa. Two drops of saliva are suspended below the dog's visible tongue, action lines trail behind each paw, and a small cloud of dust hovers behind the hind paws. Seventy-five percent of the Western subjects knew the dog was supposed to be moving, as compared to only 1 percent of the Zulus.

*Strategy 3: The postaction picture.*   The author-artist may choose to 32 show the concluding frame of the narrative, although this option seemed to be less popular among the Hawaiian sample than the previous two strategies. The most notable example showed a monster all in red (Figure 2–10). The child's commentary: "Monster. It has bloody eyes. Red ears. It has blood right there. It has a bloody nose. It has blood right there too. It got bloody eating little kids."

*Strategy 4: Multiple frames.*   A fourth way to subvert the static quality of 33 the picture is to use more than one picture to show what happens over a period of time. A child may show the movement of a kicked soccer ball by drawing a series of balls along the line of trajectory. Children also reinvent the cartoon, using a series of pictures to create the effect of a narrative.

Two teachers at Mast Way School in Lee, New Hampshire, Florence Damon 34 and Pat McLure, began to encourage children to use multiple frames to show a sequence of actions. Children regularly are asked to sequence someone else's pictures but rarely to draw their own. I borrowed the idea and asked Abby (then age six) to try it. She drew nine frames (Figure 2–11) showing a bird building a nest, then feeding a baby bird in the final frame. In fact, there is yet another time sequence in her early frames, which show the tree losing its leaves and becoming bare.

As Hubbard (1987) has noted, there are several variations on this technique. 35 In Figure 2–12, Abby attempts to show the back-and-forth movement of a Christmas tree ornament by indicating the central position with firm lines and using lighter lines to illustrate the ornament's position as it sways back and forth. Figure 2–13, the Happy Puppy Machine, is another attempt to show a process that process that occurs over time. Here she drew a long conveyer tube that processed the raw material—undifferentiated trapezoids—into happy puppies.

**FIGURE 2–10** *Postaction picture:* "*Monster. It has bloody eyes. Red ears. It has blood right there. It has a bloody nose. It has blood right there too. It got bloody eating little kids.*"

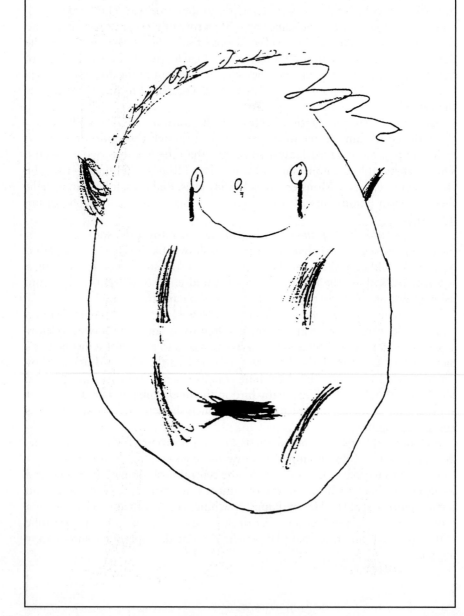

FIGURE 2–11 *Multiple frames: Building a bird's nest.*

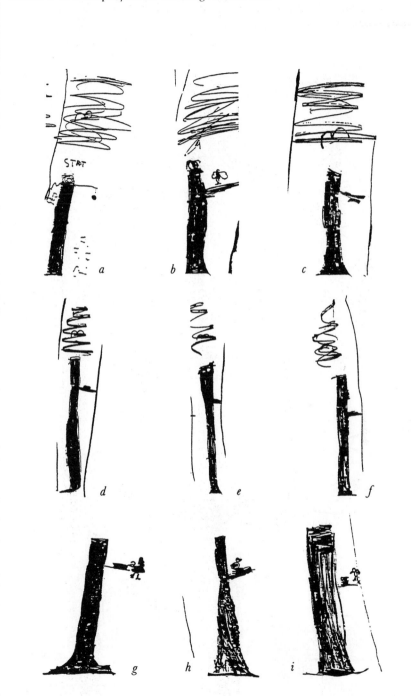

FIGURE 2–12 *Moving ornament.*

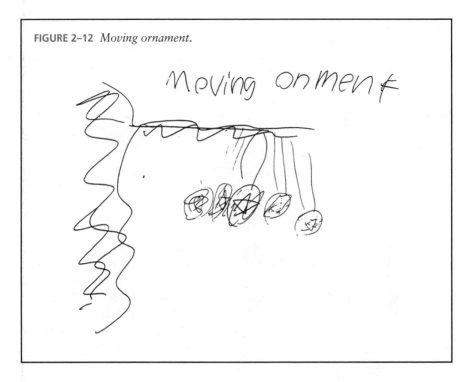

FIGURE 2–13 *Steps in a process: The Happy Puppy Machine.*

## Expository Pictures

Whereas the narrative picture stresses the continuity of action, the expository 36
picture examines the child's world removed from the stream of events. The
emphasis is on what is, not on what happens. Where the commentary on narrative pictures invariably includes an action verb, the verb used for expository
pictures is a form of *to be* or *to have*—"this is," "these are," "I have," and so
on. It could even be argued that the simple one-word label includes an understood "this is." The *label*, then, can be defined as a "to be" statement; the *caption* (which has the same root as *capture*) seizes a moment in a series of actions.

In the expository pictures, we see children confronting two graphic chal- 37
lenges that have clear counterparts in expository writing: inclusiveness and
specificity. Probably the best example of inclusiveness in drawing are the many
Richard Scarry books, which I did not enjoy reading although they were favorites of all my children. Mem Fox (1988), the best-selling Australian children's
author, says that she needs to throw in a few "winks" to parents to keep their
attention. The Scarry books did not cast any winks my way; the story lines
seem weak, unimaginative, and utterly predictable. Their phenomenal popularity arises, I believe, from the almost encyclopedic completeness of the illustrations. The books play to the child's love of lists, though the lists are primarily
visual. Some children's drawings aim for this kind of inclusiveness.

FIGURE 2–14 *Expository picture: Family portrait.*

The most common visual lists were the many family portraits. Crystal's pic- 38
ture (Figure 2–14) is typical. The text reads, "My family. I have three sister and
I have one brother in my house." She also names each of the figures: "My mom-
my and me. Pani and Joy." In Figure 2–15, we have something that approaches
the Richard Scarry formula; the child suggests action with the caption "I'm
playing at my house" but also labels, Scarry style, the elements in the picture.

One decision that the child makes when drawing expository pictures is 39
whether to concentrate on inclusiveness (getting everybody or everything into
the picture) or specificity (creating detail within the picture). It's the difference
between a wide-angle and a telephoto lens.

Teachers can promote pictorial exposition by nudging students in the two 40
directions that I have indicated. We can encourage the child to add more
elements—for example, by asking "Who else is in your family?" "What other
pets do you have?" "What other things do you have in your yard?" Or we can
prompt the child to add details, asking "How big is your father?" "Does he
wear glasses?" Susan Bridge (1988) offers the following example of an elaborating conference with her three-year-old nephew. Kevin has already drawn
one mask and appears to be starting another (Figure 2–16a).

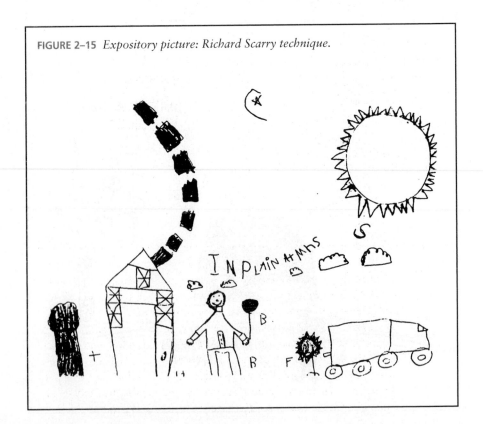

**FIGURE 2–15** *Expository picture: Richard Scarry technique.*

**FIGURE 2–16** *Expository sequence: Focus on detail—Kevin's self-portrait (from Bridge 1988, 87).*

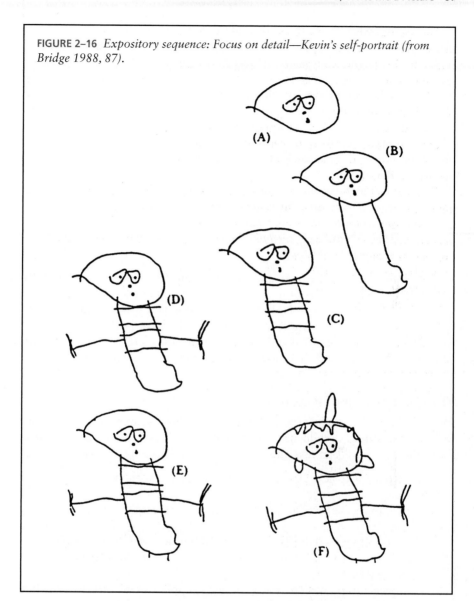

KEVIN [*drawing, begins to laugh*]: It's a funny face. It's MY face! [*Quickly he draws a tadpole body, revising the mask—Figure 2—16b*]. That's me! [*Pointing to the picture.*] That's my shirt! [*Pointing to the body he has drawn. He looks down at his own shirt, touches the fabric.*] I have stripes on it. [*Makes stripes on the shirt, —Figure 2–16c—pats stripes he has just made.*] That's part of him. [*Without hesitation he draws the arms, adding four fingers to each—Figure 2–16d.*] I don't know where the feet are. There's no room [*Directed toward me—he had drawn the figure close to the bottom of the page.*]

SUSAN: What do you think you could do if there's no more room?

KEVIN: Put it down here. [*Draws two straight lines from the tadpole body to the end of the paper —Figure 2—16e*] Feet! [*At this point Kevin appears to be finished.*]

SUSAN: Tell me about your drawing.

KEVIN: It's me!

SUSAN: It *is* you! I can see your face, and your arms —here are your fingers, and your shirt with stripes on it, and your feet. It certainly looks like you. Is there anything else you want to add to make it look just like Kevin?

KEVIN [*Looks at his picture, puts his hand up and touches his ears*]: Ears. [*Draws ears. Puts hand on the top of his head.*] Point. [*Draws a point on top of the head, making a quick motion. Touches his head again.*] Hair. [*Draws hair carefully. Looks at picture, appearing satisfied—Figure 2–16f.*] (85–87)

Bridge's comments urge Kevin to add specific details to his picture. She carefully 41 acknowledges what he has done and then asks the question that sparks that last round of elaboration—"Is there anything else you want to add to make it look just like Kevin?" Another time, she might have pushed him toward inclusiveness by asking, "Are you by yourself in this picture or are you with somebody?"—a question that might encourage him to include other figures.

## The Relationship of Picture to Text

Imagine that written language and drawing are both sources of information. What options does a child have when facing a blank piece of paper? How many different ways can text and drawing relate? There are at least seven:

1. Text only. The text carries the only message, with no accompanying picture.
2. Picture only. The picture, unaided by text, represents the event, person, or object.
3. Picture and text—redundant. The text duplicates what is in the picture.
4. Imbalance—pictorial. The picture is far more specific and informative than the written text.
5. Complementary. Both text and drawing supply specific information, but the child decides which medium provides which information.
6. Imbalance—textual. The text provides most of the information.
7. General-specific relationship. The text identifies a general category, and the picture shows specific items in that category. For example, a child could draw a candy bar and label it "candy bar" (what I would call a redundant relationship) or he or she could call it "junk" (a general-specific relationship).

I'm sure that this list underestimates the options, but it does suggest the range of choices available to children and, indirectly, to teachers, once they step outside a word-centered mindset.

The problem inherent in dealing with children's drawing-writing is deter-  42
mining which option the child has chosen. I remember one first-grade conference where the child, a reticent boy, had drawn a picture and written a
two-word label. The child began, somewhat reluctantly, to explain the story
represented in the picture. The teacher would ask, "Where did you put that
(meaning where did you write that?"), and the boy would point to his picture
to answer the questions. As far as he could see, it was all there *in the picture.*
The teacher, however, was expecting the text-picture relationship at least to be
redundant, an expectation that probably mystified the boy.

The expectation that meaning will be explicit in the text is both understand-  43
able and, in the long run, desirable. But exclusive focus on the text may not be
a good short-term strategy, because it assumes, perhaps incorrectly, that a child
is adopting a particular view of written language. Moreover, it tends to ignore
the work that the child has done in his preferred system of representation—
drawing. The teacher in this conference might have worked more effectively
within the intent of the child if she had urged an even *greater* imbalance by
asking the child to talk about and maybe elaborate on the drawing. If we are to
encourage decision making in the writing classroom, we need to view writing
in the broadest possible way, as the interweaving of various symbol systems,
which is how children tend to see it.

## Picture Only

Some children (like Jason, Gregg, and Alan, or the boy discussed above) de-  44
velop such skill at drawing that a written commentary seems almost superfluous. Ironically, *because* of their skill, these children may resist the idea that
text and picture can be coequal, because making them coequal would take
time and energy away from their drawing and require considerable text—
more than they would feel comfortable producing—to do any kind of justice
to their drawing. Figure 2–17 is an impressive example of an explicit picture.
At the center front of the picture is a clown, to the right of him a lion tamer; in
the air are four performers, two on the trapezes and two waiting on the platform. Below the trapeze is a net. At the far left of the picture, a man is setting
off a cannon, and we can trace the trail of a cannonball across the page. The
child has "written" nothing, and indeed one wonders how children with such
drawing ability view the implied request to attach written labels to creations
such as this.

## Picture and text—redundant

Sometimes, the written message seems to convey exactly the same information  45
as the picture. Children's drawing often is schematic, with no attempt to be
individually explicit. The child's house is the standard house (with the chimney
perpendicular to the slant of the roof). The sun that shines in the pictures is
not the sun that children see in the sky, but a circle radiating lines. The children do not seem to draw reality and then label or describe it; rather, they use
two sets of conventionalized symbols (words and schematic drawings), one

FIGURE 2–17 *Picture without written text.*

to label the other. This is the impression we get from Figure 2–18, where the child has drawn virtually the same schematic drawing—the person drawing—to represent Shanna, her mother, her father, and her cousin. The fish are the conventional circle-plus-triangle fish, the sun the conventional sun, and so on. The picture is adequate to identify each referent—we recognize the sun as a sun—but it conveys no more information than that.

### Imbalance–pictorial

If we contrast Figure 2–18 with Figure 2–19, we notice a shift toward a more fully informative picture. The text, "I see a Rock Foot," serves as a general label, but the picture is more than a conventionalized schema. We can also see carefully drawn fire (red in the original) coming out of the rear of the train and smoke (blue) coming out of the top stack. The door has a clearly drawn handle and what look like rivets in the smokestack are drawn at painstaking right angles. I have found that children who produce these kinds of drawings, like the children in our first category, also often resist implied requests to extend their written descriptions, although they will gladly add visual detail until the picture is virtually clogged with it. They're not particularly interested in quitting while they're ahead, because, for them, it is the activity of drawing and not drawing and not the final product that matters most.

46

**FIGURE 2–18** *Picture and text—redundant.*

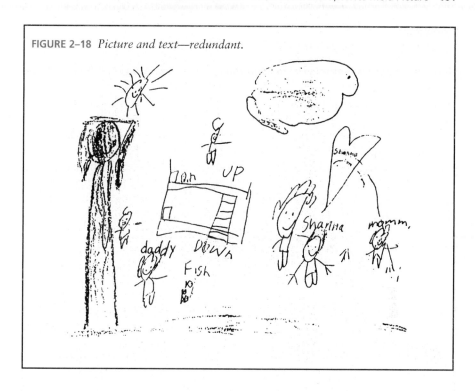

**FIGURE 2–19** *Imbalance—pictorial.*

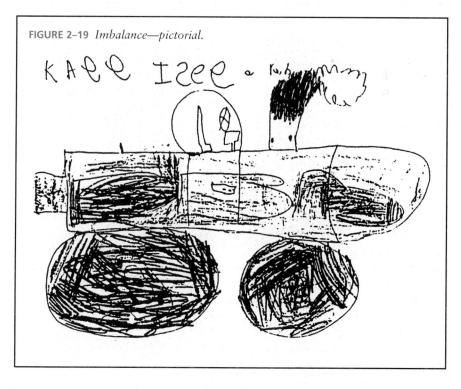

## Complementary

Maurice Sendak, the noted children's author, claims that "you must never    47
illustrate exactly what is written. You must find a space in the text so that the
pictures can do the work. Then you must let the words take over where words
do it best" (quoted in Hubbard, 1987, 60). In Figure 2–20 we see an example
of a complementary relationship where the text does not duplicate what is in
the picture. From the picture, we learn several things that the text does not tell
us: We see how long the "funny thing's" tail is, we see that the man fed him
outside his house shown at two points in the action: inside the house getting
the food and outside the house feeding the animal. And from the expressions
on their faces, we know that both the man and the funny thing are happy. From
the text, however, we learn something that would have been very difficult to
illustrate—that the man fed the funny thing plenty of times. Thus, we learn that
the action in the picture was repeated several times.

## Imbalance—textual

Often, near the end of first grade or the beginning of second grade, several    48
forces work to minimize the importance of the drawing and shift attention

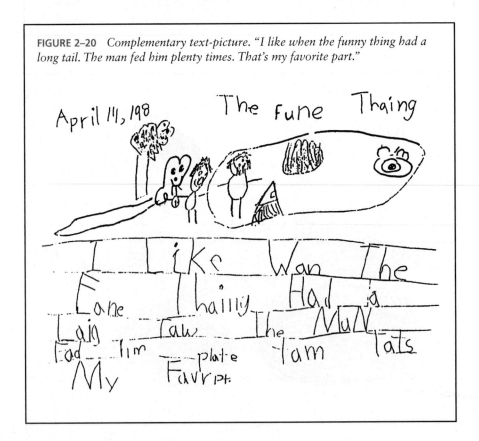

FIGURE 2–20   *Complementary text-picture. "I like when the funny thing had a long tail. The man fed him plenty times. That's my favorite part."*

to the written text. The child becomes more fluent; letter formation is easier and fewer words need to be sounded out. Sometimes this fluency is pushed to an extreme—students compete to see who can write the longest books, books as long as the ones they read. At the same time, children can become self-conscious about their illustrations. Second grade, after all, has been called the adolescence of elementary school. How one appears to others becomes suddenly important. As Gardner (1980) has shown, children begin to ask if their drawings are realistic representations—do they look right? This newfound fluency—combined with a more critical perspective on artwork, combined with a newly developed fear of appearing childish, combined with the pressure from the school to attend more to written elaboration and less to artistic elaboration—inevitably shifts the order of priorities. The writing, now, is completed first. The lined paper provides only a small space at the top for the illustration. Written language does the work.

## General-specific Relationship

Another way in which texts come to do more than duplicate pictures is through 49 the introduction of more general terms, with pictures used to provide instances or examples. (I have been using illustrations this way in this chapter.) In one such drawing, my daughter Sarah drew a schematic whale above a small fish, with the inevitable sun in the upper right-hand corner of the page. The drawing was fairly typical, but the text was not: "Whales are mammals and they are big. They live in the water. They eat all the fish." With the word "mammal," the child introduced a superordinate noun that names the class of animals to which whales belong. While "whale" is drawable, "mammal" is not. We cannot draw a mammal, only an example of a mammal. In another drawing that Sarah, age six, did at about this age, she wrote "Junk" at the top of her page and then drew several examples of junk—candy bars, gum, and so on. These clearly are early explorations of the genus-species relationship.

Of course, we want children to become skilled at producing explicit writ- 50 ten texts. We want writing to be more than a hurried formality completed quickly at the end of writing period. But, as teachers and parents, we dismiss too easily the value and complexity of the children's drawing. Although we pay lip service to the idea that a picture is worth a thousand words, we don't really believe it. It's the thousand words that really interest us. Once the golden age of drawing has passed (around the second or third grade), art gives way to a predominantly, if not exclusively, word-centered school culture, and children no longer allocate informativeness between the two systems.

One question worth asking, though, is whether word-centeredness reflects 51 the absolute superiority of written language as a system of representation or, instead, outmoded assumptions about the difficulty of including pictures in texts. For most of printing history, pictures included in books had to be engraved, a process far more time-consuming and costly than setting type. In other words, there was an *economic* advantage to being print centered. But the advent of photographic printing (as opposed to letterpress) makes chapters like this one, which intersperses drawing with text, relatively easy to do. Computer technology has increased our capacity for integrating graphics and text. Newspapers like *USA Today* look radically different from their predecessors in part because the visual and the verbal are so interwoven. I'm suggesting then that an exclusively word-centered view of literacy may not prepare students for the graphic and design opportunities that will be available to them. Ironically, we all may need to alter our view of "writing" to include these opportunities. We may need to think of composing more as the children in this chapter do—as symbol-weaving.

But there's an even more basic reason not to neglect the contribution that  52 drawing can make to the development of language learners. Drawing can help develop perceptual ability—the ability to make refined observations, which is useful for more than artwork. Consider the story about Louis Agassiz's anatomy class, where, for the first three days, he asked his students to look at a fish and draw what they saw. Elliot Eisner (1983) elaborates on this connection:

> Art education and art educators in particular have a special interest in differentiating the sensory abilities of individuals. When those abilities—call them sensory intelligence if you like—are well differentiated, the qualities to be experienced available, and an interest in experiencing those qualities high, the amount of new information an individual is able to secure from the world is increased. (23)

My own experience with artists convinces me that Eisner is right. My neighbor  53 is an artist, and, sometimes, when we sit outside at dusk and admire the way the light hits the buildings flush, I know that she is seeing something more complex and differentiated than I am. She might make some comment about shadows or lines or textures that I don't even see until she points them out. For I am one of those who never progressed beyond the schematic house and tree and cloud—though my chimneys no longer slant off the roof.

....................

## Questions for Discussion and Journaling

1. Consider the words "drawing" and "writing." Why *don't* we call "writing" a kind of "drawing"? Why don't we call "drawing" a kind of "writing"? What's different between the two activities? What if kids never learned that difference?

2. Newkirk argues that "schools are far more concerned about verbal competence than graphical competence" (para. 3). Why? Given the screen-driven, graphics-driven era we've entered in the past two decades, is this wise?

3. What kinds of decisions do you make about your writing? Because Newkirk argues that "if we are to encourage decision-making in the writing classroom, we need to view writing in the broadest possible way, as the interweaving of various symbol systems, which is how children tend to see it" (para. 43). Do your decisions about writing usually involve how to integrate visual material with your print text? Why or why not?

4. In paragraphs 9 through 19, Newkirk takes some trouble to demonstrate how disadvantaged children can be in school if their home experience has not already had them practicing the activities that are asked of them in school—in this case, using words to "label" the material in pictures. What does this line of argument have to do with the rest of this chapter? What meaning or points would be lost if it weren't here?

5. A significant portion of this chapter is concerned with disjuncts between what teachers want and what children are (probably) trying to achieve in their drawing/writing. Do you remember an experience from early school where you were trying to write one thing and your teacher wanted you to do something else? Did any of them involve drawings?

6. Look at this article from the perspective of a writing researcher: Newkirk wouldn't be able to do this work of analyzing children's drawings if he hadn't procured a stack of drawings to begin with. Suppose you wanted to do a similar study with high-schoolers' doodles (like in their class notes): where and how would you come up with the doodles?

7. Do you accept Newkirk's distinction between "narrative" and "expository" drawings? Explain your answer, and consider whether there are other kinds of drawings as well.

8. Near the end of his piece, Newkirk asks whether school is so word-centered because words are actually superior to images, or because it's still assuming that images are as difficult to incorporate into writing as they were before the computer revolution. What's your answer to his question, and why?

9. Do you think Newkirk is advocating that we pay more attention to kids' drawing and not push them so quickly to take up alphabetic writing? What's the basis for your answer?

## Applying and Exploring Ideas

1. Find a short essay you've written, either for college or, if you haven't yet written one, something from high school. Illustrate it. See if you can follow Maurice Sendak's advice (that Newkirk quotes) on not illustrating exactly what's written, but rather finding ways for pictures to do their own work while the alphabetic text does what it's good at.

2. Look around your everyday life and collect a portfolio of "grown-up" writing that uses both drawings and alphabetic writing. How much did you find? To what purposes are such writings put? Are there any that incorporate image and alphabet but don't really "need" to—they could get by with one or the other?

3. Newkirk says that his list of seven different ways that text and drawing can relate "underestimates the options" (para. 41). Try expanding his list of relationships between alphabetic text and images: what's missing?

4. Make a list of all the ways that your culture associates written language with intelligence or maturity, and the use of pictures with childishness or simple-mindedness. Then, see if you can make a list of the ways that, culturally, the use of pictures is associated with intelligence. Compare your lists and, based on them, write an argument about how your culture understands the relationship between pictures and language. What cultural roles seem to be assigned to each?

5. Suppose that grade schools committed themselves to maintaining, rather than eliminating, children's apparent instinct to "allocate informativeness between the two systems" of drawing and lettering (para. 5). Remembering what you can of your early school experiences, say second through fourth grade, how might such a commitment have changed the work you were asked to create and the writing you were asked to do? What would assignments in these new classes look like?

---

**Meta Moment**

Take a look at your own communication habits: would you consider yourself "word-centered" or "symbol-weaving"? Whichever you are, how well does that fit your current culture?

# Excerpt from *Bootstraps: From an Academic of Color*

## VICTOR VILLANUEVA

■ Villanueva, Victor. Excerpt from *Bootstraps: From an Academic of Color*. Urbana, IL: NCTE, 1993. 66–77. Print.

## Framing the Reading

No matter what races or ethnicities or nationalities you as a reader of this book identify with, it's probably not news that in any given setting, some languages or styles of a language seem dominant and others seem marginalized. Whether you have thought about this or not, you have the ability to change your language and tone for different audiences and purposes—that is, to "code-switch." The ability to move among different versions of your language, or different languages altogether, in order to match different social circumstances is an important one for successfully engaging with others. For some of you, this code-switching might mean using a different language and sound in a place of worship than you do in a place of work or school. For some of you, it might mean using the languages characteristic of ethnicities other than your own. Some of you are international students who are multilingual, while others might be second-generation students who speak one language with your families and another at school. One way or another, to be human is to be aware of the interplay among languages and how they mark identity, status, and potential. And to be human is to be aware that in circumstances where you use a form of language that is not the one most commonly used in broader society, one of your struggles is learning the language used by the majority and deciding what of it to use—when, where, how much. Making decisions about what language practices to use is not just a matter of learning something new, but of deciding who to be.

Victor Villanueva's book *Bootstraps: From an Academic of Color* is a narrative and an analysis of his own experience with this struggle. Villanueva grew up as a Puerto Rican in the Hell's Kitchen area of New York City, with parents who had emigrated from Puerto Rico with Spanish as their first language. He grew up to be a very successful professor of rhetoric, focusing on questions of race, language, and power. *Bootstraps* tells the story of his evolution, and the excerpt that you'll read here focuses specifically on his movement from the U.S. Army into an English degree and graduate school. It's a literacy narrative that captures the feelings of confusion and frustration, as well as elation and satisfaction, experienced by one member of a group whose language and

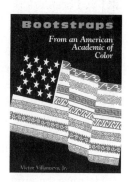

ethnicity are not in the majority as he learns to participate in an academic community that required using very different language practices. We include it because we think that, like the other literacy narratives included in this chapter, it speaks to students who have experienced trying out new language practices in a new place; it also describes the frustrations of learning to write in school settings like the one you are in now.

Villanueva is Regents Professor at Washington State University. In his work, he describes and theorizes the ways cultural systems, including universities, use language and rhetoric to reinforce or to resist ethnic and racial oppression. He made another major contribution to the study of rhetoric and writing with his anthology *Cross-Talk in Comp Theory*, a reader which gathered a wide range of composition research and theory and made it accessible to students. He's headed the Conference on College Composition and Communication and won a wide range of honors both from the field of writing studies and the universities in which he's taught, researched, and administered.

## Getting Ready to Read

*Before you read*, do at least one of the following activities:

- Find out more about this writer. You can begin at his school Web page, **http://www.libarts.wsu.edu/english/Villanueva.htm**, and also Google-search more broadly.
- Think back to when you first considered going to college, whatever age that was. Did you think, back then, you could do it? If you didn't feel confident, what prevented that confidence?

*As you read*, consider the following questions:

- What school-writing experiences have you encountered that resemble any described by Villanueva?
- What do you know about affirmative action in higher education, and how is this reading matching up with that knowledge?

I wanted to try my hand at college, go beyond the GED. But college scared me. 1 I had been told long ago that college wasn't my lot.

He drives by the University District of Seattle during his last days in the 2 military and sees the college kids, long hair and sandals, baggy short pants on the men, long, flowing dresses on the women, some men in suits, some women in high heels, all carrying backpacks over one shoulder. There is both purpose and contentment in the air. Storefronts carry names like Dr. Feelgood and Magus Bookstore, reflecting the good feelings and magic he senses. A block away is the University, red tiles and green grass, rolling hills and tall pines, apple and cherry blossoms, the trees shading modern monoliths of gray concrete and gothic, church-like buildings of red brick. And he says to himself, "Maybe in the next life."

He must be content with escaping a life at menial labor, at being able to 3 bank on the skills in personnel management he had acquired in the Army. But there are only two takers. The large department-store chain would hire him as a management trainee—a shoe salesman on commission, no set income, but a trainee could qualify for GI Bill benefits as well as the commissions. Not good enough, not getting paid beyond the GI Bill; and a sales career wasn't good enough either, the thought of his mother's years as a saleslady, years lost, still in memory. A finance corporation offers him a job: management trainee. The title: Assistant Manager. The job: bill collector, with low wage, but as a trainee, qualified to supplement with the GI Bill. The combined pay would be good, but he would surely lose his job in time, would be unable to be righteously indignant like the bill collectors he has too often had to face too often are, unable to bother people like Mom and Dad, knowing that being unable to meet bills isn't usually a moral shortcoming but most often an economic condition.

The GI Bill had come up again, however, setting the "gettinover" wheels in 4 motion. The nearby community college charges ninety dollars a quarter tuition, would accept him on the strength of his GED scores. That would mean nearly four hundred dollars a month from the GI Bill, with only thirty dollars a month for schooling ("forgetting" to account for books and supplies). What a get-over! There would be immediate profit in simply going to school. And if he failed, there would be nothing lost. And if he succeeded, an Associate degree in something. He'd be better equipped to brave the job market again.

So he walks onto the community college campus in the summer of 1976. It's 5 not the campus of the University of Washington. It's more like Dominguez High School in California. But it is a college. Chemistry: a clumsiness at the lab, but relative grace at mathematical equations and memorization. French is listening to audiotapes and filling out workbooks. History is enjoyable stories, local lore from a retired newsman, easy memorization for the grade.

Then there is English. There are the stories, the taste he had always had for 6 reading, now peppered with talk of philosophy and psychology and tensions and textures. Writing is 200 words on anything, preceded by a sentence outline. He'd write about Korea and why *The Rolling Stone* could write about conspiracies of silence, or he'd write about the problems in trying to get a son to understand that he is Puerto Rican when the only Puerto Ricans he knows are his grandparents; he'd write about whatever seemed to be on his mind at the time. The night before a paper would be due, he'd gather pen and pad, and stare. Clean the dishes. Stare. Watch an "I Love Lucy" rerun. Stare. Then sometime in the night the words would come. He'd write; scratch something out; draw arrows shifting paragraphs around; add a phrase or two. Then he'd pull out; the erasable bond, making changes even as he typed, frantic to be done before school. Then he'd use the completed essay to type out an outline, feeling a little guilty about having cheated in not having produced the outline first.

The guilt showed one day when Mrs. Ray, the Indian woman in traditional 7 dress with a Ph.D. in English from Oxford, part-time instructor at the community college, said there was a problem with his writing. She must have been able to tell somehow that he was discovering what to write while writing, no prior thesis statement, no outline, just a vague notion that would materialize, magically, while writing. In her stark, small office she hands him a sheet with three familiar sayings mimeoed on it; instructs him to write on one, right there, right then. He writes on "a bird in the hand is worth two in the bush." No memory of what he had written, probably forgotten during the writing. Thirty minutes or so later, she takes the four or five pages he had written; she reads; she smiles; then she explains that she had suspected plagiarism in his previous writings. She apologizes, saying she found his writing "too serious," too abstract, not typical of her students. He is not insulted; he is flattered. He knew he could read; now he knew he could write well enough for college.

English 102, Mr. Lukens devotes a portion of the quarter to Afro-American  8 literature. Victor reads Ishmael Reed, "I'm a Cowboy in the Boat of Ra." It begins,

> *I am a cowboy in the boat of Ra,*
> *sidewinders in the saloons of fools*
> *bit my forehead like      O*
> *the untrustworthiness of Egyptologists*
> *Who do not know their trips. Who was that*
> *dog faced man? they asked, the day I rode*
> *from town.*
>
> *School marms with halitosis cannot see*
> *the Nefertitti fake chipped on the run by slick*
> *germans, the hawk behind Sonny Rollins' head or*
> *the ritual beard of his axe; a longhorn winding*
> *its bells thru the Field of Reeds.*

There was more, but by this point he was already entranced and excited. Poetry  9 has meaning, more than the drama of Mark Antony's speech years back.

Mr. Lukens says that here is an instance of poetry more for effect (or maybe *affect*) than for meaning, citing a line from Archibald MacLeish: "A poem should not mean / But be." But there *was* meaning in this poem. Victor writes about it. In the second stanza, the chipped Nefertitti, a reference to a false black history, with images from "The Maltese Falcon" and war movies. The "School marms" Reed mentions are like the schoolmasters at Hamilton, unknowing and seeming not to know of being unknowing. Sonny Rollins' axe and the Field of Reeds: a saxophone, a reed instrument, the African American's links to Egypt, a history whitewashed by "Egyptologists / Who do not know their trips." He understood the allusions, appreciated the wordplay. The poem had the politics of Bracy, the language of the block, TV of the fifties, together in the medium Mr. D had introduced to Victor, Papi, but now more powerful. This was fun; this was politics. This was Victor's history, his life with language play.

Years later, Victor is on a special two-man panel at a conference of the Mod-  10 ern Language Association. He shares the podium with Ishmael Reed. Victor gives a talk on "Teaching as Social Action," receives applause, turns to see Ishmael Reed looking him in the eye, applauding loudly. He tries to convey how instrumental this "colleague" had been in his life.

He'll be an English major. Mr. Lukens is his advisor, sets up the community  11 college curriculum in such a way as to have all but the major's requirements for a BA from the University of Washington out of the way. The University of Washington is the only choice: it's relatively nearby, tuition for Vietnam veterans is $176 a quarter. "Maybe in this life."

His AA degree in his back pocket, his heart beating audibly with exhilara- 12
tion and fear, he walks up the campus of the University of Washington, more
excited than at Disneyland when he was sixteen. He's proud: a regular transfer
student, no special minority waivers. The summer of 1977.

But the community is not college in the same way the University is. The 13
community college is torn between vocational training and preparing the un-
prepared for traditional university work. And it seems unable to resolve the
conflict (see Cohen and Brawer). His high community-college GPA is no measure of what he is prepared to undertake at the University. He fails at French
103, unable to carry the French conversations, unable to do the reading, unable
to do the writing, dropping the course before the failure becomes a matter of
record. He starts again. French 101, only to find he is still not really competitive
with the white kids who had had high school French. But he cannot fail, and he
does not fail, thanks to hour after hour with French tapes after his son's in bed.

English 301, the literature survey, is fun. Chaucer is a ghetto boy, poking fun 14
at folks, the rhyming reminding him of when he did the dozens on the block;
Chaucer telling bawdy jokes: "And at the wyndow out she putte hir hole . . .
'A berd, a berd!; quod hende Nicholas." So this is literature. Chaucer surely
ain't white. At least he doesn't sound white, "the first to write poetry in the vernacular," he's told. Spenser is exciting: images of knights and damsels distress-
ing, magic and dragons, the *Lord of the Rings* that he had read in Korea paling
in the comparison. Donne is a kick: trying to get laid when he's Jack Donne,
with a rap the boys from the block could never imagine; building church floors
with words on a page when he's Dr. John Donne. Every reading is an adventure, never a nod, no matter how late into the night the reading. For his first
paper, Victor, the 3.8 at Tacoma Community College, gets 36 out of a possible
100—"for your imagination," written alongside the grade.

I was both devastated and determined, my not belonging was verified but I was 15
not ready to be shut down, not so quickly. So to the library to look up what
the Professor himself had published: *Proceedings of the Spenser Society.* I had
no idea what the Professor was going on about in his paper, but I could see
the pattern: an introduction that said something about what others had said,
what he was going to be writing about, in what order, and what all this would
prove; details about what he said he was going to be writing about, complete
with quotes, mainly from the poetry, not much from other writers on Spenser;
and a "therefore." It wasn't the five-paragraph paper Mr. Lukens had insisted
on, not just three points, not just repetition of the opening in the close, but the
pattern was essentially the same. The next paper: 62 out of 100 and a "Much
better." Course grade: B. Charity.

I never vindicated myself with that professor. I did try, tried to show that I 16
didn't need academic charity. Economic charity was hard enough. I took my
first graduate course from him. This time I got an "All well and good, but
what's the point?" alongside a "B" for a paper. I had worked on that paper all
summer long.

I have had to face that same professor, now a Director of Freshman Writ- 17
ing, at conferences. And with every contact, feelings of insecurity well up from

within, the feeling that I'm seen as the minority (a literal term in academics for those of us of color), the feeling of being perceived as having gotten through *because* I am a minority, an insecurity I face often. But though I never got over the stigma with that professor (whether real or imagined), I did get some idea on how to write for the University.

Professorial Discourse Analysis became a standard practice: go to the library; see what the course's professor had published; try to discern a pattern to her writing; try to mimic the pattern. Some would begin with anecdotes. Some would have no personal pronouns. Some would cite others' research. Some would cite different literary works to make assertions about one literary work. Whatever they did, I would do too. And it worked, for the most part, so that I could continue the joy of time travel and mind travel with those, and within those, who wrote about things I had discovered I liked to think about: Shakespeare and work versus pleasure, religion and the day-to-day world, racism, black Othello and the Jewish Merchant of Venice; Dickens and the impossibility of really getting into the middle class (which I read as "race," getting into the white world, at the time), pokes at white folks (though the Podsnaps were more likely jabs at the middle class); Milton and social responsibility versus religious mandates; Yeats and being assimilated and yet other (critically conscious with a cultural literacy, I'd say now); others and other themes. And soon I was writing like I had written in the community college: some secondary reading beforehand, but composing the night before a paper was due, a combination of fear that nothing will come and faith that something would eventually develop, then revising to fit the pattern discovered in the Professorial Discourse Analysis, getting "A's" and "B's," and getting comments like "I never saw that before."

> *I was both devastated and determined, my not belonging was verified but I was not ready to be shut down, not so quickly. So to the library to look up what the Professor himself had published:* Proceedings of the Spenser Society. *I had no idea what the Professor was going on about in his paper, but I could see the pattern.* 18

There were failures, of course. One professor said my writing was too formu- 19 laic. One professor said it was too novel. Another wrote only one word for the one paper required of the course: "nonsense." But while I was on the campus I could escape and not. I could think about the things that troubled me or intrigued me, but through others' eyes in other times and other places. I couldn't get enough, despite the pain and the insecurity.

School becomes his obsession. There is the education. But the obsession is as 20 much, if not more, in getting a degree, not with a job in mind, just the degree, just because he thinks he can, despite all that has said he could not. His marriage withers away, not with rancor, just melting into a dew. The daily routine has him taking the kid to a daycare/school at 6:00 a.m., then himself to school, from school to work as a groundskeeper for a large apartment complex; later, a maintenance man, then a garbage man, then a plumber, sometimes coupled with other jobs: shipping clerk for the library, test proctor. From work to pick up the kid from school, prepare dinner, maybe watch a TV show with the kid, tuck him into bed, read. There are some girlfriends along the way, and he studies them too: the English major who won constant approval from the same professor who had given him the 36 for being imaginative; the art major who had traveled to France (French practice); the fisheries major whose father was an executive vice president for IBM (practice at being middle class). Victor was going to learn—quite consciously—what it means to be white, middle class. He didn't see the exploitation; not then; he was obsessed. There were things going on in his classes that he did not understand and that the others did. He didn't know what the things were that he didn't understand, but he knew that even those who didn't do as well as he did, somehow did not act as foreign as he felt. He was the only colored kid in every one of those classes. And he hadn't the time nor the racial affiliation to join the Black Student Union or Mecha. He was on his own, an individual pulling on his bootstraps, looking out for number one. He's not proud of the sensibility, but isolation—and, likely, exploitation of others—are the stuff of racelessness.

There were two male friends, Mickey, a friend to this day, and Luis el Loco.   21 Luis was a *puertoriceño*, from Puerto Rico, who had found his way to Washington by having been imprisoned in the federal penitentiary at MacNeal Island, attending school on a prison-release program. Together, they would enjoy talking in Spanglish, listening to *salsa*. But Luis was a Modern Languages major, Spanish literature. Nothing there to exploit. It's a short-lived friendship. Mickey was the other older student in Victor's French 101 course, white, middle class, yet somehow other, one who had left the country during Vietnam, a disc jockey in Amsterdam. The friendship begins with simply being the two older men in the class, longer away from adolescence than the rest; the friendship grows with conversations about politics, perceptions about America from abroad, literature. But Victor would not be honest with his friend about feeling foreign until years later, a literary bravado. Mickey was well read in the literary figures Victor was coming to know. Mickey would be a testing ground for how Victor was reading, another contact to be exploited. Eventually, Mickey and his wife would introduce Victor to their friend, a co-worker at the post office. This is Carol. She comes from a life of affluence, and from a life of poverty, a traveler within the class system, not a journey anyone would volunteer for, but one which provides a unique education, a path not unlike Paulo Freire's. From her, there is the physical and the things he would know of the middle class, discussed explicitly, and there is their mutual isolation. There is love and friendship, still his closest friend, still his lover.

But before Carol there is simply the outsider obsessed. He manages the BA. He   22 cannot stop, even as the GI Bill reaches its end. He will continue to gather credentials until he is kicked out. Takes the GRE, does not do well, but gets into the graduate program with the help of references from within the faculty—and with the help of minority status in a program decidedly low in numbers of minorities. "Minority," or something like that, is typed on the GRE test results in his file, to be seen while scanning the file for the references. His pride is hurt, but he remembers All Saints, begins to believe in the biases of standardized tests: back in the eighth grade, a failure top student; now a near-failure, despite a 3.67 at the competitive Big

University of State. Not all his grades, he knew, were matters of charity. He had earned his GPA, for the most part. Nevertheless, he is shaken.

More insecure than ever, there are no more overnight papers. Papers are written 23 over days, weeks, paragraphs literally cut and laid out on the floor to be pasted. One comment appears in paper after paper: "Logic?" He thinks, "Yes." He does not understand. Carol cannot explain the problem. Neither can Mickey. He does not even consider asking the professors. To ask would be an admission of ignorance, "stupid spic" still resounding within. This is his problem.

Then by chance (exactly how is now forgotten), he hears a tape of a con- 24 ference paper delivered by the applied linguist Robert Kaplan. Kaplan describes contrastive rhetoric. Kaplan describes a research study conducted in New York City among Puerto Ricans who are bilingual and Puerto Ricans who are monolingual in English, and he says that the discourse patterns, the rhetorical patterns which include the logic, of monolingual Puerto Ricans are like those of Puerto Rican bilinguals and different from Whites, more Greek than the Latin-like prose of American written English. Discourse analysis takes on a new intensity. At this point, what this means is that he will have to go beyond patterns in his writing, become more analytical of the connections between ideas. The implications of Kaplan's talk, for him at least, will take on historical and political significance as he learns more of rhetoric.

About the same time as that now lost tape on Kaplan's New York research 25 (a study that was never published, evidently), Victor stumbles into his first rhetoric course.

The preview of course offerings announces a course titled "Theories of Inven- 26 tion," to be taught by Anne Ruggles Gere. His GRE had made it clear that he was deficient in Early American Literature. Somewhere in his mind he recalls reading that Benjamin Franklin had identified himself as an inventor; so somehow, Victor interprets "Theories of Invention" as "Theories of Inventors," an American lit course. What he discovers is Rhetoric.

Not all at once, not just in that first class on rhetoric, I discover some things 27 about writing, my own, and about the teaching of writing. I find some of modern composition's insights are modern hindsights. I don't mind the repetition. Some things bear repeating. The repetitions take on new significance and are elaborated upon in a new context, a new time. Besides, not everyone who teaches writing knows of rhetoric, though I believe everyone should.

I read Cicero's *de Inventione*. It's a major influence in rhetoric for centuries. 28 The strategies he describes on how to argue a court case bears a remarkable resemblance to current academic discourse, the pattern I first discovered when I first tried to figure out what I had not done in that first English course at the University.

Janet Emig looks to depth psychology and studies on creativity and even 29 neurophysiology, the workings of the brain's two hemispheres, to pose the case that writing is a mode of learning. She explains what I had been doing with my first attempts at college writing, neither magic nor a perversion. Cicero had said much the same in his *de Oratore* in the first century BCE (Before the Common Era, the modern way of saying BC):

*Writing* is said to be *the best and most excellent modeler and teacher of oratory;*
and not without reason; for if what is meditated and considered easily surpasses sudden and extemporary speech, a constant and diligent habit of writing will surely
be of more effect than meditation and consideration itself; since all the arguments
relating to the subject on which we write, whether they are suggested by art, or by a
certain power of genius and understanding, will present themselves, and occur to
us, while we examine and contemplate it in the full light of our intellect and all the
thoughts and words, which are the most expressive of their kind, must of necessity
come under and submit to the keenness of our judgment while writing; and a fair
arrangement and collocation of the words is effected by writing, in a certain rhythm
and measure, not poetical, but oratorical. (*de Oratore* I.cxxxiv)

Writing is a way of discovering, of learning, of thinking. Cicero is arguing the
case for literacy in ways we still argue or are arguing anew.

David Bartholomae and Anthony Petrosky discuss literary theorists like 30
Jonathan Culler and the pedagogical theorist Paulo Freire to come up with a
curriculum in which reading is used to introduce basic writers, those students
who come into the colleges not quite prepared for college work, to the ways
of academic discourse. Quintilian, like others of his time, the first century CE,
and like others before his time, advocates reading as a way to come to discover
the ways of language and the ways of writing and the ways to broaden the
range of experience.

Kenneth Bruffee, Peter Elbow, and others, see the hope of democratizing the 31
classroom through peer-group learning. So did Quintilian:

But as emulation is of use to those who have made some advancement of learning,
so, to those who are but beginning and still of tender age, to imitate their school-
fellows is more pleasant than to imitate their master, for the very reason that it
is more easy; for they who are learning the first rudiments will scarcely dare to
exalt themselves to the hope of attaining that eloquence which they regard as the
highest; they will rather fix on what is nearest to them, as vines attached to trees
fain the top by taking hold of the lower branches first (23–24).

Quintilian describes commenting on student papers in ways we consider
new:

[T]he powers of boys sometimes sink under too great severity in correction; for they
despond, and grieve, and at last hate their work; and what is most prejudicial, while
they fear everything; they cease to attempt anything. . . . A teacher ought, therefore,
to be as agreeable as possible, that remedies, which are rough in their nature, may
be rendered soothing by gentleness of hand; he ought to praise some parts of his
pupils' performances, tolerate some, and to alter others, giving his reasons why the
alterations are made. (100)

Richard Haswell recommends minimal scoring of student papers, sticking
to one or two items in need of correction per paper. Nancy Summers warns
against rubber-stamp comments on student papers, comments like "awk;" she
says comments ought to explain. Both have more to say than Quintilian on
such matters, but in essence both are Quintilian revisited.

Edward P. J. Corbett looks to Quintilian, Cicero, and others from among   32
the ancients, especially Aristotle, to write *Classical Rhetoric for the Modern Student*. In some ways, the book says little that is different from other books on student writing. But the book is special in its explicit connections to ancient rhetorical traditions.

Without a knowledge of history and traditions, we risk running in circles   33
while seeking new paths. Without knowing the traditions, there is no way of knowing which traditions to hold dear and which to discard. Self evident? Maybe. Yet the circles exist.

For all the wonders I had found in literature—and still find—literature   34
seemed to me self-enveloping. What I would do is read and enjoy. And, when it was time to write, what I would write about would be an explanation of what I had enjoyed, using words like *Oedipal complex* or *polyvocal* or *anxiety* or *unpacking,* depending on what I had found in my discourse-analytical journeys, but essentially saying "this is what I saw" or "this is how what I read took on a special meaning for me" (sometimes being told that what I had seen or experienced was nonsense). I could imagine teaching literature—and often I do, within the context of composition—but I knew that at best I'd be imparting or imposing one view: the what I saw or the meaning for me. The reader-response theorists I would come to read, Rosenblatt, Fish, Culler, and others, would make sense to me, that what matters most is what the reader finds. Bakhtin's cultural and political dimension would make even more sense: that all language is an approximation, generated and understood based on what one has experienced with language. In teaching literature, I thought, there would be those among students I would face who would come to take on reading, perhaps; likely some who would appreciate more fully what they had read. But it did not seem to me that I could somehow make someone enjoy. Enjoyment would be a personal matter: from the self, for the self.

And what if I did manage a Ph.D. and did get a job as a professor? I would   35
have to publish. A guest lecturer in a medieval lit course spoke of one of the important findings in his new book: medieval scribes were conscious of the thickness of the lozenge, the medieval version of the comma. He found that thinner lozenges would indicate a slight pause in reading; thicker lozenges, longer pauses. Interesting, I reckon. Surely of interest to a select few. But so what, in some larger sense? What would I write about?

Then I stumbled onto rhetoric. Here was all that language had been to me.   36
There were the practical matters of writing and teaching writing. There were the stylistic devices, the tricks of language use that most people think about when they hear the word *rhetoric;* "Let's cut through the rhetoric." It's nice to have those devices at one's disposal—nice, even important, to know when those devices are operating. But there is more. Rhetoric's classic definition as the art of persuasion suggests a power. So much of what we do when we speak or write is suasive in intent. So much of what we receive from others—from family and friends to thirty-second blurbs on TV—is intended to persuade. Recognizing how this is done gives greater power to choose. But rhetoric is still more.

Rhetoric is the conscious use of language: "observing in any given case the   37
available means of persuasion," to quote Aristotle (I.ii). As the conscious use of
language, rhetoric would include everything that is conveyed through language:
philosophy, history, anthropology, psychology, sociology, literature, politics—"the
use of language as a symbolic means of inducing cooperation in beings that by
nature respond to symbols," according to modern rhetorician Kenneth Burke (46).
The definition says something about an essentially human characteristic: our pre-
dilection to use symbols. Language is our primary symbol system. The ability to
learn language is biologically transmitted. Burke's definition points to language as
ontological, part of our being. And his definition suggests that it is epistemological, part of our thinking, an idea others say more about (see Leff).

So to study rhetoric becomes a way of studying humans. Rhetoric becomes for   38
me the complete study of language, the study of the ways in which peoples have
accomplished all that has been accomplished beyond the instinctual. There were
the ancient greats saying that there was political import to the use of language.
There were the modern greats saying that how one comes to know is at least mediated by language, maybe even constituted in language. There were the pragmatic
applications. There was the possibility that in teaching writing and in teaching
rhetoric as conscious considerations of language use I could help others like myself: players with language, victims of the language of failure.

---

## Questions for Discussion and Journaling

1. This account shifts back and forth between the first person ("I") and the third person
   ("Victor," "he"). What effects does that shifting create? Does it break any rules you've
   been taught?

2. How does Villanueva define *rhetoric*? What else does he say that studying rhetoric
   helps you study?

3. Have you ever tried observing and imitating the writing moves that other writers
   make, as Villanueva describes doing with his English teachers ("Professorial Discourse
   Analysis")? If so, what was your experience doing so? If not, what would you need to
   look for in order to do the kind of imitation Villanueva describes?

4. In paragraph 6, Villanueva describes his college writing process as, "The night before a
   paper was due, he'd gather pen and pad, and stare. Clean the dishes. Stare. Watch an
   'I Love Lucy' rerun. Stare. Then sometime in the night the words would come." (A few
   more sentences finish his description.) What elements of this process resemble your
   own? How is yours different?

5. Villanueva is describing his own experience of encountering affirmative action—how
   he benefited from it, and how it also had some negative effects. Was this an account
   you might have expected to hear? If not, how did it differ from your perceptions of
   affirmative action?

6. In telling the story of his writing process and being called into Mrs. Ray's office
   (para. 7), Villanueva suggests that he expected Mrs. Ray would take issue with his

writing style of "discovering what to write by writing, no prior thesis statement, no outline, just a vague notion of what would materialize, magically, while writing." How does that story reflect your own experience of being taught how writing is supposed to happen?

7. Did you attend other colleges before attending the one at which you're using this book? Villanueva describes the difference between his community college and the University of Washington (paras. 5–21). If you've attended both two-year and four-year schools, what differences do you see? If you've attended different schools of the same sort, what were the differences? Can you see your experiences at different schools as acquiring different "literacies"?

8. In a number of places in this excerpt, Villanueva talks not just about "literacy sponsors" but about authors whose ideas about writing and teaching writing shaped his own. Before coming to college, what authors had you read that shaped your thinking about writing?

## Applying and Exploring Ideas

1. Villanueva writes that "school became my obsession," and yet he describes struggling with writing for school. In other words, he ran the risk of being barred from doing the thing he loved because of his writing. Consider the activities you most love being part of: was there ever a moment where language or writing threatened to (or did) bar your access to them? Or where language or writing provided your gateway to them? Write a two- to three-page descriptive narrative (imitate Villanueva's style, if you like) about that situation.

2. Analyze Villanueva's piece here using Brandt's notion of literacy sponsorship. What literacy sponsors appear in Villanueva's literacy narrative? (Start by making as complete a list as you can.) What did these sponsors allow and limit?

3. Do some Professorial Discourse Analysis of two college or high school teachers you've had. What did they each expect from your writing? Did they agree or differ in their expectations? Desribe their expectations in two to three pages, and give specific examples of what each expected.

4. Look up information about Robert Kaplan's "contrastive rhetoric." Write a two-to three-page explanation describing contrastive rhetoric and explaining why might it have helped a student like Villanueva make sense of his own experiences in college.

### Meta Moment
Do you think differently about anything (ideas about writing, social issues) after reading Villanueva than you did coming into it? What, and how?

*Library of Congress*

# Learning to Read

## MALCOLM X

■ X, Malcolm. *The Autobiography of Malcolm X*. Ed. Alex Haley. New York: Ballantine, 1965. Print.

## Framing the Reading

Malcolm X was born Malcolm Little in Omaha, Nebraska, in 1925. Essentially orphaned as a child, he lived in a series of foster homes, became involved in criminal activity, and dropped out of school in eighth grade after a teacher told him his race would prevent him from being a lawyer. In 1945, he was sentenced to prison, where he read voraciously. After joining the Nation of Islam, he changed his last name to "X," explaining in his autobiography that "my 'X' replaced the white slavemaster name of 'Little.'" A strong advocate for the rights of African Americans, Malcolm X became an influential leader in the Nation of Islam but left the organization in 1964, becoming a Sunni Muslim and founding an organization dedicated to African American unity. Less than a year later, he was assassinated.

In this chapter we excerpt a piece from *The Autobiography of Malcolm X*, which he narrated to Alex Haley shortly before his death. We see Malcolm X's account as exemplifying many of the principles that Deborah Brandt introduces in "Sponsors of Literacy" (pp. 44–61). For example, Malcolm X's account of how he came to reading is remarkable for how clearly it shows the role of motivation in **literacy** and learning: when he had a reason to read, he read, and reading fed his motivation to read further. His account also demonstrates the extent to which literacies shape the worlds available to people and the experiences they can have, as well as how **literacy sponsors** affect the kinds of literacy we eventually master.

We expect that reading Malcolm X's experiences in coming to reading will bring up your own memories of this stage in your life, which should set you thinking about what worlds your literacies give you access to and whether there are worlds in which you would be considered "illiterate." We think you'll find a comparison of your experiences and Malcolm X's provocative and telling.

## Getting Ready to Read

*Before you read*, do at least one of the following activities:

- Do some reading online about Malcolm X and his biography.
- Start a discussion with friends, roommates, family, or classmates about whether, and how, "knowledge is power."

*As you read*, consider the following questions:

- How would Malcolm X's life have been different if his literacy experiences had been different?
- How was Malcolm X's literacy inextricably entangled with his life experiences, his race, and the religion he chose?
- How do Malcolm X's early literacy experiences and literacy sponsors compare to your own?

---

It was because of my letters that I happened to stumble upon starting to 1 acquire some kind of a homemade education.

I became increasingly frustrated at not being able to express what I wanted to convey in letters that I wrote, especially those to Mr. Elijah Muhammad. In the street, I had been the most articulate hustler out there—I had commanded attention when I said something. But now, trying to write simple English, I not only wasn't articulate, I wasn't even functional. How would I sound writing in slang, the way I would *say* it, something such as "Look, daddy, let me pull your coat about a cat, Elijah Muhammad—"

> In the street, I had been the most articulate hustler out there—I had commanded attention when I said something. But now, trying to write simple English, I not only wasn't articulate, I wasn't even functional.

2

Many who today hear me somewhere in person, or on television, or those 3 who read something I've said, will think I went to school far beyond the eighth grade. This impression is due entirely to my prison studies.

It had really begun back in the Charlestown Prison, when Bimbi first made 4 me feel envy of his stock of knowledge. Bimbi had always taken charge of any conversation he was in, and I had tried to emulate him. But every book I picked up had few sentences which didn't contain anywhere from one to nearly all of the words that might as well have been in Chinese. When I just skipped those words, of course, I really ended up with little idea of what the book said. So I had come to the Norfolk Prison Colony still going through only book-reading motions. Pretty soon, I would have quit even these motions, unless I had received the motivation that I did.

I saw that the best thing I could do was get hold of a dictionary—to study, 5 to learn some words. I was lucky enough to reason also that I should try to improve my penmanship. It was sad. I couldn't even write in a straight line. It was both ideas together that moved me to request a dictionary along with some tablets and pencils from the Norfolk Prison Colony school.

I spent two days just riffling uncertainly through the dictionary's pages. I'd 6 never realized so many words existed! I didn't know *which* words I needed to learn. Finally, just to start some kind of action, I began copying.

In my slow, painstaking, ragged handwriting, I copied into my tablet every- 7
thing printed on that first page, down to the punctuation marks.

I believe it took me a day. Then, aloud, I read back, to myself, everything 8
I'd written on the tablet. Over and over, aloud, to myself, I read my own
handwriting.

I woke up the next morning, thinking about those words—immensely proud 9
to realize that not only had I written so much at one time, but I'd written
words that I never knew were in the world. Moreover, with a little effort, I also
could remember what many of these words meant. I reviewed the words whose
meanings I didn't remember. Funny thing, from the dictionary first page right
now, that "aardvark" springs to my mind. The dictionary had a picture of it,
a long-tailed, long-eared, burrowing African mammal, which lives off termites
caught by sticking out its tongue as an anteater does for ants.

I was so fascinated that I went on—I copied the dictionary's next page. And 10
the same experience came when I studied that. With every succeeding page, I
also learned of people and places and events from history. Actually the dictionary is like a miniature encyclopedia. Finally the dictionary's A section had filled
a whole tablet—and I went on into the B's. That was the way I started copying
what eventually became the entire dictionary. It went a lot faster after so much
practice helped me to pick up handwriting speed. Between what I wrote in my
tablet, and writing letters, during the rest of my time in prison I would guess I
wrote a million words.

I suppose it was inevitable that as my word-base broadened, I could for 11
the first time pick up a book and read and now begin to understand what the
book was saying. Anyone who has read a great deal can imagine the new world
that opened. Let me tell you something: from then until I left that prison, in
every free moment I had, if I was not reading in the library, I was reading on
my bunk. You couldn't have gotten me out of books with a wedge. Between
Mr. Muhammad's teachings, my correspondence, my visitors—usually Ella and
Reginald—and my reading of books, months passed without my even thinking
about being imprisoned. In fact, up to then, I never had been so truly free in
my life.

The Norfolk Prison Colony's library was in the school building. A variety of 12
classes was taught there by instructors who came from such places as Harvard
and Boston universities. The weekly debates between inmate teams were also
held in the school building. You would be astonished to know how worked up
convict debaters and audiences would get over subjects like "Should Babies Be
Fed Milk?"

Available on the prison library's shelves were books on just about every gen- 13
eral subject. Much of the big private collection that Parkhurst had willed to the
prison was still in crates and boxes in the back of the library—thousands of old
books. Some of them looked ancient: covers faded, old-time parchment-looking
binding. Parkhurst, I've mentioned, seemed to have been principally interested
in history and religion. He had the money and the special interest to have a
lot of books that you wouldn't have in general circulation. Any college library
would have been lucky to get that collection.

As you can imagine, especially in a prison where there was heavy emphasis 14
on rehabilitation, an inmate was smiled upon if he demonstrated an unusually
intense interest in books. There was a sizable number of well-read inmates, especially the popular debaters. Some were said by many to be practically walking encyclopedias. They were almost celebrities. No university would ask any
student to devour literature as I did when this new world opened to me, of
being able to read and *understand*.

I read more in my room than in the library itself. An inmate who was known 15
to read a lot could check out more than the permitted maximum number of
books. I preferred reading in the total isolation of my own room.

When I had progressed to really serious reading, every night at about ten 16
P.M. I would be outraged with the "lights out." It always seemed to catch me
right in the middle of something engrossing.

Fortunately, right outside my door was a corridor light that cast a glow into 17
my room. The glow was enough to read by, once my eyes adjusted to it. So when
"lights out" came, I would sit on the floor where I could continue reading in
that glow.

At one-hour intervals the night guards paced past every room. Each time 18
I heard the approaching footsteps, I jumped into bed and feigned sleep. And
as soon as the guard passed, I got back out of bed onto the floor area of that
light-glow, where I would read for another fifty-eight minutes—until the guard
approached again. That went on until three or four every morning. Three or
four hours of sleep a night was enough for me. Often in the years in the streets
I had slept less than that.

The teachings of Mr. Muhammad stressed how history had been "whitened"— 19
when white men had written history books, the black man simply had been
left out. Mr. Muhammad couldn't have said anything that would have struck
me much harder. I had never forgotten how when my class, me and all of those
whites, had studied seventh-grade United States history back in Mason, the
history of the Negro had been covered in one paragraph, and the teacher had
gotten a big laugh with his joke, "Negroes' feet are so big that when they walk,
they leave a hole in the ground."

This is one reason why Mr. Muhammad's teachings spread so swiftly all 20
over the United States, among *all* Negroes, whether or not they became fol-
lowers of Mr. Muhammad. The teachings ring true—to every Negro. You can
hardly show me a black adult in America—or a white one, for that matter—
who knows from the history books anything like the truth about the black
man's role. In my own case, once I heard of the "glorious history of the black
man," I took special pains to hunt in the library for books that would inform
me on details about black history.

I can remember accurately the very first set of books that really impressed 21
me. I have since bought that set of books and have it at home for my children
to read as they grow up. It's called *Wonders of the World*. It's full of pictures of
archeological finds, statues that depict, usually, non-European people.

I found books like Will Durant's *Story of Civilization*. I read H. G. Wells' *Out-* 22
*line of History*. *Souls of Black Folk* by W. E. B. Du Bois gave me a glimpse into
the black people's history before they came to this country. Carter G. Woodson's
*Negro History* opened my eyes about black empires before the black slave was
brought to the United States, and the early Negro struggles for freedom.

J. A. Rogers' three volumes of *Sex and Race* told about race-mixing before 23
Christ's time; about Aesop being a black man who told fables; about Egypt's
Pharaohs; about the great Coptic Christian Empires; about Ethiopia, the
earth's oldest continuous black civilization, as China is the oldest continuous
civilization.

Mr. Muhammad's teaching about how the white man had been created led 24
me to *Findings in Genetics* by Gregor Mendel. (The dictionary's G section was
where I had learned what "genetics" meant.) I really studied this book by the
Austrian monk. Reading it over and over, especially certain sections, helped
me to understand that if you started with a black man, a white man could be
produced; but starting with a white man, you never could produce a black
man—because the white gene is recessive. And since no one disputes that there
was but one Original Man, the conclusion is clear.

During the last year or so, in the *New York Times*, Arnold Toynbee used 25
the word "bleached" in describing the white man. (His words were: "White
(i.e., bleached) human beings of North European origin. . . .") Toynbee also
referred to the European geographic area as only a peninsula of Asia. He said
there is no such thing as Europe. And if you look at the globe, you will see
for yourself that America is only an extension of Asia. (But at the same time
Toynbee is among those who have helped to bleach history. He has written that
Africa was the only continent that produced no history. He won't write that
again. Every day now, the truth is coming to light.)

I never will forget how shocked I was when I began reading about slavery's 26
total horror. It made such an impact upon me that it later became one of my
favorite subjects when I became a minister of Mr. Muhammad's. The world's
most monstrous crime, the sin and the blood on the white man's hands, are
almost impossible to believe. Books like the one by Frederick Olmstead opened
my eyes to the horrors suffered when the slave was landed in the United States.
The European woman, Fannie Kimball, who had married a Southern white slave-
owner, described how human beings were degraded. Of course I read *Uncle
Tom's Cabin*. In fact, I believe that's the only novel I have ever read since I
started serious reading.

Parkhurst's collection also contained some bound pamphlets of the Aboli- 27
tionist Anti-Slavery Society of New England. I read descriptions of atrocities,
saw those illustrations of black slave women tied up and flogged with whips;
of black mothers watching their babies being dragged off, never to be seen by
their mothers again; of dogs after slaves, and of the fugitive slave catchers,
evil white men with whips and clubs and chains and guns. I read about the
slave preacher Nat Turner, who put the fear of God into the white slavemaster.
Nat Turner wasn't going around preaching pie-in-the-sky and "non-violent"

freedom for the black man. There in Virginia one night in 1831, Nat and seven other slaves started out at his master's home and through the night they went from one plantation "big house" to the next, killing, until by the next morning 57 white people were dead and Nat had about 70 slaves following him. White people, terrified for their lives, fled from their homes, locked themselves up in public buildings, hid in the woods, and some even left the state. A small army of soldiers took two months to catch and hang Nat Turner. Somewhere I have read where Nat Turner's example is said to have inspired John Brown to invade Virginia and attack Harper's Ferry nearly thirty years later, with thirteen white men and five Negroes.

I read Herodotus, "the father of History," or, rather, I read about him. 28 And I read the histories of various nations, which opened my eyes gradually, then wider and wider, to how the whole world's white men had indeed acted like devils, pillaging and raping and bleeding and draining the whole world's non-white people. I remember, for instance, books such as Will Durant's story of Oriental civilization, and Mahatma Gandhi's accounts of the struggle to drive the British out of India.

Book after book showed me how the white man had brought upon the 29 world's black, brown, red, and yellow peoples every variety of the sufferings of exploitation. I saw how since the sixteenth century, the so-called "Christian trader" white man began to ply the seas in his lust for Asian and African empires, and plunder, and power. I read, I saw, how the white man never has gone among the non-white peoples bearing the Cross in the true manner and spirit of Christ's teachings—meek, humble, and Christ-like.

I perceived, as I read, how the collective white man had been actually nothing 30 but a piratical opportunist who used Faustian machinations to make his own Christianity his initial wedge in criminal conquests. First, always "religiously," he branded "heathen" and "pagan" labels upon ancient non-white cultures and civilizations. The stage thus set, he then turned upon his non-white victims his weapons of war.

I read how, entering India—half a *billion* deeply religious brown people— 31 the British white man, by 1759, through promises, trickery and manipulations, controlled much of India through Great Britain's East India Company. The parasitical British administration kept tentacling out to half of the subcontinent. In 1857, some of the desperate people of India finally mutinied—and, excepting the African slave trade, nowhere has history recorded any more unnecessary bestial and ruthless human carnage than the British suppression of the non-white Indian people.

Over 115 million African blacks—close to the 1930s population of the 32 United States—were murdered or enslaved during the slave trade. And I read how when the slave market was glutted, the cannibalistic white powers of Europe next carved up, as their colonies, the richest areas of the black continent. And Europe's chancelleries for the next century played a chess game of naked exploitation and power from Cape Horn to Cairo.

Ten guards and the warden couldn't have torn me out of those books. Not 33 even Elijah Muhammad could have been more eloquent than those books were in providing indisputable proof that the collective white man had acted like a devil in virtually every contact he had with the world's collective non-white man. I listen today to the radio, and watch television, and read the headlines about the collective white man's fear and tension concerning China. When the white man professes ignorance about why the Chinese hate him so, my mind can't help flashing back to what I read, there in prison, about how the blood forebears of this same white man raped China at a time when China was trusting and helpless. Those original white "Christian traders" sent into China millions of pounds of opium. By 1839, so many of the Chinese were addicts that China's desperate government destroyed twenty thousand chests of opium. The first Opium War was promptly declared by the white man. Imagine! Declaring *war* upon someone who objects to being narcotized! The Chinese were severely beaten, with Chinese-invented gunpowder.

The Treaty of Nanking made China pay the British white man for the 34 destroyed opium; forced open China's major ports to British trade; forced China to abandon Hong Kong; fixed China's import tariffs so low that cheap British articles soon flooded in, maiming China's industrial development.

After a second Opium War, the Tientsin Treaties legalized the ravaging 35 opium trade, legalized a British-French-American control of China's customs. China tried delaying that Treaty's ratification; Peking was looted and burned.

"Kill the foreign white devils!" was the 1901 Chinese war cry in the Boxer 36 Rebellion. Losing again, this time the Chinese were driven from Peking's choicest areas. The vicious, arrogant white man put up the famous signs, "Chinese and dogs not allowed."

Red China after World War II closed its doors to the Western white world. 37 Massive Chinese agricultural, scientific, and industrial efforts are described in a book that *Life* magazine recently published. Some observers inside Red China have reported that the world never has known such a hate-white campaign as is now going on in this non-white country where, present birth-rates continuing, in fifty more years Chinese will be half the earth's population. And it seems that some Chinese chickens will soon come home to roost, with China's recent successful nuclear tests.

Let us face reality. We can see in the United Nations a new world order being 38 shaped, along color lines—an alliance among the non-white nations. America's U.N. Ambassador Adlai Stevenson complained not long ago that in the United Nations "a skin game" was being played. He was right. He was facing reality. A "skin game" *is* being played. But Ambassador Stevenson sounded like Jesse James accusing the marshal of carrying a gun. Because who in the world's history ever has played a worse "skin game" than the white man?

Mr. Muhammad, to whom I was writing daily, had no idea of what a new 39 world had opened up to me through my efforts to document his teachings in books.

When I discovered philosophy, I tried to touch all the landmarks of philo- 40 sophical development. Gradually, I read most of the old philosophers, Occidental and Oriental. The Oriental philosophers were the ones I came to prefer; finally, my impression was that most Occidental philosophy had largely been borrowed from the Oriental thinkers. Socrates, for instance, traveled in Egypt. Some sources even say that Socrates was initiated into some of the Egyptian mysteries. Obviously Socrates got some of his wisdom among the East's wise men.

I have often reflected upon the new vistas that reading opened to me. I knew   41
right there in prison that reading had changed forever the course of my life. As I see it today, the ability to read awoke inside me some long dormant craving to be mentally alive. I certainly wasn't seeking any degree, the way a college confers a status symbol upon its students. My homemade education gave me, with every additional book that I read, a little bit more sensitivity to the deafness, dumbness, and blindness that was afflicting the black race in America. Not long ago, an English writer telephoned me from London, asking questions. One was, "What's your alma mater?" I told him, "Books." You will never catch me with a free fifteen minutes in which I'm not studying something I feel might be able to help the black man.

Yesterday I spoke in London, and both ways on the plane across the Atlantic   42
I was studying a document about how the United Nations proposes to insure the human rights of the oppressed minorities of the world. The American black man is the world's most shameful case of minority oppression. What makes the black man think of himself as only an internal United States issue is just a catch-phrase, two words, "civil rights." How is the black man going to get "civil rights" before first he wins his *human* rights? If the American black man will start thinking about his *human* rights, and then start thinking of himself as part of one of the world's great peoples, he will see he has a case for the United Nations.

I can't think of a better case! Four hundred years of black blood and sweat   43
invested here in America, and the white man still has the black man begging for what every immigrant fresh off the ship can take for granted the minute he walks down the gangplank.

But I'm digressing. I told the Englishman that my alma mater was books, a   44
good library. Every time I catch a plane, I have with me a book that I want to read—and that's a lot of books these days. If I weren't out here every day battling the white man, I could spend the rest of my life reading, just satisfying my curiosity—because you can hardly mention anything I'm not curious about. I don't think anybody ever got more out of going to prison than I did. In fact, prison enabled me to study far more intensively than I would have if my life had gone differently and I had attended some college. I imagine that one of the biggest troubles with colleges is there are too many distractions, too much panty-raiding, fraternities, and boola-boola and all of that. Where else but in a prison could I have attacked my ignorance by being able to study intensely sometimes as much as fifteen hours a day?

## Questions for Discussion and Journaling

1. Who seems to be Malcolm X's intended audience? How do you know?

2. How does Malcolm X define *literacy*? How does this definition compare to school-based literacy?

3. Drawing on Deborah Brandt's definition of *literacy sponsor*, list as many of Malcolm X's literacy sponsors as you can find. (Remember that sponsors don't have to be people, but can also be ideas or institutions, which can withhold literacy as well as provide it.) Which sponsors were most influential? What were their motivations?

4. Brandt explains that people often subvert or misappropriate the intentions of their sponsors (see pp. 46, 56–57, paras. 7 and 27). Was this ever the case with Malcolm X? If so, how?

5. Like Malcolm X, many readers have memories in which a reference work like a dictionary or an encyclopedia figures significantly. Did his account bring back any such memories for you? If so, what were they?

6. Malcolm X asserts that his motivation for reading—his desire to understand his own experiences—led him to read far more than any college student. Respond to his claim. Has a particular motivation helped you decide what, or how much, to read?

7. What was the particular role for *writing* that Malcolm X describes in his account of his literacy education? How do you think it helped him read? Can you think of ways that writing helped *you* become a better reader?

## Applying and Exploring Ideas

1. Both Deborah Brandt and Malcolm X wrote before much of the technology that you take for granted was invented. How do you think technologies such as the World Wide Web, text messaging, Skype, and the like shape what it means to be "literate" in the United States today?

2. Write a one-page narrative about the impact of an early literacy sponsor on your life. Recount as many details as you can and try to assess the difference that sponsor made in your literate life.

3. Malcolm X turned to the dictionary to get his start in acquiring basic literacy. If you met a person learning to read today, what primary resource would you suggest to them? Would it be print (paper) or electronic? How would you tell them to use it, and how do you think it would help them?

---

### Meta Moment

What do you think your teacher might say is the most important idea in the Malcolm X text? Do you agree, or do you have a different opinion on what the most important idea is? Explain.

# The Joy of Reading and Writing: Superman and Me

## SHERMAN ALEXIE

■ Alexie, Sherman. "The Joy of Reading and Writing: Superman and Me." *The Most Wonderful Books: Writers on Discovering the Pleasures of Reading.* Minneapolis: Milkweed Editions, 1997. 3–6. Print.

## Framing the Reading

Sherman Alexie was born in 1966 and grew up on the Spokane Indian Reservation in Wellpinit, Washington. Although he was born with water on the brain and not expected to survive, he learned to read by the time he was three and became a voracious reader at an exceptionally young age. His classmates ridiculed him for this, but he nonetheless made reading and education a priority, attending college on a scholarship and finding a poetry teacher who encouraged him to write. Since then, he has published over twenty books, including novels, short story and poetry collections, and screenplays. He has written screenplays for three movies, including *Smoke Signals*, for which he won numerous awards. Among his other numerous awards, Alexie won the World Heavyweight Poetry Bout title in 1998 and kept the title for four years. On top of all that, Alexie also frequently performs stand-up at comedy festivals.

Clearly, Alexie's life story has been an unusual one. Coming from a world of poverty, he managed to become successful and critically acclaimed. In the short essay included here, Alexie discusses how he came to literacy, through what Deborah Brandt would call the "sponsorship" of Superman comics and his father's love of books. He notes that if he had been "anything but an Indian boy living on the reservation, he might have been called a prodigy." Instead, he was considered "an oddity" (para. 5).

## Getting Ready to Read

*Before you read*, do at least one of the following activities:

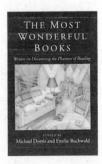

- Research the Spokane Indian Reservation where Alexie grew up: Learn what you can about its location, culture, and history.
- Alexie mentions in his essay that most Native Americans now would not willingly attend Catholic school: Try to find out why this is the case by researching the history of Catholic education of Native American groups. For help, you might look at the *Journal of American Indian Education*, which is online.

- Consider when you learned to read. What texts and events were central to your learning?

*As you read*, consider the following questions:

- What claims and assumptions does Alexie make that you don't understand? (Take notes as you read. If, for example, you don't know why he would claim that "a smart Indian is a dangerous person," make a note about this to bring up in class.)
- Why does Alexie repeatedly assert that he was "lucky"?

........................................................................................................

I learned to read with a Superman comic book. Simple enough, I suppose. I cannot recall which particular Superman comic book I read, nor can I remember which villain he fought in that issue. I cannot remember the plot, nor the means by which I obtained the comic book. What I can remember is this: I was 3 years old, a Spokane Indian boy living with his family on the Spokane Indian Reservation in eastern Washington state. We were poor by most standards, but one of my parents usually managed to find some minimum-wage job or another, which made us middle-class by reservation standards. I had a brother and three sisters. We lived on a combination of irregular paychecks, hope, fear, and government surplus food.

My father, who is one of the few Indians who went to Catholic school on purpose, was an avid reader of westerns, spy thrillers, murder mysteries, gangster epics, basketball player biographies, and anything else he could find. He bought his books by the pound at Dutch's Pawn Shop, Goodwill, Salvation Army, and Value Village. When he had extra money, he bought new novels at supermarkets, convenience stores, and hospital gift shops. Our house was filled with books. They were stacked in crazy piles in the bathroom, bedrooms, and living room. In a fit of unemployment-inspired creative energy, my father built a set of bookshelves and soon filled them with a random assortment of books about the Kennedy assassination, Watergate, the Vietnam War, and the entire 23-book series of the Apache westerns. My father loved books, and since I loved my father with an aching devotion, I decided to love books as well.

> *I still remember the exact moment when I first understood, with a sudden clarity, the purpose of a paragraph. I didn't have the vocabulary to say "paragraph," but I realized that a paragraph was a fence that held words.*

I can remember picking up my father's books before I could read. The words themselves were mostly foreign, but I still remember the exact moment when I first understood, with a sudden clarity, the purpose of a paragraph. I didn't have the vocabulary to say "paragraph," but I realized that a paragraph was a fence that held words. The words inside a paragraph worked together for a common purpose. They had some specific reason for being inside the same fence. This knowledge delighted me. I began to think of everything in terms of paragraphs. Our reservation was a small paragraph within the United States. My family's house was a paragraph, distinct from the other paragraphs of the LeBrets to the north, the Fords to our South, and the Tribal School to the west. Inside our house, each family member existed as a separate paragraph but still had genetics and common experiences to link us. Now, using this logic, I can see my changed family as an essay of seven paragraphs: mother, father, older brother, the deceased sister, my younger twin sisters, and our adopted little brother.

At the same time I was seeing the world in paragraphs, I also picked up 4 that Superman comic book. Each panel, complete with picture, dialogue, and narrative was a three-dimensional paragraph. In one panel, Superman breaks through a door. His suit is red, blue, and yellow. The brown door shatters into many pieces. I look at the narrative above the picture. I cannot read the words, but I assume it tells me that "Superman is breaking down the door." Aloud, I pretend to read the words and say, "Superman is breaking down the door." Words, dialogue, also float out of Superman's mouth. Because he is breaking down the door, I assume he says, "I am breaking down the door." Once again, I pretend to read the words and say aloud, "I am breaking down the door." In this way, I learned to read.

This might be an interesting story all by itself. A little Indian boy teaches 5 himself to read at an early age and advances quickly. He reads "Grapes of Wrath" in kindergarten when other children are struggling through "Dick and Jane." If he'd been anything but an Indian boy living on the reservation, he might have been called a prodigy. But he is an Indian boy living on the reservation and is simply an oddity. He grows into a man who often speaks of his childhood in the third person, as if it will somehow dull the pain and make him sound more modest about his talents.

A smart Indian is a dangerous person, widely feared and ridiculed by Indi- 6 ans and non-Indians alike. I fought with my classmates on a daily basis. They wanted me to stay quiet when the non-Indian teacher asked for answers, for volunteers, for help. We were Indian children who were expected to be stupid. Most lived up to those expectations inside the classroom but subverted them on the outside. They struggled with basic reading in school but could remember how to sing a few dozen powwow songs. They were monosyllabic in front of their non-Indian teachers but could tell complicated stories and jokes at the dinner table. They submissively ducked their heads when confronted by a non-Indian adult but would slug it out with the Indian bully who was 10 years older. As Indian children, we were expected to fail in the non-Indian world. Those who failed were ceremonially accepted by other Indians and appropriately pitied by non-Indians.

I refused to fail. I was smart. I was arrogant. I was lucky. I read books late 7 into the night, until I could barely keep my eyes open. I read books at recess, then during lunch, and in the few minutes left after I had finished my classroom assignments. I read books in the car when my family traveled to powwows or basketball games. In shopping malls, I ran to the bookstores and read bits and pieces of as many books as I could. I read the books my father brought home from the pawnshops and secondhand. I read the books I borrowed from the library. I read the backs of cereal boxes. I read the newspaper. I read the bulletins posted on the walls of the school, the clinic, the tribal offices, the post office. I read junk mail. I read auto-repair manuals. I read magazines. I read anything that had words and paragraphs. I read with equal parts joy and desperation. I loved those books, but I also knew that love had only one purpose. I was trying to save my life.

Despite all the books I read, I am still surprised I became a writer. I was go- 8 ing to be a pediatrician. These days, I write novels, short stories, and poems. I visit schools and teach creative writing to Indian kids. In all my years in the reservation school system, I was never taught how to write poetry, short stories, or novels. I was certainly never taught that Indians wrote poetry, short stories, and novels. Writing was something beyond Indians. I cannot recall a single time that a guest teacher visited the reservation. There must have been visiting teachers. Who were they? Where are they now? Do they exist? I visit the schools as often as possible. The Indian kids crowd the classroom. Many are writing their own poems, short stories, and novels. They have read my books. They have read many other books. They look at me with bright eyes and arrogant wonder. They are trying to save their lives. Then there are the sullen and already defeated Indian kids who sit in the back rows and ignore me with theatrical precision. The pages of their notebooks are empty. They carry neither pencil nor pen. They stare out the window. They refuse and resist. "Books," I say to them. "Books," I say. I throw my weight against their locked doors. The door holds. I am smart. I am arrogant. I am lucky. I am trying to save our lives.

························································································································

## Questions for Discussion and Journaling

1. Alexie claims that Indian children were "expected to be stupid" (para. 6). Explain in a paragraph or two how expectations can impact children's literacy learning. Can you think of examples from your own childhood where expectations of you—positive or negative—shaped what you did or didn't do?

2. Alexie lists a variety of ways that Indian children failed inside of school but excelled outside of school. Using this list, consider what it meant to be "literate" on the Indian reservation where Alexie grew up. What literacy skills did the Indian children have that were not valued or seen inside school?

3. Who and what do you consider to be Alexie's most important literacy sponsors? What do you think his life might have been like if he had had access to more powerful literacy sponsors when he was growing up, or if he had grown up in a different setting?

4. Alexie claims that he "read with equal parts joy and desperation." He tells us that he "loved those books," but that this love "had only one purpose. I was trying to save my life" (para. 7). What does he mean? What would it mean to read with desperation? Why did he feel that reading books could save his life? Do you think that he was right?

## Applying and Exploring Ideas

1. The stories of Malcolm X and Sherman Alexie might lead you to believe that anyone can overcome poverty and discrimination if they just have enough determination to read and write. Do you think that this is, in fact, the case? How can you use Deborah Brandt's research to help you think through this question? You might also look to history, or even to your own experiences, to help you consider this question.

2. Informally interview a couple of your classmates about their early literacy experiences. How frequently, if at all, do comic books and drawing show up in their early literacy experiences? In what ways did such texts impact them? If you are interested in exploring this topic further, you might look at Thomas Newkirk's studies of young children's writing (including *More than Stories* and *Misreading Masculinity: Boys, Literacy, and Popular Culture*).

# Writing for Their Lives:
## THE NON-SCHOOL LITERACY OF CALIFORNIA'S URBAN, AFRICAN AMERICAN YOUTH

## JABARI MAHIRI and SORAYA SABLO

■ Mahiri, Jabari and Soraya Sablo. "Writing for Their Lives: The Non-School Literacy of California's Urban, African American Youth." *Journal of Negro Education* 65.2 (1996): 164–246. Print.

## Framing the Reading

Jabari Mahiri earned a Ph.D. in English (Language, Literacy, and Rhetoric) from the University of Illinois at Chicago and is now Professor of Language and Literacy, Society and Culture in the Graduate School of Education at the University of California, Berkeley. He directs the TEACH Project (Technology, Equity, And Culture for High-performance schools), a research initiative that collaborates with urban schools and community partners on uses of new media for increasing student achievement and educational equity, and for improving teacher professional development. He is the Faculty Director for the Bay Area Writing Project, a Senior Scholar for the National Urban Alliance for Effective Education, and he has won several mentoring awards. Mahiri has authored or co-authored six books, including *What They Don't Learn in Schools: Literacy in the Lives of Urban Youth*, as well as many peer-reviewed journal articles like the one you are about to read.

Soraya Sablo (now Sablo-Sutton) was Mahiri's graduate student at UC–Berkeley and has been teaching elementary school for five years. She now teaches at Washington Elementary School in Alameda County, California. Her students are 65% Latino and 15% African American. She says that her research and work as an educational consultant taught her "that the most successful teachers were those who found ways to bring the curriculum to life for their students. Student engagement proved to be one of the most critical factors in predicting student success."

In this article, Mahiri and Sablo look at the complex relationship between in- and out-of-school literacy practices of African American students in two urban San Francisco Bay Area high schools. They discover that although many African American and Latino students in these urban settings perform poorly on standardized tests, have high drop-out rates, and are generally disinclined to participate in or value academic literacy tasks, many of these students had extremely rich out-of-school literacy practices. These literacy practices (poems, raps, plays, etc.) play important roles in helping students reconcile some of the serious difficulties they faced in their daily lives. However, Mahiri and Sablo found that there was no recognition or valuing of these complex out-of-school literacy practices within the students' school settings.

## Getting Ready to Read

*Before you read*, do at least one of the following activities:

- Think of some literacy practices you have outside of school. Are these valued by your teachers? Your parents? Your friends? You?
- Have you ever had a school experience where teachers tried to draw on your out-of-school literacy experiences to engage you in literacy learning?

*As you read*, consider the following questions:

- How do your background and school and community contexts compare to those being described in the study? How do you think that your attitudes about literacy have been impacted by your personal history?

................................................................................................................

This article reports on an investigation into the literacy practices of urban [1] African American youth, many of whom were found to be unmotivated to engage in school-based literacy events because they do not see the relevance of the school curriculum to their lives or, based on prior experiences, they actually fear having to write in school. The voluntary out-of-school literacy practices of two African American high school students are analyzed and their writings critiqued. Conclusions are drawn about the complex and provocative ways these youth use literate behaviors and strategies to gain voice in and make sense of their social worlds. Recommendations are offered for using African American and youth culture as a bridge to writing development.

## Non-School Literacy Practices

An emerging line of research has attempted to explore and explain the nature [2] of youth and adult language and literacy experiences that take place in an array of social settings outside of schools. Pioneers in this field include researchers such as Heath (1980, 1982, 1983), Scribner and Cole (1981, 1988), and Street (1984, 1993), whose work has contributed to a framework for viewing literacy in conjunction with specific practices and functions of language use inside particular social contexts. A number of subsequent studies have also operated within and contributed to this framework (Camitta, 1993; Dyson, 1993; Farr, 1994; Goodman & Wilde, 1992; Guerra, 1992; Heath & McLaughlin, 1991, 1993; Lee, 1991, 1993; Mahiri, 1991, 1994a, 1994b; Moss, 1994; Shuman, 1986; Taylor & Dorsey–Gaines, 1988).

Based on the findings of cross-cultural research, Street (1984) argued that  3
literacy is ultimately political and that it has different implications within
different sociocultural contexts. As he claimed, "what the particular practices and concepts of reading and writing are for a given society depends upon
the context" (p. 1); moreover, these concepts are "already embedded in an
ideology and cannot be isolated or treated as 'neutral' or merely 'technical'"
(p. 1). These contentions are echoed by Scribner and Cole's (1988) research,
conducted among the Vai people of Liberia, which illuminates and critiques
the "frailty of the evidence for generalizations about dependency of certain
cognitive skills on writing, and . . . the restricted model of the writing process from which hypotheses about cognitive consequences tend to be generated" (p. 58). Their findings challenged the restricted models of writing that
are reflected in the formulations of theorists who narrowly define literacy
and value school-based literacy as the only authentic type. As they note:

> The assumption that logicality is in the text and the text is in the school can
> lead to a serious underestimation of the cognitive skills involved in non-school,
> non-essay writing, and reciprocally, to an overestimation of the intellectual skills
> that the essayist text "necessarily" entails. . . . It tends to promote the notion that
> writing outside of the school is of little importance and has no significant conse-
> quences for the individual. (p. 61)

Heath's (1983) research focused on literacy practices in different sociocultural  4
settings in the United States. Heath found that the residents of two different
working-class communities—one White and one Black, located only a few miles
apart—had "a variety of literate traditions" that were "interwoven in different
ways with oral uses of language" (p. 234). She noted, however, that "neither community's ways with the written word [prepared] it for the school's ways" (p. 235).

Shuman's (1986) analysis of the everyday oral and written narratives of  5
working-class adolescent girls as part of the unofficial school curriculum provides additional understandings of the ways that school and youth cultures
both intersect and disconnect. As she argues:

> . . . oral fight stories, written diary accounts, written petitions, letters, and play-
> ful forms—are part of a single community's repertoire. These discourse forms
> represent choices among channels and styles of communication, and although
> they might be judged deficit when compared to standard forms, they must be
> examined as appropriate (or inappropriate) within the adolescent communica-
> tion system. (p. 12)

> In more recent work, Lee (1991) has focused on linking the oral talk of Afri-
> can American students to literary language and critique by emphasizing the use of
> rhetorical devices common to African American literature. Noting that research
> provides "meaningful insights into the texture and nuances of the interplay of
> culture and cognition," she maintains that "what is missing . . . in terms of enrich-
> ing the links between everyday practice and schooling are specific descriptions of
> the knowledge structures taught in school as they relate to the knowledge struc-
> tures constructed within nonschool social settings" (pp. 292–293).

Camitta (1993) uses the term "vernacular writing" to describe the liter- 6 acy practice of urban African American adolescents that "conforms, not to the norms of educational institutions, but to those of social life and culture" (p. 229). She concludes that writing is actually an important and valued activity for a number of these youths, whose vernacular writing, she notes, consists of "a range of significant and meaningful literate skills and resources that are artificially disconnected from the process of literacy education as it is officially conducted" (p. 229). Relatedly, in a community ethnography conducted at a school site prior to her 1993 study, Camitta (1987) identified music, sports, and fashions as three significant aspects of African American youth culture. That study also described a curriculum intervention organized around these themes that she, her teacher–collaborators, and co-researchers designed and instituted in the school's language arts program. By drawing on more authentic sources to motivate these students to write, Camitta concluded, she and her colleagues were able to mitigate the discontinuity between these students' real lives and their lives in school.

Mahiri (1994b) asserts that some African American youth have both inten- 7 sive engagements and significant competencies in a variety of literacy practices in out-of-school settings, specifically settings within their home communities. He argues, however, that "a better link must be made between what schools hold as important and meaningful and what . . . youths find meaningful in their daily lives" (p. 144).

## Purpose of the Study

This article discusses and analyzes the voluntary writings of two urban Afri- 8 can American high school students whose work we—the researchers and our cooperating focal teachers—believe reflect significant types and uses of nonschool literacy. This study was initiated because, in our overall quest to look at ways that African American and youth culture could be used as a bridge to writing development, we wanted to learn more about the kinds of writing these students do for their own purposes outside of school. Thus, one of the key objectives of this research was to explore aspects of the motivations, functions, genres, and themes of these students' voluntary writing and of the knowledge they bring to it.

> This study was initiated because, in our overall quest to look at ways that African American and youth culture could be used as a bridge to writing development, we wanted to learn more about the kinds of writing these students do for their own purposes outside of school.

Five questions guided this research. Two of these questions came directly 9 from Street's (1993) discussion of considerations that much previous research on literacy acquisition has failed to take into account. First, it "has failed to

take account of how the people themselves 'actually think about literacy'";
and second, Street maintains, it has failed to consider "how they apply their
literacy skills in their day-to-day lives" (p. 3). Although Street was addressing research on literacy acquisition in previously nonliterate cultures, critical
questions for the present research study were what the two focal students
actually thought about their productions and performances of various kinds
of texts, and how these literacy events actually functioned in their daily lives.
Additionally, we wanted to know what specific genres and themes patterned
their literacy practices and what kinds of oral/written connections were revealed in their choices of genres and themes (i.e., the nature of the "mix" of
oral and written texts). Finally, we sought to assess the implications these voluntary, out-of-school literacy practices could have for instruction and schooling in the classroom setting.

## Researching Writing beyond School

Our basic lens for looking at out-of-school literacy production was Heath's    10
(1982) concept of "literacy events" as "any occasion in which a piece of writing is integral to the nature of participants' interactions and their interpretive
processes" (p. 350). Street's (1993) concept of "literacy practices" widened
our focus to include "both behaviour and conceptualizations related to the
use of reading and/or writing" (p. 12). According to Street, "'Literacy practices' incorporate not only 'literacy events' as empirical occasions to which
literacy is integral, but also 'folk models' of those events and the ideological
preconceptions that underpin them" (pp. 12–13). Therefore, our focus on the
out-of-school production of written texts attempts to account for literacy
skills and literate behaviors associated with those productions as well as
the value, conceptions, and functions of those productions inside specific
sociocultural contexts. Augmenting this focus, we suggest a conception of
literacy in sociocultural contexts as skills applied to the production of meaning in or from text in a context. In this conception, the nature and function
of skill, production, meaning, and text may vary significantly within different
contexts.

Given this framework, we designed our study to explore and explain the spe-    11
cific nature, interrelationships, functions, and cultural/contextual connections
of these constituents of literacy practice. Data were to be collected through various means including: (a) descriptive and reflective fieldnotes from participant
observations; (b) personal interviews with focal student-writers, their teachers,
and peers; and (c) solicited samples of students' voluntary and school-based
writing, along with other associated artifacts. But first we had to identify our
focal students.

## Identifying the Focal Students

Because the practices that are the focus of this research took place primarily    12
in non-school or extracurricular settings, we needed a way to identify which

students were doing writing on their own beyond school work. Thus, we enlisted the help of two African American English teachers, Ms. Brown and Ms. Parks,[1] who assisted us in this aspect of the study and lent many valuable insights into the students, schools, and settings in which these practices evolve.

Some background on the contributions of these two focal teachers, and on   13
the general nature and thrust of our work in and outside of the California public schools, is important here. For two years prior to this investigation, we had been working with English teachers in two urban high schools in the San Francisco Bay Area on curriculum interventions that utilize the authentic life experiences of urban African American youth. These efforts were aimed at leading teachers to explore ways to build on these students' backgrounds and competencies in order to facilitate their learning and literacy development.[2] Our observations revealed that while there were many similarities between the students, the school sites, and the urban settings of the two schools, important differences were evident as well.

For example, in both schools, the African American and Latino students   14
were predominantly placed in the lower-tracked classes; most were performing well below the national norms on standardized tests. Indeed, both groups' suspension and dropout rates were significantly higher than those of students of other racial/ethnic backgrounds in their respective schools. Statistics provided to us by an administrator at one school indicated that 66% of the African American students who started as freshman would never finish there. The 1995 annual report for the other school revealed that 79% of the student body came from families that received AFDC (Aid for Families with Dependent Children) funding, and 43% received free or reduced-price lunches. The dropout statistics for African American students at the second site were similarly stark.

Differences were noted in the teaching styles and personas of the two fo-   15
cal teachers, both of whom taught at different school sites. On the one hand, Ms. Brown, an elegant and commanding woman, was a veteran teacher with 20 years' experience. Throughout her career, she had been widely recognized for her successes in working with urban African American and Latino high school students. Despite her years of experience, however, she informed us that the school knowledge she had been positioned and sanctioned to teach was increasingly being questioned, resisted, or even rejected by her students. One of the reasons she agreed to participate in our research project was to explore ways that she could be more successful with the students she was currently teaching.

Ms. Parks was a dynamic young woman with only about eight years' experi-   16
ence as an English teacher. In explaining why she became a teacher, she stated, "I saw what was happening in the school system, and it was appalling to me that many students were having continual conflict, and I thought: I could do something about that." Ms. Parks was attracted to our research project because

---

[1]Pseudonyms are used to protect the identities of the students and teachers who participated in this study.
[2]This research project was funded by a grant from the National Center for the Study of Writing and Literacy.

of her belief that the prevailing curriculum did not allow teachers to teach students what they needed to know to "survive in life." She was quite aware that preaching the value and importance of literacy alone would have little effect on her students, who were confronted with starkly different realities outside the classroom. As she admonished her students during a classroom discussion: "Just because you're not in a classroom, doesn't mean you're not being educated.... But that's not an argument to drop out of school, either. You know what I'm saying. You need it all."

Both these teachers realized that, to many of these students, the procla-  17 mation "you need it all" merely echoed the African American adage which suggests that Blacks need to be twice as good as Whites to achieve the same recognition, or that Black people's achievements must be held to a different standard. The teachers were also aware that many African American students in inner-city schools simply did not see the relevance of the school curriculum for their lives. Yet, as Parks's comments reveal, they recognized that education does not take place solely in the classroom. Most important to our study, these teachers also knew which of their students were engaging in voluntary literacy practices outside of school.

A few of their students, Brown and Parks noted, were literally producing  18 volumes of written work on their own, but were reluctant to share their writings with their teachers or in the classroom. Several of these students, both recalled, had engaged in disputes with them about the differences between the kinds of writing they produced and preferred and the writing they were required to do in class. Still others, they maintained, were prolific authors whose work completely escaped their notice. With regard to the latter group, Ms. Parks explained that every other Friday at her school several of these students participated in informal lunchtime gatherings where they gave lively impromptu performances of rap songs they had written themselves. She further claimed that students who rarely participated in her English classes during the week were highly engaged and active contributors to these Friday sessions.

As researchers observing these teachers and their classes, we became  19 acquainted with some of the students Ms. Parks and Ms. Brown identified as prolific voluntary writers. As our familiarity and comfort levels with these students increased, we began asking them about their writing. We anticipated that it would not be difficult to get them to share some of their work with us, but we were wrong. Some students summarily refused to share their work with us. Others stated that it was too personal, or that they would first have to determine which pieces we could see. Some of the students who wrote rap verse claimed that the only real file of their work existed in their heads. Despite the cooperation of a few, the resistance and caution of the majority made it clear that we would never be able to completely capture the range of voluntary writing that the African American students in this urban setting were actually doing.

Other distinctions became evident as the study took shape and progressed.  20 Although all of the researchers and teachers participating in this project were

African Americans, substantive differences were evident between the lives of these adults and the lives of the students who were the objects of our research. From time to time, glimpses of students' day-to-day realities outside of school made these stark contrasts inescapably obvious. For example, returning from travel to a conference or vacation, one of us decided to take the city bus home from the airport. This bus meanders through the students' neighborhoods on its way to the more affluent communities that are closer to the city's central business district. An inescapable sense of apprehension, rooted in the desolation of the ravaged urban surroundings, permeates this phase of the ride. During one such trip, a man got on the bus a couple of stops from the airport. He was almost immediately challenged by another rider sitting across from him, who claimed that the new passenger was staring at him. "Do you do these?" the rider said, holding up his fists like a boxer. "Yeah, I do these," said the new passenger, returning the same defiant gesture. They dared each other to get off the bus. At the next stop, they disembarked and squared off right there on the street—to the apparent disregard of most passers-by and the obvious disdain of most of the remaining passengers on the bus, which continued its lumbering toward more auspicious environs.

To the students who were the focus of this investigation, such commonplace 21 incidents of violence—and the crime, drugs, and devastation that often accompany or instigate them—are almost as visible in the streets of their neighborhoods as city buses. These young people are intimately aware of the conditions that surround them, and, as we later found out, their writings reveal as much and more. In their own distinctive way, they engage in literacy practices to help them come to terms with these conditions and with their experiences. In effect, they are writing for their lives.

## Keisha

Keisha, a 15-year-old African American female in the 10th grade, was per- 22 haps one of the most prolific and versatile writers that we encountered during our research project. We were surprised to find that she carried lots of her work with her wherever she went. After agreeing to share her work with us, Keisha immediately reached into her backpack and pulled out three thick notebooks full of poems, songs, and rap lyrics. Then she said, "Oh yeah, and here's my play," and pulled out a thick sheaf of papers bound together by rubber bands.

Keisha informed us that she had been writing voluntarily since the sixth 23 grade. By her estimation, she had written more than 40 songs, poems, and plays. In addition to being prolific, Keisha was also a very thoughtful and careful writer. However, she claimed that writing came rather easily for her and noted that it took only a few minutes for her to formulate and organize the ideas for her pieces. She also explained that her inspiration came from her friends and other people with whom she had come into contact during her life.

When asked about the themes of her writing, Keisha told us that she wrote 24 "mostly about love and society, things around me." Our reading of her work suggests that this appraisal was somewhat euphemistic. Instead, a clear pattern of focus on the harsh realities of the everyday life of low-income, inner-city African Americans is evident in her choice of topics and themes. Striking metaphors and intense emotions also characterize much of her work. For example, one of her notebooks, titled "Words of Feelings and Desires," contained the following verse:

### Shallow Thought

*Looking out into a fiery hell,*
*seeing increasing amounts of young bystanders thrown away*
*because of someone else's humiliation and agony.*
*Looking into a world of animosity,*
*bullets flying, babies crying*
*and no one is to blame.*

According to Keisha's own analysis, the "fiery hell" in this poem referred to her neighborhood, which she described as the site of increasing gang violence. The "humiliation and agony" related to the circumstances she believed were often behind much of that violence. As she explained, when a gang member was killed by someone from another gang, the violence would escalate because, among other things, one group had been humiliated; thus, her use of the term "thrown away" rather than "killed" to emphasize the unnecessary loss of life which was a regular occurrence in her world. In Keisha's view, many of the young people who found themselves caught up in these situations were in "agony" because they were constantly losing loved ones and believed there was no way out.

Two other poems, "Dreams" and "Black Reign," are also representative of 25 Keisha's prolific literary output:

### Dreams

*I have so many dreams to remember,*
*so many moments to cherish.*
*My life had no light until . . .*
*you, burning upon the sun;*
*To kiss you is a dream come true,*
*a moment to cherish.*
*To have the pleasure of being*
*around you is a blessing.*
*When you simply speak,*
*I am speechless.*
*When you smile,*
*I am paralyzed with life.*
*There isn't a word in the world*
*to express the way I feel for you,*
*not one.*
*But you, you are like the ocean*
*that glimmers in the night,*

*like the birds that cry in the morning*
*I wish I could hold you forever,*
*but I dream you will stay with*
*and hold me*
*with incredible strength.*
*Your features are so beautiful*
*they would blind the*
*normal eye,*
*but not mine.*
*You are a dream and I*
*want to have you*
*and dream over,*
*and over,*
*again.*

**Black Reign**

*Mysteriously she wanders*
*through the night,*
*trying to find*
*a way out of the clouds*
*of darkness.*
*She's lost in the rain*
*without a doubt, she's*
*lost in a love*
*of which she's been bought.*
*She's so lost she cries,*
*to let out the hurt*
*through her eyes.*
*The rain is falling and*
*constantly moving her*
*in the wrong direction.*
*After she cries, the sun appears,*
*then she sees the rain disappear.*
*The bells start to ring,*
*and the birds begin to sing.*
*She realizes she's thy Black Queen,*
*and she shouldn't let*
*anything stand in her way*
*for she is thou Black Queen*
*with thy Black Reign.*

In both poems, Keisha shows competence in the use of sophisticated descrip- 26
tive techniques to paint provocative mental images. For example, in "Dreams,"
she begins by acknowledging the difficulties inherent in expressing feelings of
intense emotion ("There isn't a word in the world to express the way I feel for
you"), but goes on to capture some aspects of those feelings using metaphor
and hyperbole (e.g., "you are like the ocean that glimmers in the night, like the

birds that cry in the morning," "your features are so beautiful they would blind the normal eye, but not mine"). This poem also reveals her skill in employing other rhetorical devices such as oxymorons (e.g., "When you smile, I am paralyzed with life").

"Black Reign" demonstrates other aspects of Keisha's emerging literary 27 aptitude. For example, the poem cleverly links the images of rain and tears. The rain, which "is falling and constantly moving her heart in the wrong direction," is likened to a flow of tears so copious that they prevent a distraught person from thinking clearly. The "night" and the "clouds of darkness" are subsequently linked to the confused emotions that prevent the subject of the poem from seeing the "sun" or the light of reason. Keisha additionally uses the homonyms "rain" and "reign" to enact the counterposing themes in this poem. Once the rain is gone—that is, once the subject has finished crying and can see her situation clearly—then she is once again able to reign or take control of her life.

This tension between chaos and the desire for control, so evident in Keisha's 28 work, was reflective of her desire to make sense of and rise above the circumstances of her own life, which were similarly chaotic. The first stanza of one of her songs, "Jus' Living," sheds some insight on her personal story:

### Jus' Living

*Jus' livin' on the eastside taking a chill,*
*watchin' young brothas being shot and killed.*
*Coming up fast, clocking Kash,*
*niggaz be having dreams, getting shot,*
*but it can't last.*
*But at the same time they doing the crime,*
*sitting behind bars without a nickel or a dime,*
*can't come out and kick it,*
*but I'mma wicked old fe-mac and that's how I'm living.*

Keisha's four-act play, which also bears the title "Jus' Living," echoes similar 29 themes. The play offers an intricate plot, well-rounded characters, and complex thematic considerations. For each scene, Keisha provides precise directorial notes and even specifications for appropriate background music. This suggests that Keisha apparently thought out every movement and emotion that she wants her characters to feel and her readers/audience to see.

The play begins with the narrator setting the scene and tone: "It starts as 30 an early morning in Oakland, California. A mother and her two sons, Robert, 16, and Rocheed, 15, struggle to survive in the heart of the ghetto." Readers soon learn that this family is living in the midst of gang violence and drugs. The mother, Ms. G, wants to move her family to a better neighborhood but is unable to do so for financial reasons. Robert, being the "man" of the house, attempts to get a job to help his mother out. When he is not successful finding employment because he has no work experience, he turns to what appears to be a more viable option: selling drugs and "gang-banging" or becoming involved in gang-related illegal activities. As one of his friends advises, "A job?! ... You betta get yo' grind on, fool!"—that is, seek work on the black market rather than routine employment.

"Jus' Living" depicts the intense peer pressure Robert faces as he grapples 31 with the decision to join or not join a gang. On one hand, it shows how grinding and gang-banging in poor communities are viewed not only as quick ways to make cash but also as a respected route to manhood. When Robert begins to have second thoughts about this type of lifestyle, his friends press him ("I thought you was a real old school gangsta"), and Robert opts to join and to live with the consequences. The play continues, noting that to be initiated into the gang, Robert must participate in the drive-by shooting of Dino, a rival gang member. In retaliation for Dino's murder, the rival gang comes to Robert's neighborhood with the intent of killing him. However, in an effort to protect her son, Robert's mother gets caught in the cross-fire and is killed.

As in her poems and songs, "Jus' Living" reveals Keisha's adeptness in the 32 use of sophisticated rhetorical devices. For example, she uses foreshadowing to provide subtle clues to the drama's tragic ending. For example, at one point Ms. G says to Robert: "You and Rocheed always act like ya' handicapped and always looking for me to do everything. Well one day I ain't gon' be here, then who you gon' be danging and telling it ain't no milk?" Later, when Robert informs his friends of his decision to start gang-banging, his brother's girlfriend, Shyra, responds with "Why you gon' do yo' momma like this?" Although she is suggesting that Robert's gang association will bring disgrace to his mother, Shyra's comment prefigures Ms. G's death.

"Jus Living" is a remarkable dramatic piece. The real drama, as we later 33 learned from interviews with Keisha, was the extent to which this play's scenes were collateral to scenes from Keisha's life. As she later informed us, her own older brother was very much like the character Robert in her play, and Robert's mother was based on her mother.

## Troy

Troy, a 17-year-old African American male in the 11th grade, had been com- 34 posing and performing rap verses and songs since sixth grade. He told us that he aspired to become a professional rapper some day. When we met him, he was performing his raps individually and as a member of a group called Realism. When asked approximately how many raps he had written, he replied: "Too many to count." Troy shared some of his compositions with us orally and, when we requested it, he also brought in transcribed lyrics for a few of his favorites.

Like many rappers, Troy stored a lot of his songs in his head, but he was 35 able to recall and recite an amazing number of raps—his own and others by professional rappers—on demand. Although he engaged in a mix of oral and written literacy practices, Troy considered himself a writer. He signed all his work "writer/lyricist, TROY." As a result, to more fully understand and position Troy's compositions within the framework of this study, we as researchers had to revisit our notions of what constitutes writing. The fact that the texts stored in Troy's mind could easily and consistently be transformed into oral and/or written texts led us to define their creation and performance as literacy events. Just as a writer can compose and store a text in a computer and afterwards select among several options and formats to print or reproduce it in another material form, we concluded that Troy composed and stored his texts in the microprocessors of his mind and selected among several options—oral, audiotape, or written text—for their material reproduction. In the process of producing meaning in these texts, Troy's raps evidenced a number of literacy skills and literate behaviors that reveal how literacy is actually construed and used in the context of urban African American youths' everyday lives.

One of Troy's favorite compositions was an autobiographical rap titled 36 "Family Fam," which he shared with us in its complete written form (below) as well as the audio-taped version[3]:

### Family Fam

*Can't nothing take me from my ken folk my blood,*
*even when I sold drug I still got love.*
*never was there any discrimination,*
*when I had the homelessness, at my lowest,*
*just reality conversation.*
*they pushed into my brain that crime is slavery, Troy,*
*but, ain't no freedom in having no money, just hate.*
*I be gettin' all emotional when I be broke,*
*you don't feel me doe,*

*It may look like I'm havin a good day,*
*but that's a cover-up for my quick-to-flash skanless way.*
*they took their time wit me and said that I needed peace,*
*but that's impossible when we ain't even got a piece,*
*of bread to split-n-half and be happy,*
*a brotha ain't even got no pappy,*
*hurt from bein' nappy.*
*never been spooked of the streets so,*
*I got two families that love me doe.*

*But the house where my momma stayed at is the spot 4 real,*
*eat fat, still have skrill, automobile,*
*and better chances of not gettin' killed.*
*I will, lay my head for any one of my family members,*
*even get my leg chopped off by white boys yellin' timber.*
*I love each and every best friend of mine,*
*that other family that I have on my flowamatic grind.*
*kan't nothing take me from my ken folk my blood,*
*cuz, even when I sold drug I still got love.*

---

[3]We realize that focusing solely on the written text version of Troy's raps limits our ability to adequately portray aspects of other forms of their production. Indeed, having to describe this type of literacy event within the medium of the written word—that is, via the confines of a scholarly article—is somewhat limiting. Mahiri (1996) details many of the problematic links between rap and written representation.

"Family Fam" exemplifies one of the central themes running through most 37 of Troy's lyrics—namely, the tension between the realities of life in the inner city and the survival strategies one has to adopt in order to cope with them. This particular rap describes the tensions between the biological family's desire that their young adopt more traditional life choices and the designs of the peer group to lead youth toward a "skanless" (scandalous) life on the streets. It begins by describing the unconditional love of the former, "my ken folk my blood," who stood by the rap's protagonist even when he "sold drug." The lyrics also offer a hard look at, and perhaps come to terms with, the lifestyle of youth in gangs. Although it goes on to note that the author listened to the advice of his family and knew that they were right ("they pushed into my mind that crime is slavery, Troy"), his "reality conversation," or talk with and among his peers, was just as influential. Ultimately, the rap claims, the latter convinced him that poverty was also a form of slavery, and the young man began to sell drugs because there "ain't no freedom in being broke, just hate." Later in the rap, Troy revisits these contradictions with a skillful play on the homonyms "peace" and "piece."

The structure of this rap does not follow the *AB AB* rhyme scheme found in 38 many raps; indeed, some lines do not rhyme at all. Notwithstanding, "Family Fam" demonstrates Troy's prolific use of highly figurative African American language styles such as call-and-response and signifying (Kochman, 1981). It also reveals his mastery of other rhetorical devices reflective of African American language styles along with an expert knowledge of contemporary African American slang terminology and its use. As Troy explained, "skrill" was a combination of the terms "scratch"—a somewhat dated slang term for money—and "mill" or million; the term could also refer to a meal ticket, he indicated.[4] For example, he uses the slang term "doe" (for "though") to emphasize his points in a way that simulates elements of African American preaching style ("you don't feel me doe," "I got two families that love me doe"). In effect, "doe" redirects readers' (or listeners') attention to and intensifies the importance of the thematic points made in the preceding lines of their respective stanzas. Additionally, Troy's use of a second-person reference ("you") in these two lines is reflective of the dialogicality, or multivoicedness, Duncan (1997; this issue) suggests is an essential part of African American youth discourse. This technique drives home the meaning of Troy's words to persons outside of the two families who feel for and love him—persons who may not know or understand the particular "family values" of these two groups.

As we came to know more about Troy personally, we found out how closely 39 this rap paralleled his life. One of the most telling lines is the one in which he describes his mother's house ("the spot 4 real") as a safe haven where he could always get a hot meal, access to a car, and some spending money. In one of our many conversations, Troy shared how important his own mother's home was to him, noting mat her house provided him a refuge from the temptations he faced in real life to sell drugs and commit other crimes for money.

---

[4]Kochman (1981) notes that within African American language styles, new words and phrases are often created in this fashion as users of the language constantly experiment with ways to better express themselves.

## Thinking about Voluntary Writing

The question of how and what Keisha, Troy, and their peers actually thought 40 about literacy can be examined on two levels. As we noted earlier, many of the students we observed at these two school sites resisted or refused to participate in most of their in-class writing assignments. One example that characterized this resistance occurred when Ms. Brown was attempting to get her students to develop good thesis statements by joking that her previous students used to "just eat them up." One of her current students joked back that it was easy for her because she had lots of college degrees, but that he personally hated working on thesis statements. In response to her food metaphor, he replied, "Yeah . . . we're not that hungry." This got a big laugh from the class and caused additional corroborative responses from other students. Indeed, discontent and frustration with writing in school were often voiced by students in both Brown's and Parks's classes. However, these same students clearly valued the out-of-school writing of their peers, voluntary writers like Keisha and Troy. Thus, it is erroneous to conclude that writing, in and of itself, was unimportant or "uncool" to these students; rather, they resisted what they viewed as the unauthentic nature of many of their experiences with academic writing.

By contrast, the literacy practices of our focal students were found to fulfill 41 a number of related and authentic functions in their day-to-day lives. Engaging in literacy practices helped them make sense of both their lives and social worlds, and provided them with a partial refuge from the harsh realities of their everyday experiences. Writing was also an important aspect of their processes of identity construction. Their literacy activities gave both these youths a sense of personal status as well as personal satisfaction.

In their writings, both Keisha and Troy probed for meaning and sought to 42 bring order to the mercurial flow of their lives. Like so many adolescents living in their community, they had seen more violence and pain than many adults will ever see. When those experiences are combined with the difficulties that nearly every teenager faces while growing up, it becomes difficult to understand how they coped at all. Yet, they tried to come to terms with their worlds by actively conceiving and critiquing the nature of their experiences through their own poetry, prose, plays, songs, and raps.

This idea of writing as refuge—of textual space as a sort of safe haven from 43 trauma—deserves further exploration in the case of Keisha and Troy. For Troy, writing was akin to the refuge of his mother's house: a "spot 4 real." This reality must be contrasted, however, to the chaos brought upon the mother's house in Keisha's play, and to the fact that Troy's poem spoke of intense divisions between his two families. These conflicts, so evident in written form, attest that ultimately for these two youths, there was no spot in their lives that could guarantee refuge. Nonetheless, for Keisha, the time she spent writing was time spent away from the streets. Her writing gave her a constructive way to avoid and address the violent and drug-ridden forces rampant in her neighborhood by exposing the futileness of those lifestyles in her texts. Similarly, Troy's voluntary writing, rehearsing, and performance of rap gave him constructive alternatives to a life on the streets. For both, writing outside of school provided a shelter within which they could freely express their feelings without encountering the anxiety that often results from school-based, teacher-sanctioned responses.

Other researchers have explored and documented the ways that literacy practices can function as a refuge for students like Keisha and Troy. McLaughlin, Irby, and Langman (1994), for example, offer the case of an inner-city youth named Rosa, whose realities included poverty, an abusive father, and a gang- and drug-infested neighborhood. They note that rather than languish in despair or withdrawal, Rosa became very active in the drama group at a boys and girls club in her community. She would spend about half her free time there writing and rehearsing scripts about her experiences of growing up in a difficult environment, and the other half performing and directing these dramas at other youth centers, churches, and schools. Like the focal students in our study, Rosa used her writing to validate and give voice to her perceptions and feelings in a constructive way. 44

Carroll's (1995) interviews with African American male authors reveal other examples of writing as a refuge for troubled youth and of its constructive functions. A poignant example can be found in the text of her interview with Nathan McCall, the author of *Makes Me Wanna Holler* (1994), an autobiographical work in which he describes the youthful gang involvement that led him to prison. As McCall relates, it was in prison that he began writing: 45

> It made me feel better sometimes to get something down on paper just like I felt it. It brought a kind of relief to be able to describe my pain. It was like, if I could describe it, it lost some of its power over me. I jotted down inner most thoughts I couldn't verbalize to anyone else, recorded what I saw around me, and expressed feelings inspired by things I read. (Carroll, 1995, p. 182)

For McCall, the product of a neighborhood much like that of Keisha and Troy, the idea that naming and describing his pain through writing could bring "a kind of relief" yielded a profound insight. Further, writing helped him to become critically aware of his experiences. As he maintains in another part of the interview: "[I]t felt different when I had to take it [a thought or feeling] to another level of understanding and actually put it down on paper. Before, I didn't have to make a commitment to thinking about it" (Carroll, 1995, p. 143). We found that our two focal students used literacy in a similar fashion. However, rather than keeping their perceptions and pain bottled up for years and then retrospectively writing about the problems of doing so, they were expressing themselves more immediately in their voluntary writing during their adolescent years. 46

Through their writing, much of which, like McCall's, was autobiographical, Keisha and Troy were also actively engaging in a process of identity construction. Without question, their senses of themselves are reflected in the experiences and scenes they portray in their poems, plays, stories, and songs. Sometimes this depiction is capsulized in a flat claim such as Keisha's poetic statement: "I'mma wicked old fe-mac and that's how I'm living." Other times it is conveyed in a rap line that reveals a telling behavior such as Troy's claim: 47

"but that's a cover-up for my quick-to-flash skanless way." Notwithstanding, these two students' writing identities in and outside of school were clearly and disturbingly different. Despite the strength and confidence with which Keisha and Troy defined themselves as writers based on their voluntary literary output, neither student was willing to embrace a similar identity based on their in-school writing. This disparity was of particular interest to us as researchers, and we discovered that it was linked to the role their voluntary writing played in helping the two students gain a sense of personal satisfaction and status. When interviewed, both Keisha and Troy indicated that they enjoyed their voluntary writing far more than did they their school writing assignments. Moreover, Keisha noted that while her family and friends outside of school praised her writing for both its style and content, her teachers often demanded that she alter both the style and content of her writing significantly. The latter, she claimed, made her feel highly uncomfortable about the prospect of conforming to school-based literary standards.

Troy informed us that he too enjoyed lots of praise and affirmation for his   48 rap work in the settings in which he performed or otherwise shared it. However, he also hinted at possibilities for establishing connections between the kinds of writing he did on his own and the written work requested by the school:

> I mean, I could write in school, you know what I'm sayin'. The essays, they don't be all that cool, but, you know what I'm sayin', I can be creative with anything I write, 'cuz I'm a writer, period.

Despite the mild affirmation, this statement characterizes the gulf students like Troy and Keisha see between their voluntary writing and school writing. For them, there is something in the nature of in-school writing that is definitely not "cool."

Perhaps the essence of what is not cool about school-based writing is most   49 directly relevant to our third research question, which addresses the specific genres and themes students like Keisha and Troy choose, and how these youths perceive the limits on their expression imposed by schools in contrast to their voluntary writing. As Rose (1989) maintains, writing instruction in schools often "teaches [students] . . . that the most important thing about writing—the very essence of writing—is grammatical correctness, not the communication of something meaningful" (p. 211). Rose cites the example of one of his students, who was an avid listener of rap music and in whom he had observed a considerable appreciation for linguistic complexity; yet, for this student, he claims, "[t]he instruction of language use he confronts strips away the vibrancy and purpose, the power and style, the meaning of the language that swirls around him" (p. 212). Relatedly, most teachers' assessments of Troy's "Family Fam" would no doubt focus almost exclusively on the rap work's nonstandard style and fail to examine his use of a number of intricate comparison/contrast strategies and complex interwoven thematic considerations. A great deal of research has challenged the viability of teaching that emphasizes disconnected drill work and other kinds of writing assignments focused on discreet components of the process that are often divorced from their contexts and the more holistic considerations of meaning in texts (Applebee, 1984; Atwell, 1987; Calkins, 1986; Poplin, 1988). However, the classroom continues to have difficulty accommodating certain culturally specific genres and provocative themes that form the axis of meanings that turn in many students' lives.

Unlike the adolescents in Camitta's (1993) study, who identified music, fashion, and sports as significant themes from African American youth culture for incorporation into the school curriculum, Keisha and Troy used literacy to focus on issues such as violence, crime, drugs, and relationships—topics that normally do not get addressed in the school curriculum. The incorporation of such sensitive issues into the official school curriculum could be extremely problematic. For instance, how could a teacher frame a discussion around drug activity when there might be young men such as Troy in the classroom who believe drug activity is a viable and necessary survival strategy? Teachers would also have to deal with considerations raised by researchers like Sola and Bennett (1994), who note the contradictions inherent in discussions of the poverty and crime that might be prevalent in some students' lives. According to Sola and Bennett, "schools cannot easily offer ethnic minorities something meaningful, because that would require those who govern the schools to acknowledge the marginality of minority communities as well as the political and economic reasons for that marginality" (p. 136). In other words, beyond recognition that these issues are difficult or even painful to discuss for both students and teachers, the dominant ideology surrounding schools acts to ignore or dismiss them. 50

Even further, Fine (1992) suggests that this ideology works to "silence" students' authentic voices, issues, and concerns. She defines silencing as "the practices by which contradictory evidence, ideologies, and experiences find themselves buried, camouflaged, and discredited" (p. 117). In the Harlem, New York, high school where she conducted her research, Fine notes how teachers resisted "naming" issues like drugs, racism, poverty, and abortion that they felt would be too political for the classroom. Instead, she claims, they engaged in a "systematic expulsion of dangerous topics" (p. 123). Especially in low-income schools, Fine alleges, "the process of inquiring into students lived experience is assumed, a priori, unsafe territory for teachers and administrators" (p. 118). 51

These practices of silencing devalue the lives and concerns of students like Keisha and Troy. They also deny such students the opportunity to take a critical look at the conditions of their communities in the context of their schooling. Therein lies part of the irony in the thematic considerations and functions of literacy practices for writers like Keisha and Troy. At various levels and in powerful ways, their voluntary writings critically examine the state of their surroundings. Moreover, these youths evidence considerable skill in the specific kinds of literacy practices and processes needed to encode and decode culturally significant information and themes as well as values and beliefs. 52

Key characteristics of our focal students' literacy practices relate to our fourth research question addressing the nature of the mix of their oral and written texts. Although Keisha's compositions were more traditionally formed written texts, they also presented interesting oral–written connections. As she informed us, her poems achieved their fullest effect when spoken rather than read. Similarly, she claimed that her plays were more meaningful when 53 performed. On a personal level, she indicated, she used her poems and plays as pretexts for conversations with her family, friends, or boyfriend around the various issues raised in her works.

Troy's focus, on the other hand, was first and foremost on the creation of oral 54 texts. For him, the spoken version of the rap is the ultimate product—a product intended and designed for aural rather than visual consumption. When he did write down his raps, he claimed, they were still formed as writing to be spoken rather than read. Notwithstanding, as we have earlier argued, the production and performance of rap are viable and valued literacy practices that reveal Troy's mastery over some of the processes through which culturally significant meanings are coded. These practices further identify Troy as a producer and not merely a consumer of culturally relevant texts that are appropriate for his audiences in both informal conversation as well as formal performance form. In effect, Troy-the-rapper is a living text, displaying his compositions through the software of sound, in real time, on the variegated screens of urban streets.

## Changing Life in Schools

Our focal teachers, Ms. Parks and Ms. Brown, recognized that life in urban 55 schools was changing dramatically. They were also aware that these changes would require them to change as well, and they were struggling to do so. Despite the best intentions of teachers, however, the question remains: Are the nation's schools capable of making the changes required to effectively link learning to the cultural identity and backgrounds of diverse groups of students? More specifically, is it realistic to suggest that teachers incorporate the non-school literacy practices of urban African American students into the curriculum, despite the difficulties involved? As the present study reveals, these students' voluntary out-of-school writing has important implications for schooling.

We acknowledge that merely including more culturally relevant topics and 56 issues in the curriculum does not constitute fundamental change. Further, we realize that our finding that culturally relevant material was not often addressed or included as a part of the in-school literacy activities at Keisha's and Troy's schools is only part of the problem. Researchers such as Gordon (1993) and Bartolome (1994) have warned against the pitfalls of attempting to use culturally relevant curriculum materials as "the solution to the current underachievement of students from subordinated cultures" when this approach is "often reduced to finding the 'right' teaching methods, strategies, or prepackaged curricula that will work with students who do not respond to so-called 'regular' or 'normal' instruction" (Bartolome, 1994, p. 174). After explaining why including culturally relevant material will not result in any magical transformation in the classroom, Gordon calls for a more liberatory education in which "students do not learn to read and write; they read and write in order to learn. They learn how to make problematic commonsense understandings and to question what is not being said as well as what is stated" (p. 457). In essence, Gordon suggests that students must learn how to take an active part in the construction of knowledge. Our findings suggest that their writing can be a valuable tool in this process.

This is where our earlier-noted conception of literacy as skills in the pro- 57
duction of meanings in or from texts becomes instrumental. We contend that
whether the literacy activity is reading or writing, meaning is actively produced, not merely consumed. One bridge, then, between the voluntary writing
of students like Keisha and Troy and school-based writing assignments can be
found in efforts to help teachers gain insights into the nature of their students'
out-of-school literate behaviors and literacy skills. Teachers need to be shown
how the behaviors and skills students demonstrate in the construction of their
voluntary texts correspond to some of the behaviors and skills they need to
develop and display in school.

If the education urban African American students receive is to be a libera- 58
tory one, the specific kinds of materials to which their literacy skills are applied is also significant. Further, these students' writing must name and link
the issues that schools have difficulty addressing, including racism, poverty,
gang violence, and drugs. However, Sola and Bennett's (1994) as well as Fine's
(1992) work, noted earlier, suggest that schools and other institutional power
structures inherently have difficulty addressing these critical issues because
they also expose the contradictions in these institutions with respect to their
roles in contributing to these issues. As Macedo (1994) notes:

> Terms that encapsulate the drug culture, daily alienation, the struggle to survive
> the substandard and inhumane conditions of ghettos: these constitute a discourse
> black Americans find no difficulty in using. It is from this raw and sometimes
> cruel reality that black students can begin to unveil the obfuscation that charac-
> terizes their daily existence inside and outside the schools. (p. 120)

Similarly, Fine (1992) maintains that naming these issues can "facilitate
critical conversation about social and economic arrangements, particularly
about inequitable distributions of power and resources by which these students and their kin suffer disproportionately" (p. 120). The paradox is that
the very issues that could be used to facilitate the discourse and development
of students like Keisha and Troy are also the issues most often resisted in the
discourse in schools. Consequently, teachers who really want to affect the lives
and learning of these students must develop a pedagogy that works to resolve
this paradox.

Clearly, Keisha and Troy are already naming and, to some extent, linking 59
many provocative issues in their voluntary writing. If, however, their writing and naming, and that of other African American inner-city youth, is only
able to offer them temporary refuge or relief from the problems and pain of
their realities, then it is only functioning like another of the mind-numbing
drugs available on the streets of their neighborhoods. Therefore, in utilizing
this material from these students' authentic experiences, teachers must help
them refine and profit from it in other ways. They must develop pedagogical
strategies for a critical literacy that help and inspire these students to truly
understand first how their reality is constructed by forces beyond their immediate neighborhood and school, and then to gain control of an agency in
their lives.

Ms. Parks and Ms. Brown were developing such strategies. Yet, in addition to recognizing their students' unique writing skills and being open to a wider range of possible texts as suitable for classroom use and review, they were gaining much, much more. With their reassessment of the goals and methods of writing instruction came increased sensitivity to the nature and importance of the meanings urban African American students seek to communicate in their voluntary and school writing. By examining and assessing the writing these students do on their own, the two teachers gained significant insights into how youth struggle to manage the complex situations in their lives. They also learned how those situations could connect to and motivate African American students in urban settings to write more both in and outside of school. Their efforts and openness to let their pedagogy be informed by the voluntary writing practices of students like Keisha and Troy should be commended and replicated in other settings.

## References

Applebee, A. (1984). *Contexts for learning to write: Studies of secondary school instruction.* Norwood, NJ: Ablex.

Atwell, N. (1987). *In the middle: Writing, reading, and learning with adolescents.* Portsmouth, NH: Heineman-Boynton/Cook.

Bartolome, L. (1994). Beyond the methods fetish: Toward a humanizing pedagogy. *Harvard Educational Review, 64*(3), 173–194.

Calkins, L. (1986). *The art of teaching writing.* Portsmouth, NH: Heineman-Boynton/Cook.

Camitta, M. (1987). *Invented lives: Adolescent vernacular writing and the construction of experience.* Philadelphia: University of Pennsylvania Press.

Camitta, M. (1993). Vernacular writing: Varieties of literacy among Philadelphia high school students. In B. Street (Ed.), *Cross-cultural approaches to literacy* (pp. 228–246). Cambridge: Cambridge University Press.

Carroll, R. (1995). *Swing low: Black men writing.* New York: Crown.

Duncan, G. (1997). Space, place, and the problematic of race: Black adolescent discourse as mediated action. *Journal of Negro Education, 65*(2), 133–150.

Dyson, A. (1993). *Social worlds of children learning.* New York: Teachers College Press.

Farr, M. (1994). In los idiomas: Literacy practices among Chicano Mexicanos. In B. Moss (Ed.), *Literacy across communities* (pp. 9–47). Cresskill, NY: Hampton Press.

Fine, M. (1992). *Disruptive voices: Transgressive possibilities of feminist research.* Ann Arbor, MI: University of Michigan Press.

Goodman, Y., & Wilde, S. (1992). *Literacy events in a community of young writers.* New York: Teachers College Press.

Gordon, B. (1993). African American cultural knowledge and liberatory education: Dilemmas, problems, and potentials in a postmodern American society. *Urban Education, 27*(4), 448–470.

Guerra, J. (1992). *An ethnographic study of the literacy practices of a Mexican immigrant family in Chicago.* Unpublished doctoral dissertation. The University of Illinois at Chicago.

Heath, S. B. (1980). The functions and uses of literacy. *Journal of Communication, 30,*123–133.

Heath, S. B. (1982). Protean shapes in literacy events: Ever-shifting oral and literate traditions. In D. Tannen (Ed.), *Spoken and written language: Exploring orality and literacy* (pp. 91–117). Norwood, NJ: Ablex.

Heath, S. B. (1983). *Ways with words: Language, life, and work in communities and classrooms.* Cambridge: Cambridge University Press.

Heath, S. B., & McLaughlin, M. (1991). Community organizations as family. *Phi Delta Kappan, 72*, 623–627.

Heath, S. B., & McLaughlin, M. (Eds.). (1993). *Identity and inner-city youth: Beyond ethnicity and gender*. New York: Teachers College Press.

Kochman, T. (1981). *Black and White in conflict*. Chicago: The University of Chicago Press.

Lee, C. D. (1991). Big picture talkers /Words walking without masters: The instructional implications of ethnic voices for an expanded literacy. *Journal of Negro Education, 60*(3), 291–304.

Lee, C. (1993). *Signifying as a scaffold for literary interpretation: The pedagogical implications of an African American discourse genre*. Urbana, IL: National Council of Teachers of English.

Macedo, D. (1994). *Literacies of power: What Americans are not allowed to know*. Boulder, CO: Westview Press.

Mahiri, J. (1991). Discourse in sports: Language and literacy features of preadolescent African American males in a youth basketball program. *Journal of Negro Education, 60*(3), 305–313.

Mahiri, J. (1994a). African American males and learning: What discourse in sports offers schools. *Anthropology & Education Quarterly, 25*(3), 1–13.

Mahiri, J. (1994b). Reading rites and sports: Motivation for adaptive literacy of young African American males. In B. Moss (Ed.), *Literacy across communities* (pp. 121–146). Cresskill, NY: Hampton Press.

Mahiri, J. (1996). Writing, rap, and representation: Problematic links between text and experience. In P. Mortensen & G. Kirsch (Eds.), *Ethics and representation in qualitative studies of literacy* (pp. 228–240). Urbana, IL: National Council of Teachers of English.

McCall, N. (1994). *Makes me wanna holler: A young Black man in America*. New York: Vintage Books.

McLaughlin, M., Irby, M., & Langman, J. (1994). *Urban sanctuaries: Neighborhood organizations in the lives and futures of inner-city youth*. San Francisco: Jossey–Bass.

Moss, B. (1994). Creating a community: Literacy events in African American churches. In B. Moss (Ed.), *Literacy across communities* (pp. 147–178). Cresskill, NY: Hampton Press.

Poplin, M. S. (1988). Holistic constructivist principles of the teaching/learning process: Implications for the field of learning disabilities. *Journal of Learning Disabilities, 21*(7), 401–416.

Rose, M. (1989). *Lives on the boundary: A moving account of the struggles and achievements of America's educationally underprepared*. New York: Penguin Books.

Scribner, S., & Cole, M. (1981). *The psychology of literacy*. Cambridge, MA: Harvard University Press.

Scribner, S., & Cole, M. (1988). Unpackaging literacy. In E. Kintgen, B. Kroll, & M. Rose (Eds.), *Perspectives on literacy* (pp. 57–70). Carbondale, IL: Southern Illinois University Press.

Shuman, A. (1986). *Storytelling rights: The uses of oral and written texts by urban adolescents*. Cambridge: Cambridge University Press.

Sola, L., & Bennett, M. (1994). The struggle for voice: Narrative, literacy and consciousness in an East Harlem school. In J. Maybin (Ed.), *Language and literacy in social practice* (pp. 117–138). Clevedon Avon, England: Multicultural Matters.

Street, B. (1984). *Literacy in theory and practice*. Cambridge: Cambridge University Press.

Street, B. (Ed.). (1993). *Cross-cultural approaches to literacy*. Cambridge: Cambridge University Press.

Taylor, D., & Dorsey–Gaines, C. (1988). *Growing up literate: Learning from inner-city families*. Portsmouth, NH: Heinemann–Boynton/Cook.

## Questions for Discussion and Journaling

1. What was the authors' motivation for conducting this study? What were their research questions? What were they hoping to learn from doing this study? What data did they collect in order to answer their research questions?

2. Why do you think Ms. Parks felt it was important to affirm to her students that "education does not take place solely in the classroom" (para. 17), that "just because you are not in a classroom, doesn't mean you aren't being educated" (para. 16)?

3. What is a "literacy event"? What are some examples of literacy events in your own experience?

4. In your experience, is school learning disconnected from the things you find meaningful in your daily life?

5. What were some of the students' non-school literacy practices? Why were these practices so meaningful to them? And why were so many of the students resistant to sharing their non-school writing with the researchers?

6. Why were so many students in this study resistant to academic writing? What specific aspects of school literacy made them uncomfortable?

7. The authors argue that Keisha and Troy's "writing identities in and outside of school were clearly and disturbingly different" (para. 47). How were their identities different in the two settings? And why do the authors find these differences "disturbing"?

8. Keisha used her out-of-school writing to balance the "tensions between chaos and the desire for control" and "make sense of and rise above the circumstances of her own life" (para. 28), while Troy used his raps to describe "the tension between the realities of life in the inner city and the survival strategies [he] had to adopt in order to cope with them" (para. 37). What other purposes did their writing have for them? Do you think it "brought a kind of relief" as it did for Nathan McCall (para. 46)? Have you ever used any sort of literacy practices to similarly help you balance tensions or find relief in your own life? If so, how did this literacy experience compare to your school literacy experiences?

9. What do the authors mean when they argue that "the dominant ideology surrounding schools acts to ignore or dismiss" what Sola and Bennet call the "marginality of minority communities as well as the political and economic reasons for that marginality" (para. 50)? And how does this orientation of schooling affect the ability of teachers to connect school literacy learning to their students' lives?

10. How have your personal experiences (including your class, race, where you live, type of school you attended, religion, etc.) shaped your literacy practices and your sense of self as a literate person? Have they encouraged you to embrace school literacies, or made you feel alienated from school literacies? Why?

## Applying and Exploring Ideas

1. Go to the e-Pages (**bedfordstmartins.com/writingaboutwriting/epages**) and read Shirley Brice Heath's study, which Mahiri and Sablo cite as a precursor to their own study. Look more deeply at the relationship between oral and written literacy practices

(para. 35). What do these authors think constitutes "writing"? Is "writing" the best term for many of the literacy events described here and in the Heath study, and in your own life? Look ahead to the last chapter of this book.

2. Compare the "writing for their lives" (para. 21) statement with Sherman Alexie's statement that the "Indian kids . . . are trying to save their lives" (para. 7, p. 131).

3. Mike Rose argues that school writing instruction "teaches [students] . . . that the most important thing about writing—the very essence of writing—is grammatical correctness, not the communication of something meaningful" (quoted in para. 49). Collect school assignments and teacher feedback from your or your classmates' schooling history and decide what message you think these were communicating to you about what "counts," what "matters," and what writing is.

4. Gordon calls for a literacy education in which "students do not learn to read and write; they read and write in order to learn. They learn how to make problematic commonsense understandings and to question what is not being said as well as what is stated" (para. 57). Work with your classmates to imagine what such a literacy education might actually look like, and how it would differ from the kind of education you have received. Is this a good idea? Why or why not?

**Meta Moment**

How does your literacy identity reflect your school, home, and community history and contexts? Why might this be a question worth thinking about?

# Tracing Trajectories of Practice:
## REPURPOSING IN ONE STUDENT'S DEVELOPING DISCIPLINARY WRITING PROCESSES

## KEVIN ROOZEN

■ Roozen, Kevin. "Tracing Trajectories of Practice: Repurposing in One Student's Developing Disciplinary Writing Processes." *Written Communication* 27.3 (2010): 318–54. Print.

## Framing the Reading

Kevin Roozen earned his Ph.D. in Composition and Rhetoric from the University of Illinois at Urbana–Champaign in 2005. He is currently Associate Professor at The University of Central Florida where he directs the Composition Program. Roozen's research is **ethnographic** and **longitudinal**, which means that he focuses in-depth on a few research participants and follows them closely over a long period of time. Roozen has published in most of his field's top **peer-reviewed journals**, including publishing recently with Elizabeth Wardle, one of the co-editors of this textbook.

Roozen is especially interested in how what he calls "literate learners" make connections between and among their various and varied **literacy practices** in seemingly very different contexts. For example, in the article you are about to read, he looks at the connections between one student's use of prayer journals, visual designs in graphic arts, and writing in English literature classes.

## Getting Ready to Read

*Before you read*, do at least one of the following activities:

- Think of all the different kinds of "literacies" that you possess—not just reading and writing for school, but maybe also writing fan fiction, drawing graphs for your engineering classes, or reading baseball statistics.
- Make a list of all of the different "literate practices" you engage in regularly in different aspects of your life. For example, do you keep a journal, or write poetry, or make lists of classic cars you are interested in? Do you regularly read *Vogue* or *AMP Magazine*? Do you participate in *World of Warcraft* as a game, or on message boards related to the game?

*As you read*, consider the following questions:

- Look in the glossary for the definitions of some words in this reading that might be new to you: intertext, repurpose, disciplinary writing expertise, discourse community, rhetorical moves, genre, semiotic, polycontextual, heterochronic, qualitative.

- Do you see an overlap among your own various literacies and literate practices? Do you see that some of your own literate practices in one context influence your literate practices in another context?

........................................................................................................

## Abstract

An extensive body of scholarship has documented the way disciplinary texts 1 and activities are produced and mediated through their relationship to a wide array of extradisciplinary discourses. This article seeks to complement and extend that line of work by drawing upon Witte's (1992) notion of intertext to address the way disciplinary activities repurpose, or reuse and transform, extradisciplinary practices. Based on text collection and practice-oriented retrospective accounts of one writer's processes for a number of textual activities, the article argues that the writer's developing disciplinary writing process as a graduate student in English literature is mediated by practices she repurposed from previous engagements with keeping a prayer journal as a member of a church youth group and generating visual designs for an undergraduate graphic arts class. Ultimately, the article argues for increased theoretical, methodological, and pedagogical attention to the discursive practices persons recruit and reinvigorate across multiple engagements with reading, writing, making, and doing.

## Keywords

Writing practice, disciplinary practices, repurposing, writing process, writing 2 transfer, disciplinary writing expertise

Over the past three decades, studies of writing development throughout the 3 college years have outlined a constellation of knowledge and abilities that contribute to disciplinary writing expertise. Along with advanced knowledge of a discipline's subject matter, research has indicated that writing expertise also involves knowledge of the particular discipline's discourse community (Bartholomae, 1985; Beaufort, 1999) as well as its rhetorical moves (Geisler, 1994; Haas, 1994), features of its genres (Artemeva, 2009; Berkenkotter, Huckin, & Ackerman, 1988, 1991), and the writing processes involved in accomplishing disciplinary tasks (Beaufort, 2004, 2007; Flower & Hayes, 1981; Perl, 1979; Sommers, 1980).

In addition to highlighting the types of knowledge that comprise disciplin- 4 ary writing expertise, research has also outlined the processes through which such knowledge develops. One prominent body of scholarship has documented the development of disciplinary knowledge through learners' increasingly deeper and fuller participation in a discipline's activities (Beaufort, 2004, 2007; Berkenkotter, Huckin, & Ackerman, 1988, 1991; Geisler, 1994; Haas, 1994; Herrington & Curtis, 2000; McCarthy, 1987). In addition, a growing body of work has mapped how knowledge emerges from the repurposing, or "the reuse and transformation of some text/semiotic object" (Prior & Shipka, 2003, p. 17), of extradisciplinary discourse into disciplinary texts and action. One set of situated studies, for example, has documented learners' efforts to repurpose discourses from one disciplinary setting to another. Gold (1989) and Rivers (1989) traced the tensions and synergies writers encounter as they repurpose discourse from coursework in English literature to accomplish tasks as technical communicators. Prior (1998) mapped one graduate student's repurposing of discourse from an American Studies course into writing for sociology. Ivanic (1998) traced one graduate student's efforts to recontextualize linguistic structures from sociology into her writing tasks for social work.

Extending the scope of inquiry to include contexts beyond the disciplinary ⁵ worlds of school and work, another body of scholarship has documented the way disciplinary knowledge emerges from learners' repurposing of intertexts from their local communities into their disciplinary activities. Research has documented how the learners' engagement with engineering (Artemeva, 2009; Winsor, 1990), architecture (Medway, 2002), political science (Spack, 1997), and American Studies (Prior, 1998) is enhanced by the talk and texts repurposed from home, family, and local community. Other studies have documented learners' repurposing of talk, texts, and images from popular culture into their engagements with biology (Kamberelis, 2001; Kamberelis & De La Luna, 2004); and English Studies (Roozen, 2009). Expanding the range of discoursal elements to a broader range of semiotic modes, other studies have traced the way activities for gender studies (Herrington & Curtis, 2000), sociology (Casanave, 2002), social work (Ivanic, 1998), art history (Chiseri-Strater, 1991), and African Studies (Buell, 2004) were informed by persons' orientations to gender and sexuality, ideological positions, and life philosophies.

This article complements and extends scholarship addressing the develop- ⁶ ment of disciplinary writing expertise by investigating the repurposing of extradisciplinary practices in the development of disciplinary activities. More specifically, I trace how one student, Lindsey Rachels (a pseudonym), draws upon practices developed for extradisciplinary engagements, particularly keeping a prayer journal as a member of a church youth group and generating visual designs for an undergraduate graphic arts class, in order to enrich and extend her writing for English Studies. Based on text collection and a series of practice-oriented retrospective accounts of Lindsey's writing practices and processes for a number of engagements, this article addresses the following research questions:

*Research Question 1:* What extradisciplinary practices does Lindsey repurpose into her disciplinary writing for English Studies?

*Research Question 2:* How are extradisciplinary practices repurposed for use in disciplinary activities?

*Research Question 3:* What role does the repurposing of extradisciplinary practices play in the development of Lindsey's disciplinary writing expertise for English Studies?

One way to understand the repurposing of textual practice across contexts 7 is via Witte's (1992) construct of "intertext" (p. 264). Developed as one means of addressing the boundary problems inherent in situating writing tightly within a particular setting, Witte's (1992) notion of "intertext" calls attention to person's experiences with a wide range of texts (broadly conceived to include a range of semiotic modes including written texts, talk, action, and so on as well as major and minor forms of those texts) that feed into and emanate from the production of text in the immediate present. Textual production, then, is informed by practices and processes associated offered up by the immediate setting as well as practices and processes repurposed from memorial texts, texts involved with previous encounters, and projected texts, texts involved in anticipated events. In this sense, the practices and processes employed in the invention and production of semiotic texts are not solely a product of a particular disciplinary setting, but rather from multiple engagements with texts. In this sense, the practices and processes that a writer might employ in producing a text and, hence, whatever features a given text may be said to have are ultimately determined not only by the particular setting in which a writer works, but rather from practices and processes associated with previous and anticipated textual engagements as well. In this manner, texts and activities can be said to be linked not just through streams of discourse, but trajectories of practice as well.

> I trace how one student, Lindsey Rachels (a pseudonym), draws upon practices developed for extradisciplinary engagements, particularly keeping a prayer journal as a member of a church youth group and generating visual designs for an undergraduate graphic arts class, in order to enrich and extend her writing for English Studies.

As a means of understanding the development of writing expertise, Witte's 8 (1992) notion of "intertext" draws attention to a number of key concerns. First, it illuminates the broad range of encounters with texts beyond the immediate context that are relevant to textual production, the way textual production is informed by different encounters with texts woven from different semiotic materials. Second, it illuminates the creative repurposing of practices and processes involved in textual invention, production, and use across contexts, the way practice is both situated in specific activities and repurposed for use in other engagements. Third, it calls attention to the transformation of practice not only across contexts but across a range of semiotic modes and representational media as well. Finally, it foregrounds the extensive array of "minor" forms of writing and texts, including lists, labels, and notes, involved in textual production and use.

Including the repurposing of extradisciplinary practice more fully into our 9 investigations of disciplinary writing expertise is important for a number of reasons. First, attending to the repurposing of practice across contexts can help us to develop broader and multidimensional conceptions of expertise that address the polycontextual and heterochronic dimensions of development (Beach, 2003; Engestrom, Engestrom, & Karkkainen, 1995; Tuomi-Grohen, Engestrom, & Young, 2003; Wenger, 1998). Furthermore, attention to the repurposing of practice across contexts responds to a number of recent calls for less bounded approaches to writing and literate practice (Brandt & Clinton, 2002; Collins & Blot, 2003; Guerra, 2007; Kells, 2007; Leander & Sheehy, 2004; Prior & Shipka, 2003; Reder & Davilla, 2005; Zachry, 2007). Attending to the repurposing of practice across contexts is important for pedagogical reasons as well. A number of studies have noted that weaving together of discourses is a key strategy for learners to scaffolding participation in advanced disciplinary activities (Bizzell, 1999; Campbell, 1997; Kamberelis, 2001; McCrary, 2005). It seems reasonable to suspect that repurposing everyday discursive practices into disciplinary activities might serve a similar function. In addition, attending to the repurposing of practice can help us develop pedagogical approaches that facilitate transfer of writing practice across contexts. Although writing instruction is predicated on the fundamental assumption that practices developed in one context can be imported into others, a number of scholars have observed that the transfer of writing skills has received relatively little attention (Beaufort, 2007; Downs & Wardle, 2007; Fishman & Reiff, 2008; Smit, 2004; Bergmann & Zepernick, 2007; Wardle, 2009).

## Method

### Participant and Setting

This manuscript reports a study exploring the interplay among the various kinds of literate activities that Lindsey had been involved in. When I met Lindsey, a white female in her mid-20s, in May of 2008, she was working toward her MEd in secondary education English language arts at a large public university in the southeast and teaching middle school Language Arts at a rural school in the area. As an undergraduate, Lindsey had initially pursued a double major in graphic design and English before concentrating solely on English during her final year and then, immediately after earning her BA, entered an MA program in English literature at another public university in the same area. After her 1st year of graduate school, Lindsey took a position teaching middle school English language arts and began taking classes to earn her teaching certificate and then continued coursework toward her MEd. I met Lindsey during a brief talk I had given during a workshop for local educators. Lindsey had been attending both as a current middle-school language arts teacher and as one of the graduate students leading the workshop. My talk had focused on the kinds of literate activities that often go unnoticed by teachers, and as an example I had drawn from a case study of one undergraduate's rich history with autobiographical journaling. Following the session, Lindsey approached me to talk about her various types of journaling for a number of literate activities, including documenting the events of her life, understanding religious texts, working on papers for her English, generating material for her blog, and taking notes for her creative writing. Earlier that year, I had received approval from my university's Internal Review Board to study persons' engagement with a broad range of literate activities. Because of her extensive engagement with journaling for a wide variety of activities, I asked Lindsey if she would be interested in participating in a research study focusing on her journaling, and she volunteered to do so.

## Data Collection

Like much qualitative inquiry, the research design emerged as the study pro- 11 gressed. Initially, I began this case study to get a sense of Lindsey's journaling practices, and I had planned to conduct text-based interviews and ethnographic observation of her journaling activities. To this end, our initial interview addressed Lindsey's journaling for a number of purposes. While discussing her tendency to copy Bible verses into her prayer journal, a process she referred to as "verse copying," Lindsey mentioned that she had stopped keeping a prayer journal during her late teen years, but then commented that she still did a form of verse copying when taking notes for her college and graduate school literature papers. This seeming reuse and transformation between seemingly divergent writing activities struck me as interesting not only because of the contrast between keeping a prayer journal and doing literary analysis but also because linking these activities involved the repurposing of discursive practice across contexts rather than the recontextualization of discourse itself. At this point, then, I shifted the inquiry from Lindsey's journaling activities to understanding the connections she forged among different literate engagements.

Lindsey's comment about repurposing her practice of verse copying into 12 the process of taking notes for her literature papers suggested a method of data collection sensitive to the repurposing of practice across her processes of invention, production, and use for a variety of different engagements. To this end, I conducted a series of process-tracing interviews (Emig, 1971; Flower & Hayes, 1981; Prior, 2004; Prior & Shipka, 2003) focused on texts and materials Lindsey provided me with from a number of her different textual activities. Process tracing involves having participants create retrospective accounts of the processes involved in the production of a particular writing project. In addition to providing a means to generate detailed accounts of discursive processes and practices used for specific tasks, these retrospective tracings also have the potential to illuminate activities and practices drawn from a wide array of engagements from the near and distant past. Rather than have Lindsey draw pictures of her process, as Prior (2004) and Prior and Shipka (2003) have done, I asked her to describe the process involved in the invention and production of various projects by showing me how various texts and materials were employed. In addition to helping trigger and support Lindsey's memory of the processes and practices she employed in the production and use of these materials, some of which had occurred 10 years before, this form of "stimulated elicitation" (Prior, 2004) during the interviews also helped to make visible Lindsey's tacit knowledge of text invention and production. It was frequently the case that we delayed scheduling interviews for weeks or months in order to give Lindsey time to locate and retrieve materials she had stored in her home or at her parents' home in a neighboring state. In addition to the focal texts for the process-tracing interviews, I made all of the other materials I collected available to Lindsey by placing them in stacks within reach of the table where we conducted the face-to-face interviews.

The initial process-tracing interview focused on the materials Lindsey 13 provided me for what she referred to as the feminine ideal project[1] for a graduate English course, one of the first papers she had written as a graduate student about 17 months before we began the study. Written in response to an assignment in her graduate American literature course that invited students to analyze two major novels and support their analysis with information from secondary sources, the paper explored F. Scott Fitzgerald and William Faulkner's treatment of the feminine ideal in *The Great Gatsby* and *The Sound and the Fury.*

Successive interviews over the next 12 months focused on the materials I 14 collected for any engagements that Lindsey mentioned were relevant to the invention and production of the feminine ideal paper, particularly the two that from her perspective played the most prominent role in shaping the paper: keeping her prayer journal and creating visual designs for an undergraduate course in graphic arts. The initial process-tracing interviews tended to focus on one of these three engagements, but later interviews tended to move recursively back and forth across the materials for all of those engagements as well as others Lindsey had mentioned. Multiple interviews over a period of 12 months provided opportunities for the kinds of "longer conversations" and "cyclical dialogue around texts over a period of time" that Lillis (2008, p. 362) identifies as crucial for understanding practice within the context of the participant's history. Lindsey's references to discursive practices and inscriptional tools from the stacks and her tendency to pick through them to select sample texts and tools as a way to make a point or provide an example prompted me to start videotaping interviews and taking still photos in order to keep track of specific texts she indicated. I examined all of the materials that were not employed as the focal texts for the process-tracing interviews in order to confirm or disconfirm the use of the practices Lindsey described.

In all, I conducted seven formal process-tracing interviews, which resulted 15 in just over 12 hours of video- and audiotape data, one process-tracing interview conducted via email, and took 60 still photographs during interviews or while I was examining Lindsey's materials between interviews. I supplemented the interviews with dozens of follow-up questions I developed while examining the interview recordings, my notes, and texts that Lindsey had brought to the interviews or had provided at other times. I emailed these follow-up questions to Lindsey after the formal interviews and she emailed her responses, which usually arrived within the week and which I then printed and archived. I also supplemented process-tracing interviews with dozens of informal conversations throughout the data collection period. I kept notes on eight of these informal conversations, which occurred during chance meetings on campus or when Lindsey stopped by my office. In all, I read approximately 600 pages of inscriptions (collected texts, key sections of transcripts of audio- and video-recordings of interviews, interview notes, and analytic notes), listened to and viewed more than a dozen hours of audio- and video-recordings, and examined dozens of photographs in order to develop a sense of Lindsey's various literate practices and how she might be repurposing them across engagements (see Table 1 below).

## Table 1

Texts Collected from Lindsey's Engagements with Religious Activities, Art and Design, and English Studies

| Literate Activity | Task and Materials Collected | How Analyzed |
|---|---|---|
| Religious Activities | Prayer Journal I: Approximately 130 pages of journaling (June 1998 to February 1999) | PTI |
| | Prayer Journal 2: Approximately 90 pages of journaling (February 1999 to July 1999) | PTI |
| | Prayer Journal 3: Approximately 40 pages of journaling (July 1999 to August 1999) | C/D |
| | Other materials: 4 of Lindsey's Bibles and documents from religious services Lindsey had attended including church bulletins, sermon outlines, and notes (1997–2002) | PTI |
| Art and Design | Rings project: Assignment sheet, evaluation chart, Lindsey's sketches in her sketchbook, and the final design. Two-dimensional Design (Fall 2002) | PTI |
| | Gradation project: Assignment sheet, evaluation chart, Lindsey's sketches in her sketchbook, and the final design. Two-dimensional Design (Fall 2002) | PTI |
| | Natural informalities project: Assignment sheet, evaluation chart, Lindsey's sketches in her sketchbook, and the final design. Two-dimensional Design (Fall 2002) | PTI |
| | Color harmonies project: Assignment sheet, evaluation chart, Lindsey's sketches in her sketchbook, and the final design. Two-dimensional Design (Fall 2002) | PTI |
| | Final project: Assignment sheet, evaluation chart, Lindsey's sketches in her sketchbook, and the final design. Two-dimensional Design (Fall 2002) | C/D |
| English Studies (Undergraduate) | Prufrock project: Notes, two outlines, and final paper. Introduction to Poetry (Fall 2002) | C/D |
| | Auden project: Notes, one outline, and final paper. Introduction to Poetry (Fall 2002) | C/D |

**Table 1** *(continued)*

| | | |
|---|---|---|
| | Cummings project: Notes, one outline, and final paper. Introduction to Poetry (Fall 2002) | C/D |
| | Odyssey project: Notes, two outlines, final draft. Introduction to Literature II (Fall 2002) | PTI |
| | Conrad and Dante project: Notes, two outlines, final draft. Introduction to Literature II (Fall 2002) | C/D |
| | Egerton project: Notes from primary and secondary sources, three outlines, final draft. Personal statement. Early British Literature (Spring 2003) | C/D |
| | Stoppard project: Notes, outline, final draft. Survey of American Literature (Fall 2003) | C/D |
| | Relevance of Art project: Notes, outline, final draft. Survey of American Literature (Fall 2003) | C/D |
| | Virginia Woolf project: Notes from primary and secondary sources, three outlines, and final draft. Gender in Literature (Spring 2004) | C/D |
| English Studies (Graduate) | The Piano project: Notes from secondary sources, copies of six journal articles used for the paper with Lindsey's marginal comments, rough draft, final draft. Literary Theory (Fall 2005) | PTI |
| | Feminine Ideal project: Class notebook, notes from primary and secondary sources, note cards, two outlines, rough draft, and final draft. American Literature (Spring 2006) | PTI |

Note: In the column at right, PTI indicates materials that served as the focus of one or more process-tracing interviews. C/D indicates materials that were examined with an eye toward confirming and/or disconfirming the use of the practices Lindsey mentioned during the process tracing interviews.

## Analysis

Goodwin (1994) notes that his analysis of the discursive practices employed by archaeologists and lawyers made extensive use of the very same practices that he was examining. In the same manner, my own analysis of Lindsey's discursive practices employed many of the same practices she described. To identify instances of practice being spun-off, or reused and transformed to meet the demands of a new or different activity, I analyzed these data interpretively and holistically (Miller, Hengst, & Wang, 2003). I first arranged data inscriptions (i.e., sample texts, sections of interview transcripts, interpretive notes, printed versions of digital photographs and still images captured from video, etc.) chronologically. I then examined those data inscriptions for instances where Lindsey had indicated or where it appeared that practices were being repurposed across contexts. For example, in addition to the repurposing of her verse copying and design practices into her writing process for literary analysis (which I elaborate in detail below), Lindsey also mentioned a practice of writing down verbatim some key phrases she heard during church sermons that informed her note-taking for several of her college courses. From my perspective, it also appeared that Lindsey's encounters with different uses of outlines for religious engagements, including the ones her father crafted each Sunday morning in preparation for teaching his Sunday-school class and also her engagement with sermon outlines that were printed in the bulletins, both informed and were informed by her use of outlining for a number of school activities.

Based on that analysis, I then constructed brief initial narratives (e.g., usu- 17 ally quick sketches in the form of an extended flow chart, but sometimes short written paragraphs. I tended to supplement both with copies of the texts and tools Lindsey had indicated during previous interviews) describing the use of a practice for one activity and then being redeployed for a different activity. I then reviewed and modified those initial narratives by checking those constructions against the data inscriptions (to ensure accuracy and to seek counter instances) and by submitting them to Lindsey for her examination. At these times I often requested additional texts from Lindsey, and frequently she volunteered to provide me with additional materials and insights that she thought might be useful in further detailing the repurposing of discursive practices across contexts. It was frequently the case that my understanding of the relationship between her different literate activities needed significant modification as a result of closer inspection of the data, identification of additional relevant data, or discussions with Lindsey during interviews or via email. I modified accounts of these interactions according to Lindsey's feedback. For example, I initially assembled a narrative that described Lindsey's physical manipulation of texts in the production of visual designs for her undergraduate design class and her repurposing of that practice in order to develop a general sense of her argument for the feminine paper. Upon showing this narrative to Lindsey, she pointed out that her physical manipulation of texts also figured prominently much later in the writing process as she created detailed outlines of her discussion. Her comments prompted an additional process-tracing interview and a revision to the narrative based on that interview. Finally, I asked Lindsey to member check (Lather, 1991; Stake, 1995, 2000) final versions of the trajectories in order to determine if they seemed valid from her perspective.

The analysis produced a number of instances of repurposing among 18 Lindsey's multiple textual engagements. To represent the dynamic interplays between Lindsey's multiple textual engagements and also to make my own analytic practices more visible, I present the results of my analysis as a series of documented narratives rather than as a structuralist analysis, as Becker (2000) and Prior (1998) suggest. In addition to following the reuse of practice from earlier to later activities, the use of documented narrative allows me to present these repurposings in a coherent fashion without flattening out the richness, complexity, and dynamics of how practices are reused and transformed across contexts. I selected the two narratives presented below for a number of reasons. First, these narratives address the repurposings of practice that Lindsey

considered to be most significant in the invention and production of the feminine ideal paper. Second, these two narratives allow me to illustrate, even if
briefly, several other repurposing of discursive practices, including writing on
the back of the door of her family's summer cottage and using note cards for
a fourth-grade science project. Third, these two narratives interanimate one
another and thus permit me to provide readers with a sense of the complexity,
richness, and density of the repurposings at play, including how they are transformed across contexts and semiotic mode.

The first narrative elaborates Lindsey's repurposing of discursive practices    19
from her extensive engagement with keeping a prayer journal into the reading-
to-write process she employs for the feminine ideal paper. The second narrative details Lindsey's repurposing of discursive practices involved in generating
visual texts for an undergraduate design class into her process for developing
and structuring the paper's argument. I separate these narratives for analytic
purposes only; in reality, and as the reader will come to see, they are deeply
intertwined.

## Findings

### Narrative I: Learning the Texts and Talk of American Literature

In this narrative, I elaborate how Lindsey's understanding of literary texts and    20
her acquisition of the voice of literary criticism are prominently shaped by
discursive practices from her religious activities, particularly in regard to the
prayer journal she kept. First, I describe the verse-copying practice she used to
understand religious texts. I then elaborate how verse copying informs Lindsey's engagement with the primary and secondary sources she used for the
feminine ideal paper.

During her teen years, Lindsey was an active member of a number of differ-    21
ent churches near her home. She attended services and youth group meetings
at two and sometimes three different churches each Sunday and Wednesday.
At the suggestion of a church youth leader, Lindsey began keeping a journal to reflect on Bible passages and her religious growth. Sitting cross-legged
on her bed each evening, Lindsey would open her Bible to the verses she'd
underlined as she encountered them while attending sermons or Sunday school
and then copy those verses into a special journal[2] she had bought for that purpose (Figure 1). The verses she underlined in her Bible "sometimes came from
those mentioned during a church sermon, or maybe I would hear somebody
reference them, and then I would go home and look those up in my Bible"
(R. Lindsey, personal interview, December 16, 2008). For Lindsey, verse copying served two key functions. First, it served as a means of understanding God's
word. As she described,

> I really liked copying scripture. If I am trying to get inside a text, it helps me to
> copy it verbatim. When I am stepping into the Bible, it helps me to write out, not
> type but write out, exactly verbatim what it says. (R. Lindsey, personal interview,
> December 16, 2008)

Elaborating during a follow-up interview, she added that, "A lot of me 22 copying the verses was me trying to analyze the Bible, like what does this verse mean, and different interpretations were interesting. It was really important to me" (R. Lindsey, personal interview, July 13, 2009). In addition to helping her understand the text, Lindsey remarked that verse copying also helped her to take up the language of the religious texts she was working with. Discussing this function, she noted that, "When I stepped into the Bible passage, it helped me to understand it better when I wrote out exactly what it said. That's the only way I can understand it and also own the language" (R. Lindsey, personal interview, December 16, 2008).

In addition to Bible passages, she would also copy into her journal quotes 23 from other religious texts (i.e., C. S. Lewis's *The Screwtape Letters* and *Mere Christianity;* Max Lucado's *Life Lessons;* etc.) she kept in the nightstand by her bed, song lyrics from religious groups such as Jars of Clay, quotes she found on inspirational calendars she had in her room or from a book of famous quotes she kept, and so on, often writing brief reflections on these passages as well. The quote from Emerson that Lindsey inscribed on the top of the October 10, 1998 journal entry (see image at left in Figure 1), for example, was copied from the book of famous quotations she owned.

The daily entries in her early prayer journals, like the entries from October 10, 24 1998 at left in Figure 1, were comprised mostly of verses copied from her Bible, with Lindsey occasionally writing brief reflections on some of those verses. Entries in later instantiations of the prayer journal, however, like the entry from June 17, 1999 at the right of Figure 1, tended to feature fewer verses but more of Lindsey's reflections. Explaining the entries in her later journals, she offered, "I would copy Bible verses word for word, and then I would write about what I thought it meant. I would basically do close readings of Bible verses" (R. Lindsey, personal interview, July 30, 2009). Her later journals also tended to include the brief prayers she would write at the close of each journaling session. According to Lindsey, after she felt like she had understood what the passage meant,

> Then I would write a prayer. This was for me an accessible way to pray. Saying a prayer, to me, just didn't feel right. That's something I really struggled with. So writing a note to God, that was something more tangible. (R. Lindsey, personal interview, July 30, 2009)

In writing these prayers, Lindsey stated that she tended to incorporate some 25 of the language of the passage she had copied that evening: "So my journaling for the night would end with a prayer, where I am iterating, well reiterating, the language that I've been using" (R. Lindsey, personal interview, December 16, 2009).

As a discursive practice, of course, Lindsey's verse copying is linked into a 26 broad array of other practices relevant to her understanding of and engagement with religious texts and activities. Importantly, however, Lindsey also reappropriated this practice into the invention and production of the feminine ideal paper she crafted for a graduate *American Literature* course. Thus, in

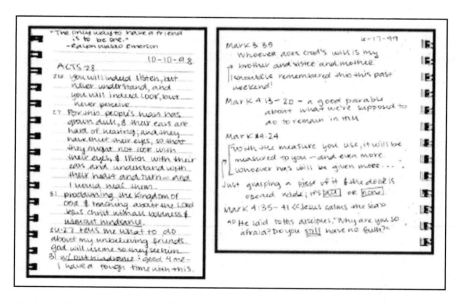

**Figure 1**  Representative pages from two of Lindsey's prayer journals showing samples of her "verse copying."
Note: At left, the entry from October 10, 1998 from Prayer Journal I. At right, the June 17, 1999 entry from Prayer Journal 2.

addition to shaping her religious engagements, then, Lindsey's verse-copying practice played a key role in her coming to understand the source materials she was working with for the feminine ideal paper.

The process Lindsey employed to accomplish the feminine ideal paper began 27 the same way she had approached the majority of her literature papers as an undergraduate, by taking copious notes as she read and reread the source texts she was working with. Most of her note-taking involved what she referred to as "passage copying," copying and recopying in longhand onto pages of loose leaf paper potentially useful passages from her primary and secondary sources. As Lindsey stated, "Before I write a paper, I just wrote quotes from sources or anything I thought that I might want to use out in longhand. I copy out passages from the text and then start to ask questions about it" (R. Lindsey, personal interview, August 26, 2008). According to Lindsey, she'd begun using this practice for a paper on the *Odyssey* in an *Introduction to Literature* course she had taken early in her 2nd year of college. Prior to that, the writing tasks she encountered in her English courses in college and in high school before that had not required a focused, in-depth analysis or the use of outside sources and thus did not require extensive passage copying for Lindsey to immerse herself in the material.

As a strategy for engaging with texts, Lindsey's passage copying rested par- 28 tially in her experiences at school reaching all the way back to the writing activities she did in the primary grades. Discussing her earliest encounters with this practice, for example, she indicated,

> Every paper that involved any kind of outside sources that I ever did for school, they made us copy quotes onto something, usually those index cards. So you'd have the title of the source at the top, and that would be source A, and then A1, A2 would be certain quotes that came from that source. I remember that the first time I had to do this was for a fourth grade science project. (R. Lindsey, personal interview, May 13, 2009)

Lindsey, then, had copied passages from texts before doing so for her 29 prayer journal. However, she characterized those early uses of copying passages for school as being aimed at learning the basic format for documenting information from outside sources accurately and organizing it effectively rather than as a means of furthering inquiry or deepening engagement with complex texts. Her use of copying passages to that effect rested more centrally with her history of copying Bible verses into the numerous prayer journals she had kept during her teen years. In fact, Lindsey initially described the passage copying for her literature papers by claiming, "It was like me re-writing scripture as a way to get into the Bible" (R. Lindsey, personal interview, August 26, 2008).

Lindsey's repurposing of her verse-copying practice shaped her engagement 30 with source texts for the feminine ideal paper in a number of key ways. In the initial stage, Lindsey read through the two novels and the six journal articles (three for each novel) she had chosen to focus on. As she did so, Lindsey filled 23 pages of notebook paper with passages from the novels (see image at left in Figure 2), approximately 250 passages in all, copied using MLA style in anticipation of potentially incorporating them into the paper. These copyings, Lindsey claimed, helped her to familiarize herself with the novels: "I copied [passages] out in longhand, and then I remembered them better, to the point that I could place any quote into where it came from in the book" (R. Lindsey, personal interview, August 12, 2008). She mentioned that this was also a way to "gain momentum," (R. Lindsey, personal interview, August 26, 2008) both in terms of a way to get started with the seemingly "epic" task of completing this project and to get her pen and brain moving as she began each session of reading and writing. Reading through her six journal articles, Lindsey filled 12 single-spaced pages of notebook paper with approximately 300 passages (see image at right in Figure 2). Besides helping her learn the subject matter of the articles, Lindsey also credited her repurposing of verse copying with helping her to acquire the language of literary criticism. As she described during one of our interviews,

> Once I'd scanned the lit[erature] on the women figures I was studying, Daisy and Caddy, and jotted down fragments from those passages, I began to feel like I could talk about the texts with some authority— I got a feel for how people talked about them. (R. Lindsey, personal interview, November 17, 2008)

Elaborating, she offered,

> By writing important lines over and over again, I become more familiar with the words. It's almost like writing them over and over again gives me ownership

**Figure 2**    Examples of Lindsey's extensive passage copying in the production of the feminine ideal paper.
Note: At left, the third of six pages of passages Lindsey copied from *The Great Gatsby.* At right, the second of the two pages of passages she copied from an *American Literature* article written by Glenn Settle.

of them, and I am better able to use the words as though they are my own. I can manipulate them in ways that enable me to piece together a cohesive paper. (R. Lindsey, personal interview, November 17, 2008)

During her early readings for the feminine ideal paper, then, Lindsey repur- 31 posed a literate practice she had previously employed to understand the Bible and to help her "own the language" (R. Lindsey, personal interview, November 17, 2008) of her religious activities as a means of understanding the novels and journal articles and appropriating the language of literary criticism. Lindsey's repurposing of practices for understanding religious texts as a way to come to terms with the content and language of the novels and journal articles, however, was not limited to her initial readings of these sources. She also redeployed this repurposed version of her verse copying at a number of other points in the paper's production, often linking it together with practices from an even broader array of literate engagements.

Lindsey's reuse of her verse copying, for example, also informed her ef- 32 forts to narrow the scope of her discussion and reduce the massive volume of passages from the novels, articles, and multiple versions of notes she was working with, a key complication that had not been an issue in previous tasks where she was only dealing with one primary text and a small set of related journal articles. In fact, for Lindsey, one of the main reasons that the feminine ideal paper gave her so much trouble was that the overwhelming volume of copied passages she had to sort through seriously complicated her strategy for narrowing the focus of the paper. The frustration this caused Lindsey came through clearly during one of our interviews when she heaved a sigh and stated that dealing with so many passages "was really a stretch for me. I just could not do it, doing two texts. Just doing Faulkner would have been manageable, but doing two just felt like too much" (R. Lindsey, personal interview, August 26, 2008). As a remedy, Lindsey recopied key passages from the journal articles onto a series of five-by-seven inch note cards to decrease the number of passages she had to deal with from the articles. This move, Lindsey indicated, was the result of

> getting really desperate. I had too many notes and I just couldn't see how they were all going to fit together, so I started using formal note cards for the articles. I learned how to do that in fourth grade, and it was funny that I was now using them in grad school. It was also another opportunity for me to write the passages over again, and to make better sense of the article. (R. Lindsey, personal interview, August 26, 2008)

In this manner, recopying the smaller set of pertinent passages onto the note cards helped Lindsey to narrow the scope of the paper and further enhance her engagement with both the content and discourse of the articles.

The reading-to-write process Lindsey employed to address the feminine 33 ideal task is informed by a number of practices associated with English Studies. Her extensive copying of passages from source texts, for example, reflects a sense that privileged literary texts are complicated and thus understanding them involves careful unraveling, translating, decoding, interpreting, and analyzing, which Fahnestock and Secor (1988; see also Warren, 2006; Wilder, 2005, 2002) identify as the fundamental assumption underlying literary criticism (p. 89). Importantly, though, in unraveling, interpreting, and analyzing those texts, Lindsey also drew heavily upon memorial practices she had accumulated from a number of literate activities. Her engagement with the novels and journal articles for the task was mediated by a nexus that includes literate practices from American literature, her religious activities, a fourth-grade science project, and experiences with source-based writing stretching back through elementary school. The verse copying, for example, is a practice originally linked into a nexus that included sermons and Sunday school lessons, the Bible and other religious and inspirational texts, and Lindsey's written prayers that Lindsey redeployed into a nexus that includes novels and journal articles, lectures, and index cards to learn the texts and talk of American literature. In this sense, Lindsey's ability to engage with the novels and the journal articles for the feminine ideal paper is not just a product of discursive practices unique to literary criticism but from both disciplinary and extradisciplinary engagements.

The heterogeneity of practices created by Lindsey's repurposing of verse 34 copying had important consequences for her work on the feminine ideal paper and previous literary analysis papers as well. Faced with tasks demanding a deep engagement with source texts but not having been exposed to practices as an English major that she felt afforded such engagement, Lindsey recontextualized her verse-copying practice and purposefully linked it into a range of practices associated with English Studies as a way to learn the texts and talk of literary analysis. Later, as a graduate student in American literature, Lindsey's verse copying continued to afford her engagement with key disciplinary texts for the feminine ideal paper. However, because the task demanded that she deal with twice the number of source texts she had previously been asked to address, and perhaps many more texts than she negotiated while keeping her prayer journal, her verse copying also introduced a constraint to her process of narrowing the focus of her argument. Lindsey addressed this limitation by repurposing yet another practice into the nexus: the use of note cards she had employed in her fourth-grade science project. The linking together of the verse copying with the use of the note cards gave the action a laminated character as Lindsey determined a more narrowed approach to the paper while simultaneously "mak[ing] better sense of the article[s]" (R. Lindsey, personal interview, August 26, 2008).

## Narrative II: Visualizing the Argument

In this second narrative, I elaborate Lindsey's repurposing of practices for 35 fashioning visual design projects in order to develop and structure the argument for her feminine ideal paper. First, I describe the practices she employed to generate visual designs for an undergraduate graphic arts class she took during her 2nd year of college. I then detail how those design practices inform Lindsey's efforts to develop both a broad and more fine-grained organization for the paper's argument. In addition to addressing how Lindsey's passage copying described in the previous narrative is incorporated into an array of practices for visualizing her argument, this narrative also traces repurposing of design practices across semiotic modes as well as disciplinary borders.

Lindsey began college as a double major in graphic design and English. Her 36 first course toward her graphic design major was *Two-dimensional Design,* a class she took concurrently with *Introduction to Literature* during her 2nd year of college. A demanding and time-consuming studio course that introduced basic principles by having students plan and execute a series of projects, *Two-dimensional Design* required students to do everything by hand using paper, pencils, and pens for sketching and inking, glue, tape, scissors, and X-acto knives. Discussing the process she employed in her projects for the course, Lindsey stated that she relied heavily on a practice of physically manipulating texts until she found a workable design.

In order to get a clearer sense of the practices involved in this type of semi- 37 otic performance, I asked Lindsey to select one particular project that would serve as the focus of one of our process-tracing interviews. She chose what she referred to as the "rings project," a task that explored ways of depicting the spatial relationships between two shapes by arranging two rings in relation to one another in a series of different orientations (Figure 3). According to Lindsey, the initial steps toward generating her design involved sketching various panes and configurations of panes in her sketchbook, experimenting with different ways to orient the rings in relation to one another within each pane and different combinations of panes (see image at top of Figure 3). "For the first week or so [after getting the assignment]," Lindsey recalled, "I was constantly sketching panes and rearranging them in every imaginable sequence in sketches in my sketchbook" (R. Lindsey, personal interview, May 5, 2009). Once she had sketched some panes that seemed to "work," Lindsey's next step involved physically arranging panes on her table in the studio and the kitchen table, desk, and walls of her apartment.[3] Describing during one of our interviews the process of arranging and rearranging sequences of panes, and quickly sketching the diagram at the bottom of Figure 3 while she did so, Lindsey stated,

> I cut some of the panes out of the sketchbook or redid them larger on other pieces of paper. Then I rearranged them in different combinations on my desk. When I saw something that worked, I taped the pieces of the project up on the wall above my drafting table and then continued to rearrange the pieces over the course of the next few days. When I liked a certain sequence or arrangement, I sketched it out on a piece of paper, or if it was a series of only four panes or so, I numbered them and recorded the various combinations that worked. Every now and then I sketched a new pane to replace one of the ones on the wall. (R. Lindsey, personal interview, May 5, 2009)

Executing the final version of the project was basically a matter of creating a much neater version in ink of what was taped up on her wall. Although each of the class's other projects emphasized different design concepts, Lindsey indicated that she employed a similar process of sketching, cutting, taping, arranging, and rearranging to complete those projects as well. 38

As a discursive practice for the production of visual designs, Lindsey's physical manipulation of elements of her projects is linked into a broad array of other practices and inscriptional tools relevant to the *Two-dimensional Design* class she was taking and to graphic design as a discipline. Importantly, however, Lindsey also redeployed this practice into the invention and production of her feminine ideal paper for *American Literature*, repurposing and resemiotizing it from a means of creating visual arguments to means of fashioning a written one. 39

Having familiarized herself with the content and language of the novels and journal articles and identified the feminine ideal as a workable, if still somewhat broad, focus for the paper, Lindsey turned her attention to developing a framework that could serve as an initial structure for the paper. In order to do so, she employed a practice she had used for every literature paper since the *Odyssey* essay for her *Introduction to Literature* class, a paper which demanded that she assemble a complex argument from multiple sources and the same paper for which she began her extensive copying of passages from source texts. Her strategy involved taking the pages of passages she had copied, starting with the entire pages and then individual passages torn from them, and physically 40

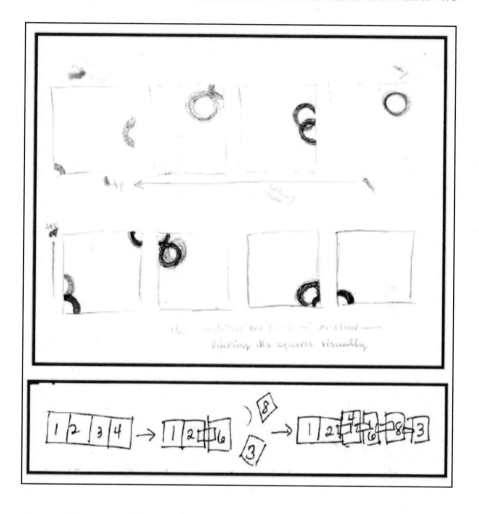

**Figure 3**  Documents illuminating Lindsey's invention and production of the rings project for *Two-dimensional Design*.
Note: At top, one of Lindsey's early pencil and pen sketches for the rings project showing various panes of rings. At bottom, a diagram Lindsey sketched during our January 5, 2009 interview to indicate her process of numbering various panes, cutting them apart, arranging different sequences, and then taping workable sequences together.

arranging them on the floors, tables, walls, and windows around her apartment. In addition to helping her take stock of the wealth of information she had gleaned from the source texts, Lindsey acknowledged that

> being able to physically manipulate the arrangement of an argument makes it easier for me to figure out which pieces fit with the whole and where they belong, how they're related. When I am able to physically manipulate the arrangement of an argument, I can more easily visualize the argument I want to make and how each piece fits into that argument. (R. Lindsey, personal interview, November 17, 2008)

As an overall initial structure began to emerge, Lindsey would then begin creating a series of increasingly detailed handwritten outlines based on the arrangements she had generated.

In arranging her argument, Lindsey stated that she drew upon a number 41 of encounters with arranging texts. She indicated, for example, the various encounters she'd had with organizing texts for school tasks stretching from elementary through high school, especially to learning to follow a rigidly structured outline for the analyses of poetry, novels, and plays beginning in fifth grade. Her engagement with this type of structured outlining intensified during 10th grade when her language arts coursework focused on preparing students for the Advanced Placement (AP) English exam. As Lindsey recalled, the instruction emphasized "how to do a really structured outline and how to work from that to write the AP essay" (R. Lindsey, personal interview, May 13, 2009). Elaborating, Lindsey stated that the preparation tried to reproduce

> the testing format, where you had a little booklet with the prompt on the front and a poem to read. And the outline you had to write had to have, like, Roman numeral one, your intro[duction], and then you had the three paragraphs and the conclusion. And each paragraph had a different function. The first paragraph had to describe style. The next one had to describe tone, and the third had to be about syntax. They hammered us with this. (R. Lindsey, personal interview, May 13, 2009)

Much like documenting the quotes she had been required to do for source- 42 based school projects, Lindsey characterized this use of outlining as merely using a prefabricated form to produce an organized essay under timed conditions rather than a means of figuring out the best way to structure the analysis of some literary work. As she put it, "doing the outlines was all about the format of it. It wasn't like a tool for thinking about the poem. It was just what you had to do to organize the essay" (R. Lindsey, personal interview, May 13, 2009).

In terms of a "tool for thinking" about how an analysis might be arranged, 43 Lindsey stated that she found the practice she employed for creating visual designs in *Two-dimensional Design* to be much more productive at this stage in her writing process. Repurposing this practice to develop a workable structure for her argument about the feminine ideal, Lindsey's first step involved spreading pages of her notes and note cards out on the floor of her room and then reorganizing them into different piles that addressed a common theme or point. Once she had organized her notes loosely by topic, she began arranging them into a tentative framework for the structure of the paper, working to determine in which order she might talk about the recurring topics she had identified while browsing her notes. For Lindsey, this was one of the most difficult aspects of working on the paper:

> The feminine ideal idea applied to both novels, so it would work for the overall focus. But, I couldn't get how to structure the paper. I just kept getting messed up when I had to keep jumping back and forth to talk about Daisy, then Caddy, then Daisy, then Caddy again. (R. Lindsey, personal interview, May 13, 2009)

Lindsey acknowledged that this kind of arrangement would have been much easier had she done it on a computer, but stated that working on the screen did not allow her to get a broad sense of the various parts she had to work with or develop a sense of the various ways they might be fitted together. As she offered,

> It's hard for me to work on a screen. I can't manipulate things the way that I can when they're on pieces of paper. If it's on a screen, I could not see both the pages of notes and all of these note cards [at the same time]. In order to see everything I would have to be opening and closing a bunch of different windows and what-ever, and my brain just doesn't work that way. (R. Lindsey, personal interview, May 13, 2009)

What eventually emerged from Lindsey's sorting and shuffling on the floor was a broad framework organized around the tripartite structure indexed in her outlines for AP English that first addressed the notions of the feminine ideal operating in the novels, then how those ideals were dismantled, and then the crises that resulted from that disruption.

Developing and supporting the three subsections of this initial frame-work required an even more nuanced organizing the passages she had copied. To accomplish this, Lindsey drew again on her design practice and began sorting quotes from primary and secondary sources by tearing off specific passages and assembling those pieces of paper[4] together in smaller groups "like a puzzle" on her table and desk (R. Lindsey, personal inter-view, August 12, 2008). Demonstrating during a process-tracing interview how this process helped her to assemble a section of the paper about Daisy Buchanan's voice (Figure 4), Lindsey ripped and sorted sections from her notes while explaining,

> I just took it [a page full of passages] like that [tearing a section from bottom of page] and laid it out and then I went through my notes and said "okay her voice, her voice, where is the quote about her voice?" So it talks about her voice right here [indicating a different page of passages], how her voice is "sad and lovely." And here [indicating the second page of passages] it says "it was held by her voice." So I took this [indicating again the second page of passages] like that [tearing a section from it] and put all these together. Then I knew that Person [author of one of the articles Lindsey used] had said something about Daisy's voice [shuffling through notecards]. Right here [indicating a passage written on a note card containing passages from the Person article]. And so that [indicating the torn sections of notes] would go, with what Leland Person said about "the essence of her promise represented by her voice." (R. Lindsey, personal interview, December 16, 2008)

Lindsey would repeat this process, which she claimed "had a hands-on patchwork feel that I associate with the crafting of a piece of artwork" (R. Lindsey, personal interview, November 17, 2008) as she experimented with how the information she had in her notes might support the initial framework she developed.

Figure 4 Lindsey, during our December 16, 2008 interview, demonstrating the process of tearing a page of her handwritten notes into smaller sections and then assembling sections torn from different pages.
Note: At top left and right, Lindsey tears apart and combines passages from different pages of *The Great Gatsby* notes. At bottom, Lindsey looks through her note cards trying to locate a quotation from Leland Person that relates to the passages from *The Great Gatsby*.

In preparation for making a series of increasingly detailed and elaborate 48 handwritten outlines at an even later point in the production of the paper, Lindsey taped combinations that "worked or felt right" (R. Lindsey, personal interview, January 5, 2009) up on the walls and windows around her desk. Describing this process of stabilizing workable sequences, at least for the moment, Lindsey stated,

> What I did is fold and then rip the notes and then I took masking tape, not clear tape but masking tape because I knew it would come off the wall, and I just taped them up all over the place. I had my textual evidence taped up in order on the walls and windows so that I could start doing my outlining. (R. Lindsey, personal interview, August 26, 2008)

In this sense, Lindsey stated, the process was like "graphic design" in that it was "just working with pieces of things and arranging them until they make sense" (R. Lindsey, personal interview, July 30, 2009).

While the rigid outlines from Lindsey's experience with literary analysis in    49
AP English may have been only faintly visible in the early stages of arranging
her argument, they played a much more prominent role as she entextualized the
assemblages of passages on her walls and windows into the precise sequence
they would appear in the text of her paper. If she felt fairly certain of how a
passage was going to function in her discussion, she would position it within
a structured outline and assign it a number or letter designating its position in
the argument: "I am very particular about keeping it organized, like Roman
numeral, capital A, number one, lower-case a. That's a big deal" (R. Lindsey,
personal interview, May 13, 2009). For the passages that she was as yet unsure
of, she would indicate them by writing their page number in parentheses in no
particular order in the pertinent section of the outline, indicating to herself that
she needed to revisit those passages to determine which ones to omit and then
play around with the physical arrangement of the remaining ones to determine
how they could help her develop her point. Once she had reread the passages
to understand them more thoroughly, and had physically manipulated the passages enough to develop a sequence that worked, she would write another outline, recopying the material from the previous one that still worked and then
making the additions or deletions she thought necessary. Discussing how she
wove all of these activities and practices together as she fashioned her outlines
for each paper, Lindsey mentioned she thought of the process in terms of using
the "rigid form" she'd used in AP English and then

> combin[ing] it with what I was doing in the 2-d Design where I was doing more
> manipulation of those materials, and then I applied it to the papers. This sort of
> allowing myself to physically shift things around but still maintain a kind of rigid
> form. (R. Lindsey, personal interview, August 26, 2008)

The excerpt from one of Lindsey's early outlines of the feminine ideal paper    50
in Figure 5 evidences Lindsey's purposeful weaving together of arrangement
practices from both AP English and *Two-dimensional Design* with the reading-
to-write practices that included her verse copying. The discussion regarding
Daisy Buchanan's voice, which Lindsey felt certain would serve some function
in her argument, is positioned as Part B of the paper's third major section.
While she knew that she wanted to have a section about Daisy's voice, she was
not at all clear at this point in her process regarding how she would develop
that discussion or even the main point she wanted to make in relation to her
argument about the feminine ideal. Not knowing in which order the passages
from *Gatsby* might appear, Lindsey just jotted down their page numbers, including the parentheses associated with MLA citation style, in the "Daisy's
Voice" section of the outline. Pointing to the array of page numbers and brief
phrases clustered around this section of the outline in Figure 5, Lindsey stated,

> This would have been just a bunch of passages on different pieces of paper. I just    51
> jotted all the page numbers down in a section of the outline where I thought they
> fit. There were way too many quotes to ever use them all, but I just wanted them
> all together so I could know which ones to work with later. (R. Lindsey, personal
> interview, July 30, 2009)

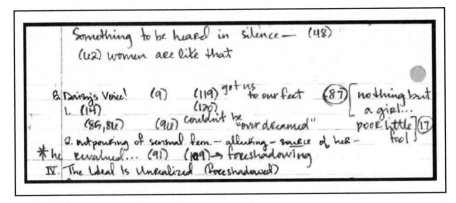

Figure 5   Portion of Lindsey's early outline for the feminine ideal paper showing her efforts to assemble the section about Daisy's voice.

Lindsey continued to weave these practices together as she refined her argu- 51 ment further, gradually creating a detailed outline that charted her discussion passage by passage. Although time consuming, she regarded assembling her paper in this precise manner as central to creating and sustaining a coherent argument. In addition to providing her with a means of coming to understand how she might best organize her analysis, crafting these outlines and the passage copying it involved also served as a way for her to deepen her understanding of the material. According to Lindsey, this process

> where I would write almost the exact outline several times, a lot of that was again me learning this stuff. So as I am organizing the paper, I am also learning the material, and for me, in order to learn it, I have to copy it a couple of times. (R. Lindsey, personal interview, May 13, 2009)

Lindsey's efforts to assemble her argument are informed by a number of 52 practices fairly specific to literary analysis. Chief among them might be her use of the special topoi that Fahnestock and Secor (1988) identify as the distinct sources of argument employed by literary scholars. Lindsey's thesis, for example, suggests her use of what Fahnestock and Secor (1988) refer to as the "paradigm" topoi, which involves scholars bringing together many apparently diverse works under a single definition. In coming to understand that topoi as a viable framework for her analysis and in structuring her analysis accordingly, Lindsey draws upon a far-flung nexus of practice that extends far beyond the disciplinary landscape of American literature or literary studies more broadly. Her efforts are mediated by some practices that are not only relatively unique to literary analysis but also by others that have been repurposed from other sites of engagement, particularly textual practices for generating visual designs and those for keeping her prayer journal. The practice for generating visual designs is repurposed and linked into a nexus of practice for arranging written argument for literary analysis, a nexus that includes the disciplinary texts for the feminine ideal paper, previous encounters organizing literary analyses, the structured AP outlines Lindsey learned in 10 grade, the computer screen, Lindsey's repurposed verse copying practice, and perhaps others as well. The arrangement of her argument, as well as her deepening knowledge of the novels and articles, emerges from Lindsey's efforts to coordinate and stabilize a dense network of diverse texts and practices.

The nexus of practice resulting from Lindsey's repurposings had important consequences for Lindsey's efforts toward literary analysis and the feminine ideal paper in particular. Encountering tasks in her English classes during her 2nd year of college that asked her to develop more complex ways to organize her arguments, Lindsey recognized what she regarded as two key limitations with the practices she had previously employed: the rigid outline she had used for literary analyses in high school, which she saw as overly simplistic and inadequate for discovering an effective organization for an argument, and composing on the computer, which she felt did not allow her a broad enough perspective of the materials she had assembled. To address these constraints, Lindsey repurposed the arrangement practices from *Two-dimensional Design*, linking it purposefully with her recontextualized verse-copying practice as well as other more ranges of disciplinary-specific practices and tools. Later in the process, those practices that she regarded as limiting her efforts to organize the argument were reintegrated as elements that afforded the invention and production of the paper. Once she had developed a workable structure for her paper as a whole and for particular sections of her discussion, she incorporated the formal outline format as a means of developing a precise sequence for the passages she decided to use. Later, as Lindsey ironed out precisely how and where she would use her textual evidence, she turned to the computer to type her paper and fine-tune some of the sections without having to recopy entire versions of her outline.

## Discussion

In light of this practice-oriented tracing of Lindsey's writing processes for the feminine ideal paper, what does attending closely and carefully to the repurposing of discursive practice across activities bring to our understanding of disciplinary development? Doing so, I argue, renders visible the enormously complex aggregation of practices that inform the production of disciplinary writing processes and thus illuminates how Lindsey's writing process for *American Literature* and her English Studies courses more broadly is enriched and enhanced by practices from her religious activities, her participation with graphic design, and a number of other literate engagements as well, including her encounters with the writing on the closet door of her family's New Hampshire cottage and her fourth-grade science project. Encountering tasks in her English classes that demand engagement with primary and secondary sources, Lindsey assembled a reading-to-write process by drawing upon memorial practices that included verse copying, her use of note cards from her fourth-grade science project, and, somewhat more remotely, jotting notes on the back of the closet door. In need of a means of inventing and organizing complex arguments, Lindsey assembled a process by combining her verse copying, her physical manipulation of texts, and her use of rigid outlines from *AP English* with more local practices from English Studies.

This practice-oriented analysis also illuminates the work involved in recruit- 55 ing discursive practice across contexts, the linking and coordinating with combinations of other practices and with new sets of inscriptional tools as well as the reconfiguring across semiotic modes necessary to repurpose practice for use in new activities. Lindsey repurposed her verse copying for literary criticism by linking it into a new set of practices that include the use of MLA citation style and the interpretation of novels and journal articles. Repurposing her physical manipulation practice from the design class involved retooling it as a means of inventing written arguments rather than visual ones as well as coordinating it with her verse copying and a number of other practices. Thus, attending to the repurposing of textual practice across activities, to paraphrase Latour (2005), foregrounds Lindsey's innovations in weaving together so many seemingly disparate practices, the ways that she fit them together, and the new associations she was prompted to establish among them (p. 12).

In addition to enhancing her writing process for English Studies, Lindsey's 56 repurposing of discursive practices enhanced the development of other key domains of disciplinary expertise: discourse community knowledge, subject-matter knowledge, genre knowledge, and rhetorical knowledge. Consider, for example, how Lindsey's reuse of verse copying as a discursive practice to engage with the Faulkner and Fitzgerald novels provided her with a way to deepen her understanding of the subject matter of these central American literary texts, and how her reuse of that practice to engage the journal articles helped her to acquire the rhetorical moves and the linguistic forms typical of literary criticism. Consider as well how the physical manipulation of portions of her notes allowed Lindsey to come to see what Fahnestock and Secor (1988) state is one of the major special topoi of literary criticism as well as a way to determine which content to include and how that content might be sequenced and organized in her analysis. In short, Lindsey's developing disciplinary expertise in American literature and English Studies more broadly is profoundly enhanced by the discursive practices she repurposed from her religious and artistic engagements.

## Conclusions

Findings from this study contribute to scholarship addressing the development 57 of disciplinary writing expertise, and literate development more broadly, in at least three ways. First, tracing the linkages Lindsey forges among these seemingly different engagements illuminates extradisciplinary practice as a key element informing disciplinary writing and activity. In other words, disciplinary writing expertise is informed not just by extradisciplinary texts and discourses but also by the practices involved in their production and use. Lindsey's writing process as a literary scholar is enriched and enhanced not by the visual images she creates or the Bible verses she copies, but rather by the practices and processes used in the production of those texts. Accounting for the trajectories of practice that inform Lindsey's disciplinary writing process demands that conceptual maps of how persons develop disciplinary writing expertise need to include the rich repertoires of memorial practices from persons' reading, writing, making and doing from a broad array of semiotic performances as well as how such practices are repurposed into disciplinary engagements.

This study also contributes to the development of methods for making persons' repertoires and repurposings of practice more visible. Such methods seem especially important to the study of writing transfer. The seemingly radically different activities that Lindsey links together and the lengthy spans of time separating them suggest the need to broaden the scope of inquiry in two key dimensions. First, data collection needs to address a wide range of participants' semiotic performances, not just activities that involve the production of seemingly similar kinds of texts (e.g., extended prose essays). Also, data collection needs to address the temporal distance separating performances, either by extending inquiry for longer spans of time and/or by collecting data from different periods in participants' lives. In essence, rather than relying on official maps to identify what activities are relevant to the production of disciplinary texts, researchers need to follow participants' mappings of relevant activities, regardless of how different they seem or how distant they are temporally. Second, data collection needs to focus on illuminating the practices and processes of textual invention that obtain in those activities. In addition to collecting the finished products of participants' semiotic performances, text collection should involve collecting a wide range of what Witte (1992) refers to as "minor" texts, texts created and used to mediate activity rather than for publication. However, because even the closest analysis of the features of texts, regardless of whether they are produced for public consumption or serve only to mediate activity, alone do not tell the whole story of the practices involved in their invention, production, and use, text-based interviews are essential.

Finally, this study contributes to the development of pedagogical approaches that can enhance disciplinary writing processes. A number of scholars have argued that an awareness of the broad range of discourses and discoursal tools learners have in their repertoires (Bazerman, 2004; Dominguez Barajas, 2007; Guerra, 2007; Ivanic, 1998; Kells, 2007; McCrary, 2005) is a key factor in literate development. In addition to the discourses at their disposal, this study suggests that students could benefit from developing an awareness of the broad range of practices they possess. In this sense, in addition to a methodological tool, detailed tracings of the practices and processes from which semiotic performances emerge can serve as a valuable pedagogical tool as well. Teachers might invite students at a number of educational levels to produce detailed accounts of the processes they employ for a number of their own activities and then compare the practices at play in each. Such examinations across seemingly divergent performances may reveal shared practices that may not be commonly recognized at first.

Perhaps more important, engaging students in these kinds of tracings might help teachers to reenvision how we think about the literate experiences that learners bring with them to their disciplinary activities. Based on her study of a doctoral student in physics, Blakeslee (1997) argues that teachers and mentors need to "acknowledge and work more with the residual practices that get carried over from students' previous experiences and training, particularly those carried over from traditional schooling" (p. 158). Given this partial tracing of the literate network from which Lindsey draws, Blakeslee's point about acknowledging and working with the practices learners bring with them is well taken, even if Lindsey's case suggests that we might not necessarily want to privilege those practices that originate in formal instruction. Blakeslee's (1997) statement does, however, raise questions regarding precisely what we acknowledge those practices as and thus the kind of work to ask learners to do with them. Whether practices are encountered through engagement with other disciplines or literate activities beyond school altogether, to characterize them as "residual" or "unproductive" (Blakeslee, 1997, p. 158) is to cast them as impediments to disciplinary expertise. At best, this might encourage educators to conclude, as Blakeslee (1997) does, that "rather than completely setting aside their old, comfortable strategies, students can continue to rely on those strategies while gradually replacing them with new and perhaps more productive ones given the tasks they must now perform" (p. 158). The binaries here—old and new, comfortable and more productive—and the unexamined assumption that the ideal is full replacement are oriented toward the notion of discrete and autonomous territories of practice. Based on this research with Lindsey, I simply do not see the validity of such views.

What might it mean, on the other hand, to acknowledge learners' existing practices as elements of expertise, and how might that inform the work we and our students do with them? To echo Witte (1992), once extradisciplinary practices are regarded as elements of expertise, "the issue becomes one of navigation, not one of separation" (p. 292). Casting extradisciplinary practices, whether from other disciplines or beyond formal schooling, in such a manner recognizes the wide range of literate knowledge and abilities that learners bring to disciplinary endeavors and thus as potentially useful for developing mastery in a focal discipline. From this perspective, the work we need to invite learners to do seems less about employing extradisciplinary practices only with an eye toward replacing them at the first opportunity and more about encouraging learners to view them as flexible resources for creating maintaining, coordinating, extending, altering, and perhaps even productively disrupting networks that provide access to disciplinary expertise; to develop a sense of the linkages and the incommensurabilities and affordances and constraints that animate those networks; and even to consider not just what textual practices were in previous *thens* and *theres*, but how they might function here and now as well as in the near and distant future.

## Declaration of Conflicting Interests

The author(s) declared no potential conflicts of interest with respect to the authorship and/or publication of this article.

## Funding

The author(s) received no financial support for the research and/or authorship of this article.

## Notes

1. Lindsey chose this particular paper primarily because she was proud of how she overcame the significant challenges the assignment posed to her writing abilities as a new graduate student: a minimum page limit that, at 16 pages, was approximately twice as long as those she had written for previous undergraduate and graduate English classes; an analysis that needed to address two primary texts rather than the single text analyses she had grown accustomed to; and the need to address the pertinent scholarship for two novels, which meant engaging with twice as many sources as she was used to. In addition, Lindsey stated that the two Cs she had received on two short papers she had written for a graduate class she had taken the previous term, which was quite a departure from the As and Bs she had received as an undergraduate, had shaken her faith in her abilities to do literary analysis. According to Lindsey, both the A she earned on the paper and the professor's single-sentence comment declaring that "this is actually a rather good essay that makes cogent use of the critical sources as well as the original texts" had gone a long way toward restoring that confidence.

2. Lindsey's copying of Bible verses and passages from other religious or inspirational texts was not limited to the pages of her journal; she also copied passages from these texts on the inside of her closet door. When I asked if she could tell me more about this practice, she replied,

    > I would write it just like I did in my prayer journals. I would put the quote in quotation marks and then indicate where it came from. I had seen this [writing on the back of a door] at the cottage. My family has a cottage in New Hampshire and there is a closet door, and the cottage was built back in 1897 or something like that, and from the day it was built, every time anybody ever visits the cottage or if anything ever happens at the cottage they keep a running record of whatever happens at the cottage on the back of the closet door. And I thought that that was so cool. (R. Lindsey, personal interview, January 5, 2009)

3. Lindsey indicated that this practice of taping sketches and other texts up on the walls surrounding a workspace was a common practice among members of her design class. However, she also stated that one reason she began to employ it was to keep her cat from scattering the arrangements she was working with on her table:

    > I would start with it here on the table, but my cat kept getting in the way, so I started taping it up on the wall, and then when I had finished pieces, I would tape the finished pieces up. (R. Lindsey, personal interview, August 26, 2008)

4. The materials that Lindsey gave me from her literature papers as an undergraduate and graduate student often included in the small sections

of passages she had torn from the full pages of loose leaf paper. These ripped sections from assembling the feminine ideal paper, however, were not among the materials she'd saved for that task.

## References

Artemeva, N. (2009). Stories of becoming: A study of novice engineers learning genres of their profession. In C. Bazerman, A. Bonini, & D. Figueiredo (Eds.), *Genre in a changing world* (pp. 158–178). Fort Collins, CO: WAC Clearinghouse.

Bartholomae, D. (1985). Inventing the university. In M. Rose (Ed.), *When a writer can't write: Studies in writer's block and other composing process problems* (pp. 134–165). New York: Guilford.

Bazerman, C. (2004). Intertextualities: Voloshinov, Bakhtin, literary theory, and literacy studies. In A. F. Ball & S. W. Freedman (Eds.), *Bakhtinian perspectives on language, literacy, and learning* (pp. 53–65). Cambridge, UK: Cambridge University Press.

Beach, K. (2003). Consequential transitions: A developmental view of knowledge propagation through social organizations. In T. Tuomi-Grohn & Y. Engestrom (Eds.), *Between school and work: New perspectives on transfer and boundary crossing* (pp. 39–61). New York: Pergamon.

Beaufort, A. (1999). *Writing in the real world: Making the transition from school to work.* New York: Teachers College Press.

Beaufort, A. (2004). Developmental gains of a history major: A case for building a theory of disciplinary writing expertise. *Research in the Teaching of English, 39,* 136–185.

Beaufort, A. (2007). *College writing and beyond.* Logan: Utah State University Press.

Becker, H. (2000). Cases, causes, conjectures, stories, and imagery. In R. Gromm, M. Hammersley, & P. Foster (Eds.), *Case study method: Key issues, key texts* (pp. 223–333). London: Sage.

Bergmann, L., & Zepernick, J. (2007). Disciplinarity and transfer: Students' perceptions of learning to write. *WPA Journal, 31,* 124–149.

Berkenkotter, C., Huckin, T., & Ackerman, J. (1991). Social context and socially constructed texts: The initiation of a graduate student into a writing research community. In C. Bazerman & J. Paradis (Eds.), *Textual dynamics of the professions: Historical and contemporary studies of writing in professional communities* (pp. 191–215). Madison: University of Wisconsin Press.

Berkenkotter, C., Huckin, T., & Ackerman, J. (1988). Conventions, conversations, and the writer: Case study of a student in a rhetoric Ph.D. program. *Research in the Teaching of English, 22,* 9–43.

Bizzell, P. (1999). Hybrid academic discourses: What, why, and how. *Composition Studies, 27,* 7–21.

Blakeslee, A. (1997). Activity, context, interaction, authority: Learning to write scientific papers in situ. *Journal of Business and Technical Communication, 11,* 125–169.

Brandt, D., & Clinton, K. (2002). Limits of the local: Expanding perspectives on literacy as a social practice. *Journal of Literacy Research, 34,* 337–356.

Buell, M. (2004). Code-switching and second language writing: How multiple codes are combined in a text. In C. Bazerman & P. Prior (Eds.), *What writing does and how it does it* (pp. 97–122). New York: Lawrence Erlbaum.

Campbell, K. (1997). Real niggaz's don't die: African American students speaking themselves into their writing. In C. Severino, J. Guerra, & J. Butler (Eds.), *Writing in multicultural settings* (pp. 67–78). New York: Modern Language Association.

Casanave, C. (2002). *Writing games: Multicultural case studies of academic literacy practices in higher education.* Mahwah, NJ: Lawrence Erlbaum.

Chiseri-Strater, E. (1991). *Academic literacies: The public and private discourses of university students.* Portsmouth, NH: Boynton/Cook.

Collins, J., & Blot, R. (2003). *Literacy and literacies: Texts, power, and identity.* Cambridge, UK: Cambridge University Press.

Dominguez Barajas, E. (2007). Parallels in academic and nonacademic discursive styles: An analysis of a Mexican Woman's Narrative Performance. *Written Communication, 24,* 140–167.

Downs, D., & Wardle, E. (2007). Teaching about writing, righting misconceptions: (Re)envisioning "first-year composition" as "introduction to writing studies." *College Composition and Communication, 58,* 552–584.

Emig, J. (1971). The composing processes of twelfth graders. Urbana, IL: National Council of Teachers of English.

Engestrom, Y., Engestrom, R., & Karkkainen, M. (1995). Polycontextuality and boundary crossing in expert cognition: Learning and problem solving in complex work activities. *Learning and Instruction, 5,* 319–336.

Fahnestock, J., & Secor, M. (1988). The rhetoric of literary criticism. In C. Bazerman & J. Paradis (Eds.), *Textual dynamics of the professions: Historical and contemporary studies of writing in professional communities* (pp. 77–96). Madison: University of Wisconsin Press.

Fishman, J., & Reiff, M. J. (2008, Summer). Taking the high road: Teaching for transfer in an FYC program. *Composition Forum, 18.*

Flower, L., & Hayes, J. (1981). A cognitive process theory of writing. *College Composition and Communication, 32,* 365–387.

Geisler, C. (1994). *Academic literacy and the nature of expertise.* Hillsdale, NJ: Erlbaum.

Gold, E. (1989). Bridging the gap: In which the author, an English major, recounts his travels in the land of the techies. In C. Matelene (Ed.), *Worlds of writing: Teaching and learning in discourse communities of work* (pp. 335–342). New York: Random House.

Goodwin, C. (1994). Professional vision. *American Anthropologist, 96,* 606–633.

Guerra, J. (2007). Out of the valley: Transcultural repositioning as a rhetorical practice in ethnographic research and other aspects of everyday life. In C. Lewis, P. Enciso, & E. Moje (Eds.), *Reframing sociocultural research on literacy: Identity, agency, and power* (pp. 137–162). Mahwah, NJ: Erlbaum.

Haas, C. (1994). Learning to read biology: One student's rhetorical development in college. *Written Communication, 11,* 43–84.

Herrington, A., & Curtis, M. (2000). *Persons in process: Four stories of writing and personal development in college.* Urbana, IL: National Council of Teachers of English.

Ivanic, R. (1998). *Writing and identity: The discoursal construction of identity in academic writing.* Amsterdam, Netherlands: John Benjamins.

Kamberelis, G. (2001). Producing heteroglossic classroom (micro)cultures through hybrid discourse practice. *Linguistics and Education, 12,* 85–125.

Kells, M. (2007). Writing across communities: Deliberation and the discursive possibilities of WAC. *Reflections, 6,* 87–108.

Lather, P. (1991). *Getting smart: Feminist research and pedagogy within the postmodern.* New York: Routledge.

Latour, B. (2005). *Reassembling the social: An introduction to actor network theory.* Oxford, UK: Oxford University Press.

Leander, K., & Sheehy, M. (2004). *Spatializing literacy research and practice.* New York: Peter Lang.

Lillis, T. (2008). Ethnography as method, methodology, and "deep-theorizing": Closing the gap between text and context in academic writing research. *Written Communication, 25,* 353–388.

Medway, P. (2002). Fuzzy genres and community identities: The case of architecture students' sketchbooks. In R. Coe, L. Lingard, & T. Teslenko (Eds.), *The rhetoric and ideology of genre* (pp. 123–153). Cresskill, NJ: Hampton Press.

McCarthy, L. (1987). Stranger in strange lands: A college student writing across the curriculum. *Research in the Teaching of English, 21,* 233–265.

McCrary, D. (2005). Represent, representin', representation: The efficacy of hybrid texts in the writing classroom. *Journal of Basic Writing, 24(2),* 72–91.

Miller, P., Hengst, J., & Wang, S. (2003). Ethnographic methods: Applications from developmental cultural psychology. In P. Camic, J. Rhodes, & L. Yardley (Eds.), *Qualitative research in psychology: Expanding perspectives in methodology and design* (pp. 219–242). Washington, DC: American Psychological Association.

Perl, S. (1979). The composing processes of unskilled college writers. *Research in the Teaching of English, 13,* 317–336.

Prior, P. (1998). *Writing/disciplinarily: A sociohistoric account of literate activity in the academy.* Mahwah, NJ: Lawrence Erlbaum.

Prior, P. (2004). Tracing process: How texts come into being. In C. Bazerman & P. Prior (Eds.), *What writing does and how it does it: An introduction to analyzing texts and textual practices* (pp. 167–200). New York: Lawrence Erlbaum.

Prior, P., & Shipka, J. (2003). Chronotopic lamination: Tracing the contours of literate activity. In C. Bazerman & D. Russell (Eds.), *Writing selves/writing societies* (pp. 180–238). Fort Collins, CO: WAC Clearinghouse. Retrieved May 4, 2010, from http://wac.colostate.edu/books/selves_societies.

Reder, S., & Davilla, E. (2005). Context and literacy practices. *Annual review of Applied Linguistics, 25,* 170–187.

Rivers, W. (1989). From the garret to the fishbowl: Thoughts on the transition from literary to technical writing. In C. Matelene (Ed.), *Worlds of writing: Teaching and learning in discourse communities of work* (pp. 64–80). New York: Random House.

Roozen, K. (2009). "Fan fic-ing" English Studies: A case study exploring the interplay of vernacular literacies and disciplinary engagement. *Research in the Teaching of English, 44,* 136–169.

Smit, D. (2004). *The end of composition studies.* Carbondale: Southern Illinois University Press.

Sommers, N. (1980). Revision strategies of student writers and experienced adult writers. *College Composition and Communication, 31,* 378–388.

Spack, R. (1997). The acquisition of academic literacy in a second language: A longitudinal case study. *Written Communication, 10,* 235–261.

Stake, R. (1995). *The art of case study research.* Thousand Oaks, CA: Sage.

Stake, R. (2000). Case studies. In N. Denzin & Y. Lincoln (Eds.), *Handbook of qualitative research* (pp. 435–454). Thousand Oaks, CA: Sage.

Tuomi-Grohn, T., Engestrom, Y., & Young, M. (2003). From transfer to boundary crossing between school and work as a tool for developing vocational education: An introduction. In T. Tuomi-Grohn & Y. Engestrom (Eds.), *Between school and work: New perspectives on transfer and boundary crossing* (pp. 1–12). New York: Pergamon.

Wardle, E. (2007). Understanding "transfer" from FYC: Preliminary results of a longitudinal study. *WPA Journal, 31,* 65–85.

Wardle, E. (2009). "Mutt genres" and the goal of FYC: Can we help students write the genres of the university? *College Composition and Communication, 60,* 765–789.

Warren, J. (2006). Literary scholars processing poetry and constructing arguments. *Written Communication, 23,* 202–226.

Wenger, E. (1998). *Communities of practice: Learning, meaning, and identity.* New York: Cambridge University Press.

Wilder, L. (2005). "The rhetoric of literary criticism" revisited: Mistaken critics, complex contexts, and social justice. *Written Communication, 22,* 76–119.

Wilder, L. (2002). "Get comfortable with uncertainty": A study of the conventional values of literary analysis in an undergraduate literature course. *Written Communication, 19,* 175–221.

Winsor, D. (1990). Engineering writing/writing engineering. *College Composition and Communication, 41*, 58–70.

Witte, S. (1992). Context, text, intertext: Toward a constructivist semiotic of writing. *Written Communication, 9*, 237–308.

Zachry, M. (2007). Regulation and communicative practices. In Zachry, M., & Thralls, C. (Eds.), *Communicative practices in workplaces and the professions* (pp. v–xv). Amityville, NY: Baywood.

........................................................................................

## Questions for Discussion and Journaling

1. Roozen begins by outlining some findings of other researchers regarding how newcomers (students like you) learn to write in their disciplines. He pulls together a number of lines of research to suggest that learning to write in the ways a discipline requires (your major, for example) entails learning its subject matter and understanding its discourse community, its rhetorical moves, its genres, and the writing processes that are required in order to write the texts required (paras. 3–5). The rest of this book will teach you more about each of these elements, but spend a few minutes thinking through what each of them might mean and might entail for you in your own major. Be sure to use the glossary at the back of the book to help you define terms that are new to you.

2. Roozen first outlines other related research, and then says "This article complements and extends scholarship addressing . . ." (para. 6). This is a clear example of one of the common "moves" that researchers make when they introduce their research articles, as John Swales described in the introduction to this textbook (p. 12). The rest of Roozen's introduction engages in the "moves" with equal clarity, so this piece provides a nice example for you to analyze. Reread the Swales "CARS Model" and then find the "moves" he describes in Roozen's introduction. Then consider how and why these "moves" help researchers like Roozen create credibility for themselves.

3. Roozen argues his main claim very early on: that the "practices and processes" a writer employs to produce a particular text are not just determined by the current setting, but also by the "practices and processes associated with previous and anticipated textual engagements" (para. 7). Maybe the best way to imagine what he means is to use your own experience as an example. Think of the most recent text you wrote (maybe for school, or maybe outside of school), and create a visual map, if possible, of all the other experiences and texts that you think influenced it. What else have you written that is like it? What else have you done that helped you know how to write that text? What other writing settings have been similar? What do you anticipate writing in the future that you think will be similar, or that might be influenced by what you did when you wrote that text? Don't forget to include what Roozen and Witte call the "extensive array of 'minor' forms of writing and texts, including lists, labels, and notes" (para. 8).

4. Roozen spends a fairly extensive amount of time explaining his "method of data collection" (para. 11–15). Explain how he went about collecting and analyzing data from Lindsey and what he collected, and then speculate about why you think he felt it

was important to describe his research methods in such detail. Who was his audience, and why do you think he felt they needed to know so much about his data collection and data analysis methods?

5. In the "Discussion" section, Roozen asks what "attending closely and carefully to the repurposing of discursive practice across activities bring[s] to our understanding of disciplinary development" (para. 54). What is his answer to this question?

## Applying and Exploring Ideas

1. In his conclusion, Roozen notes that some researchers suggest that we need to help students "replace" what he calls "extradisciplinary practices" (reading and writing practices from outside their major, for example) and *instead* learn disciplinary practices. He argues against this view of "replacing" old ways with new ones, and instead argues for "encouraging learners to view [extradisciplinary practices] as flexible resources for creating, maintaining, coordinating, extending, altering, and perhaps even productively disrupting networks that provide access to disciplinary expertise" (para. 61). Explain what this means, and then give an example of what this could look like in your own life as you learn to write for your major and profession.

2. In Table 1, Roozen provides a list of literate activities in which Lindsey engaged, and all of the related texts he collected for each literate activity. Try to brainstorm a similar list for yourself. Make two columns, and in the left list three to four literate activities in which you engage now or in which you have engaged in the past. In the right column, list all of the texts you can think of that you composed for that literate activity. What can you learn from making and looking at this list for yourself?

3. In Chapter 3 of this book, James Porter describes what he calls "intertextuality," the idea that all texts contain "traces" of other texts and that there can be no texts that don't draw on some ideas from other texts. Do you think this idea relates to the ideas outlined here by Roozen? Write a brief one-page response in which you apply Porter's notion of intertextuality to Roozen's claims and findings.

### Meta Moment

Do you think about your regular activities with reading, writing, and composing differently now than you did before reading Roozen? How do you think this enriched understanding of literate activity can help you be a more successful writer and reader?

# Past Experiences and Future Attitudes in Literacy

## ERIKA J. PETERSEN

■ Petersen, Erika. "Past Experiences and Future Attitudes in Literacy." *Young Scholars in Writing* 5 (2007): 131–36. Print.

## Framing the Reading

Erika J. Petersen wrote this piece as a first-year student at Utah Valley State College in 2007. It began as an assignment for her College Writing II course, which used a writing-about-writing approach. This piece was Erika's major research project for the semester. Erika's interest, obviously, was in how people's previous experiences with reading and writing influence their attitudes toward it, and she wound up pulling together a diverse range of research on motivation in learning, psychology, and literacy education to interpret data gathered from her primary research, which included both a set of literacy narratives and interviews with people of a range of ages and life circumstances, from high school students to college graduates.

Erika's professor in the course was Doug Downs (co-editor of this book), who on seeing the final version of her project in class encouraged her to submit the piece to the journal *Young Scholars in Writing*, which publishes undergraduate research, like Erika's, on subjects related to writing, literacy, and rhetoric. As is the case with other pieces in this book published in *YSW*, Erika revised her essay in preparation for submission, and then sent it to the editor. The piece was then peer-reviewed both by other college students and by a professor at another college (on the *YSW* editorial board), and then Erika was asked to make some further revisions and development to the piece, refining and polishing it in ways that closely resemble the revising process every other article in this textbook went through when it was submitted for publication.

L earning how to read and write is universal and personal all at once. We all have memories of how we obtained literacy, but did those experiences shape the basis of how

> We all have memories of how we obtained literacy, but did those experiences shape the basis of how we feel toward literacy in the future? Did the praise or discouragement we obtained lead us to certain attitudes?

1

we feel toward literacy in the future? Did the praise or discouragement we obtained lead us to certain attitudes? While there have been studies done in this area, none seem to focus on people's actual physical experiences of praise versus discouragement. This distinction became clear in my own study of written literacy narratives and interviews, thus creating a clearer picture of the role of praise in literacy attainment that both supports and extends previous research findings.

It's easy to overlook and take for granted the complexity of the process 2 of learning how to read and write and ultimately become literate. At such a young age we learn to do such incredible things. There are usually many people playing different roles in teaching literacy to young children: mothers, fathers, grandparents, siblings, teachers, and so on. In *Language and Literacy in the Early Years*, Marian R. Whitehead argues that we make associations with books and the people reading them to us at those early stages in life. In "Child Development and Emergent Literacy," Grover Whitehurst, the first director of the Institute of Education Sciences, and Christopher Lonigan, a leading researcher in the areas of preschool literacy instruction and assessment, describe the labyrinth of processes taking place from before preschool into kindergarten that children go through when learning literacy. Starting with gaining knowledge of the alphabet and progressing to inventive spelling and associating written words with meanings, the acquisition of literacy is a highly complicated process indeed.

As you can imagine, everyone goes through the learning process differently 3 and, in turn, runs across different experiences when doing so. Learning how to do anything involves emotional development, and at such a young age children are sensitive toward doing things right or wrong. Critiquing children with the sincerity and outspokenness you would adults or teens could potentially crush their fragile egos, making them feel less able. Being aware of the emotional and delicate side of learning literacy is vital.

If we can find similarities existing within a substantial sample of literacy 4 histories, then it would help us gain a clearer picture of if and how our past experiences in literacy have influencing capabilities. Two researchers who have conducted studies like this are Rick Evans and Alisa Belzer. In Evans's study he gained a knowledge of numerous middle-class college students' literacy histories through detailed questionnaires and interviews about how and what they read and wrote in the past. He focused mainly on three different types of reading and writing, analyzing how students encounter them and how their feelings toward them differ. Belzer's study focused on in-depth interviews with five African American women. She wanted to compare their past experiences with their present attitudes toward literacy as adults to look for patterns and gain ideas for more effective adult literacy education.

While I didn't want to reproduce the same study as Evans and Belzer, I did 5 use similar methods. To begin my study, I acquired eight "literacy reflections" from other students in English 2010 at Utah Valley University (UVU). In these literacy reflections students were asked to reflect on their literacy pasts and presents, to explore how they read and write different assignments, and their feelings and attitudes toward reading and writing. As with Evans's and Belzer's studies, the intent was to get students thinking about the different kinds of reading and writing they do and why they do it. I was hoping that by studying these students' reflections I would be able to see patterns of past experiences playing an influential role in how these college students felt toward different literacy tasks.

I then interviewed twelve other people of all different ages, ranging from 6 eleven to forty-four. I did this because I wanted not only college students' perspectives on writing but also those of children at all levels of learning and adults at different points in their lives. I wanted to interview people who were not given the assignment to write a paper on their literacy histories in order to remove bias from the study. Evans's and Belzer's articles both inter-view relevant groups of people (mainstream college students around eighteen years old and middle-aged African American women), but I wanted to show that no matter what stage of life we are in, we all have a literacy past that potentially affects our future, even well past the schooling part of our lives. Therefore, I interviewed two girls in the fifth grade, four kids in high school, and three people in college (I interviewed fewer college students because I felt that I had a good representation of them from the literacy reflections). I also interviewed three people who were thirty-three and older and out of college because I hypothesized that even when you're out of school, your literacy past still plays a role in your life. I began each interview by asking about the participants' earliest memories of reading and whom they remembered teaching them. I asked them about their favorite and least favorite teachers and why they liked or disliked them. I also got an idea of how their reading styles had changed—for example, what their favorite kinds of books were when they were children compared to their favorites now. I asked the same kinds of questions concerning writing, too. We talked about what kinds of writing they enjoyed in the past compared to now, what kinds of writing they make time for in their schedule, etc. I wanted to get a good feel for which experiences with literacy learning the interviewees remembered most clearly in order to determine if a lot of people remembered the same kinds of expe-riences. I also asked them about any awards or recognition they received in classes in certain subjects to see if that affected their subsequent aptitude and interest in them. I wanted to know not only how they responded to recogni-tion in literacy but also how they pursued it, so I asked them if they showed what they'd written to teachers and friends or talked about what they were reading to others.

After reading through all the literacy reflections and reviewing the inter- 7 views, it became clear that there was one event that everyone seemed to have gone through in one way or another. It was also addressed in both Belzer's and Evans's interviews within their studies. All interviewees talked about an experience with a teacher—either one that had influenced them to continue using their successful literacy skills, or one that had made them feel lost and hopeless about reading or writing. The students who had teachers discourage them suffered a loss in their confidence and became weary about their writing. One of the women Belzer interviewed talked about an embarrassing situation in which she read in front of the class, revealing how badly it affected her emotionally and physically. Something Evans's and Belzer's articles didn't do was examine in depth what occurs in your body, chemically, when you are praised and feeling good versus being discouraged and feeling bad. It's a valid thing to think about when looking into praise and how it may motivate you. Your body is responding to your situation, and I don't know about you, but if my body is responding in a way that's negative I doubt I will want to do whatever is causing it again. Dr. David Yells, associate professor and chair of the Department of Behavioral Science at UVU, said that while we have plenty of research results on the body's response to positive experiences, there is little data available on negative responses because it would be inhumane to test on people or animals. He did say that the central nervous system's response to situations like being called on in class could be looked at as bad if it is a particularly embarrassing situation. Your central nervous system reacts and you blush, get sweaty palms, stutter, etc.

I also noticed that everyone's really bad or really good experiences with literacy were recalled with great detail, as if they had happened yesterday. How could they remember them so clearly? In "Getting the Brain's Attention," Ingrid Wickelgren argues that dopamine is "a neurotransmitter supposed to react on the brain's reward system to produce feelings of pleasure" (1). It is released into the nucleus accumbens, which is known to be activated by pleasurable behaviors. Wickelgren also states that there is new data suggesting that dopamine released in the brain draws attention to certain significant or surprising events and that dopamine cells respond to reward only when it happens unpredictably. Some scientists believe dopamine causes frontal neurons to hold onto some temporary memories for longer, which may make them easier to remember in the future. Could the dopamine released during our experiences of learning literacy be why we remember those experiences so well? These good or bad experiences the students had with literacy probably stuck with them because of the impact they had on their self-confidence: good or bad. In fact, dopamine delivers a message while other parts of the brain respond with emotion; whether that be pleasure, excitement, or fear depends on the situation (6).

From my study of multiple literacy narratives, I have found a recurring pattern: when students were good at certain literacy skills and it was brought to theirs and others' attention, it resulted in positive literacy growth. The following pages highlight some of those occurrences.

The fifth grade girls I interviewed talked about being most interested in reading and writing that involved everyone and showed them to shine above others. One of the girls talked excitedly about her reading skills and accomplishments, but when I asked her about writing her attitude changed. She said she has not received feedback about her writing but that her teachers and friends always talked about how well and how much she reads.

One of the Brigham Young University students I interviewed is minoring in editing, so you can imagine what her literacy skills are like. She loves to read and write and is very skilled at both. She's received abundant amounts of praise in the form of words and awards. She entered a story into a Disney writing contest when she was in her teens; although she didn't win, she was praised immensely by her family for entering the contest. Her award-winning poems are framed and hanging up in her grandparents' and parents' homes. She loves to read history books and has always been described by her parents and friends as "a reader."

The older people I interviewed were very enthusiastic and excited to look 12 back at their literacy pasts. Although sometimes it took a little longer for them to remember details, their answers were very similar to those I had gotten from the younger students. All of them grew up in homes where reading was encouraged greatly. One of them even said that her mom would buy her a book at the store instead of candy. Another said that he couldn't remember having any bad experiences with reading when he was younger and was quite good at it. His writing wasn't as important to himself and others until he got into college, where he learned and excelled in writing for communications. He makes time in his busy schedule today for reading books and writing in his journal, both of which he enjoys doing very much. He also covers sports for the *Deseret Morning News,* a local paper in Utah.

It was very apparent after reading the literary reflections and reviewing 13 the interviews that following a discouraging event when learning to read or write, most students felt incompetent or felt like something was wrong until an encouraging teacher or event came along. In contrast, one college student from the literacy reflections and three high schoolers from the interviews seemed never to have had a bad experience with reading or writing. The college student excelled in literacy at a young age and was awarded and praised for it continually. He still loves both reading and writing and is very confident in his abilities to do so. The three high schoolers are all very avid readers and writers. They all had been given awards for their proficient reading skills and creative writing. When I looked over the questions I had asked them dealing with their literacy pasts, I found a pattern of praise, starting from childhood and continuing through the rest of their schooling up to this point in their education. All of them had had different experiences, of course, but all of them were very positive. Their family and friends were all very supportive. Something else I noticed that was interesting was that all three of them had gotten an early start with their literacy skills, from either a phonics program, a computer program, or homeschooling. This enabled them to have teaching opportunities with other kids in their classes who may have been struggling, therefore making them feel happy and good about their advantage in literacy skills. Dopamine release could play a part here as well as praise received for their accomplishments.

An article by Jennifer Henderlong, an assistant professor of psychology 14 at Reed College, and Mark Lepper, a professor of psychology at Stanford University, both supported most of my findings and contradicted a few. They talk about the negative and positive effects of praise, motivation, and sincerity on children. When children sense insincerity in praise, it is disregarded and turned into negative motivation. Henderlong and Lepper stated that the older the child is, the more likely he or she is to think about what the praise could mean and take it wrong, while younger kids do not really look into complexities of praise (778). According to Henderlong and Lepper, praise could be motivating if it's guiding children to feel capable and not comparing them to others' progress (785), but in my research the students seemed to enjoy being compared to others. The students highlighted some kind of class progress chart for reading, explaining that being ahead of others felt very rewarding and influenced them to pursue energetic reading. It seems that effective praise depends on how it is delivered and the situation and people it involves. Praise can lead to motivation and be a great tool when done right. You have to consider the environment and factors that could alter your desired effect on the child you are praising.

Belzer concluded in her study that schoolwork needs to be applicable in and   15 out of school. Students should be able to find connections with their schoolwork and how it may apply in their own lives. Out of my interviewees and Belzer's, there was only one person who enjoyed or looked forward to reading things that she was assigned to read at school, or writing things that she was assigned to write (on topics not of her choosing). This particular person said that what she read from her textbooks was interesting and it did not bother her to read them. In her family they are expected to do very well in all their classes and be honor students. She's the youngest in her family, and all of her brothers and sisters have been 4.0 students. It doesn't surprise me that she's more willing to read and learn from the material she is given in classes than the other high schoolers. If other students were in her position, I'm sure they'd feel that if they didn't get good grades they would be performing inadequately or disappointing their parents and might be teased or pressured by siblings. Two of the college students I interviewed, like the high school girl above, grew up in homes where doing very well was an expectation as well. They were both praised and encouraged for their achievements in literacy while growing up, but it was more of a requirement than an accomplishment.

The rest of the high schoolers and college students said they would do the   16 assigned work, and most of them got good grades for their efforts, but they did not enjoy it and considered it almost irrelevant to their lives. Students in Evans's interviews and my own were similar in that they tended to write things that they knew their teachers would want and not what they really thought. During a good portion of our schooling, we're learning how to write the kinds of papers that we would never use in our everyday lives. Yet the experiences we have while learning how to write those kinds of papers can discourage us from reading and writing throughout the rest of our lives.

During the process of writing this essay, I found my own experience rep-   17 resenting exactly what I have been researching. I've never thought of myself as being a writer. Back in elementary school was the only time I remember being excited about writing. My first grade teacher loved my stories and always shared them with my parents during parent-teacher conferences. She made me feel like writing was something special and I was very good at it. Other than that, I wasn't really encouraged to write or praised for my efforts as much as my siblings were. Parents are supposed to support you in your endeavors, so it was harder for me to take their opinions as seriously as teachers or peers. So I dropped that off of my list of things that I was good at. When I wrote papers for classes, I was always self-conscious about them and hated other people reading them. I assumed they just were not very good or had anything special about them compared to those of other students. I never received bad grades on papers, but I never had feedback, either. Therefore, I assumed my teachers probably were not really reading them or, frankly, just passed out As to almost everyone in class. Only when I continued getting As for my college papers and started getting positive feedback from my college professors did I begin to believe I actually could write. Then, during the process of writing this paper, I received a lot of compliments, encouragement, and praise for my writing abilities from my professor as well as my relatives, friends, and peers. This made me start feeling even better and a lot more confident in my writing. The dopamine in my brain was definitely flowing. I felt a rush of energy and happiness whenever I got papers back that had positive feedback, which encouraged me further. Now I want to write more and make time to do further research on this subject as well as others.

Assessing the research, literacy reflections, and interviews, it's apparent that past experiences with learning literacy appeared to play a role in these people's future attitudes toward reading and writing and that praise continues to change your attitudes throughout your entire learning experience. 18

I wonder how parents and teachers can sometimes be careless toward something so obvious but so consequential, like praise. Praise and encouragement should be taken into more consideration when teaching literacy. As I said before, parents and teachers play a huge role in helping their child develop a healthy relationship with writing. Literacy is an integral part of a successful future for everyone. Something like that should be handled with as much care as other aspects of life. Literacy really does affect us emotionally, physically, and socially. The experiences we have with it growing up create a strong literacy backbone and good attitude that we may not be able to gain later on in life. It may even affect how we teach it to our future children. 19

Many thanks to Dr. Downs, who encouraged and changed my attitude toward writing, and Shannon Carter, for the friendly help and encouragement with the editing process.

## Works Cited

Belzer, Alisa. "I Don't Crave to Read: School Reading and Adulthood." *Journal of Adolescent and Adult Literacy* 46 (2002): 104–13.

Evans, Rick. "Learning Schooled Literacy: The Literate Life Histories of Mainstream Student Readers and Writers." *Discourse Processes* 16 (1993): 317–40.

Henderlong, Jennifer, and Mark Lepper. "The Effects of Praise on Children's Intrinsic Motivation: A Review and Synthesis." *Psychological Bulletin* 128.5 (2002): 774–95.

Whitehead, Marion R. *Language and Literacy in the Early Years.* 2nd ed. London: Paul Chapman, 1997.

Whitehurst, Grover J., and Christopher J. Lonigan. "Child Development and Emergent Literacy." *Child Development* 69 (1998): 848–72.

Wickelgren, Ingrid. "Getting the Brain's Attention." *Science Magazine* 278.5335 (1997).

## Questions for Discussion and Journaling

1. Notice how Petersen weaves various sources together with her discussion of her findings from her own primary research, so that with each page we seem to be encountering new sources or discussion of them. At the same time we're learning about what Petersen learned in her interviews. How does this weaving of sources and primary data compare with other pieces you've read so far?

2. What would you say Petersen's central finding is? Is it surprising? (Why or why not?)

3. How does Petersen justify her research—that is, what does she give as reasons why this research was worth doing, or why it covered ground not already covered by previous research?

4. Petersen writes in a very personable, conversational manner, including using "I" frequently when describing her own experiences, and writing fairly informally with lines like "I also noticed that everyone's really good or bad experiences with literacy were recalled with great detail" (para. 8). How does this compare to other pieces you've read from the book? Do you appreciate this personability or wish the piece were written more formally?

## Applying and Exploring Ideas

1. Petersen's findings suggest that most of us have indelible memories of very good or very bad moments relating to reading or writing, and that these often center around teachers and schooling. Interview members of your family and several of your friends and see if the pattern that Petersen saw holds among people you know.

2. List three things that, when you've finished Petersen's article, you wish she'd explained more thoroughly or said more about. Is there any pattern to the items on your list?

### Meta Moment

Do you think you could do a study like Petersen's and publish it? Write about the reasons for your answer.

Photo by Lisa Fischoff

# Writing What Matters: A Student's Struggle to Bridge the Academic/ Personal Divide

## EMILY STRASSER

■ Strasser, Emily. "Writing What Matters: A Student's Struggle to Bridge the Academic/Personal Divide." *Young Scholars in Writing* 5 (2007): 146–50. Web.

## Framing the Reading

Downs (a co-author of this book), in the entertainment room in his house, has a rug with the words "Partying" and "Studying" written upside down to each other. Leave the rug lying in one direction, and you read "Partying"; spin it 180 degrees and it reads "Studying." It's possible Emily Strasser would not think much of this rug, as she argues for an integration of personal and school lives, of a "whole being" that is at once scholarly and intensely personal. The rug, she might argue, should say both "Partying" and "Studying" all the time, at the same time.

Strasser wrote her piece on how to achieve this melding of personal and academic in her first year at Vassar College. She was, at the time, a tutor in Vassar's Writing Center, and as such spent a notable portion of her time reading other students' writing and working to give them advice on it. This piece was written in her College Writing class with instructor Lee Rumbarger. Strasser took what might seem like an obvious point—"without the personal, emotional, and the exciting, writing will never mean anything"—and opposed it to a controversial opinion piece by über-professor Stanley Fish, which advocated that writing courses should focus purely on the mechanics of syntax and principles of logical reasoning. If a professor of the prestige of Fish was not able to see the importance of the personal value in writing, Strasser, even as a first-year college student, was willing to argue back.

Stanley Fish, in a 2002 *Chronicle of Higher Education* article titled "Say 1 It Ain't So," writes, "No composition course should have a theme, especially not one the instructor is interested in. Ideas should be introduced not for their own sake, but for the sake of the syntactical and rhetorical points they help illustrate, and once they serve this purpose, they should be sent away."

He argues that beginning writing courses should teach grammar and style only, while students' opinions and experiences should be dispensed with immediately. If, in fact, the purpose of writing education is to produce grammatically adept writers, Fish's boot-camp approach may do a fine job. Yet I would argue that writing can and should be much more than so-phisticated sentence structure and nuanced word choice. The devices of grammar and rhetoric remain superfi-cial skills until a writer employs them to express important and powerful feel-ings, thoughts, and ideas. Students leaving Fish's course will never love what they are writing, and so their abilities to construct complicated grammatical structures will not be put to meaningful purposes. Other writers do advocate, in marked contrast to Fish's grammar-centered approach, methods centered on students' experiences, interests, and ideas. Gerald Graff and bell hooks, for example, each present a vision of writing as a marriage of the personal and the intellectual, enabling self-empowerment and the possibility of challenging in-stitutions and inspiring communities. In advocating a pedagogy that values the personal as essential to the academic, I draw extensively on my own experience as a student writer: in my own development as a writer, the assignments that mattered most were those in which I used persuasive and analytical skills in personally meaningful writing. Writing and education are useless tools if they fail to speak to a student's life, experience, and passions; therefore, teachers in all settings should value their students' voices, encouraging them to write and claim their own stories and expressions.

> *Writing can and should be much more than sophisticated sentence structure and nuanced word choice. The devices of grammar and rhetoric remain superficial skills until a writer employs them to express important and powerful feelings, thoughts, and ideas.*

My own love affair with writing began with just such a teacher—my eighth grade language arts teacher, Janna. In her class, I learned to value writing as a way of telling my own stories and expressing my thoughts. Throughout the year, we moved through units of myths, fairy tales, Shakespeare, and super-heroes. We read selections from Ovid's *Metamorphosis* and were assigned to write our own stories about transformation. We explored alternate versions of popular fairy tales, and then wrote our own retellings. We wrote essays ad-dressing questions such as "What are the essential elements of a superhero? Why do we create these superhuman beings?" I was excited to write about these topics—to express my voice and create my own story in response to what we were studying. Fairy tales and myths were not written and owned by famous authors and intellectuals, but passed down orally from generation to generation, told around the fire on dark midwinter nights, embellished and altered by each subsequent teller to express personal creativity and the values of the times. As eighth graders, we, too, had stories to tell and values to express within the timeless and ancient forms of myths. As if we were just storytellers in a long succession, Janna made us believe that our voices mattered.

Today we have moved beyond the oral tradition into a written one, yet 3 even though our books are copyrighted by single authors, ideas and stories are built from myriad voices who have come before. No work is completely original and isolated. Writers must enter previously existing discourses with their own voices. Gerald Graff, in his book *Clueless in Academe*, criticizes the way the academy perpetuates "cluelessness" by making intellectual discourse appear opaque, specialized, and inaccessible, and by accentuating a false divide between popular and intellectual culture (1). Graff asserts that argument in academic discourse is not so different from argument in popular culture, the media, or daily life, yet that higher education manages to obscure these similarities. He proposes that to mend that divide, teachers should teach students to incorporate their street smarts and common skills of argumentation and persuasion into academic writing, illuminating their similarities rather than their differences. If students can learn first to write analytically about superheroes, something that they know, they can learn how to apply those critical thinking skills to loftier subjects in the academy. Graff points out that one of the foremost ways academia perpetuates a divide between popular and intellectual culture, between outsiders and insiders, is by discouraging simple outsider questions such as "So what?" and "What's the point?" as naive. Instead, Graff encourages his students to address basic "So what?" questions in their writing, thereby situating their argument within an academic conversation, responding to real voices and ideas. Just as academics will have to propose and defend their points within the context of what other academics have said, Graff's students will learn to claim their arguments within a previously existing conversation. In Janna's class, we learned to write stories that responded to and built off of other stories, adding our versions to the long histories of tellings. Like Graff, Janna believed that her students had something worthwhile to say, and she encouraged us to say it.

Just as Graff criticizes how the academy makes intellectual life appear for- 4 eign to students' lives and experiences, bell hooks disparages the separation of mind, body, and spirit that she sees prevalent in the academy. She writes, "I learned that far from being self-actualized, the university was seen more as a haven for those who are smart in book knowledge but who might be otherwise unfit for social interaction" (16). Indeed, students and professors in higher education are often expected to value academic and intellectual pursuits over personal health or a balanced lifestyle, as if academic and personal life cannot coexist. In my experience as a college student, I see the image of the sleepless, caffeine-crazed student glorified. Professors and peers expect students to stay up all night to finish a paper, and then stay out all night on the weekends partying. Fellow students are surprised if I tell them that I get at least six hours of sleep a night and make some time to read for pleasure. College culture, as I have seen it both at college and as portrayed in the media, does not encourage a well-balanced, healthy lifestyle, but values extreme separations of "study" from "party," mind from body, and work from play. In *Teaching to Transgress*, hooks advocates a holistic pedagogy that reintroduces fun, excitement, and pleasure into the classroom. She argues that teachers should be fully "self-actualized" human beings, both intellectually and emotionally, who care not only for the analytical abilities of their students, but for their emotional and spiritual well-being. She says that students and professors should regard one another as "'whole' human beings, striving not just for knowledge in books, but knowledge about how to live in the world" (14–15). Students cannot be expected to care about learning and writing if they themselves are unloved and unfulfilled.

Janna was one of those teachers who nurtured both her students' intellec- 5 tual and emotional well-being. She cared deeply for each of us who passed through her classroom, feeling for our poor, mixed-up adolescent selves. Some days, she would sense that our spirits were down, or our bodies were restless, so she would read to us, or let us play outside. Janna saw us as people, not nameless students, and because she respected us as such, we respected her endeavor to teach us. Now, five years later, I still look to Janna as a teacher, mentor, and friend.

Those who suffer most from the separation of popular and academic culture 6 that Graff describes are those who have limited access to academic institutions—the impoverished, the illiterate, the marginalized. Working at a summer program last year for underprivileged and at-risk minority middle school students—Katrina evacuees, children of alcoholics and convicts—I saw this firsthand. Attending the worst schools in the state of Georgia, these particular students had not had teachers like Janna, teachers who valued their voices and encouraged their personal expression, teachers who understood that the academic is lifeless without the personal. From their experiences, the students understood school as an endless memorizing of dates, writing of expository essays, and reading of literature, that was completely alien from their lives. As Graff calls it, "the same old 'school stuff'" (6). bell hooks writes that students should "rightfully expect that my colleagues and I will not offer them information without addressing the connection between what they are learning and their overall life experiences" (19). Without a community that valued their voices, or an understanding of how the academic could and should connect to their lives, these students did not see that expression through writing could be self-empowering.

Despite this, there was one girl in the program, Danielle, who surprised and 7 impressed me with her dream to one day become a writer and publish her own autobiographies. Danielle had a difficult home life, with an absent father and overworked mother. In some ways, she was overly mature for her age, carrying herself like a woman, making sophisticated observations. On the other hand, she was often absent, or came to the program moody and irritable, purposely causing problems in the classroom; her behavior was perhaps a reflection of her troubled home life. Yet despite her difficult childhood and marginalized position in an unequal and racist system, Danielle understood that her experiences were important and relevant. She had the desire to share her voice with the world, and to add her stories to the public discourse.

As in the cases of eighth graders writing their own fairy tales, Danielle writ- 8 ing her life story shows that writing can be important and powerful in all settings when it is based on the interests, needs, and desires of writers. My mother, telling me of her experience teaching ESL writing, spoke of how any small accomplishment could be hugely empowering for a student: for an illiterate Haitian woman, learning how to write a grocery list helped her become more self-sufficient in a foreign country, while for a Mexican mother, learning enough to read and respond to notes from her son's teacher allowed her to be actively engaged in her child's school life. Graff speaks of the way that the academy creates a division between public and intellectual life, while hooks criticizes the mind/body/spirit division. Our society too often values only a small group of voices, marking divisions by age, class, race, gender, and language. I am arguing that the voices of every age, class, race, gender, and language are important and valuable, and writing can be a tool for self-empowerment and expression, no matter where it falls on the spectrum—from grocery lists to dissertations. Teachers of writing everywhere, from ESL to the academy, should bring the intellectual closer to the personal, to encourage their students to express their voices through writing what matters to their lives.

I have struggled all of my life to find the overlap between the ideas that in- 9 trigue and stimulate me, and my emotions, experiences, and the world. I grappled with this issue especially in my freshman high school English course. My teacher, Mark, presented writing as an intellectual challenge, a skill to be mastered. His demanding assignments and incisive questions challenged me like never before. Yet while I loved the class, the books we read, and the ideas we explored, I often wondered how they could be applicable to the world. During class discussions, or while writing a paper, I was excited by the moments when ideas came together, or opened up to show a spectrum of possibilities, yet at the end of the day, I had homework, was tired and hungry, and my world seemed very distant from Odysseus's adventures, or Miranda and Prospero's enchanted island.

That same year, Janna was diagnosed with breast cancer. It was a complete 10 surprise, and everyone who loved her was shocked and scared. I was frightened and disoriented; I wanted to show my love and support for her, but I didn't know how. During that time, we had been studying Shakespearean sonnets in Mark's class. He assigned us to write a Petrarchan or Shakespearean sonnet, with optional meter. I knew that this would be the perfect gift for Janna—for the woman who had taught me to love writing, I would write a poem from my heart. I chose a Petrarchan sonnet because they tend to end more optimistically. Incidentally, they also have the hardest rhyme scheme. I had to put all of my intellectual abilities to work to write this sonnet—figuring out rhyme, meter, and metaphor so that it would fit into the seamless, loving, supportive poem I wanted to give her. In "Soaring the Tempest," I made Janna a mockingbird, to reflect her love of languages and stories, and her cancer a storm she had to fly through:

> She sings as sweetly as a mockingbird,
> Well-versed and wise in ev'ry tongue and lore.
> For ev'ry bird, she is the troubadour.
> When she is near all other birds are spurred
> To sing so bold and sweet that all are heard,
> Inspired by her brave shining inner core
> Shimmering quietly without a roar.
> She soared the sea of sky and her wings whirred.

*So small a bird to fly the windy weather.*
*She found a way to safely sail rough sky.*
*But tempest comes, air dense with gale to pour.*
*This small bird doesn't know how she will fly.*
*All loved ones flock to take it together*
*Our dear one will be strong and she shall soar.*[1]

That sonnet was the hardest thing I had ever written, and it mattered the 11 most. I had to blend intellectual abilities with deeply personal feelings. Indeed, my sonnet is my argument made manifest—when struggling to express what I cared deeply about, only the demands of a stringent form would do. Yes, Stanley Fish, students do need to learn the mechanics of writing, yet without the personal, emotional, and the exciting, writing will never mean anything.

Fish argues that writing should be taught first with rigorous grammar in 12 complete isolation from interesting content and student expression. Yet this type of teaching increases the division between the privileged and the underprivileged, and between the intellectual and the personal (and produces writing that is intellectual to the exclusion or loss or denial of the personal). I believe that writing should be taught with the purpose of empowering individuals across divides such as age, class, race, and language. When students write what matters to them, they write better, more passionately, and more strongly; claiming agency in their expressions, they take on the power to affect change in their lives and in the world. Teachers of writing in all settings should strive to help their students write what matters to their lives, and encourage them to express their voices and tell their stories.

## Notes

1. After some scary months of uncertainty, Janna did recover. Today, she is healthy and still teaches eighth graders.

   For their influence, directly and indirectly, on this paper, I would like to thank Janna and Mark, Stanley Fish, bell hooks, Gerald Graff, Doug Downs, and Lee Rumbarger, for whose class I wrote it.

## Works Cited

Fish, Stanley. "Say It Ain't So." *Chronicle of Higher Education*, 21 June 2002. 25 Jan. 2007 <http://chronicle.com/jobs/2002/06/2002062101c.htm>.

Graff, Gerald. *Clueless in Academe: How Schooling Obscures the Life of the Mind.* New Haven, CT: Yale UP, 2003. hooks, bell. *Teaching to Transgress: Education as the Practice of Freedom.* New York: Routledge, 1994.

## Questions for Discussion and Journaling

1. Strasser writes that "The devices of grammar and rhetoric remain superficial skills until a writer employs them to express important and powerful feelings, thoughts, and ideas" (para. 1). Why? And do you agree?

2. What seems to be at issue for Strasser is creating "personally meaningful writing" in response to school assignments. Is there actually anything in Stanley Fish's advocacy of a writing course that teaches reasoning which would seem to rule out such personally meaningful writing? In other words, is Strasser right to assume that Fish's insistence on writing in order to exercise one's grammar will actually lead to meaningless writing?

3. In your experience, does school create a separation of mind, body, and spirit that Strasser quotes bell hooks as identifying (para. 4)?

## Applying and Exploring Ideas

1. Write your own explanation of how the "academic" and the "personal" interrelate. In what sense is your schoolwork *personal*, and in what sense do you bring your "personal" into your schoolwork? How does one shape the other?

2. If you have also read Erika Petersen's *YSW* piece on literacy in this chapter (p. 191), compare the ways the two articles use sources. How does their treatment of use of sources look similar, and how does it differ? Write an analysis of the effects that differing uses create.

---

### Meta Moment

Strasser's argument about the importance of connecting the personal and the academic seems to treat the academic as *not temporary*, not "just" four or five years of one's life that is removed and isolated from the rest. Do you view your college education as a part of your life, or as something disconnected from your life that is simply to be gotten through so you can get on with your life? Would Jackson's reasoning work if you understood academics as the latter?

---

**:e** In e-Pages at bedfordstmartins.com/writingaboutwriting

Shirley Brice Heath, "Protean Shapes in Literacy Events: Ever-Shifting Oral and Literate Traditions" (from *Spoken and Written Language*, 1982).

*Discussion of Heath's landmark ethnographic study of children and adults from "non-mainstream" backgrounds in the Piedmont Carolinas.*

# Writing about Literacies: Major Writing Assignments

To help you learn and explore the ideas in this chapter, we are suggesting three Assignment Options for larger writing projects: Literacy Narrative, Group Analysis of Literacy History, and Analysis of Literate Repurposing.

## Assignment Option 1. Literacy Narrative

Drawing on what you have read in this chapter, examine your own literacy history, habits, and processes. The purpose of this inquiry is to get to know yourself better as a reader and writer. As Malcolm X argued, awareness gives power and purpose: the more you know about yourself as a reader and writer, the more control you are likely to have over these processes.

*Invention, Research, and Analysis:* Start your literacy narrative by considering your history as a reader and writer. Try to get at what your memories and feelings about writing/reading are and how you actually write/read now. Do not make bland generalizations ("I really love to write"), but go into detail about how you learned to write/read. Mine your memory, thinking carefully about where you've been and where you are as a reader and writer. You might begin by answering questions such as:

- How did you learn to write and/or read?
- What kinds of writing/reading have you done in the past?
- How much have you enjoyed the various kinds of writing/reading you've done?
- What are particularly vivid memories that you have of reading, writing, or activities that involved them?
- What is your earliest memory of reading and your earliest memory of writing?
- What sense did you get, as you were learning to read and write, of the *value* of reading and writing, and where did that sense come from?
- What frustrated you about reading and writing as you were learning and then as you progressed through school? By the same token, what pleased you about them?
- What kind of writing/reading do you do most commonly?
- What is your favorite kind of writing/reading?
- What are your current attitudes, feelings, or stance toward reading and writing?
- Where do you think your feelings about and habits of writing and reading come from? How did you get to where you are as a writer/reader? What in your past has made you the kind of writer/reader you are today?
- Who are some people in your life who have acted as literacy sponsors?
- What are some institutions and experiences in your life that have acted as literacy sponsors?
- What have any of the readings in this chapter reminded you about from your past or present as a reader and writer?

Questions like these help you start thinking deeply about your literate past. You should try to come up with some answers for all of them, but it's unlikely that you'll actually include all the answers to all those questions in your literacy narrative itself. Right now you're just thinking and writing about what reading and writing was like for you. When you plan the narrative, you'll select from among all the material you've been remembering and thinking about. The question then becomes, how will you decide what to talk about out of everything you *could* talk about? This depends in part on your analysis of what you're remembering.

As you consider what all these memories and experiences suggest, you should be looking for an overall "so what?"—a main theme, a central "finding," an overall conclusion that your consideration leads you to draw. It might be an insight about why you read and write as you do today based on past experience. It might be an argument about what works or what doesn't work in literacy education, on the basis of your experience. It might be a resolution to do something differently, or to *keep* doing something that's been working. It might be a description of an ongoing conflict or tension you experience when you read and write—or the story of how you resolved such a conflict earlier in your literacy history. (It could also be a lot of other things.)

*Planning and Drafting:* Your consideration and analysis of your previous experience, one way or another, will lead you to a *main point* that your literacy narrative will demonstrate and support. That main point is what you've learned in your analysis; the literacy narrative then explains why you think what you do about that main point. It draws in whatever stories, experiences, moments, and descriptions, that help explain the point. Because your literacy narrative tells the particular story of a particular person—you—its shape will depend on the particular experiences you've had and the importance you attach to them. Therefore, it's difficult to suggest a single structure for the literacy narrative that will work for all writers. The structure that you use should support your particular intention and content.

Headings or sections (like Part I or Act I or "Early Literacy Memories"), might be helpful, but your content may better lend itself to write one coherent, unbroken essay. Do what works for you, given the material you want to include. Just be sure to organize and make some sort of point (or points).

Because your literacy narrative is about you, you may find it difficult to write it without talking about yourself in the first person. Using "I" when you need to will make the piece feel somewhat informal, which is appropriate to this kind of writing.

If you wish, include pictures or artifacts with your narrative. You could bring in your first spelling test or the award you won for the essay contest or the article in the school newspaper about your poem. If your circumstances make it appropriate, write this narrative in some mode other than alphabet-on-paper: for example, write it as a blog entry on your Web site and incorporate multimedia, or write it as a performed or acted presentation, or make it a PowerPoint presentation, a YouTube video, a poster, or whatever else works to reach the audience you want to and to help you make your point.

*What Makes It Good?:* This assignment asks you to carefully think about your history as a reader and writer, to tell a clear story that helps make a point, and to write a readable piece. So, be sure your piece a) tells a story or stories about your literacy history, b) talks about where you are now as a writer and reader and how your past has shaped your present, and c) makes some overall point about your literacy experiences. Of course, this essay should also be clear, organized, interesting, and well-edited. The strongest literacy narratives will incorporate ideas and concepts from the readings in this unit to help frame and explain your experiences.

# Assignment Option 2. Group Analysis of Literacy History

Collaborate with a group of classmates on a formal research study of some theme that emerges when everyone's literacy experiences are compared. You can use the following instructions to guide the writing of this kind of study, which lends itself to answering "bigger" questions or making larger points than a single literacy narrative really can.

*Conduct a Self-Study:* Post your answers to the following questions on the class blog, wiki, or Web site:

- How did you learn to write and/or read?
- What kinds of writing/reading have you done in the past?
- How much have you enjoyed the various kinds of writing/reading you've done?
- What are particularly vivid memories that you have of reading, writing, or activities that involved them?
- What is your earliest memory of reading and your earliest memory of writing?
- What sense did you get, as you were learning to read and write, of the *value* of reading and writing, and where did that sense come from?
- What frustrated you about reading and writing as you were learning and then as you progressed through school? By the same token, what pleased you about them?
- What kind of writing/reading do you do most commonly?
- What is your favorite kind of writing/reading?
- What are your current attitudes, feelings, or stance toward reading and writing?
- Where do you think your feelings about and habits of writing and reading come from?
- How did you get to where you are as a writer/reader? What in your past has made you the kind of writer/reader you are today?
- Who are some people in your life who have acted as literacy sponsors?
- What are some institutions and experiences in your life that have acted as literacy sponsors?
- What have any of the readings in this chapter reminded you about from your past or present as a reader and writer?

*Discuss and Code the Self-Studies:* In your group, read the answers to the self-interviews. Look together for common themes, recurring trends, or unique experiences, and determine which of these might be most interesting to further research and write about. What data will you need to collect to explore these themes? (For example, do you need to interview some classmates further? Interview people outside the class?) Common themes which emerge from this sort of study include the role of technology in literacy, hobbies as literacy sponsors, motivations for literacy learning, privilege and access, and help overcoming literacy struggles.

*Collaborate to Write about Emergent Themes:* You'll pair up with another student by choosing an emergent theme to write a paper about. As a pair, pinpoint a specific research question related to your theme and gather whatever further data is necessary. Drawing on terms and ideas from this chapter's readings, you can then write your analysis of and findings on this theme.

***Planning and Drafting:*** Before beginning to write, the group as a whole should consider audience and genre appropriate for this paper. Discuss the following questions together:

- Who should be the audience for what you write? And how can you best reach them?
- How would you like to write about your findings? In a somewhat formal, scholarly way? In a more story-telling, narrative way?
- What content/format would make this narrative most effective? Paper, text-only? Paper, text, and images? Online text and images? Online text, images, and video?

As you analyze and begin to write with your partner, you should consider the following questions:

- What is your research question?
- What answers to this question do your research and analysis suggest?
- What data support each of these answers?

Those questions will actually help you arrange your paper, too, in most cases. That is, the paper includes an introduction that poses your research question and explains the value of it. It goes on to explain how you attempted to answer the question—what methods you used to gather the data you used to try to reach answers. Next, you talk about that data and what answers it led you to. The paper concludes with your sense of "so what?," the implications that your findings seem to suggest. What have you learned about this emergent theme from your research, and what does it mean for the rest of us?

If you haven't written collaboratively before, you may find it a bit of a challenge to co-ordinate schedules with your co-writer, to decide how to break up the work of writing the piece, and to make sure you both always have current information and the other writer's most up-to-date ideas so that you can write the part of the piece you need to when you need to. You'll also find that you rewrite each other's material a bit—this will help it sound like the piece was written by a single voice or mind rather than two people.

***What Makes It Good?:*** A good analysis of an issue emerging from your group's literacy history may take a number of different shapes but will tend to have these traits in common:

- A clear, directly stated research question
- A detailed description of what methods you used to try to answer the question
- Clear explanation of what you found in your research and what conclusions it leads you to
- An explanation of "so what?"—why your findings might matter
- The usual: readable, fluent prose; transitions that make the paper easy to follow; and editing and proofreading that keep the paper from distracting readers with typos and goofs

# Assignment Option 3. Analysis of Literate Repurposing

Using Kevin Roozen's article as a model, write a research report about yourself (or a classmate, if your teacher prefers), in which you provide the information about your own literate experiences and literate repurposing that Roozen provides about Lindsey. This text should do two things: a) explain what some of your important literate practices are and b) look at the connections you "[forge] among different literate engagements" (p. 162).

*Gather Data:* In preparation for this research project, you will collect examples of texts you have written, and look at similarities across them.

First, write a short, informal literacy history that considers what you think are some of the most formative moments in your literate life—where and when you learned to read and write, what kinds of texts surrounded you growing up, what kinds of texts were valued, what textual practices you were taught at home and at school. This text can be an informal list of notes, bulleted lists, or freewriting, because it is just a way to gather some information about yourself for this project.

Next, conduct a literacy inventory of sorts on yourself specifically focusing on texts. What have been some of the most important literate practices in your past? For example, have texts written and read in church been important for you, as they were for Lindsey? Maybe hobbies or games have provided a means in which to engage in important literacy practices. Identify what some of those practices are, and collect some of the texts you have read and produced in that setting.

Then, look at the texts you produce in school settings. Pick a few that are recent enough to remember, or some that have been important or memorable in some way.

Sit down with the texts you collected and take some notes about them and about how you produced them. For example:

- How did you prepare for them?
- How did you compose them?
- What other people or resources were involved?
- What do they look like?
- How are they organized?
- What language and tone do they use?
- What is each text "like" or "not like" (in other words, what other texts have you read or written before that these resemble or definitely do not resemble)?

*Analyze Data:* As you look at the texts you collected and the notes that you have written, do you see any patterns developing? Do you see similarities across texts or settings? Do you see connections or "repurposing" of ideas, processes, formats, etc., from one setting or text to another?

Look back at the notes you made about your literacy history. Do you see any information here that could explain why you do what you do when you write texts?

*Planning and Drafting:* Rather than attempting to recreate an entire article as Roozen does, write a "narrative" modeled after the narratives that he includes in his "Findings" sections. To prepare, decide what your main points will be in this narrative. To do this, remember the two tasks you should complete here: a) explain what some of your important literate practices are, and b) determine what connections you "[forge] among different literate engagements" (Roozen, p. 162).

Write a first draft in which you just quickly try to respond to each of the above. What are your most important literate practices, as evidenced by the data you collected for this project? And what connections do you see across your literate practices?

Share those notes with a classmate and ask for his or her feedback about what you should further develop. What questions does your classmate have? What does he or she want to know more about? What sample texts should you include in the revision in order to illustrate or support claims that you make?

Take your classmate's feedback and revise your draft, also drawing on Kevin Roozen's "narratives" to help you determine tone, level of detail, and so forth.

Talk with your teacher about whether you should write about your data in first person or third person, and what effects and purposes each might serve.

*What Makes It Good?:* Did you learn something from writing this? Did you learn something from reading what your classmates wrote? Did you write about your data in a way that others can read and understand your point without too much difficulty? Do you feel that what you have produced contributes in some way to the conversation that Kevin Roozen is engaging in? If teachers and administrators read all of the narrative written by your classmates, will they understand you differently and perhaps think differently about how to teach writing?

If your text accomplishes these things, then you've done a good job.

# chapter 2

# Individual in Community:
## How Do Texts Mediate Activities?

In the above photo, Muhsid Muhammad, former wide receiver for the Carolina Panthers and Chicago Bears football teams, helps deliver food to the Second Harvest Food Bank of Metrolina in Charlotte, North Carolina, as part of the Kraft Foods Huddle to Fight Hunger campaign.

In the previous chapter, you explored your own literacy history and considered how individuals' literate pasts influence their current literacy practices and attitudes. In this chapter, you will broaden your scope to consider how groups and communities influence readers, writers, and texts. People don't write in a vacuum. Their literate histories influence their current writing practices, but their purposes for writing texts, and the people to and with whom they write, also influence how they write, what they write, how their texts are used, and how users make meaning of their texts. The central idea (the threshold concept; see the Introduction) in this chapter is that people use texts in order to *do something*, and the texts they create **mediate** mean-

ingful activities. (*Mediate* here means something like "intervene to shape an experience"— see the Glossary entry (p. 798) for more.) People construct meaning through texts, and texts construct meaning as people use them.

Consider an example. If a nonprofit food bank needs money to help feed poor families at Christmas, their fundraiser might write a fundraising letter that they send out to all past volunteers and donors. How the staff person who writes the letter does so is influenced by her understanding of the ideas and interests of the people reading it—what they need, want, and value—as well as by her own training as a fundraiser, all of her past writing

212

experiences, her supervisor's expectations, and her own and other staff members' experiences with past fundraising letters. The letter the staff person writes mediates the activities of fundraising and feeding the poor. It is read by many people who have very different reactions to it (some will throw it away, others will set it aside and forget about it, others will volunteer but not donate money, others will donate money). Readers' responses will continue to shape the work of the food bank and also how future fundraising letters are written. The food bank and its donors and volunteers and clients all shape how this and future fundraising letters are written, and the fundraising letter, in turn, shapes the work of the food bank—how it is understood, or whether it can be done at all. If this letter is not effective, the food bank might have to cut back services, and it will surely revise how future fundraising letters are written or distributed. The people who read the letter might start thinking about hunger and poverty differently as a result of what they read. Meaning and activities about hunger, poverty, fundraising, and so on are constructed through the fundraising letter.

This chapter asks you to take a close look at how texts are constructed as a result of the needs and activities of various groups. In this chapter, you'll learn two terms for looking at and understanding groups: **discourse communities** and **activity systems**. And then, in turn, how the texts construct meaning for the people who read, write, and otherwise use them. You'll consider the expectations, norms, histories, and people who inuence, construct, and interpret texts, and you'll consider how texts help groups get work done and achieve shared goals—or impede work when they are not successful.

As you examine texts through the analytical lenses described in this chapter, you'll want to begin thinking of texts as **genres**, a term discussed here by several of the authors and then used explicitly by Victoria Marro, a student writer in this chapter. Genres are discussed in more detail in Chapter 3. In "Speech Acts," writing scholar Charles Bazerman describes genres as "patterned, typical, and therefore intelligible forms" (para. 5, p. 368). In other words, if you see a particular text and you recognize it as having a particular name and expected characteristics or conventions, it is a "genre." Scholar Carolyn Miller tells us that genres arise in response to repeated rhetorical situations. As a familiar example, people do nice things for you repeatedly and you need to do something in return, so the genre of thank you cards comes into being. These cards make easier the task of responding the next time someone does something nice for you; instead of having to think through all the ways you could respond, you can just buy a thank you card and write the sorts of things your mother taught you to write when you were a child. Syllabi are another example you'll recognize: each time you go into a new classroom, you need to know what is expected of you. Teachers over time came to respond to this situation similarly by providing students with a syllabus. Genres are interesting because a genre is recognizable due to its common features across texts. Yet, no two examples of a genre are ever exactly the same and features change over time. So one teacher's syllabus is not exactly like the next teacher's syllabus. And the syllabi teachers give out today are different than the ones teachers gave hundred years ago. The document that teachers gave out hundred years ago might not even have been called a "syllabus." The point is that genres help people get things done as they engage in different activities. Having a syllabus means that students have to guess a lot less than they would without a syllabus, and teachers don't have to repeat instructions as much. In other words, genres help mediate the activities in which groups of people (in that example, teachers and students) engage.

As we said earlier, this chapter presents two lenses for analyzing how texts mediate work in communities: discourse community theory and activity theory. For each theory, you will first read a straightforward explanation and description, and then examples of how scholars and students use that theory.

## Chapter Goals

- To understand how language and texts (genres) mediate group activities
- To gain tools for examining the discourse and texts used by various communities
- To gain tools for conducting primary research
- To conduct research and write about it for various audiences
- To understand writing and research as processes
- To improve as readers of complex, research-based texts

# The Concept of Discourse Community

## JOHN SWALES

▪ Swales, John. "The Concept of Discourse Community." *Genre Analysis: English in Academic and Research Settings.* Boston: Cambridge UP, 1990. 21–32. Print.

......................................

## Framing the Reading

John Swales is a professor of linguistics and codirector of the Michigan Corpus of Academic Spoken English at the University of Michigan. He received his Ph.D. from Cambridge University and has spent most of his career in linguistics working with nonnative speakers of English on strategies to help them succeed as readers and writers in the university. His publications include *English in Today's Research World* (2000) and *Academic Writing for Graduate Students* (2004) (both coauthored with Christine Feak), *Research Genres* (2004), and *Episodes in ESP* (1985; **ESP** stands for English for Specific Purposes, a research area devoted to the teaching and learning of English for specific communities).

This excerpt is a chapter of a book Swales wrote called *Genre Analysis*. In it, he refers to concepts discussed previously in his book, which will be somewhat confusing since you have not read his book's preceding chapters. In the beginning of this chapter, Swales also refers to an ongoing academic argument over the social (**constructed**) nature of language use and to arguments about what a **discourse community** is and how it is different from a **speech community**. You likely will not fully understand this discussion, since you may not be familiar with the academic debates to which he refers. What's important for you to understand is simply that a lot of people think that *discourse community* is an important enough concept to argue about. Once Swales gets through this background/framing material, he goes on to define the term himself in section 2.3, since he thinks other people's definitions have not been clear and specific enough. This is where you should really start paying attention. As Swales defines his six characteristics of a discourse community, you should try to imagine groups you belong to that exhibit all six of these characteristics.

Discourse community is the first of two frames for analysis that this chapter provides in order to help you consider how people use texts and language to accomplish work together. Swales gives you some things to look for and consider when trying to figure out what is happening in any situation where language and texts play a part: What are people doing here? Do they have shared goals? How do they communicate with one another? How do newcomers learn what to do here?

CAMBRIDGE

**Genre Analysis**
English in academic and research settings
John M. Swales

CAMBRIDGE APPLIED LINGUISTICS
Series editors: Carol A. Chapelle and Susan Hunston

Be aware that Swales's style of writing is a little dry and formal, and he may use specialized linguistic terms that you don't understand. He is good, however, at highlighting his main claims and defining his terms, so if you pay close attention, he should clear up most of your confusion. If he uses terms that he does not define, and with which you are not familiar (for example, **lexis**), be sure to take a moment to look them up in a dictionary. You need to use the six characteristics he describes to analyze communities you are familiar with, so it is important that you understand his definition.

One of the most important—and complex—of Swales's characteristics is **genre**. Unfortunately, Swales does not spend much time defining this term because he assumes that his readers are familiar with it. As we discussed in the introduction to this chapter, genres are types of texts that are recognizable to readers and writers, and that meet the needs of the **rhetorical situations** in which they function. So, for example, we recognize wedding invitations and understand them as very different from horoscopes. We know that, when we are asked to write a paper for school, our teacher probably does not want us to turn in a poem instead.

Genres develop over time in response to recurring **rhetorical** needs. We have wedding invitations because people keep getting married and we need an efficient way to let people know and to ask them to attend. Rather than making up a new rhetorical solution every time the same situation occurs, we generally turn to the genre that has developed—in this case, the genre of the wedding invitation.

Swales demonstrates that discourse communities all use genres, many of which are recognizable to people outside the group (for example, memos or reports), but he notes that groups develop their own **conventions** for those genres in light of their desired goals. So memos written within AT&T, for example, might look very different from memos written by the members of the local school board.

It might be helpful to think of genres as textual tools used by groups of people as they work toward their desired ends; genres and the conventions that guide them change as the community discovers more efficient adaptations, as group membership changes, or as the group's desired ends change. For example, consider a team of biologists studying the effect of industrial pollutants on the cell structure of microorganisms in a particular body of water. In doing their research and reporting on it, the team of biologists will use many genres that are recognized outside of their discourse community, including research logs, notebooks, lab reports, conference presentations, and published scholarly papers; in many cases, however, they will have developed discourse-specific conventions guiding the production of these genres (for example, the Council of Science Editors' rules for documentation in published papers). As is the case in every discourse community, the genres and conventions that biologists use continue to change, in part as a result of new technologies (the Internet, computerized data analysis tools) that help them analyze and disseminate information in ever more efficient ways.

## Getting Ready to Read

*Before you read,* do at least one of the following activities:

- Look up Swales's book *Genre Analysis* on a book-buying Web site or Wikipedia and read at least two reviews of it. See if you can find a listing of its table of contents.

How much do you think you're missing by reading only a single chapter? (Do you feel inspired to find the book and read the rest?)

* Write a brief description of a time you've felt "out of place." What made you feel that way?

*As you read*, consider the following questions:

* How does what Swales describes relate to your own experience moving among different groups or communities?
* What are potential problems with Swales's explanations—places that *don't* line up with your own experiences?
* How would you describe the audience Swales seems to imagine himself writing to?

........................................................................................................................

## 2.1 A Need for Clarification

Discourse community, the first of three terms to be examined in Part II, has so 1 far been principally appropriated by instructors and researchers adopting a "Social View" (Faigley, 1986) of the writing process. Although I am not aware of the original provenance of the term itself, formative influences can be traced to several of the leading "relativist" or "social constructionist" thinkers of our time. Herzberg (1986) instances Perelman and Olbrechts-Tyteca's *The New Rhetoric* (1969), Kuhn's *The Structure of Scientific Revolutions* (1970) and Fish's *Is There a Text in This Class?* (1980). Porter (1988) discusses the significance of Foucault's analysis of "discursive formations" in *The Archaeology of Knowledge* (1972); other contributors are Rorty (*Philosophy and the Mirror of Nature*, 1979) and Geertz (*Local Knowledge*, 1983), with Wittgenstein's *Philosophical Investigations* (1958) as an earlier antecedent (Bruffee, 1986), particularly perhaps for the commentary therein on "language games" (3.5).

Whatever the genealogy of the term discourse community, the relevant point 2 in the present context is that it has been appropriated by the "social perspectivists" for their variously applied purposes in writing research. It is this use that I wish to explore and in turn appropriate. Herzberg (1986) sets the scene as follows:

> Use of the term "discourse community" testifies to the increasingly common assumption that discourse operates within conventions defined by communities, be they academic disciplines or social groups. The pedagogies associated with writing across the curriculum and academic English now use the notion of "discourse communities" to signify a cluster of ideas: that language use in a group is a form of social behavior, that discourse is a means of maintaining and extending the group's knowledge and of initiating new members into the group, and that discourse is epistemic or constitutive of the group's knowledge.
>
> (Herzberg, 1986:1)

Irrespective of the merits of this "cluster of ideas," the cluster is, I suggest, *consequential* of the assumption that there are indeed entities identifiable as discourse communities, not *criterial* for establishing or identifying them. They point us towards asking *how* a particular discourse community uses its discoursal conventions to initiate new members or *how* the discourse of another reifies particular values or beliefs. While such questions are well worth asking, they do not directly assist with the logically prior ones of how we recognize such communities in the first place.

Herzberg in fact concedes that there may be a definitional problem: "The idea   3 of 'discourse community' is not well defined as yet, but like many imperfectly defined terms, it is suggestive, the center of a set of ideas rather than the sign of a settled notion" (1986:1). However, if discourse community is to be "the center of a set of ideas"—as it is in this book—then it becomes reasonable to expect it to be, if not a settled notion, at least one that is sufficiently explicit for others to be able to accept, modify or reject on the basis of the criteria proposed.

Several other proponents of the "social view," while believing that discourse   4 community is a powerful and useful concept, recognize it currently raises as many questions as it answers. Porter (1988:2), for instance, puts one set of problems with exemplary conciseness: "Should discourse communities be determined by shared objects of study, by common research methodology, by opportunity and frequency of communication, or by genre and stylistic conventions?" Fennell et al. (1987) note that current definitions have considerable vagueness and in consequence offer little guidance in identifying discourse communities. They further point out that definitions which emphasize the reciprocity of "discourse" and "community" (community involves discourse and discourse involves community) suffer the uncomfortable fate of ending up circular.

We need then to clarify, for pro-   5 cedural purposes, what is to be understood by discourse community and, perhaps in the present circumstances, it is better to offer a set of criteria sufficiently narrow that it will eliminate many of the marginal, blurred and controversial contenders. A "strong" list of criteria will also avoid the circularity problem, because in consequence it will certainly follow that not all communities—as defined on other criteria—will be discourse

> *We need then to clarify, for procedural purposes, what is to be understood by discourse community and, perhaps in the present circumstances, it is better to offer a set of criteria sufficiently narrow that it will eliminate many of the marginal, blurred and controversial contenders.*

communities, just as it will follow that not all discourse activity is relevant to discourse community consolidation. An exclusionary list will also presumably show that the kind of disjunctive question raised by Porter is misplaced. It is likely to show that neither shared object of study nor common procedure nor interaction nor agreed discoursal convention will themselves individually be necessary and sufficient conditions for the emergence of a discourse community, although a combination of some or all might. Conversely, the absence of any one (different subject areas, conflicting procedures, no interaction, and multiple

discourse conventions) may be enough to prevent discourse community formation—as international politics frequently reminds us.

It is possible, of course, that there is no pressing need to clarify the con-  6
cept of *discourse community* because, at the end of the account, it will turn
out to be nothing more than composition specialists' convenient translation of
the long-established concept of *speech community* common to sociolinguistics
and central to the ethnography of communication. This view, for example,
would seem to be the position of Freed and Broadhead (1987). After a couple
of opening paragraphs on *speech community* in linguistics and on audience
analysis, they observe, "only recently have compositional studies begun to investigate communities of writers and readers, though the terminology seems
to be changing to "discourse communities" in order to signal the focus on
the written rather than the spoken" (1987:154). Whether it is appropriate to
identify *discourse community* with a subset of *speech community* is the topic
of the next section.

## 2.2 Speech Communities and Discourse Communities

Speech community has been an evolving concept in sociolinguistics and the  7
consequent variety of definitional criteria has been discussed—among others—
by Hudson (1980), Saville-Troike (1982) and especially by Braithwaite (1984).
At the outset, a speech community was seen as being composed of those who
share similar *linguistic rules* (Bloomfield, 1933), and in those terms we could
legitimately refer to, say, the speech community of the English-speaking world.
Later, Labov will emphasize "shared norms" rather than shared performance
characteristics but still conclude that "New York City is a single speech community, and not a collection of speakers living side by side, borrowing occasionally from each other's dialects" (Labov, 1966:7). Others, such as Fishman
(1971), have taken as criterial patterned regularities in the *use* of language.
In consequence, a speech community is seen as being composed of those who
share functional rules that determine the appropriacy of utterances. Finally,
there are those such as Hymes who argue for multiple criteria:

> A speech community is defined, then, tautologically but radically, as a community
> sharing knowledge of rules for the conduct and interpretation of speech. Such
> sharing comprises knowledge of at least one form of speech, and knowledge also
> of its patterns of use. Both conditions are necessary.

> (Hymes, 1974:51)

There are a number of reasons why I believe even a tight definition of speech
community (shared linguistic forms, shared regulative rules and shared cultural
concepts) will not result in making an alternative definition of discourse community unnecessary. The first is concerned with medium; not so much in the trivial sense that "speech" just will not do as an exclusive modifier of communities
that are often heavily engaged in writing, but rather in terms of what that literary activity implies. Literacy takes away locality and parochiality, for members

are more likely to communicate with other members in distant places, and are more likely to react and respond to writings rather than speech from the past.

A second reason for separating the two concepts derives from the need to distinguish a *sociolinguistic* grouping from a *sociorhetorical* one. In a sociolinguistic speech community, the communicative needs of the *group*, such as socialization or group solidarity, tend to predominate in the development and maintenance of its discoursal characteristics. The primary determinants of linguistic behavior are social. However, in a sociorhetorical discourse community, the primary determinants of linguistic behavior are functional, since a discourse community consists of a group of people who link up in order to pursue objectives that are prior to those of socialization and solidarity, even if these latter should consequently occur. In a discourse community, the communicative needs of the *goals* tend to predominate in the development and maintenance of its discoursal characteristics. 8

Thirdly, in terms of the fabric of society, speech communities are centripetal (they tend to absorb people into that general fabric), whereas discourse communities are centrifugal (they tend to separate people into occupational or speciality-interest groups). A speech community typically inherits its membership by birth, accident or adoption; a discourse community recruits its members by persuasion, training or relevant qualification. To borrow a term from the kind of association readers of this book are likely to belong to, an archetypal discourse community tends to be a *Specific Interest Group*. 9

## 2.3 A Conceptualization of Discourse Community

I would now like to propose six defining characteristics that will be necessary and sufficient for identifying a group of individuals as a discourse community. 10

1. *A discourse community has a broadly agreed set of common public goals.* These public goals may be formally inscribed in documents (as is often the case with associations and clubs), or they may be more tacit. The goals are *public,* because spies may join speech and discourse communities for hidden purposes of subversion, while more ordinary people may join organizations with private hopes of commercial or romantic advancement. In some instances, but not in many, the goals may be high level or abstract. In a Senate or Parliament there may well exist overtly adversarial groups of members, but these adversaries may broadly share some common objective as striving for improved government. In the much more typical non-adversarial discourse communities, reduction in the broad level of agreement may fall to a point where communication breaks down and the discourse community splits. It is commonality of goal, not shared object of study that is criterial, even if the former often subsumes the latter. But not always. The fact that the shared object of study is, say, the Vatican, does not imply that students of the Vatican in history departments, the Kremlin, dioceses, birth control agencies and liberation theology seminaries form a discourse community. 11

2. *A discourse community has mechanisms of intercommunication among*  12
   *its members.*
   The participatory mechanisms will vary according to the community:
   meetings, telecommunications, correspondence, newsletters, conversations and so forth. This criterion is quite stringent because it produces
   a negative answer to the case of "The Café Owner Problem" (Najjar,
   personal communication). In generalized form, the problem goes as follows: individuals A, B, C and so on occupy the same professional roles in
   life. They interact (in speech and writing) with the same clienteles; they
   originate, receive and respond to the same kind of messages for the same
   purposes; they have an approximately similar range of genre skills. And
   yet, as Café owners working long hours in their own establishments, and
   not being members of the Local Chamber of Commerce, A, B and C never
   interact with one another. Do they form a discourse community? We can
   notice first that "The Café Owner Problem" is not quite like those situations where A, B and C operate as "point." A, B and C may be lighthouse
   keepers on their lonely rocks, or missionaries in their separate jungles,
   or neglected consular officials in their rotting outposts. In all these cases,
   although A, B and C may never interact, they all have lines of communication back to base, and presumably acquired discourse community
   membership as a key element in their initial training.
      Bizzell (1987) argues that the café owner kind of social group will be  13
   a discourse community because "its members may share the social-class-
   based or ethnically-based discursive practices of people who are likely to
   become café owners in their neighborhood" (1987:5). However, even if
   this sharing of discursive practice occurs, it does not resolve the logical
   problem of assigning membership of a community to individuals who
   neither admit nor recognize that such a community exists.
3. *A discourse community uses its participatory mechanisms primarily to*  14
   *provide information and feedback.*
   Thus, membership implies uptake of the informational opportunities.
   Individuals might pay an annual subscription to the *Acoustical Society
   of America* but if they never open any of its communications they cannot be said to belong to the discourse community, even though they are
   formally members of the society. The secondary purposes of the information exchange will vary according to the common goals: to improve
   performance in a football squad or in an orchestra, to make money in a
   brokerage house, to grow better roses in a gardening club, or to dent the
   research front in an academic department.
4. *A discourse community utilizes and hence possesses one or more genres*  15
   *in the communicative furtherance of its aims.*
   A discourse community has developed and continues to develop discoursal
   expectations. These may involve appropriacy of topics, the form, function
   and positioning of discoursal elements, and the roles texts play in the operation of the discourse community. In so far as "genres are how things get
   done, when language is used to accomplish them" (Martin, 1985:250), these

discoursal expectations are created by the *genres* that articulate the operations of the discourse community. One of the purposes of this criterion is
to question discourse community status for new or newly-emergent groupings. Such groupings need, as it were, to settle down and work out their
communicative proceedings and practices before they can be recognized
as discourse communities. If a new grouping "borrows" genres from other
discourse communities, such borrowings have to be assimilated.

5. *In addition to owning genres, a discourse community has acquired some* 16
*specific lexis.*
This specialization may involve using lexical items known to the wider
speech communities in special and technical ways, as in information technology discourse communities, or using highly technical terminology as
in medical communities. Most commonly, however, the inbuilt dynamic
towards an increasingly shared and specialized terminology is realized
through the development of community-specific abbreviations and acronyms. The use of these (ESL, EAP, WAC, NCTE, TOEFL, etc.) is, of course,
driven by the requirements for efficient communication exchange between
experts. It is hard to conceive, at least in the contemporary English-
speaking world, of a group of well-established members of a discourse
community communicating among themselves on topics relevant to the
goals of the community and not using lexical items puzzling to outsiders.
It is hard to imagine attending perchance the convention of some group of
which one is an outsider and understanding every word. If it were to happen—as might occur in the inaugural meeting of some quite new grouping—then that grouping would not yet constitute a discourse community.

6. *A discourse community has a threshold level of members with a suitable* 17
*degree of relevant content and discoursal expertise.*
Discourse communities have changing memberships; individuals enter as
apprentices and leave by death or in other less involuntary ways. However, survival of the community depends on a reasonable ratio between
novices and experts.

## 2.4 An Example of a Discourse Community

As we have seen, those interested in discourse communities have typically sited 18
their discussions within academic contexts, thus possibly creating a false impression that such communities are only to be associated with intellectual paradigms or scholarly cliques. Therefore, for my principal example of a discourse
community, I have deliberately chosen one that is not academic, but which
nevertheless is probably typical enough of many others. The discourse community is a hobby group and has an "umbrella organization" called the Hong
Kong Study Circle, of which I happen to be a member. The aims of the HKSC
(note the abbreviation) are to foster interest in and knowledge of the stamps
of Hong Kong (the various printings, etc.) and of their uses (postal rates,
cancellations, etc.). Currently there are about 320 members scattered across
the world, but with major concentrations in Great Britain, the USA and Hong

Kong itself and minor ones in Holland and Japan. Based on the membership list, my guess is that about a third of the members are non-native speakers of English and about a fifth women. The membership varies in other ways: a few are rich and have acquired world-class collections of classic rarities, but many are not and pursue their hobby interest with material that costs very little to acquire. Some are full-time specialist dealers, auctioneers and catalogue publishers, but most are collectors. From what little I know, the collectors vary greatly in occupation. One standard reference work was co-authored by a stamp dealer and a Dean at Yale; another was written by a retired Lieutenant-Colonel. The greatest authority on the nineteenth century carriage of Hong Kong mail, with three books to his credit, has recently re-tired from a lifetime of service as a signalman with British Rail. I mention these brief facts to show that the members of the discourse community have, superficially at least, nothing in common except their shared hobby interest, although Bizzell (1992) is probably correct in pointing out that there may be psychological predispositions that attract particular people to collecting and make them "kindred spirits."

The main mechanism, or "forum" (Herrington, 1985) for intercommunica- 19 tion is a bi-monthly Journal and Newsletter, the latest to arrive being No. 265. There are scheduled meetings, including an Annual General Meeting, that takes place in London, but rarely more than a dozen members attend. There is a certain amount of correspondence and some phoning, but without the Journal/ Newsletter I doubt the discourse community would survive. The combined pe-riodical often has a highly interactive content as the following extracts show:

2. Hong Kong, Type 12, with Index
No one has yet produced another example of this c.d.s. that I mentioned on J.256/7 as having been found with an index letter "C" with its opening facing downwards, but Mr. Scamp reports that he has seen one illustrated in an auc-tion catalogue having a normal "C" and dated MY 9/59 (Type 12 is the 20 mm single-circle broken in upper half by HONG KONG). It must be in someone's collection!

3. The B.P.O.'s in Kobe and Nagasaki
Mr. Pullan disputes the statement at the top of J.257/3 that "If the postal clerk had not violated regulations by affixing the MR 17/79 (HIOGO) datestamp on the front, we might have no example of this c.d.s. at all." He states that "By 1879 it was normal practice for the sorter's datestamp to be struck on the front, the change from the back of the cover occurring generally in 1877, though there are isolated earlier examples"; thus there was no violation of regulations.

My own early attempts to be a full member of the community were not marked by success. Early on I published an article in the journal which used a fairly com-plex frequency analysis of occurrence—derived from Applied Linguistics—in order to offer an alternative explanation of a puzzle well known to members of the HKSC. The only comments that this effort to establish credibility elicited were "too clever by half" and "Mr. Swales, we won't change our minds without a chemical analysis." I have also had to learn over time the particular terms of approval and disapproval for a philatelic item (cf. Becher, 1981) such as "significant," "useful," "normal," and not to comment directly on the monetary value of such items.

Apart from the conventions governing articles, queries and replies in the  20 Journal/Newsletter, the discourse community has developed a genre-specific set of conventions for describing items of Hong Kong postal history. These occur in members' collections, whether for display or not, and are found in somewhat more abbreviated forms in specialized auction catalogues, as in the following example:

> 1176   1899 Combination PPC to Europe franked CIP 4 C canc large CANTON
> dollar chop, pair HK 2 C carmine added & Hong Kong index B cds. Arr
> cds. (1) (Photo) HK $1500.

Even if luck and skill were to combine to interpret PPC as "picture postcard," CIP as "Chinese Imperial Post," a "combination" as a postal item legitimately combining the stamps of two or more nations and so on, an outsider would still not be in a position to estimate whether 1500 Hong Kong dollars would be an appropriate sum to bid. However, the distinction between insider and outsider is not absolute but consists of gradations. A professional stamp dealer not dealing in Hong Kong material would have a useful general schema, while a member of a very similar discourse community, say the China Postal History Society, may do as well as a member of the HKSC because of overlapping goals.

The discourse community I have discussed meets all six of the proposed de-  21 fining criteria: there are common goals, participatory mechanisms, information exchange, community specific genres, a highly specialized terminology and a high general level of expertise. On the other hand, distance between members geographically, ethnically and socially presumably means that they do not form a speech community.

## 2.5 Remaining Issues

If we now return to Herzberg's "cluster of ideas" quoted near the beginning  22 of this section, we can see that the first two (language use is a form of social behaviour, and discourse maintains and extends a group's knowledge) accord with the conceptualization of discourse community proposed here. The third is the claim that "discourse is epistemic or constitutive of the group's knowledge" (Herzberg, 1986:1). This claim is also advanced, although in slightly different form, in a paper by Bizzell:

> In the absence of consensus, let me offer a tentative definition: a "discourse com-
> munity" is a group of people who share certain language-using practices. These
> practices can be seen as conventionalized in two ways. Stylistic conventions regu-
> late social interactions both within the group and in its dealings with outsiders:
> to this extent "discourse community" borrows from the sociolinguistic concept
> of "speech community." Also, canonical knowledge regulates the world-views of

group members, how they interpret experience; to this extent "discourse community" borrows from the literary-critical concept of "interpretive community."

(Bizzell, 1992:1)

The issue of whether a community's discourse and its discoursal expectations are constitutive or regulative of world-view is a contemporary reworking of the Whorfian hypothesis that each language possesses a structure which must at some level influence the way its users view the world (Carroll, 1956). The issue is an important one, because as Bizzell later observes "If we acknowledge that participating in a discourse community entails some assimilation of its world view, then it becomes difficult to maintain the position that discourse conventions can be employed in a detached, instrumental way" (Bizzell, 1992:9).

However, this is precisely the position I wish to maintain, especially if *can be* 23 *employed* is interpreted as *may sometimes be employed*. There are several reasons for this. First, it is possible to deny the premise that participation entails assimilation. There are enough spies, undercover agents and fifth columnists in the world to suggest that non-assimilation is at least possible. Spies are only successful if they participate successfully in the relevant speech and discourse communities of the domain which they have infiltrated; however, if they also *assimilate* they cease to be single spies but become double agents. On a less dramatic level, there is enough pretense, deception and face-work around to suggest that the acting out of roles is not that uncommon; and to take a relatively innocuous context, a prospective son-in-law may pretend to be an active and participating member of a bridge-playing community in order to make a favorable impression on his prospective parents-in-law.

Secondly, sketching the boundaries of discourse communities in ways that 24 I have attempted implies (a) that individuals may belong to several discourse communities and (b) that individuals will vary in the number of discourse communities they belong to and hence in the number of genres they command. At one extreme there may be a sense of discourse community deprivation— "Cooped up in the house with the children all day." At the other extreme, there stand the skilled professional journalists with their chameleon-like ability to assume temporary membership of a wide range of discourse communities. These observations suggest discourse communities will vary, both intrinsically and in terms of the member's perspective, in the degree to which they impose a world-view. Belonging to the Hong Kong Study Circle is not likely to be as constitutive as abandoning the world for the seclusion of a closed religious order.

Thirdly, to deny the instrumental employment of discourse conventions is to 25 threaten one common type of apprenticeship and to cast a hegemonical shadow over international education. Students taking a range of different courses often operate successfully as "ethnographers" of these various academic milieux (Johns, 1988a) and do so with sufficient detachment and instrumentality to avoid developing multiple personalities, even if, with more senior and specialized students, the epistemic nature of the discourse may be more apparent, as the interesting case study by Berkenkotter et al. (1988) shows. I would also like to avoid taking a position whereby a foreign student is seen, via participation, to assimilate inevitably the world-view of the host discourse community. While this may happen, I would not want to accept that discourse conventions cannot be successfully deployed in an instrumental manner (see James, 1980 for further discussion of variability in foreign student roles). Overall, the extent to which discourse is constitutive of world-view would seem to be a matter of investigation rather than assumption.

Just as, for my applied purposes, I do not want to accept assimilation of 26 world-view as criterial, so neither do I want to accept a threshold level of personal involvement as criterial. While it may be high in a small business, a class or a department, and may be notoriously high among members of amateur dramatic discourse communities, the fact remains that the active members of the Hong Kong Study Circle—to use an example already discussed—form a successful discourse community despite a very low level of personal involvement. Nor is centrality to the main affairs of life, family, work, money, education, and so on, criterial. Memberships of hobby groups may be quite peripheral, while memberships of professional associations may be closely connected to the business of a career (shockingly so as when a member is *debarred*), but both may equally constitute discourse communities. Finally, discourse communities will vary in the extent to which they are norm-developed, or have their set and settled ways. Some, at a particular moment in time, will be highly conservative ("these are things that have been and remain"), while others may be norm-developing and in a state of flux (Kuhn, 1970; Huckin, 1987).

The delineation of these variable features throws interesting light on the 27 fine study of contexts for writing in two senior college Chemical Engineering classes by Herrington (1985). Herrington concluded the Lab course and Design Process course "represented distinct communities where different issues were addressed, different lines of reasoning used, different writer and audience roles assumed, and different social purposes served by writing" (1985:331). (If we also note that the two courses were taught in the same department at the same institution by the same staff to largely the same students, then the Herrington study suggests additionally that there may be more of invention than we would like to see in our models of disciplinary culture.) The disparities between the two courses can be interpreted in the following way. Writing in the Lab course was central to the "display familiarity" macro-act of college assignments (Horowitz, 1986a)—which the students were accustomed to. Writing in the Design course was central to the persuasive reporting macro-act of the looming professional world, which the students were not accustomed to. The Lab course was *norm-developed,* while the Design course was *norm-developing.* As Herrington observes, in Lab both students and faculty were all too aware that the conceptual issue in the assignments was *not* an issue for the audience—the professor knew the answers. But it was an issue in Design. As a part consequence, the level of *personal involvement* was much higher in the Design course where professor and student interacted together in a joint problem-solving environment.

The next issue to be addressed in this section is whether certain groupings, 28 including academic classes, constitute *discourse* communities. Given the six criteria, it would seem clear that shareholders of General Motors, members of the Book of the Month Club, voters for a particular political party, clienteles of restaurants and bars (except perhaps in soap-operas), employees of a university, and inhabitants of an apartment block all fail to qualify. But what about academic classes? Except in exceptional cases of well-knit groups of advanced students already familiar with much of the material, an academic class is unlikely to be a discourse community at the outset. However, the hoped-for outcome is that it will form a discourse community (McKenna, 1987). Somewhere down the line, broad agreement on goals will be established, a full range of participatory mechanisms will be created, information exchange and feedback will flourish by peer-review and instructor commentary, understanding the rationale of and facility with appropriate genres will develop, control of the technical vocabulary in both oral and written contexts will emerge, and a level of expertise that permits critical thinking be made manifest. Thus it turns out that providing a relatively constrained operational set of criteria for defining discourse communities also provides a coign of vantage, if from the applied linguist's corner, for assessing educational processes and for reviewing what needs to be done to assist non-native speakers and others to engage fully in them.

Finally, it is necessary to concede that the account I have provided of discourse community, for all its attempts to offer a set of pragmatic and operational criteria, remains in at least one sense somewhat removed from reality. It is utopian and "oddly free of many of the tensions, discontinuities and conflicts in the sorts of talk and writing that go on everyday in the classrooms and departments of an actual university" (Harris, 1989:14). Bizzell (1987) too has claimed that discourse communities can be healthy and yet contain contradictions; and Herrington (1989) continues to describe composition researchers as a "community" while unveiling the tensions and divisions within the group. The precise status of conflictive discourse communities is doubtless a matter for future study, but here it can at least be accepted that discourse communities can, over a period of time, lose as well as gain consensus, and at some critical juncture, be so divided as to be on the point of splintering. 29

## References

Becher, Tony. 1981. Towards a definition of disciplinary cultures. *Studies in Higher Education* 6:109–22.

Berkenkotter, Carol, Thomas N. Huckin, and John Ackerman. 1988. Conventions, conversations and the writer: Case study of a student in a rhetoric Ph.D. program. *Research in the Teaching of English* 22:9–44.

Bizzell, Patricia. 1987. Some uses of the concept of "discourse community." Paper presented at the Penn State Conference on Composition, July, 1987.

Bizzell, Patricia. 1992. "What Is a Discourse Community?" *Academic Discourse and Critical Consciousness*. U. Pittsburgh P. 222–237.

Bloomfield, L. 1933, *Language*. New York: Holt & Company.

Braithwaite, Charles A. 1984. Towards a conceptualization of "speech community." In *Papers from the Minnesota Regional Conference on Language and Linguistics*: 13–29.

Bruffee, K. A. 1986. Social construction, language, and the authority of knowledge: A bibliography. *College English* 48:773–90.

Carroll, John B. (ed.). 1956. *Language, thought and reality: selected writings of Benjamin Lee Whorf*. New York: John Wiley.

Faigley, Lester. 1986. Competing theories of process: a critique and a proposal. *College English* 48:527–42.

Fennell, Barbara, Carl Herndl, and Carolyn-Miller. 1987. Mapping discourse communities. Paper presented at the CCC Convention, Atlanta, Ga, March, 1987.

Fish, Stanley. 1980. *Is there a text in this class?* Harvard, Mass: Harvard University Press.

Fishman, Joshua (ed.) 1971. *Sociolinguistics: A brief introduction.* Rowley, Mass: Newbury House.

Foucault, Michel. 1972. *The archaeology of knowledge.* New York: Harper & Row.

Freed, Richard C. and Glenn J. Broadhead. 1987. Discourse communities, sacred texts, and institutional norms. *College Composition and Communication* 38:154–65.

Geertz, Clifford. 1983. *Local knowledge: Further essays in interpretive anthropology.* New York Basic Books.

Harris, Joseph. 1989. The idea of community in the study of writing. *College Composition and Communication* 40:11–22.

Herrington, Anne. 1985. Writing in academic settings: A study of the context for writing in two college chemical engineering courses. *Research in the Teaching of English* 19:331–61.

Herrington, Anne. 1989. The first twenty years of *Research in the Teaching of English* and the growth of a research community in composition studies. *Research in the Teaching of English* 23:117–38.

Herzberg, Bruce. 1986. The politics of discourse communities. Paper presented at the CCC Convention, New Orleans, La, March, 1986.

Horowitz, Daniel M. 1986a. What professors actually require: Academic tasks for the ESL classroom. *TESOL Quarterly* 20:445–62.

Huckin, Thomas N. 1987. Surprise value in scientific discourse. Paper presented at the CCC Convention. Atlanta, Ga, March, 1987.

Hudson, R.A. l980. *Sociolinguistics.* Cambridge: Cambridge University Press.

Hymes, Dell. 1974. Foundations in *sociolinguistics: Ethnographic approach.* Philadelphia: University of Pennsylvania Press.

James, Kenneth. l980. Seminar overview. In Greenall and Price (eds.):7–21.

Johns, Ann M. 1988a. The discourse communities dilemma: Identifying transferable skills for the academic milieu. *English for Specific Purposes.* 7:55–60.

Kuhn, Thomas S. 1970. *The structure of scientific revolutions* (second edition). Chicago University of Chicago Press.

Labov, William. 1966. *The social stratification of English in New York City.* Washington, D.C.: Center for Applied Linguistics.

Martin, J. R. 1985. Process and text: Two aspects of human semiosis. In Benson and Greaves (eds.): 248–74.

McKenna, Eleanor. 1987. Preparing foreign students to enter discourse communities in the U.S. *English for Specific Purposes* 6:187–202.

Perelman, Chaim and L. Olbrechts-Tyteca. 1969. *The new rhetoric; A treatise on argumentation.* Notre Dame, IN: Notre Dame University Press.

Porter, James E. 1988. The problem of defining discourse communities. Paper presented at the CCC Convention, St. Louis, March, 1988.

Rorty, Richard. 1979. *Philosophy and the mirror of nature.* Princeton, NJ: Princeton University Press.

Saville-Troike, Muriel. 1982. *The ethnography of communication.* Oxford: Basil Blackwell.

Wittgenstein, Ludwig. 1958. *Philosophical investigations.* Oxford: Basil Blackwell.

## Questions for Discussion and Journaling

1. Use your own words to describe each of the six characteristics of a discourse community according to Swales. Can you find examples of each from your own experience?

2. Swales discusses his own attempt to join the Hong Kong Study Circle. What went wrong? Which of the six characteristics did he have trouble with?

3. According to Swales, would a first-year college classroom count as a discourse community? What about a graduate class? Why or why not?

4. Swales argues that it is possible to participate in a discourse community without being assimilated in it. What does this mean?

5. Consider a discourse community you belong to, and describe how it meets the six characteristics of a discourse community. For example, what are its shared goals? What is its lexis? What are its genres?

6. Consider a time when you participated in a discourse community but resisted it or were not assimilated into it. What happened?

## Applying and Exploring Ideas

1. Write a short narrative in which you dramatize Swales's problems joining the HKSC or in which you imagine the problems a newcomer has in learning the ropes in any new discourse community you can imagine, from *World of Warcraft* to medical school to a sorority.

2. Write a one-page letter to an incoming student in which you explain what discourse communities are and how knowing about them will be helpful to that student in college.

3. Spend a few hours hanging out with or near a discourse community of your choice— dorm, store, gaming community, and so forth. Write down every use of specialized language that you hear—whether it is an unusual word or phrase, or simply an unusual use of a fairly common word or phrase. And note on your "lexis list" when a term you were familiar with was being used with a new meaning or in a new way.

> **Meta Moment**
> Do you understand anything differently about your own writing experiences after reading Swales's description of how discourse communities work? If so, consider a way that this understanding can help you navigate discourse communities in the future.

# A Stranger in Strange Lands:
## A COLLEGE STUDENT WRITING ACROSS THE CURRICULUM

### LUCILLE P. MCCARTHY

■ McCarthy, Lucille P. "A Stranger in Strange Lands: A College Student Writing across the Curriculum." *Research in the Teaching of English* 21.3 (1987): 233–65. Print.

## Framing the Reading

Lucille McCarthy earned her Ph.D. from the University of Pennsylvania, and she is currently a professor of English at the University of Maryland–Baltimore County, where she has taught since 1988. Her many articles and books demonstrate her interest in pedagogies that help promote student learning and writing. Five of her six books and many of her articles focus on student classroom experiences and have won awards such as the James N. Britton Award for Research in the English Language Arts and a National Council of Teachers of English award for Research Excellence in Technical and Scientific Communication. Her books include *John Dewey and the Challenge of Classroom Practice* (1998), *John Dewey and the Philosophy and Practice of Hope* (2007), and *Whose Goals? Whose Aspirations? Learning to Teach Underprepared Writers across the Curriculum* (2002), all co-authored with her frequent collaborator, philosopher Stephen Fishman; and *Thinking and Writing in College: A Naturalistic Study of Students in Four Disciplines* (1991; with Barbara Walvoord).

McCarthy published the article reprinted here in 1987. At that time, researchers in other fields had used **case studies** and **ethnographic research** extensively, but researchers in the field of Writing Studies had only begun to consider what we could learn about writing by using those methods. In writing this article, McCarthy notes that researchers know that writing is strongly influenced by **social context**—that, for example, some people write well in one setting (e.g., at home alone) and not very well in another (e.g., on a timed exam), or that some people write well in one **genre** (e.g., poetry) but not very well in another genre (e.g., a literary criticism essay). But McCarthy wanted to know more about *how* writing is influenced by social settings; in particular, she wanted to know how college writers and their writing are influenced by their different classroom settings.

At the time that McCarthy conducted her study, no one else had followed individual students as they wrote across the university. Since McCarthy published her study, a number of such

**longitudinal studies** have been published. While no single case study can produce **generalizable** results, a number of case studies taken together can do so. Thus, if you are interested in making claims about how writers write in college, you should read the longitudinal studies that followed McCarthy.

McCarthy followed a student named "Dave" as he wrote in three different classes—composition, biology, and poetry. Dave got good grades in the first two classes, but struggled in poetry. McCarthy tried to find out why Dave was so unsuccessful in poetry and ultimately concluded that even though the writing tasks across all the classes had some similarities, Dave *thought* they were very different, and he had very different kinds of support for the writing in each of the classes.

We have included McCarthy's study here because she demonstrates one way to look at how individuals participate in community activities (like courses) through the use of texts and language. In particular, she demonstrates what can happen when newcomers do or don't understand and share the values and conventions of a new community in which they are participating. She also demonstrates what happens when the "oldtimers" in a community (like teachers) aren't able to successfully share conventions, strategies, and values with "newcomers" (like students). If you've read Swales on discourse communities, you can consider how Dave's experiences across various classes is like visiting a variety of discourse communities, some of which use texts in ways that seem very strange to him.

## Getting Ready to Read

*Before you read*, try the following activity:

- Consider a class where you have an easy time writing, and a class where the writing is hard for you. Think about why you might have different levels of success with these writing tasks.

*As you read*, consider the following questions:

- What research question(s) does McCarthy set out to answer?
- What major findings does McCarthy discover in answer to her research question(s)?

.........................................................................................................................

Dave Garrison, a college junior and the focus of the present study, was asked how he would advise incoming freshmen about writing for their college courses. His answer was both homely and familiar.

"I'd tell them," he said, "first you've got to figure out what your teachers want. And then you've got to give it to them if you're gonna get the grade." He paused a moment and added, "And that's not always so easy."

No matter how we teachers may feel about Dave's response, it does reflect his sensitivity to school writing as a social affair. Successful students are those who can, in their interactions with teachers during the semester, determine what constitutes appropriate texts in each classroom: the content, structures, language, ways of thinking, and types of evidence required in that discipline and by that teacher. They can then produce such a text. Students who cannot do this, for whatever reason—cultural, intellectual, motivational—are those who fail, deemed incompetent communicators in that particular setting. They are unable to follow what Britton calls the "rules of the game" in each class (1975, p. 76). As students go from one classroom to another they must play a wide range of games, the rules for which, Britton points out, include many conventions and presuppositions that are not explicitly articulated.

In this article, writing in college is viewed as a process of assessing and adapting to the requirements in unfamiliar academic settings. Specifically, the study examined how students figured out what constituted appropriate texts in their various courses and how they went about producing them. And, further, it examined what characterized the classroom contexts which enhanced or denied students' success in this process. This study was a 21-month project which focused on the writing experiences of one college student, Dave, in three of his courses, Freshman Composition in the spring of his freshman year, and, in his sophomore year, Introduction to Poetry in the fall and Cell Biology in the spring. Dave, a biology/pre-med major, was typical of students at his college in terms of his SAT scores (502 verbal; 515 math), his high school grades, and his white, middle-class family background.

> *Successful students are those who can, in their interactions with teachers during the semester, determine what constitutes appropriate texts in each classroom: the content, structures, language, ways of thinking, and types of evidence required in that discipline and by that teacher.*

As I followed Dave from one classroom writing situation to another, I came to see him, as he made his journey from one discipline to another, as a stranger in strange lands. In each new class Dave believed that the writing he was doing was totally unlike anything he had ever done before. This metaphor of a newcomer in a foreign country proved to be a powerful way of looking at Dave's behaviors as he worked to use the new languages in unfamiliar academic territories. Robert Heinlein's (1961) science fiction novel suggested this metaphor originally. But Heinlein's title is slightly different; his stranger is in a *single* strange land. Dave perceived himself to be in one strange land after another.

## Background to the Study

The theoretical underpinnings of this study are to be found in the work of sociolinguists (Hymes, 1972a, 1972b; Gumperz, 1971) and ethnographers of communication (Basso, 1974; Heath, 1982; Szwed, 1981) who assume that language processes must be understood in terms of the contexts in which they occur. All language use in this view takes place within speech communities and accomplishes meaningful social functions for people. Community members share characteristic "ways of speaking," that is, accepted linguistic, intellectual, and social conventions which have developed over time and govern spoken interaction. And "communicatively competent" speakers in every community recognize and successfully employ these "rules of use," largely without conscious attention (Hymes, 1972a, pp. xxiv–xxxvi).

A key assumption underlying this study is that writing, like speaking, is  7  a social activity. Writers, like speakers, must use the communication means considered appropriate by members of particular speech or discourse communities. And the writer's work, at the same time, may affect the norms of the community. As students go from one class to another, they must define and master the rules of use for written discourse in one classroom speech community after another. And their writing can only be evaluated in terms of that particular community's standards.

Some recent practical and theoretical work in writing studies has empha-  8  sized that writers' processes and products must be understood in terms of their contexts, contexts which are created as participants and settings interact (Bazerman, 1981; Bizzell, 1982; Cooper, 1986; Faigley, 1985; Whiteman, 1981). Studies of writing in non-academic settings have shown just how complex these writing environments are and how sophisticated the knowledge—both explicit and tacit—is that writers need in order to operate successfully in them (Odell & Goswami, 1985). And classrooms offer no less complex environments for writing. As Ericson (1982) points out, the classroom learning environment includes not only the teacher and the student, but also the subject matter structure, the social task structure, the actual enacted task, and the sequence of actions involved in the task. In addition, in many classrooms students may be provided with too few instructional supports to help them as they write (Applebee, 1984). Specifically, college classroom contexts for writing, Herrington (1985) argues, must be thought of in terms of several speech communities, viewed "in relation not only to a school community, but also to the intellectual and social conventions of professional forums within a given discipline" (p. 333). These overlapping communities influence the ways students think and write and interact in college classrooms, and will shape their notions of what it means to be, for example, an engineer or a biologist or a literary critic.

Research which has directly examined particular classroom contexts for  9  writing has provided insight into their diversity (Applebee, 1984; Calkins, 1980; Florio & Clark, 1982; Freedman, 1985; Herrington, 1985; Kantor, 1984). Though these studies suggest that an individual student is likely to encounter a number of quite different classroom writing situations, there is also evidence that individual student writers may employ consistent patterns across tasks as they interpret assignments, reason, and organize their knowledge (Dyson, 1984; Langer, 1985, 1986).

What has not yet been done, however, is to follow individual college students  10  as they progress across academic disciplines. In this study I offer information about how one college student fares in such a journey across the curriculum. That is, I detail how this student's behavior changed or remained constant across tasks in three classroom contexts and how those contexts influenced his success. Though this study is limited in scope to the experiences of a single student as he wrote for three college courses, it addresses questions central to much writing across the curriculum scholarship:

1. What are the tasks students encounter as they move from one course to another?
2. How do successful students interpret these tasks? Further, how do students determine what constitutes appropriate texts in that discipline and for that teacher, and how do they produce them?
3. What are the social factors in classrooms that foster particular writing behaviors and students' achievement of competence in that setting?

The ultimate aim of this study is to contribute to our understanding of how students learn to write in school. Findings from this study corroborate the notion that learning to write should be seen not only as a developmental process occurring within an individual student, but also as a social process occurring in response to particular situations.

## Methods

The research approach was naturalistic. I entered the study with no hypotheses to test and no specially devised writing tasks. Rather, I studied the writing that was actually being assigned in these classrooms, working to understand and describe that writing, how it functioned in each classroom, and what it meant to people there. My purpose was to get as rich a portrait as possible of Dave's writing and his classroom writing contexts. To this end I combined four research tools: observation, interviews, composing-aloud protocols, and text analysis. The data provided by the protocols and text analysis served to add to, crosscheck, and refine the data generated by observation and interviews. Using this triangulated approach (Denzin, 1978), I could view Dave's writing experiences through several windows, with the strengths of one method compensating for the limitations of another. 11

## The Courses

The college is a private, co-educational, liberal arts institution located in a large, northeastern city. Of its 2,600 students nearly half are business, accounting, and computer science majors. Yet over half of students' courses are required liberal arts courses, part of the core curriculum. Two of Dave's courses in this study are core courses: Freshman Composition and Introduction to Poetry. The third, Cell Biology, is a course taken by biology majors; it was Dave's third semester of college biology. All three were one-semester courses. In the descriptions of these courses that follow, I use pseudonyms for the teachers. 12

In Freshman Composition, which met twice a week for 90 minutes, students were required to write a series of five similarly structured essays on topics of their choice. These two- or four-page essays were due at regular intervals and 13 were graded by the professor, Dr. Jean Carter. Classes were generally teacher-led discussions and exercises, with some days allotted for students to work together in small groups, planning their essays or sharing drafts. Dr. Carter held one individual writing conference with each student at mid semester.

Introduction to Poetry is generally taken by students during their sopho-    14
more year, and it, like Freshman Composition, met for 90 minutes twice a week. In this class students were also required to write a series of similar papers. These were three-to-six page critical essays on poems that students chose from a list given them by their professor, Dr. Charles Forson. These essays, like those in Freshman Composition, were due at regular intervals and were graded by the professor. The Poetry classes were all lectures in which Dr. Forson explicated poems. However, one lecture early in the semester was devoted entirely to writing instruction.

Cell Biology, which Dave took in the spring of his sophomore year, met three    15
times a week, twice for 90-minute lectures and once for a three-hour lab. In this course, like the other two, students were required to write a series of similar short papers, three in this course. These were three-to-five page reviews of journal articles which reported current research in cell biology. Students were to summarize these articles, following the five-part scientific format in which the experiment was reported. They were then to relate the experiment to what they were doing in class. These reviews were graded by the professor, Dr. Tom Kelly.

## The Participants

The participants in this study included these three professors, Drs. Carter,    16
Forson, and Kelly. All were experienced college teachers who had taught these courses before. All talked willingly and with interest about the writing their students were doing, and both Dr. Carter and Dr. Forson invited me to observe their classes. Dr. Kelly said that it would not be productive for me to observe in his Cell Biology course because he spent almost no time talking directly about writing, so pressed was he to cover the necessary course material.

The student participants in this study were Dave and two of his friends. I    17
first met these three young men in Dr. Carter's Freshman Composition class where I was observing regularly in order to learn how she taught the course, the same one I teach at the college. As I attended that course week after week, I got to know the students who sat by me, Dave and his friends, and I realized I was no longer as interested in understanding what my colleague was teaching as I was in understanding what these students were learning. As the study progressed, my focus narrowed to Dave's experiences, although none of the three students knew this. The contribution of Dave's friends to this study was to facilitate my understanding of Dave. At first, in their Freshman Composition class, these students saw my role as a curious combination of teacher and fellow student. As the study progressed, my role became, in their eyes, that of teacher/inquirer, a person genuinely interested in understanding their writing. In fact, my increasing interest and ability to remember details of his writing experiences seemed at times to mystify and amuse Dave.

At the beginning of this study Dave Garrison was an 18-year-old freshman, 18
a biology pre-med major who had graduated the year before from a parochial
boys' high school near the college. He described himself as a "hands-on" person
who preferred practical application in the lab to reading theory in books.
Beginning in his sophomore year, Dave worked 13 hours a week as a techni-
cian in a local hospital, drawing blood from patients, in addition to taking a
full course load. He "loved" his hospital work, he said, because of the people
and the work, and also because difficulties with chemistry has made him worry
about being accepted in medical school. In the hospital he was getting an idea
of a range of possible careers in health care. The oldest of four children, Dave
lived at home and commuted 30 minutes to campus. He is the first person in
his family to go to college, though both of his parents enjoy reading, he said,
and his father writes in his work as an insurance salesman. When Dave and
I first met, he told me that he did not really like to write and that he was not
very good, but he knew that writing was a tool he needed, one that he hoped
to learn to use better.

### Instrumentation and Analytic Procedures

I collected data from February 1983, through November 1985. A detailed, 19
semester by semester summary is presented in Table 1.

### *Observation*

I observed in all three classes in order to help me understand the contexts for 20
writing in which Dave was working. During the observation I recorded field
notes about the classroom activities and interactions I was seeing, and as soon
as possible after the observation I read my notes and fleshed them out where
possible. Returning to fill out the notes was particularly important when I had
participated in the classroom activities as I did in Freshman Composition. In
that class I participated in Dave's small group discussions of drafts and did
the in-class writing exercises along with the students. I wrote my field notes
on the right-side pages of a spiral notebook, leaving the pages opposite free
for later notes.

### *Interviews*

I interviewed Dave, his two friends, and the three professors in order to elicit 21
their interpretations of the writing in each class. Questions were often suggested
by the participants' earlier comments or by emerging patterns in the data that
I wanted to pursue. Interviews with professors generally took place in their
offices and centered on their assignments, their purposes for having students
write, and the instructional techniques they used to accomplish their purposes.

The interviews with the students took place in my office on campus and 22
lasted one hour. I chose to interview Dave and his friends together in a series
of monthly interviews because I believed I could learn more from Dave in this
way. The students often talked to and questioned each other, producing more

**Table 1**

Data Collection Record

OBSERVATION

Freshman Composition (Freshman year. Spring, 1983)
- Participant observation in 1 class per week for 9 weeks.
- All class documents were collected and analyzed.

Introduction to Poetry (Sophomore year. Fall, 1983)
- Observation of the 90-minute lecture devoted to writing instruction.
- All class documents were collected and analyzed.

Cell Biology (Sophomore year. Spring, 1984)
- Observation of a lab session for 15 minutes.

INTERVIEWS

Freshman Composition
- Frequent conversations and 2 hour-long interviews with the professor, Dr. Carter.
- Frequent conversations with the students before and after class.

Poetry
- 1 hour-long interview with the professor, Dr. Forson.
- 4 hour-long interviews with the students at one-month intervals.

Cell Biology
- 2 hour-long interviews with the professor, Dr. Kelly.
- 4 hour-long interviews with the students at one-month intervals.

Junior Year Follow-up (Fall, 1984)
- 2 hour-long interviews with the students.

PROTOCOLS WITH RETROSPECTIVE INTERVIEWS

Freshman Composition
- 1 protocol and interview audiotaped as Dave composed the first draft of his fourth (next to last) essay.

Poetry
- 1 protocol and interview audiotaped as Dave composed the first draft of his third (last) paper.

Cell Biology
- 1 protocol and interview audiotaped as Dave composed the first draft of his third (last) review.

TEXT ANALYSIS

Freshman Composition
- Dave's fourth essay with the teacher's responses was analyzed. All drafts of all essays were collected.

Poetry
- Dave's third paper with the teacher's responses was analyzed. All drafts of all essays were collected.

Cell Biology
- Dave's third review with the teacher's responses was analyzed. All drafts of all essays were collected.

from Dave than I believe I ever could have gotten from one-on-one sessions with him. I did on two occasions, however, interview Dave alone for one hour when I wanted to question him in a particularly intensive way.

During all interviews I either took notes or made audiotapes which I later 23 transcribed and analyzed. All hour-long interviews with the students were taped.

## Analysis of the Observation and Interviews

I read and reread my field notes and the interview transcripts looking for patterns 24 and themes. These organized the data and suggested the salient features of writing in each context, its nature and meaning, and of Dave's experiences there. These patterns and themes then focused subsequent inquiry. I was guided in this process by the work of Gilmore and Glatthorn (1982) and Spradley (1979, 1980).

## Composing-Aloud Protocols and Retrospective Interviews

Late in each of the three semesters, I audiotaped Dave as he composed aloud 25 the first draft of a paper for the course we had focused on that semester. Dave wrote at the desk in my office, his pre-writing notes and his books spread out around him, and I sat nearby in a position where I could observe and make notes on his behaviors. The protocols lasted 30 minutes and were followed by a 30-minute retrospective interview in which I asked Dave to tell me more about the process he had just been through. I reasoned that in the retrospective interviews Dave's major concerns would be reemphasized, whereas the smaller issues that may have occupied him during composing would be forgotten. Because I followed Dave across time and collected all his written work for each assignment, I could examine what preceded and what followed the composed-aloud draft. I could thus see how the protocol draft related to Dave's entire composing process for a task.

The information provided by the protocols generally corroborated what he 26 had said in the interviews. Of particular interest, however, were the points at which the protocol data contradicted the interview data. These points spurred further inquiry. Though composing-aloud was never easy for Dave, who characterized himself as a shy person, he became more and more comfortable with it as the semesters progressed. He did produce, in each of the protocol sessions, a useful first draft for his final paper in each course.

## Analysis and Scoring of the Protocols and Retrospective Interviews

I analyzed the transcripts of the protocols and interviews, classifying and 27 counting what I called the *writer's conscious concerns*. These concerns were identified as anything the writer paid attention to during composing as expressed by (1) remarks about a thought or behavior or (2) observed behaviors. I chose to focus on Dave's conscious concerns because I expected that they would include a broad range of writing issues and that they would reflect the nature and emphases of the classrooms for which he was writing. The protocols would thus provide the supporting information I needed for this study. In identifying and classifying the writer's conscious concerns, I was guided by the work of Berkenkotter (1983), Bridwell (1980), Flower and Hayes (1981), Perl (1979), and Pianko (1979).

The analysis of the transcripts was carried out in a two-part process. First I read them several times and drew from them four general categories of writer's concerns, along with a number of subcategories. Then, using this scheme, I classified and counted the writer's remarks and behaviors. The first protocol was, of course, made during Dave's writing for Freshman Composition. The categories from that composing session were used again in analyzing the protocols from Poetry and Cell Biology. To these original categories were added new ones to describe the concerns Dave expressed as he composed for the later courses. In this way I could identify both concerns that were constant across courses as well as those that were specific to particular classroom writing situations.

I carried out the analyses of the protocols alone because of the understanding of the writing context that I brought to the task. I viewed this knowledge as an asset in identifying and classifying Dave's writing concerns. Thus, instead of agreement between raters, I worked for "confirmability" in the sense of agreement among a variety of information sources (Cuba, 1978, p. 17).

### Text Analysis

The final window through which I looked at Dave's writing experiences was text analysis. I analyzed the completed papers, with the professors' comments on them, of the assignments Dave had begun during the protocol sessions. If Dave is understood to be a stranger trying to learn the language in these classroom communities, then his teachers are the native-speaker guides who are training him. In this view, students and teachers in their written interactions share a common aim and are engaged in a cooperative endeavor. Their relationship is like that of people conversing together, the newcomer making trial efforts to communicate appropriately and the native speaker responding to them.

Thus, in order to examine the conventions of discourse in each classroom and get further insight into the interaction between Dave and his professors, I drew upon the model of conversation proposed by Grice (1975). Grice says that conversants assume, unless there are indications to the contrary, that they have a shared purpose and thus make conversational contributions "such as are required . . . by the accepted purpose or direction of the talk exchange in which they are engaged" (p. 45). He terms this the "Cooperative Principle." From the Cooperative Principle Grice derives four categories or conditions which must be fulfilled if people are to converse successfully: Quality, Quantity, Relation, and Manner. When conversation breaks down, it is because one or more of these conditions for successful conversation have been violated, either accidentally or intentionally. On the other hand, people conversing successfully fulfill these conditions, for the most part without conscious attention. Grice's four conditions for conversational cooperation provided my text analysis scheme. They are

1. *Quality.* Conversants must speak what they believe to be the truth and that for which they have adequate evidence.

2. *Quantity.* Conversants must give the appropriate amount of information, neither too much nor too little.
3. *Relation.* The information that conversants give must be relevant to the aims of the conversation.
4. *Manner.* The conversants must make themselves clear, using appropriate forms of expression.

In my examination of Dave's last paper for each course, I considered both his 32 work and his professor's response as conversational turns in which the speakers were doing what they believed would keep the Cooperative Principle in force. Dave's written turns were taken to display the discourse he believed was required in each setting so he would be deemed cooperative. I identified which of Grice's four conditions for successful conversation Dave paid special attention to fulfilling in each context. In this process I drew from the interview and protocol data as well as from the texts. I then counted and categorized Dave's teachers' written responses to his papers according to these same four conditions. A response was identified as an idea the teacher wanted to convey to Dave and could be as short as a single mark or as long as several sentences. Of particular interest were, first, the extent to which Dave and each teacher agreed upon what constituted cooperation, and, second, what the teacher pointed out as violations of the conditions of cooperation, errors that jeopardized the Cooperative Principle in that setting. Further, the form and language of each teacher's response provided insight into the ways of speaking in that particular discipline and classroom.

The text analysis data added to and refined my understanding of Dave's 33 classroom writing situations. And, conversely, my analyses of Dave's texts were informed by what I knew of the classroom writing situations. For this reason, I again elected to work alone with the texts.

Validity of the findings and interpretations in this study were ensured by 34 employing the following techniques. (1) Different types of data were compared. (2) The perspectives of various informants were compared. (3) Engagement with the subject was carried on over a long period of time during which salient factors were identified for more detailed inquiry. (4) External checks on the inquiry process were made by three established researchers who knew neither Dave nor the professors. These researchers read the emerging study at numerous points and questioned researcher biases and the bases for interpretations. (5) Interpretations were checked throughout with the informants themselves. (See Lincoln & Guba, 1985, for a discussion of validity and reliability in naturalistic inquiry.)

## Results and Discussion

Information from all data sources supports three general conclusions, two 35 concerning Dave's interpretation and production of the required writing tasks and one concerning social factors in the classrooms that influenced him as he wrote. First, although the writing tasks in the three classes were in many ways similar, Dave interpreted them as being totally different from each other and totally different from anything he had ever done before. This was evidenced in the interview, protocol, and text analysis data.

Second, certain social factors in Freshman Composition and Cell Biology       36
appeared to foster Dave's writing success in them. Observation and interview
data indicated that two unarticulated aspects of the classroom writing contexts
influenced his achievement. These social factors were (1) the functions that
writing served for Dave in each setting, and (2) the roles that participants and
students' texts played there. These social factors were bound up with what
Dave ultimately learned from and about writing in each class.

Third, Dave exhibited consistent ways of figuring out what constituted ap-       37
propriate texts in each setting, in his terms, of "figuring out what the teacher
wanted." Evidence from the interviews and protocols shows that he typically
drew upon six information sources, in a process that was in large part tacit.
These information sources included teacher-provided instructional supports,
sources Dave found on his own, and his prior knowledge.

## The Writing Assignments: Similar Tasks, Audiences, and Purposes

My analysis of the assignments, combined with the observation and interview       38
data, showed that the writing in the three classes was similar in many ways. It
was, in all cases, informational writing for the teacher-as-examiner, the type of
writing that Applebee found comprised most secondary school writing (1984).
More specifically, the task in Cell Biology was a summary, and in Freshman
Composition and Poetry it was analysis, closely related informational uses of
writing. Dave's audiences were identified as teacher-as-examiner by the fact
that all assignments were graded and that Dave, as he wrote, repeatedly wondered how his teacher would "like" his work.

Further similarities among the writing in the three courses included the pur-       39
pose that the professors stated for having their students write. All three said
that the purpose was not so much for students to display specific information,
but rather for students to become competent in using the thinking and language of their disciplines. Dr. Kelly, the biologist, stated this most directly when
he explained to me why he had his students write reviews of journal articles:
"I want students to be at ease with the vocabulary of Cell Biology and how
experiments are being done. . . . Students need to get a feeling for the journals,
the questions people are asking, the answers they're getting, and the procedures
they're using. It will give them a feeling for the excitement, the dynamic part
of this field. And they need to see that what they're doing in class and lab is
actually *used* out there." Students' summaries of journal articles in Cell Biology were, in other words, to get them started speaking the language of that
discourse community.

Learning the conventions of academic discourse was also the purpose of stu-       40
dents' writing in Freshman Composition. Dr. Carter was less concerned with
the content of the students' five essays than she was with their cohesiveness.
She repeatedly stated that what would serve these students in their subsequent
academic writing was the ability to write coherent prose with a thesis and subpoints, unified paragraphs, and explicitly connected sentences. In an interview
she said, "Ideas aren't going to do people much good if they can't find the

means with which to communicate them. . . . When these students are more advanced, and the ability to produce coherent prose is internalized, then they can concentrate on ideas. That's why I'm teaching the analytic paper with a certain way of developing the thesis that's generalizable to their future writing." Dr. Carter's goal was, thus, to help students master conventions of prose which she believed were central to all academic discourse.

And likewise in Poetry the purpose of students' writing was to teach them how people in literary studies think and write. In his lecture on writing, early in the semester, Dr. Forson stated this purpose and alluded to some of the conventions for thinking and writing in that setting. He told students, "The three critical essays you will write will make you say something quite specific about the meaning of a poem (your thesis) and demonstrate how far you've progressed in recognizing and dealing with the devices a poet uses to express his insights. You'll find the poem's meaning in the poem itself, and you'll use quotes to prove your thesis. Our concern here is for the *poem*, not the poet's life or era. Nor are your own opinions of the poet's ideas germane." 41

Dr. Forson then spent 20 minutes explaining the mechanical forms for quoting poetry, using a model essay that he had written on a poem by Robert Herrick. He ended by telling students that they should think of their peers as the audience for their essays and asking them not to use secondary critical sources from the library. "You'll just deal with what you now know and with the poetic devices that we discuss in class. Each group of poems will feature one such device: imagery, symbolism, and so forth. These will be the tools in your tool box." 42

Thus in all three courses Dave's tasks were informational writing for the teacher-as-examiner. All were for the purpose of displaying competence in using the ways of thinking and writing appropriate to that setting. And in all three courses Dave wrote a series of similar short papers, due at about three-week intervals, the assumption being that students' early attempts would inform their subsequent ones, in the sort of trial-and-error process that characterizes much language learning. Further, the reading required in Poetry and Cell Biology, the poems and the journal articles, were equally unfamiliar to Dave. We might expect, then, that Dave would view the writing for these three courses as quite similar, and, given an equal amount of work, he would achieve similar levels of success. This, however, is not what happened. 43

### Dave's Interpretation of the Writing Tasks

***The Writer's Concerns While Composing.*** In spite of the similarities among the writing tasks for the three courses, evidence from several sources shows that Dave interpreted them as being totally different from each other and totally different from anything he had ever done before. Dave's characteristic approach across courses was to focus so fully on the particular new ways of thinking and writing in each setting that commonalities with previous writing were obscured for him. And interwoven with Dave's conviction that the writing for these courses was totally dissimilar was his differing success in 44 them. Though he worked hard in all three courses, he made B's in Freshman Composition, Ds and Cs in Poetry, and As in Cell Biology.

The protocol data explain in part why the writing for these classes seemed   45
so different to Dave. Dave's chief concerns while composing for each course were very different. His focus in Freshman Composition was on textual coherence. Fifty-four percent of his expressed concerns were for coherence of thesis and subpoints, coherence within paragraphs, and sentence cohesion. By contrast, in Poetry, though Dave did mention thesis and subpoints, his chief concerns were not with coherence, but with the new ways of thinking and writing in that setting. Forty-four percent of his concerns focused on accurately interpreting the poem and properly using quotes. In Cell Biology, yet a new focus of concerns is evident. Seventy-two percent of Dave's concerns deal with the new rules of use in that academic discipline. His chief concerns in Biology were to accurately understand the scientific terms and concepts in the journal article and then to accurately rephrase and connect these in his own text, following the same five-part structure in which the published experiment was reported. It is no wonder that the writing for these classes seemed very different to Dave. As a newcomer in each academic territory, Dave's attention was occupied by the new conventions of interpretation and language use in each community. (See Table 2.)

The same preoccupations controlled his subsequent work on the papers. In   46
each course Dave wrote a second draft, which he then typed. In none of these second drafts did Dave see the task differently or make major changes. He is, in this regard, like the secondary students Applebee (1984) studied who were unable, without teacher assistance, to revise their writing in more than minor ways. And Dave revised none of these papers after the teachers had responded.

We can further fill out the pictures of Dave's composing for the three classes   47
by combining the protocol findings with the observation and interview data. In his first protocol session, in April of his freshman year, Dave composed the first draft of his fourth paper for Freshman Composition, an essay in which he chose to analyze the wrongs of abortion. To this session Dave brought an outline of this thesis and subpoints. He told me that he had spent only 30 minutes writing it the night before, but that the topic was one he had thought a lot about. As he composed, Dave was most concerned with and apparently very dependent upon, his outline, commenting on it, glancing at it, or pausing to study it 14 times during the 30 minutes of composing. Dave's next most frequently expressed concerns were for coherence at paragraph and sentence levels, what Dr. Carter referred to as coherence of mid-sized and small parts. These were the new "rules of use" in this setting. Dave told me that in high school he had done some "bits and pieces" of writing and some outlines for history, but that he had never before written essays like this. The total time Dave spent on his abortion essay was five hours.

In Dave's Poetry protocol session seven months later, in November of his   48
sophomore year, he composed part of the first draft of his third and last paper for that class, a six-page analysis of a poem called "Marriage" by contemporary poet Gregory Corso. To this session he brought two pages of notes and

**Table 2**

Concerns Expressed During Composing-Aloud Protocols and
Retrospective Interviews

| | PERCENT OF COMMENTS | | |
|---|---|---|---|
| | FRESHMAN COMPOSITION | POETRY | CELL BIOLOGY |
| Concerns Expressed in All Three Courses | | | |
| Features of Written Text | | | |
| Coherent thesis/ subpoint structure | 22 | 18 | 0 |
| Coherent paragraph structure | 15 | 13 | 3 |
| Cohesive sentences | 17 | 8 | 3 |
| Editing for mechanical correctness | 9 | 3 | 3 |
| Communication Situation (assignment, reader-writer roles, purpose) | 8 | 6 | 5 |
| On-Going Process | 18 | 6 | 12 |
| Emerging Text | 11 | 2 | 2 |
| Concerns Specific to Poetry | | | |
| Appropriately using quotes from poem | 0 | 32 | 0 |
| Making a correct interpretation of the poem | 0 | 12 | 0 |
| Concerns Specific to Cell Biology | | | |
| Following the 5-part scientific guidelines | 0 | 0 | 20 |
| Correctly understanding the content of the article being summarized | 0 | 0 | 37 |
| Rephrasing & connecting appropriate parts of the article | 0 | 0 | 15 |
| Total | 100 | 100 | 100 |
| Number of comments | 64 | 62 | 60 |

his *Norton Anthology of Poetry* in which he had underlined and written notes
in the margins beside the poem. He told me that he had spent four hours (of
an eventual total of 11) preparing to write: reading the poem many times and
finding a critical essay on it in the library. During his pre-writing and composing, Dave's primary concern was to get the right interpretation of the poem,
"the true meaning" as he phrased it. And as Dave wrote, he assumed that his
professor knew the true meaning, a meaning, Dave said, that "was there, but

not there, not just what it says on the surface." Further, Dave knew that he must argue his interpretation, using not his own but the poet's words; this was his second most frequently expressed concern.

As Dave composed, he appeared to be as tied to the poem as he had been    49
to his outline in Freshman Composition the semester before. He seemed to be almost *physically* attached to the *Norton Anthology* by his left forefinger as he progressed down the numbers he had marked in the margins. He was, we might say, tied to the concrete material, the "facts" of the poem before him. Dave never got his own essay structure; rather, he worked down the poem, explicating from beginning to end. In the retrospective interview he said, "I didn't really have to think much about my thesis and subs because they just come naturally now. . . . But anyway it's not like in Comp last year. Here my first paragraph is the introduction with the thesis, and the stanzas are the subpoints." Dave's preoccupation with the poem and the new conventions of interpreting and quoting poetry resulted in a paper that was not an analysis but a summary with some interpretation along the way. His focus on these new rules of use appeared to limit his ability to apply previously learned skills, the thesis-subpoint analytical structure, and kept him working at the more concrete summary level.

This domination by the concrete may often characterize newcomers' first    50
steps as they attempt to use language in unfamiliar disciplines (Williams, 1985). Dave's professor, Dr. Forson, seemed to be familiar with this phenomenon when he warned students in his lecture on writing: "You must remember that the poet ordered the poem. *You* order your essay with your own thesis and subtheses. Get away from 'Next. . . . Next'." But if Dave heard this in September, he had forgotten it by November. Dave's experience is consonant with Langer's (1984) finding that students who know more about a subject as they begin to write are likely to choose analysis rather than summary. And these students receive higher scores for writing quality as well.

In his writing for Cell Biology the following semester, Dave's concerns were    51
again focused on the new and unfamiliar conventions in this setting. Before writing his last paper, a four-page review of an experiment on glycoprotein reported in *The Journal of Cell Biology,* Dave spent three hours preparing. (He eventually spent a total of eight hours on the review.) He had chosen the article in the library from a list the professor had given to students and had then read the article twice, underlining it, making notes, and looking up the definitions of unfamiliar terms. To the protocol session Dave brought these notes, the article, and a sheet on which he had written what he called "Dr. Kelly's guidelines," the five-part scientific experiment format that Dr. Kelly wanted students to follow: Background, Objectives, Procedures, Results, and Discussion.

In his composing aloud, Dave's chief concerns in Biology were, as in Poetry    52
the semester before, with the reading, in this case the journal article. But here, unlike Poetry, Dave said the meaning was "all out on the table." In Poetry he had had to interpret meaning from the poem's connotative language; in Biology, by contrast, he could look up meanings, a situation with which Dave was far more comfortable. But as he composed for Biology, he was just as tied to the journal article as he had been to the poem or to his outline in previous

semesters. Dave paused frequently to consult the article, partially covering it at times so that his own paper was physically closer to what he was summarizing at that moment.

Dave's first and second most commonly expressed concerns during the Biology protocol session were for rephrasing and connecting parts of the article and for following Dr. Kelly's guidelines. These were, in essence, concerns for coherence and organization, what Dave was most concerned with in Freshman Composition. But the writing for Biology bore little relation in Dave's mind to what he had done in Freshman Composition. In Biology he was indeed concerned about his organization, but here it was the five-part scientific format he had been given, very different, it seemed to him, than the thesis/subpoint organization he had had to create for his freshman essays. In fact, until I questioned him about it at the end of the semester, Dave never mentioned the freshman thesis/subpoint structure. And the concerns for coherence at paragraph and sentence levels that had been so prominent as he wrote for Freshman Composition were replaced in Biology by his concern for rephrasing the article's already coherent text. In Freshman Composition Dave had talked about trying to get his sentences and paragraphs to "fit" or "flow" together. In Biology, however, he talked about trying to get the article into his own words, about "cutting," "simplifying," and "combining two sentences." Again, it is no wonder that Dave believed that this writing was totally new. It took one of Dave's friend's and my prodding during an interview to make Dave see that he had indeed written summaries before. Lots of them.

**The Nature of Cooperation in the Three Courses.**   The text analysis data provide further insight into why Dave perceived the writing in these courses as so dissimilar. The data provide information about what was, in Grice's terms, essential to maintaining the Cooperative Principle in these written exchanges. Analyses of the teachers' responses to Dave's papers show that his concerns in each class generally did match theirs. Put differently, Dave had figured out, though not equally well in all classes, what counted as "cooperation" in each context, and what he had to do to be deemed a competent communicator there. (See Table 3.)

Analysis of Dave's finished essay for Freshman Composition suggests that his concerns for textual coherence were appropriate. Dave knew that to keep

**Table 3**

Teachers' Responses to Dave's Papers

| | NUMBER OF RESPONSES INDICATING VIOLATIONS OF CONDITIONS FOR COOPERATION | | | | |
| --- | --- | --- | --- | --- | --- |
| | QUALITY | QUANTITY | RELEVANCE | MANNER | GRADE |
| Composition | 0 | 0 | 0 | 2 | 18/20 |
| Poetry | 8 | 0 | 0 | 11 | C+ |
| Cell Biology | 0 | 0 | 0 | 14 | 96 |

the Cooperative Principle in force in Dr. Carter's class, he had to pay special attention to fulfilling the condition of *Manner,* to making himself clear, using appropriate forms of expression. He succeeded and was deemed cooperative by Dr. Carter when she responded to his contribution with a telegraphic reply on the first page: "18/20." Apart from editing two words in Dave's text, she made no further comments, assuming that Dave and she shared an understanding of what constituted cooperation in her class and of what her numbers meant. (She had explained to students that she was marking with numbers that semester in an attempt to be more "scientific," and she had defined for them the "objective linguistic features of text" to which her numbers referred.) Dave did understand the grade and was, of course, very pleased with it.

In an interview, Dr. Carter explained her grade to me. "Though his content 56 isn't great," she said, "his paper is coherent, not badly off at any place. . . . He gave a fair number of reasons to develop his paragraphs, he restated his point at the end, and there is no wasted language. It's not perfectly woven together, but it's good." Though Dr. Carter mentioned the "reasons" Dave gave as evidence for his contentions, she was concerned not so much with their meaning as with their cohesiveness. Cooperation in this setting thus depended upon fulfilling the condition of *Manner.* Dave knew this and expected only a response to how well he had achieved the required form, not to the content of his essay.

In his writing for Poetry the following semester, Dave was attempting to 57 keep the Cooperative Principle in force by paying special attention to two conditions, *Quality* and *Manner.* That is, first he was attempting to say what was true and give adequate evidence, and, second, he was attempting to use proper forms of expression. This is evidenced in the interview and protocol as well as the text data. Analysis of Dr. Forson's 19 responses to Dave's paper shows that Dave's concerns matched those of his teacher, that Dave had figured out, though only in part, what counted as cooperation in that setting. Dr. Forson's responses all referred to violations of the same conditions Dave had been concerned with fulfilling, *Quality* and *Manner.* In seven of his eight marginal notes and in an endnote, Dr. Forson disagreed with Dave's interpretation and questioned his evidence, violations of the *Quality* condition. Mina Shaughnessy (1977) says that such failure to properly coordinate claims and evidence is perhaps the most common source of misunderstanding in academic prose. The ten mechanical errors that Dr. Forson pointed out were violations of the condition of *Manner,* violations which may jeopardize the Cooperative Principle in many academic settings. Dave's unintentional violations in Poetry of the *Quality* and *Manner* conditions jeopardized the Cooperative Principle in that exchange, resulting in the C+ grade.

Dr. Kelly's responses to Dave's writing in Biology were, like those in Freshman 58 Composition, much briefer than Dr. Forson's. Dr. Kelly's 14 marks or phrases all pointed out errors in form, unintentional violations of the Gricean condition of *Manner.* But these were apparently not serious enough to jeopardize the aims of the written conversation in Biology; Dave's grade on the review was 96.

This application of Grice's rubric for spoken conversation to student-teacher 59 written interaction gives further insight into the differences in these classroom contexts for writing. It is evident that successfully maintaining the Cooperative Principle was a more complicated business in Poetry than in Freshman Composition or Biology. In Biology, Dave was unlikely to violate the condition of *Quality*, as he did in Poetry, because he was only summarizing the published experiment and thus only had to pay attention to the condition of *Manner*. In Poetry, by contrast, he was called upon to take an interpretive position. This assumed that he had already summarized the poem. He had not. Thus his analytical essay took the form of a summary, as we have seen. In Biology, on the other hand, the writing was supposed to be a summary that then moved to a comparison of the summarized experiment to what was going on in class.

For Dave, the latter assignment was more appropriate. Novices in a field 60 may need the simpler summary assignment that helps them understand the new reading, the new language that they are being asked to learn. They may then be ready to move to analysis or critique. One wonders if Dave's success in Poetry would have been enhanced if he had been asked to write out a summary of the poem first. He could then have worked from that summary as he structured his own critical essay.

Similarly, in Freshman Composition, Dave was unlikely to violate the condi- 61 tion of *Quality*, to say something untrue or provide inadequate evidence for his claim. Though Dave did have to provide evidence for his subpoints, he was not evaluated for his content, and thus he concentrated on the condition of *Manner*. Further, the writing in Freshman Composition did not require Dave to master unfamiliar texts as it did in both Poetry and Biology. And for Dave the task of integrating new knowledge from his reading into his writing in those courses was his salient concern, as we have seen.

The apparent absence of attention paid in any of these classes to fulfilling 62 the conditions of *Quantity* or *Relation* is puzzling. Perhaps Dave's prior school writing experience had trained him to include the right amount of information (*Quantity*) and stay on topic (*Relation*).

The text analysis data, then, show that what counted as cooperation in these 63 three classes was indeed quite different. Dr. Forson, in his extensive responses, apparently felt it necessary to reteach Dave how people think and write in his community. This is understandable in light of Dave's numerous unintentional violations of the Cooperative Principle. Further, though Dr. Forson told students that he was being objective, finding the meaning of the poem in the text, he told me that his responses to students' papers were to argue his interpretation of the poem and, thus, to justify his grade.

The differing language and forms of these professors' responses probably 64 also added to Dave's sense that in each classroom he was in a new foreign land. Response style may well be discipline-specific as well as teacher-specific, with responses in literary studies generally more discursive than in the sciences. Further, Dr. Forson's responses were in the informal register typically used by an authority speaking to a subordinate (Freedman, 1984). His responses to Dave's paper included the following: "You misfire here." "I get this one. Hurrah for me!" "Pardon my writing. I corrected this in an automobile." The informality, and the word "corrected" in particular, leave little doubt about the authority differential between Dr. Forson and Dave. By contrast, Dave seemed to interpret the numerical grade in Biology as more characteristic of a conversation between equals. In a comment that may say more about their classroom interaction than their written interaction, Dave spoke of Dr. Kelly's brief responses to his review: "Yeah. He's like that. He treats us like adults. When we ask him questions, he answers us." Dave's apparent mixing of his spoken and written interaction with Dr. Kelly emphasizes the point that students' and teachers' writing for each other in classrooms is as fully contextualized as any other activity that goes on there.

Before Dave turned in his last papers in Poetry and Biology, I asked him   65
to speculate about the grade he would get. When he handed in his six-page paper on the Corso poem, "Marriage," on which he had spent eleven hours, he told me that he hoped for an A or B: "I'll be really frustrated on this one if the grade's not good after I've put in the time on it." A week later, however, he told me in a resigned tone and with a short laugh that he'd gotten a C+. By contrast, when he turned in his last review in Biology, he told me he knew he would get an A. When I questioned him, he replied, "I don't know how I know. I just do." And he was right: his grade was 96. Dave obviously understood far better what constituted cooperation in Biology than he did in Poetry.

## Social Aspects of the Classrooms That Influenced Dave's Writing

Why was Dave's success in writing in these classrooms so different? The   66
answers to this question will illuminate some of the dimensions along which school writing situations differ and thus influence student achievement. It would be a mistake to think that the differing task structure was the only reason that Dave was more successful in Biology and Freshman Composition than he was in Poetry. Assignments are, as I have suggested, only a small part of the classroom interaction, limited written exchanges that reflect the nature of the communication situation created by participants in that setting. Two unarticulated qualities in the contexts for writing in Freshman Composition and Biology appeared to foster Dave's success in those classes. These were (1) the social functions Dave's writing served for him in those classes, and (2) the roles played by participants and by students' texts there.

***The Functions Dave Saw His Writing as Accomplishing.***   It has been argued   67
that the social functions served by writing must be seen as an intrinsic part of the writing experience (Clark & Florio, 1983; Hymes, 1972a, 1972b; Scribner & Cole, 1981). Evidence from interviews and observations indicate that the writing in Freshman Composition and Biology was for Dave a meaningful social activity, meaningful beyond just getting him through the course. Further, Dave and his teachers in Freshman Composition and Biology mutually understood and valued those functions. This was not the case in Poetry. The data show a correlation not only between meaningful social functions served by the writing and Dave's success with it, but also between the writing's social meaning and Dave's ability to remember and draw upon it in subsequent semesters.

In Freshman Composition Dave's writing served four valuable functions for    68
him. He articulated all of these.

1. Writing to prepare him for future writing in school and career
2. Writing to explore topics of his choice
3. Writing to participate with other students in the classroom
4. Writing to demonstrate academic competence

In Biology Dave also saw his writing as serving four valuable functions:    69

1. Writing to learn the language of Cell Biology, which he saw as necessary
   to his career
2. Writing to prepare him for his next semester's writing in Immunology
3. Writing to make connections between his classwork and actual work
   being done by professionals in the field
4. Writing to demonstrate academic competence

Evidence from interviews and observation shows that Dr. Carter and Dr. Kelly
saw writing in their classes as serving the same four functions that Dave did.

On the other hand, in Poetry, though Dave's professor stated four func-    70
tions of student writing, Dave saw his writing as serving only one function
for him: writing to demonstrate academic competence. Dave, always the
compliant student, did say after he had received his disappointing grade in
Poetry that the writing in Poetry was probably good for him: "Probably any
kind of writing helps you." Though he may well be right, Dave actually saw
his writing for Poetry as serving such a limited function—evaluation of his
skills in writing poetry criticism for Dr. Forson—that he was not really convinced (and little motivated by the notion) that this writing would serve him
in any general way.

Dave contended that any writing task was easy or difficult for him accord-    71
ing to his interest in it. When I asked him what he meant by interesting, he said,
"If it has something to do with my life. Like it could explain something to me
or give me an answer that I could use now." Writing must have, in other words,
meaningful personal and social functions for Dave if it is to be manageable,
"easy," for him. These functions existed for Dave in Freshman Composition
and Biology, providing the applications and personal transaction with the material that may be generally required for learning and forging personal knowledge (Dewey, 1949; Polanyi, 1958).

Dave's Poetry class, however, served no such personally meaningful func-    72
tions. Six weeks after the Poetry course was finished, I asked Dave some further
questions about his last paper for that course, the discussion of the Corso poem
on which he had worked 11 hours. He could remember almost nothing about
it. When I asked him to speculate why this was, he said, "I guess it's because
I have no need to remember it." By contrast, when I asked Dave in the fall of
his junior year if his Cell Biology writing was serving him in his Immunology
course as he had expected, he said, "Yes. The teacher went over how to write
up our labs, but most of us had the idea anyway from last semester because
we'd read those journal articles. We were already exposed to it."

Of course the functions of his writing in Biology served Dave better than 73 those in Poetry in part because he was a biology major. The writing for Cell Biology fit into a larger whole: his growing body of knowledge about this field and his professional future. The material in Cell Biology was for Dave a comprehensible part of the discipline of Biology which was in turn a comprehensible part of the sciences. Dave was, with experience, gradually acquiring a coherent sense of the language of the discipline, how biologists think and speak and what it is they talk about. And his understanding of the language of biology was accompanied by an increasing confidence in his own ability to use it. Both of these are probably necessary foundations for later, more abstract and complex uses of the language (Piaget, 1952; Perry, 1970; Williams, 1985).

In the required one-semester Poetry class, however, the poems seemed to 74 Dave to be unrelated to each other except for commonly used poetic devices, and his writing about them was unrelated to his own life by anything at all beyond his need to find the "true meaning" and get an acceptable grade. Dave's different relationship to the languages of these disciplines was shown when he said, "In Biology I'm using what I've *learned*. It's just putting what I've learned on paper. But in Poetry, more or less each poem is different, so it's not *taught* to you. You just have to figure it out from that poem itself and hope Dr. Forson likes it." Nor, in Poetry, was Dave ever invited to make personally meaningful connections with the poems. And he never did it on his own, no doubt in part because he was so preoccupied with the new ways of thinking and speaking that he was trying to use.

In Freshman Composition the social function of writing that was perhaps 75 most powerful for Dave was writing to participate with other students in the classroom. In his peer writing group Dave, for the first time ever, discussed his writing with others. Here he communicated personal positions and insights to his friends, an influential audience for him. That an important social function was served by these students' work with each other is suggested by their clear memory, a year and a half later, both of their essays and of each others' reactions to them.

The four social functions that Dave's writing in Freshman Composition accomplished for him enhanced his engagement with and attitude toward the 76 writing he did in that class. This engagement is reflected in Dave's memory not only of his essays and his friends' reactions to them, but also in his memory and use of the ideas and terms from that course. When Dave talked about his writing during his sophomore and junior years, he used the process terms he had learned in Freshman Composition: prewriting, revision, and drafts. He also used other language he had learned as a freshman, speaking at times about his audience's needs, about narrowing his topic, about connecting his sentences, providing more details, and choosing his organizational structure. This is not to say that Dave had mastered these skills in every writing situation nor that he always accurately diagnosed problems in his own work. In fact, we know that he did not. It is to say, however, that Dave did recognize and could talk about some of the things that writing does involve in many situations. Thus, the value of this course for Dave lay not so much in the thesis/subpoint essay structure. Rather, Dave had, as a result of his experiences in Freshman Composition, learned that writing is a process that can be talked about, managed, and controlled.

Thus the social functions that writing served for Dave in each class were viewed as an intrinsic part of his writing experiences there. Where these functions were numerous and mutually understood and valued by Dave and his teacher, Dave was more successful in figuring out and producing the required discourse. And then he remembered it longer. In Poetry, where his writing served few personally valued ends, Dave did less well, making a C on the first paper, a D on the second, and a C+ on the third. It should be noted, in addition, that grades themselves serve a social function in classrooms: defining attitudes and roles. Dave's low grades in Poetry probably further alienated him from the social communication processes in that classroom community and helped define his role there.

*The Roles Played by the Participants and by Students' Texts.* Other social aspects of these classroom contexts for writing which affected Dave's experiences were the roles played by the people and texts in them. Such roles are tacitly assigned in classroom interaction and create the context in which the student stranger attempts to determine the rules of language use in that territory. Here we will examine (1) Dave's role in relation to the teacher, (2) Dave's role in relation to other students in the class, and (3) the role played by students' texts there.

*Dave's Role in Relation to the Teacher.* This is a particularly important role relationship in any classroom because it tacitly shapes the writer-audience relation that students use as they attempt to communicate appropriately. In all three classes Dave was writing for his teachers as pupil to examiner. However, data from several sources show that there were important variations in the actual "enactments" (Goffman, 1961) of this role-relationship.

In Composition, both Dave and his professor played the role of writer. Throughout the semester Dr. Carter talked about what and how she wrote, the long time she spent in prewriting activities, the eight times she typically revised her work, and the strategies she used to understand her audience in various situations. She spoke to students as if she and they were all writers working together, saying such things as "I see some of you write like I do," or "Let's work together to shape this language." And, as we have seen, she structured the course to provide opportunities for students to play the role of writer in their peer groups. She also asked them to describe their writing processes for several of their essays. Dave told me in an interview during his junior year, "In high school I couldn't stand writing, but in Comp I started to change because I knew more what I was doing. I learned that there are steps you can go through, and I learned how to organize a paper." As a freshman, Dave understood for the first time something of what it feels like to be a writer.

In Biology both Dave and his teacher, Dr. Kelly, saw Dave as playing the role of newcomer, learning the language needed for initiation into the profession. Dr. Kelly played the complementary role of experienced professional who was training Dave in the ways of speaking in that discipline, ways they both assumed Dave would learn in time.

In Poetry, on the other hand, Dave played the role of outsider in relationship to his teacher, the insider who knew the true meanings of poetry. And Dave stayed the outsider, unable ever to fully get the teacher's "true meaning." This outsider/insider relationship between Dave and Dr. Forson was created by a number of factors: (1) Their spoken and written interaction, (2) the few meaningful social functions served for Dave by the writing in that class, (3) the demanding nature of the analytic task, combined with (4) the limited knowledge Dave commanded in that setting, (5) the limited number of effective instructional supports, and (6) the low grades Dave got, which further alienated him from the communication processes in that class. (To the instructional supports provided in Poetry we will return below.) Because Dave's outsider role was not a pleasant one for him, he seemed increasingly to separate his thinking from his writing in Poetry, saying several times that he had the right ideas, the teacher just did not like the way he wrote them.

**Dave's Role in Relationship to Other Students.**   Students' relationships with each other, like those between students and teachers, are created as students interact within the classroom structures the teacher has set up. These classroom structures grow out of teachers' explicit and tacit notions about writing and learning. What specifically were the relationships among students in Freshman Composition, Biology, and Poetry?

In Composition, as we have seen, students shared their writing and responded to each other's work. The classroom structure reflected Dr. Carter's perhaps tacit notion that writing is a social as well as intellectual affair. However, in neither Poetry nor Biology was time built into the class for students to talk with each other about their writing. Dave lamented this as he wrote for Poetry early in his sophomore year, because, he said, he now realized how valuable the small group sessions had been in Freshman Composition the semester before.

In Biology, Dave told me students did talk informally about the journal articles they had selected and how they were progressing on their summaries. Dr. Kelly, who circulated during lab, was at times included in these informal talks about writing. And it is no surprise that students discussed their writing in this way in Biology in light of Dr. Kelly's notions about writing. It is, he believes, an essential part of what scientists do. He told me that it often comes as a rude shock to students that the way biologists survive in the field is by writing. He said, "These students are bright, and they can memorize piles of facts, but they're not yet good at writing. They know what science *is*," he told me, "but they don't know what scientists *do*." Thus, writing up research results is seen by Dr. Kelly as an integral part of a biologist's lab work. No wonder his students talked about it.

In Poetry, however, there was little talk of any kind among students. Classes were primarily lectures where Dr. Forson explicated poems and explained poetic devices. Only occasionally did he call on one of the 22 students for an opinion. This lack of student interaction in Poetry was in line with the image of the writer that Dr. Forson described for students, an image that may be widely shared in literary studies: A person alone with his or her books and thoughts. Dr. Forson did, however, tell students that he himself often got his ideas for writing from listening to himself talk about poems in class. Yet, in conversation with me, he said that he did not want students discussing the poems and their writing with each other because he feared they would not think for themselves. Dave picked up on this idea very clearly. It was not until the fall of his junior year that he admitted to me that he and his girlfriend had worked together on their papers. They had discussed the interpretations of the poems and how they might best write them, but, he told me, they had been careful to choose different poems to write about so that Dr. Forson wouldn't know they had worked together. This absence of student interaction in Poetry may have contributed to the outsider role that Dave played in that class.

Throughout this study I was amazed at the amount of talk that goes on all the time outside class among students as they work to figure out the writing requirements in various courses. What Dave's experience in Poetry may suggest is that where student collaboration in writing is not openly accepted, it goes on clandestinely. 87

**The Roles Played by Students' Texts.**   What were students' texts called and how were they handled? Interview and observation data show that students' texts were treated quite differently in these three courses, and this affected how Dave saw the assignments, and, perhaps more important, how he saw himself as writer. 88

In Freshman Composition Dave wrote what he referred to as "essays"; in Biology, "reviews"; in Poetry, "papers." This latter term is commonly used, of course, but it is one that Emig (1983, p. 173) says suggests a low status text: "Paper"—as if there were no words on the sheet at all. In Poetry the high status texts, the ones that were discussed and interpreted, were the poems. Students' works were just more or less successful explications of those. Furthermore, in Poetry the one model essay the students read was written by the teacher. Though students were told they should think of their peers as their audience, in fact they never read each other's essays at all. Students' texts were, rather, passed only between student and teacher as in a private conversation. 89

In Biology, student texts enjoyed a higher status. Excellent student reviews were posted and students were encouraged to read them; they were to serve as models. Some student writers were thus defined as competent speakers in this territory, and the message was clear to Dave: This was a language that he too could learn given time and proper training. 90

And in Freshman Composition, of course, student texts were the *objects* of study. The class read good and flawed student texts from former semesters and from their own. This not only helped Dave with his writing, it also dignified student writing and elevated his estimation of his own work. Student texts were not, in short, private affairs between teacher and student; they were the subject matter of this college course. 91

Thus the roles that were enacted by teachers, students, and students' texts   92
were quite different in each classroom and were an integral part of Dave's
writing experiences there. The participants' interaction and the social functions that writing serves are important factors working to create the communication situation. And this communication situation, it has been suggested, is
the fundamental factor shaping the success of writing instruction (Langer &
Applebee, 1984, p. 171).

### The Information Sources Dave Drew Upon

In a process that was in large part tacit, Dave drew upon six sources for infor-   93
mation about what constituted successful writing in Freshman Composition,
Poetry, and Biology. These included teacher-provided instructional supports,
sources Dave found on his own, and his prior experience. Many of these have
been mentioned above. They are summarized in Table 4.

Of particular interest are the information sources Dave drew upon (or failed   94
to draw upon) in Poetry, the course in which the writing assignment was the

### Table 4

Information Sources Dave Drew Upon in Assessing Required Discourse

| INFORMATION SOURCES | FRESHMAN COMPOSITION | POETRY | CELL BIOLOGY |
|---|---|---|---|
| What teachers said in class about writing | Constant lectures & exercises about process & products | • One lecture<br>• General statements to the class about their papers when returning them | • Ten minutes giving "guidelines" when returning 1st set of reviews of reviews<br>• Informal comments in lab |
| Model texts | Many, including flawed models | • One, written by teacher<br>• One, written by professional (from library) | • The articles being summarized served as models.<br>• Posted student reviews |
| Talk with other students | Frequent groups in class | With friend outside class | Informal, in class |
| Teachers' written responses to writing | Read responses & revised early essays accordingly | Read. No revision required | Read. No revision required |
| Dave's prior experience | The extent to which Dave drew upon prior experience is difficult to say. In each class he believed he had no prior experience to draw from. However, we know he had had related prior experience. | | |
| Personal talk with teacher | One conference with teacher | None | None |

most demanding and in which Dave did least well in assessing and producing the required discourse. The information source that Dr. Forson intended to be most helpful to students, the instructional support on which he spent a great deal of time, was his response to their papers. However, his extensive comments did not help Dave a great deal in learning how to communicate in that setting. Dave said that the comments on his first paper did help him some with his second, but he really did not refer to Dr. Forson's responses on the second paper as he wrote the third. Nor did Dave use the comments on the third paper when preparing for the essay question on the final exam. Dr. Forson required no revision in direct response to his comments, and the expected carry-over of his responses from one paper to the next did not occur. Rather, Dave repeated similar mistakes again and again. The assumption that trial and error will improve students' writing across a series of similar tasks did not hold true for Dave's work in Poetry.

Neither was the model text in Poetry, Dr. Forson's analysis of the Herrick 95 poem that he went over in lecture, as useful an information source for Dave as Dr. Forson had hoped it would be. Dave told me that though he had looked at Dr. Forson's model critical essay as he wrote his first paper, it had not helped him a great deal. "Seeing how someone else did it," he said, "is a lot different than doing it yourself." In Freshman Composition and Biology, however, the model texts, both excellent and flawed ones, were more numerous. And in Biology, the model provided by the article Dave was summarizing was virtually inescapable. Model texts are, it seems reasonable, particularly important to newcomers learning the conventions of discourse in a new academic territory.

An information source which Dave was not adept at using in any course 96 was direct questioning of the professor, the native-speaker expert in each setting. Dave never voluntarily questioned a teacher, though in October of his sophomore year, when he was doing poorly in Poetry, he did make an attempt to speak with Dr. Forson at his office. But when Dr. Forson was not there, Dave waited only a short time and then left—relieved, he said. He did not return. In Freshman Composition, however, Dave was required to interact with Dr. Carter individually in his mid-semester conference. That interview provided an additional information source upon which Dave could draw as he assessed and adapted to the writing requirements in that class.

## Discussion

What, then, can we learn from Dave's experiences? First, this study adds to 97 existing research which suggests that school writing is not a monolithic activity or global skill. Rather, the contexts for writing may be so different from one classroom to another, the ways of speaking in them so diverse, the social meanings of writing and the interaction patterns so different, that the courses may be for the student writer like so many foreign countries. These differences were apparent in this study not only in Dave's perceptions of the courses but in his concerns while writing and in his written products.

Second, the findings of this study have several implications for our under-  98
standing of writing development. This study suggests that writing development
is, in part, context-dependent. In each new classroom community, Dave in many
ways resembled a beginning language user. He focused on a limited number of
new concerns, and he was unable to move beyond concrete ways of thinking
and writing, the facts of the matter at hand. Moreover, skills mastered in one
situation, such as the thesis-subpoint organization in Freshman Composition,
did not, as Dave insisted, automatically transfer to new contexts with differing
problems and language and differing amounts of knowledge that he controlled.
To better understand the stages that students progress through in achieving
competence in academic speech communities, we need further research.

Dave's development across his freshman and sophomore years, where he  99
was repeatedly a newcomer, may also be viewed in terms of his attitude toward
writing. Evidence over 21 months shows that his notion of the purpose of
school writing changed very little. Though there were, as we have seen, other
functions accomplished for Dave by his writing in Freshman Composition and
Biology, he always understood the purpose of his school writing as being primarily to satisfy a teacher-examiner's requirements. A change that did occur,
however, was Dave's increased understanding of some of the activities that
writers actually engage in and an increased confidence in his writing ability.
As a freshman, he had told me that he did not like to write and was not very
good, but by the fall of his junior year he sounded quite different. Because of
a number of successful classroom experiences with writing, and an ability to
forget the less successful ones, Dave told me, "Writing is no problem for me. At
work, in school, I just do it."

Whether Dave will eventually be a mature writer, one who, according to  100
Britton's (1975) definition, is able to satisfy his own purposes with a wide range
of audiences, lies beyond the scope of this study to determine. We do know,
however, that Dave did not, during the period of this study, write for a wide
range of audiences. Nor did he, in these classes, define his own audiences, purposes, or formats, though he did in Freshman Composition choose his topics
and in Poetry and Biology the particular poems and articles he wrote about.
What this study suggests is that college undergraduates in beginning-level
courses may have even less opportunity to orchestrate their own writing occasions than do younger students. Balancing teachers' and students' purposes
is indeed difficult in these classrooms where students must, in 14 weeks, learn
unfamiliar discourse conventions as well as a large body of new knowledge.

The findings of this study have several implications for the teaching of  101
writing. They suggest that when we ask what students learn from and about
writing in classrooms, we must look not only at particular assignments or at
students' written products. We must also look at what they learn from the social contexts those classrooms provide for writing. In Freshman Composition,
Dave learned that writer was a role he could play. In Biology, writing was for
Dave an important part of a socialization process; he was the newcomer being initiated into a profession in which, he learned, writing counts for a great
deal. From his writing in Poetry, Dave learned that reading poetry was not for

him and that he could get through any writing task, no matter how difficult or foreign. This latter is a lesson not without its value, of course, but it is not one that teachers hope to teach with their writing assignments.

This study also raises questions about how teachers can best help student 102 "strangers" to become competent users of the new language in their academic territory. Because all writing is context-dependent, and because successful writing requires the accurate assessment of and adaptation to the demands of particular writing situations, perhaps writing teachers should be explicitly training students in this assessment process. As Dave researched the writing requirements in his classroom, he drew upon six information sources in a process that was for him largely tacit and unarticulated. But Dave was actually in a privileged position in terms of his potential for success in this "figuring out" process. He had, after all, had years of practice writing in classrooms. Furthermore, he shared not only ethnic and class backgrounds with his teachers, but also many assumptions about education. Students from diverse communities may need, even more than Dave, explicit training in the ways in which one figures out and then adapts to the writing demands in academic contexts.

For teachers in the disciplines, "native-speakers" who may have used the 103 language in their discipline for so long that it is partially invisible to them, the first challenge will be to appreciate just how foreign and difficult their language is for student newcomers. They must make explicit the interpretive and linguistic conventions in their community, stressing that theirs is one way of looking at reality and not reality itself. As Fish (1980) points out, "The choice is never between objectivity and interpretation, but between an interpretation that is unacknowledged as such and an interpretation that is at least aware of itself" (p. 179). Teachers in the disciplines must then provide student newcomers with assignments and instructional supports which are appropriate for first steps in using the language of their community. Designing appropriate assignments and supports may well be more difficult when the student stranger is only on a brief visit in an academic territory, as Dave was in Poetry, or when the student comes from a community at a distance farther from academe than Dave did.

Naturalistic studies like the present one, Geertz says, are only "another 104 country heard from . . . nothing more or less." Yet, "small facts speak to large issues" (1973, p. 23). From Dave's story, and others like it which describe actual writers at work in local settings, we will learn more about writers' processes and texts and how these are constrained by specific social dynamics. Our generalizations and theories about writing and about how people learn to write must, in the final analysis, be closely tied to such concrete social situations.

## References

Applebee, A. (1984). *Contexts for learning to write: Studies of secondary school instruction.* Norwood, NJ: Ablex.

Basso, K. (1974). The ethnography of writing. In R. Bauman and J. Sherzer (Eds.), *Explorations in the ethnography of speaking* (pp. 425–432). New York: Cambridge University Press.

Bazerman, C. (1981). What written knowledge does: Three examples of academic discourse. *Philosophy of the Social Sciences, 11*, 361–387.

Berkenkotter, C. (1983). Decisions and revisions: The planning strategies of a publishing writer. *College Composition and Communication, 34*, 156–169.

Bizzell, P. (1982). Cognition, convention, and certainty: What we need to know about writing. *PRE/TEXT, 3*, 213–243.

Bridwell, L. (1980). Revising strategies in twelfth grade students' transactional writing. *Research in the Teaching of English, 14*, 197–222.

Britton, J., Burgess, T., Martin, N., McLeod, A., & Rosen, H. (1975). *The development of writing abilities 11–18.* London: Macmillan.

Calkins, L. (1980). Research update: When children want to punctuate: Basic skills belong in context. *Language Arts, 57*, 567–573.

Clark, C., & Florio, S., with Elmore, J., Martin, J., & Maxwell, R. (1983). Understanding writing instruction: Issues of theory and method. In P. Mosenthal, L. Tamor, & S. Walmsley (Eds.), *Research on writing: Principles and methods* (pp. 236–264). New York: Longman.

Cooper, M. (1986). The ecology of writing. *College English, 48*, 364–375.

Denzin, N. (1978). *Sociological methods.* New York: McGraw-Hill.

Dewey, J. (1949). *The child and the curriculum and the school and society.* Chicago: University of Chicago Press.

Dyson, A. (1984). Learning to write/learning to do school: Emergent writers' interpretations of school literacy tasks. *Research in the Teaching of English, 18*, 233–264.

Emig, J. (1983). *The web of meaning: Essays on writing, teaching, learning, and thinking.* Upper Montclair, NJ: Boynton/Cook.

Ericson, F. (1982). Taught cognitive learning in its immediate environments: A neglected topic in the anthropology of education. *Anthropology & Education Quarterly, 13*(2), 148–180.

Faigley, L. (1985). Nonacademic writing: The social perspective. In L. Odell & D. Goswami (Eds.), *Writing in nonacademic settings* (pp. 231–248). New York: Guilford Press.

Fish, S. (1980). Interpreting the Variorium. In J. Tompkins (Ed.), *Reader response criticism: From formalism to post-structuralism.* Baltimore: Johns Hopkins University Press.

Florio, S., & Clark, C. (1982). The functions of writing in an elementary classroom. *Research in the Teaching of English, 16*, 115–130.

Flower, L., & Hayes, J. (1981). The pregnant pause: An inquiry into the nature of planning. *Research in the Teaching of English, 15*, 229–244.

Freedman, S. (1984). The registers of student and professional expository writing: Influences on teachers' responses. In R. Beach & L. Bridwell (Eds.), *New directions in composition research* (pp. 334–347). New York: Guilford Press.

Freedman, S. (1985). *The acquisition of written language: Response and revision.* New York: Ablex.

Geertz, C. (1973). *The interpretation of cultures.* New York: Basic Books.

Gilmore, P., & Glatthorn, A. (1982). *Children in and out of school: Ethnography and education.* Washington, DC: Center for Applied Linguistics.

Goffman, E. (1961). *Encounters: Two studies in the sociology of interaction.* New York: Bobbs-Merrill.

Grice, H. (1975). *Logic and conversation.* 1967 William James Lectures, Harvard University. Unpublished manuscript, 1967. Excerpt in Cole and Morgan (Eds.), *Syntax and semantics, Vol. III: Speech acts* (pp. 41–58). New York: Academic Press.

Guba, E. (1978). *Toward a method of naturalistic inquiry in educational evaluation.* Los Angeles: Center for the Study of Evaluation, University of California at Los Angeles.

Gumperz, J. (1971). *Language in social groups.* Stanford, CA: Stanford University Press.

Heath, S. B. (1982). Ethnography in education: Defining the essentials. In P. Gilmore & A. Glatthorn (Eds.), *Children in and out of school: Ethnography and education* (pp. 33–55). Washington, DC: Center for Applied Linguistics.

Heinlein, R. (1961). *Stranger in a strange land*. New York: Putnam.

Herrington, A. (1985). Writing in academic settings: A study of the contexts for writing in two college chemical engineering courses. *Research in the Teaching of English, 19*, 331–359.

Hymes, D. (1972a). Introduction. In C. Cazden, V. P. John, & D. Hymes (Eds.), *Functions of language in the classroom* (pp. xi–lxii). New York: Teachers College Press.

Hymes, D. (1972b). Models of the interaction of language and social life. In J. Gumperz & D. Hymes (Eds.), *Directions in sociolinguistics* (pp. 35–71). New York: Holt, Rinehart, & Winston.

Kantor, K. (1984). Classroom contexts and the development of writing intuitions: An ethnographic case study. In R. Beach & L. Bridwell (Eds.), *New directions in composition research* (pp. 72–94). New York: Guilford.

Langer, J. (1984). The effects of available information on responses to school writing tasks. *Research in the Teaching of English, 18*, 27–44.

Langer, J. (1985). Children's sense of genre: A study of performance on parallel reading and writing tasks. *Written Communication, 2*, 157–188.

Langer, J. (1986). Reading, writing, and understanding: An analysis of the construction of meaning. *Written Communication, 3*, 219–267.

Langer, J., & Applebee, A. (1984). Language, learning, and interaction: A framework for improving the teaching of writing. In A. Applebee (Ed.), *Contexts for learning to write: Studies of secondary school instruction* (pp. 169–182). Norwood, NJ: Ablex.

Lincoln, Y., & Guba, E. (1985). *Naturalistic inquiry*. Beverly Hills, CA: Sage Publications.

Odell, L., & Goswami, D. (1985). *Writing in nonacademic settings*. New York: Guilford Press.

Perl, S. (1979). The composing process of unskilled college writers. *Research in the Teaching of English, 13*, 317–336.

Perry, W. G. (1970). *Forms of intellectual and ethical development in the college years*. New York: Holt, Rinehart, and Winston.

Piaget, J. (1952). *The origins of intelligence in children*. New York: International Universities Press.

Pianko, S. (1979). A description of the composing processes of college freshman writers. *Research in the Teaching of English, 13*, 5–22.

Polanyi, M. (1958). *Personal knowledge: Towards a post-critical philosophy*. Chicago: University of Chicago Press.

Scribner, S. & Cole, M. (1981). Unpackaging literacy. In M. F. Whiteman (Ed.), *Variation in writing: Functional and linguistic-cultural differences* (pp. 71–88). Hillsdale, NJ: Lawrence Erlbaum.

Shaughnessy, M. (1977). *Errors and expectations*. New York: Oxford University Press.

Spradley, J. (1979). *The ethnographic interview*. New York: Holt, Rinehart and Winston.

Spradley, J. (1980). *Participant observation*. New York: Holt, Rinehart and Winston.

Szwed, J. (1981). The ethnography of literacy. In M. F. Whiteman (Ed.), *Variation in writing: Functional and linguistic-cultural differences* (pp. 13–23). Hillsdale, NJ: Lawrence Erlbaum.

Whiteman, M. F. (1981). *Variation in writing: Functional and linguistic-cultural differences*. Hillsdale, NJ: Lawrence Erlbaum.

Williams, J. (1985, March). *Encouraging higher order reasoning through writing in all disciplines*. Paper presented at the Delaware Valley Writing Council-PATHS Conference, Philadelphia.

## Questions for Discussion and Journaling

1. What are McCarthy's research questions? What research methods did she use to find answers to these questions? What were her primary findings? How might her findings have been shaped by her methods? What other methods might she have used, and how might they have altered her findings?

2. McCarthy analyzed Dave's experiences using Grice's "Cooperative Principle." Explain what this principle is and how it helped McCarthy understand Dave's struggles and successes.

3. Why did Dave struggle in his poetry class? What might Dave and his teacher have done to improve Dave's chances of success in that class?

4. In this chapter, John Swales described the importance of discourse communities for the ways that people do—and don't—use language. How does the concept of discourse community shed light on Dave's experiences?

5. How does Dave's experience writing in college compare to your own? What aspects of writing in college frustrate or puzzle you? What has been hardest for you about writing in college? Why?

6. Do you find the same variance in expectations of your writing from class to class that Dave experiences, or are the expectations you encounter more consistent? What have been your strategies so far for handling any differing expectations you're finding? Does McCarthy's work give you any ideas for different strategies?

## Applying and Exploring Ideas

1. For several weeks, keep a writer's journal about your experiences writing in different classrooms. What are you asked to write? What instruction are you given? What feedback are you given? Do you talk with others about the assignments? What genres are you asked to write? How well do you do? Do you understand the grades and comments your teachers give you? At the end of the weeks of journaling, write about your findings and share them with the class.

2. Write a plan for setting up a study like McCarthy's that examines your own experiences across classrooms. Draw on Swales to help you think about designing the study. What do you want to know? What data will you collect and analyze? Write a two-page paper in which you outline the answers to these questions. Note that you aren't *conducting* a study, just imagining how you would *plan* to do so.

# Coaches Can Read, Too:
## AN ETHNOGRAPHIC STUDY OF A FOOTBALL COACHING DISCOURSE COMMUNITY

### SEAN BRANICK

## Framing the Reading

Sean Branick was a first-year student in Elizabeth Wardle's composition class at the University of Dayton when he wrote this paper. He was enrolled in a special pilot two-semester composition sequence that allowed him to work on this ethnography for a full academic year. His paper was chosen as one of the best from two such courses and published in a one-time-only university publication called *Looking for Literacy: Reporting the Research*. Branick's interest in the discourse community of football coaches arose from his own experience as a high school football player and as a student coach in college. He later served as a student football coach at the University of Hawai'i at Manoa, a defensive line intern at Ohio State University, and is now student teaching.

We are including Branick's paper here because he applies Swales's concept of discourse community to a community that many people do not immediately think of as including literacy: football. He begins by explaining the characteristics of effective football coaches, and then explains in detail why he believes that coaches do constitute a discourse community. But he doesn't stop there. He goes on to identify some special "literacies" that he believes effective coaches possess.

## Getting Ready to Read

*Before you read*, do the following activity:

- Ask yourself whether you agree that football coaches constitute a discourse community according to Swales's definition.

*As you read*, consider the following question:

- In his introduction, Branick includes the three "moves" that Swales identifies in his CARS model of research introductions (see pp. 12–15)—establishing the territory, establishing a niche, and explaining how he will fill that niche. Can you identify where Branick makes those moves?

The profession of coaching football is one of the most influential profes- 1 sions that exists in today's world. It is a profession essential to the game whether it is a third-grade team or a pro team. Coaches may range from parents volunteering with a child's youth program to people who dedicate every waking hour to the game. Coaches are made up of both everyday Joes and legends that will live in memory as long as the game is played. It is a profession that requires putting the athletes first: "The main responsibility of the coach is to enable their athletes to attain levels of performance not otherwise achievable" (Short "Role," S29). It is a profession very visible to the public yet it has many behind-the-scenes factors that may be often overlooked that directly relate to success. Among these are the idea of goal-focused coaching, coaching with confidence, and the characteristics of effective coaches.

## Goal-Focused Coaching

Whether on the football field or off the football field, people have always  2
used the process of setting and chasing goals to achieve a desired outcome. A goal is often the universal starting point in many things, including football. Anthony Grant, a sport psychologist, takes an in-depth look at the process of effectively setting a goal in order to achieve a desired result. He talks about how the coach should help facilitate the entire process of using goals, which consists of the following: "an individual sets a goal, develops a plan of action, begins action, monitors his or her performance (through observation and self-reflection), evaluates his or her performance (thus gaining insight) and, based on this evaluation, changes his or her actions to further enhance performance, and thus reach his or her goal" (751).

Grant explains that there are five important parts to this goal-focused  3
coaching concept. The first part is setting good goals. The coach must help the player set goals that coincide with his values, are well defined, and are realistically achievable. The second part is developing a strong working relationship between the coach and player. This means that a coach must work to develop an honest relationship to help create an environment conducive to growth where the player will feel comfortable being open and honest with the coach. The third aspect is developing a solution focus, which means helping the athlete develop solutions to help him achieve his goals. The fourth part is managing process. This includes developing actions steps and holding the athlete accountable for completing the agreed steps. The fifth and final aspect is achieving the desired outcome.

## Characteristics of an Effective Coach

While successful coaches have been exposed to the spotlight throughout his-  4
tory, certain personal qualities of these coaches have emerged as essential to success in the coaching business. Sports psychologist Sandra Short explores five specific qualities of effective coaches. The first of these qualities is being a teacher. This is important because coaches must be able to teach their players about the game and what to do during competition.

The second quality is being organized. Being organized is typically a  5
behind-the-scenes job but it is important because a coach must be organized

to keep track of players, competitions, and practice schedules. It is important to organize a plan for success and be able to stick to it. Coaches in team sports must be organized before stepping onto the playing field so that they will know how to handle specific situations such as substitutions and timeout management.

The third quality is being competitive. Coaches must have an inner desire 6 to compete and work to instill that desire to compete in their athletes. Being competitive must be a foundational quality in athletes. It doesn't matter how gifted an athlete is or how much he knows, if he does not have the desire to compete then he will not be successful.

The fourth quality is being a learner. Coaches must continue to learn every 7 day they are on the job. They must learn about their players' personality and they must learn about the newest trends, philosophies, and strategies in the sport that they coach.

The fifth and final quality mentioned is being a friend and mentor. It is 8 important to be a positive role model for their players to look up to. A coach should also offer support and counseling when a player may need it. Fulfilling this role can bring about a deeper level of satisfaction for both the coach and the athlete.

## Confidence in Coaching

Another aspect of coaching that has been studied is coaching confidence and its 9 relationship with imagery. Sports psychologist Sandra Short argues that imagining being confident helps increase real confidence and the feeling of effectiveness. During pregame preparations, if a coach pictures himself as a confident, successful coach, he is more likely to exude real confidence.

Another point Short made is that coaches who use imagery to put together 10 game plans feel more comfortable with the plans that they come up with. Coaches who make their plans and play out the game using their imaginations are more likely to see strengths and weaknesses in their plans and adjust their plans accordingly.

A third point made is that coaches who imagine in a "cognitive specific 11 way," that is through clear specific examples, will have more confidence in their teaching abilities. In other words, coaches who specifically imagine teaching skills and techniques will acquire confidence in teaching these attributes and therefore be more effective teachers: "The confidence a coach portrays affects the confidence athletes feel . . . . The coach acting confident is one of the most effective strategies coaches can use to increase athletes' 'feelings of efficacy'" (Short, "Relationship" 392).

There have been many articles written on the X's and the O's (specific strat- 12 egies) of the game. Seminars have been held on the newest strategies. Books have been written on the characteristics of good coaches. Studies have been done on confidence in coaching, the method of setting goals, and the role of the coach in coach-athlete relationships; however scholars have yet to study a coach's ability to read his players and the game as a form of literacy. Many people may think that literacy is not part of the responsibilities that go with coaching. However, they couldn't be farther from the truth. Tony Mirabelli gives an unorthodox definition of literacy, arguing that "Literacy extends beyond individual experiences of reading and writing to include the various modes of communication and situations of any socially meaningful group" (146). He talks about reading people and knowing when to do something to help them as forms of literacy.

This idea of multiple literacies can be applied to football coaching staff as 13 well. Coaches need to be able to do so much more than just read. They need to know how to read people. They need to know how to read their players so that they can find out how to get the most out of them. They must also know how to read and teach the plays. The coaches must know their plays because many plays have certain "reads" or "progressions" that the coach must be able to teach the players. Coaches also must be able to read the game so that they can call the best plays that suit certain situations properly.

Coaching as a complex literacy practice has not been examined. How do 14 football coaches, as members of a specific discourse community, go about reading their players and the game in order to get optimal performance and a positive end result? To figure this out, I conducted an ethnographic study on how the coaches at the University of Dayton go about reading people and reading the game.

## Methods

I recorded football coaches at the University of Dayton during their pregame 15 speeches and interviewed those coaches afterwards; I also interviewed a coaching graduate assistant at the University of Cincinnati via email. The recording of the pregame speeches took place before a home game on a Saturday afternoon. In the pregame speeches, Coach Kelly and Coach Whilding attempted to bring out the best in their players. I conducted an interview with Coach Whilding, the offensive coordinator, the following week, and with Coach Kelly, the head coach at the time, during the winter of the following season. Each interview took place in the coachs' offices. The email interview with Coach Painter, the graduate assistant at the University of Cincinnati, took place in the winter as well. In it, I asked similar questions to those used for the University of Dayton coaches. (Interview questions are attached as Appendix A.) I asked questions about how coaches go about reading their players and the game and also about the coach's personal history and motivation for coaching.

I used these methods because they allowed me to take a direct look at what 16 the coaches were saying and then get a look at the thought process behind it. The interviews involved open-ended questions that helped bring out coaching philosophies on many different issues, including the issue of reading their players and the game. This idea of reading players and the game is directly reflective of Tony Mirabelli's idea of multiple literacies.

I analyzed the data collected by applying John Swales's six characteristics of 17 a discourse community. The characteristics I focused on are the set of common goals, the genres, and the specific lexis used.

## Results

Because we are studying the multiple literacies of football coaches by looking 18 at coaching as a discourse community, it will be clearest to separate the results for the characteristics of a discourse community and the results for multiple literacies.

### Characteristics of a Discourse Community

A football coaching staff is an excellent example of a discourse community. 19 The characteristics are clearly defined and easy to recognize. The clearest characteristics to pick up on are the goals, lexis, and genres.

*Goals.* Coach Kelly and Coach Whilding helped make up one of the most 20 successful coaching staffs in the history of division 1 college football. This is mainly due to their ability to set and achieve goals, both team and personal goals. There is always the goal of winning the game. The University of Dayton had goal charts with a list of about 10 goals for every game, for offense, defense, and special teams. They use these charts with stickers to help monitor how well they achieve these goals and figure out the goals they need to work on.

Coaches also have many individual goals. Many of these goals include get- 21 ting the most out of their players physically and mentally. Coaches always strive to make their players push themselves to heights that they never thought they could reach. Coaches also have the goal of seeing their players develop as people. Coach Whilding talked about how he enjoyed seeing his players succeed in real-life situations after football: "It's good to see those guys mature and go on and get good jobs and raise families and be very responsible people in their communities."

Along with these goals, there are many rewards. While many big time college 22 coaches may receive a hefty paycheck, Coach Whilding explained that some of the rewards are not monetary: "I know guys who just hate to get up in the morning and hate to go to work, and I have just never felt that way."

*Lexis.* Another important characteristic of discourse communities is that 23 there is a specialized lexis, or set of terms that is unique to the community. There are many terms that are involved in football coaching communities that may not make sense to most people but, among a team, make perfect sense and help the community better do its work and achieve it goals.

Some of the more common terms might make more sense to the public, such 24 as touchdown or tackle. There are, however, terms that might not make sense to anybody outside the team. Examples of these may be passing routes such as "Y corner," "Follow," or "Green Gold." They could also be things like blocking schemes such as "Bob," "Sam," or "Combo." There are terms for everything, and it takes many repetitions during practice to learn all of this lexis. The lexis helps save time because one word may describe several actions. This lexis is also important because the lexis varies from team to team, so if the opposing team hears it, they will not know what it means. Without many hours spent preparing and practicing, the players and the coaches would not have this advantage in communication.

*Genres.* A genre is a text that helps facilitate communication between 25 people, and in this example all communication takes place within the discourse community. There are certain genres that help a football team and football coaching staff operate efficiently. Genres often use the unique lexis that was previously mentioned.

Perhaps the most essential genre is the playbook. The playbook is created by 26 the coaches and shows all the plays that they plan on running and the proper way that the players are supposed to run them. The players get the playbooks at the beginning of the season and need to learn the plays before they are "installed" during practice. The players must guard these books and make sure that no members from opposing teams get the information. The playbook is essential to success because there are many plays and without a playbook the players would become confused and make mistakes that could be disastrous to the outcome of the football game.

Another genre is a scouting report. The scouting report is also made up by 27 the coaches for the players. It shows the other team's personnel, what plays they like to run, and when they like to run them. It helps the players know what to expect going into the game so they can prepare accordingly. The coaches will usually spend the day after a game putting together a scouting report and distribute the report to their players at the beginning of the week.

A third genre is a play-calling sheet. This is made up by the coaches and is 28 only for the coaches, mainly the offensive coordinator. The play-calling sheet helps the coach remember all the plays that they have and what situation that the plays are favorable in. Without a play-calling sheet, the coach would have to remember the names of all the plays on his own, and that is something that could be a distraction to calling the proper plays, and could effectively cost a team a game.

Now that we understand what exactly a football coaching discourse com- 29 munity is and what it is made up of, we can learn exactly how the concept of literacy applies to this group.

## Multiple Literacies

Many people do not see the concept of literacy as something that would apply 30 to a football coaching staff. However, Mirabelli defines literacy as not just reading and writing but things such as reading people. He uses the example of a waiter reading his customers in his article. This same idea can be applied to a football coaching discourse community.

## *Interpersonal Literacies*

One of the literacies for a football coach is the ability to read the players. This 31 can be described as an interpersonal literacy. There are two types of reading the coach needs to do. First, coaches must be able to read players to know when they are ready to play; second, coaches must be able to read their players to know how to motivate them properly to get the most out of them.

There are different characteristics to look for when it comes to knowing 32 when players are ready to play. Two are comfort and knowledge. Coach Painter from Cincinnati emphasized player comfort: "Knowing their personality is a big part of reading them. When a player is ready to play they will be in a comfortable mode. Whether that is listening to music, jumping around, or even reading, when a player is loose and comfortable they are ready to compete." Coach Kelly emphasized knowledge of the game: "Do they have the knowledge to perform? What we try to do is put them in as many stressful situations as possible from a mental point of view to see if they can handle that in practice. If they can handle that in practice . . . then we cut 'em loose and let 'em play." He went on to state that another way of finding out whether or not a player has that knowledge and is ready to play is by sitting down one on one with him. Coach Kelly elaborates, "I can get a good feel for a young man when I'm sitting in a room with him, watching practice or game tape, asking him questions. . . . If there is a lot of hesitation or if they are totally off then I know we're not there yet."

Coaches must be able to read their players in order to motivate them prop- 33 erly. Every coach emphasized that each player is unique and will respond to different types of motivation in different ways. This can be done by taking an emotional, fiery approach or a calm and collected approach. Coach Kelly emphasized the importance of motivation, explaining,

> That's a key element in becoming a coach. Can they motivate? Can they identify what makes this guy go? Can you hit that button and how fast can you hit that button? The sooner you find that motivational tool the better off you're going to be. You can tell immediately if it works or not.

Finding out what motivates each individual is no easy task, but Coach 34 Whilding explains, "You have to be able to understand 'How do I reach that player . . . that young man?' And there are a lot of ways to do that. Through the years, you figure it out." He went more in depth and explained that you have to be able to reach everybody as an individual player and that there are many types of players: "There are some that like to yell and scream and get excited. There are others who don't play well like that, who are a little quieter and keep it within themselves but are still very motivated." Coach Painter from Cincinnati points out the balance between these two opposing motivational styles: "You have to use both and know when to use them. . . . Too much fire and you will lose the team and its effectiveness. Too much calm and you will lose control over the environment."

These explanations show that reading players to know when they are ready 35 to play and reading players to know how to motivate them are two very difficult parts of the coaching profession. They require balance, patience, and perseverance. Coach Whilding sums it up, saying, sometimes "it just doesn't work and you find out you have to just use another method."

### Situational Literacies

A second essential coaching literacy is being able to read a game. The coaches    36
must be able to actively read a game in order to put their players in the best possible situations to attempt to win the game. Reading a game can be broken down into two categories: pregame and in-game.

The week leading up to a game is a week filled with preparation. Preparation    37
is important because it "will allow you the ability to put players in the places they need to be at the times they need to be there to make plays. From there it's out of your hands" (Painter). Coaches study the opposing team in and out and then formulate a game plan. They consolidate this game plan along with infor-mation on the opposition into a packet, make copies of the packet, and distribute the copies to the team. This helps players stay on the same page as the coaches and prepare mentally for the game. This mental preparation will make players feel more comfortable as to what to expect during the game: "You do a lot of preparation during the week, getting ready for the week. We watch a lot of tape. You have to have an idea of what their base defense is, what their coverage is going to be, when they're going to blitz, what down they're going to blitz, what are their favorite ones" (Whilding). Coach Kelly elaborated on the importance of preparation by explaining that you have to get a good idea of what the coach likes to do in certain situations and when you feel like you know the opposing coach, it becomes a game of feel: "It's really important to me to know what's going on in that coach's mind" (Kelly).

It is also important to be able to read the game in real time. Ways of read-    38
ing and reacting during the game may be as simple as knowing when to call timeouts, call certain plays, or make substitutions, or may be more complicated such as knowing what type of halftime adjustments to make. Coach Whilding explains that a key aspect of making these adjustments is that "You have to get a feel on the field for what is working, and I think that's something you develop through the years . . . and it changes from week to week, from year to year sometimes, depending on your personnel. You have to know your person-nel. What you're good at, what you're not good at."

Because coaches don't always have the best view and are not in a position    39
to be heard by all the players when they are on the field, sometimes they will delegate this responsibility to their players. Coach Painter explains, "Our play-ers are allowed a small amount of freedom on the fly. We ask our quarterback to check us out of plays when necessary, but we have established what and when he can make such checks." These checks (changing the play at the line) give the team a better chance of calling a play that will be more likely to be successful.

Halftime adjustments are also very important. Sometimes a team will come    40
out in the first half and do something that was not expected or maybe a certain

strategy is not working the way the coach expected it to. The coaches will come together at the end of the half and discuss possible changes that might help the team. They then use halftime to explain these changes and make sure everyone is on the same page. This can turn into a chess match because sometimes one team will adjust to something that another team does, but at the same time the other team changes up what they were doing. Coach Painter explains it best by saying, "Your opponent is going to adjust, if you do not then you will be at a disadvantage. No matter how much preparation you have put in, there are going to be things you did not expect. This is where your on the field adjustments give you the final edge."

### Relationship Between Textual, Situational, and Interpersonal Literacies

Coaching functions as a discourse community that uses a variety of complex   41 literacies—textual, interpersonal, and situational. All of these literacies can be seen functioning together in a game situation.

Before the game the coach had to spend time evaluating his players and deciding who was going to play. To do this he used interpersonal literacies. Now fast forward to a game situation. Let's say that the team we are looking at is on offense. While the players are playing the game, there are assistant coaches in the press box watching to see how the defense reacts to what the offense does. They are looking for any keys or tips that could give the offense an advantage. This is an example of situational literacies. The assistant coaches in the press box will then communicate what they see to the coach calling the offense. This process involves using lexis. The coach will then process what the assistant coaches told him and will look at his play-calling sheet and decide what play to run. The play-calling sheet is an example of a genre. He will then tell the quarterback what play to run. The name of the play consists of lexis as well. The quarterback will tell the team the play and then they will line up. The quarterback will then look at the defense and see if anything needs to be changed. This is an example of situational literacies. If he decides to "check" (change) the play based on what he sees in the defense, he will use lexis to do so. The quarterback will then call "hike" (lexis) and the ball will be snapped and the play will be run with the hopes of scoring a touchdown, which is the goal on any given play.

## Conclusion

The world of coaching is more complicated than it may seem to the public   42 eye. Whether it is looking at some of the characteristics of a coaching community or looking at the tasks that coaches partake in, such as reading players and the game, there are still many characteristics and responsibilities that are unexplored to those outside of these communities. After looking in depth at some of the behind-the-scenes factors that go into coaching, I hope to have helped increase knowledge on the literacy aspects involved in coaching. I hope this helps spark interest in the connection between literacy and sports. This connection will now help people have a better sense of empathy with what the coaches are thinking when they make a specific call on the field or partake in an action off the field, and hopefully I have brought people closer to being able to answer the common question asked at any sporting event: "What was that coach thinking?!"

## Works Cited

Grant, Anthony M. "The Goal-Focused Coaching Skills Questionnaire: Preliminary Findings." *Social Behavior & Personality: An International Journal* 35.6 (2007): 751–60. Print.

Hasbrouck, Jan and Carolyn Denton. "Student-Focused Coaching: A Model for Reading Coaches." *Reading Teacher* 60.7 (2007): 690–93. Print.

Mirabelli, Tony. "Learning to Serve: The Language and Literacy of Food Service Workers." *What They Don't Learn in School*. Ed. Jabari Mahiri. New York: Peter Lang, 2004: 143–62. Print.

Short, Sandra E. "Role of the Coach in the Coach-Athlete Relationship." Spec. issue of *Lancet* 366 (2005): S29–S30. Print.

———. "The Relationship Between Efficacy Beliefs and Imagery Use in Coaches." *The Sport Psychologist* 19.4 (2005): 380–94. Print.

Swales, John. "The Concept of Discourse Community." *Genre Analysis: English in Academic and Workplace Settings*. Boston: Cambridge UP, 1990: 21–32. Print.

## Appendix A: Interview Questions for Coaches

### Interpersonal Literacies

1. How do you tell when a player is ready or not ready to play? Are there specific things that you look for (body language and attitude, etc.) or is it more intuitive?

2. In what ways do you go about motivating your players? Do you prefer a calm or a fiery approach? How did your coaches go about motivating you when you played? Do you feel like you have become an effective motivator?

3. Do you focus more on motivating players during the week or during a pregame speech? When do you think it is more effective? Are there any specific examples that stick out of when you made an attempt to motivate a player and it was either very successful or unsuccessful? If you were unsuccessful how did you change your approach?

4. Would you consider your approach to correcting athletes more of positive reinforcement or negative reinforcement? Do you think that players respond better to one method better than the other? Is it better to correct mistakes publicly or privately? How do the players react to each method?

### Situational Literacies

1. What do you feel are the most important factors to reading and calling a game? Do you use any specific methods to help you mediate reading the game (scripting plays, play-calling sheet with specific situations)?

2. Do you put any of this on your players (system of checks or audibles, plays that are run differently depending on the defense's look)?
3. How much of the outcome of a game do you feel is attributed to pregame coaching preparations (game planning, watching film)?
4. How important are in-game decisions such as halftime adjustments, substitutions, and when to gamble on big plays? Do you go with the overall feel of the game or do you look for specific details when it comes to making a game-time decision?

## Questions for Discussion and Journaling

1. Before you read, you were asked to consider whether you think football coaches are a discourse community. After reading Branick's paper, have you changed your opinion in any way? If so, what did he say that got you to think differently?

2. Branick's methods include analyzing the coaches' discourse community using Swales's six characteristics. How effectively does he conduct this analysis? What, if anything, would you change or expand, and why?

3. Branick claims, "There have been many articles written on the X's and O's . . . of the game . . . however scholars have yet to study a coach's ability to read his players and the game as a form of literacy" (para. 12). Does Branick convince you that these abilities are, in fact, a form of literacy? Explain why or why not.

## Applying and Exploring Ideas

1. Brainstorm some groups that you think might be discourse communities but which, like football coaches, might not immediately come to mind as such.

2. Pick one of the groups you listed in question 1 and try to sketch out quickly, with a partner or by yourself, whether they meet Swales's six characteristics of a discourse community.

3. Listing characteristics of a discourse community is only the first step in a project. The next step is identifying a genuine question about some aspect of the discourse community, as Branick does here. What else would you like to explore about the discourse community you identified in question 2, directly above.

# Activity Theory: An Introduction for the Writing Classroom

## DONNA KAIN and ELIZABETH WARDLE

## Framing the Reading

Elizabeth Wardle is one of the editors of *Writing about Writing* as well as a Professor at the University of Central Florida. Donna Kain is an Associate Professor at East Carolina University. Wardle and Kain were Ph.D. candidates together at Iowa State University, where they wrote this piece for their undergraduate students around 2001 or 2002. At the time, they taught writing classes in which they asked students to consider how texts worked in context—who used them, how they got written, what they accomplished or didn't, how people learned to write them. Kain and Wardle found that activity theory was often a helpful lens for thinking about writing, but that there was no explanation of activity theory appropriate for undergraduates. So they wrote this for their own students, and they have been using it ever since. In 2005 they published an article together in the journal *Technical Communication Quarterly* describing how they use activity theory with their students; that article won the 2006 NCTE Best Article of the Year in Teaching of Technical and Scientific Communication.

Activity theory, as you will learn in the following reading, "was originally a psychological theory that sees all aspects of activity as shaped by people's social interactions with each other and the tools [including writing and language] that they use" (para. 1 of the reading). Activity theory gives you a lens for looking at an object or happening and understanding it in new ways, just as all theories do. Scholars in many different fields, as well as workplace consultants, use the lens of activity theory to look at groups of people doing work together, which they call **activity systems**, and consider what their common motives are and how they try to achieve those common motives. When people are unable to achieve their common motives, activity theory provides a method for examining where the breakdowns might have happened. Activity theory takes into account not only what is happening now, but also the histories that impact what is happening now. In other words, activity theory helps you consider what a particular group (like people creating and using the food bank we mentioned in the chapter introduction) is trying to accomplish, how it has gone about trying to accomplish that work in the past, and how it is doing so now. In looking at the food bank's activities, the lens of activity theory encourages us to look at the rules or conventions adhered to by the group, how the work (the labor) is divided up within the group, and the tools (including texts and language) that help (or impede) the group in working toward their shared motives.

Activity theory is a useful lens because it acknowledges the importance of the histories, including literacy histories that you studied in Chapter 1, that individuals bring with them when they act as part of an activity system. It is also useful because it helps you take a close look at the actual texts that you or others are writing, reading, and using and ask questions like: How do these work? What are they doing? Who created them? Why are they like this? Activity theory can give you a perspective on texts and groups of people using texts that can assist you in your school, professional, and extracurricular literate lives. You'll learn even more about how to analyze texts in the next chapter on rhetoric. Victoria Marro's student essay in this chapter uses activity theory to look at the genres of her sorority in new ways. In Chapter 3, Charles Bazerman discusses the relationship between activity systems and the genres people use to accomplish work in activity systems.

Both Kain and Wardle use activity theory in their own research. In the next article in this chapter ("Identity, Authority, and Learning to Write in New Workplaces") you will see how Wardle used activity theory to understand the difficulties that a new employee experienced when writing and working. In her current work, she uses activity theory to help explain how and why students do or do not learn and transfer writing-related knowledge learned in school settings. Donna Kain uses activity theory to further her understanding of emergency communication and risk management (particularly related to hurricanes), as well as accommodations for people with disabilities.

## Getting Ready to Read

*Before you read*, do at least one of the following activities:

- List a few groups (formal or informal) in which you participate, and ask yourself what your shared common goal(s) is/are.
- Pick one of those groups and make a quick list of all of the texts you read, write, or use in order to try to achieve the goals of that group.
- Pick one of those texts, and make a quick list of all of the people who have a hand in or an influence on how it is written and used.

(If you can do the above, you are already on your way to being able to conduct an activity analysis!)

*As you read*, consider the following questions:

- Are there unfamiliar terms here that you need to spend a little more time thinking about? Are there familiar terms that seem to be used in new or unfamiliar ways? If so, make a list of these terms and try to define them for yourself before your next class.
- Keep in mind the groups you listed before you started reading, and use them to help you imagine examples as Kain and Wardle explain the components of an activity system.

People meet social needs by working and learning together over time to  1
achieve particular goals or to act on particular motives. To facilitate their
activities, people also develop and use tools. These tools include not only thing
like hammers or computers, but also language—probably the most complex
tool of all. As people refine their tools and add new ones to solve problems
more effectively, the activities they perform using those tools can change—
and vice versa: as their activities change, people use their tools differently and
modify their tools to meet their changing needs. Activity theory, which has its
roots in Russia in the early 20th century, was originally a psychological theory
that sees all aspects of activity as shaped over time by people's social interactions with each other and the tools they use.

As a society, we differentiate types of activities by the specific knowledge,  2
tools, and repertoires of tasks that people use to achieve particular outcomes.
For instance, we recognize the practice of medicine by its goal of meeting people's health-care needs; its participants, including doctors, nurses, and patients;
its body of knowledge about human physiology, disease, and treatment options; and its tools, for instance medicines and surgical instruments. We recognize the university by its goal of facilitating learning, its participants, including
teachers, students, and administrators; and its tools, including textbooks and
chalkboards.

Activity theory gives us a helpful lens for understanding how people in dif-  3
ferent communities carry out their activities. For those of us interested in rhetorical theory, the most helpful aspect of activity theory is the way it helps us
see more fully all the aspects of a situation and community that influence how
people use the tools of language and genre. While it is easy enough to say that
"context" influences how people write, saying this does not particularly help
us know how to write differently when we find ourselves in a new situation.
Activity theory provides us with very specific aspects of context to look at as
we consider the various factors that influence and change the tool of writing.

## What are Activity Systems?

The most basic activity theory lens, or unit of analysis, is the *activity system*,  4
defined as a group of people who share a common object and motive over time,
as well as the wide range of tools they use together to act on that object and
realize that motive. David Russell
(1997) describes an activity system
as "any ongoing, object-directed,
historically conditioned, dialectically structured, tool-mediated human interaction" (p. 510). That's
a mouthful to be sure; let's look a
bit more closely at what Russell
means:

> Activity theory provides us with very
> specific aspects of context to look at
> as we consider the various factors
> that influence and change the tool of
> writing.

- **Ongoing.** The study of activity systems is concerned with looking at how systems function over time. For instance, the university is an activity system of long duration that began in the past and will continue into the future. We can trace the university's activity over time and consider how it might evolve in the future.

- **Object-directed.** The types of activities that activity theory is concerned with are directed toward specific goals. Continuing with the example of the university, the object of its activity is learning, which is accomplished through instruction and research.

- **Historically conditioned.** Activity systems come into being because of practices that have a history. At any point that we begin to study how a system works, we need to consider how it came to function in a particular way. For instance, ways that the university carries out its activities developed over time. Many things we do today can be explained by the history of the university's mission as well as the history of western educational institutions.

- **Dialectically structured.** The term "dialectic" describes a type of relationship in which aspects of a process, transaction, or system are mutually dependent. When one aspect changes, other aspects change in response. Some of these changes we can anticipate; others we can't. For example, when the university began to use computers as a tool in education, the ways that teachers, researchers, and students accomplished tasks related to the activity of learning began to change in response.

- **Tool-mediated.** People use many types of tools to accomplish activities. These may be physical objects, such as computers, or systems of symbols, such as mathematics. At the university, we use textbooks, syllabi, lab equipment, computers, and many other tools to accomplish our goal of learning. The types of tools we use mediate, or shape, the ways we engage in activity and the ways we think about activity. For example, if we think about the course syllabus as a tool, we might say that it organizes the work in the classroom for both the instructor and the students, which affects how we participate in learning activities.

- **Human interaction.** Studies of activity systems are concerned with more than the separate actions of individuals. Activity theory is concerned with how people work together, using tools, toward outcomes. In the university, teachers, students, researchers, administrators, and staff interact with each other and with tools to achieve the outcomes of learning.

Activity systems are also constrained by divisions of labor and by rules. In  5 the university, for instance, the labor is divided among the participants—students are responsible for completing assignments; instructors are responsible for grading assignments; administrators are responsible for making sure grades appear on students' transcripts. In the university, we also operate with a set of rules for participating in classroom and laboratory learning. The rules in many respects are our mutual agreement about how the activity will be carried out so we can all progress toward the outcome of learning.

One way that activity theory helps you more fully understand the "context" 6 of a community and its tools is by providing a diagram outlining the important elements and their relationships. Figure 1 shows the conventions activity theory researchers use to present what they view as the critical components of every activity system. The "nodes" in the system are the points on the triangle—think of these as the specific aspects of a "context" that activity theory can help you consider more fully. The arrows indicate the reciprocal relationships among these various aspects. The labels we've provided describe some of the components of each node in the system.

## How are Parts of an Activity System Related?

The **Subject(s)** of an activity system is the person or people who are directly 7 participating in the activity you want to study. The subject provides a point of view for studying the activity. The **Motives** direct the subject's activities. Motives include the **Object** of the activity, which is fairly immediate, and the **Outcome,** which is more removed and ongoing. The **Subject(s)** use **Tools** to accomplish their **Object(ives)** and achieve their intended **Outcomes.** They are motivated to use these tools because they want to accomplish something and the tools will help them do so. The **Tools** that mediate the activity system include both physical tools such as computers, texts, and other artifacts, as well as non-physical tools such as language (written and oral) and skills. Activity theorists also refer to this category as "artifacts." When people first learn to use

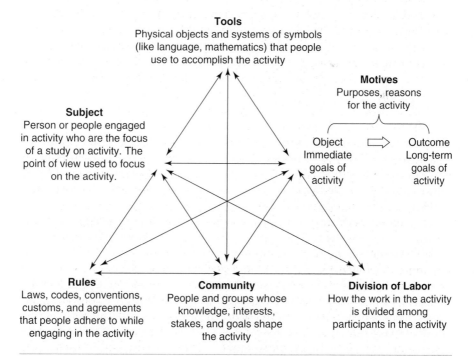

**Figure 1 Activity System**

a particular tool, they use it on the level of conscious *action;* they must think about how to use the tool and what they want it to accomplish. Once they have used the tool to perform a particular action over a period of time, the use of that tool becomes *operationalized,* largely unconscious. Tool use only moves back to the realm of conscious action if something goes wrong or if the user is presented with a new action to perform with that tool.

The terms at the base of the triangle, **Rules, Community,** and **Division of** 8 **Labor,** make up what Engestrom (1999) refers to as the "social basis" of the activity system. The social basis situates the activity in a broader context that allows us to account for the influences that shape the activity.

The **Community** is the larger group which the subject is a part of and from 9 which participants "take their cues." The community's interests shape the activity. Community members divide up the work needed to accomplish their object(ives). The **Division of Labor** describes how tasks are distributed within the activity system. People might disagree about how labor should be divided or how valuable various positions within that division are, causing conflicts within the activity system. **Rules** are one way of attempting to manage or minimize these conflicts within activity systems. Rules are defined not only as formal and explicit dos and don't, but also as norms, conventions, and values. "Rules shape the interactions of subject and tools with the object" (Russell, "Looking"). These rules understandably change as other aspects of the system change—or as the rules are questioned or resisted—but the rules allow the system to be stabilized-for-now in the face of internal conflicts. These rules affect how people use tools. Of most interest to you will be the ways in which the rules affect how people use the tool of written language.

To provide an example that we're familiar with, Figure 2 depicts the class 10 as an activity system.

## How do Activity Systems change?

Activity systems consist of the interactions among all of the factors that come 11 to bear on an activity at a given point in time. Cole and Engeström (1994; see also Engeström 1999) suggest that the relationship among the factors in an activity system is a "distribution of cognition," or a sharing of knowledge and work, across the all the elements in the system. In this way, activity systems can be thought of as communal.

But activity systems are also very dynamic and, as Russell points out, "best 12 viewed as complex formations" (1997 p. 9). Change is the quality that makes activity systems—and really all human interactions—dynamic. As people participating in activity systems learn, and as new people join the activity, they refine their tools and create new ones. Or one activity system may be influenced by developments in other activity systems. For instance tools developed by computer science may be adopted in others system, for instance the university or the health care system. As people change the tools they use, or the ways they use existing tools, changes ripple through their activity systems. Change in activity systems can also come about for other reasons. Social needs many change and activity systems may need to refine their outcomes or goals to meet those needs.

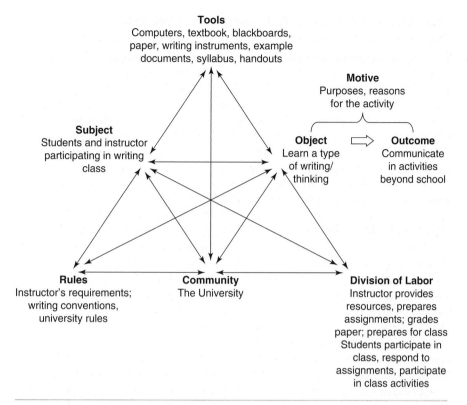

**Figure 2  Class as an Activity System**

Change produces advances and improvements, but also complications and challenges that need to be addressed and resolved by participants within activity systems. Sometimes activity systems are even abandoned or absorbed into other systems when changes make them obsolete (consider for example the fate of the pony express). 13

## What Purposes Does Activity Theory Serve?

Researchers use activity theory to study how people engage in all kinds of activities from learning at a university, to working in a manufacturing company, to shopping in a grocery store. Researchers who use activity theory want to understand the relationships among people participating in activities, the tools people use to accomplish their activities, and the goals that people have for the activity. In addition, researchers use activity theory to understand how historical and social forces shape the way people participate in activities and how change affects activities. Three important goals of activity theory include: 14

- Accounting for aspects of a system to better understand the nature of activity.
- Analyzing how the parts of a system work together to better anticipate participants' needs and goals.
- Isolating problems to develop solutions.

## How Can You Use Activity Theory to Analyze Texts?

You can use the basic tenets of activity theory and the activity theory triangle 15
to help you better understand not only how texts function but also why texts
used within a particular system of activity contain certain content and specific
conventions, such as formatting, style, and organization. For example, if you
are in a business communication course, you may be interested in learning
how grant proposals are constructed in your field. You may want to ask,
"What are grant proposals like in non-profit social service organizations?
What kinds of information do they include? How are they formatted?" If
you were performing a rhetorical analysis, you could look at a proposal and
name its textual features—length, content, layout, type of language used—
and name the rhetorical situation as far as you were able to understand it
from looking at the document: writer, audience, purpose. While this sort of
analysis is quite useful, there are many things it cannot tell you. For example,
it cannot tell you *why* the document is a particular length, *why* it contains
certain types of content and not others. A rhetorical analysis also doesn't
help you understand who does what tasks pertaining to the document: does
only one person write it? Do several people contribute information? Why do
certain people become involved in writing the proposal and not others? A
rhetorical analysis also won't remind you that the proposal genre has likely
changed within a specific social service organization—or suggest that you explore whether the features of the proposal genre as embodied in the text you
are examining are uncontested.

So how do you begin your activity theory analysis? First, consider the activity 16
theory triangle (we've included a worksheet-type triangle [p. 282] for you
to work with). Of the aspects on the triangle where you could begin your
analysis, you (as a rhetorician) will likely begin with specific texts used within
a specific activity system; for example, you might gather all the examples of
proposals you can find written by people at a particular company or working
within a particular field. These texts, then, are tools for achieving goals. At
this point, using the triangle, a number of questions should present themselves
to you:

- What is the immediate object(ive) of using this tool? Do all the members
  of the community seem to agree on this/these objects?
- What is the long-term purpose (outcome) of using this tool and others
  like it?
- Why are the people here doing what they are doing? What is motivating them to take the time to use this tool and achieve their short-term
  object(ives) and long-term outcomes?
- Which people (subjects) are directly involved in using this tool?
- What world does this tool function for? Who constitutes the community
  that uses and benefits from the use of this tool? Are the readers part of this
  community or are they participants in a different (but obviously related)
  activity system?

- If the readers of the text (the tool) are not part of the community/activity system, does this cause conflict or misunderstanding? Do the readers have different expectations about the object(ives) of the tool than the writers do?
- Who is responsible for what part of this tool? How is the work pertaining to this tool divided up? Are there conflicts about how the work is divided up?
- What seem to be the rules, guidelines, conventions (spoken and unspoken, formal and informal) governing the use of this tool? Does everyone in the community seem to have the same idea about what these rules are? What happens when people break any of these rules?

Clearly, you won't be able to answer all these questions (and others that 17 occur to you) just by looking at the text. You are going to need to talk with people who use the tool of proposals and possibly even watch them at work. Often, people can't tell you what the rules governing tool use are in their community because they are only aware of them subconsciously. Remember that when a person uses a tool for a long time, it becomes operationalized, unconscious—what is often called "tacit knowledge." So in order for you to begin to see how and why the tool gets used, you may have to do some watching and guessing, in addition to asking.

As you fill in the triangle, remember that some things about activity theory 18 aren't obviously present on the triangle: remember, for example, that actions are ongoing—they have occurred in the past and will likely continue in some form in the future. Remember that actions are historically conditioned and dialectically structured—texts look the way they do because past events have shaped them and they will continue to change as the other aspects of the activity system change. So, as you write your activity theory analysis, you may also want to see what you can find out about your document's history and see if you can identify aspects of the activity system that could be sources of conflict. Sources of conflict pertaining to the creation or use of the document will likely cause the documents to change again.

When you are finished with your activity theory analysis, you should have 19 a better understanding not only of what particular tools (in this case texts, genres, language) look like, but also why they look that way, what they are being used to accomplish, who uses them, how they have changed over time, and how they might continue to change in the future. Keep in mind, however, that an outsider—someone who is not a part of a particular activity system—can never fully grasp the hows and whys of that system. Some things will remain a mystery to you; some things, in fact, even remain a mystery to insiders. Perhaps you've heard people say, "I don't know why we do it that way, we just do." However, if you are constantly asking the questions activity theory presents to you, you will be far less likely to say something like this. You will be more likely to recognize rules (whether stated or not) and to understand why you are doing something. In this way, you will become a much savvier communicator.

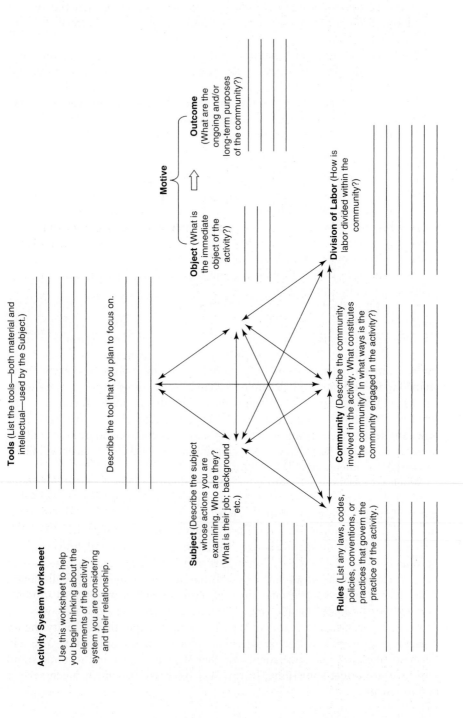

**Activity System Worksheet**

Use this worksheet to help you begin thinking about the elements of the activity system you are considering and their relationship.

**Tools** (List the tools—both material and intellectual—used by the Subject.)

_____
_____
_____
_____
_____

Describe the tool that you plan to focus on.

**Subject** (Describe the subject whose actions you are examining. Who are they? What is their job; background etc.)

_____
_____
_____
_____
_____

**Object** (What is the immediate object of the activity?)

_____
_____

**Motive**

⇧

**Outcome** (What are the ongoing and/or long-term purposes of the community?)

_____
_____
_____
_____

**Community** (Describe the community involved in the activity. What constitutes the community? In what ways is the community engaged in the activity?)

_____
_____
_____

**Rules** (List any laws, codes, policies, conventions, or practices that govern the practice of the activity.)

_____
_____
_____
_____
_____

**Division of Labor** (How is labor divided within the community?)

_____
_____
_____
_____
_____

## Works Cited

Cole, M., & Engestrom, Y. (1993). A cultural-historical approach to distributed cognition. In G. Salomon (Ed.), Distributed cognitions: Psychological and educational considerations (pp. 1–46), Cambridge, UK: Cambridge University Press.

Engeström, Y. (1999). "Activity theory and individual and social transformation." In *Perspectives on Activity Theory.* Eds. Yrjö Engström, Reijo Miettinen, and Raija-Leena Punämaki. New York: Cambridge UP.

Russell, D. (1997). "Rethinking genre in school and society: An activity theory analysis." *Written Communication, 14(4),* 504–554.

Russell, David. Looking Beyond the Interface. Forthcoming.

## Questions for Discussion and Journaling

1. Explain in your own words what an activity system is, and give three examples of activity systems with which you are familiar. For each of these systems, explain what its common motives and goals are.

2. Pick one of the activity systems you chose in response to question 1, and explain how its activities are "ongoing," "object-directed," and "historically conditioned" (para. 4).

3. Focus on that same activity system, and make a list of all of the tools that are used to help the participants in the system achieve their common goals. Remember that tools can be physical objects or symbol systems (para. 4).

4. Can you think of times when one of these tools you listed in response to question 3 was not effective in helping the group achieve its goals? What happened? Did the group change the tool or the way they use the tool?

## Applying and Exploring Ideas

1. Work with a partner to choose an activity system that interests you and to which you have access. Using the activity triangle worksheet (p. 282), and the questions in paragraph 16 of the reading, try to discern the object, purpose, tools, community, division of labor, and rules for this activity system. In particular, focus on the textual tools that this group uses in order to try to accomplish its common purposes. In order to do this task, you will need to speak to members of the activity system and collect some examples of the texts (tools) the activity system participants use.

2. Present your activity triangle worksheet to the class, and explain how this analysis has helped you understand differently about writing and how texts are used to accomplish work (mediate meaningful activity).

### Meta Moment

What has reading about and applying activity theory helped you see differently? How can you use this lens to understand your own current and future experiences?

# Identity, Authority, and Learning to Write in New Workplaces

## ELIZABETH WARDLE

■ Wardle, Elizabeth. "Identity, Authority, and Learning to Write in New Work-places." *Enculturation* 5.2 (2004): n. pag. Web. 18 Feb. 2010.

## Framing the Reading

Elizabeth Wardle is a Professor at the University of Central Florida, where she also serves the chair of the Department of Writing and Rhetoric. She was finishing her Ph.D. at about the time that Ann Johns was retiring; thus, you can think of her work as growing from the work of the scholars you have read so far. She is interested in how people learn to write, not as children but as adults moving among different **discourse communities**. The following article is one that she researched as a Ph.D. student. While in graduate school, Wardle was asked to use language that did not feel "right" or "natural" to her. She struggled to find the right register and lexis for her writing, and writing in "academic" ways seemed to stifle her creative voice. You can see, then, why she would be interested in researching someone else who was struggling to enculturate in a new activity system.

This article is the result of that study. It describes a new employee, fresh out of college, trying to communicate with a new workplace community and failing—miserably. The reasons he failed included a lack of authority in the new activity system, a specific form of rebellion against the values of that activity system that Wardle calls nonparticipation, and a sense of identity that conflicts with the new activity system. Wardle applies the frame of activity theory explained in the previous reading, "Activity Theory: An Introduction for the Writing Classroom." If you haven't read that piece, you might find this reading easier if you went back and skimmed that piece first. Here, Wardle uses the frame provided by activity theory to help explain the problems that the new employee, Alan, had when he began a new job.

## Getting Ready to Read

*Before you read,* do at least one of these activities:

- Think over your time in college so far and write a few paragraphs about whether your identity has been changed by your college experiences to date, and, if it has, *how* it has changed. How can you explain the changes (or lack of change)?

- Make a list of terms or phrases you're using now that you weren't at the beginning of your college experience. Do you associate any of this new language with participation in new groups (discourse communities or activity systems)?

*As you read*, consider the following questions:

- How does Wardle describe being a "newcomer" to an activity system? Is there anything familiar about her description that you recognize from your own experience?
- How are Wardle's *activity systems* different from *discourse communities*, as discussed in the previous readings?

D espite the media's continued representation of communication as "utili- 1 tarian and objective" (Bolin), and the acceptance of this view by much of the public and even by many academics, research in rhetoric and composition over the past twenty years has moved toward a much more complex view of communication. Of particular interest to professional communication specialists is research suggesting that learning to write in and for new situations and workplaces is complex in ways that go far beyond texts and cognitive abilities. This research posits that for workers to be successfully enculturated into new communities of practice[1] (Lave and Wenger) or activity systems (Engeström; Russell, "Rethinking" and "Activity Theory"), including learning to write in ways that are appropriate to those new communities, neophytes must learn and conform to the conventions, codes, and genres of those communities (Bazerman; Berkenkotter, Huckin, and Ackerman; Berkenkotter and Huckin; Bizzell). However, *when and how much* each neophyte must conform largely depends on how much authority and cultural capital[2] the neophyte possesses or cultivates to accomplish work effectively. Additionally, issues of identity and values are important factors in neophytes' abilities and willingness to learn to write in and for new workplaces, as they must choose between ways of thinking and writing with which they are comfortable and new ways that seem foreign or at odds with their identities and values (Doheny-Farina; Doheny-Farina and Odell). Researchers who examine issues of identity and authority as important aspects of communicating in workplace settings find that workers' identities are bound up in myriad ways with the genres they are asked to appropriate (Dias et al.; Dias and Paré; Paré). According to Anis Bawarshi, "a certain genre replaces or . . . adds to the range of possible selves that writers have available to them" (105).

> *Learning to write in and for new situations and workplaces is complex in ways that go far beyond texts and cognitive abilities.*

As composition widens its focus beyond academic writing, it is increasingly 2 important to consider what it means to write in the workplace. Not only will such knowledge help us prepare students for the writing beyond the classroom, but, as Bolin points out, those of us working in rhetoric and composition must continue to respond to complaints by the media and general public that we have not fulfilled our responsibilities and "polished" students' language use so that they can convey information "clearly." We can respond to these complaints more effectively when we better understand the ways in which writing is bound up with issues of identity and authority. While we recognize the importance of identity and authority issues in the process of enculturating new workers, we do not always fully understand how these issues influence their writing.

Here I first outline theories of identity and authority that are useful in 3 understanding how newcomers learn to write in and for new situations. The socio-historic theoretical perspective I offer draws on research from two groups: compositionists who focus on cultural-historical activity theory[3] (Russell, "Rethinking" and "Activity Theory"; Prior; Dias et al.) and sociologists who study apprenticeship (Lave and Wenger; Wenger). Combined, these lines of research expand genre theory (Bawarshi; Russell, "Rethinking") and describe the complexities of learning to write, both in school and the workplace (Dias, et al.; Dias and Paré; Prior). The socio-historic view usefully illuminates the construction of subject positions and subjectivities specifically within institutions and disciplines.

Second, I illustrate some of the difficulties inherent in writing and identity 4 formation by telling the story of one new worker who struggled with written conventions and codes in his new workplace largely because of issues of identity and authority: how he saw himself versus how other members of this workplace community saw him. Most importantly, I argue that rather than assisting in the new worker's enculturation, members of the community expected a type of servitude: they perceived him not as a community member but as a tool, an identity that he fought strongly against.

## Identity

To tease out relationships between identity and writing in the workplace, we 5 need theories that consider the workplace as a legitimate and important influence on subject formation. Socio-historic theories provide one such perspective and describe identity construction within institutions. Like other postmodern theories, socio-historic theories see identity—the "subject"—as a complex "construction of the various signifying practices . . . formed by the various discourses, sign systems, that surround her" (Berlin 18). However, socio-historic theories view the subject as not only *constructed* by signifying practices but also as *constructing* signifying practices: "writers' desires are [not] completely determined, as evidenced by the fact that textual instantiations of a genre are rarely if ever exactly the same" (Bawarshi 91). Socio-historic theories also provide specific tools for analyzing the "levers" within institutions, allowing for a detailed examination of power and the formation of subject positions. Activity theory (Cole; Cole and Engeström; Cole and Scribner; Engeström; Russell, "Rethinking" and "Activity Theory"), for example, which focuses on the relationships among shared activities within communities and individual participants' sometimes competing understandings of motives, conventions, and divisions of labor for carrying out the activities, provides a framework for understanding the interactions of individuals, groups, and texts that enables researchers to illustrate the complex interactions among various aspects of an activity system (see Figure 1).

Activity theorists such as David Russell have also argued the importance 6 of the relationship between writing and identity: as we encounter genres mediating new activity systems, we must determine whether we can and/or must appropriate those genres, thus expanding our involvement within those systems. We must also consider whether expanding involvement in one system forces us away from other activity systems we value—away from "activity systems of family, neighborhood, and friends that construct ethnic, racial, gender, and class identit(ies)" ("Rethinking" 532). Writers can sometimes "challenge the genre positions and relations available to them," thus changing genres rather than choosing between the genres and their various activity systems (Bawarshi 97). However, socio-historic theories do not view such resistance as the result of self-will or "inherent forces within each human being that love liberty, seek to enhance their own powers or capacities, or strive for emancipation" (Rose 35), but rather suggest that "resistance arises from the contradictions individuals experience in their multiple subject positions" (Bawarshi 100). As writers shape and change genres, the power of those genres also shapes and enables writers' identities (Bawarshi 97).

Sociologist Etienne Wenger's theory of communities of practice (shaped, 7 initially, with Jean Lave) is particularly useful for describing workplace enculturation as it is affected by and as it affects written practices. Wenger

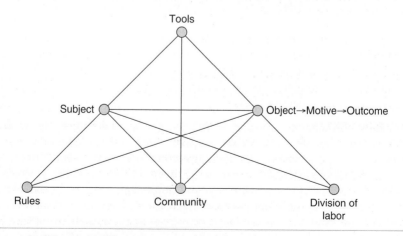

**Figure 1 Activity System Triangle**
(*Based on Engeström: Learning by Expanding*)

specifically focuses on matters of identity within *workplace* groups and activities, describing identity as a "negotiated experience . . . a layering of events of participation and reification by which our experience and its social interpretation inform each other" (149). According to Wenger, "layers build upon each other to produce our identity as a very complex interweaving of participative experience and reificative projections" (151). To "find their own unique identities" within new organizations (Wenger 156), newcomers must choose levels and types of engagement; they must find modes of belonging. Wenger describes three interrelated modes of belonging: engagement, imagination, and alignment.

- *Engagement* entails defining a "common enterprise" that newcomers and old-timers pursue together to develop "interpersonal relationships" and "a sense of interacting trajectories that shape identities in relation to one another" (184). While engagement can be positive, "a lack of mutuality in the course of engagement creates relations of marginality that can reach deeply into [newcomers'] identities" (193).
- *Imagination*, "a process of expanding . . . self by transcending . . . time and space and creating new images of the world and [self]" (176), entails newcomers "locating [their] engagement in a broader system . . . defining a trajectory that connects what [they] are doing to an extended identity . . . [and] assuming the meaning of foreign artifacts and actions" (185). While imagination can lead to a positive mode of belonging, it can also "be disconnected and ineffective . . . it can be so removed from any lived form of membership that it detaches [newcomers'] identit[ies] and leaves [them] in a state of uprootedness." Newcomers can lose "touch with the sense of social efficacy by which [their] experience of the world can be interpreted as competence" (178).
- *Alignment* entails "negotiating perspectives, finding common ground . . . defining broad visions and aspirations . . . [and] walking boundaries . . . reconciling diverging perspectives" (186–87). Alignment "requires shareable artifacts/boundary objects able to create fixed points around which to coordinate activities. It can also require the creation and adoption of broader discourses that help reify the enterprise and by which local actions can be interpreted as fitting within a broader framework" (187). However, alignment "can be a violation of [a person's] sense of self that crushes [their] identity" (181).

To fully participate, according to Wenger, new workers must find ways to engage in the work that other community members do, including the writing they do; newcomers must be able to imagine their own work—and writing—as being an important part of a larger enterprise. And they must be comfortable that the larger enterprise and its smaller components—down to the writing conventions of that community—are compatible with the identities they envision for themselves. Joining new workplace communities, then, is not simply a matter of learning new skills but also of fielding new calls for identity construction. This understanding of identity suggests that people *enact* and *negotiate* identities in the world over time: "Identity is dynamic (Hecht, 1993), and it is something that is presented and re-presented, constructed and reconstructed in interaction (including written communication)" (Rubin 9).

At times, however, participation in new communities requires accepting for oneself identities that are at odds with the values of other communities to which one belongs (Lave and Wenger; Russell, "Rethinking"). One way new-comers reconcile the competing demands of various communities is to choose to participate in some aspects of a new community and not others. Such choices are a source of power in that "power derives from belonging as well as from exercising control over what we belong to" (Wenger 207). In addition, choices about participation impact newcomers' emerging identities within communi-ties of practice. For example, the choice of non-participation can lead to mar-ginalization within the workplace (Wenger 167). Identity formation in any new community, then, is a negotiation in which newcomers have some measure of "control over the meanings in which [they] are invested" and can "assert [their] identities as productive of meaning" (Wenger 188, 208)—even if they do so by refusing to participate in some workplace activities.

Achieving enculturation in workplace communities requires neophytes to engage in new practices—including new *written* practices. Some new written practices may be opposed to newcomers' values and ethics; others may sim-ply be foreign to them; still others may ask them to give up some measure of authority to which they believe they are entitled. The resultant struggles will often be visible in their written practices. If new workers fail to write in ways that a workplace community of practice recognizes as effective and appropri-ate, the reasons may be related to identity rather than ability: "Stylistic options 'leak' clues about writers' social identities. Rhetorical choices help writers construct the social identities they wish to project in given writing episodes" (Rubin 4). Thus, failing to write in ways communities establish as appropri-ate can be a form of resistance that "does not arise from ignorance of stan-dard forms [but rather] entails considerable language awareness" (Rubin 7). On the other hand, new workers may not be consciously aware that their writ-ing choices are matters of identification: "marking social identity in writing is . . . oftentimes quite below the focal awareness of the writer" (8). Because each individual "is heterogeneously made up of various competing discourses, conflicted and contradictory scripts . . . our consciousness [is] anything but unified" (Berlin 18).

## Authority

As Wenger's theory implies, authority (like identity) is continually negotiated within communities of practice. Authority is bestowed by institutions, can be just as easily withdrawn by those same institutions or its members, and must be maintained through appropriate expressions of authority (Bourdieu). Bruce Lincoln argues that authority is best understood in relational terms "as the effect of a posited, perceived, or institutionally ascribed asymmetry between speaker and audience that permits certain speakers to command not just the attention but the confidence, respect, and trust of their audience, or . . . to make audiences act *as if* this were so" (4). When speakers possess authority, exercising that authority "need not involve argumentation and may rest on the naked assertion that the identity of the speaker warrants acceptance of the speech" (5). Those listening accept the speaker's pronouncement because the speaker *is who she is*. At any given time, however, faith in a speaker's authority can be suspended (either momentarily or forever) if "an explanation is requested . . ." because "the relation of trust and acceptance characteristic of authority is suspended, at least temporarily, in that moment" (6). Authority, then, is an intangible quality granted to persons through institutions, which renders their pronouncements as accepted by those in that institution's communities of practice, but which must be maintained through individuals' speech and actions.

Conversely, a person can understand clearly how to speak in ways that are acceptable in particular circumstances, but if not endowed with some recognized institutional authority, all the relevant and appropriate words in the world will not command it: "authority comes to language from outside. . . . Language at most represents this authority, manifests and symbolizes it" (Bourdieu 109). Bourdieu, while not specifically explaining enculturation, suggests that authority may be a kind of "social magic," dependent upon the "social position of the speaker," and reinforced by her ability to appropriately adjust her speech acts:

> Most of the conditions that have to be fulfilled in order for a performative utterance to succeed come down to the question of the appropriateness of the speaker—or, better still, his social function—and of the discourse he utters . . . it must be uttered by the person legitimately licensed to so do . . . it must be uttered in a legitimate situation . . . in front of legitimate receivers . . . [and] it must be enunciated according to the legitimate forms (syntactic, phonetic, etc.). (Bourdieu 111–12)

Thus, if the neophyte is granted some measure of authority by an institution but does not quickly learn the appropriate speech conventions of her new community of practice, she may soon lose the authority with which she began. While newcomers to a community normally experience a "grace period" for adopting community practices, it does not last forever and soon the neophyte must express her authority in her new community appropriately: "[L]earning to become a legitimate participant in a community involves learning how to talk (and be silent) in the manner of full participants" (Lave and Wenger 105).

If we understand writing as one tool among many through which knowledge, identity, and authority are continually negotiated, then we must view learning to write in new ways as a complex and often messy network of tool-mediated human relationships best explored in terms of the social and cultural practices that people bring to their shared uses of tools. If we accept these assumptions, we find ourselves faced with several questions: What happens when new workers find that to "get along" in a new workplace they must accept basic assumptions about what is valuable and appropriate that are contrary to their own—or that, in fact, degrade them to the status of an object or tool? What happens when a new worker's assumptions are frequently made obvious to the community, and those assumptions fly in the face of accepted ways of doing things?

## Learning to Write in a New Workplace: Alan's Story

My story of "Alan"—a computer support specialist who did not learn/choose  15 to write in ways his humanities department colleagues (primarily professors and graduate students) found appropriate and legitimate—illustrates answers to some of the questions about identity and authority as they intersect with writing in the workplace. For seven months, I observed and interviewed Alan, a new computer specialist in a humanities department at a large Midwestern university. I also collected 140 email messages he wrote and many others that were written to him and spent time in public computer labs listening as people discussed their computer problems with Alan. Finally, near the end of the study, I conducted a written survey with all members of the humanities department regarding their use of computers and technology and their awareness of various initiatives Alan had discussed with them via email.

Alan and the other members of the humanities department were constantly  16 at cross purposes—he did not write in ways the community members saw as appropriate, and he did not view their conventions as ones he should adopt, given his position in the community. Most importantly, the community of practice did not appear to view him as a fledging member but rather as an object—a tool enabling them to get work done. His discursive choices can be viewed as an attempt to reject the identity of tool and to appropriate authority for himself. Thus, Alan's story serves to illustrate some of the complexities associated with learning to write in new workplaces.

### Who Is Alan and What Is His Place in the Humanities Department?

Alan was a 23-year-old white male who received a B.A. in art and design from  17 a large Midwestern university. He became interested in computers as an undergraduate and as his interest in computers grew, he performed two computer-related work-study jobs on campus. He decided he liked working with computers and looked for a computer job when he graduated. Alan's first professional position was as computer support specialist responsible for several thousand "users" in various locations at the same university from which he graduated. He was unhappy in this position, primarily because he felt his supervisor did not give him enough responsibility, instead assigning the most difficult tasks to student workers who had been in the department for a long time. He left this job for another in an academic humanities department within the same university, again as a computer support specialist.

In the academic department, Alan was the sole computer support special-  18 ist, surrounded by faculty members with varying computer abilities. While no one else performed a job similar to his, the department included other support staff—all women, primarily administrative assistants—and Alan supervised one student worker several hours per week. Alan's supervisor, the department chair (a white male in his early fifties with a Ph.D. and numerous publications and awards), initially left most computer-related decisions to Alan, though the chair's collaborative administrative style made the division of labor unclear to newcomers. A Computer Resources Committee also interacted regularly with Alan, but whether they had authority over him was unclear. The mentoring he received was fairly hands-off, resembling what Lave and Wenger call "benign community neglect" (93), a situation that left Alan to find his own way, which he saw as a vote of confidence.

## What Was Alan's View of Himself and His Authority?

Alan's sense of what it meant to fill a support staff position was very different 19 from the faculty's sense. He left his previous position because it had not allowed him much responsibility, his supervisors "relied on students' work more than" his, and he felt he "was getting no respect." This previous experience strongly informed his understanding of his current job. Because Alan had some measure of institutional authority by way of the cultural capital associated with technical knowledge, Alan did not initially have to prove himself knowledgeable or competent in the ways many new workers do. He was immediately ascribed authority and respect due to his assumed technical expertise in a place where such expertise was rare. When I asked Alan to name and describe his position he replied: "I am basically a systems administrator, which means I am God here. Anywhere in this department. Except for with the department chair." This continued to be Alan's attitude during his tenure in the department. He often indicated that there was no one "above him" but the department chair. During his fourth week in the position, Alan told me he "couldn't believe how much authority" he had, "how high up in the computer world responsibility-wise" he was. He stressed that his title put "only one other person above" him in the university or the department.

Alan's sense of his level of authority was evident in the way he talked about 20 the faculty members in the department. He described the faculty members as "just users; nobodies [who] use the computers I set up." He indicated they were beneath him: "I put myself down on their level." To Alan, the faculty were simply "users" of his tools. He did not seem to understand—or care about—the faculty members' work or how his tools enabled them to do that work. His focus was on what *he* did: making machines work. His comments illustrate his attempt to find a mode of belonging through imagination; unfortunately, he imagined an identity for himself fairly removed from the reality of the situation.

In reality, he was hired in a support staff position, as a "tool" to fix things 21 the faculty needed. The faculty clearly viewed Alan as support personnel. They were happiest when things worked smoothly and when Alan's work hummed along invisibly and successfully behind the scenes. When his assistance was required, they expected him to appear immediately; some faculty even went so far as to copy email messages to the chair and computer resources committee to ensure that Alan knew there would be repercussions if he did not appear when called upon. Alan's view of everyone else as "just users" came across clearly in his writing (which primarily took place via email) and eventually called his competence into question such that department members often failed to respond to him, were ignorant of his initiatives to help them, and laughed at him and his emails. This misalignment between Alan's imagined role for himself and the role imagined for him by others led to a lack of the positive engagement Wenger argues may help newcomers enculturate; Alan and the other members of the humanities department were not actively engaging or mutually negotiating their work together.

## How Did Alan Relate to the Department in Writing?

A number of discourse conventions existed in the department that could have 22 afforded Alan further authority. Had he adopted these conventions, Alan could have achieved alignment with the department, for example using emails as "boundary objects able to create fixed points around which to coordinate activities" (Wenger 187). Alan did not adopt the conventions of the department, however. Although it is possible for writers "to enact slightly different intentions" and "resist the ideological pull of genres in certain circumstances," their resistance will only be "recognized and valued as resistance and not misinterpretation, or worse, ignorance" if it is "predicated on one's knowledge of a genre" (Bawarshi 92). Alan's written interactions with the department were seen not as resistance but as ignorance, and identified him as an outsider without authority.

One of the conventions Alan did not follow when he wrote involved the de- 23 partment's approximately 15 or 20 listservs, each reaching a specific audience. Tailoring emails to a particular audience was an accepted writing convention in the activity system. During the beginning of each fall semester, listserv addresses were sent out and department members were encouraged to use the list that most directly reached their message's audience. Alan chose to use the list that reached all department members for nearly every email he wrote—despite the fact that he administered all the lists and knew lists more tailored to his messages existed. His email activity did not "fit within [the] broader structures," demonstrating his lack of alignment with the department (Wenger 173).

A survey of the department I conducted indicated that Alan's lack of audi- 24 ence awareness and tailoring had negative consequences for his identity in the department: most people were unaware of his efforts to better their computer system because they either did not read or did not remember reading the information he sent out via email. In other words, the members of the department did not see Alan as engaged in work with and for them. For example, much of his time was spent setting up a new departmental computer network that would benefit all department members by providing them private, disk-free storage space. He discussed this in emails many times, but usually in emails that mentioned a number of other items directed at more specialized audiences.

As a result, over half the survey respondents did not know he was setting up a new network. People indicated on the survey that they stopped reading an email if the first item of business did not relate to them.

Other accepted departmental conventions governed the content and style of emails. The community members were highly literate, hyper-aware language users, in the traditional sense of the terms, who valued professional, grammatically correct, Standard English in written communication. The unspoken convention that email within the department be grammatically correct was pervasive and widely practiced in the community. Abiding by this convention was difficult for Alan, who explicitly said on several occasions that he felt his writing abilities were not good. His emails show a number of grammatical errors including sentence fragments, double negatives, and misplaced punctuation. In addition, Alan's emails often contained directives about the use of computers and labs; he frequently implied that people should respect his authority and position in the department by doing what he asked. His utterances were intended to be *"signs of authority . . . to be believed and obeyed"* (Bourdieu 66). However, he sent these emails to many irrelevant audiences and his grammar, punctuation, and sentence structure often undermined his authority as understood by audience members.

Although Alan was institutionally authorized to speak about technology, and recognized as a technical authority, he was not able to "speak in a way that others . . . regard[ed] as acceptable in the circumstances" (Thompson 9). Survey respondents' comments suggested that people dismissed Alan's legitimacy because of his writing choices. While he appeared to feel this dismissal, he did not change his writing behavior and his institutional authority began to erode.

## What Was the Outcome?

The fact that Alan, a newcomer, used email in ways that old-timers saw as inappropriate—and that this use of email caused conflict—is not surprising; after all, newcomers are expected to make missteps. But rather than adapting and changing to communicate more effectively in his new workplace, Alan resisted and clung to his own ways of writing, causing conflict and breakdowns in the community of practice. Members of the department were similarly unwilling to change their view of what they found acceptable in email. They insisted on what Bourdieu calls "the dominant competence" and imposed their idea of linguistic competence as "the only legitimate one" (56). The community didn't negotiate or compromise its idea of linguistic competence for Alan; the only real possibility for negotiation had to come from Alan—and it did not.

Because our identities are shaped to some extent by the communities in which we choose to participate—as well as by those settings we inhabit and in which we choose *not* to participate (Wenger 164)—workers such as Alan may also be demonstrating their desire to identify with communities of practice other than the primary ones in which they work by refusing to appropriate new ways of writing. By refusing to participate in communication conventions adopted by the majority of members of the community, Alan attempted to assert the identity he imagined for himself (powerful network administrator) and to resist the one imposed on him by the workplace. Pushing past resistance to work effectively with others requires people to relinquish aspects of their desired primary identities: "[L]egitimate participation entails the loss of certain identities even as it enables the construction of others" (Hodges 289). Clearly, Alan did not feel this was an acceptable proposition. The result for Alan, as Wenger might predict, was increasing marginalization. His emails were not only the butt of cruel and constant jokes in the department, but they also failed to garner support and convey necessary information. People ignored his emails or laughed at them, and neither response was conducive to getting work done. Ultimately, Alan's choice of non-participation resulted in "disturbances and breakdowns in work processes" (Hasu and Engeström 65).

Socio-historic activity theory argues that such situations can lead to posi- 29 tive developments because breakdowns can potentially serve as catalysts for change: "Discoordination and breakdown often lead to re-mediation of the performance and perspectives, sometimes even to re-mediation of the overall activity system in order to resolve its pressing inner contradictions" (Hasu and Engeström 65). However, for a breakdown to lead to positive change, those involved must be willing to consider and negotiate various perspectives and everyone must be willing to appropriate some new ways of seeing and doing. This did not happen in Alan's case. He clung to his own ways of writing and communicating, which demonstrated that he was not engaging, aligning, and imagining a role for himself as a member of the humanities department. Other members of the humanities department no more changed to accommodate Alan than Alan did to fit in with them.

After a year and a half, Alan left and found employment elsewhere.   30

## Discussion

Clearly, Alan's enculturation into the humanities department was not success- 31 ful. He was an outsider, a worker unlike the other community members in age, education, occupation, linguistic abilities, and concern for conventions. Since new workers are often different in these ways and still manage to negoti- ate communication strategies that are effective and acceptable enough so that work can be done, what might account for Alan's resistance to writing in ways that his new community saw as legitimate and appropriate?

One reason for his resistance was that Alan and other members of his de- 32 partment had a different understanding of the division of labor in the depart- ment and, thus, a different view of Alan's authority. Alan might have viewed changing his writing habits as an admission that he did not play the role he imagined for himself within the department. Despite his vocal assertions to the contrary, he was not "God" in the department. While he entered the de- partment with some measure of authority by virtue of his technical expertise, he had to prove himself and create his *ethos* continually through language— perhaps even more than through action for this particular workplace. This was something he could not or would not do.

However, a socio-linguistic analysis I conducted of Alan's writing suggests 33 that he did not feel as much authority as he claimed to have, even from the beginning of his time in the department when he had the most cooperation and respect because of his technical capital. Of 150 sentences I studied for the analysis, only 39 were directives. While all of Alan's emails were usually sent to department-wide listservs, the overwhelming majority of his directives (28 of the 39) were addressed to graduate students alone. Only 3 were written to faculty or staff members, and 6 were written to the department as a whole. Alan's use of directives suggests that while he claimed to have authority and see the faculty as simply "users," he did not, in fact, feel much authority over them, so he confined most of his directives to graduate students. Even then, Alan used hedges over two-thirds of the time, suggesting that his felt sense of authority was shaky. This understanding best matched the department's understanding. He could make technical changes and monitor and limit operations; however, he could not force people to act in the ways he wanted them to or prohibit them from using equipment, as he threatened in more than one email.

Given the limitations of his actual authority—which conflicted with his 34 desired authority—Alan's refusal to change his writing might have been one way of claiming an identity he wanted, one that included the authority and autonomy to which he felt entitled. However, his refusal to write in ways seen as acceptable by the department had the opposite effect: his method of writing stripped him of the institutional authority originally invested in him. Although Alan's words could be understood, they were not "likely to be listened to [or] recognized as acceptable." He lacked "the competence necessary in order to speak the legitimate language," which could have granted him "linguistic capital . . . a profit of distinction" (Bourdieu 55). Since authoritative language is useless "without the collaboration of those it governs," Alan's initial authority was lessened with each utterance seen by the department as illegitimate (Bourdieu 113). We should keep in mind that Alan's choices are unlikely to have been conscious; quite often linguistic action is not "the outcome of conscious calculation" (Thompson 17).

A second reason for Alan's failure to adopt community writing conventions 35 might have been his resistance to being used as a tool. As a support person, Alan joined this activity system as one of its tools, not as a community member. As a technical worker with a B.A. in a university humanities department filled with people who had M.A.s and Ph.D.s, he and the other members of the workplace were not mutually engaged. Rather, the community members used him as a tool to help achieve goals Alan did not share or value. Computer system administrators (like many other workers) are used as tools to do work that others cannot. As a result of his position, Alan was not part of the community of practice; rather, his ability to maintain computer networks figured in as one of many pieces of the humanities community: the community members needed him and his activity to use their computers.

Though Alan was hired to function as a tool, he did not sit quietly like a 36 hammer or wrench until he was needed, he did not perform exactly the same way each time he was needed, and he did not remain silent when his work was complete. As a person, Alan didn't always choose to perform his tasks when and how community members wanted. In addition, he initiated and responded to dialogue, and (most frustrating for members of the humanities department) chose to do so in ways contrary to the community expectations. Alan's refusal to write in ways that the faculty felt he should was, perhaps, one means of flouting their linguistic authority, demonstrating that he was not a servant or tool to be used at will. Rather than quietly performing the tasks asked of him, and writing about them in the ways the community members saw as legitimate, Alan resisted the department by seeing *them* as *his* tools and by choosing non-participation over acquiescence to their written conventions. Alan's method of resistance did bring him to the conscious attention of department members; they quickly came to see him as a human being who did not silently serve them in response to their every need or desire. However, his method of resistance did not enable Alan to complete his own work successfully, nor did it lead the humanities department to include him as a human member of their community. Thus, Alan's method of resistance in this case was successful on one level, but detrimental to both himself and the workplace on other levels.

Alan's example illustrates that learning to write in new communities entails 37 more than learning discrete sets of skills or improving cognitive abilities. It is a process of involvement in communities, of identifying with certain groups, of choosing certain practices over others; a process strongly influenced by power relationships—a process, in effect, bound up tightly with identity, authority, and experience. Alan's case also suggests that enculturation theories have overlooked an important point: not all new workers are expected, or themselves expect, to enculturate into a community. Some, perhaps many in our service-oriented society, are present in communities of practice not as members but as tools. Given these points, those of us interested in how people learn to write in new environments, in school and beyond, and those of us struggling to teach new ways of writing to students who resist what we ask of them, must continue to study and consider the importance of factors beyond texts and cognitive ability.

## Acknowledgments

Thanks to Rebecca Burnett (Iowa State University) and Charie Thralls (Utah State University) for encouraging this study and responding to early drafts; to David Russell (Iowa State University) and Donna Kain (Clarkson University) for responding to later drafts; and to Lisa Coleman and Judy Isaksen, *Enculturation* guest editor and board member respectively, for their helpful reviews.

## Notes

1. "A community of practice is a set of relations among persons, activity, and world, over time and in relation with other tangential and overlapping communities of practice" (Lave and Wenger 98).
2. "Knowledge, skills, and other cultural acquisitions, as exemplified by educational or technical qualifications" (Thompson 14).

3. Though relatively new to many in our field, activity theory is used more and more widely within composition studies; see, for example, Bazerman and Russell; Berkenkotter and Ravotas; Dias, et al.; Dias and Paré; Grossman, Smagorinsky and Valencia; Harms; Hovde; Kain; Russell, "Rethinking" and "Activity Theory"; Smart; Spinuzzi; Wardle; Winsor. Activity theory's implications for composition instruction are outlined in Russell's "Activity Theory and Its Implications for Writing Instruction" and in Wardle's *Contradiction, Constraint, and Re-Mediation: An Activity Analysis of* FYC and "Can Cross-Disciplinary Links Help Us Teach 'Academic Discourse' in FYC?"

## Works Cited

Bawarshi, Anis. *Genre and the Invention of the Writer: Reconsidering the Place of Invention in Composition*. Logan: Utah State UP, 2003. Print.

Bazerman, Charles. *Shaping Written Knowledge: The Genre and Activity of the Experimental Article in Sciences*. Madison: U of Wisconsin P, 1988. Print.

Bazerman, Charles, and David Russell. *Writing Selves/Writing Societies: Research from Activity Perspectives*. Fort Collins: The WAC Clearinghouse and *Mind, Culture, and Activity*, 2002. Print.

Berkenkotter, Carol, Thomas Huckin, and Jon Ackerman. "Conversations, Conventions, and the Writer." *Research in the Teaching of English* 22 (1988): 9–44. Print.

Berkenkotter, Carol, and Thomas Huckin. "Rethinking Genre from a Sociocognitive Perspective." *Written Communication* 10 (1993): 475–509. Print.

Berkenkotter, Carol, and Doris Ravotas. "Genre as a Tool in the Transmission of Practice and across Professional Boundaries." *Mind, Culture, and Activity* 4.4 (1997): 256–74. Print.

Berlin, James. "Poststructuralism, Cultural Studies, and the Composition Classroom: Postmodern Theory in Practice." *Rhetoric Review* 11 (1992): 16–33. Print.

Bizzell, Patricia. "Cognition, Convention, and Certainty: What We Need to Know about Writing." *Pre/Text* 3 (1982): 213–43. Print.

Bolin, Bill. "The Role of the Media in Distinguishing Composition from Rhetoric." *Enculturation* 5.1 (Fall 2003): n. pag. Web. 1 July 2004.

Bourdieu, Pierre. *Language and Symbolic Power*. Ed. John B. Thompson. Trans. Gino Raymond and Matthew Adamson. Cambridge: Harvard UP, 1991. Print.

Cole, Michael. *Cultural Psychology*. Cambridge: Harvard UP, 1996. Print.

Cole, Michael, and Yrgo Engeström. "A Cultural-Historical Approach to Distributed Cognition." Ed. Gavriel Salomon. *Distributed Cognitions: Psychological and Educational Considerations*. Cambridge: Cambridge UP, 1993. 1–46. Print.

Cole, Michael, and Sylvia Scribner. *The Psychology of Literacy*. Cambridge: Harvard UP, 1981. Print.

Dias, Patrick, and Anthony Paré, eds. *Transitions: Writing in Academic and Workplace Settings*. Cresskill: Hampton, 2000. Print.

Dias, Patrick, Aviva Freedman, Peter Medway, and Anthony Paré. *Worlds Apart: Acting and Writing in Academic and Workplace Contexts*. Mahwah: Lawrence Erlbaum, 1999. Print.

Doheny-Farina, Stephen. "A Case Study of an Adult Writing in Academic and Non-Academic Settings." *Worlds of Writing: Teaching and Learning in Discourse Communities at Work*. Ed. Carolyn B. Matalene. New York: Random, 1989. 17–42. Print.

Doheny-Farina, Stephen, and Lee Odell. "Ethnographic Research on Writing: Assumptions and Methodology." *Writing in Nonacademic Settings*. Eds. Lee Odell and Dixie Goswami. New York: Guilford, 1985. 503–35. Print.

Engeström, Yrgo. *Learning by Expanding: An Activity-Theoretical Approach to Developmental Research*. Helsinki: Orienta-Konsultit, 1987. Print.

Grossman, Pamela L., Peter Smagorinsky, and Sheila Valencia. "Appropriating Tools for Teaching English: A Theoretical Framework for Research on Learning to Teach." *American Journal of Education* 108 (1999): 1–29. Print.

Harms, Patricia. *Writing-across-the-Curriculum in a Linked Course Model for First-Year Students: An Activity Theory Analysis.* Ames: Iowa State UP, 2003. Print.

Hasu, Mervi, and Yrgo Engeström. "Measurement in Action: An Activity-Theoretical Perspective on Producer-User Interaction." *International Journal of Human-Computer Studies* 53 (2000): 61–89. Print.

Hodges, Diane. "Participation as Dis-Identification With/In a Community of Practice." *Mind, Culture, and Activity* 5 (1998): 272–90. Print.

Hovde, Marjorie. "Tactics for Building Images of Audience in Organizational Contexts: An Ethnographic Study of Technical Communicators." *Journal of Business and Technical Communication* 14.4 (2000): 395–444. Print.

Kain, Donna J. *Negotiated Spaces: Constructing Genre and Social Practice in a Cross-Community Writing Project.* Ames: Iowa State UP, 2003. Print.

Lave, Jean, and Etienne Wenger. *Situated Learning: Legitimate Peripheral Participation.* New York: Cambridge UP, 1991. Print.

Lincoln, Bruce. *Authority: Construction and Corrosion.* Chicago: U of Chicago P, 1994. Print.

Paré, Anthony. "Genre and Identity: Individuals, Institutions, and Ideology." *The Rhetoric and Ideology of Genre.* Eds. Richard Coe, Lorelei Lingard, and Tatiana Teslenko. Cresskill: Hampton, 2002. Print.

Prior, Paul. *Writing/Disciplinarity: A Sociohistoric Account of Literate Activity in the Academy.* Mahwah: Lawrence Erlbaum, 1998. Print.

Rose, Nikolas. *Inventing Ourselves: Psychology, Power, and Personhood.* Cambridge: Cambridge UP, 1996. Print.

Rubin, Donald L. "Introduction: Composing Social Identity." *Composing Social Identity in Written Language.* Ed. Donald Rubin. Hillsdale: Lawrence Erlbaum, 1995. 1–30. Print.

Russell, David. "Rethinking Genre in School and Society: An Activity Theory Analysis." *Written Communication* 14 (1997): 504–39. Print.

———. "Activity Theory and Its Implications for Writing Instruction." *Reconceiving Writing, Rethinking Writing Instruction.* Ed. Joseph Petraglia. Mahwah: Lawrence Erlbaum, 1995. 51–77. Print.

Smart, Graham. "Genre as Community Invention: A Central Bank's Response to Its Executives' Expectations as Readers." *Writing in the Workplace: New Research Perspectives.* Ed. Rachel Spilka. Carbondale: Southern Illinois UP, 1993. 124–40. Print.

Spinuzzi, Clay. "Pseudotransactionality, Activity Theory, and Professional Writing Instruction." *Technical Communication Quarterly* 5.3 (1996): 295–308. Print.

Thompson, John B. "Editor's Introduction." *Language and Symbolic Power.* By Pierrie Bourdieu. Cambridge: Harvard UP, 1999. 1–31. Print.

Wardle, Elizabeth. *Contradiction, Constraint, and Re-Mediation: An Activity Analysis of FYC.* Ames: Iowa State UP, 2003. Print.

———. "Can Cross-Disciplinary Links Help Us Teach 'Academic Discourse' in FYC?" *Across the Disciplines* 1 (2004): n. pag. Web. 1 July 2004.

Wenger, Etienne. *Communities of Practice: Learning, Meaning, and Identity.* New York: Cambridge UP, 1998. Print.

Winsor, Dorothy. "Genre and Activity Systems: The Role of Documentation in Maintaining and Changing Engineering Activity Systems." *Written Communication* 16.2 (1999): 200–24. Print.

## Questions for Discussion and Journaling

1. Drawing on Wardle (who cites Wenger), what are the three ways that newcomers try to belong in a new community? Give a specific example to illustrate each "mode of belonging." Then consider why a newcomer might choose *not* to participate in some aspect of a new community.

2. Wardle quotes Rubin as saying that "stylistic options 'leak' clues about writers' social identities" (para. 10). Explain what this means. Do you have examples from your own experience?

3. Wardle quotes Hasu and Engeström, well-known activity theory scholars, as saying that conflict and breakdown can actually be positive (para. 29), helping to reshape how a community does things in ways that are more productive. However, the conflicts between Alan and his work community did not have positive results. Why do you think this is? How could his conflicts have been handled so that they *did* result in positive change?

4. Toward the end of the article, Wardle quotes Thompson as saying that the choices we make with language are very often unconscious (para. 34); that is, we might be using language in resistant ways unintentionally. Do you agree that this is possible, or do you think that people are usually making conscious choices when they use language?

5. Wardle seems to be arguing that Alan did not successfully join his new workplace community because he was resisting it: He did not want to adopt the identity that people in that community imagined for him. James Gee, in an article included in the e-Pages for this book, would likely have a very different opinion; he would most likely argue that Alan could not have joined the Humanities Department activity system even if he had wanted to. Take a look at the Gee article and then consider whether you agree more with Wardle or Gee.

6. When Wardle was drafting this article, several readers objected to her claim that people like Alan are used as tools, not seen as community members. What do you think?

7. Think of all the people you know who have some sort of institutionally ascribed authority. (Hint: One of them probably assigned this reading!) Can you think of a time when one or more of them lost their authority in your eyes or someone else's through their linguistic actions or behaviors? If so, what happened?

## Applying and Exploring Ideas

1. Write a reflective essay of just a few pages in which you (first) define what it means to have authority over texts and within activity systems, and (second) discuss your feelings about your own authority (or lack of it) within any activity system you would like to focus on. Consider, for example, how you know whether you have authority there and how you gained text and discourse authority there (if you did); alternatively, consider how it feels to be at the mercy of someone else's authority in an activity system.

2. Make a list of all the tools that mediate the activities of this writing class. How do they help you do the work of the class? How would the work be different if the tools were different? Do you think there are tools that could make the class more effective that are currently not used?

> **Meta Moment**
>
> Why do you think the readings in this chapter seem to refer to *authority* so much? How might thinking about sources of authority help you as a writer on the job, in college, or in your personal writing?

# The Genres of Chi Omega:
# An Activity Analysis

## VICTORIA MARRO

■ Marro, Victoria. "The Genres of Chi Omega: An Activity Analysis." *Stylus: A Journal of First-Year Writing* 3.1 (2012): 25–32. Web. 11 Sept. 2013.

## Framing the Reading

Victoria "Tori" Marro was a student in Elizabeth Wardle's Honors Composition II course at the University of Central Florida (UCF) in Fall 2011. In that class, the students worked on research projects related to literacies in their own lives. Tori was actively involved with her sorority and interested in the ways that her sorority used texts to help chapters in different states achieve some consistent identities and activities. She wrote a draft of the text you see here as her final project, and then later submitted it to UCF's peer-reviewed journal of first-year writing, *Stylus*. The paper was accepted and underwent additional revision with help from the *Stylus* editors prior to publication in the Spring 2012 issue. The version you see here is the version published in *Stylus*. This article received an award during UCF's 3rd Annual Knights Write Showcase (which you can read about on the First-Year Writing Web site: http://writingandrhetoric.cah.ucf.edu/showcase.php). Tori is currently majoring in microbiology and molecular biology and is applying to medical schools.

## Getting Ready to Read

*Before you read*, do at least one of the following activities:

- Jot down the definition of *genre* as you understand it.
- Quickly consider what you think genres do, why they exist.

*As you read*, consider the following question:

- Does your initial understanding of genres matches Marro's understanding?

## Introduction

Sororities have existed for over 100 years and have maintained their values even as time passes and chapters become farther apart. One way these organizations have been able to keep these traditions is through the 1 use of various genres. According to the work of writing researchers such as Amy Devitt, genres are flexible responses to fit the needs of a discourse community or social setting. A discourse community is a group with agreed upon goals, communication, the use of genres, feedback, a threshold level of membership and specified language (Johns). Researchers Amy Devitt, Anis Bawarshi and Mary Jo Reiff have looked at the way that genres serve the needs of juries, doctors' offices, and classrooms. According to these researchers, "genre study allows students and researchers to recognize how 'lived textuality' plays a role in the lived experience of a group" (Bawarshi, Devitt, and Reiff 542).

One community that plays a big part in my life and in the lives of 300,000 2 other women is my sorority, Chi Omega. Usually, research done on Greek life involves eating disorders and problems with hazing, but such issues should not define these organizations. Not enough research has been done on the complex genre systems, or genre sets, used by sororities and fraternities. A genre set, as defined by Charles Bazerman, is a group of several genres that predictably recur inside a domain-specified community (Honig 91). A genre system, as defined by Amy Devitt, is a "set of genres interacting to achieve an overarching function within an activity system" (Bawarshi and Reiff 87). Genre sets and systems are important with regard to social action and interact to further the purposes of a group. By analyzing these, social roles and progress become much clearer within activity systems: "A genre system includes genres from multiple genre sets, over time, and can involve the interaction of users with different levels of expertise and authority, who may not all have equal knowledge of or access to all" (Bawarshi and Reiff 88). In an organization as large as Chi Omega, this is incredibly important because the levels of authority and expertise of members varies so greatly. Bazerman has previously looked at the use of genre systems in classrooms and in the US patent application process (Bawarshi and Reiff 88). In this paper, I will look at the genres used within Chi Omega and how the use of genre systems help the 173 collegiate chapters of Chi Omega function both independently and together as one activity system. For the purposes of this paper, an activity system functions in a similar fashion to a discourse community, with laid out purposes, tools, rules, subject, community and a division of labor. This will be further explained in my discussion. I will look at the different genres that are used, as well as the different ways that the same genre may be used by different chapters, examining the ways that the same tool can serve completely different purposes for different chapters. I will specifically look at the genres we use in my chapter today, and how these genres are utilized to further the goals of Chi Omega.

> *I will look at the genres used within Chi Omega and how the use of the genre systems help the 173 collegiate chapters of Chi Omega function both independently and together as one activity system.*

## Methods

I interviewed two sisters in other Chi Omega chapters, including Emily, an 3 active sister in the Eta Delta chapter at the University of Florida and Summer, an active sister of the Psi Kappa chapter at Clemson University. Their names have been changed. These sisters were asked what technologies their executive boards used to communicate with them; about genres used by chapters such as a weekly newsletter, Billhighway and the GIN system; and their opinion on the effectiveness of said genres. These sisters were asked their opinions on the importance of writing and ritual to Chi Omega nationally, and about the national magazine, *The Eleusis*.

An interview was also conducted with Brittany, an alum from the Psi Mu 4 chapter of Chi Omega at the University of Central Florida. Her name has been changed as well. She was asked how the executive board communicated with the sisters during her time in the chapter, about a weekly newsletter, the GIN system, and her opinion on the effectiveness of these genres. She was asked about her involvement in an alumnae chapter and the genres that were used within that chapter. She was also asked about the national magazine, *The Eleusis*.

The Psi Mu chapter secretary, Allison, was interviewed about the writing she 5 does for the chapter and the way she became versed in these genres. She was asked her opinion on the effectiveness of the GIN system and the problems with this system. Other questions included her opinions on the importance of writing to the national organization and whether or not she reads *The Eleusis*.

I also interviewed Psi Mu chapter president, Nicole. Nicole was asked about 6 how the GIN system came into effect and what methods of communication were used prior to this system. She was asked about the ritual text, but at the request of the chapter secretary, these responses will not be included. Like in all of the other interviews, she was asked if she read *The Eleusis*. As the chapter president, she was asked about her communication with other chapters and with nationals, and her opinion on the importance of writing and written communication to the organization as a whole.

Over twenty genres were collected and analyzed including the GIN system, 7 *The Eleusis*, the weekly newsletter, announcements, files and others. The importance of genres that could not be accessed, such as the written rituals and the Book of Rules, were analyzed as well. Activity triangles were constructed for Chi Omega as a national organization, as well as for individual chapters and genres. Database searches were conducted and previous research was synthesized to support findings.

Activity triangles were constructed to analyze the activity systems, Chi 8 Omega nationally, the Psi Mu, Psi Kappa, and Eta Delta chapters, and the GIN system. Activity theory, which says that people write as part of an activity system, can be displayed in a triangle, with tools at the top, subject on the middle left, object on the middle right, rules in the lower left, the community in the lower middle, and division of labor in the lower right-hand corner. A series of arrows inside the triangle shows how each portion is connected to the others (see Figure 1).

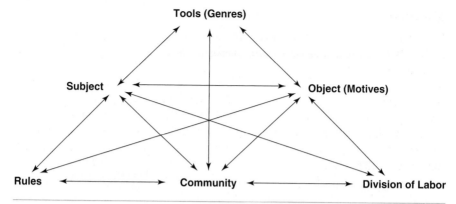

**Figure 1**   Organization of an Activity System

## Results and Discussion

Through activity analysis, I found that the chapters of Chi Omega all write 9
in different genres; however, all of the chapters share the same goals, which
are laid out in the mission statement, a shared genre. I found that this mission
statement is broken up into six parts, and each of those has a director, which
makes up the cardinal cabinet. Each director works with a specific genre set,
and these together make up a genre system. In the Psi Mu chapter, one super-
genre encompasses all of these genres sets and works as a genre system within
that genre.

Chi Omega sorority was founded in 1895 by Dr. Charles Richardson, Ina 10
May Boles, Jean Vincenhcller, Jobelle Holcombe, and Alice Simonds. Chi
Omega has initiated over 300,000 members and has 173 collegiate chapters.
The tools used by Chi Omega nationally are the written rituals, established by
Dr. Charles Richardson when the sorority was founded; the Book of Rules,
which lists all rules for members; the Chi Omega Symphony and mission
statement, which summarize the organization's purposes; the chapter rosters;
ChiOmega.com; and *The Eleusis,* the national magazine. In a letter from the
national president that came with the latest issue of *The Eleusis,* she states
the purpose of the magazine is "to connect our members to the national organization by sharing experiences, spotlighting successes, and providing tools
for the development of our members" (Fulkerson). The written ritual provides
the lexis, or specialized language, of the discourse community. The rituals are
confidential and therefore will not be further explained. The motives or objects
of the activity system are to promote friendship, integrity, scholarship, community service, involvement in the community and career and personal development. These purposes make up the mission statement of Chi Omega. The rules
are determined by the Book of Rules and, in individual chapters, the bylaws.
The community is all of the sisters and new members of Chi Omega in all of
the chapters, both collegiate and alumni. The division of labor in each chapter
is determined by the slating process, in which sisters nominate other sisters for

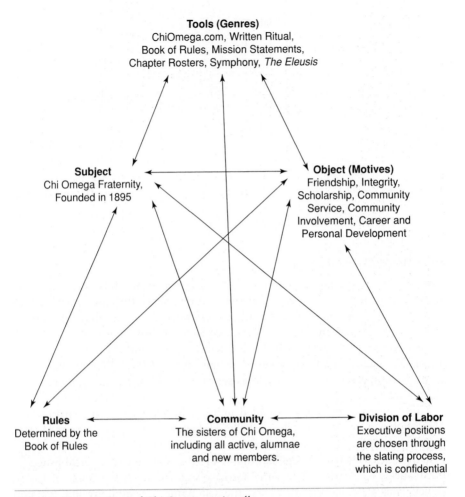

**Tools (Genres)**
ChiOmega.com, Written Ritual,
Book of Rules, Mission Statements,
Chapter Rosters, Symphony, *The Eleusis*

**Subject**
Chi Omega Fraternity,
Founded in 1895

**Object (Motives)**
Friendship, Integrity,
Scholarship, Community
Service, Community
Involvement, Career and
Personal Development

**Rules**
Determined by the
Book of Rules

**Community**
The sisters of Chi Omega,
including all active, alumnae
and new members.

**Division of Labor**
Executive positions
are chosen through
the slating process,
which is confidential

**Figure 2**   Organization of Chi Omega nationally

a position, other sisters give their input, and then another sister is nominated for that position as well. All of the input is recorded along with all of the sisters nominated for positions and at the end of the day the executive board is chosen based on that information. The idea of slating is that the position seeks the woman, not the other way around. Those who tell people they would like to be slated are ineligible to hold an executive position (see Figure 2). This activity system can be applied to each of the 173 collegiate chapters, and although in most cases more genres are used as well, it keeps all of the chapters in line with the same values and purposes.

## Using Different Tools to Achieve the Same Motives

Chi Omega is such a large organization that it would be incredibly difficult to 11
use only a few genres and have every chapter using the same genres. According to Carolyn Miller, the amount of genres used by a group is dependent on how

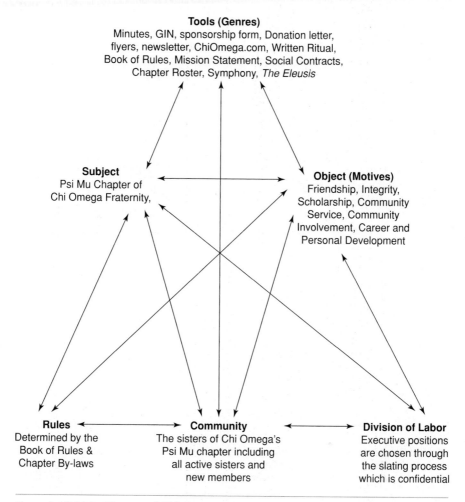

**Tools (Genres)**
Minutes, GIN, sponsorship form, Donation letter,
flyers, newsletter, ChiOmega.com, Written Ritual,
Book of Rules, Mission Statement, Social Contracts,
Chapter Roster, Symphony, *The Eleusis*

**Subject**
Psi Mu Chapter of
Chi Omega Fraternity,

**Object (Motives)**
Friendship, Integrity,
Scholarship, Community
Service, Community
Involvement, Career and
Personal Development

**Rules**
Determined by the
Book of Rules &
Chapter By-laws

**Community**
The sisters of Chi Omega's
Psi Mu chapter including
all active sisters and
new members

**Division of Labor**
Executive positions
are chosen through
the slating process
which is confidential

Figure 3   Psi Mu Chapter of Chi Omega

complex and diverse the group is (Devitt 575). This statement in itself shows the complexity and diversity of Chi Omega, and the reasoning behind how different chapters use different genres to mediate the same goals. In UCF's Psi Mu chapter (see Figure 3) alone, there are over twenty genres, with more being added all the time. These genres function together as a genre system to make the organization work. Some of these genres have been used since the sorority's founding in 1895 and others have come into being much more recently in response to situations in which the genres being used were not working efficiently. For example, one new genre used is the GIN system, which can be looked as a genre system within itself. The Eta Delta chapter also uses the GIN system (see Figure 4). The GIN system as a genre will be looked at in more detail later.

   In Brittany's interview, she explained to me that when she was in the chapter, they had a website, but nothing like the GIN system. She told me that the   12

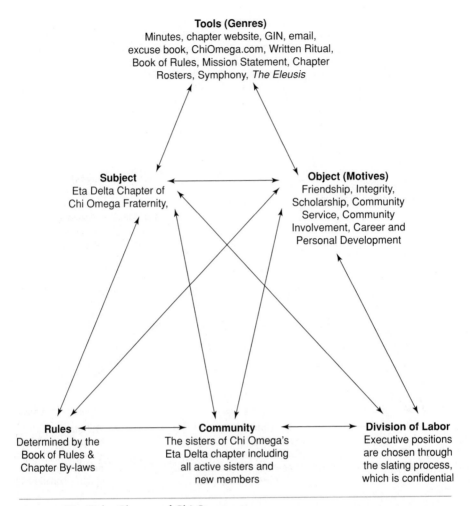

**Figure 4** Eta Delta Chapter of Chi Omega

executive board would rarely post to the chapter website because they did not believe it was secure. Announcements were sent through mass emails. Summer told me that her chapter does not use the GIN system and, like Brittany's chapter, the executive board rarely uses the chapter website. The Psi Kappa (see Figure 5) chapter uses Survey Monkeys, an online type of questionnaire, in the way that the Psi Mu chapter uses the question function on the GIN system. This shows how different genres are able to mediate the same goal for different chapters. As was the case when Brittany was a sister, Summer's chapter sends mass emails for announcements.

## A Genre System within a Genre

The activity triangle laid out simply for the GIN system (see Figure 6) shows 13 that even inside one genre, an entire genre system can be taking place. The

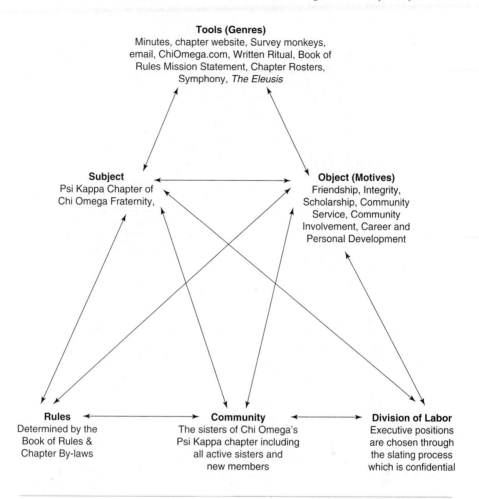

**Tools (Genres)**
Minutes, chapter website, Survey monkeys, email, ChiOmega.com, Written Ritual, Book of Rules Mission Statement, Chapter Rosters, Symphony, *The Eleusis*

**Subject**
Psi Kappa Chapter of Chi Omega Fraternity,

**Object (Motives)**
Friendship, Integrity, Scholarship, Community Service, Community Involvement, Career and Personal Development

**Rules**
Determined by the Book of Rules & Chapter By-laws

**Community**
The sisters of Chi Omega's Psi Kappa chapter including all active sisters and new members

**Division of Labor**
Executive positions are chosen through the slating process which is confidential

Figure 5  Psi Kappa Chapter of Chi Omega

Psi Mu chapter's GIN system uses are announcements, questions, files, and an event calendar. These tools help the chapter to accomplish its goals. The system even categorizes the information posted based on the urgency indicated by the person posting. If the message should be read immediately, it is posted on the wall and a text message is sent to all the sisters. If it should be read soon, an email is sent and it is posted on the wall. If it just needs to be read before the next chapter meeting, it is only posted on the wall.

The GIN system contains questions regarding purchasing merchandise and announcements about money that is due, which then function as a genre set with BillHighway.com, a website through which sisters pay their dues, fees, and also pay for any merchandise they order from the chapter. This genre set is particularly important because the chapter would not be able to accomplish its goals without a budget. Another genre set is formed by the GIN questions and announcements regarding volunteer events and the spreadsheet

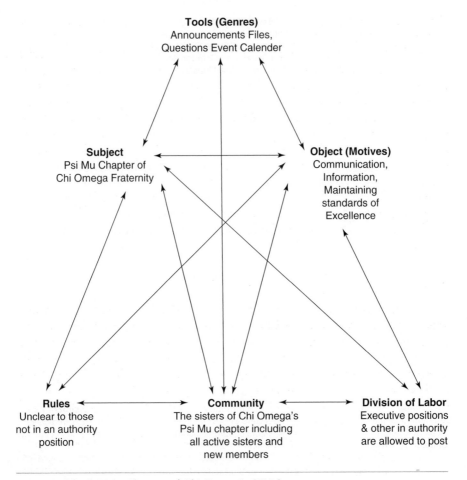

**Tools (Genres)**
Announcements Files,
Questions Event Calender

**Subject**
Psi Mu Chapter of
Chi Omega Fraternity

**Object (Motives)**
Communication,
Information,
Maintaining
standards of
Excellence

**Rules**
Unclear to those
not in an authority
position

**Community**
The sisters of Chi Omega's
Psi Mu chapter including
all active sisters and
new members

**Division of Labor**
Executive positions
& other in authority
are allowed to post

**Figure 6**　The Psi Mu Chapter of Chi Omega's GIN System

that keeps track of the community service hours, which is posted on the GIN system as a file. This genre set is mediated by the director of community service. Another genre set is made up by the questions, announcements and calendar posts regarding study sessions, a goal GPA, and the spreadsheet posted with all of the scholarship points. This set is mediated by the vice-president, who also serves as the scholarship chair. A question is posted weekly about how often sisters work out. This question, along with links posted to internships and gym classes, makes up the genre set used by the directors of career and personal development. GIN questions and announcements posted about socials function in a genre set with social contracts, mediated by the director of friendship and social. The announcements on GIN as well as in the weekly newsletter about sisterhood events function with the attendance questions in the genre set mediated by the direct of sisterhood and personnel. The campus activities director mediates a genre set which includes interest questions about the events put on by other organizations, as well as files and announcements about these events. All of these genre sets together make the genre system within the GIN system.

The Psi Mu chapter began using the GIN system in the spring of 2009. Prior 15 to this system, the chapter was contacted through emails and signup sheets in chapter. Consistent with activity theory, which "illuminates the afforances offered to us by technology" (Levine), the GIN system was found to be a better alternative. By utilizing the GIN system, the chapter was able to keep everything organized and in one place. This genre came into being to "respond appropriately to situations that writers encounter repeatedly" (Devitt 576). The writers of Chi Omega, meaning the sisters in positions of authority, found a new genre that could work more efficiently in the situations they constantly found themselves in, such as how to announce a meeting to the entire chapter, and how to remind sisters to pay their dues. The GIN system provides a means of feedback and communication, two of the defining characteristics of a discourse community (Johns).

## Some Final Thoughts

In the words of Amy Devitt, "all genres exist through and depend on human 16 action" (Bawarshi, Devitt and Reiff 548). The genres I described in the previous paragraphs are able to further the goals of the chapter because they are well maintained. The chapter secretary checks every post on the GIN system to make sure they are appropriate and the treasurer constantly checks BillHighway to make sure sisters have paid the money they owe to the chapter. Without this maintenance, these genres would not be what they are. For example, I was once shown a fraternity's GIN system. The layout of the website was the same. There was a section for files, announcements, questions, and a calendar; however, where on the Chi Omega GIN system these sections would have many links, their GIN system was quite empty. The brother showing me this GIN system told me that nobody ever used the website and he rarely checked it. The only thing that was really used on this fraternity's GIN system was the list of phone numbers and emails for the brothers. Their announcements were sent out in mass emails and text messages, and their questions were asked in chapter, answers were recorded after a show of hands. This shows how the same tool can serve completely different purposes for different chapters. Most genres are fluid rather than rigid, and can be modified to fit the situation (Devitt 579).

As I said earlier, one of the six characteristics of a discourse community is 17 a threshold level of membership (Johns). In Chi Omega, members go through a recruitment process specific to their university and are given a bid. Upon acceptance of this bid, they become new members. In order "to be successfully enculturated into new communities of practice or activity systems ... [one] must learn and conform to the conventions, codes and genres of those communities" (Wardle). As a new member, things such as the GIN system and the other genres used by the chapter can be quite confusing, and generally require observation before using them regularly. In her research, Devitt acknowledges that "knowing the genre . . . means knowing such things as appropriate subject matter, level of detail, tone and approach as well as the usual layout and organization" (Devitt 577). This explains the need for observation when becoming enculturated into a community, to learn things such as tone, level of detail, approach and subject matter.

Without various genres, large organizations such as Chi Omega would not be able to function the way that they do. There is a different genre for everything: a spreadsheet to keep track of volunteer hours, a GIN system for questions and announcements, formal letters for donations, and most importantly, the written ritual that has been used to initiate over 300,000 Chi Omega sisters. Having this genre connects each sister to all of the others, even if they've never met. Similar genres mediate the activity of Chi Omega chapters everywhere so that they are able to work together as a whole. 18

## Works Cited

Bawarshi, Anis, Amy J. Devitt, and Mary Jo Reiff, "Materiality and Genre in the Study of Discourse Communities." *College English* 65 (2003): 541–58. *EBSCOhost*. Web. 2 Nov. 2011.

Bawarshi, Anis S., and Mary Jo Reiff. *Genre: An Introduction to History, Theory, Research, and Pedagogy.* Ed. Charles Bazerman. West Lafayette: Parlor, 2010. Print.

Berkenkotter, Carol, and Thomas N. Huckin. "Rethinking Genre from a Sociocognitive Perspective." *Written Communication* 10 (1993): 475–509. *EBSCOhost*. Web. 2 Nov. 2011.

"Quick Facts about Chi Omega." *Chi Omega*. Chi Omega. Web. 16 Oct. 2011.

Devitt, Amy. "Generalizing About Genre: New Conceptions of an Old Concept." *College Composition and Communication* 44.4 (1993): 573–86. Eric EBSCOhost. Web. 2 Nov. 2011.

Fulkerson, Letitia. Letter to Chi Omega Parents. Oct. 2011. MS. 3395 Players Club Parkway, Memphis, TN.

Honig, Sheryl. "What Do Children Write in Science? A Study of the Genre Set in a Primary Science Classroom." *Written Communication* 27.1 (2010): 87–119. *EBSCOhost*. Web. 7 Nov. 2011.

"Interview of Psi Mu Chapter President." E-mail interview. 24 Oct. 2011.

"Interview of Psi Mu Chapter Secretary." E-mail interview. 24 Oct. 2011.

"Interview of Psi Kappa sister." E-mail interview. 24 Oct. 2011.

"Interview of Eta Delta sister." E-mail interview. 24 Oct. 2011.

"Interview of Psi Mu sister alum." E-mail interview. 24 Oct. 2011.

Johns, Ann M. "Discourse Communities and Communities of Practice: Membership, Conflict, and Diversity." *Text, Role, and Context: Developing Academic Literacies.* Cambridge: Cambridge UP, 1997. 51–70. Print.

Levine, Thomas H. "Tools for the Study and Design of Collaborative Teacher Learning: the Affordances of Different Conceptions of Teacher Community and Activity Theory." *Teacher Education Quarterly* 37.1 (2010): 109. Print.

Wardle, Elizabeth. "Identity, Authority, and Learning to Write in New Workplaces." *Enculturation* 5.2 (2004): n. pag. Web. 2 Nov. 2011.

## Questions for Discussion and Journaling

1. Return to the definition of *genre* that you wrote before you read this piece, and then consider how Marro's definitions of *genre, genre sets*, and *genre systems* compare to that understanding. How has your understanding of genre changed in reading this piece? (If you want, you can look ahead to the section of Bazerman's piece in the next chapter, where he defines these terms.)

2. Marro defines activity systems and gives the example of her sorority as an activity system. List some activity systems that you participate in and make a list of the important genres that those activity systems use and produce to mediate their activities and goals.

## Applying and Exploring Ideas

1. What are the texts involved in the genre set of a typical classroom in your major? What are the sorts of goals and activities that these texts help students and teachers accomplish?

2. Marro seems to suggest that the genres used by various Chi Omega chapters help the sisters across those chapters maintain a consistent identity. She does not tell you what that identity is, though. By considering the genres they use, the way they use them, and their motives and rules, can you make an informed guess about their values and identities?

## :e: In e-Pages at bedfordstmartins.com/writingaboutwriting

1. Tony Mirabelli, "Learning to Serve: The Language and Literacy of Food Service Workers" (*What They Don't Learn in School*, 2004).

   *Draws on theories about language in communities in order to examine how workers and patrons in a diner interact through language and texts.*

2. James Paul Gee, "Literacy, Discourse, and Linguistics: Introduction" (*Journal of Education* 1989).

   *Introduces the concepts of dominant, nondominant, primary, and secondary discourses in order to discuss how people are socialized through language.*

# Writing about Individuals in Community: Major Writing Assignments

To help you learn and explore the ideas in this chapter, we are suggesting two assignment options for larger writing projects: Discourse Community Ethnography and Activity Analysis.

## Assignment Option 1. Discourse Community Ethnography

Choose a discourse community that has made an impact on you or one that interests you and explore its goals and characteristics. Then choose a particular point of interest within that discourse community to consider in more detail. Write a five- to eight-page report that describes the discourse community and explores the particular point of interest (or research question) that you want to focus on. Use the data you collect to make and support your claims.

### Data Collection

- *Observe members of the discourse community* while they are engaged in a shared activity; take detailed notes. (What are they doing? What kinds of things do they say? What do they write? How do you know who is "in" and who is "out"?)
- *Collect anything people in that community read or write* (their genres)—even very short things like forms, sketches, notes, IMs, and text messages.
- *Interview at least one member of the discourse community.* Tape record and tran-scribe the interview. You might ask questions like: How long have you been here? Why are you involved? What do X, Y, and Z words mean? How did you learn to write A, B, or C? How do you communicate with other people (on your team, at your restaurant, etc.)?

***Data Analysis:*** First, try analyzing the data you collect using the six characteristics of Swales's discourse community (p. 220):

- What are the shared goals of the community? Why does this group exist? What does it do?
- What mechanisms do members use to communicate with each other (meetings, phone calls, e-mail, text messages, newsletters, reports, evaluation forms, etc.)?
- What are the purposes of each of these mechanisms of communication (to improve performance, make money, grow better roses, share research, etc.)?
- Which of the above mechanisms of communication can be considered *genres* (textual responses to recurring situations that all group members recognize and understand)?
- What kinds of specialized language (*lexis*) do group members use in their conver-sation and in their genres? Name some examples—ESL, on the fly, 86, etc. What communicative function does this lexis serve? (e.g., why say "86" instead of "we are out of this")?
- Who are the "old-timers" with expertise? Who are the newcomers with less expertise? How do newcomers learn the appropriate language, genres, knowledge of the group?

The above will give you an overall picture of the discourse community. Now you want to focus in on what you've learned to find something that is especially interesting, confusing, or illuminating. You can use Swales and Wardle and Kain to assist you in this. In trying to determine what to focus on, you might ask yourself questions such as:

- Are there conflicts within the community? If so, what are they? Why do the conflicts occur? Do texts mediate these conflicts and make them worse in some way?
- Do any genres help the community work toward its goals especially effectively—or keep the community from working toward its goals? Why?
- Do some participants in the community have difficulty speaking and writing there? Why?
- Who has authority here? How is that authority demonstrated in written and oral language? Where does that authority come from?
- Are members of this community stereotyped in any way in regard to their literacy knowledge? If so, why?

**Planning and Drafting:** As you develop answers to some of these questions, start setting some priorities. Given all you have learned above, what do you want to focus on in your paper? Is there something interesting regarding goals of the community? conflicts in the community? lexis and mediating genres? verbal and written evidence of authority/enculturation in the community? At this point you should stop and write a refined research question for yourself that you want to address in your paper. Now that you have observed and analyzed data, what question(s) would you like to explore in your paper? (Consult the articles by Wardle and McCarthy in this chapter for examples of how you might do this (pp. 231 and 285). The Mirabelli article in the e-Pages provides another example.)

If your teacher has assigned you to write a fairly formal research paper, then your paper ought to have the following parts, or make the following moves (unless there's a good reason not to):

- Begin with a very brief review of the existing literature (published research) on the topic: "We know X about discourse communities" (cite Swales, Wardle and Kain, and others as appropriate).
- Name a niche ("But we don't know Y" or "No one has looked at X").
- Explain how you will occupy the niche.
- Describe your research methods.
- Discuss your findings in detail (Use Wardle, McCarthy, and Mirabelli as examples of how to do this—quote from your notes, your interview, the texts you collected, etc.)
- Include a works cited page.

**What Makes It Good?:** Your assignment will be most successful if you've collected and analyzed data and explored the way that texts mediate activities within a particular discourse community. The assignment asks you to show a clear understanding of what discourse communities are and to demonstrate your ability to analyze them carefully and thoughtfully. It also asks that you not simply list the features of your discourse community but also explore in some depth a particularly interesting aspect of that community. Since this assignment asks you to practice making the moves common to academic research articles, it should be organized, readable, fluent, and well edited.

# Assignment Option 2. Activity Analysis

For this assignment, you will continue the analysis of activity systems that you engaged in after reading the Kain and Wardle and Marro articles. You will focus on and gather additional data from a specific activity system in order to examine how the primary and minor genres of those systems mediate activity, create and reinforce particular identities and values, and create authority for particular individuals. Write a description of the system, analyzing its motives and tools, and then reflect on what you have learned from doing so.

**Data Collection:** Begin by choosing an activity system of importance to you (currently, in the past, or potentially in the future) to focus on. This might be a church group, sorority, family, profession, classroom, club, football team, gaming community, or dorm floor. Just ensure that the activity system holds a personal interest for you and that you have access to its members and its texts.

Next, using the activity triangle worksheet from Kain and Wardle (p. 262) and the questions from paragraph 16 of that article, try to sketch out the object, purpose, tools, community, division of labor, and rules for this activity system. In particular, focus on the textual tools that this group uses in order to try to accomplish its common purposes.

Now determine what data you need to collect.

- You will likely need to interview several members of that activity system and ask them about their activities, purposes, conventions, texts, and so on.
- You will also need to collect some texts that the members commonly read, write, or use in other ways.
- And you will likely need to conduct text-based interviews with some of the system participants in order to ask them about the texts they use. For example, you might ask why they organize the texts as they do, why they use certain phrases or tones instead of others, who writes the texts, who reads them, and so on.

You will also need to set up several opportunities to observe the system members in action, either through observation, shadowing, or in some cases, participant-observation. (For example, if you are a member of the football team, you might participate as you normally do but then take frequent breaks to jot down notes about what you see.)

We suggest taking time with your teacher and classmates to plan out the data collection in more detail. For example, you and your teacher might want to discuss the specific interview questions you will ask. Also, before you contact members of the activity system, talk with your teacher about appropriate ways to approach research participants and gain their permission to engage in your research project.

**Data Analysis:** Once you have collected all your data, go back to the activity system worksheet that you drafted before you collected the data. It is now time to rethink what you wrote there. Work through the data that you collected in order to consider anew the motives of the system, the genres (tools) that mediate their work, the rules (conventions) of the system, and so on. As you work through these, make notes about where in your data you found the answers. Was it from what interview subjects said? From the texts you examined? From what you saw while you observed?

Now is also the time to analyze the genres you collected. What are they? Who writes them? Who uses them? What specialized lexis do you see in them? How are they organized? How are they distributed?

Once you feel you have solidly considered the components of the activity system, focus on what is interesting or complicated here. Do community members agree on the motives and purpose of their activities? Do the genres being used effectively facilitate the work of that community? What sorts of values do the genres suggest that the system has? Who has authority in this system? How is that authority affirmed (or questioned) in the genres and activities?

**Planning and Drafting:** Step back from the data analysis that you just did and ask yourself what you learned. What's interesting here? What's complicated? What's puzzling? What do you know now that you did not know before you collected and analyzed data? Who would care about this?

Now consider the text you want to write. What do you want to focus on? And who do you want to share your information with? Given the answers to these questions, talk with your teacher and classmates about what your text should look like. Do you want to write a formal research report that adds to the conversations that scholars have had about activity systems and texts? Do you want to write to your sister and let her know that the profession she thinks she's interested in probably doesn't suit her? Do you want to write an analysis for the activity system itself that demonstrates why some genres are less effective than others in meeting the system's goals? Do you want to write a reflection to yourself that considers what you've learned and what that means to you personally?

The text you write, and even how you go about planning and writing it, will depend on the answers to the previous questions. Consider the main claim(s) you want to make and the evidence that you need to make that claims(s) and the conventions of the genre you want to write, relevant to the audience you want to write for. Next, make a plan and start drafting. You might need to make an outline first, or you might just want to write down all of the ideas you have and then go back and try to organize it.

Once you feel you have a readable draft, share it with your teacher and classmates. Tell them your point, your desired audience, and the type of genre you were trying to write. Ask them to provide feedback on how well you accomplished your goals and how you might improve. Then revise.

**What Makes It Good?:** This text will be good if you learned to collect and analyze data, and then used that data to learn something new and share it in a manner that is engaging and appropriate for your audience and text type. Have you framed your claims and supported them? Do you cite sources where you need to? Do your readers know what your "so what?" is?

# Rhetoric
## How Is Meaning Constructed in Context?

In Chapter 1, we looked at how our individual literacy histories impact our conceptions and habits of writing. In Chapter 2, we studied how groups use texts to mediate activity. Now in Chapter 3, we'll examine how texts and their meanings are constructed in response and relation to **context**. A central theoretical lens that writing studies uses to understand writing is **rhetorical theory**, which helps explain these aspects of writing:

- how writers, texts, readers, and contexts interact
- how writers come up with what to say
- how texts construct knowledge
- how people make up their minds, and change them

Because rhetorical theory is so central to building accurate conceptions of writing as well as resisting misconceptions of it, this chapter works to introduce you to rhetorical theory and help build your understanding of it.

To be clear, when we talk about a "**theory**," we're referring to a framework of ideas that offers a systematic explanation for some aspect of our lived experience and observation. The better or stronger a theory is, the more completely it accounts for

---

Texts take much, if not all, of their meaning from context. If you're a North American reader of this text, you're probably very familiar with the upper image and the meaning it represents. But look at how a similar sign changes meaning in the lower image. The same familiar sign, but now appearing in a completely different context, one complete with a Grim Reaper and very serious looking minions. Now the sign doesn't mean "bring your vehicle to a halt at this sign." The wording on the lower sign translates to "new Higher Education Act." So what does the sign mean in its new context, and how does the Reaper costume provide further context for the sign's meaning?

existing phenomena (experiences, events, and objects) and the more accurately it makes testable predictions about future events. For example, a theory that tries to explain how people make up or change their minds has to be able to account for existing cases of this and predict how future cases will work. **Rhetoric** attempts to explain or help us understand how people interact through language and other symbols, and to predict what will create more and less successful interaction in the future.

## Overview of Rhetorical Principles

The first reading in this chapter, Covino and Jolliffe's "What is Rhetoric?" offers a broad overview of rhetorical theory, including several definitions of rhetoric. You'll quickly realize that *rhetoric* is an extremely hard term to define because it means so many different things! To try to help you keep it all in perspective, we want to outline a few principles for you to use when trying to define rhetoric.

The term *rhetoric* actually refers to one of three different things, depending on how it is used: a *field of knowledge*, a *theoretical construct*, and a *performance art*.

- *Rhetoric as a field of knowledge* refers to a body of principles about human interaction and persuasion (that makes it a field of knowledge, like chemistry or history are).
- *Rhetoric as a theoretical construct* refers to a theory (as defined above) that provides a systematic explanation of human interaction through language and other symbols.
- *Rhetoric as performance art* refers to how people perform rhetorical principles and concepts in their acts of communication. In this last sense, any human interaction follows principles of rhetoric and is thus an "act of" rhetoric.

**Rhetoric** is thus both the *art* of human interaction (including persuasion) through language and other **symbols**, as well as the *study* of that interaction. Saying that human action happens through symbols might sound confusing, but it's a fairly simple idea. Humans often take one idea and have it "stand" for another idea; for example, a red light hanging in the street is literally just a red light hanging in the street, but in our culture we have made it into a symbol that we all understand to mean "stop." Language and words are also symbols where we have determined that signs mean something else. For example, the letters "d-o-g" don't necessarily and literally mean or stand for anything—they are just inscriptions on a page. However, we have determined that these three inscriptions form a word that we all understand to represent a four-legged creature that barks. Rhetoric both describes and enables the interaction that people have when using symbols.

The use of symbols to make meaning involves at least two people, and both of them are involved in the act of making meaning. In other words, rhetoric does not just involve one person (for example, a textbook author) conveying symbols and meaning to another person; rhetoric also involves the other person (for example, the student reading the textbook) making meaning, too. A **rhetor** (any person interacting with other people) can use rhetoric to *create* interaction and meaning, and to *understand* interaction. An **interlocutor** (a person who is being interacted with; for example, a reader or audience member) also creates interaction and meaning.

You might already guess, then, that rhetoric has to do with behavior broadly, not just oral or written communication. Rhetoric is also about being and doing particular things that help contribute to the overall message and meaning a person is trying to create. For instance, when you wanted to be admitted to your college and needed to convince the Admissions office that you'd do well at that school, you had to present an overall image of someone who would be a good fit for the school. Part of presenting that image was in what you *said* in your admissions essay, but a larger part was in knowing who and how you needed to appear to be in your application. The principles of rhetoric let us predict this.

This principle of rhetoric as being and doing as well as saying and writing is even more obvious in oral interactions. Think about the president giving a state of the union address. What does he wear? Where does he stand? How does he speak? All of these things contribute to the effectiveness of his message (or not). He is trying to *be* presidential, not just *speak as* a president. Whether he does that successfully, of course, depends a lot on his audience and the meaning they make of what he does and says.

Rhetors' attempts to make meaning with their audience through both words and actions requires them to find common ground with their audience; in other words, it requires them to think of what both they and their audience might share as common *foundational values*. Maybe you're trying to convince your city to expand its homeless shelter. In order to solve that problem, you'll first need to find out what values you share (like limiting human suffering or taking care of the indigent) that will build common ground with the city in order to solve shared problems or meet shared needs (which we'll talk about as **exigence** later on). In the previous example of the president's state of the union address, he might need to think of goals that everyone shares in order to emphasize places where he and the opposing party share some common values (maybe, for example, good education for all or the ability for all college graduates to find good jobs).

# Rhetoric: Explaining How People Communicate and Make Meaning

Rhetoric attempts to explain how people communicate, how they make up their minds through interacting with each other, and how they change their minds. We can see some of rhetoric's explanatory principles when we look at examples of such communication. We'll talk about five explanatory principles here: meaning depends on context, meaning is purposeful and motivated, readers and writers interact to make meaning, readers and writers actually make knowledge, and principles for good communication are contingent on situation, not universal. These principles are some of the core "threshold concepts" about writing, which we explained in the Introduction to the book.

## Meaning Depends on Context

You've probably been in situations where the same words had different meanings. If your mom is unloading groceries from the car and says, "Help me," you know what that means because the meaning is clear in the situation. Now suppose you're at the pool and your mom has been swimming laps and you know she's been feeling sick the last couple days and suddenly she stops in the lane and says, "Help me." You know right away that the same words mean something completely different, and you will respond differently. Why is that? It's because the situations in which we use language shape the meaning of the language we use.

Situations also influence what it makes sense to say: It would be a very strange thing for you to go up to the counter at the Department of Motor Vehicles and say, "I need your permission to join a circus." The words don't seem to fit the situation. Because the meaning of language and the things we choose to say depend so much on what situation we're in, one explanatory principle of rhetoric is that human interaction and discourse is **situated** (in time and in space). That's an important principle in rhetoric: when we say something is **rhetorical**, part of what we mean is that it is *situated*. If you've read texts from Chapters 1 or 2 of this book, you already know that discourse communities and activities are also situated. So discourse communities are, in this sense, rhetorical. You can learn more about why it's important that communication is always situated by reading, in this chapter, Keith Grant-Davie's article "Rhetorical Situations and Their Constituents," and Sarah Kate Magee's article on "College Admissions Essays."

## Meaning Is Purposeful and Motivated

When was the last time you saw someone write or say something when they *truly* had no point or purpose? You know that guy who's always at your parties who talks on and on about stuff and yet never seems to have any reason for saying it? It's like he just can't stop talking even though everybody wants him to. Even then, to him, his talk has a purpose—he's trying to say something funny or interesting, he's trying to fill a silence, he's trying to get attention, he's trying to impress people. Even when people don't seem to have a point in what they say, they still have *motives* for saying it. There pretty much isn't any speech or writing in the world, in fact, that doesn't have *some* motive. (As a challenge: Can you think of any?) There's always *some* reason a person decides to say something.

This is even more true of writing, because writing takes a lot more effort than speaking; it's much less natural. When you see a piece of writing, you can bet the writer had some motive in producing it. (And remember, if you've read any of the Chapter 1 or 2 readings on activity systems or literacy histories, that there are goals, objectives, and motives in people's actions more broadly.)

A major principle of rhetoric, then, for explaining human interaction, is that it is always **motivated** by particular purposes, needs, and values. And because a given discourse (talk or writing) always has specific motivations, it won't be able to be "objective" in the sense of "neutral" or "unbiased." A discourse's motives always give it a slant. So one thing you know, if you know rhetoric, is that when people claim not to have any motive in saying something, it isn't actually true. You can learn more about how communication is always motivated: read, in this chapter, Charles Bazerman's piece on "Speech Acts, Genres, and Activity Systems" and Margaret Kantz's article on "Helping Students Use Textual Sources Persuasively."

## Readers and Writers Interact to Make Meaning

So far, then, two central principles of rhetoric are that communication is always *situated* and *motivated*. What can be easy to overlook is how these two principles suggest a third, which is that speech or writing gets its meaning not just from the writer and not just from the reader, but in the *interaction* between a writer and reader. That's not too hard to see in speech, as Maria Post's article in this chapter shows us. She analyzes Barack Obama's 2007 speech at Howard University as a presidential candidate. Post describes language that Obama used and associations he raised that didn't actually *mean anything* until or unless his audience added *its* knowledge of civil rights history and biblical references. The meaning of the speech came from Obama's *interaction with* that particular audience.

This interaction between rhetors and interlocuters can be harder to see in writing because the "interaction" isn't physical and immediate—a piece can be read a long time after it's written, in a completely different place. Yet it is exactly this principle of *interaction* that explains why a text can be understood one way if it is read near to the time and place where the author writes it, but will usually be understood differently when it's read in a different time and place. The text's meaning is established by how the writer (through the text) interacts with the reader and his or her situation; neither the writer nor the reader alone makes meaning.

So rhetoric reminds us that the meaning made in communication is always **interactional**. There's a further, special kind of interaction in meaning-making that happens *between texts themselves*, an interaction scholars call **intertextuality**. You'll find more about interaction and intertextuality in this chapter in James Porter's article "Intertextuality and the Discourse Community," as well as in Brian Martin's "Plagiarism: A Misplaced Emphasis."

## Readers and Writers Make Knowledge

So far, these ideas suggest that texts don't "contain" meaning and knowledge; readers and writers of texts interact to *construct* meaning and knowledge *from* them. Now we're approaching a fourth central principle of rhetoric: Human interaction and communication don't simply pass existing knowledge from place to place; they actually make new knowledge. You can see this happen when you're reading a text or listening to someone talk and something they say gives you a new idea—you find yourself thinking something *because* of what they said that *isn't* what they said. If you've ever had an argument with your parents or your own children, this knowledge-creating effect was probably happening: They said, "You have to do this thing you don't want to!" and you thought instead of all the reasons why you really *don't* have to do it. Your interaction created ideas that neither of you had had until the moment of that interaction. Or think of the last really difficult piece of writing you did for school. Did you have exactly the same ideas before you wrote it as you had after you wrote it? Probably not. What happens in writing moments like that is that as we write we think of things to say that we didn't know *before* we started writing.

There's a technical term for activities that create new knowledge: **epistemic.** Rhetorical activities are epistemic—they have to do with making new knowledge. You can read more about this idea in this chapter in Christina Haas and Linda Flower's "Rhetorical Reading Strategies and the Construction of Meaning," and in Ann Penrose and Cheryl Geisler's piece "Reading and Writing without Authority" in the e-Pages. They explain why your conception about "what writing is and how it works" matters. You do different things when you think "writing is just putting down ideas you already had" versus when you think "writing is *building* knowledge that didn't yet exist when you began writing."

## "Good" Writing and Communication is Contingent

The last principle of rhetoric we want to highlight here doesn't show up in just one or two readings; you can actually find it in nearly every reading in this book. It comes from putting these other four principles together. You'll see it in play when we ask this question: Which writing is better, the Declaration of Independence or the Gettysburg Address? Your first reaction might well be, "How is that question even *answerable*? Doesn't it *depend* on what criteria you use?" That's a reasonable response. Whether a piece of writing or oral communication is good does depend; the word for that is **contingent**. You've probably heard people use that word: "Our weekend plans are contingent on the weather" or "You're admitted to this college contingent on completing your high school degree." In these uses, *contingent* means almost literally *depending on*.

If you walk through one of your buildings on campus and ask various people, "What makes writing good?," you're likely to get a range of answers. Some will say that good proofreading and no errors makes writing good. Others might say active verbs, or conciseness, or descriptive language, or clear organization, or a strong thesis. But the ones who are being *really* thoughtful will say something like, "That depends on what you're writing" or "That depends on what it's being used for." What would lead them to say that? All of the principles we've just outlined above: Communication is situated in particular circumstances, motivated by specific goals, interactional by nature, and epistemic, creating new knowledge through that interaction. Thus, the quality of any instance of rhetoric really must depend on all those factors. What makes it good will depend on its circumstances and context, and *that* means there can be few universal rules for what makes communication good. This is perhaps rhetoric's most significant principle: Qualities of good communication are contingent, not universal.

We've included a more compact statement of these principles in the definition of *rhetoric* in the glossary (p. 801) so that you can reference it quickly whenever you find yourself needing to return to these ideas. It will take a long time to think through all the implications of these principles—your class will only be the beginning of your understanding of rhetoric, because it's too big to understand all at once. Expect your understanding to be initially hazy and a bit confused; that's okay. More understanding will emerge with more reading, more examples, and more time.

# Why Study Rhetoric?

You might be wondering how any of this helps you as a writer. Why is it useful to understand principles of rhetoric like these? What will you know after you read these articles and consider these ideas? Here are some reasons why principles of rhetoric matter to writers:

- The principles that writing is *situated* and *contingent* remind us to always be asking, "What in this situation and context will help me predict what will make this writing good?" These principles will also keep you from believing that criteria for writing that worked in *some other* situation will automatically work in your current one.
- The principle that writing is always *motivated* will help you remember, when you read texts, that they were designed specifically to accomplish something, and that their purpose gives them a slant and bias. It will help you remember as a writer to

make sure you've considered your own motives in writing the piece, and that you're writing a piece that best embodies and enacts those motives.

- The principle that writing makes meaning through *interaction* will keep you from believing that just because you've written something, your readers should or must understand it easily and without complication. It helps you remember that your readers are always bringing their own background, experiences, and language to your writing, and that to know how they'll make meaning of the text, you have to try to anticipate what it is they bring. This principle also reminds you that texts make meaning by connecting to other existing texts, and helps you think about to what extent you're required to be "original" in a given piece of writing.

- The principle that writing (as a form of rhetoric) is *epistemic* helps you remember that you'll never just be "transmitting information" by writing ideas that your readers "receive" unaltered. As you think more about this principle, you'll learn to anticipate ways that you'll learn from your own writing, and that it will build new ideas even as you're drafting.

The readings in this chapter help you see *why* and *how* these principles work, and they therefore push you to change any conceptions of writing you have that are inconsistent with them. If you believe there's one right way or one best way to write, these readings will challenge you; if you already answer every writing question with "it depends," these readings will give you reasons with which you can explain that answer to others. If you believe that the best way to write is to figure out everything you want to say *before* you write and then just get it all written down unaltered, never looking back, some of the readings in this chapter show that you might write more successfully if you think about writing as making meaning rather than just transmitting it.

Because rhetoric offers a systematic explanation of how people make knowledge from interaction through language—helping us see how we make up our minds and how we change them—it's excellent for helping writers know what to write, and helping us as humans better understand how we *actually* work to persuade each other to accept our ideas. There's great power in this kind of knowledge. As you start seeing the rhetorical principles these readings demonstrate in action in the world around you, you'll understand better why your writing works as it does.

## Chapter Goals

- To understand the basic outlines of rhetorical theory and its relation to writing and human interaction
- To understand the concept of *rhetorical situation* and be able to apply it to reading and writing situations
- To understand how writers construct texts persuasively (or not)
- To understand how readers construct meaning from texts
- To understand what it means to say that knowledge is *constructed*
- To understand some approaches to rhetorically analyzing texts

# What Is Rhetoric?

## WILLIAM COVINO and DAVID JOLLIFFE

■ Covino, William, and David Jolliffe. "What Is Rhetoric?" *Rhetoric: Concepts, Definitions, Boundaries*. Ed. William Covino and David Jolliffe. Boston: Allyn & Bacon, 1995. 3–26. Print.

## Framing the Reading

*Rhetoric* is an incredibly difficult word to define because it refers to several different but related concepts. Covino and Jolliffe created an anthology of readings to try to build a big picture of what rhetoric is (and what it's about), as a way of trying to give the most complete picture. And to introduce that anthology, they wrote the introductory chapter "What is Rhetoric?" to answer that question from several different angles. That is the reading we have included here.

Covino and Jolliffe are well qualified to attempt to answer this big question. William Covino is currently President of California State University–Los Angeles, having spent his career researching persuasive writing and rhetorical theory. He's been very good at explaining some of the relationships between imagination, argument, and how writing can be most persuasive. Covino shares with David Jolliffe an interest also in **literacy**, with its focus on how people learn and use the systems of argument in their cultures. Jolliffe, who holds the Brown Chair in English Literacy at the University of Arkansas–Fayetteville, focuses extensively on the teaching of rhetoric, as well as the history of rhetorical theory.

Their chapter offers a set of comparative definitions of rhetoric from rhetorical theorists throughout time, and in discussing these definitions, a sense of the term starts to emerge. Covino and Jolliffe also give an overview of some central principles or concepts of rhetorical theory that were first codified by Greek and Roman rhetors such as Isocrates, Aristotle, and Cicero from the fourth through the first centuries BCE. Readers who aren't familiar with rhetoric can experience this chapter as a difficult whirlwind of information. However, those who study rhetoric see it as a compact review of key concepts.

This selection won't tell you everything you need to know about rhetoric. Instead, its purpose is to introduce you to key concepts that other rhetoric scholars use and assume their readers will understand. This is a first opportunity to read about rhetoric and have key concepts explained. This reading will serve as a reference; you can return to it for explanations of terms you'll encounter in other articles.

## Getting Ready to Read

*Before you read*, do at least one of the following activities:

- Write a definition of *rhetoric* as you understand it right now. What does the word mean to you? How do you usually hear it used?
- Google the two authors and find lists of what they've written. How do the titles of their books and articles change your sense of what rhetoric might be about?

*As you read*, consider the following questions:

- How is Covino and Jolliffe's discussion of rhetoric different than what you expected?
- Can you think of any aspects of persuasion that *don't* get discussed in this chapter?
- Which concepts do you wish you could learn more about right away?

........................................................................................................................................

*I specify now that rhetoric is the functional organization of discourse, within its social and cultural context, in all its aspects, exception made for its realization as a strictly formal metalanguage—in formal logic, mathematics, and in the sciences whose metalanguages share the same features. In other words: rhetoric is all of language, in its realization as discourse.*

—PAOLO VALESIO

NOVANTIQUA (1980)

*[The function of rhetoric] is not to persuade but to see the available means of persuasion in each case.*

—ARISTOTLE

RHETORIC (C. 350 BCE)

*Here then we have in popular use two separate ideas of Rhetoric: one of which is occupied with the general end of the fine arts—that is to say, intellectual pleasure; the other applies itself more specifically to a definite purpose of utility, viz. fraud.*

—THOMAS DE QUINCEY

"RHETORIC" (1828)

*A rhetorician, I take it, is like one voice in a dialogue. Put several such voices together, with each voicing its own special assertion, let them act upon one another in cooperative competition, and you get a dialectic that, properly developed, can lead to the views transcending the limitations of each.*

—KENNETH BURKE

"RHETORIC—OLD AND NEW" (1950)

*Rhetoric in the most general sense may perhaps be identified with the energy inherent in communication: the emotional energy that impels the speaker to speak, the physical energy expended in the utterance, the energy level coded in the message, and the energy experienced by the recipient in decoding the message.*
—GEORGE KENNEDY
"A HOOT IN THE DARK" (1992)

*Nearly the entire history of writing is confounded with the history of reason, of which it is at once the effect, the support, and one of the privileged alibis. It has been one with the phallocentric tradition. It is indeed that same self-admiring, self-stimulating, self-congratulatory phallocentricism.*
—HELENE CIXOUS
"THE LAUGH OF THE MEDUSA" (1975)

"What is Rhetoric?" This a difficult question for which there is no short 1 answer. The difficulty begins with the fact that rhetoric is not a *content* area that contains a definite body of knowledge, like physics: instead, rhetoric might be understood as the study and practice of shaping content. This is a common definition that has informed the vilification of rhetoric since antiquity. When rhetoric is regarded as the manipulation of the linguistic features of a text, it becomes associated by some with fraud, by others with the maintenance of institutional hierarchies. In this connection, studying rhetoric means studying how people get fooled, and rhetoric is understood as the opposite of truth. The rhetoric of a text is seen as its use of ornamental, pretentious, carefully calculated, sometimes bombastic language, through which the writer or speaker seeks power over listeners or readers.

If we consider rhetoric as the study and practice of featuring rather than 2 shaping content, we foreground its function as a tool for "special-interest groups." The special-interest-group rhetor selects and configures language so that certain terms are privileged and endorsed, and others are ignored. In literary studies, for example, the rhetoric of the New Criticism appreciates unity, continuity, and coherence in literary works, and directs our attention to these elements; by contrast, the rhetoric of deconstruction finds literary value in the *breakdown* of these same elements. These two groups adopt different critical lexicons that strike us as mutually exclusive:

> It will be sufficient if [the reader] will understand the unit meanings with which the poet begins—that is, that he understands the meanings of the words which the poet uses—and if he will so far suppress his convictions or prejudices as to see how the unit meanings or partial meanings are built into a total context. (Cleanth Brooks, *The Well Wrought Urn*, 252)

> In this ideal text, the networks are many and interact, without any one of them being able to surpass the rest; this text is a galaxy of signifiers, not a structure

of signifieds; it has no beginning; it is reversible; we gain access to it by several entrances, none of which can be authoritatively declared to be the main one; the codes it mobilizes extend *as far as the eye can reach* . . . based as it is on the infinity of language. (Roland Barthes, *S/Z*, 5–6)

Brooks employs the lexicon of units and unity, Barthes of multiplicity and infinity. Analyzing the connection of lexical and syntactic choices to the special-interest group that an author represents has become a common academic and journalistic enterprise, so that there are numerous studies of, for instance, the rhetoric of advertising and marketing, the rhetoric of political movements, and the rhetoric of religious institutions, as well as the rhetoric of academic language itself, such as literary criticism and philosophy. However, to the extent that the meaning of rhetoric is restricted in such studies to the linguistic features of the text, they evade a fuller—and, in fact, classical—portrayal of rhetoric.

The power of eloquence, as defined in 55 CE by the Roman orator Marcus Tullius Cicero, indicates the scope of rhetoric: "The real power of eloquence is such that it embraces the origin, the influence, the changes of all things in the world, all virtues, duties, and all nature, so far as it affects the manners, minds, and lives of mankind" (*De Oratore* 3.20). Eloquence, which is for Cicero another word for rhetoric, is activated by and affects changing manners, minds, and lives as it constructs our knowledge of the world. Taking as our cue this representative classical view, we would like to present the practice of rhetoric here as much more than verbal ornamentation, and the study of rhetoric as much more than a catalog of ideological buzz words.

*Rhetoric is a primarily verbal, situationally contingent, epistemic art that is both philosophical and practical and gives rise to potentially active texts.* As we explicate this definition, we will attempt to interrogate it as well, recognizing that any conception of rhetoric—no matter how broad—entails ambiguities and limitations. As twentieth-century rhetorician and philosopher Kenneth Burke said, "A way of seeing is also a way of not seeing" (*Permanence and Change*, 49).

The word *text* in our definition of rhetoric can be understood in both its conventional, quite limited sense, and its ambiguous, more rhetorical sense. In the former sense, we mean by *text* any instance of spoken or written language that could be considered in isolation as a self-sufficient entity. Thus, a book, an essay, an editorial, a song's lyrics, a joke, and a speech are texts, but so are a chapter, a section of an article, a refrain in a song or poem, and a contribution to a conversation. This definition of *text* may remind you of the definition of *sentence* that you learned in elementary school: "a statement that can stand alone." You probably realize now that this is an inadequate definition of a sentence, because no statement can "stand alone"; every utterance depends for its meaning on extrinsic factors. This fact is epitomized by a famous passage from Kenneth Burke's *Philosophy of Literary Form*:

Imagine that you enter a parlor. You come late. When you arrive, others have long preceded you, and they are engaged in a heated discussion, a discussion too heated for them to pause and tell you exactly what it is about. In fact, the discussion had already begun long before any of them got there, so that no one present is qualified to retrace for you all the steps that had gone before. You listen for a while, until you decide that you have caught the tenor of the argument; then you put in your oar. Someone answers; you answer him; another comes to your defense; another aligns himself against you, to either the embarrassment or gratification of your opponent, depending upon the quality of your ally's assistance. However, the discussion is interminable. The hour grows late, you must depart. And you do depart, with the discussion still vigorously in progress. (110–111)

If we imagine a text as the momentary entry into an unending conversation 7 connected to what Burke calls (after anthropologist Bronislaw Malinowski) shifting "contexts of situation," we see that defining it as an independent and self-contained entity is something of a convenience.

We will use the term *rhetor* here to indicate an individual involved in 8 the production of a text, usually a speaker or writer; we will call readers and listeners who attend to and interpret a text *auditors*, or, as a group, the *audience*. A text is *potentially active* when the rhetor intends it to *do* something, to affect or change the auditors' minds or actions or environments. *Rhetorical analysis* is the study of whether and how texts actually do affect, influence, or change auditors. The term *potentially active* bears some scrutiny here, as one of our students, Ulrike Jaeckel, indicated in her review of this Introduction:

> Does a rhetor ever NOT intend a text to do something? Since you include "a contribution to conversation" under "texts," pretty much any utterance can become a text, . . . even (specific instances of) "hello" or "thank you." Aren't these "potentially active"—capable of producing an effect on a hearer—just by being uttered?

We agree that all utterances are texts, and all texts have the potential to change auditors. As Ulrike Jaeckel's response indicates, our term *potentially active* had effects that we did not anticipate; that is, we did not assess its potential fully enough to predict that it might activate her questions. With this admission, we might draw a distinction between the *intended* potential activity of a text and its *unintended* potential activity. Rhetorical analysis is interested in both kinds of potential.

As a primarily verbal art, rhetoric has as its medium the written and spo- 9 ken word, although many scholars study how visual images and nonverbal sounds can complement the effect of a text's words. Some use the term *rhetoric* metaphorically and speak of the rhetoric of, for instance, gestures, paintings, or films. The elocutionary movement of the eighteenth and nineteenth centuries attempted an exhaustive analysis of the communicative effects of bodily movements in order to advise orators about what kinds of body language suited what kinds of speeches. But the elocutionists made clear that gestures do not themselves constitute rhetoric; rather, the visual image of the rhetor produced linguistic understanding in the auditors. For instance, a certain contortion of the facial features would have them think and feel "pity." Following this understanding, we may say that rhetoric *inheres* in the words that a visual image *activates*, so that the rhetoric of a painting, for instance, may be understood as the verbal understanding that accompanies its viewing.

As a situationally contingent art, rhetoric guides prospective writers and speakers to consider the timeliness and suitability for the particular situation of any text they might produce. Ancient Greek philosophers and rhetoricians had a useful term for this abstract concept: *kairos*. Inherent in *kairos* is a sensitivity to the belief that in any situation where the potential for active communication exists, rhetors must consider whether, from the point of view of potential auditors, the time, the circumstances, and the intellectual and ideological climate are right. These are factors that are very difficult to control, let alone predict. In recent years, scholarship in the humanities and the social sciences has begun to recognize the difficulty of maintaining "stable" texts with determinate meaning; this recognition accounts for the difference in the statements by Brooks and Barthes above, written in 1947 and 1970, respectively. Barthes's statement suggests that—given infinite possibilities for meaning—*kairos* is an unachievable ideal. Adding to this view our recognition that the public realm any text enters is today more politically, ethnically, and intellectually diversified than ever, the contingent nature of rhetoric becomes a very prominent and formidable consideration. 10

As an epistemic art, rhetoric leads prospective auditors to see "truth" neither as something that exists in their own minds before communication nor as something that exists in the world of empirical observation that they must simply report "objectively." Instead, rhetorical truth is something achieved *transactionally* among the rhetor and the auditors whenever they come to some shared understanding, knowledge, or belief. As coparticipants in a verbal exchange, all the parties involved are knowledge-makers. 11

Philosophical rhetoric is primarily concerned with the exploratory construction of knowledge. The philosophical rhetor is less concerned with the composition of a particular text than with exploring ways of knowing and defining a subject. Plato attempts to illustrate philosophical rhetoric in *Phaedrus*, in which Socrates engages in a question-and-answer exchange with Phaedrus about the nature of love, of rhetoric, and of writing, working through different possible meanings of each term. Ann E. Berthoff has recently tried to engage writing students in a kind of philosophical rhetoric through the use of a "double-entry notebook," in which they write about a subject in one column and then return to that writing at a later date, reconsider it, and write a critique of their prior thinking/writing in a facing column. In this way, writers engage in a dialectical exchange with themselves as they try to "think, and think again," as Berthoff puts it. Another form of philosophical rhetoric might be called *topical* rather than dialectical, originating in Aristotle's definition of rhetoric as "seeing the available means of persuasion" (*Rhetoric* 1355b) through the subjection of an issue to *topoi* or "topics," which are strategies 12 (such as comparison or analogy) that contribute to full investigation. As a philosophical art, rhetoric guides rhetors to think and observe deeply—intuitively, systematically, and empirically. Philosophic or exploratory rhetoric can also be seen as the foundation for practical rhetoric. That is, systematic exploration leads prospective rhetors to find what they *could* say or write in specific situations when they plan a potentially active text, even if they do not actually produce it.

Rhetoric is not logic, but they are related fields of inquiry. Logic studies   13 the way a chain of reasoning leads from premises to incontrovertible conclusions. Rhetoric also studies how rhetors and auditors reason from premises to conclusions, but it is located in the realm of uncertainty and *probable* truth, in which conclusions are arguable rather than incontrovertible.

Rhetoric is not dialectic, although Aristotle calls rhetoric the *antistrophos*   14 (counterpart) to dialectic, and the examples from Plato and Berthoff above suggest that rhetorical exploration can take on a dialectical—question-answer or comment-response—form. In its classical sense, dialectic is a system of reasoning about subjects for which there are few or no "hard," scientific data or proven premises. Rhetoric also addresses such subjects, but because the practice and study of rhetoric take into account how rhetors actually shape their reasoning processes into texts that appeal to a potential auditor's understanding and emotions, it is a more expansive, inclusive, and socioculturally alert art than dialectic.

Rhetoric is not poetics, but they are related fields as well. Poetics studies   15 literary texts—poetry, fiction, drama, and so forth—as linguistic artifacts, examining such features as imagery, diction, textual organization, and rhythm. In his *Poetics*, Aristotle discusses the ways in which tragic drama affects its audience, and this perspective suggests that both rhetoric and poetics are audience-oriented. The decisive distinction between rhetoric and poetics rests on rhetoric's concern with the *invention* of an effective text: whereas poetics regards the elements of an effective live composition, rhetoric is additionally a body of resources for composing.

To anyone who would hold that rhetoric is merely an empty display of verbal ornamentation or a facile use of one-sided terms and concepts, we would   16 offer a broader view of rhetoric's scope: Certainly, the rhetoric of a text is the selection and organization of language it uses to move potential readers and listeners to consider its ideas and conclusions. But the rhetoric of a text is also the intellectual, cognitive, affective, and social considerations that guide the writer or speaker to use the language as he or she does, *and* the rhetoric of a text is the effect it actually has on people who listen to it or read it.

## The Elements of Rhetoric

Over the centuries, scholars have produced works that explain principles, tech-   17 niques, and guidelines for practicing the art of rhetoric. Because they have generally been used to teach prospective rhetors, these works have often been called *rhetorica docens*, the Latin term for a "teaching" rhetoric book. In addition, scholars over the centuries have studied what they regarded as excellent and effective texts—often speeches—produced by renowned rhetors, trying to infer principles that other rhetors could follow. Collectively, the exemplary texts have been called *rhetorica utens*, Latin for *rhetoric in use*. The traditional body of concepts that we know as rhetorical theory is derived from both the works of *rhetorica docens* and *rhetorica utens*.

The major elements of rhetorical theory are the *rhetorical situation*, the *audience*, the *pisteis* or "proofs" (and their subdivisions), and the five canons of rhetoric: *invention, arrangement, style, memory*, and *delivery*. 18

Although the concept of the rhetorical situation is inherent in the history of rhetoric from antiquity to the present, it is most clearly explicated in an essay written in 1968 by Lloyd Bitzer titled "The Rhetorical Situation" (reprinted in Part III). According to Bitzer, a situation is rhetorical when three elements are present: an exigence, an audience, and rhetorical constraints. An exigence is a need, a gap, something wanting, that can be met, filled in, or supplied *only* by a spoken or written text. We can say that the exigence of a situation calls forth a text. Thus, exigence is related to *kairos* as a kind of "generative timeliness": The death of a famous person creates an exigence that calls forth a eulogy. Receiving lousy service from a public utility company creates an exigence that calls forth a letter of complaint. The discovery of a new concept by researchers—for example, the discovery of the double-helix structure of DNA by James Watson and Francis Crick—creates an exigence that calls forth an article reporting the discovery and arguing for its importance. 19

The audience, according to Bitzer, is not simply the aggregation of people who listen to or read the text called forth by the exigence. More specifically, the audience comprises the people who have a reason to be concerned about the exigence and who are capable of acting on it or being acted upon by it. The audience for a eulogy is the people who were connected, however remotely, to the deceased person and who are in the position to have their feelings of grief assuaged by the text. The audience for the letter of complaint is the people connected with the utility company who are in some position to see that the lousy service improves in the future. The audience for the report of the new discovery is the people who are concerned about the state of knowledge in the field and who believe that future research projects should be built on the foundations of newly validated concepts, whether they actually conduct those research projects themselves or simply keep informed of others who do. 20

Rhetorical constraints, according to Bitzer, are the features of the audience's—and perhaps the speaker's or writer's—frames of mind, belief systems, and ways of life that lead the audience to accept the speaker's or writer's ideas and to act upon the exigence. Rhetorical constraints include the audience's presuppositions and beliefs about the subject of the text as well as the patterns of demonstration or proof that the audience will accept. In 21 other words, the constraints are ideas and attitudes that exist between the rhetor—motivated to create discourse by the exigence—and the auditors, who ideally will act upon this exigence. Constraints upon a eulogy include the facts about the deceased person's life and works that the audience can be expected to know, as well as the audience's beliefs about the thoughts and sentiments that are comforting in a time of grief. Constraints upon the letter of complaint include the writer's conception of what would constitute good service, the facts of the situation that amount to lousy service, and the types of appeals the writer believes she can make—appeals to her status as a good customer who regularly pays her bill, say, or appeals to the company's image as a truthworthy provider of service—that will induce the company to improve. Constraints upon the research report include the beliefs, shared by the writers and the audience, about the nature of an experiment or research project in the field, presumptions about the "objective" roles of the researchers themselves, the facts of the experiment or project that the researchers are reporting, and the patterns of reasoning they use (and fully expect their audience to "buy") in order to argue for their discovery as something significant in the intellectual community.

Although Bitzer's article brought together concepts that had already been 22 developed in rhetorical theory, some scholars found his characterization of exigence, audience, and constraints a bit too passive. Thus, his work was very productively revised in an article written eight years later by Richard Vatz, titled "The Myth of the Rhetorical Situation" (reprinted in Part IV). The problem with Bitzer's depiction of the rhetorical situation, Vatz maintains, lies in Bitzer's tacit suggestion that exigences, audiences, and constraints exist as *a priori* categories, before a rhetor chooses to produce a text. It's not that exigences, audiences, and constraints are simply there, Vatz argues, and a rhetor simply trips over them and uses them. On the contrary, says Vatz, exigences, audiences, and constraints are created by rhetors who choose to activate them by inscribing them into their texts. In other words, a situation becomes rhetorical only when a speaker or writer evokes an audience within a text, embodies an exigence within the text that the evoked audience is led to respond to, and handles the constraints in such a way that the audience is convinced that they are true or valid. Bitzer's and Vatz's articles represent two major contributions to an important debate within rhetorical theory about whether texts simply recognize and make use of certain conditions or whether texts actually create those conditions.

## Audience

At first glance, the concept of audience in rhetorical theory seems simple 23 to illustrate, but that simplicity is deceptive. The term *audience* embodies a metaphor from the theater, and indeed when a speech is given before an assembly, we can say that that collection of people is an audience for the speech. In other words, the term *audience* can refer exclusively to those who *hear* a speech or performance, as suggested by a strict translation of *audire*, to hear. But the definition of audience becomes considerably tangled when we consider three complications: First, spoken texts are often recorded for later listening or transmitted electronically beyond the setting where they are performed. Second, spoken texts are often performed versions of previously written texts or are transcribed into written form after they are spoken, and are thus available for audiences completely removed in both time and space from the person who delivered the speech. Third, most of the texts we encounter are never spoken or intended to be spoken, but instead are written and, like transcribed spoken texts, may be read by anyone who happens to pick them up.

Scholars have tried to accommodate these complications by reconsidering 24 the definition of audience. They have, for instance, distinguished the *primary* audience for a text from various *subsidiary* audiences; this distinction has also been drawn using the terms *immediate audience* and *mediated audiences*. Consider an example: The governing council of an economically developing city commissions an ecologist to write a report on the environmental implications of opening up a certain region of the city for commercial real estate development. The primary, immediate audience for the ecologist's report would be the city council members. The report, however, would probably have at least several subsidiary or mediated audiences: the aides to the council members, who read important documents for their bosses and help them digest the material; potential real estate developers, who want to see whether their entrepreneurial plans are favored or foiled by the document; writers for the local media, who are responsible for reporting such issues in newspapers, magazines, radio, and television; and members of environmental protection groups, who want to maintain the ecological viability of the region in the face of what they consider threats posed by commercial development plans. The ecologist's text, to be most effective, would have to address the concerns of all these audiences in some way.

Drawing on canonical works from antiquity through the eighteenth century, 25 traditional rhetorical theory has conceived a text's audience as some individual or collective "other" whom the rhetor must identify, analyze in psychological and emotional terms, and then, by means of the text, "change" in some way so that they will adhere to the rhetor's central idea or thesis. This traditional view has three drawbacks. First, it largely limits attention to the primary, immediate auditors in a rhetorical situation, and generally ignores any subsidiary, mediated audiences. Second, the traditional view tends to assume an antagonistic relation between the rhetor and the audience; it tacitly posits that there is some ideological, emotional, or psychological condition that must be changed within the auditors before they can accept the rhetor's ideas. Third, the traditional view ignores the shared, dialectical nature of communication by characterizing the rhetorical interaction as moving in one direction, from the rhetor to the auditor: The rhetor is the sender and the auditor is the receiver.

Clearly, real communication does not operate on such an immediate, one- 26 way, agonistic street. Some theorists have conflated the concept of audience, as traditionally treated in rhetorical theory, with the concept of speech; *community*, as developed in sociolinguistics. The result has been the forging of a new concept, *discourse community*, an entity defined by Martin Nystrand in 1982. A discourse community, according to Nystrand, comprises people who "may very well *never* speak or write to each other," but who "*could effectively so interact if required* since they know the ways-of-speaking of the group" (15; emphasis in original). In a 1991 work, John Swales provides a more comprehensive definition of discourse community: It comprises people who strive to achieve a "broadly agreed set" of epistemological or social goals by means of their spoken or written texts, who employ "mechanisms of intercommunication among members," who use "participatory mechanisms" to provide information and feedback concerning one another's texts, who use one or more genres "in the communicative furtherance of [the common] aims," and who conventionally use "some specific lexis" (24–27). Consider, for example, the kind of discourse community that has developed in many contemporary industrial settings as quality control operations have been shifted from a single department to the production workforce as a whole. Instead of having a company inspector examining the products as they are being made, the workers themselves assess the products and they document, in writing, what is working well, what is not working, and what needs to be done differently in future shifts. They meet regularly, usually in "quality control teams," to go over the quality control documents they are writing and to plan modifications to both production and the documentation system; they produce a common genre, the "quality management report," which embodies their common knowledge of appropriate content, diction, and format. These workers form a discourse community.

The concept of a discourse community allows rhetorical theorists to analyze  27 interactions among rhetors and both primary and subsidiary audiences, and to illustrate how audiences and speakers and writers influence each other's texts. A clear example of such an analysis is provided by the work of Greg Myers, a linguist at Lancaster University in Great Britain. In the early 1980S, Myers studied how two academic biologists—one a well-known researcher in his field and the other attempting to publish his first article in what for him was a new area—shaped their personae as they wrote grant proposals and articles for professional journals. Myers was able to analyze how the two biologists reacted differently to the responses by the grant proposal reviewers, as well as how the biologists tried to shape their articles to accommodate the range of auditors in their discourse community, which included the reviewers, the journal editors, and the readership of the journal.

The concept of audience is further complicated by the question whether the  28 audience in mind is "addressed" or "evoked." As noted previously, rhetorical theory has traditionally conceived the audience as an isolated, usually antagonistic other whom rhetors have to "address" and "accommodate" in their texts. Clearly, there are some rhetorical situations in which the transaction between the rhetor and the auditors happens in exactly that way. But as early as 1975, with the publication of Walter Ong's essay, "The Writer's Audience is Always a Fiction," rhetorical theorists began to characterize the writer–reader interaction in some texts as constructive rather than adaptive. In other words, in some rhetorical situations, writers cannot know with any certainty who their readers are; accordingly, writers work to *construct* an audience, playing on the assumptions and operating within the rhetorical constraints to which they presume the constructed audience would adhere. For example, when writing a letter to a friend or colleague, discussing common ideas or experiences, a writer addresses an auditor personally and immediately as a known entity. On the other hand, when writing an article for mass publication, a writer must *inscribe* or *invoke* the interests, knowledge, and needs of a presumed audience. In either case, the rhetor determines the *role* of the audience as part of the process of composing. A full explanation of this conception of audience is offered by Lisa Ede's and Andrea Lunsford's 1984 article, "Audience Addressed/Audience Invoked: The Role of Audience in Composition Theory and Pedagogy."

## Means of Persuasion

An ancient term for the kinds of appeals that may affect an audience is *pisteis*.  29
The concept of the *pisteis* is Aristotelian, and the singular term *pistis*, usually understood as "proof," "appeal," or "means of persuasion," is one of those classical Greek terms for which we have no precise English equivalent. In his *Rhetoric*, Aristotle discusses three sorts of textual appeals: to the authority of the rhetor (*ethos*), to the emotions or "stages of life" of the audience (*pathos*), and to systems of reasoning (*logos*) that the rhetor and the audience share. Although Aristotle categorizes the appeals separately, examining their operation clearly shows that they intersect and interact.

*Ethos* is generally defined as the good character and the consequent cred-  30
ibility of the rhetor. Theorists in ancient Greece and Rome did not agree among themselves whether *ethos* exists solely in the text a rhetor creates, or whether the rhetor must evince *ethos* in his or her life as well as in his or her texts. Aristotle maintained the former position: He taught that a text must demonstrate that the rhetor is a person of good sense (*phronesis*), virtue (*arete*), and good will (*eunoia*). A rhetor could not depend, according to Aristotle, on the audience's knowing more about the rhetor's *ethos* than the text itself established. The text must do the job. The theorists who translated and adapted Greek rhetoric for Roman life, notably Cicero and later Quintilian, tended to take the externalist position. Quintilian, who referred to *ethos* with the Latin term *auctoritas*, maintained that the character of a speaker or writer was as vital as the representations of it within a text. Thus, Quintilian taught that the expert at rhetoric was the *vir bonus dicendi peritus:* the *good man* [sic] skilled at speaking.

Although there are clearly instances where the *ethos* of a rhetor is dem-  31
onstrated by actions and examples in life, because texts are today so frequently disseminated and consumed at a remove from the author, it is sensible to examine the ways the texts themselves inscribe a rhetor's *ethos*.

Consider, for example, the convention in published academic papers of using footnotes and bibliographies to cite previously published studies. Why does a writer do this? Surely, some readers could use these citations to check the accuracy and validity of the writer's intellectual antecedents, and some readers might use them to guide their own reading or research on the same subject. Actually, however, such citations operate to invest the writer—and thus the text—with *phronesis:* good sense or "practical" wisdom. The writer becomes more credible because she has done the required homework in the field and shown it through the citations. Consider, to continue using the published academic paper as an example, the tradition of listing the author's academic affiliation in a byline, an address line, or a biographical paragraph; here is an example recently published to accompany an article by William Covino:

> William A. Covino is professor of English at the University of Illinois, Chicago, where he teaches in the graduate program in language, literacy, and rhetoric. His articles on rhetorical theory and history have appeared in several journals, and his books include *The Art of Wondering: A Revisionist Return to the History of Rhetoric, Forms of Wondering: A Dialogue on Writing for Writers,* and *Magic, Rhetoric, and Literacy: An Eccentric History of the Composing Imagination.*

Although certainly some readers might want to correspond with the author or  32
read something else he has written, for most such a listing amounts to a display of *arete*, a demonstration of affiliations and activities that amount to "virtue" in an academic context. Consider, to take a final example from this genre, the degree of deference an author shows to previous studies, even if his or her work will diverge radically from them, and the amount of polite hedging the author of an academic paper demonstrates when setting out the significance of his or her own thesis.

> The pioneering histories of rhetoric produced early in the current revival (Kennedy, Corbett, and Kinneavy) have served virtually to bring into existence for a twentieth-century audience authors and text ignored under the philosophic tradition. The task at hand now is to examine more closely the method of reading we bring to those texts and, more broadly, to the whole discursive field within which they take their places. The result will be different readings of canonical texts, as well as the identification of new significant sites of "rhetoric" in its more comprehensive sophistic definition. (Susan Jarratt, *Recreating the Sophists*, xix).

Jarratt might conceivably have been more dismissive of previous scholar-  33
ship and more brash in asserting the importance of her own. Maintaining *eunoia*—good will toward the discourse community she hopes to engage with her work—requires the more respectful tone struck here, a tone we recognize as a strategic appeal at the same time that we presume it to be sincere.

We have already alluded to the second traditional *pistis* in our discussion  34
of audience. This is the appeal to *pathos*, sometimes called the *pathetic* or

the *emotional* appeal. The central idea underlying *pathos* is that an effective text will somehow activate or draw upon the sympathies and emotions of the auditors, causing them to attend to and accept its ideas, propositions, or calls for action. As with *ethos*, the source of most later rhetorical theory concerning *pathos* is Aristotle's *Rhetoric*. In Book 1, Aristotle describes in detail the emotions he believes a text, depending on the rhetorical situation, could activate in order to persuade one's audience: anger, calmness, friendship, enmity, fear, confidence, shame, shamelessness, kindness, unkindness, pity, indignation, envy, and emulation. In addition, he categorizes potential audiences into social groupings according to character types—the young, the elderly, people in their prime, aristocrats, the wealthy, and the powerful—and analyzes the dominant emotions inherent in each of these character types that a text might try to animate.

Two points about Aristotle's view of *pathos* are noteworthy for understand- 35 ing the role of this appeal in rhetorical theory. First, his catalog of emotions and characters is thoroughly ethnocentric, tied to his purpose of providing instruction in rhetoric to young men who strove to gain political influence in fourth-century BCE Athens. There is little to suggest that rhetors in all, or even most, current rhetorical situations would find it wise to appeal to the emotions as Aristotle defines them. Nor would it probably be wise for rhetors to stereotype their auditors into Aristotle's categories. Nonetheless, the basic move that Aristotle's treatment illustrates—fitting one's text to the character types and states of mind that make up one's audience—remains legitimate in current rhetorical activity. Second, Aristotle assumes a neutral stance toward ethical issues related to pathetic appeals. Certainty current rhetorical theorists, as well as rhetors, need to distinguish between texts that indiscriminately titillate and pander to an audience's emotions and texts in which *pathos* is tied to a virtuous *ethos*, in which a rhetor of goodwill seeks to evoke the same in the audience.

The third *pistis* is *logos*, the appeal to patterns, conventions, and modes of 36 reasoning that the audience finds convincing and persuasive. Although it is common to translate *logos* into its cognate, the "logical" appeal, such a translation is imprecise and potentially misleading. *Logos* in ancient Greek means more than simply logic or reasoning; it means something like "thought plus action." Thus, just as *ethos* moves an audience by activating their faith in the credibility of the rhetor and *pathos* stimulates their feelings and seeks a change in their attitudes and actions, so *logos*, accompanied by the other two appeals, mobilizes the powers of reasoning.

Although *logos* has been explained using different terminology by rhetorical 37 theorists over the centuries, the "logical" transaction they describe can always be characterized in the same general way. A rhetor enters a rhetorical situation either knowing, or prepared to discover, what she and her audience hold as common assumptions about the subject that she will discuss. Knowing that she will have to invoke these common assumptions either implicitly or explicitly in her text, she proceeds to offer a premise or observation about the situation at hand, about the subject of the text. With the common assumptions invoked and the premise or observation put into play, the speaker can then posit a conclusion that follows from the assumption and the premise; this conclusion is, in general terms, the central idea or thesis that the speaker or writer hopes the audience will believe or act upon. The key feature of this basic "logical" transaction of rhetoric is that none of its constituent elements is always, or even frequently, certain and beyond argument. That is, the speaker or writer might find herself in a wrangle with the audience about (1) what they do believe, think, or feel in common; (2) whether the premise or observation is just and appropriate; or (3) whether the conclusion—the central idea or thesis—actually does follow from the assumptions and premise, and even if it does, whether there are other circumstances that would prevent the audience from accepting the conclusion. Conversely, the speaker or writer might find the audience in perfect agreement with some or all of the constituents, in which case the "logical" rhetorical transaction succeeds grandly. . . .

This basic transaction of *logos*—assumptions, assertion or observation, and  38
claim—is called an *enthymeme.* According to Aristotle, speakers or writers arguing a case either construct enthymemes or cite examples; those are the only two persuasive devices available. Unfortunately, Aristotle's own definition of the enthymeme is quite sketchy. He explains that the enthymeme is to rhetoric what the syllogism is to logic. A syllogism offers an incontrovertible proposition as its major premise, an empirically verifiable observation as its minor premise, and a necessary, logical conclusion; an enthymeme, however, might be contentious at all three points. It is a "rhetorical syllogism" that depends for acceptance upon the context in which it occurs. In the centuries since Aristotle, rhetorical theorists have tried to flesh out his suggestive definition. Some have seen the enthymeme as a materially deficient syllogism because neither its premises or conclusions are provable; some have seen it as formally deficient because the major premise—what the rhetor believes that the audience presumes to be true—often goes unstated, and the minor premise—the assertion or observation—is occasionally implicit as well. Contemporary rhetoricians have largely stopped trying to distinguish the enthymeme from the syllogism, simply accepting that the two logical devices have some formal and material similarities but are essentially different.

The other logical device Aristotle describes, the example, might initially  39
seem the converse of the enthymeme, but actually the two devices are related. Anyone who has ever argued a case knows the value of citing a precedent. If you are campaigning for a Republican presidential candidate and arguing that he or she will act decisively to protect American economic interests in the oil-rich Middle East, you might cite the precedent of George Bush's actions in the Gulf War and claim that your candidate will be equally decisive. To Aristotle, however, an example is more than a single instance that acts as a precedent. The Greek word Aristotle uses for example is *paradeigma*, from which English draws the cognate *paradigm.* To be rhetorically effective, an example must offer a *repeated pattern* of precedents. For example, if a rhetor is arguing

that, despite its advocates' claims to the contrary, the "Star Wars" defense system will probably be used aggressively and offensively, she might cite the example of previous weapons systems: "They said the incendiary bomb would be used only for defense and it was used offensively; they said the hydrogen bomb would be used only for defense and it was used offensively; they said the atomic bomb would be used only for defense and it was used offensively. Shouldn't we expect, then, that the 'Star Wars' system will be used offensively?"

Although the enthymeme looks like what a logician would call a deduction 40 and the example looks logically like an induction, they are similar in their effect rhetorically. As James Raymond has perceptively noted, the example is itself a kind of enthymeme. Its major premise, the unstated assumption, is that history tends to repeat itself. Its observation, its assertion about the situation at hand, consists of the pattern of precedent-setting instances. Its claim is the conjecture about the future that follows from this premise and the cited instances.

Although the enthymeme and example are usually discussed in rhetorical 41 theory under the rubric of *logos,* these two tools of argument are not devoted exclusively to appealing to the logic and reasoning of the audience. Indeed, in order to move an audience to believe what the rhetor holds as a communal assumption, to accept her observation about the subject at hand as valid and legitimate, and to adhere to the conclusion that she claims follows from the assumption and the observation, she may need to deploy *pathos* and *ethos* as well. That is, arguing enthymematically may require her to appeal to the audience's reasoning, emotions, interests, and to her own credibility and character.

## The Canons of Rhetoric

In addition, although the enthymeme and example are often discussed in rhe- 42 torical theory as elements of *logos,* they are also central elements in the first of what the Roman rhetoricians proposed as the five *canons* of rhetoric: invention, arrangement, style, memory, and delivery. Each of these canons is considered separately later in Part II, but conceptual definitions of each at this point will suggest how they have been developed as general features within rhetorical theory.

*Invention* is the art of generating effective material for a particular rhe- 43 torical situation. Some rhetorical theorists have argued that *invention* is not a completely appropriate term for this canon because the rhetor often does not generate *new* material, but simply calls it forth from memory. Invention requires the rhetor to assess the audience in order to determine what they feel, think, and know about the subject he intends to speak or write about; to determine, at least provisionally, what purpose he hopes his text will accomplish; and thus to decide what kinds of material—facts, propositions, ideas, and so on—he will inscribe in the text. For many rhetors, these determinations are made subconsciously, simultaneously, and perhaps even randomly.

Nonetheless, such decisions allow the rhetor to probe his thoughts, knowledge base, and experiences and the data in the world around him, and to generate material he believes will be effective for the particular audience and purposes he will invoke. Some rhetors effect this search for material using techniques specific to their particular discipline. For example, a writer constructing an argument in literary criticism may search a novel, poem, or play for some apparently anomalous or distinct feature of plot, character, theme, or diction, with a view to explicating it. Some rhetors, on the other hand, invent material by using some form of structured heuristic (derived from the Greek for *finding*) technique, such as an abbreviated form of Aristotle's *topoi*, Kenneth Burke's dramatistic pentad (which investigates human action as the interaction of Act, Agent, Scene, Agency, and Purpose), the common "journalist's questions," or the tagmemic matrix (which adapts terms from physics—particle, wave, field—as categories for understanding the nature of a unit of information). Finally, some rhetors may generate material using a relatively unstructured, even intuitive, heuristic such as freewriting, brainstorming, and drawing tree diagrams.

*Arrangement*, sometimes called "disposition," is the art of ordering the material in a text so that it is most appropriate for the needs of the audience and the purpose the text is designed to accomplish. Every effective rhetor understands, at least intuitively, that in most conventional situations a text must have a beginning, a middle, and an end but methods of producing this order differ widely. Some speakers and writers considering arrangement may use principles drawn from ancient rhetoric; in general terms, these principles suggest that an effective argument is specifically ordered first to capture the audience's attention, second to provide necessary background information, third to state and prove the text's thesis or central idea, fourth to anticipate and address possible countertheses, and finally to conclude by appealing to the audience's emotions. Rather than relying on any general laws, however, most rhetors derive principles of arrangement from the genres their discourse community values and expects from speakers and writers within it. For example, a writer of scientific research reports knows that for her text to command the attention of people in the discipline, she must write an introduction that frames a research question, a section outlining the methods and materials involved in her research, a section detailing the results of the specific project, and a section arguing that these results actually mean something significant.

Some rhetorical theorists have included under the rubric of arrangement not only principles for ordering entire texts, but also guidelines for arranging information within smaller units, such as paragraphs. The work of the Scottish rhetorician Alexander Bain, for example, led many scholars in the late nineteenth and early twentieth centuries to describe the arrangement of material in both whole texts and paragraphs according to the *mode of discourse* they were supposed to display: narration, description, exposition (often subdivided into such "methods of exposition" as cause-and-effect, definition, comparison–contrast, and so on), and argumentation. Finally, some rhetorical theorists have treated issues of the relative importance of information under arrangement. One mode of arrangement-by-importance is Nestorian order, named after the clear-voiced orator of the Greeks in the Trojan War. Nestor, according to legend, would begin a speech with the next-to-most important information, then provide the least important, and close with the most important.

The canon of arrangement has been called into question with the advent 46 of postmodernism, in particular through the insistence that no text ever really "begins" or "ends"; rather, as Burke's "conversation in the parlor" above suggests, all texts enter into a larger text. The artificiality of beginnings and endings has been explored by postmodern writers such as Roland Barthes, as the excerpt above from *S/Z* indicates. For an audience of postmodern literary theorists, then, the rhetor might deliberately create a discourse that violates the conventions of arrangement, one that accepts and welcomes the disorderliness of open intellectual play.

*Style*, sometimes called elocution, is the art of producing sentences and 47 words that will make an appropriately favorable impression on readers or listeners. Traditionally, the canon of style has included discussions of levels of language—the grand, the middle, and the low, for example—as well as explanations of *tropes*, or figures of thought, and *schemes*, or figures of actual expression. To cite just three examples: Under the rubric of tropes, rhetorical theorists have explained the nature and uses of metaphor (implied comparison), personification (the attribution of human qualities to nonhuman entities), and synechdoche (the substitution of the part for the whole). Under schemes, rhetorical theorists have catalogued such devices as parallelism (creating a similarity of structure in a set of related words, phrases, or clauses), ellipsis (a deliberate omission of words that are readily supplied by the context), and anaphora (the repetition of the same words at the beginning of successive phrases or clauses). A great debate in the history of rhetoric has surrounded the question of whether style is simply an ornamentation of thought and speech, or whether style is "organic" to the specific text and represents, as Thomas De Quincey proposed, the "incarnation of thought."

Most modern rhetorical theorists have adopted some version of the latter 48 position and see style as the process of "giving presence" to ideas that rhetors want their audiences to attend to. Chaim Perelman, among others, has discussed presence in terms of the emphasis that the rhetor gives to "events which, without his intervention, would be neglected but now occupy our attention." The rhetor can do this by presenting images that will affect an audience— "Caesar's bloody tunic as brandished by Antony, the children of the victim of the accused"—or by applying techniques of *amplification* (e.g., "repetition, accumulation, accentuation of particular passages") that highlight the "reality" that the rhetor would like to present (Perelman, *The Realm of Rhetoric*, 35–37).

*Memory*, the fourth traditional canon of rhetoric, seems to bear the most 49 residue of the oral culture in which rhetorical theory has its ancient roots;

however, memory is undergoing something of a revival in contemporary theory. In classical periods, rhetors were expected to commit their speeches to memory. In later periods, the art of memory was taught to young rhetors as a means of mental discipline, even though they most often read texts that had been written out. The most commonly taught mnemonic method was for rhetors to associate the parts of the speech with visual images in some specific physical setting. For example, a rhetor could mentally connect the introduction of his speech to the porch of a house, the background narration to the foyer, the thesis and proof to the arch and the grand ballroom, and the conclusion to the antechamber. As rhetoric over the centuries became more and more an art of crafting and delivering written texts, the canon of memory diminished in importance. In current rhetorical theory, however, computers are being used to store monumental databases and rhetors arc devising increasingly inventive ways to manipulate these data, so memory is becoming a vital canon once again.

*Delivery*, the final traditional canon of rhetorical theory, once constituted   50 the art of using one's voice and body effectively when speaking. Elaborate theory and pedagogy, in both classical periods and later in the eighteenth and nineteenth centuries, was developed to teach rhetors how to pronounce words, project their voices, and move their faces, arms, hands, and even legs and feet. In departments offering courses in public speaking today, contemporary principles of delivery are still being developed; where rhetorical theory and pedagogy are more concerned with written texts, the canon of delivery has come to embrace the study of *graphemics*, the display of material on the printed page or screen.

When one teaches rhetoric, either its theory or its effective practice, one   51 can teach principles of invention, arrangement, style, memory, and delivery as general tenets, applicable in varying degrees to discourse in all fields. However, as suggested earlier, rhetoric has developed during the second half of this century as the study and practice of the featuring of specific content that is vital to the epistemological and social functions of special-interest groups. The title of a 1983 book by Christopher Norris, *The Deconstructive Turn: Essays in the Rhetoric of Philosophy*, suggests what might have been regarded as a heretical idea in centuries past—that philosophy is rhetorical. The "rhetoricizing" of academic subjects that were once regarded as objective, and whose scholars regarded themselves as disinterested, comes along with the postmodern recognition that all discourse serves to advance certain interests, certain versions of truth and facts that serve individual and institutional biases and motives. One of the projects of rhetoric has become the investigation of how such biases and motives are inscribed into academic and scholarly discourses, and so we see increasing attention by humanists, scientists, and social scientists to the *pisteis* of the writing that defines their fields. The presence of rhetoric in other fields is addressed extensively in Part IV of this book in order to suggest what a global art rhetoric has become in our time.

## Works Cited

Aristotle. *Rhetoric*. Trans. George Kennedy. New York: Oxford UP, 1991.

——. *Poetics*. Trans. W. Hamilton Fyfe. Cambridge: Harvard UP, 1932.

Barthes, Roland. *S/Z*. Trans. Richard Miller. New York: Hill and Wang, 1974.

Berthoff, Ann E. *The Making of Meaning: Metaphors, Models, and Maxims for Writing Teachers.* Portsmouth, NH: Boynton/Cook, 1981.

Bitzer, Lloyd. "The Rhetorical Situation." *Philosophy and Rhetoric* 1.1 (1968): 1–14.

Brooks, Cleanth. *The Well Wrought Urn: Studies in the Structure of Poetry.* New York: Harcourt, 1947.

Burke, Kenneth. *Permanence and Change*, 3rd ed. 1935. Berkeley: U of California P, 1984.

——. *The Philosophy of Literary Form*, 3rd ed. Berkeley: U of California P, 1973.

——. "Rhetoric—Old and New." *New Rhetorics*. 1950. Ed. Martin Steinmann. New York: Scribner's, 1967.

Cicero, *On Oratory and Orators (De Oratore)*. Trans. J. S. Watson. Carbondale: Southern Illinois UP, 1970.

Cixous, Helene. "The Laugh of the Medusa." *Critical Theory Since 1965*. Ed. Hazard Adams and Leroy Searle. Tallahassee: Florida State UP, 1986, 309–320.

Ede, Lisa, and Andrea Lunsford. "Audience Addressed/Audience Invoked: The Role of Audience in Composition Theory and Pedagogy." *College Composition and Communication* 35 (1984): 155–71.

De Quincey, Thomas. "Rhetoric." *Selected Essays on Rhetoric*, Ed. Frederick Burwick. Carbondale: Southern Illinois UI, 1967. 81–133.

Eagleton, Terry. *Literary Theory: An introduction*. Minneapolis: U of Minnesota P, 1983.

Jarratt, Susan. *Rereading the Sophists.*, Carbondale, Southern Illinois UI, 1991.

Kennedy, George. "A Hoot in the Dark: The Evolution of General Rhetoric." *Philosophy and Rhetoric* 25.1 (1992): 1–21.

Myers, Greg. "The Social Construction of Two Biologists' Proposals." *Written Communication* 2 (1985): 219–45.

Norris, Christopher. *The Deconstructive Turn: Essays in the Rhetoric of Philosophy.* London: Methuen, 1983.

Nystrand, Martin. "Rhetoric's 'Audience' and Linguistics' 'Speech Community': Implications for Understanding Writing, Reading, and Text." *What Writers Know: The language, Process, and Structure of Written Discourse.* Ed. Martin Nystrand. New York: Academic, 1982. 1–30.

Ong, Walter. "The Writer's Audience Is Always a Fiction." *PMLA* 90 (1975): 9–21.

Perelman, Chaim. *The Realm of Rhetoric*. Notre Dame: U of Notre Dame P, 1982.

Plato, *Phaedrus*. Trans. Harold North Fowler. Cambridge, MA: Harvard UP, 1914.

Quintilian. *The Institutio Oratoria of Quintilian*. Trans. H. E. Butler, 4 vols. Cambridge, MA: Harvard UP, 1921.

Raymond, James. "Enthymemes, Examples, and Rhetorical Method." *Essays in Classical Rhetoric and Modern Discourse*. Eds. Robert J. Connors, Lisa Ede, and Andrea Lunsford. Carbondale: Southern Illinois UP, 1984. 140–51.

Swales, John. *Genre Analysis: English in Academic and Research Settings*. Cambridge: Cambridge UP, 1990.

Valesio, Paolo. *Novantiqua*. Bloomington: Indiana UP, 1980.

Vatz, Richard. "The Myth of the Rhetorical Situation." *Philosophy and Rhetoric* 6 (1972): 154–61.

## Questions for Discussion and Journaling

1. Compare how you've thought of rhetoric in the past to how it appears to you after this reading. What differences are most obvious?

2. Using your own words, explain what the term *epistemic* means. What is the difference if rhetoric is epistemic versus if it is not?

3. What do Covino and Jolliffe list as the major elements of rhetorical theory?

4. Do you understand the distinction Covino and Jolliffe are trying to draw between "philosophical" and "practical" rhetoric? Try giving examples of each of these two aspects.

5. It seems important to think of texts as "active" (para. 8), in Covino and Jolliffe's words. What do they mean by using this term, and if a text is active, what would it *not* be?

6. Covino and Jolliffe state that rhetoric is not "dialectic" (para. 14). Look up *dialectic*: what is it? Why is rhetoric not dialectic?

7. In "The Fields of Rhetoric" section, Covino and Jolliffe argue that rhetoric is not solely about "persuad[ing] people to take a specific action." If rhetoric isn't just an explanation for how *persuasion* works, what else is it about?

8. When Aristotle laid out five canons of rhetoric, public speaking was more common than public writing (because writing was expensive and time-consuming). If you were coming up with a list of "canons of rhetoric" today, from scratch, what do you think they would be?

9. Why isn't audience included as a part of rhetorical situation? Could you make an argument that it *should* be?

10. In discussing *logos*, the writers generalize that in the "'logical' transaction of rhetoric," nothing is "certain or beyond argument" (para. 37). Rhetoric deals only with the *probable*, not the *certain*—with what is *likely*, rather than with what is *absolutely true*. Do you think, then, that rhetoric is very widely used or very rarely used?

## Applying and Exploring Ideas

1. Take an aspect of rhetorical theory (for example, one of the canons) and apply it to the hottest topic of discussion in the news today. For example, how is the information about that topic delivered? Or how do the people talking about that topic try to persuade through the use of emotional appeals?

2. Covino and Jolliffe argue that rhetoric is "primarily verbal" (para. 9). What alternatives are there—what else could rhetoric be but verbal, and would it be possible to have a rhetoric that *wasn't* primarily verbal?

3. Rhetoric is "situationally contingent" (para. 5), meaning that its use, what works best, or what it looks like, will vary depending on the situation. Make a list of implications of that principle: What does it mean for human communication to be contingent on the situation? For example, what does it mean for *teaching and learning* rhetoric if rhetoric varies by the situation?

4. Get a circle of three fellow students together and have this discussion: Of the three *pisteis* (appeals), which seems most important? Keep lists of the reasons each might be argued to be most important; then make a separate list of which reasons allow all of you to reach consensus.

---

**Meta Moment**

Can you think of a moment in which two people are interacting that wouldn't use rhetoric (wouldn't be rhetorical)?

---

# Rhetorical Situations and Their Constituents

## KEITH GRANT-DAVIE

■ Grant-Davie, Keith. "Rhetorical Situations and Their Constituents." *Rhetoric Review* 15.2 (1997): 264–79. Print.

## Framing the Reading

Keith Grant-Davie is an English professor at Utah State University in Logan, "a rural town in the Rocky Mountains." He has studied how readers and writers interact from a number of angles: what readers say writers are trying to do, how writers repeat themselves to make themselves clearer to readers, and how writing and speech are shaped by the context in which they take place and the context(s) to which they respond. When he wrote this article, Grant-Davie was directing the graduate program in USU's English department.

We've referenced the term **rhetorical situation** in earlier chapters and it appears in this chapter's introduction as well as in the previous selection by Covino and Jolliffe. You'll encounter it frequently throughout the rest of this chapter. The term is not an easy one to pin down, however, so you may still be wondering exactly what a rhetorical situation is. Composition theorists like Grant-Davie call an activity, an event, or a situation *rhetorical* when it's shaped by language or communication—also called **discourse**—that tries to get people to *do* something. In order to understand rhetoric, it's necessary to understand the motivations—the purposes, needs, values, and expectations—of the **rhetors**—that is, the people who generate it.

Advertisements are prime examples of rhetorical communication. In advertising, a business communicates with its **audience**—potential customers—in order to persuade them to buy a product: for example, the Coca-Cola corporation hires basketball star Kobe Bryant to command us, "Obey your thirst—drink Sprite!" But rhetorical situations don't have to be strategically planned and constructed *as* rhetoric: in fact, we encounter them every day, in ordinary, unplanned, un-self-conscious interactions. Imagine, for example, sitting in your kitchen with a friend who says, "Boy, I'm really cold." In both the advertisement and your friend's declaration, language *does* things: it convinces us to buy something or to turn up the heat. Such communication is therefore *rhetorical*—that is, it's persuasive or *motivated* communication—and the situations in which it happens would be *rhetorical situations*.

Grant-Davie's article examines the elements of rhetorical situations and may help you better understand and respond to their rhetoric. Why, for example, didn't the Coca-Cola corporation simply bypass the celebrity and the ad agency and issue a statement telling us they'd like us to drink Sprite? Why didn't your chilly friend ask directly, "Can you please turn up the heat?" We need to explore the rhetorical situations of both examples in order to respond intelligently. To use an everyday example: if your little sister walks into your room yelling at the top of her lungs, you won't know how to respond until you understand what's happened and why she's yelling—is she angry, hurt, or excited? Understanding the rhetorical situation of her outburst will help you understand what's at stake and guide you in making an appropriate response.

The idea of a rhetorical situation might not be completely clear to you right away—most people need to encounter the idea in several different ways before they really start to get a handle on it. (If you remember the idea of **threshold concepts** from the introduction to this book, you'll realize that *rhetorical situation* is just such a threshold concept. It takes some time to understand and completely changes your understanding of writing once you do.) In particular, it might take you a few tries to understand the idea of **exigence**. Grant-Davie explains this term a few different ways, but the simplest explanation for it is a *problem* or *need* that can be addressed by communication. In the case of the Sprite ad, the exigence of the communication is complex: it includes the corporation's desire to sell and the consumer's desire for a product that will fill one or more needs (thirst quenching but also identification with a popular celebrity). In the case of your chilly friend, the exigence is more straightforward: Your friend wants to be warmer, but doesn't want to appear pushy or offend you by directly stating her desire for a thermostat adjustment.

You'll also encounter the term **stases**, which is a pattern or set of questions that helps explain what's at issue in a given rhetorical situation—a problem of *fact*, of *value*, or of *policy*. (The classic journalist's questions—Who? What? Where? When? How? Why?—are actually stases that attempt to establish fact.) Finally, you'll encounter the concept of **constraints**, which are factors that limit or focus the response to the exigence (problem or need) in a given situation. (In the case of your chilly friend, her desire to be perceived as friendly, not pushy, is a primary constraint.) These and other concepts in Grant-Davie's article will become clearer as you see them used in other readings.

Remember, when we identify language or communication as rhetorical, we're saying that it is *doing* something. So we could ask of Grant-Davie's article, what does it *do*? Keep that question in mind as you read.

## Getting Ready to Read

*Before you read*, do at least one of the following activities:

- Ask one or more roommates or friends to describe the last serious argument or debate they had. Get them to describe the situations in which the debates took place in as much detail as they can. Make a list of what was "in the situation," following the reporter's "five Ws": Who was there? What was it about? When and where did it happen? Why did it happen (that is, what were the motivations of the arguers)?
- Watch a television commercial and look for how it "sets the scene"—how it very quickly puts viewers in the middle of one situation or another (like a family riding in a car or people eating in a restaurant or a sick person talking with a doctor). Make some notes about how the commercial uses scenery, particular language, or text to help explain "where you are" as a viewer, and ask yourself how important understanding that "scene" or situation is to understanding what's being advertised.

*As you read*, consider the following questions:

- What rhetorical situation gave rise to Grant-Davie's article—that is, why did he write it in the first place? Who is his intended audience? Who else has been talking about this problem/question? What text(s) is he responding to?
- How does the article move from its introduction through the defining work it does to its concluding example? Why is it divided into sections?
- Can you use the examples Grant-Davie gives to help you find examples of rhetorical situations and their components (*exigence, rhetors, audience,* and *constraints*) in your own life?

Ken Burns's documentary film, *The Civil War*, has mesmerized viewers since 1 it first aired on PBS in 1990. Among its more appealing features are the interviews with writers and historians like Shelby Foote and Barbara Fields, who provide the background information and interpretation necessary to transform battles, speeches, and letters from dry historical data into a human drama of characters, intentions, and limitations. In effect, their commentaries explain the rhetorical situations of the events, pointing out influential factors within the broader contexts that help explain why decisions were made and why things turned out as they did. Their analyses of these rhetorical situations show us that some events might easily have turned out otherwise, while the outcomes of other events seem all but inevitable when seen in light of the situations in which they occurred. When we study history, our first question may be "what happened?" but the more important question, the question whose answer offers hope of learning for the future as well as understanding the past, is "why did it happen?" At a fundamental level, then, understanding the rhetorical situations of historical events helps satisfy our demand for causality—helps us discover the extent to which the world is not chaotic but ordered, a place where actions follow patterns and things happen for good reasons. Teaching our writing students to examine rhetorical situations as sets of interacting influences from which rhetoric arises, and which rhetoric in turn influences, is therefore one of the more important things we can do. Writers who know how to analyze these situations have a better method of examining causality. They have a stronger basis for making composing decisions and are better able, as readers, to understand the decisions other writers have made.

> When we study history, our first question may be "what happened?" but the more important question, the question whose answer offers hope of learning for the future as well as understanding the past, is "why did it happen?"

Scholars and teachers of rhetoric have used the term *rhetorical situation* 2 since Lloyd Bitzer defined it in 1968. However, the concept has remained largely underexamined since Bitzer's seminal article and the responses to it by Richard Vatz and Scott Consigny in the 1970s. We all use the term, but what exactly do we mean by it and do we all mean the same thing? My purpose in this essay is to review the original definitions of the term and its constituents, and to offer a more thoroughly developed scheme for analyzing rhetorical situations. I will apply the concept of a rhetorical situation to reading or listening situations as well as to writing or speaking situations, and to what I call "compound" rhetorical situations—discussions of a single subject by multiple rhetors and audiences.[1]

Bitzer defines a rhetorical situation generally as "the context in which 3 speakers or writers create rhetorical discourse" (382).[2] More specifically he defines it as "a complex of persons, events, objects, and relations presenting an actual or potential exigence which can be completely or partially removed if discourse, introduced into the situation, can so constrain human decision or action as to bring about the significant modification of the exigence" (386).[3] In other words, a rhetorical situation is a situation where a speaker or writer sees a need to change reality and sees that the change may be effected through rhetorical discourse. Bitzer argues that understanding the situation is important because the situation invites and largely determines the form of the rhetorical work that responds to it. He adds that "rhetorical discourse comes into existence as a response to situation, in the same sense that an answer comes into existence in response to a question, or a solution in response to a problem" (385–86). Richard Vatz challenges Bitzer's assumption that the rhetor's response is controlled by the situation. He contends that situations do not exist without rhetors, and that rhetors create rather than discover rhetorical situations (154). In effect, Vatz argues that rhetors not only answer the question, they also ask it.[4]

Scott Consigny's reply to Bitzer and Vatz suggests that each of them is both 4 right and wrong, that a rhetorical situation is partly, but not wholly, created by the rhetor. Supporting Vatz, Consigny argues that the art of rhetoric should involve "integrity"—the ability to apply a standard set of strategies effectively to any situation the rhetor may face. On the other hand, supporting Bitzer, he argues that rhetoric should also involve "receptivity"—the ability to respond to the conditions and demands of individual situations. To draw an analogy, we could say that carpentry has integrity inasmuch as carpenters tackle most projects with a limited set of common tools. They do not have to build new tools for every new task (although the evolution of traditional tools and the development of new ones suggest that integrity is not a static property). Conversely, carpentry might also be said to have receptivity if the limited set of tools does not limit the carpenter's perception of the task. A good carpenter does not reach for the hammer every time.

Looking at these articles by Bitzer, Vatz, and Consigny together, we might 5 define a rhetorical situation as a set of related factors whose interaction creates and controls a discourse. However, such a general definition is better understood if we examine the constituents of situation. Bitzer identifies three: exigence, audience, and constraints. Exigence is "an imperfection marked by urgency; it is a defect, an obstacle, something waiting to be done, a thing which is other than it should be" (386). A rhetorical exigence is some kind of need or problem that can be addressed and solved through rhetorical discourse. Eugene White has pointed out that exigence need not arise from a problem but may instead be cause for celebration (291). Happy events may create exigence, calling for epideictic rhetoric. Bitzer defines the audience as those who can help resolve the exigence: "those persons who are capable of being influenced by discourse and of being mediators of change" (387), while constraints are "persons, events, objects, and relations which are parts of the situation because they have the power to constrain decision and action needed to modify the exigence" (388).

Bitzer's three-way division of rhetorical situations has been valuable, but to 6 reveal the full complexity of rhetorical situations, I think we need to develop his scheme further. I propose three amendments. First, I believe exigence, as the motivating force behind a discourse, demands a more comprehensive analysis. Second, I think we need to recognize that rhetors are as much a part of a rhetorical situation as the audience is. Bitzer mentions in passing that when a speech is made, both it and the rhetor become additional constituents of the situation (388), but he does not appear to include the rhetor in the situation that exists *before* the speech is made. And third, we need to recognize that any of the constituents may be plural. Bitzer includes the possibility of multiple exigences and constraints, but he seems to assume a solitary rhetor and a single audience. In many rhetorical situations, there may be several rhetors, including groups of people or institutions, and the discourse may address or encounter several audiences with various purposes for reading. The often complex interaction of these multiple rhetors and audiences should be considered. What follows, then, are definitions and discussions of the four constituents I see in rhetorical situations: exigence, rhetors, audiences, and constraints.

## Exigence—The Matter and Motivation of the Discourse

Bitzer defines rhetorical exigence as the rhetor's sense that a situation both calls 7 for discourse and might be resolved by discourse. According to this definition, the essential question addressing the exigence of a situation would be "Why is the discourse needed?" However, in my scheme I propose that this question be the second of three that ask, respectively, what the discourse is about, why it is needed, and what it should accomplish. I derive the logic for this order of questions from the version of stasis theory explained by Jeanne Fahnestock and Marie Secor, who argue that the stases provide a natural sequence of steps for interrogating a subject. This sequence proceeds from questions of fact and definition (establishing that the subject exists and characterizing it) through questions of cause and effect (identifying the source of the subject and its consequences) and questions of value (examining its importance or quality) to questions of policy or procedure (considering what should be done about it)

("The Stases in Scientific and Literary Argument" 428–31; "The Rhetoric of Literary Criticism" 78–80). Sharon Crowley, too, has suggested stasis theory as a good tool for analyzing rhetorical situations (33).

**What is the discourse about?** This question addresses the first two stases, 8 fact and definition, by asking what the discourse concerns. The question may be answered at quite a concrete level by identifying the most apparent topic. A speech by a politician during an election year may be about mandatory school uniforms, Medicare, an antipollution bill, the fight against terrorism, or any of a host of other topics. However, what the discourse is about becomes a more interesting and important question, and a source of exigence, if asked at more abstract levels—in other words, if the question becomes "What fundamental issues are represented by the topic of the discourse?" or "What values are at stake?" Political speeches often use specific topics to represent larger, more enduring issues such as questions of civil rights, public safety, free enterprise, constitutionality, separation of church and state, morality, family values, progress, equality, fairness, and so forth. These larger issues, values, or principles motivate people and can be invoked to lead audiences in certain directions on more specific topics. A speech on the topic of requiring school uniforms in public schools may engage the larger issue of how much states should be free from federal intervention—an issue that underlies many other topics besides school uniforms. In the first episode of *The Civil War,* historian Barbara Fields draws a distinction between the superficial matter of the war and what she sees as the more important, underlying issues that gave it meaning:

> For me, the picture of the Civil War as a historic phenomenon is not on the battlefield. It's not about weapons, it's not about soldiers, except to the extent that weapons and soldiers at that crucial moment joined a discussion about something higher, about humanity, about human dignity, about human freedom.

On the battlefield, one side's ability to select the ground to be contested has often been critical to the outcome of the engagement. In the same way, rhetors who can define the fundamental issues represented by a superficial subject matter—and persuade audiences to engage in those issues—is in a position to maintain decisive control over the field of debate. A presidential candidate may be able to convince the electorate that the more important issues in a debate about a rival's actions are not the legality of those specific actions but questions they raise about the rival's credibility as leader of the nation ("He may have been exonerated in a court of law, but what does the scandal suggest about his character?"). Attorneys do the same kind of thing in a courtroom, trying to induce the jury to see the case in terms of issues that favor their client. Granted, these examples all represent traditional, manipulative rhetoric—the verbal equivalent of a physical contest—but I believe the same principle is critical to the success of the kind of ethical argument Theresa Enos describes, where the aim is not victory over the opponent but a state of identification, where writer and reader are able to meet in the audience identity the writer has created within the discourse (106–08). In these kinds of argument, establishing acceptable issues would seem to be an essential stage, creating an agenda that readers can agree to discuss.

I am proposing stasis theory be used as an analytic tool, an organizing 9 principle in the sequence of questions that explore the exigence of a situation, but defining the issues of a discourse also involves determining the stases that will be contested in the discourse itself. The presidential candidate in the example mentioned above is abandoning the stasis of definition and choosing instead to take a stand at the stasis of value. Asking what the discourse is about, then, involves identifying the subject matter or topic at the most obvious level, but also determining issues that underlie it and the stases that should be addressed—in short, asking "what questions need to be resolved by this discourse?"

**Why is the discourse needed?** The second question about exigence ad- 10 dresses both the third and fourth stases (cause and value). It addresses cause by asking what has prompted the discourse, and why *now* is the right time for it to be delivered. This aspect of exigence is related, as Bill Covino and David Jolliffe have observed, to the concept of *kairos*—"the right or opportune time to speak or write" (11, 62). Exigence may have been created by events that precede the discourse and act as a catalyst for it; and the timing of the discourse may also have been triggered by an occasion, such as an invitation to speak. A presidential speech on terrorism may be prompted both by a recent act of terrorism but also by a timely opportunity to make a speech. In the case of letters to the editor of a newspaper, the forum is always there—a standing invitation to address the newspaper's readership. However, letter writers are usually prompted by a recent event or by the need to reply to someone else's letter.

While addressing the stasis of cause, the question "why is the discourse 11 needed?" also addresses the value stasis in the sense that it asks why the discourse matters—why the issues are important and why the questions it raises really need to be resolved. The answer to this question may be that the issues are intrinsically important, perhaps for moral reasons. Alternatively, the answer may lie in the situation's implications. Exigence may result not from what has already happened but from something that is about to happen, or from something that might happen if action is not taken—as in the case of many speeches about the environment.

**What is the discourse trying to accomplish?** Finally, exigence can be re- 12 vealed by asking questions at the stasis of policy or procedure. What are the goals of the discourse? How is the audience supposed to react to the discourse? I include objectives as part of the exigence for a discourse because resolving the exigence provides powerful motivation for the rhetor. The rhetor's agenda may also include primary and secondary objectives, some of which might not be stated in the discourse. The immediate objective of a presidential campaign speech might be to rebut accusations made by a rival, while a secondary objective might be to clarify the candidate's stance on one of the issues or help shape his image, and the broader objective would always be to persuade the audience to vote for the candidate when the time comes.

## Rhetor(s)—Those People, Real or Imagined, Responsible for the Discourse and Its Authorial Voice

Bitzer does not include the rhetor as a constituent of the rhetorical situation 13
before the discourse is produced, although he includes aspects of the rhetor under the category of constraints. Vatz only points out the rhetor's role in defining
the situation, yet it seems to me that rhetors are as much constituents of their
rhetorical situations as are their audiences. Their roles, like those of audiences,
are partly predetermined but usually open to some definition or redefinition.
Rhetors need to consider who they are in a particular situation and be aware
that their identity may vary from situation to situation. Neither Bitzer nor Vatz
explores the role of rhetor in much depth, and an exhaustive analysis of possible roles would be beyond the scope of this essay, too; but in the following
paragraphs, I will touch on some possible variations.

First, although for syntactic convenience I often refer to the rhetor as sin- 14
gular in this essay, situations often involve multiple rhetors. An advertisement
may be sponsored by a corporation, written and designed by an advertising
agency, and delivered by an actor playing the role of corporate spokesper-
son. Well-known actors or athletes may lend the ethos they have established
through their work, while unknown actors may play the roles of corporate
representatives or even audience members offering testimony in support of
the product. We can distinguish those who originated the discourse, and who
might be held legally responsible for the truth of its content, from those who
are hired to shape and deliver the message, but arguably all of them involved
in the sales pitch share the role of rhetor, as a rhetorical team.

Second, even when a rhetor addresses a situation alone, the answer to the 15
question "Who is the rhetor?" may not be simple. As rhetors we may speak in
some professional capacity, in a volunteer role, as a parent, or in some other
role that may be less readily identifiable—something, perhaps, like Wayne
Booth's "implied author" or "second self"—the authorial identity that readers
can infer from an author's writing (70–71). Roger Cherry makes a contrast
between the ethos of the historical author and any persona created by that
author (260–68). Cherry's distinction might be illustrated by the speech of a
presidential candidate who brings to it the ethos he has established through his
political career and uses the speech to create a persona for himself as president
in the future. Then again, a rhetor's ethos will not be the same for all audiences.
It will depend on what they know and think of the rhetor's past actions, so the
"real" or "historical" author is not a stable "foundation" identity but depends
partly on the audience in a particular rhetorical situation. Like exigence, then,
audience can influence the identity of the rhetor.

Rhetors may play several roles at once, and even when they try to play just 16
one role, their audience may be aware of their other roles. A Little League
baseball umpire might, depending on his relationship with local residents,
receive fewer challenges from parents at the game if he happens also to be
the local police chief. The range of roles we can play at any given moment is
certainly constrained by the other constituents of the rhetorical situation and
by the identities we bring to the situation. However, new rhetorical situations

change us and can lead us to add new roles to our repertoire. To use Consigny's terms, rhetors create ethos partly through integrity—a measure of consistency they take from situation to situation instead of putting on a completely new mask to suit the needs of every new audience and situation; and they also need receptivity—the ability to adapt to new situations and not rigidly play the same role in every one.

## Audience—Those People, Real or Imagined, with Whom Rhetors Negotiate through Discourse to Achieve the Rhetorical Objectives

Audience as a rhetorical concept has transcended the idea of a homogenous body    17
of people who have stable characteristics and are assembled in the rhetor's presence. A discourse may have primary and secondary audiences, audiences that are present and those that have yet to form, audiences that act collaboratively or as individuals, audiences about whom the rhetor knows little, or audiences that exist only in the rhetor's mind. Chaïm Perelman and Lucie Olbrechts-Tyteca point out that unlike speakers, writers cannot be certain who their audiences are, and that rhetors often face "composite" audiences consisting either of several factions or of individuals who each represent several different groups (214–17).

In Bitzer's scheme audience exists fairly simply as a group of real people    18
within a situation external to both the rhetor and the discourse. Douglas Park has broadened this perspective by offering four specific meanings of audience: (1) any people who happen to hear or read a discourse, (2) a set of readers or listeners who form part of an external rhetorical situation (equivalent to Bitzer's interpretation of audience), (3) the audience that the writer seems to have in mind, and (4) the audience roles suggested by the discourse itself. The first two meanings assume that the audience consists of actual people and correspond to what Lisa Ede and Andrea Lunsford have called "audience addressed" (Ede and Lunsford 156–65). Park's third and fourth meanings are more abstract, corresponding to Ede and Lunsford's "audience invoked." Park locates both those meanings of audience within the text, but I would suggest that the third resides not so much in the text as in the writer before and during composing, while the fourth is derived from the text by readers. Since writers are also readers of their own texts, they can alternate between the third and fourth meanings of audience while composing and rereading; so they might draft with a sense of audience in mind, then reread to see what sense of audience is reflected in the text they have created. In some instances writers may be their own intended audiences. One example would be personal journals, which writers may write for themselves as readers in the future, or for themselves in the present with no more awareness of audience as separate from self than they have when engaging in internal dialogue.

Instead of asking "Who is the audience?," Park recommends we ask how a    19
discourse "defines and creates contexts for readers" (250). As an example of such a context, he offers Chaïm Perelman's notion of the universal audience, which Perelman defines in *The New Rhetoric* as an audience "encompassing

all reasonable and competent men" (157). Appealing to the universal audience creates a forum in which debate can be conducted. Likewise, Park argues, a particular publication can create a context that partly determines the nature of the audience for a discourse that appears in it.

Like the other constituents of rhetorical situations, the roles of rhetor and 20 audience are dynamic and interdependent. As a number of theorists have observed, readers can play a variety of roles during the act of reading a discourse, roles that are not necessarily played either before or after reading. These roles are negotiated with the rhetor through the discourse, and they may change during the process of reading (Ede and Lunsford 166–67; Long 73, 80; Park 249; Perelman and Olbrechts-Tyteca 216; Phelps 156–57; Roth 182–83). Negotiation is the key term here. Rhetors' conceptions of audiences may lead them to create new roles for themselves—or adapt existing roles—to address those audiences. Rhetors may invite audiences to accept new identities for themselves, offering readers a vision not of who they are but of who they could be. Readers who begin the discourse in one role may find themselves persuaded to adopt a new role, or they may refuse the roles suggested by the discourse. I may open a letter from a charity and read it not as a potential donor but as a rhetorician, analyzing the rhetorical strategies used by the letter writer. In that case I would see my exigence for reading the letter, and my role in the negotiation, as quite different from what the writer appeared to have had in mind for me.[5]

Rhetorical situations, then, are not phenomena experienced only by rhetors. 21 As Stephen Kucer and Martin Nystrand have argued, reading and writing may be seen as parallel activities involving negotiation of meaning between readers and writers. If reading is a rhetorical activity too, then it has its own rhetorical situations. So, if we prefer to use *writing situation* as a more accessible term than *rhetorical situation* when we teach (as some textbooks have—e.g., Pattow and Wresch 18–22; Reep 12–13), we should not neglect to teach students also about "reading situations," which may have their own exigencies, roles, and constraints.

## Constraints—Factors in the Situation's Context That May Affect the Achievement of the Rhetorical Objectives

Constraints are the hardest of the rhetorical situation components to define 22 neatly because they can include so many different things. Bitzer devotes just one paragraph to them, defining them as "persons, events, objects, and relations which are parts of the situation because they have the power to constrain decision and action needed to modify the exigence." Since he assumes that rhetors are largely controlled by situations and since he observes "the power of situation to constrain a fitting response" (390), his use of the term *constraints* has usually been interpreted to mean limitations on the rhetor—prescriptions or proscriptions controlling what can be said, or how it can be said, in a given situation. A rhetor is said to work within the constraints of the situation. However, this commonly held view of constraints as obstacles or restrictions has obscured the fact that Bitzer defines constraints more as aids to the rhetor than as handicaps. The rhetor "harnesses" them so as to constrain the audience to take the desired action or point of view. This view of constraints seems useful, so I see them as working either for or against the rhetor's objectives. I refer to the kind that support a rhetor's case as positive constraints, or assets, and those that might hinder it as negative constraints, or liabilities.

Bitzer goes on to divide constraints along another axis. Some, which he 23 equates with Aristotle's inartistic proofs, are "given by the situation." These might be "beliefs, attitudes, documents, facts, traditions, images, interests, motives and the like"—presumably including beliefs and attitudes held by the audience. Other constraints, equivalent to Aristotle's artistic proofs, are developed by the rhetor: "his personal character, his logical proofs, and his style" (388). To paraphrase, Bitzer defines constraints very broadly as all factors that may move the audience (or disincline the audience to be moved), including factors in the audience, the rhetor, and the rhetoric. Such an all-inclusive definition would seem to threaten the usefulness of constraints as a distinct constituent of rhetorical situations, so I propose excluding the rhetor and the audience as separate constituents and making explicit the possibility of both positive and negative constraints. I would define constraints, then, as all factors in the situation, aside from the rhetor and the audience, that may lead the audience to be either more or less sympathetic to the discourse, and that may therefore influence the rhetor's response to the situation—still a loose definition, but constraints defy anything tighter.

With the rhetor and the audience excluded from the category of constraints, 24 it is tempting to exclude the other artistic proofs too, thereby simplifying the category further by drawing a distinction between the rhetorical situation and the discourse that arises from it. However, clearly the situation continues after the point at which the discourse begins to address it. A rhetor continues to define, shape, reconsider, and respond to the rhetorical situation throughout the composing process, and at any given point during that process, the rhetor may be highly constrained by the emerging discourse. If we are to be coherent, what we have already written must constrain what we write next.

If constraints are those other factors in rhetorical situations, besides rhetors 25 and audiences, that could help or hinder the discourse, what might they be? I have already included the emerging text of the discourse as a constraint on what a rhetor can add to it. To this we can add linguistic constraints imposed by the genre of the text or by the conventions of language use dictated by the situation. Other constraints could arise from the immediate and broader contexts of the discourse, perhaps including its geographical and historical background. Such constraints could include recent or imminent events that the discourse might call to readers' minds, other discourses that relate to it, other people, or factors in the cultural, moral, religious, political, or economic climate—both local and global—that might make readers more or less receptive to the discourse. Foreign trade negotiations, a domestic recession, a hard winter, civil disturbances, a sensational crime or accident—events like these might act as constraints on the rhetorical situation of an election campaign speech, suggesting appeals to make or avoid making. Every situation arises within a context—a background of time, place, people, events, and so forth. Not all of the context is directly relevant to the situation, but rhetors and audiences may be aware of certain events, people, or conditions within the context that *are* relevant and should be considered part of the situation because they have the potential to act as positive or negative constraints on the discourse. The challenge for the rhetor is to decide which parts of the context bear on the situation enough to be considered constraints, and what to do about them—for instance, whether the best rhetorical strategy for a negative constraint would be to address it directly and try to disarm it—or even try to turn it into a positive constraint—or to say nothing about it and hope that the audience overlooks it too.

Some of my examples have complicated the roles of rhetor and audience, 26 but all so far have looked at discourses in isolation and assumed that situations are finite. It seems clear that a situation begins with the rhetor's perception of exigence, but when can it be said to have ended? Does it end when the exigence has been resolved or simply when the discourse has been delivered? I favor the latter because it establishes a simpler boundary to mark and it limits rhetorical situations to the preparation and delivery of discourses, rather than extending them to their reception, which I consider to be part of the audience's rhetorical situation. Also, as I have tried to show, exigence can be quite complex and the point at which it can be said to have been resolved may be hard to identify. The same exigence may motivate discourses in many quite different situations without ever being fully resolved. Major sources of exigence, like civil rights, can continue to motivate generations of rhetors.

To say that a rhetorical situation ends when the discourse has been delivered 27 still leaves us with the question of how to describe discourse in a discussion. Dialogue challenges the idea of rhetorical situations having neat boundaries. When participants meet around a table and take turns playing the roles of rhetor and audience, are there as many rhetorical situations as there are rhetors—or turns? Or should we look at the whole meeting as a single rhetorical situation? And what happens when the participants in a discussion are not gathered together at one place and time, engaged in the quick give and take of oral discussion, but instead debate a topic with each other over a period of weeks— for example, by sending and replying to letters to the editor of a newspaper? To look at a meeting as a single rhetorical situation recognizes that many of the constituents of the situation were common to all participants, and it emphasizes Bitzer's view that situations are external to the rhetor; whereas to look at each person involved in the discussion as having his or her own rhetorical situation— or each contribution to the discussion having its own situation—would seem to lean toward Vatz's view that rhetorical situations are constructed by rhetors. Both views, of course, are right. Each rhetor has a different perspective and enters the debate at a different time (especially in the case of a debate carried on through a newspaper's editorial pages), so each addresses a slightly different rhetorical situation; but the situations may interlace or overlap extensively with those addressed by other rhetors in the discussion. It may be useful, then, to think of an entire discussion as a compound rhetorical situation, made up of a group of closely related individual situations. Analyzing a compound situation involves examining which constituents were common to all participants and which were specific to one or two. For example, some sources of exigence may have motivated all participants, and in these common factors may lie the hope of resolution, agreement, or compromise. On the other hand, the divisive heat of a debate may be traced to a fundamental conflict of values—and thus of exigence—among the participants.

Examples of this kind of compound rhetorical situation can be found when- 28 ever public debate arises, as it did recently in the editorial pages of a local newspaper in a rural community in the Rocky Mountains. The debate was sparked when the newspaper printed a front-page story about a nearby resort hotel, Sherwood Hills, that had erected a 46-foot, illuminated Best Western sign at the entrance to its property. Such a sign on a four-lane highway would not normally be remarkable, but the setting made this one controversial. Sherwood Hills lies hidden in trees at the end of a long driveway, off a particularly scenic stretch of the highway. There are no other residences or businesses nearby, and the area is officially designated a forest-recreation zone, which usually prohibits businesses and their signs. Several months earlier, the resort owners had applied to the county council for a permit and been told that some kind of sign on the road might be allowed, but the application had not been resolved when the sign went up.

The newspaper ran several stories reporting the resort owners' rationale 29 (they felt they had applied in good faith and waited long enough) and the council members' reaction (they felt indignant that the owners had flouted the law and were now seeking forgiveness rather than permission). The newspaper also berated the resort owners' actions in an editorial. What might have been a minor bureaucratic matter resolved behind closed doors turned into a town debate, with at least 15 letters to the editor printed in the weeks that followed. From a rhetorical perspective, I think the interesting question is why the incident sparked such a brushfire of public opinion, since not all controversial incidents covered by the newspaper elicit so many letters to the editor. Looking at the debate as a compound rhetorical situation and examining its constituents helps answer that question.

The rhetors and audiences included the resort owners, the county council, 30 the county planning commission, the Zoning Administrator, the newspaper staff, and assorted local citizens. Their debate was nominally about the sign— whether it was illegal (a question at the stasis of definition) and what should be done about it (a question at the policy stasis). These questions were sources of exigence shared by all participants in the debate. However, even greater exigence seems to have come from questions at the stasis of cause/effect—what precedent might the sign create for other businesses to ignore local ordinances?—and at the stasis of value—were the sign and the act of erecting it without a permit (and the ordinance that made that act illegal) good or bad? For most of the letter writers, the debate revolved around the issue of land use, one of the more frequently and hotly contested issues in the western United States, where the appropriate use of both public and private land is very much open to argument.

Critics of the sign generally placed a high value on unspoiled wilderness. For 31 them the sign symbolized the commercial development of natural beauty and challenged laws protecting the appearance of other forest-recreation zones in the area. Those in favor of the sign, on the other hand, saw it not as an eyesore but as a welcome symbol of prosperity erected in a bold and justified challenge to slow-moving bureaucracy and unfair laws, and as a blow struck for private property rights. Underlying the issue of land use in this debate, then, and providing powerful exigence, was the issue of individual or local freedom versus government interference—another issue with a strong tradition in the western U.S. (as in the case of the "sagebrush rebellions"—unsuccessful attempts to establish local control over public lands). The tradition of justified—or at least rationalized—rebellion against an oppressive establishment can of course be traced back to the American Revolution, and in the 1990s we have seen it appear as a fundamental source of exigence in a number of antigovernment disputes in various parts of the nation.

Exigence and constraints can be closely related. For the critics of Sherwood 32 Hills, the breaking of the law was a source of exigence, motivating them to protest, but the law itself was also a positive constraint in the situation, giving them a reason to argue for the removal of the sign. Certainly the law constrained the council's response to the situation. On the other hand, the law was apparently a less powerful constraint for the owners of Sherwood Hills and for many of their supporters who felt that the law, not the sign, should be changed. For many on that side of the debate, the tradition of rebelling against what are perceived to be unfair government restrictions provided both exigence and a positive constraint. The feeling that private property owners' rights had been violated was what motivated them to join the discussion, but it also gave them an appeal to make in their argument. The rhetor's sense of exigence, when communicated successfully to the audience, can become a positive constraint, a factor that helps move the audience toward the rhetor's position.

Precedents always create constraints. In the Sherwood Hills debate, sev- 33 eral participants mentioned comparable business signs, including one recently erected at another local resort, also in a forest-recreation area. The existence of that sign was a positive constraint for supporters of the Sherwood Hills sign. However, it was also a negative constraint since the other resort had followed the correct procedure and received a permit for its sign, and since the sign was smaller and lower than the Sherwood Hills sign, had no illumination, and had been designed to harmonize with the landscape.

Other constraints emerged from local history. The highway past Sherwood 34 Hills had recently been widened, and the dust had not yet settled from the dispute between developers and environmentalists over that three-year project. Even before the road construction, which had disrupted traffic and limited access to Sherwood Hills, the resort had struggled to stay in business, changing hands several times before the present owners acquired it. The sign, some supporters suggested, was needed to ensure the new owners' success, on which the prosperity of others in the community depended too. The owners were also praised as upstanding members of the community, having employed local people and contributed to local charities. Two letter writers argued from this constraint that the community should not bite the hand that feeds.

This analysis of the Sherwood Hills sign debate as a compound situation only scratches the surface, but understanding even this much about the situation goes a long way toward explaining why the incident generated such an unusual wave of public opinion. The conclusion of a compound rhetorical situation may be harder to determine than the end of a single-discourse situation, particularly if the subject of discussion is perennial. This particular dispute ended when the exchange of letters stopped and the Sherwood Hills owners reached a compromise with the county council: Both the sign and the ordinance remained in place, but the sign was lowered by ten feet.

As my discussion and examples have shown, exigence, rhetor, audience, and constraints can interlace with each other, and the further one delves into a situation the more connections between them are likely to appear. However, while the boundaries between the constituents will seldom be clear and stable, I do think that pursuing them initially as if they were discrete constituents helps a rhetor or a rhetorician look at a situation from a variety of perspectives. My efforts in the preceding pages have been to discuss the possible complexities of rhetorical situations. Teaching student writers and readers to ask the same questions, and to understand why they are asking them, will help them realize their options, choose rhetorical strategies and stances for good reasons, and begin to understand each other's roles.[6]

## Notes

1. I thank *Rhetoric Review* readers John Gage and Robert L. Scott, whose careful reviews of earlier drafts of this essay helped me improve it greatly.
2. Bitzer's definition does not distinguish *situation* from *context*. The two terms may be used interchangeably, but I prefer to use *context* to describe the broader background against which a rhetorical situation develops and from which it gathers some of its parts. I see situation, then, as a subset of context.
3. In "The Rhetorical Situation" and "Rhetoric and Public Knowledge," Bitzer uses the terms *exigence* and *exigency* synonymously. I have used *exigence* in this essay mostly for reasons of habit and consistency with the original Bitzer/Vatz/Consigny discussion. I consider it an abstract noun like *diligence*, *influence*, or *coherence*. While cohesion can be located in textual features, coherence is a perception in the reader. In the same way, exigence seems to me to describe not so much an external circumstance as a sense of urgency or motivation within rhetors or audiences. It is they who recognize (or fail to recognize) exigence in a situation and so the exigence, like the meaning in literary works, must reside in the rhetor or audience as the result of interaction with external circumstances. Although Bitzer calls those circumstances exigences, I prefer to think of them as *sources* of exigence.
4. This fundamental disagreement between Bitzer and Vatz parallels the debate within literary theory over the location of meaning: whether meaning exists in the text, independent of the reader, or whether it is largely or entirely brought by the reader to the text. Bitzer's view looks toward formalism, Vatz's toward reader-response theories, and mine toward the position that meaning is a perception that occurs in the reader but is (or should be) quite highly constrained by the text.
5. Taking poststructuralist approaches to the roles of rhetor and audience, Louise Wetherbee Phelps and Robert Roth further challenge any assumption of a static, divided relationship between the two. Phelps uses Mikhail Bakhtin's idea of heteroglossia to deconstruct the idea of

a boundary between author and audience. She argues that the other voices an author engages through reading and conversation while composing are inevitably present in the text, inextricably woven with the author's voice, and that this intertextuality of the text and the author makes a simple separation of text and author from audience impossible (158–59). Roth suggests that the relationship between writers and readers is often cooperative, not adversarial (175), and that a writer's sense of audience takes the form of a shifting set of possible reading roles the writer may try on (180–82). Neither Phelps nor Roth argue that we should abandon the terms *rhetor* and *audience*. Phelps acknowledges that although author and audience may not be divisible, we routinely act as if they were (163), and she concludes that we should retain the concept of audience for its heuristic value "as a usefully loose correlate for an authorial orientation—whoever or whatever an utterance turns toward" (171). Like Phelps, Roth recognizes that the free play of roles needs to be grounded. "What we really need," he concludes, "is a continual balancing of opposites, both openness to a wide range of potential readers and a monitoring in terms of a particular sense of audience at any one moment or phase in the composing process" (186).

6. I have summarized my analysis in a list of questions that might be used by writers (or adapted for use by audiences) to guide them as they examine a rhetorical situation. Space does not allow this list to be included here, but I will send a copy to anyone who mails me a request.

## Works Cited

Bitzer, Lloyd F. "The Rhetorical Situation." *Philosophy and Rhetoric* 1 (1968): 1–14. Rpt. *Contemporary Theories of Rhetoric: Selected Readings*. Ed. Richard L. Johannesen. New York: Harper, 1971. 381–93.

———. "Rhetoric and Public Knowledge." *Rhetoric, Philosophy, and Literature: An Exploration*. Ed. Don M. Burks. West Lafayette, IN: Purdue UP, 1978. 67–93.

Booth, Wayne C. *The Rhetoric of Fiction*. 2nd ed. Chicago: U of Chicago P, 1983.

Cherry, Roger D. "Ethos Versus Persona: Self-Representation in Written Discourse." *Written Communication* 5 (1988): 251–76.

Consigny, Scott. "Rhetoric and Its Situations." *Philosophy and Rhetoric* 7 (1974): 175–86.

Covino, William A., and David A. Jolliffe. *Rhetoric: Concepts, Definitions, Boundaries*. Boston: Allyn, 1995.

Crowley, Sharon. *Ancient Rhetorics for Contemporary Students*. New York: Macmillan, 1994.

Ede, Lisa, and Andrea Lunsford. "Audience Addressed/Audience Invoked: The Role of Audience in Composition Theory and Pedagogy." *College Composition and Communication* 35 (1984): 155–71.

Enos, Theresa. "An Eternal Golden Braid: Rhetor as Audience, Audience as Rhetor." Kirsch and Roen 99–114.

Fahnestock, Janne, and Marie Secor. "The Rhetoric of Literary Criticism." *Textual Dynamics of the Professions*. Ed. Charles Bazerman and James Paradis. Madison: U of Wisconsin P, 1991. 76–96.

———. "The Stases in Scientific and Literary Argument." *Written Communication* 5 (1988): 427–43.

Fields, Barbara. Interview. *The Civil War*. Dir. Ken Burns. Florentine Films, 1990.

Kirsch, Gesa, and Duane H. Roen, eds. *A Sense of Audience in Written Communication*. Newbury Park, CA: Sage, 1990.

Kucer, Stephen L. "The Making of Meaning: Reading and Writing as Parallel Processes." *Written Communication* 2 (1985): 317–36.

Long, Russell C. "The Writer's Audience: Fact or Fiction?" Kirsch and Roen 73–84.

Moore, Patrick. "When Politeness Is Fatal: Technical Communication and the Challenger Accident." *Journal of Business and Technical Communication* 6 (1992): 269–92.

Nystrand, Martin. "A Social-Interactive Model of Writing." *Written Communication* 6 (1988): 66–85.

Park, Douglas. "The Meanings of 'Audience.' " *College English* 44 (1982): 247–57.

Pattow, Donald, and William Wresch. *Communicating Technical Information: A Guide for the Electronic Age*. Englewood Cliffs, NJ: Prentice, 1993.

Perelman, Chaïm. *The New Rhetoric: A Theory of Practical Reasoning*. Trans. E. Griffin-Collart and O. Bird. *The Great Ideas Today*. Chicago: Encyclopedia Britannica, Inc., 1970. Rpt. *Professing the New Rhetorics: A Sourcebook*. Ed. Theresa Enos and Stuart C. Brown. Englewood Cliffs, NJ: Prentice, 1994, 145–77.

Perelman, Chaïm, and L. Olbrechts-Tyteca. *The New Rhetoric*. Trans. John Wilkinson and Purcell Weaver. U. of Notre Dame P, 1969: 1–26. Rpt. *Contemporary Theories of Rhetoric: Selected Readings*. Ed. Richard L. Johannesen. New York: Harper, 1971, 199–221.

Phelps, Louise Wetherbee. *Audience and Authorship: The Disappearing Boundary*. Kirsch and Roen 153–74.

Reep, Diana C. *Technical Writing: Principles, Strategies, and Readings*. 2nd ed. Boston: Allyn, 1994.

Roth, Robert G. *Deconstructing Audience: A Post-Structuralist Rereading*. Kirsch and Roen 175–87.

Vatz, Richard. "The Myth of the Rhetorical Situation." *Philosophy and Rhetoric* 6 (1973): 154–61.

White, Eugene E. *The Context of Human Discourse: A Configurational Criticism of Rhetoric*. Columbia: U of South Carolina P, 1992.

## Questions for Discussion and Journaling

1. Have you ever thought of writers as negotiating with their audiences? As a writer, what is the difference between imagining yourself *talking* to and *negotiating* with your audience? What would you do differently if you were doing the latter?

2. How would you define *exigence*? Why does exigence matter in rhetorical situations? (What difference does it make?)

3. Grant-Davie opens with a discussion of historical documentaries and the difference between asking "What happened?" and asking "Why did it happen?" Which question, in your view, does analyzing rhetorical situations answer? What makes you think so?

4. What are *constraints*? To help you work this out, consider what Grant-Davie's constraints might have been in drafting this piece. Bitzer, you learned in this piece, argues that we should think of constraints as *aids* rather than *restrictions*. How can that be?

5. As a writer, how would it help you to be aware of your rhetorical situation and the constraints it creates?

6. Grant-Davie seems to want us to use the idea of rhetorical situation mostly in an *analytical* way, to understand why existing discourses have taken the shape they have. In other words, he seems to be talking to us as *readers*. In what ways is the idea also useful for writers? That is, how is it useful to understand the rhetorical situation you're "writing into"?

7. Grant-Davie suggests that we have to ask three questions to understand the exigence of a rhetorical situation: what a discourse is about, why it's needed, and what it's trying to accomplish. What's the difference between the second question and the third question?

8. What happens if we imagine everyone in a rhetorical situation to be *simultaneously* a rhetor and an audience? How does imagining a *writer* as simultaneously rhetor and audience make you think differently about writing?

9. Based on the rhetorical situation for which Grant-Davie was writing, would you say you are part of the audience he imagined, or not? Why?

10. Other writers (Bitzer, Vatz, Consigny) have tried to explain the concept of the *rhetorical situation* before. Why does Grant-Davie think more work is needed?

## Applying and Exploring Ideas

1. a) Write a brief (one- to two-page) working definition of *rhetorical situation*. Be sure to give some examples of rhetorical situations to illustrate your definition.

   b) Complicate your working definition by examining how Grant-Davie, Bitzer, Vatz, and Consigny see the rhetorical situation similarly or differently from one another. You may write this as a straightforward compare-and-contrast discussion if you would like, or, to spice things up a little, write it as a dialogue and create the situation in which it occurs. (Is it an argument? A dinner-table discussion? A drunken brawl?) Where does it happen, how does it go, and what do the participants say?

2. Write a two- to three-page analysis of the rhetorical situation of Grant-Davie's own article, using the elements the article explains.

3. Identify an argument that's currently going on at your school. (Check your school newspaper or Web site if nothing springs to mind.) In a short (two- to three-page) analysis, briefly describe the argument. After describing the argument, analyze the rhetorical situation. Then conclude by noting whether or how your understanding of the argument changed after you analyzed the rhetorical situation.

4. Look at three course syllabi and/or three academic handouts you've received this semester or in previous semesters. What rhetorical situation does each instructor seem to be imagining? Why do you think so? Do the instructors seem to imagine their rhetorical situations differently? If so, why do you think they do this?

5. Watch a few TV commercials and notice how quickly they establish a rhetorical situation *within* the ad. (Not, that is, the rhetorical situation of you as audience and the company as rhetor, but the rhetorical situation inside the commercial, where actors or characters play the roles of rhetors and audiences.) Write a two- to three-page analysis that describes three commercials, the rhetorical situations they create, and whether or not you consider them to be persuasive.

### Meta Moment

Why do you think that your teacher assigned this article? How might this article help you achieve the goals of this chapter? How can understanding the concept of *rhetorical situation* potentially be useful to you in school and in your life?

# Speech Acts, Genres, and Activity Systems: How Texts Organize Activity and People

## CHARLES BAZERMAN

■ Bazerman, Charles. "Speech Acts, Genres, and Activity Systems: How Texts Organize Activity and People." *What Writing Does and How It Does It: An Introduction to Analyzing Texts and Textual Practices*. Ed. Charles Bazerman and Paul Prior. London: Routledge, 2004. 309–39. Print.

## Framing the Reading

Charles Bazerman is a widely published scholar of writing and the teaching of writing. He serves as Professor in the Department of Education at the University of California, Santa Barbara. If you read the introduction to Chapter 2, and any of the selections in Chapter 2, you will be well prepared to understand his claims in this reading. He tells you immediately that "people using text create new realities of meaning, relations, and knowledge" (para. 1). The introduction to Chapter 2 gave a simple example of how this might happen through a fundraising letter written by a food bank staff person. Bazerman provides a more complex example in the first part of this selection, describing how a written university policy influences what he calls "social facts," "those things people believe to be true" (para. 8).

Bazerman provides a lot of new vocabulary for you in this chapter, including **genre,** *genre sets, genre systems, systems of human activity*, and *speech act*. This might seem overwhelming at first. However, he is extremely careful about defining all of these terms and he always gives examples of what the terms mean. Students can usually grasp these ideas fairly quickly by applying them to situations that are familiar to them, as Victoria Marro's paper showed in Chapter 2. Early on, Bazerman gives you a number of reasons why understanding this material will help you in very practical ways: by responding effectively as a writer to new situations, by helping you understand when texts you or someone else wrote don't work as you had hoped, by helping you figure out when a group's activities are not working as planned and then revising texts so that the group can better accomplish its work. Being able to do these things will help you right away, in situations as varied as your sorority and fraternity or a job internship.

Bazerman has authored at least eighteen books, edited at least eleven other books, and written over 120 articles and book chapters on a variety of aspects of writing, including the history of scientific writing and the use of writing in advancing technology and developing academic disciplines.

## Getting Ready to Read

*Before you read*, do at least one of the following activities:

- Read or reread the introduction to Chapter 2.
- If your teacher asks you to do so, quickly read the short Wardle and Kain selection defining activity theory in Chapter 2.

*As you read*, consider the following question:

- What examples from your own experience can you call upon to help illustrate the terms that Bazerman is defining?

.................................................................................................

Part I of this book provides conceptual and analytic tools to show how texts evoke worlds of meaning by representing content and using the resources of language, including relations with other texts, and other media, such as graphics. Part II to this point provides tools to examine how texts arise within and influence the living world of people and events. This final chapter proposes one more set of conceptual and analytic tools for viewing the work that texts do in society. This chapter provides means to identify the conditions under which they accomplish this work; to notice the regularity of texts in carrying out recognizably similar tasks; and to see how specific professions, situations, and social organizations can be associated with a limited range of text types. Finally, it provides methods to analyze how the orderly production, circulation, and use of these texts in part constitutes the very activity and organization of social groups. The analytical approach of this chapter relies on a series of concepts: social facts, speech acts, genres, genre systems, and activity systems. These concepts suggest **how people using text create new realities of meaning, relation, and knowledge.**

Consider a typical academic situation. One university's faculty senate after much debate passes a regulation requiring students to pass six writing intensive courses in order to be granted a B.A. The regulation defines several criteria that a course must meet before it can be approved by the curriculum committee as writing intensive, such as a minimum number of writing assignments with a minimum number of total required words across the term. This requirement then gets written into various administrative documents including the university catalogue and various student advisement documents. Students read these documents (or are reminded by advisors at critical junctures) and know they have to locate and register for courses that will fulfill those requirements if they hope to graduate. Memos and other administrative documents are sent to the faculties of various departments to encourage them to offer such courses. The faculty of those departments write syllabi indicating that students will be required to write the requisite number of assignments and words. Further, the faculty are likely to shape those assignments in relation to the intellectual challenges of their subject matter and the goals of the course such as improving students' ability to understand and use economic models or to interpret 17th-century Spanish verse. The faculty then submit these syllabi for review by faculty committees, according to procedures set out in other administrative documents. Once the appropriate committee approves, the approval is noted in the minutes of the committee, in future editions of the catalogue, and each term's schedule of courses available for registration. Students then register and take these courses using typical registration forms and procedures; at the end of the term the teacher submits grades on an official grade sheet to be inscribed on the student's permanent record. When students get near graduation, these records will be reviewed by some official who will, among other things, add up whether six of these writing intensive courses have been taken. If all graduation requirements have been met, students gain diplomas useful for graduate school admissions, employment, and hanging on a wall. If not, students will be notified they need to take more courses.

In this sequence of events, many texts have been produced. But even more 3 significantly, many social facts have been produced. These facts wouldn't have existed except that people have made them so by creating texts; graduation requirements, course syllabi defining the work of the various courses, criteria for courses to be labeled writing intensive, lists of approved courses, each student's record of writing intensive courses, and so on. In this cycle of texts and activities, we see well articulated organizational systems within which specific kinds of texts flow in anticipatable paths with easily understood and familiar consequences (at least to those people who are familiar with university life). We have highly typified genres of documents and highly typified social structures within which those documents create social facts that affect the actions, rights, and obligations of others.

When we look inside the courses where the required writing is actually 4 done, we see even more typified structures in which writing takes place. In each course we have identifiable cycles of texts and activities, shaped by the syllabus, plans, assigned textbooks and readings, and assignment sheets which structure expectations and consequences. Typically, much of the first class of each course is taken up by laying out these expectations defined in the syllabus. Students then typically project how the course will unfold, how much work will be required, and whether the experience will be interesting and/or worthwhile in order to decide whether to stay in the course or replace it with another. Later in this chapter we look more closely at courses as structured activity systems built upon an infrastructure of genred texts.

This extended example suggests how each text is embedded within struc- 5 tured social activities and depends on previous texts that influence the social activity and organization. Further, this example suggests how each text establishes conditions that somehow are taken into account in consequent activities. The texts within this example create realities, or facts, for students and teachers live both in what they explicitly state and in the structures of relationship and activity they establish implicitly simply by fitting together in an organized way of life. Each successful text creates for its readers a **social fact.** The social facts consist of meaningful social actions being accomplished through language, or

**speech acts.** These acts are carried out in patterned, typical, and therefore intelligible textual forms or **genres**, which are related to other texts and genres that occur in related circumstances. Together the text types fit together as **genre sets** within **genre systems**, which are part of **systems of human activity.** I explain more precisely what I mean by each of these terms in the next section.

Understanding these genres and how they work in the systems and circumstances they were designed for, can help you as a writer fulfill the needs of the situation, in ways that are understood and speak to the expectations of others. Understanding the acts and facts created by texts can also help you understand when seemingly well-written texts go wrong, when those texts don't do what they need to do. Such an understanding can also help you diagnose and redesign communicative activity systems—to determine whether a particular set of document used at certain moments is redundant or misleading, whether new documents need to be added, or whether some details of a genre might be modified. It can also help you decide when you need to write innovatively to accomplish something new or different.

Understanding the form and flow of texts in genre and activity systems can even help you understand how to disrupt or change the systems by the deletion, addition, or modification of a document type. While this may tempt textual mischief, it also provides the tools for thinking about social creativity in making new things happen in new ways. If, for example, you are sitting around with friends after dinner, you may have a choice of pulling out the TV listings, mentioning the newspaper's lead political story, taking out the book of photos of your last trip, or turning on the computer to look at the latest Web site. By introducing these different texts not only are you introducing different topics, you are introducing different activities, interactional patterns, attitudes, and relationships. The choice of a text may influence whether you make bets and wisecracks over a football game, debate politics, admire or envy each others' adventures, or make schemes for your own shared projects. Once one of these patterned activities are taken up they can shape opportunities of interaction until the mood is broken and a new activity is installed. In a classroom, a teacher's lessons often serve to define genres and activities, thereby shaping learning opportunities and expectations.

> *Each text is embedded within structured social activities and depends on previous texts that influence the social activity and organization. . . . Each text establishes conditions that are somehow taken into account in consequenct activities. The texts . . . create realities.*

## Basic Concepts

***Social Facts and the Definition of the Situation.*** **Social facts** are those things people believe to be true, and therefore bear on how they define a situation.

6

7

8

People then act as though these facts were true. The sociologist W. I. Thomas (1923) states it so: "If [people] define situations as real, they are real in their consequences." If people believe that their country has been offended or threatened by another country, they may even go to war over what they believe to be fact. Sometimes these social facts bear on our understanding of the physical world. As long as some people believe Elvis is around they will act as though it were true, even though most people accept his burial as definitive. Even statements that are socially held as scientifically verified, may not be recognized by some people as true. So even though it is well established that airplanes do fly and have safety records far better than land vehicles, many people do not securely believe such facts and prefer to go by train.

More often though social facts bear on subjects that are primarily matters 9 of social understanding, such as whether or not a mayor has authority to make certain decisions and act in a certain way. That authority is based on a series of historically developed political, legal, and social understandings, arrangements, and institutions. As long as people continue to believe in the legitimacy of those understandings, arrangements, and institutions, they will accept the mayor's authority in appropriate circumstances. These social facts are a kind of self-fulfilling prophecy, for the more the mayor seems to exercise legitimate authority, the more people are likely to recognize and grant that authority. Under certain conditions, however, such as after a conviction for felony or after the violent overthrow of a government, people may no longer respect the authority of that mayor.

Very often social facts bear on the words people speak or write and on 10 the force the utterance carries. If all the students in the class understand the teacher's syllabus to require a paper to be turned in on a certain day, they will act on this. If, on the other hand, they all understand him to have said during one class that the deadline can be extended, many will likely pursue what they perceive as a new option. The professor may or may not share this social belief about what was said, with consequences for conflict or cooperation. Similarly, if my friend and I believe we have made a bet by saying the right verbal formulas in the right situation, then one of us will pay up the other at the appropriate moment. On the other hand, if I believe a bet was being made, and my friend only believes we were making a joke, then there is no shared social fact and conflict may result.

Similarly, my right to attend a college may depend on whether I had en- 11 rolled properly, whether I had sent in a check to pay back tuition, whether I had received a diploma from high school, and a whole list of other social facts determined by texts. In order to be allowed to attend, I need to respect the institution's definition of required social facts and then be able to produce acceptable textual tokens of each. If, for example, I claim that in fact I had taken a course at another school but there is no record of it, or the new school rejects the record of that course, we do not share that course as a social fact. For institutional purposes it might as well have been a figment of my imagination.

As discussed in chapter 4, intertextuality often seeks to create a shared un- 12 derstanding of what people have said before and what the current situation is. That is, intertextual reference can attempt to establish the social facts upon which the writer is attempting to make a new statement. In making a plea to the registrar of my school I will need to bring transcripts from the prior institution, perhaps copies of syllabi, and maybe letters from current professors indicating I have the skills that would come from having taken that course.

Many of the social facts, such as the ones described in the last several examples hinge on speech acts, whether certain verbal formulations were accurately and properly done. If properly accomplished, these words are to be taken as fully completed acts that should be respected as having been done.　13

**Speech Acts.**　The philosopher John Austin in his book, *How to Do Things with Words*, argued that words not only mean things, they do things. His argument builds on such examples as two friends making a promise or a preacher declaring a pair of people married. These acts are done just by the words themselves. As a result of a set of words said at the proper time in the proper circumstances by the proper person, someone will be obligated to do something, or the life arrangements of two people will change. In considering written documents, you might equally say that applying for a bank loan is carried out purely in the words and numbers you use to fill out and submit the application. Equally, the bank's approval is simply accomplished by a letter being issued saying you have been approved. From such striking examples Austin goes on to argue that every statement does something, even if only to assert a certain state of affairs is true. Thus, all utterances embody **speech acts.**　14

Of course for our words to carry out their acts these words must be said by the right people, in the right situation, with the right set of understandings. If two potential bettors were strangers likely not to meet after the football game, if no stakes were set, if the event wagered upon had already passed, if the context and intonation suggested a joke rather than a formal bet, or if a thousand other things were not right, one or another of the parties might not believe a real and proper bet had been made. Similarly, if the person making a marriage declaration were not a member of the clergy or judiciary with power in this jurisdiction, or if the people were not legally eligible for marriage with each other, or if they were taking part in a dramatic performance, there would be no real and binding marriage. A loan application by someone under 18 is not a legal application and a letter of approval signed by the night janitor at the bank or that does not set terms of repayment is not a real approval. All these represent **"felicity" conditions** that must be right in order for the speech act to succeed. Without the felicity conditions being met, the act would not be an act, or at least the same sort of act. Austin and John Searle, who continued the analysis of speech acts, pointed out that speech acts operate at three levels. First is the **locutionary act**, which includes a **propositional act.** The locutionary act is literally what is said. So in saying that "it is a bit chilly in this room," I am reporting on a state of affairs and making a certain proposition about the temperature in the room.　15

Quite possibly the act I was attempting to accomplish, however, was to request my host to raise the thermostat. Or perhaps I was disagreeing with　16 the rather "cold" remarks being made about someone. By speaking indirectly I intended my words to have a specific illocutionary force, which I assume others would recognize given the immediate circumstances and the manner of delivery of the sentence. The act I intend my hearer to recognize is the **illocutionary act.**

The listeners, however, may take my comments to mean something else en- 17 tirely, such as a complaint about the stinginess of the host or an attempt to change the subject of an unpleasant discussion. Their own further responses will take into account what *they* thought I was doing, and not necessarily what *I* thought I was doing, or even what I literally said. How people take up the acts and determine the consequences of that act for future interaction is called the **perlocutionary effect.** To make the issue even more complicated, listeners may not be happy or cooperative with what they understand me to be doing, and in their further utterances and acts they may not go along with it. I may intend to request an adjustment of the thermostat, and the host may even understand my request, but still might then say something like, "I have been reading how energy shortages may lead to international economic instability." Where did that come from? Why is the host reporting on his economics reading? Perhaps he is trying to tell me that he does not want to waste fuel and intends to keep the thermostat low.

This **three-leveled analysis of speech acts**—what was literally stated, the in- 18 tended act, and actual effect—is also applicable to written texts. You may write a letter to a friend telling of the latest events in your life, but your illocutionary intent may be to maintain a low-key friendship or to trigger an answering letter that would reveal whether a certain problem had been resolved. And the reader's perlocutionary uptake may be that she believes that you miss her greatly and are trying to rekindle an intense romance. So as not to encourage you, she may never write back.

This three-leveled analysis of speech acts also allows us to understand the 19 status of claims or representations made within texts about states of affairs in the world—the propositional acts, as Searle calls them. Many texts assert propositions, such as a new scientific finding about the health value of chocolate, or the news "facts" of a public demonstration, or the "true meaning" of a poem. Thus the illocutionary force is to gain acceptance of the propositional act. However, only under some conditions will the readers believe these assertions as fact. In the case of the wondrous effects of chocolate, if there are contrary scientific findings or obvious flaws in the procedures followed, or the authors have no medical credentials, or if it becomes known they received major funding from the chocolate manufacturer's association, the proposition may well not be accepted by enough relevant readers to achieve status as a "fact." Other conditions may effect how people take up the assertions about news events or literary interpretation. The only perlocutionary effect may remain that the proposition is seen only as a dubious assertion. With only that more limited act accomplished, the resulting social fact will only be that the authors are trying to convince certain people of this or that claim. If, however, the authors do gain wide acceptance, new social facts about the value of chocolate, an historical event, or the meaning of a poem will be established until someone undermines those facts or replaces them with new "truths." When viewed through this analysis, the matter of arguing for the truth of propositions becomes a matter of meeting those felicity conditions that will lead the relevant audiences to accept your claims as true, thus matching the perlocutionary effect with your illocutionary intent.

***Typification and Genres.*** The three-leveled distinction among what we say or 20 write, what we intend to accomplish by what we say or write, and what people understand us to be attempting points out how much our intentions may be misunderstood and just how difficult may be coordinating our actions with each other. The lack of coordination is potentially much worse when we are communicating by writing, for we cannot see each other's gestures and mood, nor can we immediately see the other's uptake in a perlocutionary effect that does not match our illocutionary intent. That is, we can't notice our host immediately saying, "Oh, I didn't realize that you were uncomfortable" and step toward the thermostat, when we only wished to be ironic about the nasty turn in the conversation. If we spot misunderstandings in face-to-face situations, then we can always repair the damage with a comment like, "Oh, I was just joking." But in writing the opportunities for repair are usually extremely limited, even if we have enough information to suspect we may have been misunderstood.

One way we can help coordinate our speech acts with each other is to act 21 in typical ways, ways easily recognized as accomplishing certain acts in certain circumstances. If we find a certain kind of utterance or text seems to work well in a situation and be understood in a certain way, when we see another similar situation we are likely to say or write something similar. It we start following communicative patterns that other people are familiar with, they may recognize more easily what we are saying and trying to accomplish. Then we can anticipate better what their reactions will be if we followed these standardized, recognizable forms. These patterns are mutually reinforcing. Recognizable, self-reinforcing forms of communication emerge as **genres.**

In creating typified forms or genres, we also come to typify the situations 22 we find ourselves in. If we recognize that when a guest in someone else's house comments about bodily discomfort, the host typically understands that as an obligation to make the guest feel comfortable, then we can adjust our comments so as not to say things that would mistakenly put our host in a state of obligation. The typification gives a certain shape and meaning to the circumstances and directs the kinds of actions that will ensue.

This process of moving to standardized forms of utterances that are recog- 23 nized as carrying out certain actions in certain circumstances and to standard understandings of situations is called **typification.** Thus in some professions if we wish to seek a position, we need to prepare a resume on curriculum vitae to list all the relevant facts and professional accomplishments of our life and to highlight our desirable qualities for the potential employer. Standard formats direct us toward what information to present, such as address, education, and prior experience. The standard format also directs us how to present that information. Following the standard format, as well, helps the employer find and interpret the information. Further, there are standard differences in format for different professions. In academic employment, publications and research take a central role, whereas in business listing responsibilities in each prior position and a record of specific training and skills are often important. Of course, even within the standard forms people try to express their particular characteristics and make their resume distinctive and memorable, so as to stand out from the others. Yet as soon as someone invents a new element or format that seems to work, it is likely to be picked up by others and become fairly standard within that field. Such, for example, is the newly established practice on resumes for a number of professions of listing computer programs one is familiar with.

The definition of genre presented here is a little different from the everyday sense we have of genres, but is consistent with it. As we walk through life we recognize very rapidly texts as being one or another familiar kind, usually because we recognize some features of the text that signal us what kind of message to expect. On an envelope, bulk rate postage and slogans signal us about junk mail advertisements and solicitations; a memo format signed by someone high up in the organization signals an announcement or directive. So we tend to identify and define genres by those special signaling features, and then all the other textual features that we expect to follow. 24

This identification of genres through features is very useful knowledge for us to interpret and make sense of documents, but it gives us an incomplete and misleading view of genres. By seeing genres as only characterized by a fixed set of features we come to view genres as timeless and the same for all viewers. Everybody always knows what we know—right? Wrong. Common knowledge changes over time as genres and situations change; "common knowledge" even varies from person to person, or even the same person in different situations and moods. The definition of genres only as a set of textual features ignores the role of individuals in using and making meaning. It ignores differences of perception and understanding, the creative use of communications to meet perceived novel needs in novel circumstances, and the changing of genre understanding over time. 25

We can reach a deeper understanding of genres if we understand them as **psycho-social recognition phenomena** that are parts of processes of socially organized activities. Genres are only the types individuals recognize as being used by themselves and others. Genres are what we believe they are. That is, they are social facts about the kinds of speech acts people can make and the ways they can make them. Genres arise in social processes of people trying to understand each other well enough to coordinate activities and share meanings for their practical purposes. 26

Genres typify many things beyond textual form. They are part of the way that humans give shape to **social activity.** When you are at a football game and recognize that the crowd is taking up a chant for your team, as you join in you are being drawn into the spectacle and emotions of the community athletic event. As you read and are convinced by the political pamphlet of a candidate for Congress you are being drawn into a world of politics and citizenship. As you learn to read and use research articles of your field you are drawn into 27 a professional way of being and work. When a new Web site develops and attracts attention, your local community service organization may evolve into a clearinghouse for corporate donation of excess products. You and your fellow volunteers may then find yourselves drawn into an entirely new set of activities and roles.

To characterize how genres fit into and comprise larger organizations, roles, 28 organizations, and activities, several overlapping concepts have been proposed, each grabbing a different aspect of this configuration: genre set, source system and activity system.

A **Genre Set** is the collection of types of texts someone in a particular role 29 is likely to produce. In cataloging all the genres someone in a professional role is likely to speak and write, you are identifying a large part of their work. If you find out a civil engineer needs to write proposals, work orders, progress reports, quality test reports, safety evaluations, and a limited number of other similar documents, you have gone a long way toward identifying the work they do. If you then can figure out what skills are needed to be able to write those reports (including the mathematical, measuring, and testing skills that are needed to produce the figures, designs, calculations, etc., in the reports) you will have identified a large part of what a civil engineer has to learn to do that work competently. If you identify all the forms of writing a student must engage in to study, to communicate with the teacher and classmates, and to submit for dialogue and evaluation, you have defined the competences, challenges, and opportunities for learning offered by that course.

A **Genre System** is comprised of the several genre sets of people working to- 30 gether in an organized way, plus the patterned relations in the production, flow, and use of these documents. A genre system captures the regular sequences of how one genre follows on another in the typical communication flows of a group of people. The genre set written by a teacher of a particular course might consist of a syllabus, assignment sheets, personal notes on readings, notes for giving lectures and lesson plans for other kinds of classes, exam questions, email announcements to the class, replies to individual student queries and comments, comments and grades on student papers, and grade sheets at the end of the term. Students in the same course would have a somewhat different genre set: notes of what was said in lectures and class, notes on reading, clarifications on assignment sheets and syllabus, email queries and comments to the professor and/or classmates, notes on library and data research for assignments, rough drafts and final copies of assignments, exam answers, letters requesting a change of grade. However, these two sets of genres are intimately related and flow in predictable sequences and time patterns. The instructor is expected to distribute the syllabi on the first day and assignment sheets throughout the term. Students then ask questions about the expectation in class or over email, and then write clarifications on the assignment sheets. The assignment sheets in turn guide student work in collecting data, visiting the library, and developing their assignments. The pace of their work picks up as the assignment deadline approaches. Once assignments are handed in, the professor comments on and grades them. Similarly the instructor prepares, then delivers lectures and classes. Students are expected to take notes on readings beforehand and then on what the instructor says in class; then they study those notes on class and readings before the various quizzes and exams. Typically the instructor looks at the lectures and assigned readings in order to write questions for quizzes and exams. The students then take the exam and the teacher grades them. At the end of the term the instructor calculates by some formula the sum of all the grades to produce the content of the grade sheet, which is submitted to the registrar to enter into an institutional system of genres.

This **system of genres** is also part of the **system of activity** of the class. In  31 defining the system of genres people engage in you also identify a framework which organizes their work, attention, and accomplishment. In some situations spoken genres dominate, but as you move up the educational ladder and into the professional world, the system of written genres become especially important. In some activities physical aspects take on a highly visible and central role, and the spoken and written genres are peripheral or supportive rather than central. Playing basketball may be mostly about moves and ball handling, but there are rules, strategies, cheers, league organization, and newspaper reporting which engage spoken and written genres. Factory production similarly is closely tied to orders, control and quality reports, production records, machine instructions, and repair manuals. In knowledge-based fields, such as medicine, and especially fields where the primary product is making and distributions of symbols, such as journalism, then the activity system is centrally organized around written documents.

Considering the activity system in addition to the genre system puts a fo-  32 cus on what people are doing and how texts help people do it, rather than on texts as ends in themselves. In educational settings, activity puts the focus on questions such as how students build concepts and knowledge through solving problems, how instructional activities make knowledge and opportunities for learning available, how instructors support and structure learning, and how and for what purposes student abilities are assessed.

## Methodological Issues

The textual analysis in this chapter aims at genre and the larger aggregations  33 (genre sets, genre systems, and activity systems) that genres are part of. The concepts of social fact and speech act provide a basis for understanding the analytical approach of this chapter. We do not, however, in this chapter provide focused analytic tools for investigating social facts and speech acts. Empirical research and analysis of social facts and speech acts would raise many additional methodological concerns of sociology, anthropology, and linguistics than we have space for here. To keep our task simpler, we will keep our analytical focus at the level of genre, and particularly genres of written texts, setting aside methodological issues that pertain primarily to spoken utterances.

Before getting to methods of studying written genres, however, we need to  34 address one issue that arises from considering extended written genres as speech acts. The concept of speech acts was developed by Austin and Searle using brief utterances, for the most part spoken. Linguists and linguistic anthropologists who have used the concept of speech act in their investigations typically have stayed with brief spoken utterances—typically of the length of a short sentence. The shortness of the utterance makes the task of identifying distinct propositional and illocutionary acts simple. A single sentence can be seen as making a single request, or a single bet, or a single claim, and little more. And the immediate response possible in spoken interaction gives strong clues about the perlocutionary uptake of the listener. Further the initial speaker's response can give evidence of whether he or she felt the intent or force of the initial statement was understood correctly (i.e., whether the perlocutionary force was close or distant from the illocutionary intent).

Written texts typically do not have these advantages for analysis. Written 35 texts are typically longer than a single sentence. The sentences within the texts themselves are typically longer and more complex. So that each sentence may contain many acts, and the many sentences of a text compound the problem infinitely. Nonetheless, we usually see the overall text as having a single or few dominant actions that define its intent and purpose, that we take up as the perlocutionary effect or the fact of social accomplishment for the text. An application to graduate school can be seen as the aggregate of writing numerous identifying and descriptive facts about ourselves, boasting about our accomplishments, presenting our thoughts about our professional goals, photocopying a paper completed earlier in our schooling, requesting several people to write letters of recommendation, filling out forms to several institutions to forward our scores and record, and writing a check to cover the application fee. How do we as analysts recognize this aggregate genre, with the actions and contexts implied?

Further, written texts usually provide little immediate evidence of the read- 36 er's uptake. That uptake may be more complex and considered than in response to spoken utterances because the reader may find varying meanings and develop multiple responses in reading through the long text. The reader then may ponder the text for some longer period. Because the reader's response is usually separated in time and space from the moment of writing, and is often buried within the privacy of silent reading, the writer may gain little evidence of any reader's uptake. Furthermore, even with knowledge of readers' uptake, the writer usually has few opportunities for corrections, repairs, or elaborations to resolve misunderstandings or differences between illocutionary intent and perlocutionary effect. Finally, a written text more easily than a spoken utterance can travel into entirely new situations where it may serve unanticipated uses for new readers, as when a private email gets spread around the Internet, or a politician's medical records get into the press.

**This methodological dilemma of identifying speech acts in written texts is** 37 **similar to the dilemma we face as readers and writers of texts.** How do we make sense out of the complexity, indeterminacy, and contextual multiplicity that a text presents us with? We use genre and typifications to help us with just this sort of dilemma. As readers and writers we use whatever we have learned through our lives about texts, text types, and situation types to get a sense of the text at hand and to attribute a dominant action for each text. But there are serious methodological difficulties with relying totally on our "native speaker intuitions" as anything more than a first approximation. Technically, relying on our intuitions already makes us assume many of the things we want to investigate. We are already assuming that everybody understands these texts exactly as we understand them—that they share exactly the same kind and level of textual and social knowledge, and that we all share the same textual culture. This in a sense assumes the problem of genre understanding is always trivial and always solved—and in fact requires no education, socialization, or acculturation. If we all understood each other's texts so easily and well, many teachers would be out of a job. But mutual understanding of texts is not so easily achieved. Genre studies are needed precisely because we do not understand the genres and activities of unfamiliar fields that are important to us or to our students. Even those genres and activity systems that we already are to some degree familiar with could bear more analysis, so that we can act more effectively and precisely with a more articulated sense of what is going on.

So how do we get out of this dilemma of multiple understandings of genres 38 and acts? How do we move beyond our "naturalized" user's view of genres and activity systems to a more carefully researched, observed, analyzed knowledge? How do we incorporate an understanding of the practices and knowledge of others—and then understand how these very practices come about and are learned? This is essentially the methodological problem of genre studies to which there is no simple and quick answer. Rather we have only a bootstrapping operation of increasing our knowledge and perspective through research such as examining more texts in a more regularized way; interviewing and observing more writers and readers, and ethnographically documenting how texts are used in organizations. The richer and more empirical a picture develops, the less we are dependent on the limitations of our own experience and training. The following methodological comments are aimed precisely at expending our perspective on genres and the systems they are part of.

### Methodological Issues and Analytic Tools: What Is a Genre and How Do You 39
### Know One? Over the last few pages I have developed a complicated answer
to something we recognize every day in fairly straightforward ways. When we look at documents we notice certain features that seem to signal them to us as belonging to one genre or another and therefore attempting to accomplish a certain kind of interaction with us.

You get a mail offer for a credit card. You immediately recognize what it 40 is, perhaps without even opening the envelope. How do you do this? It is in a standard envelope, but with the glassine window for the address, so we recognize it as business or institutional. We recognize the bulk rate postage, and know it is some kind of impersonal solicitation. We notice the offer to lower our interest rates. We already know that inside the envelope we will find an application for a credit card along with a letter. Even more we know whether we want to have anything to do with what they are offering.

You walk into a cafeteria and glance at a newspaper lying on a table. You 41 immediately know many things about what it will contain and what the articles will look like, the style they will be in, how they will be organized, and even where in the newspaper different kinds of articles will be found. Again, this quickly assessed knowledge helps us structure what we do with that newspaper.

Most genres have easy to notice features that signal you about the kind of 42 text it is. And often these features are closely related to major functions or activities carried out by the genre. The bold newspaper headlines mentioning major events are designed to grab your attention by pointing out the exciting news that you will want to read more about. The date and place of the story lets you know where in the world the news comes from (of course this really only became an important feature after telegraph and other forms of distant communication made the newspaper more than a local report). The lead sentence typically gives you *who, what, where,* and *when* so you can decide whether to read on about the details. The cheap paper is chosen because the paper's content gets old fast, and newspapers are usually thrown out within a couple of days. These features direct how we attend to the newspaper and even how long we keep it.

Because genres are recognizable by their distinctive features and those fea- 43 tures seem to tell us so much about the function, it is tempting to see genres just as a collection of these features. We then are tempted to analyze the genres by picking out those regular features we notice and tell a story about the reason for these features, based on our knowledge of the world. Much, in fact, can be learned about familiar genres current in our time and community by proceeding in this way, but only because they are part of our immediate cultural world. There are, however, limitations and problems with identifying and analyzing genres by making up plausible reasons for easily spotted features.

First, it limits us to understanding those aspects of genre we are already 44 aware of.

Second, it ignores how people may see each text in different ways, because 45 of their different knowledge of genres, the different systems they are part of, the different positions and attitudes they have about particular genres, or their different activities at the moment. A wanted poster, for example, is read very differently by and has very different meanings for an FBI agent, a parent nervous about the safety of children, and the fugitive. Researchers in a particular field, for another example, may be able to distinguish many different kinds of articles that appear in the journals of their field, while graduate students may only recognize a few, which they will not understand the full implications of. How is a review of the literature at a research front that appears in a top research journal different from a textbook review or a seminar-assigned review of literature? First-year undergraduates may not even know research literatures exist and may think all scientific writing looks like the textbooks they are familiar with. In the business world, someone familiar with the texts that circulate in an insurance company may not be so familiar with those in a wholesale hardware operation. Even within the same industry sets of typical documents may vary in significant respects from one company to another.

Third, such a collecting of features may make it appear that these features of the text are ends in themselves, that every use of a text is measured against an abstract standard of correctness to the form rather than whether it carries out the work it was designed to do. If a news article is printed on high quality paper is it less a news article? If it does not list the "who, what, where, and when" in the opening paragraph is it seriously faulted? Of course, every example of a genre may vary in particulars of content, situation, and writer intent, which may lead to differences in the form. Yet we still use our genre knowledge to understand it. We may even use multiple genre models to understand and use it. The features and genres invoked have their only justification and motive in the understanding and activity that occurs between people, and finally whatever works, counts. 46

Fourth, consequently, the view of genre that simply makes it a collection of features obscures how these features are flexible in any instance or even how the general understanding of the genre can change over time, as people orient to evolving patterns. Students writing papers for courses have a wide variety of ways of fulfilling the assignment, and may even bend the assignment as long as they can get their professor or grader to go along will the change. Newspaper stories now have a different "feel" than those of a century ago—which can be attributed to changes in the understanding of articles—such as the expectation of rapid communication, the quick dating of stories, the recognition of the role of celebrity and famous people, the critical culture. 47

To deal with these issues, then, we can suggest several different approaches to identifying and analyzing genres that go beyond the cataloging of features of genres that we already recognize. 48

First, **to go beyond those features we are already aware of,** we can use a variety of less obvious linguistic, rhetorical, or organizational analytical concepts to examine a collection of texts in the same genre. In that way we can discover if there are consistencies within a genre that go beyond the most obvious identifying features. By examining typical patterns of subject and verbs, we may, for example, consider whether or not state education standards attribute agency, and of what sort to students, or whether those documents put most of the decision making in the hands of teachers, or administrators, or abstract principles of knowledge. Or we may see how science textbooks use graphic images and tables and compare those uses to those in more professional scientific documents to see whether students are being given the opportunity to become familiar with scientific practices of graphic representation. Most of the methods of textual analysis in this book can be considered with respect to genre, although not all of them will necessarily reveal a pattern in any particular genre. 49

Second, **to consider variation in different situations and periods,** we can extend the sample to include a larger number and range of texts that still might be considered within the same genre. More examples allow us to see how the form of the text varies. Even more importantly, if you are able to gain information about the rhetorical situation of each of the examples, you can analyze 50 how those variations are related to differences in the situation and the interaction being carried out in the situation.

We may further consider how there may be patterned differences between 51 what is called the same genre in different areas or fields. If we start looking at experimental research articles in biology and psychology we can notice characteristic differences between them. We may then consider the way in which these are the same genres and the extent to which you might consider them different. And we can then consider how differences in the form are related to differences in the social and activity organization of the fields.

Similarly, we can compare front-page news articles in different countries to 52 consider the different roles news takes within the differing political, economic, and social lives found in those countries. Or we can compare front-page stories in a national paper of record like the *New York Times* and a tabloid or a local paper. These kinds of investigations will reveal how expectation of genres can become highly specialized in different areas, how what people recognize is very much a local cultural matter, and how news enters into the complex of organized life activities.

Another way to extend your sample is to look historically. With sufficient 53 examples of the genre over time, we can get a sense of how the genre understandings change as a field and historical context change. These changes may be so great that the names of the genres change or very different things count as a genre. The earliest scientific articles look more like letters than anything we see now in *Physics Review*. The more we hold all other aspects of the situation constant, the more we can see how much of the change is due to changes in genre understanding. To compare news stories from a century ago to today, it helps to look at newspapers from the same size town with the same level of readership in a similar region, so as to identify what differences are likely to result from historical changes in newspaper format rather than differences of the audience served.

Third, to deal with the problem of characterizing **genres that you may not be** 54 **familiar with or that others may understand differently than you do,** you need to gather information not just about the texts, but about other people's understanding of them. One broad way is to ask people in a certain field to name the kinds of texts they work with (i.e., to identify their genre set). If you find that all people in a field make a similar list of kinds of texts that accountants or insurance claims adjusters use, then you may have some sense that they do have common understandings. The existence of a well-known name for a genre within a world of practice suggests that this is indeed common knowledge to practitioners, but people may in fact understand somewhat different things by a single shared name. To check the degree of agreement as to understand the particulars of the genre, collecting samples of what they would consider each of those named genres gives you a chance to examine how similar they are in form and in function they are. Sometimes professional or legal or administrative documents define and specify what must go into various documents and how they are to be used. Procedures and regulations manuals, for example, may identify 12 kinds of forms to be filled out, the occasions on which they are to be filled out, and the manner of completion. However, be careful, because people do not always do things exactly as the regulations tell them to or they interpret the regulations differently, or they try to accomplish other things beyond the mandate of the regulations.

Fourth, to extend beyond the explicit understanding of what people in a  55 field name, in order **to see the full range of implicit practice,** you can do ethnographic research in the workplace, classroom, or other site of text production, distribution, or use. By collecting every text people use over a day, or a week, or a month, as well as noting on what occasions they use them, for what purposes, and how they produce, work with, and interpret these texts, you will get a more complete picture of their textual worlds. If you do this, make sure you are as complete as possible, including such things as email messages, personal notes jotted on the margins of other forms, or other things people might not consider formal documents worth noting. Interviewing people in the process of using texts can give you further insight into the meanings, intentions, uptakes, and activity of the participants.

In the course of this ethnographic work you may also record the sequence  56 particular documents come in, in relation to which activities, and which documents are referred to in the course of reading and writing each new document. This data will help you document and understand the genre set, genre system, and activity system. Examining the genre set allows you **to see the range and variety of the writing work** required within a role, and to identify the genre knowledge and writing skills needed by someone to accomplish that work. Examining the genre system allows you **to understand the practical, functional, and sequential interactions of documents.** Understanding these interactions also allows you to see how individuals writing any new text are intertextually situated within a system and how their writing is directed by genre expectations and supported by systemic resources. Finally, considering the activity system enables you **to understand the total work accomplished by the system and how each piece of writing contributes to the total work.** Analysis of genre and activity systems also allows you to evaluate the effectiveness of the total systems and the appropriateness of each of the genred documents in carrying forward that work. This analysis could help you determine whether any change in any of the documents, distribution, sequence, or flow might improve the total activity system.

## Methodological Guidelines: How to Frame and Pursue a Genre Investigation

1. *Frame your purposes and questions to limit your focus.* As with any form  57 of research and analysis the first and most important task is knowing **why you are engaged** in the enterprise and **what questions you hope to answer** by it. Depending on your purposes, what you have access to, the amount of time and energy you can commit to the project, you may carry out an investigation at any of the levels discussed in the previous section. Each

level has its problems and benefits. No one is right or wrong. You just need to be aware of the limits and values of each.

2. *Define your Corpus.* Once you know what you are looking for and why, 58 the next task is to **identify the specific texts or collections you want to examine,** making them extensive enough to provide substantial evidence in making claims, but not too broad to become unmanageable. There is no magic equation to determine what gives you adequate evidence of a genre or stability, but a good rule of thumb is the point of diminishing returns plus a couple more. That is, the sample size should be large enough that adding additional samples will be unlikely to give you major new news or variations. Once you have found that point, add a couple more just to make sure.

On the other hand, if you are examining the history of a journal, or 59 a comparison across several subspecialties, your sample should be rich enough to include more than a few from each period or domain.

If you are gathering the genres from a genre set or a genre system, 60 again the point of "diminished returns plus a couple" is a good guideline. If the genres and work are organized within a limited and coherent cycle, then you can use that cycle to organize and limit your collecting. For example, in looking at a class, you may look at the entire cycle of the term's work; or you may examine the cycle of texts involved in a single unit or assignment sequence. You need not examine every student's paper for every assignment, but you should have a reasonable sample of all assignments, all sets of notes, etc. If you are working with a small peer editing group in the class, all the texts they work with could define your sample of collected work.

3. *Select and apply your analytic tools.* Based on the purposes of your 61 investigation, you need to **select appropriate analytic tools** to examine the consistencies and variations of features, functions, or relations over the collection. These are the tools discussed in the previous section on how to recognize a genre. As you carry out the analysis, it should be evident whether you are tapping into some fairly stable patterns of text and activity.

After extensive collecting and analysis, **if no stable patterns emerge** 62 this may be because of one of two difficulties.

- The collection does not reflect the actual practices of users or a coherent flow of documents. For example, if you collect all texts looked at or worked on by students sitting in the student center lounge, you may be tapping into so many different activity systems brought there by students who are just passing through, that you will find no coherence. If you wanted to get a sense of the many genres that pass through a student's life, you might do better to follow a single student around over a day or several days.

- The analytical focus may be misplaced. For example, if you are looking at television advertisements assuming the purpose is to give information about the product, you may find in many ads little product information to consider. You may be stymied, because ads often seek variety and novelty in order to gain the attention of jaded viewers and give little information. Sometimes the ads withhold even identifying the product until the end to keep you wondering. Perhaps, therefore, your analysis might be better framed around novelty and attention gaining devices. The drive for attention gaining novelty may be so strong that the recognizable features of ads change very rapidly, which your analysis will need to take into account.

## Applied Analysis

The following case demonstrates the value of considering genre, genre sets, 63 genre systems, and activity systems in evaluating the learning potential and consequences of a set of classroom activities. I would like to thank Chris Carrera and Kambiz Ebraham for their help in collecting the data.

Over a 6-week period during the late fall of 1998 in a sixth-grade class 64 in a suburban California public elementary school, students engaged in a social studies learning unit on the Maya, which was to some degree integrated with simultaneous learning units an mathematics, language arts, and video production. As part of this unit they read and wrote a variety of texts. Texts they wrote included worksheet and outline completions, notes on the readings, quizzes, exams, informational reports (with drafts), collaboratively written scripts (with drafts) for an adventure story about an expedition to the land of the Maya, and final reflections on what they learned from the unit. These documents are the genre set of student writing during this unit. Each student's **genre set** was collected in a file of the student's work. The student work also included art on Mayan sports, a map of an imagined Mayan city, collaboratively built models of the imagined cities, a board game about the Maya which incorporated words and text (produced by pairs of collaborating students), and videos of their adventure stories (collaboratively produced in teams of about four students each). We can call this **an extended graphic genre set**, although all parts were not collected and placed within the student file of work—suggesting a difference in the evaluation of these productions. Among their readings were a number of assignment sheets and blank worksheets, packets of information about the Maya, supplementary reference books and Web sites, each other's reports and drafts of reports, and drafts of their mutually constructed projects and scripts. Many of these were collected in the student work files.

In traditional terms the aim of this unit could be described as learning social 65 studies facts and concepts with some reinforcement activities. The inclusion of the final reports, the worksheets, outlines, exams, and information sheets in the work file reinforces that impression. The final reports of most students were collections of facts gleaned from handouts, textbooks, encyclopedias, and online reference materials, presented with only minimal organization and no transition between different topics and the fact sheets, quizzes, and exams equally show only the accumulation of fragmentary facts and ideas. Only a few students were able to achieve a level of articulated synthesis that gave a sense of totality of vision to their papers. On the other hand, students seemed to have understood the expectations of the genre as to require a collection of information. One student, Maria, in the opening sentences of her paper articulates exactly this understanding of what she has to do.

> Okay, before I pour all this information on you, let me introduce you to the Maya. They had six prosperous cities: Tulum, Chichen Itza, Uxmal, Mayapan, Tikal, and Palenque. Got that? Great.
> Here comes the rest . . .
> They were the first people in the New World to have written records. They also had numbers. One was a dot. • Two was two dots. ••

This goes on for about 500 words presenting information on chronicles, calendars, ball games, human sacrifice, geographic and historical extent, trading, and demise. In fact, almost all the papers from the class were similar to Maria's in content, organization, and diction, varying mostly in length and amount of information reported.

That students had such an understanding of the task and the genre is not 66 surprising given that the original assignment packet for this unit described this assignment only as a "three-page typed report describing the Mayan culture." This was embedded within a much more elaborate set of activities, described shortly, but the specific genre of this assignment was very narrow. The narrow information collection focus of this assignment was reinforced and supported by a number of other activities that occurred between the original assignment and the due date of the paper (December 4). First, with the assignment packet and in the days after several handouts were distributed to the class photocopied from reference works covering history, calendar, religion, number system, sports, cities, sacrifice, geography, art, and similar topics. Second, each week in class specific topics of the information were reviewed, with an informational quiz; on Friday. Third, on November 9, students had to fill out a preprinted informational outline on the Mayan civilization providing four points of information for each of three categories: The Land and Region; Classic Period; Mayan Knowledge (see Fig. 11.1 for Janine's response). Fourth, due November 30 just before the final reports was a research chart to be filled out by students working in pairs, first by hand on the worksheet, and then transcribed on a spreadsheet. For five cities, each pair of students had to identify the location, record an important discovery, describe the region and select an interesting cultural fact. Figure 11.2 is the research chart produced by Maria and Sau-lin.

The product here is a mechanically organized set of factual fragments, 67 selected and transcribed from the distributed informational sheets. The further transcription of this material onto a spreadsheet beyond providing new technical skills, reinforces the idea that information (and research) consists of such fragments organized into formal categories. Thus it is not surprising that

# Ancient Maya
## Outline
## November 9, 1998

You are to complete this outline with information from our Maya packet, classroom discussions, and research materials. Remember to keep the information brief and to the point.

I. Maya Civilization
    A. The Land and Region
        1. Harsh living conditions
        2. Jungle, rain forest
        3. Mountains
        4. Mexican southeastern states, Yucatan Peninsula Guatemala, south into Guatemala, northern Honduras
    B. Classic Period
        1. Beginnings of Mayan greatness 300 AD
        2. Flourished until 900 AD
        3. Schools
        4. Markets for trading goods Centers for practicing religion.
    C. Maya Knowledge
        1. Master astronomers
        2. " " mathematicians
        3. " " architecture
        4. " " writing
           " time & calendars

---

Figure 11.1 Informational outline for students to fill in.

students understand the final research report as they do and do not feel challenged to rise to a higher level of synthesis, analysis, or discussion.

The apparently student-produced genres of outlines, worksheets, and quiz- 68 zes are in fact collaboratively produced with the teacher in the very specific sense that the words on the final page include words produced by the teacher and the students. The teacher produces the topics and categories and structure for the outline and chart and the questions for the quiz. He further produces the instructions on each of the assignment sheets. In this latter sense,

| CITY NAME | CITY LOCATION | RESEARCH INFORMATION | REGION DESCRIPTION | INTERESTING FACTS |
|---|---|---|---|---|
| Uxmal | Northwestern part of the Mexican Yucatan. | The magnificent architecture here is adorned with many elaborate decorations and bright colors. | Rugged terrain, and hot ground | The Magician's Pyramid has been said to be built in one night. |
| Tikal | The middle of dense jungle, north of Guatemala. | This sprawling city consists of numerous residences, temples, pyramids, and ball courts. | Viny, and very colorful | Played a soccer type game called Pok-a-tok. |
| Tulum | The coast of the Caribbean Sea | Tulum prospers because it can acquire trade goods from the sea. | Water, coast, and very colorful | Sacrificed humans to Gods. |
| Chichen Itza | North-central part of the Mexican Yucatan | Chichen Itza has grown to great wealth and power because of its central location among the Maya trade routes. | North-central rain forest | Attempted to kill other cities. |
| Palenque | East part of Mexico | Human sacrifices were located here. | Thick Mexican Jungle | They had special ceremonies. |

**Figure 11.2** The research chart produced by Maria and Sau-lin.

and also by structuring the intermediate informational assignments we can also see the teacher's hand in the final reports. Thus these genres are strongly shaped by the teacher's decisions of what should be written and how. The students' recognition of the teacher's speech act of assignment shapes their further actions in fulfillment of the assignment, just as the teacher's further assignments are dependent on his recognition of the students' completion of prior acts. And each new student production is dependent on them having completed earlier acts, turning them into facts which they could then rely on and build upon.

In two collaboratively produced teacher–student genres, however, the teacher's decisions structure a very different kind of work for the students. First is the unit final exam, given on December 11, with three questions.

1. What qualities do you think gave strength to the Mayan Empire?
2. In what ways can trade between cities help to create good relationships?
3. Why do you think the Mayan Empire did not go on forever?

Each of the three questions requires students to think evaluatively, causally, and critically, and most of them did so. Maria provided one of the more elaborated set of answers, but not all that different from that of most of her classmates. In answer to Question 1, "What qualities do you think gave strength to the Mayan Empire?" she wrote:

> I think that the accuracy in their calendars, their knowledge of the movements of the stars, their ability to create their own letters gave strength to the Mayan Empire. I also think that no matter what role you had, or what you did, you were Important to the Mayan Empire, and that gave strength to the Mayan Empire.

How did such questions and answers count as an appropriate test of what the students had learned if the earlier activities were primarily transcription of fragmented information? And where did the students get the ideas and stance from which they could answer these questions?

Before we answer that let us examine another end-of-the-sequence document, the "Final Thoughts" worksheet filled out 2 days before the final exam. The following example from Desmond covers typical themes (see Figs. 11.3 and 11.4). Only the first question really evokes in Desmond (and most of the other students) any reference to the factual information, and even then the information is subordinated to an evaluative conclusion. All his remaining responses (as were the responses of most of his classmates) referred to the other activities of building models, the play production and videotaping, And key themes were working together, doing things better, and having fun—all issues of participation and engagement. Given the predominant flavor of the work we have examined so far, how did students glean such learning and develop such attitudes toward the unit?

The answers on these two sets of documents reflect some class discussion about the factual material they were learning, but they also reflect the wider system of activity built into the unit. The unit was built around two sets of activities organized by the teacher, each with their own set of supportive and assigned genres that developed and rehearsed orientation, creativity, and thought. The informational content was embedded within these activities that engaged the students and that they found fun. But even more these activities gave students the opportunity to think about and use the factual content, and thus to develop significant meanings from the content.

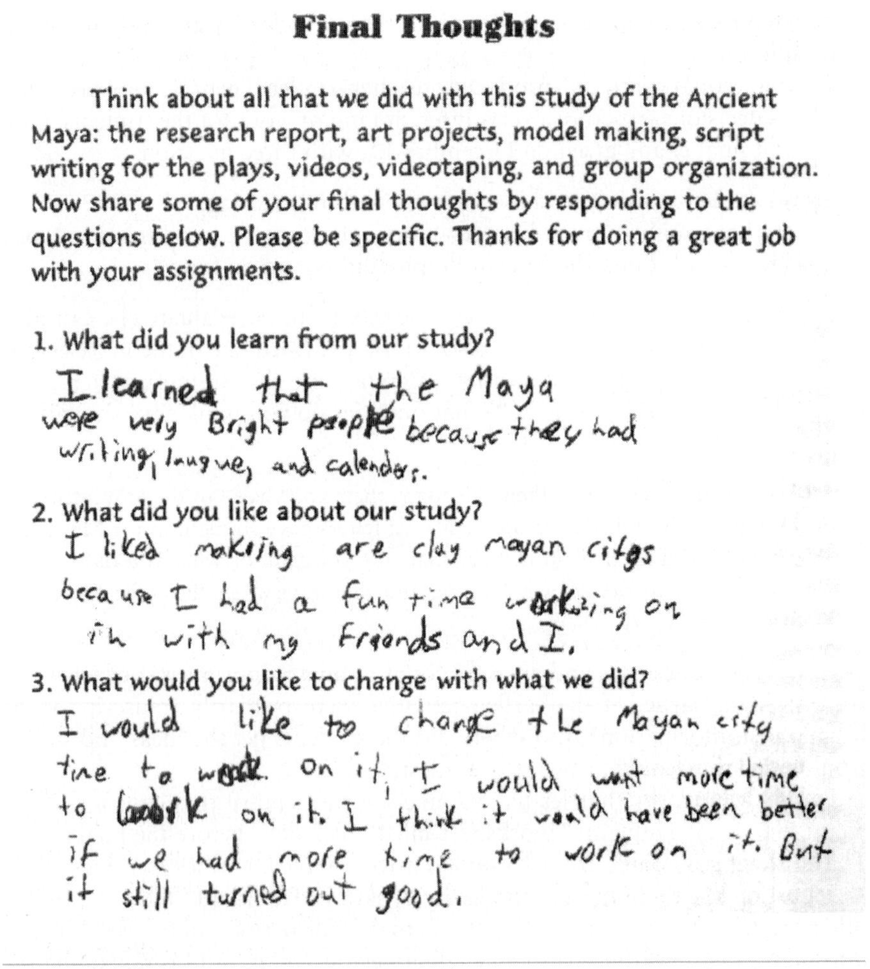

# Final Thoughts

Think about all that we did with this study of the Ancient Maya: the research report, art projects, model making, script writing for the plays, videos, videotaping, and group organization. Now share some of your final thoughts by responding to the questions below. Please be specific. Thanks for doing a great job with your assignments.

1. What did you learn from our study?

I learned that the Maya were very Bright people because they had writing, laugue, and calendas.

2. What did you like about our study?

I liked makeing are clay mayan citys because I had a fun time working on ih with my Friends and I.

3. What would you like to change with what we did?

I would like to change the Mayan city time to work. On it. I would want more time to work on it. I think it would have been better if we had more time to work on it. But it still turned out good.

Figure 11.3

The activities were set in motion by the original assignment sheet at the beginning unit, which set out the following simulation frame: 72

> Project: You are a member of an ancient Maya people and you have been assigned the task of establishing a new site to design and build a great city. The name of the city will be chosen from one of the following: Tulum, Chichen Itza, Uxmal, Mayapan, Tikal, or Palenque. The task is to be done individually, but you may confer with others to get ideas or give suggestions. Good luck and begin immediately, because the king is not a patient man and needs the city built before invaders arrive.

The sheet goes on to specify three parts of the project: a "three-page typed report on Mayan Culture, an illustration/graphic, and a blueprint of the Mayan City with everything labeled." A fourth final activity is mentioned of group

4. What would have made it better and more interesting?

*Are play would have been better if we had more cumaperation.*

5. How could we have improved our video productions?

*It would be better if we were orgenzed.*

\* Include some of your own personal thoughts below that may not be asked for in the five questions.

*It was very fun.*

Figure 11.4

creation of a play with script and costumes and videotaping. Each of these four parts was modified and elaborated in the ensuing 6 weeks.

The original situation frame of designing a new Mayan city gave motive 73 and purpose to the informational and other activities of the first half of the unit. The factual information is what you need in order to be able to know what a Mayan city is and how you should design one to include its typical buildings, institutions, and places for its usual activities. That work became most fully and directly expressed in the map/design each produced, which then became the basis for a scale model. Two additional art projects, however, reflected the same kind of civilization building thinking. One was a board game each had to design to reflect the daily life of residents of the city and the other was to act as the chief Maya artist commissioned to create a design that reflects the style of the culture (students were also learning to use graphic software as part of this assignment). Finally there was a sequence of Mayan math exercises (from a prepared unit) that used standard word and logic problems using objects and situations relevant to the Mayan agriculture, social structure, and culture and that also gave some experience using Mayan number system and calendar. These immersions in Mayan life through simulations did more that rehearse some factual material about the Maya, they drew sixth graders into thinking about the material and how the facts reflected a way of life.

The second half of the unit transformed the situational frame from design 74 into inquiry and the mode of work from individual into collaborative. This shift was initiated by an assignment sheet handed out 4 weeks into the unit on November 20, just after the designs and scale models were finished. The assignment sheet informs the students that they are archeologists who have found an artifact with a map to an undiscovered Mayan City. They are to organize in teams to search for the city and its treasures; they will then script and produce a video documentary of their adventures. The assignment sheet then provides space for the students to sketch out preliminary ideas about setting, characters, events, and story summary for the initial work sessions with the collaborative group (about five students in each group). Also provided is a follow-up framework for the script, in which the characters, setting for each scene, the props and costumes and the production team roles, and other notes are to be listed. These assignment sheets scaffold the work of script writing and production for the students as they make decisions in filling out the blanks and then do the additional work implied in each of their answers.

The research chart discussed earlier finds its meaning within this archeologi- 75 cal frame of action. The instructions for the chart describe it as reported from field archeologists back to their colleagues to let them know what has been found. So now the material is not just information to be tested on—it is something the students, in their simulated roles as archeologists, know to be shared with others. The knowledge they have found also becomes subject and material of their videos (which were also produced as live plays).

The scripts for the videos are pretty basic, involving archeologists walking 76 through the city with local informants pointing out aspects of the culture, with lots of dwelling on the ball game with a death penalty for losing and other moments of human sacrifice. Nonetheless, the stories are larded with the facts and names that have cropped up in the various reading and writing genres throughout the unit, so that the students have learned to inhabit the informational space even while engaged in imaginative play. Looking at the limitations of the scripts, one could well understand why a number of students commented that the videos would have been much better if they had learned to work together and everyone learned to do their part. It also becomes evident that the teacher used the lesson of cooperation within successful civilizations to help students reflect on the difficulties of their own collaboration—and thus comments about cooperation being essential to Mayan success turn up as well on the final exam.

When we look at **the total activity system of the classroom** as students par- 77 ticipated in each unit, and the kind of work and learning accomplished in the production of each of the teacher-directed genres, we can see that students were doing more than reproducing facts from handouts and books. They were thinking about the material and using the material to engage in other activities, which required understanding and elicited motivated engagement. These various activities were coordinated in a mutually supported sequential system that ended with classroom presentation of reports, airing of the videos produced by each of the several small groups, reflective observations on the activity, and analytical thought on the final exam. The activities each were centrally engaged with well-known, **typified textual and graphic genres**, which afforded students anticipateable access to information, challenges and problem solving, and opportunities for learning. The end result included familiarity with some factual information about the Maya but also a sense of what Mayan life was like, an experience of being an inquirer into another culture, increased skill in synthesizing and presenting information, using knowledge creatively for imaginative productions, and a sense of the practical import of the information. There was also learning and practice of many computing and video media skills. Such complex learning with multiple, varied formal products and such varied forms of cognition and learning could only be evoked and coordinated because of the teacher's practical understanding of the complex interrelated activities set in motion by the assignments and of the roles of specific genres in establishing and focusing activities. Although interviews and conversations with the teacher provided no indication of an awareness of the theoretical framework presented in the chapter, in a practical way the teacher managed precisely the concrete realizations of the concepts presented here.

## Activities

1. Textbooks
   a. Describe the features, functions, and student activity of a textbook for a single field, such as American History. Write a paper analyzing the genre.
   b. Compare the features, functions, and student activities of the first set of textbooks (e.g., in American History) to the features, functions, and student activities of textbooks in a very different field (such as mathematics). Write a paper comparing the two related genres.
   c. Compare the features, functions, and reader activities of either of the set of textbooks with the features, functions, and reader activities of professional research articles or books in the same field. Write a paper comparing the genre of textbook and research contribution in that field.

2. A Class

   Identify and collect samples of the entire genre set produced by you in a recent class you have taken or are now taking. Then consider the entire genre and activity and system of the class. You may wish to interview the instructor and other students; you may also wish to take observational notes on how texts are produced, distributed, used, and related in the class.

3. A Genre Set of a Professional

   Interview a professor or other professional to determine what kinds of texts receives and writes in the course of a typical day. If possible, collect samples. You may wish to shadow them for a day to notice what kinds of texts they receive and produce. Write a paper analyzing the genre set you have found.

4. Student Assignments

To examine the range of variation within a genre or the differing understandings of a genre, examine a set of papers of all the students in a class responding to a single assignment. (Be sure to get a copy of the original assignment.) What features are in common? What is the range of variation? How much commonality and variation seems invited by the assignment? By the assignment's place within the course? By the overall nature of schooling? By other cultural factors? How much variation seems to reflect student differences in interests, personality, resources, skills, or resources? You may interview the instructor to determine how much of the variation is acceptable to the instructor, which variations seem to reduce the instructor's evaluation, and which variations seem to violate the expectations or genre of the assignment. You may also interview the other students to find out what they thought the genre of the assignment asked for, how much they thought they were varying the genre, and what motivated the particular way they varied their paper from what they viewed as the standard response. In a paper report your findings and analysis.

## For Further Reading

In sociology the classic statement on social facts is from Emile Durkheim's (1982) *The Rules of Sociological Method*, and the classic discussion of the social definition of the situation is in a brief passage (pp. 41–44) of W. I. Thomas' (1923) *The Unadjusted Girl*. Robert King Merton's (1968) essay on "The Self Fulfilling Prophecy" brings the two concepts together in a readable and convincing way.

The standard philosophic discussions of speech acts are two thin but dense books, John Austin's (1962) *How to Do Things with Words* and John Searle's (1969) *Speech Acts*. The former opens up very broadly the ways words perform actions, while the latter attempts to identify a more focused and limited system of acts. Within linguistics and linguistic anthropology this performative approach to language has created the basis for the area of study known as pragmatics. A good introduction to pragmatics is Allessandro Duranti's (1997) *Linguistic Anthropology*. A somewhat more difficult but rewarding presentation is William Hanks' (1996b) *Language and Communicative Practice*.

The sociological and phenomenological concept of typification has its source in the work of Alfred Schutz, particularly *The Structures of the Life World* (Schutz & Luckman, 1973). A very approachable and influential elaboration of his approach is the work of his students Peter Berger and Thomas Luckmann, *The Social Construction of Reality* (1966).

Schutz's phenomenological approach to typification was brought together with rhetorical studies and applied specifically to the concept of genre by Carolyn Miller (1984) in "Genre as a Social Act." There is now an extensive literature on genre as typification in rhetoric and writing studies, including Charles Bazerman, *Shaping Written Knowledge* (1988); Berkenkatter and

Huckin, *Genre Knowledge* (1995); Freedman and Medway, eds. *Genre and the New Rhetoric* (1994); and Bazerman and Paradis, eds. *Textual Dynamics of the Professions* (1991).

Bazerman's *Shaping Written Knowledge* also links genre-as-typification to activity theory growing out of the work of Vygotsky, *Thought and Language* (1986) and *Mind in Society* (1978), particularly in relation to Vygotsky's interest in the history of cultural forms. David Russell's two essays (1997a, 1997b) elaborate the ways genre theory is enriched by considering it in an activity theory frame. Bazerman and Russell have edited a special issue of *Mind, Culture and Activity* (1997) as well as *Writing Selves/Writing Society* (2003), an edited electronic collection devoted to activity approaches to writing. Bazerman's (1999) *The Languages of Edison's Light* is an extensive study using the concepts set out in this chapter.

Other related approaches to genre come out of functional linguistics, including Swales (1990), Bhatia (1993), and Cope and Kalantzis (1993). Within literary theory, the history of the way genre has traditionally been handled is in Hernadi (1972); Mikhael Bakhtin (1986) and Ralph Cohen (1986) have developed approaches consistent with the approaches here; and Thomas Beebee (1994) has considered how genres are associated with ideology.

· · · · · · · · · · · · · · · · · · · · · · · · · · · · · · · · · · · · · · · · · · · · · · · · · · · · · · · · · · · · · · · · · · · · ·

## Questions for Discussion and Journaling

1. Explain what Bazerman means by a "social fact," and then provide a few examples of social facts that have had consequences for you recently.

2. What do Bazerman and John Austin mean by "words not only mean things, they do things" (para. 14)? Think of a few recent examples in your own experience where speech acts "did something," had some consequence. What had to happen for those speech acts to succeed?

3. Give an example from your own experience in which you trace out a locutionary speech act (what literally got said), the illocutionary act (what the speaker actually intended the hearer to recognize), and the perlocutionary effect (how listeners took up the act and determined the consequences of the act for future interaction). For help, review Bazerman's own example (paras. 15–19).

4. Now do the same kind of thing you did in response to question 3, but for a written act in which you have recently engaged. Then consider why Bazerman says that coordinating your intended meaning with your audience's reception of what you've written is so much more difficult "when we are communicating by writing" (para. 20).

5. After having answered questions 3 and 4 above, reflect on why it might be useful for you to be able to think about written and spoken acts in this way.

6. Bazerman defines genres as "recognizable, self-reinforcing forms of communication" (para. 21), as "patterned, typical, and therefore intelligible textual forms" (para. 5), and as "standardized forms of utterances that are recognized as carrying out certain actions in certain circumstances" (para. 23). Pick a genre that is familiar to you

(for example, a course syllabus) and explain how it fits these defining characteristics. For example, what actions does it carry out? What makes it recognizable? What are its recognizable patterns? What about a syllabus is typical across situations? How do you know a syllabus when you see one? Why is this form used repeatedly? Why is it helpful that people (in the syllabus example, teachers) have a common way of communicating in a particular recurring situation (in the syllabus example, of conveying expectations every time they teach a new group of students)?

7. Explain the difference between genre sets and genre systems (paras. 29–30), and then give some examples.

8. Bazerman points out that we usually try to understand new genres through our intuition, by considering what we already know and guessing about what is required. However, he says that we "do not understand the genres and activities of unfamiliar fields that are important to us," and that we can't always figure them out through our "intuition" (para. 37). Think of a time when you were asked to write a new genre and made your best guess about what was required, but did not succeed.

## Applying and Exploring Ideas

1. Bring to class several examples of common textual genres that you encounter on a regular basis, but that other people in your class may not necessarily be very familiar with. (You might look for some texts from a hobby or a social or academic group in which you participate; for example, meeting minutes or a transcript from a chat room for a game you play online.) Get into a small group and choose a text that not everyone in the group is familiar with. First, ask members of your small group who are not familiar with this genre to analyze the text. What do they see when they look at it? What is strange to them? What is their response to it? Next, ask the people who are familiar with a particular text to list its identifying features—the features that help them immediately know what this genre is and what it asks you to do when you use it/participate in the group that uses it. As a group, discuss how the genre appears to people who are familiar and unfamiliar with it. Were those in the group who were familiar with the genre surprised by the reactions of the people in the group who were not familiar with it?

2. Next, ask the people in the small group to share one of the familiar texts they brought. They should quickly outline the features that are consistent in that text and that enable them to recognize it, and then describe aspects of the texts where writers have some freedom to do things differently (features that are not always the same). Finally, they should explain some features of the text that they think might have changed over time.

3. For further activities, complete some of the tasks suggested by Bazerman on page 391.

---

**Meta Moment**

How can you think about and approach new texts differently now than you did before you read this article and tried doing some genre analysis? How can this help you in various aspects of your life?

# Intertextuality and the Discourse Community

## JAMES E. PORTER

■ Porter, James E. "Intertextuality and the Discourse Community." *Rhetoric Review* 5.1 (1986): 34–47. Print.

## Framing the Reading

Two of the deepest conceptions of writing that our culture holds are (1) that writing must be *original* and (2) that if a writer "borrows" ideas from other writing without acknowledging that borrowing, the writer is *plagiarizing*. In the following study, James Porter argues that these common ideas about originality and plagiarism don't account for how texts actually work and how writers actually write. Porter calls into question how original writers can actually be in constructing texts and, following from that question, also wonders how we should define plagiarism if true originality is so difficult to find.

The principle Porter explores in asking these questions is **intertextuality**—that is, the idea that *all* texts contain "traces" of other texts and that there can be no text that does not draw on *some* ideas from some other texts. You may rightly be skeptical of a claim so broad, so follow along carefully as Porter explains why he thinks this is true. You may be particularly interested in the section in which Porter demonstrates his argument by looking at how the Declaration of Independence was written, as he claims, collaboratively, by a number of different authors.

The implications of Porter's study are significant for how you understand writing and how you understand yourself as a writer. Most of us have been taught that writers are *autonomous*—that is, that they're free do to whatever they want with their texts, and also that they're solely responsible for what's in those texts. Porter's research on actual writing and writers challenges this construct. If Porter is correct, then we need a *different* construct of the *author*, one that acknowledges the extent to which communities shape what a writer chooses to say; the extent to which writers say things that have already been said (even when they believe they're being original); and the extent to which texts are constructed by many different people along the way, as readers feed ideas back to the writer.

### Getting Ready to Read

*Before you read*, do at least one of the following activities:

- Write a paragraph on what, in your mind, the difference between an *author* and a *writer* is. When would you choose the first term to describe the person/people behind a text, and when would you choose the second?

- Make a list of all the ways you get "help," of any kind, in your writing. Where do you get ideas, advice, feedback, and assistance?
- Find one or two friends or family members who write a great deal, either for a living, as a major part of their jobs, or as a hobby. Interview them about who or what they see contributing to their writing. To what extent do they see themselves doing their writing "on their own"?

*As you read*, consider the following questions:

- Watch for how Porter poses questions about writers' *autonomy* and *originality*. Does he finally decide that autonomy and originality are impossible?
- Do you think Porter is *criticizing* the Declaration of Independence? Thomas Jefferson? Explain your answer.
- If you haven't seen the Pepsi commercial that Porter discusses, try to find a version of it to watch online. Does Porter's reading of the commercial match yours, or do you understand it differently?

---

At the conclusion of Eco's *The Name of the Rose*, the monk Adso of     1
Melk returns to the burned abbey, where he finds in the ruins scraps of parchment, the only remnants from one of the great libraries in all Christendom. He spends a day collecting the charred fragments, hoping to discover some meaning in the scattered pieces of books. He assembles his own "lesser library . . . of fragments, quotations, unfinished sentences, amputated stumps of books" (500). To Adso, these random shards are "an immense acrostic that says and repeats nothing" (501). Yet they are significant to him as an attempt to order experience.

We might well derive our own order from this scene. We might see Adso as     2
representing the writer, and his desperate activity at the burned abbey as a model for the writing process. The writer in this image is a collector of fragments, an archaeologist creating an order, building a framework, from remnants of the past. Insofar as the collected fragments help Adso recall other, lost texts, his experience affirms a principle he learned from his master, William of Baskerville: "Not infrequently books speak of books" (286). Not infrequently, and perhaps ever and always, texts refer to other texts and in fact rely on them for their meaning. All texts are interdependent: We understand a text only insofar as we understand its precursors.

> *All texts are interdependent: We understand a text only insofar as we understand its precursors.*

This is the principle we know as intertextuality, the principle that all writ-     3
ing and speech—indeed, all signs—arise from a single network: what Vygotsky called "the web of meaning"; what poststructuralists label Text or Writing (Barthes, *écriture*); and what a more distant age perhaps knew as *logos*.

Examining texts "intertextually" means looking for "traces," the bits and pieces of Text which writers or speakers borrow and sew together to create new discourse.[1] The most mundane manifestation of intertextuality is explicit citation, but intertextuality animates all discourse and goes beyond mere citation. For the intertextual critics, Intertext is Text—a great seamless textual fabric. And, as they like to intone solemnly, no text escapes intertext.

Intertextuality provides rhetoric with an important perspective, one currently neglected, I believe. The prevailing composition pedagogies by and large cultivate the romantic image of writer as free, uninhibited spirit, as independent, creative genius. By identifying and stressing the intertextual nature of discourse, however, we shift our attention away from the writer as individual and focus more on the sources and social contexts from which the writer's discourse arises. According to this view, authorial intention is less significant than social context; the writer is simply a part of a discourse tradition, a member of a team, and a participant in a community of discourse that creates its own collective meaning. Thus the intertext *constrains* writing. 4

My aim here is to demonstrate the significance of this theory to rhetoric, by explaining intertextuality, its connection to the notion of "discourse community," and its pedagogical implications for composition. 5

## The Presence of Intertext

Intertextuality has been associated with both structuralism and poststructuralism, with theorists like Roland Barthes, Julia Kristeva, Jacques Derrida, Hayden White, Harold Bloom, Michel Foucault, and Michael Riffaterre. (Of course, the theory is most often applied in literary analysis.) The central assumption of these critics has been described by Vincent Leitch: "The text is not an autonomous or unified object, but a set of relations with other texts. Its system of language, its grammar, its lexicon, drag along numerous bits and pieces—traces—of history so that the text resembles a Cultural Salvation Army Outlet with unaccountable collections of incompatible ideas, beliefs, and sources" (59). It is these "unaccountable collections" that intertextual critics focus on, not the text as autonomous entity. In fact, these critics have redefined the notion of "text": Text *is* intertext, or simply Text. The traditional notion of the text as the single work of a given author, and even the very notions of author and reader, are regarded as simply convenient fictions for domesticating discourse. The old borders that we used to rope off discourse, proclaim these critics, are no longer useful. 6

We can distinguish between two types of intertextuality: iterability and presupposition. Iterability refers to the "repeatability" of certain textual fragments, to citation in its broadest sense to include not only explicit allusions, references, and quotations within a discourse, but also unannounced sources and influences, clichés, phrases in the air, and traditions. That is to say, every discourse is composed of "traces," pieces of other texts that help constitute its meaning. (I will discuss this aspect of intertextuality in my analysis of the Declaration of Independence.) Presupposition refers to assumptions a text makes about its 7 referent, its readers, and its context—to portions of the text which are read, but which are not explicitly "there." For example, as Jonathan Culler discusses, the phrase "John married Fred's sister" is an assertion that logically presupposes that John exists, that Fred exists, and that Fred has a sister. "Open the door" contains a practical presupposition, assuming the presence of a decoder who is capable of being addressed and who is better able to open the door than the encoder. "Once upon a time" is a trace rich in rhetorical presupposition, signaling to even the youngest reader the opening of a fictional narrative. Texts not only refer to but in fact *contain* other texts.[2]

An examination of three sample texts will illustrate the various facets of 8 intertextuality. The first, the Declaration of Independence, is popularly viewed as the work of Thomas Jefferson. Yet if we examine the text closely in its rhetorical milieu, we see that Jefferson was author only in the very loosest of senses. A number of historians and at least two composition researchers (Kinneavy, *Theory* 393–49; Maimon, *Readings* 6–32) have analyzed the Declaration, with interesting results. Their work suggests that Jefferson was by no means an original framer or a creative genius, as some like to suppose. Jefferson was a skilled writer, to be sure, but chiefly because he was an effective borrower of traces.

To produce his original draft of the Declaration, Jefferson seems to have 9 borrowed, either consciously or unconsciously, from his culture's Text. Much has been made of Jefferson's reliance on Locke's social contract theory (Becker). Locke's theory influenced colonial political philosophy, emerging in various pamphlets and newspaper articles of the times, and served as the foundation for the opening section of the Declaration. The Declaration contains many traces that can be found in other, earlier documents. There are traces from a First Continental Congress resolution, a Massachusetts Council declaration, George Mason's "Declaration of Rights for Virginia," a political pamphlet of James Otis, and a variety of other sources, including a colonial play. The overall form of the Declaration (theoretical argument followed by list of grievances) strongly resembles, ironically, the English Bill of Rights of 1689, in which Parliament lists the abuses of James II and declares new powers for itself. Several of the abuses in the Declaration seem to have been taken, more or less verbatim, from a *Pennsylvania Evening Post* article. And the most memorable phrases in the Declaration seem to be least Jefferson's: "That all men are created equal" is a sentiment from Euripides which Jefferson copied in his literary commonplace book as a boy; "Life, Liberty, and the pursuit of Happiness" was a cliché of the times, appearing in numerous political documents (Dumbauld).

Though Jefferson's draft of the Declaration can hardly be considered his 10 in any exclusive sense of authorship, the document underwent still more expropriation at the hands of Congress, who made eighty-six changes (Kinneavy, *Theory* 438). They cut the draft from 211 lines to 147. They did considerable editing to temper what they saw as Jefferson's emotional style: For example, Jefferson's phrase "sacred & undeniable" was changed to the more restrained "self-evident." Congress excised controversial passages, such as Jefferson's condemnation of slavery. Thus, we should find it instructive to note, Jefferson's few attempts at original expression were those least acceptable to Congress.

If Jefferson submitted the Declaration for a college writing class as his own  11
writing, he might well be charged with plagiarism.[3] The idea of Jefferson as author is but convenient shorthand. Actually, the Declaration arose out of a cultural and rhetorical milieu, was composed of traces—and was, in effect, team written. Jefferson deserves credit for bringing disparate traces together, for helping to mold and articulate the milieu, for creating the all-important draft. Jefferson's skill as a writer was his ability to borrow traces effectively and to find appropriate contexts for them. As Michael Halliday says, "[C]reativeness does not consist in producing new sentences. The newness of a sentence is a quite unimportant—and unascertainable—property and 'creativity' in language lies in the speaker's ability to create new meanings: to realize the potentiality of language for the indefinite extension of its resources to new contexts of situation. . . . Our most 'creative' acts may be precisely among those that are realized through highly repetitive forms of behaviour" (*Explorations* 42). The creative writer is the creative borrower, in other words.

Intertextuality can be seen working similarly in contemporary forums.  12
Recall this scene from a recent Pepsi commercial: A young boy in jeans jacket, accompanied by dog, stands in some desolate plains crossroads next to a gas station, next to which is a soft drink machine. An alien spacecraft, resembling the one in Spielberg's *Close Encounters of the Third Kind*, appears overhead. To the boy's joyful amazement, the spaceship hovers over the vending machine and begins sucking Pepsi cans into the ship. It takes *only* Pepsis, then eventually takes the entire machine. The ad closes with a graphic: "Pepsi. The Choice of a New Generation."

Clearly, the commercial presupposes familiarity with Spielberg's movie or, at  13
least, with his pacific vision of alien spacecraft. We see several American clichés, well-worn signs from the Depression era: the desolate plains, the general store, the pop machine, the country boy with dog. These distinctively American traces are juxtaposed against images from science fiction and the sixties catchphrase "new generation" in the coda. In this array of signs, we have tradition and counter-tradition harmonized. Pepsi squeezes itself in the middle, and thus becomes the great American conciliator. The ad's use of irony may serve to distract viewers momentarily from noticing how Pepsi achieves its purpose by assigning itself an exalted role through use of the intertext.

We find an interesting example of practical presupposition in John Kifner's  14
*New York Times* headline article reporting on the Kent State incident of 1970:

> Four students at Kent State University, two of them women, were shot to death this afternoon by a volley of National Guard gunfire. At least 8 other students were wounded.
>
> The burst of gunfire came about 20 minutes after the guardsmen broke up a noon rally on the Commons, a grassy campus gathering spot, by lobbing tear gas at a crowd of about 1,000 young people.

From one perspective, the phrase "two of them women" is a simple statement  15
of fact; however, it presupposes a certain attitude—that the event, horrible
enough as it was, is more significant because two of the persons killed were
women. It might be going too far to say that the phrase presupposes a sexist
attitude ("women aren't supposed to be killed in battles"), but can we imagine
the phrase "two of them men" in this context? Though equally factual, this
wording would have been considered odd in 1970 (and probably today as
well) because it presupposes a cultural mindset alien from the one dominant
at the time. "Two of them women" is shocking (and hence it was reported)
because it upsets the sense of order of the readers, in this case the American
public.

Additionally (and more than a little ironically), the text contains a num-  16
ber of traces which have the effect of blunting the shock of the event. Notice
that the students were not shot by National Guardsmen, but were shot "by a
volley of . . . gunfire"; the tear gas was "lobbed"; and the event occurred at a
"grassy campus gathering spot." "Volley" and "lobbed" are military terms, but
with connections to sport as well; "grassy campus gathering spot" suggests a
picnic; "burst" can recall the glorious sight of bombs "bursting" in "The Star-
Spangled Banner." This pastiche of signs casts the text into a certain context,
making it distinctively American. We might say that the turbulent milieu of the
sixties provided a distinctive array of signs from which John Kifner borrowed
to produce his article.

Each of the three texts examined contains phrases or images familiar to its  17
audience or presupposes certain audience attitudes. Thus the intertext exerts
its influence partly in the form of audience expectation. We might then say that
the audience of each of these texts is as responsible for its production as the
writer. That, in essence, readers, not writers, create discourse.

## The Power of Discourse Community

And, indeed, this is what some poststructuralist critics suggest, those who pre-  18
fer a broader conception of intertext or who look beyond the intertext to the
social framework regulating textual production: to what Michel Foucault calls
"the discursive formation," what Stanley Fish calls "the interpretive community," and what Patricia Bizzell calls "the discourse community."

A "discourse community" is a group of individuals bound by a common  19
interest who communicate through approved channels and whose discourse
is regulated. An individual may belong to several professional, public, or
personal discourse communities. Examples would include the community
of engineers whose research area is fluid mechanics; alumni of the University of Michigan; Magnavox employees; the members of the Porter family;
and members of the Indiana Teachers of Writing. The approved channels
we can call "forums." Each forum has a distinct history and rules governing
appropriateness to which members are obliged to adhere. These rules may be
more or less apparent, more or less institutionalized, more or less specific to
each community. Examples of forums include professional publications like

*Rhetoric Review, English Journal,* and *Creative Computing;* public media like *Newsweek* and *Runner's World;* professional conferences (the annual meeting of fluid power engineers, the 4C's); company board meetings; family dinner tables; and the monthly meeting of the Indiana chapter of the Izaak Walton League.

A discourse community shares assumptions about what objects are appro- 20 priate for examination and discussion, what operating functions are performed on those objects, what constitutes "evidence" and "validity," and what formal conventions are followed. A discourse community may have a well-established *ethos;* or it may have competing factions and indefinite boundaries. It may be in a "pre-paradigm" state (Kuhn), that is, having an ill-defined regulating system and no clear leadership. Some discourse communities are firmly established, such as the scientific community, the medical profession, and the justice system, to cite a few from Foucault's list. In these discourse communities, as Leitch says, "a speaker must be 'qualified' to talk; he has to belong to a community of scholarship; and he is required to possess a prescribed body of knowledge (doctrine). . . . [This system] operates to constrain discourse; it establishes limits and regularities. . . . who may speak, what may be spoken, and how it is to be said; in addition [rules] prescribe what is true and false, what is reasonable and what foolish, and what is meant and what not. Finally, they work to deny the material existence of discourse itself" (145).

A text is "acceptable" within a forum only insofar as it reflects the commu- 21 nity episteme (to use Foucault's term). On a simple level, this means that for a manuscript to be accepted for publication in the *Journal of Applied Psychology,* it must follow certain formatting conventions: It must have the expected social science sections (i.e., review of literature, methods, results, discussion), and it must use the journal's version of APA documentation. However, these are only superficial features of the forum. On a more essential level, the manuscript must reveal certain characteristics, have an *ethos* (in the broadest possible sense) conforming to the standards of the discourse community: It must demonstrate (or at least claim) that it contributes knowledge to the field, it must demonstrate familiarity with the work of previous researchers in the field, it must use a scientific method in analyzing its results (showing acceptance of the truth-value of statistical demonstration), it must meet standards for test design and analysis of results, it must adhere to standards determining degree of accuracy. The expectations, conventions, and attitudes of this discourse community—the readers, writers, and publishers of *Journal of Applied Psychology*—will influence aspiring psychology researchers, shaping not only how they write but also their character within that discourse community.

The poststructuralist view challenges the classical assumption that writ- 22 ing is a simple linear, one-way movement: The writer creates a text which produces some change in an audience. A poststructuralist rhetoric examines how audience (in the form of community expectations and standards) influences textual production and, in so doing, guides the development of the writer.

This view is of course open to criticism for its apparent determinism, for de-  23
valuing the contribution of individual writers and making them appear merely
tools of the discourse community (charges which Foucault answers in "Discourse on Language"). If these regulating systems are so constraining, how can
an individual emerge? What happens to the idea of the lone inspired writer and
the sacred autonomous text?

Both notions take a pretty hard knock. Genuine originality is difficult within  24
the confines of a well-regulated system. Genius is possible, but it may be constrained. Foucault cites the example of Gregor Mendel, whose work in the
nineteenth century was excluded from the prevailing community of biologists
because he "spoke of objects, employed methods and placed himself within
a theoretical perspective totally alien to the biology of his time.... Mendel
spoke the truth, but he was not *dans le vrai* (within the true)" (224). Frank
Lentricchia cites a similar example from the literary community: Robert Frost
"achieved magazine publication only five times between 1895 and 1912, a
period during which he wrote a number of poems later acclaimed . . . [because]
in order to write within the dominant sense of the poetic in the United States
in the last decade of the nineteenth century and the first decade of the twentieth, one had to employ a diction, syntax, and prosody heavily favoring Shelley
and Tennyson. One also had to assume a certain stance, a certain world-weary
idealism which took care not to refer too concretely to the world of which one
was weary" (197, 199).

Both examples point to the exclusionary power of discourse communities  25
and raise serious questions about the freedom of the writer: chiefly, does the
writer have any? Is any writer doomed to plagiarism? Can any text be said to
be new? Are creativity and genius actually possible? Was Jefferson a creative
genius or a blatant plagiarist?

Certainly we want to avoid both extremes. Even if the writer is locked  26
into a cultural matrix and is constrained by the intertext of the discourse
community, the writer has freedom within the immediate rhetorical context.[4]
Furthermore, successful writing helps to redefine the matrix—and in that way
becomes creative. (Jefferson's Declaration contributed to defining the notion
of America for its discourse community.) Every new text has the potential
to alter the text in some way; in fact, every text admitted into a discourse
community changes the constitution of the community—and discourse
communities can revise their discursive practices, as the Mendel and Frost
examples suggest.

Writing is an attempt to exercise the will, to identify the self within the  27
constraints of some discourse community. We are constrained insofar as we
must inevitably borrow the traces, codes, and signs which we inherit and
which our discourse community imposes. We are free insofar as we do what
we can to encounter and learn new codes, to intertwine codes in new ways,
and to expand our semiotic potential—with our goal being to effect change
and establish our identities within the discourse communities we choose to
enter.

## The Pedagogy of Intertextuality

Intertextuality is not new. It may remind some of Eliot's notion of tradi- 28
tion, though the parameters are certainly broader. It is an important concept,
though. It counters what I see as one prevailing composition pedagogy, one
favoring a romantic image of the writer, offering as role models the creative
essayists, the Sunday Supplement freelancers, the Joan Didions, E. B. Whites,
Calvin Trillins, and Russell Bakers. This dashing image appeals to our need
for intellectual heroes; but underlying it may be an anti-rhetorical view: that
writers are born, not made; that writing is individual, isolated, and internal;
not social but eccentric.

This view is firmly set in the intertext of our discipline. Our anthologies 29
glorify the individual essayists, whose work is valued for its timelessness and
creativity. Freshman rhetorics announce as the writer's proper goals personal
insight, originality, and personal voice, or tell students that motivations for
writing come from "within." Generally, this pedagogy assumes that such a
thing as the writer actually exists—an autonomous writer exercising a free,
creative will through the writing act—and that the writing process proceeds
linearly from writer to text to reader. This partial picture of the process can all
too readily become *the* picture, and our students can all too readily learn to
overlook vital facets of discourse production.

When we romanticize composition by overemphasizing the autonomy of the 30
writer, important questions are overlooked, the same questions an intertextual
view of writing would provoke: To what extent is the writer's product itself a
part of a larger community writing process? How does the discourse community influence writers and readers within it? These are essential questions, but
are perhaps outside the prevailing episteme of composition pedagogy, which
presupposes the autonomous status of the writer as independent *cogito*. Talking about writing in terms of "social forces influencing the writer" raises the
specter of determinism, and so is anathema.

David Bartholomae summarizes this issue very nicely: "The struggle of the 31
student writer is not the struggle to bring out that which is within; it is the
struggle to carry out those ritual activities that grant our entrance into a closed
society" (300). When we teach writing only as the act of "bringing out what
is within," we risk undermining our own efforts. Intertextuality reminds us
that "carrying out ritual activities" is also part of the writing process. Barthes
reminds us that "the 'I' which approaches the text is already itself a plurality of
other texts, of codes which are infinite" (10).

Intertextuality suggests that our goal should be to help students learn to 32
write for the discourse communities they choose to join. Students need help
developing out of what Joseph Williams calls their "pre-socialized cognitive
states." According to Williams, pre-socialized writers are not sufficiently im-
mersed in their discourse community to produce competent discourse: They do
not know what can be presupposed, are not conscious of the distinctive intertextuality of the community, may be only superficially acquainted with explicit
conventions. (Williams cites the example of the freshman whose paper for

the English teacher begins "Shakespeare is a famous Elizabethan dramatist.") Our immediate goal is to produce "socialized writers," who are full-fledged members of their discourse community, producing competent, useful discourse within that community. Our long-range goal might be "post-socialized writers," those who have achieved such a degree of confidence, authority, power, or achievement in the discourse community so as to become part of the regulating body. They are able to vary conventions and question assumptions—i.e., effect change in communities—without fear of exclusion.

Intertextuality has the potential to affect all facets of our composition peda- 33 gogy. Certainly it supports writing across the curriculum as a mechanism for introducing students to the regulating systems of discourse communities. It raises questions about heuristics: Do different discourse communities apply different heuristics? It asserts the value of critical reading in the composition classroom. It requires that we rethink our ideas about plagiarism: Certainly *imitatio* is an important stage in the linguistic development of the writer.

The most significant application might be in the area of audience analysis. Cur- 34 rent pedagogies assume that when writers analyze audiences they should focus on the expected flesh-and-blood readers. Intertextuality suggests that the proper focus of audience analysis is not the audience as receivers per se, but the intertext of the discourse community. Instead of collecting demographic data about age, educational level, and social status, the writer might instead ask questions about the intertext: What are the conventional presuppositions of this community? In what forums do they assemble? What are the methodological assumptions? What is considered "evidence," "valid argument," and "proof"? A sample heuristic for such an analysis—what I term "forum analysis"—is included as an appendix.

A critical reading of the discourse of a community may be the best way to 35 understand it. (We see a version of this message in the advice to examine a journal before submitting articles for publication.) Traditionally, anthologies have provided students with reading material. However, the typical anthologies have two serious problems: (1) limited range—generally they overemphasize literary or expressive discourse; (2) unclear context—they frequently remove readings from their original contexts, thus disguising their intertextual nature. Several recently published readers have attempted to provide a broader selection of readings in various forums, and actually discuss intertextuality. Maimon's *Readings in the Arts and Sciences*, Kinneavy's *Writing in the Liberal Arts Tradition*, and Bazerman's *The Informed Writer* are especially noteworthy.

Writing assignments should be explicitly intertextual. If we regard each 36 written product as a stage in a larger process—the dialectic process within a discourse community—then the individual writer's work is part of a web, part of a community search for truth and meaning. Writing assignments might take the form of dialogue with other writers: Writing letters in response to articles is one kind of dialectic (e.g., letters responding to *Atlantic Monthly* or *Science* articles). Research assignments might be more community oriented rather than topic oriented; students might be asked to become involved in communities of researchers (e.g., the sociologists examining changing religious attitudes in American college students). The assignments in Maimon's *Writing in the Arts and Sciences* are excellent in this regard.

Intertextual theory suggests that the key criteria for evaluating writing 37
should be "acceptability" within some discourse community. "Acceptability"
includes, but goes well beyond, adherence to formal conventions. It includes
choosing the "right" topic, applying the appropriate critical methodology, ad-
hering to standards for evidence and validity, and in general adopting the community's discourse values—and of course borrowing the appropriate traces.
Success is measured by the writer's ability to know what can be presupposed
and to borrow that community's traces effectively to create a text that contributes to the maintenance or, possibly, the definition of the community. The
writer is constrained by the community, and by its intertextual preferences and
prejudices, but the effective writer works to assert the will against those community constraints to effect change.

The Pepsi commercial and the Kent State news article show effective uses of 38
the intertext. In the Kent State piece, John Kifner mixes picnic imagery ("grassy
campus gathering spot," "young people") with violent imagery ("burst of gunfire") to dramatize the event. The Pepsi ad writers combine two unlikely sets
of traces, linking folksy depression-era American imagery with sci-fi imagery
"stolen" from Spielberg. For this creative intertwining of traces, both discourses
can probably be measured successful in their respective forums.

## Coda

Clearly much of what intertextuality supports is already institutionalized (e.g., 39
writing-across-the-curriculum programs). And yet, in freshman comp texts and
anthologies especially, there is this tendency to see writing as individual, as
isolated, as heroic. Even after demonstrating quite convincingly that the Declaration was written by a team freely borrowing from a cultural intertext, Elaine
Maimon insists, against all the evidence she herself has collected, that "Despite
the additions, deletions, and changes in wording that it went through, the Declaration is still Jefferson's writing" (*Readings* 26). Her saying this presupposes
that the reader has just concluded the opposite.

When we give our students romantic role models like E. B. White, Joan 40
Didion, and Lewis Thomas, we create unrealistic expectations. This type of
writer has often achieved post-socialized status within some discourse community (Thomas in the scientific community, for instance). Can we realistically expect our students to achieve this state without first becoming socialized,
without learning first what it means to write within a social context? Their
role models ought not be only romantic heroes but also community writers
like Jefferson, the anonymous writers of the Pepsi commercial—the Adsos of
the world, not just the Aristotles. They need to see writers whose products are
more evidently part of a larger process and whose work more clearly produces
meaning in social contexts.

## Notes

1. The dangers of defining intertextuality too simplistically are discussed by Owen Miller in
   "Intertextual Identity," *Identity of the Literary Text*, ed. Mario J. Valdés and Owen Miller

(Toronto: U of Toronto P, 1985), 19–40. Miller points out that intertextuality "addresses itself to a plurality of concepts" (19).

2. For fuller discussion see Jonathan Culler, *The Pursuit of Signs* (Ithaca: Cornell UP, 1981), 100–16. Michael Halliday elaborates on the theory of presupposition somewhat, too, differentiating between exophoric and endophoric presupposition. The meaning of any text at least partly relies on exophoric references, i.e., external presuppositions. Endophoric references in the form of cohesive devices and connections within a text also affect meaning, but cohesion in a text depends ultimately on the audience making exophoric connections to prior texts, connections that may not be cued by explicit cohesive devices. See M. A. K. Halliday and Ruqaiya Hasan, *Cohesion in English* (London: Longman, 1976).

3. Miller cautions us about intertextuality and *post hoc ergo propter hoc* reasoning. All we can safely note is that phrases in the Declaration also appear in other, earlier documents. Whether or not the borrowing was intentional on Jefferson's part or whether the prior documents "caused" the Declaration (in any sense of the word) is not ascertainable.

4. Robert Scholes puts it this way: "If you play chess, you can only do certain things with the pieces, otherwise you are not playing chess. But those constraints do not in themselves tell you what moves to make." See *Textual Power* (New Haven: Yale UP. 1985), 153.

## Works Cited

Barthes, Roland. *S/Z.* Trans. Richard Miller. New York: Hill and Wang, 1974.

Bartholomae, David. "Writing Assignments: Where Writing Begins." *fforum.* Ed. Patricia L. Stock. Upper Montclair, NJ: Boynton/Cook, 1983.

Bazerman, Charles. *The Informed Writer.* 2nd ed. Boston: Houghton Mifflin, 1985.

Becker, Carl. *The Declaration of Independence.* 2nd ed. New York: Random, Vintage, 1942.

Bizzell, Patricia. "Cognition, Convention, and Certainty: What We Need to Know about Writing." *PRE/TEXT* 3 (1982): 213–43.

Culler, Jonathan. *The Pursuit of Signs.* Ithaca: Cornell UP, 1981.

Dumbauld, Edward. *The Declaration of Independence.* 2nd ed. Norman: U of Oklahoma P, 1968.

Eco, Umberto. *The Name of the Rose.* Trans. William Weaver. San Diego: Harcourt Brace Jovanovich, 1983.

Fish, Stanley. *Is There a Text in This Class?* Cambridge: Harvard UP, 1980.

Foucault, Michel. *The Archaeology of Knowledge and the Discourse on Language.* Trans. A. M. Sheridan Smith. New York: Harper & Row, 1972.

Halliday, M. A. K. *Explorations in the Functions of Language.* New York: Elsevier, 1973.

Halliday, M. A. K., and Ruqaiya Hasan. *Cohesion in English.* London: Longman, 1976.

Kifner, John. "4 Kent State Students Killed by Troops." *New York Times* 5 May 1970: 1.

Kinneavy, James L. *A Theory of Discourse.* Englewood Cliffs: Prentice-Hall, 1971.

———, et al. *Writing in the Liberal Arts Tradition.* New York: Harper & Row, 1985.

Kuhn, Thomas S. *The Structure of Scientific Revolutions.* 2nd ed. Chicago: U of Chicago P, 1970.

Leitch, Vincent B. *Deconstructive Criticism.* New York: Cornell UP, 1983.

Lentricchia, Frank. *After the New Criticism.* Chicago: U of Chicago P, 1980.

Maimon, Elaine P., et al. *Readings in the Arts and Sciences.* Boston: Little, Brown, 1984.

———, *Writing in the Arts and Sciences.* Cambridge: Winthrop, 1981.

Miller, Owen. "Intertextual Identity." *Identity of the Literary Text.* Ed. Mario J. Valdés and Owen Miller. Toronto: U of Toronto P, 1985, 19–40.

Scholes, Robert. *Textual Power.* New Haven: Yale UP, 1985.

Williams, Joseph. "Cognitive Development, Critical Thinking, and the Teaching of Writing." Conference on Writing, Meaning, and Higher Order Reasoning, University of Chicago, 15 May 1984.

## Appendix

### *Forum Analysis*

### Background

—Identify the forum by name and organizational affiliation.

—Is there an expressed editorial policy, philosophy, or expression of belief? What purpose does the forum serve? Why does it exist?

—What is the disciplinary orientation?

—How large is the forum? Who are its members? Its leaders? Its readership?

—In what manner does the forum assemble (e.g., newsletter, journal, conference, weekly meeting)? How frequently?

—What is the origin of the forum? Why did it come into existence? What is its history? Its political background? Its traditions?

—What reputation does the forum have among its own members? How is it regarded by others?

### Discourse Conventions

#### *Who Speaks/Writes?*

—Who is granted status as speaker/writer? Who decides who speaks/writes in the forum? By what criteria are speakers/writers selected?

—What kind of people speak/write in this forum? Credentials? Disciplinary orientation? Academic or professional background?

—Who are the important figures in this forum? Whose work or experience is most frequently cited?

—What are the important sources cited in the forum? What are the key works, events, experiences that it is assumed members of the forum know?

#### *To Whom Do They Speak/Write?*

—Who is addressed in the forum? What are the characteristics of the assumed audience?

—What are the audience's needs assumed to be? To what use(s) is the audience expected to put the information?

—What is the audience's background assumed to be? Level of proficiency, experience, and knowledge of subject matter? Credentials?

—What are the beliefs, attitudes, values, prejudices of the addressed audience?

#### *What Do They Speak/Write About?*

—What topics or issues does the forum consider? What are allowable subjects? What topics are valued?

—What methodology or methodologies are accepted? Which theoretical approach is preferred: deduction (theoretical argumentation) or induction (evidence)?

—What constitutes "validity," "evidence," and "proof" in the forum (e.g., personal experience/observation, testing and measurement, theoretical or statistical analysis)?

## How Do They Say/Write It?

### Form

—What types of discourse does the forum admit (e.g., articles, reviews, speeches, poems)? How long are the discourses?

—What are the dominant modes of organization?

—What formatting conventions are present: headings, tables and graphs, illustrations, abstracts?

### Style

—What documentation form(s) is used?

—Syntactic characteristics?

—Technical or specialized jargon? Abbreviations?

—Tone? What stance do writers/speakers take relative to audience?

—Manuscript mechanics?

## Other Considerations?

.........................................................................................................

## Questions for Discussion and Journaling

1. After reading the first page of the article, define *intertextuality*. When you're finished reading the entire article, define it again. How, if at all, do your two definitions differ?

2. Do you agree with Porter that *intertext*—the great web of texts built on and referring to each other—makes individual writers less important? Why or why not?

3. Why does Porter call the idea of an autonomous writer "romantic"?

4. Porter argues that the key criterion for evaluating writing should be its "acceptability" within the reader's community. How is this different from the way you might have assumed writing should be evaluated prior to reading his article? How is it different from the way(s) your own writing has been evaluated in the past?

5. If Porter is right about intertextuality and its effects on originality, then his article must not be "original," and he must not be writing as an "autonomous individual." How does his own work reflect—or fail to reflect—the principles he's writing about?

6. What harm is there, according to Porter, in imagining writing "as individual, as isolated, as heroic" (para. 39)? What problems does it cause?

## Applying and Exploring Ideas

1. Choose a commercial or advertisement you've seen recently and search for traces of intertextuality in it. How many texts can you find represented in it? How do you find *cultural* intertext represented in it?

2. If we accept Porter's argument, then the typical school definition of *plagiarism* seems oversimplified or inaccurate. Rewrite the plagiarism policy for the course you're in now so that it accounts for Porter's notion of plagiarism but still keeps students from cheating. When you're finished, compare the original and your revised version. How much and in what ways do they differ?

> ### Meta Moment
> Many of us have been taught to imagine "writers" as people who work more or less alone to get their ideas down in print. Has Porter's study changed the way *you* imagine writers and writing? Would adopting his notion of writers and writing change the way you write?

Linda Flower

# Rhetorical Reading Strategies and the Construction of Meaning

## CHRISTINA HAAS

## LINDA FLOWER

■ Haas, Christina, and Linda Flower. "Rhetorical Reading Strategies and the Construction of Meaning." *College Composition and Communication* 39.2 (1988): 167–83. Print.

## Framing the Reading

In the late 1980s and early 1990s, Christina Haas and Linda Flower were doing research on how reading contributes to writing at Carnegie Mellon University's Center for the Study of Writing. Specifically, they were trying to understand what experienced readers do differently from less-experienced ones. What they found was that more-experienced readers used what they called **rhetorical** reading strategies to more efficiently come to an understanding of difficult texts.

Haas and Flower's research makes use of a somewhat imperfect method of investigation called a *think-aloud protocol*. Because we can't see what people think, we can at least try to hear some of what they're thinking by asking them to "think out loud." So research participants are asked first to read aloud and then to describe what they're thinking while they try to understand what the text means. The researchers make tapes of this talk, which are later transcribed for further study. The method is a good way of capturing some of what's going on in people's heads, but you may be able to see potential drawbacks to it as well.

If you read Keith Grant-Davie's article on rhetorical situations, you'll remember our discussion of the term **rhetoric** as descriptive of texts that *accomplish* or *do* things (like get you to buy a car or get you married or get you into war). Haas and Flower help us think about another angle of rhetoric: the *motivation* of the **rhetors** (speakers and writers) and the **context** in which the texts they create are written and read.

It may help you to know, in reading this piece, that Carnegie Mellon has been the scene of a lot of research on artificial intelligence—how to make machines able to think like humans. In research conducted around the time the article was written, human brains were often thought of as "information processors" much like

computers—working with memory, central processors, inputs and outputs, and sensory data. Because this way of understanding the human mind was "in the air" (everyone was talking more or less this way) at that time, Haas and Flower's article carries some of that sense, too, and they tend to talk about minds as quite machine-like (for better or for worse). Knowing that, you understand a little more of the context of this article, and (Haas and Flower would say) that means you're a little better equipped to make sense of it.

## Getting Ready to Read

*Before you read*, do at least one of the following activities:

- Ask a couple of friends how they read: When do they pay attention to who is the writer of what they're reading? When do they look up information like definitions or background on the subject? What strategies do they use to keep track of what they're reading, like highlighting, notes in the margins, or a reading notebook? When they encounter material they don't understand, what do they do to try to understand it? Keep notes of your friends' answers and compare them to what you do as a reader.
- Make an audio or video recording of yourself reading an unfamiliar and hard-to-read text aloud and talking aloud as you try to figure out what it means. When you play back the recording, make notes about what you heard that you didn't expect to and what you learn about yourself as a reader from doing this.
- Make a quick self-assessment of your reading abilities by answering the following questions: What are you good at, as a reader? What do you think you're not good at when it comes to reading? Is there anything you wish you had been taught better or differently?

*As you read*, consider the following questions:

- How does the reading style that Haas and Flower recommend compare to your own habits of reading and understanding texts?
- What does it mean to *construct* the meaning of a text rather than to "extract" it or find it "in" the text?
- What, according to Haas and Flower, are more-experienced readers doing that less-experienced readers aren't?
- How do Haas and Flower actually study their question? What do you think of their methods?

There is a growing consensus in our field that reading should be thought 1 of as a constructive rather than as a receptive process: that "meaning" does not exist in a text but in readers and the representations they build. This constructive view of reading is being vigorously put forth, in different ways, by both literary theory and cognitive research. It is complemented by work in rhetoric which argues that reading is also a discourse act. That is, when readers construct meaning, they do so in the context of a discourse situation, which includes the writer of the original text, other readers, the rhetorical context for reading, and the history of the discourse. If reading really is this constructive, rhetorical process, it may both demand that we rethink how we teach college students to read texts

> *There is a growing consensus in our field that reading should be thought of as a constructive rather than as a receptive process: that "meaning" does not exist in a text but in readers and the representations they build.*

and suggest useful parallels between the act of reading and the more intensively studied process of writing. However, our knowledge of how readers actually carry out this interpretive process with college-level expository texts is rather limited. And a process we can't describe may be hard to teach.

We would like to help extend this constructive, rhetorical view of reading, 2 which we share with others in the field, by raising two questions. The first is, how does this constructive process play itself out in the actual, thinking process of reading? And the second is, are all readers really aware of or in control of the discourse act which current theories describe? In the study we describe below, we looked at readers trying to understand a complex college-level text and observed a process that was constructive in a quite literal sense of the term. Using a think-aloud procedure, we watched as readers used not only the text but their own knowledge of the world, of the topic, and of discourse conventions, to infer, set and discard hypotheses, predict, and question in order to construct meaning for texts. One of the ways readers tried to make meaning of the text was a strategy we called "rhetorical reading," an active attempt at constructing a rhetorical context for the text as a way of making sense of it. However, this valuable move was a special strategy used only by more experienced readers. We observed a sharp distinction between the rhetorical process these experienced readers demonstrated and the processes of freshman readers. It may be that these student readers, who relied primarily on text-based strategies to construct their meanings, do not have the same full sense of reading as the rhetorical or social discourse act we envision.

Some of the recent work on reading and cognition gives us a good starting 3 point for our discussion since it helps describe what makes the reading process so complex and helps explain how people can construct vastly different interpretations of the same text. Although a thinking-aloud protocol can show us a great deal, we must keep in mind that it reveals only part of what goes on as a reader is building a representation of a text. And lest the "constructive" metaphor makes this process sound tidy, rational, and fully conscious, we should emphasize that it may in fact be rapid, unexamined, and even inexpressible. The private mental representation that a reader constructs has many facets: it is likely to include a representation of propositional or content information, a representation of the structure—either conventional or unique—of that information, and a representation of how the parts of the text function. In addition, the reader's representation may include beliefs about the subject matter, about the author and his or her credibility, and about the reader's own intentions in reading. In short, readers construct meaning by building multifaceted, interwoven representations of knowledge. The current text, prior texts, and the reading context can exert varying degrees of influence on this process, but it is the reader who must integrate information into meaning.

We can begin to piece together the way this constructive, cognitive pro- 4 cess operates based on recent research on reading and comprehension, and on reading and writing. Various syntheses of this work have been provided by Baker and Brown; Bransford; Flower ("Interpretive Acts"); and Spivey. To begin with, it is helpful to imagine the representations readers build as complex networks, like dense roadmaps, made up of many nodes of information, each related to others in multiple ways. The nodes created during a few minutes of reading would probably include certain content propositions from the text. The network might also contain nodes for the author's name, for a key point in the text, for a personal experience evoked by the text, for a striking word or phrase, and for an inference the reader made about the value of the text, or its social or personal significance. The links between a group of nodes might reflect causality, or subordination, or simple association, or a strong emotional connection.

The process of constructing this representation is carried out by both highly 5 automated processes of recognition and inference *and* by the more active problem-solving processes on which our work focuses. For instance, trying to construct a well-articulated statement of the "point" of a text may require active searching, inferencing, and transforming of one's own knowledge. The reason such transformations are constantly required can be explained by the "multiple-representation thesis" proposed by Flower and Hayes ("Images" 120). It suggests that readers' and writers' mental representations are not limited to verbally well-formed ideas and plans, but may include information coded as visual images, or as emotions, or as linguistic propositions that exist just above the level of specific words. These representations may also reflect more abstract schema, such as the schema most people have for narrative or for establishing credibility in a conversation. Turning information coded in any of these forms into a fully verbal articulation of the "point," replete with well-specified connections between ideas and presented according to the standard conventions of a given discourse, is constructive; it can involve not only translating one kind of representation into another, but reorganizing knowledge and creating new knowledge, new conceptual nodes and connections. In essence, it makes sense to take the metaphor of "construction" seriously.

It should be clear that this image of "meaning" as a rich network of dispa- 6 rate kinds of information is in sharp contrast to the narrow, highly selective and fully verbal statement of a text's gist or "meaning" that students may be asked to construct for an exam or a book review. Statements of that sort do, of course, serve useful functions, but we should not confuse them with the multi-dimensional, mental structures of meaning created by the cognitive and affective process of reading.

If reading, then, is a process of responding to cues in the text and in the 7
reader's context to build a complex, multi-faceted representation of meaning, it
should be no surprise that different readers might construct radically different
representations of the same text and might use very different strategies to do
so. This makes the goals of teacher and researcher look very much alike: both
the teacher and the researcher are interested in the means by which readers
(especially students) construct multi-faceted representations, or "meaning." The
study we are about to describe looks at a practical and theoretical question
that this constructive view of reading raises: namely, what strategies, other than
those based on knowing the topic, do readers bring to the process of understanding difficult texts—and how does this translate into pedagogy?

Seeing reading as a constructive act encourages us as teachers to move from 8
merely *teaching texts* to *teaching readers*. The teacher as co-reader can both
model a sophisticated reading process and help students draw out the rich possibilities of texts and readers, rather than trying to insure that all students interpret
texts in a single, "correct" way—and in the same way. Yet this goal—drawing out
the rich possibilities of texts and of readers—is easier to describe than to reach.

## What Is "Good Reading"?

The notion of multiple, constructed representations also helps us understand a 9
recurring frustration for college teachers: the problem of "good" readers who
appear to miss the point or who seem unable or unwilling to read critically.
Many of our students are "good" readers in the traditional sense: they have
large vocabularies, read quickly, are able to do well at comprehension tasks involving recall of content. They can identify topic sentences, introductions and
conclusions, generalizations and supporting details. Yet these same students
often frustrate us, as they paraphrase rather than analyze, summarize rather
than criticize texts. Why are these students doing less than we hope for?

To interpret any sophisticated text seems to require not only careful reading 10
and prior knowledge, but the ability to read the text on several levels, to build
multi-faceted representations. A text is understood not only as content and
information, but also as the result of someone's intentions, as part of a larger
discourse world, and as having real effects on real readers. In an earlier study,
we say that experienced readers made active use of the strategy of rhetorical
reading not only to predict and interpret texts but to solve problems in comprehension (Flower, "Construction of Purpose.") Vipond and Hunt have observed a related strategy of "point-driven" (vs. "story-driven") reading which
people bring to literary texts.

If we view reading as the act of constructing multi-faceted yet integrated 11
representations, we might hypothesize that the problem students have with
critical reading of difficult texts is less the representations they *are* constructing
than those they *fail to construct*. Their representations of text are closely tied
to content: they read for information. Our students may believe that if they
understand all the words and can paraphrase the propositional content of a
text, then they have successfully "read" it.

While a content representation is often satisfactory—it certainly meets the   12
needs of many pre-college read-to-take-a-test assignments—it falls short with
tasks or texts which require analysis and criticism. What many of our students *can* do is to construct representations of content, of structure, and of
conventional features. What they often *fail to do* is to move beyond content
and convention and construct representations of texts as purposeful actions,
arising from contexts, and with intended effects. "Critical reading" involves
more than careful reading for content, more than identification of conventional features of discourse, such as introductions or examples, and more
than simple evaluation based on agreeing or disagreeing. Sophisticated, difficult texts often require the reader to build an equally sophisticated, complex
representation of meaning. But how does this goal translate into the process
of reading?

As intriguing as this notion of the active construction of meaning is, we really   13
have no direct access to the meanings/representations that readers build. We
cannot enter the reader's head and watch as the construction of meaning proceeds. Nor can we get anything but an indirect measure of the nature, content,
and structure of that representation. What we can do, however, is to watch the
way that readers go about building representations: we can observe their use of
*reading strategies* and so infer something about the representations they build.

In order to learn something about the construction of meaning by readers,   14
we observed and analyzed the strategies of ten readers. Four were experienced
college readers, graduate students (aged 26 to 31 years), three in engineering
and one in rhetoric; six were student readers, college freshmen aged 18 and 19,
three classified "average" and three classified "above average" by their freshman composition teachers.

We were interested in how readers go about "constructing" meaning and   15
the constructive strategies they use to do so. However, we suspected that many
academic topics would give an unfair advantage to the more experienced
readers, who would be able to read automatically by invoking their knowledge of academic topics and discourse conventions. This automaticity would,
however, make their constructive reading harder for us to see. We wanted a
text that would require equally active problem solving by both groups. So, in
order to control for such knowledge, we designed a task in which meaning
was under question for all readers, and in which prior topic knowledge would
function as only one of many possible tools used to build an interpretation.
Therefore, the text began *in medias res*, without orienting information about
author, source, topic, or purpose. We felt that in this way we could elicit the
full range of constructive strategies these readers could call upon when the
situation demanded it.

The text, part of the preface to Sylvia Farnham-Diggory's *Cognitive Processes*   16
*in Education,* was like many texts students read, easy to decode but difficult to
interpret, with a high density of information and a number of semi-technical
expressions which had to be defined from context. The readers read and
thought aloud as they read. In addition, they answered the question "how do
you interpret the text now?" at frequent intervals. The question was asked of

readers eight times, thus creating nine reading "episodes." The slash marks indicate where the question appeared, and also mark episode boundaries, which we discuss later. To see the effect of this manipulation on eliciting interpretive strategies, you might wish to read the experimental text before going further. (Sentence numbers have been added.)

But somehow the social muddle persists.[s1] Some wonderful children come from appalling homes; some terrible children come from splendid homes.[s2] Practice may have a limited relationship to perfection—at least it cannot substitute for talent.[s3] Women are not happy when they are required to pretend that a physical function is equivalent to a mental one.[s4] Many children teach themselves to read years before they are supposed to be "ready."[s5] / Many men would not dream of basing their self-esteem on "cave man" prowess.[s6] And despite their verbal glibness, teenagers seem to be in a worse mess than ever.[s7] /

What has gone wrong?[s8] Are the psychological principles invalid?[s9] Are they too simple for a complex world?[s10] /

Like the modern world, modern scientific psychology is extremely technical and complex.[s11] The application of any particular set of psychological principles to any particular real problem requires a double specialist: a specialist in the scientific area, and a specialist in the real area.[s12] /

Not many such double specialists exist.[s13] The relationship of a child's current behavior to his early home life, for example, is not a simple problem—Sunday Supplement psychology notwithstanding.[s14] / Many variables must be understood and integrated: special ("critical") periods of brain sensitivity, nutrition, genetic factors, the development of attention and perception, language, time factors (for example, the amount of time that elapses between a baby's action and a mother's smile), and so on.[s15] Mastery of these principles is a full-time professional occupation.[s16] / The professional application of these principles—in, say a day-care center—is also a full-time occupation, and one that is foreign to many laboratory psychologists.[s17] Indeed, a laboratory psychologist may not even recognize his pet principles when they are realized in a day care setting.[s18] /

What is needed is a coming together of real-world and laboratory specialists that will require both better communication and more complete experience.[s19] / The laboratory specialists must spend some time in a real setting; the real-world specialists must spend some time in a theoretical laboratory.[s20] Each specialist needs to practice thinking like his counterpart.[s21] Each needs to practice translating theory into reality, and reality into theory.[s22]

The technique of in-process probing tries to combine the immediacy of con-  17
current reporting with the depth of information obtained through frequent questioning. It can of course give us only an indirect and partial indication of the actual representation. What it does reveal are gist-making strategies used at a sequence of points during reading, and it offers a cumulative picture of a text-under-construction.

Aside from our manipulation of the presentation, the text was a typical  18
college reading task. Part of the author's introduction to an educational psychology textbook, it presented an array of facts about the social reality of

learning, problems of education, and the aims of research. *Our* reading of the text, obviously also a constructed one, but one constructed with the benefit of a full knowledge of the source and context, included two main facts and two central claims. In a later analysis, we used these facts and claims to describe some of the transactions of readers and text.

Fact: Social problems exist and psychological principles exist, but there's a mismatch between them.

Fact: There are two kinds of educational specialists—real-world and laboratory.

Claim (explicit in text): The two kinds of specialists should interact.

Claim (implicit): Interaction of the two specialists is necessary to solve social problems.

The differences in "readings" subjects constructed of the text were striking  19 and were evidenced immediately. For instance, the following descriptions of three readers' readings of the text suggest the range of readers' concerns and begin to offer hints about the nature of their constructed representations of the text. These descriptions were what we called "early transactions" with the text—an analysis based on readers' comments during reading of the first two paragraphs, or ten sentences, of the text.

Seth, a 27-year-old graduate student in Engineering, by his own account  20 a voracious reader of literature in his own field, of travel books, history, and contemporary novels, is initially confused with the concepts "physical function and mental one" (sentence 4). He then explains his confusion by noting the nature of the materials: "Well, that's got some relationship with something that came before this business."

Kara, a freshman who does average college work, also thinks the text is con-  21 fusing; specifically, she says "I don't know what glibness means" (sentence 7). But whereas Seth sets up a hypothesis about both the content of the text and its source—"I think it's part of an article on the fact that the way you turn out is not a function of your environment"—and reads on to confirm his hypothesis, Kara's reading proceeds as a series of content paraphrases—"It's talking about children coming from different homes . . . and women not being happy." She continues to interpret the text a chunk at a time, paraphrasing linearly with little attempt to integrate or connect the parts. She reacts positively to the text—"I love the expression 'what has gone wrong'" (sentence 8)—and, despite her initial confusion with "glibness," she seems satisfied with her simple reading: "I just feel like you're talking about people—what's wrong with them and the world."

Not all the freshman student readers' transactions with the text were as  22 superficial and oversimplified as Kara's—nor were they all as contented with their readings of the text. Bob—an above-average freshman with a pre-med major—paraphrases content linearly like Kara, but he also sets up a hypothetical structure for the text: "It seems that different points are being brought out and each one has a kind of a contradiction in it, and it seems like an introduction . . . ." Unlike Kara, however, he becomes frustrated, unable to reconcile his own beliefs with what he's reading: "Well, I don't think they're too simple for a complex world. I don't think these are very simple things that are being said here. I think the situations—women, children, and men—I think they're pretty complex . . . so I don't understand why it said 'too simple for a complex world'" (sentence 10).

Our more experienced reader, Seth, also sets up a hypothesis about the text's structure: "Maybe he's [the author] contrasting the verbal glibness with caveman instinct." But Seth goes further: "I think the author is trying to say that it's some balance between your natural instinct and your surroundings but he's not sure what that balance is." These hypotheses try to account for not only the propositional content of the text, but also the function of parts ("contrasting"), the author's intent, and even the author's own uncertainty. 23

Seth continues to read the text, noting his own inexperience with the area of psychology—"I'm thinking about Freud and I really don't know much about psychology"—and trying to tie what he has just read to the previous paragraph: "I guess the psychological principles have something to do with the way children turn out. But I don't know if they are the physical, environmental things or if they're a function of your surroundings and education." 24

In these "early transactions" with the text, we see a range of readings and vast differences in the information contained in the readers' representations: Kara is uncertain of the meaning of a word and somewhat confused generally; she paraphrases content and is satisfied with the text and her reading of it. If we have a hint about the representations of text that Kara is building it is that they are focused primarily on content and her own affective responses and that they are somewhat more limited than those of the other readers. Bob's comments suggest that he may be building representations of structure as well as content, and that he is trying to bring his own beliefs and his reading of the text into line. 25

Seth is concerned with the content, with possible functions—both for parts of the text and for the text as a whole—with the author's intentions, with the experimental situation and with missing text; he also attends to his own knowledge (or lack of it) and to his prior reading experiences. What this suggests is that Seth is creating a multi-dimensional representation of the text that includes representations of its content, representations of the structure and function of the text, representations of author's intention and his own experience and knowledge as a reader of the text. 26

The "texts" or representations of meaning that the readers created as they were wrestling with the text and thinking aloud were dramatically different in both quantity—the amount of information they contained—and quality—the kinds of information they contained and the amount of the original text they accounted for. However, with no direct access to the internal representations that readers were building, we looked instead at the overt strategies they seemed to be using. 27

## Strategies for Constructing Meaning

The initial transactions with text suggested some differences among readers. Our next move was to more systematically analyze these differences. Each protocol contained two kinds of verbalizations: actual reading of the text aloud 28 and comments in which the readers were thinking aloud. About half of these comments were in response to the question, "How do you interpret the text now?" and the rest were unprompted responses. Each comment was sorted into one of three categories, based on what the readers seemed to be "attending to." This simple, three-part coding scheme distinguished between Content, Function/Feature, and Rhetorical reading strategies. These strategies are readily identifiable with some practice; our inter-rater reliability, determined by simple pair-wise comparisons, averaged 82%. Later, after about 20 minutes' instruction in the context of a college reading classroom, students could identify the strategies in the reading of others with close to 70% reliability.

Comments coded as *content strategies* are concerned with content or topic   29
information, "what the text is about." The reader may be questioning, interpreting, or summing content, paraphrasing what the text "is about" or "is saying." The reader's goal in using content strategies seems to be getting information from the text. Some examples of comments coded as content strategies:

> "So we're talking about psychological principles here."

> "I think it's about changing social conditions, like families in which both parents work, and changing roles of women."

> "I don't know what glibness is, so it's still confusing."

As Table 1 shows, both student and more experienced readers spent a large proportion of their effort using content strategies. On the average, 77% of the reading protocol was devoted to content strategies for students, 67% for the older readers. Building a representation of content seems to be very important for all of the readers we studied.

*Function/feature strategies* were used to refer to conventional, generic func-   30
tions of texts, or conventional features of discourse. These strategies seemed closely tied to the text: readers frequently named text parts, pointing to specific words, sentences, or larger sections of text—"This is the main point." "This must be an example," "I think this is the introduction." While content strategies seemed to be used to explain what the text was "saying," function/feature strategies were often used to name what the text was "doing": "Here he's contrasting," "This part seems to be explaining. . . ." In short, the use of these strategies suggests that readers are constructing spatial, functional, or relational structures for the text. Some examples of comments coded as function/feature strategies:

## Table 1

Mean Proportion of Strategies Used

|  | STUDENTS | | EXPERIENCED READERS | |
|---|---|---|---|---|
| Content Strategies | 77% | (58.1) | 67% | (58.0) |
| Feature Strategies | 22% | (15.8) | 20% | (18.0) |
| Rhetorical Strategies | 1%* | (.3) | 13%* | (9.3) |

*Difference significant at .05 level. Numbers in parentheses indicate the mean number of protocol statements in each category.

"I guess these are just examples."

"Is this the introduction?"

"This seems to be the final point."

Predictably, these strategies accounted for less of the protocol than did the content strategies: 22% for students, 20% for more experienced readers (see Table 1). And the groups of readers looked similar in their use of this strategy. This, too, may be expected: Identifying features such as introductions, examples, and conclusions is standard fare in many junior high and high school curricula. In addition, these students are of at least average ability within a competitive private university. We might ask if more basic readers—without the skills or reading experiences of these students—might demonstrate less use of the function/feature strategies. Further, these readers were all reading from paper; people reading from computer screens—a number which is rapidly increasing—may have difficulty creating and recalling spatial and relational structures in texts they read and write on-line (Haas and Hayes 34–35).

*Rhetorical strategies* take a step beyond the text itself. They are concerned  31
with constructing a rhetorical situation for the text, trying to account for author's purpose, context, and effect on the audience. In rhetorical reading strategies readers use cues in the text, and their own knowledge of discourse situations, to re-create or infer the rhetorical situation of the text they are reading. There is some indication that these strategies were used to help readers uncover the actual "event" of the text, a unique event with a particular author and actual effects. One reader likened the author of the text to a contemporary rhetorician: "This sounds a little like Richard Young to me." Readers seem to be constructing a rhetorical situation for the text and relating *this* text to a larger world of discourse. These examples demonstrate some of the range of rhetorical strategies: comments concerned with author's purpose, context or source, intended audience, and actual effect. Some examples of rhetorical reading strategies:

"So the author is trying to make the argument that you need scientific specialists in psychology."

"I wonder if it [the article] is from *Ms*."

"I don't think this would work for the man-in-the-street."

"I wonder, though, if this is a magazine article, and I wonder if they expected it to be so confusing."

While the groups of readers employed content and function/feature strate-  32
gies similarly, there is a dramatic difference in their use of the rhetorical strategy category. Less than 1% (in fact, one statement by one reader) of the students' protocols contained rhetorical strategies, while 13% of the experienced readers' effort went into rhetorical strategies. This is particularly striking when we consider the richness and wealth of information contained in these kinds of comments. For instance, setting this article into the context of *Ms.* magazine brings with it a wealth of unstated information about the kind of article that appears in that source, the kind of writers that contribute to it, and the kind of people who read it.

Rhetorical reading appears to be an "extra" strategy which some readers   33
used and others did not. Mann-Whitney analyses show no significant differences in the use of content or function/feature strategies, and an interesting—
$p < 0.5$—difference between the two groups in use of rhetorical strategies. The
small numbers in parentheses indicate the mean number of protocol statements
in each category for each group of readers; the significance tests, however, were
performed on the proportions of strategies used by each reader.

An example of two readers responding to a particularly difficult section of   34
text reveals the differences in the use of strategies even more clearly than do
the numbers.

> *Student Reader*: Well, basically, what I said previously is that there seems to be a
> problem between the real-world and the laboratory, or ideal situation versus
> real situation, whatever way you want to put it—that seems to be it.
>
> *Experienced Reader*: Ok, again, real world is a person familiar with the social
> influences on a person's personality—things they read or hear on the radio. . . .
> And laboratory specialists are more trained in clinical psychology. And now I
> think this article is trying to propose a new field of study for producing people
> who have a better understanding of human behavior. This person is crying out
> for a new type of scientist or something. (Ph.D. Student in Engineering)

While the student reader is mainly creating a gist and paraphrasing content,
the experienced reader does this and more—he then tries to infer the author's
purpose and even creates a sort of strident persona for the writer. If readers can
only build representations for which they have constructive tools or strategies,
then it is clear that this student reader—and in fact all of the student readers
we studied—are not building rhetorical representations of this text. In fact,
these student readers seem to be focused almost exclusively on content. The
student reader above is a case in point: her goal seems to be to extract information from the text, and once that is done—via a simple paraphrase—she
is satisfied with her reading of the text. We called this type of content reading "knowledge-getting," to underscore the similarity to the knowledge-telling
strategy identified by Bereiter and Scardamalia (72) in immature writers. In
both knowledge-getting and knowledge-telling, the focus is on content; larger
rhetorical purposes seem to play no role.

It is useful to see rhetorical reading not as a separate and different strat-   35
egy but as a progressive enlargement of the constructed meaning of a text.
These student readers seldom "progressed" to that enlarged view. Reading
for content is usually dominant and crucial—other kinds of strategies build
upon content representations. Functions and features strategies are generic and
conventional—easily identified in texts and often explicitly taught. Rhetorical strategies include not only a representation of discourse as discourse but
as *unique* discourse with a real author, a specific purpose, and actual effects.
This possible relationship between strategies may point to a building of skills,
a progression which makes intuitive sense and is supported by what we know
about how reading is typically taught and by teachers' reports of typical student reading problems.

The difference in the use that experienced and student readers make of 36
these strategies does not in itself make a convincing case for their value. Rhetorical reading strategies certainly *look* more sophisticated and elaborate, but
an important question remains: What does rhetorical reading *do* for readers?
We might predict that constructing the additional rhetorical representation—
requiring more depth of processing—would be an asset in particularly problematic reading tasks: texts in a subject area about which the reader knows
little, or texts complex in structure. It might also be important in those reading
tasks in which recognizing author's intention is crucial: propaganda, satire,
even the interpretation of assignments in school.

However, let us consider a rival hypothesis for a moment: maybe rhetorical 37
strategies are simply "frosting on the cake." Maybe good readers use these
strategies because reading for information is easier for them, and they have
extra cognitive resources to devote to what might be largely peripheral concerns
of the rhetorical situation.

We suspect that this was not the case, that rhetorical reading is not merely 38
"frosting on the cake" for several reasons: first, in the absence of a rhetorical situation for the text, *all* experienced readers constructed one. Second, the
more experienced readers seemed to be using all the strategies in tandem; i.e.,
they used the rhetorical strategies to help construct content, and vice versa.
They did not "figure out" the content, and then do rhetorical reading as an
"embellishment." Rhetorical reading strategies were interwoven with other
strategies as the readers constructed their reading of the texts.

And third, in the "tug of war" between text and reader which characterizes 39
constructive reading (Tierney and Pearson 34), we found that the rhetorical
readers seemed to recognize and assimilate more facts and claims into their
reading of the text. Recall that there were two facts and two claims which we
felt constituted a successful reading of this text. We used readers' recognition
of these facts and claims to gauge and to describe the kind of representation
they had constructed.

Fact: Social problems exist and psychological principles exist, but there's
a mismatch between them.

Fact: There are two kinds of educational specialists—real-world and
laboratory.

Claim (explicit in text): The two kinds of specialists should interact.

Claim (implicit): Interaction of the two specialists is necessary to solve
social problems.

In recognizing facts in the text, both groups of readers did well. But there 40
were very interesting differences in the patterns of recognition of claims in the
text. Readers who used the rhetorical strategies, first, recognized more claims,
and second, identified claims sooner than other readers. As we described earlier, our presentation of the text to the readers created nine reading episodes;
each asked for the readers' interpretation of "the text so far" at the end of the
episode. This allowed us some measure of constructed meaning by plotting
the points at which readers recognized each fact or claim. We said that readers

recognized a claim when they mentioned it as a possibility. This "recognition" was often tentative; readers made comments such as "So maybe this section is saying the two kinds of scientists should communicate," or "I guess this could solve the stuff at the beginning about social muddle."

The "episode line" in Figure 1 shows the points at which two readers (a student and a more-experienced reader) recognized Claim 1, plotted in relation to the point at which the text would reasonably permit such recognition. Figure 2 shows this information for the same readers recognizing Claim 2. Claim 2 is never explicitly stated, it only becomes easy to infer in the final episode. Of all the implicit meanings the text *could* convey, we saw this second claim as central to the coherence of the argument.

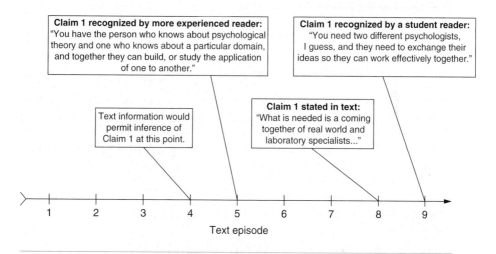

**Figure 1** When did a reader recognize Claim 1? "The two kinds of specialists should interact."

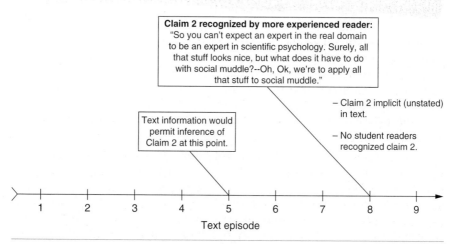

**Figure 2** When did a reader recognize Claim 2? "Interaction of two kinds of specialists is necessary to solve social problems."

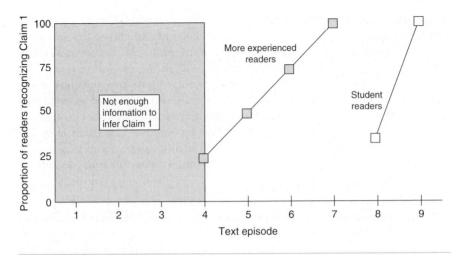

**Figure 3** Readers' Recognition of Claim 1

As Figure 3 illustrates, all student readers got Claim 1, but only at episode 9, 42 where it was explicitly stated—for the second time—in the text. (Claim 1 is first stated in episode 8.) More experienced readers, on the other hand, had all inferred Claim 1 much earlier—by episode 7. In addition, student readers did not recognize the unstated second claim at all, although all experienced readers inferred it, some as early as episode 8.

At episode 4 (the first point at which it would be possible to infer Claim 1), 43 25% of the experienced readers had inferred and mentioned this idea. At episode 5, 50% of these readers recognized it, at episode 6, 75% saw it, and by episode 7, all of the experienced readers had inferred Claim 1. In contrast, none of the student readers recognized this claim until episode 8, when it was cued in the text. At that point, 33% of the students noted it. At episode 9, when Claim 1 was restated, the rest of the students recognized it.

Claim 2 was never explicitly stated in the text, but half the experienced 44 readers had inferred this claim at episode 8 and all had inferred it at episode 9. None of the student readers offered any hints that they had recognized this implicit claim. It seems that the rhetorical readers were better able to recognize an important claim that was *never explicitly spelled out in the text*. In sophisticated texts, many important high-level claims—like Claim 2—remain implicit, but are crucial nonetheless.

This study, because it is observational rather than experimental, does not 45 allow us to conclude that the rhetorical reading we observed in the more experienced readers—and only in the more experienced readers—was the only or even the dominant cause for their ability to recognize claims. However, it makes sense that readers who are trying to make inferences about author, context, purpose, and effect, who are trying to create a representation of the text as the result of a purposeful action, would be more likely to recognize the claims—both implicit and explicit—within a text.

## The Role of Rhetorical Reading

This study suggests that the strategy of rhetorical reading may be an impor-  46
tant element in the larger process of critical reading. The constructive process
we observed in readers actively trying to understand the author's intent, the
context, and how other readers might respond appears to be a good basis for
recognizing claims, especially unstated ones the reader must infer. Speaking
more generally, this act of building a rich representation of text—larger than
the words on the page and including both propositional content and the larger
discourse context within which a text functions—is the kind of constructive
reading we desire our students to do.

However, is rhetorical reading a strategy students could easily adopt if cued  47
to do so? Being able to see one's own text and the texts of others as *discourse
acts*—rather than bodies of facts and information—is desirable, useful, and important for reading and writing of all kinds. This is the kind of meaning building we would like students to do, and rhetorical reading is one strategy that
may help them do it. In saying this, however, we recognize that this knowledge
will do us little good if we can't use it to help students. People must be *able* to
construct elaborate representations of meaning, and they must have the strategies to do so. How this is to come about is not clear.

Our first attempt at "suggestive" teaching—introducing the students to the  48
concept of rhetorical reading and encouraging them to use it—found that while
students could identify the rhetorical reading strategy in the reading of others,
they were less successful at using it. Can we expect merely to hand students
tools for building rich representations of text and set them to work? Or will
rhetorical reading require active teaching—teaching by direct instruction, by
modelling, and by encouraging students to become contributing and committed members of rhetorical communities?

Although the answers to these questions are not yet clear, we offer here our  49
own reading of these results: first, some readers are actively concerned with the
situations from which texts arise. These readers seemed to expend some effort
in representing the rhetorical situation of a text they are reading. However,
reading is a complex cognitive activity. It involves constructing representations
on several levels, and student readers, even good students, seem to be bogged
down in content: they focus on knowledge-getting while reading.

We believe that teaching students to read rhetorically is genuinely difficult. It  50
is difficult in the way that teaching students to *write* rhetorically is difficult. In
fact, this work with student and experienced *readers* provides a potential parallel to research results with student and expert *writers*. While expert writers,
like those Flower, Hayes, Shriver, Carey, and Haas have studied, work within a
rhetorical framework—imagining audience response, acknowledging context,
and setting their own purposeful goals—student writers often concentrate on
content and information—they "knowledge tell," in Bereiter and Scardamalia's
terms. Similarly, these student readers seem to concentrate on knowledge, content, what the text is about—not taking into account that the text is the product of a writer's intentions and is designed to produce an effect on a specific
audience.

While experienced readers may understand that both reading and writing 51 are context-rich, situational, constructive acts, many students may see reading and writing as merely an information exchange: knowledge-telling when they write, and "knowledge-getting" when they read. Helping students move beyond this simple, information-exchange view to a more complex rhetorical model—in both their reading and their writing—is one of the very real tasks which faces us as teachers. And research with real readers and writers continues to offer insights into the equally complex ways all of us construct meaning.

## Works Cited

Baker, Linda, and Ann L. Brown. "Metacognitive Skills and Reading." *Handbook of Reading Research*. Ed. R. Barr, Michael L. Kamil, and Peter Mosenthal. New York: Longman, 1984. 353–94.

Bereiter, Carl, and Marlene Scardamalia. "Cognitive Coping Strategies and the Problem of Inert Knowledge." *Learning and Thinking Skills: Research and Open Questions*. Ed. Susan Chipman, J. Segal, and Robert Glaser. Hillsdale, NJ: Lawrence Erlbaum Associates, 1985. 65–80.

Bransford, John. *Cognition: Learning, Understanding and Remembering*. Belmont, CA: Wadsworth Publishing Company, 1979.

Farnham-Diggory, Sylvia. *Cognitive Processes in Education: A Psychological Preparation for Teaching and Curriculum Development*. New York: Harper and Row, 1972.

Flower, Linda. "The Construction of Purpose in Writing and Reading." *College English* 50 (1988): 528–50.

Flower, Linda. "Interpretive Acts: Cognition and the Construction of Discourse." *Poetics* 16 (April 1987): 109–30.

Flower, Linda, and John R. Hayes. "Images, Plans, and Prose: The Representation of Meaning in Writing." *Written Communication* 1 (January 1984): 120–60.

Flower, Linda, John R. Hayes, Karen Shriver, Linda Carey, and Christina Haas. *Planning in Writing: A Theory of the Cognitive Process*. ONR Technical Report # 1. Pittsburgh: Carnegie Mellon, 1987.

Haas, Christina, and John R. Hayes. "What Did I Just Say? Reading Problems in Writing with the Machine." *Research in the Teaching of English* 20 (February 1986): 22–35.

Scardamalia, Marlene. "How Children Cope with the Cognitive Demands of Writing." *Writing: The Nature, Development, and Teaching of Written Communication (Vol. 2)*. Ed. Carl Frederiksen, M. F. Whiteman, and J. F. Dominic. Hillsdale, NJ: Lawrence Erlbaum Associates, 1981. 81–103.

Spivey, Nancy N. "Construing Constructivism: Reading Research in the United States." *Poetics* 16 (April 1987): 169–93.

Tierney, Robert, and P. David Pearson. "Toward a Composing Model of Reading." *Composing and Comprehending*. Ed. Julie M. Jensen. Urbana, IL: NCTE, 1984. 33–45.

Vipond, Douglas, and Russell Hunt. "Point-driven Understanding: Pragmatic and Cognitive Dimensions of Literary Reading." *Poetics* 13 (June 1984): 261–77.

..................................................................................................

## Questions for Discussion and Journaling

1. What are Haas and Flower trying to find out by doing this research? Why do they want to find it out?

2. Haas and Flower spend a lot of time pointing out that readers "construct" "representations" of a text's content and what it means. Why is this particular language of

construction and representation so important to them? How is it different from the ways in which we usually talk about what happens when readers read?

3. One claim this article makes is that when readers try to understand texts, they bring their own knowledge to them. What kinds of knowledge did you bring to this article that helped you make sense of it?

4. Haas and Flower seem to criticize reading that's merely for "information exchange." Why? What do they consider inadequate about using readings simply to convey information?

5. What does it mean to see texts "as purposeful actions" (para. 12)? What are some examples you've seen of texts that serve as actions?

6. Consider how Haas and Flower went about answering their research questions. What were some advantages and some drawbacks to their methods? What do you think might be the biggest weakness of their approach? How would you have done it?

7. Think back to the last time someone gave you some instruction in how to read. When was it? What were you taught? What differences are there between what you were taught and what Haas and Flower say is important to teach about reading?

8. Can you identify instances in the past where you've been a rhetorical reader? If so, what were you reading? How was it similar to and different from your usual reading practice?

## Applying and Exploring Ideas

1. Use a text your teacher gives you to conduct your own read-aloud/think-aloud experiment. After recording yourself reading the text and stopping at predetermined points to talk about how you understand the text at that moment, listen to your recording and try to find patterns that describe how you read and understand while reading. Then write a three- to four-page report discussing what you've learned.

2. Write a summary of Haas and Flower's article that discusses the following: Why was it written? Who was meant to read it (and how can you tell)? What do Haas and Flower seem to be trying to *do* with the article? If you have read Grant-Davie, you will recognize that part of what you are being asked to do here is identify the *rhetorical situation*. How can your understanding of the text be improved by identifying the rhetorical situation?

3. Make a list of the rhetorical reading strategies that Haas and Flower discuss, trying to include even those they only imply without explicitly stating. Use this list to help you write a set of instructions on reading rhetorically for the next group of students who will take the class you're in now. What should they look for in texts? What questions should they ask about texts to ensure they're reading rhetorically?

4. Locate a text that seems to be purely *informational* (like an instruction manual or directions for taking the SAT). Reading it rhetorically—that is, trying to understand the motivation of the writer and the audience's needs—can you find aspects of the text that go beyond information to claims, opinion, and argument?

### Meta Moment

How can you benefit from knowing the results of Haas and Flower's study? How does reading and understanding this article help you achieve the goals of this chapter?

# Helping Students Use Textual Sources Persuasively

## MARGARET KANTZ

■ Kantz, Margaret. "Helping Students Use Textual Sources Persuasively."
*College English* 52.1 (1990): 74–91. Print.

## Framing the Reading

Given this chapter's focus on rhetoric, several of its pieces suggest writing and reading are not just about transmitting and receiving information. Texts don't mean the same thing to every reader because, as rhetorical theory shows, readers *construct* meaning by *interacting* with texts, putting something of themselves into the text and drawing meaning from the text's **context**.

Margaret Kantz's work takes us to the next logical step, in discussing how it is that we write a new text from other existing texts. In Kantz's article we follow the learning experiences of a particular student, Shirley. Whereas Shirley had been taught in high school that "research" meant compiling facts and transmitting them to a teacher, she must now learn to use a variety of conflicting sources to make an original **argument** on the subject she's researching. Kantz analyzes how Shirley has moved from the realm of *reporting* "just the facts" to the more sophisticated world of *arguing about what the facts might be*, and she shows readers how many new ideas are involved in that change.

A key concept in this change is learning to recognize that facts aren't so much inherently true statements as they are **claims**—that is, assertions that most of a given **audience** has *agreed* are true because for that audience sufficient proof has already been given. You, like most people, would probably classify the statement "the Earth is round" as a "fact." Its status as a fact, however, depends on our mutual agreement that "round" is an adequate description of the Earth's actual, imperfectly spherical shape. What Kantz wants us to see is that what makes the statement a fact is not how "true" the statement is but that most people have *agreed* that it's true and treat it as true. Statements about which we haven't reached this consensus remain *claims*, statements that people *argue* about. Kantz's work here demonstrates why it's so important to read texts—even "factual" works like textbooks and encyclopedias—as consisting of claims, not facts.

This idea that textbooks and other "factual" texts aren't inherently true but instead simply represent a *consensus of opinion* is a major conceptual change from the way most students are taught in school before college. It is also a major implication of rhetorical theory. Like the ideas that writing is always personal

(not purely factual and objective), which you encountered if you read Murray's article in Chapter 1 (p. 66), and Haas and Flower's findings (in this chapter, p. 411) about how different readers construct their own meanings from texts, the idea of truth built through consensus stems from rhetoric's qualities of being **situated** and **epistemic**, knowledge-*making*. Rhetorical theory suggests that people are limited to subjective, partial knowledge formed through consensus because we are embedded in particular moments—we can never see an issue from every angle or perspective simultaneously, leaving our knowledge incomplete and provisional. It is this idea that Kantz is working on in exploring the difference between facts and claims.

While Kantz wrote this piece as a professor at Central Missouri State University, she conducted the research for it as a graduate student at Carnegie Mellon University. One of her professors there was Linda Flower and one of her classmates was Christina Haas, whose names you might have noticed earlier in this chapter (and, if you pay close attention, in Kantz's Works Cited list). We make this point to remind you that texts are authored by real people, and these people are often connected both inside and outside of their texts.

## Getting Ready to Read

*Before you read*, do at least one of the following activities:

- Think about an argument you've had recently in which people disagreed about the facts of the issue. How did you resolve the factual dispute? Did the arguers ever agree on what the facts were? If not, how was the argument resolved?
- Write down, in a few quick sentences, how *you* define these terms: *fact, claim, opinion*, and *argument*.
- Watch three TV commercials (you might want to record them) and count the number of *facts* and the number of *claims* in each. Then think about what's most persuasive in the ads: the facts, the claims, or the combination of the two?

*As you read* Kantz's article, consider the following questions:

- How does Kantz know what she knows? What is the basis for her claims?
- What is Kantz's research question or problem? What does she want to know, or what is she trying to solve?
- What challenges do the students about whom Kantz writes face in making sense of conflicting sources?

Although the researched essay as a topic has been much written about, it has been little studied. In the introduction to their bibliography, Ford, Rees, and Ward point out that most of the over 200 articles about researched essays published in professional journals in the last half century describe classroom methods. "Few," they say, "are of a theoretical nature or based on research, and almost none cites even one other work on the subject" (2). Given Ford and Perry's finding that 84% of freshman composition programs and 40% of advanced composition programs included instruction in writing research papers, more theoretical work seems needed. We need a theory-based explanation, one grounded in the findings of the published research on the nature and reasons for our students' problems with writing persuasive researched papers. To understand how to teach students to write such papers, we also need a better understanding of the demands of synthesis tasks.

> *We need a theory-based explanation, one grounded in the findings of the published research on the nature and reasons for our students' problems with writing persuasive researched papers.*

As an example for discussing this complex topic, I have used a typical college sophomore. This student is a composite derived from published research, from my own memories of being a student, and from students whom I have taught at an open admissions community college and at both public and private universities. I have also used a few examples taken from my own students, all of whom share many of Shirley's traits. Shirley, first of all, is intelligent and well-motivated. She is a native speaker of English. She has no extraordinary knowledge deficits or emotional problems. She comes from a home where education is valued, and her parents do reading and writing tasks at home and at their jobs. Shirley has certain skills. When she entered first grade, she knew how to listen to and tell stories, and she soon became proficient at reading stories and at writing narratives. During her academic life, Shirley has learned such studying skills as finding the main idea and remembering facts. In terms of the relevant research, Shirley can read and summarize source texts accurately (cf. Spivey; Winograd). She can select material that is relevant for her purpose in writing (Hayes, Waterman, and Robinson; Langer). She can make connections between the available information and her purpose for writing, including the needs of her readers when the audience is specified (Atlas). She can make original connections among ideas (Brown and Day; Langer). She can create an appropriate, audience-based structure for her paper (Spivey), take notes and use them effectively while composing her paper (Kennedy), and she can present information clearly and smoothly (Spivey), without relying on the phrasing of the original sources (Atlas; Winograd). Shirley is, in my experience, a typical college student with an average academic preparation.

Although Shirley seems to have everything going for her, she experiences difficulty with assignments that require her to write original papers based on textual sources. In particular, Shirley is having difficulty in her sophomore-level writing class. Shirley, who likes English history, decided to write about the Battle of Agincourt (this part of Shirley's story is biographical). She found half a dozen histories that described the circumstances of the battle in a few pages each. Although the topic was unfamiliar, the sources agreed on many of the facts. Shirley collated these facts into her own version, noting but not discussing discrepant details, borrowing what she assumed to be her sources' purpose of retelling the story, and modelling the narrative structure of her paper on that of her sources. Since the only comments Shirley could think of would be to agree or disagree with her sources, who had told her everything she knew about the Battle of Agincourt, she did not comment on the material; instead, she concentrated on telling the story clearly and more completely than her sources had done. She was surprised when her paper received a grade of C–. (Page 1 of Shirley's paper is given as Appendix A.)

Although Shirley is a hypothetical student whose case is based on a real 4 event, her difficulties are typical of undergraduates at both private and public colleges and universities. In a recent class of Intermediate Composition in which the students were instructed to create an argument using at least four textual sources that took differing points of view, one student, who analyzed the coverage of a recent championship football game, ranked her source articles in order from those whose approach she most approved to those she least approved. Another student analyzed various approaches taken by the media to the Kent State shootings in 1970, and was surprised and disappointed to find that all of the sources seemed slanted, either by the perspective of the reporter or by that of the people interviewed. Both students did not understand why their instructor said that their papers lacked a genuine argument.

The task of writing researched papers that express original arguments pre- 5 sents many difficulties. Besides the obvious problems of citation format and coordination of source materials with the emerging written product, writing a synthesis can vary in difficulty according to the number and length of the sources, the abstractness or familiarity of the topic, the uses that the writer must make of the material, the degree and quality of original thought required, and the extent to which the sources will supply the structure and purpose of the new paper. It is usually easier to write a paper that uses all of only one short source on a familiar topic than to write a paper that selects material from many long sources on a topic that one must learn as one reads and writes. It is easier to quote than to paraphrase, and it is easier to build the paraphrases, without comment or with random comments, into a description of what one found than it is to use them as evidence in an original argument. It is easier to use whatever one likes, or everything one finds, than to formally select, evaluate, and interpret material. It is easier to use the structure and purpose of a source as the basis for one's paper than it is to create a structure or an original purpose. A writing-from-sources task can be as simple as collating a body of facts from a few short texts on a familiar topic into a new text that reproduces the structure, tone, and purpose of the originals, but it can also involve applying abstract concepts from one area to an original problem in a different area, a task that involves learning the relationships among materials as a paper is created that may refer to its sources without resembling them.

Moreover, a given task can be interpreted as requiring an easy method, a 6 difficult method, or any of a hundred intermediate methods. In this context, Flower has observed, "The different ways in which students [represent] a 'standard' reading-to-write task to themselves lead to markedly different goals and strategies as well as different organizing plans" (*Role* iii). To write a synthesis,

Shirley may or may not need to quote, summarize, or select material from her sources; to evaluate the sources for bias, accuracy, or completeness; to develop original ideas; or to persuade a reader. How well she performs any of these tasks—and whether she thinks to perform these tasks—depends on how she reads the texts and on how she interprets the assignment. Shirley's representation of the task, which in this case was easier than her teacher had in mind, depends on the goals that she sets for herself. The goals that she sets depend on her awareness of the possibilities and her confidence in her writing skills.

7 Feeling unhappy about her grade, Shirley consulted her friend Alice. Alice, who is an expert, looked at the task in a completely different way and used strategies for thinking about it that were quite different from Shirley's.

8 "Who were your sources?" asked Alice. "Winston Churchill, right? A French couple and a few others. And they didn't agree about the details, such as the sizes of the armies. Didn't you wonder why?"

9 "No," said Shirley. "I thought the history books would know the truth. When they disagreed, I figured that they were wrong on those points. I didn't want to have anything in my paper that was wrong."

10 "But Shirley," said Alice, "you could have thought about why a book entitled *A History of France* might present a different view of the battle than a book subtitled *A History of British Progress*. You could have asked if the English and French writers wanted to make a point about the history of their countries and looked to see if the factual differences suggested anything. You could even have talked about Shakespeare's *Henry V*, which I know you've read—about how he presents the battle, or about how the King Henry in the play differs from the Henrys in your other books. You would have had an angle, a problem. Dr. Boyer would have loved it."

11 Alice's representation of the task would have required Shirley to formally select and evaluate her material and to use it as proof in an original argument. Alice was suggesting that Shirley invent an original problem and purpose for her paper and create an original structure for her argument. Alice's task is much more sophisticated than Shirley's. Shirley replied, "That would take me a year to do! Besides, Henry was a real person. I don't want to make up things about him."

12 "Well," said Alice, "You're dealing with facts, so there aren't too many choices. If you want to say something original you either have to talk about the sources or talk about the material. What could you say about the material? Your paper told about all the reasons King Henry wasn't expected to win the battle. Could you have argued that he should have lost because he took too many chances?"

13 "Gee," said Shirley, "That's awesome. I wish I'd thought of it."

14 This version of the task would allow Shirley to keep the narrative structure of her paper but would give her an original argument and purpose. To write the argument, Shirley would have only to rephrase the events of the story to take an opposite approach from that of her English sources, emphasizing what she perceived as Henry's mistakes and inserting comments to explain why his decisions were mistakes—an easy argument to write. She could also, if she wished, write a conclusion that criticized the cheerleading tone of her British sources.

As this anecdote makes clear, a given topic can be treated in more or less 15
sophisticated ways—and sophisticated goals, such as inventing an original purpose and evaluating sources, can be achieved in relatively simple versions of a
task. Students have many options as to how they can fulfill even a specific task
(cf. Jeffery). Even children can decide whether to process a text deeply or not,
and purpose in reading affects processing and monitoring of comprehension
(Brown). Pichert has shown that reading purpose affects judgments about what
is important or unimportant in a narrative text, and other research tells us that
attitudes toward the author and content of a text affect comprehension (Asch;
Hinze; Shedd; Goldman).

One implication of this story is that the instructor gave a weak assignment 16
and an ineffective critique of the draft (her only comment referred to Shirley's
footnoting technique; cf. Appendix A). The available research suggests that
if Dr. Boyer had set Shirley a specific rhetorical problem such as having her
report on her material to the class and then testing them on it, and if she had
commented on the content of Shirley's paper during the drafts, Shirley might
well have come up with a paper that did more than repeat its source material
(Nelson and Hayes). My teaching experience supports this research finding.
If Dr. Boyer had told Shirley from the outset that she was expected to say
something original and that she should examine her sources as she read them
for discrepant facts, conflicts, or other interesting material, Shirley might have
tried to write an original argument (Kantz, "Originality"). And if Dr. Boyer
had suggested that Shirley use her notes to comment on her sources and make
plans for using the notes, Shirley might have written a better paper than she
did (Kantz, *Relationship*).

Even if given specific directions to create an original argument, Shirley might 17
have had difficulty with the task. Her difficulty could come from any of three
causes: 1) Many students like Shirley misunderstand sources because they read
them as stories. 2) Many students expect their sources to tell the truth; hence,
they equate persuasive writing in this context with making things up. 3) Many
students do not understand that facts are a kind of claim and are often used
persuasively in so-called objective writing to create an impression. Students
need to read source texts as arguments and to think about the rhetorical contexts in which they were written rather than to read them merely as a set of
facts to be learned. Writing an original persuasive argument based on sources
requires students to apply material to a problem or to use it to answer a question, rather than simply to repeat it or evaluate it. These three problems deserve
a separate discussion.

Because historical texts often have a chronological structure, students believe 18
that historians tell stories, and that renarrating the battle casts them as a historian. Because her sources emphasized the completeness of the victory/defeat and
its decisive importance in the history of warfare, Shirley thought that making
these same points in her paper completed her job. Her job as a reader was thus
to learn the story, i.e., so that she could pass a test on it (cf. Vipond and Hunt's
argument that generic expectations affect reading behavior. Vipond and Hunt
would describe Shirley's reading as story-driven rather than point-driven).

Students commonly misread texts as narratives. When students refer to a text-book as "the story," they are telling us that they read for plot and character, regardless of whether their texts are organized as narratives. One reason Shirley loves history is that when she reads it she can combine her story-reading strat-egies with her studying strategies. Students like Shirley may need to learn to apply basic organizing patterns, such as cause-effect and general-to-specific, to their texts. If, however, Dr. Boyer asks Shirley to respond to her sources in a way that is not compatible with Shirley's understanding of what such sources do, Shirley will have trouble doing the assignment. Professors may have to do some preparatory teaching about why certain kinds of texts have certain char-acteristics and what kinds of problems writers must solve as they design text for a particular audience. They may even have to teach a model for the kind of writing they expect.

The writing version of Shirley's problem, which Flower calls "writer-based 19 prose," occurs when Shirley organizes what should be an expository analysis as a narrative, especially when she writes a narrative about how she did her research. Students frequently use time-based organizing patterns, regardless of the task, even when such patterns conflict with what they are trying to say and even when they know how to use more sophisticated strategies. Apparently such common narrative transitional devices such as "the first point" and "the next point" offer a reassuringly familiar pattern for organizing unfamiliar ma-terial. The common strategy of beginning paragraphs with such phrases as "my first source," meaning that it was the first source that the writer found in the library or the first one read, appears to combine a story-of-my-research struc-ture with a knowledge-telling strategy (Bereiter and Scardamalia, *Psychology*). Even when students understand that the assignment asks for more than the fill-in-the-blanks, show-me-you've-read-the-material approach described by Schwegler and Shamoon, they cling to narrative structuring devices. A rank ordering of sources, as with Mary's analysis of the football game coverage with the sources listed in an order of ascending disapproval, represents a step away from storytelling and toward synthesizing because it embodies a persuasive evaluation.

In addition to reading texts as stories, students expect factual texts to tell 20 them "the truth" because they have learned to see texts statically, as descriptions of truths, instead of as arguments. Shirley did not understand that nonfiction texts exist as arguments in rhetorical contexts. "After all," she reasoned, "how can one argue about the date of a battle or the sizes of armies?" Churchill, however, described the battle in much more detail than Shirley's other sources, apparently because he wished to persuade his readers to take pride in England's tradition of military achievement. Guizot and Guizot de Witt, on the other hand, said very little about the battle (beyond describing it as "a monotonous and lamentable repetition of the disasters of Crecy and Poitiers" [397]) because they saw the British invasion as a sneaky way to take advantage of a feud among the various branches of the French royal family. Shirley's story/study skills might not have allowed her to recognize such arguments, especially because Dr. Boyer did not teach her to look for them.

When I have asked students to choose a topic and find three or more sources 21 on it that disagree, I am repeatedly asked, "How can sources disagree in different ways? After all, there's only pro and con." Students expect textbooks and other authoritative sources either to tell them the truth (i.e., facts) or to express an opinion with which they may agree or disagree. Mary's treatment of the football coverage reflects this belief, as does Charlie's surprise when he found that even his most comprehensive sources on the Kent State killings omitted certain facts, such as interviews with National Guardsmen. Students' desire for truth leads them to use a collating approach whenever possible, as Shirley did (cf. Appendix A), because students believe that the truth will include all of the facts and will reconcile all conflicts. (This belief may be another manifestation of the knowledge-telling strategy [Bereiter and Scardamalia, *Psychology*] in which students write down everything they can think of about a topic.) When conflicts cannot be reconciled and the topic does not admit a pro or con stance, students may not know what to say. They may omit the material altogether, include it without comment, as Shirley did, or jumble it together without any plan for building an argument.

The skills that Shirley has practiced for most of her academic career— 22 finding the main idea and learning content—allow her to agree or disagree. She needs a technique for reading texts in ways that give her something more to say, a technique for constructing more complex representations of texts that allow room for more sophisticated writing goals. She also needs strategies for analyzing her reading that allow her to build original arguments.

One way to help students like Shirley is to teach the concept of rhetorical situ- 23 ation. A convenient tool for thinking about this concept is Kinneavy's triangular diagram of the rhetorical situation. Kinneavy, analyzing Aristotle's description of rhetoric, posits that every communicative situation has three parts: a speaker/ writer (the Encoder), an audience (the Decoder), and a topic (Reality) (19). Although all discourse involves all three aspects of communication, a given type of discourse may pertain more to a particular point of the triangle than to the others, e.g., a diary entry may exist primarily to express the thoughts of the writer (the Encoder); an advertisement may exist primarily to persuade a reader (the Decoder). Following Kinneavy, I posit particular goals for each corner of the triangle. Thus, the primary goal of a writer doing writer-based discourse such as a diary might be originality and self-expression; primary goals for reader-based discourse such as advertising might be persuasion; primary goals for topic-based discourse such as a researched essay might be accuracy, completeness, and mastery of subject matter. Since all three aspects of the rhetorical situation are present and active in any communicative situation, a primarily referential text such as Churchill's *The Birth of Britain* may have a persuasive purpose and may depend for some of its credibility on readers' familiarity with the author. The term "rhetorical reading," then (cf. Haas and Flower), means teaching students to read a text as a message sent by someone to somebody for a reason. Shirley, Mary, and Charlie are probably practiced users of rhetorical persuasion in non-academic contexts. They may never have learned to apply this thinking in a conscious and deliberate way to academic tasks (cf. Kroll).

The concept of rhetorical situation offers insight into the nature of students' 24 representations of a writing task. The operative goals in Shirley's and Alice's approaches to the term paper look quite different when mapped onto the points on the triangle. If we think of Shirley and Alice as Encoders, the topic as Reality, and Dr. Boyer as the Decoder, we can see that for Shirley, being an Encoder means trying to be credible; her relationship to the topic (Reality) involves a goal of using all of the subject matter; and her relationship to the Decoder involves an implied goal of telling a complete story to a reader whom Shirley thinks of as an examiner—to use the classic phrase from the famous book by Britton et al.—i.e., a reader who wants to know if Shirley can pass an exam on the subject of the Battle of Agincourt. For Alice, however, being an Encoder means having a goal of saying something new; the topic (Reality) is a resource to be used; and the Decoder is someone who must be persuaded that Alice's ideas have merit. Varying task representations do not change the dimensions of the rhetorical situation: the Encoder, Decoder, and Reality are always present. But the way a writer represents the task to herself does affect the ways that she thinks about those dimensions—and whether she thinks about them at all.

In the context of a research assignment, rhetorical skills can be used to read 25 the sources as well as to design the paper. Although teachers have probably always known that expert readers use such strategies, the concept of rhetorical reading is new to the literature. Haas and Flower have shown that expert readers use rhetorical strategies "to account for author's purpose, context, and effect on the audience . . . to recreate or infer the rhetorical situation of the text" (176; cf. also Bazerman). These strategies, used in addition to formulating main points and paraphrasing content, helped the readers to understand a text more completely and more quickly than did readers who concentrated exclusively on content. As Haas and Flower point out, teaching students to read rhetorically is difficult. They suggest that appropriate pedagogy might include "direct instruction . . . modeling, and . . . encouraging students to become contributing and committed members of rhetorical communities" (182). One early step might be to teach students a set of heuristics based on the three aspects of the communicative triangle. Using such questions could help students set goals for their reading.

In this version of Kinneavy's triangle, the Encoder is the writer of the source 26 text, the Decoder is the student reader, and Reality is the subject matter. Readers may consider only one point of the triangle at a time, asking such questions as "Who are you (i.e., the author/Encoder)?" or "What are the important features of this text?" They may consider two aspects of the rhetorical situation in a single question, e.g., "Am I in your intended (primary) audience?"; "What do I think about this topic?"; "What context affected your ideas and presentation?" Other questions would involve all three points of the triangle, e.g., "What are you saying to help me with the problem you assume I have?" or "What textual devices have you used to manipulate my response?" Asking such questions gives students a way of formulating goals relating to purpose as well as content.

If Shirley, for example, had asked a Decoder-to-Encoder question—such as 27 "Am I in your intended audience?"—she might have realized that Churchill and the Guizots were writing for specific audiences. If she had asked a Decoder-to-Reality question—such as "What context affected your ideas and presentation?"—she might not have ignored Churchill's remark, "All these names [Amiens, Boves, Bethencourt] are well known to our generation" (403). As it was, she missed Churchill's signal that he was writing to survivors of the First World War, who had vainly hoped that it would be a war to end all wars. If Shirley had used an Encoder-Decoder-Reality question—such as "What are you saying to help me with the problem you assume I have?"—she might have understood that the authors of her sources were writing to different readers for different reasons. This understanding might have given her something to say. When I gave Shirley's source texts to freshmen students, asked them to use the material in an original argument, and taught them this heuristic for rhetorical reading, I received, for example, papers that warned undergraduates about national pride as a source of authorial bias in history texts.

A factual topic such as the Battle of Agincourt presents special problems  28
because of the seemingly intransient nature of facts. Like many people, Shirley believes that you can either agree or disagree with issues and opinions, but you can only accept the so-called facts. She believes that facts are what you learn from textbooks, opinions are what you have about clothes, and arguments are what you have with your mother when you want to stay out late at night. Shirley is not in a position to disagree with the facts about the battle (e.g., "No, I think the French won"), and a rhetorical analysis may seem at first to offer minimal rewards (e.g., "According to the Arab, Jewish, and Chinese calendars the date was really . . .").

Alice, who thinks rhetorically, understands that both facts and opinions are  29
essentially the same kind of statement: they are claims. Alice understands that the only essential difference between a fact and an opinion is how they are received by an audience. (This discussion is derived from Toulmin's model of an argument as consisting of claims proved with data and backed by ethical claims called warrants. According to Toulmin, any aspect of an argument may be questioned by the audience and must then be supported with further argument.) In a rhetorical argument, a fact is a claim that an audience will accept as being true without requiring proof, although they may ask for an explanation. An opinion is a claim that an audience will not accept as true without proof, and which, after the proof is given, the audience may well decide has only a limited truth, i.e., it's true in this case but not in other cases. An audience may also decide that even though a fact is unassailable, the interpretation or use of the fact is open to debate.

For example, Shirley's sources gave different numbers for the size of the  30
British army at Agincourt; these numbers, which must have been estimates, were claims masquerading as facts. Shirley did not understand this. She thought that disagreement signified error, whereas it probably signified rhetorical purpose. The probable reason that the Guizots give a relatively large estimate for the English army and do not mention the size of the French army is so that their French readers would find the British victory easier to accept. Likewise, Churchill's relatively small estimate for the size of the English army and his

high estimate for the French army magnify the brilliance of the English victory. Before Shirley could create an argument about the Battle of Agincourt, she needed to understand that, even in her history textbooks, the so-called facts are claims that may or may not be supported, claims made by writers who work in a certain political climate for a particular audience. She may, of course, never learn this truth unless Dr. Boyer teaches her rhetorical theory and uses the research paper as a chance for Shirley to practice rhetorical problem-solving.

For most of her academic life, Shirley has done school tasks that require her  31 to find main ideas and important facts; success in these tasks usually hinges on agreeing with the teacher about what the text says. Such study skills form an essential basis for doing reading-to-write tasks. Obviously a student can only use sources to build an argument if she can first read the sources accurately (cf. Brown and Palincsar; Luftig; Short and Ryan). However, synthesizing tasks often require that readers not accept the authors' ideas. Baker and Brown have pointed out that people misread texts when they blindly accept an author's ideas instead of considering a divergent interpretation. Yet if we want students to learn to build original arguments from texts, we must teach them the skills needed to create divergent interpretations. We must teach them to think about facts and opinions as claims that are made by writers to particular readers for particular reasons in particular historical contexts.

Reading sources rhetorically gives students a powerful tool for creating a  32 persuasive analysis. Although no research exists as yet to suggest that teaching students to read rhetorically will improve their writing, I have seen its effect in successive drafts of students' papers. As mentioned earlier, rhetorical read-ing allowed a student to move from simply summarizing and evaluating her sources on local coverage of the championship football game to constructing a rationale for articles that covered the fans rather than the game. Rhetori-cal analysis enabled another student to move from summarizing his sources to understanding why each report about the Kent State shootings necessarily expressed a bias of some kind.

As these examples suggest, however, rhetorical reading is not a magical  33 technique for producing sophisticated arguments. Even when students read their sources rhetorically, they tend merely to report the results of this analy-sis in their essays. Such writing appears to be a college-level version of the knowledge-telling strategy described by Bereiter and Scardamalia (*Psychology*) and may be, as they suggest, the product of years of exposure to pedagogical practices that enshrine the acquisition and expression of information without a context or purpose.

To move students beyond merely reporting the content and rhetorical orien-  34 tation of their source texts, I have taught them the concept of the rhetorical gap and some simple heuristic questions for thinking about gaps. Gaps were first described by Iser as unsaid material that a reader must supply to infer from a text. McCormick expanded the concept to include gaps between the text and the reader; such gaps could involve discrepancies of values, social conven-tions, language, or any other matter that readers must consider. If we apply the concept of gaps to Kinneavy's triangle, we see that in reading, for example, a gap may occur between the Encoder-Decoder corners when the reader is not a member of the author's intended audience. Shirley fell into such a gap. Another gap can occur between the Decoder-Reality corners when a reader disagrees with or does not understand the text. A third gap can occur between the Encoder-Reality points of the triangle if the writer has misrepresented or misunderstood the material. The benefit of teaching this concept is that when a student thinks about a writer's rhetorical stance, she may ask "Why does he think that way?" When a student encounters a gap, she may ask, "What effect does it have on the success of this communication?" The answers to both questions give students original material for their papers.

Shirley, for example, did not know that Churchill began writing *The Birth*   35
*of Britain* during the 1930s, when Hitler was rearming Germany and when the British government and most of Churchill's readers ardently favored disarmament. Had she understood the rhetorical orientation of the book, which was published eleven years after the end of World War II, she might have argued that Churchill's evocation of past military glories would have been inflammatory in the 1930s but was highly acceptable twenty years later. A gap between the reader and the text (Decoder-Reality) might stimulate a reader to investigate whether or not she is the only person having this problem; a gap between other readers and the sources may motivate an adaptation or explanation of the material to a particular audience. Shirley might have adapted the Guizots' perspective on the French civil war for American readers. A gap between the author and the material (Encoder-Reality) might motivate a refutation.

To discover gaps, students may need to learn heuristics for setting rhetorical   36
writing goals. That is, they may need to learn to think of the paper, not as a re-hash of the available material, but as an opportunity to teach someone, to solve someone's problem, or to answer someone's question. The most salient questions for reading source texts may be "Who are you (the original audience of Decoders)?"; "What is your question or problem with this topic?"; and "How have I (the Encoder) used these materials to answer your question or solve your problem?" More simply, these questions may be learned as "Why," "How," and "So what?" When Shirley learns to read sources as telling not the eternal truth but a truth to a particular audience and when she learns to think of texts as existing to solve problems, she will find it easier to think of things to say.

For example, a sophomore at a private university was struggling with an as-   37
signment that required her to analyze an issue and express an opinion on it, using two conflicting source texts, an interview, and personal material as sources. Using rhetorical reading strategies, this girl discovered a gap between Alfred Marbaise, a high school principal who advocates mandatory drug testing of all high school students, and students like those he would be testing:

> Marbaise, who was a lieutenant in the U.S. Marines over thirty years ago . . . makes it very obvious that he cannot and will not tolerate any form of drug abuse in his school. For example, in paragraph seven he claims, "When students become involved in illegal activity, whether they realize it or not, they are violating other students . . . then I become very, very concerned . . . and I will not tolerate that."

Because Marbaise has not been in school for nearly forty years himself, he does not take into consideration the reasons why kids actually use drugs. Today the social environment is so drastically different that Marbaise cannot understand a kid's morality, and that is why he writes from such a fatherly but distant point of view.

The second paragraph answers the So what? question, i.e., "Why does it matter that Marbaise seems by his age and background to be fatherly and distant?" Unless the writer/reader thinks to ask this question, she will have difficulty writing a coherent evaluation of Marbaise's argument.

The relative success of some students in finding original things to say about    38
their topics can help us to understand the perennial problem of plagiarism. Some plagiarism derives, I think, from a weak, nonrhetorical task representation. If students believe they are supposed to reproduce source material in their papers, or if they know they are supposed to say something original but have no rhetorical problem to solve and no knowledge of how to find problems that they can discuss in their sources, it becomes difficult for them to avoid plagiarizing. The common student decision to buy a paper when writing the assignment seems a meaningless fill-in-the-blanks activity (cf. Schwegler and Shamoon) becomes easily understandable. Because rhetorical reading leads to discoveries about the text, students who use it may take more interest in their research papers.

Let us now assume that Shirley understands the importance of creating an    39
original argument, knows how to read analytically, and has found things to say about the Battle of Agincourt. Are her troubles over? Will she now create that A paper that she yearns to write? Probably not. Despite her best intentions, Shirley will probably write another narrative/paraphrase of her sources. Why? Because by now, the assignment asks her to do far more than she can handle in a single draft. Shirley's task representation is now so rich, her set of goals so many, that she may be unable to juggle them all simultaneously. Moreover, the rhetorical reading technique requires students to discover content worth writing about and a rhetorical purpose for writing; the uncertainty of managing such a discovery task when a grade is at stake may be too much for Shirley.

Difficult tasks may be difficult in either (or both of) two ways. First, they    40
may require students to do a familiar subtask, such as reading sources, at a higher level of difficulty, e.g., longer sources, more sources, a more difficult topic. Second, they may require students to do new subtasks, such as building notes into an original argument. Such tasks may require task management skills, especially planning, that students have never developed and do not know how to attempt. The insecurity that results from trying a complex new task in a high-stakes situation is increased when students are asked to discover a problem worth writing about because such tasks send students out on a treasure hunt with no guarantee that the treasure exists, that they will recognize it when they find it, or that when they find it they will be able to build it into a coherent argument. The paper on Marbaise quoted above earned a grade of D because the writer could not use her rhetorical insights to build an argument presented

in a logical order. Although she asked the logical question about the implications of Marbaise's persona, she did not follow through by evaluating the gaps in his perspective that might affect the probable success of his program.

A skillful student using the summarize-the-main-ideas approach can set 41 her writing goals and even plan (i.e., outline) a paper before she reads the sources. The rhetorical reading strategy, by contrast, requires writers to discover what is worth writing about and to decide how to say it as or after they read their sources. The strategy requires writers to change their content goals and to adjust their writing plans as their understanding of the topic develops. It requires writers, in Flower's term, to "construct" their purposes for writing as well as the content for their paper (for a description of constructive planning, see Flower, Schriver, Carey, Haas, and Hayes). In Flower's words, writers who construct a purpose, as opposed to writers who bring a predetermined purpose to a task, "create a web of purposes . . . set goals, toss up possibilities . . . create a multidimensional network of information . . . a web of purpose . . . a bubbling stew of various mental representations" (531–32). The complex indeterminacy of such a task may pose an intimidating challenge to students who have spent their lives summarizing main ideas and reporting facts.

Shirley may respond to the challenge by concentrating her energies on a famil- 42 iar subtask, e.g., repeating material about the Battle of Agincourt, at the expense of struggling with an unfamiliar subtask such as creating an original argument. She may even deliberately simplify the task by representing it to herself as calling only for something that she knows how to do, expecting that Dr. Boyer will accept the paper as close enough to the original instructions. My students do this frequently. When students decide to write a report of their reading, they can at least be certain that they will find material to write about.

Because of the limits of attentional memory, not to mention those caused by 43 inexperience, writers can handle only so many task demands at a time. Thus, papers produced by seemingly inadequate task representations may well be essentially rough drafts. What looks like a bad paper may well be a preliminary step, a way of meeting certain task demands in order to create a basis for thinking about new ones. My students consistently report that they need to marshal all of their ideas and text knowledge and get that material down on the page (i.e., tell their knowledge) before they can think about developing an argument (i.e., transform their knowledge). If Shirley's problem is that she has shelved certain task demands in favor of others, Dr. Boyer needs only to point out what Shirley should do to bring the paper into conformity with the assignment and offer Shirley a chance to revise.

The problems of cognitive overload and inexperience in handling complex 44 writing tasks can create a tremendous hurdle for students because so many of them believe that they should be able to write their paper in a single draft. Some students think that if they can't do the paper in one draft that means that something is wrong with them as writers, or with the assignment, or with us for giving the assignment. Often, such students will react to their drafts with anger and despair, throwing away perfectly usable rough drafts and then coming to us and saying that they can't do the assignment.

The student's first draft about drug testing told her knowledge about her sources' opinions on mandatory drug testing. Her second draft contained the rhetorical analysis quoted above, but presented the material in a scrambled order and did not build the analysis into an argument. Only in a third draft was this student able to make her point:

> Not once does Marbaise consider any of the psychological reasons why kids turn away from reality. He fails to realize that drug testing will not answer their questions, ease their frustrations, or respond to their cries for attention, but will merely further alienate himself and other authorities from helping kids deal with their real problems.

This comment represents Terri's answer to the heuristic "So what? Why does the source's position matter?" If we pace our assignments to allow for our students' thoughts to develop, we can do a great deal to build their confidence in their writing (Terri raised her D+ to an A). If we treat the researched essay as a sequence of assignments instead of as a one-shot paper with a single due date, we can teach our students to build on their drafts, to use what they can do easily as a bridge to what we want them to learn to do. In this way, we can improve our students' writing habits. More importantly, however, we can help our students to see themselves as capable writers and as active, able, problem-solvers. Most importantly, we can use the sequence of drafts to demand that our students demonstrate increasingly sophisticated kinds of analytic and rhetorical proficiency.

Rhetorical reading and writing heuristics can help students to represent tasks in rich and interesting ways. They can help students to set up complex goal structures (Bereiter and Scardamalia, "Conversation"). They offer students many ways to think about their reading and writing texts. These tools, in other words, encourage students to work creatively.

And after all, creativity is what research should be about. If Shirley writes a creative paper, she has found a constructive solution that is new to her and which other people can use, a solution to a problem that she and other people share. Creativity is an inherently rhetorical quality. If we think of it as thought leading to solutions to problems and of problems as embodied in questions that people ask about situations, the researched essay offers infinite possibilities. Viewed in this way, a creative idea answers a question that the audience or any single reader wants answered. The question could be, "Why did Henry V win the Battle of Agincourt?" or, "How can student readers protect themselves against nationalistic bias when they study history?" or any of a thousand other questions. If we teach our Shirleys to see themselves as scholars who work to find answers to problem questions, and if we teach them to set reading and writing goals for themselves that will allow them to think constructively, we will be doing the most exciting work that teachers can do, nurturing creativity.

## Appendix A: Page 1 of Shirley's paper

The battle of Agincourt ranks as one of England's greatest military triumphs. It was the most brilliant victory of the Middle Ages, bar none. It was fought on October 25, 1414, against the French near the French village of Agincourt.

Henry V had claimed the crown of France and had invaded France with an army estimated at anywhere ~~between~~ *from* 10,000[1] ~~and~~ *to* 45,000 men[2]. During the seige of Marfleur dysentery had taken (1/3) of them[3], his food supplies had been depleted[4], and the fall rains had begun. In addition the French had assembled a huge army and were marching toward him. Henry decided to march to Calais, where his ships were to await him[5]. He intended to cross the River Somme at the ford of Blanchetaque[6], but, falsely informed that the ford was guarded[7], he was forced to follow the flooded Somme up toward its source. The French army was shadowing him on his right. Remembering the slaughters of Crecy and Poictiers, the French constable, Charles d'Albret, hesitated to fight[8], but when Henry forded the Somme just above Amiens[9] and was just

---

1. Carl Stephinson, Medieval History, p. 529.
2. (Guizot, Monsieur and Guizot, Madame) World's Best Histories-France, Volume II, p. 211.
3. Cyrid E. Robinson, England-A History of British Progress, p. 145.
4. Ibid.
5. Winston Churchill, A History of the English-Speaking Peoples, Volume I: The Birth of Britain, p. 403.
6. Ibid.
7. Ibid.
8. Robinson, p. 145.
9. Churchill, p. 403.

*You footnote material that does not need to be footnoted.*

## Works Cited

Asch, Solomon. *Social Psychology.* New York: Prentice, 1952.

Atlas, Marshall. *Expert-Novice Differences in the Writing Process.* Paper presented at the American Educational Research Association, 1979. ERIC ED 107 769.

Baker, Louise, and Ann L. Brown. "Metacognitive Skills and Reading." *Handbook of Reading Research*. Eds. P. David Person, Rebecca Barr, Michael L. Kamil, and Peter Mosenthal. New York: Longman, 1984.

Bazerman, Charles. "Physicists Reading Physics: Schema-Laden Purposes and Purpose-Laden Schema." *Written Communication* 2.1 (1985): 3–24.

Bereiter, Carl, and Marlene Scardamalia. "From Conversation to Composition: The Role of Instruction in a Developmental Process." *Advances in Instructional Psychology*. Ed. R. Glaser. Vol. 2. Hillsdale, NJ: Lawrence Erlbaum Associates, 1982. 1–64.

———. *The Psychology of Written Composition*. Hillsdale, NJ: Lawrence Erlbaum Associates, 1987.

Briscoe, Terri. "To test or not to test." Unpublished essay. Texas Christian University, 1989.

Britton, James, Tony Burgess, Nancy Martin, Alex McLeod, and Harold Rosen. *The Development of Writing Abilities (11–18)*. Houndmills Basingstoke Hampshire: Macmillan Education Ltd., 1975.

Brown, Ann L. "Theories of Memory and the Problem of Development: Activity, Growth, and Knowledge." *Levels of Processing in Memory*. Eds. Laird S. Cermak and Fergus I. M. Craik. Hillsdale, NJ: Laurence Erlbaum Associates, 1979. 225–258.

———, Joseph C. Campione, and L. R. Barclay. *Training Self-Checking Routines for Estimating Test Readiness: Generalizations from List Learning to Prose Recall*. Unpublished manuscript. University of Illinois, 1978.

——— and Jeanne Day. "Macrorules for Summarizing Texts: The Development of Expertise." *Journal of Verbal Learning and Verbal Behavior* 22.1(1983): 1–14.

——— and Annmarie S. Palincsar. *Reciprocal Teaching of Comprehension Strategies: A Natural History of One Program for Enhancing Learning*. Technical Report #334. Urbana, IL: Center for the Study of Reading, 1985.

Churchill, Winston S. *The Birth of Britain*, New York: Dodd, 1956. Vol. 1 of *A History of the English-Speaking Peoples*. 4 vols. 1956–58.

Flower, Linda. "The Construction of Purpose in Writing and Reading." *College English* 50.5 (1988): 528–550.

———. *The Role of Task Representation in Reading to Write*. Berkeley, CA: Center for the Study of Writing, U of California at Berkeley and Carnegie Mellon. Technical Report, 1987.

———. "Writer-Based Prose: A Cognitive Basis for Problems in Writing." *College English* 41 (1979): 19–37.

Flower, Linda, Karen Schriver, Linda Carey, Christina Haas, and John R. Hayes. *Planning in Writing: A Theory of the Cognitive Process*. Berkeley, CA: Center for the Study of Writing, U of California at Berkeley and Carnegie Mellon. Technical Report, 1988.

Ford, James E., and Dennis R. Perry. "Research Paper Instruction in the Undergraduate Writing Program." *College English* 44 (1982): 825–31.

Ford, James E., Sharla Rees, and David L. Ward. *Teaching the Research Paper: Comprehensive Bibliography of Periodical Sources*, 1980. ERIC ED 197 363.

Goldman, Susan R. "Knowledge Systems for Realistic Goals." *Discourse Processes* 5 (1982): 279–303.

Guizot and Guizot de Witt. *The History of France from Earliest Times to 1848*. Trans. R. Black. Vol. 2. Philadelphia: John Wanamaker (n.d.).

Haas, Christina, and Linda Flower. "Rhetorical Reading Strategies and the Construction of Meaning." *College Composition and Communication* 39 (1988): 167–84.

Hayes, John R., D. A. Waterman, and C. S. Robinson. "Identifying the Relevant Aspects of a Problem Text." *Cognitive Science* 1 (1977): 297–313.

Hinze, Helen K. "The Individual's Word Associations and His Interpretation of Prose Paragraphs." *Journal of General Psychology* 64 (1961): 193–203.

Iser, Wolfgang. *The act of reading: A theory of aesthetic response*. Baltimore: The Johns Hopkins UP, 1978.

Jeffery, Christopher. "Teachers' and Students' Perceptions of the Writing Process." *Research in the Teaching of English* 15 (1981): 215–28.

Kantz, Margaret. "Originality and Completeness: What Do We Value in Papers Written from Sources?" Conference on College Composition and Communication. St. Louis, MO, 1988.

———. *The Relationship Between Reading and Planning Strategies and Success in Synthesizing: It's What You Do with Them that Counts.* Technical report in preparation. Pittsburgh: Center for the Study of Writing, 1988.

Kennedy, Mary Louise. "The Composing Process of College Students Writing from Sources," *Written Communication* 2.4 (1985): 434–56.

Kinneavy, James L. *A Theory of Discourse.* New York: Norton, 1971.

Kroll, Barry M. "Audience Adaptation in Children's Persuasive Letters." *Written Communication* 1.4 (1984): 407–28.

Langer, Judith. "Where Problems Start: The Effects of Available Information on Responses to School Writing Tasks." *Contexts for Learning to Write: Studies of Secondary School Instruction.* Ed. Arthur Applebee. Norwood, NJ: ABLEX Publishing Corporation, 1984. 135–48.

Luftig, Richard L. "Abstractive Memory, the Central-Incidental Hypothesis, and the Use of Structural Importance in Text: Control Processes or Structural Features?" *Reading Research Quarterly* 14.1 (1983): 28–37.

Marbaise, Alfred. "Treating a Disease." *Current Issues and Enduring Questions.* Eds. Sylvan Barnet and Hugo Bedau. New York: St. Martin's, 1987. 126–27.

McCormick, Kathleen. "Theory in the Reader: Bleich, Holland, and Beyond." *College English* 47.8 (1985): 836–50.

McGarry, Daniel D. *Medieval History and Civilization.* New York: Macmillan, 1976.

Nelson, Jennie, and John R. Hayes. *The Effects of Classroom Contexts on Students' Responses to Writing from Sources: Regurgitating Information or Triggering Insights.* Berkeley, CA: Center for the Study of Writing, U of California at Berkeley and Carnegie Mellon. Technical Report, 1988.

Pichert, James W. "Sensitivity to Importance as a Predictor of Reading Comprehension." *Perspectives on Reading Research and Instruction.* Eds. Michael A. Kamil and Alden J. Moe. Washington, D.C.: National Reading Conference, 1980. 42–46.

Robinson, Cyril E. *England: A History of British Progress from the Early Ages to the Present Day.* New York: Thomas Y. Crowell Company, 1928.

Schwegler, Robert A., and Linda K. Shamoon. "The Aims and Process of the Research Paper." *College English* 44 (1982): 817–24.

Shedd, Patricia T. "The Relationship between Attitude of the Reader Towards Women's Changing Role and Response to Literature Which Illuminates Women's Role." Diss. Syracuse U, 1975. ERIC ED 142 956.

Short, Elizabeth Jane, and Ellen Bouchard Ryan. "Metacognitive Differences between Skilled and Less Skilled Readers: Remediating Deficits through Story Grammar and Attribution Training." *Journal of Education Psychology* 76 (1984): 225–35.

Spivey, Nancy Nelson. *Discourse Synthesis: Constructing Texts in Reading and Writing.* Diss. U Texas, 1983. Newark, DE: International Reading Association, 1984.

Toulmin, Steven E. *The Uses of Argument.* Cambridge: Cambridge UP, 1969.

Vipond, Douglas, and Russell Hunt. "Point-Driven Understanding: Pragmatic and Cognitive Dimensions of Literary Reading." *Poetics* 13, (1984): 261–77.

Winograd, Peter. "Strategic Difficulties in Summarizing Texts." *Reading Research Quarterly* 19 (1984): 404–25.

## Questions for Discussion and Journaling

1. Kantz writes that Shirley "believes that facts are what you learn from textbooks, opinions are what you have about clothes, and arguments are what you have with your mother when you want to stay out late at night" (para. 28). What does Kantz contend that facts, opinions, and arguments *actually* are?

2. Make a list of the things Kantz says students don't know, misunderstand, or don't comprehend about how texts work. Judging from your own experience, do you think she's correct about student understanding? How many of the things she lists do you feel you understand better now?

3. As its title indicates, Kantz's article has to do with using sources *persuasively*. Did her article teach you anything new about the persuasive use of sources to support an argument? If so, what?

4. Do you think Kantz contradicts herself when she says that we should think of sources neither as stories nor as repositories of truth? Explain why or why not.

5. Which of the students in Kantz's article do you most identify with, and why?

6. Do you think Kantz's ideas will change your own approach to doing research and writing with sources? If so, how?

## Applying and Exploring Ideas

1. Kantz places some blame for students' writing difficulties on poorly written assignments that don't clearly explain what teachers want. Conduct your own mini review of college writing assignments you've received. How many do you think gave sufficient explanation of what the professor was looking for? As you look at assignments that did give good directions, what do they have in common? That is, based on those assignments, what did you need to be told in order to have a good understanding of what you were being asked to write? Write one to two pages about what you find, and share what you write in class.

2. Write a short reflection on the relationship between creativity and research as you've learned to understand it prior to this class, and as Kantz talks about it. Where do your and her ideas overlap? Where does her thinking influence yours? And where does it not seem to work for you?

---

**Meta Moment**

One of our goals for this book is to have you consider constructs or conceptions of writing that don't hold up under close scrutiny. How would you name the constructs that Kantz is calling into question? Why would it be useful for you as a writer in college or in professional settings to understand her findings and claims?

# Plagiarism:
# A Misplaced Emphasis

## BRIAN MARTIN

■ Martin, Brian. "Plagiarism: A Misplaced Emphasis." *Journal of Information Ethics* 3.2 (Fall 1994): 36–47. Print.

## Framing the Reading

A number of readings in *Writing about Writing* ask you to look at things differently than you might have in the past. As the introduction to this chapter explained, we are asking you to look at social constructions—the ideas we have about things—and reexamine them where appropriate. Of all of the social constructions this book asks you to reconsider, we think that the construction of plagiarism as discussed by Brian Martin in this article might be one of the most difficult, simply because the idea of plagiarism is widespread in American society and our public discussions of plagiarism tend to assume that this word means one thing and that we all understand what that one thing is and agree that it is wrong. Brian Martin asks us to reconsider all of that—what plagiarism means and whether different kinds of plagiarism matter in different ways than we commonly assume.

If Martin's ideas throw you for a loop, you might remember that he has a Ph.D. in theoretical physics from Sydney University. He writes about a broad range of topics, from nonviolence to whistleblowing to controversies over pesticides and AIDS, and he is the vice president of an organization called Whisteblowers Australia. He says on his Web site that the "central theme" in his research is "the dynamics of power, with special attention to strategies for challenging repression and exploitation." In other words, Martin thinks broadly about a range of ideas and seems committed to thinking outside the box and asking others to do the same. He is professor of social sciences at the University of Wollongong, Australia.

## Getting Ready to Read

*Before you read*, do at least one of the following activities:

- Jot down what you have been taught in school (implicitly or explicitly) about plagiarism: what it is, why it is wrong, how to avoid it.
- Ask yourself how your ideas about plagiarism have been socially constructed: Who do you see talking about this? Where have you been taught about it? What are the common messages about it? Have you been exposed to any alternate conceptions about plagiarism?

*As you read*, consider the following questions:

- How do Martin's definitions of plagiarism compare to what you have been taught about plagiarism?
- Are you struggling to understand or imagine what Martin is outlining? If so, do you think it is because he is constructing plagiarism differently than you have been taught?

## The Problem as Normally Conceived

Among intellectuals, plagiarism is normally treated as a grievous sin. In higher education, which is both the central training ground and a key employer of intellectuals, students are warned of the seriousness of the offense. Some teachers have developed laborious or sophisticated means of detecting it. The authors of one paper on the subject recommend reading essays four times as part of the process of rooting out plagiarism (Bjaaland and Lederman, 1973). Meanwhile, computer scientists have studied complex algorithms for assessing likely cases (Faidhi and Robinson, 1987). An alternative is to prevent plagiarism by designing assessment procedures appropriately, for example, by getting students to use their own experiences in creative writing (Carroll, 1982). Academics can set a good example by giving appropriate credit for sources used in preparing their lectures and notes (Alexander, 1988). At the institutional level, plagiarism is normally addressed through formal policies, including penalties for transgressions (Thomley, 1989). Another approach is to introduce an honor system in which students pledge to not cheat and to report cheating by other students (Fass, 1986). The problem of plagiarism can also lead to a reconsideration of educational philosophy (Malloch, 1976). 1

In spite of the seriousness with which student plagiarism is treated by academics, their collective efforts seem to be inadequate to the size of the problem (Baird, 1980; Connell, 1981; Galles, 1987; Stavisky, 1973; but see Karlins, Michaels, and Podlogar, 1988). Undoubtedly no more than a small fraction of student plagiarism is ever detected and, of that which is detected, serious penalties are imposed on only a minority of offenders. It is safe to say that if rules against cheating were able to be strictly and effectively enforced, failure rates would skyrocket. But this is unlikely. The introduction of word processing and computer networks makes plagiarism easier to execute and even harder to detect. Computer sampling of music recordings and incorporation of samples (copied portions) in other music is already an established practice, with associated problems of credit and copyright (Keyt, 1988). 2

At this point it may be useful to make a few distinctions (Martin, 1984: 183–184). The most obvious and provable plagiarism occurs when someone copies phrases or passages out of a published work without using quotation marks, without acknowledging the source, or both. This can be called word-for-word plagiarism. When some of the words are changed, but not enough, the 3 result can be called paraphrasing plagiarism. This is considered more serious when the original source is not cited. A more subtle plagiarism occurs when a person gives references to original materials and perhaps quotes them, but never looks them up, having obtained both from a secondary source—which is not cited (Bensman, 1988: 456–457). This can be called plagiarism of secondary sources. Often it can be detected through minor errors in punctuation of citation which are copied from the secondary material. More elusive yet is the use of the structure of the argument in a source without due acknowledgment. This includes cases in which the plagiarizer does look up the primary documents but does not acknowledge a systematic dependence on the citations in the secondary source. This can be called plagiarism of the form of a source. More general than this is plagiarism of ideas, in which an original thought from another is used but without any dependence on the words or form of the source. Finally there is the blunt case of putting one's name to someone else's work, which might be called plagiarism of authorship.

Most of the plagiarism by university students that is challenged by their 4 teachers is word-for-word plagiarism, simply because it is easiest to detect and prove. One of the most serious types, plagiarism of authorship—which occurs when a student gets someone else to write an essay—can be extremely difficult to detect and prove. This creates a suspicion that most of the concern is about the least serious cases. Undoubtedly, much of the word-for-word plagiarism by students is inadvertent. They simply do not know or understand proper acknowledgment practice. Sometimes they are taught in high school to copy from sources without acknowledgment (Dant, 1986; Schab, 1972) and the problem persists in higher education. Students are apprentices, and some of them learn the scholarly trade slowly.

Academic institutions have the power to fail and even expel student plagia- 5 rizers, although this power is seldom exercised (Mawdsley, 1986; Reams, 1987). But colleagues are a different matter. Plagiarism among practicing intellectuals is widely considered to be completely unacceptable, but doing something about it is another matter. As in the case of students, word-for-word plagiarism is easiest to prove, and it might be expected that most blatant plagiarizers would be weeded out during their student years. There are some dramatic cases in which word-for-word plagiarizes have been exposed and penalized, but there are plenty of contrary cases in which plagiarizers have fashioned successful careers (Broad and Wade, 1982; Mallon, 1989; Spender, 1989: 140–194).

For example, Martin Luther King, Jr.'s plagiarism seemed to provide no hin- 6 drance to his career as a preacher and leader of a social movement, but the subsequent exposure of the plagiarism caused anguished reconsideration among scholars sympathetic to King's role in the civil rights movement (Thelen, 1991). This case illustrates both the ease with which plagiarizers can escape detection or penalty and the enormous impact on a person's reputation of exposure of plagiarism (in this case, posthumously). As for those who plagiarize ideas, it is virtually impossible to take action. Among many academics and scientists, there is a great fear that one's ideas will be stolen by unscrupulous competitors. This often results in an unwillingness to share ideas.

The standard view, subscribed to by most intellectuals, is that plagiarism     7
is a serious offense against scholarship and should be condemned and penalized. It is strongly discouraged among students. It is thought to be rare among
scholars. The revisionist picture, subscribed to especially by those who have
studied plagiarism, is that it is much more common among both students and
scholars than usually recognized
and hence infrequently punished.
Both the standard and revisionist
views agree on the seriousness of
plagiarism and the need to be vigilant against it. They also agree that
the problem of plagiarism is largely due to inexperienced or errant
individuals—on the psychology
of plagiarists, see Shaw's (1982)
insightful account—and that penalties and policies should be designed to encourage individuals to
avoid plagiarism.

> *Both the standard and revisionist pictures [of plagiarism] are inadequate because they deal only with a particular type of plagiarism in the scholastic world, where credit for ideas is of great significance, because it is the currency for status and advancement.*

The argument in this paper is that both the standard and revisionist pictures     8
are inadequate because they deal only with a particular type of plagiarism in
the scholastic world, where credit for ideas is of great significance, because it is
the currency for status and advancement.

## Institutionalized Plagiarism

In a number of social circumstances, plagiarism is such a pervasive and ac-     9
cepted practice that it is seldom considered worthy of concern or mention. A
few examples are given here before turning to the significance of this type of
plagiarism. Ghostwriting is commonplace in the popular press (Posner, 1988).
When a politician, famous sports figure, business executive, or movie star gives
a speech or writes a book or newspaper column, frequently the actual writing is done by someone else. Sometimes, in books, this is acknowledged, as
in the case of *The Autobiography of Malcolm X* written by "Malcolm X with
the assistance of Alex Haley" (X, 1965). The "with" in such cases precedes the
person who did the writing. (Haley was later accused of plagiarism over his
book *Roots*; the question of authorship is seldom a simple one!) But in many
cases the writer is listed only in small print on an acknowledgments page, or
not at all. Ghostwriting is a type of plagiarism of authorship; a failure to appropriately acknowledge contributions. The weirdest development along this
line is the use of ghostwriters by famous journalists who are too busy to write
their own columns (Posner, 1988).

In scientific research, the phenomenon of "honorary authorship" is common-     10
place. In typical cases, a supervisor or laboratory director, who has done little
or none of the research, is listed as co-author of a research paper (LaFollette,
1992: 91–107). For some academic textbooks, the official authors are chosen

for their market value, but do relatively little work. The actual writers of such "managed texts" may receive little or no credit (Coser, Kadushin, and Powell, 1982; Fischer and Lazerson, 1977). This is not to mention all the books—fiction and nonfiction—that are virtually rewritten by in-house editors before reaching the public.

Another type of ghostwriting is political speechwriting. A few politicians 11 write their own speeches, but most rely on speechwriters, who are seldom acknowledged in an appropriate way. The same situation applies to big-name comedians, few of whom write the bulk of their routines. An even more common misrepresentation of authorship occurs in government, corporate, church and trade union bureaucracies. Work that is done by junior workers is commonly signed by higher officials. The official justification is that the person whose name goes on a document is organizationally responsible for that work, but he or she also is commonly considered to be "responsible" in terms of gaining credit for doing the work, especially by outsiders.

This phenomenon is so commonplace that it is seldom mentioned in discus- 12 sions of either plagiarism or bureaucracy. (For a forthright discussion of cases in university administrations, see Moodie [1993].) It is not difficult to confirm the widespread occurrence of this misattribution of authorship by simply talk-ing to junior bureaucrats. Typically, they may not worry very much about the formalities of authorship but are likely to be aggrieved if they do not receive aknowledgment within the organization for work done. Needless to say, a sys-tem that officially misattributes formal authorship makes it extremely easy for superiors to appropriate credit for the work of subordinates.

From the point of view of outsiders, there is widespread misunderstand- 13 ing of the operation of the system. Many people treat the official structures as reflecting the underlying reality. For example, in parliamentary systems a minister is an elected parliamentarian in charge of a government department. When someone writes a letter to a minister, he or she receives in reply a letter from the minister that is almost always written by someone in the department and seldom seen by the minister at all. The letter writer seldom thinks of the interaction as having been one with a junior bureaucrat. This type of plagia-rism of authorship is built into the structures and operations of bureaucracies and is hardly ever categorized as plagiary. Yet it undoubtedly satisfies the usual formal definitions of plagiarism.

The widespread plagiary in bureaucracies and the ghostwriting prevalent in 14 many fields may be called "institutionalized plagiarism," which is to be distin-guished from the "competitive plagiarism" found in academic and intellectual circles. In the latter situation, claiming credit for ideas is the basis for status and advancement in a system conceived to be based on autonomous and individual intellectual production. In this context, plagiarism is breaking the rules of the game, gaining undue credit in a competitive intellectual endeavor. Institutional-ized plagiarism is a feature of systems of formal hierarchy, in which credit for intellectual work is more a consequence than a cause of unequal power and position. In bureaucracies, workers are conceived of as cogs in a formal sys-tem rather than independent intellectual producers: their work contributes to products of the bureaucracy; putting it in the name of bureaucratic elites is the formal procedure by which this occurs. Institutionalized plagiarism can also be categorized as an aspect of the systematic misrepresentation that is a feature of mass institutions, especially the mass media (Mitroff and Bennis, 1988).

These two types of plagiary, competitive and institutionalized, can also be 15 called retail and wholesale plagiarism, respectively, by analogy with Chomsky and Herman's (1979) distinction between retail and wholesale terrorism, namely small-scale killing by limited groups and large-scale killing by major governments. Retail plagiarism typically exploits the intellectual labor of a few people at a time; wholesale plagiarism involves the systematic exploitation of large numbers of workers as a matter of standard procedure.

Most studies of terrorism focus on the retail form and ignore or down- 16 play the wholesale. Similarly, most studies of plagiarism focus exclusively on the competitive variety and ignore its institutionalized forms. The example of Joseph R. Biden, Jr. illustrates this. Biden was a U.S. presidential aspirant who in 1987 was exposed for having plagiarized the speeches of some other politicians, such as British Labour Party leader Neil Kinnock. This caused much moralizing in the media (some of it ghostwritten) and contributed to Biden dropping out of the race. Yet the dependence of almost all leading politicians on speechwriters was little remarked. Biden was caught out in the sin of plagiarizing from other politicians (a type of competitive plagiarism), whereas plagiarizing from speechwriters was treated as acceptable because it was plagiary of workers in a subordinate position (institutionalized plagiarism). Indeed, when Biden copied from Robert Kennedy's speeches, it was actually the words of Kennedy's speechwriter Adam Walinsky that both used (Posner, 1988:19).

A closer examination of the competitive and institutionalized types of pla- 17 giary would show many overlaps and inconsistencies rather than a uniformly clear distinction. For example, some heads of university laboratories demand their name on every publication (institutionalized plagiarism in a competitive setting) and some corporate and government bureaucracies allow or even foster conventional individual authorship. Nonetheless, the generalization that most studies of plagiarism focus on violations of competitive etiquette and downplay misattributions in hierarchical organizational settings still applies.

One explanation for the preoccupation with competitive plagiarism is that 18 those who write about plagiary work in the competitive sector themselves. Another explanation is that this preoccupation serves the interests of those elites — bureaucrats, politicians and others—who benefit from institutionalized plagiarism. As in the case of crime (Collins, 1982: 86–118), the definition of an offense is a form of politics that serves particular interest groups. Stigmatizing petty thieves serves to protect the big criminals from scrutiny. Occasionally the double standard becomes apparent and a preoccupation with plagiarism becomes a threat to elites. For example, the implications for university administrations are suggested by the following: "From a broader philosophical perspective, 'ghostwriting'—a long accepted practice in the political arena—raises some rather thorny questions. As one student in the present study commented, 'If the [university] President can use a ghostwriter, why can't I?' Indeed, the problem of using one standard for college students and another standard for public officials at the very least imposes a rather perverse situational ethics on the whole idea of literary honesty" (Hawley, 1984:35). Generally, though, university presidents can plagiarize from speechwriters with impunity. Only when they plagiarize from scholars (e.g., Piliawsky, 1982:13–15)—competitive plagiarism—are they likely to be called to task.

## Does It Matter?

In correspondence with sociologist Deena Weinstein, I once asked about other 19 scholars who seemed to cover similar ideas to her own but who never cited her work. She replied (personal communication, 7 October 1982) by saying "Unless I am hiding something from myself, I believe that I don't give a hoot about priority. Ideas are not property so they cannot be stolen. But . . ." (her ellipsis). She went on to describe how other scholars had had early access to her ideas. This seems to be a standard dilemma. From the point of view of the abstract "advancement of knowledge," plagiarism is not a particular problem, since the knowledge is disseminated whoever gets credit for it. But from the point of view of individual scholars, credit for ideas is vital in career terms and, typically, even more so in terms of self-image.

Kroll, in a study of college freshmen, found that the arguments against pla- 20 giarism considered most important were "fairness to authors and other students, the responsibility of students to do independent work, and respect for ownership rights" (Kroll, 1988:203). Fairness to authors and responsibility to do independent work are moral arguments. So too is respect for ownership rights since, for students and most academics, the economic advantages of plagiarism, in terms of gaining financially from copyright violation, are negligible. None of these arguments show that plagiarism is a significant hindrance to the "quest for truth."

A pragmatic argument against plagiarism is that it enables second-rate intel- 21 lectuals to get ahead (Cranberg, 1992). With greater access to status and funds, they can thus hinder intellectual advancement by doing less well than the presumably superior intellects for whose work they may have stolen credit. This argument sounds plausible, but it has some flaws. In many cases, plagiarism is carried out by undoubtedly talented and experienced people, as in the case of D. H. Lawrence plagiarizing from various women (Spender, 1989:151–160) or, more prosaically, in the case of academics who plagiarize from their students. Furthermore, there is no evidence that plagiarizers are less able as administrators or intellectual leaders than those from whom they copy. Indeed, there is little evidence at all relevant to this argument. It may simply be an attractive view because plagiarism is considered to be a bad thing: therefore it *must* have bad effects.

A resolution to this problem—the apparent lack of any pragmatic reason 22 to be concerned about plagiarism—begins by observing that the arguments discussed so far in this context all concern competitive plagiarism, which is relatively rare and highly stigmatized. Very different considerations apply to institutionalized plagiarism, which is standard procedure. At least two important arguments can be leveled against institutionalized plagiarism. First, it reinforces the power and position of elites. By gaining official credit for the work of others, the status and authority of elites is enhanced, while giving relatively little status and authority to subordinates whose work has been given less than its fair share of credit. If a president were to introduce a speech by saying, "I'm now going to read a speech written by . . . ," this would undoubtedly reduce the president's aura and the status of the office. Similarly, if an important institutional policy were openly acknowledged to be the work of junior employees, it might be asked why they were not the ones launching and explaining the policy. Second, institutionalized plagiarism reduces the accountability of subordinates, who do not have to take formal blame for inadequacies in their work. They are less likely to take extreme care with their work when they know that others will be officially responsible. Of course, those at the top have greater formal responsibility and officially are accountable for inadequacies. But this accountability has limited scope: bureaucratic elites are typically only held accountable by others at a similar level.

In structures of unequal power, subordinates and clients seldom have the resources to challenge the elites. Weinstein (1979) characterizes bureaucracies as authoritarian political systems, in which dissent or apposition is stamped out. In essence, the system is responsive only at the top to pressures of similarly powerful elites; the workers in the bureaucracy are expected to respond only to bureaucratic elites, not to a wider array of concerns. 23

There are other arguments that could be made against institutionalized plagiarism, such as that it reduces innovation, causes alienation and represents inefficient use of the talents of the workers. For the purposes here, the arguments that institutionalized plagiarism reinforces hierarchies and reduces accountability are sufficient. 24

The next question is, does it matter that institutionalized plagiarism is linked to hierarchy and unaccountability? That of course depends on one's assessment of major social institutions, especially state and corporate bureaucracies. If these are seen as functional for the best interests of society, then institutionalized plagiarism presumably must be considered valuable; on the other hand, if these institutions are seen as contrary to the best interests of society, then institutionalized plagiarism is undesirable. 25

## Plagiarism in a Self-managed Society

Imagine a society in which formal hierarchy has been eliminated: a "self-managed" society (Benello and Roussopoulos, 1971; Burnheim, 1985; Herbst, 1976; Ward, 1982). The basis for social organization might include direct decision-making by consensus or voting in small groups. Decisions that affect people on the job or in local communities would be made collectively by those people. Higher-order coordination might be organized through delegates and federations or through random selection for functional groups. The details vary, but certainly in any self-managed society, the state and large corporate or 26

government bureaucracies would be replaced by more democratic and resp
sive social forms. In a self-managed society, power is dispersed and decentra
ized. Furthermore, a self-managed society would not have vast inequalities in
wealth, since these are typically linked to inequalities of power. Would there be
plagiarism in such a society, and what would be done about it?

It should be obvious that most institutionalized plagiarism would be 27
eliminated along with the institutions that fostered it. Within a collective
enterprise, such as designing and building transport systems, what would
be the rationale for allocating credit? Would credit for ideas even matter? It
seems reasonable to suppose that a key consideration would be to allocate
credit for the purposes of future work or involvement. For example, it would
be useful to know who developed or checked an idea or did some work in
order to build on successes and learn from failures. This suggests a pragmatic,
utilitarian allocation of credit. The aim would not be to glorify or advance
the individual but to make best use of the skills of each person and achieve
maximum benefit for society within the framework of self-management.
Although self-management would reduce the problem of institutionalized
plagiarism, the problem of competitive plagiarism could well persist.
Recognition for contributions to society as well as concern about fairness are
likely to remain important to most people. Although it is possible to imagine
a society in which no one cared about credit for ideas, it is also possible—and
possibly easier—to imagine "free" societies in which there is recognition of
creativeness, such as applause for a musical composition, even if this did not
lead to special privileges.

So plagiarism might occur but, on the other hand, it would be less likely to 28
be considered such a serious offence; it would probably be discussed on terms
of etiquette (on the development of manners, see Elias, 1978). Since credit for
ideas would not be important for career advancement and because contributions to collective well-being would be considered highly, it is even possible
that creative workers would decline to claim full credit for their work, allowing
plagiarism to occur by default rather than by commission.

Supporters of self-management often point out the collective nature of so- 29
cial life. No single person can make a contribution without relying extensively
on the prior and ongoing work of others. Producing goods in a factory depends
on systems of education and transport, prior inventions, markets, etc. Similarly,
intellectual creativity always relies and builds on upbringing, prior ideas, culture, communications media, audiences, and the like. Claims to exclusive credit
for originality, as well as to ownership of intellectual property, are characteristic of the system of capitalist individualism. The myth of the autonomous
creator would be much harder to sustain under self-management.

Today, even inadvertent plagiarism can be a matter of extreme embarrass- 30
ment (Perrin, 1992). False allegations of plagiarism can cause severe trauma to
the accused (Klass, 1987) and can be used to attack scholars who are opposed
for some other reasons (St. Onge, 1988). On the other hand, plagiarism is such
a serious charge that often the accusers may be attacked as a way of ward-
ing off valid concerns (Adnavourin, 1988; Mazur, 1989: 190). One benefit of

455

r competitive plagiarism would be that these high stakes and
ences of plagiary allegations would be reduced.

about the role of plagiarism in a hypothetical self-managed    31
ce for the assessment of plagiarism today. They imply that
ortant issue, but not for the reasons usually put forward.
competitive plagiarism is given too much attention and con-
in far too extreme terms. Given the pervasiveness of plagiarism, it
should be treated as a common, often inadvertent problem, rather like speeding
on the road or cheating on income taxes. Most cases should be dealt with as
matters of etiquette rather than "theft." Otherwise, the danger is that plagiarism allegations can be a way of mounting unscrupulous attacks on individuals
who are targeted for other reasons.

Contrary to the case of competitive plagiarism, the issue of institutionalized    32
plagiarism deserves *more* attention. It serves as a focus on power inequality
and intellectual exploitation. The term "plagiarism" needs to be brought into
common use to describe ghostwriting and attribution of authorship to top
bureaucrats and officials, as a way of challenging those practices. In situations
of intellectual exploitation, the demand for proper acknowledgment of work
can be a subversive one. Since hierarchical and bureaucratized work structures
foster institutionalized plagiarism, demanding fair credit for work done exposes and challenges these structures. In summary, concern about plagiarism
has been diverted from the most serious and pervasive problems and channeled
into excessive concern about less serious problems. This process is clearly one
that serves the interests of the biggest intellectual exploiters.

## Acknowledgments

I thank Randall Collins, Al Higgins, Gavin Moodie, and Deena Weinstein for
helpful comments on the text, as well as untold others for creating the cultural
context that made this work possible.

## References

Adnavourin, Avi. 1988. "Academic assassination and a three-university plagiarism coverup: the
case of Robert M. Frumkin." *Philosophy and Social Action* 14(1): 15–19.

Alexander, James D. 1988. "Lectures: the ethics of borrowing." *College Teaching* 36: 21–24.

Baird, Jr., John S. 1980. "Current trends in college cheating." *Psychology in the Schools* 17: 515–
522.

Benello, C. George, and Dimitrios Roussopoulos, eds. 1971. *The Case for Participatory Democracy: Some Prospects for a Radical Society.* New York; Grossman.

Bensman, Joseph. 1988. "The aethetics and politics of footnoting." *Politics, Culture, and Society.*
1: 443–470.

Bjaaland, Patricia C., and Arthur Lederman. 1973. "The detection of plagiarism." *Educational
Forum* 37: 201–206.

Broad, William, and Nicholas Wade. 1982. *Betrayers of the Truth: Fraud and Deceit in the Halls of
Science.* New York: Simon and Schuster.

Bumheim, John. 1985. *Is Democracy Possible? The Alternative to Electoral Politics.* London: Polity
Press.

Carroll, Joyce Armstrong. 1982. "Plagiarism: the unfun game." *English Journal* 71: 92–94.

Chomsky, Noam, and Edward S. Herman. 1979. *The Political Economy of Human Rights.* Boston: South End Press.

Collins, Randall. 1982. *Sociological Insight: An Introduction to Nonobvious Sociology.* New York: Oxford University Press.

Connell, Christopher. 1981. "Term paper mills continue to grind." *Educational Record* 62: 19–28.

Coser, Lewis, Charles Kadushin, and Walter W. Powell. 1982. *Books: The Culture and Commerce of Publishing.* New York: Basic Books.

Cranberg, Lawrence. 1992. "The plague of plagiarism persists in modern science." *The Scientist* 6 (3 February): 11, 14.

Dant, Doris R. 1986. "Plagiarism in high school: a survey." *English Journal* 75: 81–84.

Elias, Norbert. 1978. *The Civilizing Process: The History of Manners. Volume 1. Sociogenetic and Psychogenetic Investigations.* Oxford: Basil Blackwell.

Faidhi, J. A. W., and S. K. Robinson. 1987. "An empirical approach for detecting program similarity and plagiarism within a university programming environment." *Computers and Education* 11: 11–19.

Fass, Richard A. 1986. "By honor bound: encouraging academic honesty." *Education Record* 67: 32–35.

Fischer, Kurt W., and Arlyne Lazerson. 1977. "Managing a book versus plagiarizing it." *Teaching of Psychology* 4: 198–199.

Galles, Gary M. 1987. "Professors are woefully ignorant of a well-organized market inimical to learning: the big business in research papers." *Chronicle of Higher Education* 39 (28 October): B1, B3.

Hawley, Christopher S. 1984. "The thieves of academe: plagiarism in the university system." *Improving College and University Teaching* 32: 35–39.

Herbst, Ph. G. 1976. *Alternatives to Hierarchies.* Leiden, Netherlands: Martinus Nijhoff.

Karlins, Marvin, Charles Michaels, and Susan Podlogar. 1988. "An empirical investigation of actual cheating in a large sample of undergraduates." *Research in Higher Education* 29: 359–364.

Keyt, Aaron. 1988. "An improved framework for music plagiarism litigation." *California Law Review* 76: 421–464.

Klass, Perri. 1987. "Turning my words against me." *New York Times Book Review* 5 April: 1, 45–46.

Kroll, Barry M. 1988. "How college freshmen view plagiarism." *Written Communication* 5: 203–221.

LaFollette, Marcel C. 1992. *Stealing into Print: Fraud, Plagiarism, and Misconduct in Scientific Publishing.* Berkeley: University of California Press.

Malloch, A. E. 1976. "A dialogue on plagiarism." *College English* 38: 165–174.

Mallon, Thomas. 1989. *Stolen Words: Forays into the Origins and Ravages of Plagiarism.* New York: Ticknor and Fields.

Martin, Brian. 1984. "Plagiarism and responsibility." *Journal of Tertiary Educational Administration* 6: 183–190.

Mawdsley, Ralph D. 1986. "Plagiarism problems in higher education." *Journal of College and University Law* 13: 65–92.

Mazur, Allan. 1989. "Allegations of dishonesty in research and their treatment by American universities," *Minerva* 27: 177–194.

Mitroff, Ian I., and Warren Bennis. 1989. *The Unreality Industry: The Deliberate Manufacturing of Falsehood and What It Is Doing to Our Lives.* New York: Carol.

Moodie, Gavin. 1993. "Bureaucratic plagiarism." *Campus Review* (Australia) (25–31 March): 10, 19.

Perrin, Noel. 1992. "How I became a plagiarist." *American Scholar* 61: 257–259.

Piliawsky, Monte. 1982. *Exit 13: Oppression and Racism in Academia*. Boston: South End Press.

Posner, Ari. 1988. "The culture of plagiarism." *The New Republic*, 18 April: 19–24.

Reams, Jr., Bernard D. 1987. "Revocation of academic degrees by colleges and universities." *Journal of College and University Law* 14: 283–302.

Schab, Fred. 1972. "Cheating in high school: a comparison of behavior of students in the college prep and general curriculum," *Journal of Youth and Adolescence* 1: 251–256.

Shaw, Peter. 1982. "Plagiary," *American Scholar* 51: 325–337.

Spender, Dale. 1989. *The Writing or the Sex?: Or Why You Don't Have to Read Women's Writing to Know It's No Good*. New York: Pergamon.

Stavisky, Leonard Price. 1973. "Term paper 'mills,' academic plagiarism, and state regulation." *Political Science Quarterly* 88: 445–461.

St. Onge, K. R. 1988. *The Melancholy Anatomy of Plagiarism*. Lanham: University Press of America.

Thelen, David, ed. 1991. "Becoming Martin Luther King, Jr.—plagiarism and originality: a round table." *Journal of American History* 78: 11–123.

Thomley, Patsy W. 1989. "In search of a plagiarism policy." *Northern Kentucky Law Review* 16: 501–519.

Ward, Colin. 1982. *Anarchy in Action*. London: Freedom Press.

Weinstein, Deena. 1979. *Bureaucratic Opposition: Challenging Abuses at the Workplace*. New York: Pergamon.

X, Malcolm, with the assistance of Alex Haley. 1965. *The Autobiography of Malcolm X*. New York: Grove Press.

## Questions for Discussion and Journaling

1. Martin outlines different kinds of plagiarism: word-for-word plagiarism, paraphrasing plagiarism, plagiarism of secondary sources, plagiarism of the form of a source, plagiarism of ideas, and plagiarism of authorship (para. 3). Briefly define each of these (in your own words, not Martin's!), and for each one try to think of an example that you have seen or experienced.

2. Of the types of plagiarism that Martin outlines, which have you most commonly heard discussed in school settings (even if the teachers used a different name to describe it)?

3. What do you think Martin means when he says that "students are apprentices" (para. 4)? If your former teachers saw you as an apprentice, how do you think they would have talked and taught about plagiarism differently (if at all)?

4. Martin gives a number of examples of what he calls "institutionalized plagiarism" or "wholesale plagiarism." What does he mean by these phrases? Have you ever thought about this kind of plagiarism before you read this article?

5. Martin calls institutionalized plagiarism "the systematic exploitation of large numbers of workers as a matter of standard procedure" (para. 15), arguing that it "reinforces the power and position of elites" and "reduces the accountability of subordinates" (para. 22). Do you agree with his assessments about this type of plagiarism? Why or why not?

6. What does Martin mean by "competitive plagiarism" or "retail plagiarism" and how is it different from institutionalized plagiarism?

7. Martin argues against what he calls "the myth of the autonomous creator" (writer) (para. 29). What does he mean by this phrase? The other readings in this chapter should help you understand this, although he uses slightly different terminology than some of the other authors. Do you think that your experiences in school and society have taught you to believe in an autonomous creator/writer?

8. Martin argues that competitive plagiarism currently receives too much attention, while institutionalized plagiarism does not receive enough attention. Explain why he believes this, and then explain whether or not you agree with him, and why.

## Applying and Exploring Ideas

1. Do a little research on Turnitin. What is this service? Which of Martin's types of plagiarism is it intended to prevent? Now do some research on the arguments against Turnitin (you can find many of these through a quick Internet search). Who argues against Turnitin and why? Although Martin's article was written in 1994, long before the advent of Turnitin, you can imagine that he would argue strongly against it. Why? What would his arguments about it be?

2. Martin tells you that Martin Luther King Jr. plagiarized. Do some research to find out what he plagiarized. Which of the kinds of plagiarism that Martin outlines did King engage in? Draw on some of the other readings in this chapter (for example, Porter on intertextuality, p. 395) in order to make an argument about how we should react to/understand King's use of other sources.

3. Do a little exploration of the writing requirements of the job you are hoping to find after graduating. What do people in this position write? Do others write for them? Do they revise or put their names on texts others have written? To learn as much as possible, see if you can locate someone currently in this position and briefly interview him or her. Once you've learned as much as you can, consider whether any of Martin's criticisms regarding "institutionalized plagiarism" will be relevant to your work in this position. Draw on other readings in this chapter to consider how the people doing this job construct meaning together. Does anything you've learned change your opinion about this profession?

### Meta Moment

Are you thinking differently about plagiarism now than you were before you read this article? How can you challenge social constructions you encounter commonly, such as constructions of "good writing"?

# College Admissions Essays: A Genre of Masculinity

## SARAH-KATE MAGEE

■ Magee, Sarah-Kate. "College Admissions Essays: A Genre of Masculinity." *Young Scholars in Writing* 7 (2009): 116–21. Print.

## Framing the Reading

Sarah-Kate Magee wrote this piece while a first-year student at the College of Charleston, where she was double-majoring in arts management and economics and minoring in dance. She wrote it in a course titled Advanced Academic Writing, a first-year writing course (like the one you're probably in while using this book) taught by Chris Warnick.

The question that Magee takes on in her research is part of a larger issue that has long motivated inquiry in writing studies: the role of gender in writing. Sociolinguists like Deborah Tannen have long argued that there are differences in how masculine and feminine genders use language, and scholars of feminist rhetorical theory assert differences in ways of knowing reflected in feminine/women's discourses versus masculine/men's discourses. Given such indications, an obvious question is how gender might express itself in writing. Magee begins her essay by referencing a major existing essay on this question, Elizabeth Flynn's 1988 *College Composition and Communication* article "Composing as a Woman." Magee's contribution is to consider whether an entire genre—in this case, college admissions essays—might be understood as gendered. Might a genre's conventions (the patterns of qualities and characteristics that allow a given genre to be recognized *as a genre* to begin with) actually render the genre more "masculine" or "feminine" as Flynn's work defined these terms?

As you read this article, pay particular attention to its parts or sections: What does each do, and how does each contribute to building Magee's line of reasoning? How would you characterize the methods she uses to address her research question, and do you think you could replicate those methods with other genres or other research questions similar to Magee's?

I have often heard and been skeptical of supposed intellectual or emotional differences between men and women. For example, Lawrence Summers, the past president of Harvard University, suggested that men are better at math and science than women, but my

1

own experience refutes this generalization; I'm better at science and math than many men I know. Others I have encountered expect women to be much more emotional and believe they always and automatically want to share their feelings; I am female, and that statement does not describe me. Recently, I read an article that made me think more deeply about gender differences than I had before. I had not considered that men and women might be different in their writing styles until I read Elizabeth Flynn's "Composing as a Woman." In this article, Flynn suggests that women write differently than men.

Flynn's arguments intrigued me and made me wonder if gender differences 2 do, in fact, exist, and if so, how these are expressed. Flynn explores gender differences in students' personal writing; her findings made me curious about the role gender differences play in college admissions essays. College essays, while personal in nature, are different from the student writing Flynn examined. Will Flynn's argument explain my own college admissions writing? Is my writing really different from that of my male counterparts? Do other young women write differently from their male classmates? Is their style similar to mine?

> *Will Flynn's argument explain my own college admissions writing? Is my writing really different from that of my male counterparts? Do other young women write differently from their male classmates? Is their style similar to mine?*

## Flynn's Exploration of Gender Differences in Writing

In "Composing as a Woman," Flynn surveys "feminist research on gender dif- 3 ferences in social and psychological development" and theorizes on how such research could be used in examining student writing (425). Flynn drew from Nancy Chodorow's *The Reproduction of Mothering*, Carol Gilligan's *In a Different Voice*, and Mary Belenky, Blythe Clinchy, Nancy Goldberger, and Jill Tarule's *Women's Ways of Knowing* to build a framework for a feminist consideration of student writing. These writers looked at the differences between men and women, but Flynn took it a step further and applied the differences to writing styles. Flynn describes how Chodorow and the other writers she cites contend that the social and psychological development of men and women is different: men and women "have different conceptions of self and different modes of interaction with others as a result of their different experiences" (426). They argue that men and women interact with the world and view themselves in different ways. Since writing is often personal and can be a reflection of self, it makes sense that such differences would manifest in composing and writing.

In greater depth, Flynn examines Chodorow's *The Reproduction of Moth-* 4 *ering*, in which Chodorow explains the differences between the male and female identification processes: "Feminine identification processes are relational, whereas masculine identification processes tend to deny relationships"

(176). Women are dependent on other human beings and have no problem admitting it, but men deny those relationships, even if they are dependent on others. Chodorow's claim holds true in the student writing Flynn examined. The narratives of female students are relational—"stories of interaction, of connection, or of frustrated connection." Conversely, men's narratives are "stories of achievement, of separation, or of frustrated achievement" (428). Flynn goes on to characterize female writing in several distinct ways. In women's writing, the emphasis is placed on a shared experience where something relational informs the woman's identity. The conception of self is based on the relationships within the group. For men, she claims, emphasis is placed on achievement on an individual level. The conception of self is based on the individual and his accomplishments, not anything gained from a relational experience.

## Exploring Gender Characteristics in My Writing

As a result of my experiences and many mixed impressions I had about the 5 differences between the genders, I did not automatically believe Flynn's argument about the different characteristics of women's and men's writing styles. I figured that Flynn might be one more person who exaggerates or distorts the differences between men and women. However, her points did not seem as unrealistic as the broad statements I had heard in other conversations, like the mischaracterization that men are superior in math. Flynn was able to convince me that women's narratives are "stories of interaction, or connection" because I see myself focused on forming relationships and connections (428). These connections are more important to me than achieving great accomplishments; my self-image is consistent with Flynn's argument. In order to explore her claims further, I decided to look at a piece of my own writing and see whether and how it fit into her categorization of feminine composition styles. The only example I had of recent narrative-based writing was my college admissions essay. Did my writing fit the feminine qualities Flynn suggests are present in student composition? How did the genre of the piece affect feminine characteristics that might be present in my writing?

My essay begins with my fanciful wish that if I were not bound by space 6 and time, I would reclaim the imagination of a six-year-old and spend twenty-four hours as a Disney princess, specifically Belle. In my narrative, I express my desire for a fairy godmother who would make the objects of my wildest dreams appear while also wondering how "magic" could positively impact our world. Next, I discuss the problem of hunger, both across the globe and down the street. I highlight what I have done as a recruiter for a local Christian Rural Overseas Program (CROP) Hunger Walk to combat the problem. I explain that I would use my princess magic to safely and sustainably feed the world. The essay ends with a revelation that magic or a fairy godmother is not what we need to change the world. It is my compassion, imagination, hard work, determination, and commitment that will make a difference.

If Flynn is correct, and my essay was similar to the female student writing she examined, my college admissions essay—because it has some 7 narrative-like characteristics—would tell a story of interaction. However, there are no interactions, no relationships, and no bonding experiences in my admissions essay. The essay does not exhibit the characteristics Flynn suggests are typical of feminist composition. Instead, I write in a manner consistent with masculine composition. I made sure to emphasize my achievements as a recruiter for the CROP Hunger Walk; highlighting accomplishments is typical in the narratives of men, according to Flynn. I could have dismissed Flynn as wrong and misguided; however, her characterization of feminine writing as one focused on relationships fits exactly with my own personal feelings. I was curious why this piece of writing lined up with the masculine characterization since I view myself as a relationship-focused person, instead of one focused on achievements. Since writing can often be a reflection of self, I expected my writing to mirror me as a person and be relationship-focused as well.

I considered the nature and purpose of my personal narrative versus 8 the student writing Flynn studied. There were differences; the essays she examined were exploratory assignments written for school. The students in her study were instructed to write "narrative descriptions of learning experiences" (430). The motivation behind their writing was to write for the classroom; as a college admissions essay, my writing had a very different distinct and specific purpose. It was designed to show myself as more than SAT scores and grades to admissions counselors at schools I wanted to attend. I had to sell myself so that someone at School X would want me to attend his or her institution. It was the genre that influenced both the lack of relationships and the focus on achievements. I had limited words to convince the counselor that I was an impressive person. There was not space for me to talk about the friends I made while recruiting for the CROP Hunger Walk; what was important was that I was a leader and worked hard for a social cause. Those friends were not the ones seeking admission so they should not be included in the essay, and our relationship said nothing about my achievements, or why I would be a valuable addition to School X's student population.

## Exploring Gender Characteristics in Others' Writing

Was I alone in my neglect of interactions when writing my essay? Did the es- 9 says of other college-bound young women lack relationships and interactions with others while emphasizing achievements? I have examined the admissions essays of two friends, Rosie and Amy, who both have worked hard in high school and want to get into good colleges. I chose them because they value being accepted at prestigious institutions while also having developed very strong relationships and connections with their family and friends. Rosie and Amy gave me permission to use their essays in my study of college admissions essays as a gendered genre and they have reviewed the analyses of their writing that I am presenting. Rosie's college essay focuses on her mantra "Today, we can conquer the world" and how she applies it to her life daily.

> I could conquer the world. At seventeen, conquering the world is not wiping out whole nations and being the newest and most powerful dictator. Conquering the world means learning as much as I can, and pushing myself to be a better, more independent, loving, passionate person. . . . When it came time to choose senior year classes, I didn't look at how often classes met, or ask around about the easy classes. I chose classes like classical mythology, world religions, and explorations in advanced geometry because those sounded interesting to me. Mythology ended up being the hardest class I had ever taken. It was hard, but I was learning with such intensity and in a way I had never done before. I felt like I was conquering the world.

Rosie's essay is also missing relationships and interactions with others. There is no mention of her roommate at the North Carolina School of Science and Math who is her best friend and constant companion. Instead, she highlights how she challenged herself academically and then explains how satisfactory it felt to succeed. She does not include the friend who took the mythology class with her and how they worked together to overcome the challenge. Rosie's only implicit reference to others, "ask around," is not relationship-based, but serves to separate herself from those who might ask others for advice in order to determine the easy classes. Like my narrative, her essay lacks elements of feminine composition and showcases a frustrated achievement, an element of masculine composition.

Amy's admission essay mentions her relationship with others more than   10
either Rosie's or mine; however, she still composes in a masculine style.

> I choreographed and taught my first full-length dance this year and I was able to watch my feelings flow through other people's bodies. I also had my first poem published and I have been able to see my words affect other people as they read what I wrote. . . . Other teachers have shown me that sometimes I have to teach myself—such as physics, where I struggled to understand what my teacher was trying to explain, but painstakingly read my textbook, worked extra problems and asked questions until I finally grasped what was going on. . . . So in a word, I am a dreamer. But in many words I am a writer, a reader, a dancer, a planner, and a teacher—because my dreams are not just ideas, they are actions.

Amy underscores her artistic achievements and her frustrated achievements with understanding physics. All of her accomplishments are given in relation to their impact on others, so it would seem that her essay includes interaction. However, the interactions in Amy's essays serve more to emphasize her achievements rather than show her strong bond and connection with others. For example, her choreography is so successful that the dancers are able to show the feelings she intended in their movements. The physics teacher's inability to explain physics gave Amy the opportunity to teach herself, where she struggled and overcame her confusion. Although there are some references to interactions with others, an element of feminine composition, Amy's essay is very much masculine in style because of its heavy emphasis on actions and achievements.

## College Admissions Essays as a Genre

All of us wrote about topics that made us stand out as leaders and appear  11
independent. Responses that included relationships with others would not present us as independent thinkers ready to embark on new chapters in our lives,
which was something we felt we should show in our essays. Some might argue
that students could write college admissions essays about experiences where
they worked well with others to show that they are team players. Although collaboration is valued in the workforce and in college, admissions counselors are
looking for applicants who exhibit leadership while working in groups. Colleges explicitly state that they desire students who demonstrate these qualities.

According to Lafayette College, a prestigious institution of higher education  12
in Easton, Pennsylvania, that is ranked as the thirty-fifth best liberal arts college in the nation by *US News and World Report*, the factors administrators
consider in evaluating applications include "the candidate's personal character
such as motivation, social awareness, ambition, individualism, and potential
for leadership as exhibited through involvement in the community and extracurricular activities" ("Requirements and Class Profile"). Lafayette is not
the only institution of higher education that includes personal qualities and
leadership in what it is looking for in applicants. Institutions such as Davidson
College, Kenyon College, University of North Carolina–Chapel Hill, Virginia
Tech, and Harvey Mudd College use a "holistic review" process to evaluate applications and explicitly say they are looking for students who have exhibited
leadership experiences.

The application process and application standards make connections, a  13
characteristic of feminine composition, less significant and achievements more
significant. Applying to college is in essence a competition—a competition of
achievements. The admission process has become lengthy and in-depth because
education is valued culturally. Test scores are stressed, extracurricular activities
are seen as résumé-builders, and the all-important essay can make or break an
application. Strategists and educational experts have cashed in on the market
of college admissions. Guidebooks have been written and schools have been
thoroughly ranked. When applying to college, I read through several of the
essays deemed especially excellent in *50 Successful Harvard Admission Essays*
and consulted George Ehrenhaft's *Writing a Successful College Application
Essay*.

Pointers Ehrenhaft gives include writing about something important, picking  14
something unique that only you can write about, and managing to boast about
your accomplishments without sounding like you are boasting (19). Ehrenhaft
advises against writing about summer mission trips because those experiences
have become the norm. He suggests that an appropriate topic should relate to
an activity you are passionate about, something that "comes from the heart"
(16) and, most importantly, should highlight your leadership experience: those
two things together make you a competitive applicant. Neither book addresses
the difference in how men and women compose or how this difference could
influence writing college admission essays. Each book is so specific about what

to write about, accomplishments and achievements, that it eliminates the opportunity to talk about relationships. Those who want to write a successful admissions essay abandon connections even if those relationships are important in their lives.

## Exploring Genre, Purpose, and Gender

Analyzing Rosie's, Amy's, and my college admissions essays, I realized that 15 the college admissions essay genre is more masculine than others. The writing of female writers in this genre has masculine characteristics. In other words, the *genre* seems to influence women's writing style, perhaps in a way that is different from what Flynn accounted for. College essays require students to tell "stories of achievement, separation, or frustrated achievement," no matter what their gender (Flynn 428). A successful college admissions essay must be personal and highlight an achievement or tell how the student struggled and learned something while overcoming that obstacle. The implied expectations of college essays are inherently masculine; "men become the standard against which women are judged" (425).

Does it have to be this way, or has this occurred because of assumptions we 16 have about what is persuasive in an admissions essay? No considerations are made for the differences in how men and women might compose. Should they be? What is considered well done is consistent with the ways men compose; the college admissions essay genre subconsciously requires a masculine style of composition. Why did three young women, who are very connected with others, neglect their relationships and focus only on their achievements when they wrote their college admissions essay? Where did they get the impression that they needed to do that? For that matter, why do *all* writers of admissions essays assume that they must focus only on their achievements?

Interestingly, the prompts for the genre do *not* preclude a wider variety of 17 approaches. A writer's impression of an appropriate focus for his or her essay does not come from the essay questions themselves. The questions are not inherently biased towards masculine composition. The question I responded to was, "If you could go anywhere for twenty-four hours, not limited by time or space, where would you go, what would you do, and why?" I could have written about spending a day with my closest friends and traveling back to Elizabeth Bennet's time. I could have told how such an experience would connect us for years and share how much I value knowing people I can count on. But what would such an essay say about me? I love my friends and *Pride and Prejudice?* It does not say anything about what I could contribute to School X's student population, and why I am a competitive applicant. Rosie's and Amy's essays were free responses and had no guiding prompt. They could have literally written about anything, yet there is no mention of friends or the important relationships in their lives. The *purpose* of college admissions essays—another crucial aspect of the writing context—*does* preclude certain responses.

The admission process is a giant competition, so in one way it makes 18 sense that the college admission essay genre caters to masculine composition because, traditionally, competition is associated with masculine values. It almost fits that female students have to write an essay that makes use of masculine qualities, such as achievement. While achievements are important for an admissions counselor to know, they do not describe the overall personality or character of the applicant when an essential aspect of life is ignored. If the point of an essay is to show the applicant as more than just an SAT score or GPA, then the counselor should get the whole picture of the essay's author. Without even realizing it, female students have allowed their writing to mimic masculine composition because the institutions of higher education and the educational experts have clearly told us that accomplishments and achievements are what matters. The college admission genre only furthers the "danger of immasculation" (Flynn 434) by ignoring the differences between masculine and feminine thinking and writing styles and overemphasizing the style that Flynn names as "masculine." Unintentionally, the college admissions essay genre limits what can be written. Unspoken rules guide a successful essay's focus towards achievements. Other experiences, particularly relationship-based experiences, are deemed not appropriate subject matter. There is no awareness of the expectation solely to highlight achievements in college admissions essays, a style of composition Flynn describes as masculine. Such awareness needs to exist to allow for a wider range of experiences to write about in a successful essay. The unintentional bias in the college admissions essays genre only furthers and perpetuates the suppression of women's own ways of thinking and composing.

## Works Cited

Chodorow, Nancy. *The Reproduction of Mothering: Psychoanalysis and the Sociology of Gender.* Berkeley: U of California P, 1978. Print.

Ehrenhaft, George. *Writing a Successful College Application Essay.* Hauppauge: Barron's Educational Press, 2008. Print.

Flynn, Elizabeth A. "Composing as a Woman." *College Composition and Communication* 39 (1988): 423–35. Print.

"Requirements and Class Profile." *Lafayette College's Website.* Lafayette College, n.d. Web. 3 Dec. 2008.

Staff of the *Harvard Crimson*, eds. *50 Successful Harvard Admission Essays.* New York: St. Martin's Griffin, 1999. Print.

............................................................................................................

## Questions for Discussion and Journaling

1. Notice how in many places Magee is deciding what she thinks about various gender claims by comparing a given argument to her own experience. How closely do your own experiences with writing and language fit broadly held gender stereotypes? In which aspects do your experiences break the stereotypes?

2. How long does it take Magee to set up, or explain the origins of, her specific research question and methods of addressing it? What major "moves" does her essay

make in order to get there (what different lines of thought does she pursue one after the next)?

3. Magee is arguing that because women—who, it is theorized, would ordinarily write in a more "feminine" style that emphasized relationships over self and independence— are shown in the essays she examined to be writing in a more "masculine," non-relational style, that therefore the genre of admissions essays is itself masculinized. What other interpretations of this data could explain it?

## Applying and Exploring Ideas

1. An obvious question about Magee's study is whether a look at a bigger sample of students and essays would demonstrate the same patterns she found. Write a research proposal that explains how you would "scale up" this research in order to test Magee's findings with a wider range of writers.

2. Write a retrospective account of how you wrote your own college admission essay(s). How did you decide on what to write about? What factors influenced how you wrote? What process did writing the document take from when you read the prompt(s) for it to when you submitted it? Who else worked on it with you, and what did they contribute? Does your own experience, both in writing and in what you wrote, bear out Magee's thinking on the admissions essay as a masculinized genre?

### Meta Moment

Using the description Magee provides (based on Flynn's work) of what would count as a "masculine" or "feminine" writing style, can you identify which you tend toward?

# Obama's Speech at Howard: Becoming King

## MARIA POST

■ Post, Maria. "Obama's Speech at Howard: Becoming King." *Young Scholars in Writing* 6 (2008): 150–56. Print.

## Framing the Reading

Maria Post was a student of Elizabeth Vander Lei's at Calvin College when she wrote this piece in her English 101 course. She was majoring in English and Spanish and minoring in sociology. In her writing course, Post decided to take up the question of "how Barack Obama overcame the barrier of his racial identity to win the acceptance of the African American community" and what that suggests about how he was able to be a successful presidential candidate (para. 3).

Post focuses her inquiry on Obama's September 28, 2008, speech at Howard University, a historically black college, in which the candidate used religious themes and civil rights history to address the problem of achieving social justice. Post's rhetorical analysis examines ways Obama tried to associate himself, through themes, language, and rhetorical style, with Martin Luther King Jr., and in so doing build identification with African American voters.

Because rhetorical theory is so rich and has so many aspects and elements, the sort of textual analysis we often refer to as *rhetorical analysis* can actually take a wide variety of shapes. Rhetorical analysis might focus on any of the five canons of rhetoric, on some persuasive element such as the pisteis (logos, ethos, and pathos), on analysis of context and situation (including kairos), or any other aspect of rhetorical theory that interests the writer. In this case, Post chooses to conduct her rhetorical analysis from the perspectives of *style* and *identification*. You can easily follow both her headings and conclusion for a compact list of the specific elements she looks at.

O n Father's Day, 2008, Barack Obama asked the congregation of the Apostolic Church of God in Chicago to recall one of the early struggles of his campaign. "You remember at the beginning," he asked, "people were wondering, how come he doesn't have all the support in the African-American community? You remember that? That was when I wasn't black enough—now I'm too black." It is true that early in his campaign, Obama struggled to rally blacks to his side.

1

In fact, throughout 2007, more blacks said they preferred Hillary Clinton than said they preferred Obama for the Democratic nomination (Saad).

Some critics even questioned whether Obama, as a biracial man, was "black 2 enough" to authentically represent African American interests. Ron Walters, an expert on African American leadership and politics, writes that since Obama's mother was a white American and his father was Kenyan, and since he was raised in Hawaii and Indonesia, "his identity omitted many of the cultural markers with which Blacks are more familiar to the extent that it has promoted a curiosity of 'cultural fit' that in turn has become an issue of political trust" (13). Walters also quotes Debra Dickerson, a black writer with the online magazine *Salon*, as suggesting that since Obama's father was a voluntary immigrant from Kenya, Obama is not black in the traditional sense. She said in 2006 that "'Black', in our political and social reality, means those descendants from West African slaves. Voluntary immigrants of African descent . . . are just that, voluntary immigrants of African descent with markedly different outlooks on the role of race in their lives and politics" (9). Also, since Obama's candidacy arose from the center of the electorate rather than from within the black community (16), Obama has had to prove to African Americans that he can represent their interests.

The story of how Barack Obama overcame the barrier of his racial identity 3 to win the acceptance of the African American community does much to answer the question of why Obama has been a successful candidate. Throughout the presidential race, he has used flamboyant rhetoric to present himself as a representative of the people. Obama persuades voters to project themselves onto him and to see themselves in him, thus establishing an ethos as a candidate who speaks for all. By looking at his speech on 28 September 2007, at Howard University, we can see how Obama established himself as a member and a leader of the black community, and thus understand better how Obama has connected with the American people throughout the race.

> *The story of how Barack Obama overcame the barrier of his racial identity to win the acceptance of the African American community does much to answer the question of why Obama has been a successful candidate.*

When Obama, then a contender for the Democratic presidential nomina- 4 tion, spoke at Howard University, he aimed to establish himself as the next great leader of the African American community. Since Howard is a historically black college, Obama's speech offered an opportunity to convince African Americans that he could represent them and their interests as president. His themes—injustice and the fight for civil rights, both past and present—also seem tailored to his audience. Obama compares past injustices to present-day injustices and past civil rights workers to the activists of his and his audience's generations. The main idea of his speech is that no matter the risk, "we" (by which Obama means either the American people in general or the African

American community of which he claims he is a part) must fight for justice. Obama elevates his audience members by telling them that by working to correct today's societal injustices, they can be the successors to civil rights activists of the past. Through his implication that his past work to fight injustice qualifies him to represent and lead his audience, he also elevates himself to the level of a civil rights leader. He elevates himself and his audience further by using sacred and heroic association and the traditional Moses typology to compare his audience to the biblical Israelites, past civil rights activists to Moses, and both himself and the audience to Moses's successor, Joshua. Since Obama is aiming in his speech to gain credibility as a black leader, it is interesting to note that Martin Luther King Jr. frequently used elevation, sacred and heroic association, and the Moses typology. Also, by claiming to be Joshua, Obama suggests that he is a successor to past civil rights leaders such as King. Thus, when Obama imitates King by using repetition, sacred and heroic association, elevation, and the Moses typology, Obama reminds his audience of King's rhetoric and connects himself with past leaders of the African American community. By using language reminiscent of King to speak to African Americans about civil rights, Obama attempts to prove not only his "blackness" but also his ability to represent the black community as King had done before him.

## In the Style of Martin Luther King

Obama, in his speech at Howard, consistently uses the stylistic techniques of  5
Martin Luther King to establish himself as King's successor. Obama uses King's stylistic strategies to captivate the people in his audience so they will accept him as a leader in the fight for civil rights. According to Richard Lischer, a professor at Duke University's Divinity School, King promoted civil rights by appealing to his audience's sense of beauty: he "pursued his high and serious purpose with a style whose first principle was the achievement of pleasure." King used repetition and rhyme to create pleasure in his audience (120). Obama uses language reminiscent of King for the same purpose of captivation. He repeats sounds and words to delight his audience, emphasize important ideas, and establish an ethos as King's successor.

### Repetition

In the first major section of repetition in his speech at Howard, Obama  6
strengthens his comparison of himself to King by repeating ideas that tie past civil rights activists and their leaders to himself and his audience. He compares the injustice of the civil rights era to present-day inequality, explaining that if King and other activists of the past could fight injustice, modern Americans can as well. This section of the speech focuses on the idea that "those who came before us did not strike a blow against injustice only so that we would allow injustice to fester in our time." Repeating this idea, Obama invokes King's name to talk about Hurricane Katrina, saying, "Dr. King did not take us to the mountaintop so that we would allow a terrible storm to ravage those

who were stranded in the valley." Obama expounds on the theme of past and present injustice by comparing the success of *Brown v. Board of Education* to the failure of today's school system, and by comparing the Little Rock Nine with the Jena Six. Obama also appeals to his audience by comparing everyday people struggling against civil rights era injustice to those struggling against current injustice:

> The teenagers and college students who left their homes to march in the streets of Birmingham and Montgomery; the mothers who walked instead of taking the bus after a long day of doing somebody else's laundry and cleaning somebody else's kitchen—they didn't brave fire hoses and Billy clubs so that their grand-children and their great-grandchildren would still wonder at the beginning of the 21st century whether their vote would be counted; whether their civil rights would be protected by their government; whether justice would be equal and op-portunity would be theirs.

Obama's frequent use of the "They didn't . . . so we would" pattern effectively employs King's technique of repetition to appeal to Obama's audience and heighten his comparison of himself with King. By repeatedly citing both ex-amples of civil rights victories and persisting inequalities, Obama appeals both to his audience's pride in their forebears, including King, and to their sense that they can be successors to their heroes, joining with Obama to fight injustice. Thus, Obama lays the groundwork for his later use of elevation and sacred and heroic association as well as the implication that he can lead African Ameri-cans as both a Joshua figure and a successor to King. Obama continues to use language reminiscent of King in the rest of the speech. He repeats sounds, us-ing stylistic techniques that King used, to establish that he knows how to lead the black community. One of King's repetition strategies that Obama uses is *anaphora*. Anaphora is the repetition of the same word or group of words at the beginning of successive clauses. King used anaphora in his speech "Our God Is Marching On!", saying:

> How long? Not long, because no lie can live forever.
>
> How long? Not long, because you still reap what you sow.
>
> How long? Not long, because the arc of the moral universe is long but it bends toward justice.
>
> How long? Not long, 'cause mine eyes have seen the glory . . . (qtd. in Lischer 128)

Obama echoes King's use of anaphora after describing his risk-taking as an Illinois state senator reforming the death penalty system. He says, "I believed that it was too risky not to act," and then repeats the phrase "What's risky": "What's too risky is keeping quiet. What's too risky is looking the other way." When Obama uses language reminiscent of King's rhetoric in this passage, he also strengthens his comparison of himself and his audience to past civil rights activists, boldly confronting institutional injustice.

Obama continues to echo King's rhetoric and strengthen his claim to be   7 King's successor by using both anaphora and *epistrophe*. He uses anaphora again after promoting the idea of drug rehabilitation programs: "Let's reform this system. Let's do what's smart. Let's do what's just." He also repeats the phrase "It will take a movement" to inspire the audience to action, saying, "It will take a movement to finish what began in Topeka, Kansas and Little Rock, Arkansas. It will take a movement of Americans from every city and town." After explaining the injustice of sentencing of drug offenders, he uses epistrophe, ending a series of sentences with the same words. He says, "Judges think that's wrong. Republicans think that's wrong. Democrats think that's wrong." He also repeats the word "possible" in another example of epistrophe to convince his audience that change can come about: "I would not have driven out to Chicago after college to organize jobless neighborhoods if I didn't believe this was possible. . . . I would not be standing here today if I didn't believe this was possible. . . . And I know that you believe it's possible too." This repetition, in addition to engaging and inspiring his audience, also connects Obama, once more, with King.

At the end of his speech, Obama uses anaphora again both to encourage   8 his audience and to establish himself, through the use of King's stylistic strategies, as King's successor. The same passage contains rhyme meant to delight Obama's listeners, inspire them, and remind them of King's rhetoric. The type of rhyme that Obama uses in the passage is *homoioteleuton*, the similarity of endings of adjacent or parallel words. The passage reads: "Be strong and have courage in the face of joblessness and helplessness and hopelessness. Be strong and have courage, in the face of our doubts and fears, in the face of skepticism, in the face of cynicism, in the face of a mighty river." The words "Be strong and have courage" are taken from the biblical book of Joshua. This quotation is indicative of Obama's use of sacred and heroic association and also strengthens his ultimate comparison of himself to Joshua, and consequently to Moses and King. Thus, in this passage Obama connects himself with King not only by using similar language to King but also by using the Moses typology to imply that he is King's successor.

## Elevation

Another of King's methods that Obama uses to connect himself and his audi-   9 ence with the historic fight against injustice, and thus with King and fellow civil rights workers, is elevation. According to Lischer, King sought "to *elevate* the cause he represented to one of noble and historic proportions" (121). For example, speaking of the struggle for civil rights in the United States, King said, "We must see the tension in this nation is between *injustice* and *justice*, between the forces of *light* and the forces of *darkness*" (122). Obama uses this strategy of elevation to remind the members of his audience that the fight for justice is significant, historic, and heroic. He also elevates both them and himself to convince them that they are capable of fighting for justice and that he can lead them in that fight. He says, "I'm not just running to make history. I'm running because I believe that together, we can change history's course." Obama also speaks of the potential of the United States to fight injustice: "No one leader . . . can . . . make real the promise of opportunity and equality for every citizen. Only a country can do these things. Only this country can do these things."

With this last sentence, Obama has effectively elevated the United States to be the only country in the entire world with a chance to create a just society. He invites his audience to join him in the historic fight for justice. By elevating the struggle for civil rights to epic proportions, and by doing so in the context of a campaign speech, Obama is also elevating the cause of his candidacy.

## Sacred and Heroic Association

A method Obama uses to elevate both his audience and himself is sacred and    10 heroic association. In this rhetorical strategy, speakers use allusions to both religious texts and significant events and people to elevate both the audience and their cause (Lischer 129–30). King used this strategy to allow his audience to identify with heroes of the past. For example, in his final sermon, after speaking of justice and brotherhood, King quoted from the biblical book of Job: "And that day the morning stars will sing together and the sons of God will shout for joy" (qtd. in Lischer 130). This sacred association gave a sense of holiness to King's cause. Obama imitates this strategy of elevation. First, he elevates his audience to the level of history-makers and heroes. He says, "I believe it's time for this generation to make its own mark—to write our own chapter in the American story." Obama elevates both his audience and himself by convincing the members of his audience that together, he and they can change the course of history, as their predecessors in the civil rights movement did. By claiming that the members of his audience can be as heroic as civil rights demonstrators of the past, and by also claiming that he can lead them in the fight for civil rights, Obama is elevating himself by suggesting that he can be a heroic civil rights leader in the mold of King. Obama uses sacred and heroic association again just before the conclusion of the speech. He compares his audience to the biblical hero Joshua, saying, "You are members of the Joshua generation." In this reference, Obama is also using the Moses/Joshua typology, another strategy employed by King.

## Moses/Joshua Typology

According to prominent Martin Luther King Jr. scholar Keith Miller, since the    11 time of slavery, African American speakers have used the Moses typology in their rhetoric. African American rhetoric has traditionally employed the concept of "sacred time," unrestricted by limits of geography or chronology, which allows them to see biblical characters as recurring archetypes. This means that characters from the Old Testament could appear in the New Testament and also in the present day ("Alabama as Egypt" 20). In his book *Voice of Deliverance*, Miller explains that slaves often identified themselves with the Hebrew slaves in Egypt, and they also often combined Moses and Jesus into a common deliverer (20). In Christian typology, Moses and Jesus can also be related to Joshua. Archbishop Desmond Tutu said that "Jesus is but the Greek from of Joshua who led the Israelites across the Jordan River into the Promised Land. . . . Matthew sees Jesus as a second but greater Moses" (qtd. in Miller, "Alabama as Egypt" 20).

Miller demonstrates that King used the Moses typology to identify himself   12
with Moses and African Americans with the Hebrews. In King's speech "Death
of Evil on the Seashore," he compares the fight for civil rights to the struggle of
Israelite slaves. For example, he says that after the Civil War, the "pharaohs of
the South" made an "Egypt of segregation." Now, he says, blacks can escape
from Egypt and by striving "shall reach the Promised Land" (qtd. in Miller,
"Alabama as Egypt" 27–28). In his speech "I've Been to the Mountaintop,"
King again uses the Moses typology. He portrays himself as Moses, who
climbed a mountain to look out over the Promised Land that he would never
reach. King says, "I just want to do God's will. And He's allowed me to go up
to the mountain. And I've looked over. And I've seen the Promised Land. I may
not get there with you. But I want you to know tonight that we as a people
will get to the Promised Land" (qtd. in Miller, *Voice of Deliverance* 182). King
clearly plays the part of Moses in this speech. But just as Moses died before he
could lead his people into the Promised Land, King died one day after his "I've
Been to the Mountaintop" speech, with the fight for civil rights still raging.
Who, then, is left to finish his work, to play Joshua to King's Moses?

In his speech at Howard, Obama both poses this question and answers it.   13
He expands the Moses/Joshua typology to include civil rights demonstrators
and leaders of the past and present. He honors past civil rights workers who
played the role of Moses, saying, "Everyone in this room stands on the shoulders of many Moses. They are the courageous men and women who marched
and fought and bled for the rights and freedoms we enjoy today." He also
shows the need for a Joshua, a new leader to carry on the struggle. He continues where King left off in "I've Been to the Mountaintop," saying, "It was not
in God's plan to have Moses cross the river. Instead He would call on Joshua
to finish the work that Moses began. He would ask Joshua to take his people
that final distance." Obama at first appears to appoint his audience as Joshua.
He calls them "members of the Joshua Generation," and he says to them, "It
is up to you to cross the river." However, when he actually gave his speech,
Obama added a few sentences to his prepared remarks that make clear who
the real Joshua is. He says, "When Joshua discovered the challenge he faced, he
had doubts and he had worries. He told God: 'Don't choose me; I'm not strong
enough; I'm not wise enough; I don't have the training; I don't have enough
experience.'" Here Obama refers to the fact that he himself has been criticized
for not having enough political experience, a joke that the audience obviously
appreciated, given their laughter. However, by saying that Joshua didn't have
"enough experience," Obama is doing more than joking: he is drawing a parallel between himself and Joshua. Joshua did not have experience, but God still
ordained him to lead his people to the Promised Land. It has been said that
Obama does not have experience; however, he can still be the leader of the
Joshua Generation. He can, in fact, be Joshua. He can continue the work of his
people's Moses, Dr. King. As president, he can be King's successor and lead his
people to the Promised Land.

By comparing himself to Joshua, Obama is implying that he is not merely a   14
politician but a hero, ordained by God to lead his people. The question of how

Obama is able to claim to be a successor to King and a Joshua figure without being labeled presumptuous has two possible answers. One could be that, although Obama uses King's rhetorical strategies, overall his comparison of himself to King is fairly subtle. For instance, he only actually mentions King a few times in his speech. However, using the Moses/Joshua typology ensures that once his listeners have identified past civil rights leaders with Moses and Obama with Joshua, they will take the next logical step and identify Obama with King. However, Obama's claim is still quite bold, and the question of how he was able to make it while avoiding the charge of presumption is still a vexing one.

I believe that the answer to this question ultimately lies in Obama's use of elevation. Obama connects with voters, convincing them to project themselves and their dreams onto him. Thus, Obama becomes in effect more than a representative of them; to the audience members, they and Obama become almost one and the same. Thus, when Obama elevates his audience, he also elevates himself. When Obama compares his listeners to those who marched in civil rights era demonstrations, he, as their representative, also implicitly compares himself to the leaders of those marches. When Obama, then, calls his audience the "Joshua Generation," he, as a representative of his audience, is logically also a member of the Joshua Generation. If Obama's listeners accept the claim that they are analogous to the Israelites, God's chosen people, and if they accept Obama as their leader, then it would logically follow that they see Obama as Joshua, a leader of the Israelites. Since Martin Luther King Jr. is Moses, and since Obama is Joshua, Moses's successor, Obama is clearly King's successor. Obama will continue where King left off; Obama will lead African Americans in the continued struggle for civil rights; Obama will lead his people into the Promised Land. 15

## Conclusion

In his speech at Howard, Obama made one of the bold moves that have shifted his image from that of a man who, as Obama said at the Apostolic Church of God, "wasn't black enough," to that of an African American who can authentically lead the black community as its representative. By using King's rhetorical strategies of repetition, elevation, heroic and sacred association, and the Moses/Joshua typology, Obama establishes the ethos he needs to win the black vote: he shows that he is a man who understands both the African American experience and how to lead blacks as a successor to King. By using language reminiscent of King, Obama establishes himself as a leader who will continue the struggle for civil rights and who will lead America to the Promised Land of justice and equality. 16

### Works Cited

Lischer, Richard. *The Preacher King: Martin Luther King Jr. and the Word That Moved America.* New York: Oxford UP, 1995.

I would like to thank my faculty mentor, Elizabeth Vander Lei, and my *Young Scholars* advising editor, Doug Downs, for all the encouragement, guidance, and ideas which they shared with me throughout the process of writing and revising this paper.

Miller, Keith D. "Alabama as Egypt: Martin Luther King, Jr., and the Religion of Slaves." *Martin Luther King, Jr., and the Sermonic Power of Public Discourse*. Ed. Carolyn Calloway-Thomas and John Louis Lucaites. Tuscaloosa: U of Alabama P, 1993. 18–32.

——, *Voice of Deliverance: The Language of Martin Luther King, Jr. and Its Sources*. New York: Free Press, 1992. Obama, Barack. "Remarks of Senator Barack Obama: Apostolic Church of God." Apostolic Church of God, Chicago. 15 June 2008.

——, "Remarks of Senator Barack Obama: Howard University Convocation." Howard University, Washington, DC. 28 Sept. 2007.

Saad, Lydia. "Black Democrats Move into Obama's Column." *Gallup* 15 Jan. 2008. 9 Oct. 2008. <http://www.gallup.com/poll/103756/Black-Democrats-Move-Into-Obamas-Column.aspx>.

Walters, Ron. "Barack Obama and the Politics of Blackness." *The Barack Obama Phenomenon*. Spec. issue *of Journal of Black Studies* 38.1 (2007): 7–29.

## Questions for Discussion and Journaling

1. A reader analyzing a text can only match moves the text is making to existing categories (for example, as Post finds instances in Obama's speech of "elevation" or "typology") if they already know that those categories exist. What did Post need to already know to do this analysis, and what are some ways she might have learned that knowledge?

2. Use *Silva Rhetoricae* (**rhetoric.byu.edu**) to look up other kinds of stylistic repetition besides *anaphora*. How many kinds does the site list, and which ones do you see used in everyday language?

3. Do you buy, ultimately, Post's argument that Obama was deliberately trying to echo the style, sound, and role of Martin Luther King Jr.? Explain your answer, and, if you think he was, offer an opinion on how successful you think that association was.

## Applying and Exploring Ideas

1. Find a copy of Obama's 2007 Howard University speech online. For each of Post's categories, see if you can locate additional examples in the speech to those she already points out. Then, examine the speech for other style moves Obama makes. (Use *Silva Rhetoricae* to identify terms and moves you might want to look for specifically.) Write a short paper that extends Post's analysis of the speech with the additional examples and additional style moves you've found.

2. Write an analysis of the rhetorical situation of Obama's Howard speech using Grant-Davie's definition of *rhetorical situation* (see page 350), emphasizing kairos, exigence, and context.

### Meta Moment
How does Post's article change your understanding of rhetoric? What do you understand better about rhetoric after reading it?

# Writing about Rhetoric: Major Writing Assignments

To help you learn and explore the ideas in this chapter, we suggest four Assignment Options for larger writing projects: Rhetorical Analysis of a Writing Experience, Rhetorically Analyzing an Activity to Understand What Users Need from a Text, Building an Activity Genre Set, and Analysis of Science Accommodation.

## Assignment Option 1. Rhetorical Analysis of a Writing Experience

Think back: What's the most memorable piece of writing you've ever done? What was the situation? And how did that situation help shape the writing? In this four-to-five page rhetorical analysis of a memorable writing experience, your task as a writer is to reflect on how that particular writing experience was a result of the particular situation it was related to—how the situation helped determine what you wrote and why.

Writers are always responding to the situations they're writing in, from, and for, more or less consciously. But even when you're not aware of it, you're responding to rhetorical situations (even before you knew that term or concept). This assignment can show you how you've already been doing that and spur your thinking about what possibilities writing holds if you do it more consciously.

*Analysis Description and Object of Study:* Your rhetorical analysis will be based on some significant piece of writing or writing experience that you've had in the last several years. That writing could have been for school, work, family, or your personal life. It could have been completely private (like a journaling experience) or all-the-way public, like a blog or other online post. It could have been a single short document, like a poem or song lyrics, or it could have been an extended project or experience that involved multiple pieces of writing. The key requirement here is that it has to have been a memorable or important enough experience that you can *clearly remember the circumstances surrounding the writing*.

Once you know what experience and writing you want to focus on, you need to *reflect on and analyze that experience and writing from a rhetorical perspective*. What's that mean? Remember that your overall research question—what you're trying to find out that you don't already know—is *how did your rhetorical situation help shape that piece of writing?* Based on the principles Grant-Davie demonstrates as well as work you do in class, consider the following about the experience you had and the circumstances surrounding it:

- Why did you *need to write* to begin with (**exigence**)? Since it's easier not to write than it is to write, there had to be some reason or purpose behind your writing, some problem to be solved or addressed. What was that?
- Where did that need *come from* (**context**)? What gave rise to it? This is a *historical* question: To understand the circumstances that demanded writing, you need to know what led to those circumstances.
- What **constraints** did you face as a writer? What were the *givens* in your situation—the aspects of it you could not change that controlled what you could do with your writing?

- Who was meant to *read and use your writing* and *what did you want them to do with it* (**audience**)? How was your writing supposed to do something for, to, or with the readers you imagined it for?

The answers to all of these questions, and others, will help you talk about *why* this piece of writing took the shape that it did.

*Planning, Drafting, and Developing through Revision:* In order to make your analysis most meaningful and clear both to you and to other readers, it will need to include at least the following features:

- An *introduction* explaining what inquiry your piece does by posing your research question.
- Some *description of the writing you're focusing on and the experience itself*. You might even include an electronic copy of the writing you're talking about, if one is still available, but in many cases that may not be possible. Whether you can do that or not, take whatever space is necessary in your analysis to describe as clearly as possible what this writing and experience were.
- An *extended discussion of the questions above* in order to describe and analyze the rhetorical situation in which the writing or experience occurred.
- A *conclusion including implications* of your reflection: What did you learn from this? What principles can you draw to help you in future writing situations?

*What Makes It Good?:* While your rhetorical analysis of a writing experience may take a number of different shapes, it will tend to include these traits:

- Meaningful and accurate use of rhetorical terms such as *exigence, constraints, audience* (or *readers*), *purpose, motivation*, and *context*
- A focus on and clear account of how the writing you're analyzing was shaped by the situation and circumstances in which you were writing it
- A main point about the writing, the situation, or rhetorical principles more broadly
- Readable and usable flow through main parts of the piece (such as a description of the writing itself and the experience of writing it, to the aspects of the rhetorical situation that shaped it)
- Evidence that you understand how rhetorical situations constrain writing (in the broad sense of *constrain* that Grant-Davie offers)

## Assignment Option 2. Rhetorically Analyzing an Activity to Understand What Users Need from a Text

In this project, you'll create an analysis of an activity system (see Chapter 2, and Bazerman in this chapter) which will be specifically directed at figuring out what users' needs are for a particular text that mediates some aspect of the activity. This kind of analysis is one you would use in the early planning stages of creating a document in a very high-stakes situation.

This assignment is designed to let you consider some ways in which readers *use* a text or document to meet a given need, how the need for a text emerges in a rhetorical situation that constrains the text, and how rhetorical situations come from larger systems of people-doing-things—activity systems—that shape the need for and use of the text and therefore its rhetorical constraints. Given these principles, in this assignment you'll attend to the categories you should consider when you enter new rhetorical situations.

Remember that to better understand, and find examples of, the idea of *rhetorical situations*, you can review Grant-Davie's article in this chapter (p. 347). To review the basic principles of activity systems, you can return to Bazerman in this chapter (p. 365), Wardle in Chapter 2 (p. 284), or Kain and Wardle in Chapter 2 (p. 273). Terms you'll need to be familiar with for this project include *exigence*, *rhetors*, *constraints*, *objects*, *goals/motives*, *subjects*, *tools*, and *rules/norms*.

*Choose Your Objects for Analysis:* To begin this project, you'll need to select both an activity system and a particular genre of document to analyze. You'll probably find this easiest to do with a genre you actually have some experience writing and an activity system you're somewhat familiar with (if not a participant in), but you can also do this project with less familiar genres and activities. It's also possible that if you're doing this assignment, your teacher will already have selected the genres and actvities the class will work on. If the choice is up to you, be careful to select a genre and activity where you can get unfettered access to examples of the genre and to participants in the activity who would regularly *encounter* that genre (both its writers and its readers/users), as you'll need to interview some of these subjects about how they make use of the genre in question.

Some examples of genre/activity combinations could include:

- Timed writing exams for high-school learning-outcomes assessment or college admissions (such as the SAT or ACT writing exams)
- Appeals to substitute a course to fulfill a college curriculum requirement
- Grant proposals to fund travel abroad for college students
- Proposal memos to alter policies at your place of employment
- Training documents for volunteers at a nonprofit community organization
- Airplane safety information cards ("located in the seat pocket in front of you" on commercial airliners)
- Codes/Covenant/Restrictions documents for a subdivision or homeowners association

*Data Collection:* Your *research question* for this project should (unless your teacher suggests otherwise) probably be in three parts, something like:

1. What rhetorical situation(s), particularly exigence(s), is this kind of document a response to?
2. What needs do a document's users have for this kind of document in order to accomplish some part of the activity they're participating in?
3. How should these needs constrain and shape the document?

Therefore, once you've selected a genre and activity to analyze, you need a plan to collect data on the genre, its typical rhetorical situations, users, and activity system.

We recommend that the class brainstorm methods for building information on each of these elements, following your teacher's guidance. At a minimum, you'll usually need to do these kinds of research:

- Collect at least two *examples of the genre* in question (textual data)
- Develop descriptions of the rhetorical situations that (1) create the exigence for the document and (2) constrain the circumstances in which the document is actually read or used. (For example, if a video recording were made of a reader using this document, what would it record about the time, space, circumstances, and context of the reading?)
- Collect material that helps you understand the *nature of the activity system* itself. (What are its goals/objects, values, subjects/participants, tools, and rules/norms?)
- Interview at least one person who *receives, reads, and uses documents* of this genre to play their part in the activity. (Notice that you'll need to develop a list of interview questions for them.)
- Interview at least one person who has written (or, ideally, regularly writes) or contributed to documents in this genre (and, again, prepare interview questions for them beforehand)
- Don't neglect to check for research that's already been done on this genre or activity by searching the Web and your library's databases. If you do this as a first step and find existing research, you can use it as a guide for designing your own.

When you've completed data collection, you should have examples of the genre to work with and perspectives of people in the activity who use this tool (the document itself) to participate in the activity system. Remember, what you're trying to find out is how the activity's objects and values come together with the rhetorical situation of the document's *use* to create constraints that help shape successful documents.

***Principles and Questions for Analysis:*** With data collected, you'll turn to analysis, which will be guided by a few particular assumptions. As you've seen explained in a variety of readings in the book, any text we write serves as a tool in some activity system, which can help us better understand what we need to write and why. Rhetorical situations present writers with readers who expect a given text to meet a certain need (exigence), and the particulars of that need, those readers, and the writer's own motivations will constrain the resulting text in various ways. So, considering the elements of the activity system(s) in which the rhetorical situation occurs will usually help us better understand that situation/ in these ways:

- Knowing the object(s) of the system helps the writer understand how the text, its exigence, and their own motivations fits within the broader goals of the system.
- Knowing who participates in the system (its "subjects") will give the writer a better sense of the text's readers and their needs, values, and expectations.
- Knowing the textual tools of the system will help the writer better understand what genre(s) the situation requires and the particular forms those genres take in this situation.
- Knowing the rules and norms of the system will help the writer more fully understand both the readers who will use the text, how they'll use it, and what shape the text is expected to take.

Given those principles, when you turn to actually analyze your data, you should let some of the following questions guide you. Activity systems and the networks of genres that they create are often too complex to be completely analyzed, and these questions may give you far more to look at than you can use in a single project. It's okay to choose just a few, in consultation with the rest of the class and/or your instructor. There are also many more questions than these that *could* be asked; we've offered these because they're fairly intuitive, arising from your own typical experiences with texts.

### Objects and Exigence of the Activity Systems

- What activity system(s) use the texts you collected?
- What are the goals (objects) and values of the system(s)?
- What specific rhetorical situation are you analyzing?
- How does the rhetorical situation relate to the goals and values of these activity systems?

### Writer Motivations

- Who are the writers?
- What are the writer's purpose and goals for the text?
- What does the writer imagine the text accomplishing?
- How will the writer know if the text is effective?

### Tool Use (Genre/Text Use)

- What genres did you collect?
- What are these genres a tool for doing?
- What use will and must readers make of the genre?
- In what actual (physical) circumstances will the genre be used?
- What values and expectations will readers bring to the genre based on their *need* for it, the rules and norms of the activity, their planned use of the text, and the activity-values they share?

When you, your class, and instructor have settled on what questions to ask, from this list as well as others you've come up with, look to the data you've collected for answers. Take a lot of notes in order to connect various moments or portions of data to particular questions. As you analyze, responses to questions, particular patterns, and insights about what's happening should begin to emerge. Be sure you're taking careful notes to keep track of all these ideas. If you've been able to locate existing research on the activity or genre you're studying, you can compare your results to those in that research and consider the results of that comparison as well.

*Planning, Drafting, and Development through Revision:* As always, writing requires both coming up with what to say and getting it said. You can try to break those two elements apart by *planning* as much of your analysis report as possible before you begin writing the report itself. Deciding on the major sections of the report, listing or outlining ideas to be covered in each section, or even writing a sentence-outline that lists ideas in great detail without putting them into prose will all make your drafting itself go more smoothly.

At the same time, when you have difficulty coming up with the ideas that would go in such outlining, it's often useful to freewrite or just strike out on your writing expedition "unplanned," seeing what you have to say. This approach will usually make your drafting take much longer, both because you're trying to do two mental operations (composing and inscribing) at once and because the results will need a lot of development through revision in order to transform from "ideas about what I want to say" to "what I want to say." But, writing can be a powerful tool for *finding* what you want to say, so don't hesitate to use it for that as long as you understand that the first thing you write is *the thing that helps you write the thing you're supposed to write*, not the thing you're supposed to write itself.

One of the first major considerations in planning and drafting a piece is its overall structure and flow: What major parts will it have and what order will they come in? Your analysis report could follow the traditional social-science reporting pattern of Introduction (see Swales), Background, Methods, Analysis and Discussion, and Implications/Conclusion. Or, in looking at the points you need to make, you might see a different organization working more effectively. You might find it useful to participate in a short class workshop where you compare your own organizational plans with those of other students to generate ideas and other possibilities for flowing your report.

Even if you've planned your piece thoroughly and carefully, *expect* that a project this large and complex will require development through revision. This is because of the **epistemic** nature of writing: No matter what you know before you start writing, the act of writing will itself give you new realizations and take you to unexpected places, even when you're following an outline. So anticipate that what you want to say at the end of your first draft will be a bit different than what was important to you when you started drafting, and be willing and prepared (especially with time) to take what you learned *while writing* your initial draft and incorporate it back into the whole piece, not just the last page.

*What Makes It Good?:* A good project and analysis report on it may take a number of different shapes but will tend to have these traits in common:

- Lots of concrete data drawn from real examples and informative interviews with people using the texts you're studying (with that data used as examples of the points you're making and conclusions you're drawing in the text)
- Careful attention to the needs and values of those people using the texts you're studying to participate in the activity you're studying
- A main point that's made clearly and is in some way novel, unexpected, or valuable to readers wanting to learn more about the activity and genre you analyzed or about how rhetorical situations and reader use within activities shape a given genre
- Organization/flow that makes your report highly readable and usable
- Evidence that you understand the relationships among between rhetorical situations, reader needs and values, activity systems, and genres

# Assignment Option 3. Building an Activity Genre Set

Here's a big, interesting project: Create a catalog of all the genres that a given participant in a professional or work-related activity system writes and reads (based on the similar work Bazerman does on p. 381). Then write an introduction to the catalog that speaks to other students interested in that profession or job, summarizing the implications your catalog suggests about:

- What the common texts in this profession or job are
- What someone doing this job needs to know in order to read and write these texts and thus do their work

- What the work of this profession seems to be
- What this profession's values and priorities seem to be
- What knowledge, abilities, and skills students should acquire and hone in order to be successful at this profession

*Object of Study and Data Collection:* Pick a person who performs a job that you think you might be interested in, and find out what texts they produce and read on a regular basis for that job (their genre set). Interview the person and ask them about all of the texts they read and write; collect examples of as many of them as they are able to provide you with (some may be confidential).

Remember Bazerman's advice on page 381: Be clear about why you are engaging in this research, and outline clearly for yourself what questions you hope to answer by engaging in it. Make a list of all the data you plan to collect, including texts, interviews, observations, etc., and where and how you will get this data.

*Analyzing Texts and Building Your Catalog:* This is a very complex assignment: First you have to compile the various genres your interviewee writes and reads; then you have to infer from the compilation what work is being done and what knowledge, abilities, and skills that work requires. Either in class discussions or in separate discussions with your teacher, you'll need to consider how to analyze the data that you collect. (Review the example analysis that Bazerman provides on pp. 383–91.)

We can predict at least some of the questions you'll need to ask about your data already:

- What are the common characteristics of these texts?
- What work do these texts perform or allow, and how does this work relate to the goals of the overall actvities these texts are tools in mediating?
- What do these texts suggest are the values and priorities of the people who write and use them?

*Designing, Drafting, and Revising Your Catalog Summary:* Remember that what you're actually *doing* in creating this catalog is preparing it and a summary to be used by students curious about this profession or job and wondering what it involves and how to do well at it. That's your exigence and purpose, and it tells you something about your readership; together, those elements will help you understand the constraints that should shape the document you produce. What should it look like? What material, design, and arrangement will make it most usable for these readers? Participate in class workshops where you consider various design alternatives for the piece. Keep in mind, too, that various pieces all the students in the class produce could be combined into a single, multi-profession genre catalog as a resource for later students. What designs would contribute to such combining?

Look to the beginning of this assignment description to see again the questions your summary of your catalog should address. Are they listed in the best order, or might there be a better flow? How long do you think your summary will need to be in order to discuss each of those? (What happens if your summary is longer than your catalog? How would you suggest modifying the assignment?)

In order to revise your early drafts, you might *user-test* your summary and catalog by asking other students to use it as it's intended. What questions does it leave them with? Where do they want more information? Where do they wish you'd explained things more clearly or changed the order of what you write about?

*What Makes It Good?:* Think from your readers' perspectives: What does this catalog and summary need to be?

- Accurate: Don't misinform your readers; take care that what you say about what writing is done in a profession and the knowledge it requires are correct.
- Readable: Information needs to be laid out in a format that readers can easily access and follow.
- Perceptive: The difference between a good catalog and a great one might come down to how well you infer what knowledges, abilties, and skills a professional must have from the documents they're reading and writing.
- Thorough: A catalog that includes the most genres a given writer is using beats a catalog that only includes a few of them.
- Helpful: Can another student read your catalog, get a feel for the work being done in that profession, and draw conclusions about how interesting it would be to them and how they could prepare themselves for that job?

# Assignment Option 4. Analysis of Science Accommodation

One way to better understand the kinds of writing and thinking valued in the university is to compare them to more popular forms of writing and thinking with which you are familiar. Toward this end, your task will be to find a mass media report or discussion about a scientific finding, and then trace it back to the original report from which it was taken, in order to analyze the differences between the two types of discourse.

*Object of Study:* Find an interesting mass media report or discussion about science (e.g., a CNN headline, a blog entry, etc.). Trace the science back to the original research report from which it was taken. Make some initial observations about how they're different. Are there any obvious similarities?

*Researching and Analyzing:* Analyze the differences between the original scientific report and the mass media report of the scientific finding. The technical name for what happens when a scholarly source becomes popularized is **accommodation**. (If you would like to read more about the accommodation of science before you begin, check out Jeanne Fahenstock's article "Accommodating Science" from *Written Communication*, 1998.)

As you analyze each text, consider questions such as these:

- What is the rhetorical situation—**exigence, rhetors, audiences, context, constraints**—for each text?
- What is the **genre** of each text? (For instance, is one a peer-reviewed research article and the other a two-minute news report?) Is there a genre shift between the

original presentation of the scientist's work and its popularization? Why was one genre not appropriate or useful in the other rhetorical situation?

- How subtly or obviously are claims stated in each (and how accurately)? How do the scientists state the significance of their claims? How does this compare to how the media account states the significance of the scientific claims?
- How are non-specialists accommodated in the mass media piece—through language change, tone change, more overt statement of significance, the use of more sweeping claims (e.g., "the only kind" or "the first kind"), placement of information in the paragraph or sentence, removal of qualifiers or hedges (taking out "appears" or "suggests"), changes in phrasing that are more removed from the observed results of the study by leaping to results? Why are these changes made? Does the meaning change when these rhetorical changes are made?
- What sources are used in the original science report and in the media accommodation of it? Does the accommodation go beyond the published research to include interviews for quotations from the scientists not found in the original article? Do these interview quotations include observations and conclusions not found in the original published article? Why are these changes made? What is the effect of these changes?
- Is contradictory evidence omitted in the accommodation? Why?
- Are unsupportable or unsupported claims included in the accommodation? Why?
- Is there any evidence that the scientists tried to refute claims in the accommodation? Given your analysis of information published about this research, did the scientist succeed in changing the claims made about his/her work?
- To your knowledge, did other scientists refute the claims of the original scientists after the original publication? If so, were those counterarguments ever publicized?

Now step back and consider what values the scientists' language suggest they adhere to, and what values are suggested by the news media's language. For example, do scientists value objectivity and caution more than news media? What do news media seem to value? Can you explain the difference in terms of activity systems, audience needs and values, or other concepts from this chapter?

*Planning:* Consider what you found by asking yourself the following:

- What are the differences between the writing done by scientists and the writing done by those in the popular media? What do these differences tell us about the values of academic writers?
- What is hard or unfamiliar to you about the scientific writing?
- How do scientists support their claims? How does this compare to how the media supports their claims?
- What are the strengths and weaknesses of each type of writing?

Now plan an essay written for incoming first-year college students in which you outline how academic discourse differs from more popular discourse. In this essay, you should note various levels of difference, from values to length to tone to sources used. It might be helpful to frame your advice in terms of the values, conventions, and purposes of different

**activity systems** or **discourse communities**. Why and how is language used differently in the university, and particularly in the sciences?

*Drafting and Development through Revision:* You have a variety of options for presenting the information you have gathered to your audience of incoming students.

- You might consider writing a fairly formal and traditional research paper, making the three "moves" that John Swales outlines at the beginning of your paper. (See the CARS model, p. 12.)
- You might present your information in a less formal way, perhaps as a magazine article that includes tables or visual representations of some of the differences you've found. You might consider creating an interactive Web site where you and your classmates can share your findings.

As always, discuss your options with your instructor.

As you and your classmates consider each other's drafts along the way, see if you've answered this question effectively: How and why does academic discourse differ from more popular discourse?

*What Makes It Good?:* Once you know the differences between the science article and its accommodation, your job is to educate other students about what you have learned. You should be able to explain to them how scientific academic writing differs from more popular kinds of writing, and you should be able to help them understand *why* these two kinds of writing are so different (remember everything that you have learned about **discourse** in reading (see p. 215, and others). A really good analysis will not just explain *what* is different, but *why* those differences exist, and *what they mean*.

## chapter 4

# Processes

## How Are Texts Composed?

While we often think of writing as a solitary activity, the reality is that writers—who are creating texts that help mediate activities—are constantly working with readers and other writers as they write. In this photo, writer Rodes Fishburne hangs his ideas in an office shared by a group of freelancers. The shared office space provides lots of readers and helps the writers' ideas progress.

So far in this book, we have considered how individuals' literate histories influence their current literacy practices and attitudes, how the texts individuals create are constructed and influenced by other people, and how texts are constructed and make meaning. Now we will focus on how people create texts: the processes by which individuals put words on a page and attempt to make meaning—for themselves as well as for and with others. How do writers' individual writing processes vary to respond to changing contexts? Are there aspects of writing process which are typical across many contexts for most writers?

Answering the question, "How do I write?" isn't as easy as it seems. How well do you really understand how you get things written? How would you describe your writing process if asked to do so right now? And is what you *think you do* actually *what you do?*

While many people are quite conscious of "what works for them" in order to get a text written, they tend to have more difficulty explaining *why* it works—or even what they're doing, beyond some basic details like "I write down a lot of ideas until I feel like I know what I want to say and then I just start typing it up." Such a description doesn't actually tell us a lot. Yet it would seem that if you want to become a more versatile, capable, powerful writer, you need to be pretty aware of what activities, behaviors, habits, and approaches lead to your strongest writing—and which don't.

Understanding yourself as a writer is complicated by popular conceptions (or misconceptions) of what writing is and how it gets done. As you've seen in each earlier chapter of the book, many of our conceptions related to writing (like imagining it to have universal rules, or cultural attitudes toward originality in writing) are inaccurate. These misconceptions are not harmless; they can impact what we do and don't do, what we are willing to try or not, and how we feel about ourselves and our writing. In the case of writing processes, three popular but incorrect conceptions seem to be that some people are born writers and others are not, that good writers write alone, using mysterious "inspiration," and that for good writers, writing is easy. If we believe these things about writing, we might be less likely to try to write better, assuming that if we struggle we simply aren't "natural writers." Or we might not ask other people for feedback, assuming that good writers should be able to produce something by themselves without feedback from readers.

This chapter draws on research about writing processes in order to demonstrate how these and other popular misconceptions about writing are inaccurate, and to replace them with concrete ideas about what writers do when they write. Writing researchers have collected useful data on what people are doing when they write, so that they can show novice writers what experienced writers are doing, get them to practice doing similar things, and help them find their own writing groove along the way.

Writing researchers and writers themselves are fascinated by where a writer's ideas come from and how they develop over time. So studies of composing processes seriously examine **invention**, or how writers (or **rhetors**) think up ideas over time, whether through multiple drafts, or outlines, or lots of mulling and percolating and interaction with other people. Most readings in this chapter have a lot to say about **planning** and **revision**. Perhaps the most important idea, raised in the first reading by Paul Prior, is that writing is only partly the "transcribing" act of writing down an idea—what he calls **inscription**. Instead, writing also includes the act of coming up with the ideas to be inscribed—this he calls **composition**. In many cases, writers do both at once, writing what they know at the moment in order to look at what they've written later and see what it tells them about what they need to write in a new version. (In these moments, writing works like driving in the dark with headlights: You can only see two hundred yards at a time, and to see the next two hundred, you have to drive the first two hundred.) Prior's piece also overviews for us what most of the rest of the pieces in this chapter do: Use a variety of methods to try to trace what writers' processes actually are, and from that tracing principles that can help us write more effectively.

One group of readings in the chapter gets us to think about invention and drafting. For example, Anne Lamott gets at a way to use inscription (drafting) to aid composition (coming up with what to say) in her piece "Shitty First Drafts"—insisting that as writers we have permission to write badly at first, as a necessary step in finding our way to better later drafts. Mike Rose helps us think about some reasons why getting words onto the page can be difficult: Compared with writers who treat rules flexibly and say what they want before thinking about following rules, other writers are so busy trying not to break any rules that they have difficulty thinking of anything to say. Peter Elbow suggests writers try to draft in ways that make us comfortable, such as "speaking" or talking our writing onto the page, and then finding ways through rewriting to turn that talk into more carefully crafted writing. Nancy Sommers, in the first of two of her pieces in this chapter, works on the problem of how writers incorporate sources in their writing while keeping their own writerly voices primary.

The weight that each of these writers puts on revision and their belief that meaning emerges through multiple drafts leads us to wonder about revision itself and how it works. The second group of readings in this chapter carries this focus, beginning with Sommers's piece on the revising strategies of student and experienced writers. Sommers finds that student writers often don't understand that ideas emerge through the act of writing, and thus they tend to see revision as changing words rather than as a chance to continue to find their ideas. Carol Berkenkotter looks closely at the revision processes of one professional writer, Donald Murray (who also responds briefly to Berkenkotter's study), finding that Murray actually blends revision and planning, or invention, into the same activity. Murray, like the experienced writers in Sommers's study, sees revision as a chance to make meaning, not "fix" words. The next reading allows us to directly hear about Murray's perspective on rewriting in "The Maker's Eye" (actually originally written several years before Berkenkotter invited him to participate in her study). We also include, in the e-Pages, Barbara Tomlinson's research examining metaphors that writers use to describe revision. The language we choose to describe the activity of revision reveals our assumptions about what revision is, how it works, and its purposes.

Like any piece of writing itself, people's writing processes develop over time and change depending on context (as the previous chapters suggested). You will be able to see that in many of the readings in this chapter; for example, Donald Murray writes differently for his job than he does when he is given a timed writing task (similar to the ones that you might receive for school testing). The students in Sommers's study have learned a way to revise that seems to work for them in school, but the professional writers she talks to feel they need very different strategies. The last pair of readings in the chapter focus on writers moving from place to place in their education. Sondra Perl examines the composing processes of unskilled writers, who are both new to college and struggling with the conventions and goals of college-level writing. Dorothy Winsor looks to the other end of college education in studying how engineers develop as writers when they begin working in professional practice, comparing how they learn on the job to how they were taught while earning their engineering degrees. For a broader view of development as a writer, look to the e-Pages for Junot Díaz's short piece, "Becoming a Writer" (**bedfordstmartins.com/writingaboutwriting/epages**).

There are a number of other ways to understand and group the readings in this chapter as well, depending on what aspects of the writing process you are focusing on. For example, because writing is in the realm of thought and ideas, we're dealing with the mental or **cognitive** aspect of writing when we think about process. You'll see a number of the researchers in this chapter thinking about, theorizing about, modeling, and testing problem-solving patterns, or **heuristics,** and other guesses at how our brains process ideas in order to construct meaning in texts (both as writers and readers). (See, for example, Rose [p. 532], Berkenkotter [p. 590], and Sommers [p. 565].) Along with the cognitive, some researchers consider the *affective* domain—that is, what goes on with the body and with emotions. (Berkenkotter [p. 590], Winsor [p. 640], Lamott [p. 527], Perl [p. 615], Elbow [p. 547], and Murray [p. 610] think about these issues.) This is where **context** comes in: Writing depends not only on the ideas in your brain, but on whether you're trying to write in a journal under a tree on a gorgeous sunny afternoon, or in a fluorescent-lit cubicle with a boss who needs your memo on budget cuts right away breathing over your shoulder. It also depends on the history of the writer (think about what you learned in Chapter 1) and his or her previous experiences with writing, with the ideas currently under consideration, with the

**genre** being written, etc. Our environment and **rhetorical situation** shape our thoughts, so the cognitive domain never stands apart from what's outside our brains and bodies.

Still, writing is ultimately the meaning we make in our heads, so to understand composing processes, we have to somehow look inside our heads. This is the tricky part of writing research, as you'll see reflected in the numerous **methodologies** (procedures for conducting research) the research studies in this chapter use and demonstrate. (See, for example, Perl [p. 615], Rose [p. 532], Berkenkotter [p. 590], Sommers [p. 576], Tomlinson [e-Pages], and Prior [p. 492]). The basic problem is this: Researchers can't directly access what's happening in your brain; they have to infer what's happening by looking for external signs. You could *tell* researchers what you're thinking, although (1) you can't talk as fast as you think, and (2) the talking inevitably *changes* what you're thinking. Researchers could look at the mistakes you make and try to explain the rules you're following (which you're probably not even aware of). They could interview you and study the words you use to express yourself. They could ask you to draw about your processes and all of the resources on which you rely while writing. But they would still never know *exactly* what's going on in there. (Not even you know that, really.) So, in these readings, you'll see researchers working to get at something that we can't access directly.

The people who wrote the articles in this chapter not only study writing, but they also see themselves as writers, and sometimes think about the ways in which their own research applies to their own writing. If you're interested in watching how this happens, be sure to look at Lamott [p. 527], Berkenkotter [p. 590], Murray [p. 610], Elbow [p. 547], Rose [p. 532], and Sommers [p. 565].

This chapter emphasizes these threshold concepts: writing is *knowledge-making*, it requires ongoing and repeating *processes*, and it is *not perfectible*. Ultimately, this chapter prompts you to be reflective about yourself as a writer; if you really engage in the material, you should attain some **mindfulness** about your writing process, some in-the-moment self-awareness and strategizing about what you're doing. Researchers have learned that mindfulness is one of the practices that will help you to use later what you are learning now—that is, to **transfer** your writing-related knowledge to new situations. Some of the activities you will be asked to engage in here might seem strange—keeping a log of all your writing in a week, talking out loud while you write, and so on. If you can suspend your cynicism about these activities, though, we think you will come out a more aware—and hopefully a more capable—writer on the other end.

This chapter will also invite you to explore how other writers write—or don't—and what helps them be successful—or not. We hope, in short, that the work you do in this chapter will help you thoughtfully explore both your own writing processes and those of others around you, so that you continue to get a better sense of how writing works, what processes and practices promote effective writing, and who you are as a writer.

## Chapter Goals

- To acquire vocabulary for talking about writing processes and yourself as a writer
- To actively consider your own writing processes and practices and shift them if you wish
- To understand writing and research as processes requiring planning, incubation, revision, and collaboration
- To improve as a reader of complex, research-based texts

# Tracing Process: How Texts Come into Being

## PAUL PRIOR

- Prior, Paul. "Tracing Process: How Texts Come Into Being." *What Writing Does and How It Does It*. Ed. Charles Bazerman and Paul Prior. Mahwah, NJ: Lawrence Erlbaum, 2004. 167–200. Print.

## Framing the Reading

It's easy to ask, casually, "What is your writing process?" And to give a casual answer: "Well, I spend some time figuring out what to write and then when I'm ready to start writing—or when I can't put it off any longer—I sit down and start drafting, and then when I have a first draft I edit it to make sure it's what I actually want to say." If you give this sort of answer, it is likely because that is what you think you do when you write, and you might not remember (or ever even consider) what you might do beyond that. But, as Paul Prior demonstrates in this chapter from his book, there is much more involved in the act of composing, and Prior helps us understand how to learn more about what actually happens when we write.

Prior is an English professor at the University of Illinois, Urbana–Champaign. He made a major mark on the field of writing studies with his 1998 book *Writing/Disciplinarity: A Sociohistoric Account of Literate Activity in the Academy*. In everyday terms, Prior studies how members of academic disciplines (like history, mathematics, astrophysics, or writing studies) use language and writing to accomplish their activities. He uses both **activity theory** and **genre theory** (you can find more on these in Chapters 2 and 3) in his analyses. Part of studying this subject is looking very closely at "how texts come into being"—how people actually produce them. Due to his interest in studying how writing works, Prior directs the University of Illinois's Center for Writing Studies, which brings together faculty from several departments to work on questions related to the nature and activity of writing. He is also currently co-editor of the scholarly journal *Research in the Teaching of English*.

In the book chapter reprinted here, Prior helps readers think carefully through the many aspects of writing a text, and takes an equally close look at authorship, even differentiating between people who *instigate* the writing of a text and those who actually *write* it. (In American culture both can be identified as authors.) In addition to considering the nature of the writing process itself, Prior also creates a primer on *how to study* the writing process, including tracing the networks of texts that stand behind any other text (an idea that might seem familiar

if you read Kevin Roozen's work in Chapter 1 [p. 157] or James Porter's piece in Chapter 3 [p. 395]), collecting writers' accounts of their writing processes, and directly observing those processes. By the time you finish this chapter, you'll have a much richer sense of what it is to create (compose, write) a text (and why it's not always easy!) and a set of strategies for doing your own investigations of writing processes, both your own and others'. As we mentioned in the introduction to this chapter and to this book, your conceptions about writing and how writing happens make a difference to how you write and what you are willing to think about and do differently when you write. If you can learn to consider how writing happens and think about your own writing practices, you might be able to change the way you think about writing and be able to write with greater success in a variety of situations.

Note in the citation above that Prior is also a co-editor of the book from which this chapter is taken, along with Charles Bazerman (author of a reading in Chapter 3 as well).

## Getting Ready to Read

*Before you read,* do at least one of the following activities:

- List all the different parts of your own typical writing process that you can think of. What are all the things you have to do to compose a piece of writing?
- Do your homework on the author: what else can you learn about Paul Prior via Google or a scholarly database like CompPile (**comppile.org/search/comppile_ main_search.php**)?

*As you read,* consider the following questions:

- Make notes regarding the new terms that Prior provides to describe writing. For example, how does he define the *animator* versus the *principal*? As you make notes about these new terms, try to think of how to apply them to your own writing experiences.
- Prior says that writing is an "embodied activity"—one you conduct with your entire body, not just your brain and fingers. As you read, try to think of examples of how your writing is embodied.
- How much do you interact with others while you write a text? (And remember that "writing a text," as defined in this chapter, includes invention, or coming up with ideas, not just transcribing words on a page.)

## Preview

Why is it important to study writing processes? The first and central reason is that writing processes are where texts come from. If you want to understand why a text is written as it is, how it might have been written differently, how it came to meet some goals but not others, how it could have been written better, then it makes sense to look not just at the text itself, but at the history of work and the varied materials from which the text was produced. In the 1970s, a number of researchers and teachers came to the conclusion that processes of writing are fundamental to understanding, teaching, and learning writing, that writing is not about learning and applying formulas for making fixed kinds of texts, but about ways of working—ways of acting—that align writers, readers, texts, and contexts.

In this chapter, we take up the central issue of how to study writing processes, 2 the actual activities that people engage in to produce texts. As was discussed in the book's Introduction, the process of writing obviously includes the immediate acts of putting words on paper (or some other medium) and the material text or series of texts thus produced. However, the words have to come from some-where. Thus, tracing the writing process also means tracing the inner thoughts, perceptions, feelings, and motives of the writer(s) as well as tracing exchanges (spoken or written) between people, exchanges in which the content and pur-poses of a text may be imagined and planned, in which specific language may even be "drafted" out in talk as we see in chapters 8 and 9. Thinking and inter-action about a text may happen at any point, may be fleeting rather than sus-tained, may be planned or unplanned, recognized at the time or made relevant only later. A text may be drafted and written in less than a minute (as in a quick email response) or may represent the work of an entire lifetime. Many writers describe ideas arising when they are jogging, riding on a bus, watching TV, tak-ing a shower, in the midst of an apparently unrelated conversation, waking up from a dream, and so on. A key issue in tracing the process is how a text gets initiated. Many accounts of writing processes bracket off the task, taking it as a given—perhaps because the researcher often gives it. However, all the elements of initiation and motivation—the emergence of some text as write-able in some context—are central to tracing the process. Finally, writers do not make texts up out of thin air. As chapter 4 emphasizes, writers must always draw on other texts, most obviously through quotation and citation, but also as models (direct and indirect) and dialogic partners. The role of these other texts must be considered as central parts of the process. When we understand the writing process in this way, there is clearly no single way to study writing processes and certainly no way of actually capturing everything that goes into producing even a single text. In this chapter, **we will consider a toolkit of methods for tracing writing, includ-ing intertextual analysis, think-aloud protocols, different types of interviews, use of existing accounts, and observation.**

## Basic Concepts

*Inscription, Composing, and Text.* In everyday usage, "writing" signifies two 3 distinct acts, **inscription** and **composing**, that are treated as one. Writing is a process of inscription, of inscribing text onto or into some medium. We usu-ally think first of writing on paper, but in fact the **media** can be diverse. People also inscribe text on t-shirts, on electronic media, in stone, into tree trunks, on or in metal, in the dirt, and so on. **Tools of inscription** include pens, brushes, and pencils, computers and printing presses, lithographs and keyboards, knives and sticks. In any case, when we think of writing, our first image is probably of an act of inscription, of writing with pen in hand on paper or typing with keyboard on an electronic screen. In tracing the history of a text, it may be that we are tracing a series of material inscriptions, using several tools, sometimes layered together. For example, I first wrote parts of this text in pencil on unlined paper in a spiral notebook. I then used a keyboard to enter the text, revising as

> *. . . writers do not make texts up out of thin air.*

I typed, onto an electronic disk displayed on a screen. I printed that text and revised by editing and writing with a pen onto the printed page (sometimes writing longer revisions on the blank back surface).

In general, we may think of a writer as a person who is composing the 4 text as she is inscribing it. However, **composing and inscription are separable**. For example, a photocopy machine, a machine pressing words into a piece of metal, and a secretary typing up a hand-written manuscript without editing it are involved in inscription but not composing. Likewise, composing can, and often does happen, without inscription of a text, as when a person plans a text or even drafts out language mentally or in conversation with others.

When people talk about "**text**," there are several different senses that we 5 should be aware of to avoid confusion. *Text* sometimes means a unique material inscription. In this sense, tracing the writing process might involve tracing a series of, perhaps diverse, texts that are linked together from the perspective of some final product. Writing a paper for a class then might involve many texts, not only drafts, but also notes of many kinds (including marginal notes in readings), raw and transformed data that will be discussed, written responses to drafts, the assignment itself, and so on. *Text* is sometimes taken more expansively, to refer as well to the various mental and oral representations of the material texts, regardless of whether they are ever written out. For example, what if a writer formulates a sentence verbally, either when writing alone or when composing collaboratively with other people, and then rejects that sentence? Is this moment of composing and revision fundamentally different because the sentence wasn't inscribed and erased? Sometimes, all of these material inscriptions (and perhaps the ideational representations) are idealized in retrospect as "the text," uniting all moments in the production under a unified label. It is common to say that I read a book; say *Harry Potter and the Philosopher's Stone*, regardless of which copy of it I read, whether in hardback or paper, on the Web, or as a handwritten manuscript whether in English, Spanish, or Arabic. Likewise, I might say "I spent a month writing that paper" meaning not that I slowly wrote a *single* document over a month, but that I worked toward the final product for a month, during which period I produced a whole series of texts in the first sense (drafts, notes, editorial marginalia, revisions, email messages to friends about the ideas, summaries of key readings). How we understand text—as a unique material object, as a representation regardless of medium (including thought and speech), as the ideal that unifies varied acts and objects in a processes—is not the issue; the issue is being aware of the different senses, not shifting, from one to the other unconsciously.[1]

---

[1] In some technical uses, a text is understood as any specific semiotic object that we might reflect on and analyze. Thus, people can also talk about the text of a film, of the body, of clothing, of a conversation, of a cityscape, and so on.

*Authorship.*    When we see that tracing the composing of a text, what classical  6
rhetoric termed **invention**, involves the contributions of multiple people, it becomes
clear that tracing the writing process also implicates tracing authorship. Goffman
(1981) analyzed the everyday notion of the speaker/writer, suggesting that three
roles are typically collapsed within that term: the **animator**, who actually utters/
inscribes the words; the **author**, who selects the sentiments and words; and the
**principal**, whose positions are being represented in the words. In many instances of
situated discourse, however, these roles are divided, not fused. For example, a presidential press secretary (the animator) might make an announcement of an environmental initiative that the President (the principal) intends to enact, reading words
written by an EPA speech writer (author). This simple division suggests that tracing
the writing process also means tracing a **structure of participation**, of examining
who is involved in making the text and in what ways.

Even Goffman's analysis of authorship, however, oversimplifies the com-  7
plexities of the participation structure. If we return to the hypothetical example
of the press secretary's announcement of an environmental initiative, it is unlikely that a lone speech writer in the EPA would produce such a text. Studies
of writing in institutions have routinely found complex processes of collaborative planning and writing. Documents are cycled to various parties in the
organization for comment, revision, and/or review. This chain of participants
may also include editors who alter the text and word processors who inscribe
written or taped drafts. In these chains, the history of a single text (in the idealized sense) is likely to involve multiple writers.

Even this more typical scenario, with authorship distributed among a number  8
of people, oversimplifies, for we also need to consider **inter-textuality** (see Bazerman, chap. 4, this volume) and the **dialogic influences** of real and imagined audiences. Each participant involved in making the text is recalling anticipating, pre-
supposing, or actually sounding out others (in this case, perhaps the president,
the press, the public, special interests). In the government, public hearings of
various sorts are often required parts of the process. In other domains (advertising, politics, public relations, marketing), focus groups and experiments are often
used to test out ideas and products as they are in development. Each participant
in the writing process also consults, draws on, takes text from, responds to, and
argues with other texts. These complex structures of participation in authorship also complicate the notion of the principal (the one whose views are represented). Our hypothetical announcement may explicitly represent the president's
position. However, through its history of production and intertextual influences,
it will have come to represent the voices of many people. And, of course, whenever a government announcement of this type is made, it is read and analyzed in
terms of whose voices, interests, ideas, and influences it reveals.

From this perspective, some form of **co-authorship** is unavoidable. To take  9
another familiar example, in this view, every teacher is very actively co-authoring
her students' texts, taking up key roles in the production of the text through initiating and motivating it, setting important parameters (the type of text to write,
the length, what kinds of sources to use, the timing of the process), and often
contributing to content (whether through class discussion or specific response).

This role is not diminished because our cultural models of authorship do not acknowledge that teachers co-author their students' texts or because the quality of the text and problems with the text are usually attributed, especially in grades, solely to the student's knowledge or effort. Understanding how people represent the process and authorship and understanding how a text is actually produced in practice are related but distinct issues; it is important to explore both.

*Writing as Practice.*   When we look closely at situated composing, we do not   10
find a smooth easy activity. Writing moves forward (and backward) in fits and starts, with pauses and flurries, discontinuities and conflicts. Situated **acts of composing/inscription** are themselves complex composites. Writers are not only **inscribing text**. They are also repeatedly **rereading** text that they've written, **revising** text as they write as well going back later to revise, pausing **to read other texts** (their own notes, texts they have written, source materials, inspirations), pausing **to think and plan**. In fact, if we look at actual **embodied activity,** we also see that writers are doing many other things as well—drinking coffee, eating snacks, smoking, listening to music, tapping their fingers, pacing around rooms talking to themselves, and so on. Many of these behaviors seem related to the writing, to managing the emotions as well as the creative process. Writers may also be engaged in **selecting text**—using boilerplate, drawing on prior texts, choosing quotations, and paraphrasing a source. And, of course, in many cases, composing also involves talking to other people while doing all these things—whether continuously at the time of inscribing the text as when people compose collaboratively or periodically as when writers seek input or feedback on what they are writing.

A text does not fully or unambiguously display its history—even the most   11
insightful of interpretations and analyses are only likely to recover some elements of its fuller history, to notice some textual features that allow for uncertain guesses about their origins. Many texts (but not all) are produced across multiple moments of composing and inscription and involve a trail of related texts. Many (but not all) texts involve the active participation of two or more people. All texts build on and respond to other texts, which means that the history of any text is linked to histories of others. All writing draws on writers' knowledge, beliefs, and practices, built up through experiences of socially and historically situated life events. Writers themselves are only very partially aware of the many debts they owe to these intertextual and intercontextual influences. To understand how a text comes into being requires, looking broadly at contexts as well as closely at specific situated activity. There is, it should be clear, no way to get the whole story of any text. However, there are ways to get much more of the story than the text itself can offer, and there is much to be learned from these additional insights.

## Methods and Applied Analyses

This section discusses methods of analysis and presents a number of exam-   12
ples. Its headings, subheadings, and particular analyses can serve as a map

of some of the kinds of analyses you might find it productive to pursue. Not incidentally, the examples also suggest some ways of displaying data, of making analysis visible.

## Collecting and Keeping Track of Texts

One of the key steps for researchers in tracing writing processes is collecting 13 and keeping track of the textual inscriptions themselves. In many cases, it is not possible to collect every text produced. Some are thrown out or get lost. Electronic texts may be deleted.[2] Marginal notes on readings are forgotten. However, the more relevant texts you are able to collect, the fuller the view you can develop of the process and its contexts. You might ask participants in a research study to maintain and make available not just drafts, but also drafts that they or others have written on, separate responses, notes or doodling, other texts that they have written and used or that were closely related, and so on.

As a practical matter, it is important to ask participants what the texts are 14 and to add explanatory labels for yourself that include when the text was given to you, what it is, who wrote it, perhaps who wrote on it (it is not unusual for writing in different ink or pencil on a text to mark different writers—different respondents and authors—or different episodes of composing). These kinds of details may seem obvious when you get the text, but weeks, months, or years later when you are analyzing the data, it is easy to find yourself mystified when you pick up a text without this kind of **contextual record** attached.

For teachers interested in tracing the process for pedagogical reasons, many 15 of the same concerns apply. A student's final draft often makes more sense if you have available a clear record of the texts that were produced along the way, by you and other respondents as well as the student. The student's own story of the process, the text, and the contexts written at the end of the process and/or along the way (e.g., as a series of memos reporting thoughts, questions, and progress) can aid a teacher's reading and response.

## Intertextual Analysis

One of the central ways of tracing writing processes is to analyze how the text 16 itself is related to other written texts or to instances of talk. In many cases, intertextual analysis reveals much about the structure of participation as well as about the sources of a text.

---

[2]Some researchers have used programs that provide a full record of keyboard typing. Bridwell-Bowles, Parker, and Brehe (1987) offered a detailed analysis of keystroke data. Tracking periods of pauses, forward text production, cursor movements, revisions, editing, and various combined operations, they captured some of the fine-grained differences between the writers they were studying, both in terms of total time spent in each type of activity and the distribution of the activities over the episode of text production. Even in controlling settings, it is a challenging task to read and interpret such data. Movie screen capture programs can provide a more readable view of the changing electronic screen and the actions it indexes. Geisler (2001, 2003) has extended this method to naturalistic research on writing and reading with a PDA.

***Relating Text to an Initiating Text.***  A classroom assignment leads to a stu-  17
dent's text. An organization's call for conference paper proposals prompts
and shapes an abstract that is submitted. A company's request for a proposal
leads to a proposal tightly linked to the request. A client's request for information leads first to a letter and eventually to a change in a product's instructional manual. A letter to a senator leads—through complex channels—to a
bill sponsored by the senator. Texts often respond to other texts that may be
treated as initiators.

**An initiating text** does not simply control what follows. It has to go through  18
processes of interpretation and negotiation. For example, in an education
seminar, Professor Mead made the following assignment on the syllabus:

1. A proposal for a study, with bibliography. The proposal should contain a tentative title, statement of the problem, background to the study, statement of
   research questions or hypotheses, method (to include procedures for data collection and data analysis), and significance of the study as major headings.
   The details will get worked out as the proposal is adapted to the individual
   problem. The proposal should be no longer than four to six pages, exclusive
   of bibliography.

In a seminar session, Mead discussed this assignment, elaborating on the content and goals of each section of the research proposal. As he talked through
the "method" section, he suggested a somewhat different, more specific set of
topics and outlined them on the blackboard as follows:

5. Methodology
   –population
   –instruments
   –procedures
   –data analysis

All 12 students whose research proposals I received followed the outline
Mead had given, using headings identical or nearly identical to those given in
the syllabus or written on the board in the second week of class. Of course,
assignments do not automatically lead to matching texts. In fact, Mead provided equally explicit directions for the organization of a second assignment,
a critique of a research article, and the students did not closely follow that
outline.

***Relating Text to Source Texts.***  Sometimes "writing" is simply using others'  19
texts, what we call either boilerplate or plagiarism depending on the context. As
Hendrickson (1989) noted, accountants writing a proposal to audit a company
are expected to simply fill in the names and dates and make no other changes
because any change would create legal uncertainties. In academic settings, there
may also be boilerplate. For example, a sociology student (Moira) in a research
seminar was writing a report based on a common data set from a research project. Professor West, who had designed the research, had already written a careful

description of the data collected. When Moira asked West in an early draft if she could just use that description in her report, West said it would be fine. Moira then simply pasted the 3½ page description into her paper.

In other cases, writers may copy text in ways that would not be so readily  20
sanctioned. For example, when I analyzed use of sources in the master's thesis of an education student (Mai), I found a number of examples of source use that looked like the following (the bold print marks the text that Mai copied into her thesis from a book):

> Besides the assumption of distinguishable underlying abilities, **advocates of a communicative competence approach make** <u>assumptions</u> **about** <u>language</u> **that have been largely ignored in traditional approaches to language assessment.** Joan Good **Erickson (1981) argued that an appropriate** <u>model of language assessment</u> **assumes:**
>
> - <u>Language is a symbolic, generative process that does not lend itself easily to formal assessment.</u>
> - <u>Language is synergistic, so that any measure of the part does not give a picture of the whole.</u>
> - <u>Language is a part of the total experience of a child and is difficult to assess as an isolated part of development.</u>
> - <u>Language use (quality and quantity) varies according to the setting, interactors, and topic.</u>
>
> Erickson maintained that <u>language assessment should reflect the nature of the communication process and evaluate the major use of language—that of a verbal/ social communicative interaction in a natural setting.</u>

As you can see, Mai copied a lot and made few changes. Had the professors on her thesis committee realized that she was using source text this way, I am fairly sure they would have identified it as a problematic use of sources, possibly plagiarism, and required her to revise it. Oh, and by the way, the underlined text above is language that the author of the book Mai copied from—it wasn't Erickson's book—had copied from Erickson's book. Here too, I suspect that Erickson and her publisher would not have considered such copying appropriate.

***Tracing a Series of Texts.***    I mentioned earlier the case of Moira and her writing  21
in the sociology seminar. When I asked Moira for copies of texts related to her work in the seminar, she provided me with 12 separate documents produced over a period of 10 months. Three were drafts of her preliminary examination. Seven were drafts of a conference paper (which I refer to as *Arenas*). One was a memo Professor West had written in response to Moira's first draft of the conference paper (*Arenas 1*). The final text, put together to share with the seminar, included a different draft of her preliminary examination and a part of one of the seven drafts of her conference paper. In addition, eight of the texts included handwritten editing, comments and suggested revisions (in seven cases, this response text was written by West, in one case by a professor at another

university whose theories Moira was employing in her research). Finally, some of the texts also included handwritten notes, editing, and revisions that Moira had added.[3]

**Tracing language across multiple drafts** requires a careful and close com- 22 parison of texts. Figure 7.1 displays an example of one way that West's words ended up in Moira's conference paper. In addition to responses written on the text of *Arenas 1*, West also responded with a separate 2-page memo. Moira incorporated parts of that memo fairly directly into her next draft, *Arenas 2*. In Figure 7.1 the arrows between the two columns point to how closely Moira's text echoes West's. For example, in Point A on the left West says "whether objective change leads to subjective discomfort (dissatisfaction)" and in Point 1 in *Arenas 2* on the right, Moira says "whether objective change leads to subjective discomfort, represented by path A." If you compare B to 2, D to 3, E to 4, and G to 5, you will see additional examples of this borrowing. While these comparisons do reveal some deviations from West's words, those deviations seem relatively minor and one case, the addition of "and psychological" after "behavioral" in Points 2 and 5 of *Arenas 2*, could be traced to West's responses in other parts of the text. A fuller analysis (Prior, 1998) of the ways that Moira did *not* take up West's memo suggested that she was resisting West's argument, as in Points c and f, that objective change in social environments had a direct effect on adolescents' behavior (without mediation of the adolescent's subjective response to that change).

In some cases, such **intertextual tracing** was less straightforward. For 23 example, in responding to *Arenas 1*, West only crossed out the "s" in "adolescents" in the second sentence of Moira's abstract; however, in *Arenas 2*, that sentence was extensively revised.

*Arenas 1* (Abstract, sentence 2)

It is hypothesized that objectively measured transitions in multiple contexts will have an adverse impact on adolescents adjustment, and this response will depend on the actor's subjective perceptions and interpretation of the changes as negative.

*Arenas 2* (Abstract, sentence 2; underlining added to mark changes)

It is hypothesized that change in any given life arena will have less adverse psychological and behavioral consequences if the adolescent has an "arena of comfort" in another domain, characterized by lack of change and satisfaction.

---

[3]This kind of complexity does not appear to be unusual. Geoffrey Cross (1994) describes how eight primary writers and several other contributors took 77 days to complete an eight-paragraph executive letter for an insurance company's annual report. The letter was signed by the CEO and the President, two of the eight primary participants, though their contributions were primarily oral planning and final approval of the text. In this period, the writers produced two conceptual outlines and seven primary drafts. Late in the process, earlier drafts were rejected and an entirely new draft was written more or less from scratch. Altogether, Cross collected 18 documents, six of which had handwritten comments and editing on them, including one document with the handwritten editing and comments of three different individuals.

**Extract from West's memo of March 7**

You need to be more specific about what is being tested. As I understand it, the arena of comfort hypothesis suggests the following model:

Objective change ——a—→ subjective discomfort (dissatisfaction? low self-esteem? lack of control?)

c

b

behavioral maladjustment

arena of comfort may possibly act as a moderator of a, b, c (c is the direct path from objective change to behavioral maladjustment)

In other words, you are investigating

a) Whether objective change leads to subjective discomfort (dissatisfaction)

b) Whether subjective discomfort leads to behavioral maladjustment ——

c) Whether objective change influences behavioral maladjustment directly (without mediation by discomfort or dissatisfaction with respect to the changing domain).

d) Whether the presence of an arena of comfort (where there is no change and satisfaction) moderates (decreases) the effect of objective change on subjective dissatisfaction

e) Whether the arena of comfort moderates (decreases) the effect of subjective dissatisfaction on behavioral maladjustment

f) Whether the arena of comfort moderates (decreases) the effect of objective change on behavioral maladjustment

g) You could also test whether a context constitutes an arena of comfort merely by satisfaction, or the absence of objective change, or whether both conditions are necessary.

\* Arrows between columns added to clarify intertextual borrowing.

**Moira's AN INTERCONTEXT MODEL OF RISK from Arenas 2 dated March 11**

The general model, diagrammed below (Figure 1), investigates (1) whether objective change leads to subjective discomfort, represented by path A, (2) whether subjective discomfort leads to behavioral and psychological maladjustment, represented by path B, (3) whether the presence of an arena of comfort moderates (decreases) the effect of objective change on subjective dissatisfaction, (4) whether the arena of comfort moderates (decreases) the effect of subjective discomfort on behavioral and psychological maladjustment, and finally, (5) whether a context constitutes an arena of comfort merely by lack of discomfort, or the absence of objective change, or whether both conditions are necessary.

(Figure 1.) General Intercontext Model of Risk

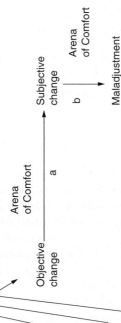

Arena of Comfort

Objective ——a—→ Subjective change            change

b

Arena of Comfort

Maladjustment

Figure 7.1.  Professor West's memo as intertextual resource for the second draft of Moira's conference paper.\*

The bold print represents words inserted from West's written response to Moira's sentence 5 on page 3 of *Arenas 1*. The double-underlined text represents words inserted from the original language of Moira's sentence 5 on page 3 of *Arenas 1*.

*Arenas 1* (p. 3, sentence 5)

The revised hypothesis is that simultaneous change in all life arenas will have adverse (any given) (less)

consequences if the adolescent ~~perceives the changes to be undesirable and~~ (psych & behavioral) (has an arena of comfort in another)

~~disruptive~~. (domain, characterized by lack of change and satisfaction.)

*Arenas 2* (p. 3, sentence 11)

The revised hypothesis is that change in **any given** life arena will have **less** adverse **psychological and behavioral** consequences if the adolescent **has an "arena of comfort" in another domain, characterized by lack of change and satisfaction.**

*Arenas 2* (Abstract, sentence 2)

It is hypothesized that <u>change in</u> **any given** <u>life arena</u> will have **less** adverse **psychological and behavioral** <u>consequences if the adolescent</u> **has an "arena of comfort" in another domain, characterized by lack of change and satisfaction**

**Figure 7.2.** From text to text—Tracing West's words in Moira's texts.

Had Moira initiated the major revision of this sentence? At first, I thought so. However, West's response to another sentence—from page 3 of *Arenas 1*—suggested a different story. That response is represented at the top of Figure 7.2. West's revision was incorporated without change in *Arenas 2*, as shown in the bottom left of Figure 7.2—the bold print indicating West's words. The sentence on the bottom right of Figure 7.2 is the second sentence from the abstract again, the same as the one above, only now the bold print and underlining highlight the borrowing from the page 3 sentence, revealing a complex blend of Moira's and West's words. This example makes it clear that changes at one textual site sometimes triggered changes at another site. It also reveals the apparently seamless and uniform abstract of *Arenas 2* as a textured, dialogic, historic construction, something directly crafted by at least two people.[4]

Another crucial lesson for analysis from this example is that some of the language that ended up in Moira's final draft of the preliminary examination was actually written by West in response to early drafts of the conference paper, then copied by Moira into that paper, then later pasted by Moira into drafts of

24

---

[4]The problem of who is talking in sentences like this one is similar to the problem Wittgenstein (1958) noted with regard to recognizing the diverse functions of language: "Of course, what confuses us is the uniform appearance of words when we hear them spoken or meet them in script and print" (p. 6).

her preliminary examination. For example, the following sentence (compare to Fig. 7.2) appeared in the last draft of Moira's preliminary examination:

> Following Simmons' formulation, it may be hypothesized that change in any given life arena will have less adverse psychological and behavioral consequences if the adolescent has an "arena of comfort" in another domain, characterized by stability (lack of change) and satisfaction.

This example points to the potential limits of looking only at successive drafts of *one* text. Consider how my analysis would have been limited, and likely misleading had I looked only at the four drafts of the preliminary examination and treated sentences like the one above as new composing by Moira.

***Relating Text to Talk.*** It is also possible to **trace intertextual relations between talk and text.** These relations are explored in greater depth in the next chapter. In some cases, those relations are very close indeed, as in the examples of Sean's hypotheses and Tony's arguments against Huck Finn that are described in chapter 8. In other cases, the effects may be less direct. For example, Lilah, a graduate student in American Studies was doing research on ethnicity in the United States for several courses, focusing, especially on a study of local Cinco de Mayo celebrations in a northern city. Lilah noted that her choice for one paper came from watching a Bill Moyers' interview of Sam Keen on TV. She also noted in her own reflections, and displayed in her papers, that her analysis of the local history of Cinco de Mayo was strongly influenced by interviews with community activists. The activists' talk appeared not only in specific quotes in her paper, but in her rejection of an argument that the centrality of food, especially tacos, represented the commodification and hence diminishment of Chicano/a culture. Instead, with the activists, she focused on the visibility of the event and its economic benefits to the neighborhood. [25]

Phelps (1990) observed that writing researchers had been caught up in "the textual and the psychologized rhetorics where abstractions like the fictive audience (textual representation) and the cognitive audience (mental representation) are more salient than the actual exchanges of talk and text by which people more or less publicly draft and negotiate textual meanings" (p. 158). Intertextual analysis of such exchanges of talk and text can provide much data on writing processes and on the structure of participation, the varied forms of co-authorship realized through the exchanges. [26]

## Eliciting Writers' Accounts

Intertextual analysis can provide much data on the writing process; however, there is much that cannot be captured by these methods: exchanges that are missed; the writer's thoughts, feelings, and sense-making; contexts that do not appear in the text. In particular, it useful to elicit writers' accounts of their goals, their contexts, their processes, their feelings, the meanings they see in their texts, the influences they are aware of or can reflectively construct for what they've written and done. Broadly, **participant accounts** can be divided [27] into concurrent accounts, those that are made immediately with the writing, and retrospective accounts made after the fact.

***Concurrent Accounts (Think-Aloud Protocols).***   When you look at writers com-  28
posing and inscribing text alone, it is difficult to see what is happening because much of it is locked up in the silent thinking, reading, and composing the writer engages in. Early researchers (e.g., Emig, 1971; Flower & Hayes, 1981) faced with this problem drew on a technique developed by psychologists to study other cognitive processes: the use of **concurrent, or think-aloud, protocols**. The use of think-aloud protocols was particularly central to writing research in the 1970s and 1980s when this methodology was the key way researchers explored the writing process. The methodology has been less central in the last decade for several reasons. There are questions about how thinking aloud affects the writing process. There also have been questions about the value of the cognitive models typically associated with this line of inquiry. In addition, think-aloud protocols have usually been attempted only in laboratory conditions while there has been an intense interest in studies of writing in naturalistic conditions. And finally, attention to composing in naturalistic conditions also suggested that many of the key processes were social as well as cognitive. These questions are real and important (see Smagorinsky, 1994, for more on these issues). However, it is also important to recognize that concurrent protocols for the first time began to crack open the notion of "writing," to reveal the complex, fine-grained, and diverse nature of the acts that are combined under that label. There is a wide gap between an everyday representation of writing, as in "I wrote a paper last night," and the image of writing that a think-aloud protocol makes available, and filling that gap remains a critical project for writing research.

The following is an example of instructions for a reading-to-write task.[5]     29

> For this assignment, you should do the reading-writing task described in the envelope, talking aloud and recording your thoughts <u>from the time the envelope is opened</u>. Do not open the envelope until you are ready to do and record this exercise. You should be able to do the exercise in about 30 minutes.
>
> Talking aloud means:
>
> 1. **reading aloud** whenever you read anything (including the task instructions) inside the envelope as well as your own text
> 2. **vocalizing the words you write** down as you write them
> 3. **saying aloud what you are thinking about,** remembering, imagining, visualizing, hearing—questions that come to mind, plans you are making, expectations, reactions, memories, images you see, conversations you recall or imagine, internal dialogues, etc.
>
> Try to provide as complete a description of your thoughts as possible <u>while</u> you are doing the writing task. The idea is to provide a kind of stream-of-consciousness

---

[5]For another example of think-aloud instructions see Appendix A in Penrose and Sitko (1993).

commentary on your thinking, not an explanation or account of your thinking. Obviously, you should not say aloud anything that will be embarrassing or uncomfortable for yourself or others.

In a seminar I taught in 1993, we all produced think-aloud protocols on a reading-to-write task (see Flower et al., 1990). I will present three brief segments out of the 21-page transcript that came out of my engagement with this 30-minute task and consider the varied ways this kind of data might be analyzed. In the first segment below, I am reading aloud (ALL CAPITALS) a paragraph on literacy from Hunter and Harmen and I begin commenting (plain text), questioning their definition by asking *which* texts one must be able read, write, and understand to be literate. The stress when reading the word "whatever" continued that line of doubt and the final comment shown, "like physics," was said ironically, as an example of a kind of text that many highly-educated people could *not* understand.

> ... WITHIN THE GENERAL TERM LITERACY [clearing my throat], WE SUGGEST THE FOLLOWING DISTINCTIONS, ONE CONVENTIONAL LITERACY, THE ABILITY TO READ, WRITE, AND COMPREHEND TEXTS, // it's like what texts are you talking about? // ON FAMILIAR SUBJECTS, AND TO UNDERSTAND **WHATEVER** SIGNS, LABELS, INSTRUCTION, // like physics, // AND DIRECTIONS ARE NECESSARY TO GET ALONG WITH ONE'S ENVIRONMENT ... // that seems like a ... // it seems like it means something, // but (I do) have questions there, // TWO. FUNCTIONAL LITERACY,

After reading brief passages from five different texts, I reread the directions and began to ask how I was going to "summarize and synthesize the ideas." In the following segment, I am moving from a plan to look for themes to considering Hunter and Harmen's passage, labeling it for the first time as a "traditional" view and again questioning their lack of specification and contextualization for understanding signs.

> ... I could summarize and synthesize the ideas presented in the quotations // so I could be looking here for themes in terms of um, what, literacy is and what—what themes are there here, // drinking some coffee— // hmm— // what theme would I like to pull out? // I mean conventional and functional literacy, Hunter and Harmen is just the— // it's-hm, it's the least interesting, // it's just the very traditional kind of—discussion // and and, I read it as being very empty, // you know, UNDERSTAND SIGNS, // which signs? // in which contexts? // at what level of understanding? // um, either conventional or functional literac— // and and there— there's an interesting ideological thing going on here, // where the functional literacy is is, um, stated in terms of what people want for themselves, // but what people want for themselves is shaped by their social environment too.

After more thinking and reading, and jotting down a few brief notes, I began writing. Here is the transcript where I compose the second sentence. I begin writing (<u>the underlined words</u>), thinking (plain text), rereading what I had written (**<u>UNDERLINED, ALL CAPITALS</u>**), and orally composing (quotes).

Literacy is a highly contested . . . . politically charged [7 second pause] // CHARGED term//ok [13 second pause] // um Traditional notions of literacy [8 second pause] whether . . . conventional. .or. .functional [7 second pause] // hm, I'm looking for a word here // "tend to" // "ought to" // right // TRADITION-AL NOTIONS OF LITERACY WHETHER CONVENTIONAL OR FUNC-TIONAL, //um . . aw. I had a word in my head, which I didn't say aloud, // LITERACY IS A HIGHLY CONTESTED POLITICALLY CHARGED TERM // TRADITIONAL NOTIONS OF LITERACY WHETHER CONVENTIONAL OR FUNCTIONAL . . // . ."tend to be framed" // tend to be framed, // ok, I'm write-// framed in terms of // TEND TO BE FRAMED OF IN TERMS OF // skills and competence often . . viewing . . . . competence . . . as a . . . binary trait // ok // "something you have or don't have," //yeah,// thinking about treating this [as] a draft // something you have or don't have, //ok

**Text produced:** Literacy is a highly contested, politically charged term. Traditional notions of literacy, whether conventional or functional, tend to be framed in terms of skills and competence, often viewing competence as a binary trait, something you have or don't have.

To date, concurrent protocols have primarily been analyzed in categorical 31 and quantitative terms. Thus for example, I would take the transcribed protocol and divide it into units. (Units are typically some kind of phrasal or clausal utterance as opposed to sentences, for reasons that should be obvious when you look at the preceding transcripts. I have roughly **parsed** these transcripts, using double back slashes // to mark the divisions.) I would then begin **coding** these units. The most basic codes are already indicated in the transcript, which distinguishes **reading the sources** (all capitals), **thinking** (plain text), **inscribing text** (underlined), **rereading the text written** (all capitals and underlined), and **orally composing text** (quotes). (**Pauses** could also be measured precisely, though they aren't in these transcripts.)

A basic analysis might consist of simply counting up the number of units 32 (or the size of the units in terms of number of words, for example) for each of these categories. Typically analysts will want to go beyond these very basic classifications of the protocol, to identify more specific activities. For example, thinking may be subdivided into categories like **setting goals, generating ideas,** and **responding to other texts.** And these categories might be further subdivided. Setting goals might be divided into goals for content, procedure, style, organization, and rhetorical situation. Responding to texts may be divided in terms of how close the comment is staying to the text (e.g., summary vs. transformation), stance toward the text (e.g., agreement vs. rejection), or some other feature that seems salient in the data. Geisler (1994), for example, noticed that Ph.D. students in philosophy were regularly responding to texts in terms of what the authors were arguing while freshmen writing in response to the same texts rarely did so, focusing mainly on the ideas. Thus, she coded her transcripts for **author mentions,** which became a key element of her analysis.

With the think-aloud transcript divided into units and classified in these 33 ways, analyses might focus on the overall activity, especially on comparisons between individuals or groups, between tasks, between conditions, and so on. This kind of coding and counting can provide a sense of what proportion of time is spent in each type of activity. It might also focus on the sequential pattern of the activity, addressing such questions as at what points in the process the writers read texts or how goal-setting is distributed across the process. It might identify sequential patterns over the session (as in the shift seen in the three extracts above from early reading with limited commentary, to mid-session thinking and planning, to late session composing and inscribing) or types of repeated sequences (e.g., write-evaluate-write or write-reread-comment-write as seen in the last extract).[6]

However, these think-aloud transcripts could be analyzed from other discourse perspectives. For example, drawing on Bakhtin's (1981, 1986) theories of language as dialogic and intertextual and Vygotsky's (1987) understanding of development as fundamentally social, I might instead look for traces of, and responses to others. The underlying notion of internalization was articulated by Vygotsky (1987): "An operation that initially represents an external activity is reconstructed and begins to occur internally . . . Every function in the child's cultural development appears twice: First, on the social level, and later on the individual level; first, *between* people (*interpsychological*) and then *inside* the child (*intrapsychological*). . . ." (pp. 56–57). Wertsch (1991) emphasizes the contribution of Bakhtin's notion of **hidden dialogue** (dialogue with the second voice missing) to understanding internalized speech. Analyzing parent-child interactions around a puzzle, he traced the shift from the parent's verbal and nonverbal scaffolding to the child's own self-regulation of the activity. **Inner speech,** like intertextuality, can involve **repetition** and **presupposition.** In general, it does not involve full inner dialogue (e.g., a person mentally asking herself "What does that piece look like?" and then answering "It looks like the bus"). Inner dialogue will typically appear as the answer that presupposes a question or even the shift to regulated attention without words (just looking at the pieces with a particular puzzle-making orientation).

> Bakhtin's account of dialogicality . . . suggests that what comes to be incorporated into, or presupposed by, an utterance are voices that were formerly represented explicitly in intermental functioning. The issue is how one voice comes into contact with another, thereby changing the meaning of what it is saying by becoming increasingly dialogical, or multivoiced. (Wertsch, 1991, pp. 90–91)

The notion of inner speech and hidden dialogicality, of inner speech as incorporating iteration and presupposition, could be used as a framework for analyzing think-aloud protocols.

For example, in the extracts I have presented from my think-aloud, I am directly adopting (without quotation or citation) a categorical scheme (conventional vs. functional literacy) from Hunter and Harmen, a clear example of intertextual uptake. In the second segment, I identify Hunter and Harmen's

---

[6]Flower et al. (1990) would suggest ways of linking an analysis of the text I wrote (classified in terms of how I used sources and added in other Ideas), the strategies displayed in the text and protocol, and the think-aloud protocol comments.

views as traditional, setting up a contrast between traditional and other (modern) views of literacy. In making this contrast, I am not echoing any particular text, but am acting in response to many texts I have encountered that tell a metanarrative of progress. In other words, this contrast and the organizational structuring it affords is another trace of intertextual influence. When I question Hunter and Harmen in the first two segments, I am echoing a repeated experience, a request for specifics, that I have experienced in school and out, directed at others' texts and my own. The form of this practice—that incessant questioning of what, how, where, when, and why, that demand for precision and detail—is again intertextual. However, it is also a presuppositional stance taken up in relation to texts: At no point in the transcript did I consider what stance I should take to these texts. (And, of course, there are other stances. I might have approached the text as a poem, perhaps saying the words aloud to savor their sounds and rhythms or working to learn them by heart.) Finally, there is my use of "tend to." Here I see hidden dialogicality (presupposition), a response to the repeated questioning from teachers and readers, "Always?" that has crystallized into the kind of carefully qualified stance toward claims typical of many academic texts. With this brief analysis, I mean to suggest that other forms of discourse analysis could be employed when looking at think-aloud protocols. These kinds of analysis would be particularly useful when accompanied by other intertextual analysis and by interviews.

***Retrospective Accounts of Writing.*** Retrospective accounts of writing rely on people's memory, and it appears clear that people remember relatively little of the moment-to-moment thinking and action they have engaged in. Retrospective accounts must also be considered as reflections and constructions tuned to the social situation and time in which they are produced. The farther the separation between the event and the recall, the more likely that the account will contain the familiar **conventionalization** and **simplification** that Bartlett (1932) first described. Details drop out and new ones are added. 36

***Using Naturalistic Accounts.*** Some of the earlier theories and research on writing were inspired by writers', typically professional writers', accounts of their processes. Such accounts might appear in **autobiographical or biographical narratives or in interviews.** The series of *Paris Review* interviews with literary authors represented one key source, often presenting images of manuscript texts in progress as well as close accounts of writers' habits. Ernest Hemingway, for example, reported (see Plimpton, 1963) writing in the morning, standing up at a reading board, writing in pencil on onionskin paper. His interview begins with an image of one of his handwritten manuscript pages. In some cases, people have set out to document in great detail institutional processes of writing. For example, a publicist, Terry Erdman, wrote a book on the production of Star Trek TV shows and films, *Star Trek Action* (1998). The book includes richly detailed observations of writers at work, including recorded dialogue and texts from writers' brainstorming meetings, sample scripts and storyboards, and examinations of transformations that occur during production 37

A **process log** is a journal in which you discuss what you are writing, what you are reading in relation to your written work, and how writing for this class relates to other writing you are doing or have done. I ask that you spend about 15 minutes four times a week writing in your process log. I also ask that you maintain copies of notes and drafts of your writing that I can collect from you.

**What should I write about in my logs?**

**1)** Keep track of any writing you have done for this course since your last entry. If you have not done any writing, say so. (By writing, I mean not only substantial work on a draft of a paper or other assignment, but also notes you write to yourself about what you need to do, email exchanges about course writing tasks, fragments of ideas or neat sentences that you scribble on a scrap of paper, whatever . . . .) I am interested in the stories and scenes of your writing: in what you wrote, how long, when and where.

**2)** Keep track of what you are **reading that relates to your writing.** I am interested in how you approach and read texts in your field. I am particularly interested in hearing about instances where reading something triggers thoughts about your writing, even if the reading was not obviously related, even if the reading was not academic (e.g., reading a newspaper, a novel for pleasure, surfing the web).

**3)** Keep track of **discussions** you have with professors, other students, friends, family, co-workers, or whoever that relate to your writing. These discussions may be anything from a conference with a professor to a casual conversation on a bus. You may include lectures you attend, discussion in this or other classes.

**4)** I am interested in **what you think and how you feel** about the writing you are doing, how you are understanding the task, imagining the text, facing particular problems, feeling frustrated or excited.

**5)** If you do not have much to write about some days, I would be interested in ways the writing you do for this class relates to past writing you have done as well as to future projects or work, in your writing processes (e.g., How do you write? Where? Who reads your writing? How do you get ideas? Do you think about your writing during other activities? How do you experience ideas when you write—as words in your heads, voices, images or pictures? What are your attitudes toward writing? How do you evaluate your writing?)

**What texts should I keep track of?** As #1 above suggests, I am interested in <u>any</u> writing you do in relation to this course. I would also be interested in papers you have written in the past that relate to your writing here, anything you are writing that relates but is not for this course. I am interested in scribbled notes, outlines, lists of things to do, ideas you write in the margins of books or articles, data that you are using, email exchanges, listserv discussions, and, of course, drafts you print out (including ones with handwritten editing or responses from your instructor). The more you provide me, the better. Please do not be concerned about issues of correctness, clarity, neatness. I will show you my early drafts of papers, which have many misspellings, typos, errors, incomplete ideas. For many people, myself included, writing is a messy process. We tend to keep the messy pieces to ourselves, but I hope you will be willing to share them because they are essential to the process. (Of course, if you are one of those people who sit down and write a single final draft, that is fine too.) If you are writing on a computer, keeping electronic copies of your work in a separate folder for this research might be easiest. You could photocopy paper texts or give them to me temporarily so that I can photocopy them.

---

Figure 7.3. Sample instructions for a process log.

and post-production. Here again, naturalistic accounts can provide valuable information.

***Process Logs.*** You can also ask writers to keep a log on a daily basis (or so 38 many times a week) of the activities they engage in and their thoughts on the writing process. See Figure 7.3 for an example of instructions for a **process log**

in relation to a study of writing in a class. The instructions could be modified in varied ways to fit other settings, to vary the regularity or form of the log (e.g., entries could be sent as emails), to address other kinds of participants (e.g., instructions for a 10-year-old would need to be quite different), and to highlight different questions. Nelson (1993) reported on process logs as a window into undergraduate students' research processes. Log entries varied from longish discussions of sources and writing activities on days of intense activity (usually close to deadlines) to brief, telegraphic, somewhat whimsical entries such as the following:

> *November 2: Thought about my paper with a feeling of dread. Decided I had to go to the library that day. Didn't* (p. 107)

In a research project I conducted (see Prior, 1998), one graduate student (Lilah) agreed to keep a log (out of some 60 who were invited to do so). During a 10-week quarter, Lilah provided 23 entries of varying length and format (from essay-like, paragraphs on focused topics to telegraphic lists of ideas for papers), totaling 73 handwritten pages of text. In an early log entry, after she has decided to study the history of the local Cinco de Mayo celebration, Lilah recounts a conversation from another seminar:

> *One woman is writing her paper on Tex-Mex cuisine. As it happens, the year Tex-Mex became big was also the year when illegal aliens and cracking down on border control was the hot political issue. She thinks it has something to do with imperialist nostalgia—desire for cultural artifacts of destroyed or subjugated peoples. It's also a commodification of culture—a way of getting "goods" from another culture without the people.*
>
> *Someone mentioned that she should go to the International Festival and look at how that is commodified. Suddenly, ethnicity = food, i.e., something consumable. This is what I'm wondering about with Cinco de Mayo. What's used to present ethnicity? And is the festival really about ethnicity or more about commodification of an ethnic community that makes it more palatable to the larger <u>American</u> community? I've always felt a little disappointed with these events that claim to be international and end up just featuring different dances, clothes, foods. But until today I didn't know why. Really, they lose their cultural differentness by putting it into a shape Americans can buy.*

In both cases, the logs display key points in the history of the text, reveal much about affect and motivation, and facilitate interviewing. A question about the class where Tex-Mex food and imperialism were discussed is more likely to trigger a rich response than an open-ended question about whether class discussions influenced the paper (especially weeks or months after the event).

***Semi-Structured Interviewing.*** Semi-structured interviewing essentially consists of asking questions that have been worked out to some degree in advance, but also involves leaving the script behind to follow up on the interview. For example, when I first interviewed Sean, a sociology graduate student whose dissertation prospectus is discussed in Chapter 8, I asked a standard question—whether his papers were related to personal interests:

> Paul: um, is this related to personal interests at all? Is this something you expect, something that that you might have been interested in four years ago, before you got involved in the project?
>
> Sean: no, no, definitely not, no, it was more of looking at the five variables and deciding what I was going to do, basically the three, biggies as far as I could see were self-esteem, self-efficacy, and depression, self-esteem I know first hand was just a very complicated literature, it's gigantic, and there are some very serious complications with the whole idea of self-esteem, so I didn't want to get into that, and um the, and also there's a lot of good work that's been done on self-esteem, so if it would be difficult for me to make a contribution in that area, not only in terms of getting on top of the huge literature trying to cirumvent the fundamental problems but also in trying to come up with something new and that you know people would be interested in, very difficult variable to work with I think, self-efficacy was actually a very good variable, but someone already took it.

Sean quickly responded "no" to the question of whether he was personally interested in his topic (depressive affect). However, he immediately went on, beyond the question, to talk about the five variables in the data set and how he judged which one would be the best for him. This information provided insights about the research project he was working on and about the rhetorical character of topic selection. When he mentioned (in the last line of the quote) that "someone" had already taken his first choice, I followed up with another (unplanned) question:

> Paul: somebody else here or . . .?
>
> Sean: well, Dave Lynch, the Professor Lynch, he already had self-esteem, or self-efficacy, and so I felt as though depression would be my best shot, so that's what I {I laugh} I but you know I've thought about this often, you're supposed to, like an author, you're supposed to write what you know right? well, I don't know any depressed teen-agers {I laugh}, this has all been a very library oriented thing.
>
> Paul: yeah, not a personal experience
>
> Sean: not at all {he laughs, I laugh}

The follow-up told me more about how different members of the research team had carved out personal niches and about Sean's motivations for his research. Discursively, his shift in interpersonal representations—from "someone" to "Dave Lynch" to "Professor Lynch" (perhaps after starting to say "the professor")—was also interesting, perhaps a sign of the multiple social footings for graduate students working on the sociology research project, perhaps also a sign of his negotiating my status as researcher in relation to the group. In the end, Sean returned to my initial question, with a sense of irony.

These exchanges illustrate the way **semi-structured interviews move be-** 40
**tween scripted questions and open-ended conversations.** The initial questions
can be fairly generic (like the question I asked Sean at first) or grounded in
specific knowledge you have built up through earlier research. As an example
of the latter, in an interview with Lilah (the American Studies student who did
the process log), I drew on several comments she had made in the process log
about her efforts for the three professors she was writing papers for that quarter and asked if she had a sense of why she had put more effort into her paper
for Nash than for Marini, and more for Marini than Kohl.

*Stimulated Elicitation Interviewing.*   When asking a question in typical semi- 41
structured interviews, you are depending on the person's memory as the basis
for a response. Many researchers have found that an interviewee's responses
become richer when the person interviewed has some **external stimulus, some**
**object that can trigger and support memory as well as serving as a source**
**for new reflection.** The specific props and directions can be varied. The prop
might be a text or specific highlighted parts of a text (in original form or transformed), photographs of certain scenes, an audiotape of some interaction, or
a videotape of some action. The directions for how to respond to the prop can
also be quite varied. Let me give several examples here of ways that texts might
be used as props in text-based interviewing.

In interviewing a NNES sociology student who had provided only a single 42
draft of one paper with the professor's responses on it, I went through the text
and highlighted a number of the editorial marks, corrections, and marginal
comments the professor had made and asked the student in the interview to
read the comment aloud, explain what it meant, and state what action if any
he had taken in response to the comment. From this interview, I learned much
about which comments the student seemed to understand and which he didn't.
It also became clear that, although he was supposed to be revising the document, he had not thought through the responses and had not begun revision at
the point of the interview.

In an early interview with West (the sociology professor), I asked her to 43
look at each student's text and tell me a bit about the history of that text and
the student. She would glance through the texts as she was talking, sometimes
stopping to read bits of text and especially any of her own written responses.

In another study (Prior, Hawisher, Gruber, & MacLaughlin, 1997), we were 44
interviewing teaching assistants and faculty on how they had implemented
writing-across-the-curriculum practices in their courses. We would ask them to
talk through their syllabi and explain specific assignments. In some cases, when
instructors had brought copies of the assignments, their talking from those assignments combined with questions by the interviewer (who also could use the
assignment text to form new questions) resulted in very detailed discussion of
the instructor's motivations and expectations for the assignment.

One form of **text-based interviewing** that has been used often in writing 45
research is called **discourse-based interviewing.** Discourse-based interviewing
(Odell, Goswami, & Herrington, 1983) was developed to help uncover writers'

tacit knowledge of, and motivations for, texts. It is a method that involves some transformations to the original texts. This technique typically involves: (1) presenting one or more alternatives for some passage(s) of a text to the writer (or possibly someone else), (2) asking if she would accept the alternative(s), and (3) asking her to explain why or why not. For example, in a discourse-based interview on an email message, I might cross out the salutation "Dear Professor Hujwiri," and write in a proposed alternative salutation "Anisa." Of course, alternatives could involve any transformation: deleting text, adding new text, moving text around, changing the font or the medium (e.g., from handwriting to print). It is important to make it clear to the writer that the alternative is *not* intended to be a correction or a proposed improvement, that it might be better, worse, or no different.

Here again, this basic method can be varied.[7] In some cases, I made similar 46 transformations to a professor's written comments and then asked the student whether she would prefer the original comment or the alternative and why. In a case study of Moira and West, I made extensive use of parallel discourse-based interviews on Moira's texts with both Moira and West. I chose this approach because I wanted to gauge whether Moira had accepted West's revisions because West was the authority and to see whether Moira and West would agree on the reasons for and against specific alternatives—in other words, to see if Moira was just making the changes or if she was learning from them.

In this case, I included alternatives taken from Moira's earlier drafts that 47 had been revised. Most of these prior draft alternatives were ones that Moira had authored, West had rewritten in her response, and Moira had accepted in her revision. I prepared three texts for the discourse-based interviews. Using clean copies of the three texts (*Arenas 4* and *7* and *Prelim 4*), I introduced 36 alternatives (in some cases two alternatives in a single sentence). Moira responded to the full set of alternatives in her interview. However, because I was interviewing West about other students' texts and her time was limited, I only presented 21 of those alternatives to West. In this interview, I offered Moira 16 opportunities to replace revisions West had written and she had copied with her original language. In seven of the 16 cases, Moira chose to return to her original language, not realizing that that was what she was doing. In five cases, she chose to retain West's revisions. She expressed no preference in two cases and rejected both in two others. Evidently, when West's authority was removed from the revisions, some became much less compelling, while others appeared to have become internally persuasive. In a separate interview, West was offered nine of the same alternatives (changes that placed Moira's original texts against West's revisions). West chose to keep her own revisions seven times, to return to Moira's wording once, and to reject both once.

Although the quantitative data were suggestive, I was especially interested 48 in comparing the reasons they offered and the extent to which those reasons

---

[7]Although she does not name the technique, Nancie Atwell (1987) describes using discourse-based interview questions during her "evaluation conferences" with middle-school students.

operationalized, this becomes tricky.
However, [the relationship between objective change and subjective discomfort, and their implications for psychological and behavioral adjustment, remain problematic].

| Moira | West |
|---|---|
| . . . ok, hm, I like change, because this was so wordy, but I don't know if it gets at it ( ) because I don't know if it was necessarily in her operationalization I mean because it- the article I was reading was more theoretical argument than an operationalization, so er uh, or empirical work, so since she's never tested it herself, I don't think that "operationalize" would be the right word but I would definitely accept revamping this sentence and simplifying it, I like this because of the "tricky" but "operationalize" is probably not the right word . . . | . . . here I would think that the new wording is simpler, so that's a benefit of it, but the referent to "this" is unclear because uh, and I think that the revision changes the meaning of the sentence, because what you're initially talking about here are the relationships among variables, a theoretical connection whereas the new wording introduces the issue of measurement, and, uh, and and it's a- it's ano- it's another issue, so I think I would reject that alternative... |

Figure 7.4. Moira and West reply to a proposed change in *Arenas 4*.

matched. That analysis revealed complex patterns of convergence and divergence. Figure 7.4 displays an example. The sentence at the top represents the prompt I constructed. The proposed alternative, "operationalized, this becomes a bit tricky," is actually Moira's language from *Arenas 1;* the printed, crossed-out text is a substitution West had written in and Moira then included in all subsequent drafts of *Arenas*. Moira rejected both the alternative and West's revised language, whereas West rejected the alternative and kept her wording. However, Moira made it clear that she no longer felt comfortable describing the issue as one of "operationalization," as she had in *Arenas 1*, seeing it instead as "theoretical." In fact, in spite of their different decisions, comparing the transcripts from West's and Moira's interviews made it clear that both agreed that the real issue was theory, not operationalization. Thus, on that issue, we see clear convergence. Both Moira and West also mentioned some benefits to "simplifying" the language. However, Moira seemed more attached to her original tone, particularly preferring the word "tricky" to "problematic." In other words, Moira had found the content of West's words persuasive, but was resisting the kind of language and style that West employed.

Another way to elicit accounts is to **ask writers to draw their writing processes and contexts** (and then describe that drawing). In a current research project that Jody Shipka and I are conducting (see Prior & Shipka, 2003), we ask writers to draw two pictures of their processes for a specific writing project. The drawing of the first image is prompted by something like the following directions:

> The first picture should represent how you actually engaged in writing this particular piece. That picture might show a place or places where you wrote, a kind of sustained espisode of writing, what resources you use, other people who are involved, how you vary your activities as you engage in a specific episode of writing, how you feel during the writing, and so on.

In addition, we show the participant examples of several other writers' drawings produced in response to this prompt (intentionally choosing drawings that are quite different in detail and style). The second image is elicited with something like the following directions, aided once again by several examples of other writers' drawings:

> The second picture should represent the whole writing process for this project from start to finish (or to the current stage). The picture might show how this writing project got started, interactions with other people and other texts, experiences that have shaped the project over time, the history of drafts and responses to drafts, your evaluations of and emotions about this project at different times, and so forth.

For the first image, writers typically draw rooms in their homes where they write and some of the objects and people they interact with there. For the second, they typically draw a chain of events across a variety of sites. (One drew the continent of Africa with a small village hut in the middle because that was where her field research occurred.) In both drawings, participants often produce visual metaphors to depict thought processes and emotions. The task of doing these drawings in response to our prompts and examples seems to encourage participants to provide detailed descriptions of the scenes and resources of their writing, of the "procrastinating" downtime behaviors they engage in as well as the focused work, and of the emotions they experience (and how they manage those emotions). While participants are doing the drawing, we also have an opportunity to look at the text or texts that they have brought in. We ask them to bring to the interview whatever would help us to understand their writing on this task. Participants have brought draft and final texts (sometimes, with written comments from others, such as instructors), notes, assignments, personal journals, photocopies of articles marked up by the writer, and so on. While the participants are drawing, we look over the texts. The interview then is semi-structured, with some general questions about writing, a request to talk through (and possibly amend) the drawing, and questions prompted by our reading of the texts.

Figure 7.5 presents two drawings that an undergraduate student, Laura, 50 produced as we talked about a paper she wrote for a non-fiction writing class. The scene of writing at the bottom of the figure represents her apartment. With the drawing as prop, Laura described her movements between her upstairs bedroom, where the computer was, and the downstairs couch, where the TV was (for breaks). She explained why she normally wrote at night because of her class schedule and talked about a number of the conditions of her typical writing: eating pizza, listening to instrumental jazz, being interrupted by telephone calls, reading texts that lay around the room, and so on. In talking through the drawing of the overall process, Laura began with reading the book that she would write about, getting an idea (a light bulb in the drawing) and then going to the main library stacks. She went on to represent her process over the next 7 weeks as she researched and wrote the paper, turned it in, got back her draft with a grade of C, and then went through a process of working through her sadness over the grade, revising the paper, and finally turning it in and getting a better grade. (Laura also brought the final paper with the instructor's handwritten response and the draft she had turned in, with her instructor's comments as well as some extensive handwritten notes and drafting she later added to it.) What is critical here again is not the specific images on the drawing, but the ways that the drawing is described and elaborated on in the interview and the follow-up questions that those descriptions support.

**Using videotaped or audiotaped records of composing as a basis for interview-** 51 **ing** is another type of stimulated elicitation. Rose (1984), in his study of writer's block, asked people to write in a laboratory session. He used two cameras, one focused tightly on the page so that it would display what was being written and the second on the person. Immediately after the writing was over, Rose presented the images on split-screen TV and asked the writers to talk through what they were seeing on the tape, stopping it sometimes to explain in more detail. DiPardo (1994) describes a similar use of audiotaped records of peer response groups.

## Observation of Writing

**Participant observation** of sites of writing offers researchers additional resources 52 that support data collection. Being at sites of composing can result in getting greater access to basic data (e.g., texts that are being produced), in building a knowledge of the histories and typical processes of writing and review, and it can allow direct observation of interactions. Of course, some of these benefits can also be achieved by asking participants to audiotape or videotape themselves (or perhaps to turn on their Web cameras).

***Field Notes on Writing Processes.***   Latour and Woolgar (1986) describe an eth- 53 nographic field study of a biochemistry lab at the Salk Institute. Although their focus was on science, much of their data looked at processes of inscription. Through **field notes and photographs** of the lab, they developed a fine-grained

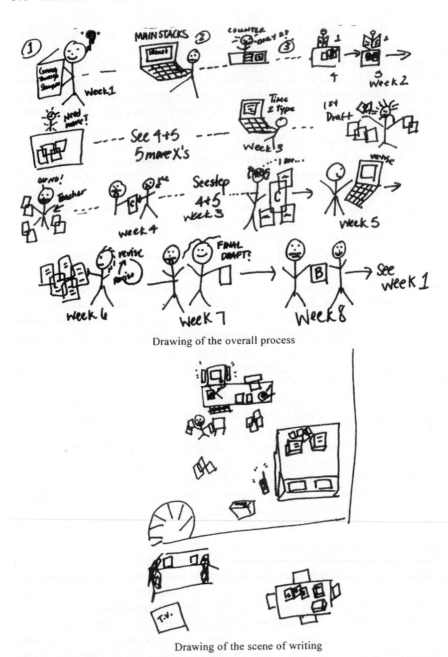

Drawing of the overall process

Drawing of the scene of writing

Figure 7.5. Drawings of the writing process.

account of the ways that data were produced (which involved much labeling of samples, the keeping of meticulously detailed laboratory notebooks, and computer printouts), the ways that raw data were transformed into table and graphs, the ways that those tables and graphs then became the data and were moved to the biochemists' offices where they were used, along with articles, books, grant proposals, and already written articles, to produce new articles, which were circulated to colleagues, submitted to journals, revised, sometimes becoming publications which were then resources for new publications and citations to add to articles, grant proposals, and vitae. Their study suggests some of the key values of participant observation.

*Recording Events Related to Writing.*   Matsuhashi (1987a) provides close 54 analysis of revising based on **videotaped recording of participants writing** in a research setting. With the videotaped record, she was able to examine pauses, noting the quite diverse temporal patterns of inscription, and also to trace the precise details of revision during the process. In her data, she focused entirely on what was happening on the page; however, videotaped records could provide for detailed analyses of writing practices more broadly.

A number of researchers have used or created **settings where people have to** 55 **collaborate on their writing** and then recorded those interactions. (For example, see Kamberelis and de la Luna's example of the owl pellet report in chapter 9.) Although such recording could be used for stimulated elicitation interviewing, it can also be used for direct analysis. Syverson (1999) describes a study in which she asked a collaborative group in her class to audiotape their meetings. By listening to the discussion in the dorm rooms, Syverson learns much about the conditions of composing (e.g., late nights, regular interruptions) as well as about the details of collaborative planning and composing of the text.

## Integrating Data From Multiple Sources

Dyson (1997) suggests the richness of mixing participant observation, inter- 56 viewing, text collection, and recording in her accounts elementary students planning, writing, and performing story-plays for writers' theatre. She is able to trace individual and group patterns over weeks and even across years and, to explore in detail ways that students incorporated mass media in their texts.

Through participant-observation, text analysis, and interviewing, Kamberelis 57 and Scott (1992) analyzed the complex origins of two elementary students' texts. One fourth-grade student, Lisa, wrote "Living in the Black Life," which read in part:

> Its nice living in the black life. I haven't been harmed in Detroit. Back then black was treated bad and beaten and spat at. . . . We communicate, with each other but it is a wonderful life that my life being black. And I don't hate for being black and other blacks shouldn't hate being black. They should be happy who they are. And no matter what whites do to blacks we are good people still. So love who you are don't hate yourself and thank God for making you a person.

Kamberelis and Scott found that, given the opportunity, Lisa had creatively adopted the utterances and ideologies of many others.

> . . . for example, Lisa told members of a peer editing group that "it's [the title] from a song I like called "Back in the High Life Again" [by Steve Winwood] that's about having a good life after some down times." Similarly, Lisa noted in an interview that "I got the idea to say 'it's a wonderful life' from a movie I saw at Christmas about a guy who wanted to kill his self' cause his life was really a mess and how an angel told him he should like himself and go back and be with his family."(p. 377)

In interviews about her writing, Lisa describes what Jesse Jackson said on TV, a guest from a local university (Professor L.) said in class, and her mother and people in her church said regularly about the need for Blacks to be proud even if they face hatred or mistreatment from Whites. Kamberelis and Scott note: "This message is re-envoiced in *Living in the Black Life* in a way that seems to preserve both the urgency of the message and the ministerial cant in which it was originally delivered by Jackson and Professor L."(p. 378). Here again, Kamberelis and Scott (1992) were able to unpack many specific intertextual influences because of the intense longitudinal collection of multiple types of data (see also Kamberelis & de la Luna, chap. 9).

## Conclusion

The naturalistic study of writing processes is complex; however, it is also criti-  58
cal. **We can only understand where texts come from—in terms of their author-ship and social contexts as well as their content and textual organization—by careful tracing of their histories.** The richest histories will emerge from multiple methods, with intertextual analysis, participant accounts, and observation of activity working together to produce a fuller portrait of the process. When we trace such histories, we are studying not cognition alone or social context alone, but rather the intersection of the cognitive and the social in activity that is distributed across individual acts, collaborative interactions, and many socially and historically developed tools (from technologies of inscription and distribution to discourse genres for communication). Research on writing processes has already led to major shifts, not only in our understanding of how writing gets done, but also in our practical sense of how to manage our own writing and how to teach others to write. Various process-influenced pedagogies of writing have become the dominant model for teaching writing at all levels, though many older practices not informed by process research certainly remain in place. Much remains to be learned in this field. We have, for example, just begun to explore writers' everyday practices—the embodied, situated, mediated, and dispersed processes out of which specific texts emerge. There is every reason to suppose that what we find through this line of research will continue to contribute to our practical work as writers—and, for some of us, as teachers of writing—just as it will continue to enlarge our understanding and propel our theories of people's literate practices.

## Activities

This section presents some activities you might engage in to begin exploring 59 methodologies for tracing the writing process.

1. Consider a paper you have recently written. Make a drawing that represents the key concrete activities you engaged in as part of this writing process. Be sure to include activities involved in invention (like reading, talking to others, coming up with ideas about the paper—wherever that might happen) as well as inscription (like the actual production of the text, your drafts and notes). Then draw another visual representation in which you create a visual metaphor (or metaphors) that represents key elements of your process of writing the paper. Compare the two representations. Do they tell you different things about the process? What does each include? What does each exclude?

2. First, write a general account, based on your memory, of how you write summaries. Second, do a think-aloud protocol, following the instructions presented earlier in this chapter in the section on concurrent protocols. Your task will be to summarize and respond to the discussions of the nature of "texts" found in the following passages of this book: Wysocki's discussion of the visual nature of text in the second section of *Basic Concepts*, p. 124, the first two paragraphs of Kamberelis and de la Luna's *Texts: Forms of Writing and Formal Characteristics of Written Language*, pp. 240–241; and the second paragraph of *Three critical issues* in the Introduction by Bazerman and Prior, pp. 6–7. Immediately after the protocol, sit down and write about the experience. Pay attention to the relationship between what you said aloud and what you experienced in your head. Also note how thinking aloud affected the way you read and wrote. Then transcribe the protocol (using the conventions discussed in chap. 8). Now compare your initial account of writing with the think-aloud protocol and the immediate account. Note differences as well as similarities across these accounts.

3. Using the instructions for process logs provided in Figure 7.3, keep a process log of your writing in relation to a class assignment or some other writing project. (While you are doing the writing project, don't begin to review and study your log.) When the writing is completed, first write up an account from your memory of your process for this project and then begin to look through your log and materials (any drafts, notes, email, etc.) you maintained. Consider the following questions.

   - Compare the account of the process you wrote up with the log and materials. Are there differences? (I would expect the log and materials to include evidence of specific events and decisions that would not appear in the final account, though the opposite is also possible. You may also find points on which the two accounts disagree about what happened.)
   - How complete do you feel the record is? Are there important events, certain types of information, or certain types of materials that are not included in your process log? Also, are there log entries or materials that you have kept that you might not be comfortable sharing with a researcher?

- Examine the development of a few selected passages from your text. Using any drafts or notes, try to trace the precise changes that occurred in the texts through the writing process. Then consider what evidence you have *in the process log* (entries and materials) for why these changes happened. (You probably have memories that go beyond what is in the process log, but as a researcher of others' writing, memories would only be available through additional participant accounts, e.g., from interviewing.)
- Finally, from these comparisons, what do you see as the benefits of process logs and their limits or problems?

4. Look at writing in a specific site (a school classroom, at home, at a work-place). Using observation, intertextual analysis, and interview methods, examine where, when, and how writing is typically done in that site, who participates in writing and at what points in the process, why people engage in writing, how texts (including drafts and notes) are produced and kept (or discarded), who reads the texts produced and why they do, and how texts draw on other texts.

## For Further Reading

Early research on writing processes continues to be of value. Janet Emig's (1971) study is a seminal work in the field and introduced think-aloud methodologies. It also points to earlier literatures, such as the *Writers at Work* series of interviews from *Paris Review* (e.g., Plimpton, 1963). Donald Graves' (1983) collection features several early studies of the composing processes of young children. A series of studies (see, e.g., Flower & Hayes, 1981, 1984) that was associated with the Rhetoric program at Carnegie Mellon pursued writing processes in laboratory-like conditions (i.e., writers writing in an institutional space, like a classroom, for short periods of time on assigned research tasks). Analyses in this line of research drew heavily on cognitive processing models for studying differences in expert and novice knowledge.

Rymer (1989) attempted to extend the think-aloud design to naturalistic composing processes in a study of biologists writing (but found few were willing to engage in this approach while doing their actual work). Geisler (1994) extended the think-aloud design by asking paid participants to write more extensive texts over multiple episodes and by assigning tasks that sought to simulate typical academic writing tasks. Various later studies have employed other methodologies aimed at getting writers to externalize their thinking, either by setting up and recording peer group or collaborative writing situations in relation to course assignments (e.g., Flower et al., 1990; Syverson, 1999) or by taking advantage of naturally occurring discussions of texts in progress (e.g., Cross, 1994; Prior, 1998).

Matsuhashi's (1987b) collection brought together a variety of early observational studies of writing processes. This type of research seemed to recede in the late 1980s as researchers shifted to studying social contexts of writing and talk about texts. However, studies of workplace cognition, communication, and action have begun to present very close observational analyses of the functions and temporal character of writing. Goodwin and Goodwin (1996), Heath and

Luff (2000) and several studies presented in Luff, Hindmarsh, and Heath (2000) offer detailed observations and recording of operations centers, tracing the complex interplay of talk and text across multiple channels and media.

A number of ethnographic and historical accounts of scientific knowledge have included rich observations of writing processes. Latour and Woolgar's (1986) account of experimental practices in biochemistry at the Salk Institute focuses on the ways chains of inscription are produced and transformed in laboratories. In another biochemistry laboratory, Amann and Knorr-Cetina (1990) offer a more detailed look at ways that talk mediates the reading and interpretation of raw data and how interpretations are then transformed in writing. Gooding (1990) offers detailed mapping of experimental practice and writing. Bazerman (1999) offers close accounts of the ways laboratory notebooks mediated invention and led to other genres including patents and publicity. Myers (1990) traces chains of genres in scientific work, especially the move from grant proposals to technical articles to popular reports.

Over the last decade, research on writing processes has shifted toward naturalistic studies of writing processes in diverse settings: communities (e.g., Kalman, 1999), schools (e.g., Dyson, 1997; Finders, 1997; Kamberelis, 2001), and workplaces (e.g., Beaufort, 1999; Cross, 1994). Most of these studies rely heavily on externalized collaborative activity as a window into the process. Some have also provided detailed tracing of series of texts. Finally, I would note that Kress (1997) offers a fascinating view of, and theoretical framework for, literacy development as part of a general multimodal, multimedia development of sign-using and sign-making. Several of his observations bear on processes by which children make semiotic objects, including texts.

## References

Amann, Klaus, & Knorr-Cetina, Karin. (1990). The fixation of (visual) evidence. In Michael Lynch & Steve Woolgar (Eds.), *Representation in scientific practice* (pp. 85–122). Cambridge, MA: MIT Press.

Atwell, Nancie. (1987). *In the middle: Writing, reading, and learning with adolescents.* Portsmouth: Boynton/Cook Heinemann.

Bakhtin, Mikhail. (1981). *The dialogic imagination: Four essays by M. M. Bakhtin.* (Caryl Emerson & Michael Holquist, Trans.; Michael Holquist, Ed.). Austin: University of Texas Press.

Bakhtin, Mikhail. (1986). *Speech genres and other late essays.* (Vern McGee, Trans.; Caryl Emerson & Michael Holquist, Eds.). Austin: University of Texas Press.

Bartlett, Francis. (1932). *Remembering: A study in experimental and social psychology.* Cambridge, England: Cambridge University Press.

Bazerman, Charles. (1999). *Language of Edison's light.* Cambridge, MA: MIT Press.

Bazerman, Charles. (2004). Intertextuality: How texts rely on other texts. In Charles Bazerman & Paul Prior (Eds.), *What writing does and how it does it: An introduction to analyzing texts and textual practices* (pp. 83–96). Mahwah, NJ: Lawrence Erlbaum Associates.

Bazerman, Charles, & Prior, Paul. (2004). Introduction. In Charles Bazerman & Paul Prior (Eds.), *What writing does and how it does it: An introduction to analyzing texts and textual practices* (pp. 1-10). Mahwah, NJ: Lawrence Erlbaum Associates.

Beaufort, Anne. (1999). *Writing in the real world: Making the transition from school to work.* New York: Teachers College Press.

Bridwell-Bowles, Lillian, Johnson, Parker, & Brehe, Steven. (1987). Composing and computers: Case studies of experienced writers. In Ann Matsuhashi (Ed.), *Writing in real time: Modeling production processes* (pp. 81–107). Norwood, NJ: Ablex.

Cross, Geoffrey. (1994). *Collaboration and conflict: A contextual exploration of group writing and positive emphasis.,* Cresskill, NJ: Hampton Press.

DiPardo, Anne. (1994). Stimulated recall in research on writing: An antidote to "I don't know, it was fine." In Peter Smagorinsky (Ed.), *Speaking about writing: Reflections on research methodology* (pp. 163–184). Thousand Oaks, CA: Sage.

Dyson, Anne. (1997). *Writing superheroes: Contemporary childhood, popular culture, and classroom literacy.* New York: Teachers College Press.

Emig, Janet. (1971). *The composing processes of twelfth graders.* Urbana, IL: The National Council of Teachers in English.

Erdman, Terry. (1998). *Star Trek action.* New York: Pocket Books.

Finders, Margaret. (1997). *Just girls: Hidden literacies and life in junior high.* Urbana, IL & New York: National Council of Teachers of English & Teachers College Press.

Flower, Linda, & Hayes, John. (1981). Plans that guide the composing process. In Carl Frederiksen & Joseph Dominic (Eds.), *Writing: The nature, development, and teaching of written communication* (pp. 39–58). Hillsdale, NJ: Lawrence Erlbaum Associates.

Flower, Linda, & Hayes, John. (1984). Images, plans, and prose: The representation of meaning in writing. *Written Communication, 1,* 120–160.

Flower, Linda, Stein, Victoria, Ackerman, John, Kantz, Margaret, McCormick, Kathleen, & Peck, Wayne. (1990). *Reading-to-write: Exploring a cognitive and social process.* New York: Oxford University Press.

Geisler, Cheryl. (1994). *Academic literacy and the nature of expertise: Reading, writing, and knowing in academic philosophy.* Hillsdale, NJ: Lawrence Erlbaum Associates.

Geisler, Cheryl. (2001). Textual objects: Accounting for the role of texts in the everyday life of complex organizations. *Written Communication, 18,* 296–325.

Geisler, Cheryl. (2003). When management becomes personal: An activity-theoretic analysis of Palm technologies. In Charles Bazerman & David Russell (Eds.), *Writing selves/writing societies: Research from activity perspectives* (pp. 125–158). For Collins, CO: The WAC Clearinghouse and Mind, Culture and Activity. (Available at http://wac.colostate.edu/books/selves_society/)

Goffman, Erving. (1981). *Forms of talk.* Philadelphia: University of Pennsylvania Press.

Gooding, David. (1990). *Experiment and the making of meaning.* Boston: Kluwer.

Goodwin, Charles, & Goodwin, Marjorie. (1996). Seeing as situated activity: Formulating planes. In Yrjo Engstrom & David Middleton (Eds.), *Cognition and communication at work* (pp. 61–95). Cambridge, England: Cambridge University Press.

Graves, Donald. (1983). *Writing: Teachers and children at work.* Exeter, NH: Heinemann.

Heath, Christian, & Luff, Paul. (2000). *Technology in action.* Cambridge, England: Cambridge University Press.

Hendrickson, Althea. (1989). How to appear reliable without being liable: C.P.A. writing in its rhetorical context. In Carolyn Matalene (Ed.), *Worlds of writing: Teaching and learning in everyday family activities.* Unpublished manuscript. University of Illinois at Urbana.

Kalman, Judy. (1999). *Writing on the plaza: Mediated literacy practices among scribes and clients in Mexico City.* Cresskill, NJ: Hampton Press.

Kamberelis, George. (2001). Producing heteroglossic classroom (micro)cultures through hybrid discourse practice. *Linguistics and Education, 4,* 359–403.

Kamberelis, George, & de la Luna, Lenora. (2004). Children's writing: How textual forms, contextual forces, and textual politics co-emerge. In Charles Bazerman & Paul Prior (Eds.), *What writing does and how it does it: An introduction to analyzing texts and textual practices* (pp. 239–278). Mahwah, NJ: Lawrence Erlbaum Associates.

Kamberelis, George, & Scott, Karla. (1992). Other people's voices: The coarticulation of texts and subjectivities. *Linguistics and Education, 4,* 359-403.

Kress, Gunther. (1997). *Before writing: Rethinking the paths to literacy.* London: Routledge.

Latour, Bruon, & Woolgar, Steve. (1986). *Laboratory life: The social construction of scientific facts.* Princeton, NJ: Princeton University Press.

Luff, Paul, Hindmarsh, Jon, & Heath, Christian. (2000). *Workplace studies: Recovering work practice and informing system design.* Cambridge, England: Cambridge University Press.

Matsuhashi, Ann. (1987a). Revising the plan and altering the text. In Ann Matsuhashi (Ed.), *Writing in real time: Modeling production processes* (pp. 197–223). Norwood, NJ: Ablex.

Matsuhashi, Ann. (1987b). *Writing in real time: Modeling production processes.* Norwood, NJ: Ablex.

Myers, Greg. (1990). *Writing biology: Texts in the social construction of scientific knowledge.* Madison: University of Wisconsin Press.

Nelson, Jennie. (1993). The library revisited: Exploring students' research processes. In Anne Penrose & Barbara Sitko (eds.), *Hearing ourselves think: Cognitive research in the college writing classroom* (pp. 102–122). New York: Oxford University Press.

Odell, Lee, Goswami, Dixie, & Herrington, Anne. (1983). The discourse-based interview: A procedure for exploring the tacit knowledge of writers in non-academic settings. In Peter Mosenthal, Lynne Tamor, & Sean Walmsley (Eds.), *Research on writing* (pp. 221–236). New York: Longman.

Penrose, Ann, & Sitko, Barbara. (Eds.). (1993). *Hearing ourselves think: Cognitive research in the college writing classroom*. New York: Oxford University Press.

Phelps, Louse. (1990). Audience and authorship: The disappearing boundary. In Gesa Kirsch & Duane Roen (Eds.), *A sense of audience in written communication* (pp. 153–174). Newbury Park, CA: Sage.

Plimpton, George. (Ed.). (1963). *Writers at work: The Paris Review interviews*. (Second Series). New York: The Viking Press.

Prior, Paul, Hawisher, Gail, Gruber, Sibylle, & MacLaughlin, Nicole. (1997). Research and WAC evaluations: An in-progress reflection. In Kathleen Blake Yancey & Brian Huot (Eds.), *WAC and program assessment: Divers methods of evaluating writing across the curriculum programs* (pp. 185–216). Norwood, NJ: Ablex.

Prior, Paul. (1998). *Writing/disciplinarity: A sociohistoric account of literate activity in the academy*. Mahwah, NJ: Lawrence Erlbaum Associates.

Prior, Paul, & Shipka, Jody. (2003). Chronotopic lamination: Tracing the contours of literate activity. In Charles Bazerman & David Russell (Eds.), *Writing selves/writing societies: Research from activity perspectives* (pp. 180–238). Fort Collins, CO: The WAC Clearinghouse and Mind, Culture and Activity. (Available at http://wac.colostate.edu/books/selves_society/)

Rose, Mike. (1984). *Writer's block: The Cognitive dimension*. Carbondale, IL: Southern Illinois University Press.

Rymer, Jone. (1989). Scientific composing processes: How eminent scientists write journal articles. In David Joliffe (Ed.), *Advances in writing research volume 2: Writing in academic disciplines* (pp. 211–250). Norwood, NJ: Ablex.

Smagorinsky, Peter. (Ed.). (1994). *Speaking about writing: Reflections on research methodology*. Thousand Oaks, CA: Sage.

Syverson, Margaret. (1999). *The wealth of reality: An ecology of composition*. Carbondale, IL: Southern Illinois University Press.

Vygotsky, Lev. (1987). *Thinking and speech*. (Norris Minick, Ed. & Trans.). New York: Plenum.

Wertsch, James. (1991). *Voices of the mind: A sociocultural approach to mediated action*. Cambridge, MA: Harvard University Press.

Wittgenstein, Ludwig. (1958). *Philosophical investigations*. (Gertrude Anscombe, Trans.). Oxfords, England: Basil Blackwell.

Wysocki, Anne Frances. (2004). The multiple media of texts: How onscreen and paper texts incorporate words, images, and other media. In Charles Bazerman & Paul Prior (Eds.), *What writing does and how it does it: An introduction to analyzing texts and textual practices* (pp. 123-163). Mahwah, NJ: Lawrence Erlbaum Associates.

## Questions for Discussion and Journaling

1. Why do you suppose it would be useful for you to think about and research how you or others actually write? This might seem like a strange question, but try to think of some ways that learning about writing processes could be helpful.

2. Adding up the various aspects of process Prior writes about, make a list of everything involved with tracing the writing process. (Hint: Your list probably should include most of the terms and ideas Prior uses as headings throughout the part of the chapter called "Methods and Applied Analysis.")

3. Using your own words, explain the difference between composition and inscription. Does one always or usually seem to come first?

4. Why is it important to distinguish different kinds of authorship as Prior does with animator, author, and principal?

5.  What does Prior mean when he argues that to trace process you have to trace the *structure of participation* in the text? What sorts of participation in creating the text does he include?

6.  If you were to trace the network of texts that stand behind a text whose process you're investigating, what kinds of texts would you have to look for? (To help you, you might read or revisit Kevin Roozen's article in Chapter 1 [p. 157].)

7.  Summarize the strengths and weaknesses of the several kinds of writer accounts Prior discusses (concurrent, retrospective, naturalistic, process logs, and semi-structured and stimulated-elicitation interviewing). In reading about them, do you find you have a favorite?

8.  To record observations of writing, Prior suggests video-recording. What other ways can you think of to observe how you or someone else writes?

9.  Prior offers the suggestion of integrating multiple sources of research on process, which is also known as triangulation. A reason for his suggestion is that research that tells you *what* a writer did may not tell you *why* the writer did what she did. Which of the research methods Prior reviews here seem more suited to showing *what* happened to a text, and which seem better suited to explaining *why*?

## Applying and Exploring Ideas

1.  Suppose you were given the task of comparing the writing processes of two different writers who were working on the same kind of writing task. Create a short research plan that describes what methods you would use to conduct this analysis and explain your plan.

2.  Describe a writing situation in which composition and inscription seem inextricably mixed together. Do you think such mixing happens often?

3.  Think of the last big writing project you worked on for school (you can decide what counts as "big") and do an intertextual tracing of it—what were its initiating text(s), source texts, draft series, and other texts it touches? (Again, if you read Roozen in Chapter 1 [p. 157], you already have some ideas for how to start this.)

4.  Make a drawing of your writing process on that "last big writing project" from the preceding question. If you can't remember it in enough detail, make a drawing of a writing process a friend describes to you.

5.  Suppose you wanted to interview another writer on his or her writing process. Draft a list of questions that would solicit the information you are seeking about how the writer composes texts.

6.  While Prior's chapter provides ideas for studying *others'* writing processes, consider the value of using some of the same methods to study your own. What aspects of your process would you benefit from being more aware of or having more control over?

> **Meta Moment**
> Are you thinking differently now about how writing happens than you were before reading this selection? If so, how? And how can thinking about and consciously studying writing processes assist you in improving as a writer?

# Shitty First Drafts

## ANNE LAMOTT

■ Lamott, Anne. "Shitty First Drafts." *Bird by Bird: Some Instructions on Writing and Life*. New York: Anchor, 1994. 21–27. Print.

## Framing the Reading

Anne Lamott is most people's idea and, perhaps, stereotype of a successful writer. She has published fourteen novels and nonfiction books since 1980, probably the best known of which is the book this excerpt comes from, *Bird by Bird: Some Instructions on Writing and Life*. She is known for her self-deprecating humor and openness (much of her writing touches on subjects such as alcoholism, depression, spirituality and faith, and motherhood). This piece is no exception. Characteristically, Lamott's advice in "Shitty First Drafts" draws extensively on her personal experience with writing (it was her sixth book). And you'll probably find it makes its arguments not only reasonably, but entertainingly. Not many writers would disagree with either her overall point or her descriptions in making it. Thus, it's become one of the most widely anthologized pieces of contemporary advice on writing process.

## Getting Ready to Read

*Before you read*, do at least one of the following activities:

- Think back through your writing experiences and education, and make a list of the times you've been told it's okay to write badly, and who told you.
- What advice would you typically give someone who's having a hard time getting started writing?

*As you read*, considering the following questions:

- Can you imagine what the shitty first draft of *this piece itself* looked like? Reading the finished prose, can you make any guesses about what the second and third drafts changed from the first?
- How does this piece make you feel about writing?

Now, practically even better news than that of short assignments is the idea 1
of shitty first drafts. All good writers write them. This is how they end up
with good second drafts and terrific third drafts. People tend to look at successful writers, writers who are getting their books published and maybe even doing well financially, and think that
they sit down at their desks every
morning feeling like a million dollars, feeling great about who they
are and how much talent they have
and what a great story they have
to tell; that they take in a few deep
breaths, push back their sleeves,
roll their necks a few times to get
all the cricks out, and dive in, typing fully formed passages as fast as
a court reporter. But this is just the fantasy of the uninitiated. I know some very
great writers, writers you love who write beautifully and have made a great deal
of money, and not *one* of them sits down routinely feeling wildly enthusiastic and
confident. Not one of them writes elegant first drafts. All right, one of them does,
but we do not like her very much. We do not think that she has a rich inner life
or that God likes her or can even stand her. (Although when I mentioned this to
my priest friend Tom, he said you can safely assume you've created God in your
own image when it turns out that God hates all the same people you do.)

> *I know some very great writers, writers you love who write beautifully and have made a great deal of money, and not one of them sits down routinely feeling wildly enthusiastic and confident.*

Very few writers really know what they are doing until they've done it. Nor 2
do they go about their business feeling dewy and thrilled. They do not type
a few stiff warm-up sentences and then find themselves bounding along like
huskies across the snow. One writer I know tells me that he sits down every
morning and says to himself nicely, "It's not like you don't have a choice, because you do—you can either type or kill yourself." We all often feel like we are
pulling teeth, even those writers whose prose ends up being the most natural
and fluid. The right words and sentences just do not come pouring out like
ticker tape most of the time. Now, Muriel Spark is said to have felt that she was
taking dictation from God every morning—sitting there, one supposes, plugged
into a Dictaphone, typing away, humming. But this is a very hostile and aggres-
sive position. One might hope for bad things to rain down on a person like this.

For me and most of the other writers I know, writing is not rapturous. In 3
fact, the only way I can get anything written at all is to write really, really shitty
first drafts.

The first draft is the child's draft, where you let it all pour out and then let 4
it romp all over the place, knowing that no one is going to see it and that you
can shape it later. You just let this childlike part of you channel whatever voices
and visions come through and onto the page. If one of the characters wants to
say, "Well, so what, Mr. Poopy Pants?" you let her. No one is going to see it.
If the kid wants to get into really sentimental, weepy, emotional territory, you
let him. Just get it all down on paper, because there may be something great in
those six crazy pages that you would never have gotten to by more rational,

grown-up means. There may be something in the very last line of the very last paragraph on page six that you just love, that is so beautiful or wild that you now know what you're supposed to be writing about, more or less, or in what direction you might go—but there was no way to get to this without first getting through the first five and a half pages.

I used to write food reviews for *California* magazine before it folded. (My writing food reviews had nothing to do with the magazine folding, although every single review did cause a couple of canceled subscriptions. Some readers took umbrage at my comparing mounds of vegetable puree with various ex-presidents' brains.) These reviews always took two days to write. First I'd go to a restaurant several times with a few opinionated, articulate friends in tow. I'd sit there writing down everything anyone said that was at all interesting or funny. Then on the following Monday I'd sit down at my desk with my notes, and try to write the review. Even after I'd been doing this for years, panic would set in. I'd try to write a lead, but instead I'd write a couple of dreadful sentences, xx them out, try again, xx everything out, and then feel despair and worry settle on my chest like an x-ray apron. It's over, I'd think, calmly. I'm not going to be able to get the magic to work this time. I'm ruined. I'm through. I'm toast. Maybe, I'd think, I can get my old job back as a clerk-typist. But probably not. I'd get up and study my teeth in the mirror for a while. Then I'd stop, remember to breathe, make a few phone calls, hit the kitchen and chow down. Eventually I'd go back and sit down at my desk, and sigh for the next ten minutes. Finally I would pick up my one-inch picture frame, stare into it as if for the answer, and every time the answer would come: All I had to do was to write a really shitty first draft of, say, the opening paragraph. And no one was going to see it.

So I'd start writing without reining myself in. It was almost just typing, just making my fingers move. And the writing would be *terrible*. I'd write a lead paragraph that was a whole page, even though the entire review could only be three pages long, and then I'd start writing up descriptions of the food, one dish at a time, bird by bird, and the critics would be sitting on my shoulders, commenting like cartoon characters. They'd be pretending to snore, or rolling their eyes at my overwrought descriptions, no matter how hard I tried to tone those descriptions down, no matter how conscious I was of what a friend said to me gently in my early days of restaurant reviewing. "Annie," she said, "it is just a piece of *chicken*. It is just a bit of *cake*."

But because by then I had been writing for so long, I would eventually let myself trust the process—sort of, more or less. I'd write a first draft that was maybe twice as long as it should be, with a self-indulgent and boring beginning, stupefying descriptions of the meal, lots of quotes from my black-humored friends that made them sound more like the Manson girls than food lovers, and no ending to speak of. The whole thing would be so long and incoherent and hideous that for the rest of the day I'd obsess about getting creamed by a car before I could write a decent second draft. I'd worry that people would read what I'd written and believe that the accident had really been a suicide, that I had panicked because my talent was waning and my mind was shot.

The next day, though, I'd sit down, go through it all with a colored pen, 8
take out everything I possibly could, find a new lead somewhere on the second
page, figure out a kicky place to end it, and then write a second draft. It always
turned out fine, sometimes even funny and weird and helpful. I'd go over it one
more time and mail it in.

Then, a month later, when it was time for another review, the whole process 9
would start again, complete with the fears that people would find my first draft
before I could rewrite it.

Almost all good writing begins with terrible first efforts. You need to start 10
somewhere. Start by getting something—anything—down on paper. A friend
of mine says that the first draft is the down draft—you just get it down. The
second draft is the up draft—you fix it up. You try to say what you have to
say more accurately. And the third draft is the dental draft, where you check
every tooth, to see if it's loose or cramped or decayed, or even, God help us,
healthy.

What I've learned to do when I sit down to work on a shitty first draft is 11
to quiet the voices in my head. First there's the vinegar-lipped Reader Lady,
who says primly, "Well, *that's* not very interesting, is it?" And there's the emaci-
ated German male who writes these Orwellian memos detailing your thought
crimes. And there are your parents, agonizing over your lack of loyalty and
discretion; and there's William Burroughs, dozing off or shooting up because
he finds you as bold and articulate as a houseplant; and so on. And there are
also the dogs: let's not forget the dogs, the dogs in their pen who will surely
hurtle and snarl their way out if you ever *stop* writing, because writing is, for
some of us, the latch that keeps the door of the pen closed, keeps those crazy
ravenous dogs contained.

Quieting these voices is at least half the battle I fight daily. But this is better 12
than it used to be. It used to be 87 percent. Left to its own devices, my mind
spends much of its time having conversations with people who aren't there. I
walk along defending myself to people, or exchanging repartee with them, or
rationalizing my behavior, or seducing them with gossip, or pretending I'm on
their TV talk show or whatever. I speed or run an aging yellow light or don't
come to a full stop, and one nanosecond later am explaining to imaginary cops
exactly why I had to do what I did, or insisting that I did not in fact do it.

I happened to mention this to a hypnotist I saw many years ago, and he 13
looked at me very nicely. At first I thought he was feeling around on the floor
for the silent alarm button, but then he gave me the following exercise, which
I still use to this day.

Close your eyes and get quiet for a minute, until the chatter starts up. Then 14
isolate one of the voices and imagine the person speaking as a mouse. Pick it up
by the tail and drop it into a mason jar. Then isolate another voice, pick it up
by the tail, drop it in the jar. And so on. Drop in any high-maintenance parental units, drop in any contractors, lawyers, colleagues, children, anyone who is
whining in your head. Then put the lid on, and watch all these mouse people
clawing at the glass, jabbering away, trying to make you feel like shit because
you won't do what they want—won't give them more money, won't be more

successful, won't see them more often. Then imagine that there is a volume-control button on the bottle. Turn it all the way up for a minute, and listen to the stream of angry, neglected, guilt-mongering voices. Then turn it all the way down and watch the frantic mice lunge at the glass, trying to get to you. Leave it down, and get back to your shitty first draft.

A writer friend of mine suggests opening the jar and shooting them all in the 15 head. But I think he's a little angry, and I'm sure nothing like this would ever occur to you.

---

## Questions for Discussion and Journaling

1. Why is it so hard for many people (maybe you) to knowingly put bad writing on paper?

2. What are your own "coping strategies" for getting started on a piece of writing? Do you have particular strategies for making yourself sit down and start writing?

3. What would you say is the funniest line in this piece? Why did it make you laugh?

4. Most readers find that Lamott sounds very down-to-earth and approachable in this piece. What is she doing with language and words themselves to give this impression?

5. Lamott talks, toward the end of this piece, about all the critical voices that play in her mind when she's trying to write. Most, maybe all, writers have something similar. What are yours?

## Applying and Exploring Ideas

1. Lamott obviously knows well what the weaknesses in her SFDs are likely to be. Are you aware yet of any patterns in your first-draft writing—places or ways in which you simply expect that the writing will need work once you actually have words on paper?

2. As you read other "process" pieces in this chapter, what do you find makes Lamott different (from, say, Elbow or Rose or Sommers)? What is she saying (or how is she saying it) that others don't—or what does she not say that others do?

3. The introduction to this chapter uses a "driving with headlights" analogy to say what Lamott says this way: "There may be something on the very last line of page six that you just love . . . but there was no way to get to this without first getting through the first five and a half pages" (para. 4). Make your own metaphor or analogy to explain this phenomenon.

### Meta Moment

Lamott gives you permission to write badly in order to write well. What else would you like permission to do with/in your writing?

# Rigid Rules, Inflexible Plans, and the Stifling of Language: A Cognitivist Analysis of Writer's Block

## MIKE ROSE

■ Rose, Mike. "Rigid Rules, Inflexible Plans, and the Stifling of Language: A Cognitivist Analysis of Writer's Block." *College Composition and Communication* 31.4 (1980): 389–401. Print.

## Framing the Reading

All of the readings in this chapter focus on aspects of how writers compose—that is, how they walk through the process of actually producing a text, from coming up with ideas for it to finalizing the piece. Some selections pay more attention to elements or functions of composing (like planning, prewriting, drafting, and revising); others focus on the **constraints** and rules—audiences, situations, grammar rules—that writers must navigate. Mike Rose's study of writer's block brings these elements together by asking what's happening when writers are literally incapable of writing the next sentence.

Rose's career has been one of studying, teaching, and helping writers who have a difficult time writing. Currently a faculty member in the UCLA Graduate School of Education and Information Studies, Rose has taught for nearly 40 years at many levels of education, including kindergarten and adult literacy programs. Some of his earliest research involved problems of writers block, and the article you're reading here eventually became part of his 1984 book *Writer's Block: The Cognitive Dimension*. More broadly, Rose has worked throughout his career on problems of literacy and access to education. His most widely recognized book is 1989's *Lives on the Boundary*, and he has published many since dealing with access to education and the opportunities it provides.

At the time Rose wrote this article, the dominant approach to understanding writing problems was to consider them to be *thinking* problems—problems of **cognition**, or mental operation. If we could understand how writers *think*, how their brains process information, the theory was, we would be able to teach writing more effectively because we could understand and teach the mental operations that lead to good writing.

Some proponents of cognitive analysis seemed to want to reduce human thinking to machine processing. They ignored everything going on *outside* a writer's head—that is, the **rhetorical situation** and **context**—and assumed that situation had nothing to do with the rules by which brains process information and thus generate writing. Like other critics of this position, Rose suspected that other rules—cultural rules, school rules—might need more study and critique. Trained in psychological counseling, he applied a different set of cognitivist ideas to this problem of cultural rules and their negative effect on some people's writing. You'll read the results in this article.

It's worth noting that writer's block is a technical term that we tend to overuse. In the same way that anyone who finds focusing for more than ten seconds difficult is likely to claim they have "ADHD" when in fact few people really do, too many writers who can't think of what to say next are likely to claim, jokingly or seriously, that they have "writer's block." Rose is talking about a rarer, more serious problem.

## Getting Ready to Read

*Before you read*, do at least one of the following activities:

- Quickly make a list of rules that seem to always be in your mind when you are writing for school.
- Make a short list of things that make it hard for you to write.
- Write one paragraph about a person or event that negatively impacted your ability to write.

*As you read*, consider the following questions:

- What kinds of rules seem to keep people from writing, and what kinds of rules seem to enable people to write?
- What are the relationships among **heuristics**, plans, rules, algorithms, set, and perplexity?
- Where do you see yourself, if anywhere, among the various writers Rose describes?

..............................................................................................................

R uth will labor over the first paragraph of an essay for hours. She'll write a 1 sentence, then erase it. Try another, then scratch part of it out. Finally, as the evening winds on toward ten o'clock and Ruth, anxious about tomorrow's deadline, begins to wind into herself, she'll compose that first paragraph only to sit back and level her favorite exasperated interdiction at herself and her page: "No. You can't say that. You'll bore them to death."

Ruth is one of ten UCLA undergraduates with whom I discussed writer's 2 block, that frustrating, self-defeating inability to generate the next line, the right phrase, the sentence that will release the flow of words once again. These ten people represented a fair cross-section of the UCLA student community: lower-middle-class to upper-middle-class backgrounds and high schools, third-world and Caucasian origins, biology to fine arts majors, C+ to A− grade point averages, enthusiastic to blasé attitudes toward school. They were set off from the community by the twin facts that all ten could write competently, and all were currently enrolled in at least one course that required a significant amount of writing. They were set off among themselves by the fact that five of them wrote with relative to enviable ease while the other five experienced moderate to nearly immobilizing writer's block. This blocking usually resulted in rushed, often late papers and resultant grades that did not truly reflect these students' writing ability. And then, of course, there were other less measurable but probably more serious results: a growing distrust of their abilities and an aversion toward the composing process itself.

What separated the five students who blocked from those who didn't? It wasn't skill; that was held fairly constant. The answer could have rested in the emotional realm—anxiety, fear of evaluation, insecurity, etc. Or perhaps blocking in some way resulted from variation in cognitive style. Perhaps, too, blocking originated in and typified a melding of emotion and cognition not unlike the relationship posited by Shapiro between neurotic feeling and neurotic thinking.[1] Each of these was possible. Extended clinical interviews and testing could have teased out the answer. But there was one answer that surfaced readily in brief explorations of these students' writing processes. It was not profoundly emotional, nor was it embedded in that still unclear construct of cognitive style. It was constant, surprising, almost amusing if its results weren't so troublesome, and, in the final analysis, obvious: the five students who experienced blocking were all operating either with writing rules or with planning strategies that impeded rather than enhanced the composing process. The five students who were not hampered by writer's block also utilized rules, but they were less rigid ones, and thus more appropriate to a complex process like writing. Also, the plans these non-blockers brought to the writing process were more functional, more flexible, more open to information from the outside.

> It was constant, surprising, almost amusing if its results weren't so troublesome, and, in the final analysis, obvious: the five students who experienced blocking were all operating either with writing rules or with planning strategies that impeded rather than enhanced the composing process.

These observations are the result of one to three interviews with each student. I used recent notes, drafts, and finished compositions to direct and hone my questions. This procedure is admittedly non-experimental, certainly more clinical than scientific; still, it did lead to several inferences that lay the foundation for future, more rigorous investigation: (a) composing is a highly complex problem-solving process[2] and (b) certain disruptions of that process can be explained with cognitive psychology's problem-solving framework. Such investigation might include a study using "stimulated recall" techniques to validate or disconfirm these hunches. In such a study, blockers and non-blockers would write essays. Their activity would be videotaped and, immediately after writing, they would be shown their respective tapes and questioned about the rules, plans, and beliefs operating in their writing behavior.

This procedure would bring us close to the composing process (the writers' recall is stimulated by their viewing the tape), yet would not interfere with actual composing.

In the next section I will introduce several key concepts in the problem-solving literature. In section three I will let the students speak for themselves. Fourth, I will offer a cognitivist analysis of blockers' and non-blockers' grace or torpor. I will close with a brief note on treatment.

## Selected Concepts in Problem Solving: Rules and Plans

As diverse as theories of problem solving are, they share certain basic assumptions and characteristics. Each posits an *introductory period* during which a problem is presented, and all theorists, from Behaviorist to Gestalt to Information Processing, admit that certain aspects, stimuli, or "functions" of the problem must become or be made salient and attended to in certain ways if successful problem-solving processes are to be engaged. Theorists also believe that some conflict, some stress, some gap in information in these perceived "aspects" seems to trigger problem-solving behavior. Next comes a *processing period,* and for all the variance of opinion about this critical stage, theorists recognize the necessity of its existence—recognize that man, at the least, somehow "weighs" possible solutions as they are stumbled upon and, at the most, goes through an elaborate and sophisticated information-processing routine to achieve problem solution. Furthermore, theorists believe—to varying degrees—that past learning and the particular "set," direction, or orientation that the problem solver takes in dealing with past experience and present stimuli have critical bearing on the efficacy of solution. Finally, all theorists admit to a *solution period,* an end-state of the process where "stress" and "search" terminate, an answer is attained, and a sense of completion or "closure" is experienced.

These are the gross similarities, and the framework they offer will be useful in understanding the problem-solving behavior of the students discussed in this paper. But since this paper is primarily concerned with the second stage of problem-solving operations, it would be most useful to focus this introduction on two critical constructs in the processing period: rules and plans.

### Rules

Robert M. Gagné defines "rule" as "an inferred capability that enables the individual to respond to a class of stimulus situations with a class of performances."[3] Rules can be learned directly[4] or by inference through experience.[5] But, in either case, most problem-solving theorists would affirm Gagné's dictum that "rules are probably the major organizing factor, and quite possibly the primary one, in intellectual functioning."[6] As Gagné implies, we wouldn't be able to function without rules; they guide response to the myriad stimuli that confront us daily, and might even be the central element in complex problem-solving behavior.

Dunker, Polya, and Miller, Galanter, and Pribram offer a very useful dis- 9 tinction between two general kinds of rules: algorithms and heuristics.[7] Algorithms are precise rules that will always result in a specific answer if applied to an appropriate problem. Most mathematical rules, for example, are algorithms. Functions are constant (e.g., pi), procedures are routine (squaring the radius), and outcomes are completely predictable. However, few day-to-day situations are mathematically circumscribed enough to warrant the application of algorithms. Most often we function with the aid of fairly general heuristics or "rules of thumb," guidelines that allow varying degrees of flexibility when approaching problems. Rather than operating with algorithmic precision and certainty, we search, critically, through alternatives, using our heuristic as a divining rod—"if a math problem stumps you, try working backwards to solution"; "if the car won't start, check x, y, or z," and so forth. Heuristics won't allow the precision or the certitude afforded by algorithmic operations; heuristics can even be so "loose" as to be vague. But in a world where tasks and problems are rarely mathematically precise, heuristic rules become the most appropriate, the most functional rules available to us: "a heuristic does not guarantee the optimal solution or, indeed, any solution at all; rather, heuristics offer solutions that are good enough most of the time."[8]

## Plans

People don't proceed through problem situations, in or out of a laboratory, 10 without some set of internalized instructions to the self, some program, some course of action that, even roughly, takes goals and possible paths to that goal into consideration. Miller, Galanter, and Pribram have referred to this course of action as a plan: "A plan is any hierarchical process in the organism that can control the order in which a sequence of operations is to be performed" (p. 16). They name the fundamental plan in human problem-solving behavior the TOTE, with the initial T representing a *test* that matches a possible solution against the perceived end-goal of problem completion. O represents the clearance to *operate* if the comparison between solution and goal indicates that the solution is a sensible one. The second T represents a further, post-operation, *test* or comparison of solution with goal, and if the two mesh and problem solution is at hand the person *exits* (E) from problem-solving behavior. If the second test presents further discordance between solution and goal, a further solution is attempted in TOTE-fashion. Such plans can be both long-term and global and, as problem solving is underway, short-term and immediate.[9] Though the mechanicality of this information-processing model renders it simplistic and, possibly, unreal, the central notion of a plan and an operating procedure is an important one in problem-solving theory; it at least attempts to metaphorically explain what earlier cognitive psychologists could not—the mental procedures underlying problem-solving behavior.

Before concluding this section, a distinction between heuristic rules and 11 plans should be attempted; it is a distinction often blurred in the literature, blurred because, after all, we are very much in the area of gestating theory and preliminary models. Heuristic rules seem to function with the flexibility of plans. Is, for example, "If the car won't start, try x, y, or z" a heuristic or a plan? It could be either, though two qualifications will mark it as heuristic rather than plan. (A) Plans subsume and sequence heuristic and algorithmic rules. Rules are usually "smaller," more discrete cognitive capabilities; plans can become quite large and complex, composed of a series of ordered algorithms, heuristics, and further planning "sub-routines." (B) Plans, as was mentioned earlier, include criteria to determine successful goal-attainment and, as well, include "feedback" processes—ways to incorporate and use information gained from "tests" of potential solutions against desired goals.

One other distinction should be made: that is, between "set" and plan. Set, 12 also called "determining tendency" or "readiness,"[10] refers to the fact that people often approach problems with habitual ways of reacting, a predisposition, a tendency to perceive or function in one way rather than another. Set, which can be established through instructions or, consciously or unconsciously, through experience, can assist performance if it is appropriate to a specific problem,[11] but much of the literature on set has shown its rigidifying, dysfunctional effects.[12] Set differs from plan in that set represents a limiting and narrowing of response alternatives with no inherent process to shift alternatives. It is a kind of cognitive habit that can limit perception, not a course of action with multiple paths that directs and sequences response possibilities.

The constructs of rules and plans advance the understanding of prob- 13 lem solving beyond that possible with earlier, less developed formulations. Still, critical problems remain. Though mathematical and computer models move one toward more complex (and thus more real) problems than the earlier research, they are still too neat, too rigidly sequenced to approximate the stunning complexity of day-to-day (not to mention highly creative) problem-solving behavior. Also, information-processing models of problem-solving are built on logic theorems, chess strategies, and simple planning tasks. Even Gagné seems to feel more comfortable with illustrations from mathematics and science rather than with social science and humanities problems. So although these complex models and constructs tell us a good deal about problem-solving behavior, they are still laboratory simulations, still invoked from the outside rather than self-generated, and still founded on the mathematico-logical.

Two Carnegie Mellon researchers, however, have recently extended the 14 above into a truly real, amorphous, unmathematical problem-solving process— writing. Relying on protocol analysis (thinking aloud while solving problems), Linda Flower and John Hayes have attempted to tease out the role of heuristic rules and plans in writing behavior.[13] Their research pushes problem-solving investigations to the real and complex and pushes, from the other end, the often mysterious process of writing toward the explainable. The latter is important, for at least since Plotinus many have viewed the composing process as unexplainable, inspired, infused with the transcendent. But Flower and Hayes are beginning, anyway, to show how writing generates from a problem-solving process with rich heuristic rules and plans of its own. They show, as well, how many writing problems arise from a paucity of heuristics and suggest an intervention that provides such rules.

This paper, too, treats writing as a problem-solving process, focusing, how- 15 ever, on what happens when the process dead-ends in writer's block. It will further suggest that, as opposed to Flower and Hayes' students who need more rules and plans, blockers may well be stymied by possessing rigid or inappropriate rules, or inflexible or confused plans. Ironically enough, these are occasionally instilled by the composition teacher or gleaned from the writing textbook.

## "Always Grab Your Audience"—The Blockers

In high school, *Ruth* was told and told again that a good essay always grabs 16 a reader's attention immediately. Until you can make your essay do that, her teachers and textbooks putatively declaimed, there is no need to go on. For Ruth, this means that beginning bland and seeing what emerges as one generates prose is unacceptable. The beginning is everything. And what exactly is the audience seeking that reads this beginning? The rule, or Ruth's use of it, doesn't provide for such investigation. She has an edict with no determiners. Ruth operates with another rule that restricts her productions as well: if sentences aren't grammatically "correct," they aren't useful. This keeps Ruth from toying with ideas on paper, from the kind of linguistic play that often frees up the flow of prose. These two rules converge in a way that pretty effectively restricts Ruth's composing process.

The first two papers I received from *Laurel* were weeks overdue. Sections 17 of them were well written; there were even moments of stylistic flair. But the papers were late and, overall, the prose seemed rushed. Furthermore, one paper included a paragraph on an issue that was never mentioned in the topic paragraph. This was the kind of mistake that someone with Laurel's apparent ability doesn't make. I asked her about this irrelevant passage. She knew very well that it didn't fit, but believed she had to include it to round out the paper, "You must always make three or more points in an essay. If the essay has less, then it's not strong." Laurel had been taught this rule both in high school and in her first college English class; no wonder, then, that she accepted its validity.

As opposed to Laurel, *Martha* possesses a whole arsenal of plans and rules 18 with which to approach a humanities writing assignment, and, considering her background in biology, I wonder how many of them were formed out of the assumptions and procedures endemic to the physical sciences.[14] Martha will not put pen to first draft until she has spent up to two days generating an outline of remarkable complexity. I saw one of these outlines and it looked more like a diagram of protein synthesis or DNA structure than the time-worn pattern offered in composition textbooks. I must admit I was intrigued by the aura of process (vs. the static appearance of essay outlines) such diagrams offer, but for Martha these "outlines" only led to self-defeat: the outline would become so complex that all of its elements could never be included in a short essay. In other words, her plan locked her into the first stage of the composing process. Martha would struggle with the conversion of her outline into prose only to scrap the whole venture when deadlines passed and a paper had to be rushed together.

Martha's "rage for order" extends beyond the outlining process. She also 19 believes that elements of a story or poem must evince a fairly linear structure and thematic clarity, or—perhaps bringing us closer to the issue—that analysis of a story or poem must provide the linearity or clarity that seems to be absent in the text. Martha, therefore, will bend the logic of her analysis to reason ambiguity out of existence. When I asked her about a strained paragraph in her paper on Camus' "The Guest," she said, "I didn't want to admit that it [the story's conclusion] was just hanging. I tried to force it into meaning."

Martha uses another rule, one that is not only problematical in itself, but 20 one that often clashes directly with the elaborate plan and obsessive rule above. She believes that humanities papers must scintillate with insight, must present an array of images, ideas, ironies gleaned from the literature under examination. A problem arises, of course, when Martha tries to incorporate her myriad "neat little things," often inherently unrelated, into a tightly structured, carefully sequenced essay. Plans and rules that govern the construction of impressionistic, associational prose would be appropriate to Martha's desire, but her composing process is heavily constrained by the non-impressionistic and non-associational. Put another way, the plans and rules that govern her exploration of text are not at all synchronous with the plans and rules she uses to discuss her exploration. It is interesting to note here, however, that as recently as three years ago Martha was absorbed in creative writing and was publishing poetry in high school magazines. Given what we know about the complex associational, often non-neatly-sequential nature of the poet's creative process, we can infer that Martha was either free of the plans and rules discussed earlier or they were not as intense. One wonders, as well, if the exposure to three years of university physical science either established or intensified Martha's concern with structure. Whatever the case, she now is hamstrung by conflicting rules when composing papers for the humanities.

*Mike's* difficulties, too, are rooted in a distortion of the problem-solving 21 process. When the time of the week for the assignment of writing topics draws near, Mike begins to prepare material, strategies, and plans that he believes will be appropriate. If the assignment matches his expectations, he has done a good job of analyzing the professor's intentions. If the assignment *doesn't* match his expectations, however, he cannot easily shift approaches. He feels trapped inside his original plans, cannot generate alternatives, and blocks. As the deadline draws near, he will write something, forcing the assignment to fit his conceptual procrustian bed. Since Mike is a smart man, he will offer a good deal of information, but only some of it ends up being appropriate to the assignment. This entire situation is made all the worse when the time between assignment of topic and generation of product is attenuated further, as in an essay examination. Mike believes (correctly) that one must have a plan, a strategy of some sort in order to solve a problem. He further believes, however, that such a plan, once formulated, becomes an exact structural and substantive blueprint that cannot be violated. The plan offers no alternatives, no "subroutines." So, whereas Ruth's, Laurel's, and some of Martha's difficulties seem to be rule-specific ("always catch your audience," "write grammatically"), Mike's troubles are more global. He may have strategies that are appropriate for various writing situations (e.g., "for this kind of political science assignment write a compare/contrast essay"), but his entire approach to formulating plans and carrying them through to problem solution is too mechanical. It is probable that Mike's behavior is governed by an explicitly learned or inferred rule: "Always try to 'psych out' a professor." But in this case this rule initiates a problem-solving procedure that is clearly dysfunctional.

While Ruth and Laurel use rules that impede their writing process and Mike 22 utilizes a problem-solving procedure that hamstrings him, *Sylvia* has trouble deciding which of the many rules she possesses to use. Her problem can be characterized as cognitive perplexity: some of her rules are inappropriate, others are functional; some mesh nicely with her own definitions of good writing, others don't. She has multiple rules to invoke, multiple paths to follow, and that very complexity of choice virtually paralyzes her. More so than with the previous four students, there is probably a strong emotional dimension to Sylvia's blocking, but the cognitive difficulties are clear and perhaps modifiable.

Sylvia, somewhat like Ruth and Laurel, puts tremendous weight on the 23 crafting of her first paragraph. If it is good, she believes the rest of the essay will be good. Therefore, she will spend up to five hours on the initial paragraph: "I won't go on until I get that first paragraph down." Clearly, this rule—or the strength of it—blocks Sylvia's production. This is one problem. Another is that Sylvia has other equally potent rules that she sees as separate, uncomplementary injunctions: one achieves "flow" in one's writing through the use of adequate transitions; one achieves substance to one's writing through the use of evidence. Sylvia perceives both rules to be "true," but several times followed one to the exclusion of the other. Furthermore, as I talked to Sylvia, many other rules, guidelines, definitions were offered, but none with conviction. While she *is* committed to one rule about initial paragraphs, and that rule is dysfunctional, she seems very uncertain about the weight and hierarchy of the remaining rules in her cognitive repertoire.

## "If It Won't Fit My Work, I'll Change It"—The Non-blockers

Dale, Ellen, Debbie, Susan, and Miles all write with the aid of rules. But their 24 rules differ from blockers' rules in significant ways. If similar in content, they are expressed less absolutely—e.g., "*Try* to keep audience in mind." If dissimilar, they are still expressed less absolutely, more heuristically—e.g., "I can use as many ideas in my thesis paragraph as I need and then develop paragraphs for each idea." Our non-blockers do express some rules with firm assurance, but these tend to be simple injunctions that free up rather than restrict the composing process, e.g., "When stuck, write!" or "I'll write what I can." And finally, at least three of the students openly shun the very textbook rules that some blockers adhere to: e.g., "Rules like 'write only what you know about' just aren't true. I ignore those." These three, in effect, have formulated a further rule that expresses something like: "If a rule conflicts with what is sensible or with experience, reject it."

On the broader level of plans and strategies, these five students also differ 25 from at least three of the five blockers in that they all possess problem-solving plans that are quite functional. Interestingly, on first exploration these plans seem to be too broad or fluid to be useful and, in some cases, can barely be expressed with any precision. Ellen, for example, admits that she has a general "outline in [her] head about how a topic paragraph should look" but could not describe much about its structure. Susan also has a general plan to follow, but, if stymied, will quickly attempt to conceptualize the assignment in different ways: "If my original idea won't work, then I need to proceed differently." Whether or not these plans operate in TOTE-fashion, I can't say. But they do operate with the operate-test fluidity of TOTEs.

True, our non-blockers have their religiously adhered-to rules: e.g., "When 26 stuck, write," and plans, "I couldn't imagine writing without this pattern," but as noted above, these are few and functional. Otherwise, these non-blockers operate with fluid, easily modified, even easily discarded rules and plans (Ellen: "I can throw things out") that are sometimes expressed with a vagueness that could almost be interpreted as ignorance. There lies the irony. Students that offer the least precise rules and plans have the least trouble composing. Perhaps this very lack of precision characterizes the functional composing plan. But perhaps this lack of precision simply masks habitually enacted alternatives and sub-routines. This is clearly an area that needs the illumination of further research.

And then there is feedback. At least three of the five non-blockers are an 27 Information-Processor's dream. They get to know their audience, ask professors and T.A.s specific questions about assignments, bring half-finished products in for evaluation, etc. Like Ruth, they realize the importance of audience, but unlike her, they have specific strategies for obtaining and utilizing feedback. And this penchant for testing writing plans against the needs of the audience can lead to modification of rules and plans. Listen to Debbie:

> In high school I was given a formula that stated that you must write a thesis paragraph with *only* three points in it, and then develop each of those points. When I hit college I was given longer assignments. That stuck me for a bit, but then I realized that I could use as many ideas in my thesis paragraph as I needed and then develop paragraphs for each one. I asked someone about this and then tried it. I didn't get any negative feedback, so I figured it was o.k.

Debbie's statement brings one last difference between our blockers and non- 28 blockers into focus; it has been implied above, but needs specific formulation: the goals these people have, and the plans they generate to attain these goals, are quite mutable. Part of the mutability comes from the fluid way the goals and plans are conceived, and part of it arises from the effective impact of feedback on these goals and plans.

## Analyzing Writer's Block

### Algorithms Rather Than Heuristics

In most cases, the rules our blockers use are not "wrong" or "incorrect"—it is   29
good practice, for example, to "grab your audience with a catchy opening" or
"craft a solid first paragraph before going on." The problem is that these rules
seem to be followed as though they were algorithms, absolute dicta, rather
than the loose heuristics that they were intended to be. Either through instruction, or the power of the textbook, or the predilections of some of our blockers
for absolutes, or all three, these useful rules of thumb have been transformed
into near-algorithmic urgencies. The result, to paraphrase Karl Dunker, is that
these rules do not allow a flexible penetration into the nature of the problem. It is this transformation of heuristic into algorithm that contributes to the
writer's block of Ruth and Laurel.

### Questionable Heuristics Made Algorithmic

Whereas "grab your audience" could be a useful heuristic, "always make three   30
or more points in an essay" is a pretty questionable one. Any such rule, though
probably taught to aid the writer who needs structure, ultimately transforms a
highly fluid process like writing into a mechanical lockstep. As heuristics, such
rules can be troublesome. As algorithms, they are simply incorrect.

### Set

As with any problem-solving task, students approach writing assignments   31
with a variety of orientations or sets. Some are functional, others are not.
Martha and Jane (see footnote 14), coming out of the life sciences and social
sciences respectively, bring certain methodological orientations with them—
certain sets or "directions" that make composing for the humanities a difficult, sometimes confusing, task. In fact, this orientation may cause them to
misperceive the task. Martha has formulated a planning strategy from her
predisposition to see processes in terms of linear, interrelated steps in a system. Jane doesn't realize that she can revise the statement that "committed"
her to the direction her essay has taken. Both of these students are stymied
because of formative experiences associated with their majors—experiences,
perhaps, that nicely reinforce our very strong tendency to organize experiences temporally.

### The Plan That Is Not a Plan

If fluidity and multi-directionality are central to the nature of plans, then the   32
plans that Mike formulates are not true plans at all but, rather, inflexible and
static cognitive blueprints.[15] Put another way, Mike's "plans" represent a restricted "closed system" (vs. "open system") kind of thinking, where closed system thinking is defined as focusing on "a limited number of units or items, or
members, and those properties of the members which are to be used are known

to begin with and do not change as the thinking proceeds," and open system thinking is characterized by an "adventurous exploration of multiple alternatives with strategies that allow redirection once 'dead ends' are encountered."[16] Composing calls for open, even adventurous thinking, not for constrained, no-exit cognition.

### Feedback

The above difficulties are made all the more problematic by the fact that they    33 seem resistant to or isolated from corrective feedback. One of the most striking things about Dale, Debbie, and Miles is the ease with which they seek out, interpret, and apply feedback on their rules, plans, and productions. They "operate" and then they "test," and the testing is not only against some internalized goal, but against the requirements of external audience as well.

### Too Many Rules—"Conceptual Conflict"

According to D. E. Berlyne, one of the primary forces that motivate prob-    34 lem-solving behavior is a curiosity that arises from conceptual conflict—the convergence of incompatible beliefs or ideas. In *Structure and Direction in Thinking*,[17] Berlyne presents six major types of conceptual conflict, the second of which he terms "perplexity":

> This kind of conflict occurs when there are factors inclining the subject toward each of a set of mutually exclusive beliefs. (p. 257)

If one substitutes "rules" for "beliefs" in the above definition, perplexity becomes a useful notion here. Because perplexity is unpleasant, people are motivated to reduce it by problem-solving behavior that can result in "disequalization":

> Degree of conflict will be reduced if either the number of competing . . . [rules] or their nearness to equality of strength is reduced. (p. 259)

But "disequalization" is not automatic. As I have suggested, Martha and Sylvia hold to rules that conflict, but their perplexity does *not* lead to curiosity and resultant problem-solving behavior. Their perplexity, contra Berlyne, leads to immobilization. Thus "disequalization" will have to be effected from without. The importance of each of, particularly, Sylvia's rules needs an evaluation that will aid her in rejecting some rules and balancing and sequencing others.

### A Note on Treatment

Rather than get embroiled in a blocker's misery, the teacher or tutor might in-    35 terview the student in order to build a writing history and profile: How much and what kind of writing was done in high school? What is the student's major? What kind of writing does it require? How does the student compose? Are there rough drafts or outlines available? By what rules does the student operate? How would he or she define "good" writing? etc. This sort of interview reveals an incredible amount of information about individual composing processes. Furthermore, it ofen reveals the rigid rule or the inflexible plan that may lie at the base of the student's writing problem. That was precisely what happened with the five blockers. And with Ruth, Laurel, and Martha (and Jane) what was revealed made virtually immediate remedy possible. Dysfunctional rules are easily replaced with or counter-balanced by functional ones if there is no emotional reason to hold onto that which simply doesn't work. Furthermore, students can be trained to select, to "know which rules are appropriate for which problems."[18] Mike's difficulties, perhaps because plans are more complex and pervasive than rules, took longer to correct. But inflexible plans, too, can be remedied by pointing out their dysfunctional qualities and by assisting the student in developing appropriate and flexible alternatives. Operating this way, I was successful with Mike. Sylvia's story, however, did not end as smoothly. Though I had three forty-five minute contacts with her, I was not able to appreciably alter her behavior. Berlyne's theory bore results with Martha but not with Sylvia. Her rules were in conflict, and perhaps that conflict was not exclusively cognitive. Her case keeps analyses like these honest; it reminds us that the cognitive often melds with, and can be overpowered by, the affective. So while Ruth, Laurel, Martha, and Mike could profit from tutorials that explore the rules and plans in their writing behavior, students like Sylvia may need more extended, more affectively oriented counseling sessions that blend the instructional with the psychodynamic.

## Notes

1. David Shapiro, *Neurotic Styles* (New York: Basic Books, 1965).
2. Barbara Hayes-Ruth, a Rand cognitive psychologist, and I are currently developing an information-processing model of the composing process. A good deal of work has already been done by Linda Flower and John Hayes (see para. 14 of this article). I have just received—and recommend—their "Writing as Problem Solving" (paper presented at American Educational Research Association, April 1979).
3. *The Conditions of Learning* (New York; Holt, Rinehart and Winston, 1970), p. 193.
4. E. James Archer, "The Psychological Nature of Concepts," in H. J. Klausmeier and C. W. Harris, eds., *Analysis of Concept Learning* (New York: Academic Press, 1966), pp. 37–44; David P. Ausubel, *The Psychology of Meaningful Verbal Behavior* (New York: Grune and Stratton, 1963); Robert M. Gagné, "Problem Solving," in Arthur W. Melton, ed., *Categories of Human Learning* (New York: Academic Press, 1964), pp. 293–317; George A. Miller, *Language and Communication* (New York: McGraw-Hill, 1951).
5. George Katona, *Organizing and Memorizing* (New York: Columbia Univ. Press, 1940); Roger N. Shepard, Carl I. Hovland, and Herbert M. Jenkins, "Learning and Memorization of Classifications," *Psychological Monographs*, 75, No. 13 (1961) (entire No. 517); Robert S. Woodworth, *Dynamics of Behavior* (New York: Henry Holt, 1958), chs. 10–12.
6. *The Conditions of Learning*, pp. 190–91.
7. Karl Dunker, "On Problem Solving," *Psychological Monographs*, 58, No. 5 (1945) (entire No. 270); George A. Polya, *How to Solve It* (Princeton: Princeton University Press, 1945); George A. Miller, Eugene Galanter, and Karl H. Pribram, *Plans and the Structure of Behavior* (New York: Henry Holt, 1960).
8. Lyle E. Bourne, Jr., Bruce R. Ekstrand, and Roger L. Dominowski, *The Psychology of Thinking* (Englewood Cliffs, N.J.: Prentice-Hall, 1971).

9. John R. Hayes, "Problem Topology and the Solution Process," in Carl P. Duncan, ed., *Thinking: Current Experimental Studies* (Philadelphia: Lippincott, 1967), pp. 167–81.

10. Hulda J. Rees and Harold E. Israel, "An Investigation of the Establishment and Operation of Mental Sets," *Psychological Monographs*, 46 (1925) (entire No. 210).

11. Ibid.; Melvin H. Marx, Wilton W. Murphy, and Aaron J. Brownstein, "Recognition of Complex Visual Stimuli as a Function of Training with Abstracted Patterns," *Journal of Experimental Psychology*, 62 (1961), 456–60.

12. James L. Adams, *Conceptual Blockbusting* (San Francisco: W. H. Freeman, 1974); Edward DeBono, *New Think* (New York: Basic Books, 1958); Ronald H. Forgus, *Perception* (New York: McGraw-Hill, 1966), ch. 13; Abraham Luchins and Edith Hirsch Luchins, *Rigidity of Behavior* (Eugene: Univ. of Oregon Books, 1959); N. R. F. Maier, "Reasoning in Humans. I. On Direction," *Journal of Comparative Psychology*, 10 (1920), 115–43.

13. "Plans and the Cognitive Process of Writing," paper presented at the National Institute of Education Writing Conference, June 1977; "Problem Solving Strategies and the Writing Process," *College English*, 39 (1977), 449–61. See also footnote 2.

14. Jane, a student not discussed in this paper, was surprised to find out that a topic paragraph can be rewritten after a paper's conclusion to make that paragraph reflect what the essay truly contains. She had gotten so indoctrinated with Psychology's (her major) insistence that a hypothesis be formulated and then left untouched before an experiment begins that she thought revision of one's "major premise" was somehow illegal. She had formed a rule out of her exposure to social science methodology, and the rule was totally inappropriate for most writing situations.

15. Cf. "A plan is flexible if the order of execution of its parts can be easily interchanged without affecting the feasibility of the plan . . . the flexible planner might tend to think of lists of things he had to do; the inflexible planner would have his time planned like a sequence of cause-effect relations. The former could rearrange his lists to suit his opportunities, but the latter would be unable to strike while the iron was hot and would generally require considerable 'lead-time' before he could incorporate any alternative sub-plans" (Miller, Galanter, and Pribram, p. 120).

16. Frederic Bartlett, *Thinking* (New York: Basic Books, 1958), pp. 74–76.

17. *Structure and Direction in Thinking* (New York: John Wiley, 1965), p. 255.

18. Flower and Hayes, "Plans and the Cognitive Process of Writing," p. 26.

......................................................................................................

## Questions for Discussion and Journaling

1. Create a list of all the rules that, according to Rose, interfere with "the blockers'" writing. What rules, if any, do you find yourself forced to follow that seem to get in the way of your writing?

2. Describe the difference between the rules that blockers in Rose's study were following and those that non-blockers were following. What accounts for the difference?

3. What's the difference between an *algorithm* and a *heuristic*? Give a couple of examples of each that you use on an everyday basis.

4. Based on Rose's study and descriptions of writers and their rules, write a "rule" explaining what makes a rule good for writers, and what makes a rule bad for writers. You'll get bonus points if you can tell whether your rule is an algorithm or a heuristic.

5. Can you think of mutually exclusive rules that you've tried to follow in your writing? If you can't easily or quickly think of any, comb through the rules that you follow for writing, and see if they're consistent with each other.

## Applying and Exploring Ideas

1. Find the origins of the rules you follow. Start by listing the ten rules that most power-
   fully impact your writing, whether good or bad. Now stop and think. Where, and
   when, did you learn each rule? Did it come from personal experience? Teachers?
   Parents? Observation of what other people were doing? Are there any rules you follow
   that you *don't* like? What would happen if you abandoned them?

2. Stop and think: Do you encounter rules in writing that flatly contradict your experience
   as a writer or reader? (For example: we're aware of a rule against beginning a sentence with "and." And we see good, professional writers do it all the time.) Describe
   one or two of these rules that you know of.

3. Rose concludes his article with a discussion of the difference between *knowing* a rule
   is ineffective and *acting* on that knowledge. If you find yourself following a rule that
   Rose suggests has a negative impact on writing, reflect on these questions: If you had
   permission to, would you stop following this rule? What is the risk of setting aside
   one rule and starting to use another? Is it possible that, rather than setting aside a rule
   completely, you might simply treat it more flexibly and have the best of both worlds?

---

### Meta Moment

Has anyone ever talked to you about *blocking* before? How might understanding this concept and knowing how to actively deal with it be useful to you in your life?

# The Need for Care: Easy Speaking onto the Page Is Never Enough

## PETER ELBOW

■ Elbow, Peter. "The Need for Care: Easy Speaking onto the Page Is Never Enough." *Vernacular Eloquence: What Speech Can Bring to Writing*. London: Oxford UP, 2012. 198–211. Print.

## Framing the Reading

Peter Elbow is one of the most well-known of the scholars who study writing and writing instruction. He is a Professor of English Emeritus at the University of Massachusetts Amherst, where he directed the writing program for many years. He is best known for his ideas about how to get writing done through a process called **freewriting**, and for his ideas about how to help students respond to one another's work and write, in his words, "without teachers." In his book by that name, *Writing without Teachers*, Elbow describes his struggles with writer's block and how his inability to write caused him to drop out of an English Ph.D. program at Harvard. Perhaps because of his own experiences as a struggling writer, Elbow devotes most of his published work to helping writers write, and helping teachers help students write. In addition to *Writing without Teachers*, Elbow has written *Writing with Power: Techniques for Mastering the Writing Process*, *Embracing Contraries: Explorations in Learning and Teaching*, *What is English?*, and *Everyone Can Write: Essays toward a Hopeful Theory of Writing and Teaching Writing*. The selection you are about to read is from his newest book, *Vernacular Eloquence: What Speech Can Bring to Writing*, published in January 2012 (and, unlike most academic books, reviewed by the *Boston Globe* in March 2012). Elbow made a video for students called "On Writing" that is available on YouTube, in which he talks about (among other things) needing to give himself permission to "make a mess" when he writes, instead of writing an outline like he was taught to do in school.

In the book from which the following selection is drawn, Elbow discusses ways that writers can use speaking to help them write. He argues for "speaking onto the page" and drawing on our ability to speak clearly and directly in order to write with more ease, clarity, and directness. In the selection you will read (which is Chapter 10 of *Vernacular Eloquence*), he points out that we should give up "care" (which he defines as "conscious conceptual thinking") in the early stages of writing in order to be more spontaneous and direct, but that this does not mean "we have to give up care entirely." In other words, he suggests we dictate and speak in order to get ideas formed and onto the page, but that we then use care in examining and revising what we have initially drafted. In essence, he argues, no one can write well without exercising "vigilant, cold, sharp-eyed care"; yet "few can write well unless they also know how to *relinquish* care, especially during the early stages of a writing project."

## Getting Ready to Read

*Before you read*, do at least one of the following activities:

- Think about what you usually do when you first try to write something. Do you labor over every word and sentence, or do you quickly get any and all ideas on paper? Do you think what you usually do is working effectively for you?
- Has any teacher ever told you that you can "make a mess" as you draft and go back and revise later?

*As you read*, consider the following questions:

- How much of this advice have you heard before?
- If you have not heard this advice before, do you think it would have helped you to hear it before?
- What pieces of advice from Elbow could you begin using immediately to help you as you write?

Y ou could call this book one sided. There's only one chapter on care while I  1
devote all the rest, in effect, to non-care: to what the tongue can do without planning. But I've made it one sided because the need for care is old news and doesn't need my help.

Yet I also imagine a very different critique. Someone might make fun of my  2
main argument in this way:

> *You're pretending to be radical, but your whole argument is just a disguised rehash of a venerable old tradition. Aristotle and Hazlitt speak for it—a tradition that says good writing <u>should</u> look like unstudied speech. But these folks had the wisdom and honesty to insist that it takes care and hard work to produce what looks like it came without trying. They don't naively pretend we can get this kind of good writing by trusting what comes for free.*

## The Venerable Tradition of Care

I don't disagree with that venerable goal in itself. In fact I'll spell it out a bit  3
more. But then I'll argue against some thinking associated with this tradition.

So here is Aristotle:  4

> We can now see that a writer must disguise his art and give the impression of speaking naturally and not artificially. Naturalness is persuasive, artificiality is the

contrary; for our hearers are prejudiced and think we have some design against them, as if we were mixing their wines for them. (*Rhetoric* Book III, 1404b)

Richard Graff summarizes this tradition in the Classical period:

Throughout antiquity, spontaneity or apparent spontaneity, was held out as an ideal for oratory, an ideal embodied in the famous doctrine that "art should conceal art." For the orator, this demand for naturalness could be fulfilled in at least two ways, either by perfecting his skill in true oral improvisation or by mastering the ability to compose a written text and manage his oral delivery of it so as to make the whole performance seem spontaneous.

In the first sentence of perhaps his most famous essay, Hazlitt in the eighteenth 5 century asks us "to write as any one would speak in common conversation":

It is not easy to write a familiar style. Many people mistake a familiar for a vulgar style, and suppose that to write without affectation is to write at random. On the contrary, there is nothing that requires more precision, and, if I may so say, purity of expression, than the style I am speaking of. It utterly rejects not only all un-meaning pomp, but all low, cant phrases, and loose, unconnected, slipshod allu-sions. It is not to take the first word that offers, but the best word in common use; it is not to throw words together in any combinations we please, but to follow and avail ourselves of the true idiom of the language. To write a genuine familiar or truly English style, is to write as any one would speak in common conversation who had a thorough command and choice of words, or who could discourse with ease, force, and perspicuity, setting aside all pedantic and oratorical flourishes. ("Essay VIII. On Familiar Style")

I agree that it often takes great care to produce language that *looks* spon- 6 taneous. Novelists and dramatists testify as much. Alan Bennett writes plays that brilliantly render spontaneous careless speech, and his "Talking Heads" are masterful and touching monologues. I'd gotten to know Bennett a bit when I studied at Oxford and have had the occasional tea with him since then; so a few years ago I proudly sent him an article of mine about freewrit-ing or speech in writing. He thanked me on a postcard saying something like this: "I read with grateful pleasure your interesting words about quicker easier writing. Meanwhile, I'm afraid I spend all day trying to write just a sentence or two."

When I listen to the radio or watch TV, I sometimes like to think about all 7 the *writing* in what I hear. Writers produced that text for Diane Sawyer to say—text that is supposed to sound completely unplanned and "naturally" spo-ken. Not easy; it can't be tossed off. We notice when the writer says something "off" or stumbles with a sentence that's too complicated for natural speech. (At Stanford University, Andrea Lunsford teaches a course on writing for radio.) Consider writers for *Glamour* or teen magazines. They are often highly educated and exert self-conscious sophisticated skill to produce unself-conscious-sounding gushy "teenspeak." When you call up the bus company and ask for help with schedules, you sometimes get the pre-recorded voice of a perky young woman who starts out, "Okay, let's see. I'll do my best to help you." Someone had to write those words. A good critic, Louis Menand, writes:

> [C]hattiness, slanginess, in-your-face-ness, and any other features of writing that are conventionally characterized as "like speech" are usually the results of laborious experimentation, revision, calibration, walks around the block, unnecessary phone calls, and recalibration." ("Bad Comma" 104)

So I'm not fighting the argument for care. The need for care is the theme  8
of this chapter and a premise for the whole book. And I understand why teachers and stylists advise care so relentlessly. Think of all the careless writing in our email boxes, online, in rushed daily newspapers—not to mention careless writing in scholarly articles and student papers.

> *"No one can get sustained good writing without vigilant, cold, sharp-eyed care. Still, my larger message is that few can write well unless they also know how to relinquish care."*

## The Doctrine of Eternal Vigilance

Eternal vigilance may be the price of liberty, but not, I'd argue, the price of  9
good writing. Eternal vigilance may help some people write well; more power to them. But I'm fighting against the doctrine of eternal vigilance as a monopoly, the feeling made to live in so many people's heads that it's the *only* way to write well: *never* let down your guard. As a monopoly it does considerable harm.

Yes, someone like Ian McEwan can make eternal vigilance work. He says  10
that he writes

> without a pen in my hand, framing a sentence in my mind, often losing the beginning as I reached the end, and only when the thing was secure and complete would I set it down. I would stare at it suspiciously. Did it really say what I meant? Did it contain an error or an ambiguity that I could not see? Was it making a fool of me? (quoted in Zalewski 55)

He wrote *Atonement* this way, and many other good and successful novels.

But it strikes me that eternal vigilance will only work if you have what  11
McEwan has: enormous skill, a highly developed conscious taste, limitless stamina—*and* what might be even *more* crucial: the gift of full faith in yourself to believe that you actually *can* find the right thoughts and words. Otherwise, you join the ranks of so many people of talent who give up before they manage to write what they could write. Some teachers and writers will respond, "Of course. No one should pick up a pen unless they have great skill, stamina, and

faith in themselves." But that dictum excludes me and it excludes many others who could otherwise write well.

Most of us need *relief* from vigilance if we want to write productively— some time for *no care* in putting down words. Otherwise we choke off the rich supply that is actually available to us all. Most of us write better when we allow ourselves to write down words and ideas before knowing whether they are acceptable or good. I like to tell students that eternal vigilance makes sense in driving; every other car might have a drunk driver who will kill you. But while you write each sentence, it's not so helpful to assume that it could get you in trouble. No one can harm you for a draft you never show them. Wait till revising for that kind of vigilance.

My point in this chapter is that we don't have to choose between vigilance and unplanned vernacular language. Carelessness alone leads to sloppy bad writing. Vigilance alone—staying always on guard even while we are trying to find words and ideas—can lead to unsuccessful writing and it also drags many people down to where they hate or even stop writing.

---

Here is some writing that was surely produced with unrelenting care. The writer manages to say with complete precision exactly what she wants to say in flawless grammar. Indeed, she is a leading authority on grammar in writing. She's saying that writing is more "developed" if we use a "writtenlike, dense clausal structure." But do we want to read prose like this when she could have said it so much more clearly by using some of the "undeveloped" capacities of speech?

This view of syntactic complexity, capturing the insight that more developed writing packs more information into each clause, and that this density of information is achieved by taking information that might be presented by a less mature writer in a whole clause and constructing it as a modifying element or subordinate clause, became very influential, stimulating other researchers to investigate syntactic complexity. Haswell's (2000) recent large-scale study, a reanalysis of 80 variables from studies of undergraduate writing using factor analysis to develop clusters of features that demonstrate maturity and development, also found increased length and density associated with postnominal modification, prepositional strings, and other structural features. The characterization of written language development as a movement from a more oral-like clause-chaining style to a more writtenlike, dense clausal structure has been useful for researchers in analyzing the written language of developing writers. (Schleppergrell 554)

---

Yet cold vigilance is exactly what we all need during the revising and editing stages. And we need plenty of it, because revising and editing almost always take *longer* than generating. I spend many more of my writing hours revising than unplanned speaking onto the page. But I need speaking onto the page not only in order to get things written in the first place, but also because it is a mysterious doorway to all the linguistic and rhetorical virtues that I'm trying to show in this book.

My overall goal is to find what's best about speaking and bring it to what's 15
best about writing. One of the *best* things about writing is how it invites care.
It gives us time for detached scrutiny and slow, careful, conscious, decision
making. When we speak with natural spontaneity or use our speaking gear to
write, we mostly *give up* the linguistic virtues of care. But just because we give
up care during early stages of the writing process, that doesn't mean we have
to give it up entirely. It's not either/or when it comes to care and carelessness.
If we want to create good writing, we need *both* mental processes. In fact if we
use both, we get a powerful dialectical benefit. That is, it's easier to relinquish
careful planning and be creatively and fruitfully generative if we know we are
going to come back tomorrow or next month and apply single-minded, scrutinizing care. And it's easier to be rigorously and indeed *negatively* careful when
nonplanning has given us a rich fund of words and diverse ideas to choose
from—even wild and wrong ideas.

## Why Care Is Indispensable

So it's a very traditional view that I affirm: if we want something good, we can't get 16
along without cold scrutinizing vigilance and careful decision making. That is,
even though easy freewriting, emailing, and blogging *can* yield short stretches
of smart, powerful, charming, and rhetorically effective pieces of writing—
even though Darwin *could* sometimes get better sentences with blurting than
with care—nevertheless we can't get *sustained* pieces of good writing without
the use of deliberate conscious care. Care is particularly needed if you accept
my invitation in Part Two to *relinquish* care during the early stages of writing.

In truth, care is *more* essential than carelessness. That is, quite a number of 17
people have written brilliantly using *only* vigilant care, while very few have
written well without it. Perhaps it looked in Chapter 8 as though Buckley
and Trollope and Woolf learned to write well without care: they became so
practiced and skilled as native writers of careful skilled writing that they could
produce it as fluently as most of us can speak. Perhaps these writers were so
practiced that they could make decisions at lightning speed, or perhaps they
knew how to get into an almost tranced "flow" condition where "decisions get
made" without any need for conscious attention. Nevertheless, if they wanted
to be sure their writing was good, they could not avoid *reviewing with care*
what they had written so quickly and well. And even if that review didn't
result in any change, it involved a cold careful *decision not to change,* based
on a shrewd expert examination. In Chapter 6, I pointed to the good writing
that Michael Dyson and many others have produced from spoken interviews
where much of the language was surely uncareful speech. But Dyson had to
use careful deliberation to choose and organize the good bits—and cut or edit
the rest.

Note that careful reviewing is not so much a process of *producing* language 18
as of *examining* it—from the outside as it were—with a detached monitoring,
critical mentality. The problem with the doctrine of eternal vigilance for many
of us is that it asks us, in effect, to generate language from the outside.

## Two Procedures for Using Care to Bring Coherence Out of Chaos

When people first try freewriting or speaking onto the page, they sometimes   19
terrify themselves with the results. They feel overwhelmed by too many informal, inexact words. All these ideas, memories, and images are in the order they
came to mind—some of them wrong and some inappropriate for the piece
in hand. Ideas, arguments, memories, or plot events are sometimes tangled
together and seem inseparable or unorganizable.

For this situation I will suggest two ways to harness care for creating co-   20
herence. The first procedure—using collage form—is the quickest and easiest; it
leads to a coherent and pleasing piece of writing but not a fully explicit and logically organized essay. It yields a "collage essay"—often an effective way to present thinking or even an argument. But collages are also ideal for stories, memoirs,
poems, travel pieces, and interviews. (Dyson's interview essays that I referred to
in Chapter 6 border on being collages. See also the collage obituary from *The
New Yorker* that I've put at the end of this chapter.) The second procedure is
what I call the skeleton process: it's a more consciously conceptual process and a
powerful way to create a careful and more traditionally organized essay.

✳　　　✳　　　✳

## Using the *Collage* to Get from Chaos to Coherence

A "collage" in the original sense—as used by painters and other artists—is   21
a picture produced not by painting or drawing but by gluing actual objects
on the canvas: bits of colored paper or cardboard or metal or even things
like theater tickets. (*Kolla* is Greek for "glue.") For a *written* collage, writers
bring together separate, disconnected bits of writing rather than one continuous, connected piece. Often there are spaces or asterisks or decorative dingbats
between the separate bits. (Dingbats are the decorative text-separators that you
see just above this section.) That may not sound like good writing, but finished
collages are often remarkably satisfying and rhetorically effective. At a symposium on fiction, Donald Barthelme said, "The principle of collage is one of the
central principles of art in this century and it seems also to me to be one of the
central principles of literature" (Menand "Saved" 74).

You'll find many written collages in the world—even though lots of them   22
are not labeled as such. Many articles in newspapers or magazines are really
collages. They contain many quick changes of focus but those nontransitions
are not marked except with a change of paragraph—yet readers take these
jumps in stride. Feature stories in newspapers and magazines lend themselves
particularly to collage form. We've all read something like "A Portrait of Lower
Manhattan" where the article skips from street scenes to clothing shops to
atmosphere to history—from wide-shot overviews to close-up portraits—all
with no clunky transition sentences. TV documentaries are almost always collages: they continually jump us from one clip to the next with no transition,
and we take this in stride. The collage form is alive and works well. Interviews

and interview-based essays are often not so far from the associative, somewhat random collage structure.

A collage can serve as a quick and simple way to produce a finished piece. 23 That is, after you have done a lot of freely and carelessly generated writing, you can just pick out the passages you like best, do minimal revising or editing, and put them together in whatever order strikes you as intuitively interesting or fruitful. Mark Twain thought he was making a joke, but really he was describing the collage: "Writing is easy. All you have to do is cross out the wrong words."

Creating a written collage is fairly quick and painless. It has the added ben- 24 efit of showing you that there was good stuff buried in all that unplanned, unorganized speaking onto the page that might be discouraging you. It helps you clear away all the distracting clutter and see the virtues.

In truth, the collage form lets us *avoid* the hardest jobs in writing: 25

- Revising weak passages. For a collage, just throw them away. (You can "cheat" and improve a couple of passages that are weak but seem indispensable.)
- Figuring out the main point and stating it clearly. A collage can work very well even if you haven't figured out your main point or what you are actually saying!
- Figuring out the best logical order for the bits. Instead, let yourself decide intuitively on an order that seems fruitful or intriguing.
- Making good transitions between the sections. The collage dispenses with transitions. (Actually there *are* transitions—invisible but effective: gaps that function by surprise, opposition, juxtaposition, or sly allusion.)

Here are the concrete steps that will yield a collage: 26

1. Look through all the rough writing (speaking onto the page) that you have written for this piece and choose the bits you like best. Some will be as short as a sentence or two, some as long as a page. If you are working on paper, cut them out with scissors. On a computer, put these passages into a new file and put asterisks or dingbats between them. (Be sure to keep the original file unchanged; you may want to raid it again.)
2. Lay them out in front of you so you can see them all. If you've been working onscreen, print them out and cut them into pieces that you can physically rearrange. Then read through them—slowly, respectfully, even meditatively.
3. Then arrange them in what feels like a pleasing or compelling or interesting order.
4. At this point, you may see you need a couple more bits: missing thoughts or images or stories you want to add. Fine. Perhaps you see your core idea better now and can say it with clarity; or you are moved to write a reflection on it. Or you remember a badly written bit you threw away and see that it's needed. Or maybe you see a good way to write something for an opening or closing bit. But remember that good collages can get along without "introductions" or "conclusions": you simply need a bit that works as a way to "jump into" your piece and another to "close the door" at the end.

5. Next, revise it all—but invite a kind of minimal and purely "negative" approach. See how much you can do by just *leaving out* words, phrases, sentences, or passages that don't work. Omission usually adds energy; addition usually saps it. Of course you'll do some rephrasing, perhaps for clarity or energy, but see how far you can get without heavy rewriting (unless there's some particular section you really want to rework). Reading your words out loud is best for this process.

6. Instead of trying to make nice connections or transitions between your pieces, just leave spaces for asterisks or dingbats.

7. If you want a finished piece, copy edit your collage carefully and type and format it to make it look its best.

By the way, there's a continuum that stretches between collage and essay, so   27
one option is to start with a bare, scanty, and merely suggestive collage—and then revise it *in the direction of* an explicit essay.

---

Collage is an ideal form for collaborative writing—particularly for people who are scared of writing with others. The collage invites an interesting mix of individual and cooperative tasks. Individually, each person is wholly in charge of her passages; no one has to bend her ideas or style to fit the others; there's no need for any of those frustrating arguments over single words or phrases. (These arguments are often what make people give up collaborative writing. However, solo authors can get feedback on their bits from the others—if they want it.) But everyone collaborates in deciding which pieces to use and what order to put them in. A collaborative collage is often stronger and more interesting if it shows sharp contrasts or even conflicts between different people's visions, points of view, ideas—and even voices and writing styles. It becomes a dialogue or conversation, not a monologue. (See my "Collaborative Collage.")

---

## Using the Skeleton Process for Building a Coherent, Well-Organized Essay from Disorganized Exploratory Writing

With my metaphor of "skeleton," I'm suggesting a process where you start by   28
looking for stray bones lying around on the ground and then gradually build them into a strong coherent "skeleton" that's actually alive. The process leads gradually from chaos to order and uses an especially productive kind of outlining.

1. *Find promising passages.* Read slowly through all the rough writing that pertains to the topic. Read it in whatever random order you find it. Look for any passages that somehow feel pertinent or important. They may be long or short—occasionally just a sentence. Many will be important because they contain a thought or idea or point (big or small); but some will be important because they contain *stories* or *examples* rather than ideas or reasons.

2. *Create bones.* For each important passage, create a tiny summary *germ sentence.* Make it as brief and pithy as possible. If a passage contains

more than one idea or point (perhaps it's a longer passage), summarize
them all. You can write germ sentences when you choose each passage or
wait till you've chosen them all.

In writing these summary sentences, you may need to spell out a point or idea
that's not clear or perhaps only implied in your rough writing. If the important
passage tells not a thought but rather an illustrative story or example, summarize it too. But try to *say* what it is "about." For example, don't just say "The ad
for Coca-cola"; say "The Coke ad implies that Coke will improve your health."

The main thing is this: if a passage of rough fast writing *feels* important in
some way for the topic you are writing about, force it to yield a germ sentence.
You are creating bones.

Insist that you summarize them in *sentences—with verbs*—not just in single
words or phrases. Don't just write "blue-collar salaries"; write "some blue-collar
workers earned more than some white-collar workers." The goal of this activity is to create ingredients that will later help you see the *logic* of your thinking.
You won't be able to see the *logic* if you just write "the Coke ad" or "blue-collar
salaries." Germ sentences might well be questions: "How come some blue collars
earned more than some white collars?" It's particularly valuable to make a germ
sentence out of an implied perplexity—something you don't understand. Single
words or short phrases are mute and merely *point* to an *implied* concept or idea.
A little sentence *says something* and has conceptual or semantic energy that helps
get you from one idea to the next. Verbs strong-arm you into thinking.

Most of all, germ sentences will help you later when you are trying to figure out a sequence or organization. And short is good. That's why I find that
informal language is good—even better. To make these ideas as *pointed* as possible, I try to turn them into *blurted speech*. I find that the mental energy I need
to crunch my points into *short* kernel sentences with verbs makes my ideas
stronger and clearer. Even if a particular "point" is nothing but an example or
illustration, the sentence still helps; for example, "he spoke monotone—but his
words had power." If you come across the same idea or example again (which
often happens with freewriting or easy speaking onto the page), there's no need
to write another sentence—except that sometimes a better, more pointed germ
sentence springs to mind.

This process will yield a long list of short sentences. They'll be in random
order. Fine. You aren't worrying about sequence or organization yet. You aren't
even trying to figure out your main point yet—nor decide which other ideas to
keep or drop. (If you write these on index cards, it's easy to arrange them in
different orders—but I usually get along just writing them on regular paper—
which makes it easier to see them all at once.)

3. *Figure out a main idea.* Now look through this long list of kernel sentences or bones—in the order you find them. First just mark or underline
   the ones that feel important or central. This will help you if you still don't
   know your main idea—and in fact if you think you know your main idea,
   you may change your mind if you start by just marking the passages that
   feel important.

Look through these marked ones and figure out your main idea. Maybe it's obvious at this point. But maybe you still can't figure it out. This happens to me a lot. Maybe all that exploratory writing and thinking has led you through ideas you've thought of before, but now you can see that these ideas are taking you on a journey toward an idea that you've never had before. But you *still* don't quite have it. Maybe there's a kind of *felt but absent* main idea that's been gently tugging at you, tickling you, driving you in your exploratory writing. It's an idea that's trying to hold all this interesting material together, but it isn't here yet. That's a good sign; you are on your way to a piece of new thinking.

But now you have to figure it out. Perhaps *now* you can write out this implied main idea in a crude short germ sentence. But that may be difficult even now. You can sort of feel it—sense the shape of the hole where it belongs—but you can't yet *say* it. In that case then, freewrite some more out of this *feeling* so you can work your way to it. Or talk it through with someone. When you finally have it, you can move on to step four.

Notice, by the way, that if you had made an outline *before* doing the exploratory writing, you never would have come up with this interesting new idea you're now trying to figure out. We're often advised to start off a writing project by making an outline, but that's almost never worked for me. I can never make a useful outline till *after* I've done a lot of exploratory writing. And even then, outlines don't become useful for me till I learn to build them out of germ sentences instead of single words or phrases.

4. *Build the skeleton*—a sequence. Now that you have a sentence for your main point (and of course your main point *can* change later as you write—which can also be a good sign), you can begin to work out a good sequence for your bones, that is, for your ideas, reasons, examples, or stories.

Start by just looking at your main idea and the germ sentences that seem most important. Because you forced yourself to write your points in the form of *sentences,* it will be much easier to figure out how to string those sentences together so they make good sense or tell a good story. More ideas may well come to you during this process—ideas for more germ sentences.

You could call this an outline, but I find it helpful to think of it as a *story outline*. It's made of sentences that tell a kind of *story of thinking*—a story that feels coherent and sensible. It's an outline of *thoughts,* not just single words or single phrases that point to mere *topics* or *areas*. The idea of "story outline" helps me realize that there's no "correct" sequence for my ideas. I'm not trying to write a perfect piece of geometry. I'm trying to build a good sequence of sentences where each point *follows* the previous one naturally, and where the whole sequence is going somewhere and has a felt shape—like a good story.

Most good essays are actually more like stories of thinking than pieces of lockstep logic. There are lots of ways to tell a story well. Good stories can start in the beginning of the events, the middle, or the end. So too with good stories of thinking and good essays. They can start at the beginning, but they can also work well if you start in the middle or with some random interesting story—or even start with the conclusion and then tell the story of how you got there.

As you arrange your sentences to tell a good story of thinking, you may find that there are some gaps—some ideas or points that are missing if you want them all to follow each other in a coherent way. If so, you'll have to write these missing sentences now. It's very common to need more examples and illustrations, though you may not see that need till you actually start to write a coherent draft.

> 5. *Create a coherent draft.* When I used to make conventional outlines of words or phrases instead of sentences, I always had a hard time writing a draft from them. Somehow the "points" wouldn't "go" into prose. I've found that a story outline of actual sentences works much better. Some germ sentences can even serve as little titles or subheads for a section.

*Using the skeleton process for revising or feedback.* I've been describing the skel-  29 eton process as an early procedure for creating a draft. But it can also be useful late in the process for *revising* a draft essay that you've already worked on or even finished—but which somehow doesn't work. Perhaps you gave the draft to readers and they are dissatisfied, but they gave you all kinds of suggestions that conflict with each other or that you mostly don't trust. If you use the skeleton process this way, it becomes a way to revise a draft or even an already finished piece.

✳    ✳    ✳

The collage form and the skeleton process are disciplined ways to use *care*—  30 not the tongue but conscious cognitive critical scrutiny. They involve standing back and figuring out what we are *trying* to say or *ought* to say, figuring out what order things should go in, and changing or cutting what doesn't work or doesn't belong. They help us come at language with critical detachment from the outside—extricating ourselves from being caught up inside the language and thinking we are generating.

## Applying Care and Planning to the *Process* of Writing

I see this chapter as the conceptual hinge of the whole book: no one can get  31 sustained good writing without vigilant, cold, sharp-eyed care. Still, my larger message is that few can write well unless they also know how to *relinquish* care, especially during the early stages of a writing project. Most of us need to welcome unplanned, unvetted, probably-wrong words and ideas onto the page if we want to find rich enough fodder for the vigilance and care we need later. But we can't give up care.

The practical problem then is this: how can we plan and not plan?—be  32 careful and careless? How can we harness the best of both? It's hard enough to learn to pat the top of your head and rub your belly at the same time—and these activities don't fully exclude each other. But when processes exclude each other, like care and carelessness, *time* comes to the rescue: we can be careless and careful at different moments or stages of a writing process.

It turns out that many people who rail against carelessness are not actu-  33 ally very careful about the *process* they use for writing. Some even scorn attention to "process" (just as professors of a disciplinary subject sometimes scorn attention to "pedagogy"). They just carry on writing the way they've always done ("carefully" they'd say) without really thinking it through from a position of critical consciousness. In this final section of the chapter, I want to argue for more conscious care about the very *process* we use for getting things written. Process is a realm where thoughtful deliberation is particularly appropriate.

Conscious conceptual thinking has shown me a writing process in which  34 carelessness and care can interact in a fruitful way. It's a process that is implicit throughout the book.

1. *Generating.* This stage is for exploring on paper and early drafting, speaking onto the page or freewriting in whatever language comes most easily and comfortably to the mind and mouth. The goal is to get down as much material as possible in one way or another.

2. *Substantive revising.* This is often a slow, difficult process of digging in and thinking hard. It's likely to involve plenty of slow pondering. I often find a story outline helpful at this point (rather than at the beginning). In substantive revising, we deal with issues of organization and even genre. For many genres, we need to think about the expectations of those who feel they "own" the genre. As an essay, for example, is this more argument or analysis? As a piece about scientific or sociological process, is it a lab report or an analytical or even argumentative essay about research procedures? As a memoir or personal essay, is it trying to fit a particular tradition or just take its own path—and is it trying for facts and verisimilitude or a purely subjective point of view?

   As narrative, how explicitly present do you want to be as teller? In this book, I mostly neglect substantive revising since I don't see a special role there for the tongue. A big exception, however, is my plea for story outlines. They are built out of spoken sentences rather than static words or phrases. And the notion of *story* outline acknowledges that readers are operating in time, whereas conventional outlines imply the space dimension. (See Chapter 15 for more on this.)

3. *Late revising.* This is for clarity and style. I'll focus on this stage next in Part Three (in Chapters 11 through 14).

4. *Final editing of surface features.* Such features are usually matters of convention. So if the piece needs to end up in "correct" Edited Written English, this is the time to make the changes that are needed. How formal or informal should it be in register or tone? Even if a piece doesn't have to be in Edited Written English, this final editing step is still needed for typing mistakes and other oversights like inconsistent spelling. (But keep your

eye out for the point that emerges in the next section—the Introduction to Part Three: "correct writing" doesn't require knowing *everything* in the rule books; it only requires knowing the relatively small number of no-no's that set off the "error alarm" in the heads of mainstream readers.)

This is the process I've learned to use for writing essays for publication and 35 for this book. Of course when I want to do certain other kinds of writing— diary or journal writing, emailing, and exploratory writing—I can settle for the first step alone. And when I want to write informal pieces that don't matter so much—some letters, quick memos, slightly more important emails, and the like—I can skimp on steps 3 and 4.

In listing four linear steps, I don't mean to sound too simplistic or rigid. If 36 writing is going well, there may be no need to follow this sequence. That is, in the middle of loose freewriting or easy talking onto the page, you might find that you don't get too distracted from your thinking if you stop and do some revising or editing: fix some spelling; completely rewrite some sentences or paragraphs to make them clearer or logical; ponder at length to revise a thought that is elusive or seems wrong. If that works for you, fine.

But if you are not satisfied with your experience of writing—if you are hav- 37 ing what feels like too much trouble or anxiety or even pain—what you need may be some genuine rigidity. As you generate words and thoughts, you may need to forcibly *stop* yourself from fixing spelling, improving phrases, or trying to get your thinking clear. For me, unless my writing is going perfectly, I often need to hold a kind of gun to my head and rigidly prevent myself from trying to rewrite a sentence that is positively ugly or stupid sounding when I'm trying to generate ideas or even draft. Otherwise I lose all momentum or even grind to a halt. The thing that slows most writers down—discourages, frustrates, and sometimes swamps them altogether—is the process of continually becoming distracted or derailed by a problem that they could forget for now. Just keep going.

What's most damaging (except for the Ian McEwans of the world) is trying 38 to perfect each sentence before moving on to the next. Face it; you can't know till later how this sentence ought to look. Indeed, you may well have to cut it later, so why struggle now to improve it. Worse yet, you may find later that you really *should* cut it—but you can't bring yourself to do that because you sacrificed so much effort on it and have come to love it as your baby.

It often happens as we write that we come up with an idea (or memory or 39 turn of the story)—but then suddenly suspect that it's not quite right, and this leads us to write a different version or idea. We can't quite figure out which is right. Unless you are feeling very good about your process at the moment, I'd suggest *not* stopping to try to ponder it out. Better, usually, to leave both versions there. Just keep writing out what you are writing. This may even lead to a third version. At this generating stage of things, you are not in a good position even to *know* whether the first, second, or third idea is better. Wait till the revising stage to fix all matters of careful thinking and organization. And wait till the late revising stage for all matters of style and phrasing and tone; *and* wait till the editing stage for all issues of grammar and spelling. I consciously try to stay pretty well within these linear stages and advise others to do the same. I sometimes turn off the automatic spell check and use it only at the end.

Note however: this linear rigidity is only needed in *one direction*. That is, my main problems come from jumping *forward* into revising and editing as I generate. Jumping *backward*—from some kind of revising back into generating—is useful at any point. That is, during any later stages of writing—even when I thought I had finished—I've found it useful to allow myself to notice problems in thinking, organizing, or style. At these moments, I have to be willing to plunge back into the chaos of new generating or organizing—either by talking onto the page or by slow deliberate revisionary thinking. It sometimes takes a page of exploratory writing to help me simply clarify the logic in a single paragraph that's "off." Here then is why all writers tend to breathe a sigh of relief to discover there's no more time left. Without deadlines it's hard to finish anything.

40

A mainstream journal once turned down an article I submitted because they complained that I seemed to advocate a writing process that was "simplistically linear" and too one-step-at-a-time. Hadn't I heard of all the research about experienced and professional writers using a more "recursive" writing process?

I admit that this overall writing process might seem too much like "cookbook" writing. The skeleton process in particular is a refinement of what I described in *Writing Without Teachers* as a way to get something written when my mind had shut down—because of the panic of a deadline or my sense that I could never figure out my thoughts. I called it "desperation writing" (60ff). Some folks never need this kind of deliberate care over process; occasionally I don't. But scholars and psychologists have often noted how *many* different mental processes need to go on for writing to occur—not to mention halfway decent writing. So maybe it's a useful fiction to proceed as though the task of writing makes it hard to fire on all eight cylinders at once.

Besides, when scholars scorn any talk about "linear steps" in the writing process and wave the banner of recursiveness among "skilled practitioners," they are invoking a misleading empiricism. Are "skilled practitioners" always our best models for the writing process? Many of them experience unnecessary pain and delay—and plenty of them write pretty sad, clunky articles or essays (I remember research involving writers for *Seventeen* magazine). And should we all try to write like Ian McEwan? If I were researching "the practices of skilled writers," I'd explore a practice that's probably more central to success in good writing: the courage to *throw away* what one has labored over with sweat and blood.

The former first violinist of the Juilliard String Quartet, Robert Mann, played brilliantly, but it would be crazy for any student to imitate the ungainly inefficient physical technique he somehow managed to wield. Sondra Perl did foundational research showing how recursiveness tends to be a huge *problem* with novice writers: they tended to stop after almost every sentence or two to read back over what they had written and worry that it might be wrong.

# LITERACY STORY

## *An Example of a Collage from* The New Yorker *(July 5, 1982)*

### ROBERT BINGHAM (1925–82)

HE was a tall man of swift humor whose generally instant responses reached far into memory and wide for analogy. Not much missed the attention of his remarkably luminous and steady eyes. He carried with him an education from the Boston Latin School, Phillips Exeter Academy, Harvard College—and a full year under the sky with no shelter as an infantryman in France in the Second World War. Arriving there, he left his rifle on the boat.

One of his lifelong friends, a popular novelist, once asked him why he had given up work as a reporter in order to become an editor.

"I decided that I would rather be a first-rate editor than a second-rate writer," he answered.

The novelist, drawing himself up indignantly, said, "And what is the matter with being a second-rate writer?"

Nothing, of course. But it is given to few people to be a Robert Bingham.

To our considerable good fortune, for nearly twenty years he was a part of *The New Yorker*, primarily as an editor of factual writing. In that time, he addressed millions of words with individual attention, giving each a whisk on the shoulders before sending it into print. He worked closely with many writers and, by their testimony, he may have been the most resonant sounding board any sounder ever had. Adroit as he was in reacting to sentences before him, most of his practice was a subtle form of catalysis done before he saw a manuscript.

Talking on the telephone with a writer in the slough of despond, he would say, "Come, now, it can't be that bad. Nothing could be *that* bad. Why don't you try it on me?"

"But you don't have time to listen to it."

"We'll make time. I'll call you back after I finish this proof."

"Will you?"

"Certainly."

*

"In the winter and spring of 1970, I read sixty thousand words to him over the telephone."

*

"If you were in his presence, he could edit with the corners of his mouth. Just by angling them down a bit, he could erase something upon which you might otherwise try to insist. If you saw that look, you would be in a hurry to delete the cause of his disdain. In some years, he had a mustache. When he had a mustache, he was a little less effective with that method of editing, but effective nonetheless."

*

"I turned in a story that contained a fetid pun. He said we should take that out. He said it was a terrible line. I said, 'A person has a right to make a pun once in a while, and even to be a little coarse.' He said, 'The line is not on the level of the rest of the piece and therefore seems out of place.' I said, 'That may be, but I want it in there.' He said, 'Very well. It's your piece.' Next day, he said, 'I think I ought to tell you I haven't changed my mind about that. It's an unfortunate line.' I said, 'Listen, Bobby. We discussed that. It's funny. I want to use it. If I'm embarrassing anybody, I'm embarrassing myself.' He said, 'O.K. I just work here.' The day after that, I came in and said to him, 'That joke. Let's take that out. I think that ought to come out.' 'Very

well,' he said, with no hint of triumph in his eye."

*

"As an editor, he wanted to keep his tabula rasa. He was mindful of his presence between writer and reader, and he wished to remain invisible while representing each. He deliberately made no move to join the journeys of research. His writers travelled to interesting places. He might have gone, too. But he never did, because he would not have been able to see the written story from a reader's point of view."

*

"Frequently, he wrote me the same note. The note said, 'Mr. —, my patience is not inexhaustible.' But his patience *was* inexhaustible. When a piece was going to press, he stayed long into the evening while I fumbled with prose under correction. He had pointed out some unarguable flaw. The fabric of the writing needed invisible mending, and I was trying to do it with him in a way satisfactory to him and to the over-all story. He waited because he respected the fact that the writing had taken as much as five months, or even five years, and now he was giving this or that part of it just another five minutes."

*

"Edmund Wilson once said that a writer can sometimes be made effective 'only by the intervention of one who is guileless enough and human enough to treat him, not as a monster, nor yet as a mere magical property which is wanted for accomplishing some end, but simply as another man, whose sufferings elicit his sympathy and whose courage and pride he admires.' When writers are said to be gifted, possibly such intervention has been the foremost of the gifts."

Copyright © 1982 Condé Nast. All rights reserved. Originally published in *The New Yorker*. Reprinted by permission.

## Questions for Discussion and Journaling

1. Elbow claims that careless speech has some virtues or positive qualities that we should seek to integrate into our writing. What are some of these?

2. Elbow draws a distinction between "vigilant care" and "unrelenting care" in writing and revising. The first he says is necessary. The second he says is dangerous. What does he mean?

3. How does Elbow define a "written collage"?

4. What does Elbow mean when he says that it is important at some point when we are drafting to "harness detachment, scrutiny, and correction . . . extricating ourselves from being caught up inside the language and thinking we are generating"?

5. Elbow points out that careful decision-making in writing is "necessary, but it's not sufficient." Decisions about writing and revising can be careful but still be bad. Can you think of some times when you made writing decisions carefully, but they turned out not to be good decisions? How do you know whether a writing decision is good or bad?

6. What does Elbow mean when he says that we should practice and learn to "write by ear"?

7. Elbow draws a distinction between types of revising (substantive and late, for example) and editing. What are these differences? Have you ever thought before about revising and editing as different? Do you normally engage in both revising and editing, or do you tend toward editing alone?

## Applying and Exploring Ideas

1. Elbow says that when writing is not going well and you are experiencing anxiety or pain about your writing, you might benefit from "forcibly [stopping] yourself from fixing spelling, improving phrases, or trying to get your thinking clear" (para. 37). He suggest that we should "[j]ust keep going" instead of allowing ourselves to become "distracted or derailed by a problem that [you] really should forget for now" (para. 37). The next time you draft something difficult, try this approach and see what it does for you.

2. Elbow suggests that we shouldn't get too invested in what we write so that we have "the courage to throw away" what we "labored over." Try writing something as quickly as you can, without stopping, and then just throwing it away and starting all over again. Do this three or four times and see what happens. If you can't think of something to write about, try writing an e-mail to a friend about something interesting you have seen or heard in the past few days.

3. Can you find some examples of what Elbow calls "written collage"?

4. Follow Elbow's directions and write a collage (para. 26). To do that, either take something you have started drafting in another context, or "speak onto the page" for a few minutes about something interesting that happened to you recently. Whichever you choose, then follow his direction for writing a collage: Choose the bits you like the best and cut them out, lay them in front of you, arrange them in a pleasing or

compelling order, fill in missing thoughts or images, take out any pieces you don't like, put spaces or asterisks where transitions go. Once you've done this, take a minute to reflect on the experience and the collage itself. This was really just an exercise in trying to draft. Was it helpful, interesting, or productive for you in any way? Would you ever try it again?

5. The next time you are given a writing assignment for a class that requires you to draw on outside texts, try using Elbow's "skeleton process" (para. 28) to get you started: Look for passages that seem interesting, create a germ sentence for each, then look through the list of germ sentences you've written to see which ones seem central, write what seems to be your main point, and then begin to work on a story outline. Consider this a drafting experiment, just like the collage was a drafting experiment. Does doing this help you in any way? How is it different from your normal drafting process?

## Meta Moment

How did you think about composing/drafting before you read this piece, and how do you think about it now? Is there anything about your composing process(es) that you think you should try to change based on Elbow's advice?

# I Stand Here Writing

## NANCY SOMMERS

■ Sommers, Nancy. "I Stand Here Writing." *College English* 55.4 (1993): 420–28. Print.

## Framing the Reading

Nancy Sommers teaches and researches at Harvard University, where she has served a number of roles over nearly three decades, including directing Harvard's Expository Writing Program and several other programs, and launching the Harvard Study of Undergraduate Writing, which tracked four hundred students throughout their college experience in order to investigate what they were writing and how.

Throughout her career, Sommers's work has focused on the development of high school and college students' literacies and writing. She has been a significant advocate and practitioner of empirical research on writing: interviewing writers directly, getting them to write about writing, and studying what they say, and collecting (often at great expense) and reading the writing they actually produce. Her work has been of tremendous value to other writing researchers. In this piece, however, Sommers works more reflectively, examining her own practices as a reader, thinker, and writer in order to consider the role of reading and "sources" in **invention**, how writers come up with what to say in their writing.

Depending on what you've already read in this book, you might also get a strong sense of déjà vu as you read Sommers's thinking on how we read sources, how we make meaning of sources, how we use sources in our own writing, and how we find the balance between *our* words and *others'* words. Particularly, you might recognize parallels (or at least a shared subject matter) with Murray's, Kantz's, Porter's, and Haas and Flower's work. If you hadn't already stopped to think about it, this question about where our words come from seems to be an important one for writers—so important (and complicated) that many researchers can study that question from many angles for many years without fully answering it.

## Getting Ready to Read

*Before you read,* do at least one of the following activities:

- Review any of the above mentioned authors/pieces you've already read.
- Do you think differently about the place of personal opinion and experience in academic writing than you did when you began this class? If so, what has changed in your thinking?

*As you read,* consider the following question:

- Is Sommers discussing any familiar ideas? What ideas are new to you? Is she looking in a new or different way at some ideas you've thought about before?

...........................................................................................................

*I* stand in my kitchen, wiping the cardamom, coriander, and cayenne off my 1
fingers. My head is abuzz with words, with bits and pieces of conversation. I hear a phrase I have read recently, something about "a radical loss of certainty." But, I wonder, how did the sentence begin? I search the air for the rest of the sentence, can't find it, shake some more cardamom, and a bit of coriander. Then, by some play of mind, I am back home again in Indiana with my family, sitting around the kitchen table. Two people are talking, and there are three opinions; three people are talking, and there are six opinions. Opinions grow exponentially. I fight my way back to that sentence. Writing, that's how it begins: "Writing is a radical loss of certainty." (Or is it uncertainty?) It isn't so great for the chicken when all these voices start showing up, with all these sentences hanging in mid-air, but the voices keep me company. I am a writer, not a cook, and the truth is I don't care much about the chicken. Stories beget stories. Writing emerges from writing.

The truth. Has truth anything to do with the facts? All I know is that no 2
matter how many facts I might clutter my life with, I am as bound to the primordial drama of my family as the earth is to the sun. This year my father, the son of a severe Prussian matriarch, watched me indulge my daughters, and announced to me that he wished I had been his mother. This year, my thirty-ninth, my last year to be thirty-something, my mother—who has a touch of magic, who can walk into the middle of a field of millions of clovers and find the *one* with four leaves—has begun to think I need help. She sends me cards monthly with four-leaf clovers taped inside. Two words neatly printed in capital letters—GOOD LUCK!! I look at these clovers and hear Reynolds Price's words: "Nobody under forty can believe how nearly everything's inherited." I wonder what my mother knows, what she is trying to tell me about the facts of my life.

When I was in high school studying French, laboring to conjugate verbs, the 3
numerous four-leaf clovers my mother had carefully pressed inside her French dictionary made me imagine her in a field of clovers lyrically conjugating verbs of love. This is the only romantic image I have of my mother, a shy and conservative woman whose own mother died when she was five, whose grandparents were killed by the Nazis, who fled Germany at age thirteen with her father and sister. Despite the sheer facts of her life, despite the accumulation of grim knowable data, the truth is my mother is an optimistic person. She has the curious capacity always to be looking for luck, putting her faith in four-leaf clovers, ladybugs, pennies, and other amulets of fortune. She has a vision different from mine, one the facts alone can't explain. I, her daughter, was left, for a long time, seeing only the ironies; they were my defense against the facts of my life.

In this world of my inheritance in which daughters can become their fathers' 4
mothers and mothers know their daughters are entering into a world where
only sheer good luck will guide them, I hear from my own daughters that I am
not in tune with their worlds, that I am just like a 50s mom, that they are 90s
children, and I should stop acting so primitive. My children laugh uproariously
at my autograph book, a 1959 artifact they unearthed in the basement of my
parents' home. "Never kiss by the garden gate. Love is blind, but the neighbors
ain't," wrote one friend. And my best friend, who introduced herself to me
on the first day of first grade, looking me straight in the eye—and whispering
through her crooked little teeth "the Jews killed Jesus"—wrote in this autograph book: "Mary had a little lamb. Her father shot it dead. Now she carries
it to school between two slices of bread."

My ten-year-old daughter, Rachel, writes notes to me in hieroglyphics and 5
tapes signs on the refrigerator in Urdu. "Salaam Namma Man Rachaal Ast"
reads one sign. Simply translated it means "Hello, my name is Rachel." Alex,
my seven-year-old daughter, writes me lists, new lists each month, visibly reminding me of the many things I need to buy or do for her. This month's list
includes a little refrigerator filled with Coke and candy; ears pierced; a new
toilet; neon nail polish and *real* adult make-up.

How do I look at these facts? How do I embrace these experiences, these texts 6
of my life, and translate them into ideas? How do I make sense of them and the
conversations they engender in my head? I look at Alex's list and wonder what
kind of feminist daughter I am raising whose deepest desires include neon nail
polish and *real* adult make-up. Looking at her lists a different way, I wonder if
this second child of mine is asking me for something larger, something more permanent and real than adult make-up. Maybe I got that sentence wrong. Maybe
it is that "Love (as well as writing) involves a radical loss of certainty."

Love is blind, but the neighbors ain't. Mary's father shot her little lamb 7
dead, and now she carries it to school between two slices of bread. I hear these
rhymes today, and they don't say to me what they say to my daughters. They
don't seem so innocent. I hear them and think about the ways in which my
neighbors in Indiana could only see my family as Jews from Germany, exotic
strangers who ate tongue, outsiders who didn't celebrate Christmas. I wonder
if my daughter Rachel needs to tell me her name in Urdu because she thinks
we don't share a common language. These sources change meaning when I ask
the questions in a different way. They introduce new ironies, new questions.

I want to understand these living, breathing, primary sources all around me. 8
I want to be, in Henry James's words, "a person upon whom nothing is lost."
These sources speak to me of love and loss, of memory and desire, of the ways
in which we come to understand something through difference and opposition.
Two years ago I learned the word *segue* from one of my students. At first the
word seemed peculiar. Segue sounded like something you did only on the Los
Angeles freeway. Now I hear that word everywhere, and I have begun using it. I
want to know how to segue from one idea to the next, from one thought to the
fragment lying beside it. But the connections don't always come with four-leaf
clovers and the words GOOD LUCK neatly printed beside them.

My academic need to find connections sends me to the library. There are eleven million books in my University's libraries. Certainly these sanctioned voices, these authorities, these published sources can help me find the connections. Someone, probably some three thousand someones, has studied what it is like to be the child of survivors. Someone has written a manual on how the granddaughter of a severe Prussian matriarch and the daughter of a collector of amulets ought to raise feminist daughters. I want to walk into the fields of writing, into those eleven million books, and find the one book that will explain it all. But I've learned to expect less from such sources. They seldom have the answers. And the answers they do have reveal themselves to me at the most unexpected times. I have been led astray more than once while searching books for the truth.

Once I learned a lesson about borrowing someone else's words and losing 10 my own.

I was fourteen, light years away from thirty-something. High school de- 11 bate teams across the nation were arguing the pros and cons of the United States Military Aid Policy. It all came back to me as I listened to the news of the Persian Gulf War, as I listened to Stormin' Norman giving his morning briefings, an eerie resonance, all our arguments, the millions of combative words— sorties—fired back and forth. In my first practice debate, not having had enough time to assemble my own sources, I borrowed quote cards from my teammates. I attempted to bolster my position that the U.S. should limit its military aid by reading a quote in my best debate style: "W. W. Rostow says: 'We should not give military aid to India because it will exacerbate endemic rivalries.'"

> I want to walk into the fields of writing, into those eleven million books, and find the one book that will explain it all. But I've learned to expect less from such sources. They seldom have the answers.

Under cross-examination, my 12 nemesis, Bobby Rosenfeld, the neighbor kid, who always knew the right answers, began firing a series of questions at me without stopping to let me answer:

> Borrowing words from authorities had left me without words of my own.

"Nancy, can you tell me who W. W. Rostow is? And can you tell me why he 13 might say this? Nancy, can you tell me what 'exacerbate' means? Can you tell me what 'endemic rivalries' are? And exactly what does it mean to 'exacerbate endemic rivalries'?"

I didn't know. I simply did not know who W. W. Rostow was, why he might 14 have said that, what "exacerbate" meant, or what an "endemic rivalry" was. Millions of four-leaf clovers couldn't have helped me. I might as well have been speaking Urdu. I didn't know who my source was, the context of the source, nor the literal meaning of the words I had read. Borrowing words from authorities had left me without any words of my own.

My debate partner and I went on that year to win the Indiana state championship and to place third in the nationals. Bobby Rosenfeld never cross-examined me again, but for twenty years he has appeared in my dreams. I am not certain why I would dream so frequently about this scrawny kid whom I despised. I think, though, that he became for me what the Sea Dyak tribe of Borneo calls a *ngarong*, a dream guide, someone guiding me to understanding. In this case, Bobby guided me to understand the endemic rivalries within myself. The last time Bobby appeared in a dream he had become a woman.

I learned a more valuable lesson about sources as a college senior. I was the kind of student who loved words, words out of context, words that swirled around inside my mouth, words like *exacerbate, undulating, lugubrious,* and *zeugma.* "She stained her honour or her new brocade," wrote Alexander Pope. I would try to write zeugmas whenever I could, exacerbating my already lugubrious prose. Within the English department, I was known more for my long hair, untamed and untranslatable, and for my long distance bicycle rides than for my scholarship.

For my senior thesis, I picked Emerson's essay "Eloquence." Harrison Hayford, my advisor, suggested that I might just get off my bicycle, get lost in the library, and read all of Emerson's essays, journals, letters. I had picked one of Emerson's least distinguished essays, an essay that the critics mentioned only in passing, and if I were not entirely on my own, I had at least carved out new territory for myself.

I spent weeks in the library reading Emerson's journals, reading newspaper accounts from Rockford and Peoria, Illinois, where he had first delivered "Eloquence" as a speech. Emerson stood at the podium, the wind blowing his papers hither and yon, calmly picking them up, and proceeding to read page 8 followed by page 3, followed by page 6, followed by page 2. No one seemed to know the difference. Emerson's Midwestern audience was overwhelmed by this strange man from Concord, Massachusetts, this eloquent stranger whose unit of expression was the sentence.

As I sat in the library, wearing my QUESTION AUTHORITY T-shirt, I could admire this man who delivered his Divinity School Address in 1838, speaking words so repugnant to the genteel people of Cambridge that it was almost thirty years before Harvard felt safe having him around again. I could understand the Midwestern audience's awe and adulation as they listened but didn't quite comprehend Emerson's stunning oratory. I had joined the debate team not to argue the U.S. Military Aid Policy, but to learn how to be an orator who could stun audiences, to learn a personal eloquence I could never learn at home. Perhaps only children of immigrant parents can understand the embarrassing moments of inarticulateness, the missed connections that come from learning to speak a language from parents who claim a different mother tongue.

As an undergraduate, I wanted to free myself from that mother tongue. Four-leaf clovers and amulets of oppression weighed heavy on my mind, and

I could see no connection whatsoever between those facts of my life and the untranslatable side of myself that set me in opposition to authority. And then along came Emerson. Like his Midwest audience, I didn't care about having him whole. I liked the promise and the rhapsodic freedom I found in his sentences, in his invitation to seize life as our dictionary, to believe that "Life was not something to be learned but to be lived." I loved his insistence that "the one thing of value is the active soul." I read that "Books are for the scholar's idle time," and I knew that he had given me permission to explore the world. Going into Emerson was like walking into a revelation; it was the first time I had gone into the texts not looking for a specific answer, and it was the first time the texts gave me the answers I needed. Never mind that I got only part of what Emerson was telling me. I got inspiration, I got insight, and I began to care deeply about my work.

21     Today I reread the man who set me off on a new road, and I find a different kind of wisdom. Today I reread "The American Scholar," and I don't underline the sentence "Books are for the scholar's idle time." I continue to the next paragraph, underlining the sentence "One must be an inventor to read well." The second sentence doesn't contradict the one I read twenty years ago, but it means more today. I bring more to it, and I know that I can walk into text after text, source after source, and they will give me insight, but not answers. I have learned too that my sources can surprise me. Like my mother, I find myself sometimes surrounded by a field of four-leaf clovers, there for the picking, waiting to see what I can make of them. But I must be an inventor if I am to read those sources well, if I am to imagine the connections.

22     As I stand in my kitchen, the voices that come to me come by way of a lifetime of reading, they come on the waves of life, and they seem to be helping me translate the untranslatable. They come, not at my bidding, but when I least expect them, when I am receptive enough to listen to their voices. They come when I am open.

23     If I could teach my students one lesson about writing it would be to see themselves as sources, as places from which ideas originate, to see themselves as Emerson's transparent eyeball, all that they have read and experienced—the dictionaries of their lives—circulating through them. I want them to learn how sources thicken, complicate, enlarge writing, but I want them to know too how it is always the writer's voice, vision, and argument that create the new source. I want my students to see that nothing reveals itself straight out, especially the sources all around them. But I know enough by now that this Emersonian ideal can't be passed on in one lesson or even a semester of lessons.

24     Many of the students who come to my classes have been trained to collect facts; they act as if their primary job is to accumulate enough authorities so that there is no doubt about the "truth" of their thesis. They most often disappear behind the weight and permanence of their borrowed words, moving their pens, mouthing the words of others, allowing sources to speak through them unquestioned, unexamined.

25     At the outset, many of my students think that personal writing is writing about the death of their grandmother. Academic writing is reporting what

Elizabeth Kübler-Ross has written about death and dying. Being personal, I want to show my students, does not mean being autobiographical. Being academic does not mean being remote, distant, imponderable. Being personal means bringing their judgments and interpretation to bear on what they read and write, learning that they never leave themselves behind even when they write academic essays.

Last year, David Gray came into my essay class disappointed about every-  26
thing. He didn't like the time of the class, didn't like the reading list, didn't seem to like me. Nothing pleased him. "If this is a class on the essay," he asked the first day, "why aren't we reading real essayists like Addison, Steele, and Lamb?" On the second day, after being asked to read Annie Dillard's "Living Like Weasels," David complained that a weasel wasn't a fit subject for an essay. "Writers need big subjects. Look at Melville. He needed a whale for *Moby-Dick*. A weasel—that's nothing but a rodent." And so it continued for a few weeks.

I kept my equanimity in class, but at home I'd tell my family about this  27
kid who kept testing me, seizing me like Dillard's weasel, and not letting go. I secretly wanted him out of my class. But then again, I sensed in him a kindred spirit, someone else who needed to question authority.

I wanted my students to write exploratory essays about education, so I  28
asked them to think of a time when they had learned something, and then a time when they had tried to learn something but couldn't. I wanted them to see what ideas and connections they could find between these two very differ-ent experiences and the other essays they were reading for the class. I wanted the various sources to work as catalysts. I wanted my students to find a way to talk back to those other writers. The assigned texts were an odd assortment with few apparent connections. I hoped my students would find the common ground, but also the moments of tension, the contradictions, and the ambigui-ties in those sources.

David used the assigned texts as a catalyst for his thinking, but as was his  29
way, he went beyond the texts I offered and chose his own. He begins his essay, "Dulcis Est Sapientia," with an account of his high school Latin class, suggesting that he once knew declensions, that he had a knack for conjuga-tions, but has forgotten them. He tells us that if his teacher were to appear suddenly today and demand the perfect subjunctive of *venire*, he would stut-ter hopelessly.

About that Latin class, David asks, "What is going on here? Did I once  30
know Latin and forget it through disuse? Perhaps I never learned Latin at all. What I learned was a bunch of words which, with the aid of various ending sounds, indicated that Gaius was either a good man delivering messages to the lieutenant or a general who struck camp at the seventh hour. I may have known it once, but I never learned it." The class never gave David the gift of language. There was something awry in the method.

What is learning? That's what David explores in his essay as he moves  31
from his Latin lesson to thinking about surrealist paintings, to thinking about

barriers we create, to Plato, to an airplane ride in which he observed a mother teaching her child concepts of color and number, all the time taking his readers along with him on his journey, questioning sources, reflecting, expanding, and enriching his growing sense that learning should stress ideas rather than merely accumulating facts and information.

David draws his essay to a close with an analysis of a joke: A man goes to a 32 cocktail party and gets soused. He approaches his host and asks, "Pardon me, but do lemons whistle?"

The host looks at him oddly and answers, "No, lemons don't whistle." 33

"Oh dear," says the guest, "then I'm afraid I just squeezed your canary into 34 my gin and tonic."

David reflects about the significance of this joke: "One need not be an orni- 35 thologist to get the joke, but one must know that canaries are yellow and that they whistle. . . . What constitutes the joke is a connection made between two things . . . which have absolutely nothing in common except for their yellow-ness. It would never occur to us to make a comparison between the two, let alone to confuse one with the other. But this is the value of the joke, to force into our consciousness the ideas which we held but never actively considered. . . . This knocking down of barriers between ideas is parallel to the process that occurs in all learning. The barriers that we set . . . suddenly crumble; the boundaries . . . are extended to include other modes of thought." Learning, like joking, David argues, gives us pleasure by satisfying our innate capacity to recognize coherence, to discern patterns and connections.

David's essay, like any essay, does not intend to offer the last word on its 36 subject. The civilizing influence of an essay is that it keeps the conversation go-ing, chronicling an intellectual journey, reflecting conversations with sources. I am confident that when David writes for his philosophy course he won't tell a joke anywhere in his essay. But if the joke—if any of his sources—serves him as a catalyst for his thinking, if he makes connections among the sources that circulate within him, between Plato and surrealism, between Latin lessons and mother-child lessons—the dictionaries of *his* life—then he has learned some-thing valuable about writing.

I say to myself that I don't believe in luck. And yet. Not too long ago Rachel 37 came home speaking with some anxiety about an achievement test that she had to take at school. Wanting to comfort her, I urged her to take my rabbit's foot to school the next day. Always alert to life's ironies, Rachel said, "Sure, Mom, a rabbit's foot will really help me find the answers. And even if it did, how would I know the answer the next time when I didn't have that furry little claw?" The next day, proud of her ease in taking the test, she remained perplexed by the one question that seized her and wouldn't let go. She tried it on me: "Here's the ques-tion," she said. "Can you figure out which of these sentences cannot be true?"

(a) We warmed our hands by the fire.
(b) The rain poured in and around the windows.
(c) The wind beckoned us to open the door.

Only in the mind of someone who writes achievement tests, and wants to close the door on the imagination, could the one false sentence be "The wind beckoned us to open the door." Probably to this kind of mind, Emerson's sentence "Life is our dictionary" is also not a true sentence.

But life *is* our dictionary, and that's how we know that the wind can beckon  38 us to open the door. Like Emerson, we let the wind blow our pages hither and yon, forcing us to start in the middle, moving from page 8 to page 2, forward to page 7, moving back and forth in time, losing our certainty.

Like Emerson, I love basic units, the words themselves, words like carda-  39 mom, coriander, words that play around in my head, swirl around in my mouth. The challenge, of course, is not to be a ventriloquist—not to be a mouther of words—but to be open to other voices, untranslatable as they might be. Being open to the unexpected, we can embrace complexities: canaries and lemons, amulets and autograph books, fathers who want their daughters to be their mothers, and daughters who write notes in Urdu—all those odd, unusual conjunctions can come together and speak through us.

The other day, I called my mother and told her about this essay, told her that  40 I had been thinking about the gold bracelet she took with her as one of her few possessions from Germany—a thin gold chain with three amulets: a mushroom, a lady bug, and, of course, a four-leaf clover. Two other charms fell off years ago—she lost one, I the other. I used to worry over the missing links, thinking only of the loss, of what we could never retrieve. When I look at the bracelet now, I think about the Prussian matriarch, my grandmother, and my whole primordial family drama. I think too of Emerson and the pages that blew in the wind and the gaps that seemed not to matter. The bracelet is but one of many sources that intrigues me. Considering them in whatever order they appear, with whatever gaps, I want to see where they will lead me, what they tell me.

With writing and with teaching, as well as with love, we don't know how  41 the sentence will begin and, rarely ever, how it will end. Having the courage to live with uncertainty, ambiguity, even doubt, we can walk into all of those fields of writing, knowing that we will find volumes upon volumes bidding *us* enter. We need only be inventors, we need only give freely and abundantly to the texts, imagining even as we write that we too will be a source from which other readers can draw sustenance.

......................................................................................................

## Questions for Discussion and Journaling

1. How would you state the "problem" that this article addresses? In other words, why is Sommers writing it? What issue is she taking up here, and why?

2. When Sommers says that texts "will give me insight, but not answers" (para. 21), what distinction is she drawing between the two things? In your own experience, have you been encouraged to look at texts as sources of insight or sources of answers? Why do you think this is?

3. Consider Sommers's distinctions among *personal*, *academic*, and *autobiographical*: "Being personal, I want to show my students, does not mean being autobiographical. Being academic does not mean being remote, distant, imponderable . . ." (para. 25). What's your understanding of the distinctions she's making between these terms? Do you feel like you know how to be "personally academic" or "academically personal" or how to be personal without being autobiographical? How academic does Sommers's piece itself feel to you? Why?

4. If you haven't already done so, read the following piece by Sommers as well (p. 578). How does reading her words encourage you to imagine her? What would you expect Sommers to be like in person? How do the two pieces invite you to imagine her differently? How does her language, tone, style, organization, etc., suggest things about her as an author and person?

5. In paragraph 23, Sommers starts a new section with the line, "If I could teach my students one lesson about writing it would be to see themselves as sources, as places from which ideas originate, to see themselves as Emerson's transparent eyeball, all that they have read and experienced—the dictionaries of their lives—circulating through them." Do you see yourself like this, as a source of ideas with all that you "have read and experienced . . . circulating" through you? If you read Chapter 1 of this book, including Roozen's article, did that help you see yourself like this? If you don't see yourself like this, how do you see yourself?

6. Sommers describes reading a text by Emerson at two widely different times in her life and finding different lines in the text to be meaningful to her at each time. How have you seen the passage of time affecting what *you* find most meaningful in the things you read?

7. Early in the essay, we get Sommers's account of "a lesson about borrowing someone else's words and losing my own" (para. 10). Has this ever happened to you? If so, explain how. If not, you might consider Winsor's discussion (p. 642) about the use of models. While we need models in order to know what to write, is it possible that using models might also make you lose your own words, at least for a time?

8. Reread the first paragraph of the piece again, especially this part: "Writing is a radical loss of certainty . . . Stories beget stories. Writing emerges from writing." Given what you learned in the rest of Sommers's essay, what now seems meaningful, important, or interesting about these lines? What do they mean to you?

9. How would you connect Sommers's statement that "I must be an inventor if I am to read those sources well" (para. 21) to Margaret Kantz's and Haas and Flower's arguments about *constructing meaning* in reading in Chapter 3 (if you've read those)?

## Applying and Exploring Ideas

1. Choose another reading that you've encountered in this book that reminds you most of Sommers's piece. What connections (sometimes we say *resonances*) do you find between the pieces? Now get in a small group and see how other students answered this question and why. What connections are you all seeing across the readings in this book so far?

2. As a writer, would you consider yourself "open to the unexpected" (para. 39)? If so, how? If not, why not? Why does Sommers seem to value this possibility of openness and discovery in writing?

3. Where does *your* writing usually come from? In other words, how do you tend to come up with ideas? Look at the last two or three memorable writing projects you've done and write two to three pages explaining where your ideas come from. Then get into a small group with other students and compare your findings. What is similar across your various experiences, and what is different?

4. If you read Donald Murray's "All Writing Is Autobiography" in Chapter 1, compare his argument about the role of *autobiography* in writing to Sommers's argument about the role of *the personal* in writing. Do these pieces together help you further distinguish between "autobiographical" and "personal"? Or do they confuse the issue? Try to freewrite for a page or so and describe the differences between these two.

5. Sommers gives an example of how puzzled her daughter was about a question on a standardized achievement test, and argues that "only in the mind of someone who writes achievement tests, and wants to close the door on imagination, could the one false sentence be 'The wind beckoned us to open the door'" (para. 37). How does this experience compare with your own experiences on standardized writing tests you took throughout school? In what ways did those tests encourage or discourage your imagination? Were there any ways in which those tests were helpful to your thinking and writing?

6. Review the pieces you've read so far in this book. How many of them seem to be making some use of "the personal," as Sommers describes it in their work? Write two to three pages in which you describe some of the pieces in this book that use "the personal" and try to identify patterns in when, or to what purposes, the personal perspective appears in those pieces.

## Meta Moment

What would change about your invention process for writing if you took Sommers's argument seriously that writers should value their own experiential and reading knowledge by "mak[ing] connections among the sources that circulate within [us]" (para. 36)?

# Revision Strategies of Student Writers and Experienced Adult Writers

## NANCY SOMMERS

■ Sommers, Nancy. "Revision Strategies of Student Writers and Experienced Adult Writers." *College Composition and Communication* 31.4 (1980): 378–88. Print.

## Framing the Reading

We've already introduced you to Nancy Sommers in the preceding reading (so if you didn't read that piece, take a moment and read the first paragraph of its "Framing the Reading" section to get a sense of who Sommers is). Now we move from Sommers's investigation of how writers work on the **invention** phase of their writing to her questioning about how writers handle revision, or coming up with what to say in their writing. This article came when Sommers worked at the University of Oklahoma and at New York University in the late 1970s and early 1980s, long before her current work at Harvard.

If you've read the first Sommers piece, one of the first things you might notice about this piece, in contrast, is a much different, possibly more "scientific" feel to the writing (especially in this piece's "Methods" section). It's worth thinking about how the same writer can handle two very different styles of writing and have both appear in scholarly journals. That makes Sommers's articles an excellent example of the range of work that can count as scholarly to begin with.

This study is one of the most widely anthologized articles in the field (meaning that it is very frequently reprinted in a variety of collections about the study of writing and writing process—including the book you are reading now), and it won a major award. Sommers's basic research question is whether there are differences in how student writers talk about and implement revision in their writing compared with how experienced professional writers do so. The need for this research, she argued in 1980, was that while other aspects of the writing process were being studied quite carefully, revision wasn't being studied in the same detail; she attributed this lack of research to definitions of the writing process that were dominant at the time—definitions that imagined revision as almost an afterthought to writing. So Sommers studied revision and reached the conclusions you'll read here, finding that revision is central to writing, and that professional and experienced writers understand revision differently than most student writers.

Something you want to keep in mind while reading this piece (which you will already have encountered if you've read other chapters in this book): Context is important. Remember, for example, that the composing and revising Sommers observed *was not* happening on word-processors, because those largely didn't exist in 1980. Whatever you think of revision today, however you do it, unless you're writing with pencil/pen and paper, you're not experiencing revision the same way that the people Sommers interviewed in 1980 did. (And you're probably aware how much drafting on computer is different than drafting on paper.) Be sure that you're attending to these kinds of contextual differences between a nearly 35-year-old study and how you write today, and keep an eye out for others. Still, part of the reason Sommers's article is still so widely read is because it suggested something that all of us involved in the study of writing should look out for as we think about writing process. See if you can get a feel for the importance of this subject as you're reading.

## Getting Ready to Read

*Before you read,* do at least one of the following activities:

- Read the "Framing the Reading" for Sommers's preceding article (p. 565) if you haven't already.
- Make a list of words you use to describe the process of changing what you've written to improve it. What do you call this kind of changing? Do you use different terms for the changing that you do at different times (for example, changes you make to a sentence while you're finishing writing it, changes you make after you finish an entire draft of what you're writing, or changes you make as you're getting ready to turn a draft in for grading or give your final version to readers)?
- Think about where revision fits in your writing process: At what points do you do it? How much, usually?

*As you read,* consider the following question:

- At what moments in the piece does Sommers's discussion of principles lead to clear, straightforward statements of differences between the student and experienced writers? Make a list of these statements.

......................................................................................................................................

Although various aspects of the writing process have been studied exten-   1
sively of late, research on revision has been notably absent. The reason for this, I suspect, is that current models of the writing process have directed attention away from revision. With few exceptions, these models are linear; they separate the writing process into discrete stages. Two representative models are Gordon Rohman's suggestion that the composing process moves from prewriting to writing to rewriting and James Britton's model of the writing process as a series of stages described in metaphors of linear growth, conception—incubation—production.[1] What is striking about these theories of writing is that they model

themselves on speech: Rohman defines the writer in a way that cannot distinguish him from a speaker ("A writer is a man who . . . puts [his] experience into words in his own mind"—p. 15); and Britton bases his theory of writing on what he calls (following Jakobson) the "expressiveness" of speech.[2] Moreover, Britton's study itself follows the "linear model" of the relation of thought and language in speech proposed by Vygotsky, a relationship embodied in the linear movement "from the motive which engenders a thought to the shaping of the thought, *first* in inner speech, *then* in meanings of words, and *finally* in words" (quoted in Britton, p. 40). What this movement fails to take into account in its linear structure—"first . . . then . . . finally"—is the recursive shaping of thought by language; what it fails to take into account is *revision*. In these linear conceptions of the writing process revision is understood as a separate stage at the end of the process—a stage that comes after the completion of a first or second draft and one that is temporally distinct from the prewriting and writing stages of the process.[3]

The linear model bases itself on speech in two specific ways. First of all, it 2 is based on traditional rhetorical models, models that were created to serve the spoken art of oratory. In whatever ways the parts of classical rhetoric are described, they offer "stages" of composition that are repeated in contemporary models of the writing process. Edward Corbett, for instance, describes the "five parts of a discourse"—*invertio, dispositio, elocutio, memoria, pronuntiatio*—and, disregarding the last two parts since "after rhetoric came to be concerned mainly with written discourse, there was no further need to deal with them,"[4] he produces a model very close to Britton's conception [*inventio*], incubation [*dispositio*], production [*elocutio*]. Other rhetorics also follow this procedure, and they do so not simply because of historical accident. Rather, the process represented in the linear model is based on the irreversibility of speech. Speech, Roland Barthes says, "is irreversible":

> "A word cannot be retracted, except precisely by saying that one retracts it. To cross out here is to add: if I want to erase what I have just said, I cannot do it without showing the eraser itself (I must say: 'or rather . . .' 'I expressed myself badly . . .'); paradoxically, it is ephemeral speech which is indelible, not monumental writing. All that one can do in the case of a spoken utterance is to tack on another utterance."[5]

What is impossible in speech is *revision:* like the example Barthes gives, revision in speech is an afterthought. In the same way, each stage of the linear model must be exclusive (distinct from the other stages) or else it becomes trivial and counterproductive to refer to these junctures as "stages."

By staging revision after enunciation, the linear models reduce revision in 3 writing, as in speech, to no more than an afterthought. In this way such models make the study of revision impossible. Revision, in Rohman's model, is simply the repetition of writing; or to pursue Britton's organic metaphor, revision is simply the further growth of what is already there, the "preconceived" product. The absence of research on revision, then, is a function of a theory of writing which makes revision both superfluous and redundant, a theory which does not distinguish between writing and speech.

What the linear models do produce is a parody of writing. Isolating revi-  4 sion and then disregarding it plays havoc with the experiences composition teachers have of the actual writing and rewriting of experienced writers. Why should the linear model be preferred? Why should revision be forgotten, superfluous? Why do teachers offer the linear model and students accept it? One reason, Barthes suggests, is that "there is a fundamental tie between teaching and speech," while "writing begins at the point where speech becomes *impossible*."[6] The spoken word cannot be revised. The possibility of revision distinguishes the written text from speech. In fact, according to Barthes, this is the essential difference between writing and speaking. When we must revise, when the very idea is subject to recursive shaping by language, then speech becomes inadequate. This is a matter to which I will return, but first we should examine, theoretically, a detailed exploration of what student writers as distinguished from experienced adult writers *do* when they write and rewrite their work. Dissatisfied with both the linear model of writing and the lack of attention to the process of revision, I conducted a series of studies over the past three years which examined the revision processes of student writers and experienced writers to see what role revision played in their writing processes. In the course of my work the revision process was redefined as *a sequence of changes in a composition—changes which are initiated by cues and occur continually throughout the writing of a work.*

## Methodology

I used a case study approach. The student writers were twenty freshmen at  5 Boston University and the University *of* Oklahoma with SAT verbal scores ranging from 450–600 in their first semester of composition. The twenty experienced adult writers from Boston and Oklahoma City included journalists, editors, and academics. To refer to the two groups, I use the terms *student writers* and *experienced writers* because the principal difference between these two groups is the amount of experience they have had in writing.

Each writer wrote three essays, expressive, explanatory, and persuasive, and  6 rewrote each essay twice, producing nine written products in draft and final form. Each writer was interviewed three times after the final revision of each essay. And each writer suggested revisions for a composition written by an anonymous author. Thus extensive written and spoken documents were obtained from each writer.

The essays were analyzed by counting and categorizing the changes made.  7 Four revision operations were identified: deletion, substitution, addition, and reordering. And four levels of changes were identified: word, phrase, sentence, theme (the extended statement of one idea). A coding system was developed for identifying the frequency of revision by level and operation. In addition, transcripts of the interviews in which the writers interpreted their revisions were used to develop what was called a *scale of concerns* for each writer. This scale enabled me to codify what were the writer's primary concerns, secondary concerns, tertiary concerns, and whether the writers used the same scale of concerns when revising the second or third drafts as they used in revising the first draft.

## Revision Strategies of Student Writers

Most of the students I studied did not use the terms *revision* or *rewriting*. In   8
fact, they did not seem comfortable using the word *revision* and explained that revision was not a word they used, but the word their teachers used. Instead, most of the students had developed various functional terms to describe the type of changes they made. The following are samples of these definitions:

> *Scratch Out and Do Over Again:* "I say scratch out and do over, and that means what it says. Scratching out and cutting out. I read what I have written and I cross out a word and put another word in; a more decent word or a better word. Then if there is somewhere to use a sentence that I have crossed out, I will put it there."
>
> *Reviewing:* "Reviewing means just using better words and eliminating words that are not needed, I go over and change words around."
>
> *Reviewing:* "I just review every word and make sure that everything is worded right. I see if I am rambling; I see if I can put a better word in or leave one out. Usually when I read what I have written, I say to myself, 'that word is so bland or so trite,' and then I go and get my thesaurus."
>
> *Redoing:* "Redoing means cleaning up the paper and crossing out. It is looking at something and saying, no that has to go, or no, that is not right."
>
> *Marking Out:* "I don't use the word rewriting because I only write one draft and the changes that I make are made on top of the draft. The changes that I make are usually just marking out words and putting different ones in."
>
> *Slashing and Throwing Out:* "I throw things out and say they are not good. I like to write like Fitzgerald did by inspiration, and if I feel inspired then I don't need to slash and throw much out."

The predominant concern in these definitions is vocabulary. The students un-   9
derstand the revision process as a rewording activity. They do so because they perceive words as the unit of written discourse. That is, they concentrate on particular words apart from their role in the text. Thus one student quoted above thinks in terms of dictionaries, and, following the eighteenth century theory of words parodied in *Gulliver's Travels*, he imagines a load of things carried about to be exchanged. Lexical changes are the major revision activities of the students because economy is their goal. They are governed, like the linear model itself, by the Law of Occam's razor that prohibits logically needless repetition: redundancy and superfluity. Nothing governs speech more than such superfluities; speech constantly repeats itself precisely because spoken

words, as Barthes writes, are expendable in the cause of communication. The aim of revision according to the students' own description is therefore to clean up speech; the redundancy of speech is unnecessary in writing, their logic suggests, because writing, unlike speech, can be reread. Thus one student said, "Redoing means cleaning up the paper and crossing out." The remarkable contradiction of cleaning by marking might, indeed, stand for student revision as I have encountered it.

The students place a symbolic importance on their selection and rejection 10 of words as the determiners of success or failure for their compositions. When revising, they primarily ask themselves: can I find a better word or phrase? A more impressive, not so clichéd, or less hum-drum word? Am I repeating the same word or phrase too often? They approach the revision process with what could be labeled as a "thesaurus philosophy of writing"; the students consider the thesaurus a harvest of lexical substitutions and believe that most problems in their essays can be solved by rewording. What is revealed in the students' use of the thesaurus is a governing attitude toward their writing: that the meaning to be communicated is already there, already finished, already produced, ready to be communicated, and all that is necessary is a better word "rightly worded." One student defined revision as "redoing"; "redoing" meant "just using better words and eliminating words that are not needed." For the students, writing is translating: the thought to the page, the language of speech to the more formal language of prose, the word to its synonym. Whatever is translated, an original text already exists for students, one which need not be discovered or acted upon, but simply communicated.[7]

The students list repetition as one of the elements they most worry about. 11 This cue signals to them that they need to eliminate the repetition either by substituting or deleting words or phrases. Repetition occurs, in large part, because student writing imitates—transcribes—speech: attention to repetitious words is a manner of cleaning speech. Without a sense of the developmental possibilities of revision (and writing in general) students seek, on the authority of many textbooks, simply to clean up their language and prepare to type. What is curious, however, is that students are aware of lexical repetition, but not conceptual repetition. They only notice the repetition if they can "hear" it; they do not diagnose lexical repetition as symptomatic of problems on a deeper level. By rewording their sentences to avoid the lexical repetition, the students solve the immediate problem, but blind themselves to problems on a textual level; although they are using different words, they are sometimes merely restating the same idea with different words. Such blindness, as I discovered with student writers, is the inability to "see" revision as a process: the inability to "re-view" their work again, as it were, with different eyes, and to start over.

The revision strategies described above are consistent with the students' un- 12 derstanding of the revision process as requiring lexical changes but not semantic changes. For the students, the extent to which they revise is a function of their level of inspiration. In fact, they use the word *inspiration* to describe the ease or difficulty with which their essay is written, and the extent to which the essay needs to be revised. If students feel inspired, if the writing comes easily, and if they don't get stuck on individual words or phrases, then they say that they cannot see any reason to revise. Because students do not see revision as an activity in which they modify and develop perspectives and ideas, they feel that if they know what they want to say, then there is little reason for making revisions.

The only modification of ideas in the students' essays occurred when they 13 tried out two or three introductory paragraphs. This results, in part, because the students have been taught in another version of the linear model of composing to use a thesis statement as a controlling device in their introductory paragraphs. Since they write their introductions and their thesis statements even before they have really discovered what they want to say, their early close attention to the thesis statement, and more generally the linear model, function to restrict and circumscribe not only the development of their ideas, but also their ability to change the direction of these ideas.

Too often as composition teachers we conclude that students do not will- 14 ingly revise. The evidence from my research suggests that it is not that students are unwilling to revise, but rather that they do what they have been taught to do in a consistently narrow and predictable way. On every occasion when I asked students why they hadn't made any more changes, they essentially replied, "I knew something larger was wrong, but I didn't think it would help to move words around." The students have strategies for handling words and phrases and their strategies helped them on a word or sentence level. What they lack, however, is a set of strategies to help them identify the "something larger" that they sensed was wrong and work from there. The students do not have strategies for handling the whole essay. They lack procedures or heuristics to help them reorder lines of reasoning or ask questions about their purposes and readers. The students view their compositions in a linear way as a series of parts. Even such potentially useful concepts as "unity" or "form" are reduced to the rule that a composition, if it is to have form, must have an introduction, a body, and a conclusion, or the sum total of the necessary parts.

The students decide to stop revising when they decide that they have not 15 violated any of the rules for revising. These rules, such as "Never begin a sentence with a conjunction" or "Never end a sentence with a preposition," are lexically cued and rigidly applied. In general, students will subordinate the demands of the specific problems of their text to the demands of the rules. Changes are made in compliance with abstract rules about the product, rules that quite often do not apply to the specific problems in the text. These revision strategies are teacher-based, directed towards a teacher-reader who expects compliance with rules—with pre-existing "conceptions"—and who will only examine parts of the composition (writing comments about those parts in the margins of their essays) and will cite any violations of rules in those parts. At best the students see their writing altogether passively through the eyes of former teachers or their surrogates, the textbooks, and are bound to the rules which they have been taught.

## Revision Strategies of Experienced Writers

One aim of my research has been to contrast how student writers define revi-   16
sion with how a group of experienced writers define their revision processes.
Here is a sampling of the definitions from the experienced writers:

> *Rewriting:* "It is a matter of looking at the kernel of what I have written, the con-
> tent, and then thinking about it, responding to it, making decisions, and actually
> restructuring it."

> *Rewriting:* "I rewrite as I write. It is hard to tell what is a first draft because it is
> not determined by time. In one draft, I might cross out three pages, write two,
> cross out a fourth, rewrite it, and call it a draft. I am constantly writing and re-
> writing. I can only conceptualize so much in my first draft—only so much infor-
> mation can be held in my head at one time; my rewriting efforts are a reflection of
> how much information I can encompass at one time. There are levels and agenda
> which I have to attend to in each draft."

> *Rewriting:* "Rewriting means on one level, finding the argument, and on another
> level, language changes to make the argument more effective. Most of the time I
> feel as if I can go on rewriting forever. There is always one part of a piece that I
> could keep working on. It is always difficult to know at what point to abandon
> a piece of writing. I like this idea that a piece of writing is never finished, just
> abandoned."

> *Rewriting:* "My first draft is usually very scattered. In rewriting, I find the line
> of argument. After the argument is resolved, I am much more interested in word
> choice and phrasing."

> *Revising:* "My cardinal rule in revising is never to fall in love with what I have
> written in a first or second draft. An idea, sentence, or even a phrase that looks
> catchy, I don't trust. Part of this idea is to wait a while. I am much more in love
> with something after I have written it than I am a day or two later. It is much
> easier to change anything with time."

> *Revising:* "It means taking apart what I have written and putting it back together
> again. I ask major theoretical questions of my ideas, respond to those questions,
> and think of proportion and structure, and try to find a controlling metaphor. I
> find out which ideas can be developed and which should be dropped. I am con-
> stantly chiseling and changing as I revise."

The experienced writers describe their primary objective when revising as   17
finding the form or shape of their argument. Although the metaphors vary, the
experienced writers often use structural expressions such as "finding a framework," "a pattern," or "a design" for their argument. When questioned about
this emphasis, the experienced writers responded that since their first drafts are
usually scattered attempts to define their territory, their objective in the second
draft is to begin observing general patterns of development and deciding what
should be included and what excluded. One writer explained, "I have learned
from experience that I need to keep writing a first draft until I figure out what I
want to say. Then in a second draft, I begin to see the structure of an argument
and how all the various sub-arguments which are buried beneath the surface

of all those sentences are related." What is described here is a process in which the writer is both agent and vehicle. "Writing," says Barthes, unlike speech, "develops like a seed, not a line,"[8] and like a seed it confuses beginning and end, conception and production. Thus, the experienced writers say their drafts are "not determined by time," that rewriting is a "constant process," that they feel as if (they) "can go on forever." Revising confuses the beginning and end, the agent and vehicle; it confuses, *in order to find*, the line of argument.

After a concern for form, the experienced writers have a second objective: 18 a concern for their readership. In this way, "production" precedes "conception." The experienced writers imagine a reader (reading their product) whose existence and whose expectations influence their revision process. They have abstracted the standards of a reader and this reader seems to be partially a reflection of themselves and functions as a critical and productive collaborator—

> . . . . experienced writers say their drafts are "not determined by time," that rewriting is a "constant process," that they feel as if (they) "can go on forever."

a collaborator who has yet to love their work. The anticipation of a reader's judgment causes a feeling of dissonance when the writer recognizes incongruities between intention and execution, and requires these writers to make revisions on all levels. Such a reader gives them just what the students lacked: new eyes to "re-view" their work. The experienced writers believe that they have learned the causes and conditions, the product, which will influence their reader, and their revision strategies are geared towards creating these causes and conditions. They demonstrate a complex understanding of which examples, sentences, or phrases should be included or excluded. For example, one experienced writer decided to delete public examples and add private examples when writing about the energy crisis because "private examples would be less controversial and thus more persuasive." Another writer revised his transitional sentences because "some kinds of transitions are more easily recognized as transitions than others." These examples represent the type of strategic attempts these experienced writers use to manipulate the conventions of discourse in order to communicate to their reader.

But these revision strategies are a process of more than communication; they 19 are part of the process of *discovering meaning* altogether. Here we can see the importance of dissonance; at the heart of revision is the process by which writers recognize and resolve the dissonance they sense in their writing. Ferdinand de Saussure has argued that meaning is differential or "diacritical," based on differences between terms rather than "essential" or inherent qualities of terms. "Phonemes," he said, "are characterized not, as one might think, by their own positive quality but simply by the fact that they are distinct."[9] In fact, Saussure bases his entire *Course in General Linguistics* on these differences, and such differences are dissonant; like musical dissonances which gain their significance from their relationship to the "key" of the composition which itself is determined by the whole language, specific language (parole) gains its meaning from the system of language (langue) of which it is a manifestation and part. The musical composition—a "composition" of parts—creates its "key" as in an overall structure which determines the value (meaning) of its parts. The analogy with music is readily seen in the compositions of experienced writers: both sorts of composition are based precisely on those structures experienced writers seek in their writing. It is this complicated relationship between the parts and the whole in the work of experienced writers which destroys the linear model; writing cannot develop "like a line" because each addition or deletion is a reordering of the whole. Explicating Saussure, Jonathan Culler asserts that "meaning depends on difference of meaning."[10] But student writers constantly struggle to bring their essays into congruence with a predefined meaning. The experienced writers do the opposite: they seek to discover (to create) meaning in the engagement with their writing, in revision. They seek to emphasize and exploit the lack of clarity, the differences of meaning, the dissonance, that writing as opposed to speech allows in the possibility of revision. Writing has spatial and temporal features not apparent in speech—words are recorded in space and fixed in time—which is why writing is susceptible to reordering and later addition. Such features make possible the dissonance that both provokes revision and promises, from itself, new meaning.

For the experienced writers the heaviest concentration of changes is on the 20 sentence level, and the changes are predominantly by addition and deletion. But, unlike the students, experienced writers make changes on all levels and use all revision operations. Moreover, the operations the students fail to use—reordering and addition—seem to require a theory of the revision process as a totality—a theory which, in fact, encompasses the *whole* of the composition. Unlike the students, the experienced writers possess a non-linear theory in which a sense of the whole writing both precedes and grows out of an examination of the parts. As we saw, one writer said he needed "a first draft to figure out what to say," and "a second draft to see the structure of an argument buried beneath the surface." Such a "theory" is both theoretical and strategical; once again, strategy and theory are conflated in ways that are literally impossible for the linear model. Writing appears to be more like a seed than a line.

Two elements of the experienced writers' theory of the revision process are 21 the adoption of a holistic perspective and the perception that revision is a recursive process. The writers ask: what does my essay as a *whole* need for form, balance, rhythm, or communication. Details are added, dropped, substituted, or reordered according to their sense of what the essay needs for emphasis and proportion. This sense, however, is constantly in flux as ideas are developed and modified; it is constantly "re-viewed" in relation to the parts. As their ideas change, revision becomes an attempt to make their writing consonant with that changing vision.

The experienced writers see their revision process as a recursive process—a 22 process with significant recurring activities—with different levels of attention and different agenda for each cycle. During the first revision cycle their attention is primarily directed towards narrowing the topic and delimiting their ideas. At this point, they are not as concerned as they are later about vocabulary and style. The experienced writers explained that they get closer to their meaning by not limiting themselves too early to lexical concerns. As one writer commented to explain her revision process, a comment inspired by the summer 1977 New York power failure: "I feel like Con Edison cutting off certain states to keep the generators going. In first and second drafts, I try to cut off as much as I can of my editing generator, and in a third draft, I try to cut off some of my idea generators, so I can make sure that I will actually finish the essay." Although the experienced writers describe their revision process as a series of different levels or cycles, it is inaccurate to assume that they have only one objective for each cycle and that each cycle can be defined by a different objective. The same objectives and sub-processes are present in each cycle, but in different proportions. Even though these experienced writers place the predominant weight upon finding the form of their argument during the first cycle, other concerns exist as well. Conversely, during the later cycles, when the experienced writers' primary attention is focused upon stylistic concerns, they are still attuned, although in a reduced way, to the form of the argument. Since writers are limited in what they can attend to during each cycle (understandings are temporal), revision strategies help balance competing demands on attention. Thus, writers can concentrate on more than one objective at a time by developing strategies to sort out and organize their different concerns in successive cycles of revision.

It is a sense of writing as discovery—a repeated process of beginning over  23 again, starting out new—that the students failed to have. I have used the notion of dissonance because such dissonance, the incongruities between intention and execution, governs both writing and meaning. Students do not see the incongruities. They need to rely on their own internalized sense of good writing and to see their writing with their "own" eyes. Seeing in revision—seeing beyond hearing—is at the root of the word *revision* and the process itself; current dicta on revising blind our students to what is actually involved in revision. In fact, they blind them to what constitutes good writing altogether. Good writing disturbs: it creates dissonance. Students need to seek the dissonance of discovery, utilizing in their writing, as the experienced writers do, the very difference between writing and speech—the possibility of revision.

## Notes

1. D. Gordon Rohman and Albert O. Wlecke, "Pre-writing: The Construction and Application of Models for Concept Formation in Writing," Cooperative Research Project No. 2174, U.S. Office of Education, Department of Health, Education, and Welfare; James Britton, Anthony Burgess, Nancy Martin, Alex McLeod, Harold Rosen, *The Development of Writing Abilities (11–18)* (London: Macmillan Education, 1975).

2. Britton is following Roman Jakobson, "Linguistics and Poetics," in T. A. Sebeok, *Style in Language* (Cambridge, Mass: MIT Press, 1960).

3. For an extended discussion of this issue see Nancy Sommers, "The Need for Theory in Composition Research," *College Composition and Communication*, 30 (February 1979), 46-49.

4. *Classical Rhetoric for the Modern Student* (New York: Oxford University Press, 1965), p. 27.

5. Roland Barthes, "Writers, Intellectuals, Teachers," in *Image-Music-Text*, trans. Stephen Heath (New York: Hill and Wang, 1977), pp. 190-191.

6. "Writers, Intellectuals, Teachers," p. 190.

7. Nancy Sommers and Ronald Schleifer, "Means and Ends: Some Assumptions of Student Writers," *Composition and Teaching*, II (in press).

8. *Writing Degree Zero* in *Writing Degree Zero and Elements of Semiology*, trans. Annette Lavers and Colin Smith (New York: Hill and Wang, 1968), p. 20.

9. *Course in General Linguistics*, trans. Wade Baskin (New York, 1966), p. 119.

10. Jonathan Culler, *Saussure* (Penguin Modern Masters Series; London: Penguin Books, 1976), p. 70.

*Acknowledgment:* The author wishes to express her gratitude to Professor William Smith, University of Pittsburgh, for his vital assistance with the research reported in this article and to Patrick Hays, her husband, for extensive discussions and critical editorial help.

## Questions for Discussion and Journaling

1. Sommers says that the language students use to describe revision is about *vocabulary*, suggesting that they "understand the revision process as a rewording activity" (para. 9). How is that different from the way she argues that revision *should* be understood?

2. Is it important that Sommers elected to identify her two groups of writers as *student* and *experienced* writers rather than as, for example, *novice* and *professional* writers? What alternative terms might *you* choose to identify these groups? Do the terms make a difference? (In order to help you think about this question, you might take a look at Marissa Penzato's piece at the end of this chapter.)

3. In her introduction and in analyzing students' descriptions of revision, Sommers focuses quite a lot on the difference between speech and writing. In your words, what is she saying that difference is between the two, and why is this difference relevant to how we understand revision?

4. In paragraph 19, Sommers writes that for experienced writers, revision is "a process of more than communication; they are a part of the process of *discovering meaning* altogether." What does she seem to mean by "discovering meaning"? How is "discovering meaning" different from "communication"? Does Sommers's emphasis on writing as an act of making meaning relate to anything else you've encountered in this book?

5. What do you think Sommers means when she says that for experienced writers, revision is based on a non-linear theory in which a sense of the whole writing both precedes and grows out of an examination of the parts? What does she mean by "the whole writing"? What does it mean for writing processes to be non-linear (not a straight line of progress from beginning to end)? And why do you think that experienced writers see writing as non-linear but student writers tend to see writing as linear (pre-write → write → edit)?

6. One of the experienced writers that Sommers interviews talks about having an "editing generator" and an "idea generator." What do you think that means? Can you

think about your own writing experiences and identify any kinds of mental "genera-tors" that help you come up with ideas, edit, etc.? If you haven't had the experience of an "idea generator," why do you think that is?

7. Sommers's research, she says, makes her believe that student revision practices don't reflect a *lack* of engagement, "but rather that they do what they have been taught to do in a consistently narrow and predictable way." Where do you think students got the idea that they should see writing as transcribing and revising as changing words? Does this match what you have been taught about writing and revising? If not, what has been different in your experience?

8. In the closing lines of her article, Sommers asserts that "good writing disturbs; it cre-ates dissonance." What does that mean? Do you think that is always true? Can you think of good writing that *doesn't* disturb, create dissonance, or try to resist other ideas? Sommers is really making a claim about what counts as "good" writing. How does her definition here of good writing compare to those of other scholars you've read in this book? How does it compare to your own idea of good writing?

9. Sommers contrasts writing with a "predefined meaning" (para. 19) versus "writing as discovery" (para. 23). How are these two understandings of writing different? Why does she claim that these are opposing? What does writing as discovery seem to allow that writing with a predefined meaning doesn't? Can you think of examples where you've done each? Was one kind of experience better than the other?

## Applying and Exploring Ideas

1. Create a one- to two-paragraph summary of Sommers's report on what student writers say about revision, gathering up her main points about what the students she interviewed thought about revision. Then compare it with your own ideas about revision. How much do these students sound like you? Where your ideas about revi-sion sound different, do they sound more like the professional writers' ideas, or like something else altogether?

2. Sommers begins her article by looking at research by Rohman and Wlecke and Britton that imagines writing as happening in linear *stages*. By the end of her article, she describes research suggesting that writers seem to be concerned with most stages of writing (coming up with ideas, composing text, revising ideas, editing, etc.) all at the same time (see para. 22). Explain each of these views and then argue for one of these views (or a combination of the two) that best explains how you write.

3. Look up the word *recursive* and get a sense of its various definitions. Based on that, and about how you typically think about writing, write an explanation for the class of why writing is a recursive activity. Then stop and think: how is *your* typical writing process *actually* recursive? What does that recursivity look like in your own writing?

4. Suppose you wanted to follow up on Sommers's research about what students believe about, and how they perform, revision. How would you do it? Before you answer this question, you might want to take a look at student Marissa Penzato's essay at the end of this chapter (p. 653), noting that Penzato found that students' revision for non-school activities was quite different than their revision for school activities. Write a

one- to two-page research plan that explains who or what you would study, and how you would gather information in order to compare what students and professional writers think about revision. (Hint: Penzato's finding suggests that you might consider how people revise for different contexts and genres.)

5. Sommers identifies four "levels of change" in revision: word, phrase, sentence, and theme—"the extended statement of one idea" (by which she seems to mean, when a single sentence doesn't express a "complete thought" but when rather a couple or several sentences or even a paragraph are required to express an idea). Find two pieces of writing you've completed recently which you revised before submitting, and examine what you actually changed between the first draft and the last. Do you see any changes that aren't accounted for by Sommers's four levels—any levels "higher" than theme, or different from *sentence structure* (which basically contains all her levels)? Write a report on your analysis that focuses specifically on this question.

> ### Meta Moment
> Can you think of things you can do, and ways you can imagine writing differently, so that you revise more like an experienced writer and less like the student writers in Sommers's study?

# Decisions and Revisions: The Planning Strategies of a Publishing Writer

## CAROL BERKENKOTTER

*and*

# Response of a Laboratory Rat—or, Being Protocoled

## DONALD M. MURRAY

- Berkenkotter, Carol. "Decisions and Revisions: The Planning Strategies of a Publishing Writer." *College Composition and Communication* 34.2 (1983): 156–69. Print.
- Murray, Donald M. "Response of a Laboratory Rat—or, Being Protocoled." *College Composition and Communication* 34.2 (1983): 169–72. Print.

## Framing the Readings

In 1979, Sondra Perl, in a study of "unskilled college writers" that you will find later in this chapter, used a "think-aloud" or "talk-aloud" protocol, a technique that at the time was very popular among psychology researchers. This method solved a very basic problem of research on mental operations—that is, how we know what thoughts people are having that lead them to write certain things—by proposing the following simple solution: Have them talk while they think. Another aspect of Perl's design, a "laboratory" setting where students came to the researcher and wrote in response to specific prompts the researcher provided, was quite common in this time and style of research on writing processes. Most researchers publishing studies on writers' processes, including Carol Berkenkotter, author of one of the pieces you are about to read, used such methods.

But there are real problems with this kind of research, chief among them the artificiality of the setting and the writing tasks. In the following selection, you will read Berkenkotter's account of how she engaged a professional writer, Donald Murray, as a participant for a different kind of research, one that tried to keep the writer in his own context—normal surroundings, real projects—rather than bringing him into a lab. Like

Perl's article, then, Berkenkotter's has two focuses: a test of a particular methodology and a question about a particular aspect of composing—in this case, the revision process of a professional writer.

Berkenkotter and Murray did something else uncharacteristic of research on writing in the era: Murray was given the opportunity to write a reflection on the experience of being a research subject, his thoughts on what Berkenkotter's study found, and observations on the methodology. For this reason, we strongly recommend that you read the pieces back-to-back; the experience of reading Berkenkotter isn't complete without Murray's rejoinder and the interplay between the two pieces.

While you should pay close attention to any researcher's methods and context, the most interesting part of this article for you will likely be what you can learn about how a professional and award-winning writer goes about writing. His processes are odd, and you likely don't go about writing like he does. (Keep in mind that in 1981, when Berkenkotter and Murray undertook the study, cell phones, the Internet, and personal computers were not in widespread use. It was a very different time.) Pay close attention, though, to how Murray invents things to say, how he learns from his writing, how he writes for his audience, and how he revises, and ask yourself what his writing gains from his complex planning, drafting, and revising.

Carol Berkenkotter is currently a professor in the University of Minnesota's Department of Writing Studies. At the time she wrote this piece, about 30 years ago, she was teaching at Michigan Technological University. Over that span of time, her research shifted from the kinds of writing-process questions that shaped this article, to extensive focus on **genre** theory. One of her most significant works is her 1995 book with Thomas Huckin, *Genre Knowledge in Disciplinary Communication: Cognition/Culture/Power.* Her research subject and co-author here, Donald Murray, has two articles of his own in this book. You can read more about him in Chapter 1 with his article "All Writing Is Autobiography."

## Getting Ready to Read

*Before you read*, do at least one of the following activities:

- Take fifteen minutes and write in response to this prompt: "Explain death to an eleven-year-old." Then consider how it felt to write this. Was it easy? Hard? What did you wonder or think about while you were writing? Set this aside and come back to it after you have read this article.
- Consider whether you have any writing rituals. For example, do you have to have a cup of coffee while you write? Do you need to write on paper before typing? Do you have to take a nap or clean the house?

*As you read*, consider the following questions:

- What discoveries do Berkenkotter and Murray make that contradict their expectations?
- What are strengths and weaknesses of this particular way of studying writing processes?
- What have you learned about writing from reading this article that you didn't know before?

# Decisions and Revisions: The Planning Strategies of a Publishing Writer

## CAROL BERKENKOTTER

The clearest memory I have of Donald M. Murray is watching him writing 1
at a long white wooden table in his study, which looks out on the New
Hampshire woods. Beside his desk is a large framed poster of a small boy sitting on a bed staring at a huge dragon leaning over the railing glowering at
him. The poster is captioned, "Donald imagined things." And so he did, as he
addressed the problems writers face each time they confront a new assignment.
During the summer of 1981, as I listened to him daily recording his thoughts
aloud as he worked on two articles,
a short story, and an editorial, I
came to understand in what ways
each writer's processes are unique
and why it is important that we
pay close attention to the setting
in which the writer composes, the
kind of task the writer confronts, and what the writer can tell us of his own
processes. If we are to understand *how* writers revise, we must pay close attention to the context in which revision occurs.

> *If we are to understand how writers
> revise, we must pay close attention to
> the context in which revision occurs.*

Janet Emig, citing Eliot Mishler, has recently described the tendency of writ- 2
ing research toward "context stripping."[1] When researchers remove writers
from their natural settings (the study, the classroom, the office, the dormitory
room, the library) to examine their thinking processes in the laboratory, they
create "a context of a powerful sort, often deeply affecting what is being observed and assessed."[2] Emig's essay points to the need to examine critically the
effects of these practices.

The subject of the present study is not anonymous, as are most subjects, 3
nor will he remain silent. I began the investigation with a critical eye regarding
what he has said about revision, he with an equally critical attitude toward
methods of research on cognitive processes. To some extent our original positions have been confirmed—yet I think each of us, researcher and writer,
has been forced to question our assumptions and examine our dogmas. More
important, this project stirs the dust a bit and suggests a new direction for research on composing processes.

I met Mr. Murray at the Conference on College Composition and Commu- 4
nication meeting in Dallas, 1981. He appeared at the speaker's rostrum after
my session and introduced himself, and we began to talk about the limitations
of taking protocols in an experimental situation. On the spur of the moment

I asked him if he would be willing to be the subject of a naturalistic study. He hesitated, took a deep breath, then said he was very interested in understanding his own composing processes, and would like to learn more. Out of that brief exchange a unique collaborative research venture was conceived.

To date there are no reported studies of writers composing in natural (as opposed to laboratory) settings that combine thinking-aloud protocols with the writers' own introspective accounts. Recently, researchers have been observing young children as they write in the classroom. In particular, we have seen the promising research of Donald Graves, Lucy Calkins, and Susan Sowers, who have worked intimately with children and their teachers in the Atkinson Schools Project.[3] By using video tapes and by actively working in the classroom as teachers and interviewers, these researchers were able to track the revising processes of individual children over a two-year period. Studies such as these suggest that there may be other ways of looking at writers' composing processes than in conventional research settings.

There remains, however, the question: to what extent can a writer's subjective testimony be trusted? I have shared the common distrust of such accounts.[4] There is considerable cognitive activity that writers cannot report because they are unable to compose and monitor their processes simultaneously. Researchers have responded to this problem by taking retrospective accounts from writers immediately after they have composed,[5] or have studied writers' cognitive activity through the use of thinking-aloud protocols.[6] These protocols have been examined to locate the thoughts verbalized by the subjects while composing, rather than for the subjects' analysis of what they said. Typically, subjects were instructed to "say everything that comes to mind no matter how random or crazy it seems. Do not analyze your thoughts, just say them aloud." The effect of these procedures, however, has been to separate the dancer from the dance, the subject from the process. Introspective accounts made *in medias res* have not been possible thus far because no one has developed techniques that would allow a subject to write and comment on his or her processes between composing episodes. For this reason I had begun to entertain the idea of asking a professional writer to engage in a lengthy naturalistic study. When Donald Murray introduced himself, I knew I wanted him to be the subject.

## Methodology

The objectives that I began with are modifications of those Sondra Perl identified in her study of five unskilled writers.[7] I wanted to learn more about the planning and revising strategies of a highly skilled and verbal writer, to discover how these strategies could be most usefully analyzed, and to determine how an understanding of this writer's processes would contribute to what we have already discovered about how skilled writers plan and revise.

The project took place in three stages. From June 15th until August 15th, 1981 (a period of 62 days), Mr. Murray turned on the tape recorder when he entered his study in the morning and left it running during the day wherever he happened to be working: in his car waiting in parking lots, his university office, restaurants, the doctor's office, etc. This kind of thinking-aloud protocol differs from those taken by Linda Flower and John R. Hayes since the subject's composing time is not limited to a single hour; in fact, during the period of time that Mr. Murray was recording his thoughts, I accumulated over one hundred and twenty hours of tape. The writer also submitted photocopies of all text, including notes and drafts made prior to the study. Thus I was able to study a history of each draft.

In the second stage, during a visit to my university, I gave the writer a task 9 which specified audience, subject, and purpose. I asked him to think aloud on tape as he had previously, but this time for only one hour. Between the second and third stages, Mr. Murray and I maintained a dialogue on audiotapes which we mailed back and forth. On these tapes he compared his thoughts on his composing in his own environment over time to those on giving a one-hour protocol in a laboratory setting.

During the third stage of the study, I visited the writer at his home for two 10 days. At this time I observed him thinking aloud as he performed a writing task which involved revising an article for a professional journal. After two sessions of thinking aloud on tape for two and one-half hours, Mr. Murray answered questions concerning the decisions he had made. Over the two-day period we taped an additional four hours of questions and answers regarding the writer's perceptions of his activities.

Another coder and I independently coded the transcripts of the protocols 11 made in the naturalistic and laboratory settings. Using the same procedure I employed in my study of how writers considered their audience (i.e., first clas-sifying and then counting all audience-related activities I could find in each protocol), my coder and I tallied all planning, revising, and editing activities, as well as global and local evaluations of text[8] that we agreed upon. I was particu-larly interested in Murray's editing activities. Having listened to the tapes I was aware that editing (i.e., reading the text aloud and making word- and sentence-level changes) sometimes led to major planning episodes, and I wanted to keep track of that sequence.

The study was not conducted without problems. The greatest of these arose 12 from how the writer's particular work habits affected the gathering of the data and how he responded to making a one-hour protocol. Unlike most writers who hand draft or type, Mr. Murray spends much time making copious notes in a daybook, then dictates his drafts and partial drafts to his wife, who is an accomplished typist and partner in his work. Later, he reads aloud and edits the drafts. If he determines that copy-editing (i.e., making stylistic changes in the text) is insufficient, he returns to the daybook, makes further notes, and prepares for the next dictation. The revision of one of the articles he was work-ing on went through eight drafts before he sent it off. Two days later he sent the editor an insert.

Murray's distinctive work habits meant that all of the cognitive activity oc- 13 curring during the dictation that might ordinarily be captured in a protocol was lost since he processed information at a high speed. During these periods

I could not keep track of the content of his thoughts, and became concerned instead with the problem of why he frequently would find himself unable to continue dictating and end the session. There turned out to be considerable value in following the breakdowns of these dictations. I was able to distinguish between those occasions when Murray's composing was, in Janet Emig's terms, "extensive," and when it was "reflexive," by comparing the relative ease with which he developed an article from well-rehearsed material presented at workshops with the slow evolution of a conceptual piece he had not rehearsed. According to Emig, "The extensive mode . . . focuses upon the writer's conveying a message or communication to another. . . . the style is assured, impersonal, and often reportorial." In contrast, reflexive composing ". . . focuses on the writer's thoughts and feelings. . . . the style is tentative, personal, and exploratory."[10] In the latter case the writer is generating, testing, and evaluating new ideas, rather than reformulating old ones. I could observe the differences between the two modes of composing Emig describes, given Murray's response to the task in which he was engaged. When the writer was thoroughly familiar with his subject, he dictated with great fluency and ease. However, when he was breaking new ground conceptually, his pace slowed and his voice became halting; often the drafts broke down, forcing him to return to his daybook before attempting to dictate again.[11]

A more critical problem arose during the giving of the one-hour protocol.  14
At the time he came to my university, the writer had been working on tasks he had selected, talking into a tape recorder for two months in a familiar setting. Now he found himself in a strange room, with a specific writing task to perform in one short hour. This task was not simple; nor was it familiar. He was asked to "explain the concept of death to the ten- to twelve-year-old readers of *Jack and Jill* magazine." Under these circumstances, Murray clutched, producing two lines of text: "*Dear 11 year old. You're going to die. Sorry. Be seeing you. P. Muglump, Local Funeral Director.*" Both the transcript and later retrospective testimony of the writer indicated that he did not have pets as a child and his memories of death were not of the kind that could be described to an audience of ten- to twelve-year-old children. He also had difficulty forming a picture of his audience, since he suspected the actual audience was grandparents in Florida who send their children subscriptions to *Jack and Jill.* Toward the end of the hour, he was able to imagine a reader when he remembered the daughter of a man he had met the previous evening. The protocol, however, is rich with his efforts to create rhetorical context—he plotted repeated scenarios in which he would be asked to write such an article. Nevertheless, it seems reasonable to conclude that Mr. Murray was constrained by what Lester Faigley and Stephen Witte call "situational variables":[12] the knowledge that he had only one hour in which to complete a draft, his lack of familiarity with the format of *Jack and Jill* (he had never seen the magazine), his doubts that an audience actually existed, and finally, the wash of unhappy memories that the task gave rise to. "So important are these variables," Faigley and Witte contend, "that writing skill might be defined as the ability to respond to them."[13]

One final problem is intrinsic to the case study approach. Although the tapes 15
are rich in data regarding the affective conditions under which the writer composed (he was distracted by university problems, had to contend with numerous interruptions, encountered family difficulties that he had to resolve, not to
mention experiencing his own anxiety about his writing), as Murray reported,
the further away he was in time from what he had done, the less able he was to
reconstruct decisions he had made.

## Results

### Planning and Revising

In this study I was primarily concerned with the writer's planning, revising, and 16
editing activities. I had to develop a separate code category for the evaluation
of text or content, since the writer frequently stopped to evaluate what he had
written. Figure 1 indicates the percentage of coded activities devoted to planning, revising, and editing for three pieces of discourse.[14] These three pieces
were among the projects Murray worked on over the two-month period when
he was making the protocols.

The coded data (taken from the transcripts of the tapes he made during this 17
time) showed that up to 45%, 56%, and 35% of the writer's activities were
concerned with planning, 28%, 21%, and 18% with either global or local
evaluation, 3.0%, 3.0%, and .0% with revising (a finding which surprised me
greatly, and to which I shall return), and 24%, 20%, and 47% with editing.

Murray's planning activities were of two kinds: the first were the stating 18
of "process goals"—mentioning procedures, that is, that he developed in order to write (e.g., "I'm going to make a list of titles and see where that gets
me," or "I'm going to try a different lead.").[15] Frequently, these procedures (or
"thinking plans" as they are also called)[16] led the writer to generate a series of
sub-plans for carrying out the larger plan. The following excerpt is from the
first draft of an article on revision that Murray was writing for *The Journal of
Basic Writing*. He had been reading the manuscript aloud to himself and was
nearly ready to dictate a second draft. Suddenly he stopped, took his daybook
and began making copious notes for a list of examples he could use to make

|  | JOURNAL OF BASIC WRITING | COLLEGE COMPOSITION AND COMMUNICATION | EDITORIAL FOR CONCORD MONITOR |
| --- | --- | --- | --- |
| Planning | 45% | 56% | 35% |
| Evaluating | 28% | 21% | 18% |
| Revising | 3.0% | 3.0% | .0% |
| Editing | 24% | 20% | 47% |

**Figure 1** Percentage of Coded Activities Devoted to Planning, Evaluating, Revising,
and Editing for Three Pieces of Discourse.

the point that the wise editor or teacher should at first ignore sentence-level editing problems to deal with more substantive issues of revision (this excerpt as well as those which follow are taken from the transcript of the tape and the photocopied text of the daybook):

> Let me take another piece of paper here. Questions, ah . . . examples, and ah set up . . . situation . . . *frustration of writer. Cooks a five course dinner and gets response only to the table setting . . . or to the way the napkins are folded* or to the . . . *order of the forks.* All right. I can see from the material I have how that'll go. I'll weave in. Okay. *Distance in focus. Stand back. Read fast. Question writer.* Then *order doubles advocate. Then voice. Close in. Read aloud.* Okay, I got a number of different things I can see here that I'm getting to. I'm putting different order because that may be, try to emphasize this one. May want to put the techniques of editing and teaching first and the techniques of the writer second. So I got a one and a two to indicate that. [Italics identify words written down.]

In this instance we can see how a writing plan (taking a piece of paper and developing examples) leads to a number of sub-plans: "I'll weave in," I'm putting in different order because that may be, try to emphasize this one," "May want to put the techniques of editing and teaching first and the techniques of the writer second," etc.

A second kind of planning activity was the stating of rhetorical goals, i.e., planning how to reach an audience: "I'm making a note here, job not to explore the complexities of revision, but simply to show the reader how to do revision." Like many skilled writers, Murray had readers for his longer pieces. These readers were colleagues and friends whose judgment he trusted. Much of his planning activity as he revised his article for *College Composition and Communication* grew out of reading their responses to his initial draft and incorporating his summary of their comments directly onto the text. He then put away the text, and for the next several days made lists of titles, practiced leads, and made many outlines and diagrams in his daybook before dictating a draft. Through subsequent drafts he moved back and forth between the daybook and his edited dictations. He referred back to his readers' comments twice more between the first and last revised drafts, again summarizing their remarks in his notes in the daybook.

To say that Mr. Murray is an extensive planner does not really explain the nature or scope of his revisions. I had initially developed code categories for revising activities; however, my coder and I discovered that we were for the most part double-coding for revising and planning, a sign the two activities were virtually inseparable. When the writer saw that major revision (as opposed to copy-editing) was necessary, he collapsed planning and revising into an activity that is best described as *reconceiving*. To "reconceive" is to scan and rescan one's text from the perspective of an external reader and to continue redrafting until all rhetorical, formal, and stylistic concerns have been resolved, or until the writer decides to let go of the text. This process, which Nancy Sommers has described as the resolution of the dissonance the writer senses between his intention and the developing text,[17] can be seen in the following

19

20

episode. The writer had been editing what he thought was a final draft when he saw that more substantive changes were in order. The flurry of editing activity was replaced by reading aloud and scanning the text as the writer realized that his language was inadequate for expressing a goal which he began to formulate as he read:

> (reading from previous page)[18] *It was E. B. While who reminded us, "Don't write about Man. Write about a man."* O.K. I'm going to cut that paragraph there . . . I've already said it. *The conferences when the teacher listens to the student can be short. When the teacher listens to the student in conference . . . when the teacher listens to the student* . . . the conference is, well, *the conference can be short. The student learns to speak first of what is most important to the student at the point.* To mention first what is most *important* . . . what most concerns . . . *the student* about the draft or the process that produced it. *The teacher listens . . . listens, reads the draft through the student's eyes then reads the draft, read or rereads . . . reads or* . . . scans or re-scans the draft to confirm, adjust, or compromise the student's concerns. *The range of student response includes the affective and the cognitive . . . It is the affective that usually controls the cognitive, and the affective responses usually have to be dealt with first* . . . (continues reading down the page) *Once the feelings of inadequacy, overconfidence, despair or elation are dealt with, then the conference teacher will find the other self speaking in more cognitive terms. And usually these comments* . . . O.K. that would now get the monitor into, into the phrase. All right. Put this crisscross cause clearly that page is going to be retyped . . . I'll be dictating so that's just a note. (continues reading on next page) *Listening to students allows the teacher to discover if the student's concerns were appropriate to where the student is in the writing process. The student, for example, is often excessively interested in language at the beginning of the process. Fragmentary language is normal before there is a text.* Make a comment on the text, (writes *intervention*) Now on page ten scanning . . . my God, I don't . . . I don't think I want to make this too much a conference piece. I'm going to echo back to that . . . monitor and also to the things I've said on page two and three. O.K. Let's see what I can do . . . The biggest question that I have is how much detail needs to be on conferences. I don't think they're, I don't think I can afford too much. Maybe some stronger sense of the response that ah . . . students make, how the other self speaks. They've got to get a sense of the other self speaking.

The next draft was totally rewritten following the sentence in the draft: 21 "When the teacher listens to the student, the conference can be short." The revision included previously unmentioned anecdotal reports of comments students had made in conferences, a discussion of the relevant implications of the research of Graves, Calkins, and Sowers, and a section on how the writing workshop can draw out the student's "other self" as other students model the idealized reader. This draft was nearly three pages longer than the preceding one. The only passage that remained was the final paragraph.

Granted that Mr. Murray's dictation frees him from the scribal constraints 22 that most writers face, how can we account for such global (i.e., whole text) revision? One answer lies in the simple, yet elegant, principle formulated by Linda Flower and John R. Hayes.[19] In the act of composing, writers move back and forth between planning, translating (putting thoughts into words), and reviewing their work. And as they do, they frequently "discover" major rhetorical goals.[20] In the episode just cited we have seen the writer shifting gears from editing to planning to reconceiving as he recognized something missing from the text and identified a major rhetorical goal—that he had to make the concept of the other self still more concrete for his audience: "They've got to get a sense of the other self speaking." In this same episode we can also see the cognitive basis for alterations in the macrostructure, or "gist," of a text, alterations Faigley and Witte report having found in examining the revised drafts of advanced student and expert adult writers.[21]

## Planning and Incubation

This discussion of planning would be incomplete without some attention to the role of incubation. Michael Polanyi describes incubation as "that persistence of heuristic tension through . . . periods of time in which problems are not consciously entertained."[22] Graham Wallas and Alex Osborn agree that incubation involves unconscious activity that takes place after periods of intensive preparation.[23] 23

Given the chance to observe a writer's processes over time, we can see incubation at work. The flashes of discovery that follow periods of incubation (even brief ones) are unexpected, powerful, and catalytic, as the following episode demonstrates. Mr. Murray was revising an article on revision for the *Journal of Basic Writing*. He had begun to review his work by editing copy, moving to more global issues as he evaluated the draft: 24

> The second paragraph may be . . . Seems to me I've got an awful lot of stuff before I get into it. (Counting paragraphs) 1, 2, 3, 4, 5, 6, 7, 8, 9, 10, ten paragraphs till I really get into the text. Maybe twelve or thirteen. I'm not going to try to hustle it too much. That might be all right.

The writer then reread the first two paragraphs, making small editorial changes and considering stylistic choices. At that point he broke off and noted on the text three questions, *"What is the principle? What are the acts? How can it be taught?"* He reminded himself to keep his audience in mind. "The first audience has got to be the journal, and therefore, teachers." He took a five-minute break and returned to report,

> But, that's when I realized . . . the word hierarchy ah, came to me and that's when I realized that in a sense I was making this too complicated for myself and simply what I have to do is show the reader . . . I'm making a note here . . . *Job not to explore complexities of revision, but simply to show the reader how to do revision.*

From a revision of his goals for his audience, Murray moved quickly into planning activity, noting on his text, 25

Hierarchy of problems. O.K. What I'm dealing with is a hierarchy of problems. *First, focus/content, second, order/structure, third, language/voice* . . . O.K. Now, let's see. I need to ah, need to put that word, hierarchy in here somewhere. Well, that may get into the second paragraph so put an arrow down there (draws arrow from hierarchy to second paragraph), then see what we can do about the title if we need to. Think of things like 'first problems first' (a mini-plan which he immediately rejects). It won't make sense that title, unless you've read the piece. Ah well, come up with a new title.

Here we can observe the anatomy of a planning episode with a number of 26 goals and sub-goals generated, considered, and consolidated at lightning speed: "O.K. What I'm dealing with is a hierarchy of problems." . . . "I need to ah, need to put that word, hierarchy in here somewhere." ". . . so put an arrow down there, then see what we can do about the title . . ." ". . . 'first problems first.' It won't make sense that title . . . Ah well, come up with a new title." We can also see the writer's process of discovery at work as he left his draft for a brief period and returned having identified a single meaning-laden word. This word gave Murray an inkling of the structure he wanted for the article—a listing of the problems writers face before they can accomplish clear, effective revision. In this case, a short period of incubation was followed by a period of intense and highly concentrated planning when Murray realized the direction he wanted the article to take.

## Introspection

One of the most helpful sources in this project was the testimony of the writer 27 as he paused between or during composing episodes. Instead of falling silent, he analyzed his processes, providing information I might have otherwise missed. The following segments from the protocols will demonstrate the kinds of insights subjects can give when not constrained by time. At the time of the first, Mr. Murray had completed the tenth list of titles he had made between June 26th and July 23rd while working on the revision of his article for *College Composition and Communication*. Frequently, these lists were made recursively, the writer flipping back in his daybook to previous lists he had composed:

> I think I have to go back to titles. *Hearing the student's other self.* Hold my place and go back and see if I have any that hit me in the past. *Teaching the reader and the writer. Teaching the reader in the writer. Encouraging the internal dialogue.* I skipped something in my mind that I did not put down. *Make your students talk to themselves. Teaching the writer to read.*

At this point he stopped to evaluate his process:

> All that I'm doing is compressing, ah, compressing is, ah, why I do a title . . . it compresses a draft for the whole thing. Title gives me a point of view, gets the tone, the difference between teaching and teach. A lot of time on that, that's all right.

The following morning the writer reported, "While I was shaving, I thought 28 of another title. *Teaching the other self: the writer's first reader.* I started to think of it as soon as I got up." This became the final title for the article and led to the planning of a new lead.

Later that day, after he had dictated three pages of the fourth of eight drafts, 29 he analyzed what he had accomplished:

> Well, I'm going to comment on what's happened here . . . this is a very compli-
> cated text. One of the things I'm considering, of course, is incorporating what I
> did in Dallas in here . . . ah, the text is breaking down in a constructive way, um,
> it's complex material and I'm having trouble with it . . . very much aware of pace
> of proportion; how much can you give to the reader in one part, and still keep
> them moving on to the next part. I have to give a little bit of head to teaching. . . .
> As a theatrical thing I am going to have to put some phrases in that indicate that
> I'm proposing or speculating, speculating as I revise this . . .

This last summation gave us important information on the writer's global 30 and local evaluation of text as well as on his rhetorical and stylistic plans. It is unique because it shows Murray engaged in composing and introspecting at the same time. Generally speaking, subjects giving protocols are not asked to add the demands of introspection to the task of writing. But, in fact, as Murray demonstrated, writers *do* monitor and introspect about their writing simultaneously.

## Summary

Some of the more provocative findings of this study concern the sub-processes 31 of planning and revising that have not been observed in conventional protocols (such as those taken by Flower and Hayes) because of the time limitations under which they have been given. When coding the protocols, we noted that Mr. Murray developed intricate style goals:

> It worries me a little bit that the title is too imperative. When I first wrote, most
> of my articles were like this; they pound on the table, do this, do that. I want this
> to be a little more reflective.

He also evaluated his thinking plans (i.e., his procedures in planning): "Ah, reading through, ah, hmm . . . I'm just scanning it so I really can't read it. If I read it, it will be an entirely different thing."

Most important, the writer's protocols shed new light on the great and small 32 decisions and revisions that form planning. These decisions and revisions form an elaborate network of steps as the writer moves back and forth between planning, drafting, editing, and reviewing.[24] This recursive process was demonstrated time after time as the writer worked on the two articles and the editorial, often discarding his drafts as he reconceived a major rhetorical goal, and returned to the daybook to plan again. Further, given his characteristic habit of working from daybook to dictation, then back to daybook, we were able to observe that Donald Murray composes at the reflexive and extensive poles described by Janet Emig. When working from material he had "rehearsed" in recent workshops, material with which he was thoroughly familiar, he was able to dictate virtually off the top of his head. At other times he was unable to continue dictating as he attempted to hold too much in suspension in short-term memory. On these occasions the writer returned to the daybook and spent considerable time planning before dictating another draft.

One final observation: although it may be impolitic for the researcher to 33 contradict the writer, Mr. Murray's activity over the summer while he was thinking aloud suggests that he is wrong in his assertion that writers only consider their audiences when doing external revision, i.e., editing and polishing. To the contrary, his most substantive changes, what he calls "internal revision," occurred as he turned his thoughts toward his audience. According to Murray, internal revision includes

> everything writers do to discover and develop what they have to say, beginning with the reading of a completed first draft. They read to discover where their content, form, language, and voice have led them. They use language, structure, and information to find out what they have to say or hope to say. The audience is one person: the writer. [25]

The writer, however, does not speak in a vacuum. Only when he begins to discern what his readers do not yet know can he shape his language, structure, and information to fit the needs of those readers. It is also natural that a writer like Murray would not be aware of how significant a role his sense of audience played in his thoughts. After years of journalistic writing, his consideration of audience had become more automatic than deliberate. The value of thinking-aloud protocols is that they allow the researcher to eavesdrop at the workplace of the writer, catching the flow of thought that would remain otherwise unarticulated.

However, *how* the writer functions when working in the setting to which he 34 or she is accustomed differs considerably from how that writer will function in an unfamiliar setting, given an unfamiliar task, and constrained by a time period over which he or she has no control. For this reason, I sought to combine the methodology of protocol analysis with the techniques of naturalistic inquiry.

This project has been a first venture in what may be a new direction. Re- 35 search on single subjects is new in our discipline; we need to bear in mind that each writer has his or her own idiosyncrasies. The researcher must make a trade-off, forgoing generalizability for the richness of the data and the qualitative insights to be gained from it. We need to replicate naturalistic studies of skilled and unskilled writers before we can begin to infer patterns that will allow us to understand the writing process in all of its complexity.

## Notes

1. Janet Emig, "Inquiry Paradigms and Writing," *College Composition and Communication,* 33 (February, 1982), p. 55.
2. Emig, "Inquiry Paradigms and Writing," p. 67.
3. Donald Graves, "What Children Show Us About Revision," *Language Arts,* 56 (March, 1979), 312–319; Susan Sowers, "A Six Year Old's Writing Process: The First Half of the First Grade,"

*Language Arts*, 56 (October, 1979), 829-835; Lucy M. Calkins, "Children Learn the Writer's Craft," *Language Arts*, 57 (February, 1980), 207–213.

4. Janet Emig, *The Composing Processes of Twelfth-Graders* (Urbana, IL: National Council of Teachers of English, 1971), pp. 8–11; Linda Flower and John R. Hayes, "A Cognitive Process Theory of Writing," *College Composition and Communication*, 32 (December, 1981), 368.

5. See Janet Emig, *The Composing Processes of Twelfth-Graders*, p. 30; Sondra Perl, "Five Writers Writing: Case Studies of the Composing Processes of Unskilled College Writers," Diss. New York University, 1978, pp. 48, 387–391; "The Composing Processes of Unskilled College Writers," *Research in the Teaching of English*, 13 (December, 1979), 318; Nancy I. Sommers, "Revision Strategies of Student Writers and Experienced Adult Writers," paper delivered at the Annual Meeting of the Modern Language Association, New York, 28 December, 1978. A slightly revised version was published in *College Composition and Communication*, 32 (December, 1980), 378–388.

6. See Linda Flower and John R. Hayes, "Identifying the Organization of Writing Processes," in *Cognitive Processes in Writing*, ed. Lee W. Gregg and Erwin R. Steinberg (Hillsdale, NJ: Lawrence Erlbaum Associates, 1981), p. 4; "The Cognition of Discovery: Defining a Rhetorical Problem," *College Composition and Communication*, 32 (February, 1980), 23; "The Pregnant Pause: An Inquiry into the Nature of Planning," *Research in the Teaching of English*, 19 (October, 1981), 233; "A Cognitive Process Theory of Writing," p. 368; Carol Berkenkotter, "Understanding a Writer's Awareness of Audience," *College Composition and Communication*, 32 (December, 1981), 389.

7. Perl, "Five Writers Writing: Case Studies of the Composing Processes of Unskilled College Writers," p. 1.

8. Evaluations of text were either global or local. An example of global evaluation is when the writer says, "There's a lack of fullness in the piece." When the writer was evaluating locally he would comment, ". . . and the ending seems weak."

9. Emig, *The Composing Processes of Twelfth-Graders*, p. 4.

10. *Ibid.* See also "Eye, Hand, and Brain," in *Research on Composing: Points of Departure*, ed. Charies R. Cooper and Lee Odell (Urbana, IL: National Council of Teachers of English), p. 70. Emig raises the question, "What if it is the case that classical and contemporary rhetorical terms such as . . . extensive and reflexive may represent centuries old understandings that the mind deals differentially with different speaking and writing tasks. To put the matter declaratively, if hypothetically, modes of discourse may represent measurably different profiles of brain activity."

11. Janet Emig, observing her subject's writing processes, noted that "the *nature of the stimulus*" did not necessarily determine the response. Emig's students gave extensive responses to a reflexive task (*The Composing Processes of Twelfth-Graders*, pp. 30–31, 33). Similarly, Murray gave a reflexive response to an extensive task. Such a response is not unusual when we consider what the writer himself has observed: "The deeper we get into the writing process the more we may discover how affective concerns govern the cognitive, for writing is an intellectual activity carried on in an emotional environment, a precisely engineered sailboat trying to hold course in a vast and stormy Atlantic" ("Teaching the Other Self: The Writer's First Reader," *College Composition and Communication*, 33 [May, 1982], p. 142). For a writer as deeply engaged in his work as Murray, drafting a conceptual piece was as personal and subjective as describing a closely felt experience.

12. Lester Faigley and Stephen Witte, "Analyzing Revision," *College Composition and Communication*, 32 (December, 1981), 410–411.

13. Faigley and Witte, p. 411.

14. These three pieces of discourse were chosen because their results are representative of the writer's activities.

15. Linda Flower and John R. Hayes describe "process goals" as "instructions and plans the writer gives herself for directing her own composing process." See "The Pregnant Pause: An Inquiry Into the Nature of Planning," p. 242. However, this definition is not always agreed upon by cognitive psychologists studying problem-solvers in other fields. On one hand, Allen Newell, Herbert A. Simon, and John R. Hayes distinguish between the goals and plans of a problem-solver, considering a goal as an end to be achieved and a plan as one kind of method for reaching

that end. See John R. Hayes, *Cognitive Psychology* (Homewood, IL: The Dorsey Press, 1978), p. 192; Allen Newell and Herbert A. Simon, *Human Problem Solving* (Englewood Cliffs, NJ: Prentice-Hall, Inc. 1972), pp. 88–92, 428–429. On the other hand, George Miller, Eugene Galanter, and Karl H. Pribram use the term "plan" inclusively, suggesting that a plan is "any hierarchical process in the organism that can control the order in which a sequence of operations is to be performed." See *Plans and the Structure of Human Behavior* (New York: Holt, Rinehart, and Winston, Inc., 1960), p. 16.

16. Flower and Hayes use these terms interchangeably, as have I. "Thinking plans" are plans for text that precede drafting and occur during drafting. Thinking plans occur before the movements of a writer's hand. Because of the complexity of the composing process, it is difficult to separate thinking plans from "process goals." It is possible, however, to distinguish between *rhetorical goals and rhetorical plans*. Murray was setting a goal when he remarked, "The biggest thing is to . . . what I've got to get to satisfy the reader . . . is that point of what do we hear the other self saying and how does it help?" He followed this goal with a plan to "Probe into the other self. What is the other self? How does it function?"

17. Sommers, "Revision Strategies," pp. 385, 387. (See note 5, above.)

18. The material italicized in the excerpts from these transcripts is text the subject is writing. The material italicized and underlined is text the subject is reading that has already been written.

19. Flower and Hayes, "A Cognitive Process Theory of Writing," 365–387.

20. Berkenkotter, "Understanding a Writer's Awareness of Audience," pp. 392, 395.

21. Faigley and Witte, pp. 406–410.

22. Michael Polanyi, *Personal Knowledge: Toward a Post-Critical Philosophy* (Chicago: The University of Chicago Press, 1958), p. 122.

23. Graham Wallas, *The Art of Thought* (New York: Jonathan Cape, 1926), pp. 85–88; Alex Osborn, *Applied Imagination: Principles and Procedures of Creative Problem-Solving*, 3rd rev. ed. (New York: Charles F. Scribner and Sons), pp. 314–325.

24. For a description of the development of a writer's goal structure, see Flower and Hayes, "A Cognitive Process Theory of Writing."

25. Donald M. Murray, "Internal Revision: A Process of Discovery," *Research on Composing: Points of Departure* (See note 10), p. 91.

# Response of a Laboratory Rat— or, Being Protocoled

## DONALD M. MURRAY

## 1.

First a note on self-exposure, a misdemeanor in most communities. I have long felt the academic world is too closed. We have an ethical obligation to write and to reveal our writing to our students if we are asking them to share their writing with us. I have felt writers should, instead of public readings, give public workshops in which they write in public, allowing the search for meaning to be seen. I've done this and found the process insightful—and fun.

I have also been fascinated by protocol analysis research. It did seem a fruitful way (a way, there is no one way) to study the writing process. I was, however, critical of the assignments I had seen given, the concentration on inexperienced students as subjects, and the unrealistic laboratory conditions and time limitations.

And, in the absence of more proper academic resources, I have made a ca-   3
reer of studying myself while writing. I was already without shame. When Carol
Berkenkotter asked me to run in her maze I gulped, but I did not think I could
refuse.

## 2.

The one-hour protocol was far worse than I had expected. If I had done that   4
first there would have been no other protocols. I have rarely felt so completely
trapped and so inadequate. I have gone through other research experiences, but
in this case I felt stronger than I ever had the need to perform. That was nothing that the researcher did. It was a matter of the conditions. I had a desperate
desire to please. I thought of that laboratory experiment where subjects would
push a button to cause pain to other people. I would have blown up Manhattan
to get out of that room. To find equivalent feelings from my past I would have
to go back to combat or to public school. I have developed an enormous compassion and respect for those who have performed for Masters and Johnson.

## 3.

The process of a naturalistic study we have evolved (Can a rat be a colleague?   5
Since a colleague can be a rat, I don't see why not.) soon became a natural process. I do not assume, and neither did my researcher, that what I said reflected
all that was taking place. It did reflect what I was conscious of doing, and a bit
more. My articulation was an accurate reflection of the kind of talking I do to
myself while planning to write, while writing, and while revising. At no time
did it seem awkward or unnatural. My talking aloud was merely a question of
turning up the volume knob on the
muttering I do under my breath as
I write.

*Writing is an intellectual activity, and I do not agree with the romantics who feel that the act of writing and act of thinking are separate.*   6

I feel that if there was any self-
consciousness in the process it was
helpful. I was, after all, practicing
a craft, not performing magic. Writing is an intellectual activity, and
I do not agree with the romantics
who feel that the act of writing and the act of thinking are separate.

Having this researcher, who had earned my trust, waiting to see what I   7
wrote was a motivating factor. While the experiment was going on she was
appropriately chilly and doctoral. But I still knew someone was listening, and
I suspect that got me to the writing desk some days.

It is certainly true that debriefing by the researcher at some distance from   8
the time of writing was virtually useless. I could not remember why I had done
what. In fact, the researcher knows the text better than I do. I am concentrating almost entirely on the daily evolving text, and yesterday's page seems like
last year's. I intend to try some teaching experiments in the future that make it

possible for me to be on the scene when my students are writing. I'm a bit more suspicious now than I had been about the accounts that are reconstructed in a conference days after writing. They are helpful, the best teaching point I know, but I want to find out what happens if we can bring the composing and the teaching closer together.

## 4.

I certainly agree with what my researcher calls introspection. I am disappointed, however, that she hasn't included the term that I overheard the coders use. Rats aren't all that dumb, and I think there should be further research into those moments when I left the desk and came back with a new insight. They called them: "Bathroom epiphanies."    9

## 5.

I was surprised by:    10

1. The percentage of my time devoted to planning. I had realized the pendulum was swinging in that direction, but I had no idea how far it had swung. I suspect that when we begin to write in a new genre we have to do a great deal of revision, but that as we become familiar with a genre we can solve more writing problems in advance of a completed text. This varies according to the writer but I have already changed some of my teaching to take this finding into account by allowing my students much more planning time and introducing many more planning techniques.
2. The length of incubation time. I now realize that articles that I thought took a year in fact have taken three, four, or five years.
3. The amount of revision that is essentially planning, what the researcher calls "reconceiving." I was trying to get at that in my chapter, "Internal Revision: A Process of Discovery," published in *Research on Composing: Points of Departure,* edited by Charles R. Cooper and Lee Odell. I now understand this process far better, and much of my revision is certainly a planning or prewriting activity.

## 6.

I agree with my researcher (what rat wouldn't?) that affective conditions are important in writing. I do think the affective often controls the cognitive, and I feel strongly that much more research has to be done, difficult as it may be, into those conditions, internal and external, that make effective writing possible or impossible.    11

## 7.

I was far more aware of audience than I thought I was during some of the writing. My sense of audience is so strong that I have to suppress my conscious awareness of audience to hear what the text demands.    12

Related to this is the fact that I do need a few readers. The important role  13
of my pre-publication readers was clear when my revisions were studied. No
surprise here. I think we need more study of the two, or three, or four readers professional writers choose for their work in process. It would be helpful
for us as teachers to know the qualities of these people and what they do for
the writer. I know I choose people who make me want to write when I leave
them.

## 8.

I worry a bit about the patterns that this research revealed have been laid  14
down in my long-term memory. The more helpful they are the more I worry
about them. I fear that what I discover when I write is what I have discovered
before and forgotten, and that rather than doing the writing that must be
done I merely follow the stereotypes of the past. In other words, I worry that
the experienced writer can become too glib, too slick, too professional, too
polished—can, in effect, write too well.

## 9.

The description of working back and forth from the global to the particular  15
during the subprocesses of planning and revising seems accurate to me.

There is a great deal of interesting research and speculation about this pro-  16
cess, but we need much more. I find it very difficult to make my students aware
of the layers of concern through which the writing writer must oscillate at such
a speed that it appears the concerns are dealt with instantaneously.

Too often in my teaching and my publishing I have given the false impres-  17
sion that we do one thing, then another, when in fact we do many things simultaneously. And the interaction between these things is what we call writing.
This project reaffirmed what I had known, that there are many simultaneous
levels of concern that bear on every line.

## 10.

I realize how eccentric my work habits appear. I am aware of how fortunate  18
I am to be able to work with my wife. The process of dictation of non-fiction
allows a flow, intensity, and productivity that is quite unusual. It allows me to
spend a great deal of time planning, because I know that once the planning is
done I can produce copy in short bursts. It is not my problem but the researcher's, however, to put my eccentric habits into context.

If I am the first writer to be naked, then it is up to those other writers who  19
do not think they look the same to take off their clothes. I hope they do not
appear as I do; I would be most depressed if I am the model for other writers.
I hope, and I believe, that there must be a glorious diversity among writers.
What I think we have done, as rat and ratee, is to demonstrate that there is
a process through which experienced writers can be studied under normal

working conditions on typical writing projects. I think my contribution is not to reveal my own writing habits but to show a way that we can study writers who are far better writers than I.

## 11.

Finally, I started this process with a researcher and have ended it with a col- 20 league. I am grateful for the humane way the research was conducted. I have learned a great deal about research and about what we have researched. It has helped me in my thinking, my teaching, and my writing. I am grateful to Dr. Carol Berkenkotter for this opportunity.

---

### Questions for Discussion and Journaling

1. What was your impression of Murray's writing processes as they're described here? How do they compare to yours? What do you do the same or differently?

2. Murray's relationship with his audience seems complicated. Try to describe it, and then compare it to your own sense of audience: How much are *you* thinking about *your* audience while you write?

3. How did this study change Berkenkotter's understanding of writing processes, particularly planning and revision?

4. What problems with existing methods for studying writing process does Berkenkotter identify? If you read Perl, did you notice any of these problems in her methods? What do you think they might mean for Perl's findings? In what ways is Berkenkotter's newer approach to studying writing processes able to solve the weaknesses in other methods? Do any weaknesses remain?

5. Why do you suppose Berkenkotter often refers to Murray as "the writer" and in his response Murray calls Berkenkotter "the researcher"? Why not just use each other's names, since the audience knows them anyway?

6. What do you think of the apparent back-and-forth between the researcher and researched that occurred as Berkenkotter analyzed her data and drew conclusions? Was it good? Bad? Necessary? Irrelevant? Did anything about it surprise you?

### Applying and Exploring Ideas

1. Less-experienced writers, especially when writing for school, tend to spend comparatively little time on revision (by which we mean *developing the ideas* in a piece rather than **editing**, which is the sentence-level work that improves the style and correctness of a text). Explore your own writing habits: How do you spend your writing time? How would you characterize your level of writing experience? How do you think your level of experience relates to the amount of time you spend on various parts of the writing

process? In making these estimates, keep the following in mind: Murray, a highly professional and quite reflective writer, had an erroneous impression of how much time he spent on various aspects of his writing process.

2. Begin a writing log in which you list all the writing situations you find yourself in on a day-to-day basis: Every time you write over two weeks, note what you write, the audience for that writing, the genre, the technologies employed, and the skills used. At the end of the period, reflect on what you learned about your writing habits.

3. Try your own brief experiment, re-creating Berkenkotter and Murray's dynamic: Pair with a class partner and designate one of you as researcher and the other as researched. Have the researcher observe the researched's writing process on a short (approximately one-page) piece of writing, and then have the researcher write a brief description of that process while the researched writes a piece of similar length on the experience of doing the writing. Compare these descriptions, and negotiate the findings: What, put together, do the two accounts reveal about the writer's process?

## Meta Moment

Name one thing you learned from the Berkenkotter and Murray readings that you could use to help you write more effectively.

# The Maker's Eye: Revising Your Own Manuscripts

## DONALD M. MURRAY

■ Murray, Donald M. "The Maker's Eye: Revising Your Own Manuscripts." *Language Awareness: Readings for College Writers.* Ed. Paul Eschholz, Alfred Rosa, and Virginia Clark. Boston: Bedford/St. Martin's, 2013. 194–98. Print. (Originally published in *Writer*, 1973).

## Framing the Reading

You may have already read a piece by Donald Murray in Chapter 1. If so, you know that he was a well-known writer and writing teacher for many years up until his death in 2006; he even won a Pulitzer Prize in 1954 for his *Boston Herald* editorials about American military policy. He wrote many books about writing, including *Write to Learn, The Craft of Revision*, and *A Writer Teaches Writing*. He also wrote about many other topics, including the death of his daughter in *The Lively Shadow: Living with the Death of a Child*.

Murray, like Peter Elbow, was intensely interested in how writing happens and how to help himself, his students, and others write. Murray wrote openly and frequently about his own writing processes and habits, and he encouraged other writers to set a routine of writing every day. If you read Carol Berkenkotter's article in this chapter, you will already know a lot about how Murray wrote, since Berkenkotter studied his writing practices for her research. Like Elbow, Murray advocates initially writing for discovery, without self-censoring. He believed that invention and discovery should, in fact, take up most of the writing process.

In this short piece, originally written for a magazine called *The Writer*, in October 1973, Murray talks about the importance of seeing drafting as "possibility" and as providing "opportunities to discover." Here he provides suggestions for how to reread your own writing with an eye toward meaningful revision.

## Getting Ready to Read

*Before you read*, do at least one of the following activities:

- Think about what "revision" means to you.
- Think about what you usually do to think of ideas when you begin to write.

*As you read*, consider the following question:

- How do your ideas about invention and revision compare to the ones Murray suggests?

When students complete a first draft, they consider the job of writing 1
done—and their teachers too often agree. When professional writers
complete a first draft, they usually feel that they are at the start of the writing
process. When a draft is completed, the job of writing can begin.

That difference in attitude is the difference between amateur and professional, 2
inexperience and experience, journeyman and craftsman. Peter F. Drucker, the
prolific business writer, calls his first draft "the zero draft"—after that he can
start counting. Most writers share the feeling that the first draft, and all of
those which follow, are opportunities to discover what they have to say and
how best they can say it.

To produce a progression of drafts, each of which says more and says it 3
more clearly, the writer has to develop a special kind of reading skill. In school
we are taught to decode what appears on the page as finished writing. Writers,
however, face a different category of possibility and responsibility when they
read their own drafts. To them the words on the page are never finished. Each
can be changed and rearranged, can set off a chain reaction of confusion or
clarified meaning. This is a different kind of reading which is possibly more
difficult and certainly more exciting.

Writers must learn to be their own best enemy. They must accept the criti- 4
cism of others and be suspicious of it; they must accept the praise of others
and be even more suspicious of it. Writers cannot depend on others. They must
detach themselves from their own pages so that they can apply both their car-
ing and their craft to their own work.

Such detachment is not easy. Science-fiction writer Ray Bradbury suppos- 5
edly puts each manuscript away for a year to the day and then rereads it as a
stranger. Not many writers have the discipline or the time to do this. We must
read when our judgment may be at its worst, when we are close to the euphoric
moment of creation.

Then the writer, counsels novelist Nancy Hale, "should be critical of every- 6
thing that seems to him most delightful in his style. He should excise what he
most admires, because he wouldn't thus admire it if he weren't . . . in a sense
protecting it from criticism." John Ciardi, the poet, adds, "The last act of the
writing must be to become one's own reader. It is, I suppose, a schizophrenic
process, to begin passionately and to end critically, to begin hot and to end
cold; and, more important, to be passion-hot and critic-cold at the same time."

Most people think that the principal problem is that writers are too proud of 7
what they have written. Actually, a greater problem for most professional writers
is one shared by the majority of students. They are overly critical, think everything
is dreadful, tear up page after page, never complete a draft, see the task as hopeless.

The writer must learn to read critically but constructively, to cut what is 8
bad, to reveal what is good. Eleanor Estes, the children's book author, explains:
"The writer must survey his work critically, coolly, as though he were a stranger to it. He must be willing to prune, expertly and hard-heartedly. At the end
of each revision, a manuscript may look . . . . worked over, torn apart, pinned
together, added to, deleted from, words changed and words changed back. Yet
the book must maintain its original freshness and spontaneity."

Most readers underestimate the amount of rewriting it usually takes to pro- 9
duce spontaneous reading. This is a great disadvantage to the student writer,
who sees only a finished product and never watches the craftsman who takes the
necessary step back, studies the work carefully, returns to the task, steps back,
returns, steps back, again and again. Anthony Burgess, one of the most prolific
writers in the English-speaking world, admits, "I might revise a page twenty
times." Roald Dahl, the popular children's writer, states, "By the time I'm nearing
the end of a story, the first part will have been reread and altered and corrected
at least 150 times . . . Good writing is essentially rewriting. I am positive of this."

Rewriting isn't virtuous. It isn't something that ought to be done. It is simply 10
something that most writers find they have to do to discover what they have to
say and how to say it. It is a condition of the writer's life.

There are, however, a few writers who do little formal rewriting, primarily be- 11
cause they have the capacity and experience to create and review a large number
of invisible drafts in their minds before they approach the page. And some writers slowly produce finished pages, performing all the tasks of revision simultaneously, page by page, rather than draft by draft. But it is still possible to see the
sequence followed by most writers most of the time in rereading their own work.

Most writers scan their drafts first, reading as quickly as possible to catch 12
the larger problems of subject and form, and then move in closer and closer as
they read and write, reread and rewrite.

The first thing writers look for in their drafts is *information*. They know 13
that a good piece of writing is built from specific, accurate, and interesting information. The writer must have an abundance of information from which to
construct a readable piece of writing.

Next writers look for *meaning* in the information. The specifics must build 14
to a pattern of significance. Each piece of specific information must carry the
reader toward meaning.

Writers reading their own drafts are aware of *audience*. They put themselves 15
in the reader's situation and make sure that they deliver information which a
reader wants to know or needs to know in a manner which is easily digested.
Writers try to be sure that they anticipate and answer the questions a critical
reader will ask when reading the piece of writing.

Writers make sure that the *form* is appropriate to the subject and the audi- 16
ence. Form, or genre, is the vehicle which carries meaning to the reader, but
form cannot be selected until the writer has adequate information to discover
its significance and an audience which needs or wants that meaning.

Once writers are sure the form is appropriate, they must then look at the 17
*structure*, the order of what they have written. Good writing is built on a solid
framework of logic, argument, narrative, or motivation which runs through
the entire piece of writing and holds it together. This is the time when many
writers find it most effective to outline as a way of visualizing the hidden spine
by which the piece of writing is supported.

The element on which writers spend a majority of their time is *development*. 18
Each section of a piece of writing must be adequately developed. It must give
readers enough information so that they are satisfied. How much information
is enough? That's as difficult as asking how much garlic belongs in a salad. It

must be done to taste, but most beginning writers underdevelop, underestimating the reader's hunger for more information.

As writers solve development problems, they often have to consider questions of *dimension*. There must be a pleasing and effective proportion among all the parts of the piece of writing. There is a continual process of subtracting and adding to keep the piece of writing in balance.   19

Finally, writers have to listen to their own voices. *Voice* is the force which drives a piece of writing forward. It is an expression of the writer's authority and concern. It is what is between the words on the page, what glues the piece of writing together. A good piece of writing is always marked by a consistent, individual voice.   20

As writers read and reread, write and rewrite, they move closer and closer to the page until they are doing line-by-line editing. Writers read their own pages with infinite care. Each sentence, each line, each clause, each phrase, each word, each mark of punctuation, each section of white space between the type has to contribute to the clarification of meaning.   21

> *The maker's eye is never satisfied, for each word has the potential to ignite new meaning.*   22

Slowly the writer moves from word to word, looking through language to see the subject. As a word is changed, cut or added, as a construction is rearranged, all the words used before that moment and all those that follow that moment must be considered and reconsidered.

Writers often read aloud at this stage of the editing process, muttering or whispering to themselves, calling on the ear's experience with language. Does this sound right—or that? Writers edit, shifting back and forth from eye to page to ear to page. I find I must do this careful editing in short runs, no more than fifteen or twenty minutes at a stretch, or I become too kind with myself. I begin to see what I hope is on the page, not what actually is on the page.   23

This sounds tedious if you haven't done it, but actually it is fun. Making something right is immensely satisfying, for writers begin to learn what they are writing about by writing. Language leads them to meaning, and there is the joy of discovery, of understanding, of making meaning clear as the writer employs the technical skills of language.   24

Words have double meanings, even triple and quadruple meanings. Each word has its own potential of connotation and denotation. And when writers rub one word against the other, they are often rewarded with a sudden insight, an unexpected clarification.   25

The maker's eye moves back and forth from word to phrase to sentence to paragraph to sentence to phrase to word. The maker's eye sees the need for variety and balance, for a firmer structure, for a more appropriate form. It peers into the interior of the paragraph, looking for coherence, unity, and emphasis, which make meaning clear.   26

I learned something about this process when my first bifocals were prescribed. I had ordered a larger section of the reading portion of the glass because of my work, but even so, I could not contain my eyes within this new   27 limit of vision. And I still find myself taking off my glasses and bending my nose toward the page, for my eyes unconsciously flick back and forth across the page, back to another page, forward to still another, as I try to see each evolving line in relation to every other line.

When does this process end? Most writers agree with the great Russian 28 writer Tolstoy, who said, "I scarcely ever reread my published writings, if by chance I come across a page, it always strikes me: all this must be rewritten; this is how I should have written it."

The maker's eye is never satisfied, for each word has the potential to ignite 29 new meaning. This article has been twice written all the way through the writing process [. . .]. Now it is to be republished in a book. The editors made a few small suggestions, and then I read it with my maker's eye. Now it has been re-edited, re-revised, re-read, and re-re-edited, for each piece of writing to the writer is full of potential and alternatives.

A piece of writing is never finished. It is delivered to a deadline, torn out of 30 the typewriter on demand, sent off with a sense of accomplishment and shame and pride and frustration. If only there were a couple more days, time for just another run at it, perhaps then. . . .

## Questions for Discussion and Journaling

1. What does it mean to write for an audience? Think about several recent texts you have written both in and out of school, and consider how the audience impacted them. If you had spent more time thinking about the audience needs, how might you have revised the texts?

2. Murray here and in many of his other articles and books talks a lot about "voice." What do you think that "voice" in writing actually is? Do you feel like you have a "voice" in your own writing? Does your voice change depending on what you are writing and for whom? How so?

## Applying and Exploring Ideas

1. The next time you draft something, take Murray's advice about how to revise, and see if that changes the quality and nature of what you write.

2. Look back to the advice that Elbow gave about writing and revising in "The Need for Care." Drawing on what both he and Murray suggest, write up some advice for yourself about things you could do differently in order to write and revise more effectively.

### Meta Moment
Compare Murray's view of composing to your own, and reflect on whether you want to actively try to change anything about your process(es) as a result of hearing from Murray.

# The Composing Processes of Unskilled College Writers

## SONDRA PERL

■ Perl, Sondra. "The Composing Processes of Unskilled College Writers." *Research in the Teaching of English* 13.4 (1979): 317–36. Print.

## Framing the Reading

Writing this article in 1979, Sondra Perl argued, "To date no examination of composing processes has dealt primarily with unskilled writers. As long as 'average' or skilled writers are the focus, it remains unclear as to how process research will [help unskilled writers]" (para. 4). Much of the nature of this article is captured in that brief passage.

With the study reported here, Perl attempted to accomplish two important and quite distinct projects in advancing writing research. The first was to create a brand-new way to study writers writing. In the first few pages you'll read Perl's description of the problem with previous research on the writing process: It relied almost entirely on stories researchers told about what they observed. Perl tried to create a more objective system for describing what writers were doing.

The second was to study a group of writers that previous research had ignored. Writers who aren't very good at writing probably aren't the best test subjects for "how writing works," and so they had not been studied much by researchers trying to learn about "the composing process" (which is how composition was described in those times—as a single kind of process writers either mastered or didn't). Yet, as Perl argued, studying people who are already proficient writers would probably not "provide teachers with a firmer understanding of the needs of students with serious writing problems" (para. 4).

Like a few other articles in this chapter, Perl's is around 30 to 35 years old. It reflects a time of great interest, among writing researchers, about processes writers use to compose texts. That interest waned a few years later; even though there was still much to be discovered and understood (most process research findings were provisional at best and needed to be followed up with larger-scale studies that have never been done), the attention of writing researchers went in other directions. Thus the majority of research on the writing process tends to be at least twenty years old.

Perl's article had a particularly great impact on the field because of her combined focus on a standardized method for observing, recording, and reporting on writers' behaviors while writing and her attention to "basic" writers whose writing was difficult to read and understand. Work such as this has made Perl one of the most significant researchers the field has seen. She went on to study how writers imagine what to say before they quite *know* what they want to say. (In 2004 she published a book called *Felt Sense: Writing with the Body*, which includes a CD that offers "meditations" for writers. It's quite different from the work you'll read here, which we hope might motivate you to look it up.)

## Getting Ready to Read

*Before you read*, do at least one of the following activities:

- Ask yourself how you view yourself as a writer. Do you think you are a skilled or unskilled writer? Is writing easy or hard for you?
- Write down exactly what you think you do when you have to write something for school. Have you ever thought about this consciously before?
- Watch a roommate or friend write something for school, and make note of the things he or she does while writing.

*As you read*, consider the following questions:

- What arguments does Perl make about what research methods are necessary for good studies of writing?
- What attitudes and assumptions does Perl seem to bring to her study that you might not agree with, or at least might question?
- What conclusions is Perl able to reach about the major aspects of the composing process—prewriting, writing, and editing—that she identifies?
- How are Tony's processes as an "unskilled" writer different from those of skilled writers?

---

This paper presents the pertinent findings from a study of the composing  1 processes of five unskilled college writers (Perl, 1978). The first part summarizes the goals of the original study, the kinds of data collected, and the research methods employed. The second part is a synopsis of the study of Tony, one of the original five case studies. The third part presents a condensed version of the findings on the composing process and discusses these findings in light of current pedagogical practice and research design.

## Goals of the Study

This research addressed three major questions: (1) How do unskilled writers  2 write? (2) Can their writing processes be analyzed in a systematic, replicable manner? and (3) What does an increased understanding of their processes suggest about the nature of composing in general and the manner in which writing is taught in the schools?

In recent years, interest in the composing process has grown (Britton et al.,  3 1975; Burton, 1973; Cooper, 1974; Emig, 1967, 1971). In 1963, Braddock,

Lloyd-Jones, and Schoer, writing on the state of research in written composition, included the need for "direct observation" and case study procedures
in their suggestions for future re-
search (pp. 24, 31–32). In a section
entitled "Unexplored Territory,"
they listed basic unanswered questions such as, "What is involved
in the act of writing?" and "Of what does skill in writing actually consist?"
(p. 51). Fifteen years later, Cooper and Odell (1978) edited a volume similar
in scope, only this one was devoted entirely to issues and questions related to
research on composing. This volume in particular signals a shift in emphasis
in writing research. Alongside the traditional, large-scale experimental studies,
there is now widespread recognition of the need for works of a more modest,
probing nature, works that attempt to elucidate basic processes. The studies
on composing that have been completed to date are precisely of this kind; they
are small-scale studies, based on the systematic observation of writers engaged
in the process of writing (Emig, 1971; Graves, 1973; Mischel, 1974; Pianko,
1977; Stallard, 1974).

> How do unskilled writers write?

For all of its promise, this body of research has yet to produce work that 4
would insure wide recognition for the value of process studies of composing.
One limitation of work done to date is methodological. Narrative descriptions
of composing processes do not provide sufficiently graphic evidence for the
perception of underlying regularities and patterns. Without such evidence, it
is difficult to generate well-defined hypotheses and to move from exploratory
research to more controlled experimental studies. A second limitation pertains
to the subjects studied. To date no examination of composing processes has
dealt primarily with unskilled writers. As long as "average" or skilled writers
are the focus, it remains unclear as to how process research will provide teachers with a firmer understanding of the needs of students with serious writing
problems.

The present study is intended to carry process research forward by address- 5
ing both of these limitations. One prominent feature of the research design
involves the development and use of a meaningful and replicable method for
rendering the composing process as a sequence of observable and scorable behaviors. A second aspect of the design is the focus on students whose writing
problems baffle the teachers charged with their education.

## Design of the Study

This study took place during the 1975–76 fall semester at Eugenio Maria de 6
Hostos Community College of the City University of New York. Students were
selected for the study on the basis of two criteria: writing samples that qualified them as unskilled writers and willingness to participate. Each student met
with the researcher for five 90-minute sessions (see Table 1). Four sessions were
devoted to writing with the students directed to compose aloud, to externalize their thinking processes as much as possible, during each session. In one

additional session, a writing profile on the students' perceptions and memories of writing was developed through the use of an open-ended interview. All of the sessions took place in a soundproof room in the college library. Throughout each session, the researcher assumed a noninterfering role.

The topics for writing were developed in an introductory social science 7 course in which the five students were enrolled. The "content" material they were studying was divided into two modes: extensive, in which the writer was directed to approach the material in an objective, impersonal fashion, and reflexive, in which the writer was directed to approach similar material in an affective, personalized fashion. Contrary to Emig's (1971) definitions, in this study it was assumed that the teacher was always the audience.

## Data Analysis

Three kinds of data were collected in this study: the students' written products, 8 their composing tapes, and their responses to the interview. Each of these was studied carefully and then discussed in detail in each of the five case study presentations. Due to limitations of space, this paper will review only two of the data sets generated in the study.

### Coding the Composing Process

One of the goals of this research was to devise a tool for describing the 9 movements that occur during composing. In the past such descriptions have taken the form of narratives which detail, with relative precision and insight, observable composing behaviors; however, these narratives provide no way of ascertaining the frequency, relative importance, and place of each behavior within an individual's composing process. As such, they are cumbersome and difficult to replicate. Furthermore, lengthy, idiosyncratic narratives run the risk of leaving underlying patterns and regularities obscure. In contrast, the method created in this research provides a means of viewing the composing process that is:

1. Standardized—it introduces a coding system for observing the composing process that can be replicated;
2. Categorical—it labels specific, observable behaviors so that types of composing movements are revealed;
3. Concise—it presents the entire sequence of composing movements on one or two pages;
4. Structural—it provides a way of determining how parts of the process relate to the whole; and
5. Diachronic—it presents the sequences of movements that occur during composing as they unfold in time.

In total, the method allows the researcher to apprehend a process as it unfolds. It lays out the movements or behavior sequences in such a way that if patterns within a student's process or among a group of students exist, they become apparent.

**Table 1**

Design of the Study

| | Session 1 (S1) | Session 2 (S2) | Session 3 (S3) | Session 4 (S4) | Session 5 (S5) |
|---|---|---|---|---|---|
| Mode | Extensive | Reflexive | | Extensive | Reflexive |
| Topic | Society & Culture | Society & Culture | Interview: Writing Profile | Capitalism | Capitalism |
| Directions | Students told to compose aloud; no other directions given | Students told to compose aloud; no other directions given | | Students told to compose aloud; also directed to talk out ideas before writing | Students told to compose aloud; also directed to talk out ideas before writing |

## The Code

The method consists of coding each composing behavior exhibited by the stu-  10
dent and charting each behavior on a continuum. During this study, the coding
occurred after the student had finished composing and was done by working
from the student's written product and the audiotape of the session. It was possible to do this since the tape captured both what the student was saying and
the literal sound of the pen moving across the page. As a result, it was possible
to determine when students were talking, when they were writing, when both
occurred simultaneously, and when neither occurred.

The major categorical divisions in this coding system are talking, writing,  11
and reading; however, it was clear that there are various kinds of talk and various kinds of writing and reading operations, and that a coding system would
need to distinguish among these various types. In this study the following operations were distinguished:

1. General planning [PL]—organizing one's thoughts for writing, discussing how one will proceed.
2. Local planning [PLL]—talking out what idea will come next.
3. Global planning [PLG]—discussing changes in drafts.
4. Commenting [C]—sighing, making a comment or judgment about the
   topic.
5. Interpreting [I]—rephrasing the topic to get a "handle" on it.
6. Assessing [A(+); A(–)]—making a judgment about one's writing; may be
   positive or negative.
7. Questioning [Q]—asking a question.
8. Talking leading to writing [T→W]—voicing ideas on the topic, tenta-
   tively finding one's way, but not necessarily being committed to or using
   all one is saying.
9. Talking and writing at the same time [TW]—-composing aloud in such
   a way that what one is saying is actually being written at the same time.
10. Repeating [re]—repeating written or unwritten phrases a number of
    times.
11. Reading related to the topic:
    (a) Reading the directions [$R_D$]
    (b) Reading the question [$R_q$]
    (c) Reading the statement [$R_s$]
12. Reading related to one's own written product:
    (a) Reading one sentence or a few words [$R^a$]
    (b) Reading a number of sentences together [$R^{a-b}$]
    (c) Reading the entire draft through [$R^{W1}$]
13. Writing silently [W]
14. Writing aloud [TW]
15. Editing [E]
    (a) adding syntactic markers, words, phrases, or clauses [Eadd]
    (b) deleting syntactic markers, words, phrases, or clauses [Edel]
    (c) indicating concern for a grammatical rule [Egr]

(d)  adding, deleting, or considering the use of punctuation [Epunc]

(e)  considering or changing spelling [Esp]

(f)  changing the sentence structure through embedding, coordination or subordination [Ess]

(g)  indicating concern for appropriate vocabulary (word choice) [Ewc]

(h)  considering or changing verb form [Evc]

16.  Periods of silence [s]

By taking specific observable behaviors that occur during composing and supplying labels for them, this system thus far provides a way of analyzing the process that is categorical and capable of replication. In order to view the frequency and the duration of composing behaviors and the relation between one particular behavior and the whole process, these behaviors need to be depicted graphically to show their duration and sequence.   12

## The Continuum

The second component of this system is the construction of a time line and a numbering system. In this study, blank charts with lines like the following were designed:

```
— — — — —  — — — — — —  — — — — — — ⌐ — — — — — — —  — — — — — —  — — — — — —  — — — — — —
    10           20           30           40           50           60           70
```

A ten-digit interval corresponds to one minute and is keyed to a counter on a tape recorder. By listening to the tape and watching the counter, it is possible to determine the nature and duration of each operation. As each behavior is heard on the tape, it is coded and then noted on the chart with the counter used as a time marker. For example, if a student during prewriting reads the directions and the question twice and then begins to plan exactly what she is going to say, all within the first minute, it would be coded like this:   13

Prewriting
——————————
RdRqRdRqPLL
- - - - - - - - -
10

If at this point the student spends two minutes writing the first sentence, during which time she pauses, rereads the question, continues writing, and then edits for spelling before continuing on, it would be coded like this:

1
—————————————————————
$TW_1$ /s/Rq  $TW_1$[Esp]$TW_1$
- - - - - - - - -  - - - - - - -
20              30

At this point two types of brackets and numbering systems have appeared. The initial sublevel number linked with the TW code indicates which draft the student is working on. $TW_1$ indicates the writing of the first draft; $TW_2$ and $TW_3$ indicate the writing of the second and third drafts. Brackets such as [Esp] separate these operations from writing and indicate the amount of time the   14 operation takes. The upper-level number above the horizontal bracket indicates which sentence in the written product is being written and the length of the bracket indicates the amount of time spent on the writing of each sentence. All horizontal brackets refer to sentences, and from the charts it is possible to see when sentences are grouped together and written in a chunk (adjacent brackets) or when each sentence is produced in isolation (gaps between brackets). (See Appendix for sample chart.)

The charts can be read by moving along the time line, noting which behaviors occur and in what sequence. Three types of comments are also included in the charts. In bold-face type, the beginning and end of each draft are indicated; in lighter type-face, comments on the actual composing movements are provided; and in the lightest type-face, specific statements made by students or specific words they found particularly troublesome are noted.          15

From the charts, the following information can be determined:          16

1. the amount of time spent during prewriting;
2. the strategies used during prewriting;
3. the amount of time spent writing each sentence;
4. the behaviors that occur while each sentence is being written;
5. when sentences are written in groups or "chunks" (fluent writing);
6. when sentences are written in isolation (choppy or sporadic writing);
7. the amount of time spent between sentences;
8. the behaviors that occur between sentences;
9. when editing occurs (during the writing of sentences, between sentences, in the time between drafts);
10. the frequency of editing behavior;
11. the nature of the editing operations; and
12. where and in what frequency pauses or periods of silence occur in the process.

The charts, or *composing style sheets* as they are called, do not explain what students wrote but rather *how* they wrote. They indicate, on one page, the sequences of behavior that occur from the beginning of the process to the end. From them it is possible to determine where and how these behaviors fall into patterns and whether these patterns vary according to the mode of discourse.          17

It should be noted that although the coding system is presented before the analysis of the data, it was derived from the data and then used as the basis for generalizing about the patterns and behavioral sequences found within each student's process. These individual patterns were reported in each of the five case studies. Thus, initially, a style sheet was constructed for each writing session on each student. When there were four style sheets for each student, it was possible to determine if composing patterns existed among the group. The summary of results reported here is based on the patterns revealed by these charts.          18

## Analyzing Miscues in the Writing Process

Miscue analysis is based on Goodman's model of the reading process. Created in 1962, it has become a widespread tool for studying what students do when they          19 read and is based on the premise that reading is a psycholinguistic process which "uses language, in written form, to get to the meaning" (Goodman, 1973, p. 4). Miscue analysis "involves its user in examining the observed behavior of oral readers as an interaction between language and thought, as a process of constructing meaning from a graphic display" (Goodman, 1973, p. 4). Methodologically, the observer analyzes the mismatch that occurs when readers make responses during oral reading that differ from the text. This mismatch or miscueing is then analyzed from Goodman's "meaning-getting" model, based on the assumption that "the reader's preoccupation with meaning will show in his miscues, because they will tend to result in language that still makes sense" (Goodman, 1973, p. 9).

In the present study, miscue analysis was adapted from Goodman's model in 20 order to provide insight into the writing process. Since students composed aloud, two types of oral behaviors were available for study: encoding processes or what students spoke while they were writing and decoding processes or what students "read"[1] after they had finished writing. When a discrepancy existed between encoding or decoding and what was on the paper, it was referred to as miscue.

For encoding, the miscue analysis was carried out in the following manner: 21

1. The students' written products were typed, preserving the original style and spelling.
2. What students said while composing aloud was checked against the written products; discrepancies were noted on the paper wherever they occurred,
3. The discrepancies were categorized and counted.

Three miscue categories were derived for encoding: 22

1. Speaking complete ideas but omitting certain words during writing.
2. Pronouncing words with plural markers or other suffixes completely but omitting these endings during writing.
3. Pronouncing the desired word but writing a homonym, an approximation of the word or a personal abbreviation of the word on paper.

For decoding, similar procedures were used, this time comparing the words 23 of the written product with what the student "read" orally. When a discrepancy occurred, it was noted. The discrepancies were then categorized and counted.

Four miscue categories were derived for decoding: 24

1. "Reading in" missing words or word endings;
2. Deleting words or word endings;
3. "Reading" the desired word rather than the word on the page;
4. "Reading" abbreviations and misspellings as though they were written correctly.

A brief summary of the results of this analysis appears in the findings.

---

[1] The word "read" is used in a particular manner here. In the traditional sense, reading refers to accurate decoding of written symbols. Here it refers to students' verbalizing words or endings even when the symbols for those words are missing or only minimally present. Whenever the term "reading" is used in this way, it will be in quotation marks.

## Synopsis of a Case Study

Tony was a 20-year-old ex-Marine born and raised in the Bronx, New York. 25
Like many Puerto Ricans born in the United States, he was able to speak
Spanish, but he considered English his native tongue. In the eleventh grade,
Tony left high school, returning three years later to take the New York State
high school equivalency exam. As a freshman in college, he was also working
part-time to support a child and a wife from whom he was separated.

### Behaviors

The composing style sheets provide an overview of the observable behaviors 26
exhibited by Tony during the composing process. (See Appendix for samples
of Tony's writing and the accompanying composing style sheet.) The most salient feature of Tony's composing process was its recursiveness. Tony rarely
produced a sentence without stopping to reread either a part or the whole.
This repetition set up a particular kind of composing rhythm, one that was cumulative in nature and that set ideas in motion by its very repetitiveness. Thus,
as can be seen from any of the style sheets, talking led to writing which led to
reading which led to planning which again led to writing.

The style sheets indicated a difference in the composing rhythms exhibited 27
in the extensive and reflexive modes. On the extensive topics there was not
only more repetition within each sentence but also many more pauses and repetitions between sentences, with intervals often lasting as long as two minutes.
On the reflexive topics, sentences were often written in groups, with fewer
rereadings and only minimal time intervals separating the creation of one sentence from another.

Editing occurred consistently in all sessions. From the moment Tony began 28
writing, he indicated a concern for correct form that actually inhibited the
development of ideas. In none of the writing sessions did he ever write more
than two sentences before he began to edit. While editing fit into his overall
recursive pattern, it simultaneously interrupted the composing rhythm he had
just initiated.

During the intervals between drafts, Tony read his written work, assessed 29
his writing, planned new phrasings, transitions or endings, read the directions
and the question over, and edited once again.

Tony performed these operations in both the extensive and reflexive modes 30
and was remarkably consistent in all of his composing operations. The style
sheets attest both to this consistency and to the densely packed, tight quality of
Tony's composing process—indeed, if the notations on these sheets were any
indication at all, it was clear that Tony's composing process was so full that
there was little room left for invention or change.

### Fluency

Table 2 provides a numerical analysis of Tony's writing performance. Here 31
it is possible to compare not only the amount of time spent on the various

## Table 2

Tony: Summary of Four Writing Sessions (Time in Minutes)

| | | S1  TW$_1$ | | | | S4  T→W | |
|---|---|---|---|---|---|---|---|
| | Drafts | Words | Time | Drafts | Words | Time | |
| | | | Prewriting:  7.8 | | | Prewriting:  8.0 | |
| Extensive mode | W1 | 132 | 18.8 | W1 | 182 | 29.0 | |
| | W2 | 170 | 51.0 | W2 | 174 | 33.9 | |
| | Total | 302 | Total composing:  91.2* | Total | 356 | Total composing:  82.0* | |
| | | S2  TW$_1$ | | | | S5  T→W | |
| | Drafts | Words | Time | Drafts | Words | Time | |
| | | | Prewriting:  3.5 | | | Prewriting:  5.7 | |
| Reflexive mode | W1 | 165 | 14.5 | W1 | 208 | 24.0 | |
| | W2 | 169 | 25.0 | W2 | 190 | 38.3 | |
| | W3 | 178 | 24.2 | W3 | 152 | 20.8 | |
| | Total | 512 | Total composing:  76.0* | Total | 550 | Total composing:  96.0* | |

\* Total composing includes time spent on editing and rereading, as well as actual writing.

composing operations but also the relative fluency. For Sessions 1 and 2 the data indicate that while Tony spent more time prewriting and writing in the extensive mode, he actually produced fewer words. For Sessions 4 and 5, a similar pattern can be detected. In the extensive mode, Tony again spent more time prewriting and produced fewer words. Although writing time was increased in the reflexive mode, the additional 20 minutes spent writing did not sufficiently account for an increase of 194 words. Rather, the data indicate that Tony produced more words with less planning and generally in less time in the reflexive mode, suggesting that his greater fluency lay in this mode.

### Strategies

Tony exhibited a number of strategies that served him as a writer whether the 32 mode was extensive or reflexive. Given any topic, the first operation he performed was to focus in and narrow down the topic. He did this by rephrasing the topic until either a word or an idea in the topic linked up with something in his own experience (an attitude, an opinion, an event). In this way he established a connection between the field of discourse and himself and at this point he felt ready to write.

### Level of Language Use

Once writing, Tony employed a pattern of classifying or dividing the topic into 33 manageable pieces and then using one or both of the divisions as the basis for narration. In the four writing sessions, his classifications were made on the basis of economic, racial, and political differences. However, all of his writing reflected a low level of generality. No formal principles were used to organize the narratives nor were the implications of ideas present in the essay developed.

In his writing, Tony was able to maintain the extensive/reflexive distinction. 34 He recognized when he was being asked directly for an opinion and when he was being asked to discuss concepts or ideas that were not directly linked to his experience. However, the more distance between the topic and himself, the more difficulty he experienced, and the more repetitive his process became. Conversely, when the topic was close to his own experience, the smoother and more fluent the process became. More writing was produced, pauses were fewer, and positive assessment occurred more often. However, Tony made more assumptions on the part of the audience in the reflexive mode. When writing about himself, Tony often did not stop to explain the context from which he was writing; rather, the reader's understanding of the context was taken for granted.

### Editing

Tony spent a great deal of his composing time editing. However, most of this 35 time was spent proofreading rather than changing, rephrasing, adding, or evaluating the substantive parts of the discourse. Of a total of 234 changes made in all of the sessions, only 24 were related to changes of content and included the following categories:

1. Elaborations of ideas through the use of specification and detail;
2. Additions of modals that shift the mood of a sentence;
3. Deletions that narrow the focus of a paper;
4. Clause reductions or embeddings that tighten the structure of a paper;
5. Vocabulary choices that reflect a sensitivity to language;
6. Reordering of elements in a narrative;
7. Strengthening transitions between paragraphs;
8. Pronoun changes that signal an increased sensitivity to audience.

The 210 changes in form included the following: 36

| Additions | 19 | Verb changes | 4 |
|---|---|---|---|
| Deletions | 44 | Spelling | 95 |
| Word choice | 13 | Punctuation | 35 |
| | | Unresolved problems | 89 |

The area that Tony changed most often was spelling, although, even after completing three drafts of a paper, Tony still had many words misspelled.

### Miscue Analysis

Despite continual proofreading, Tony's completed drafts often retained a look 37 of incompleteness. Words remained misspelled, syntax was uncorrected or overcorrected, suffixes, plural markers, and verb endings were missing, and often words or complete phrases were omitted.

The composing aloud behavior and the miscue analysis derived from it provide 38 one of the first demonstrable ways of understanding how such seemingly incomplete texts can be considered "finished" by the student. (See Table 3 for a summary of Tony's miscues.) Tony consistently voiced complete sentences when composing aloud but only transcribed partial sentences. The same behavior occurred in relation to words with plural or marked endings. However, during rereading and even during editing, Tony supplied the missing endings, words, or phrases and did not seem to "see" what was missing from the text. Thus, when reading his paper, Tony "read in" the meaning he expected to be there which turned him into a reader of content rather than form. However, a difference can be observed between the extensive and reflexive modes, and in the area of correctness Tony's greater strength lay in the reflexive mode. In this mode, not only were more words produced in less time (1,062 vs. 658), but fewer decoding miscues occurred (38 vs. 46), and fewer unresolved problems remained in the text (34 vs. 55).

**Table 3**

Tony—Miscue Analysis

| | ENCODING | | | |
|---|---|---|---|---|
| | Speaking complete ideas but omitting certain words during writing | Pronouncing words with plural markers or other suffixes completely but omitting these endings during writing | Pronouncing the desired word but writing a homonym, an approximation of the word or a personal abbreviation of the word on paper | Total |
| S1 | 1 | 4 | 11 | 16 |
| S2 | 8 | 0 | 14 | 22 |
| S4 | 4 | 0 | 16 | 20 |
| S5 | 3 | 1 | 15 | 19 |
| | 16 | 5 | 56 | 77 |

| | DECODING | | | |
|---|---|---|---|---|
| | Reading in missing words or word endings | Deleting words or word endings | Reading the desired word rather than the word on the page | Reading abbreviations and misspellings as though they were written correctly | Total |
| S1 | 10 | 1 | 1 | 15 | 27 |
| S2 | 5 | 1 | 2 | 10 | 18 |
| S4 | 3 | 3 | 0 | 13 | 19 |
| S5 | 7 | 1 | 2 | 10 | 20 |
| | 25 | 6 | 5 | 48 | 84 |

When Tony did choose to read for form, he was handicapped in another    39
way. Through his years of schooling, Tony learned that there were sets of rules
to be applied to one's writing, and he attempted to apply these rules of form
to his prose. Often, though, the structures he produced were far more complicated than the simple set of proofreading rules he had at his disposal. He was
therefore faced with applying the rule partially, discarding it, or attempting
corrections through sound. None of these systems was completely helpful to
Tony, and as often as a correction was made that improved the discourse, another was made that obscured it.

## Summary

Finally, when Tony completed the writing process, he refrained from com-    40
menting on or contemplating his total written product. When he initiated
writing, he immediately established distance between himself as writer and
his discourse. He knew his preliminary draft might have errors and might
need revision. At the end of each session, the distance had decreased if not
entirely disappeared. Tony "read in" missing or omitted features, rarely perceived syntactic errors, and did not untangle overly embedded sentences. It
was as if the semantic model in his head predominated, and the distance
with which he entered the writing process had dissolved. Thus, even with his
concern for revision and for correctness, even with the enormous amount of
time he invested in rereading and repetition, Tony concluded the composing
process with unresolved stylistic and syntactic problems. The conclusion here
is not that Tony can't write, or that Tony doesn't know how to write, or that
Tony needs to learn more rules: Tony is a writer with a highly consistent
and deeply embedded recursive process. What he needs are teachers who
can interpret that process for him, who can see through the tangles in the
process just as he sees meaning beneath the tangles in his prose, and who can
intervene in such a way that untangling his composing process leads him to
create better prose.

## Summary of the Findings

A major finding of this study is that, like Tony, all of the students studied dis-    41
played consistent composing processes; that is, the behavioral subsequences
prewriting, writing, and editing appeared in sequential patterns that were recognizable across writing sessions and across students.

This consistency suggests a much greater internalization of process than has    42
ever before been suspected. Since the written products of basic writers often
look arbitrary, observers commonly assume that the students' approach is also
arbitrary. However, just as Shaughnessy (1977) points out that there is "very
little that is random . . . in what they have written" (p. 5), so, on close observation, very little appears random in *how* they write. The students observed had
stable composing processes which they used whenever they were presented

with a writing task. While this consistency argues against seeing these students as beginning writers, it ought not necessarily imply that they are proficient writers. Indeed, their lack of proficiency may be attributable to the way in which premature and rigid attempts to correct and edit their work truncate the flow of composing without substantially improving the form of what they have written. More detailed findings will be reviewed in the following subsections which treat the three major aspects of composing: prewriting, writing, and editing.

## Prewriting

When not given specific prewriting instructions, the students in this study be- 43
gan writing within the first few minutes. The average time they spent on prewriting in sessions 1 and 2 was four minutes (see Table 4), and the planning strategies they used fell into three principal types:

1. Rephrasing the topic until a particular word or idea connected with the student's experience. The student then had "an event" in mind before writing began.
2. Turning the large conceptual issue in the topic (e.g., equality) into two manageable pieces for writing (e.g., rich vs. poor; black vs. white).
3. Initiating a string of associations to a word in the topic and then developing one or more of the associations during writing.

When students planned in any of these ways, they began to write with an ar- 44
ticulated sense of where they wanted their discourse to go. However, frequently students read the topic and directions a few times and indicated that they had "no idea" what to write. On these occasions, they began writing without any secure sense of where they were heading, acknowledging only that they would "figure it out" as they went along. Often their first sentence was a rephrasing of the question in the topic which, now that it was in their own handwriting and down on paper in front of them, seemed to enable them to plan what ought to come next. In these instances, writing led to planning which led to clarifying which led to more writing. This sequence of planning and writing, clarifying and discarding, was repeated frequently in all of the sessions, even when students began writing with a secure sense of direction.

Although one might be tempted to conclude that these students began writ- 45
ing prematurely and that planning precisely what they were going to write ought to have occurred before they put pen to paper, the data here suggest:

1. that certain strategies, such as creating an association to a key word, focusing in and narrowing down the topic, dichotomizing and classifying, can and do take place in a relatively brief span of time; and
2. that the developing and clarifying of ideas is facilitated once students translate some of those ideas into written form. In other words, seeing ideas on paper enables students to reflect upon, change and develop those ideas further.

**Table 4**

Overview of All Writing Sessions

| | Prewriting Time* | | | | Total Words / Total Composing Time | | | | Editing Changes | | Unresolved Problems | Miscues During Reading |
|---|---|---|---|---|---|---|---|---|---|---|---|---|
| | S1 | S2 | S4 | S5 | S1 | S2 | S4 | S5 | Content | Form | | |
| Tony | 7.8 | 3.5 | 8.0 | 5.7 | 302 91.2 | 512 76.0 | 356 82.0 | 550 96.0 | 24 | 210 | 89 | 84 |
| Dee | 2.5 | 2.9 | 5.0 | 5.0 | 409 55.5 | 559 65.0 | 91 24.5 | 212 29.0 | 7 | 24 | 40 | 32 |
| Stan | 3.5 | 4.3 | 14.8 | 14.7 | 419 62.0 | 553 73.1 | 365 73.0 | 303 68.0 | 13 | 49 | 45 | 55 |
| Lueller | 2.0 | 1.5 | 4.0 | 13.0 | 518 90.8 | 588 96.8 | 315 93.0 | 363 77.8 | 2 | 167 | 143 | 147 |
| Beverly | 5.5 | 7.0 | 32.0 | 20.0 | 519 79.0 | 536 80.3 | 348 97.4 | 776 120.0 | 21 | 100 | 55 | 30 |

*Due to a change in the prewriting directions, only Sessions 1 and 2 are used to calculate the average time spent in prewriting.

## Writing

Careful study revealed that students wrote by shuttling from the sense of what 46
they wanted to say forward to the words on the page and back from the words
on the page to their intended meaning. This "back and forth" movement appeared to be a recursive feature: at one moment students were writing, moving
their ideas and their discourse forward; at the next they were backtracking,
rereading, and digesting what had been written.

Recursive movements appeared at many points during the writing process. 47
Occasionally sentences were written in groups and then reread as a "piece" of
discourse; at other times sentences and phrases were written alone, repeated
until the writer was satisfied or worn down, or rehearsed until the act of rehearsal led to the creation of a new sentence. In the midst of writing, editing
occurred as students considered the surface features of language. Often planning of a global nature took place: in the midst of producing a first draft,
students stopped and began planning how the second draft would differ from
the first. Often in the midst of writing, students stopped and referred to the
topic in order to check if they had remained faithful to the original intent, and
occasionally, though infrequently, they identified a sentence or a phrase that
seemed, to them, to produce a satisfactory ending. In all these behaviors, they
were shuttling back and forth, projecting what would come next and doubling
back to be sure of the ground they had covered.

A number of conclusions can be drawn from the observations of these stu- 48
dents composing and from the comments they made: although they produced
inadequate or flawed products, they nevertheless seemed to understand and
perform some of the crucial operations involved in composing with skill. While
it cannot be stated with certainty that the patterns they displayed are shared by
other writers, some of the operations they performed appear sufficiently sound
to serve as prototypes for constructing two major hypotheses on the nature of
their composing processes. Whether the following hypotheses are borne out in
studies of different types of writers remains an open question:

1. Composing does not occur in a straightforward, linear fashion. The process is one of accumulating discrete bits down on the paper and then
   working from those bits to reflect upon, structure, and then further develop what one means to say. It can be thought of as a kind of "retrospective
   structuring"; movement forward occurs only after one has reached back,
   which in turn occurs only after one has some sense of where one wants
   to go. Both aspects, the reaching back and the sensing forward, have a
   clarifying effect.
2. Composing always involves some measure of both construction and discovery. Writers construct their discourse inasmuch as they begin with a
   sense of what they want to write. This sense, as long as it remains implicit,
   is not equivalent to the explicit form it gives rise to. Thus, a process of constructing meaning is required. Rereading or backward movements become
   a way of assessing whether or not the words on the page adequately capture
   the original sense intended. Constructing simultaneously affords discovery.

Writers know more fully what they mean only after having written it. In this way the explicit written form serves as a window on the implicit sense with which one began.

## Editing

Editing played a major role in the composing processes of the students in this 49 study (see Table 5). Soon after students began writing their first drafts, they began to edit, and they continued to do so during the intervals between drafts, during the writing of their second drafts and during the final reading of papers.

While editing, the students were concerned with a variety of items: the lexi- 50 con (i.e., spelling, word choice, and the context of words); the syntax (i.e., grammar, punctuation, and sentence structure); and the discourse as a whole (i.e., organization, coherence, and audience). However, despite the students' considered attempts to proofread their work, serious syntactic and stylistic problems remained in their finished drafts. The persistence of these errors may, in part, be understood by looking briefly at some of the problems that arose for these students during editing.

## Rule Confusion

(1) All of the students observed asked themselves, "Is this sentence [or feature] 51 correct?" but the simple set of editing rules at their disposal was often inappropriate for the types of complicated structures they produced. As a result, they misapplied what they knew and either created a hypercorrection or impaired the meaning they had originally intended to clarify; (2) The students observed attempted to write with terms they heard in lectures or class discussions, but since they were not yet familiar with the syntactic or semantic constraints one word placed upon another, their experiments with academic language resulted in what Shaughnessy (1977, p. 49) calls, "lexical transplants" or "syntactic dissonances"; (3) The students tried to rely on their intuitions about language,

## Table 5

Editing Changes

|  | TONY | DEE | STAN | LUELLER | BEVERLY | TOTALS |
|---|---|---|---|---|---|---|
| Total number of words produced | 1720 | 1271 | 1640 | 1754 | 2179 | 8564 |
| Total form | 210 | 24 | 49 | 167 | 100 | 550 |
| Additions | 19 | 2 | 10 | 21 | 11 | 63 |
| Deletions | 44 | 9 | 18 | 41 | 38 | 150 |
| Word choice | 13 | 4 | 1 | 27 | 6 | 51 |
| Verb changes | 4 | 1 | 2 | 7 | 12 | 26 |
| Spelling | 95 | 4 | 13 | 60 | 19 | 191 |
| Punctuation | 35 | 4 | 5 | 11 | 14 | 69 |
| Total content | 24 | 7 | 13 | 2 | 21 | 67 |

in particular the sound of words. Often, however, they had been taught to mistrust what "sounded" right to them, and they were unaware of the particular feature in their speech codes that might need to be changed in writing to match the standard code. As a result, when they attempted corrections by sound, they became confused, and they began to have difficulty differentiating between what sounded right in speech and what needed to be marked on the paper.

## Selective Perception

These students habitually reread their papers from internal semantic or meaning models. They extracted the meaning they wanted from the minimal cues on the page, and they did not recognize that outside readers would find those cues insufficient for meaning. 52

A study of Table 6 indicates that the number of problems remaining in the students' written products approximates the number of miscues produced during reading. This proximity, itself, suggests that many of these errors persisted because the students were so certain of the words they wanted to have on the page that they "read in" these words even when they were absent; in other words, they reduced uncertainty by operating as though what was in their heads was already on the page. The problem of selective perception, then, cannot be reduced solely to mechanical decoding; the semantic model from which students read needs to be acknowledged and taken into account in any study that attempts to explain how students write and why their completed written products end up looking so incomplete. 53

## Egocentricity

The students in this study wrote from an egocentric point of view. While they occasionally indicated a concern for their readers, they more often took the reader's understanding for granted. They did not see the necessity of making their referents explicit, of making the connections among their ideas apparent, of carefully and explicitly relating one phenomenon to another, or of placing narratives or generalizations within an orienting, conceptual framework. 54

On the basis of these observations one may be led to conclude that these writers did not know how to edit their work. Such a conclusion must, however, be drawn with care. Efforts to improve their editing need to be based on an informed view of the role that editing already plays in their composing processes. Two conclusions in this regard are appropriate here: 55

1. Editing intrudes so often and to such a degree that it breaks down the rhythms generated by thinking and writing. When this happens the students are forced to go back and recapture the strands of their thinking once the editing operation has been completed. Thus, editing occurs prematurely, before students have generated enough discourse to approximate the ideas they have, and it often results in their losing track of their ideas.
2. Editing is primarily an exercise in error-hunting. The students are prematurely concerned with the "look" of their writing; thus, as soon as a

## Table 6

The Talk-Write Paradigm Miscues—Decoding Behaviors

|  | TONY | DEE | STAN | LUELLER | BEVERLY | TOTALS |
|---|---|---|---|---|---|---|
| Unresolved problems | 89 | 40 | 45 | 143 | 55 | 372 |
| "Reading in" missing words or word endings | 25 | 13 | 11 | 44 | 11 | 104 |
| Deleting words or word endings | 6 | 2 | 4 | 14 | 9 | 35 |
| "Reading" the desired word rather than the word on the page | 5 | 6 | 18 | 15 | 8 | 52 |
| "Reading" abbreviations and misspellings as though they were written correctly | 48 | 11 | 22 | 74 | 2 | 157 |
|  | 84 | 32 | 55 | 147 | 30 | 348 |

few words are written on the paper, detection and correction of errors replaces writing and revising. Even when they begin writing with a tentative, flexible frame of mind, they soon become locked into whatever is on the page. What they seem to lack as much as any rule is a conception of editing that includes flexibility, suspended judgment, the weighing of possibilities, and the reworking of ideas.

## Implications for Teaching and Research

One major implication of this study pertains to teachers' conceptions of un- 56 skilled writers. Traditionally, these students have been labeled "remedial," which usually implies that teaching ought to remedy what is "wrong" in their written products. Since the surface features in the writing of unskilled writers seriously interfere with the extraction of meaning from the page, much class time is devoted to examining the rules of the standard code. The pedagogical soundness of this procedure has been questioned frequently,[2] but in spite of the

---

[2] For discussions on the controversy over the effects of grammar instruction on writing ability, see the following: Richard Braddock, Richard Lloyd-Jones, and Lowell Schoer, *Research in Written Composition* (Urbana, Ill.: National Council of Teachers of English, 1963); Frank O'Hare, *Sentence Combining* (NCTE Research Report No. 15, Urbana, Ill.: National Council of Teachers of English, 1973); Elizabeth F. Haynes, "Using Research in Preparing to Teach Writing," *English Journal*, 1978, 67, 82–89.

debate, the practice continues, and it results in a further complication, namely that students begin to conceive of writing as a "cosmetic" process where concern for correct form supersedes development of ideas. As a result, the excitement of composing, of constructing and discovering meaning, is cut off almost before it has begun.

More recently, unskilled writers have been referred to as "beginners," implying that teachers can start anew. They need not "punish" students for making mistakes, and they need not assume that their students have already been taught how to write. Yet this view ignores the highly elaborated, deeply embedded processes the students bring with them. These unskilled college writers are not beginners in a *tabula rasa* sense, and teachers err in assuming they are. The results of this study suggest that teachers may first need to identify which characteristic components of each student's process facilitate writing and which inhibit it before further teaching takes place. If they do not, teachers of unskilled writers may continue to place themselves in a defeating position: imposing another method of writing instruction upon the students' already internalized processes without first helping students to extricate themselves from the knots and tangles in those processes. 57

A second implication of this study is that the composing process is now amenable to a replicable and graphic mode of representation as a sequence of codable behaviors. The composing style sheets provide researchers and teachers with the first demonstrable way of documenting how individual students write. Such a tool may have diagnostic as well as research benefits. It may be used to record writing behaviors in large groups, prior to and after instruction, as well as in individuals. Certainly it lends itself to the longitudinal study of the writing process and may help to elucidate what it is that changes in the process as writers become more skilled. 58

A third implication relates to case studies and to the theories derived from them. This study is an illustration of the way in which a theoretical model of the composing process can be grounded in observations of the individual's experience of composing. It is precisely the complexity of this experience that the case study brings to light. However, by viewing a series of cases, the researcher can discern patterns and themes that suggest regularities in composing behavior across individuals. These common features lead to hypotheses and theoretical formulations which have some basis in shared experience. How far this shared experience extends is, of course, a question that can only be answered through further research. 59

A final implication derives from the preponderance of recursive behaviors in the composing processes studied here, and from the theoretical notion derived from these observations: retrospective structuring, or the going back to the sense of one's meaning in order to go forward and discover more of what one has to say. Seen in this light, composing becomes the carrying forward of an implicit sense into explicit form. Teaching composing, then, means paying attention not only to the forms or products but also to the explicative process through which they arise. 60

# Appendix

## Composing Style Sheet

Name: Tony   Mode: Extensive TW₁   Date: October 31, 1975

Session: 1   Topic: Society & Culture   Time: 11:00 AM - 12:30 PM

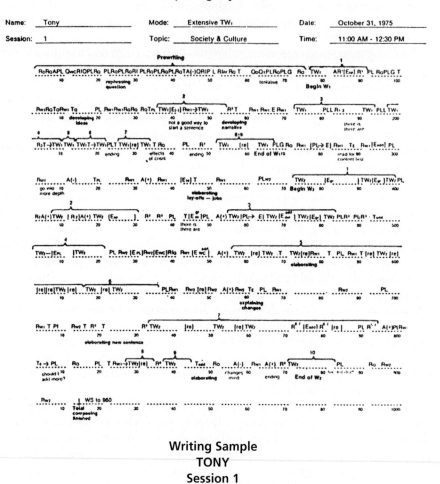

## Writing Sample
## TONY
## Session 1
## W1

All men can't be consider equal in a America base on financial situation.[1] Because their

are men born in rich families that will never have to worry about any financial difficulties.[2]

And then theyre /~~the~~ ^are^ another type of Americans that is born to a poor family and

alway / ^may^ have some kind of fina—difficulty.[3] Espeicaly nowadays in New York city With

the bugdit Crisis / ^and all^ ^If he is able^.[4] ~~He may~~ be able To get a job.[5] But are now he lose the job just

as easy as he got it.[6] So when he loses his job he'll have to try to get some fina—assistance.[7]

~~A~~ Then he'll probley have even more fin—diffuicuty.[8] So right / ^here^ you can't see that In

Ameria~~n~~, all men are not create equal in the fin—sense.[9]

## Writing Sample
## TONY
## Session 1
## W2

All men can not be consider equal in America base on financial situations.[1] Because

their are men born in rich families that will never have to worry about any financial dif-

the
fuel diffuliculties.[2] And then they're are / another type of ameicans that are born to a poor

may
family.[3] And This is the type of Americans that ~~will~~ / alway have some kind of finanical

dif*uliculty.[4] Espeical today ~~today the~~in new york The way the city has fallen ~~has fallen~~

working
into fin—debt.[5] It has become such a big crisis for the ~~people~~ people, in the [6] If the
with the                                           the                    ~~is~~
working man is able to find a job, espeicaly ~~for~~ / ~~city~~ a city The way ~~the way~~ city / fin—

sitionu is set up now, ~~h~~He'll probley lose the job a whole lot faster than what he got it.[7]

When he loses his job he'll ~~p~~ have even more fin—difficulty.[8] And then he'll be force to

go~~t~~ to the city for some fini—assi—.[9] So right here you can see that all men in America

are not create equal in the fin—sense.[10]

## References

Braddock, R., Lloyd-Jones, R., & Schoer, L. *Research in written composition.* Urbana, Ill.: National Council of Teachers of English, 1963.

Britton, J., Burgess, T., Martin, N., McLeod, A., & Rosen, H. *The development of writing abilities (11–18).* London: Macmillan Education Ltd., 1975.

Burton, D. L. Research in the teaching of English: The troubled dream. *Research in the Teaching of English*, 1973, 1, 160–187.

Cooper, C. R. Doing research/reading research. *English Journal*, 1974, 63, 94–99.

Cooper, C. R., & Odell, L. (Eds.) *Research on composing: Points of departure.* Urbana, Ill.: National Council of Teachers of English, 1978.

Emig, J. A. On teaching composition: Some hypotheses as definitions. *Research in the Teaching of English*, 1967, 1, 127–135.

Emig, J. A. *The composing processes of twelfth graders.* Urbana, Ill.: National Council of Teachers of English, 1971. (Research Report No. 13) (Ed. D. Dissertation, Harvard University, 1969).

Goodman, K. S. (Ed.) *Miscue analysis: Applications to reading instruction.* Urbana, Ill.: NCTE and ERIC, 1973.

Graves, D. H. Children's writing: Research directions and hypotheses based upon an examination of the writing process of seven year old children (Doctoral dissertation, State University of New York at Buffalo, 1973). *Dissertation Abstracts International*, 1974, 34, 6255A.

Haynes, E. F. Using research in preparing to teach writing. *English Journal*, 1978, 67, 82–89.

Mischel, T. A case study of a twelfth-grade writer. *Research in the Teaching of English*, 1974, 8, 303–314.

O'Hare, F. *Sentence-combining: Improving student writing without formal grammar instruction.* Urbana, Ill.: National Council of Teachers of English, 1973. (Research Report No. 15).

Perl, S. *Five writers writing: Case studies of the composing processes of unskilled college writers.* Unpublished doctoral dissertation, New York University, 1978.

Pianko, S. *The composing acts of college freshmen writers.* Unpublished Ed.D. dissertation, Rutgers University, 1977.

Shaughnessy, M. P. *Errors and expectations: A guide for the teacher of basic writing.* New York: Oxford University Press, 1977.

Stallard, C. K. An analysis of the writing behavior of good student writers. *Research in the Teaching of English,* 1974, *8,* 206–218.

.........................................................................................................................................

## Questions for Discussion and Journaling

1. Perl notes that Tony's writing process and resulting text were markedly different when he was writing about his own experience and when he was trying to write less personally. Describe this difference and explain whether it makes sense to you.

2. Why does Perl take it as such a positive sign that Tony and her other research participants' composing processes are "consistent" rather than scattered or random?

3. One of Perl's questions is whether writing processes can be analyzed in a "systematic, replicable" manner (para. 2). What do you think she means by those two terms?

4. Find the section of the article where Perl discusses how she developed her "code" of composing behaviors. What is your sense of how she put it together, and at what point in her research did she do so?

5. Build a list of reasons Perl is critical of previous writing-process research, and explain each of them. How well would you say her research here overcomes or eliminates those problems?

6. Do you think Perl's research methods might have actively shaped the writing her participants produced? That is, if she had changed the design of her study, is it possible she would have gotten different writing from her participants? Explain.

7. Perl appears not to count changes made while drafting sentence-by-sentence as "editing"; instead, she reserves that term for changes made between drafts. Why do you think she makes that distinction?

8. Do you see your own composing as "the carrying forward of an implicit sense into explicit form" (para. 60)? How so, and how not?

## Applying and Exploring Ideas

1. Put together a list of the problems Tony had with composing and editing—for example, his tendency to say a sentence one way but write down something else. As you review the list, do you see problems that you've had trouble with in the past, or any you still have trouble with? If so, how did you solve them—or what have you tried that hasn't worked? Discuss this question with one or more classmates: Have they encountered the problem of selective perception, for example? If so, how have they dealt with it?

2. Perl argues that it's a good thing when people don't wait to write until they know everything they want to say—rather, she wants writers to use the clarifying power of the act of writing itself to help them figure out what they want to say. To what extent does this strategy resemble your own writing process?

3. Perl was researching in a time before camcorders. Today, to do the same research, we would not only set up a camera (thus recording the participant's speech, behaviors, and writing activity simultaneously and in real time) but possibly also capture their keystrokes (assuming they composed at a computer) for a microscopically accurate record of exactly how the participant was writing. If you have a camcorder, try recording yourself or a volunteer while he or she writes, and then use the recording to help you devise a code to explain the processes you recorded. If that's not possible, consider: If you were doing Perl's study today, how would you design it to take advantage of current technology and your own ideas about the writing process? What kind of code would you devise to explain the activity that your technology recorded?

**Meta Moment**
Name one thing you now understand or will do differently after reading about Tony's process.

# Joining the Engineering Community: How Do Novices Learn to Write Like Engineers?

## DOROTHY A. WINSOR

■ Winsor, Dorothy A. "Joining the Engineering Community: How Do Novices Learn to Write Like Engineers?" *Technical Communication* 37.2 (1990): 171–72. Print.

## Framing the Reading

Dorothy A. Winsor retired from Iowa State University, where she focused her research on the writing and rhetoric of engineers. A large proportion of what the field of writing studies knows about how engineers write, we know because of Winsor's work. She had two major books in this area, *Writing Like an Engineer: A Rhetorical Education*, and *Writing Power: An Ethnographic Study of Writing in an Engineering Center*. She also was editor of the *Journal of Business and Technical Communication*, the leading scholarly journal in technical communication. Her typical method of conducting research was to interview people, gather a large corpus of their writing, and compare how they talked about writing with what they *did* when they wrote (as evidenced by the resulting texts). Winsor showed that if you want to understand how writing and texts supported or mediated an activity, you have to examine very carefully how what the texts actually *do* in making the activity what it is.

The article included here is quite short and was written fairly early in Winsor's studies of engineering writing that led to her two books. It appeared in a special section of the scholarly journal *Technical Communication*. Usually, space in journals is given to research that is already completed or at least where the writer is already reporting substantive findings from their research project. Almost everything you read in *Writing about Writing* falls in that category. But at the time Winsor's piece was published, *Technical Communication* was also making a few pages available for researchers to report on projects that *weren't* finished yet, but were instead in progress, and in their early stages, before the researcher was drawing many conclusions. The instructions the journal editors gave regarding this work were: "Readers are invited to contribute reports on in-progress research. Entries should include the rationale, methods, and preliminary results of the research and should not exceed one thousand words in

length" (about the length of a three-page, double-spaced essay). So, as you read Winsor's piece, you should consider how different her rhetorical situation was from many of the longer research-based pieces you read in *Writing about Writing*.

It may help you in reading this piece to understand that when Winsor asks whether "novice employees" learn to write "via models or mentoring" (para. 1), she engages what at the time (the end of the 1980s) was an important conversation in the field about that exact question: How much can people actually learn to write by following models? On the one hand, it seems intuitive that people learning to write should be able to take an example and "copy" or *imitate* its structure, moves, look, feel, and sound. But that is sometimes surprisingly hard to do—you have to understand a thing fairly well before you can imitate it well. And at the same time, if writers are learning mostly by imitation, when do they learn how to make their own designs for writing? So there's some discomfort with modeling, even though it looks like it should work well, and even though it's fairly difficult for most people to write a kind of text *well* if they've never seen that kind of text before. At the time Winsor wrote this piece, learning to write via models was not accepted by all writing teachers and scholars (and still isn't). While Winsor doesn't take space in her very short one thousand words to explain all this, if you read the piece with that question in mind, you'll see the places where she's thinking about it.

## Getting Ready to Read

*Before you read,* do at least one of the following activities:

- Use Wikipedia to look up the terms *tacit knowledge* and *exemplar*.
- Remember a time you were given a model of a piece of writing and asked to create another piece of writing like it.

*As you read,* consider the following questions:

- What concepts are you encountering in Winsor's work that seem to overlap with ideas you've read elsewhere in this book?
- Apart from the teacher of your current writing course, do you have any "expert" writers helping you build your writing abilities now? Have you in the past?

........................................................................................................

The current interest in discourse communities has raised the question of how novices learn the communication practices of disciplines and organizations. How and when do novice employees learn to write effectively? Do they learn to write via models or mentoring? Do they learn in their technical writing courses in school what they need to know to write effectively on the job? Or are there aspects of technical writing that can be learned only at work? This article reports on early findings of a study aimed at answering this last question and points out directions for further research which these early findings suggest.

## A Preliminary Study

As an early step in this study, I collected written statements from 190 seniors at 2 a co-operative engineering college. These students had alternated three-month periods of school and full-time work from the time they entered college. They had accumulated an average of 21 months of work experience and thus may be taken as a sample of novice engineers.

They were asked to write open-ended reports on the writing they had done 3 at work and how they learned to do it. The open-ended nature of the task meant that 13% of the students made no mention of how they had learned to write. For the students who did cite learning methods, the most commonly given one was the use of models (cited by 53% of the students), followed by advice/editing from supervisors (38%), advice/editing from co-workers (24%), a college technical writing class they all were required to take as freshmen (14%), high school training (7%), classes at work (5%), and work evaluations (5%). The descriptions students wrote of their activities also indicate that much learning took place from sink-or-swim experience.

These statistics suggest that students perceive abstract rules and training, 4 represented by various kinds of classes, as *least* useful among the cited learning methods. In contrast, the students see the embodied experience of models and interaction with experts as most productive, particularly when combined with practice and feedback.

## Students' Comments

Students' comments on their learning give further insight into what these sta- 5 tistics mean. Students indicate that a typical learning pattern is to use models and seek advice from co-workers when preparing drafts, submit the draft to a supervisor, and use the supervisor's feedback to revise.

When students comment on the use of models, they most often say that what 6 they get from the models is, as one student says, "help with the format and style that is generally used at my plant." Such models are useful, says another student, "because the audience is familiar with certain formats." As can be seen from both these comments, these novice engineers typically regard format as a matter of local convention, rather than something right or wrong. Sometimes, this understanding is explicit, as in the following remark: "As it is in most companies, they all have their set ways of doing things. Even if there is a better way of preparing a report, they don't want to hear about it."

> Students indicate that a typical learning pattern is to use models and seek advice from coworkers when preparing drafts, submit the draft to a supervisor, and use the supervisor's feedback to revise.

These comments might suggest 7 that students see formats as solely a matter of using conventional arrangement to declare themselves members of the work community. Other comments, however, suggest that this is not so and that "format" is extended to mean something more like genre, governing content as well as arrangement (Cf. Winker [I]). One non-native speaker, for instance, reports reading models repeatedly as to "understand what they have to say in these kinds of reports." Another student reports using "an earlier report as a basis for my analysis as well as an outline for my actual report." A third says he used models for "what was expected to be presented in the report and the desired report format."

To supplement these models, students often seek out the help of more experienced co-workers, who offer advice on rhetorical matter as well as on content and form. Thus one student says co-workers "taught me the essentials of writing a report," which were "writing at the level of the audience, information breakdown and organization for this audience, and basic technical report format." And another, who had to write the minutes of a volatile meeting, says that "co-workers advised me on the points of emphasis and stressed the importance of detailing the results of the meeting." 8

Supervisors provide feedback on all areas of writing but are most valued by these students for their advice on political matters. Thus one student reports, "Throughout my work experiences I have had supervisors who were kind enough to give me advice on terms to use and not to use in certain situations. This is especially important when dealing with highly political issues in which the documentation may be around for years to come." And a typical story is told by another student who, as a freshman, was asked to evaluate a software system: "In my opinion, the software really stunk, and my report reflected these feelings. Luckily, I had my boss review it before I sent it out. He got a real kick out of it, but said it had to he toned down before I sent it out." 9

Overall, students remark on the value of experience: "Communication skills cannot be learned solely from a textbook. The style of writing in a workplace can only be learned from experience"; "My skills in this area were gained less through the use of advice or examples and more through necessity"; "School can show us the reins but we won't really learn to control the horse until we ride it." 10

## Implications

While these statistics and comments are interesting, they raise more questions than they answer, particularly about what these young engineers mean when they say they use models. Precisely how did they use models and what did they learn from them? A recent study by Warren W. Werner articulates some of the problems teachers see in students' use of models in technical writing classes [2]. Werner distinguishes the abstract pattern of a model from the concrete examples in textbooks and says students often copy examples slavishly, fail to generalize to the model, and therefore do not learn anything transferrable to situations which differ from the one the example originally addressed. 11

Our understanding of the use of models is made more complicated if we see them as analogous to genres. Charles Bazerman sees many of the same limitations in textbook treatment of genre that Werner sees in student use of 12 examples. Bazerman eschews the notion "that there are simple genres that must be slavishly followed, that we must give students an appropriate set of cookie cutters for their anticipated careers" [3].

On the other hand, Bazerman does see a positive role for genres. A genre, 13 he says, represents a solution to a common rhetorical problem in an area. His definition echoes the work of Carolyn Miller, who says a genre is "typified rhetorical action" encompassing both form and substance [4]. Furthermore, Miller and Selzer have shown that in engineering documents, genre expectations are mixed with those of discipline and organization [5].

It is possible to see use of models as one way individuals interact with sur- 14 rounding socioculture to achieve assimilation into discourse communities. In this sense, models can function like Kuhnian exemplars, that is, as shared examples of acceptable work which train a student to function like an engineer in an organization [6].

If students are learning from models in this way, then a lot of their learning 15 may be tacit. H. M. Collins writes about his own experience as a participant/ observer trying to build a laser [7]. He concludes that much skill-like knowledge is unlearnable by means of rules. He claims such learning takes place only by means of actual contact between expert and novice, a conclusion which squares well with students' citing as a learning method not only imitation but also advice or editing from supervisors and co-workers.

Collins makes the interesting point that once skill has been achieved, many 16 learners perceive what they have learned as a rule and blame themselves for not having taken it in earlier. Collins claims, however, that learners have taken in far more than can be explained by rules. They have assimilated tacit knowledge which, as he says, weaves them into a social network.

If novice engineers are able to use models both as temporary crutches to 17 compensate for their own lack of experience with the complex rhetorical demands of their workplace and as aids to acquiring tacit knowledge of those demands, then it is not surprising that models are useful.

## Next Step

None of these speculations is confirmable with the data I have from students' 18 reports. My next step will be to observe a limited number of young engineers writing at work, and interview them and their supervisors about the relationship between their writing and models they work from. I hope to answer such questions as these:

1. How do novices select models? How do they recognize a good model?
2. What areas do they consciously attend to in imitating a model?
3. Do they use models early in the writing process, with consequences for invention, or late in the process, with consequences primarily for shaping?
4. How do they know when they've done a good job of imitating a model? Do their supervisors agree on which imitations arc successful?

5. How local is the knowledge they gain from models? Will it transfer to other companies or departments?
6. Which imitated areas seem most central to their roles as engineers and employees?

## References

1. Victoria M. Winkler, "The Role of Models in Technical and Scientific Writing," in *New Essays in Technical and Scientific Communication*, eds. Paul V. Anderson, R. John Brockmann, and Carolyn R. Miller (Farmingdale, N.Y.: Baywood. 1983), 111–22.
2. Warren W. Werner, "Models and the Teaching of Technical Writing," *Journal of Technical Writing and Communication* 19, 1 (1989): 69–81.
3. Charles Bazerman, *Shaping Written Knowledge* (Madison: University of Wisconsin Press, 1988), 8, 62.
4. Carolyn R. Miller, "Genre as Social Action." *Quarterly Journal of Speech* 70, 2 (1984): 151–67.
5. Carolyn R. Miller and Jack Selzer. "Special Topics of Argument in Engineering Reports," in *Writing in Nonacademic Settings*, eds. Lee Odell and Dixie Goswami (N.Y.: Guilford, 1985), 309–41.
6. Thomas S. Kuhn, *The Structure of Scientific Revolutions* (Chicago: University of Chicago Press. 1970).
7. H.M. Collins, *Changing Order* (Beverly Hills, CA: Sage, 1985).

## Questions for Discussion and Journaling

1. Winsor's opening sentence makes an assertion and an assumption: "The current interest in discourse communities has raised the question of how novices learn the communication practices of disciplines and organizations." What does Winsor assume her audience already knows and agrees with before they even begin reading her article? And how does that shape who her audience can be?

2. From the "Student Comments" section of the article, choose three comments that sound "right" to you and three that don't, and explain why.

3. If you have enough experience with writing outside school to offer your own opinion on Winsor's question in her first paragraph, what would you say? What can and can't school teach about writing outside of school (or, specifically, workplace writing)?

4. Get your Google on and search the term *Kuhnian exemplar* (para. 14). What's Winsor talking about?

5. We expect you were unsurprised that the students Winsor talked to "perceive abstract rules and training, represented by various kinds of classes, as *least* useful among the cited learning methods" (para. 4). If you wanted to make an argument *for* using and teaching some of the abstract rules and training you encounter in classes, what would you say?

6. Winsor uses Warren Werner's research to point out a potential problem with learning via models: that a writer may "copy examples slavishly" and thus not do the kind of learning which will transfer to later writing situations. Yet Winsor's research suggests that there *is* some important kind of learning happening via models. How would you summarize her explanation of how/when models can be useful?

7. Do you have any answers from your own experience to the five questions Winsor poses at the end of her article (under "Next Step") on how writers actually use models?

## Applying and Exploring Ideas

1. Write a short literacy narrative in which you focus specifically on how you've used models as you've learned to write various kinds of texts both inside and outside of school. For example, how often were you given models when you were assigned a kind of writing? How well did using models work for you—what was good and bad about having them?

2. Think of a specific kind (genre) of writing that you had to learn in one setting and then use later on in other settings. It might be a kind of essay or report (kinds of writing you probably associate with school), or a kind of writing you use out of school—letters, invitations, party flyers, newspaper stories, etc. Whatever genre you settle on, think back to how you initially learned to write it, and then think about what *changed* (if anything) when you had to use the same genre in a different setting from where/how you learned it. What did you have to do differently? What knowledge about that kind of writing "transferred" from where you learned it to other places where you used it later? What knowledge didn't transfer? Did anyone help you figure out the transition or did you have to understand it on your own?

3. Paraphrasing Collins, Winsor writes about "assimilat[ing] tacit knowledge" which "weaves [us] into a social network" (para. 16). Look up the term *tacit knowledge* (we recommend its Wikipedia page). Then, through class discussion or working in groups, talk with other students about examples from your own experiences of, first, becoming part of a social network (which is another term for activity system, which you learned in Chapter 2), and second, what tacit knowledge that social network expected you to learn in order to become a member.

4. Make a list of each specific kind (or genre) of writing Winsor mentions in the article. She talks about "writing" a lot, but she doesn't say much about particular genres. If you wanted to find out about more genres of engineering writing, how would you go about it? Write a research plan for what electronic or human resources you'd use to build a catalog of genres of writing in engineering.

### Meta Moment

If you are currently learning various kinds of writing (or writing abilities) through the use of models, how are you making sure that you learn knowledge that you'll be able to use in later writing situations?

# Late Nights, Last Rites, and the Rain-Slick Road to Self-Destruction

## THOMAS OSBORNE

■ Osborne, Thomas. "Late Nights, Last Rites, and the Rain-Slick Road to Self-Destruction." *Stylus* 2.2 (Fall 2011): 1–4. Web. 15 Jan. 2014.

## Framing the Reading

Thomas Osborne wrote this paper for Matthew Bryan's ENC 1101 class at the University of Central Florida. It was revised and subsequently published in UCF's peer-reviewed journal for first-year students, *Stylus*, and it later won him an award at the 2nd Annual Knights Write Showcase.

This is a reflective, conversational account of Osborne's struggle with writing and how what he calls the "spectacular failure" of his attempts to compose in response to the assignment led him to the ideas he describes here. One of the reasons that we have included Osborne's essay is that he describes the difficulty of letting go of his words and ideas once they are written and admitting that he needs to "just start over" (para. 3). Many of the other authors in this chapter talk about the difficulty—and necessity—of sometimes doing this. Sondra Perl, for example, describes how her case study, "Tony," simply can't get away from the words he has already put on the page, and how he labors over them without considering that he could start anew. Nancy Sommers describes the difficulty students have in seeing revision as anything more than changing words or sentences.

Another reason we have included Osborne's essay is that he analyzes his "failed" piece of writing to examine his writing style and attempt to strengthen it. He describes, for example, how his ingrained need to correct every grammar error causes him to lose ideas that never make it to the page.

## Getting Ready to Read

*Before you read*, do the following activity:

- Consider your own attitude toward revising text once you have written it.

*As you read*, consider the following questions:

- Compare yourself as a writer to Osborne's description of himself as a writer. How are you similar? How are you different?

STYLUS:
*A JOURNAL OF FIRST-YEAR WRITING*
VOLUME 2 | ISSUE 2 | FALL 2011

Late Nights, Last Rites,
and the Rain-Slick Road
to Self-Destruction
THOMAS OSBORNE

Reconceiving, Using Confirmation
and Repetition to Your Advantage
ABBEY NARRO

Disney Princess Series: More than Your
Average Fairy Tales
KRISTA BOUGGARD

Discourse Communities and Orients
CHANTENI FRAZIER

Rhetorical Criticism of Online Discourse
BRANDON JONES

The Journal of the First-Year
Writing Program at the
University of Central Florida

It's three in the morning. A rainy night on a date of no importance in par- 1
ticular. The headlights of a student just now pulling into the parking lot
grab my attention. I scoff, inwardly scolding the stranger for being up so
late. And yet, here I am, sipping coffee at three in the morning. I have been
working on this stupid essay for four days now, and, tonight, for eight hours
straight. I'm tired and frustrated to the point where I would scream if I knew
it wouldn't wake my roommates. The sentence you are reading right now
was jotted down after six arduous paragraphs of stale, rambling fluff. Most
people have written this sort of thing at one point or another. It's the kind of
writing that you want to tear out and burn so that no other human being on
the planet is able to bear witness to the catastrophic failure that has sprung
forth from your mind. In fact, that is exactly what I did: I just erased several
dozen hours of hard work from existence. Despite this, I find myself smiling
as I recline comfortably (not really) in my dorm-supplied wooden chair at
three in the morning. Perhaps, if I glanced at my reflection in the mirror, I
would not see a smile, but the face of an exhausted writer. But I'm smiling.
On the inside, at least. I can feel it. I'm smiling because I have finally figured
out what I'm doing. In the spectacular failure of my own writing, I have, in a
sense, discovered myself.

However, before I explain how I came to that revelation, one must under- 2
stand the process that has led up to this point. I have been staring at the same
six pathetic, jumbled paragraphs of text for four days now. My eyes have
passed over the words so many times that I could probably recite the entire essay by heart if I had to. It was the first paper I had written in a long time that I
felt genuinely proud of. Yet, it was only after comparing papers with a friend of
mine that I realized that my essay was completely out of whack. As my friend
put it so eloquently between bites of a barbecue chicken sandwich, "You write
weird." I do indeed, I admitted to myself upon reflection. But that isn't bad,
is it? It's a quirk. It makes me distinctive and interesting, doesn't it? I second-
guessed myself. I tend to do that a lot. His essay was immaculate: well-worded,
organized, and objective. It seemed to be the epitome of what other essays
should look like. My essay, on the other hand, looked like it was ripped from
the script of a soap opera, or from the angry last rites of some dying cancer patient. "The devil is in the details," he mentioned, while I scanned over his paper
for the second time, as if that was supposed to blow me out of the water with
some deep, philosophical resonance. I simply scowled at him. I felt awful. I felt
like my work was awful. Ideas and statements and paragraphs that I had ap-
plauded myself over now seemed bitter and loose and uninteresting. Something
had changed. I took it back to my room and stared at it. I read it twice, and
then twice more. I paced around the four feet of walking space in my room,
reading it aloud, as if that would put the text under a different light. I had to
open my window. I needed fresh air. "The devil is in the details," the voice of
my friend chimed from someplace inside my head. "What does that mean?!" I
screamed at the top of my lungs, startling a girl on the sidewalk below.

I think it was at that moment that the weight of my failure finally crushed 3
me. I had put so much heart and soul into what I had written that I didn't want

to admit to myself that it was awful. I didn't want to, but I did. I had to. I threw away the draft and deleted the copy on my computer, smiling as I did it for reasons unknown to me at the time. I had spent more time and effort on the darn thing than I care to mention, and here I was, smiling as it figuratively burned in the wastebasket. "I'll just start over," I thought to myself. The moment my fingers touched the keyboard, however, something clicked. I understood. I

> *I had put so much heart and soul into what I had written that I didn't want to admit to myself that it was awful.*

realized what made my essay so different from that of my friend. Not bad, necessarily, but different. Like snowflakes, I think. I knew exactly what to write about. I knew that the nuclear meltdown-sized failure that I had constructed for myself could be dissected, line by line. Everything that I was looking for that described me as a writer was staring daggers at me in my trash bin. I dug it out from under a half-eaten piece of pizza and an empty box of band-aids. My eyes darted over the words again and the more I read, the more I smiled. Everything that I needed was, literally, all there, in black and white, clear as crystal. I remembered what I was thinking and feeling while I wrote it and compared it to my expectations, what my essay was "supposed" to look like. I jotted notes down all over the draft and once I knew what was wrong, I took a step back and examined the changes that had to be made. Even without a single word down on paper, my new essay began to rise from the ashes like a phoenix, growing stronger and more brilliant by the second. Hoping to learn from the old paper, I began to write my analysis of the analysis of my writing style, still unsure of whether or not to allow myself to make the same mistakes twice.

The most predominant fault that I had to address (much to my dismay) was 4 the fact that on the inside I am, essentially, a senile old man. Perhaps not physically, but I write like an old man speaks. I like to tell long-winded stories that may or may not interest my audience. I tend to ramble. In fact, I'm still rambling. We are four paragraphs into this thing and I'm only just now getting to the meat and potatoes of the paper. I also use excessive detail when it's not necessary. Everything that escapes my cracked old lips is seasoned with a touch of salty, dry humor that always seems to embarrass the rest of the family, especially when guests are over for dinner. "He can't help it," the aunts and uncles will say to their children as they pass the green beans and honey-glazed ham around the table, pretending to be put off by my behavior. "He's just old and senile." However, despite their "shock" and verbal disapproval, they are laughing on the inside. Life is just far too boring without a good laugh every once in a while. I write the way I talk, and I talk with a certain unexpectedly snarky wit that's hard to maneuver around. The casual nature of my writing may stem from the fact that I can never truly take a written assignment seriously. I strive for a good grade, and will work as hard as possible to achieve one, but there is a voice in the back of my head that is effectively scoffing at the ridiculousness of some assignments and expectations that I have had to complete and live up to.

Perhaps it's because I do not want to become what my friend, and many oth- 5 ers are: cutouts of the perfect student, examples to abide by. In a sea of perfect papers and flawless dissertations, maybe I'm struggling to keep my head above water. Many of the other writers are better swimmers than I, but perhaps that is only because I am being weighted down by my own expectations. After seeing my friend's essay, I felt like my rubber dinghy was deflating, and all the signal flares in the world couldn't save me. Maybe I didn't want to admit that I was sinking. It doesn't matter now. I jumped ship instead of ignoring my failure and going down with it like a stubborn captain. Some part of me felt confident enough to kick and scream my way to the top of the torrent. In a sense, that's exactly what I did. I kicked and screamed until three in the morning, and when I reached the shore, I was smiling again.

Another big problem with my essay, I realized, was one that was not even on 6 the paper. It was in my head. On a good day, ideas flow from my mind like a raging river, with my fingers being the only floodgate. Sometimes, the current is so strong, that the ideas push through faster than my fingers can keep up. The ones that leak through are as good as lost forever, thanks to my pitiful memory and my rodent-sized attention span. I blame my mother: she was an insufferable grammar Nazi that forever ruined my ability to create fluid writing. I probably should have had some sort of lead-in transition for that statement, but I couldn't think of anything that would soften the blow. My mother would correct nearly every statement that came out of my mouth. "No, dear, it is 'My friends and I,'" she would say, or, "No, you are not 'done,' honey. You are 'finished.'" I tore my hair out for nearly a decade. She managed to drill my speech so hard that it leaked into my writing. Now every time I make a grammar or spelling mistake, I have to immediately go back and correct it, even if I'm in the middle of a word. I can't help it. I might explode if I don't.

In many cases, the sudden halt in my writing causes my figurative train of 7 thought to completely fly off the rails, sending passengers and luggage flying in every direction. Their magical journey through the valley of Well-Worded Ideas and Self-Discovery has come to a screeching, uncomfortable halt. The earth-shattering statement that I formulated in my mind moments earlier was now lost forever, strewn somewhere under an old copy of *Newsweek* and a fat woman's lingerie. I'll get frustrated. I'll get depressed. I'll start trying to force my brain to come up with an alternative idea. Many times it will work. Other times, a succulent new idea will be waiting for me, wrapped up all nice and pretty with a bow, just outside the edge of my ability to express on paper; in which case I end up having to buckle down, take a number, and submit to the waiting game that always seems to accompany my planning process. However long I end up waiting is irrelevant; the moment my number is called is the happiest five-seconds of my life . . . at which point I'll realize that there is only enough meat in the package for a sentence or two. My willingness to get back in line without grumbling is testament to my stubbornness. Why else would I have been so hesitant to throw away my original essay?

Sometimes even I wonder what drives me to keep writing. I would imagine 8 that there are not many other people who would willingly be up at three in the morning writing an essay, let alone be willing to say that he or she was having fun in the process. That's not to say I don't struggle. While writing the last essay (and even this one), I ran into more hang-ups than a telemarketing company. Those poor souls are willing to work eight hours a day, seven days a week, being yelled at over the telephone. I can't explain why anyone in the world would want to be one, but I can explain what keeps them from jumping out the window of their glass-sided office buildings. It's making the sale. Every once in a blue moon, the stars will align and all your hard work and patience pays off. As a writer, you don't have to operate phones for a living to know what that must feel like, to be vindicated in your existence after running into dead ends for days, if not weeks on end. Stumbling across a bright new idea lifts your spirits, gives you ambition, and dries your socks off long enough for you to feel comfortable slogging back into the putrid bog of despair that makes up writing the other ninety percent of the time. Even as the sludge is seeping back in, you'll still have a smile on your face (even at three in the morning) because you will be thinking of that sale.

It's part of the reason writing is so much fun. The ability to put anything down  9 in words can be oddly liberating. Several years ago, one of my friends insisted that I fill a book with my "wonderful ideas." Well, what started out as a running gag became reality: it's now four years later and I am still writing what could loosely be called my autobiography. *Kareem and Me*, as it has been colloquially dubbed, spans several hundred pages and is full of inside jokes, ranting monologues, and stories based on real events that have had the truth stretched so thin that it looks like taffy. The later chapters began to spiral out of control, becoming some sort of pseudo novel, with well-developed characters and story arcs. By this point, however, the audience had disappeared. Interest in the book faded as friends forgot the project actually existed, but I kept writing, I'm still writing, if just for my own sake. Perhaps it helps me feel grounded in my own thoughts and emotions when they may be too absurd to express outwardly. I get to tell the stories that I want to hear and access parts of myself that I am sometimes not fully aware of yet. In truth, starting my essay over was an adventure.

Two days have passed since the inception of my new essay, and after some  10 heavy revision, the paper has finally come to fruition. However, despite the fact that I felt proud of my introspective opus, I knew there was one test that I had to pass before I could truly let my guard down. With less than contained excitement, I hunted my friend down, finding him in a convenience store buying lunch, and had him give it a once-over. Besides the fact that he seemed irked by his cameo early on, he smiled the whole way through. It wouldn't matter what he said at this point; I made my sale. I had been vindicated. My mission was complete. The subtle smile that he was having such a hard time hiding completely offset the hours of hard work that I had put into it. His reaction was my entire motivation for writing. "Well?" I questioned over his shoulder, my anticipation getting the better of me. He stumbled into a display of Frito's in surprise and tried to play it off by taking a sip of coffee while picking up one of the bags. He handed me the essay back. "It's fine, I guess. You still write weird," he said, forgetting to wipe the smile off his face.

"I know!" I squealed in delight. "Isn't it great?"                                          11

My friend just rolled his eyes. To me, it was great. The weirdness that had   12
forced me to scrap hours of hard work now stood proudly by my side as an
invisible ally. Instead of fighting it, I would embrace it. It is an extension of my
personality, after all. I would like to think that the weirdness has helped me
complete this essay, but, then again, maybe I am still just staring down the rain-
slick road to self-destruction.

## Question for Discussion and Journaling

1. Think about the last time you were able to step back from something you had written
   and decided to start again. What prompted you to do this?

## Applying and Exploring Ideas

1. Try to replicate Osborne's processes here. Find something you've written recently and
   are unsatisfied with. Now throw it out (either literally or imagine doing so) and start
   again. Write about the process and practices that led you to rewrite it the way you did.

### Meta Moment

Do you think that your current approach to composing and revising is serving you well? Are
there aspects of it you could change?

# Fanfiction, Poetry, Blogs, and Journals: A Case Study of the Connection between Extracurricular and Academic Writings

## MARISSA PENZATO

■ Penzato, Marissa. "Fanfiction, Poetry, Blogs, and Journals: A Case Study of the Connection between Extracurricular and Academic Writings." *Stylus* 3.1 (Spring 2012): 10–24. Web. 15 Jan. 2014.

## Framing the Reading

Marissa Penzato conducted the study for this paper in Elizabeth Wardle's Fall 2011 ENC 1102 class. She submitted it for publication in *Stylus: A Journal of First-Year Writing* and won a prize for it at the 3rd Annual Knights Write Showcase (for more information, visit: **writingandrhetoric.cah.ucf.edu/showcase.php**). She is currently an aerospace engineering student.

## Getting Ready to Read

*Before you read*, do the following activity:

- Think about and list the kinds of literacies you enjoy outside of school.

*As you read*, consider the following question:

- How did Penzato collect and analyze her data?

There has been a recent spate of interest in the literate lives of students. 1
Numerous researchers (Grabill et al., 2010; Haven, 2009; Roozen, 2008; Roozen, 2009; Roozen, 2010; Shrum, 2011; Wardle, 2007) have researched the multiple discourse communities that students participate in and transfer, repurposing, and connection across discourse communities and genres. In his numerous studies, Kevin Roozen (2008; 2009; 2010) has studied several students and

found that the methods used in discourse communities, be it for organization, writing process, etc., have often transferred from one discourse community to another. After his study of two students, named Kate and Charles in his articles, he concluded that in many ways Kate's fanfiction (writing using the characters, setting, storyline, etc. of a movie, TV show, book, etc.) activities had helped her understand numerous assignments both as an undergraduate and a graduate in college (2009), and that Charles' activities and experience with journalism, poetry, and stand-up comedy helped him with some of his college courses (2008). Through further research (a study of two college students), Shrum has supported Roozen's findings, concluding that the experience of Nikki and Jack (pseudonyms) in their various discourse communities had aided them in other discourse communities on occasions. However, at times their outside literacy experiences didn't help with school tasks (Shrum, 2011). Other researchers (Sommers, 1980) have compared the revision strategies of student writers and experienced writers, concluding that students have poor revision strategies. However, Nancy Sommers considers student writers as not being "experienced" and her research was only done concerning academic writings. A person's experience writing varies with their discourse communities and genres, and with this varying experience come a difference in the quality of revision. In her article on the transfer from First-Year Composition in other academic writings, Elizabeth Wardle (2007) identifies what students in her study had identified as an engaging writing assignment:

- The assignment doesn't have one "right" answer but is authentic to each student.
- The prompt for the writing assignment is thought-provoking so students think about the assignment outside of class and when not writing.
- Students have some freedom while being given the necessary structure to help them succeed.
- The assignment is not simple regurgitation or summary of fact.
- The assignment relates in some way to students' interests/future.
- The assignment is challenging, not easily within reach.
- The assignment clearly relates to the rest of the course content.
- The assignment is intended to achieve a clear purpose.
- The student understands what is being asked of them in the assignment and why. (p. 77-8)

Many of these characteristics could be applied to fanfiction, and, in fact, explain why most of the participants in my study were so engaged with fanfiction.

While this research is extensive, it is lacking in some areas, bringing up 2 many questions:

- How does a person's engagement in a discourse community or genre differ depending on their motivation?
- Is there connection, repurposing and/or transfer across fanfiction and other discourse communities and genres?
- Are student writers really as "inexperienced" as Sommers makes them out to be?

- Could student writers have more complex revision strategies than Sommers found them to have?

To answer these questions, I conducted a study that examined four experi-  3
enced fanfiction authors, varying in age and location, focusing on the discourse
communities they participate in; primarily, I wanted to analyze how fanfiction may have affected their other
discourse communities and vice
versa. The study grew to include
their varying motivation, engagement, and methods of revision in
their discourse communities. The
ages of the participants varied,
ranging from a middle school student to a college student, as well
as their locations, one from the
South, the North, and the West

> . . . the results of this research have
> suggested that these young writers,
> although students, have revision
> strategies that more closely resemble
> those of the experienced adult writers
> Sommers studied.

(USA), and the fourth from Australia. The results of the study support the
findings of those researchers who have found that students participate in multiple discourse communities (Grabill et al. 2010; Haven, 2009; Roozen, 2008;
Roozen, 2009; Roozen 2010; Shrum, 2011; Wardle, 2007). There have been
few instances where the participants' discourse communities outside of fanfiction had conflicted with or transferred into fanfiction; often the participants'
fanfiction is so different from what they write in their other discourse communities that they believe none of the other discourse communities affect their
fanfiction. In contradiction to Nancy Sommers' findings in her article "Revision Strategies of Student Writers and Experienced Adult Writers," the results
of this research have suggested that these young writers, although students,
have revision strategies that more closely resemble those of the experienced
adult writers Sommers studied, rather than the student writers.

In this article, I will first explain my research methods; overview each case  4
(Elizabeth, Belinda, Laura, and Sarah), presenting their fanfiction experience
first, then discussing their other discourse communities and genres; then conclude with a brief summary of the findings.

## Methods

All four participants are fanfiction writers that I have encountered through my  5
involvement in the fanfiction community for the movie 9 on the FanFiction.net
website. Prior to the study, I sent them a message through the private messaging
system on the FanFiction.net website asking if they'd be willing to participate
in a study, briefly explaining the study and how I would conduct the interview. All four replied that they were very much willing to participate. The participants (Elizabeth, Belinda, Laura, and Sarah) are all female and vary in age
and location. Elizabeth, the youngest, is a middle-school student from Georgia;
Belinda is a high-school student from Australia; Sarah is a high-school student
from Michigan; and Laura, the eldest, is a college student from California. Each

participant signed a consent form (and in the case for those under 18, a parent signed the consent form as well) giving me permission to interview them.

This study consisted of an initial interview with open-ended questions and an optional text-based interview where the participants were asked open-ended questions concerning a fanfiction and a text from one of their other discourse communities. Due to the participants' location, the interviews were conducted through either email or the private messaging system on the FanFiction.net website. The data was collected by copying the question asked in the interview and the answer given and pasting it into a Microsoft Word document, having a Word document assigned specifically to each participant. Prior to writing each case, I created a new Word document for each participant, in which I created headings on the basis of how I wanted to organize the case and organized the participant's answers depending on which heading it fell under.

## Case Studies

In this section, I present each of my participants, describing their fanfiction, other discourse communities and genres, and their revision strategies in these discourse communities and genres.

## Case One: Elizabeth

Elizabeth is a middle-school student from Georgia who is a diligent and motivated writer. She was brought to my attention because of her well-written fanfiction for Shane Acker's feature-film 9 and the helpful advice that she has left on my first fanfiction, also for this movie. During this study, she participated in an open-ended interview and a text-based interview. In the text-based interview, I collected three texts which I analyzed and interviewed her about: two of her fanfictions and a poem she's written in her free time. She participates in multiple discourse communities and genres, including fanfiction, academic, extracurricular (non-fanfiction), journaling, and writing competitions. These communities vary greatly; each requires a set of skills that the others do not. For instance, in fanfiction the writer can write however he/she wants, but the best stories are those that are well-detailed and very descriptive with a well-developed plot whereas academic writing has a strict format and prompt to follow, and the emphasis is (more commonly) on grammar and spelling rather than the actual content.

When asked which of these discourse communities was the most important to her, she replied:

> Pushing aside the fact that getting good grades is a passion for me, I would have to say writing in my free time. I find my true talent in that, besides being given a topic and told to write on it. Not only that, but writing on your own time and ideas is much less stressful. (Personal Interview, Oct. 15, 2011)

She gave a similar answer when asked in which discourse community she had the most confidence in her writing:

I am much more confident in what I do in my free time, like what I put on Fanfiction[.net] for example. With my free time comes, of course, my own time decisions. I can choose how long I really want to think about what I've written other than given a deadline and such. I also am more comfortable with picking my own topics. I have the abilities to expand or decrease the plot as I wish, and really get into what I'm writing. With school topics I just get uninterested. (Personal Interview, Oct. 15, 2011)

As seen in these answers, Elizabeth values the writing done in her free time 11 (her fanfiction and non-fanfiction writing) above her school-related writing. This is because it conforms to her interests, she can devote all the time she needs to this writing, and can flex her writing skills where school writing may constrain them.

### Elizabeth's Fanfiction

Although involvement in the fanfiction community for the movie 9 brought 12 her to my attention, she also writes for multiple other fanfiction communities. Since she began writing fanfiction midway through 2011, she has written about ten fanfictions for around ten different fanfiction communities. Her involvement in this discourse community began with reading fanfiction for a video game she was a fan of, but grew to writing for this video game as well as other games, books, and movies she was interested in once she created an account on FanFiction.net.

For Elizabeth, the hardest part with learning to write fanfiction was learning 13 how the FanFiction.net website worked. She says that she really didn't have any difficult writing fanfiction stories other than struggling with how to get a story started, how to "get every character involved, hint what the plot could be about, and other small details that need to be in a chapter are just a few examples" (Personal interview, Oct. 20, 2011).

### *Writing Process*

Elizabeth described herself as "technically hav[ing] no process" for writing 14 fanfiction. However, her interview comments suggest that she does have one. Maybe her idea of a writing process is limited to what schools declare as a writing process: a strict order of planning, drafting, and editing. In one of our interviews through the private messaging system on FanFiction.net, she explained that she'll get ideas for potential stories from watching a movie, reading a book, or playing a game, then "jot" it down and start writing her story; after this, she will "review over it, see what is decent and what is not, and add or take away information that may or may not be needed."

An important aspect behind every writer is inspiration. Elizabeth's inspiration 15 for her fanfiction is mainly just the movie, book, or game that her stories are based off of. However, she later told me that she is also inspired by her "want to be a part of the FanFiction[.net] website" because "everyone on the site enjoys the same thing: writing" and that she is "very glad to be surrounded by that."

### Elizabeth's Versatility

Elizabeth's complex writing process and deep motivation with writing fanfic- 16
tion lead to incredible versatility in her writing. Her ability to easily shift her
tone across her stories is a remarkable gift for any writer, much less one who
is so young. This versatility became obvious in the portion of the text-based
interview concerning two of her fanfictions. Her two stories discussed during
the interview, "Armor of a Guardian" based off of the book series/movie *The
Legend of the Guardians: The Owls of Ga'Hoole* and "New Earth" based
off of the movie 9, presented two drastically different tones. The difference in
these tones was evident from the moment you start reading them. Below is the
introduction to her fanfiction "Armor of a Guardian":

> "And so they say, Naira escaped. And Kludd? Well, Kludd was never found . . .
> Should I stop?"
> Soren paused in his story, wings spread and an amusing smile on his beak.
> "Wha'?" One owlet chirped. "Please, don't stop! There must be more, there
> must be!"
> Soren was about to answer when Ezylryb entered, laughing wholeheartedly.
> "Ah, listen to them Soren." He playfully jumped at an owlet, drawing a fit of
> giggles from it.
> "They want more stories! Let's not disappoint them." He walked to the door
> in the hollow, and sighed in contentment. "There's a good storm brewing," he
> spread out his wings, the feathers slowly rocking in the breeze, "and hopefully, it
> will be chock-full of baggy wrinkles!" He lofted into the air, flying in the direc-
> tion of the Sea of Hoolemere. Soren shook his head, smiling, and swiveling his
> head to the side, nodded to his band. Together, Soren, Twilight, Digger, Gylfie, and
> Otulissa took to the skies, silently following their teacher as they met each others
> excited gaze. Everyone was content, except for one, who was lost in his thoughts.

The tone, which is evident here, is light and playful through a majority of the
story, but as hinted at the end of introduction, it does shift to a more serious tone at times. However, this tone is very different from the tone in "New
Earth," where the tone, which is held throughout the story, is a much darker
one than that of "Armor of a Guardian":

> They say that the world is a haven; that it will offer hope and survival for every-
> one and everything. No matter where you were, just like the creatures that in-
> habited the region, you could survive, because if an animal could, humans could.
> It was quickly proved false.
> In fact, the human race was wiped out . . . completely. Without mercy, pity, or
> falter, they were destroyed, leaving the Earth without a trace. The only way to tell
> it had been inhabited was by the cruel effects of the . . . war. A hole was ripped
> into the sky, and the sunlight destroyed everything. The killing of the plants lead
> to the death of the animals, the death of the plants and animals eventually killed
> off whatever lucky humans were in hiding.
> I had stumbled upon a few bunkers in my lifetime, and trust me when I say, I
> have never forgotten. The smell of deceased flesh had eventually disappeared,

fortunately, but the skeletons were never easy to get by. I couldn't imagine the fear of the unknown; of being stuck in a metal hole for years, too scared to come into the world, for the pure horror of wondering if you did, would a mechanical beast take your life?

Although this is only a portion of the introduction to "New Earth," the dark and serious tone, which is present throughout the entire story, is evident.

Elizabeth explained that many things contributed to this drastic change in tone: experience writing fanfiction (for "Armor of a Guardian" was one of her first fanfictions, while "New Earth" is her most recent one), realizing that she needed to be more patient and take her time, and the difference in theme and tone between 9 and *The Legend of the Guardians: The Owls of Ga'Hoole*.

## Elizabeth's Other Discourse Communities and Genres

Elizabeth is involved in a number of other discourse communities including  17 academic writing, extracurricular writing separate from fanfiction, writing in a journal, and writing competitions. However, her involvement in these discourse communities did not influence her fanfiction as much as previous research would lead us to expect. The only evidence found of influence of another discourse community in fanfiction was the transfer from her English teacher's (who she's had for several years) focus on improving vocabulary, grammar, spelling, and descriptiveness.

### School

As stated above, Elizabeth described her academic writing as having aided her  18 fanfiction in that her English teacher (who she's had for a few years) strongly encourages improving students' vocabulary, grammar, spelling, and descriptiveness and that she has incorporated what she's learned from her teacher into her stories the best that she can. Other than that, Elizabeth feels that there is no other transfer between her fanfiction and academic writing because she feels that there is a big difference between the topics of her fanfiction and academic writing. She feels that with her academic writing, the topics are just too bland and constrained for her to flex her true writing capabilities.

### Journal

Elizabeth was inspired to keep a journal by a story she had once read about a  19 man who had recorded every day of his life for forty years. After reading this story, she wanted to follow in his footsteps "at least a little," recording the small events in her life. Although she is inspired to keep a journal, she describes it as being very brief and not very detailed; "scribble" as she called it in an interview, the "plainest kind of writing possible." This, combined with her little mention of this activity in the interviews, leads me to believe that this genre has very little influence (if any) on her fanfiction.

### *Writing Competitions*

Elizabeth became involved with writing fairs and contests through her own in- 20
terest in the events, viewing them as a way to practice for her other stories, and
also through encouragement from her teachers (who have noticed her talent).
She described the writing done in her writing competitions as being creative
stories she can choose her own topics for. Although it is because she can choose
her own topics that she enjoys this activity, she feels that she focuses more on
what she feels the judges want to see rather than what she feels is best. There
is a very strict writing process she must follow for her writing competitions
that includes prewriting, drafting, revising/editing, and publishing, very similar
to the writing process she follows for her academic writing. There are many
similarities between this discourse community and school, including the writing process and audience. It is because of these similarities, that she feels that
her writing competitions have little influence on her fanfiction.

### Comparison of Texts

In the text-based interview, not only did I interview her about two of her fan- 21
fiction pieces but also about a poem she has written in her free time: "Harvest
Moon." Her process with writing "Harvest Moon" was very similar to her writing process for her fanfiction pieces. Her methods of planning, writing and revising her poem were similar to her fanfiction texts in that it was just a "matter
of getting all of the information down" then reviewing it to see that aspects of
the story/poem turned out the way she intended them to. Another aspect that
this poem was similar to her fanfiction was the similarity in her state of mind
while writing. She mentioned writing with a "darker state of mind" in "Harvest
Moon," very similar to her state of mind while writing "New Earth"; this was
due to both containing dark images and themes of loss, battle, and death.

### Summary

Elizabeth participates in a number of discourse communities and genres includ- 22
ing fanfiction, academic, extracurricular (non-fanfiction), journaling, and writing
competitions. Fanfiction is the discourse community she values the most and
has the highest confidence in because of her freedom in writing what she wants,
how she wants—a freedom that is rarely, if at all, present in her other discourse
communities and genres. Her deep motivation and complex writing process has
led to her fanfiction writing having great versatility and a revision process that is
more complex than Sommers' research gives student writers credit for.

The results of my interviews with the next case participant, Belinda, give 23
very similar findings. Belinda's fanfiction isn't nearly as versatile when it comes
to shifting her tone so drastically across her writings as Elizabeth does. This,
however, does not make Belinda any less of a gifted or experienced writer, nor
her stories of any less quality; for her stories normally revolve around the same
themes so the quality of her writings—as well as the development of the plot—
can be her main focus.

## Case Two: Belinda

Belinda, a motivated and punctilious writer, is a high school student from 24 Australia. As numerous researchers have already found (Grabill et al., 2010; Haven, 2009; Roozen, 2008; Roozen, 2009; Roozen, 2010; Shrum, 2011; Wardle, 2007), Belinda participates in numerous discourse communities including fanfiction, school, extracurricular, and blogging. Belinda takes great pride in her writing but feels that she has the most confidence in her fanfiction, something she also feels is her most important discourse community. During this study, she participated in an initial interview with open-ended questions and a text-based interview where she provided me with a fanfiction and a poem she had written as an assignment in her French class (translated into English).

### Belinda's Fanfiction

Belinda was brought to my attention because of her vivid and well-written fan- 25 fiction for the movie *9*, in particular her most recent story "The Apartment." Although it was because of her fanfiction for the movie *9* that I had decided to interview her, she writes for multiple other fanfiction communities, having written about 24 stories for 8 different fanfiction communities, mostly for *9* and Disney (revolving around Mickey Mouse and his friends) posted on FanFiction. net and DeviantArt. Nikki, Shrum's participant who was also a fanfiction writer, was not very attentive to her grammar and spelling in her writing; however, Belinda takes pride in being a fanfiction author who pays particular attention to the quality of her grammar and spelling, because, as she said, "the amount of stories you find on this website [FanFiction.net] these days that are practically incomprehensible due to their atrocious lack of care for grammar/spelling is really sad."

Belinda began writing fanfiction in 2007, and mostly writes stories with a 26 romantic element; however, she has touched stories that are family or friendship centered. Her involvement in this discourse community began when she heard that her cousin and a friend were writing a Harry Potter fanfiction and was inspired to write one of her own. She didn't feel too confident in the quality of this first fanfiction but as she continued to write more fanfiction, her confidence in the quality of her fanfiction increased.

The only difficulty Belinda has mentioned to have experienced while writing 27 fanfiction is that if she isn't "in the zone" she can't write. It is because of this that it could take her months to complete a story, and the reason why there could be weeks or months between updates of a story.

### *Writing Process*

Belinda states that all but two types of her fanfiction texts follow the same kind 28 of writing process:

> It all starts with a scene in my head. I usually think something up by listening to music, and once I have this one scene figured out, I'll imagine more and more scenes. If I feel motivated enough or feel as if I can come up with enough ideas to write the story, I begin to write. . . . most of my planning happens as I write each new chapter. (Personal interview, Nov. 3, 2011)

The time it takes her to write a story, or a chapter of a story depends on how 29 much inspiration she has and how deep in "the writing zone" she is. If she is not really in the mood to write, she may "just write a sentence or two and then leave it," and she may not touch a story for months before having "a light bulb moment" and writing a chapter in a "decent timeframe" (to her, this is about 2 hours).

The two types of fanfictions that she has written that don't follow this pro- 30 cess are her fanfiction "The Apartment," which is an adopted story, and when she collaborated with another writer in writing a fanfiction.

Belinda adopted the idea behind "The Apartment," a fanfiction for the movie 31 9, from a user who was posting ideas for potential fanfictions up for adoption on FanFiction.net. It was on this website that she had encountered the idea and, before contacting the user and asking to adopt the story, she first figured out the past of the main character and the events that would lead to the climax. After being given permission to adopt the story, she shared with the user some of her ideas for the story (such as the events prior to the story and the characters' personalities) prior to actually beginning to write. She again consulted with the user before posting the first few chapters to assure that she wasn't going to manipulate her original idea. However, for the most recent chapters she has taken on a "more independent approach."

Belinda has mentioned writing two fanfictions in collaboration with other 32 authors; she talks about the one that she has done for the movie 9 more so than her other one, the first one she did, in her interview. Based on how she described this first collaboration fanfiction, it sounds like either this story was not as successful as the most recent one or that she was not satisfied in the quality of her writing. In writing this fanfiction, she and the other author both contributed ideas for the story and alternated who wrote the chapters.

Belinda has said numerous times over the course of our interviews that her 33 fanfiction writing was heavily inspired by music that she listens to. She mentioned two stories in particular that involve Mickey and Minnie Mouse (along with other characters like Donald and Goofy) where the idea for the story was inspired by songs she'd listened to.

Her mood and personal experiences are also inspirations for her stories. 34 When Belinda is in a happy mood she is quoted in saying that she writes "really fluffy stuff," stories full of cute romantic moments between a pairing, whereas when she's depressed she writes "angsty" poetry. She has mentioned one story in particular, a fanfiction for the movie 9, "Her Furnace," which was inspired by a personal experience. In the story, the main character wakes up to find herself unable to get warm, only finding warmth in another character, her romantic interest, and using him as her "furnace" for the night. Belinda mentions that this story was thought up when she woke up in the middle of the night and was really cold.

## Belinda's Other Discourse Communities and Genres

Although fanfiction is Belinda's primary discourse community, she participates 35 in numerous other discourse communities and genres including school, extracurricular, posting on Facebook, and blogging. The extracurricular writing and what she posts on Facebook is poetry that she writes that "typically doesn't rhyme," mostly about how she "feels at the time."

### School

Belinda's writing for school involves creative writing assignments, a descrip- 36 tion of a school trip to see a musical, and a story which had ended up in her school's yearbook.

The piece that had made it into the yearbook was a very condensed version 37 of a story she had written for an English assignment, where she had to write a short story based on the themes of a short story they had read in class. Her teacher had liked her story and asked for a copy to put in the yearbook. Considering that this assignment sounds very similar to fanfiction, it could explain why she was so engaged in this assignment and why the quality of the writing impressed her teacher. However, upon reading her piece in the yearbook, it became obvious to Belinda that only a fraction of it had actually made it into the yearbook. This did disappoint her but she understood it was just a matter of space in the yearbook.

The writing she does in school is dependent on the task. Most of the prompts 38 she's assigned she feels are very similar to fanfiction, if you look at them "in that light." She explains what she means by this by describing a creative writing assignment she had a few years ago:

> In year 9 [9th grade] we had a creative writing elective (chosen class) in which we would write our own stories using a list of prompts throughout the year; one I have kept was 'Red Shoes,' a prompt which I used to write a short piece about a girl who is supposed to be a more modern Dorothy Gale . . . only instead it is a girl named Dot who I think had OCD and was also prone to panic attacks. Instead of ruby slippers she had sparkly red Converse shoes. (Personal interview, Nov. 2, 2011)

She may feel that the prompts for some school assignments are similar to fanfiction, but she made it clear that the planning methods that teachers force students to use conflict with how she writes and plans best, saying that they "don't understand that I don't work that way."

### Poetry

The writing that Belinda does on her free time and on Facebook is poetry. 39 These poems sometimes rhyme (however, they don't most of the time) and often reflect how she feels at the time, usually being angst poetry. She describes her method of writing poetry as just "writing down sentences that rhyme and make sense together."

### Blogging

Blogging is something that Belinda rarely does. She describes it as something 40 that "never got off the ground." In her blogging, she talked about subjects she was angry about or things that she enjoyed; it was pretty much what you'd write in a journal/diary just not her secrets. I assume that this wasn't one of her more important writing activities considering how little she mentioned it.

## A Comparison of Texts

In the text-based interview, I interviewed Belinda about two texts she had writ-  41 ten: a poem and a fanfiction text. The fanfiction she chose to be interviewed on was "The Apartment," her fanfiction for the movie 9 that, as mentioned earlier, was a story that was adopted from another writer; it is also a work-in-progress. The poem she supplied me with, "Je Voudrais Voir Votre Sourire" ("I Want to See Your Smile"), was one that she had written for an assignment in her French class; she had originally written it in French, but then translated it into English.

Belinda feels that there are no similarities between these two texts other  42 than the love theme. Her writing process differs between the two because she tries to get her school writings "as perfect as possible," whereas with fanfiction she is more laid back. I, however, do see something that is similar between her poem and her fanfictions. Although it is a little too early in "The Apartment" to see the romantic tone, the tone of the romance in her poem is very similar to the tone she has in the romance of her more developed fanfictions.

The only revisions that Belinda made to her poem were just correcting gram-  43 matical errors, no major changes to what she wrote about. However, "The Apartment" did undergo some revision in plot, based on the feedback she received from the user whose idea the story was originally. Many of her other fanfictions have undergone similar revisions as "The Apartment." Sommers (1980) claims that the revision process of students is limited to only word choice and grammar; Belinda has already proved that her revision process is beyond this by describing that she has revised the plot at times. Therefore, she has described a revision process much more complex than Sommers claims that student writers have.

## Summary

Belinda participates in a number of discourse communities and genres in-  44 cluding fanfiction, academic, poetry, and blogging. Fanfiction is the discourse community that she values the most and has the most confidence in, and, like Elizabeth, this is because of the freedom to write what she wants, how she wants. It is probably the lack of this freedom in academic writing that results in her frustration with it. Belinda manages to work against this frustration and is highly motivated and driven to write in the highest quality possible with all of her discourse communities. Since her revision process is complex and is not done merely during one time period, it is incredibly accurate, resulting in a quality of writing that she takes great pride in.

My next research participant, Laura, is just as motivated and has just as  45 complex a writing process as Elizabeth and Belinda. Unlike my other partici- pants, Laura is a college student whose involvement in art and creative writing has led her to develop an interest in pursuing a major in a relevant field. Like Elizabeth and Belinda, she highly values fanfiction; however, it is in her academic writing that she has the most confidence.

## Case Three: Laura

Laura, a college student from California, is a devoted and diligent writer. During this study, she participated in an initial interview with open-ended questions and a brief text-based interview where she provided me with a fanfiction and one of her original stories. She participates in a number of different discourse communities and genres including fanfiction, academic, extracurricular, and a journal. She has an amazing imagination, having written about 50 fanfictions and over 20 original pieces (stories and poems). 46

Laura's fanfiction is what she values the most because "it displays the largest collection of [her] writings from any community." However, this is not where she believes to have the most confidence in her writing. It is in her academic writing that she has the most confidence because her assignments also include creative writing, and she receives mostly positive feedback. 47

Not only is Laura a talented writer, but also a rather talented artist, having a large collection of fanart and other artwork posted on her DeviantArt account. Although she is unsure what she wants to major in, her experience and interest in "storytelling through print and visual media" has driven her to become interested in pursuing a degree in related major, such as illustration or creative writing. 48

## Laura's Fanfiction

Laura was brought to my attention by her vivid and well-developed fanfiction pieces for the movie *9*. Although it was her fanfiction pieces for this movie that I decided to interview her about, she has written overall 48 fanfiction pieces for about 14 different fanfiction communities. A majority of her fanfictions are written for the play *Little Shop of Horrors* and the movies *The Nightmare Before Christmas*, *Happy Feet*, and *9*. 49

Laura has been writing fanfiction for about four years, mostly in the genres of romance and family. Her involvement in this discourse community began in high school, when she became a fan of Tim Burton's film *The Nightmare Before Christmas* and became involved on the "primary fan site" for the movie. It was on this site that she had first encountered fanfiction, and it was during her sophomore year that she wrote her first fanfiction and posted it on this website. 50

She learned to write fanfiction by simply "trying it," and as she continued to write, she figured out "what worked and what didn't." Her only difficulty when it came to learning to write fanfiction was having to "learn [her] style." To explain what she meant by this, she clarified that a lot of her older stories had too much description leading to an undesirably high word count. By having to recognize her style, I can assume that she adjusted the aspects of her writing that didn't please her so to improve the quality of her writing. 51

### Writing Process

Laura's process for writing a piece of fanfiction varies. Usually she'll write 52 out a summary of the story and figure out where she wants to divide it into chapters, but sometimes she'll "jump right into writing a story with little to no planning." Before starting a story and devoting time to it, she likes to "play around" with scenes from her idea and see if the idea is interesting enough to devote a full story to. For stories that have been requested by readers and/or other authors, she returns to what the requested story is based off of and pays attention to the characters before beginning to write.

Laura has many inspirations for her fanfiction. Positive reviews, music, the 53 movie/play/book that her stories are based off of, and family all encourage her to write:

> [T]here are a lot of things that help me write and get me inspired. Encouraging reviews are my main inspiration. Music allows me to separate from life and sit down and write. Experiencing the movies, plays, or books the fics are based on usually makes the wheels in my head turn. On a more personal note, I often dedicate my fanfictions to my deceased grandmother and father, as they were both inspirations in my life. (Personal interview, Nov. 22, 2011)

### Laura's Other Discourse Communities and Genres

Besides fanfiction, Laura participates in a number of other discourse commu- 54 nities and genres including extracurricular, academic, and a journal. Laura's extracurricular writing, and sometimes her academic writing, take the form of original stories.

### Extracurricular

Laura's extracurricular writing involves the numerous original pieces she has 55 written. She has written over 20 original pieces (both stories and poems), most of these having been posted online on her Fictionpress.com (a website devoted to original creations) portfolio. Her original stories follow close to the same writing process as her fanfiction does: writing it and then reading it over and revising until she can't find any more errors. Just like with her fanfiction, music and her family are heavy inspirations in her original writing. Also, considering that most of her original stories are about animals, fantasy, and the supernatural, many things in nature, horror, and her imagination inspires her to write.

### School

Laura's experience with fanfiction and her original pieces has led her to take 56 classes revolving around her interest in creative writing. Because of this, her academic writings involve mostly essays and short stories. Like her original stories, her academic writing follows the same writing process as her fanfiction;

essentially just writing, and then reading over and revising. Considering that many of her school writings are short stories, it can be assumed that these have the same inspiration as her original projects. However, her essays are inspired only by her opinions and morals.

### Journal

The journal that Laura keeps, which can also be considered a blog of sorts, is  57 on her DeviantArt account, and most of her entries can be seen by other users. In her journal, she posts about her personal life and stories that she is working on, but also includes other topics. She is a "little less careful" with her writing in her journal since it's mainly just a social activity, but her writing process is essentially the same as her other discourse communities.

### Comparison of Texts

In our brief text-based interview, I interviewed Laura concerning two of her  58 texts: her fanfiction "Clumsy" written for the movie *The Nightmare Before Christmas* and an original story she had written for a project in her creative writing course, "The Siege of Carvak." Both stories were planned out in a similar fashion, with her starting off with just an idea or the whole plot in mind and both being inspired by her interests (interactions between the two main characters of *The Nightmare Before Christmas* for "Clumsy" and her interest in dragons and fantasy for "The Siege of Carvak"). In writing the stories, she let both go where they'd please, letting the conversations and twists and turns in the stories come as even a surprise to her. Both stories were also revised with a similar method, with her writing an early draft and proofreading it several times before asking for feedback on it from her peers. After receiving feedback and suggestions from her peers, she would then revise the piece some more before deciding that the piece was presentable. This revision process is fairly constant across all of her discourse communities and genres.

### Summary

Laura is highly motivated and engaged in writing fanfiction and original sto-  59 ries. It is because of this high interest in creative writing that she is so engaged with her academic writing, something that consists of creative writing assignments. There are many aspects of her writing that remain the same across her discourse communities and genres including her writing process and inspiration. Since she wrote a lot of fanfiction before she started writing original stories and blogging, what she has learned from writing fanfiction may have transferred a little into these discourse communities and genres.

My next case participant is different from the others; for although she has  60 written fanfiction, and actively participates in the discourse community, it is not her primary discourse community. Her primary discourse community, the one she holds the highest value in and the most confidence in, is roleplaying.

## Case Four: Sarah

Sarah is a high school student from Michigan and a highly motivated writer. 61
During this study, she participated in an initial interview consisting of open-ended questions. She participates in a number of discourse communities including fanfiction, roleplaying, and extracurricular activities. However, unlike the other participants, her activity in fanfiction has been limited as a writer; she is more active as a reader. In fact, the discourse community she values the most and has the most confidence is her roleplaying, which is done on a roleplaying website that she is very active in. She values this discourse community so highly because it is here that she spends most of her time writing and where her writing is of a higher quality.

### Sarah's Fanfiction

It was Sarah's participation in the fanfiction community for the movie 9 which 62
brought her to my attention. She has only published one fanfiction (that I am aware of): a well-written and rather deep poem for the movie 9. Although she hasn't written many fanfictions, it was because of the helpful advice she had left on the fanfiction that I have been working on that I was driven to interview her, for she spoke as an experienced writer.

Sarah has been involved with the FanFiction.net community for about three 63
years; however, her writing has been limited. She learned of fanfiction and the FanFiction.net website from a friend and decided to become involved in the community, particularly the fanfiction for a movie she had recently become a fan of, 9. She had learned how to write fanfiction by observing the fanfiction of others and how they write, and learning to incorporate her own ideas into that style.

### *Writing Process*

Sarah's fanfiction is heavily inspired by music; so, her process for writing a 64
piece of fanfiction includes listening to music "non-stop" for inspiration, and trying to "picture the entire story as a film in [her] head." From this, she'll normally have a vague idea of what she wants the story to look like, but she says that she's learned to just let her story "go where it pleases."

As mentioned, music is a heavy inspiration for Sarah's fanfiction. However, 65
she has also mentioned that many of the works of other fanfiction writers have been inspiration for her stories.

### Sarah's Other Discourse Communities and Genres

Sarah participates in a few other discourse communities and genres, including 66
the discourse community she values the most, roleplaying, and her extracurricular writing. Sarah's extracurricular writing involves stories done purely for fun between her and her friends.

### Roleplaying

Sarah described the writing done in her roleplaying as being "comical, casual,   67
or very structured." She termed this form of roleplaying that she participates
in as being "novel style": "'Novel style' is the type of roleplaying. It's posting
in larger paragraphs instead of lines of dialogue followed by a little action,"
(Personal Interview, Oct. 24, 2011). From this, it can be assumed that this style
of roleplaying follows a certain format that all, or most, participants in this
discourse community use.

Sarah's inspirations and writing process in roleplaying is essentially the   68
same as in her fanfiction. The only difference she has mentioned between her
fanfiction and roleplaying is that her roleplaying may be a "little more thought
out"; however, music still heavily inspires her and visualization and letting her
story "go where it pleases" are still her techniques for writing.

### Extracurricular

Sarah's extracurricular writing is comprised mostly of "fun, random" stories   69
involving a few of her characters and her friends' characters. Since this is
done purely for fun, her writing here is very casual and rather comical. Her
inspirations and writing process here is the same as in her other discourse communities: heavily inspired by music, and planned out through visualization and
letting her imagination take control of her writing.

### Summary

There are many aspects of Sarah's writing that connect across her discourse   70
communities and genres. Her inspirations and writing process are fairly
constant across her discourse communities and genres. Each of her discourse
communities or genres could have contributed to the other in some way—
roleplaying more so than the others because of the amount of time she spends
and the value she holds in this discourse community.

## Summary of Findings

As Wardle found in her study, a student's level of engagement on a writing as-   71
signment depends on his or her motivation. She identified the characteristics
of what the students who participated in her study considered an engaging
writing assignment. Many of the characteristics identified could be supported
by the findings of my study. One of the characteristics of an engaging assignment that all of my participants identified as what they enjoyed most about
fanfiction or the discourse community they valued the most, was having "some
autonomy/freedom while being given the necessary structure to help them succeed" (Wardle, 2007, p. 78). Most fanfiction pieces are written with the same
format/style, being very similar to a novel. However, this doesn't mean one has
to write in this format; writers have complete freedom to write about what they
want, how they want to in fanfiction. It is the lack of this freedom in academic

writing that is the reason why many of my participants, Elizabeth and Belinda in particular, have grown frustrated with academic writings. Another characteristic of an engaging writing assignment is that the "assignment relates in some way to students' interests/future" (Wardle, 2007, p. 78). This is another reason why my participants are so engaged in many of the discourse communities and genres. The fanfiction that my participants write is done purely because they are interested in creative writing and in whatever their fanfiction is based off of, be it a movie, book, play, etc. The writing relating to their interests also plays an important role in many of the other discourse communities and genres that my participants are highly engaged in, such as roleplaying, journals, poetry, and writing original stories. Many of my participants have expressed disdain for academic writing because of the lack of interesting topics; however, others, Belinda and Laura in particular, have expressed interest in academic writing because of being assigned a writing topic that relates to their interest in creative writing.

As Kevin Roozen (2008; 2009; 2010) and Autumn Shrum (2011) found in 72 their research, my cases also suggest there has been some evidence of connection, repurposing, and transfer across the discourse communities of my participants. This is mainly because many of their discourse communities and genres relate to their interest in creative writing. All of my participants have expressed that their writing processes are fairly similar across all of their discourse communities and genres. By "writing process," I mean how they plan what they're going to write and their process during actually writing. Their revision process is another thing that connects across their discourse communities, for many of the participants have expressed that their revision process is fairly constant across their discourse communities. One case of repurposing from one discourse community to the next is in the case of Laura, concerning her fanfiction and original stories. Prior to beginning to write original stories, Laura had plenty of experience writing fanfiction. Since these are both forms of creative writing, many techniques and processes that Laura used in writing fanfiction could have been repurposed to be used for her original stories. Another case of repurposing is with Sarah and her roleplaying. Sarah has expressed that the people she interacts with on her roleplaying site have helped her greatly with her writing. Considering that this is where she spends a majority of her time writing, there is a possibility that what she has learned from this discourse community has been repurposed to be used in other discourse communities and genres. A few of my participants have expressed belief that knowledge of grammar, spelling, and vocabulary they have gained from school has transferred into their numerous other discourse communities and genres.

In "Revision Strategies of Student Writers and Experienced Adult Writers," 73 Nancy Sommers researched and identified the revision strategies of twenty student writers and twenty experienced adult writers. She found that student writers had a very narrow view of revision, seeing it as only being a linear process and being constrained to only word choice; while the experienced writers viewed revision as being not defined by time (unlike the students' view of it being linear) and by finding the best way to get their point across (Sommers, 1980).

From those I have interviewed, I can assume that these young writers, although students, have the revision strategies more closely resembling those of experienced adult writers.

Revision is never a linear process to these young writers; they do most of their revision and restructuring while they are in the process of writing. This revision may pertain to only word choice or it may pertain to the whole storyline. For example, Belinda shares an experience she had while writing a chapter to one of her fanfictions where she decided that it "wasn't going anywhere and simply scrapped it and started over." This process was never reported by the student writers that Sommers had interviewed; it was only reported by the experienced adult writers.  74

In her research article "Revision Strategies of Student Writers and Experienced Adult Writers," Nancy Sommers claims that students are inexperienced writers, particularly when it comes to revision (1980). However, the findings of my study contradict this claim. My participants have complex planning methods and writing processes, and the quality of their stories suggest that their revision processes is much more efficient than Sommers gives student writers credit for. Many of the fanfiction pieces of my participants have been highly praised by readers and other writers for both their content and quality. Several of my participants have also received praise and recognition from their teachers and other writing professionals for the writing (creative writing in particular) they have done outside of fanfiction. From the recognition they have received for their writing both in and outside of fanfiction, it can be assumed that they are, in fact, much more experienced with than what Sommers claims to have found in her article.  75

## Works Cited

Grabill et. Al. (2010). Revisualizing composition: mapping the writing lives of first-year college students. Retrieved from http://wide.msu.edu/special/writinglives

Haven, C. (2009, October 12). The new literacy: Stanford study finds richness and complexity in student's writing. *Stanford Report*. Retrieved from http://news.stanford.edu/news/2009/october12/lunsford-writing-research-101209.html

Roozen, K. (2008). Journalism, poetry, stand-up comedy, and academic literacy: Mapping the interplay of curricular and extracurricular literate activities. *Journal of Basic Writing, 27(1)*, 5–34.

Roozen, K. (2009). "Fan-ficing" English studies: A case study exploring the interplay of vernacular literacies and disciplinary engagement. *Research in the Teaching of English, 44(2)*, 136–166.

Roozen, K. (2010). Tracing trajectories of practice: Repurposing in one student's developing disciplinary writing processes. *Written Communication, 27(3)*, 318–354.

Shrum, A. (2011). Case #1. In progress M.A. thesis.

Shrum, A. (2011). Case #2. In progress M.A. thesis.

Sommers, N. (1980). Revision strategies of student writers and experienced adult writers. *College Composition and Communication, 31(4)*, 378–388.

Wardle, E. (2007). Understanding 'transfer' from FYC: Preliminary results of a longitudinal study. *WPA, 31(1/2)*, 65–85.

## Questions for Discussion and Journaling

1. Are you surprised by the amount of extracurricular writing in which Penzato's subjects engage? Do you or your friends write outside of school this extensively—or have you in this past?

2. Penzato's participant Belinda describes needing to sometimes "not touch a story for months." This ability to take extensive time in drafting is a big difference from school writing. Do you think this ability to "incubate" (as Berkenkotter describes earlier in this chapter) influences the quality of writing? Why or why not?

3. Penzato begins her paper by overviewing some of the research that frames her own study. Some of these authors are included in this book and you may have read them (Roozen and Sommers). Take a look at those articles again (if you've looked at them before) and make note of which parts of their studies Penzato referenced. Are these the parts you would have referenced? Are there other articles you have read that you think could also helpfully frame Penzato's study?

4. Penzato argues that the students in her study suggest that Sommers's view of the revision of student writers is too limited. What does she suggest about student writers' revision practices that differs from Sommers? Based on your own experiences, do you think student writers are more like Sommers's depiction or more like Penzato's depiction?

5. Penzato suggests a connection between a writer's mood and the style/tone with which she writes. Do you think this connection holds true for you too? What are some examples of where you have seen this happen?

## Applying and Exploring Ideas

1. Penzato's research subjects describe a frustration with academic writing and its constraints. Work with a partner to design a research study that might look at the motivation and revision strategies of students engaging in school and non-school activities in order to see whether this frustration is widespread and whether it has an impact on quality of writing. What research questions would you ask? Whom would you study? What data would you collect? How would you analyze the data?

2. Penzato's research suggests that people can have very different kinds of writing processes depending on their motivation, audience, and purpose. Reflect on your own writing processes for school and non-school writing and see whether you observe a similar difference. If not, why do you think that is?

> **Meta Moment**
> Are there aspects of your writing processes for non-school activities that you could usefully repurpose for school writing tasks?

## :e: In e-Pages at bedfordstmartins.com/writingaboutwriting

- Junot Díaz, "Becoming a Writer" (e-Pages)
- Barbara Tomlinson, "Tuning, Tying, and Training Texts: Metaphors for Revision" (e-Pages)

# Writing about Processes: Major Writing Assignments

To help you learn and explore the ideas in this chapter, we are suggesting three assignment options for larger writing projects: Autoethnography, Portrait of a Writer, and Writer's Process Search.

## Assignment Option 1. Autoethnography

For this assignment, you will conduct a study similar to those conducted by Perl and Berkenkotter, but instead of looking at someone else, you will examine yourself and your own writing processes and write an autoethnography in which you describe them. Your method will be to record (preferably with video and audio) your complete writing process as you complete a writing assignment for a class. Your purpose is to try to learn some things about your actual writing practices that you might not be aware of and to reflect on what you learn using the terms and concepts you've read about in this chapter.

***Object of Study and Collecting Data:*** To make this assignment as useful as possible, you need to plan ahead, so figure out what you will be writing for this or other classes in the next few weeks, and make a decision about what you will study. Consider the following:

- What kinds of assignments are easiest or most difficult for you to write?
- What kinds of assignments would be the most useful to examine yourself writing?

Before beginning your project, make sure that you know how to use your computer or other device's audio and/or video recording systems.

As you write the assignment that you will study, record yourself every time that you work on it—this includes even times when you are thinking and planning for it, or when you are revising. Keep the following in mind:

- You may not be near your recording device(s) when you are planning; if that is the case, then keep a log in which you note your thoughts about the assignment.
- When you sit down to type the paper, think out loud the entire time. This will feel strange, and it will take some effort. Do your best.
- Try to externalize everything you are thinking. If you have trouble knowing what to say, go back to Perl and Berkenkotter and look at the kinds of things that Tony and Donald Murray said aloud when they were being studied.

When you have completely finished writing the assignment whose writing process you're studying, listen to or view the recording of yourself and transcribe it. This means typing everything that you said on the tape, even the "ums" and "ahs." It will be helpful to double space (or even triple space) the transcript so that you can make notes on it.

***Analyzing Your Data:*** Alone or with your class, as your teacher directs, come up with a code to help you study your transcript. To see how to make a code, return to Berkenkotter and Perl for their descriptions of how they came up with their codes. To consider what categories or elements of writing process you might want to include in your code, look back through the readings you've done in this chapter. What did our various authors choose to study about people's writing processes? Some suggestions for things you might include would be notes about context (where and when you wrote, what distractions you faced, your attitude, any deadlines, etc.), codes for planning, brainstorming, large-scale revision, small-scale revision, pausing, and so on.

What you want is a code that will help you understand what's happening when you write. Beware of the following potential pitfalls:

- If the code is too vague, you won't learn anything at all.
- If the code is too detailed (for example, if you try to do what Perl did and record the exact amount of time you took for each action), you might never get done coding.

We recommend coming up with a code with the rest of your class, and then trying to use that code on a practice transcript that your teacher provides. This will help you see if the code is useful.

Once you have settled on a code, use it to analyze your transcript.

- You might get a box of highlighters of different colors, and use each color to highlight the parts of the text that correspond to parts of the code (for example, pink is for planning).
- You could simply underline parts of the transcript and label them in shorthand (P = planning).
- If you used a computer, you could search for key phrases in the text and mark each occurrence by using the software's "reviewing" feature to insert a comment in the margin.
- You could use free or low-cost coding and data analysis software such as Dedoose to upload your transcript and label different parts of it with codes you input, which allows you to generate helpful visualizations of how your various codes interact with the data.

Once you have coded the transcript, go back and consider these questions:

- What is interesting about what you found? What immediately jumps out at you?
- Did you do some things a lot, and other things rarely or never? Which codes do you see frequently or little at all?
- How does your analysis suggest you compare to Tony or to Murray?

Like some of the authors in this chapter, you might make some charts or tables for yourself in order to visually explore what percentage of time you spent on various activities.

***Planning and Drafting:*** What are you going to write about? You don't need to go into excruciating detail about everything you coded. Instead, you should decide what you want to claim about what you found. For example:

- How would you describe your writing process?
- What are the most important take-home points from your analysis?
- Are there aspects of your process that are definitively impacted by technologies like instant messaging, social networking, Skype, or even word-processing?

Based on the patterns that emerge from your analysis of data, decide what your claims will be and then return to your analysis to select data that give evidence of those claims.

By now, from discussions in class and with your teacher you should have a sense of what genre you'll write your report in, and in deciding that, you should know your audience, purpose, and exigence as well. Will you write about your findings in an informal reflective essay in which you discuss your process and compare yourself to some of the writers in the chapter—something like Sommers does in "I Stand Here Writing"—or write a more formal, researched argument like Perl or Berkenkotter did, using an intro/background/methods/analysis/discussion structure? Or will you write in some other genre?

You'll definitely want to plan your genre before you begin drafting, since your drafting processes will vary by genre. If you are writing the reflective essay, you are most likely writing for yourself (writing to learn) and to share what you learn with fellow student writers and your teacher, for the purpose of improving your writing processes and abilities. Such reflection is often best "drafted toward" by knowing the main claims you want to make and striking out on your writing, understanding that you'll be discovering and learning along the way and will probably revise extensively in order to reach a consistent message from beginning to ending of your piece.

If you will be writing a more scholarly research article, you might begin by outlining the various sections of your paper: In your introduction, what other research will you cite? Whose work provides important background information for your study? What is the gap or niche that your study fills? How will you describe your research methods? What are the main claims you want to make in the findings? One trick that some writers use is to write headings for each section, with main claims underneath. Then the writer can go back and write one section at a time in order to break up the writing.

Once you have a "shitty first draft," revise it to make it a little more coherent. Then share it with classmates, being sure to tell them what genre you wrote and what concerns or issues you'd like them to read for.

***What Makes It Good?:*** The purpose of this assignment was for you to try to learn some things about your actual writing practices that you might not have been aware of, and to reflect on what you learned using the terms and concepts you've read about in this chapter. Does your paper demonstrate that this purpose was achieved? In addition, your readers will want to learn something from having read your paper. Does your finished text clearly convey your insights and findings?

*A caveat:* We have found that some students just go through the motions when they complete this assignment, but don't make an attempt to learn something about themselves as writers. When those students write their papers, they have very little to say about "results" or "insights." They tend to say pretty clichéd things like "I am distracted when I write. I should try to write with fewer distractions." In general, if the "insights" of the paper were obvious to you before you ever conducted the autoethnography, then you have not fully engaged in the project and are unlikely to receive a good grade on it.

***Alternative Assignment:*** Instead of studying yourself writing one assignment, compare yourself writing two very different kinds of texts (maybe in school and out of school, or humanities and science) and analyze them to see whether—or how—your process changes depending on what you write.

# Assignment Option 2. Portrait of a Writer

The various authors in this chapter clearly believe that good writing takes hard work and multiple drafts, and that many of us are hampered from being better writers by the "rules" and misconceptions we have been taught about writing.

This is true even of very famous people who write a lot every day. For example, U.S. Supreme Court Justice Sonia Sotomayor has been widely criticized for her writing. She even criticizes herself, saying, "Writing remains a challenge for me even today—everything I write goes through multiple drafts—I am not a natural writer."[1] Here she conflates being a "good" writer with being a "natural" writer; she seems to believe that some people are born good writers and some people aren't. Her conception is that a "good" writer only has to write one draft; anyone who has to write multiple drafts must be a "bad" writer. Even from this one short quotation, you can see that Justice Sotomayor's conceptions of writing are limiting, and would not hold up if closely examined by the researchers and professional writers in this chapter.

Use what you have read in this unit to consider the story you have to tell about yourself as a writer. How do you see yourself as a writer? Is that self-perception helping you be the best writer you can be? The purpose of this assignment is for you to apply what you have learned in this chapter to help you better understand why and how you write—and how you might write differently.

*Brainstorming and Planning:* Try the following to generate material for your assignment:

- Go back to the discussion and activity questions you completed as you read the articles in this chapter. What did you learn about yourself and your writing processes here?
- Consider what you write and don't write.
- Consider how you prepare—or don't prepare—to write a paper.
- Think of any kinds of writing that you enjoy, and any kinds of writing that you dread.
- Freewrite about the writing rules that block you, and the writing rules that aid you.
- Make a list of all the metaphors or similes about writing and revision that you and your friends use.

You should spend a substantial amount of time reflecting on yourself as a writer, using the concepts and ideas that you learned in this chapter. Even if some or most of your brainstorming doesn't end up in your paper, the act of reflecting should be useful to you as a writer.

Looking at all the notes and freewriting from your brainstorming so far, considering what's interesting here. What catches your interest the most? What is new or surprising to you? Settle on a few of these surprises or "ah hah!" moments as the core of what you will write for this assignment. For each of these core elements of your essay, brainstorm examples, details, and explanations that would help your reader understand what you are trying to explain about yourself.

*Drafting and Revising:* Write a three- to five-page essay in which you describe your view of yourself as a writer, using examples and explanations to strengthen your description. As appropriate, you might refer to the authors of texts in this chapter to help explain your experiences, processes, or feelings. Conclude the essay by considering how or whether the

---

[1]politico.com/blogs/joshgerstein/0609/Sotomayor_writing_a_challenge_even_today.html.

things you have learned in this chapter might change your conception of yourself as a writer or your writing behaviors. Your class should discuss potential audiences for this essay:

- Are you writing to the teacher, to demonstrate what you've learned in this chapter?
- Are you writing for yourself, to help solidify what you've learned?
- Would you like to adapt your essay to write for someone else—maybe your parents, to demonstrate who you are as a writer and what influences you can identify? Maybe to a teacher who had an impact, positive or negative, on who you are as a writer?

Of course, this choice of audience and purpose will have a significant impact on your essay—its form, content, tone, language, level of formality, and so on. You might also talk with your teacher about more creative ways to paint your self-portrait:

- Try writing a play outlining your writing process.
- Transform a metaphor about writing into a visual description—for example, a collage—of who you are as a writer or what you think "good writing" is.
- Create a hypertext essay where readers can look at pictures, watch video, listen to songs, even listen to your own voice, as you describe yourself and your conceptions of writers, the writing process, and "good writing."

Try to get readers for your piece as early in your composing process as possible, and use their feedback on their reading experience to revise for the most reader-friendly document possible. Pay particular attention to whether your readers seem to be experiencing all the ideas you want to—or whether some of what you want to say is clear in your thoughts but not in what you've composed.

**What Makes It Good?:** This purpose of this assignment is for you to step back and consider yourself as a writer, applying what you learned in this chapter to help you better understand why and how you write—and how you might write differently, or perhaps even understand yourself differently as a writer. When you've finished it, ask yourself:

- Were you able to apply what you learned in this chapter to understand yourself better? (If not, that will likely show up in the depth of your writing.)
- Did you successfully identify an audience for your piece and write appropriately for those readers?

# Assignment Option 3. Writer's Process Search

We hope the readings in this chapter have raised some questions for you about how professional writers might go about writing every day, and what language they might choose to talk about and describe writing. It is tempting to offer an assignment where you go find a handful of writers and interview them on their processes and ideas about writing, and then write the results. (And you should feel free to discuss such a project with your teacher if that's interesting to you.) But as it turns out, there are a number of venues where other researchers and reporters *already have* done these sorts of interviews, and posted them in online archives.

The presence of these archives provides the basis for this assignment option: Establish a research question on some aspect of writing process (for example, "Where do professional writers get their ideas?" or "How do professional writers talk about revision?"), and mine the interview archives we list below (and any others you might be aware of or come across in your own reading) seeking writers' accounts that relate to and can help answer your research question. Synthesize whatever commentary you find into a report on your question: What do professional writers of various kinds have to say about the aspect of writing you're wondering about? That is your focus in researching and writing this piece. We call it a "writer's process search" because you'll be searching these interview archives for data (interviews) that address your question(s) on writing processes.

**Getting to Know the Archives:** Your first task in this project will be to familiarize yourself with the data resources available to you. We collect here four repositories of interviews with writers. Certainly, more such repositories exist, which you might find with some good Internet searching, but we know these will give you a good start. Together they include interviews from literary writers, other professional writers, playwrights and screenwriters, songwriters, journalists, and research writers. Most take a question-and-answer (Q&A) format with their interview subjects. When used together with a resource like Wikipedia (since many of the people interviewed are likely to have a Wikipedia page) to gain richer background on the interviewees, these archives create a rich repository of professionally recognized writers talking about writing in their own words.

### The New York Times—Books

### "Writers on Writing"

### nytimes.com/books/specials/writers.html

Unlike the other archives we're pointing you to, in the *Times'* column "Writers on Writing," the writers were not interviewed; rather, they wrote short essays on some topic related to writing which were then published in the *Times*. What you'll find at this site, then, are writers such as Joyce Carol Oates, Saul Bellow, Barbara Kingslover, Chitra Divakaruni, David Mamet, and Susan Sontag, writing on subjects like what makes a good novel, taking a break from writing in order to have more to say (Ford), selecting music for writing (White), handwriting (Gordon), the relationship between writing and living (Gish), how running assists writing (Oates), or the role of rewriting in writing (Sontag). Because each essay is thematic, this isn't the place where a single writer will have a wide-ranging discussion on many different aspects of writing process. As is the case with most of these archives, it's easier to search by author than by subject, so you'll need to schedule enough time just to read what's there and make good notes about where you found particular information so that you can locate it again later. On the upside, most of the articles were written between 1999 and 2001 and thus don't require a *New York Times* subscription to access. When you find one that touches on your area of inquiry, it will be a rich source of information about a writer's words on the subject of writing.

### Songwriters on Process

### writersonprocess.com

This Web site contains an archive of interviews with songwriting musicians. The interviews are conducted by site author Benjamin Opipari, who asks questions of the writers about "their creative process, from beginning to end." Opipari demonstrates an eclectic taste in interview subjects, having spoken with sogwriters as diverse as Chris Difford from Squeeze to Neil Finn of Crowded House to Bechtolt and Evans of YACHT and Cohen and Emm of Tanlines. A wide range of other genres are represented as well. The interviews tend to focus on the process by which songwriters get ideas for lyrics and music, and how they move those ideas along to become finished songs. Typical questions include "When it comes to the songwriting process, how do you feel about inspiration?," "How disciplined are you as a songwriter?," and "How much revision do you do to your lyrics?" Readers can learn a lot about songwriting simply by reading the interviews, but they're also good for zooming in on particular aspects of the writing process. The site is arranged by the name of the interviewee and their band, and the format for interviews (with questions bolded and short) makes any given interview easy to glance through to get a sense of subjects covered.

### The Paris Review

#### "Interviews"

#### theparisreview.org/interviews

*The Paris Review* is a journal of literary writing (fiction, poetry, and essays) that also publishes some literary criticism. It was founded in 1953. A year later, it began running interviews with contemporary writers—and it has done so every year for the ensuing sixty years, running more than half a dozen per year. The site is searchable by author or by decade. You'll find interviews with Maya Angelou, Margaret Atwood, Ray Bradbury, Philip Larkin, Dorris Lessing, Edna O'Brien, Walker Percy . . . the list is immense, and the range of genres represented is complete (fiction, poetry, plays, essays, journalism), though many of the interviewees are novelists. These interviews are often conducted as public events with audiences, which may influence the responses the writers offer to questions. As with other interview archive sites, this one will be difficult to search by subject—but because of its arrangement by time, it might be especially useful for questions related to change in writing process through time (for example, how processes change as writing technologies do).

### The New York Times

#### "Why I Write: Q&A with Seven Times Journalists."

#### learning.blogs.nytimes.com/2011/10/17/why-i-write-q-and-a-with-seven -times-journalists/

Different from the other three archive sites, this "Learning Network" blog post in the *Times* focused narrowly on a short list of journalists writing for the *Times*, covering a range of story types, and asked each the same questions. The occasion of these interviews was the 2011 "National Day on Writing" (created by the National Council of Teachers of English). Among other questions, each of the writers (such as Web producer Jeffrey Delviscio, Styles writer Simone Oliver, and sportswriter Pete Thamel) responded to how they became a reporter, what outside forces influence their writing, what their writing process looks like, and why they write. The whole set of interviews can be read in about half an hour, and is extremely valuable for seeing less famous but very professional writers talk in down-to-earth ways about how they experience writing.

***Brainstorming and Selecting a Research Question:*** Explore each of these sites, familiarizing yourself with which writers have been interviewed by each source and considering the best ways to search the sites for material specifically related to the research question you'll choose.

Once you've read some interviews at each site in order to get your inquiry juices flowing, you should be considering what question you might like to focus your project on.

- Did you see something a given writer was talking about that you'd like to investigate further?
- Is there some "writer's problem" such as writer's block or coming up with what to write about that you'd like to find how professional writers deal with?
- Is there a larger aspect of writing process, such as revision, that you'd like to see how various writers talk about?
- Is there some subject related to writing, such as what role music can play during the writing process, that you're curious about?
- Are you seeing trends related to the kind of writing that a person does? For example, do songwriters think about process differently than journalists?
- Do writing technologies come up at all? If so, are there trends across time, genre, or type of writer?

While the focus of your particular question may be somewhat challenging to settle on, giving the variety of information in the archives, it's very likely that some of these writers will have discussed your question, whatever it turns out to be. Notice that the broader your question, the more quickly you're likely to find interviews related to it; however, a very broad question might be difficult to write about because of its breadth.

***Collecting and Analyzing Data:*** Once you have settled on a research question, you'll need to begin searching the interview archives to find a set of interviews that touch on your subject of inquiry. You will collect a number of these interviews and begin considering and synthesizing what various writers say about your question.

First you will need a plan for searching the interview archives. There are a number of approaches you could take:

- You could choose which interviews to look at based on your interest in the authors themselves. For example, you could make a list of all the authors names you already recognize in a given archive and choose all those to read; you could also briefly familiarize yourself with authors by searching their names in Wikipedia.
- You could do a "brute-force" search by opening a large number of interviews and using your browser's "Find in page" function (Ctrl-F) to search for keywords related to your subject of inquiry. This method lets you determine in just a second or two whether your subject term appears in the interview, and takes you directly to it in the page if it does. You could easily search fifty to sixty interviews per hour using this method.
- You could select interviews based on a Google search. For example, if your question is on the role of music in the composing process and you want to see which *Paris Review* interviews have landed on the subject of music, you can type *music "paris review" interview* into the search bar and Google will return a list of all the *Paris Review* interviews it finds that term in. (Of course, you will also find a million other

unrelated hits. If you use this method, be sure to include the title words of your archive in quotation marks to force Google to return hits only on that specific title rather than on any combination of words from the title.)

- You could always simply read randomly, and if you have five or six hours over a few days to devote to your research, this approach (which relies on what researchers call *serendipity*) might be a very good one, especially combined with one of the other approaches. The interviews are relatively short, quick reads, interesting in and of themselves, and you could cover quite a lot of ground simply by giving yourself some time to be curious and read actively.

You'll also need to decide which archives are the best fit for your research question. You'll find some overlap between *New York Times Book* interviews and *Paris Review* interviews but very little overlap in the others.

Once you have a stack of interviews that seem to touch on your subject of inquiry in some way, you'll analyze that data the same way that you do in many of the other projects in this book:

- Watch for patterns that emerge: What gets said repeatedly? But also, be prepared for there not to be a pattern; if writers disagree or do things in wildly different ways, that is just as much a finding as discovering that there are similarities across writers. Writing is a very individual process, so finding only one pattern might be difficult. You might also see several patterns—people might do A, B, or C rather than mostly doing A.

- Watch for outliers: Is there something that very few of the writers say? When someone does say this thing, is it striking or unusual in comparison to the emerging patterns?

- Look closely at details in language. When a writer refers to revision as "polishing" versus referring to it as "honing," for example, the terms engage different metaphors for writing that show different assumptions about its nature and how it works. (For more on this subject, read Barbara Tomlinson's article in the e-Pages. She used *Paris Review* interviews for her research, too, so she provides a nice example of how to use this interview data for your study.)

- Compare what you're reading with your own experience: Compared to your own writing experiences, what are these writers saying that sounds "normal" and what are they saying that sounds unusual to you?

Again as in other projects requiring analysis of observations or a corpus of textual data, take careful notes to keep track of the patterns and interesting ideas you're seeing, and after you've reviewed your interviews at least twice, step back and see what you have to say on your question. Now might also be a good time to do more general Web searching to see if other people have written and commented on the question you're working on.

***Planning, Drafting, and Revising:*** Ultimately, you should emerge from your data analysis with some key points to make in your Writer's Process Search report. The purpose of the project has been to discover what professional writers of various kinds have to say about the aspect of writing you're studying; the purpose of your report is to present your findings in a readable and interesting way to your classmates and instructor (or to another audience that you and your teacher might agree upon).

It might be most natural to arrange this piece in typical social-science research-report fashion, where you introduce your subject of inquiry and research question using Swales's CARS model (in the Introduction to *Writing about Writing*), detail the archive reviews you used and explain the methods by which you searched them, walk readers through the data you found and how you analyzed it, discuss what you found, and conclude with implications from your study: How do the findings of your study help us?

However, instead of using the typical social-science research report format, you might also leave your imagination open to other ways of making this report. Here are some of many possibilities that you should discuss with your classmates and teacher:

- Combine the interview subjects with similar ideas into one "composite" interview. Margaret Kantz does something like this in her "Using Textual Sources Persuasively" article in Chapter 3. In this way, you might create several "characters" who articulate the main ideas espoused by a number of the writers whose interviews you read. You could also consider drafting some friends to play these characters and produce a short documentary.
- A song, poem, or play that in some way dramatized your findings rather than merely reporting them. This might be especially relevant if you drew on the song-writers' database.
- A hypertext that included additional background information on the writers whose interviews you used and linked back to the interviews themselves.
- A (somewhat long) tweet-stream that reduced your findings to 140-character sayings.

Whatever genre and modality you write in, expect to use a fair amount of quotation from the interviews themselves in your piece. Remember, what the interviewees said is your data, and your readers need to be able to see examples of your data in order to judge for themselves how much sense the conclusions that you're drawing from the data make. Quotations from the interviews will become your *reasons* for making the claims you do about your subject of inquiry.

Revise, as always, by getting reader feedback on how much sense the piece makes, how readable it is (in terms of flow and organization, clarity of statements of ideas, and editing quality), and what would improve their experience of the piece.

***What Makes it Good?:*** The best versions of this project will do the following:

- Make a clear point or series of points about your subject of inquiry (in answer to your research question).
- Explain your research question and the sources of it precisely and clearly.
- Use a creative and reliable method of searching the archives.
- Balance use of quotation as examples with analysis of quotations. (They don't speak for themselves; you need to explain what's important about them or what they convey.)
- Report findings in a manner consistent with the genre/modality you've chosen to write in, hopefully being no less interesting and entertaining than the interviews themselves.

## chapter 5

# Multimodal Composition
## What Counts as Writing?

Because writing is happening in so many more ways than it was forty years ago—with the advent of **computer mediated communication** in the 1970s and 80s, the explosion of network-mediated writing in the 1990s, and the current ubiquity of screen-delivered texts in the present decade—more aspects of writing are being exposed now than were obvious back when the height of writing was typewritten books mass-produced by printing press. Yet our cultural and personal understandings of what counts as writing and what makes writing good still tend to be dominated by the understandings of writing we had back when the "best" writing was:

An image of writing in the 21st century: digital, networked, collaborative, screen-based, and interactive. How different is this kind of writing from that of our great-grandparents?

- entirely alphabetic (no pictures or images)
- long-form (valorizing long, thick chunks of text, as in books, rather than short, fragmented snippets of writing, as in texting, Twitter, or sampling)
- codex (arranged in book format with pages, as opposed to screen-based or sequential access, such as a scrolling document like a Web page)
- single-authored, with clear and distinct sources (as opposed to written by multiple people, or crowdsourced, or gradually emerging from collected discussion)
- published by large companies after being carefully edited (as opposed to self-published and largely unedited)
- one-way communication from author (sender) to audience (receiver) (as opposed to interactive communication among one or more writers and multiple readers, as in blogs, and electronic discussion forums)

- valued for its own sake—a neat "piece of writing" (as opposed to writing valued purely for what people can use it to accomplish, not for itself but for the way it supports some other activity)
- valued for correctness, perfection, and pristine finish (as opposed to the "rough and ready" attitude that frequently accompanies electronic writing today—"if you understood it, it was correct enough, even if it didn't follow proper rules of spelling and punctuation")
- read straight through, all the way through, without distraction, without interference from other texts, with concentration and singular focus (as opposed to how people tend to read online today, scanning in bits and pieces and "multi-tasking" across multiple documents at once)

Those now-traditional understandings of writing began to appear about six hundred years ago in the decades following the invention of the printing press. That invention had resulted in the relatively inexpensive mass-production of writing, the resulting comparative cheapness of long-form writing (like novels, which appeared in the 1700s), and the resulting need to *standardize* graphic elements of writing such as spelling and punctuation (which before the printing press were not standardized at all). The comparative difficulty and expense of mass-reproducing *images* led to mostly all-alphabetic texts. Once long-form alphabetic-print came to dominate textuality in Western cultures, it also came to dominate our definitions of what counted as writing and what made writing good. Dennis Baron's piece "From Pencils to Pixels," which opens this chapter, discusses these movements in detail. Baron frames our thinking about writing by reminding us that it has *always* been technological—without tools, there is no writing—and that new technologies of writing have always been initially feared, before being embraced so widely that their users forget they are, in fact, technology.

Technological advances over the past forty years, then, have brought us radical alternatives to long-form, print-based writing, with the result of exposing ways in which our traditional assumptions about the nature of writing and definitions of "good" writing seem to have been a bit narrow. We still assume the technology that is "invisible" to us—like the printing presses that create mass-produced long books—is "normal" writing. This chapter collects readings that focus on new, usually electronic and networked, **modalities** and genres of writing, readings which have the effect of getting us to look again at our assumptions about what writing is, how it works, and what makes it good. *Modality* refers to the senses or facilities readers use to experience a text; typical modalities are alphabetic-print, visual/image (still, like photographs, or moving, like video), aural, color, and kinesthetic/touch. In another sense, "modality" refers to our mode of access to texts or which particular technology "mediates" (or makes available) the text, with typical examples being newsprint, codex/book, and electronic/networked.

To help you make greatest use of the readings in this chapter, we will offer here some starting points in thinking about writing as more than mono-modal, alphabetic print. In fact, "writing," even when it *is* print-only, is much more than the alphabetic transcription of language into letters. Letters of the alphabet are actually themselves pictures which, in becoming fluent readers, we've forgotten how to see as pictures—we know this from work by Scott McCloud, which we've referenced below. Scholars in visual literacy such as Ann Wysocki have further shown that the visual and graphical elements of even purely alphabetical texts are unavoidably *visual* and *graphical*, not simply transmitting meaning through language represented in alphabetic print. Such research gives us ways of understanding **multimodal** texts (multimedia texts combining multiple modes, such as alphabetic, visual, and aural) as the "new normal" in writing and textuality.

This sense of multimodal texts as now-normal can conflict strongly with the cultural notion, developed during the past centuries of monomodal, alphabetic-only texts, that words are highly intelligent and pictures are for people who can't use words well—that picture-based or "illustrated" texts are usually more simplistic and for less educated or less mature readers (think children's books), or more for entertainment and less for serious intellectual work. In this chapter, Baron's article, plus Steve Bernhardt's piece on "Seeing the Text" in the e-Pages at bedfordstmartins.com/writingaboutwriting, help us understand that texts which incorporate graphic elements and images (photos, pictures, drawings, charts, etc.) are *at least* as sophisticated as print-only texts, not less "grown-up." (As simple evidence of this, open any science journal: it will be full of images doing complex intellectual work.) Images in fact used to dominate writing before the invention of the printing press. But when the least expensive way to write became printing-press based mass-reproduction, most learned texts in the humanities (where the English teachers hang out) incorporated few or no visuals, so high writing ability (and even intelligence itself) came to be associated with print-only texts, and image-driven texts came to be associated with "lower" purposes such as entertainment, or with teaching and training, or with accommodating lack of facility with written language (which was then called "illiteracy"). Now that screen-based publication and reading have made it nearly as cheap and easy to reproduce images as to reproduce alphabetic print, images once again dominate written texts, forcing us to ask questions about what counts as writing that we didn't have to ask when "writing" was dominated by print-only materials produced by printing presses.

Ironically, while the technical means to create and reproduce image-driven writing have recently become highly accessible and comparably inexpensive (consider how easy it is to create and share videos on YouTube, for example), the copyright and intellectual-property climate in developed nations, especially the U.S., has grown increasingly restrictive and even predatory. The very ease with which "non-print" (any non-alphabetic modality) material can be shared—think of music file sharing, for example, or the image-sharing and-modifying culture represented by Lolcats and similar Web sites—has provoked a hostile response from copyright holders of the works users try to share. These rights-holders are usually not actually the "authors" of the work. (Though if you read Porter's article on intertextuality in Chapter 3, you know that the idea of a text having just a single author is unlikely to begin with.) Instead, creators of content usually must sign their rights to their work over to their publishers in order to be published, and these publishers increasingly tend to be large multinational entertainment corporations. Such companies come with large legal teams who enforce copyright by threat of lawsuits (as when the Recording Industry Association of America sues individuals for hundreds of thousands of dollars for sharing a single music file without permission). This threat of lawsuit chills even the most legitimate sharing, reprinting, and licensing of multimodal writing, creating labyrinthine processes for obtaining permissions to reprint previously published material, and preventing even textbooks like this one and, in some cases, researchers themselves from using previously published material for fear of being unable to get sufficient permissions to forestall lawsuits from publishers.

This chapter, for example, was originally designed with the three readings listed below in mind. But when we pursued permissions to reprint them, due either to excessive time required or expense incurred, we were unable to obtain permissions:

- "The Vocabulary of Comics," chapter 2 of Scott McCloud's fantastic book *Understanding Comics* (1994). It's a primer on how visual rhetoric works, conducted through an analysis of comics—the book itself being written *in comics*. The fee to reprint this one chapter was thousands of dollars, hugely unaffordable.
- "The Multiple Media of Texts: How Onscreen and Paper Texts Incorporate Words, Images, and Other Media," Ann Wysocki's chapter on visual design in texts from Charles Bazerman and Paul Prior's collection *What Writing Does and How It Does It* (Lawrence Earlbaum, 2004). Wysocki creates a thorough taxonomy of elements of visual design in texts, plus several examples of analysis of visual elements in texts. The chapter incorporates a number of images, each of which required us to get separate permissions to reprint, which stood to be too complex and costly a project in the time available. And as is the nature of multimodal texts, there's no point reprinting just one of the modalities they work in (like, reprinting the words but leaving out the images).
- "Rethinking Composing in a Digital Age: Authoring Literate Identities through Multimodal Storytelling," a 2010 *Written Communication* article by Lalitha Vasude-van, Katherine Schultz, and Jennifer Bateman. The piece is an excellent account of multimodal research projects composed by fifth graders, and it includes reprints of photos from some of the projects themselves. Even though all the students whose work appears in the article had given the article's authors permission to print their work in *Written Communication*, we would have to get permission all over again from all the participants (and, because they are minors, from their parents as well) to include the article in this textbook, a process that time prohibited. And, of course, this would have been on top of getting permission from *Written Communication* itself to reprint the article for a fee.

We would encourage readers who want deep background on visual literacy and visual multimodality to gain access (legally!) to these and similar works, via interlibrary loan or other "fair use"-protected access, and we regret that we're unable to include the pieces here.

Such challenges in compiling a chapter like this are important to discuss for three reasons: First, the spirit of writing-about-writing is itself *transparency about* and *study of* how writing works and how texts come to be; these challenges are a perfect case for such transparency. Second, you, the students reading this book, are the people who in coming years will be increasingly affected by the train wreck resulting from the collision between the easy availability and composition of multimodal writing, on the one hand, versus the increasingly restrictive legal environment around the easy sharing of work on which this availability and composition depend, on the other hand. This restrictive environment won't change without the bright sunlight created by writers speaking publicly about these challenges. And third, we do wish to explain why some resources on visual literacy that would work well in a chapter and book such as this have not been included. There is much more to be said about the intersection of sharing creative content while protecting the rights of content-creators and publishers; it is indeed a significant area of discussion for future study which we encourage you to consider, maybe even as a research project for this chapter.

Happily for our chapter, many other issues exist around multimodal composition besides simply the ideas that writing is inherently visual and that new, screen-based technologies make multimodal composing available to almost any writer. Following Baron, in this chapter, the next group of readings challenge cultural stereotypes that the "best" writing is *long-form* writing and that short texts aren't really legitimate writing. Amanda Lenhart (lead researcher on this subject for the Pew Research Center) and her co-authors find that many or even most students don't believe that the short, everyday writing they do when they text, chat, or facebook even qualifies as "writing," because it's so different from the *school* writing they associate with being "what writing is." Naomi Baron, as well as Jeffrey Grabill & Stacey Pigg (lead researchers for the WIDE research group) and Michaela Cullington, each demonstrate in their work how short, fragmentary writings—texting, Twitter, lists, notes, sampling, and the like—are real, everyday forms of writing that enable communication between people and foster real work for the short or micro-texts people are writing. (And also that such forms of writing don't preclude people from participating in and valuing longer, more traditional forms of writing.) From the reading side of the writer/reader interchange, James Sosnoski's piece in the e-Pages at bedfordstmartins.com /writingaboutwriting, shows us how readers increasingly handle even longer texts by fragmenting them, chopping them up, and using them in snippets.

Many of the researchers whose work is included in this chapter—most notably Naomi Baron, Michaela Cullington, and Brandon Jones—find that this intensely *communicative*, interactional use of writing (as in texting or online discussion boards, for example) sometimes means that writers and readers can de-emphasize correctness, spelling, and punctuation, because the lack of these refinements doesn't get in the way of this kind of everyday communication as it would in longer, more formal, less personal, and more "distanced" texts.

Several of the researchers in this chapter focus heavily on this idea of interactivity—finding that these new electronic, networked modalities and genres are proving to be much more collaborative and interactive than traditional forms of writing. Christian Kohl and his coauthors show how, for example, Wikipedia articles are actually defined by the collaborative processes that create them over time—the interaction is the source (and strength) of the articles' knowledge. Baron's and Cullington's articles focus on the interactive nature and purpose of texting and "text-speak." In e-Pages, Ann Cochran's research on "recovery blogs" written by people battling eating disorders such as anorexia focuses closely on the effects of writers' interaction with each other, which is the purpose of creating such blogs in the first place. In all of these cases, writing has lost its traditional expectation of a one-way message sent from writer to reader, completed before sending and usable by the reader only as a receiver, not as a writer-back. These new "networked" texts are created with the most basic assumption that they will provoke written responses, and that such written responses in some sense "complete" them.

Some readings in this chapter also take up one of the greatest discomforts we seem to have, culturally, with the new electronic modalities: They let us skip editors altogether and instead self-publish. In the age of books, self-publication was an absolute mark of inferiority and suspicious, low-quality content. Only an extended, expensive editorial process and professional publication could guarantee, and serve as a mark of, the quality of writing enclosed between the publisher-created covers of a book, magazine, or newspaper. But almost every new electronic modality involves self-publication, in ways that have initially made many cultural authorities (teachers, librarians, cultural commentators, editors, and publishers) deeply uncomfortable. Kohl et al., in their study of Wikipedia authoring, look closely at its self-published nature; contrary to popular assumption, they find that the self-published and crowd-sourced nature of Wikipedia does not, in fact, make it any less credible than traditionally published encyclopedias. Instead, because readers can see the open process by which claims were arrived at and justified, Wikipedia articles can actually be more reliable and believable than traditional encyclopedia work. Additionally, Jones' study of online gaming bulletin boards and Cochran's study of recovery blogs both demonstrate the raw power and effect of self-publishing online.

As noted briefly above, electronic writing modalities don't simply change our conceptions of and processes of writing; they also change the ways we read. James Sosnoski, in the e-Pages at bedfordstmartins.com/writingaboutwriting, studies this shift in reading habits in great detail, arguing that some reading practices, such as skimming, are legitimately useful.

Once you've begun thinking about current forms of writing in the ways that the articles in this chapter suggest, you can look back to more "traditional" or dominant forms of writing and recognize that the characteristics of "new" forms of writing are not new at all; they were *always* in the nature of writing, but were elided (concealed or overlooked) by the dominant forms of writing for the past six hundred years. Writing has *always* been visual; we have simply forgotten to (or taught ourselves not to) see it that way. Writing has *always* been highly interactional and collaborative; only the nineteenth-century romantic myth of the lone inspired writer drove us to stop noticing how much writers have always written in the company of others and honed their writing via reader feedback. Short-form writing has *always* counted as writing; we have just thought so highly of novels for the past 150 years that we failed to realize that grocery lists are writing, too. Writing has *always* been technological, because technology is not limited to electronics; it's any use of a non-biological tool to accomplish a task. Writing always requires tools to inscribe surfaces; it is and always has been technological.

Because these traditional, dominant understandings of writing have been *so* dominant for so long, people (especially young people still in school) may be unlikely to identify their short, informal, electronic forms of written communication as "writing" at all (as Lenhart et al.'s Pew study reveals).

New, electronic, networked modalities and genres of writing have exposed more aspects of the nature of writing than traditional views. As you learn more about these aspects of writing, we would like you to keep these focusing questions in mind:

What in today's world counts as *writing* (versus visual art, photography, film, music, or speech), and what makes writing good? (Correct grammar and punctuation? The ability to communicate an idea and be used for a purpose? Catchy and well-crafted language? Good arguments?)

As you work though this chapter, we also want you to keep in mind the threshold concept that *writing is by nature a technology*. It requires *tools*, and it is not "natural" (in a biological sense). What changes about how you approach writing, what your expectations of it are, and how you go about doing it, if you truly start thinking of writing in these ways?

These are questions you have asked throughout this book, but we think that ending with a focus on characteristics of writing that have been hidden until recently will help you complicate the answers you have been working on so far. We think you will truly be working to build a new "big picture" about the nature of writing based on many of the pieces in this chapter. Not least of all, we think you will enjoy doing so because the answers to these and other related questions are so relevant right now. As a society, we are struggling to answer these questions, and you have something to contribute to the conversation.

## Chapter Goals

- understand the inevitably technological nature of writing
- consider how each different writing technology reveals some aspects or elements of writing that some other technologies elide or conceal
- learn what new electronic, networked writing technologies are now revealing about the nature of writing and what counts as good writing that older technologies tended to conceal or overlook
- become familiar with the visual, image-driven nature of writing and build comfort and facility with incorporating visual elements in your writing
- study multimodal textuality and practice producing your own multimodal compositions

# From Pencils to Pixels: The Stages of Literacy Technologies

## DENNIS BARON

■ Baron, Dennis. "From Pencils to Pixels: The Stages of Literacy Technologies." *Passions, Pedagogies, and 21st Century Technologies*. Ed. Gail Hawisher and Cynthia Selfe. Logan: Utah State UP, 1999. 15–33. Print.

## Framing the Reading

Dennis Baron is a linguist who has studied **literacy**, communication technologies, and the laws countries make about language use (like making English the "official" language of the United States). In this essay, which developed material he later used in his 2009 book *A Better Pencil: Readers, Writers, and the Digital Revolution*, Baron examines the history of a few writing technologies that we are unlikely to even recognize as "technology" anymore. In thinking, for example, about how pencils were once state-of-the-art technology, Baron suggests that writing was never *not* technological, that every writing technology has taken time to become established, and that writing technologies must be learned.

Baron's work raises more questions than it answers, but in doing so it shows us how comparatively limited the research is at the intersection of technology and literacy. According to Baron, literacy researchers have largely failed to understand writing *as a technology*; as a result, he argues, they haven't really understood what we're actually doing when we write. In using historical explanations and discussion of writing tools that many of us no longer recognize as technological to begin with, Baron raises interesting questions about the future of writing. What will happen when the computers we use now are no longer really recognized as "unnatural" technologies? How will that altered perception influence how we write?

## Getting Ready to Read

*Before you read*, do at least one of the following activities:

- Write your own definition of "technology," and provide some examples. What kinds of things count as technology, and what don't?
- Make a quick list of all the technologies you use for writing.
- Talk with a parent or grandparent about what writing technologies were dominant when they were in school. How do those technologies compare with the ones you use today?

*As you read*, consider the following questions:

- For Baron, what counts as a technology?
- How do literacy technologies empower some people and disempower others?
- What does Baron seem to want us to learn from his work?
- How does the authenticity Baron talks about relate to literacy?

The computer, the latest development in writing technology, promises, or threatens, to change literacy practices for better or worse, depending on your point of view. For many of us, the computer revolution came long ago, and it has left its mark on the way we do things with words. We take word processing as a given. We don't have typewriters in our offices anymore, or pencil sharpeners, or even printers with resolutions less than 300 dpi. We scour *MacUser* and *PC World* for the next software upgrade, cheaper RAM, faster chips, and the latest in connectivity. We can't wait for the next paradigm shift. Computerspeak enters ordinary English at a rapid pace. In 1993, "the information superhighway" was voted the word—actually the phrase—of the year. In 1995, the word of the year was "the World Wide Web," with "morph" a close runner-up. The computer is also touted as a gateway to literacy. The Speaker of the House of Representatives suggested that inner-city school children should try laptops to improve their performance. The Governor of Illinois thinks that hooking up every school classroom to the Web will eliminate illiteracy. In his second-term victory speech, President Clinton promised to have every eight-year-old reading, and to connect every twelve-year-old to the National Information Infrastructure. Futurologists write books predicting that computers will replace books. Newspapers rush to hook online subscribers. The *New York Times* will download the Sunday crossword puzzle, time me as I fill in the answers from my keyboard, even score my results. They'll worry later about how to get me to pay for this service.

I will not join in the hyperbole of predictions about what the computer will or will not do for literacy, though I will be the first to praise computers, to acknowledge the importance of the computer in the last fifteen years of my own career as a writer, and to predict that in the future the computer will be put to communication uses we cannot now even begin to imagine, something quite beyond the word processing I'm now using to produce a fairly conventional text, a book chapter.

I readily admit my dependence on the new technology of writing. Once, called away to a meeting whose substance did not command my unalloyed attention, I began drafting on my conference pad a memo I needed to get out to my staff by lunchtime. I found that I had become so used to composing virtual prose at the keyboard I could no longer draft anything coherent directly onto a piece of paper. It wasn't so much that I couldn't think of the words, but the physical effort of handwriting, crossing out, revising, cutting and pasting (which I couldn't very well do at a meeting without giving away my inattention), in short, the writing practices I had been engaged in regularly since the age of four, now seemed to overwhelm and constrict me, and I longed for the flexibility of digitized text.

When we write with cutting-edge tools, it is easy to forget that whether it consists of energized particles on a screen or ink embedded in paper or lines gouged into clay tablets, writing itself is always first and foremost a technology, a way of engineering materials in order to accomplish an end. Tied up as it is with value-laden notions of literacy, art, and science, of history and psychology, of education, of theory, and of practicality, we often lose sight of writing as technology, until, that is, a new technology like the computer comes along and we are thrown into excitement and confusion as we try it on, try it out, reject it, and then adapt it to our lives—and of course, adapt our lives to it.

> *Whether it consists of energized particles on a screen or ink embedded in paper or lines gouged into clay tablets, writing itself is always first and foremost a technology, a way of engineering materials in order to accomplish an end.*

4

New communications technologies, if they catch on, go through a number 5 of strikingly similar stages. After their invention, their spread depends on accessibility, function, and authentication. Let me first summarize what I mean, and then I'll present some more detailed examples from the history of writing or literacy technologies to illustrate.

## The Stages of Literacy Technologies

Each new literacy technology begins with a restricted communication func- 6 tion and is available only to a small number of initiates. Because of the high cost of the technology and general ignorance about it, practitioners keep it to themselves at first—either on purpose or because nobody else has any use for it—and then, gradually, they begin to mediate the technology for the general public. The technology expands beyond this "priestly" class when it is adapted to familiar functions often associated with an older, accepted form of communication. As costs decrease and the technology becomes better able to mimic more ordinary or familiar communications, a new literacy spreads across a population. Only then does the technology come into its own, no longer imitating the previous forms given us by the earlier communication technology, but creating new forms and new possibilities for communication. Moreover, in a kind of backward wave, the new technology begins to affect older technologies as well.

While brave new literacy technologies offer new opportunities for produc- 7 ing and manipulating text, they also present new opportunities for fraud. And as the technology spreads, so do reactions against it from supporters of what are purported to be older, simpler, better, or more honest ways of writing. Not only must the new technology be accessible and useful, it must demonstrate its trustworthiness as well. So procedures for authentication and reliability must be developed before the new technology becomes fully accepted. One of the greatest concerns about computer communications today involves their authentication and their potential for fraud.

My contention in this essay is a modest one: the computer is simply the latest step in a long line of writing technologies. In many ways its development parallels that of the pencil—hence my title—though the computer seems more complex and is undoubtedly more expensive. The authenticity of pencil writing is still frequently questioned: we prefer that signatures and other permanent or validating documents be in ink. Although I'm not aware that anyone actually opposed the use of pencils when they began to be used for writing, other literacy technologies, including writing itself, were initially met with suspicion as well as enthusiasm.

## Humanists and Technology

In attacking society's growing dependence on communication technology, the Unabomber (1996) targeted computer scientists for elimination. But to my chagrin he excluded humanists from his list of sinister technocrats because he found them to be harmless. While I was glad not to be a direct target of this mad bomber, I admit that I felt left out. I asked myself, if humanists aren't harmful, then what's the point of being one? But I was afraid to say anything out loud, at least until a plausible suspect was in custody.

Humanists have long been considered out of the technology loop. They use technology, to be sure, but they are not generally seen as pushing the envelope. Most people think of writers as rejecting technological innovations like the computer and the information superhighway, preferring instead to bang away at manual typewriters when they are not busy whittling new points on their no. 2 quill pens.

And it is true that some well-known writers have rejected new-fangleness. Writing in the *New York Times*, Bill Henderson (1994) reminds us that in 1849 Henry David Thoreau disparaged the information superhighway of his day, a telegraph connection from Maine to Texas. As Thoreau put it, "Maine and Texas, it may be, have nothing important to communicate." Henderson, who is a director of the Lead Pencil Club, a group opposed to computers and convinced that the old ways are better, further boasts that Thoreau wrote his anti-technology remarks with a pencil that he made himself. Apparently Samuel Morse, the developer of the telegraph, was lucky that the only letter bombs Thoreau made were literary ones.

In any case, Thoreau was not the complete Luddite that Henderson would have us believe. He was, in fact, an engineer, and he didn't make pencils for the same reason he went to live at Walden Pond, to get back to basics. Rather, he designed them for a living. Instead of waxing nostalgic about the good old days of hand-made pencils, Thoreau sought to improve the process by developing a cutting-edge manufacturing technology of his own.

The pencil may be old, but like the computer today and the telegraph in  13
1849, it is an indisputable example of a communication technology. Henderson,
unwittingly concedes as much when he adds that Thoreau's father founded
"the first quality pencil [factory] in America." In Thoreau's day, a good pencil
was hard to find, and until Thoreau's father and uncle began making pencils
in the New World, the best ones were imported from Europe. The family fortune was built on the earnings of the Thoreau Pencil Company, and Henry
Thoreau not only supported his sojourn at Walden Pond and his trip to the
Maine woods with pencil profits, he himself perfected some of the techniques
of pencil-making that made Thoreau pencils so desirable.

The pencil may seem a simple device in contrast to the computer, but al-  14
though it has fewer parts, it too is an advanced technology. The engineer Henry
Petroski (1990) portrays the development of the wood-cased pencil as a paradigm of the engineering process, hinging on the solution of two essential problems: finding the correct blend of graphite and clay so that the "lead" is not
too soft or too brittle; and getting the lead into the cedar wood case so that it
doesn't break when the point is sharpened or when pressure is applied during
use. Pencil technologies involve advanced design techniques, the preparation
and purification of graphite, the mixing of graphite with various clays, the bak-
ing and curing of the lead mixture, its extrusion into leads, and the preparation
and finishing of the wood casings. Petroski observes that pencil making also
involves a knowledge of dyes, shellacs, resins, clamps, solvents, paints, woods,
rubber, glue, printing ink, waxes, lacquer, cotton, drying equipment, impregnat-
ing processes, high-temperature furnaces, abrasives, and mixing (Petroski 12).
These are no simple matters. A hobbyist cannot decide to make a wood-cased
pencil at home and go out to the craft shop for a set of instructions. Pencil-
making processes were from the outset proprietary secrets as closely guarded
as any Macintosh code.

The development of the pencil is also a paradigm of the development of lit-  15
eracy. In the two hundred fifty years between its invention, in the 1560s, and its
perfection at John Thoreau and Company, as well as in the factories of Conté
in France, and Staedtler and Faber in Germany, the humble wood pencil underwent several changes in form, greatly expanded its functions, and developed
from a curiosity of use to cabinet-makers, artists and note-takers into a tool so
universally employed for writing that we seldom give it any thought.

## The Technology of Writing

Of course the first writing technology was writing itself. Just like the telegraph  16
and the computer, writing itself was once an innovation strongly resisted by
traditionalists because it was unnatural and untrustworthy. Plato was one
leading thinker who spoke out strongly against writing, fearing that it would
weaken our memories. Pessimistic complaints about new literacy technologies,
like those made by Plato, by Bill Henderson, and by Henderson's idol, Henry
David Thoreau, are balanced by inflated predictions of how technologies will
change our lives for the better. According to one school of anthropology, the

invention of writing triggered a cognitive revolution in human development (for a critique of this so-called Great Divide theory of writing, see Street 1984). Historians of print are fond of pointing to the invention of the printing press in Europe as the second great cognitive revolution (Eisenstein 1979). The spread of electric power, the invention of radio, and later television, all promised similar bio-cultural progress. Now, the influence of computers on more and more aspects of our existence has led futurologists to proclaim that another technological threshold is at hand. Computer gurus offer us a brave new world of communications where we will experience cognitive changes of a magnitude never before known. Of course, the Unabomber and the Lead Pencil Club think otherwise.

Both the supporters and the critics of new communication technologies like 17 to compare them to the good, or bad, old days. Jay Bolter disparages the typewriter as nothing more than a machine for duplicating texts—and as such, he argues, it has not changed writing at all. In contrast, Bolter characterizes the computer as offering a paradigm shift not seen since the invention of the printing press, or for that matter, since the invention of writing itself. But when the typewriter first began to sweep across America's offices, it too promised to change writing radically, in ways never before imagined. So threatening was the typewriter to the traditional literates that in 1938 the *New York Times* editorialized against the machine that depersonalized writing, usurping the place of "writing with one's own hand."

The development of writing itself illustrates the stages of technological 18 spread. We normally assume that writing was invented to transcribe speech, but that is not strictly correct. The earliest Sumerian inscriptions, dating from ca. 3500 BCE, record not conversations, incantations, or other sorts of oral utterances, but land sales, business transactions, and tax accounts (Crystal 1987). Clay tokens bearing similar marks appear for several thousand years before these first inscriptions. It is often difficult to tell when we are dealing with writing and when with art (the recent discovery of 10,000-year-old stone carvings in Syria has been touted as a possible missing link in the art-to-writing chain), but the tokens seem to have been used as a system of accounting from at least the 9th millennium BCE. They are often regarded as the first examples of writing, and it is clear that they are only distantly related to actual speech (see figure 1).

We cannot be exactly sure why writing was invented, but just as the gurus of 19 today's technology are called computer geeks, it's possible that the first writers also seemed like a bunch of oddballs to the early Sumerians, who might have called them cuneiform geeks. Surely they walked around all day with a bunch of sharp styluses sticking out of their pocket protectors, and talked of nothing but new ways of making marks on stones. Anyway, so far as we know, writing itself begins not as speech transcription but as a relatively restricted and obscure record-keeping shorthand.

As innovative uses for the literacy technology are tried out, practitioners 20 may also adapt it to older, more familiar forms in order to gain acceptance from a wider group. Although writing began as a tool of the bean counters,

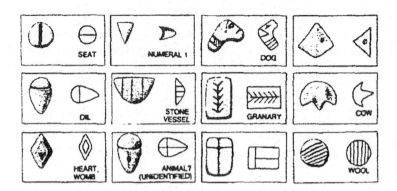

**Figure 1 Clay Tokens and Sumerian Inscriptions** Some of the commonest shapes are here compared with the incised characters in the earliest Sumerian inscriptions (only some of which have been interpreted) (Crystal 1987, 196).

it eventually added a second, magical/religious function, also restricted and obscure as a tool of priests. For writing to spread into a more general population in the ancient world, it had first to gain acceptance by approximating spoken language. Once writers—in a more "modern" sense of the word—discovered what writing could do, there was no turning back. But even today, most written text does not transcribe spoken language: the comparison of script and transcript in figure 2 makes this abundantly clear.

Of course writing never spread very greatly in the ancient world. William Harris (1989) argues convincingly that no more than ten percent of the classical Greek or Roman populations could have been literate. One reason for this must be that writing technology remained both cumbersome and expensive: writing instruments, paints, and inks had to be hand made, and writing surfaces like clay tablets, wax tablets, and papyrus had to be laboriously prepared. Writing therefore remained exclusive, until cheap paper became available, and the printing press made mass production of written texts more affordable and less labor-intensive.

21

## What Writing Does Differently

As a literacy technology like writing begins to become established, it also goes beyond the previous technology in innovative, often compelling ways. For example, while writing cannot replace many speech functions, it allows us to communicate in ways that speech does not. Writing lacks such tonal cues of the human voice as pitch and stress, not to mention the physical cues that accompany face to face communication, but it also permits new ways of bridging time and space. Conversations become letters. Sagas become novels. Customs become legal codes. The written language takes on a life of its own, and it even begins to influence how the spoken language is used. To cite an obvious

22

*Scripted dialogue:*

> *Thersites:* The common curse of mankind, folly and ignorance, be thine in great revenue! heaven bless thee from a tutor, and discipline come not near thee! Let thy blood be thy direction till thy death! then, if she that lays thee out says thou art a fair corpse, I'll be sworn and sworn upon't she never shrouded any but lazars. Amen.
>
> Shakespeare, *Troilus and Cressida,* II, iii, 30.

*Unscripted dialogue (ostensibly):*

> *Lt. Col North:* I do not recall a specific discussion. But, I mean. It was widely known within the CIA. I mean we were tracking that sensitive intelligence. I—I honestly don't recall, Mr. Van Cleve. I mean it—it didn't seem to me, at the time, that it was something that I was trying to hide from anybody. I was not engaged in it. And one of the purposes that I thought we had that finding for was to go back and ratify that earlier action, and to get on with replenishing. I mean, that was one—what I understood one of the purposes of the draft to be.
>
> from *Taking the Stand: The Testimony of Lt. Col. Oliver North,* 15

---

**Figure 2  Script and Transcript**

example, people begin to reject traditional pronunciations in favor of those that reflect a word's spelling: the pronunciation of the "l" in falcon (compare the l-less pronunciation of the cognate name Faulkner) and the "h" in such "th" combinations as *Anthony* and *Elizabeth* (compare the nicknames *Tony* and *Betty,* which reflect the earlier, h-less pronunciation).

23  In order to gain acceptance, a new literacy technology must also develop a means of authenticating itself. Michael Clanchy (1993) reports that when writing was introduced as a means of recording land transfer in 11th-century England, it was initially perceived (and often rightly so) as a nasty Norman trick for stealing Saxon land.

24  As Clanchy notes, spoken language was easily corroborated: human witnesses were interactive. They could be called to attest whether or not a property transfer had taken place. Doubters could question witnesses, watch their eyes, see whether witnesses sank when thrown bound into a lake. Written documents did not respond to questions—they were not interactive. So the writers and users of documents had to develop their own means of authentication. At first, seals, knives, and other symbolic bits of property were attached to documents in an attempt to give them credibility. Medieval English land transfers also adopted the format of texts already established as trustworthy, the Bible or the prayer book, complete with illuminations, in order to convince readers of their validity.

25  Questions of validity came up because writing was indeed being used to perpetrate fraud. Monks, who controlled writing technology in England at the time, were also responsible for some notorious forgeries used to snatch land

from private owners. As writing technology developed over the centuries, additional ways of authenticating text came into use. Individualistic signatures eventually replaced seals to the extent that today, many people's signatures differ significantly from the rest of their handwriting. Watermarks identified the provenance of paper; dates and serial numbers further certify documents, and in the absence of other authenticators, stylistic analysis may allow us to guess at authorship on the basis of comparative and internal textual evidence. In the digital age, we are faced with the interesting task of reinventing appropriate ways to validate cybertext.

## The Pencil as Technology

Just as writing was not designed initially as a way of recording speech, the 26 pencil was not invented to be a writing device. The ancient lead-pointed stylus was used to scribe lines—the lead made a faint pencil-like mark on a surface, suitable for marking off measurements but not for writing. The modern pencil, which holds not lead but a piece of graphite encased in a wooden handle, doesn't come on the scene until the 1560s.

The 16th-century pencil consists of a piece of graphite snapped or shaved 27 from a larger block, then fastened to a handle for ease of use. The first pencils were made by joiners, woodworkers specializing in making furniture, to scribe measurements in wood. Unlike the traditional metal-pointed scribing tools, pencils didn't leave a permanent dent in the wood. By the time Gesner observed the pencil, it had been adopted as a tool by note-takers, natural scientists, or others who needed to write, sketch, or take measurements in the field. Carrying pens and ink pots outdoors was cumbersome. Early pencils had knobs at one end so that they could be fastened with string or chain to a notebook, creating the precursor to the laptop computer.

Pencils were also of use to artists. In fact the word pencil means "little tail," 28 and refers not only to the modern wood-cased pencil but to the artist's brush. Ink and paint are difficult to erase: they must be scraped off a surface with a knife, or painted over. But graphite pencil marks were more easily erased by using bread crumbs, and of course later by erasers made of rubber—in fact the eraser substance (caoutchouc, the milky juice of tropical plants such as ficus) was called rubber because it was used to rub out pencil marks.

## Thoreau and Pencil Technology

It is true that Thoreau rejected modern improvements like the telegraph as 29 worthless illusions. In *Walden* he says, "They are but improved means to an unimproved end." Thoreau did not write much of pencils. He even omitted the pencil in his list of items to take into the Maine woods, though like naturalists before him, he certainly carried one on his twelve-day excursion in order to record his thoughts. Despite this silence, Thoreau devoted ten years of his life to improving pencil technology at his family's pencil factory.

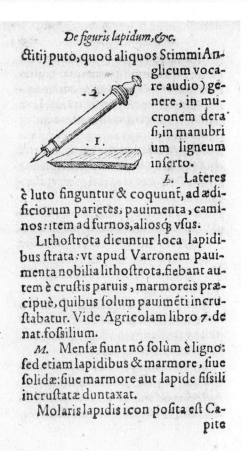

*De figuris lapidum, &c.*

ctitij puto, quod aliquos StimmiAn-
glicum voca-
re audio) ge-
nere, in mu-
cronem dera-
si, in manubri
um ligneum
inserto.

*L.* Lateres
è luto finguntur & coquunt, ad ædi-
ficiorum parietes, pauimenta, cami-
nos : item ad furnos, aliosq; vsus.

Lithostrota dicuntur loca lapidibus strata : vt apud Varronem pauimenta nobilia lithostrota, fiebant au-
tem è crustis paruis, marmoreis præ-
cipuè, quibus solum pauiméti incru-
stabatur. Vide Agricolam libro 7. de
nat. fosilium.

*M.* Mensæ fiunt nó solùm è ligno :
sed etiam lapidibus & marmore, siue
solidæ : siue marmore aut lapide fisili
incrustatæ duntaxat.

Molaris lapidis icon posita est Ca-
pite

---

**Figure 3 De Figuris Lapidum** Translation: "The stylus . . . is made . . . from a sort of lead (which I have heard some call English antimony), shaved to a point and inserted in a wooden handle." From *De rerum fossilium lapidum et gemmarum maxime, figuris et similitudinibus liber,* a book on the shapes and images of fossils, esp. those in stone and rock. Gesner wrote a Greek-Latin dictionary, was a doctor, lectured on physics, and, obviously, was a rock hound.

It was this pencil technology, not inherited wealth or publication royalties, that provided the income for one of the greatest writers of the American renaissance.

As Petroski tells it, the pencil industry in the eighteenth century was buf-  30
feted by such vagaries as the unpredictable supply of graphite, dwindling cedar forests, protective tariffs, and, for much of its history, an international
consumer preference for British-made pencils. All of this affected John Thoreau and Co., manufacturers of pencils. Until the nineteenth century, the best

pencil graphite (or plumbago, as it was often called), came from Borrowdale, in England. There were other graphite deposits around the world, but their ore was not particularly pure. Impure ore crumbled or produced a scratchy line. In the later eighteenth century, the Borrowdale deposits began to run low, and exports were curtailed. After the French Revolution, with his supply of English graphite permanently embargoed, the French pencil-maker Nicholas-Jacques Conté learned to produce a workable writing medium by grinding the local graphite, mixing it with clay and water, and forcing the mixture into wooden casings.

This process allowed the French to produce their own pencils, and it also  31 permitted manufacturers to control the hardness of the lead, which in turn controlled the darkness of the mark made by the pencil. (The more clay, the harder the lead, and the lighter and crisper the mark; less clay gives a darker, grainier mark). So successful was Conté's process that Conté became synonymous with pencil, and Conté crayons are still valued by artists. In Nuremberg, Staedtler teamed to mix ground graphite with sulfur. He and his rival, Faber, founded German pencil dynasties that also survive to this day.

The superiority of Borrowdale English graphite was evident to American  32 consumers as well, and they regularly preferred imports to domestic brands. American pencil manufacturers had a hard time convincing the public that they could make a good native pencil. In 1821 Charles Dunbar discovered a deposit of plumbago in Bristol, New Hampshire, and he and his brother-in-law, John Thoreau, went into the pencil business. By 1824 Thoreau pencils were winning recognition. Their graphite, however, was not as pure as Borrowdale, and since the Conté process was unknown in the United States, American pencils, though cheaper than imports, remained inferior.

Henry Thoreau set about to improve his father's pencil. According to  33 Petroski, Thoreau began his research in the Harvard Library. But then, as now, there was little written on pencil manufacture. Somehow, Thoreau learned to grind graphite more finely than had been done before and to mix it with clay in just the right proportion, for his improvements on the pencil-making process, combined with the high import duty imposed on British pencils after the War of 1812, led to great demand for Thoreau pencils.

Thoreau did not ascribe transcendent value to pencils. As Petroski sees it,  34 Thoreau's purpose was simply to make money. Once he developed the best pencil of the day, Thoreau saw no sense in trying to improve on his design. His pencils sold for seventy-five cents a dozen, higher than other brands, a fact which Emerson remarked on, though he still recommended Thoreau pencils to his friends. It is easy for us to think of Thoreau only as a romantic who lived deliberately, disobeyed civil authority, and turned Walden Pond into a national historic site. But to do these things, he was also an engineer and marketing expert. When pencil competition grew, shaving his profit margin, Thoreau stopped pushing pencils and sold his graphite wholesale to electrotypers because this proved more lucrative (Petroski 122).

Perhaps, then, Thoreau, despite his technological expertise, opposed Morse's  35 telegraph just to protect the family business. It is more likely, though, from the absence of references to pencil-making in any of his writings, that Thoreau honestly thought pencils were better for writing than electrical impulses, and he simply kept his business life and his intellectual life in separate compartments. In any case, Thoreau's resistance to the telegraph didn't stop the project.

## The Telephone

The introduction of the telephone shows us once again how the pattern of 36 communications technology takes shape. The telephone was initially received as an interesting but impractical device for communicating across distance. Although as Thoreau feared, the telegraph eventually did permit Maine and Texas and just about everywhere else to say nothing to one another, Samuel F. B. Morse, who patented the telegraph and invented its code, saw no use for Alexander Graham Bell's even newer device, the telephone. Morse refused Bell's offer to sell him the rights to the telephone patent. He was convinced that no one would want the telephone because it was unable to provide any permanent record of a conversation.

Indeed, although we now consider it indispensable, like writing, the uses of 37 the telephone were not immediately apparent to many people. Telephone communication combined aspects of speaking and writing situations in new ways, and it took a while to figure out what the telephone could and couldn't do. Once they became established, telephones were sometimes viewed as replacements for earlier technologies. In some cities, news and sports broadcasts were delivered over the telephone, competing with the radio (Marvin 1988). Futurologists predicted that the telephone would replace the school or library as a transmitter of knowledge and information, that medical therapy (including hypnosis) could be delivered and criminals punished over the phone through the use of electrical impulses. The telephone even competed with the clock and the thermometer: when I was growing up in New York in the 1950s, my family regularly called MEridian 6-1212 to find out the time, and WEather 7-1212 for the temperature and forecast.

Of course the telephone was not only a source of information. It also threat- 38 ened our privacy. One early fear of putting telephones in people's homes was that strangers could call up uninvited; people could talk to us on the phone whom we would never wish to converse with in person—and no one predicted then that people selling useless products would invariably call at dinner time. Today, as our email addresses circulate through the ether, we find in our electronic mailboxes not just surprise communications from long-lost acquaintances who have tracked us down using Gopher and other Web browsers, but also unwelcome communiqués from intruders offering get-rich-quick schemes, questionable deals, and shoddy merchandise. Even unsolicited religious messages are now circulating freely on net news groups.

The introduction of the telephone for social communication also required 39 considerable adaptation of the ways we talk, a fact we tend to forget because we think of the modern telephone as a reliable and flexible instrument. People had to learn how to converse on the telephone: its sound reproduction was poor; callers had to speak loudly and repeat themselves to be understood, a situation hardly conducive to natural conversation. Telephones were located centrally and publicly in houses, which meant that conversations were never private. Telephones emulated face-to-face communication, but they could not transmit the visible cues and physical gestures that allow face-to-face conversation to proceed smoothly, and this deficiency had to be overcome. Many people still accompany phone conversations with hand and facial gestures; very young children often nod into the phone instead of saying "Yes" or "No," as if their interlocutor could see them.

Initially, people were unsure of the appropriate ways to begin or end phone 40 conversations, and lively debates ensued. The terms "hello" and "good-bye" quickly became standard, despite objections from purists who maintained that "hello" was not a greeting but an expression of surprise, and that "good-bye," coming from "God be with you," was too high-toned and serious a phrase to be used for something so trivial as telephone talk. As people discovered that telephones could further romantic liaisons, guardians of the public morality voiced concern or disgust that sweethearts were actually making kissing noises over the phone. Appropriate language during conversation was also an issue, and phone companies would cut off customers for swearing (like today's computer Systems Operators, or Sysops, the telephone operators, or "hello girls" as they were called in the early days, frequently listened in on conversations and had the authority to interrupt or disconnect calls).

While the telephone company routinely monitored the contents of telephone 41 calls, when transcripts of telephone conversations were first introduced as evidence in trials, phone companies argued that these communications were just as private and privileged as doctor-patient exchanges (Marvin 68). Phone companies also tried to limit telephone access solely to the subscriber, threatening hotels and other businesses with loss of phone service if they allowed guests or customers to make calls. Telephone companies backed down from their demand that phones only be used by their registered owners once another technological development, the pay telephone, was introduced, and their continued profits were assured (this situation is analogous to the discussions of copy protection and site licensing for computer software today).

## The Computer and the Pattern of Literacy Technology

Writing was not initially speech transcription, and pencils were first made 42 for woodworkers, not writers. Similarly, the mainframe computer when it was introduced was intended to perform numerical calculations too tedious or complex to do by hand. Personal computers were not initially meant for word processing either, though that has since become one of their primary functions.

Mainframe line editors were so cumbersome that even computer programmers preferred to write their code with pencil and paper. Computer operators actually scorned the thought of using their powerful number-crunchers to process mere words. Those who braved the clumsy technology to type text were condemned to using a system that seemed diabolically designed to slow a writer down well below anything that could be done on an IBM Selectric, or even with a pencil. (Interestingly, when the typewriter was developed, the keyboard was designed to slow down writers, whose typing was faster than the machine could handle; initially computers too were slow to respond to keystrokes, and until type-ahead capability was developed, typists were frustrated by loud beeps indicating they had exceeded the machine's capacity to remember what to do.)

Early word-processing software for personal computers did little to improve the situation. At last, in the early 1980s, programs like Wordstar began to produce text that looked more like the typing that many writers had become used to. Even so, writers had to put up with screens cluttered with formatting characters. Word wrap was not automatic, so paragraphs had to be reformatted every time they were revised. Furthermore, printed versions of text seldom matched what was on the computer screen, turning page design into a laborious trial-and-error session. Adding to the writer's problems was the fact that the screen itself looked nothing like the piece of paper the text would ultimately be printed on. The first PC screens were grayish-black with green phosphor letters, displaying considerably less than a full page of text. When it came along, the amber screen offered what was seen as a major improvement, reducing eye strain for many people. Today we expect displays not only with black on white, just like real paper, and high resolution text characters, but also with color, which takes us a step beyond what we could do with ordinary typing paper.

If the initial technical obstacles to word processing on a PC weren't enough to keep writers away from the new technology, they still had to come up with the requisite $5,000 or more in start-up funds for an entry-level personal computer. Only die-hards and visionaries considered computer word processing worth pursuing, and even they held on to their Selectrics and their Bics just in case.

*If you type this:*

^BCombining Special Effects^B. To combine special effects, simply insert one control character after another. For example, your ^BWordstar^B^VTM^V cursor may look like this: H^HI^HN^HZ.

I^Ba^BI = /(a^Vx^V^T2^T + a^Vy^V^T2^T + a^Vz^V^T2^T)

*You (might) get this:*

**Combining Special Effects.** To combine special effects, simply insert one control character after another. For example, your Wordstar™ cursor may look like this: ■

|a| = / (a$_x$² + a$_y$² + a$_z$²)

Figure 4 **Instructions from a Wordstar manual**

The next generation of word-processing computers gave us WYSIWYG: 46
"what you see is what you get," and that helped less-adventurous writers make
the jump to computers. Only when Macintosh and Windows operating systems
allowed users to create on-screen documents that looked and felt like the old,
familiar documents they were used to creating on electric typewriters did word
processing really become popular. At the same time, start-up costs decreased
significantly and, with new, affordable hardware, computer writing technology
quickly moved from the imitation of typing to the inclusion of graphics.

Of course that, too, was not an innovation in text production. We'd been 47
pasting up text and graphics for ages. The decorated medieval charters of
eleventh-century England are a perfect parallel to our computerized graphics
a millennium later. But just as writing in the middle ages was able to move
beyond earlier limitations, computer word processing has now moved beyond
the texts made possible by earlier technologies by adding not just graphics,
but animation, video, and sound to documents. In addition, Hypertext and
HTML allow us to create links between documents or paths within them,
both of which offer restructured alternatives to linear reading.

The new technology also raises the specter of digital fraud, and the latest 48
literacy technology is now faced with the task of developing new methods of
authentication to ensure confidence and trust in its audience (see figure 5).

Over the years, we have developed a number of safeguards for preventing or 49
detecting fraud in conventionally produced texts. The fact that counterfeit currency still gets passed, and that document forgeries such as the *Hitler Diaries*
or hoaxes like the physicist Alan Sokal's spoof of deconstruction, "Transgress-
ing the Boundaries Toward a Transformational Hermeneutics of Quantum
Gravity," come to light from time to time shows that the safeguards, while
strong, are not necessarily foolproof. The average reader is not equipped to
detect many kinds of document falsification, and a lot of text is still accepted
on trust. A writer's reputation, or that of a publisher, predisposes readers to
accept certain texts as authoritative, and to reject others. Provenance, in the
world of conventional documents, is everything. We have learned to trust writing that leaves a paper trail.

Things are not so black and white in the world of digital text. Of course, 50
as more and more people do business on the Internet, the security of
transactions, of passwords, credit card numbers, and bank accounts becomes
vital. But the security and authenticity of "ordinary" texts is a major concern
as well. Anyone with a computer and a modem can put information into
cyberspace. As we see from figure 5, digitized graphics are easy to alter.
Someone intent on committing more serious deception can with not too
much trouble alter text, sound, graphics, and video files. Recently several former
Columbia University students were arrested for passing fake twenty-dollar
bills that they had duplicated on one of Columbia's high-end color printers.
The Treasury Department reported that while these counterfeits were easy
for a non-expert to spot, some $8,000 to $9,000 of the bad money had been
spent before the counterfeiters attracted any attention. Security experts, well
aware of the problems of digital fraud, are developing scramblers, electronic

**Figure 5 Example of Digital Fraud** From Feb. 1994 *Scientific American,* William J. Mitchell, "When is seeing believing?" (68–73). Mitchell explains the process used to create this photograph of Marilyn Monroe and Abraham Lincoln that never existed in the original. The final result can be so seamless that the forgery is undetectable. Examples of the intrusion of such false images include an ABC News broadcast in which correspondent Nina Totenberg was shown on camera with the White House in the background. In actuality, she was miles away in a studio and the montage gave the impression she was reporting from the field. Needless to say, fraudulent computer text is even easier to compose and promulgate across the bandwidth.

watermarks and invisible tagging devices to protect the integrity of digital files, and hackers are probably working just as hard to defeat the new safeguards. Nonetheless, once a file has been converted to hard copy, it is not clear how it could be authenticated.

Digitized text is even easier to corrupt accidentally, or to fiddle with on 51 purpose. Errors can be inadvertently introduced when print documents are scanned. With electronic text, it may be difficult to recover other indicators that we expect easy access to when we deal with print: the date of publication, the edition (sometimes critical when dealing with newspapers or literary texts), editorial changes or formatting introduced during the digitization process, changes in accompanying graphics (for example, online versions of the *Washington Post* and the *New York Times* use color illustrations not found in the paper editions). And of course digital text can be corrupted on purpose in ways that will not be apparent to unsuspecting readers.

Electronic texts also present some challenges to the ways we attribute 52 expertise to authors. When I read newsgroups and electronic discussion lists,

I must develop new means for establishing the expertise or authority of a poster. I recently tried following a technical discussion on a bicycle newsgroup about the relative advantages of butyl and latex innertubes. I can accept the advice of a bicycle mechanic I know, because we have a history, but posters to a newsgroup are all strangers to me. They may be experts, novices, cranks, or some combination of the three, and in the case of the two kinds of tire tubes, I had difficulty evaluating the often conflicting recommendations I received. After reading the newsgroup for a while, becoming familiar with those who post regularly, and getting a sense of the kinds of advice they gave and their attitudes toward the subject, I began to develop a nose for what was credible. My difficulty was compounded, though, because the most authoritative-sounding poster, in the conventional sense of authoritative—someone who evoked principles of physics and engineering to demonstrate that flats were no more common or disastrous with latex than butyl tubes, and who claimed to have written books on bicycle repair—was clearly outshouted by posters attesting the frequency and danger of rupturing latex inner tubes. In the end I chose to stay with butyl, since everyone seemed to agree that, though heavier than latex, it was certainly not the worst thing in the world to ride on.

My example may seem trivial, but as more and more people turn to the 53 World Wide Web for information, and as students begin relying on it for their research papers, verifying the reliability and authenticity of that information becomes increasingly important, as does revisiting it later to check quotations or gather more information. As anyone knows who's lost a file or tried to revisit a website, electronic texts have a greater tendency to disappear than conventional print resources.

## Conclusion

As the old technologies become automatic and invisible, we find ourselves more 54 concerned with fighting or embracing what's new. Ten years ago, math teachers worried that if students were allowed to use calculators, they wouldn't learn their arithmetic tables. Regardless of the value parents and teachers still place on knowing math facts, calculators are now indispensable in math class. When we began to use computers in university writing classes, instructors didn't tell students about the spell-check programs on their word processors, fearing the students would forget how to spell. The hackers found the spelling checkers anyway, and now teachers complain if their students don't run the spell check before they turn their papers in.

Even the pencil itself didn't escape the wrath of educators. One of the major 55 technological advances in pencil-making occurred in the early twentieth century, when manufacturers learned to attach rubber tips to inexpensive wood pencils by means of a brass clamp. But American schools allowed no crossing out. Teachers preferred pencils without erasers, arguing that students would do better, more premeditated work if they didn't have the option of revising. The students won this one, too: eraserless pencils are now extremely rare. Artists use them, because artists need special erasers in their work; golfers too use pencils without erasers, perhaps to keep themselves honest. As for the no-crossing-out rule, writing teachers now routinely warn students that writers never get it right the first time, and we expect them to revise their work endlessly until it is polished to perfection.

The computer has indeed changed the ways some of us do things with words, 56 and the rapid changes in technological development suggest that it will continue to do so in ways we cannot yet foresee. Whether this will result in a massive change in world literacy rates and practices is a question even more difficult to answer. Although the cost of computers has come down significantly enough for them to have made strong inroads into the American office and education environment, as well as in the American middle class home, it is still the case that not every office or every school can afford to computerize, let alone connect to the World Wide Web. And it is likely that many newly-computerized environments will not have sufficient control over the technology to do more than use it to replicate the old ways.

After more than a decade of study, we still know relatively little about 57 how people are using computers to read and write, and the number of people online, when viewed in the perspective of the total population of the United States, or of the world—the majority of whose residents are still illiterate—is still quite small. Literacy has always functioned to divide haves from have nots, and the problem of access to computers will not be easy to solve (see Moran, this volume).

In addition, researchers tend to look at the cutting edge when they examine 58 how technology affects literacy. But technology has a trailing edge as well as a down side, and studying how computers are put to use raises serious issues in the politics of work and mechanisms of social control. Andrew Sledd (1988) pessimistically views the computer as actually reducing the amount of literacy needed for the low end of the workplace: "As for ordinary kids, they will get jobs at Jewel, dragging computerized Cheerios boxes across computerized check-out counters."

Despite Sledd's legitimate fear that in the information age computers 59 will increase the gap between active text production and routine, alienating, assembly-line text processing, in the United States we live in an environment that is increasingly surrounded by text. Our cereal boxes and our soft drink cans are covered with the printed word. Our televisions, films, and computer screens also abound with text. We wear clothing designed to be read. The new computer communications technology does have ability to increase text exposure even more than it already has in positive, productive ways. The simplest one-word Web search returns pages of documents which themselves link to the expanding universe of text in cyberspace.

Computer communications are not going to go away. How the computer 60 will eventually alter literacy practices remains to be seen. The effects of writing took thousands of years to spread; the printing press took several hundred years to change how we do things with words. Although the rate of change of computer development is significantly faster, it is still too early to do significant speculating.

In the brave new world virtual text, if you chain an infinite number of monkeys to an infinite number of computers, you will eventually get, not Hamlet, but Hamlet BASIC.

We have a way of getting so used to writing technologies that we come to 61 think of them as natural rather than technological. We assume that pencils are a natural way to write because they are old—or at least because we have come to think of them as being old. We form Lead Pencil Clubs and romanticize do-it-yourselfers who make their own writing equipment, because home-made has come to mean "superior to store-bought."

But pencil technology has advanced to the point where the ubiquitous no. 2 62 wood-cased pencil can be manufactured for a unit cost of a few pennies. One pencil historian has estimated that a pencil made at home in 1950 by a hobby-ist or an eccentric would have cost about $50. It would cost significantly more nowadays. There's clearly no percentage in home pencil-making. Whether the computer will one day be as taken-for-granted as the pencil is an intriguing ques-tion. One thing is clear: were Thoreau alive today he would not be writing with a pencil of his own manufacture. He had better business sense than that. More likely, he would be keyboarding his complaints about the information superhigh-way on a personal computer that he assembled from spare parts in his garage.

Read "From Pencils to Pixels" and answer the following questions.

## Questions for Discussion and Journaling

1. Who was the Unabomber? How did he use writing? What technologies did he use for writing?

2. Sometimes Baron seems to shrug at technology and suggest that it's hard to imagine new technologies as fundamentally changing the shape or nature of writing. Do you agree that this seems to be one of his messages? If so, do you agree with it?

3. Why might the first class of people to have access to a technology be called "priestly," as Baron describes them near the beginning of his piece (para. 6)?

4. What are some other literacy technologies you can think of that, like the pencil, were once high technology but are now barely recognized as technology at all? What do these technologies have in common?

5. Why does Baron focus so much on *fraud* and *authenticity* in discussing writing technologies?

6. Look back over the illustrations and images in Baron's text. What do they contribute to it? Do you understand the illustrations and images as *writing*? Would considering them *writing* require adding to the list of technologies commonly associated with writing and literacy?

## Applying and Exploring Ideas

1. Select a writing technology Baron talks about and write a brief history of how it has spread to its current number of users since it was invented. Does Baron's account of how new literacy technologies spread seem to fit the technology you're studying?

2. Baron devotes some time to discussing the "Thoreau pencil," an improvement on previous pencils. What writing technology do you wish someone would improve? What kinds of improvement does it need?

3. Think about communication technologies that keep a record of a conversation and those that don't. What are the advantages of keeping, and not keeping, such records? Can you think of any communication technologies that *don't* keep a record that we would still recognize as writing?

4. Poll your classmates to build a list of knowledge that people need to gain about a particular new writing technology (for example, texting). What do people report needing to learn about how to use the technology, and how to be socially acceptable with it (for example, avoiding cell-yell)?

> ### Meta Moment
> Does it help you to think of writing as a technology? What, if anything, changes in how you understand writing if you think of it in these terms?

# Writing, Technology, and Teens: Summary of Findings

## AMANDA LENHART
## AARON SMITH
## ALEXANDRA RANKIN MACGILL
## SOUSAN ARAFEH

■ Lenhart, Amanda, Aaron Smith, Alexandra Rankin Macgill, and Sousan Arafeh. "Writing, Technology, and Teens: Summary of Findings." *Pew Reserach Center*. The Pew Charitable Trusts, 24 Apr. 2008, Web. 12 May 2013.

## Framing the Reading

This reading is a little different than many of the other readings in this book because it is a summary of a research report conducted by staff members at a research center. We think you will find it quite easy to read and understand, and it is worth thinking about why that might be the case. As you read this piece, ask yourself these questions: What genre is this? And who is the intended audience? If you can answer those questions, you will be able to understand why this piece might be easier for you to read than some of the other selections in this textbook.

In order to help you frame this reading a little better, go online to the Pew Research Center's "Pew Internet and American Life Project": **pewinternet.org**. There you will learn (under "About Us") that the Pew Research Center is "a nonpartisan, nonprofit 'fact tank' that provides information on the issues, attitudes and trends shaping America and the world." Explore that Web site a little in order to discover what each of Pew's seven projects is, specifically what the purpose of the "Internet and American Life Project" is. Then take a look at their "All Reports" tab; skim over all of their reports, and then find the full report that the following reading summarizes (it is from April 24, 2008). Now that you have a sense of where the following report came from, you should have a relatively easy time reading it. In addition, you now have become acquainted with an excellent online resource for your future questions or projects.

## Getting Ready to Read

*Before you read*, do at least one of the following activities:

- Make a quick list of all the technologies you use to write in a given week.
- Make a list of the kinds of writing you do on your own (including texting) and the kinds of writing you do at school.

*As you read*, consider the following questions:

- How well do the survey respondents' answers correspond with your own experiences?
- How much do you think has changed since 2008 when this research was conducted?

T eenagers' lives are filled with writing. All teens write for school, and 93% of teens say they write for their own pleasure. Most notably, the vast majority of teens have eagerly embraced written communication with their peers as they share messages on their social network pages, in emails and instant messages online, and through fast-paced thumb choreography on their cell phones. Parents believe that their children write more as teens than they did at that age.

This raises a major question: What, if anything, connects the formal writing teens do and the informal e-communication they exchange on digital screens? A considerable number of educators and children's advocates worry that James Billington, the Librarian of Congress, was right when he recently suggested that young Americans' electronic communication might be damaging "the basic unit of human thought—the sentence."[1] They are concerned that the quality of writing by young Americans is being degraded by their electronic communication, with its carefree spelling, lax punctuation and grammar, and its acronym shortcuts. Others wonder if this return to text-driven communication is instead inspiring new appreciation for writing among teens.

While the debate about the relationship between e-communication and formal writing is on-going, few have systematically talked to teens to see what they have to say about the state of writing in their lives. Responding to this information gap, the Pew Internet & American Life Project and National Commission on Writing conducted a national telephone survey and focus groups to see what teens and their parents say about the role and impact of technological writing on both in-school and out-of-school writing.[2] The report that follows looks at teens' basic definition of writing, explores the various kinds of writing they do, seeks their assessment about what impact e-communication has on their writing, and probes for their guidance about how writing instruction might be improved.

At the core, the digital age presents a paradox. Most teenagers spend a considerable amount of their life composing texts, but they do not think that a lot of the material they create electronically is real writing. The act of exchanging emails, instant messages, texts, and social network posts is communication that carries the same weight to teens as phone calls and between-class hallway greetings.

At the same time that teens disassociate e-communication with "writing," they also strongly believe that good writing is a critical skill to achieving success—and their parents agree. Moreover, teens are filled with insights and critiques of the current state of writing instruction as well as ideas about how to make in-school writing instruction better and more useful. 5

**Even though teens are heavily embedded in a tech-rich world, they do not believe that communication over the internet or text messaging is writing.** 6

The main reason teens use the internet and cell phones is to exploit their communication features.[3,4] Yet despite the nearly ubiquitous use of these tools by teens, they see an important distinction between the "writing" they do for school and outside of school for personal reasons, and the "communication" they enjoy via instant messaging, phone text messaging, email and social networking sites. 7

- 85% of teens ages 12–17 engage at least occasionally in some form of electronic personal communication, which includes text messaging, sending email or instant messages, or posting comments on social networking sites.
- 60% of teens do not think of these electronic texts as "writing."

Teens generally do not believe that technology negatively influences the quality of their writing, but they do acknowledge that the informal styles of writing that mark the use of these text-based technologies for many teens do occasionally filter into their school work. Overall, nearly two-thirds of teens (64%) say they incorporate some informal styles from their text-based communications into their writing at school. 8

- 50% of teens say they sometimes use informal writing styles instead of proper capitalization and punctuation in their school assignments;
- 38% say they have used text shortcuts in school work such as "LOL" (which stands for "laugh out loud");
- 25% have used emoticons (symbols like smiley faces ☺) in school work.

**The impact of technology on writing is hardly a frivolous issue because most believe that good writing is important to teens' future success.** 9

Both teens and their parents say that good writing is an essential skill for later success in life. 10

- 83% of parents of teens feel there is a greater need to write well today than there was 20 years ago.
- 86% of teens believe good writing is important to success in life—some 56% describe it as essential and another 30% describe it as important.

Parents also believe that their children write more now than they did when they were teens. 11

- 48% of teenagers' parents believe that their child is writing more than the parent did during their teen years; 31% say their child is writing less; and 20% believe it is about the same now as in the past.

Recognition of the importance of good writing is particularly high in black households and among families with lower levels of education. 12

- 94% of black parents say that good writing skills are more important now than in the past, compared with 82% of white parents and 79% of English-speaking Hispanic parents.
- 88% of parents with a high school degree or less say that writing is more important in today's world, compared with 80% of parents with at least some college experience.

**Teens are motivated to write by relevant topics, high expectations, an interested audience and opportunities to write creatively.** 13

Teens write for a variety of reasons—as part of a school assignment, to get a good grade, to stay in touch with friends, to share their artistic creations with others or simply to put their thoughts to paper (whether virtual or otherwise). In our focus groups, teens said they are motivated to write when they can select topics that are relevant to their lives and interests, and report greater enjoyment of school writing when they have the opportunity to write creatively. Having teachers or other adults who challenge them, present them with interesting curricula and give them detailed feedback also serves as a motivator for teens. Teens also report writing for an audience motivates them to write and write well. 14

**Writing for school is a nearly every-day activity for teens, but most assignments are short.** 15

Most teens write something nearly every day for school, but the average writing assignment is a paragraph to one page in length. 16

- 50% of teens say their school work requires writing every day; 35% say they write several times a week. The remaining 15% of teens write less often for school.
- 82% of teens report that their typical school writing assignment is a paragraph to one page in length.
- White teens are significantly more likely than English-speaking Hispanic teens (but not blacks) to create presentations for school (72% of whites and 58% of Hispanics do this).

The internet is also a primary source for research done at or for school. 94% of teens use the internet at least occasionally to do research for school, and nearly half (48%) report doing so once a week or more often. 17

**Teens believe that the writing instruction they receive in school could be improved.** 18

Most teens feel that additional instruction and focus on writing in school would help improve their writing even further. Our survey asked teens whether their writing skills would be improved by two potential changes to their school 19 curricula: teachers having them spend more time writing in class, and teachers using more computer-based tools (such as games, writing help programs or websites, or multimedia) to teach writing.

Overall, 82% of teens feel that additional in-class writing time would im- 20 prove their writing abilities and 78% feel the same way about their teachers using computer-based writing tools.

**Non-school writing, while less common than school writing, is still wide-** 21 **spread among teens.**

Outside of a dedicated few, non-school writing is done less often than school 22 writing, and varies a bit by gender and race/ethnicity. Boys are the least likely to write for personal enjoyment outside of school. Girls and black teens are more likely to keep a journal than other teens. Black teens are also more likely to write music or lyrics on their own time.

- 47% of black teens write in a journal, compared with 31% of white teens.
- 37% of black teens write music or lyrics, while 23% of white teens do.
- 49% of girls keep a journal; 20% of boys do.
- 26% of boys say they never write for personal enjoyment outside of school.

**Multi-channel teens and gadget owners do not write any more—or less—** 23 **than their counterparts, but bloggers are more prolific.**

Teens who communicate frequently with friends, and teens who own more 24 technology tools such as computers or cell phones do not write more for school or for themselves than less communicative and less gadget-rich teens. Teen bloggers, however, are prolific writers online and offline.

- 47% of teen bloggers write outside of school for personal reasons several times a week or more compared to 33% of teens without blogs.
- 65% of teen bloggers believe that writing is essential to later success in life; 53% of non-bloggers say the same.

**Teens more often write by hand for both out-of-school writing and school** 25 **work.**

Most teens mix and match longhand and computers based on tool availabil- 26 ity, assignment requirements and personal preference. When teens write they report that they most often write by hand, though they also often write using computers as well. Out-of-school personal writing is more likely than school writing to be done by hand, but longhand is the more common mode for both purposes.

- 72% of teens say they usually (but not exclusively) write the material they are composing for their personal enjoyment outside of school by hand; 65% say they usually write their school assignments by hand.

**As tech-savvy as they are, teens do not believe that writing with computers** 27 **makes a big difference in the quality of their writing.**

Teens appreciate the ability to revise and edit easily on a computer, but 28 do not feel that use of computers makes their writing better or improves the quality of their ideas.

- 15% of teens say their internet-based writing of materials such as emails and instant messages has helped improve their overall writing while 11% say it has harmed their writing. Some 73% of teens say this kind of writing makes no difference to their school writing.
- 17% of teens say their internet-based writing has helped the personal writing they do that is not for school, while 6% say it has made their personal writing worse. Some 77% believe this kind of writing makes no difference to their personal writing.

When it comes to using technology for school or non-school writing, teens believe that when they use computers to write they are more inclined to edit and revise their texts (57% say that). 29

**Parents are generally more positive than their teen children about the effect of computers and text-based communication tools on their child's writing.** 30

Parents are somewhat more likely to believe that computers have a positive influence on their teen's writing, while teens are more likely to believe computers have no discernible effect. 31

- 27% of parents think the Internet writing their teen does makes their teen child a better writer, and 27% think it makes the teen a poorer writer. Some 40% say it makes no difference.

On specific characteristics of the impact of tech-based writing, this is how parents' and teens' views match up: 32

---

THE IMPACT OF TECHNOLOGY ON WRITING

*Do you think using computers makes students more likely to . . . ?*

| | PARENTS (RESPONDING ABOUT THEIR CHILDREN) | TEENS (RESPONDING ABOUT STUDENTS IN GENERAL) |
|---|---|---|
| POSITIVE ATTRIBUTES | AGREE | AGREE |
| Write better because they can revise and edit easily | 69% | 59% |
| Present ideas clearly | 54 | 44 |
| Be creative | 50 | 44 |
| Communicate well | 43 | 36 |
| NEGATIVE ATTRIBUTES | | |
| Take short cuts and not put effort into writing | 45 | 49 |
| Use poor spelling and grammar | 40 | 42 |
| Write too fast and be careless | 40 | 41 |
| Have a short attention span | 22 | 28 |

*Source:* Pew Internet & American Life Project Teen/Parent Survey on Writing, September-November 2007. Margin of error is ±5%

Teens enjoy non-school writing, and to a lesser extent, the writing they do  33
for school.

Enjoyment of personal, non-school writing does not always translate into  34
enjoyment of school-based writing. Fully 93% of those ages 12–17 say they
have done some writing outside of school in the past year and more than
a third of them write consistently and regularly. Half (49%) of all teens
say they enjoy the writing they do outside of school "a great deal," compared with just 17% who enjoy the writing they do for school with a similar
intensity.

Teens who enjoy their school writing more are more likely to engage in  35
creative writing at school compared to teens who report very little enjoyment
of school writing (81% vs. 69%). In our focus groups, teens report being motivated to write by relevant, interesting, self-selected topics, and attention and
feedback from engaged adults who challenged them.

---

WRITING, TECHNOLOGY AND TEENS: SUMMARY OF FINDINGS AT A GLANCE

Even though teens are heavily embedded in a tech-rich world, they do not believe
that communication over the Internet or text messaging is writing.

The impact of technology on writing is hardly a frivolous issue because most believe
that good writing is important to teems' future success.

Teens are motivated to write by relevant topics, high expectations, an interested
audience and opportunities to write creatively.

Writing for school is a nearly every-day activity for teens, but most assignments are
short.

Teens believe that the writing instruction they receive in school could be improved.

Non-school writing, while less common than school writing, is still widespread
among teens.

Multi-channel teens and gadget owners do not write any more—or less—than their
counterparts, but bloggers are more prolific.

Teens more often write by hand for both out-of-school writing and school work.

As tech-savvy as they are, teens do not believe that writing with computers makes a
big difference in the quality of their writing.

Parents are generally more positive than their teen children about the effect of
computers and text based communication tools on their child's writing.

Teens enjoy non-school writing, and to a lesser extent, the writing they do for
school.

SOURCE: Lenhart, Amanda; Arafeh, Sousan; Smith, Aaron and Rankin Macgill,
Alexandra, *Writing, Technology and Teens*, Washington, DC: Pew Internet &
American Life Project, April 24, 2008.

---

## Notes

1. Dillon, Sam. "In Test, Few Students are Proficient Writers," *The New York Times*, April 3, 2008.
2. This Pew Internet & American Life Project study was carried out in partnership with the National Commission on Writing, an initiative of The College Board. This report is based on the findings of a national representative random digit dial telephone survey of teens 12–17 and a parent or guardian, and a series of focus groups with teens. All numerical data was gathered through telephone interviews conducted by Princeton Survey Research Associates between September 19 and November 16, 2007, from a sample of 700 parent child pairs. For results based on the total sample, one can say with 95% confidence that the error attributable to sampling and other random effects is +/– 4.7%. Eight focus groups were conducted by Research Images with teens 12–17 in four U.S. cities in the summer of 2007. For more details on the methods used to gather the data in this report, please see the Methodology section beginning on page 65 of the full report.
3. Analysis of daily communications choices is based on all teens, regardless of technology ownership.
4. Lenhart, Amanda, Mary Madden and Paul Hitlin, "Teens and Technology: Youth are Leading the Transition to a Fully Wired and Mobile Nation," Pew Internet & American life Project, Washington, DC, July 27, 2005.

## Questions for Discussion and Journaling

1. Sixty percent of the students surveyed for this research study said they don't consider text messaging, e-mail, or IM to be "writing." Why do you think this is the case? Do you consider these forms of communication to be writing? Why or why not?

2. Sixty-four percent of the teens surveyed for this study said that they sometimes use informal writing styles in their school writing. Do you do this? People like James Billington, the Librarian of Congress, think electronic writing that seeps into formal writing like this is "damaging the basic unit of human thought—the sentence" (para. 2). Do you agree or disagree that this is the case? Why or why not?

3. The teens surveyed for this study explained what motivates them to write. List their answers, and then add your own: What motivates *you* to write?

4. The teens in this survey said that most of their school writing assignments are quite short. Make a list of the most frequent types of writing assignments you receive now, or received in high school. Do your experiences correlate with those of the students surveyed by Pew?

## Applying and Exploring Ideas

1. Talk with some of your older relatives and ask them what they wrote, and how much they wrote, as teenagers. Then talk with some of your friends and ask them the same questions. What are the differences in the responses?

2. Think about the kinds of writing instruction you received in high school and evaluate it. Do you think it was effective? Then conduct short interviews with two friends and

ask them to describe and evaluate the writing instruction they received in high school. Write a one- to two-page synopsis of your findings.

3. After completing question 2 above, write a short letter to your high school principal suggesting some ways that high school writing instruction could be improved.

4. Do a short experiment to see if you agree with the Pew survey results regarding the impact of writing with computers. Write a short description of your high school writing experience by hand. Then do the same, but write on the computer. What were the differences? Consider some of the possibilities conveyed in the chart in the Pew study (for example, can revise and edit more easily on computer).

**Meta Moment**
What were some conceptions of writing you had prior to reading this research report? Have your conceptions of writing changed?

# Instant Messaging and the Future of Language

## NAOMI S. BARON

■ Baron, Naomi S. "Instant Messaging and the Future of Language." *Communications of the ACM* 48.7 (July 2005): 29–31. Print.

## Framing the Reading

You might think this article is about technology in writing, or about text-speak or other electronic-writing languages. We don't think so. We think this is an article about *language change* and how cultures manage it. The language in question happens to be technology-related, but the broad question here is about how cultures negotiate natural linguistic novelty while trying to preserve existing conventions of language (and writing). It is up to you as a reader to judge how successfully its writer finds a balance.

Naomi Baron is a linguist specializing in computer mediated communication (CMC), particularly writing, and the history of English. She is a professor at the American University in Washington, D.C., where she also directs the Center for Teaching, Research, and Learning. She's published seven books, including *Always On: Language in an Online and Mobile World* in 2008. It was based on some of the same research that she summarizes in this piece.

Baron's approach here is interesting in that rather than wading into ongoing arguments about the merits of the language "kids these days" use in electronic communication, she offers context for that language change in relation to language change throughout history. Furthermore, rather than taking a position in favor of tolerance toward new electronic language or against it, she suggests *both* accepting the new language and maintaining the current one. While her argument is brief as a result of genre convention (this piece is meant to be a short opinion column, a commentary—not a full scholarly article), it leaves readers with a lot to think about.

## Getting Ready to Read

*Before you read*, do at least one of the following activities:

- Recall what you've heard from teachers about the language used in texting, instant-messaging, and e-mail. Does their commentary tend to be favorable or unfavorable toward these kinds of language? Do you have the sense they actually know well the language they're commenting on?

- Quickly look up the journal this article appeared in, *Communications of the ACM*. What is the ACM, and who reads this journal? In other words, who does Baron probably think her audience is?

*As you read*, consider the following questions:

- Does Baron advocate anything that you wish she didn't?
- How much of the history of language development that Baron offers is already familiar to you?

........................................................................................................................

Computer-mediated communication (CMC) provides young users opportunities for social affinity and control over when and with whom they interact, but its long-term influence on language remains largely in the hands of parents and teachers, their traditional linguistic role models.

Are email, instant messaging (IM), and text messaging on cell phones degrading the language? This question surfaces in debates among language professionals and, perhaps more important, among parents and their teenage offspring. If some traditionalists are correct, we must take swift action now, before these children are reduced to marginal literacy. But if those celebrating linguistic innovation are correct, adults should get out of the way of normal language change. Families and educational purists have an obvious stake in the outcome of this controversy, but so, too, do the makers and marketers of computer-based software and devices—from IM platforms to predictive text programs for cell phones.

The problem with viewing CMC as linguistically either good or bad is twofold. On the one hand, such a dichotomous perspective ignores the variation in online communication, reflecting age, gender, education level, cultural background, personality, and years of experience with the CMC platform (listservs, for example, do not function like IM) or the purpose of the communiqué (a well-crafted email message applying for a job vs. a hasty blitzmail note arranging to meet at the library at 10). On the other hand, many evils attributed to CMC, especially as practiced by teens, can be traced back to ARPANET days.

Here, I highlight CMC issues in English-speaking countries, particularly the U.S. Admittedly, CMC practices vary in some respects elsewhere. For example, the international texting craze is just now taking hold in the U.S., while computer-based IM is a relatively recent phenomenon in Europe. However, the linguistic novelties cropping up in CMC are as pronounced in Stockholm and Seoul as they are in San Francisco.

If we look at the history of written English over the past 1,200 years (roughly from the time of *Beowulf*), we find shifting patterns in the roles speech and writing play in society. Up through the Middle Ages, and the Renaissance, writing was essentially a handmaiden to speech and was generally rather formal.

Preachers read the Bible aloud; written speeches were memorized and delivered orally; plays were intended to be performed, not published. Not surprisingly, orthographic conventions were not strict; even Shakespeare spelled his own name at least six different ways. Gradually, with the spread of literacy and the rise of print culture, writing became a distinct genre. Spelling began to matter, and even those with a grammar-school education knew the difference between formal and informal writing style.

Fast forward to the mid-20th century. In the U.S., pedagogy underwent a sea change, fueled by progressive education (eschewing rote learning, celebrating creativity) and by the national confusion during the Vietnam War and afterward over the relevance of existing curricula. A student-centered agenda emerged, first in grade-school education and eventually in colleges, counseling teachers to be guides on the side rather than sages on stages. Writing instructors were commonly advised to focus on content and de-emphasize mechanics, with the result that many graduates from even the finest U.S. preparatory institutions could not spell and had no clue how to use a semicolon. Add to these new educational practices a growing social trend toward informality, and you had an environment ripe for teenage innovation of the sort we now see in IM and text messaging. 6

Adolescents have long been a source of linguistic and behavioral novelty. Teens often use spoken language to express small-group identity. It is hardly surprising to find many of them experimenting with a new linguistic medium (such as IM) to complement the identity construction they achieve through speech, clothing, or hair style. IMs laced with, say, brb [be right back], pos [parent over shoulder], and U [you] are not so different from the profusion of "like" or "totally" common in the speech of American adolescents. 7

> *Adolescents have long been a source of linguistic and behavioral novelty.*

The IM behavior of many younger teens is not generally reflected in the language patterns we find in contemporary college students. For the past three years, my students and I at American University in Washington, D.C., have been investigating undergraduate use of IM on America Online Instant Messenger (AIM). Our research suggests that IM conversations serve largely pragmatic information-sharing and social-communication functions rather than providing contexts for establishing or maintaining group identity. Moreover, college students often eschew brevity. Our data contains few abbreviations or acronyms. Spelling is remarkably good, and punctuation isn't particularly bad either. Students use contractions (such as "don't" rather than "do not") only about two-thirds of the time, spelling out the full words the other third, with females significantly more likely to type full forms than males. 8

IM conversations are not always instant. An online survey we conducted in the fall of 2004 of the other activities the undergraduates engaged in while 9

IMing—surfing the Net, working on a paper, listening to music, eating, speaking face-to-face, and managing up to 12 simultaneous IM conversations—revealed considerable multitasking among survey participants. People can physically be typing in only one IM conversation at a time, rendering, the others asynchronous to varying degrees. Participants in focus groups reported feeling comfortable juggling multiple online and offline tasks. Several of them indicated that engaging in only a single IM conversation (doing nothing else online or offline) would feel odd. IMing, they suggested, was something they did under the radar of the other virtual and physical activities vying for their attention.

The most important effect of IM on language turns out to be not stylized 10 vocabulary or grammar but the control seasoned users feel they have over their communication networks. In earlier research (fall 2002), a group of my undergraduate students looked at away messages in IM that had been posted by members of their Buddy Lists. Users ostensibly post away messages to indicate that the person posting the message will be away from the computer (though still logged on to the IM system) and therefore unable to respond to incoming IMs. However, study participants used away messages for a variety of functions, including requests for virtual company ("Please disturb me") and screening incoming IMs ("Sleeping"). College students commonly read their buddies' away messages to catch up on the activities of people (such as friends from high school) they do not want to IM or call.

The shape of written language has always been as much a product of so- 11 cial attitudes and educational values as of technological developments. IM is unlikely to play a significant role in altering writing standards—unless we as parents and educators let it.

Our data suggests that when teenagers transition to college, they naturally 12 shed some of their adolescent linguistic ways in favor of more formal writing conventions (such as correct spelling and reduced use of contractions) they learned in high school. But what about these students' younger siblings who often begin IMing at nine or ten? Anecdotal evidence suggests that a number of their teachers, not wanting to be branded as troglodytes out of touch with contemporary culture, tolerate IM novelties in classroom written assignments. No harm, but only if these same teachers ensure their students develop a solid grasp of traditional writing conventions as well.

Unless society is willing to accept people spelling their names six differ- 13 ent ways or using commas, semicolons, and periods according to whim, we owe it to our children and to our students to make certain they understand the difference between creativity and normative language use. Knowledge of contemporary CMC style (and the social control IM and other media offer) is empowering. However, if today's teenagers are also to master more formal written language style, their parents and teachers must provide good models and, if necessary, even gentle sticks.

## Questions for Discussion and Journaling

1. Why does Baron suggest that the claim that IM and texting are degrading language is an oversimplification?

2. How closely does your experience of IM and texting match what Baron describes students doing (paras. 8–10)? Comparing your own answers with those of the rest of your class, can you find any pattern in responses? For example, we expect that your class has students of varying ages in it, but we also suspect that age may not be the best predictor of how much a person's experience resembles Baron's descriptions. What's the case in your class?

3. What aspects of computer-mediated communication do you think Baron is referring to when she says "the control seasoned users feel they have over their communication networks" is the most important effect of IM on language (para. 10)? She uses the example of chat statuses; what other examples can you think of?

4. Baron argues that we must teach "the difference between creativity and normative language use" (para. 13). Explain the distinction she's drawing between the two categories. Do you find anything problematic about that argument?

## Applying and Exploring Ideas

1. If you're young enough to have been a high school or elementary student after instant-messaging, texting, and e-mail became popular, it's likely you remember learning the difference between the language and writing conventions (spelling and punctuation) of these genres and those of formal school writing. Write a one- to two-page literacy narrative recounting how you learned they had different rules (to whatever extent you were aware of learning them or understanding them).

2. Would you say that "normal" conventions of formal writing are actually worth maintaining? Are there any that you would opt to let disappear through the normal course of language change? Which ones, and why?

3. Design a study that would let you compare college students' school writing to their computer-mediated communication (IM and texting) and see how much of what we associate with "text-speak" shows up in each. (This study might be too large to actually conduct in the class; the object here is to explore and plan what would be necessary to do such a study.)

> ### Meta Moment
> When you consider subjects like language change and degradation, how do you keep yourself from generalizing and stereotyping what's going on with language?

# Revisualizing Composition:

## MAPPING THE WRITING LIVES OF FIRST-YEAR COLLEGE STUDENTS

JEFF GRABILL

WILLIAM HART-DAVIDSON

STACEY PIGG    MICHAEL McLEOD

PAUL CURRAN    JESSIE MOORE

PAULA ROSINSKI    TIM PEEPLES

SUZANNE RUMSEY

MARTINE COURANT RIFE

ROBYN TASAKA    DUNDEE LACKEY

BETH BRUNK-CHAVEZ

■ Grabill, Jeff, William Hart-Davidson, Stacey Pigg, Michael McLeod, Paul Curran, Jessie Moore, Paula Rosinski, Tim Peeples, Suzanne Rumsey, Martine Courant Rife, Robyn Tasaka, Dundee Lackey, and Beth Brunk-Chavez. "Revisualizing Composition: Mapping the Writing Lives of First-Year College Students." WIDE Research Center. Michigan State University. 7 Sept. 2010. Web. 13 May 2013.

## Framing the Reading

Jeffrey Grabill is a professor and Bill Hart-Davidson is an associate professor in the Department of Writing, Rhetoric, and American Cultures at Michigan State. Stacey Pigg was a doctoral student at Michigan State when she co-authored this article and is currently an assistant professor in the Department of Writing and Rhetoric at the University of Central Florida. Together with the other authors, they are part of a large team of researchers that make up the Writing In Digital Environments Research Center, which Grabill and Hart-Davidson co-direct. This research center looks at a variety of questions about digital communication.

The study you will read here was conducted by a team of thirteen researchers from seven different schools. It explores questions about what first-year college students are writing, what writing they most value, and what technologies are mediating their writing.

## Getting Ready to Read

*Before you read*, do at least one of the following activities:

- Do a Google search for the Writing In Digital Environments (WIDE) Research Center. What is this group? Who is involved? What do they study? If you can find this paper on their Web site, take a look at the studies they published before and after this one.
- If you read the earlier article in this chapter describing a study conducted by the Pew Research Center, consider the ways in which the WIDE Research Center is similar to and different from the Pew Research Center.
- In Section 3, the authors explain that the type of college or university students attend is a good predictor of which genres students have written. You may not have thought very much before about the kind of college or university you are attending—at least not using the categories that the WIDE researchers assign: the Carnegie classification system (explained briefly in their "About this Study" section). Do a quick Google search to discover what the Carnegie classification system is, and then find out what Carnegie category your college or university falls under.

*As you read*, consider the following questions:

- How do WIDE researchers' findings compare to your own experiences?
- Keep your school's Carnegie classification in mind and see whether your experience seems to correlate with the type of school you attend, as the WIDE researchers suggest it will in sections 3.1 and 3.2.

## Summary of Findings

This white paper reports initial findings from a Writing in Digital Environments (WIDE) Research Center study entitled Revisualizing Composition: Mapping the Writing Lives of First-Year College Students. These initial findings are drawn from a survey of students enrolled in writing classes at a sample of US postsecondary institutions. 1

Writing practices and technologies have changed considerably over recent years. Given these changes, we know that contemporary college students are highly literate, but we lack clear and comprehensive portraits of how writing works in their lives. The primary aim of this study is to generate a large and uniform data set that leads to a better understanding of the writing behaviors of students across a variety of institutions and locations. Working from the assumption that students lead complex writing lives, this study is interested in a broad 2

> *Working from the assumption that students lead complex writing lives, this study is interested in a broad range of writing practices and values both for the classroom and beyond it, as well as the technologies, collaborators, spaces, and audiences they draw upon in writing.*

range of writing practices and values both for the classroom and beyond it, as well as the technologies, collaborators, spaces, and audiences they draw upon in writing. Initial findings include the following:

- SMS texts (i.e., texts using short message services on mobile devices), emails, and lecture notes are three of the most frequently written genres (or types) of writing
- SMS texts and academic writing are the most frequently valued genres
- Some electronic genres written frequently by participants, such as writing in social networking environments, are not valued highly
- Students' write for personal fulfillment nearly as often as for school assignments
- Institution type is related in a meaningful way to the writing experiences of participants, particularly what they write and the technologies used
- Digital writing platforms—cell phones, Facebook, email—are frequently associated with writing done most often
- Students mostly write alone, and writing alone is valued over writing collaboratively

These findings, along with others reported in this white paper, shed light on the writing practices and values of contemporary college students. In particular, these findings point to the pervasiveness of writing in the lives of our participants and the importance of hand-held devices like mobile phones as a writing platform.

Our findings also raise a number of questions related to how students expe-   3
rience, use, and value new writing technologies and environments in the larger context of their writing lives. We hope the findings in this report raise questions for further research and scholarship.

## About the Survey

This report is based on the findings of a survey (n = 1366) distributed to stu-   4
dents enrolled in a first-year writing class during April-June of the Spring 2010 semester. Students at seven institutions completed the survey (Elon University [Elon, North Carolina]; Indiana University-Purdue University at Fort Wayne [Ft. Wayne, Indiana]; Lansing Community College [Lansing, Michigan]; Leeward Community College [Pearl City, Hawaii]; Michigan State University [East Lansing, Michigan]; the University of North Carolina at Pembroke [Pembroke, North Carolina]; the University of Texas at El Paso [El Paso, Texas]).

These institutions represent a range of institution types according to the   5
Carnegie classification system, including Research University, very high activity, Michigan State University; Research University, high activity, the University of Texas at El Paso; Master's Colleges and University, Medium, Indiana University-Purdue University at Fort Wayne and the University of North Carolina at Pembroke; Master's Colleges and Universities, Small, Private, Elon University; Associate's Public Rural-serving, Large, Lansing Community College; and Associate's Public 2-year Colleges under 4-year Universities,

Leeward Community College. Of the 2110 students who began the survey, 1366 completed it, for a completion rate of 65% (see Methodology for more details).

The survey asked for demographic information and included a series of questions related to what participants write. Participants were first asked to identify types of writing that they do based on a list of 30 writing types. Then participants were asked to rank order the five types of writing that they do most often. Next they were asked to rank order the types of writing that they value the most. For each type of writing, participants were asked to detail why, where, with whom, for whom, and with what technologies they typically write. The meaning of "writing" in this survey included a wide range of practices, from lists to research papers to texting to multi-media compositions. . . .

## Section 1: What Are Students Writing in and out of School?

### 1.1: SMS Texts, Emails, and Lecture Notes Are Three of the Most Frequently Written Genres

The genres—or types—of writing that participants report writing most frequent are SMS text messages, emails, and lecture notes. Texting and emailing were ranked highly by participants when asked to identify all of their writing practices and by participants when asked to rank their most frequent writing practices. This finding reinforces common perceptions that texting and email have become commonplace writing practices. This finding also highlights the importance of the phone as a platform for writing. However, in highlighting the importance of a practice like texting, this finding may challenge other common perceptions of what counts as "writing."

When considering the simple ranking of writing practices, we find that 91% of participants selected texting from the thirty choices available of all writing that they have done, and 78% said that texting was one of the five kinds of writing they do most often. In fact, nearly half of all participants (46%) indicated that texting was the kind of writing that they performed more than any other. A greater percentage of participants overall (94%)

**Beyond the Data: Cell phones: The New Pencil for Personal Life?**

Cell phones have become a prominent writing technology for students for self-sponsored writing. Students use phones most often for SMS texting, but they also use them for a range of other digital writing, including emails, status message updates, instant messaging, and comments on status messages or posts. Cell phones are also frequently used for lists, and even occasionally for academic genres including lecture notes, reading notes, research papers, academic papers, and outlines. We have had students report using their phones to compose academic essays.

selected email as a type of writing practice they had performed in the past, but fewer placed in within their top five types of writing done most often (57%), and less than ten percent selected it as the genre they write the most (9%).

A number of academic writing practices were highly ranked, which is not  9 surprising given the participants and sampling approach. 78% of participants selected lecture notes as a type of writing they have done, while 93% and 82% chose research and academic papers respectively (meaning, in turn, that almost 7% and 20% respectively report having not written academic or research papers).

We utilized a statistical weighting method for the ranked fists of most fre-  10 quent and valued writing practices for our findings that accounted for the placement of a given writing practice somewhere in the top 5 listings for frequency and value. We believe that this method provides a stronger measure of both frequency and value. When considering the weighted ranking of writing practices, the top 10 most frequently written genres are as follows:

1. Texting
2. E-mail
3. Lecture notes
4. Academic paper
5. Research papers
6. Lists
7. Instant messaging
8. Comments on status messages or posts
9. Status message updates
10. Reading notes

We see in this list a range of traditional academic genres along with types of writing that we think of as "helpers" for larger tasks (e.g., notes). We see as well a number of genres that are a function of networked communication technologies. They have a clear place in the writing lives of these participants.

## 1.2: As Expected, Students Frequently Write Traditional School Genres Including Academic Papers and Research Papers

The top five most often used types of writing include the academic and re-  11 search paper, as well as more informal types of writing that often support the academic and research paper such as lecture and reading notes, lists, and even email and texting. Additional inquiry is needed to explore how, whether, and how often the more informal types of writing are used (or not) to support traditional school writing such as the academic and research paper.

## 1.3: Several Digital Genres Are Written by Almost All Participants, but Several Others Are Practiced by Less Than Half of Participants

As described above, half of the ten genres that participants report writing most  12 frequently are digital genres. Along with email and texting, which we detail above, instant messaging was practiced by 83% of participants, and status message updates (65%) and comments on status message updates (75%) were likewise prominent, indicating the importance of social media in the writing lives of these participants. However, other types of electronic communication were not as pervasive. Chat rooms had been utilized previously by just over half of all students. A total of 49% of participants reported writing for websites, and 39% of students reported writing for blogs.

### 1.4: Gender Is a Relevant Factor in What Students Write but in a Limited Number of Genres

For many types of writing, gender is not significantly related to frequency in our sample. For the fifteen genres where gender is significantly related to frequency, only three categories skewed male, and only one of these in a strong way: websites, with over half of males (53%) and less than half of females (45%) reporting writing this genre. The other, business writing, was reported by 25% of males and 20% of females. Female respondents were significantly more likely than males to use academic "helper" genres: outlines, reading notes, lecture notes, and lists. 13

## Section 2: How Do Students Value the Writing They Do?

### 2.1: SMS Texts and Academic Writing Are the Most Frequently Valued Genres

Participants were asked to rank how they valued 30 genres of writing by selecting the five most valuable types of writing to them. When considering the simple ranking of writing practices, we find that students ranked the following five genres most frequently as one of their top five most valued: Texting (47%), Academic Paper (45%), Lecture Notes (43%), Email (43%), and Research Paper (41%). 14

The weighted scores for value results in the following list of most valued genres of writing: 15

1. Texting
2. Academic Paper
3. Lecture Notes
4. Research Paper
5. Email
6. Resume
7. List
8. Letter
9. Journal/Diary
10. Forms

School-sponsored genres are valued highly by survey participants: academic paper and research paper ranked second and fourth, respectively. Lecture notes ranked third. As figure one indicates, 21% of participants ranked academic

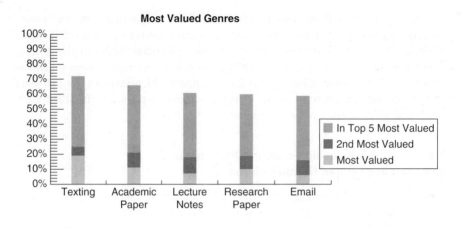

Figure 1 Display of top five most valued genres based on un-weighted rankings.

papers as their first or second most valued genre. 19% of students ranked research papers as their first or second most valued genre. Finally, for those who selected lecture notes, 19% of participants ranked lecture notes as their first or second most valued genre.

## 2.2: Some Less Frequently Written Genres Are Valued Highly by Student Writers

Among the ten most valued genres, four genres are valued highly but written   16
relatively infrequently. Resumes ranked 6th for value, but 20th for frequency. Journal/diary ranked 9th for value, but 12th for frequency. Letters ranked 8th for value, but 14th for frequency. Finally, poetry ranked 12th for value, but 15th for frequency.

## 2.3: Some Electronic Genres Written Frequently by Participants Are Not Valued Very Highly

There are a number of electronic genres that rank higher among participants   17
for use than for value. Notably, while texting ranked as most valued and most frequently used among all genres, participants do not value this form of writing at the same level that they practice it. As Figure 2 indicates, while 1049 participants (78%) selected texting as one of their top five most frequently used genres, only 641 participants (47%) ranked it in their top five most valued genres. Similarly, email was the second most frequently used genre (776 students, 57%), but it ranked 5th for value (586 students, 43%).

Several electronic genres which are used frequently did not rank in the top   18
ten most valued. Comments on status messages or posts in social software environments were ranked 8th for frequency but ranked 21st for value. Instant messaging ranked 7th for frequency but 15th for value. Finally status message updates were ranked 9th for frequency, but 18th for value.

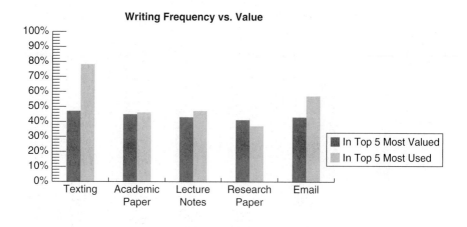

**Figure 2** Top five most valued genres compared with their frequency numbers

## Section 3: Do Students from Different Institution Types Compose and Value Different Kinds of Writing?

### 3.1: Institution Type Is a Meaningful Predictor of the Writing Experiences of Participants

In our sample, institution was statistically significant in predicting what genres   19
participants at different types of institutions had written. Participants who attended research universities were significantly more likely than participants from Master's or Associates institutions to have engaged in play/screenwriting and website writing. Survey participants who attended associate-granting institutions were significantly more likely to have written cover letters. Participants who attend master's-granting institutions were significantly more likely to have written many genres, including academic genres (academic papers, research papers, lab reports), helper academic genres (reading notes, outlines, lecture notes, peer responses), digital genres (texting, status message updates and responses, emails, instant messages), and more (poetry, journal, lists, letters, forms).

### 3.2: Use of Digital Genres Differed across Institution Types

Each institution type was significantly more likely to write a set of particular   20
digital genres. Master's University students were most likely to use email at least once, followed by Associate's College students and then Research University students. More participants enrolled in Associate's Colleges used chat rooms, but these participants were least likely to make status updates or comment on status updates. Participants enrolled in Master's Universities were most likely to email, use instant messenger, write status message updates, comment on status messages, and to text. Participants enrolled in Research

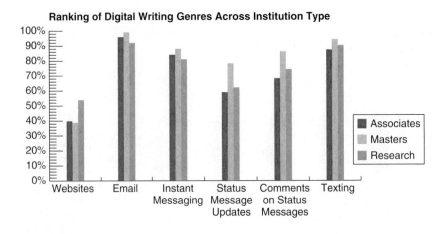

Figure 3 Percentage of students at each institution type reporting having written digital genres. Relationships shown are statistically significant.

Universities were most likely to write for websites and least likely to use instant messenger. These findings suggest that we need further investigation into how students at different kinds of institutions incorporate digital genres into their writing lives.

## Section 4: Why Do Participants Write What They Write?

### 4.1: Participants Are Most Often Motivated by the Need to Complete School Assignments

Half (50%) of all frequently written and most valued genres were associated 21 with writing for school, 97% of participants reported that one of their most valued or most often completed genres was done to fulfill a school assignment.

### 4.2: Participants Write for Personal Fulfillment Nearly as Often as for School Assignments

Nearly half (44%) of all valued and frequently written genres were associ- 22 ated with personal fulfillment. 93% of participants said that one of their most valued or most often completed genres was done for personal fulfillment. This finding is especially interesting given the fact that participants were solicited through academic avenues (e.g., college email addresses, course websites) and sometimes took the survey in college classrooms, where we might expect them to focus on school-sponsored motivations for writing.

## 4.3: Participants Associate Their Writing with Entertainment, Civic Participation, and for Their Jobs Much Less Often Than for School or Personal Fulfillment

After writing for school and personal fulfillment, writing for entertainment was the next most frequently identified motivation for the writing participants do most often and value most highly. Almost a third (31%) of the most frequently written and most valued genres were associated with entertainment. Writing for civic participation (16%) and writing to fulfill the requirements of a job (12%) were associated much less frequently with participants' writing. Notably, although writing for civic participation and for the job were related less frequently to most of the types of writing participants identified, over half of students associated these motivations with at least one of their most frequent or valued kinds of writing. 61% of participants reported writing for civic participation at least once among their most often written and valued genres, and 55% reported writing for the job at least once, suggesting that these motives are present in the lives of many participants, even if less pervasively.

## Section 5: What Are Participants Writing with Particular Technologies?

### 5.1: Participants Who Associate Particular Technologies with at Least One of Their Most Frequently or Valued Genres Use That Technology Frequently

As Figure 4 shows, 90% of participants associate word processors with at least one of their most frequently or valued written genres. Word processing technologies are used most often to write academic or research papers, but they also are used often for outlines, lecture notes, and emails. Users also rate word processing

**Beyond the Data: Facebook . . . meh** [23]

Our results show that Facebook is used frequently among first-year college students, and they use it to write a broad range of genres. The reasons why students do not report valuing this writing as highly are unclear, but it likely means that when faced with a list of types of writing, they still attach a lot of value to traditional print forms such as research papers and academic writing vs. shorter, born-digital forms such as status messages and instant messages.

Most of the writing students report doing on Facebook is directly related to interpersonal messaging. Though many think of social networking platforms as places where people write indulgently about themselves, our survey shows participants who more often comment on the posts and status updates of others than post things to their own profile. They also use Facebook to [24] send messages: texts, IM, and email. Participants also report using the platform for writing everything from lists to screenplays to poetry.

|  | % Used at Least Once | % Most Often Used |
| --- | --- | --- |
| Word Processor | 90% | 91% |
| Notebook or Paper | 89% | 94% |
| Cellphone | 86% | 98% |
| Pencil | 80% | 92% |
| Email | 76% | 90% |
| Facebook | 67% | 95% |

Figure 4 Percentage of students who associated each technology at least once with the writing they do, and the percentage of students who associated each technology with a most often written genre.

technologies as the technology most often associated with their most valued writing (79%).

**Beyond the Data:** Students are often writing alone and for personal fulfillment motives. But what does this mean?

Our findings suggest that students are doing a great deal of personal writing. They report writing alone and for personal fulfillment quite often. We hope that this finding helps us better understand the nature of personal writing for contemporary students. While they are often doing personal writing, we do not think that this writing is always private. For example, students are frequently writing alone when using cell phones, though they are frequently using them to connect to others through texting and social media platforms.

### 5.2: Blogs, Twitter, and Wikis Are Not Used by Many Participants, but Among Those Participants Who Use These Technologies, They Are Used Frequently

In contrast to how often they are associated with writing done most often, these technologies are only moderately or minimally associated with valued writing. This inverse relationship may reinforce the popular perception that a small percentage of people write the majority of blog, twitter, and wiki posts. This data also suggests that use of these technologies is not age specific or always connected to or influenced by writing in a school setting.

## Section 6: With Whom Are Participants Writing?

### 6.1: Participants Do Much of Their Most Common and Valued Writing Alone

While participants write with friends or classmates, writing with these two groups is not valued nearly as much as writing alone.

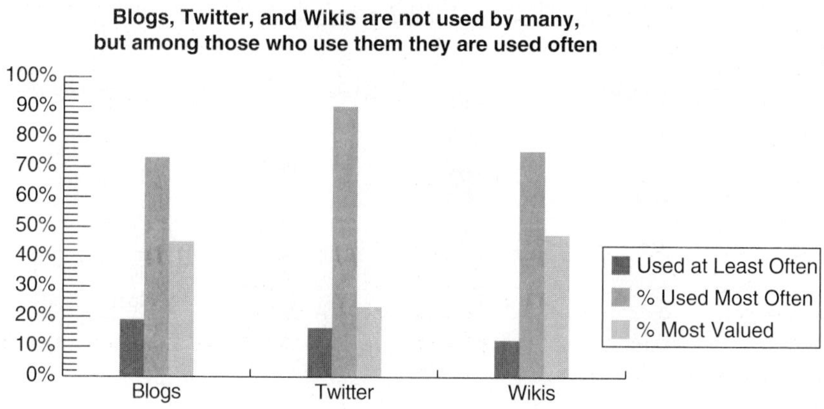
Blogs, Twitter, and Wikis are not used by many, but among those who use them they are used often
100%
90%
80%
70%
60%
50%
40%
30%
20%
10%
0%
Blogs
Twitter
Wikis
Used at Least Often
% Used Most Often
% Most Valued

Figure 5 Percentage of students who associated each technology at least once with the writing they do, and the percentage of students who associated each technology with a most often written genre.

### 6.2: Only 245 Participants Report Collaborating with Writing Center Consultants for Their Most Valued or Frequently Written Genres (One of the Lowest Ranked Collaborators, Behind Only "Other")

When compared with all of the other types of collaborators, the fewest number of participants worked with writing center consultants while writing their most frequent and valued genres. Among those participants who report working with writing center consultants, they list it as their least used collaboration. Further, participants identified collaborating with writing center consultants as least valued (second only to "Other"). 27

### 6.3: Writing with Work Colleagues Is Reported Less Often and Not Highly Valued

38% of participants report collaborating with work colleagues to write at least one of their most frequent of valued genres. While 33% associate work colleagues with one of their most often written genres, only 12% of participants associate it with a most valued genre. 28

## Methodology

### Sampling

In this study, we constructed a purposive, stratified sample in an attempt to match the demographic profile of US college students (those enrolled in both four-year and two-year institutions in 2010). We identified institutions for recruitment that had enabled us to construct a reasonable sample of US 29

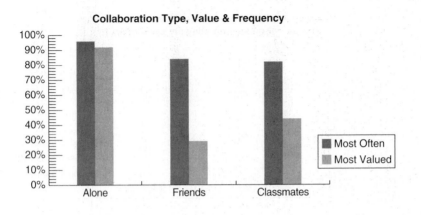

**Figure 6** Percentage of students who associate each collaborator with their most frequently written and valued genres.

institutions of higher education. With regard to data analysis, in order to arrive at the findings in this report, two similar tests were utilized. Fisher's Exact Test was used to determine relationships between variables when possible (i.e., when results formed a $2 \times 2$ contingency table). Chi-square tests were used in all other situations. Results were considered significant at the .05 level.

Our sampling resulted in the following profile:                                    30

- Age: The vast majority of participants (90%) were a "traditional" age for US institutions of higher education (18–23). Half of all participants were 19 years old, indicating that they had enrolled in college immediately after graduating from high school.
- Institution: 58% of participants attended a research university, 20% of participants attend a master's granting institution, and 11% of participants attend a Community college.
- Race and ethnicity: 43% of our sample was non-white, with 5% Black, 28% Hispanic, 8% Asian, and 2% Native American.

### Comparison to Race and Ethnicity Profiles of Students in Higher Education

To further assess our sample, we compared the demographic data of those   31
completing our survey with both the 1999–2000 and the 2003–2004 "National Postsecondary Student Aid Study: Profile of Undergraduates in U.S. Postsecondary Education institutions" report issued by the U.S. National Center for Education Statistics (NCES).

The 2003–2004 version of the NCES report included a special focus on   32
two-year institutions, and so in its 2004 report of demographic data the center breaks out community colleges and 4-year institutions. The table below shows how our sample compares with the NCES numbers:

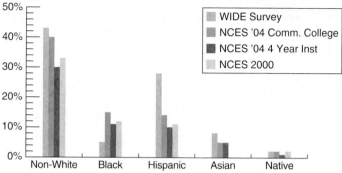

**Figure 7** Race and ethnicity breakdown for Revisualizing Composition and two National Centers for Education Statistics Studies.

As Figure 6 shows, we likely oversampled Hispanic students and, to a lesser 33 degree, Asian students. We undersampled African American students. That our sample includes a slightly higher percentage of non-white participants than the NCES demographic profile of college students reflects a concerted effort on our part to construct a diverse student profile. The participation of the University of Texas, El Paso and Leeward Community College, respectively, contributed in large measure to the numbers in all of the minority population categories above with the exception of African American students. For future surveys, we should focus more carefully on ways to sample African American students at a level consistent with their numbers in the overall demographic profile (12–15%).

## Survey Distribution

Distribution methods varied by institution based on local IRB recommendations. The survey was distributed via email to all students in first-year composition classes at Michigan State University, University of Texas, El Paso, and Leeward Community College. At Lansing Community College and the University of North Carolina, Pembroke, writing program faculty who teach first-year composition were contacted via email with the online survey link and distributed the survey link to students enrolled in their courses, some of which included first-year business and technical writing classes. At IPFW, the survey was distributed to all students enrolled in any writing course during the spring of 2010, including advanced writing and technical writing students, and a majority of students enrolled in first-year and intermediate composition courses. At Elon University, the survey was sent via email to all first-year students who matriculated in 2009 and were still enrolled in Spring 2010.

## Questions for Discussion and Journaling

1. What research questions did the WIDE researchers ask here, and what research methods did they use to answer those questions? How do their research methods differ from those used by other authors in this chapter?

2. The WIDE researchers, along with other writing scholars in this chapter and throughout this book, understand writing broadly. The WIDE authors found that 78 percent of student respondents said that texting was one of the five most common types of writing they have done. However, they note that texting challenges "common perceptions of what counts as 'writing'" (para. 7). Drawing on your own experiences with texting and considering what you have read so far in this book, write a few paragraphs in which you try to discover what your opinion is of texting and how it fits into your developing understanding of what "writing" is.

3. The WIDE authors made a list of the top ten genres most frequently written by students. Make your own top ten list based on your own experience. How does it compare to the WIDE findings? If there are differences, what do you think accounts for them?

4. The study found that writing in chatrooms, for Web sites, and for blogs was much less common than e-mailing, texting, and status updates. Why do you think this is the case? (Note that for Web site writing, the researchers found that males engage in this activity much more frequently than females.) Do you see differences in the kind of writing (including effort and knowledge) required for each of these forms?

5. The WIDE researchers found that students valued texting the most, but the next three genres they valued most were academic. When the WIDE researchers asked students what kind of writing they valued, how do you think students were defining "value"? Do you think they value texting and research papers in the same way? Consider the list of genres you write (that you made for question 3, above). How are these different genres valuable to you? What is it about them that makes them valuable? Is it easy for you to compare and rank the kinds of value that each of those genres has for you, or is it like comparing apples and oranges?

6. In addition to the genres that students write, WIDE also organizes findings by the purposes for which students write: school, work, entertainment, personal fulfillment, civic participation. Think about the genres that you and other students write. Do they take on different kinds of value and different conventions depending on the purpose and context? For example, is an e-mail always an e-mail, or do e-mails differ a lot if they are written for work, school, and entertainment?

7. The WIDE researchers found that students write alone quite frequently, but that their technologies and genres are actually linking them to others. Consider how technology has changed what it means to write alone. For example, is posting on Facebook while you are alone in your dorm room the same as writing in your diary while alone in an isolated farmhouse in 1872? How has technology changed the way writing connects people?

## Applying and Exploring Ideas

1. Because this study involves surveying college students about the kinds of writing in which they regularly engage, it immediately and obviously invites you to compare your own experiences to their findings and to follow up with your own research projects. Work with a partner to identify two or three research questions you would like to explore further as a result of what you read here. Would a survey be the best method for gathering data to answer these questions, or will you need to use other methods (methods you have seen modeled throughout this book, such as interviews, case studies, protocols, etc.)?

2. The authors state that they are "working from the assumption that students lead complex writing lives." Then they go on to all of the ways that students' writing lives are complex. Make a list of the various ways that your writing life is and has been complex, using their discussion as a model.

3. The WIDE researchers suggest that smart phones may be "the new pencil," since students use them for everything from texting to making lists to taking notes. Make a list of all the ways that you and your close friends use your phones. Then, looking at that list, decide whether you agree that the smart phone is "the new pencil." Write two to three pages making and supporting your answer to that question. If your teacher has also assigned Dennis Baron's "From Pencils to Pixels," you might bring his ideas into play here.

4. Conduct an informal survey of your classmates, your roommates, fraternity or sorority, or some other group in order to come up with a list of all the technologies they use to engage with writing, using the list in Section 5 as a starting point.

### Meta Moment

Do you define "writing" differently after reading this article? As you use technologies for writing, can you consider how they help you do things differently than you would without those technologies?

# History Now: Media Development and the Textual Genesis of Wikipedia

## CHRISTIAN KOHL   WOLF-ANDREAS LIEBERT
## THOMAS METTEN

■ Kohl, Christian, Wolf-Andreas Liebert, and Thomas Metten. "History Now: Media Development and the Textual Genesis of Wikipedia." *Language and New Media*. Ed. Charley Rowe and Eva Wyss. Creskill, NJ: Hampton Press, 2009. 165–82. Print.

## Framing the Reading

Wikis are arguably one of the three most important Web apps of the Internet revolution to date (the others being non-wiki-based blog software and video-upload and storage software), because of the ease with which they let readers of the Web *write* the Web. If you weren't there to see the Web in the mid-1990s—if you came to using it a decade later—it's hard to imagine the difference between the user-driven content we think is normal now and the static, read-only nature of Web pages when the Web became an entity in 1994 (with the invention of the Web browser). The difference was so stark that we actually think of the two times as different versions of the Web—1.0 and 2.0.

The authors of this piece are faculty at the University of Koblenz–Landau in Germany, where they study textuality and new media. In this piece, what Kohl, Liebert, and Metten specifically want to study is how writing texts for wikis differs from writing traditional texts. They choose as their object of study the most prominent wiki, Wikipedia. What, they wonder, are the differences between Wikipedia articles and traditional encyclopedia articles? Their chapter ends up considering two of the most apparent differences: Unlike paper encyclopedia articles, Wikipedia articles are written via collaborative discussion among any users who feel they have something to contribute to the article, and therefore, the articles evolve over time with an exposed history. (All the edits and versions of a page are captured in the page's History tab, and all the conversation underlying its development is captured in its Talk tab.)

An important focus of this piece is how writing for Wikipedia, because it is collaborative and happens over time, exposes the dialogue that leads to a given current page as a *knowledge-constructing process*. This is probably far from the first time you've encountered this concept in *Writing about Writing*, but wikis have the unique property of exposing that dialogue and *recording it* so that it can be studied in detail. When we look at the Talk and History tabs of a Wikipedia page, we get to actually see the knowledge the Article tab arrives at while it's being built. This is one reason that Wikipedia is not nearly as unreliable as many have claimed since it was invented: "Anybody can write anything they feel like on there and you can't tell the difference between what's true and false!" Because edits to a page are recorded (History) and discussed (Talk), any reader can always tell *how the text got that way* and how what's offered as settled knowledge on the Article tab has come to be. As readers, we can decide for ourselves to what extent the discussion and edits have led to a reliable article.

You are likely to think that this piece feels repetitive or seems to require a lot of work in making meaning only to arrive at somewhat straightforward principles (such as, Wikipedia texts have to be analyzed in light of the history of their development because they were developed over time). More than the typical academic article, this chapter does come back to the same basic set of conclusions several times. This is helpful because you get several chances to try to understand the authors' claims. However, the authors reach the same conclusions in different ways. Each time, they're giving different reasons and considering different aspects of collaborative knowledge-making as they do. Try to pay attention to the various ways they come to their conclusions.

## Getting Ready to Read

*Before you read*, do at least one of the following activities:

- Look at three Wikipedia articles of your choice very carefully. Read the entire article and note its features and organization, and any Wikipedia tags like "[citation needed]." Notice the five tabs that sit at the top of each page: Article and Talk on the left, and Read, Edit, and History on the right. Click each of those tabs, on each article, to see where they lead.
- If you have a paper or CD-ROM encyclopedia (*Britannica*, *Encarta*, etc.) available (and if you don't, your library will), read the editorial material at the front of a volume to learn about how that encyclopedia and its articles came to be.
- Make a list of readings from *Writing about Writing* that you've read which talk about knowledge construction; think back through the main points of those pieces so that you'll recognize any similar ideas that arise in this article.
- Read the abstract to this piece carefully and, from it, make a list of subjects you expect the piece to talk about.

*As you read*, consider the following questions:

- How well does the piece's abstract match what the piece actually says?
- As the writers discuss a given principle, consider what other kinds of texts and writing you've seen that seem to use or be based on the same ideas.
- Write down each main conclusion the writers seem to make, and the number of the paragraph they make it in. If they reach a conclusion that you saw earlier in the piece, add the additional paragraph number to your earlier entry.

## Abstract

This chapter argues that Wikipedia is a user-driven knowledge system and hence is able to incorporate controversies and different points of view. By an analysis of the discussion-article-relations of the main-article of the philosophy portal, we try to make explicit the internal management of collaborative writing processes and the way in which the process of article-discussion-interactions in Wikipedia leads to the incorporation of controversies and different points of view. 1

The analysis of the main article of the philosophy portal focuses on the period from July to August 2005 because this was a period of increasing collaboration. By extracting basic patterns of article-discussion-relations we expect to make clear which specific medial functions of Wikipedia were at work. These functions have an enormous impact on the process of collaborative writing because the process of writing and thinking about writing itself becomes transparent as a whole. Collaborative writing in Wikipedia thus becomes a process discussing different discourse positions and incorporating multiple aspects by rewriting and rearranging the article. These interchanges of articles and discussions along with the dynamic development are what distinguishes Wikipedia articles from classic encyclopedia articles. 2

At the moment, the most prominent example of Wiki-systems is the Internet encyclopedia Wikipedia.[1] If one looks at the Wikipedia as an encyclopedia, it is part of the long history of encyclopedias. According to Mittelstraß (1967) the *Encyclopédie* of Diderot and d'Alembert can be called the first modern encyclopedia. Two characteristic features that contrasted this encyclopedia with others were the formation of a group of authors (in contrast to the single author of earlier encyclopedias; see Elia, chap. 13, this volume) and the claim not only to present existing knowledge, but to work educationally (Haß-Zumkehr, 2001; Volpers, 2002). Subsequently, the Brockhaus, a type of encyclopedia that firmly addressed an (educated) amateur audience, was developed in Germany (Volpers, 2002).[2] Wikipedia differs from the *Encyclopédie* and the *Brockhaus* in three essential points: 3

1. The principle of *collaboration* becomes decisive: Although groups of authors and publishers are involved[3] with the *Encyclopédie* or the *Brockhaus,* there still is a conventional editorial staff process: An author is responsible for an article, the only intervention in this article can occur through the editorial staff and the publishers. In the case of Wikipedia, however, there are always several authors equally responsible for an article, there is no editorial staff, no publishers, and also no formal, fixed editorial processes.

2. In case of Wikipedia *everybody is able to be part of the authorship.* The authors are mostly anonymous and not necessarily experts. This differs from the *Encyclopédie* or the *Brockhaus.* Furthermore, the authors are not specifically selected and invited by an editorial staff, but become active on their own impulse.

3. There is *no preselection* of dictionary entries, given taxonomy, article size, deadline *or similar restrictions* of more classic editorial processes.

As Stickfort (2002) noted, the Internet medium has "added . . . a new 4 dimension to the former traditional forms of information collection and information spreading" (271). Besides the generally perceived new possibilities of searching (and finding) as well as the distribution of information, the World Wide Web (WWW) opens new possibilities for the construction of knowledge. Wikis are tools for Internet-based knowledge construction that, in comparison to classical processes of knowledge construction, as for example the writing of an article or a monograph, partly allows radical changes. Initially, Wikipedia served as a prominent example of Wiki-systems. Nevertheless, as long as Wikipedia is viewed in the tradition of encyclopedias, determining features, by which Wikis are usually marked, do not stand out clearly. Only with a representation of the media qualities does their real potential become clear.

Hence, this chapter discusses the historical development and qualities of 5 Wikis. Some basic considerations of the dynamic media are made from which the meaning of the historicity of every text becomes evident. Hence, this chapter opens two historical dimensions: the history of the Wiki technology as a media history, and the history of the origin of text as a textual history. The dimension of the textual history arises from the possibilities of the medium, and therefore from this follows the media history.

## Media History and Basic Principles

Indeed, Wikis have become popular only since about 2003, and Wiki projects 6 are often seen as an example of "Web 2.0." Nevertheless, Wikis already existed in 1994, thus since the beginning of the WWW. "Wiki" is the designation for a type of software, similar to "word processing" or "spreadsheet," which can stand for a number of different programs. The basic principles of this software are called "Wiki principles." However, the concrete applications are often called "Wiki," for example in phrases like "in our Wiki." However, in this case "Wiki" does not refer to the software type, but to the concrete application. What is meant is "in our Wiki of the lecture XY" or "our film Wiki." Another complication arises from the fact that a large number of different software products of the type "Wiki" exists, which vary in their functional circumference. The following section briefly explains what Wikis actually are, which ideas and principles are behind the technology, and the varied application possibilities.

### What Is a Wiki?

A Wiki is a Web application that enables collaborative work on the Internet 7 (Kleinz, 2003; Leuf & Cunningham, 2001; Möller, 2002). The user should be able to participate without previous knowledge and technical hurdles. Cooperation and common compiling and handling of texts are in the foreground.[4] This principle already has its reflection in the name: "Wiki" comes from the Hawaiin language and means "fast" or "informally" (Leuf & Cunningham, 2001).

The first "Wiki" was used in 1994 by Ward Cunningham for the "Portland  8
Pattern Repository,"[5] therefore, Cunningham is often said to be the "Wiki inventor." According to Leuf and Cunningham (2001) a Wiki is a "freely expand-
able collection of interlinked Web 'pages,' a hypertext system for storing and
modifying information—a database where each page is easily editable by any
user with a forms-capable Web browser client" (14). Wiki-software runs on a
Web server and enables every user to publish, change, and link texts on the Internet. The user does not need any HTML knowledge or special software. Text
is entered as rough text and a conventional browser without auxiliary modules
is sufficient. Furthermore, all contributions can be read and worked on by
all participants. This way, a large number of spatially distributed individuals
can work collaboratively on (hyper-) texts via the Internet. The low technical
requirements as well as the simple usage make it possible for "computer lay-
men" to publish and work on texts on the Internet and to provide hypertexts.
Finally, the technology is platform-independent: This means that it can be used
with any operating system that has a browser—the only condition is access to
the Internet.

On the basis of Cunningham's "Primal-Wiki," meanwhile, many variants  9
of this software exist.[6] On the one hand, these differ by the programming language in which they were written,[7] and on the other hand by their functions
and restrictions. This is how for example TWiki[8] developed, a piece of Wiki
software that was programmed for operation in enterprises and therefore has a
user administration. These different derivatives are also called "Wiki-clones."[9]
Above all, they vary in the functional range, which concerns user friendliness
and user administration. Some versions additionally have a Plugin architecture,
so that additional functionality can be added according to desire. Furthermore,
the "configurableness" of the user surface is different from Wiki to Wiki: The
spectrum ranges from rigid systems in which changes are not possible without
modifications of the source code of the software, to systems that can be based
on drafts and can easily be adapted to one's own needs.

On the basis of a collaboration platform for programmers to exchange soft-  10
ware design samples, Wikis are meantime used in the most diverse areas of
application: internally as a tool for documentation; for organization; and for
transfer of knowledge[10]; for the documentation of software[11]; in E-Learning[12];
collecting recipes, restaurant criticisms, or reports on journies[13]; to the creation
of textbooks, dictionaries, or encyclopedias.[14]

## Wiki Principles

Despite the heterogeneity of the software and the large differences concerning  11
the operational area and functionality, two core elements can be identified that
are constitutive for Wikis: simplicity and openness.[15]

### Simplicity

The demand for "simplicity" becomes clear with different aspects of the  12
software. The principle particularly becomes clear with the conditions for the

usage of the software as well as the requirements of hardware and software. Changing and providing contents takes place in the browser, either in a so-called WYSIWYG editor, or rather text-oriented with the usage of the so-called Wiki syntax. Besides the simple input and formatting of texts, similar easy productions of links are in the foreground; finally Wikis are, above all, tools for the collaborative creation of hypertext networks.[16] The user does not have to have any technical knowledge and does not have to know the programming language in order to be able to cooperate in a Wiki project.

So far, well-known Wiki surfaces are quite text laden, having none too few [13] graphic elements; the emphasis of the production of Wikis is so far clearly on content, not on the design. So far no usability studies or similar investigations concerning operability or the acceptance of different Wiki surfaces exist.

A further crucial factor for the acceptance of Wikis are the low entrance [14] hurdles: The technical facilities necessary for the operation of a Wiki are low on both the client and on the server side, the user only needs a conventional browser, the operator can exclusively use free software and does not need any special know-how for the installation and usage. By now there are providers where Wikis can be rented or used free of charge, similarly to blogs or e-mail services, so called "Wiki farms."[17] Now, even Web content management-systems and learning management-systems frequently offer Wikis besides chat and blogs.[18]

### Openness

Next to simplicity, openness is the second characteristic of Wikis. Publicly [15] accessible Wikis hardly have any barriers—in principle all users have the same right to write and read. This means that each visitor can work on pages or create new ones. However, by now, many Wikis have a more or less sophisticated user administration, so that registration may be necessary, for example certain articles on Wikipedia are only processible by signed users or by administrators. Furthermore, with an appropriate server configuration (e.g., a firewall), it is easy to ensure that a Wiki is accessible only to a certain user group, for example coworkers at a particular company. Some Wikis, for instance TWiki, enable the creation of user groups and the synchronization of persons and groups with already existing listings, such as Microsoft Active Directory.

> Next to simplicity, openness is the second characteristic of Wikis. Publicly accessible Wikis hardly have any barriers—in principle all users have the same right to read and write. This means that each visitor can work on pages or create new ones.

The principle of openness grants many rights and liberties to the Wiki [16] participants; however, at the same time it obligates them to respectful handling of the contributions of others. The "missing" write protection for contents of a Wiki does not inevitably lead to chaotic contents because for each person who deletes contributions or writes nonsense,[19] there are several others who cancel or improve this change again. Cifollili (2003) also pointed out that destroying a contribution requires more expenditure than repairing it. So far there are no comprehensive studies about this behavior of usage, so that this estimation is based only on empirical values (Hennicken & Zahiri, 2003; Leuf & Cunningham, 2001). However, Wikipedia supplies examples of the effectiveness of the Wiki principle: Viegas et al. (2004) have proven that 50% of all examined cases of vandalism on Wikipedia were repaired within 2 or 3 minutes.[20] Dworschak (2004) and Viegas et al. (2004) see this openness as a fundamental difference to other communication forms on the Internet and claim the fact that everyone can change anything to be the high "ability to reach a consensus" of Wikis. A further consequence of the openness of Wikis is the dissolution of the distinction of author and recipient: The abolition of this separation of roles is frequently stated as characteristic for Internet communication; however, only Wiki systems enable these two roles to be implemented at any time by any user. One can even go further and note that it is a constitutive characteristic of Wikis that all participants can be recipient and author at the same time: Otherwise the Wiki would not function and would appear to be a "normal" Web site. Because of this extension, not only the user's possibilities change, but the requirements also increase. Instead of a unidirectional communication in the form of bare reception, a multidirectional communication takes place: the exchange of knowledge by cooperative work with several other users. A shift away from passive reading toward more interaction and activity takes place. Critical thinking, handling different points of view, the reflection of one's own position concerning other opinions, teamwork, and the cooperative writing of texts must be learned and practiced.

### Legal Aspects: OpenSource and OpenContent

The contents of a Wiki are commonly compiled by the users. Therefore, the legal question of which license the contributions use is of great importance. Many Wikis put an emphasis on a so-called "OpenContent" license. Open-Content is an analogical formation to "OpenSource."[21] The term *OpenSource* originates from the software development and describes a license form that deviates from the classical "copyright" by assigning certain rights of usage to the users, instead of limiting them. It concerns the right for handling, the passing on, and the duplication of the source code of programs. Known software projects that follow this model of development are the operating system Linux, the office-package OpenOffice, the Web server Apache, and the browser suite Mozilla.[22] A further characteristic of OpenSource licenses is that they are so-called "virus licenses." This means that products derived from them must have the same license as the output product. Thus, free entrance and free distribution are secured durably; this not only concerns the output product, but also all conversions derived from it. [17]

Similar to the conditions of the software source code, OpenContent stands for the same license model in reference to "knowledge" or "contents."[23] The most prominent OpenContent licenses are the "license for free contents"[24] and the "Creative Commons license"[25] for the German right as well as the [18]

"GFDL"[26] for U.S.-American right. Different variants of these licenses exist. The rights of usage, passing on, and subsequent handling can be specified in detail.[27] Wiki contents, however, do not have to use such a license: Although in most Wiki projects the author uses an OpenContent license, any Wiki user can feel free to use a license preferred for the user's own project.

For scientists, there is an additional question of how the quasi-anonymous authorship in Wikis (e.g., Wikipedia) will be evaluated by consultants and employers in the future. Right now contributions in a Wiki are not suitable for addition to a publication list. For this reason, an important stimulus for writing is void (i.e., the production of appropriate reputation, or bourdieuesque "capital").   19

## Collaborative Media and Text History

The participatory possibilities on the Internet are increasing since the spreading of "Web 2.0" uses.[28] In light of the dissolution of a clear role assignment of author and reader as well as the extended technical possibilities of Wiki systems, texts on the Internet no longer appear static, but rather as dynamic forms of writing. Interactivity describes a new dimension of social interaction, which, also by means of the Wiki software, was established as specific writing practice. Texts that develop in Wiki systems are therefore not singular historical events, but possess a temporal structure. Therefore, they must be understood and analyzed as writing processes and less as final works. This results in the initially outlined second perspective: Apart from the history of the development of the medium itself, the medium's own temporalness can be described, which contributes to the possibilities of communication.   20

Landow (2003) repeatedly stressed that the majority of the web pages on the Internet are still arranged as "nonbook books." Web pages, therefore, are not understood as books, but in the long run they are designed like books. In this way, an established and antiquated sample of historical media is transferred to new, historically younger media (see McNeill, chap. 12, this volume). However, electronic documents are—against the opinion of many teachers, technologists and software developers—not books (Landow, 2003). With the paradigm of the book, three aspects in particular are connected that coin the handling of texts: Texts are to be discretely differentiated from other texts, the roles of author and reader are clearly definable, and texts are static. Landow on the other hand, suggested describing specific applications of the Internet as a "collaborative learning environment." Such a perspective offers the possibility of understanding texts in Wiki systems not as static works, but rather as dynamic processes. Therefore, the following paragraph, in consideration of the designated aspects, focuses on theoretical considerations about how a changed understanding of texts in Wiki systems affects the investigations of the texts.   21

## Text Theory 2.0

The multiple cross-linking of Web sites on the Internet led to the assumption that the discrete distinction of Web sites dissolves. We contradict this first   22 aspect: The discrete distinction of texts does not dissolve on the Internet. Instead of the limits of a book, a direct linking of sites does develop. However, regarding the historical development of media representational forms, the linking of web pages only appears to be a gradual increase in relation to other representational forms. Daily papers and encyclopedias are likewise characterized by such features as complex chaining and modular structures. Although web pages are, on the one hand, directly connected with one another, there is, on the other hand, no problem in making a clear demarcation. The switch from the web page of a car manufacturer to one of a telephone solicitor becomes immediately evident on the basis of the design. To this extent, hypertexts enable a strengthened modularity of texts whose single modules exist in different relations to each other and can be directly interconnected (see Jakobs, chap. 14, this volume). However, regarding content, organization and addressing a clear demarcation of texts takes place.

Although for the recipient, the identity of web pages remains to a large ex- 23 tent protected, the dissolution of authorship and the mixture of the roles of author and recipient have further reaching consequences. With the development of the Internet, considerations developed by among others Roland Barthes and Jacques Derrida earlier, repeatedly have re-arisen: "hypertextuality embodies poststructuralist conceptions of the open text" (see Landow, 2006:2). Barthes (2006) suggested relativizing the relationship among the writer, reader, and observer. Therefore, he understood the text from the point of view of the process of writing and stated: "[t]he theory of the 'text' can only accompany the practice of the writing" (72). The reader no longer just reads what is offered to him or her, but is actively involved in creating the text. In the context of hypertext theory, this for a long time just meant: as the reader selects his or her reading path within the complex hypertext structure, he or she develops an individual way of reception. Such a way of reading is made possible by hypertext systems; books, however, specifiy the procedure of reception to a large extent. Strongly interlaced hypertext systems, therefore, create a labyrinth with innumerable possibilities for reception.

The picture of such a labyrinth, however, only develops by means of a de- 24 scription of the structures of the hypertexts. As a result of the structural dimension of hypertexts, which is described by the metaphor of the net, hypertexts are mostly seen as nonlinear. The nonlinearity of hypertexts designates specific structures, which can only apply to certain forms of hypertext organization, and exist together with numerous others, hierarchical or linear organization forms. In each case, the recipient only perceives a linear succession of web pages, which he or she can only gradually reconstruct. Storrer (2000) prepared such a structural perspective on hypertexts for linguistics, whereby such an analysis completely corresponds to the linguistic tradition, which is strongly affected by structuralist theory. The Internet encyclopedia Wikipedia is often compared with printed encyclopedias because both media not only aim at a comparable representation of contents, but also show a strong chaining structure, therefore showing structural parallels. If one exclusively analyzes the texts and their chaining structure within the hypertext system, such a comparison seems appropriate. The kind of text (encyclopedia entry) as well as handed-down concepts of the encyclopedia determine the understanding of the Wikipedia participants as well as those who examine the Internet encyclopedia from a linguistic point of view. From this point of view it is only about the structural and thematic organization of the texts, and not about processes of writing. The view on the structural dimension of hypertexts, however, does not clarify the crucial characteristics of Wikis. An analysis of hypertext structures is important; however, it cannot clarify the processes of text emergence that are crucial for an understanding of Wikis.

Grube (2003) said it is alluring to argue from the perspective of nonlinearity 25 that hypertexts are deeply embodied in the tradition of older texts. Therefore, he suggested "that the so far leading criterion of nonlinearity to determine hypertexts should be taken back in favor of the criterion of interactivity" (83). The understanding of the texts shifts if the writing as well as the writing process moves toward the focus. It will then become clear Wikipedia's texts, due to the software, establish a changed cultural writing practice that no longer proceeds from an individual author not the author's monological expression. The result of this work is not the text as a final work. The dynamic dimension of the texts clarifies that its temporal organization is of special importance. Contributions in Wikipedia no longer represent only single texts in a net of further texts (hypertext), but also must be regarded in their history of development.

Therefore, we want to understand texts—as they develop in Wikis and also 26 occur in Wikipedia—as processes, whereas the processes of the emergence are to be analyzed regarding the temporal course of events. Although the static text appears as a unique event in a historical continuum, the dynamic text embodies the history of its emergence by the act of the participant's writing. A contribution in the Internet encyclopedia, therefore, can be understood as an embodiment of the act of writing and processes of interacting, negotiating, reformulating, and making the contribution easily understood. This dimension of text history can be described as the performative dimension, which depends on the media condition and clearly goes beyond a purely structural understanding. Therefore, three dimensions of the investigation become relevant for the analysis of the texts in Wikipedia: the structural dimension, the media dimension, and the performative dimension.

The performative dimension records the temporalness of the text with re- 27 spect to the history of text emergence. Those aspects are crucial for the understanding of collaborativly written texts.

Such an analysis stresses the eventful happening of the single text and doc- 28 uments its history as one of interaction. The idea of interactivity, therefore, marks a turning point in the participation of the recipients, who not only can select their own reading paths but also can create text by clicks in the reception. The reader in Wiki systems is also an active writer. With the computer, such a dynamic sampling of symbol structures occurred (see Krämer, 2003). Time becomes a dimension of the text with respect to text emergence; the writing opens an action area for the interaction and common text formatting. Wiki systems extend the area of action by changing the monologic writing into dialogic negotiating. That connection of negotiating and communication clarifies that the reader-text interaction is embedded in a communicative happening as well. The user interacts with the text, but does this knowing that the individual passages are to be assigned to specific participants. The result of this is the communicative connection. The writing, understood as an area of operations and perception, is therefore not only described as a medium of representation; but also as presenting an "interrelation of eye, hand, and machine" (Krämer, 2003:52). Although Krämer, with reference to the outwardness of writing, stated that these not only serve an expanded communication, they also serve the monologic solving of problems. Wikis show that writing also serves the dialogic writing of texts. Articles—as they appear in Wikipedia—represent a snapshot within a constantly progressing and unfinished process of writing of numerous authors. The current shape of a text, therefore, only can be understood because of the history of development of the respective contribution. Wiki systems enable such a text analysis because of the detailed archive of versions of texts, which makes each change of individual authors accessible. This way, the history of each contribution is completely documented from the first entry on.

## Text Emergence and Text Analysis

Collaborative processes of writing dissolve the central intention of the author. [29] The authors only work on passages and never on the entire text. Therefore, they mostly take large parts of text and supplement them with their own formulations, which can include individual words, sentences, or whole paragraphs. The statements taken over now attain the character of quotations, whereby the keeping does not guarantee that the quoter means the same thing with the rewording like the preceding person. Thus, those characteristics of the writing emerge, which Derrida (2004, and others) named particularly in his early work about the concept of script: The writing must function in absence of author and reader. The text as a unit carries the traces of all authors. At the same time the sign—the writing—is quotable (i.e., it is part of the linguistic signs to be repeatable). "I would like to insist on this possibility: The possibility of taking out and quotational grafting, which is part of the structure of each spoken or written sign [marque] . . . What would a sign be that could not be quoted? And whose origin could not be lost along the way?" (Derrida, 2004:89). The repeatability of the sign and the repetition in the writing opens up the temporal structure of the text as the practice of writing. By writing, the participants in each case react to the preceding contributions of other authors. As writers, they start a "dialogue" with the already expressed information. This thematically oriented discourse stands out within the history of development of the text and is constantly continued. The statements of other participants are quoted and varied. On the one hand, the text appears to the recipient as a unit; on the other hand the archive of versions and the documentation of discussions clarify the interactive character of the text emergence. Although texts in books are static, Wiki systems make dynamic writing processes possible. Therefore, the interlaced structure of hypertexts is not their crucial characteristic, rather, it is the temporal structure of their emergence by the practice of the writing of several authors.

An analysis of the contributions in Wikipedia should not only regard an 30 individual text, but also include further texts with reference to a topic into the analysis (Kohl & Liebert, 2004). Therefore, it is about the contribution itself, the documentation of its emergence, the archive of versions, and the discussion pages belonging to the contribution. Thus, the discussion pages offer the participants the possibility of commentating their intentions and interests as well as explanations about their own understanding of the text. Such a view includes the structures of hypertext. Apart from such a structural collection of Wikipedia contributions, an analysis of the temporal course of text emergence should take place. Therefore, the participation of participants and their interactions must trace an appropriate representation and analysis of collaboratively developed texts. The text can be examined regarding its temporal structure as well as with a view of text-constitutive actions, and the participation of the participants. An analysis should include both dimensions in order to formulate statements about the emergence and quality of texts. A comprehensive analysis that does not consider the forms of interaction of text emergence can hardly make appropriate statements about the entries in Wikipedia. Only an analysis of the action patterns and intentions of the participants can create a complete picture of text emergence if the dialogical principle of text emergence and the mutual reference of the participants are considered at the same time. This is particularly important because the appearance of the text frequently resembles a monologically written text.

Earlier we remarked that the understanding of text types of the partici- 31 pants also plays an important role. Apart from this, a stylistic analysis, which is closely bound to the conceptions of the kind of text, seems to be of special importance. On the basis of the contribution about philosophy in Wikipedia, the complexity of such an analysis is to be clarified in a few notes. Contributions in Wikipedia usually start with individual expressions and entries. The further process can take place in different kinds of ways. Some contributions only consist of few sentences for a long time, others rapidly develop, and after a short time they already offer a comprehensive overview about a topic. The text emergence does not proceed continuously. Phases of intensive revising take turns with phases in which hardly any changes are made for a long time. In short phases of intensive treatment, few participants can take part, whereas during long phases, in which hardly any changes take place, revising can be intended for many different participants. On the one hand, the development of a contribution depends on the interest of the participants and the respective constellation of participants; on the other hand, factors such as currentness of a topic in further discourses have an influence on text development. Processes of cultural change, therefore, also settle in processes of text emergence.

Wikipedia's contribution about the topic "philosophy" meanwhile belongs 32 to the so-called excellent articles. This contribution was made with the first entry on May 4, 2002. Since then and up to December 2, 2006, the contribution was worked on 1,216 times. Therefore, the contribution was changed with an average of 0.73 times a day. Within the first year, however, only 34 changes were made. However, 14 changes were made alone on August 3, 2006. This clarifies that the process of the handling does not proceed continuously. A look at the participants shows that only four people made the changes on August 3. Viewed alone, the frequency of changes or the number of the participants involved does not reveal much. If one now adds the commentating of the contribution on the discussion pages to the analysis, the result is a complex picture of the history of development of the contribution, the participation of the participants as well as their self-understanding and intentions. The text as a thematically coherent unit is only readable in an appropriate way when the different aspects are referred to each other.

Aspects that were relevant for the analysis of static (i.e., printed texts) must 33 be examined in relation to the considerations discussed. Contributions within Wikipedia appear as discourse shapes that developed within a complex process of collaborative development. The texts embody dynamics and actions of the participants in each case one at a time. An appropriate understanding of these texts, however, must regard the current status of a text with view to its prehistory. The text is an historical document, not in so far as it developed at a certain historical time, but in so far as it embodies the complex history of its emergence. Regarding Wikis in a media-historical perspective, therefore, does not only mean regarding the interrelation of different media in the historical process but also to regard the historicity of the medium as well as the developing texts. Therefore, a linguistic discourse history must—as it becomes clear by the example of the Wikis—be supplemented with its own historicity of the texts. Therefore, a text cannot exclusively be seen as a subject-bound relinquishing of an intention at a certain time, but must also be analyzed with view to its own temporal structure.

Altogether, the three levels mentioned here appear to be relevant for the 34 analysis: Apart from a structural analysis, the description of a text regarding the medium is relevant. The performative dimension of the analysis now describes the actions of the text emergence. The structural dimension of a text, the medium of its constitution, as well as the form of interaction are therefore crucial for the analysis of the texts. Although the form of interaction is mostly quasi-automatically attributed to the monological expression, interactive media, as they are present by means of the Wiki software exhibit dialogical essential structures. Therefore, the written text cannot be solely understood as an expression of a participant any longer, but must be analyzed regarding the communicative happening. The result is the construction that the contributions of Wikipedia are written conceptionally and in media writing; however, regarding the interaction form, they are arranged dialogically.

Some examples will clarify this distinction: While the kind of text of 35 the interview documents and differentiates the different expressions of the participants, the kind of text of the encyclopedia entry presupposes that the individual items of the participants are not presented as such. Both kinds of text—interview and encyclopedia entry—however, are mostly monologic expressions. The interview and the encyclopedia entry are in each case written by one participant. The kind of text and the text emergence therefore can be different from each other. Although the text emergence of the contributions in Wikipedia are based on a dialogic principle, the text appears to be written according to a monologic principle. Therefore, an interview can be understood as a monological expression of an editor, which reports on a preceding discussion that is produced in the form of a dialogic structure. An encyclopedia entry in Wikipedia, however, appears as a monological expression; however, it is based on the dialogic act of the participant's writing.

Although discourse theory regenerates the historical references of the texts 36 to each other, regarding the Wikis it becomes clear that texts themselves must be noticed in their temporal structure. The contributions in Wikipedia embody history not because they show an historical event, but because they are documents of a temporal developing process. Although the discourse notices texts as events of individual authors, the demarcation of the text dissolves in relation to the discourse in the Wikis. Contributions in Wikipedia appear as uniform texts, although they represent—often also controversial—discourses.

## Interaction and Construction of Knowledge

The historicity as well as the dynamic emergence of the text refer to two as- 37 pects regarding the generation of knowledge. On the one hand, such a text no longer serves only mediation of information. The opinions and considerations of different authors flow into a text. The obligation to create a uniform and commonly arranged text promotes a process of negotiating, which intensifies the work with the positions of other participants. In summary, it can be said that knowledge is not obtained in Wikis but designed in the tacklement with the positions of other participants during an interactive and collaborative writing process. The experiences of the participants as well as the writing processes form the basis of knowledge. Krämer (2003) expressed this aspect of the epistemological writing with the following formula: "[n]ot only communication but also cognition" (30). Krämer referred to an aspect that is part of a long tradition and is usually stated in the prominent formulation of Heinrich of Kleist of the gradual producing of thoughts while talking. The script is thus not really meant as a means of communication but rather as outward equipment or technology by which sense can be mediated. The writing itself becomes a specific practice of interactive and collaborative construction of knowledge.

Using Wikipedia as an example, Forte and Bruckman (2006) pointed out 38 that these have qualities that enable their participants to have specific experiences. The authors describe the participants of Wikipedia as a global community of learners, which is merged into a common process of constructing knowledge. As Forte and Bruckman said, Wikipedia is not suitable for learning processes only for the reason that it represents immeasurable and universally available online resources; but Wiki systems create an area of action, which make an interactive happening of knowledge construction possible. Thus, the disruption in relation to the principal book as memory and transmitting medium is carried. Although the book aims at a final work, Wikis arrange interactive and dynamic processes of writing. In most interesting applications, the Internet must be understood as dynamic and interactive because this is exactly where the specific potential is. Therefore, writing becomes a specific means of knowledge construction (Forte & Bruckman, 2006).

The basis of a culture of knowledge then, which is not only constituted with media, is fundamentally based on linguistic, interaction, formed by the controversial process of text genesis. This way writing becomes a practice of knowledge construction. From this extended epistemological understanding results the picture outlined here. Knowledge develops during a constructional, unfinished process from the individual experience, during a process of dialogic writing in the new media. Texts—as they develop in Wikis—stand in an historical continuum. They also exhibit an internal history, one of their emergence, which is unfinished and constantly continued.

## Notes

1. http://www.wikipedia.org (English original) and http://de.wikipedia.org (German version).
2. In order to prevent a retro-romanticizing of these two works, it should not be ignored that the impact to start both the *Encyclopedie* and the *Brockhaus* came from the side of the publisher, that means that economic interests were the cause.
3. According to Anger (2002) about 1,500 scientific authors are involved in *Brockhaus*.
4. This refers to the present state of the art: Theoretically it is just as conceivable to work on video or audio data with an appropriate Wiki software. This, however, means higher demands both for the software developers and the users.
5. Portland Pattern Repository Web site: http://www.c2.com/cgi/wiki?Welcome Visitors [03.12.2003].
6. Huhmann (2004) and Möller (2003) compared different Wikis. However, it is not always transparent according to which criteria the evaluations were made, partly they seem to be based on personal impressions. Under http://c2.com/cgi/wiki?Wiki Choicetree [21.07.2004] is a listing of Wiki software, arranged according to functions. For reasons of space, we do not list the different Wikis with their respective pro and cons.
7. For a more exact representation of the differences, see Leuf and Cunningham (2001).
8. http://www.twiki.org [30.07.2004]
9. See http://c2.com/cgi/wiki?WikiEngines [12.07.2004] for a list of Wiki implementation in various programming languages.
10. See Puls, Bongulielmi, and Henseler (2002), Hof (2004), and Majchrzak, Wagner, and Yates (2006).
11. See for example, the documentation about the Linux-Distribution Knoppix http://www.knoppix.net/wiki/Main_Page [11.11.2006] or about text processing LyX http://wiki.lyx.org/ [11.11.2006].
12. See Dieberger and Guzdial (2003) and Hennicken and Zahiri (2003).
13. See, for example, the restaurant- und Bar guide "DaWiki" http://www.dien-stag-abend.de/wiki/index.php/Hauptseite [11.11.2006] or WikiTravel http://wikitravel. org/en/Main_Page [11.11.2006].
14. See, for example, WikiBooks http://wikibooks.org/ [11.11.2006], Wiktionary http://wiktionary.org/ [11.11.2006] or the best known Wiki Wikipedia http://www.wikipedia.org [11.11.2006].
15. See the "Wiki Principles" (http://c2.com/cgi/wiki?WikiPrincipies [12.07.2004]) and the "Wiki Design Principles" (http://c2.com/cgi/wiki?WikiDesignPrinciples [12.07.2004]).
16. For the term *hypertext,* see Storrer (2000), Nielsen (1996), Kuhlen (1991), particularly about problems of coherence and coherency in such text networks see Storrer (1999).

17. For a commercial offerer see http:/www.etouch.net [24.11.2006], for a free offerer see http://www.wikihost.org/?lan=de [24.11.2006].
18. See http://joomla.org/ [24.11.2006] and http://moodle.org/ [24.11.2006].
19. Intentionally destroying content within the Wiki communities is also called *vandalism*. This covers the deletion of content, as well as the inserting of unreasonable, insulting content, or including passages that are not in favor of the common goal of the Wikis.
20. However this statement is based on a highly simplified operationalisation of "vandalism": Only such cases of vandalism that are determined automatically are seized; a deep content-wise analysts, as well as subtle vandalism (which goes beyond the use of dirty words), did not take place.
21. See O'Reilly & Associates (1999), Himanen (2001), and Grassmuck (2002).
22. For a detailed representation of the process of development of OpenSource projects see Kollmann (2002) and Grassmuck (2002:233–317), who also gives an overview over the different license models.
23. See: "Von freier Software zu freiem Wissen" (Grassmuck, 2002:394–404).
24. http://www.cec.nrw.de/Lizenzen/uvm-lizenzl.htm [17.07.2004]
25. http://creativecommons.org/license/ [17.07.2004]
26. Gnu Free Documentation License: http://www.gnu.org/copyleft/fdl.html [17.07.2004]
27. About the legitimation of such license models see Lessig (2002).
28. About the term Web2.0 see O'Reilly (2005).

## References

Anger, E. (2002). Brockhaus Multimedial 2002 Premium auf CD-ROM und DVD-ROM [Electronic version]. In H. Rösch (Ed.), *Enzyklopädie im Wandel: 'Schmuckstück der Bücherwand, rotierende Scheibe oder Netzangebot* [Encyclopedia evolution: Jewel of the bookshelf, rotating plane or net offer]. Köln: FH Köln, Fachbereich Informationswis-senschaft (Kölner Arbeitspapiere zur Bibliotheks- und Informationswissenschaft;32). Retrieved February 9, 2005, from http://www.fbi.fh-koeln.de/institut/papers/kabi/band. php?key=42.

Barthes, R. (2006). *Das Rauschen der Sprache* [Speech noise]. Frankfurt A.M.: Suhrkamp. Ciffolilli, A. (2004). Phantom authority, self-selective recruitment and retention of members in virtual communities: The case of Wikipedia. In *First Monday, 12, 8*. Retrieved July 21, 2003, from http://firstmonday.org/issues/issue8_12/ciffolilli/index.html.

Derrida, J. (2004). Signatur Ereignis Kontext [Signature, event, context]. In *Die différance* [The difference] (pp. 68–109). Reclam.

Dieberger, A., & Guzdial, M. (2003). CoWeb—Experiences with collaborative web spaces. In C. Lueg & D. Fisher (Eds.), *From usenet to cowebs: Interacting with social information spaces* (pp. 155–166). London: Springer.

Dworschak, M. (2004). Rapunzel bis Regenzeit. [From 'Rapunzel' to 'Rainy season'] *Der Spiegel, 10, 174–175.*

Forte, A., & Bruckman, A. (2006). From Wikipedia to the classroom: Exploring online publication and learning. *Proceedings of the International Conference of the Learning Sciences* (Vol. 1, pp. 182–188). Bloomington, IN.

Grassmuck, V. (2002). *Freie Softwere: Zwischen Privat- und Gemeineigentum* [Free software: Between private and public ownership]. Bonn: Bundeszentrale für politische Bildung.

Grube, G. (2005). Autooperative Schrift—und eine Kritik der Hyptertexttheorie [Self-writing, and a critique of hypertext theory]. In G. Grube, W. Kogge, & S. Krämet (Eds.), *Schrift. Kulturtechnik zwischen Auge, Hand und Maschine* [Writing: Cultural technology between eye, hand, and machine] (pp. 81–114). München: Wilhelm Fink.

Haß-Zumkehr, U. (2001). *Deutsche Wörterbücher—Brennpunkt von Sprach- und Kulturgeschichte* [German dictionary: Focus of linguistic and cultural history]. Berlin/New York: de Gruyter.

Hennicken, D. & Zahiri, C. (2003). *Arbeiten im Netz: Erste Erfahrungen mit der Kooperations- und Austauschplattform Wiki in der Architekten und Planer-Ausbildung / Forschungsprojekt Notebook Universität, learning to learn—mobiles Lernen und Forschen. Universität Kassel, Fachbereich 06, Architektur Stadtplanung Landplannng* [Working in the net: First experiences with the Wiki cooperation and exchange platform in the architect and planner education]. *Kassel. Arbeitspapier.* Retrieved July 26, 2004, from http://www.uni-kassel.de/notebook/publikationen/ap_arbeiten_im_netz.pdf.

Himanen, P. (2001). *The hacker ethic: A radical approach to the philosophy of business.* New York: Random House.

Iof, R. D. (2004). Something Wiki this way comes. *Business Week Online.* Retrieved November 11, 2006, from http://www.businessweek.com/magazine/content/04_23/b3886138. htm.

Huhmann, J. (2004). Noch schneller: Welches Wiki für welchen Zweck? [Even faster: Which wiki for which purpose?] *iX, 4,* 74–78.

Kleinz, T. (2003). Schreibrecht für alle! Mit Wikis Sites gemeinschaftlich betreuen [Writing rights for all! Collaborative coaching with wiki sites], *c't, 2,* 176f.

Kohl, C., & Liebert, W. A. (2004). Selbstorganisation der Wissenschaftsvermittlung: Quellentransparenz, Kontroversität und Qualitätssicherung in der Internetenzyklopädie Wikipedia [Self-organisation of the scientific sharing: Source transparency, controversy, and quality assurance in the Wikipedia internet encyclopedia]. *Fachsprache, 26*(3–4), 133–147.

Kuhlen, R. (1991). *Hypertext: Ein nicht-lineares Medium zwischen Buch und Wissensbank* [Hypertext: A nonlinear medium between book and knowledge base]. Berlin: Springer.

Krämer, S. (2005). "Operationsraum Schrift": Übereinen Perspektivenwechsel in der Betrachtung der Schrift [Operation Write: On a change in perspective in how writing is regarded]. In G. Grube, W. Kogge, & S. Krämer (Eds.), *Schrift. Kulturtechnik zwischen Auge, Hand und Maschine* [Writing: Cultural technology between eye, hand, and machine] (pp. 23–57). München: Wilhelm Fink.

Landow, G. P. (2003). The paradigm is more important than the purchase. Educational innovation and hyptertext theory. In G. Liestøl, A. Morrison, & T. Rasmussen (Eds.), *Digital media revisited. Theoretical and conceptual innovation in digital domains.* Cambridge: MIT Press.

Landow, G. P. (2006). *Hypertext 3.0. Critical theory and new media in an era of globalization.* Baltimore: John Hopkins University Press.

Leuf, B., & Cunningham, W. (2001). *The Wiki way: Collaboration and sharing on the Internet.* Boston: Addison-Wesley.

Majchrzak, A., Wagner, C., & Yates, D. (2006). Corporate Wiki users: Results of a survey. *Proceedings of the 2006 International Symposium on Wikis* (pp. 99–104). New York: ACM Press.

Mittelstraß, J. (1967). Bildung und wissenschaftliche Enzyklopädien in historischer und wissenssoziologischer Betrachtung [Education and scientific encyclopedias from the standpoint of history and sociology]. *Die wissenschaftliche Redaktion, 4,* 81–104.

Möller, E. (2002). Das Web, wie es hätte sein sollen [The Web as it should have been]. *Telepolis 30.01.2002.* Retrieved October 10, 2003, from http://www.heise.de/tp/deutsch/inhalt/te/11585/2html.

Möller, E. (2003). Schreibwerkstätten: Fünf Wiki-Engines im Vergleich [Writing workshops: Comparison of five wiki engines], *c't. 25,* 202–205.

O'Reilly, T. (2005). *What is Web 2.0?: Design patterns and business models for the next generation of software.* Retrieved December 12, 2006, from http://www.oreillynet.com/pub/a/oreilly/tim/news/2005/09/30/ what-is-web-20.html.

O'Reilly & Associates. (1999). *Open Source: kurz & gut* [Open source: Short and sweet]. Köln: Author.

Puls, C., Bongulielmi, L., & Henseler, P. (2002). *Leitfaden für den Aufbau einer unternehmensinternen Wissensbasis mit Hilfe von Wiki* [Guide to the construction of a project-internal knowledge base with the help of a wiki]. Zürich: ETH, Zentrum für Produktentwicklung. Retrieved October 29, 2003 from http://e-cellection.ethbib. ethz.ch/show?cype=bericht\&nr=217.

Stickfort, B. (2002). Das Internet als enzyklopädische Utopie [The internet as encyclopedic utopia]. In I. Tomkowiak (Ed.), *Populäre Enzyklopädien: Von der Auswahl, Ordnung und Vermittlung des Wissens* [Popular encyclopedias: On the choice, arrangement, and dissemination of knowledge] (pp. 271–295). Zürich: Chronos.

Stcorrer, A. (2000). Was ist 'hyper' am Hypertext? [What is hyper about hypertext?] In W. Kallmeyer (Ed.), *Sprache und neue Medien* [Language and new media] (pp. 223–249). Berlin: de Gruyter.

Viegas et al. (2004). Studying cooperation and conflict between authors with history flow visualizations [Electronic Version]. *Proceedings of the 2004 conference on Human factors in computing systems* (pp. 575–582). New York: ACM Press. Retrieved July 28, 2004, from http://web.media.mit.edu/~fviegas/papers/history_flow.pdf.

Volpers, H. (2002). Idee und Begriff der Enzyklopädie im Wandel der Zeit [Ideas and concepts of the encyclopedia in the course of time]. In H. Rösch (Ed.), *Enzyklopädie im Wandel: Schmuckstück der Bücherwand, rotierende Scheibe oder Netzangebot* [Encyclopedia evolution: Jewel of the bookshelf, rotating plane or net offer]. Köln: FH Köln, Fachbereich Informationswissenschaft. (Kölner Arbeitspapiere zur Bibliotheksund Informationswissenschaft;32). Retrieved February 9, 2005, from http:// www.fbi.fh-koeln.de/institut/papers/kabi/band.php?key=42.

*Wikipedia: Geprüfte Versionen*, (n.d.) Retrieved February 1, 2007, from http://de.wikipedia.org/w/index.php?t!tle=Wikipedia:Gesichtete_Versionen&oldid=2724.

*Wikipedia: Gesichtete Versionen*, (n.d.) Retrieved January 7, 2007, from http;//de.wikipedia.org/w/index.php?title=Wikipedia:Gepr%C3%BCfte_Versionen&oldid=26114070.

........................................................................................

## Questions for Discussion and Journaling

1. When you've finished the article, try outlining it in order to see its structure and main points.

2. What do Kohl et al. say are the three decisive differences between wikis and traditional encyclopedias? How do these differences illustrate the radical changes wikis make to "classical processes of knowledge construction" (para. 4)?

3. According to the authors, what are the distinctive features of wiki software? (You can look back to the "What Is a Wiki" section to find some discussion of this point.)

4. How do the wiki principles of simplicity and openness connect to the three major differences Kohl et al. identify between Wikipedia and traditional encyclopedias?

5. In paragraphs 25–28, the authors create a definition of wiki-based texts as *processes*, based on the idea that because these texts are not the work of a single author and are not a monologue, they gain a "dynamic dimension"—a quality of change or continual *emerging* from being one text to becoming another when someone else works on them—that makes being shaped over *time* ("temporal organization") one of their key features. What does it mean to writers if texts can be understood not just as *products* but as *processes*?

6. Kohl et al. argue that "the current shape of a text . . . can only be understood because of the history of" its development (para. 28). Try explaining, in your own words, how the authors reach this conclusion. (You'll probably really need to grapple with the handful of paragraphs preceding this statement.) If the authors are correct,

this idea implies that you can't fully understand a text unless you understand the history of its composition. Is this a new idea to you? Is it a comfortable one?

7. What does Kohl et al.'s analysis of changes to the "philosophy" entry on Wikipedia demonstrate about the rate at which changes to pages take place?

8. The authors are apparently fascinated that while any given Wikipedia entry *seems* "monological," that is, written by one person, it is actually written "dialogically," that is, by dialogue between at least two writers—but that dialogue is itself carried on in a series of monologues author-by-author (on the article's Talk page) (para. 35). Does that collaborative process differ at all from any group writing projects you might have done?

9. How would you put this statement in your own words: "Knowledge is not obtained in Wikis but designed in the tacklement with the positions of other participants during an interactive and collaborative writing process. The experiences of the participants as well as the writing processes form the basis of knowledge" (para. 37)? How do you think this is different for wikis than for other kinds of writing?

10. This article might have been much more difficult for you to follow and make sense of than many other pieces you've read in this book. What makes it so? What is different about this text from other, easier-to-understand pieces?

11. What main ideas do you think Kohl et al. were trying to argue for here? Why do you think they haven't said them as straightforwardly as you might have?

## Applying and Exploring Ideas

1. These authors paraphrase Landow's (2003) argument that the "book paradigm" has three rules for handling texts: "Texts are to be discreetly differentiated from other texts, the roles of author and reader are clearly definable, and texts are static" (para. 21). Compare these requirements to the workings of Web apps you regularly use—for example, YouTube or other video-upload sites, photo sites such as Flickr, social-networking sites such as Facebook, and perhaps blogs. How do these kinds of writing conform to and violate those three "book-based" principles of textuality? Take a few pages to make some lists and write an analysis of this question, perhaps in concert with a group of classmates. Note, as you do, whether and how your findings on this differ from the conclusions Kohl et al. draw.

2. Kohl et al. ultimately argue that an analysis "that does not consider the forms of interaction of text emergence can hardly make appropriate statements about the entries in Wikipedia" (para. 30)—in other words, they claim that wiki-based writing can't be accurately analyzed without considering the edits and discussion of the edits that lead to the current version of a given page. Try this for yourself: Visit a Wikipedia page that's of interest to you and evaluate just the article page itself; then evaluate the page in light of its Talk page as well. What changes in your evaluation? Write a short narrative of this experience and what you learn from it.

3. The idea that wiki-based texts should be analyzed not as a final product but as a process of development through time works particularly well since wikis usually contain

a "history" page of some sort that shows different previous versions of the page or a discussion of edits to it. But is there any reason to limit this perspective to wikis? Aren't *many* published texts collaboratively developed over time? Write an argument exploring (or defending, or rejecting) the idea that any responsible analysis of a text involves research into the history of its development.

4. As a class, discuss the meaning of Kohl et al.'s final paragraph. When you've developed a workable paraphrase of it, compare what these authors say there to principles you've read elsewhere in this book: Where else have you encountered any of these ideas? Write a summary of points of connection you find between the final paragraph and your other readings.

5. Think carefully about the difference between the open knowledge construction of a Wikipedia page and what you know about how traditional encyclopedias are developed with a "closed" model (written by experts for publishing companies in a process readers can't see). If you need to, do some searches on what that editorial process for traditional encyclopedias is. (For irony, use Wikipedia.) Write an analysis of what is different in the two ways of constructing knowledge, and for which purposes each way is preferable, and why.

---

### Meta Moment

How does it change your understanding of writing if "collaborative processes of writing dissolve the central intention of the author" and "the authors only work on passages and never on the entire text" (para. 29)?

# Rhetorical Criticism of Online Discourse

## BRANDON JONES

■ Jones, Brandon. "Rhetorical Criticism of Online Discourse." *Stylus* 2.2 (2011): 24–32. Web. 13 May 2013.

## Framing the Reading

Brandon Jones was a student in Mary Tripp's ENC 1101 class at the University of Central Florida in Spring 2011 when he wrote this paper. He submitted the paper to *Stylus*, UCF's journal for first-year students, and revised it again when it was accepted for publication in the Fall 2011 issue.

### Getting Ready to Read

*Before you read*, do at least one of the following activities:

- Read or review the introduction to Chapter 3 to familiarize yourself with the rhetorical terms that Jones uses in this essay.
  Visit **rhetorica.net/textbook** and look at the sections on rhetorical situation and the canons of rhetoric.

*As you read*, consider the following questions:

- What sorts of online discourse do you engage in?
- How would you go about conducting a study of online discourse? Would you do what Jones did?

Since the conception of the Internet, researchers from many fields have been 1 interested in its many possibilities; rhetorical critics and theorists, however, have shown relatively little interest in the Internet, and the discourse created on it, up until the early 90s. Internet discourse researchers, such as Barbara Warnick, Laura J. Gurak, and G.P. Landow, have spent the last twenty years developing the theories and methods necessary to criticize discourse on this medium. However, compared to the research on traditional rhetoric, which goes back over 2,000 years ago to the time of the Greeks, their research has barely scratched the surface of Internet rhetoric. Because of the lack of research into Internet rhetoric, not surprisingly, rhetorical criticism of Internet discourse hasn't become as mainstream as criticism of other, more traditional forms of discourse, such as political discourse.

So why is it that there has been relatively little research into this topic? 2 Barbara Warnick, who is among the first to begin researching discourse on this medium, believes that one reason for the rhetorical critics' lack of early interest in the Internet might be because they believed that the ". . . critical work and critical theory will need to be changed to suit new communication environments . . ." ("Public Discourse" 73). G.P. Landow, an early researcher of hypertext, explains that because of the way that hypertext is produced it is also read differently: "Unlike books, which contain physically isolated texts, hypertext emphasizes connections and relations, and in so doing, it changes the way the texts exist and the way we read them" (174). These differences lead to text, audience, and author dispersal, which have complicated the use of traditional methods of rhetorical criticism on Internet discourse (Warnick "Public Discourse" 73).

## Theories for a New Rhetoric

The need for theories and methods of rhetorical criticism for Internet discourse 3 was the driving force behind many of the earliest rhetorical theorists' and critics' research into this field. One fairly prominent idea for the development of rhetorical theories for Internet discourse is an analysis of discourse focused on the ethos of the author (Gurak, Mitra, and Watts). Laura J. Gurak, one of the first to support this idea, believes that traditional rhetorical characteristics like ethos, pathos, and logos still can affect the persuasiveness of an argument in an online environment, despite the dispersal of authorship so prominent in online discourse. Of these characteristics, Gurak believes that ethos, in combination with delivery, is the most pertinent to online discussion: ". . . the content of any message is inherently interwoven with a certain character, or ethos, and this ethos is a powerful determinant of whether speakers and their messages are accepted by the audience" (84). In her book, *Persuasion and Privacy in Cyberspace*, Gurak details the online protests over the Lotus Marketplace and the Clipper Chip, two of the earliest examples of large-scale online debate. What Gurak found was that certain texts (such as CSPR's petition and the "Seiler letter") were posted over and over again throughout the online discussions over the two cases. According to Gurak, the reason these texts were used repeatedly was not solely because of their content, but because they had the "appropriate character and credibility to appeal to privacy advocates and other participants across the Internet" (85). Gurak uses this fact as a basis to support her belief that ethos is the most important characteristic of online discourse: "The dominance of certain texts in the debates illustrates the power of ethos in cyberspace and complicates the liberal model of online community by illustrating that 'truth' does not always prevail, especially in the highly specialized spaces of the Internet" (85).

Similar ideas about ethos are seen in the studies of Ananda Mitra and Eric 4 Watts, both of whom argue that the analysis of discourse in cyberspace should be focused on the concept of voice, a concept very similar to ethos: "...the idea of voice...provides an alternative theoretical lens to consider how cybercommunities can and do operate within the discursive space of the Internet" (480). Mitra and Watts describe voice as the speaker's (or speakers') "authority" or "agency" (482). According to Mitra and Watts, the Internet breaks down the hierarchies of power found in traditional discourse, leaving the voice and the "eloquence" of it as the primary attributes for evaluation by the audience: "Using the metaphor of voice, along with the potential to flatten hierarchies of power on the Internet, it is possible to demonstrate that the reader must consider that the voice and its eloquence will be the key evaluative aspect in cyberspace" (493). One key difference between voice in online discourse and voice in more traditional forms of discourse is that electronic discourse is rarely ever comprised of just one voice, but rather many individual voices: "Communication on Internet sites gives play to many voices without assimilating them into a single voice . . . Web site authors [often] invite readers to contribute messages that they then post on their sites" (Warnick "New Media" 63).

What Gurak, Mitra, Warnick, and Watts' studies, along with many others, 5 have shown is that, although there are numerous differences between digital and traditional rhetoric (text, audience, and author dispersal are just a few of these differences), traditional methods of rhetorical criticism can and are being developed to suit digital discourse. What once seemed to many as an unlikely source for rhetorical activity is now believed by some to have the potential to change the way that rhetoric has been viewed for the last 2,000 years. James P. Zappen, one of the most recent researchers into digital rhetoric, proposes not only a change to the way that traditional methods and theories of rhetorical criticism are used, but to the way that rhetoric is viewed in its entirety. He argues that "dialogue—conceived not as a mode of persuasion, but as a testing of one's own ideas, a contesting of others' ideas, and a collaborative creating of ideas—is possible in any medium: oral, print, digital" (321). Warnick, Gurak, and many of the others I have mentioned have shown with their research that the Internet can indeed have a significant impact on traditional views of rhetoric.

## Characteristics and Patterns of Online Discourse

In addition to their primary goal of developing the methods and theories re- 6 quired to rhetorically criticize online discourse, many of the aforementioned researchers also detailed in their studies some of the basic characteristics and patterns of online communication and the various constraints that affect discourse. Some characteristics of Internet discourse include speed, which, according to Gurak, "encourages an oral and casual style, but it also encourages redundant and repetitive postings"; anonymity, which complicates the notion of authorship and encourages "flaming" (a strongly emotional and personal attack against another); and reach, which allows for interaction with a variety of people with varying cultures (qtd. in Zappen 321). Other characteristics, which I mentioned earlier, are text, author, and audience dispersal.

Several patterns of online discourse, which were noted by Barbara War-  7
nick, include lack of desire to distinguish between reality and the virtual world, which Warnick claims is a result of ". . . the nature of the medium itself . . ." ("Public Discourse" 80); group conformity and pressure to conform to the group's values (Gurak observed in her own studies that "in some of these discussions there was no 'other side' to be weighed, because individuals who held the minority position were not comfortable challenging the dominant ethos of the . . . community") (qtd. in Warnick "Public Discourse" 81); and "technological elitism," which, according to Warnick, results in a sort of hierarchy that the Internet is normally void of ("Public Discourse" 81). These characteristics and patterns will be useful to me in my own research into digital discourse.

## Conclusions on Past Research

Although the studies performed by each of the aforementioned researchers  8
have provided a good starting point for rhetorical critics and theorists, between them they have only provided a few small examples of rhetorical criticism of digital discourse. The Internet contains an abundance of diverse communities, each with their own unique communication styles. The critical theories and work of traditional rhetorical criticism have been developing since the conception of rhetoric several millennia ago, while researchers have only been studying digital rhetoric for about twenty years now. Because of this comparatively small amount of research, I believe that more research in some of the different online communities out there will be needed to develop a fully refined theory of digital rhetoric. Although I know full well that I would never be able study each of the millions of online communities in the world, I hope that by performing my own rhetorical study on just one of these unique communities I will be able to help contribute to the research into Internet discourse and rhetoric.

## Primary Research—Methods

For my research, I wanted to focus primarily on testing the claims of some of  9
the digital rhetoric researchers that came before me, particularly Gurak, Mitra, Watts, and Zappen. I had decided that the best place to analyze rhetoric on the Internet would be in an online forum, being that they are both extremely prominent on the Internet and full of countless examples of digital text. The first step of my research was to choose the online forum whose texts I would be analyzing. I originally planned to examine various texts from multiple forums and then compare them to one another, but due to time constraints I decided to analyze texts from just one forum. The forum I decided to examine was the Starcraft II community forums on battle.net. There are several reasons I decided on this forum; one being because I had some familiarity with the forum, the second, and most important, reason being that the posters on

the website are given publicly viewable ranks based on their performance in the game that the website is centered around. I believe that these ranks might be seen as a source of credibility for the posters on the forum and that this credibility would contribute to the overall ethos of the poster. I decided that I could then compare the ranks of thread authors on the forum to the successfulness of their thread in order to determine what effects, if any, that credibility/ethos has in this online community. Another notable characteristic of this forum is that the players are grouped into one of three groups—Terran, Protoss, and Zerg. This is also publicly viewable. I believe that this artificial grouping within the community will have some impact on the way that texts are received by their audience on the forum.

In order to determine the effects of ethos on the texts of this forum, I would   10 need numerous threads from authors of various ranks. I had originally wanted to collect a total of twenty threads using a random method of selection but due to time constraints and an unexpected discovery about the content of the threads on the forum (I will discuss this in my results section), I decided that the best approach would be to subjectively select approximately ten threads to analyze. In addition to the ten individual threads I would be examining, I also decided to do a macro level analysis of the forum as a whole. To do this I looked at the first page of each of the three discussion sections (first two pages of the General Discussion section) on the forum and sorted the threads into the following categories: argument, entertainment, gloating, inquiries, complaints/rants, commenting (statements without a noticeable argument), and strategy (related to the game). After this I began to examine individual threads and collect various data from each of them.

I started off collecting data I could use to determine the effects of ethos/   11 credibility on the forum (see Appendix A for the data table I used). That data includes: author's rank, the number of replies to the thread, and various other data pertaining to those replies—such as whether they were positive (agree at least partially with author), negative (disagree with the author), or neutral (either off topic or doesn't clearly agree or disagree) and what group the repliers belong to. To test for the effects of delivery, I rated the author on their grammar (1 bad–5 good). In addition to testing the claims of some of the previous researchers of this topic, I was also hoping that by collecting a variety of miscellaneous data from the forum that I might be able to make some discoveries of my own. Some of the other data that I collected includes the length of the author's original post, the number of views it received, the location of the thread (which section it was posted under), the number of unique posters, the number of subsequent posts by the author, the group of the author, and the number of times the author was "flamed" (viciously insulted). After I had finished collecting data from each of the threads I had examined and from the forum as a whole, I began to sort the data in different ways in an attempt to discover correlations between various sets of data.

## Results and Discussion

The first major, and somewhat surprising, finding that I made was from my analysis of the entire forum. Out of the three sections of the forum I examined (185 threads total), only 27% of threads were actually trying to make an argument. The other 73% of the threads consisted mostly of complaints/rants (mindless complaints with no suggestions for change—about 10%), questions related to community issues (22%), entertainment (such as jokes and links to videos—14%), and other miscellaneous threads about the community and the game that it revolves around. What this shows is that much of the communication that takes place on this particular forum does not revolve around persuasion. I believe that these results support Zappen's view of rhetoric as something more than just a mode of persuasion.

My next finding was on the correlation between the author's rank and the effectiveness of his or her post. What I consider an "effective" post is one with a high amount of positive replies and a low number of negative replies. Because of Gurak, Mitra, and Watts' theories revolving around the importance of ethos, I had originally expected the

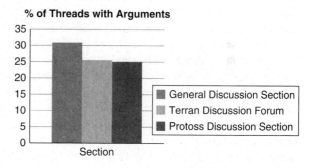

higher-ranking authors to have a significantly higher number of positive replies and far fewer negative replies. This, however, was not the case. Although the higher-ranking authors did have a higher number of positive replies on average, they also had a significantly higher amount of negative replies than the lower-ranking authors. At first these findings seem to contradict Gurak's theory on the dominance of ethos in cyberspace; however, I believe that there is an explanation for this occurrence. As shown above, low ranking authors received far more neutral responses to their posts than the higher ranking authors; in addition to this, the high ranking authors also received, on average, almost twice as many replies as the low ranking authors (an average of 33 replies for high ranked authors, 18 for low ranked authors). What I believe these statistics imply is that responders tend to be more critical of authors with higher ranks and tend to take the lower ranking authors less seriously. In light of this information, I do believe that Gurak (along with Mitra and Watts) was right about ethos being the dominant rhetorical characteristic in cyberspace. As for the other traditional rhetorical characteristics, pathos and logos, there was not any significant difference between authors who relied on logic in their arguments and those who made more emotional arguments.

Although not in the least bit surprising, it is worth noting that, on average, about 80% of the positive replies an author received were from members

12

13

14

**High Ranking Authors**

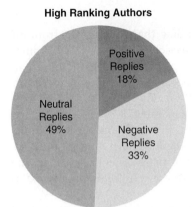

**Low Ranking Authors**

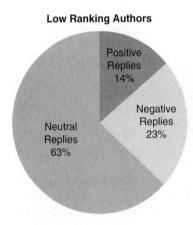

of the same group and that about 80% of the negative replies were from members of different groups (see Appendix B). Another minor discovery that I made is that grammar didn't seem to have any effect on the number of positive or negative replies an author's thread received; however, this may be due to a flaw in my method, which, admittedly, was a tad too subjective (I had no systematic method of differentiating between good and bad grammar). Unfortunately, because of this flaw in my methodology, I was unable to come to any conclusions about the effects of delivery on the Internet.

Before I conclude, I would like to address 15 some of the other flaws and limitations of my research methods. Perhaps the biggest limitation to my research is the sample size I collected. On the forum I examined there are thousands (if not tens of thousands) of threads. By closely examining only ten, it is entirely possible that the threads I examined were oddities among the more typical threads on the forum. I tried to adjust for this problem by performing a more broad examination of the forum. By knowing that only a small portion of the threads were actually arguments, I believe that my small sample size seems a little more significant. The last noteworthy flaw that I see with my research is that I did not analyze threads a consistent time after creation. The threads I examined ranged anywhere from several hours to a few days old. The amount of time that people had to respond to a thread might have had some impact on the type of responses they were receiving. In an attempt to avoid this problem, I only analyzed threads that had not been posted on within an hour of my examination time. Although there were some fairly significant flaws in my research, I do believe that, because of the steps I took to mitigate their effects, I was able to keep my results from being corrupted to a significant level.

## Conclusion

What my findings have shown is that much of what other researchers have 16 discovered about communication in online environments is true. Although the arguments of authors with stronger, more credible ethos were not vastly more successful than others, they did command much more attention than that of lower-ranking authors. What I believe is the most significant finding of my research is the fact that only a small portion of the discussions taking place on the forum I examined revolved around persuasion. I believe that Zappen is correct in believing that

> *Although the arguments of authors with stronger, more credible ethos were not vastly more successful than others, they did command much more attention than that of lower-ranking authors.*

rhetoric must evolve to include more than just persuasion; this is especially true if critics and theorists truly wish to adapt their theories of rhetoric for the Internet. For further investigation into rhetoric on the Internet, I believe that the best topic to focus on is the specific ways in which large groups of individuals communicate with one another.

## Works Cited

Dahlberg, Lincoln. "The Internet and Democratic Discourse: Exploring the Prospects of Online Deliberative Forums Extending the Public Sphere." *Information, Communication & Society* 4.4 (20011): 615–33. *Communication & Mass Media Complete*. Web. 22 Feb. 2011.

Gurak, Laura J. *Persuasion and Privacy in Cyberspace: The Online Protests over Lotus Marketplace and the Clipper Chip*. Chelsea: Yale UP, 1997. *Google Books*. Web. 21 Feb. 2011.

Landow, George P. "Hypertext in Literary Education, Criticism, and Scholarship." *Computers and the Humanities* 23.3 (1989): 173–98. *JSTOR*. Web. 22 Feb. 2011.

Mitra, Ananda and Eric Watts. "Theorizing Cyberspace: The Idea of Voice Applied to the Internet Discourse." *New Media & Society* 4.4 (2002): 479–98. *SAGE*. Web. 27 Feb. 2011.

Warnick, Barbara. "Rhetorical Criticism in New Media Environments." *Rhetoric Review* 20.1/2 (2001): 60-5. *JSTOR*. Web. 21 Feb. 2011.

———. "Rhetorical Criticism of Public Discourse on the Internet: Theoretical Implications." *Rhetoric Society Quarterly* 28.4 (1998): 73–84. *JSTOR*. Web. 21 Feb. 2011.

Yarbrough, Stephen R. "Power, Motive, and Discourse Studies." *After Rhetoric: The Study of Discourse Beyond Language and Culture*. Carbondale: Southern Illinois UP, 1999. 16–50. *NetLibrary*. Web. 8 Feb. 2011.

Zappen, James P. "Digital Rhetoric." *Technical Communication Quarterly* 14.3 (2005): 319–325. *Communication & Mass Media Complete*. Web. 21 Feb. 2011.

# APPENDIX A: DATA COLLECTION TABLE

The following are the tables I used for collecting/sorting data.

| Thread Name | Rank | Length | Location | Group | Unique Posters | Author Posts | Views |
|---|---|---|---|---|---|---|---|
| "Getting Losses Back" | Plat | 108 | General D. | Protoss | 14 | | ?? |
| "To replace Collosus . . ." | Bronze | 237 | Protoss | Zerg | 12 | | 85 |
| "Toss the race that presses 2 buttons and win" | Diamond | 379 | General D. | Terran | 24 | | 115 |
| "Nerf 6 Pool" | Master | 29 | Protoss | Protoss | 33 | 24 | 348 |
| "Zealot armor" | Master | 112 | Protoss | Terran | 10 | 1 | 113 |
| "Fix for neural parasite" | Gold | 44 | Zerg | Zerg | 7 | 0 | 76 |
| "WTF is it with Colli?" | Silver | 175 | General D. | Protoss | 29 | 1 | 207 |
| "The Fleet Beacon" | Diamond | 143 | General D. | Protoss | 18 | 1 | 123 |
| "Hey Blizzard-two units > all armies" | Gold | 13 | General D. | Terran | 27 n/a | | 186 |
| "Zerg need buff and more Units" | Silver | 296 | General D. | Zerg | 6 | 2 | 39 |

| Thread Name | # of Replies | | | (+) Replies (reposts removed) | | |
| --- | --- | --- | --- | --- | --- | --- |
| | From Same Group | From Dif. Group | Total | From Same Gr | From Dif. Group | Total |
| "Getting Losses Back" | 7 | 14 | 21 | 1 | 2 | 3 |
| "To replace Collosus . . ." | 1 | 13 | 14 | 0 | 1 | 1 |
| "Toss the race that presses 2 buttons and win" | 5 | 26 | 31 | 5 | 0 | 5 |
| "Nerf 6 Pool" | 62 | 13 | 75 | 10 | 1 | 11 |
| "Zealot armor" | 4 | 7 | 11 | 0 | 0 | 0 |
| "Fix for neural parasite" | 4 | 2 | 7 | 2 | 1 | 3 |
| "WTF is it with Colli? | 11 | 18 | 33 | 3 | 1 | 4 |
| "The Fleet Beacon" | 10 | 17 | 27 | 3 | 0 | 3 |
| "Hey Blizzard-two units > all armies" | 5 | 24 | 29 | 0 | 0 | 0 |
| "Zerg need buff and more Units" | 2 | 4 | 6 | 0 | 0 | 0 |

| Thread Name | (-)Replies From Same Group | From Dif. Group | Total | Neutral Replies | Flaming | Grammar ( ) | Creation Date |
|---|---|---|---|---|---|---|---|
| "Getting Losses Back" | 2 | 3 | 5 | 6 | | 5 | 6-Apr |
| "To replace Collosus . . ." | 1 | 2 | 3 | 5 | 1 | 4 | 4/6/2011 |
| "Toss the race that presses 2 buttons and win" | 0 | 14 | 14 | 5 | 0 | 5 | 4/7/2011 |
| "Nerf 6 Pool" | 4 | 3 | 7 | 15 | 0 | 5 | 4/4/2011 |
| "Zealot armor" | 0 | 3 | 3 | 7 | 0 | 4 | 4/9/2011 |
| "Fix for neural parasite" | 2 | 1 | 3 | 1 | 0 | 2 | 4/10/2011 |
| "WTF is it with Colli?" | 0 | 4 | 4 | 21 | 0 | 3 | 4/10/2011 |
| "The Fleet Beacon" | 0 | 4 | 4 | 11 | 0 | 4 | 4/11/2011 |
| "Hey Blizzard -two units > all armies" | 0 | 3 | 3 | 24 | 3 | 3 | 4/11/2011 |
| "Zerg need buff and more Units" | 0 | 1 | 1 | 5 | 0 | 4 | 4/10/2011 |

| General Discussion Forum | Argument | Enter-tainment | Brag | Comment | Bug/Issue | Inquiry | Com-plaint | Rant/Troll | Strategy | Total | % of Argu-ment |
|---|---|---|---|---|---|---|---|---|---|---|---|
| | 29 | 18 | | 5 | 4 | 31 | 4 | 2 | 1 | 94 | 30.85106383 |
| Protoss Discussion Forum | 11 | 6 | 2 | 1 | | 6 | 1 | 5 | 14 | 44 | 25 |
| Terran Discussion Forum | 12 | 3 | 1 | 5 | | 4 | 3 | 2 | 18 | 47 | 25.53191489 |
| | | | | | | | | | | AVG.: | 27.12765957 |

## Links

"Getting Losses Back": http://us.battle.net/sc2/en/forum/topic/2353276627

"To replace the Colossus with the Reaver": http://us.battle.net/sc2/en/forum/topic/2353267041

"Toss the race that . . .": this thread was deleted for inappropriate content after analysis

"Nerf 6 pool": http://us.battle.net/sc2/en/forum/topic/2351685355

"Zealot armor": http://us.battle.net/sc2/en/forum/topic/2369738450

"Fix for Neural Parasite": http://us.battle.net/sc2/en/forum/topic/2369738614

"WTF is it with Colli?" http://us.battle.net/sc2/en/forum/topic/2369738121

"Fleet Beacon": http://us.battle.net/sc2/en/forum/topic/2369919261

"Hey blizzard . . .": http://us.battle.net/sc2/en/forum/topic/2369879066

"Zerg need buff and more units": http://us.battle.net/sc2/en/forum/topic/2369678827

## Appendix B: Result Tables

This table shows the results I received from comparing various sets of data from the previous tables; nothing important was found regarding the response-view ratio.

| Percentage of Positive Posters | Percentage of Negative Posters | Response-View Ratio (Responses/ Views) | Responder-viewer Ratio (Posters/ Views) | Percentage of Neutral Replies |
|---|---|---|---|---|
| 21.42857143 | 35.71428571 | | | 42.85714286 |
| 8.333333333 | 25 | 16.47058824 | 14.11764706 | 41.66666667 |
| 20.83333333 | 58.33333333 | 26.95652174 | 20.86956522 | 20.83333333 |
| 33.33333333 | 21.21212121 | 21.55172414 | 9.482758621 | 45.45454545 |
| 0 | 30 | 9.734513274 | 8.849557522 | 70 |
| 42.85714286 | 42.85714286 | 9.210526316 | 9.210526316 | 14.28571429 |
| 13.79310345 | 13.79310345 | 15.94202899 | 14.00966184 | 72.4137931 |
| 16.66666667 | 22.22222222 | 21.95121951 | 14.63414634 | 61.11111111 |
| 0 | 11.11111111 | 15.59133785 | 14.51612903 | 88.88888889 |
| 0 | 16.66666667 | 15.38461538 | 15.38461538 | 83.33333333 |
| | | | Average: | 49.16768446 |

High rank = Master, Diamond, and Platinum

Low rank = Bronze, Silver, and Gold

| | Positive | Negative | Neutral |
|---|---|---|---|
| H-Rank | 18.45238095 | 33.4963925 | 48.05122655 |
| L-Rank | 14.99671593 | 21.88560482 | 63.11767926 |

## Questions for Discussion and Journaling

1. Jones begins by discussing Internet discourse broadly but then quickly narrows his focus to a study looking at the message board for a game called Starcraft II. What other
data could Jones have drawn on in order to explore online discourse? Do you think
that "online discourse" is a narrow enough term to aid a researcher? Is there any one
kind of discourse that could be termed "online discourse," or do you think there are
many kinds of online discourse?

2. Jones cites researcher Barbara Warnick's claim that the dispersal of texts, audiences,
and authors in Internet communication makes this form of communication more difficult to analyze. Many of the other articles in this chapter suggest similar findings (for
example, the WIDE researchers note that writing alone does not mean the same thing
now as it used to). Make a list of some forms of writing dispersed via the Internet and
then consider how the audiences and authors for these are connected and dispersed.

3. Jones describes *voice* and *ethos* as being similar. If you have read parts of Chapter
3 (discussing rhetoric, including *ethos*) and parts of Chapter 4 (discussing writing
process, including *voice*), then these terms will be familiar to you. Try to define each of
them and then determine whether you agree with Jones that these two concepts are
similar. You can use the glossary to help you.

4. Jones cites scholars who argue that writing online invites multiple voices. How do you
think this changes our traditional ideas about authorship and the role of the writer?
(If you read Porter or Martin in Chapter 3, you might have some especially interesting
ideas about this question.)

## Applying and Exploring Ideas

1. Jones argues that "the Internet . . . can indeed have a significant impact on . . .
rhetoric" (para. 5). Drawing on other articles you have read in this or other chapters,
write two to three pages in which you explain what you think he means, and give
some of your own examples.

2. Jones found that a majority of the discussion posts he analyzed were not "trying
to make an argument." Among those he categorized as not making an argument
were complaints or rants, questions, or jokes and links to entertaining videos. Jones
concludes, then, that the majority of the communication on this site "does not revolve
around persuasion." In a paragraph or two, try to define for yourself what *argument*
and *persuasion* are. Then decide whether you agree with Jones's conclusion and write
two or three additional paragraphs in which you either support or refute his claim. To
help you, you might consider, for example, whether a rant or joke can be persuasive.
If not, then what are they?

3. Review the idea of *discourse communities* from Chapter 2. Jones found that authors
with higher rankings on the Starcraft II forum received not only positive replies from
others but also many negative replies. Try to explain why this might be. Why do you
think that active and highly ranked members of a discourse community might receive
not only a lot of positive responses from other community members but also a lot of
positive negative responses? Why do you think that members with lower rankings

might receive more neutral responses? With a partner, try to create an explanation (come up with a theory) detailing how community membership impacts community responses to discourse.

4. Jones found that grammar did not seem to be a factor in whether the replies to a post were positive or negative (although he admits that his methods for measuring "good" and "bad" grammar were not very careful). If his findings are accurate, why do you think this might be the case? Would the same disregard for grammar also hold true for online discourse in other kinds of discourse communities (for example, professional organizations)? Why or why not?

### Meta Moment

When you engage in acts of rhetoric in online sites, how do you create credibility for yourself? How do you judge the credibility of others?

# Texting and Writing

## MICHAELA CULLINGTON

■ Cullington, Michaela. "Texting and Writing." *Young Scholars in Writing 8* (2010): 90–95. Print.

## Framing the Reading

If you've been in grade school or high school any time in the past fifteen years—or been the parent of a child who has—it's probably not news that many teachers are extremely concerned about "bad habits" in writing that kids might learn from texting and transfer to their school writing. (In these cases, "writing" is almost always defined as simply *spelling and punctuation*.) That this transfer of bad habits exists is a habitual assumption of news media and social commentary, as is the conclusion that its effects will most likely include the end of Western civilization as we know it.

But what's *really* happening when kids grow up texting and writing papers in school? This is Michaela Cullington's question—driven, as you'll see, by her own experiences and those of the people around her, who both text and write school papers and, she claims, *don't* let text-speak slip into their writing. Such dissonances often make the best **exigence** for research questions: a "common sense" or widely assumed conclusion that runs strongly counter to the researcher's own lived experience.

But what is perhaps most interesting about Cullington's research and argument here is that she refuses to accept the simple binary that texting must be having either a good or a bad effect on students' writing. By insisting on collecting her own data and deriving her own answers, she arrives at a conclusion that is neither of those common choices.

Cullington, a speech pathology major, wrote this piece in Dr. Laurie McMillan's first-year composition course at Marywood University.

### Getting Ready to Read

*Before you read*, do at least one of the following activities:

- Do a quick Google search for "texting and school writing skills"—what comes up?
- Consider your impressions of how often you or other students use text-speak in your school writing, and then ask yourself, what is the actual basis of those impressions? How much of this texting language in school writing have you actually *seen*, and how much have you simply heard about from others?

*As you read*, consider the following questions:

- What do you think of Cullington's tone in the piece—what words would you use to characterize how she sounds?
- Do Cullington's conclusions make sense based on your own experience?

It's taking over our lives. We can do it almost anywhere—walking to class, 1 waiting in line at the grocery store, or hanging out at home. It's quick, easy, and convenient. It has become a concern of doctors, parents, and teachers alike. What is it? It's texting!

Text messaging—or texting, as it is more commonly called—is the process 2 of sending and receiving typed messages via a cellular phone. It is a common means of communication among teenagers and is even becoming popular in the business world because it allows quick messages to be sent without people having to commit to a telephone conversation. A person is able to say what is needed and the other person will receive the information and respond when it's convenient to do so.

In order to more quickly type what they are trying to say, many people use 3 abbreviations instead of words. The language created by these abbreviations is called textspeak. Some people believe that using these abbreviations is hindering the writing abilities of students, some say that textspeak has no effect on student writing, and still others argue that texting is actually having a positive effect on writing. This is a great debate. Although some believe that texting has either a positive or a negative effect on writing, it in fact seems likely that texting has no significant effect on student writing.

## Concerns about Textspeak

A September 2008 article in *USA Today* entitled "Texting, Testing Destroys 4 Kids' Writing Style" summarizes many of the most common complaints about the effect of texting. It states that according to the National Center for Education Statistics, only 25% of high school seniors are "proficient" writers. The article quotes Jacquie Ream, a former teacher and author of *K.I.S.S.— Keep It Short and Simple*, a guide for writing better and more effectively. Ream states, "[W]e have a whole generation being raised without communication skills." She firmly believes that because of this lack of communication skills, students do not have the ability to write well. She blames the use of acronyms and shorthand in text messages for students' inability to spell and ultimately write. Ream also points out that students struggle to convey emotion in their writing because, as she states, in text messages "emotions are always sideways smiley faces." She also puts blame on teachers for not teaching their students good critical thinking skills. She says kids learn only to "parrot" information they're given rather than use it to develop their own thoughts and ideas. Ream concludes that "there's a whole generation that can't come up with new ideas— and even if they did have a breakthrough thought or opinion of their own, they couldn't share it with the rest of us."

This debate became prominent after some teachers began to believe they 5 were seeing a decrease in the writing abilities of their students. Many attributed this perceived decline to the increasing popularity of text messaging and its use of abbreviations. Naomi Baron, a linguistics professor at American University, worried by the rise in its popularity, blames texting for the fact that "so much of American society has become sloppy and laissez faire about the mechanics of writing" ("Should We Worry or LOL?"). Teachers report finding "2" for "to," "gr8" for "great," "dat" for "that," and "wut" for "what," among other examples of textspeak, in their students' writing. A Minnesota teacher of the seventh and ninth grades says that she has to spend extra time in class editing papers and must "explicitly" remind her students that it is not acceptable to use text slang and abbreviations in writing (Walsh). Other proponents of the argument contend that texting is interfering with standard written English: students do not learn how to write correctly because they are constantly texting their friends using textspeak. One English teacher believes that text language has become "second nature" to her students (Carey); they are so used to it that they do not even catch themselves doing it.

Many also complain that because texting does not stress the importance 6 of punctuation, students are neglecting it in their formal writing. Teachers say that their students are forgetting commas, apostrophes, and even capital letters to begin sentences. Proper usage of grammar rules is necessary for writing effectively. If it is true that students are indeed failing to follow proper punctuation rules and correct spelling as a result of constantly texting, teachers will need to make more of an effort to instruct students on proper writing.

Another complaint is that text messages lack emotion. Many argue that texts 7 lack feeling because of their tendency to be short, brief, and to the point. Communicating emotions through words is an important aspect of writing. The reader should be able to very easily understand and often even feel how the author is feeling. Because students are not able to communicate emotion effectively through texts, some teachers worry they may lose the ability to do so in writing.

To get a more personal perspective on the question of how teachers perceive 8 texting to be influencing student writing, I interviewed two of my former high school teachers—my junior-year English teacher and my senior-year theology teacher. Both teachers stress the importance of writing in their courses. They maintain that they notice text abbreviations in their students' writing often. To correct this problem, they point out when it occurs and take points off for its use. They also remind their students to use proper sentence structure and complete sentences. The English teacher says that she believes texting inhibits good writing—it reinforces simplistic writing which may be acceptable for conversation but is "not so good for critical thinking or analysis." She suggests that texting tends to generate topic sentences without emphasizing the following explanation. She also says that her students are "woefully unskilled in critical analysis and interpretation." According to these teachers, then, texting is inhibiting good writing. However, their evidence is limited, based on just a few personal experiences rather than on a significant amount of research.

## Responses to Concerns about Textspeak

In response to these complaints that texting is having a negative impact on stu- 9 dent writing, others insist that texting should be viewed as beneficial because it provides motivation to write, a chance to practice writing skills, and an opportunity for students to gain confidence in their writing. For example, Sternberg, Kaplan, and Borck argue that texting is a good way to motivate students. Teens enjoy texting, and if they frequently write through texts, they will be more motivated to write formally. Texting also helps to spark students' creativity because they are always coming up with new ways to express their ideas (417).

In addition, because they are engaging in written communication rather than oral speech, texting teens learn how to convey their message to a reader in as few words as possible. In his book *Txtng: The Gr8 Db8,* David Crystal discusses a study which concludes that texting actually helps foster "the ability to summarize and express oneself concisely" in writing (168). Furthermore, Crystal explains that texting actually helps people to "sharpen their diplomatic skills . . . [because] it allows more time to formulate their thoughts and express them carefully" (168). One language arts teacher from Minnesota believes that texting helps students to learn an "element of writing," letting students develop their own "individual voice" (Walsh). Perfecting such a voice allows the writer to offer personal insights and express feelings that will interest and engage readers.

Supporters of texting also argue that it not only teaches elements of writing but provides extra practice to those who struggle with the conventions of writing. As Crystal points out, children who struggle with literacy will not choose to use a technology that requires them to do something that is difficult for them. However, if they do choose to text, the experience will help them learn to write. Through this experience, teenagers can "overcome their awkwardness and develop their social and communication skills" (*Txtng* 171). Shirley Holm, a junior high school teacher, describes texting as a "comfortable form of communication" (Walsh). Teenagers are used to texting, enjoy doing so, and as a result are always writing. Through this experience of writing in ways they enjoy, they can learn to take pleasure in writing formally. As Derek Anderson, a composition and literature teacher, explains, "[A]ny writing is good writing, as long as you get your point across" (Walsh). Writing skills improve with time and practice. If students are continually writing in some form, they will eventually develop better skills.

Furthermore, those who favor texting explain that with practice comes the confidence and courage to try new things, which some observers believe they are seeing happen with writing as a result of texting. Teenagers have, for example, created an entirely new language—one that uses abbreviations and symbols instead of words, does not require punctuation, and uses short, incomplete phrases throughout the entire conversation. It's a way of speaking that is a language in and of itself. Crystal, among others, sees this "language evolution" as a positive effect of texting; he seems, in fact, fascinated that teenagers, who are so young, are capable of creating such a phenomenon. He describes it as the "latest manifestation of the human ability" (*Txtng* 175). David Warlick, a teacher and author of books about technology in the classroom, would agree with Crystal. He believes students should be given credit for "inventing a new language ideal for communicating in a high-tech world" (Carey).

10

11

12

## Methods

I decided to conduct my own research into this controversy. I wanted to get 13
different, more personal, perspectives on the issue. First, I surveyed seven high
school and college students on their opinions about the impact of texting on
writing, which provided a personal
account of how students believe
texting is affecting them. Second, I
questioned two high school teachers (as noted above). Finally, in an
effort to compare what students
are actually doing to people's perceptions of what they are doing, I
analyzed student writing samples
for instances of textspeak.[1]

> I decided to conduct my own research
> into this controversy. I wanted to get
> different, more personal, perspectives
> on the issue.

To let students speak for themselves about how their texting habits were 14
influencing their writing, I created a list of questions for seven high school and
college students, some of my closest and most reliable friends. Although the
number of respondents was small, I could trust my knowledge of them to help
me best interpret their responses. In addition, these students are very different
from one another, which I believed would allow for a wide array of thoughts
and opinions on the issue. I was thus confident in their answers regarding
reliability and diversity, but was cautious not to make too many assumptions
because of the small sample size.

I asked the students how long they had been texting; how often they texted; 15
what types of abbreviations they used most and how often they used them; and
whether they noticed themselves using any type of textspeak in their formal
writing. In analyzing their responses, I looked for commonalities to help me
draw conclusions about the students' texting habits and if/how they believed
their writing was affected.

I also wanted some teachers' opinions. Had they seen textspeak in their 16
students' writing? Did they believe texting is hindering their students' writing?
I created a list of questions for the teachers similar to the one for the students
and asked two of my high school teachers to provide their input. I asked if they
had noticed their students using textspeak in their writing assignments and, if
so, how they dealt with it. I also asked if they believed texting had a positive or
negative effect on writing. Next, I asked if they were texters themselves. And,
finally, I solicited their opinions on what they believed should be done to prevent teens from using text abbreviations and other textspeak in their writing.

I was surprised at how different the students' replies and opinions were 17
from the teachers'. I decided to find out for myself whose impressions were
more accurate by comparing some students' actual writing vis-à-vis students'
and teachers' perceptions of that writing. To do this I looked at twenty samples
of student writing—end-of-semester research arguments written in two first-
year college writing courses with different instructors. The paper topics varied
from increased airport security after September 11 to the weapons of the Vietnam War to autism, and ranged from eight to ten pages. This sample gave me a

firsthand look at whether or not students were in fact incorporating textspeak into their formal writing assignments. To analyze the papers for the presence of textspeak, I looked closely for use of abbreviations and other common slang terms and sayings, especially those usages which the students had stated in their surveys were most common. These included "hbu" ("How about you?"); "gtg" ("Got to go"); and "cuz" ("because"). I also looked for the numbers 2 and 4 used instead of the words "to" and "for."

## Discussion of Findings

My research suggests that texting actually has a minimal effect on student writ-   18
ing. It showed that students do not believe textspeak is appropriate in formal writing assignments. They recognize the difference between texting friends and writing formally and know what is appropriate in each situation. This was proven true in the student samples, in which no examples of textspeak were used. Many experts would agree that there is no harm in textspeak, as long as students continue to be taught and reminded that a formal language occasion is not the place for it. As Crystal explains, the purpose of creating the abbreviations used in text messages is to allow for more space, not to replace language. In a standard text message, the texter is allowed only 160 characters for a communication: abbreviations were created to shorten words and use less space in each message ("Texting" 81). Texting was not created to replace the English language, but rather to make quick communications shorter and easier.

Dennis Baron, an English and linguistics professor at the University of   19
Illinois, has done much research on the effect of technology on writing, and his findings are aligned with my own study. In his book *A Better Pencil: Readers, Writers, and the Digital Revolution*, which examines how technology has changed the way people write, he concludes that students do not use textspeak in their writing. In fact, he suggests students do not even use abbreviations in their text messages very often. The students I surveyed stated that they rarely, if ever, use abbreviations even in their texts. Barron says that college students have "put away such childish things, and many of them had already abandoned such signs of middle-school immaturity in high school" (qtd. in "A Better Pencil"). He also observes that "writers learn to adapt their style to the demands of their audience and the conventions of the genre in which they're writing." His conclusions are surprising because most people assume that texting is affecting student writing. But Baron's findings directly oppose that assumption.

In surveying the high school and college students, I found that most have   20
been texting for a few years, usually starting around ninth grade. They said they generally text between thirty and a hundred messages every day. I also found that they use abbreviations only occasionally but the most common are "lol" ("Laugh out loud"), "gtg" ("Got to go"), "hbu" ("How about you?"), "cuz" ("because"), and "jk" ("Just kidding"). Each student admitted to using abbreviations in writing on occasion but did not believe they were acceptable in formal writing. Most students, including those I surveyed, report that they do not use textspeak in formal writing. As one Minnesota high school student

says, "[T]here is a time and a place for everything," and formal writing is not the place for communicating the way she would if she were texting her friends (Walsh). Another student admits that she sometimes finds herself using these abbreviations. However, she notices and corrects them before handing in her final paper (Carey). One teacher reports that, despite texting, her students' "formal writing remains solid" (Walsh). She occasionally sees that a student has used an abbreviation; however, it is in informal, "warm-up" writing. She believes that what students choose to use in everyday types of writing is up to them as long as they use standard English in formal writing (Walsh).

In analyzing the student writing samples, I found no evidence of textspeak. 21 This contradicts suggestions that texting is having a negative influence on the writing abilities of students. This also discounts the teachers' worries that textspeak may appear in student writing. In both the reports from students and the writing samples, it is evident that students recognize context: in texting, as in conversations with their friends, they can use more casual language. However, when writing formally, they know they must use standard written English.

Also supporting my own research findings are those from a study which 22 took place at a mid-western research university. These results dispel the belief that the use of text abbreviations hinders students' spelling abilities. This study involved eighty-six students who were taking an Introduction to Education course at the university. The participants were asked to complete a questionnaire that included questions about their texting habits, the spelling instruction they had received, and how proficient they were at spelling. They also took a standardized spelling test. Before starting the study, the researchers reasoned that texting and the use of abbreviations would have a negative impact on the spelling abilities of the students. However, after analyzing the data they found that the results did not support their hypothesis. The researchers also remarked that while their study did not support the belief that texting is affecting the spelling abilities of students, the use of text messaging as a common means of communication is becoming increasingly popular; therefore, this issue should continue to be examined (Shaw, Carlson, and Waxman).

I myself am a frequent texter. I chat with my friends from home every day 23 through texting. I also use texting to communicate with my school friends, perhaps to discuss what time we are going to meet for dinner or to ask quick questions about homework. According to the cell phone bill, I send and receive around 6,400 texts a month. This may seem like a lot, but compared to many texters it is a relatively low number. In the messages I send, I rarely notice myself using abbreviations. The only time I use them is if I do not have time to write out the complete phrase. However, sometimes I find it more time consuming to try to figure out how to abbreviate something so that my message will still be comprehensible to the reader.

Since I rarely use abbreviations in my texting, I never use them in my for- 24 mal writing. I know that they are unacceptable and it would make me look unintelligent if I included acronyms and symbols instead of proper and formal language. I also have not noticed an effect on my spelling as a result of texting. I am confident in my spelling abilities and even on the occasion that I use an abbreviation, I know what it stands for and how to spell it. Based upon my own research, expert research, and personal observations, I can confidently state that texting has no effect on writing abilities.

The issue of whether texting is affecting students' writing and, if so, whether      25
it is a positive or negative influence is much debated. It is very interesting to look at the dynamics of the arguments. Teachers and parents who claim that they are seeing a decline in the writing abilities of their students and children mainly support the negative impact argument. Some teachers and researchers suggest that texting provides a way for teens to practice writing in a casual setting and thus helps prepare them to learn to write formally. Ultimately, however, experts and students themselves report that they see no effect, positive or negative, on their writing as a result of texting. Teachers' personal anecdotal experiences should not overshadow the actual evidence, which shows that texting is not interfering with students' use of standard written English.

## Note

1. All participants in the study have given permission for their responses to be published.

## Works Cited

"A Better Pencil." *Inside Higher Ed.*, 18 Sept. 2009: n. pag. Web. 9 Nov. 2009.

Baron, Dennis. *A Better Pencil: Readers, Writers, and the Digital Revolution.* Oxford: Oxford UP, 2009. Print.

Carey, Bridget. "The Rise of Text, Instant Messaging Vernacular Slips into Schoolwork." *Miami Herald* 6 Mar. 2007: n. pag. *Academic Search Elite.* EBSCO. Web. 27 Oct. 2009.

Crystal, David. "Texting." *ELT Journal* 62.1 (2008): 77–83. Wilson Web. 8 Nov. 2009.

——. *Txtng: The Gr8 Db8.* Oxford: Oxford UP, 2008. Print.

Shaw, Donita M., Carolyn Carlson, and Mickey Waxman. "An Exploratory Investigation into the Relationship between Text Messaging and Spelling." *New England Reading Association Journal* 43 (2007): 57–62. Wilson Web. 8 Nov. 2009.

"Should We Worry or LOL?" *NEA Today* Mar. 2004: 12. *Academic Search Elite.* EBSCO. Web. 27 Oct. 2009.

Sternberg, Betty, Karen A. Kaplan, and Jennifer E. Borck. "Enhancing Adolescent Literacy Achievement through Integration of Technology in the Classroom." *Reading Research Quarterly* 42 (2007): 416–20. Wilson Web. 8 Nov. 2009.

"Texting, Testing Destroys Kids' Writing Style." *USA Today* Sept. 2008: 8. *Academic Search Elite.* EBSCO. Web. 9 Nov. 2009.

Walsh, James. "Txt Msgs Creep in2 class; Some Say That's gr8." *Star Tribune* 23 Oct. 2007: n. pag. *Academic Search Elite.* EBSCO. Web. 27 Oct. 2009.

## Questions for Discussion and Journaling

1. Compare Cullington's introduction to the steps Swales delineates in his CARS model (pp. 12–15). How closely do the moves her intro makes match Swales's model?

2. If you read Naomi Baron's piece earlier in this chapter, you might have noticed her appearance in Cullington's review of literature critical of texting. How does what Cullington reports of Baron's opinion in 2004 align with Baron's 2005 article reprinted here?

3. In her description of methods, Cullington argues that a good reason for using one's best friends as data sources is because a researcher can better interpret the responses of participants she knows intimately. What are the benefits to interviewing participants a researcher *doesn't* know? Is it clear whether the advantages of interviewing one group outweigh the advantages of interviewing the other?

4. People debating an issue often forget that the issue itself can shift beneath them with the passage of time, so that what they were arguing at the beginning might be irrelevant several years on. This can be especially true in relation to issues of electronics, networks, and social interaction, because the technology itself moves so quickly—something that was a problem just last year might be a complete non-issue with the next version of software or hardware. Can you think of any ways the "texting-and-writing" issue could have shifted between 2004 (the date of Cullington's earliest source) and when she studied the problem five years later?

## Applying and Exploring Ideas

1. One of the most striking elements of Cullington's article is her straightforward attitude of "with all the conflicting opinions, I wanted to see this for myself," and her determination to go straight to the source, to teachers and students *and* student writing. Have you encountered any controversies about writing or language, either in this course or through your own experience, that would lend themselves to similar study? Write a research proposal that explains what the controversy is, why it's important, and how you could match Cullington's "I'm just going to look at it myself" ethic.

2. What further research questions emerge out of Cullington's study? That is, what questions does her work raise or leave unanswered? Make a list of those you see, and compare it with classmates to make the most complete list possible.

> **Meta Moment**
>
> What is the most important thing you learned from this article about how to write about writing research?

**e** **In e-Pages at bedfordstmartins.com/writingaboutwriting**

Steve Bernhardt, "Seeing the Text" (e-Pages)

James Sosnoski, "Hyper-Readers and Their Reading Engines" (e-Pages)

Ann Cochran, "Blogging the Recovery from Anorexia: A New Platform for the Voice of ED" (e-Pages)

# Writing about Multimodal Composition: Major Writing Assignments

To help you learn and explore the ideas in this chapter, we offer three assignment options for larger writing projects: Writing Experiences Survey, News Media Discourse Analysis, and Writing Definition.

## Assignment Option 1. Writing Experiences Survey

In this project, you'll try to replicate some of the research you encountered if you read the WIDE and Pew studies of student writing habits. The object is to survey fellow students (in your class, other classes, or across campus) about their experiences with writing. Based on your findings, you'll be writing a report for high school teachers, conveying what you think would be important for them to know about students' writing experiences.

*Brainstorming Your Object of Study and Methods:* While this is already a pretty tightly focused project, you'll need to do some thinking about what kinds of writing experiences you'd like to focus on, and you'll have to plan, concretely, *how* to do the survey.

For example, if you replicated the WIDE (p. 724) and Pew (p. 730) studies closely, you'd be asking students about:

- the kinds of writing experiences that motivate them
- the kinds of writing they do most frequently
- the kinds of writing experience and instruction they have had in school
- the technologies that mediate writing

But, you could also expand the areas you look at, or focus in more tightly on particular aspects.

As you consider what particular questions you might ask on your survey, use the Pew and WIDE studies as examples, and feel free to brainstorm other questions, especially if you decide to look at areas different than those studies already do.

In recent years, it's become reasonably easy to build and distribute surveys electronically, using Web applications such as SurveyMonkey or Google Forms. (You can google "online survey software" for a range of options.) Different apps let you have different numbers of questions and respondents in their free versions, and use different pricing structures if you want to inexpensively (or more expensively) step up the number of either. So, shop around some in selecting software.

If you replicate research questions from the Pew or WIDE studies, you know that they've already been tested and used by other respondents. If you invent your own questions, you'll need to test them on a few users to make sure that the users can make sense of the questions and possible answers before you release the survey as a whole.

Remember ethical conduct of research: At many campuses, class projects don't require review by your institution's research ethics board (or IRB), but that does not relieve you of responsibility to ensure that you protect the privacy of your respondents and the data they contribute to your study, and that you "first, do no harm" in the questions you ask or what you write about the data you collect.

*Data Analysis and Follow-up Interviews:* As is usually the case with data analysis, you'll be looking for patterns in your responses, and for responses that break or stand out from those patterns. What matters is what's interesting to *you*, as the researcher, in those responses, so you'll choose where to focus any follow-up research you do. It's very likely that your survey will leave you knowing a great deal about *what* people's experiences are but not a lot about *why* their experiences are what they are, or about what those experiences *mean* to the writers having them or to our culture more broadly.

Therefore, expect to want to conduct some follow-up interviews in which you ask those questions of specific respondents (of your choice); your interview questions will emerge from the survey responses themselves. A generally good strategy is to have a few questions you ask of each interviewee but to also make sure each interview is a free-form *conversation* that goes where you and your interviewee take it. What you hear in the interviews should help you further shape what it is you want to convey in your report about students' writing experiences.

*Planning, Drafting, and Revising:* As noted above, your research should result in a report similar to the one from the Pew Research Center and WIDE, with high school teachers (especially language arts teachers) as its audience. What do you want those teachers to know about college students' writing experiences? And what can teachers learn from students about how to improve writing instruction and students' motivation to write?

Your planning will need to cover two main elements: what points you want to make in your report, and how to structure the report in order to make those points. Depending on how closely your survey replicates the Pew or WIDE studies, your report may be able to follow a similar structure. You can certainly always adopt the standard social-science reporting model (introduction, background, methods, data analysis, implications). However, depending on your data and what points you want to make, you may find a more efficient or meaningful organization for your argument.

As you draft the piece, pay attention to new ideas that arise *while you're writing*. Make your first step in revision to compare the end of your draft with the beginning: Are they consistent? Most of the time, a writer's ideas "shift" a bit during drafting, making the original introduction and conclusion out of step with each other. Sometimes, if a writer's first try at the piece is a "discovery draft" which is deliberately intended to help him or her learn what he or she has to say, the writer may only have arrived at the main point at the end of this first draft. Revision, then, is about making sure that any ideas you discovered in the writing of one draft are fully reflected *throughout* the next draft (that the next draft is "aware of" those new ideas from its beginning and that they're carefully incorporated into the best places in the revision).

*What Makes it Good?:* Here are some things stronger reports will do better than weaker ones:

- Have a clear point or argument (or several), supported with clear reasons linked to particular data from your study
- Be highly readable by making its main findings and points visually prominent for readers and using an intuitive, effective organization of ideas
- Include discussion of what survey questions were asked, what kinds of and how many respondents completed the survey, and how respondents were made aware of the survey to begin with

- Attempt to explain and interpret findings rather than simply state what they were
- Provide some visual representations of more complicated data, as necessary for better reader comprehension
- Use a tone and present a professional ethos appropriate for an audience of high-school teachers

## Assignment Option 2. News Media Discourse Analysis

In any social or cultural revolution—such as the introduction of brand-new writing technologies like blogging, IM, texting, Twitter, Facebook, or Pinterest—there comes a time, after the initial newness has passed, for researchers to study not just the revolution itself but the *talk about* the revolution. The talk—for example, popular media accounts—tells us not just about what the technologies are and do, but about how people are *representing*, *conceiving*, and *discussing* those technologies. As we've argued from the very Introduction to *Writing about Writing*, what people *say* about (and *believe* about) a given phenomenon is nearly as important to defining what the phenomenon is as the actual nature of the phenomenon itself. Talk creates reality; conceptions about an issue or object construct meaning. Thus, all the talk is important to study. This assignment gives you a framework for analyzing some of that talk about writing.

To complete this assignment, you'll collect a **corpus** of news- or entertainment-media discourse (stories or talk from newspapers and online news sites, magazines, television news, podcasts, etc.) about the electronic writing technology(ies) of your choice. By analyzing your corpus for what themes and ideas the writers in it express, you'll be able to draw conclusions about how these technologies are represented. You should offer your conclusions in a multimodal document or presentation that visually, aurally, and alphabetically represents and analyzes both your data and your findings.

*Building and Analyzing a Corpus:* In order to get this project underway and begin collecting your corpus, you'll need to make a few decisions:

- What writing technology or technologies do you wish to focus on?
- How "deep" in time do you want to make your corpus—which years do you want it to cover? The more years, the larger the corpus; also, you can make your study more or less historical by changing its date range: studying commentary on Facebook from 2004–2007 will probably net you much different discussion than studying 2009–2012.
- What particular news media types or outlets will you want to include in your corpus? For a newer and less popular technology, you might use any story you find anywhere. But most technologies you might study are old enough to have spawned tremendous amounts of popular discourse of different sorts. The coverage of Twitter in traditional news media (for example, *The New York Times* or *ABC Nightly News*) will likely differ significantly from coverage in new-media, online formats (for example, *Gawker*, *Boing Boing*, *Gizmodo*, or *Slashdot*)—and each of these news outlets has different intended audiences. Perhaps you want to compare one kind of coverage to another (say, 24-hour cable news networks to industry blogs). You could consider looking at discourse on your technology even in entertainment itself, such as popular television sitcoms and dramas, or action films. Whatever you

choose, make sure it's *feasible* and that you can articulate your rationales for making that choice.

- How will you search for instances of the kinds of discourses you've selected to include in your corpus? If you've selected a modality and genre of discourse that automatically archives online—such as blogs, Web sites like the "fake news" *Onion* (which presents satirical discourse), or shows archived online such as Jon Stewart's also fake-news *Daily Show*, then searching the archives at those sites will be sufficient to build your corpus. If you're looking at more traditional news media such as newspapers and television broadcasts, a news database will be tremendously helpful. See if your campus library subscribes to a database such as *LexisNexis* or *ProQuest News*, databases that contain searchable full text of every major newspaper and television news broadcast in the country, updated daily.

Once you've laid these plans and developed a rationale for each choice you make in collecting your corpus, you're ready to start collecting. Consider exploring apps such as Zotero or Endnote for collecting, organizing, tagging, and documenting each item in your corpus. While answering the question "How large should my corpus be?" is rather like answering "How long should a rope be?" or "How tall should a tree be?" you can assume that your corpus should have a minimum of twenty items, but should not be too large to keep you from being able to study it carefully and in depth (see below) in whatever number of weeks you have for this project.

In order to analyze the corpus, you'll want to do both some quantitative work and some qualitative work. The quantitative work you'll do by counting instances of words or phrases or ideas that crop up in the individual texts. (For instance, if you were analyzing the news media discourse on gun control at the time we're writing this, you could count how often the phrase "law-abiding gun owner" comes up in news stories, and keep track of which particular kinds of people are most often the ones using it.) How will you know which terms to count to begin with? By first skimming your corpus and developing *impressions* of what terms come up frequently or seem to carry a lot of weight in the discourse. If you were studying texting, for instance, you might notice terms related to the concept of "degrading writing skills" coming up very frequently. You would need to see what synonyms that concept was being expressed in and then actually start counting how often the idea occurs in the discourse. Another number you'd want to develop is how many total words there are in your entire corpus (by counting the total words in each item and then adding all those counts up).

Quantitative analysis is fairly easy to understand, but what do we mean by *qualitative* analysis? We mean studying elements of the piece that can't be counted because they're not discrete, individual items in the text, but rather "topics" that emerge from the whole text overall or large parts of the text. For instance, judging who the *audience* for a given discourse was intended to be is qualitative analysis because it answers the question not *how many* (countable) but *who* (non-countable, identity-related). (Note that enough qualitative data can itself *become* countable: "In half the items in the corpus, the audience was middle-aged parents.") Similarly, trying to determine the *dominant narrative* of an item is qualitative analysis because it's a thematic question, not a question of "how many." The same is true of trying to analyze the frame of an instance of discourse. (*Frame* meaning the particular perspective, point of view, stance, or filter that is used to shape the meaning of discourse. For example, school breakfast programs can be framed as government waste, ameliorating poverty, or improving students' study abilities.) Determining the frame is a problem of definition (qualitative) rather than counting (quantitative). Very often you'll find that quantitative data lead to qualitative questions: *What does it mean that* 75 percent of articles on texting are framed in a negative light? And usually you'll find that when problems of definition, evaluation, or judgment are involved, what's required is qualitative analysis.

As you conduct both quantitative and qualitative analysis of your corpus, you'll find themes, conclusions, and interesting moments *emerge* slowly through reading and reread-ing. You'll need a good note-taking system to keep track of these moments, and each new idea that strikes you will require rereading parts of the corpus you've already read in order to see if the idea had been there in earlier pieces as well. Out of this analysis, you should be able to arrive at some conclusions characterizing the nature of the discourse you've been studying. If you're not sure what you should be looking for, perhaps some of these guiding questions will help:

- How are the technology and the activities it mediates or supports represented in your corpus?
- Are different group's uses of the technologies represented differently?
- How is the technology most often framed? Positively or negatively? In what terms?
- Does a dominant narrative about the technology emerge? Does it change over time? Is it different for different groups?
- Does one kind of narrative or frame seem to accompany discourse written for one particular audience, versus other audiences?
- What is your impression of how well the discourse on a technology matches the actualities of that technology? (This is the question, for example, that Michaela Cullington is asking in her *Young Scholars in Writing* article included in this chapter.) Are there specific inaccuracies or misconceptions in the dominant discourse?

You may wish to brainstorm other guiding questions for analysis with classmates or your teacher.

*Planning, Drafting, and Revising:* Particularly because of the possibility that the tech-nology you've chosen to analyze popular media discourse on is itself a multimodal technol-ogy (e.g., Facebook, Pinterest, etc.), you should plan from the beginning to represent your research findings in a multimodal presentation or document. That could be:

- A dedicated blog (e.g., WordPress or Tumblr) with multiple posts, images, and podcasts
- A rich-media PowerPoint or Prezi, again including alphabetic, visual, and aural elements
- A video presentation developed in Apple *iMovie* or Windows *MovieMaker* (or more sophisticated software such as Apple *FinalCut* or Adobe *Premiere*) uploaded to You-Tube or a similar Web service
- A Pinterest board where your findings are posted as a collection of images/visuals that themselves incorporate alphabetic and graphic presentations of your findings
- A rich Word, OpenOffice, or Google document (the latter having the advantage of being already online and thus networkable) with embedded graphics and aural texts as well as links out to the Web
- A Wikipedia entry

Your teacher might guide your choices based on which of these modalities your course can support or teach to begin with. (For example, Wikipedia articles face increasingly high standards in order to be kept on the site once posted, and shouldn't be launched into lightly.) However, increasingly free, quickly learnable online apps are putting even the most technically difficult of these media (probably video composition) within reach of even new users. If you use an Apple computer, for example, you already have built-in access to very high quality and user-friendly film composition software in *iMovie*. (Windows *MovieMaker* is much more basic and somewhat less user-friendly, but still serviceable for novice filmmakers using PCs.) In other words, with your teacher's permission, even if you need to learn a particular modality or software for composition on your own, it's increasingly possible to do. (There are now video tutorials for just about every imaginable writing activity and communication software readily available online.) Don't be afraid to try something brand new to you: With a little time and patience, you'll be able to make it work.

Understand, though, that as a general principle every modality you add to monomodal composition (say, alphabetic only) does not just *double* the time required to compose your piece; it *squares* it. That means if a project was going to take you five hours in alphabetic writing, it will take you not ten hours in alphabetic and graphic composition, but *twenty-five* hours. If you're working in video and thus need to manage alphabetic, graphic, *and* soundtrack modalities, you're going to spend a *lot* of time, like more than fifty hours, to get it the way you want it. Most of this time will be in editing and fine-tuning: Having multiple modes available increases your choices, the total number of possible *arrangements* of your text, and it just physically takes *time* to sift and test the possibilities. Multimodal composition, especially that involving video, also increases the importance of *planning* in order to keep *drafting* manageable. This is why most complex multimodal documents created by professionals are first *storyboarded*, drawn out page by page or frame by frame, so that the composers know exactly what elements they need before they sit down to edit them all together. (Such planning will also guide your sense of what video shots and footage or still images you'll need to gather in order to have the raw materials for composing your video.)

As an upside, however, the more modally complex your document, the shorter or "smaller" it can be while still conveying the same amount of material a monomodal text would. A twenty-page alphabetic-only essay, for example, might well equate to "just" a five-minute video or a ten-slide PowerPoint, because each "moment" of the multimodal text conveys so many more ideas through multiple channels simultaneously. For this project, do not imagine yourself making, say, a twenty-minute video. That would probably require hundreds of hours of work. Keep it small and manageable—seek your teacher's guidance on what's a reasonable scope and size for your project. In any event, in short, it is crucial to leave yourself plenty of time for multimodal composition.

As noted above, in multimodal composing, your best bet for working smoothly through a project is not to plan massive revision of drafts, but rather to plan extensively, revising *the plan*, and then building your draft text from the best plan you can make. Changes to the draft will then be accomplished through *editing*, more local and less global changes (because making global changes to a multimodal text is far more complicated and difficult than making global changes to a monomodal text). Editing will feel like "tuning" the text that results from enacting your composing plan. And it can feel endless: There will be a time in composing your piece when you say, "I could do another five hours of work on this, but it's good enough," and then you make it available to read and do any final editing based on user feedback.

*What Makes It Good?:* You'll know you're producing a high quality piece for this project if:

- You've found something in your analysis that's important to say and useful for the field to know.
- Your data collection is sensible, thorough, and well explained in your final presentation.
- Your analysis of your corpus is thoughtful and smart, reasonable and specific.
- The central point or argument of your presentation is clear and well supported.
- Your presentation or document is easy to use and all its parts contribute harmoni-ously to the overall whole (rather than being a nonunified collection of parts that don't work together or are just there for their own sakes).
- Everything in your presentation/document *works*—you've removed anything glitchy, and the overall presentation is fluent and intuitive.

# Assignment Option 3. Writing Definition

Many of the readings in this chapter present conceptions and definitions of writing that are counterintuitive at least in broader culture and, possibly, for you as an individual writer. We grow up, typically, thinking of writing as the manipulation of language that's "written down"—inscribed alphabetically in linear print texts. What does it mean when text doesn't have to be linear (Web pages and other hypertexts), when it can be mediated by images (photos, drawings, charts, etc.), when images themselves can be "texts," and when we talk about "writing" music, multimodal documents like blogs and photoessays, and speeches? So, work like Grabill and Pigg's (p. 724) on students' electronic writing experiences; Kohl et al.'s (p. 740) on collaborative, time-based writing in wikis; Baron's (p. 719) on the na-ture of writing as technological; and Bernhardt's (e-Pages) on how graphical layouts can increase the readability of alphabetic texts—all of these suggest there's something much more complicated about "what counts as writing" than just lines of language represented alphabetically.

This assignment, then, asks you to take the very big question of *what counts as writing* in an age of multimodal textuality. If you read the pieces noted above (Prior in Chapter 4, p. 492, might also be helpful), you'll be prepared to consider where you think is the line be-tween "writing" and other visual, aural, or multimodal texts. When does a collection of im-ages stop being images alone and start being "writing"? Does a YouTube video that you've composed count as writing? (What if it's a series of title screens with "writing" on them? What if it's a series of images that includes no alphabetic text and no voiceover?) When is a speech "written," and when is it just "talk"? In short, by what principles would we decide which texts are "writing," which are "film," which are "music," and which are "talking"?

*Developing a Definition of Writing:* Any time you try to define what a thing is or isn't, or define what is or isn't a particular thing (writing), you're going to be working a theoretical realm—your work will always be in the realm of argument, not absolute proof, and it will always be somewhat speculative. At the same time, you'll find yourself having to work from examples—you'll need to take specific instances and draw general principles from them. So part of your work will be choosing good examples from which to draw principles that help you in defining. For example, if you were looking at a TED Talk, you'd see a speech, a talk, that's clearly quite well "written" and highly rehearsed, incorporating projected graphics, many of the graphics themselves being multimodal, incorporating image and alphabetic in equal measures. What principles can you draw from a text like such a talk, about what counts as writing, what doesn't, or what a text would have to have in order to be a *written* text?

***Planning, Drafting, and Revising:*** Because you're likely to be developing a definition based on examples of various multimodal texts, and you're going to need to be able to show those texts and discuss them, it's likely that this definition project will work best as a multimodal composition. (See the previous assignment for a list of potential modalities and software for composing in them.)

If you're working in multimodal composition, it will probably be best to plan your argument as much as you can and storyboard how the text will make that argument before you start drafting. Part of that storyboarding will involve collecting artifacts (examples of texts that help support your claims) that you intend to incorporate or refer to in your composition. Having these examples in front of you will help you know how to best arrange your piece.

This will be a quite "argumentative" piece—it will depend heavily on claims supported by reasons backed by examples (whether of sample texts, or of arguments already made by others). So it's extremely likely that after you've got a working draft of your composition, readers will go over it and find parts of your argument that aren't yet well enough supported, examples that can be interpreted differently than you have, or moments where you jump from one idea to another and leave a gap in reasoning or just don't flow your argument well. These will be your cues for revision. Be sensitive to your readers' concerns: Even if they can't quite explain their problem with your piece well, the fact that *something* in your text stopped them suggests that there's a difficulty there which should lead to some rewriting on your part.

***What Makes It Good?:*** A definitional essay, even a multimodal one, needs to do certain things:

- Make claims and provide good reasons for your claims
- Provide appropriate and convincing examples supporting your reasons
- Make observations or connections that other people wouldn't notice until you point them out
- Break new ground: get out beyond your sources and draw conclusions based on their work that they hadn't yet seen (Many people think undergraduate students can't do this, but we completely disagree; especially when it comes to new ways of composing, you have something new to offer to the conversation.)
- Find a few defining principles that help you draw some lines between what you think counts as writing and what you think does not
- Compose a well-designed multimodal composition that works and makes sense to people when they try to read/use it

# Glossary

**accommodation**

In this book, *accommodation* is used to refer to the ways that writers from one group understand and write about texts written by another group—for example, how journalists write about ("accommodate") scientists' research articles.

**activity system**

In his 1997 article "Rethinking Genre in School and Society: An Activity Theory Analysis," David Russell describes an *activity system* as "any ongoing, object-directed, historically conditioned, dialectically structured, tool-mediated human interaction." In simpler terms, an *activity system* consists of a group of people who act together over time as they work toward a specific goal. The people in the system use many kinds of tools, both physical (like computers or books) and symbolic (like words), to do their work together. The group's behaviors and traditions are influenced by *their* history, and when one aspect of the system changes, other aspects of it change in response.

*Activity theory* "was originally a psychological theory that sees all aspects of activity as shaped by people's social interactions with each other and the tools [including writing and language] that they use" (p. 273). In Chapter 2, Kain and Wardle explain: "The most basic activity theory lens, or unit of analysis, is the activity system, defined as a group of people who share a common object and motive over time, as well as the wide range of tools they use together to act on that object and realize that motive. David Russell (1997) describes an activity system as 'any ongoing, object-directed, historically conditioned, dialectically structured, tool-mediated human interaction' (p. 510)."

**apprenticeship**

*Apprenticeship* is a term used to describe the relationship between a master and a student, or a mentor and a mentee, in which the student or mentee undergoes training in order to become an expert in a profession or group.

In his 1998 book, *Communities of Practice,* Etienne Wenger argues that apprentices move from peripheral participation to more central participation in a group as they become engaged with and more skilled at the group's practices. (See also **community of practice**.)

**argument**

*Argument* can describe any of the many ways by means of which people try to convince others of something.

Mathematically, arguments are the individual propositions of a proof. In a legal context, formal arguments are used to persuade a judge or jury to rule in favor of a particular position. In everyday use, or on talk radio or cable news shows, arguments tend to consist of people yelling at each other but rarely convincing or being convinced. We call all these forms of argument *agonistic,* meaning that they pit people against each other in a win/lose contest.

In an *intellectual* or *academic* context, argument is *inquiry-based* or *conversational*, and it describes the attempt to *build knowledge* by questioning existing knowledge and proposing alternatives. Rather than aiming simply to show who is right or wrong, inquiry-based argument aims to *cooperatively find the best explanation* for whatever is in question.

**audience**

An *audience* is anyone who hears or reads a text—but it is also anyone a writer *imagines* encountering his or her text. This means that there is a difference between *intended* or "invoked" audience and *actual* or "addressed" audience.

For example, when Aristotle composed *On Rhetoric* in about 350 BC, his intended audience was his students, and for a time they were also his actual audience. (We would also call them his *primary* audience, the ones who first encountered his text.) Today, Aristotle's actual audience—the people who read him in coursepacks, on iPads, and on Kindles—are *secondary* audiences for Aristotle's work.

## authority

An *authority* is an accepted source, an expert, or a person with power or credibility. *Authority* (as an abstract noun) denotes confidence and self-assurance.

In this book, the term is generally used to refer to people who understand the **conventions** or accepted practices of a **discourse community** and thus are able to speak, write, or act with credibility and confidence. A writer's **ethos** is based in part on his or her authority.

## authorship

To "author" a text is to create or originate it; the *authorship* of a text then is a question of *who* created or originated it. Most traditional Western notions of authorship presume that **originality** is one key component of authorship.

The term is seen by some scholars as problematic if it assumes *sole* authorship— invention by just one person—because it seems to discount the importance of social interaction and the fact that virtually every idea we can have already draws from other ideas authored by other people. The question becomes, where do we draw the line on who has authored what? For a related discussion, see **plagiarism**.

## autobiography

Literally, *autobiography* is writing about one's own life. ("Auto" = self, "bio" = life, and "graphy" = writing.) The **genre** of autobiography is a book-length text containing a retrospective account of the author's life.

More broadly, *autobiographical* means simply about, or having to do with, one's own life. Donald Murray and others contend that all writing is autobiographical—that is, that one's writing always has some connection to one's own life and that a writer can never completely remove all traces of her life from her writing.

## autoethnography

*Autoethnography* is an **ethnography**, or cultural study, of one's own experiences and interaction with the world.

## CARS ("Create a Research Space") model

John Swales's description of the three typical "moves" made in the introductions to academic research articles. Swales conducted an analysis of research articles in many disciplines and discovered that most introductions in all disciplines do the following:

1. establish a territory (by describing the topic of study);
2. establish a niche (by explaining the problem, gap, or question that prompted the current study); and
3. occupy the niche (by describing the answer to the question or problem, and/or outlining what will be done in the article).

## case studies

*Case studies* are detailed observations and analyses of an event, situation, individual, or small group of people. Case study research, according to Mary Sue MacNealy in her book *Strategies for Empirical Research in Writing*, refers to "a carefully designed project to systematically collect information about an event, situation, or small group of persons or objects for the purpose of exploring, describing, and/or explaining aspects not previously known or considered." Case studies are considered to be **qualitative research**.

## claim

A *claim* is an assertion that a writer tries to convince his or her readers of. For example, "*Wired* magazine is great." To believe or accept a claim, readers need to know the *reasons* why a writer believes the claim or wants readers to accept it. For example, "*Wired* includes really interesting articles about people in the technological world." Readers may also need *evidence* to believe the claim or its reasons, like, "Every month *Wired* has several stories that interview the people who invented netbooks, the iPhone, cloud computing, and the most cutting-edge technological innovations."

## codex

A *codex* is a text arranged in book format—with pages (or *leaves*) sharing a central binding (or *spine*). The pages of a codex can be *randomly* accessed—that is, any page can be accessed directly in the book, without a reader needing to read all the text around it. Before codexes the most common text arrangements was the scroll, a continuous sheet stored as a roll and unwrapped from one end to the other to be read. Scrolls (as well as any kind of recording tape such as audio or video cassettes or movie reels) are *sequentially accessed,* where a given point can only be reached by passing all the text that precedes it.

## cognition

*Cognition* describes anything having to do with *thought* or *mental activity*.

In Writing Studies, *cognitive* and *cognition* have to do with the internal thinking processes that writers use to write. Scholars in Writing Studies have contrasted the *internal, private, personal* nature of cognition with the *social* aspects of writing—that is, with the writer's *external* interactions with their surroundings, culture, and audience. Most research about cognition in Writing Studies was conducted in the 1980s and sought to find and describe the mental processes that writers use to solve problems related to writing.

## community of practice

*Community of practice* is a term coined by sociologists Jean Lave and Etienne Wenger to describe groups of people who participate in a shared activity or activities. In his 1998 book, *Communities of Practice,* Wenger argues that participating in a community of practice also involves "constructing *identities* in relation to these communities" (4).

This term is similar to, but not exactly the same as, the terms **activity system** and **discourse community**.

## composition

The process of designing a text and its ideas ("I'm composing my paper") or the product of that design process ("I got an A on that composition"). Paul Prior (p. 492) divides writing into two separate acts, **composition** and **inscription**, where *composing* is designing a text and its ideas, and *inscribing* is using tools and media to set the text on some object.

*Composition* sums up the first three rhetorical canons of *invention* (coming up with ideas, from memory or from research), *arrangement* (determining the line of reasoning or the flow of ideas in the text), and *style* (fine-tuning expressive choices of language and sentence syntax to best suit the text to its **exigence**, **audience**, and **context**). One of the unique powers of writing is that *inscription* is often an aid to *composition*: when you **freewrite** or do most other kinds of writing, the act of writing itself is often giving you new ideas, that is, helping you compose.

## computer mediated communication

The term given to human communication carried out via computer, and thus *mediated* or *facilitated* by it. Examples include e-mail, word-processing, blogging, Skyping, and snap-chat.

## concept

An idea or **construct**.

## conflict

*Conflicts* are disagreements, fights, struggles, clashes, or tensions, usually resulting from perceived differences in interests, needs, values, or goals.

## constraints

*Constraints* are factors that limit or otherwise influence the persuasive strategies available to the rhetor. More precisely, in "Rhetorical Situations and Their Constituents," Keith Grant-Davie defines constraints as "all factors in the situation, aside from the rhetor and the audience, that may lead the audience to be either more or less sympathetic to the discourse, and that may therefore influence the rhetor's response to the situation" (p. 357).

## construct (CONstruct, conSTRUCT)

*Construct*, the verb (pronounced conSTRUCT), means *to build or to put together* ("con" = with, and "struct" = shape or frame). By turning the verb into a noun (pronounced CONstruct), we make the word mean, literally, *a thing that has been constructed*. In everyday use, we use the noun *CONstruct* only in the realm of *ideas or concepts*. The ideas of *freedom, justice, wealth,* and *politics*, for example, are all constructs, or ideas that we have *built up* over time.

What is important to remember about constructs is that, while they may seem to be "natural" or "inevitable," they're actually unchallenged **claims** that can be questioned, contested, redefined, or reinvented.

## context

Literally, a *context* is the substructure for a woven fabric ("con" = with/together, "text" = weaving, fabric). In Writing Studies, *context* typically refers to where a text comes from or where it appears. (A *written work* first started being called a *text* because it's "woven" from words in the same way that *textiles* are woven from threads.) Contexts can consist of other text(s) as well as the circumstances or setting in which a text was created—for example, various contexts for the statement "We hold these truths to be self-evident" include the Declaration of Independence, the meeting of the Continental Congress in spring and summer of 1776, and the broader socio-historical environment that describes pre–Revolutionary War America.

## contingent

One of the claims of this book is that meaning is *contingent*; that is, it depends. In other words, meaning is conditional. For example, "good writing" depends upon the context, purpose, and audience. Ideas about meaning as being contingent, conditional, are taken up most directly in Chapter 3, where authors claim that meaning depends on context and that principles for good communication depend on the specific situation and are not universal.

## contribution

In academic contexts, one makes a *contribution* by adding to an ongoing conversation on a given research subject, issue, problem, or question.

In Writing Studies, *contribution* is commonly discussed in terms of Kenneth Burke's *parlor metaphor*, where Burke describes scholarship as an ongoing conversation at a party: You arrive late and other guests are already in conversation; you join one conversation by listening for a while and then, once you have something to add, making a contribution to the conversation; after a time, you join another conversation, while the first one continues without you.

## conventions

In Writing Studies, writing is understood to be governed by *conventions*—that is, agreements among people about the best ways to accomplish particular tasks (such as starting new paragraphs, or citing sources, or deciding how to punctuate sentences). That people have to come to agreements about such questions means that there is no "natural" or pre-existing way to accomplish the tasks; rather, people simply agreed to do *A* rather than *B*. Tabbing the first line of a paragraph one-half inch is a convention. Ending sentences with periods is a convention. Citing sources in parentheses is a convention, as are parentheses themselves.

Conventions are a kind of **construct**, and like constructs, they can be questioned, challenged, and changed, if key decision makers agree to alter them or to establish another convention in their place.

## corpus analysis

A *corpus analysis* is a detailed examination of a collection of related texts, phrases, utterances, etc. (*Corpus* means "body"—the word *corpse* derives from it.) For example, Ken Hyland conducted a *corpus analysis* of academic writing to discover how people in various fields cite their sources.

## Create a Research Space Model: see CARS ("Create a Research Space") model

## disciplinary writing expertise

The skills and knowledges required to effectively communicate in writing with members of a discipline or profession (such as history, chemistry, mathematics, engineering, or law). These "skills and knowledges" would include, but not be limited to, specialized linguistic knowledge (the jargon of the discipline), **genre** knowledge (genres specific to a discipline or disciplinary adaptations of less specialized genres like memos or reports), **epistemic** knowledge (understanding of how the discipline or field prefers to construct its arguments or what kinds of argument and evidence are most convincing in the discipline), and **activity** knowledge (understanding of what the discipline does, what it seeks to achieve, and how to perform the discipline or tasks within it).

### discourse/Discourse

At its most basic, *discourse* is *language in action*, or language being used to accomplish something. Discourse can describe either *an instance of* language (e.g., "His discourse was terse and harsh") or a collection of instances that all demonstrate some quality (e.g., "Legal discourse tries to be very precise"). Because groups of people united by some activity tend to develop a characteristic discourse, we can talk about communities that are identified *by* their discourse—thus, **discourse community**.

James Paul Gee uses *Discourse* with an uppercase D to differentiate his specialized meaning of the term.

### discourse community

Scholars continue to debate the meaning of this term, as the selections in this book suggest. For the sake of simplicity, we will use John Swales's definition from his 1990 book, *Genre Analysis: English in Academic and Research Settings*. According to Swales, a *discourse community* is a made up of individuals who share "a broadly agreed upon set of common public goals"; further, it has "mechanisms of intercommunication among its members," "uses its participatory mechanisms primarily to provide information and feedback," has and uses "one or more genres" that help the group achieve its shared goals, "has acquired some specific lexis," and has "a reasonable ratio" of "novices and experts."

### drafting

*Drafting* is the writing-process activity that involves writing down what you're thinking. While a basic description of the writing process differentiates drafting and revision, any moment in which a writer is creating text can be seen as drafting, even if it's also revising. (Some writers, in fact, report that they revise *while* they draft.)

### EAP: see ESP

### editing

*Editing* is the correction of minor errors in a written text. Editing usually comes at the end of the writing process. It should not be confused with **revision**, which involves major rethinking, rewriting, and restructuring of texts.

### enculturation

*Enculturation* refers to the process by which a newcomer learns to become a part of a group or "culture" (including an **activity system**, **discourse community**, or **community of practice**). Becoming successfully enculturated usually requires gaining some level of competence in the activities and language practices of the group. See **apprenticeship** for a definition of a similar term.

### epistemic

Having to do with the making of knowledge. Research is an *epistemic* pursuit because it is about developing new knowledge. *Epistemology* is the branch of philosophy that deals with human knowledge: where it comes from and how people know what they know. Communication, including *writing*, is also an epistemic activity—it makes new knowledge—as we can see when we read a piece and come away with a new idea that we didn't know before but also that wasn't in the text we just read.

### error

*Error* is the term for "mistakes" in grammar (e.g., subject-verb agreement, like "Dogs barks loudly"), punctuation, or usage (e.g., using *that* where some readers would prefer *which*). *Mistakes* is in quotes here because such "errors" are as often differences of opinion regarding convention or taste as they are actual problems that every English speaker or writer would agree are violations of rules.

**ESP, EAP**
*ESP* stands for "English for Specific Purposes" and refers to a subfield of Applied Linguistics that examines how people learn to use language for specialized purposes. *EAP* is a subset of ESP and stands for "English for Academic Purposes." It refers to a field of study that teaches **L2** (non-native) speakers how to use their non-native language (English) appropriately in school settings.

**ethnography, ethnographic research**
*Ethnography* is a research methodology for carefully observing and describing people participating in some activity. At its broadest, ethnography can be written of entire cultures; more narrowly, ethnographies can be written of a class of students, a church and its members, or a videogame arcade and the gamers who play there.

**ethos**
*Ethos* is a Greek word usually used to describe the credibility, expertise, or competence that a writer or speaker establishes with an audience through his or her **discourse**. At its broadest, *ethos* is a term for the sense of "personality" that readers perceive about a writer. As a persuasive appeal, ethos derives from **authority**, character (the perceived values, morals, and ethics of a writer), and goodwill (the readers' sense that the writer has the readers' best interests at heart and is not purely self-interested).

**exigence**
*Exigence* is the *need or reason* for a given action or communication. All communication exists for a reason. For example, if you say, "Please turn on the lights," we assume the *reason* you say this is that there's not enough light for your needs—in other words, the *exigence* of the situation is that you need more light.

**freewriting**
*Freewriting* is a technique for generating ideas in which the writer simply writes without stopping, without taking the pen from the paper, and without giving any thought to correcting grammatical **errors**. It is often used to get started and to overcome writer's block.

**generalizable, generalize**
*Generalizable* is a term used to refer to research findings that can apply to a larger group than the one that was studied. Generalizable research typically examines a group of statistically significant size under rigorous experimental conditions. **Qualitative research** is not generalizable, strictly speaking, while **quantitative research** may be.

**genre**
*Genre* comes from the French word for "kind" or "type" and is related to the Latin word *genus*, which you might remember from the scientific classification system for animals and plants. In the field of rhetoric, *genres* are broadly understood as *categories of texts*. For example, poetry, the short story, the novel, and the memoir are genres of literature; memos, proposals, reports, and executive summaries are genres of business writing; hiphop, bluegrass, trance, pop, new age, and electronica are genres of music; and the romantic comedy, drama, and documentary are genres of film.

Genres are types of texts that are recognizable to readers and writers and that meet the needs of the **rhetorical situations** in which they function. So, for example, we recognize wedding invitations and understand them to be different from horoscopes. We know that when we are asked to write a paper for school, our teacher probably does not want us to turn in a poem instead.

Genres develop over time in response to recurring rhetorical needs. We have wedding invitations because people keep getting married, and we need an efficient way to let people know and to ask them to attend. Rather than making up a new rhetorical solution every time the same situation occurs, we generally turn to the genre that has developed—in this case, the genre of the wedding invitation.

**Discourse** theorists have suggested that the concept of *genre* actually goes well beyond texts; accordingly, some theorists use *genre* to describe *a typified but dynamic social interaction that a group of people use to conduct a given activity*. (*Typified* means it follows a pattern, and *dynamic* means that people can change the pattern to fit their circumstances as long as it still helps them do the activity.) In "Rethinking Genre. . . . ," for example, David Russell says that genres are actually "shared expectations among some group(s) of people."

### genre theory
See **genre**. Scholars who study and discuss genre have generated a body of thinking about it that is commonly referred to as *genre theory*.

### heterochronic
This term, which appears in Kevin Roozen's article (p. 157) simply refers to things that happen at different times. However, when Roozen and others use the term they are attempting to give a name to the way that past, present, and future are folded in together. *Heterochronic* refers to the way that an event or an action is informed not just by what is going on in the immediate present, but also by what has happened in the near and distant past and what might be anticipated in the near and distant future.

### heuristics
*Heuristics* are approaches or patterns for problem solving. For example, a heuristic for deciding what to have for dinner tonight might be the following: (1) check the fridge; (2) check the pantry; and (3) eat whatever can be assembled most quickly and palatably from the ingredients there.

### identity
*Identity* comprises an individual's characteristics or personality; it consists of those factors that create a sense of "who you are." Recent theory suggests that individuals may not have one "true," stable identity but might have multiple and/or changing identities.

### inscription
The act of marking a medium in order to create writing. Paul Prior (p. 492) divides writing into two separate acts, **composition** and inscription, where *composing* is designing a text and its ideas, and *inscribing* is using tools and media to set the text on some object. While inscription can happen without composition (photocopying) and composition can happen without inscription (conversation), what we describe as *writing* cannot happen without both. Prior reminds us that *medium* (what gets inscribed) can be anything from a t-shirt to a plastic disc to a clay tablet to paper, while *inscribing tools* can be anything from knives and sticks to pencils to printers to DVD burners.

### integral citation, nonintegral citation
*Integral citation* is the term used for citation in which the source is named directly in the sentence of an article or paper. For example, "John Jones claims that water is wet" (23). *Nonintegral citation* is the term used for citation in which the source is cited only parenthetically. For example: "Water is wet (Jones 23)."

### intercommunication
*Intercommunication* refers to communication within a group (as opposed to communication between or among individuals in different groups).

### interlocutor
A person taking part in a conversation or dialogue.

### intertext, intertextuality
*Intertextuality* refers to the idea that all texts are made up of other texts—and thus, to the resulting *network* of texts that connect to any given text or idea. At the most basic level, texts share *words*: that is, every text uses words that other texts have used. Sometimes texts use words that, in their combination, are considered unique; in those cases, following Western conventions, those words must be formally marked as *quotations*. *Intertextuality* can go beyond just language, however, by referencing the *ideas and events* that other texts have focused on. If, for example, I claim that people whose governments abuse them have the right to make a better government, I haven't used a quotation from the Declaration of Independence, but most people familiar with that document could "hear it" in my statement. Intertextuality thus is an effect even more than an intention—I don't have to *intend* to be intertextual in order to *be* intertextual.

### invention
*Invention* comprises the processes, strategies, or techniques writers use to come up with what to say in their writing. While the term suggests the notion of "making things up," a significant part of invention is not saying brand-new things but rather combing one's memory and written

resources for things that have already been said that will work. Ancient rhetorical theorists such as Aristotle thought carefully about how *stock arguments* they called *common topics* could help a speaker—for instance, the idea that "that which has happened frequently before is likely to happen again," which could be recalled through invention and included in many pieces of writing.

### L1, L2

*L1* is a term used in linguistics to refer to a native (or "first") language; it is commonly applied to people who are speaking or writing in their native language ("L1 speakers") and to those who study first-language acquisition ("L1 scholars"). *L2* refers to a second (or non-native) language, and it is commonly applied to people who are speaking or writing in their second (or non-native) language ("L2 speakers") and to those who study second-language acquisition ("L2 scholars").

### lexis

*Lexis* is a term used for the specific vocabulary used by a group or field of study.

### literacy, literate

*Literacy* denotes fluency in a given practice. In its original use, *literacy* referred to *alphabetic* literacy—that is, to fluency in reading and writing "letters," or alphabetic text. This kind of literacy was contrasted with **orality**, which was characterized as a *lack* of literacy. Over time, however, in academic circles, the meaning of *literacy* and *literate* has broadened to encompass fluency in other areas; most academics therefore now use the term *literacies* (plural) and discuss *digital, electronic, musical, visual, oral, mathematical,* and *gaming* literacies, among many other kinds.

### literacy sponsor

*Literacy sponsor* is a term coined by Deborah Brandt to describe people, ideas, or institutions that help others become **literate** in specific ways. A sponsor could be a parent or sibling who taught you to read, a teacher who helped you learn to love books, or a manufacturing company that requires its employees to be able to read. The sponsors of *alphabetic* literacy in your life might be very different from the sponsors of *visual* literacy, *musical* literacy, or other forms of literacy in your life. (*Pandora,* for instance, can be a musical literacy sponsor for people who use it.)

### literature review, review of the literature

A *literature review* (or *review of the literature*) is a text that explains the existing conversation about a particular topic. Literature reviews are usually found at the beginning of research articles or books, but are sometimes written as separate projects. Note that *literature* in this case refers to published research in an area, not to novels or short stories.

### longitudinal study

A *longitudinal study* is a research study that examines an individual, group, event, or activity over a substantial period of time. For example, rather than studying a student's writing habits for just a few days or weeks, a *longitudinal study* might look at his or her habits over several years.

### mediate

People use texts in order to get things done. They read in order to learn something (for example, they read instructions in order to figure out how to put together a new desk); they write in order to communicate something (for example, a student might write an e-mail to let her mom know she is short on money). Texts, then, help things happen, they play a role in situations and enable communication and activities to take place. In the examples offered above, reading the instructions *mediates* assembly of the desk; sending Mom an e-mail *mediates* receiving $200 to buy much needed school supplies.

### metaknowledge

*Metaknowledge* is knowledge about knowledge—that is, what we can determine about our learning, its processes, and its products.

### methodologies

In an academic or scholarly context, *methodologies* are procedures for conducting research—the formalized, field-approved methods used to address particular kinds of research questions. Some examples of methodologies in Writing Studies are **case study**, **ethnography**, experiment, quasi-experiment, and **discourse analysis**. *Methodology* can also mean the particular combination of methods used in any particular study. For example, the methodologies used by Sondra Perl in "The Composing Processes of Unskilled College Writers" include case study and discourse analysis.

### mindfulness

*Mindfulness* means thinking carefully about what one is doing — that is, purposefully and carefully paying attention. This term derives from Zen Buddhism and has become a key concept in modern psychology. It is often used by researchers interested in helping writers effectively **transfer** knowledge about writing. For a writer to be mindful, for example, means not just to come up with something to say, but to *pay attention to how* she came up with something to say. In the future, she may be able to *mindfully* try that procedure again, adapting it to the new situation.

### modality

*Modality* refers to the senses or facilities readers use to experience a text; typical modalities are alphabetic-print, visual/image, aural, color, and kinesthetic/touch. In another sense, *modality* means mode of access to texts, with typical examples being paper, codex/book, or electronic/networked.

### multiliteracies

*Multiliteracies* is a term that reflects the recent, broader understanding of **literacy** as consisting of more than mastery of the "correct" use of alphabetic language. *Multiliteracies* includes the ability to compose and interpret **multimodal** texts (texts that include oral, written, and audio components, among other possibilities), as well as the ability to make meaning in various contexts. A group of scholars known as the New London Group is generally credited with coining the term *multiliteracies*.

### multimodal

*Multimodal* refers to texts combining multiple modes, such as alphabetic, visual, and aural.

### mushfake

*Mushfake* is a term used by James Paul Gee to describe a partially acquired **discourse**, a discourse that people use to "make do" when they participate in or communicate with a group to which they don't belong. Gee borrows the term from prison culture, in which *mushfake* refers to making do with something when the real thing is not available (in e-Pages).

### nonintegral citation: see integral citation, nonintergral citation

### non participation

*Non participation* is a type of rebellion in which a person chooses not to engage in an expected activity or to abide by a particular code or rule.

### orality

*Orality* is the condition of being spoken rather than written. An *oral culture* is one that has no system of writing (meaning that the language used in the culture has no alphabet or other way of being visually represented). Such cultures rely on oral **literacies** that, before being recognized as a kind of literacy, were thought by researchers such as Walter Ong to be the *opposite* of literacy.

### originality

*Originality* is the quality of being singular, unique, and entirely made up or invented, as opposed to imitative or derivative. American culture presumes that writers will have originality — that they will invent work never seen before — and judges the quality of **authorship** in part on its originality. This simplified view of **invention** is assumed by many scholars to be inaccurate in that it fails to describe how people develop ideas through social interaction. This can lead to difficulties in defining and identifying **plagiarism**.

### peer-reviewed journal

Journals are collections of relatively short articles (between 5 and thirty pages, usually) on a related topic, published periodically (monthly or quarterly, usually) — just like a magazine. Some journals are *scholarly* — meaning that their articles are written by scholars in a field or discipline to other scholars studying in the same field. Their purpose is to report on new research: scholarly journals are the main sites in which scholarly conversations (see Greene in the introduction) are carried on. Most of the articles collected in this book come from scholarly journals, such as *College Composition and*

*Communication* or *College English*. Some of these scholarly conversations can be *very* specialized—the kind that perhaps only twenty-five or fifty people in the entire world would share enough background knowledge to understand. (Imagine an article on a brand new branch of theoretical physics or a piece on a new kind of black hole: not many people study those.) That specialization poses two problems for a journal: First, how does the editor of a journal—who might be an expert on *a few* specialty areas in a field (say, on "writing process" and on "pedagogy" in composition) but can't be an expert on *all* of them—actually know whether a given article knows what it's talking about? Second, *so* many people doing research want to publish in any given journal, the journal doesn't have space for them all. In fact, it might only have space for a small percentage of what gets submitted to it. How can it choose which pieces to take and which not to publish? The answer to both questions is *peer review*: the editor sends submissions to other experts in the specialty the article is reporting on—usually between two and four other readers. They report back to the journal's editor on the relative *value* of a submission—how significant a contribution it makes, how it fits in the ongoing conversation—and on its *quality*—how well its argument is made, how good its research is. They can make suggestions to the editor about how the piece needs to be improved before publication, and thus guide revisions that most articles are required to make before finally being published. Peer review, then, is a major feature of scholarly journals, and most library databases (along with Google Scholar) let you limit searches to just peer-reviewed journals. (Almost all scholarly *books* are peer-reviewed as well.)

## plagiarism

*Plagiarism* literally means *kidnapping* in Latin; in contemporary English, the word refers to the **theft** of a text or idea. (Authors sometimes think of their writings or ideas as their "children," thus the link to kidnapping.) Definitions of plagiarism tend to come down to *taking another's ideas without giving them credit and thus pretending that you invented the ideas yourself*. In cultures that highly value *intellectual property*—the idea that one's ideas are one's *own* and that use of those ideas by others deserves either credit or payment—plagiarism is an ethical violation punishable by community sanction (such as failing a class or losing one's job). Plagiarism's cousin *copyright infringement* is an actual crime punishable by fine or imprisonment.

A significant difficulty with the idea of plagiarism is that **originality** and **authorship** are technically quite difficult to trace in ways that new digital technologies are making impossible to miss or deny. In *sampling, re-mixing,* and *mash-up* cultures where ideas are freely reused and reincorporated to make new texts, authorship becomes very difficult to trace, and it becomes difficult to tell what counts as original work.

## planning

While **invention** focuses on coming up with what to say in one's writing, *planning* focuses more broadly on *how to get a piece written*. Therefore, it includes not only invention but *arrangement*, which is the art of organizing what one has to say to present it most effectively. Planning also includes **process** considerations, such as considering what work needs to be done to complete a piece, what order to do it in, and when to do it in order to meet a deadline.

## polycontextual

Having multiple contexts, or, occurring in multiple contexts. A **rhetorical situation** is *polycontextual* if the same text is encountered in multiple contexts, or if multiple contexts (say, both one's Music History class and one's Sunday worship service) contribute to the making or interpreting of a given text.

## process

*Process* refers to the variety of activities that go into writing/composing, including, at minimum,

- **planning** (inventing and arranging ideas)
- **drafting** (creating actual text from previously unwritten ideas)
- **revising** (developing a text or a portion of a text further after an initial draft)
- **editing** (fine-tuning, polishing, or correcting problems in a text), and
- **production** (transferring a text to its final, "produced" form, whether in print, online, or in a portable digital format).

*Process theory* is the study of the methods by which various writers compose and produce texts. The *process movement*, which took place within the field of Composition Studies in the 1970s, was the widespread adoption by writing teachers of instruction that focused on teaching students successful writing processes rather than focusing solely on the quality of their written products.

### qualitative research, quantitative research

The term *qualitative* refers to an event or object's *qualities* that can't be explained or measured numerically (that is, *quantitatively*). *Qualitative research* includes studies such as **case studies** and **ethnographies** designed to explore such qualities; it typically seeks explanations or answers to questions such as *who, what, how,* and *why*—for example, how some people go about writing, or why they write as they do. *Qualitative research* usually includes small, focused samples, as opposed to the large samples in *quantitative research*. As a result of qualitative findings, researchers formulate *hypotheses* (theories), which can often in turn be tested through further qualitative research or through larger data sets gathered through quantitative research (for example, surveys of large numbers of people or laboratory experiments). It should be noted, however, that there are many aspects of reading and writing that cannot easily be studied through quantitative studies.

### rebellion

*Rebellion* is an act of defiance or a refusal to accept something (a rule, for example) that an authority or group has presented as appropriate or expected.

### register

In the field of lingustics, *register* refers to a type of language used in a particular setting. Changing one's register might mean changing the kinds of words used, as well as the way one says the words. For example, a person might say, "I've finished my homework" to her parents, using one register, while she might say (or text), "I'm finally dooooooooooone!" to her friends.

### repurpose

When writing scholars talk about *repurposing*, they are usually talking about how people draw on prior knowledge and experience to help them do something new. For example, a student who has written a five-paragraph essay needs to draw on that experience in order to write a research paper. However, she can't simply draw on the experience; she must also adapt what she knows how to do in order to accomplish something related but new. In other words, she must repurpose, reshape, what she already knows from a five-paragraph essay in order to successfully write a more complex research paper. See Kevin Roozen (p.157).

### review of the literature: see literature review

### revision

*Revision* is the act of developing a piece of writing *by* writing—that is, by adding additional material, shifting the order of its parts, or deleting significant portions of what has already been written. The purpose of revision ("re-vision") is to "see again," which is necessary because what one could see in originally drafting a piece has been changed *by* the drafting.

This might become clearer if you think of writing as driving at night. When you begin to write, you know a certain amount about where you're going in your project, just as, when you're driving at night, your headlights let you see two hundred yards (but only two hundred yards) ahead. Writing (or driving) further takes you to new places, where you continually see something different, rethink your position, and decide how to proceed.

Because revision can go on for some time, for many professional writers *most* writing time is actually spent revising, not creating the first draft. Also, it is important to distinguish revision from **editing,** the correction of minor mistakes in a near-final draft.

### rhetor

Originally (in Greek) a *public speaker, rhetor* means *one who engages in rhetoric or* **discourse**. *Writer* and *speaker* are common synonyms.

### rhetoric

*Rhetoric* is the study of human interaction and communication, or the product(s) of that interaction and communication. Because most human interaction is *persuasive* by nature—that is, we're trying to convince each other of things, even when we say something simple like "that feels nice"—one way to think of rhetoric is as the study of persuasion.

Rhetoric always has to do with these specific principles:

1. Human communication, or **discourse**, is *situated* in a particular time and place. That time and place are the **context** of the communication. A given instance of communication—say, a particular text—doesn't in a sense mean *anything* if considered in isolation from its context; knowledge of the context of the communication is necessary in order to understand its meaning. For example, "Help me!" means one thing when your mom is standing next to a van full of groceries and another when she's standing next to a van with a flat tire. Her *discourse* is *situated*.

2. Communication is *motivated* by particular *purposes*, needs, and values. There is no such thing as *un*motivated communication—no neutral, non-persuasive, "just-sayin'" discourse.

3. Communication is *interactional*—that is, it develops in the "back-and-forth" between author and **audience**. This means that readers actually *complete* a writer's text. Successful writers think carefully about who their audience is and what the audience values and needs.

4. Communication is *epistemic*, which means that it *creates new knowledge*. We often talk about "reporting" or "transmitting" information as if all we do is pass it along. But rhetoric suggests that we can't just pass along knowledge without changing it as we pass it, so our communication makes new knowledge as it goes.

5. Communication is *contingent*, meaning that what we consider *good* communication depends on the circumstances and context in which it happens. Because communication depends on context, we can't make universal rules about what makes good communication.

### rhetorical

*Rhetorical* describes an understanding of or approach to human interaction and communication as situated, motivated, interactive, epistemic, and contingent. (See the definition of **rhetoric**.) *Rhetorical study*, then, is the investigation of human communication as situated, motivated, interactive, epistemic, and contingent. *Rhetorical reading* involves reading a text as situated, motivated, etc. *Rhetorical analysis* is a way of analyzing texts to find what choices their **rhetor** (speaker or writer) made based on their purpose and motivation, their situatedness and context, and how they interact with and make new knowledge for their audience.

### rhetorical moves

Whenever a person writes or speaks, he or she is making *rhetorical moves*. In other words, the speaker is making choices about how to communicate appropriately given the **rhetorical situation**. The speaker makes choices about everything from **tone** to length, from word choice to **content**, all of which affect how successful his or her rhetoric is.

### rhetorical situation

*Rhetorical situation* is the particular circumstance of a given instance of communication or **discourse**. The rhetorical situation includes **exigence** (the *need or reason* for the communication), **context** (the *circumstances* that give rise to the *exigence*, including location in time/history and space/place/position), **rhetor** (the originator of the communication—its speaker or writer), and **audience** (the auditor, listener, or reader of the rhetor's discourse).

### semiotic

Having to do with the use and interpretation of signs and **symbols**. A red light hanging from a pole at an intersection is a "sign" because it is an object that *stands for* another meaning (in this case, "stop here").

### situated

Located at a particular place and time, and therefore dependent on a specific context and set of circumstances. In everyday language, we use *situated* to describe an object's or person's place: "The piano was situated on the left side of the great room" or "She situated herself between the two potted ferns." In a scholarly, rhetorical sense, we mean roughly the same thing, but use the term to call attention to the uniqueness of the moment and place of situation: "The President's speech is situated at a very tense time of diplomatic relations with Libya." Situatedness is a key element of *rhetorical* activities: when we say a given activity or experience is "rhetorical," we mean that it has the quality of being *situated* in time and space (among other qualities). That is the opposite of being *universal*: a universal rule is one which applies in all times and places. In contrast, most rules are situated, applying only to specific times, places, and circumstances.

### social context

*Social context* is the environment, situation, or culture in which something is embedded. Key aspects of the social context of **discourse** might include participants, goals, setting, race, class, gender, and so on.

### speech community

*Speech community* is a term from the field of sociolinguistics used to describe a group of people who share similar language patterns. According to John Swales, people are generally members of a speech community "by birth, accident, or adoption" (p. 220). A speech community thus differs from a **discourse community**, where members are recruited "by persuasion, training, or relevant qualification" (p. 220).

### stases

*Stases* (we often say *the stases*) are a problem-solving pattern (a **heuristic**) that helps writers develop arguments by asking a set of specific questions about the subject. First described in the rhetorical theory of Aristotle, the word *stases* shares the same root as the words *state*, *status*, and *stasis* (the singular of *stases*), all of which denote *condition* or *being*. Stases have to do with *the state of things*, so that when we consider the stases, we are taking stock, or asking, "What is the state of things?" The stases include (1) questions of fact, (2) questions of value, and (3) questions of policy:

1. What is the *nature* of the thing in question? How would we define or name the thing? What caused the thing? For example, if a four-legged creature with a wagging tail shows up at your back door, your first question might be "What is [the nature of] that?" Your answer might be that it's a "stray dog."
2. What is the *quality* or *value* of the thing? Is it good or bad? Desirable or undesirable? Wanted or unwanted? Happy or sad? Liked or disliked? Your answer to this will depend on a complex set of calculations, taking into account the nature of the thing and the context in which it is encountered. To extend our example, let's say you decide the stray dog is good because you like dogs and this one is appealing.
3. What should *be done* about it? What policy should we establish toward it? What is the best thing to do with respect to it? In the case of our example, you might decide that the best policy would be to take in the stray dog, at least temporarily, and feed it.

### symbol

A symbol is a thing that represents or stands for something else—usually an object standing for an idea or an abstract concept. In the U.S. flag, which is itself a symbol, white stars stand for (symbolize) individual states and the blue field in which they all rest symbolizes unity. Language is a symbol (or sign) system; all words are symbols for the objects or concepts they're associated with.

### theory

A systematic explanation for some aspect of people's lived experience and observation. For a given experience—say, an apple falling on one's head—people propose explanations, or *theories*, for why the experience happens as it does, or why it doesn't happen some other way (e.g., a theory of gravity). People then test the theory against more observed experiences, seeing if those experiences are consistent with the explanation suggested by the theory, and seeing whether the theory can predict what will happen in future experiences. Theories are, for a long time, not "right" or "wrong" but "stronger/better" or "weaker/poorer" at explaining the phenomenon in question. The better or stronger a theory is, the more completely it accounts for existing phenomena (experiences, events, and objects) and the more accurately it makes testable predictions about future events. For example, a theory that tries to explain how people make up or change their minds has to be able to account for existing cases of this and predict how future cases will work. Theories—such as the theory in Writing Studies that "writing is a process"—become treated as essentially factual when we recognize that though they are still **constructs** (made-up explanations that can only approximate the truth), they're very good explanations widely supported by many kinds of evidence.

**threshold concepts**

Some ideas literally change the way you experience, think about, and understand a subject. Researchers call these special ideas *threshold concepts*. Every specialized field of study (or discipline—like history, biology, mathematics, etc.) has threshold concepts that learners in that field must become acquainted with in order to fully understand the ideas of that field of study. Threshold concepts, once learned, help the learner see the world differently. They can be hard to learn (what researchers Jan Meyer and Ray Land call "troublesome") for a variety of reasons, including because they might directly conflict with ideas you already have. Once you're aware of these new and troublesome threshold concepts and you really start to understand them, they are hard to unlearn— Meyer and Land say they are "irreversible." Very often, learning threshold concepts doesn't just change the way you think about the subject, but also the way you think about yourself. But what makes them most powerful is that they help you understand a whole set of other ideas that are hard to imagine without knowing the threshold concept—so they let you do a whole lot of learning at once by helping entire sets of ideas "fall into place." The introduction to *Writing about Writing* spells out some of the main threshold concepts discussed in this book.

**tone**

*Tone* is a reader's *judgment* of what a text sounds like, sometimes also termed the dominant mood of a text. It is important to note that tone is not a characteristic actually *in* a text but rather one constructed in the interaction among the writer, the reader, and the text. Tone emerges not just from the language (word choice and sentence structure) of a text but also from a reader's judgment of the **rhetorical situation** and the writer's **ethos** and motivation.

**transfer**

Now often called *generalization*, *transfer* refers to the act of applying existing knowledge, learned in one kind of situation, to new situations. For example, a writer who learns how to write a summary in her College Writing I class in English is expected to *transfer* that summary-writing knowledge to her "history of the telescope" project in Astronomy. Transfer, we are learning, is not automatic—people learn many things that they forget and/or don't or can't use in different circumstances. Research suggests that learning in particular ways (for example, being **mindful**) can increase the likelihood of later transfer.

**voice**

*Voice* is the way a writer "sounds" in a text, or the extent to which you can "hear" a writer in his or her text. The definition of this term has changed over time. It has been used to refer to **authenticity** in writing, as well as to a written text that seems to be "true" to who its author is and what he or she wants to say. Author bell hooks has argued that finding a voice or "coming to voice" can be seen as an act of resistance. In *Writing about Writing* we use the term *voice* to refer to a writer's ability to speak with some **authority** and expertise deriving from his or her own experiences and knowledge. According to this view, writers have multiple voices, any one of which may find expression, depending on the precise context of utterance.

**writing Studies**

*Writing Studies* is one of the terms used to describe a field or discipline that takes writing and composing as its primary objects of study. Another term commonly used to describe this field of study is Rhetoric and Composition. Most of the readings in this book are written by Writing Studies scholars.

# Works Cited

MacNealy, Mary Sue. *Strategies for Empirical Research in Writing.* New York: Longman, 1999. Print.

Russell, David. "Rethinking Genre in School and Society: An Activity Theory Analysis." *Written Communication* 14.4 (1997): 504–554. Print.

Swales, John. *Genre Analysis: English in Academic and Research Settings.* New York: Cambridge UP, 1990. Print.

Wenger, Etienne. *Communities of Practice: Learning, Meaning, and Identity.* New York: Cambridge UP, 1998. Print.

# Acknowledgments

## Text

**Alexie, Sherman.** "Superman and Me." Original publication: *Los Angeles Times*, April 19, 1998, as part of a series, "The Joy of Reading and Writing." Copyright © 1997 Sherman Alexie. All rights reserved. Used by permission of Nancy Stauffer Associates.

**Baron, Dennis.** "From Pencils to Pixels: The Stages of Literacy," from *Passions, Pedagogies, and 21st Century Technologies*. Ed. Gail E. Hawisher and Cynthia L. Selfe. Logan: Utah State University Press, 1999 (pp.15–33). Copyright © 1999. Reprinted by permission.

**Baron, Naomi.** "Instant Messaging and the Future of Language," from *Communications of the ACM* July 2005, Vol. 28 No. 7. Copyright © 2005 Association for Computing Machinery, Inc. Reprinted by permission. http://dx.doi.org/10.1145/1070838.1070860.

**Bazerman, Charles.** "Speech Acts, Genres, and Activity Systems: How Texts Organize Activity and People." Copyright © 2004 from *What Writing Does and How It Does It*, edited by Charles Bazerman and Paul A. Prior. Reproduced by permission of Taylor and Francis Group, LLC, a division of Informa pic.

**Berkenkotter, Carol.** "Decisions and Revisions: The Planning Strategies of a Publishing Writer." *College Composition and Communication* 34 (1983):156–69. Copyright © 1983 by the National Council of Teachers of English. Reprinted with permission.

**Bernhardt, Steve.** "Seeing the Text." *College Composition and Communication* Vol. 37. No. 1 Feb. 1986. Copyright © 1986 by the National Council of Teachers of English. Reprinted with permission.

**Brandt, Deborah.** "Sponsors of Literacy." *College Composition and Communication* 49.2 (1998): 165–185. Copyright © 1998 by the National Council of Teachers of English. Reprinted by permission.

**Branick, Sean.** "Coaches Can Read, Too: An Ethnographic Study of a Football Coaching Discourse Community." Reprinted by permission of the author.

**Cline, Andrew R.** "A Rhetoric Primer." From *Rhetorica* http://rhetorica.net/textbook. *Introduction to A Rhetoric Primer: A Brief History of Ancient Greek Rhetoric, Theories of Rhetoric(s), Rhetorical Situation and Kairos, The Canons of Rhetoric, Invention Arrangement, Style, Memory, Delivery.* Reprinted by permission of the author.

**Cochran, Ann.** "Blogging the Recovery from Anorexia: A New Platform for the Voice of ED" Reprinted by permission of the author.

**Covino, William A. and David A. Jolliffe.** "What Is Rhetoric?" From *Rhetoric: Concepts, Definitions, Boundaries*, first edition, by William A. Covino and David A. Jolliffe. © 1995, pp. 3–25. Reprinted by permission of Pearson Education, Inc. Upper Saddle River, NJ.

**Cullington, Michaela.** "Texting and Writing." Reprinted by permission of the author.

**Dawkins, John.** "Teaching Punctuation as a Rhetorical Tool." *College Composition and Communication* 46.4 (1995): 533–548. Copyright © 1995 by the National Council of Teachers of English. Reprinted with permission.

**Díaz, Junot.** "Becoming a Writer." First published in *O: The Oprah Magazine* and reprinted by permission of Junot Díaz and Aragi, Inc.

**Editors of the New Yorker.** Tribute Piece to Robert Bingham, in the July 5, 1982 issue of *The New Yorker*. "An Example of a Collage from Robert Bingham (1925–82)." Copyright © 1982 Condé Nast. Reprinted by permission of the publisher.

**Elbow, Peter.** "The Need for Care: Easy Speaking onto the Page is Never Enough," from Chapter 10 of *Vernacular Eloquence* by Peter Elbow. Copyright © 2012. Reprinted by permission of Oxford University Press, USA.

**Gee, James Paul.** "Literacy, Discourse, and Linguistics: Introduction." *Journal of Education* 171.1 (1989): 5–17. Reprinted by permission of James Paul Gee, Mary Lou Fulton Presidential Professor of Literacy Studies, Arizona State University.

**Grabill, Jeff, and William Hart-Davidson, Stacey Pigg, Paull Curran, Micke McLeod, Jessie Moore, Paula Rosinski, Tim Peeples, Suzanne Rumsey, Martine Courant Rife, Robyn Taska, Dundee Lackey, Beth Brunk-Chavez.** "Revisualizing Composition: Mapping the Writing Lives of First-Year College Students." Reprinted by permission of the authors.

**Grant-Davie, Keith.** "Rhetorical Situations and Their Constituents." *Rhetoric Review* 15 (1997). 264–279. Reprinted by permission of Taylor & Francis LLC, a division of Informa pic.

**Greene, Stuart.** "Argument as Conversation: The Role of Inquiry in Writing a Researched Argument" by Stuart Greene. From *The Subject is Research: Processes and Practices* by Wendy Bishop and Pavel Zemliansky. Copyright © 2001 by Boynton/Cook Publishers, Inc. Reprinted by permission of Heinemann, Portsmouth, NH. All rights reserved.

**Hass, Christina and Linda Flower.** "Rhetorical Reading Strategies and the Construction of Meaning." *College Composition and Communication* 39:2 (1988): 167–183. Copyright © 1988 by the National Council of Teachers of English. Reprinted with permission.

**Heath, Shirley Brice.** "Protean Shapes in Literacy Events: Ever-Shifting Oral and Literate Traditions." In *Spoken and Written Language: Exploring Orality and Literacy*. Ed. Deborah Tannen. Norwood: Ablex, 1982. 91–117. Reprinted by permission of the author.

**Hyland, Ken.** "Handout on differences in different disciplines' discourse." Adapted from tables 2.1, 2.2, 2.3, and 2.4 from *Disciplinary Discourses: Social Interactions in Academic Writing*. Ann Arbor: The University of Michigan Press, 2004. Reprinted by permission.

**Jackson Peterson, Erika.** "Past Experiences and Future Attitudes in Literacy." Reprinted by permission of the author.

**Jones, Brandon.** "Rhetorical Criticism of Online Discourse." Reprinted by permission of the author.

**Kain, Donna and Elizabeth Wardle.** "Activity Theory: An Introduction for Writing in the Classroom." Reprinted by permission of the authors.

**Kantz, Margaret.** "Using Textual Sources Persuasively." College English 52.1 (1990): 74–91. (Originally published as "Helping Students Use Textural Sources Persuasively.") Copyright © 1990 by the National Council of Teachers of English. Reprinted with permission.

**Kohl, Christian, and Wolf-Andreas Liebert, Thomas Metten.** "History Now: Media Development and Textual Genesis of Wikipedia." from *Language and New Media*, eds. Rowe & Wyss, pages 165–182 (2009). Reprinted with the permission of Hampton Press.

**Lamott, Anne.** "Shitty First Drafts," from *Bird by Bird* by Anne Lamont. © 1994 by Anne Lamont. Reprinted by permission of Pantheon Books, a division of Random House, Inc., an imprint of The Random House Publishing Group, a division of Random House LLC. All rights reserved.

**Lenhard, Amanda.** "Writing, Technology, and Teens: Summary of Findings." Pew Internet and American Life Project, PEW, April 2008. http://www.pewinternet.org/Reports/2008/Writing-Technology-and-Teens/01-Summary-of-Findings.aspx.

**Magee, Sarah-Kate.** "College Admissions Essays: A Genre of Masculinity." Reprinted by permission of the author.

**Mahiri, Jabari and Soraya Sablo.** "Writing for Their Lives: The Non-School Literacy of California's Urban African American Youth." *The Journal of Negro Education*, 65, 164–180. Reprinted by permission of the publisher.

**Malcolm X.** "Learning to Read." From *Autobiography of Malcolm X*, by Malcolm X and Alex Haley. Copyright © 1964 by Alex Haley and Malcolm X. Copyright © 1965 by Alex Haley and Betty Shabazz. Used by permission of Random House, Inc., an imprint of The Random House Publishing Group, a division of Random House LLC. All rights reserved.

**Marro, Victoria.** "The Genres of Chi Omega: An Activity Analysis." Reprinted by permission of the author.

**Martin, Brian.** "Plagiarism: A Misplaced Emphasis," from *Journal of Information Ethics*, Vol. 3, No. 2 (Fall 1994) © Edited by Robert Hauptman. By permission of McFarland & Company, Inc., Box 611, Jefferson, NC 28640. www.mcfarlandpub.com.

**McCarthy, Lucille P.** "A Stranger in Strange Lands: A College Student Writing Across the Curriculum." Pages 233–65, *Research in the Teaching of English* (1987). Copyright © 1987 by the National Council of Teachers of English. Reprinted with permission.

**Mirabelli, Tony.** "The Language and Literacy of Food Service Workers." From What *They Don't Learn in School*. Jabari Mahiri, ed. NY: Peter Lang, 2004. Pages 143–162. Reprinted by permission.

**Murray, Donald M.** "The Maker's Eye: Revising Your Own Manuscripts." *The Writer*, 1973. Copyright © 1973 by Donald M. Murray. Reprinted by permission of The Rosenberg Group on behalf of the author's estate.

**Murray, Donald.** "All Writing is Autobiography." *College Composition and Communication* 42 (1991): 66–74. Copyright © 1991 by the National Council of Teachers of English. Reprinted by permission.

**Newkirk, Thomas.** "Draw Me a Word, Write Me a Picture." Chapter 2 of More Than Stories: *The Range of Children's Writing*. Portsmouth, NH: Heinemann, 1989. Pages 35–66. Reprinted by permission of the author.

**Osborne, Thomas.** "Late Nights, Last Rites, and the Rain-Slick Road to Self-Destruction." Reprinted by permission of the author.

**Penrose, Ann, and Cheryl Geisler.** "Reading and Writing Without Authority." *College Composition and Communication* 45.4 (1994): 505–520. Copyright © 1994 by the National Council of Teachers of English. Reprinted by permission.

**Penzato, Marissa.** "Fanfiction, Poetry, Blogs, and Journals: A Case Study of the Connection between Extracurricular and Academic Writings." Reprinted by permission of the author.

**Perl, Sondra.** "The Composing Processes of Unskilled College Writers." *Research in the Teaching of English* 13 (1979): 317–36. Copyright © 1979 by the National Council of Teachers of English. Reprinted with permission.

**Perry, Lauren.** "Writing with Four Senses: A Hearing Impaired Person's Writing." Reprinted by permission of the author.

**Porter, James.** "Intertextuality and the Discourse Community." *Rhetoric Review* 5.1 (1986): 34–47. Copyright © 1986. eprinted by permission of Taylor & Francis LLC, a division of Informa pic.

**Post, Maria.** "Obama's Speech at Howard: Becoming King." Reprinted by permission of the author.

**Prior, Paul A.** "Tracing Process: How Texts Come Into Being" by Paul A. Prior. Copyright © 2004 from *What Writing Does and How It Does It*, edited by Charles Bazerman and Paul A. Prior. Reproduced by permission of Taylor and Francis Group, LLC, a division of Informa pic.

**Roozen, Kevin.** "Tracing Trajectories of Practice: Repurposing in One Student's Developing Disciplinary Writing Processes." *Written Communication*, Volume 27, Issue 3, pages 318–354. Copyright © 2010 by Sage Publications. Reprinted by permission of Sage Publications.

**Rose, Mike.** "Rigid Rules, Inflexible Plans, and the Stifling of Language: A Cognitivist Analysis of Writer's Block." *College Composition and Communication* 31 (1980): 389–401. Copyright © 1980 by the National Council of Teachers of English. Reprinted with permission.

**Sommers, Nancy.** "I Stand Here Writing," from *College English* Vol. 55, No. 4, Apr. 1993, pp. 420–428. Copyright © 1993 by the National Council of Teachers of English. Reprinted with permission.

**Sommers, Nancy.** "Revision Strategies of Student Writers and Experienced Adult Writers." *College Composition and Communication* 31.4 (1980): 378–88. Copyright © 1980 by the National Council of Teachers of English. Reprinted with permission.

**Sosnoski, James.** "Hyper-Readers and Their Reading Engines." Chapter 9 of Passions, *Pedagogies, and 21st Century Technologies*, ed. Gail E. Hawisher and Cynthia L. Selfe. Logan: Utah State University Press, 1999. pp.15–33. Copyright © 1999. Reprinted by permission.

**Strasser, Emily.** "Writing What Matters: A Student's Struggle to Bridge the Academic/Personal Divide." Reprinted by permission of the author. Emily Strasser is an MFA candidate in creative nonfiction at the University of Minnesota.

**Straub, Richard.** "Responding —Really Responding—to Other Student's Writing" in *The Subject is Writing*, 4th Edition edited by Wendy Bishop and James Strickland. Copyright © 2006 by Boynton/Cook Publishers, Inc. Reprinted by permission of Heinemann, Portsmouth, NH. All rights reserved.

**Swales, John.** "The Concept of Discourse Community." In *Genre Analysis: English in Academic and Workplace Settings*, pp. 21–32. Cambridge University Press, Copyright © 1990. Reprinted with the permission of Cambridge University Press.

**Swales, John.** "CARS Model Handout Adapted from Genre Analysis: English in Academic and Research Settings" Copyright © 1990 Cambridge University Press. Reprinted with the permission of Cambridge University Press.

**Tomlinson, Barbara.** "Tuning, Tying, and Training Texts: Metaphors for Revision." *Written Communication* 5 (1988): 58–81. Reprinted by permission.

**Villanueva, Victor.** From *Bootstraps: From an Academic of Color*, pages 66–77. Urbana, IL: National Council of Teachers of English (NCTE), 1993. Copyright © 1993 by the National Council of Teachers of English. Reprinted with permission.

**Wardle, Elizabeth.** "Identity, Authority, and Learning to Write in New Workplaces." *Enculturation* 5.2 (2004). Reprinted by permission of the author.

**Winsor, Dorothy.** "Joining the Engineering Community: How Do Novices Learn to Write Like Engineers?" from Technical Communication, May, 1990, Volume 37, Issue 2. Reprinted by permission of the publisher.

## Photos

**p. 12:** Reprinted with the permission of Cambridge University Press; **p. 16:** (1) Photo courtesy of Ron Lunsford; (2) Courtesy of Heinemann; **p. 27:** (2) Courtesy of Heinemann; **p. 40:** David Cheskin/PA Wire; **p. 43:** (2) Courtesy of National Council of Teachers of English; **p. 65:** (1) Copyright ©Gary Samson, University of New Hampshire; (2) Courtesy of National Council of Teachers of English; **p. 107:** (2) Courtesy of National Council of Teachers of English; **p. 119:** (1) Library of Congress; (2) Book Cover, copyright ©1992 by Ballantine, from *Autobiography of Malcolm X*, by Malcolm X as told to Alex Haley. Used by permission of Ballantine Books, an imprint of The Random House Publishing Group, a division of Random House, LLC. All rights reserved. Any third party use of this material, outside this publication, is prohibited. Interested parties must apply directly to Random House LLC for permission. **p. 128:** (1) Ulf Andersen / Getty Images; (2) Cover art by Randy Scholis, used with permission from Milkweed Editions; **p. 133:** Photo: Ayesha Walker; **pp. 169–180:** Courtesy of Sage Publications; **p. 199:** Photo: Lisa Fischoff; **p. 212:** Jason E. Miczek / AP Images for Kraft Foods; **p. 230:** (2) Courtesy of National Council of Teachers of English; **p. 318:** (1) AP Photo / Bernd Kammerer; (2) Canadian Press via AP Images; **p. 347:** Courtesy of Keith Grant-Davie; **pp. 385–89:** Copyright ©2003. From *What Writing Does and How It Does It*, by Charles Bazerman and Paul Prior. Reproduced by permission of Taylor and Francis Group, LLC, a division of Informa plc.; **p. 395:** Photo by Kathryn King Leacock; **p. 410:** (1) Courtesy of Linda Flower; (2) Courtesy of National Council of Teachers of English; **p. 428:** Courtesy of National Council of Teachers of English; **p. 447:** (1) Photo: Sharon Beder; (2) From ©Journal of Information Ethics v.3, no. 2, 1994 by permission of McFarland & Company, Inc., Box 611, Jefferson, NC 28640. www.mcfarlandpub.com; **p. 288:** AP Photo/Marcio Jose Sanchez; **p. 518:** Courtesy of Taylor & Francis; **p. 525:** (1) Darryl Bush/Hulton Archive; (2) *Bird By Bird* cover art copyright ©1994 by Pantheon Books, a division of Random House, Inc., from *Bird by Bird: Some Instructions on Writing and Life* by Anne Lamott. Used by permission of Pantheon Books, an imprint of the Knoph Doubleday Publishing Group, a division of Random House, LLC. All rights reserved; **p. 530:** (1) Mike Rose; (2) Courtesy of National Council of Teachers of English; **p. 563:** (2) Courtesy of National Council of Teachers of English; **p. 588:** (1) Courtesy of Carol Berkenkotter; (2) ©Gary Samson, University of New Hampshire; (3) Courtesy of National Council of Teachers of English; **p. 608:** ©Gary Samson, University of New Hampshire; **p. 613:** (1) Courtesy of Sondra Perl; (2) Courtesy of National Council of Teachers of English; **p. 681:** Stephanie Pilick / picture-alliance / dpa / AP Images; **p. 688:** (1) Photograph by Rachel Baron; (2) Copyright 1999 Utah State University Press. Used by permission; **p. 694:** Reprinted with permission. Copyright ©2002 by Scientific American, Inc. All rights reserved; **p. 687:** The New York Public Library / Art Resource, NY; **p. 703:** Digital composite by Jack Harris; Photo of Marilyn Monroe courtesy of Personality Photos, Inc.; **p. 706:** Cartoon by Dennis Baron; **p. 708:** (1) Courtesy of Pew Internet & American Life Project; (2) Pew Research Center's Internet & American Life Project; (3) Pew Research Center's Internet & American Life Project; **p. 717** (1) Cover design ©Association for Computing Machinery, Inc.; artist: Lisa Haney. Used with permission; **e.-Pages:** (Spoken and Written Languages) Courtesy of ABC-CLIO LLC; (Tony Mirabelli) Courtesy of Peter Lang Publishing; (What They Don't Learn in School) Suzanne Starr; (Journal of Education) By permission of the Journal of Education; (Ann M. Penrose) Edward T. Funkhouser; (CCC) Courtesy of National Council of Teachers of English; (Ken Hyland) Courtesy of Ken Hyland; (Disciplinary Discourses) *Disciplinary Discourses: Social Interactions in Academic Writing*, by Ken Hyland (Ann Arbor: The University of Michigan Press, 2004); (Junot Diaz) ©Nina Subin (Wetlands Figure 1) Courtesy of National Council of Teachers of English; (Wetlands Table 1) Courtesy of National Council of Teachers of English; (Passions, Pedagogies, and 21st-Century Design) Copyright 1999 Utah State University Press. Used by permission.

# Index

**Missing something?** To access the online material that accompanies this text, visit **bedfordstmartins.com /writingaboutwriting**. Students who do not buy a new book can purchase access at this site.

## Inside the Bedford Integrated Media for *Writing about Writing*

Shirley Brice Heath, *Protean Shapes in Literacy Events: Ever-Shifting Oral and Literate Traditions*

Tony Mirabelli, *Learning to Serve: The Language and Literacy of Food Service Workers*

James Paul Gee, *Literacy, Discourse, and Linguistics: Introduction*

Andrew Cline, *A Rhetoric Primer*

Ann M. Penrose and Cheryl Geisler, *Reading and Writing without Authority*

Ken Hyland, From *Disciplinary Discourses: Social Interactions in Academic Writing*

John Dawkins, *Teaching Punctuation as a Rhetorical Tool*

Junot Diaz, *Becoming a Writer*

Barbara Tomlinson, *Tuning, Tying, and Training Texts: Metaphors for Revision*

Lauren Perry, *Writing with Four Senses: A Hearing Impaired Person's Writing*

Steve Bernhardt, *Seeing the Text*

James Sosnoski, *Hyper-Readers and their Reading Engines*

Ann Cochran, *Blogging the Recovery from Anorexia: A New Platform for the Voice of ED*